G000320240

THE SKY SPORTS
ULTIMATE FOOTBALL
GUIDE 1996

Incorporating the Football Club Directory

Published by: SKY BLUE PUBLICATIONS LTD

Sponsored by: SKY SPORTS

Publisher : – Bryan A Richardson
Editor : – Michael Williams
Consulting Editor : – Tony Williams
Editorial Assistants : – Kevin Pullein
Suzie Tatnell
Franky Woulds
Greg Tesser
Fergus Perry
Katy Williams
Cover Design : – Paul Fuller & Graham Watson-Thomas
Sky Introduction Text : – Chris Haynes

ISBN 0-9526904-0-3

Sky Blue Publications Ltd
King Richard Street
Coventry
CV2 4FW
Telephone No 01203 – 633823
Fax No 01203 – 633854

FOREWORD

Welcome to the new "Sky Sports Ultimate Football Guide" incorporating the Endsleigh Football Club Directory. This new and much improved edition continues to lead the field in both content and readable presentation.

The Directory concentrates on all 92 Football League Clubs. Enthusiastic statisticians from each team offered their help and a deliberate policy of publishing a month or so after the season started has a couple of major advantages.

Firstly, the players are found in the clubs with whom they started the season, (Most football annuals are printed in mid-summer and miss all the July and August transfers).

Secondly, up to date team photos with new signings and new styles of kit are included.

The "Good News Awards", are given to personalities or clubs who have brought good news stories to football. Over the ten years the awards have been made, the panel invited by the editor to choose the recipients has included some illustrious names: Bobby Robson, Graham Taylor, Terry Venables, Martin Tyler, Brian Moore, Bob Wilson and Gordon Taylor to name a few.

The life and development of the Club Directory now takes a major leap forward in its new guise as the "Sky Sports - Ultimate Football Guide." With the massive support of Sky Sports in football coverage, it is natural they should be actively supporting and involved with "the bible of football."

We will continue to improve the "Ultimate Football Guide" and ensure it remains your favourite - with the continued help and support of Sky Sports and all the professional game.

Bryan Richardson

Publisher.

Football
on
Sky Sports
in a
different
league

SKY sports

LIVE MATCH COVERAGE

Over the past three seasons Sky Sports commitment to Britain's favourite sport has continued to grow. Each season Sky Sports has shown football every day of the week, with a range of innovative support programmes, and more live coverage than ever seen before on British television.

The FA Carling Premiership with 60 live games each season, forms just part of Sky's groundbreaking football coverage. Over the past four years Sky Sports has broadcast over 400 live games taking Sky viewers to over 50 league grounds in England alone; to England internationals at home and abroad; Scottish club matches from the major competitions; and a range of other matches from schoolboy internationals to the growing women's game.

Since its first full football season in 1991-92, Sky Sports has shown more live football each successive season. In the first year, before the start of the FA Premier League contract, Sky Sports broadcast 75 live matches. But by the close of the most recent full season, Sky's football coverage featured over 140 live games, spanning 50 weeks from the FA Charity Shield in August '94 through to the final of the Copa America at the end of July '95; the new season kicked off just two weeks later with the Charity Shield exclusively live on Sky Sports.

This year Sky Sports range of live coverage again stretches way beyond England's leading league. Sky also has; live coverage of the FA Cup, sponsored by Littlewoods Pools, from the First round stage through to the Semi-Final, offering at least one live game and one replay from each stage; and every England international from Wembley Stadium exclusively live.

In Scotland, Sky has live rights for the Bell's Scottish League, Scottish Coca-Cola Cup and Tennents Cup for the next three seasons, bringing up to 17 games each year from Scotland's premier club tournaments. Each season a number of other games are shown live featuring clubs or teams in a wide range of tournaments. For the past two years only Sky Sports has shown the Final of the Women's FA Cup, alongside coverage of the FA Umbro Trophy live from Wembley Stadium. And live international coverage has encompassed England internationals at B, Under-21, Under-18, Youth and Schoolboy level as well as the full internationals.

THE FOLLOWING PAGES OUTLINE SKY'S FOOTBALL PROGRAMMES AND HELP TO EXPLAIN HOW LIVE MATCHES ARE PRODUCED

FORD ESCORT SUPER SUNDAY

Live Sunday football first came to British television in 1979, but it was Sky's regular live coverage, with major matches on most weekends right from the start of the season, that established Sunday as a footballing day throughout the year.

Ford Escort Super Sunday normally starts at 2pm with Richard Keys and his studio guests setting the scene for the afternoon's entertainment. There are highlights of every Saturday match from the FA Carling Premiership, and a reminder of the current league tables, before viewers are given a Story of the Season for each of the clubs, looking at the highlights and lowlights and analysing form, whilst outside the ground, the cameras capture the players arriving, and ask fans of the teams - home and away - for their vox-pop views on the game.

At half time, and after the game, Richard Keys and his special studio guests discuss the game, with instant replays of relevant action. And at the end of the game, Andy Gray leaves his commentary position to return to the studio and add his opinions.

The Super Sunday Outside Broadcast is the largest regular roadshow anywhere in Europe, taking five production trucks and up to ninety personnel the length of the country. Each game is produced at the ground, then sent by landline to an uplink centre which sends the pictures up to the Astra Satellite. So, although highlights packages and most of the graphics are produced at Sky's HQ in advance of the game, the production is self-sufficient and can operate independently of the facilities back at Sky's west London headquarters.

FORD ESCORT MONDAY NIGHT FOOTBALL

The 1995-96 season has brought another major step in the evolution of Ford Escort Monday Night Football. The new campaign introduced a new-look studio, deeper tactical insights, and a revolutionary graphics and replay tool for post-match analysis.

Sky's biggest transfer of the summer closed-season took elements of the popular support show Andy Gray's Boot Room over to Monday Night Football. Each week the live match is followed by half an hour of tactical talk with Andy Gray – replacing last-season's Talkback section. So whilst the post-match analysis will feature elements familiar to viewers of Andy Gary's Boot Room, the style and content have been revolutionised by Sky's major summer signing – the new Replay 2000 Graphics and action-replay system.

Replay 2000 has allowed more advanced analysis than ever before, illustrating how the game was won and lost with graphic devices that; track the movements of players and the flight of the ball, highlight individual players as they run, create three-dimensional diagrams from real footage, and draw cross-lines to help with off-side decisions. With these exclusive features the Replay 2000 is the ideal partner for Andy Gray and his intuitive coaching and instruction.

Monday Night Football first changed the face of the game in August 1992. Since then Monday night matches have become an established and popular part of the extended football weekend. Monday Night Football was launched with pre-match and half-time entertainment, live bands, and fireworks for the first season, and was soon established in football folklore with a four page story – featuring Richard Keys and Andy Gray – in the classic comic-strip Roy of the Rovers. Research at the end of the first season showed that attendances at Monday Night matches were higher on average than similar Saturday fixtures, and on television the games tended to attract higher audiences than Ford Escort Super Sunday Games.

PRODUCING LIVE GAMES

The average match is covered by a crew of up to ninety people, and with up to 100 football OB's each season the crew are well-rehearsed, work together as a team, and understand the style - and demands - of Sky's production style.

The nerve centre of the outside broadcast is a fleet of trucks and trailers parked outside the ground and linked to the cameras and microphones, by the pitch and in the presenter's studio, by up to ten miles of cable. Collectively, these form a self-sufficient production site for live games.

In the ' presentation scanner', the programme director Mike Allen oversees the build-up to the live game and controls the half-time and full-time analysis. The executive producer - Andy Melvin - is responsible for the entire operation and is seated alongside.

Next door in the 'match scanner' the match director - Tony Mills - selects the camera shots and controls the cameramen and commentators during the 90 minutes of the game.

In the 'VTR scanner' a team of technicians control a bank of eight video replay machines, monitoring and recording the game's key incidents, ready to use for instant replays or for half-time analysis.

A fourth vehicle is the British Telecom 'links truck', through which the TV and audio signals are sent.

CAMERAS

The number of cameras used varies between games and venues. At the launch of the FA Premier League coverage in August 1992 Sky's first live Premier League match was covered by 16 different camera positions. Since then new equipment has been tested, and new camera angles developed so that up to 20 cameras an be used at a televised match in the FA Carling Premiership. The greatest number of cameras installed in a ground for live coverage on Sky Sports has been 23 for the 1994 FA Charity Shield at Wembley Stadium.

SLOW-MOTION REPLAYS

With the introduction of the super-slow-mo camera in 1993, Sky broke new boundaries in televised football. By running the film faster whilst recording through a special camera, replays become sharper with viewers able to see shots, saves, and on-the-ball skills with remarkable clarity. Executive producer Andy Melvin explains; "You can get the ball revolving through the air and the picture is so sharp you can see the stitching on the ball. We can also capture great expressions on the faces of the players and the fans for reaction shots.

This season, replays can be played on screen faster than ever before, with goals and incidents shown within seconds. During live matches a team of five VT operators constantly study the live

FA Carling Premiership

exclusively live

Ford Escort Super Sunday live at 3pm
Ford Escort Monday Night Football live at 7pm

game selecting and cueing up possible replay angles. And within moments of a goal being scored the match director can show a series of replays from a range of angles.

AUDIO

For a live match, up to fifteen directional microphones are aimed at the crowd and the pitch, to pick up the sounds of the players and the fans. Andy Melvin explains; "We are producing an entertainment show, not just a sporting event, and good sound is essential. With our coverage, armchair fans should almost feel that they are there on the pitch."

Dolby Surround Sound adds to the experience, with those having Home Cinema systems or Surround Sound decoders able to sit in the middle of the crowd noise, hear the commentators talking at the front of the room, and experience sound effects - as goals are scored or replays introduced - moving around the room.

STATISTICS

There are two main sources of Sky's football statistics; a full-time team of football statisticians who collate club statistics and feed relevant facts to commentators and producers, and a member of the production team who analyses each game as it is being played.

Throughout the year two statisticians update statistics on every Premier League club, and prepare information on international squads, Scottish league teams, and the clubs that appear in the FA Cup ties. One statistician attends each match, seated alongside the producer and armed with the facts that are crucial to the game.

At each live game a member of the production team sits alongside the commentators and logs every major move of the game on a lap-top computer, recording free-kicks, throw-ins, fouls, shots on goal and the amount of possession for each team. These statistics are fed into a graphics generator and tables are created for half-time and full-time studio analysis.

GRAPHICS

All of the football graphics have a similar look, even though the images seen in Super Sunday or Monday Night Football may have been produced months in advance or just seconds before, in Sky's advanced graphics centre or out on the road in an OB truck.

For a live game, the first graphics to be developed are the opening title sequences, promotional break-bumpers, and closing credits. These are created by Sky's Creative Services department, who boast the most advanced graphics and post-production facilities of any European TV station.

In the week of a live match the On-Line department focus on creating the more urgent requirements of the next show; such as the PlayBall competition, and the opening title sequence.

A member of the studio graphics team also attends each live game, based in one of the OB trucks to input the team line-ups, on-screen information and half-time statistics, and the captions that illustrate red cards, yellow cards, and substitutions.

The on-screen clock and scoreline is a permanent presence, created on a PC and placed in the left-hand corner of the screen.

HOW THE PICTURE TRAVELS TO THE TV SET

At a live game, produced on-the-road, the sound and vision of the action on the pitch travel through a network of up to ten miles of cable into the production area; a fleet of five trucks - parked behind the stands - packed with graphics equipment, VT machines, hundreds of monitors, and two power generators.

From the 'links truck' at the stadium, the signal travels by land line to the BT Tower in the centre of London, then is transmitted back to a receiver at Sky's West London headquarters. From

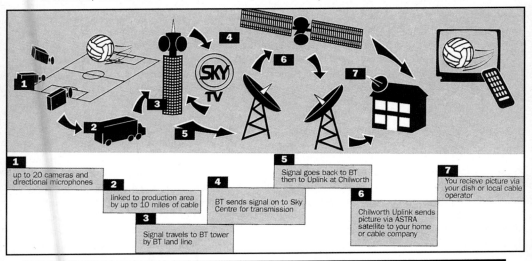

1 up to 20 cameras and directional microphones

2 linked to production area by up to 10 miles of cable

3 Signal travels to BT tower by BT land line

4 BT sends signal on to Sky Centre for transmission

5 Signal goes back to BT then to Uplink at Chilworth

6 Chilworth Uplink sends picture via ASTRA satellite to your home or cable company

7 You recieve picture via your dish or local cable operator here it travels by landline to an uplink centre in London's Docklands, where the signal is sent on to the Astra satellite, orbiting 23,500 miles above the Atlantic Ocean. Satellite viewers receive their signal direct from the Astra satellite, cabled homes receive theirs via the local cable companies larger receiving dish and a network of local cables.

From the pitch to the living room, the images from a live match travel nearly 50,000 miles in less than a quarter of a second.

SUPPORT PROGRAMMES

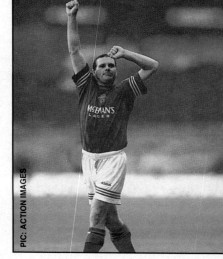

PIC: ACTION IMAGES

Last season Sky Sports covered over 140 live football matches, but there is more than the live game to Sky's football coverage. Every week the channel schedules more than 18 hours of support programming, to keep the viewers informed and entertained with a complete soccer service.

The line-up features a different football programme every day of the week, covering the game from international to grass roots level:

Tartan Extra - Monday, 18.30-19.00

With Gazza at Glasgow Rangers, the first full season of Sky's live Scottish coverage -after last year's mid-season deal with the Scottish League and SFA - has coincided with a surge of interest in the Scottish game. This season Sky Sports will show up to 17 live games from Scotland's major tournaments - the Bell's Premier Division, Coca Cola Cup, and Tennent's Scottish Cup - and there will be expanded coverage of the game throughout Sky's support programmes. Tartan Extra continues to give a complete weekly round-up of the Scottish game, with goals and highlights, results and news from across the Scottish leagues, from Aberdeen to Arbroath.

Sky Sports Centre - Weekdays 18.00-18.30 & 22.00-22.30

This unique live news show gives a complete round-up of the day's sports news. The 30-minute programme has evolved from Soccer News - last season's fifteen minute football service - and with twice the time to devote to sport, presenters Dominik Holyer and Jane Hoffen deliver an alternative to the 6 o'clock News and News at Ten for serious sports fans, with information, analysis and the latest stories from across the world of sport, as well as the evening's football results.

On Friday evenings, David Bobin and Anna Walker present an extended Sky Sports Centre, with 60-minutes of news, interviews and big match previews for the weekend ahead, as well as the day's other sports headlines.

The Footballers Football Show - Tuesday, 21.00-22.00

For the past four seasons this weekly discussion, for the dedicated football fan, has become a recognised forum for serious and topical debate and consistently hit the headlines. The first talk show of its kind, the Footballers' Football Show was described in the Daily Express at the end of its first season as "pure heaven - like the best pub conversation ever, and the level of intelligence much higher than anything you're ever likely to hear from politicians on Newsnight or poseurs on the Late Show.î The show has featured an impressive list of names in the know from the world of football; from club statisticians to the England manager, via players and coaches, writers and referees, and most of the leading club chairmen. And the topics of discussion have been equally

Sky Sports Centre

news, views
and analysis
live every weekday
at
6pm and 10pm

wide-ranging; from agents to physiotherapy, and red cards to rioting and several of its stories have hit the back pages, setting the sporting headlines for the following day.

Futbol Mundial - Wednesday evening

Futbol Mundial takes in all four corners of the globe, reviewing both the international scene and the world's leading domestic leagues.

There are results and standings across Europe, Africa, Asia and South America, and the show follows the big stories and transfers, showing action of the greatest players in the global game.

From further afield the show will keep track of major tournaments and international games across the five footballing continents in an imaginative mix of highlights, news and features. And in the build-up to Euro'96, the 60-minute show will provide a vital insight into the European nations set to challenge England in next summer's finals.

Soccer AM - Saturday, 07.00-11.00

Presented by Russ Williams and Helen Chamberlain, Soccer AM goes out early on Saturday morning, ahead of the week's main games, and its carefree attitude is the perfect way to wake-up to the weekend.

With lively chat and competitions galore it always attracts the attention of the younger audience, but there is also plenty of entertainment for older football fans.

Soccer AM gives full previews of the games ahead, with up-to-date ticket information, and road traffic reports, for those hoping to travel to games in the afternoon.

Phone-ins give the fans a chance to get involved, and armchair fans can ask to see their favourite moments from the Sky archives.

The programme also features interviews with players, plus predictions for the crunch matches of the weekend as special studio guests set the scene for the soccer action ahead.

PICS: ACTION IMAGES

Sports Saturday - Saturday, 12.00-17.30

The Saturday afternoon sports extravaganza starts at midday previewing the day's football fixtures from the Premiership, Football League and Scotland. And the show stays on-air until 5.30 to provide unrivalled coverage of the afternoon's football. Reporters are out at every Premiership game to give half-time and full time reports before an extensive results round-up begins in the ScoreLines service at 4.40. The show also has a strong news content, with sports bulletins and round-ups at midday, 1pm, 4pm and 5pm.

The start of the show is focused on football, with the likes of Mark Lawrenson, Phil Thompson and George Best previewing the day's football, from the Premiership the Endsleigh Leagues, and

Scotland, and the show will end just as it started with football news, and a round-up of the day's results and tables.

Soccer Extra - Sunday, 07.00-11.00

Soccer Extra gives Sunday's early-riser a full review of Saturday's football news and highlights, and a look at the headlines on the Sunday sports pages.

A review of the Premiership action is given a fresh approach with an in-depth look at how the goals were scored and interviews with the star performers of the day. And a look ahead to Ford Escort Super Sunday and Monday Night Football brings interviews and action from the competing players.

Studio guests provide lively debate, with Sky Sports presenters Gary O'Reilly and Helen Chamberlain acting as the referees, and the fans get their say with regular phone-ins. There are also studio appearances from members of the Football Supporters Association discussing the game's big issues in the popular Fans Forum, plus competitions and interactive TV games in a fast-moving four-hour show.

Goals on Sunday - Sunday, 12.00-13.30

Anna Walker's Goals on Sunday is placed at the centre of the three-day football weekend. The Sunday lunchtime show is in the perfect position to review Saturday's Premiership action and look ahead to the live games of Super Sunday and Monday Night Football.

This season Goals on Sunday has been extended by half an hour, so although it will focus on the FA Carling Premiership, it will not neglect the news from Scotland and the Endsleigh league. Featured in the new-look ninety-minute programme; a statistical round-up shows who is scoring goals, and where they are scored from, and gives an insight into the strengths and weaknesses of individual players and successful teams; studio guests review Saturday's matches and analyse the goals; and there is a chance to review the latest league tables in the build-up to the afternoon's game.

PIC: ACTION IMAGES

OTHER SOCCER SERVICES

Beyond the two dedicated sports channels - Sky Sports and Sky Sports 2 - football fans can keep completely up to date with two other services of Sky TV. Sky News has sports news at 20 minutes past the hour throughout the day, with live coverage of major press conferences. And on Saturdays, Sportsline provides a full results service three times a day with highlights of the day's games in Sportsline Extra at 11.30pm.

On Sky's Fastext service each club has its own dedicated page, so that anytime day or night throughout the week fans can consult the latest news from their own club. And on other pages of the interactive service are the latest results, standings and stories from across the leagues and the entire sporting world.

GOOD NEWS AWARDS

Since 1986, The Football League Directory has honoured football personalities who have brought good news to our national winter sport, and we are very pleased to continue this tradition. Perhaps we needed good news more than usual last season as the game suffered from a number of unsavoury headlines. So our thanks to the huge majority throughout the football world who conducted themselves within the games normal high standards. Our special congratulations to the seven winners of Good News Awards as described below by Tony Williams.

NEVILLE SOUTHALL Everton's experienced Welsh goalkeeper looked really uncomfortable during his club's desperate battle to find form at the beginning of last season, but as the experts were writing him off, the fortunes of the club, his defence and the keeper himself dramatically improved and it was the consistent displays of the big fellow that inspired all around him. He obviously reacted well to the appointment of Joe Royle as manager and Neville's great career produced another peak when he helped Everton beat Manchester United at Wembley in the Cup Final. His amazing nonchalance and refusal to admit that his brilliance was anything other than an ordinary day's work, certainly ensures he can never be accused of taking himself too seriously. He is celebrating his 500th game for Everton this season and has given wonderful service to his club, Wales and the game in general.

There are very few more popular players in football than **GORDON STRACHAN**. Whether it was his impish grin as he celebrated some memorable goals or his incredible energy and enthusiasm for the game, Gordon set a great example to all involved. Last season as the new Assistant Manager to Ron Atkinson at Coventry City, he shook the playing staff with his training schedule that showed he wanted all his players to obtain his own high standard of fitness. He proved his point by beating Spurs at White Hart Lane practically single handed, thus ensuring his new club's Premier League status for another year. Gordon has served all his clubs with a style and a passion that has been infectious. Scotland, Aberdeen, Manchester United, Leeds United and now Coventry City have all been successful when he has played. His career has been special and who would bet against a managerial future that will have a similar impact on the game he loves.

JACK WALKER has probably achieved what every football fan dreams about. His outstanding success as a businessman produced wealth that most people could hardly comprehend. But to successfully invest it in his beloved Blackburn Rovers has given the game a superb example of outstanding 'support'. Many self styled entrepreneurs have had their dreams but very few have actually produced success. It's more than just money. The right people, sound ideas and only good planning and hard work will ensure that results are obtained. Many will try to emulate Jack Walker but very few will succeed however wealthy they may be.

There was a lot of excitement in the north west outpost of The Endsleigh League last season, as Carlisle United stormed to the Third Division championship and attracted good attendances which created a superb atmosphere at Brunton Park. The much pub-

By far the greatest team the world has ever seen

EL LOCO
Futbol Mundial
weekly world soccer magazine

THE STOPPER
Exclusive live action on
Ford Escort Super Sunday

THE CENTRE-BACK
Rock-solid news from the
Sky Sports Centre
(Live at 6pm and 10pm weeknights)

MR.110%
Sunday morning chat and action in
Soccer Extra

THE SEASONED PRO
Verbal professional fouls in the
Footballers' Football Show

THE PLAYMAKER
Andy Gray analyses
Ford Escort Monday Night Football, exclusively live

SUPERSUB
Tartan Extra comes on for
30 glorious minutes every Monday

THE TARTAN TERRIER
Regular live coverage of the
Best of Scottish Football

THE DYNAMO
Box-to-box pre-game chat on
Soccer AM, Saturdays

THE SNIFFER
All the latest scores on
Sports Saturday

THE OUT-AND-OUT STRIKER
Goals on Sunday,
the complete round-up

Football on Sky Sports
in a different league

licised Michael Knighton proved he could run a League club on very successful lines but the appointment of **MICK WADSWORTH** as Director of Coaching brought a new type of team boss to the Endsleigh League. Previously employed by the Football Association in staff and regional coaching capabilities, his appointment must have raised a few eyebrows amongst the older professionals in the game. Mick hadn't a great playing pedigree but what a superb answer to the doubters - promotion and the championship with style! His success is also great news for all the other thousands of good coaches who just dream of getting a 'break' in full time football. They now know it's possible!

Did anyone ever doubt that **BRYAN ROBSON** would make a good manager? Very few I would imagine! But it's one thing having the attributes that make a good football leader and another to find a club who will give you the opportunity, with the right back up and a new super stadium thrown in to complete the perfect stage! Yes, the ex-England skipper is a 'winner' and his shrewd team building has already provided a sound Middlesborough squad on which he can build a challenge to his Geordie neighbours. Bryan exudes confidence on and off the field and is a fine example of our young English coaches who will hopefully be able to influence England's return to the world's top football nations in the seasons ahead.

Scotland were drawn in a tough looking group for Euro '96. The team was workmanlike rather then full of star names and the possibility of making the journey to the Euro finals looked to be full of obstacles. Following the departure of Andy Roxburgh, **CRAIG BROWN** was chosen to be his successor. Craig had joined the Scot's backroom staff for the 1986 World Cup Finals in Mexico and had made such an impression he was invited to be Roxburgh's Assistant in August 1986. Since his appointment as Manager in November 1993, Brown has steadily built a sound squad and has created a team spirit where there are no stars and no jealousies, just a very sincere determination to take their country back into contention for honours. By qualifying for the European Championships in England Craig will surely have given Scotsmen their footballing pride back and just watch that support regroup for the invasion!

Football viewing on television has taken on a completely different aspect since Sky Television won the right to show live coverage of The FA Premier League. The knowledge of the average football fan must have widened by 100% thanks to **ANDY GRAY'S** quite outstanding ability to pick out instantly, explain clearly and highlight technically, incident after incident, week in and week out. As a mature and hardened football person, I find myself positively excited by Sky's presentation and in particular Andy's obvious love of the game and its characters. Youngsters and veterans alike can now really begin to understand and 'see' so much more within his 'beautiful game'. Never has anyone in the media ever presented their sport with such skill and given so much pleasure and knowledge to fans of all ages and levels of experience. Thank you!

THE SKY SPORTS
ULTIMATE FOOTBALL
GUIDE 1996

Incorporating the
Football Club Directory

Published by: SKY BLUE PUBLICATIONS LTD

Sponsored by: SKY SPORTS

INTRODUCTION TO CLUB PAGES

Once again we have maintained, what we think to be our tried and tested format for the book, coupled together with the odd cosmetic change here and there.

One major change though for this year's publication, is the break up into Division's, ie. the club section is now broken up into the Premiership, Division One, Division Two and Division Three. Within each Divisional section you will find the clubs, in alphabetical order, who commenced the 1995-96 season in that Division.

A completely new section can be found at the back of the book, with the introduction of 'England's International Matches and Teams 1946-1995', which we hope you will find both interesting and informative.

To help you understand the notations used within this book and to give you a brief idea of the information that can be found within the club section, the following notes should be read.

FIRST PAGE:	Includes a review of the 1994-95 season; Senior club personnel; **1995-96** Playing squad photograph plus caption. *(In the case of the 1995-96 photo not being available at the time of going to press, the 1994-95 photo has been used).*
SECOND & THIRD PAGES	Complete match by match details of the 1994-95 season. Notations used: Left Hand Page: † = After extra-time. Right Hand Page: † = Player sent off; *= Player substituted by No.12. • = Player substituted by No.14; S = Non-playing substitute.
RECORDS PAGE(S)	Premier and First Division clubs' records and statistics cover two complete pages. Second and Third Division clubs' records and statistics covered on one page with details of their Manager also included.
PLAYERS PAGE	Includes players with full contracts as at the start of the 1995-96 season. Details include - Height, Weight, Birth Date and Contract Date as well as League, FA Cup, League Cup and 'other'* appearances and goals. *All European competitions and any other domestic competition, such as The Full Members Shield or Play-offs and alike, come under the heading of 'Other' Appearances and goals.
SEVENTH PAGE (Prem. & Div.1)	Overspill from the players page is then followed by details on both the top goalscorer for 1994-95 and the team manager.
GROUNDS PAGE	Contains 1995-96 matchday ticket prices along with details on the ground and easy to read directions. Also included on this page are details plus the front cover of the clubs' 1995-96 matchday programme.

Premiership

F.A. CARLING PREMIERSHIP

1995-96

F.A. Carling
Premiership 1994-95

Final League Table

		P	W	D	L	F	A	W	D	L	F	A	Pts
			Home						**Away**				
1	Blackburn Rovers	42	17	2	2	54	2	10	6	5	26	18	89
2	Manchester United	42	16	4	1	42	4	10	6	5	35	24	88
3	Nottingham Forest	42	12	6	3	36	18	10	5	6	36	25	77
4	Liverpool	42	13	5	3	38	13	8	6	7	27	24	74
5	Leeds United	42	13	5	3	35	15	7	8	6	24	23	73

Into Europe

		P	W	D	L	F	A	W	D	L	F	A	Pts
6	Newcastle United	42	14	6	1	46	20	6	6	9	21	27	72
7	Tottenham Hotspur	42	10	5	6	32	25	6	9	6	34	33	62
8	Queens Park Rangers	42	11	3	7	36	26	6	6	9	25	33	60
9	Wimbledon	42	9	5	7	26	26	6	6	9	22	39	56
10	Southampton	42	8	9	4	33	27	4	9	8	28	36	54
11	Chelsea	42	7	7	7	25	22	6	8	7	25	33	54
12	Arsenal	42	6	9	6	27	21	7	3	11	25	28	51
13	Sheffield Wednesday	42	7	7	7	26	26	6	5	10	23	31	51
14	West Ham United	42	9	6	6	28	19	4	5	12	16	29	50
15	Everton	42	8	9	4	31	23	3	4	10	13	28	50
16	Coventry City	42	7	7	7	23	25	5	7	9	21	37	50
17	Manchester City	42	8	7	6	37	28	4	6	11	16	36	49
18	Aston Villa	42	6	9	6	27	24	5	6	10	24	32	48

Relegated

		P	W	D	L	F	A	W	D	L	F	A	Pts
19	Crystal Palace	42	6	6	9	16	23	5	6	10	18	26	45
20	Norwich City	42	8	8	5	27	21	2	5	14	10	33	43
21	Leicester City	42	5	6	10	28	37	1	5	15	17	43	29
22	Ipswich Town	42	5	3	13	24	34	2	3	16	12	59	27

FA Carling Premership 1995-96

ARSENAL
(The Gunners)
F.A. CARLING PREMIERSHIP
SPONSORED BY: JVC (UK) LTD.

Back Row (L-R): Chris Kiwomya, Scott Marshall, Paul Merson, Lee Harper, Steve Bould, Andy Linighan, David Seaman, Steve Morrow, Nigel Winterburn, Vince Bartram, Ray Parlour, John Hartson, Ian Selley, George Armstrong (res. Coach). **Front Row:** Gary Lewin (Physio), Paul Dickov, Eddie McGoldrick, Lee Dixon, John Jensen, Ian Wright, Tony Adams, Bruce Rioch (Manager), Dennis Bergkamp, Glenn Helder, David Platt, Mark Flatts, David Hillier, Martin Keown, Stewart Houston (First Team Coach).

ARSENAL
FORMED IN 1886
TURNED PROFESSIONAL IN 1891
PLC IN 1990

CHAIRMAN: P D Hill-Wood
DIRECTORS:
D Dein (Vice-Chairman)
Sir Robert Bellinger CBE, DSO
R G Gibbs, C E B L Carr,
R C L Carr, K J Friar, D Fiszman.

SECRETARY/Managing Director:
Ken J Friar (0171 226 0304)
Assistant Secretary
David Miles
COMMERCIAL MANAGER
John Hazell (0171 359 0808)

MANAGER: Bruce Rioch
ASSISTANT:

RESERVE TEAM MANAGER
George Armstrong
YOUTH TEAM MANAGER
Pat Rice
PHYSIOTHERAPIST
Gary Lewin

CLUB STATISTICIAN FOR THE DIRECTORY
Chris Thompson

The 1994/95 season will probably go down in history as one of the most traumatic the club has ever experienced. Well publicised problems involving the manager and more than one of the players kept the club on the front pages throughout the season and beyond. On the pitch the problems would cause just as much anguish.

It had, however, started so brightly, Benfica's Stefan Schwarz and Eddie McGoldrick were recruited to bolster the midfield. Arsenal made a victorious return to the pre-season Makita Tournament, beating Athletico Madrid on penalties then Napoli in the final.

The season proper began well enough too with an opening day 3-0 victory over Manchester City, Kevin Campbell scoring the first Premiership goal of the new campaign.

In the League the Gunners only won six home games all season and in fact went four months without a Premiership win at Highbury between October and February.

The domestic cups did not bring much respite either. Arsenal reached the quarter final stage of the Coca-Cola cup smoothly enough before going out to old foes Liverpool.

Millwall ended the clubs' FA Cup aspirations for another year with a third round replay win at Highbury. Yet again goal scoring was the problem caused by a lack of real midfield creativity.

When George Graham did move into the transfer market his purchases surprised many. John Hartson who equalled the record fee paid by the club and Chris Kiwomya came in January followed by Dutch International Glenn Helder a month later.

The European Cup Winners Cup was again Arsenal's most productive avenue. A memorable penalty shoot-out triumph over Sampdoria in Genoa took the Gunners to a Paris final against Real Zaragosa.

A poor match was deservedly won by the Spaniards in extra-time with a stunning goal from Nayim.

Much will have changed at Highbury during the Summer. A new manager will have been installed. An ageing team will also have been overhauled. Tough decisions will have been made in letting a number of old favourites leave as well as recruiting their replacements. The team's playing style may well have changed as well.

The upheaval means the Gunners fans will probably have to wait a season or two before the team are again realistic challengers for honours. If the magnificent gates of 1994/95 are maintained a lot of people will experience a fascinating season. It will be interesting to see which way the wind of change will blow in North London during 1995/96.

CHRIS THOMPSON.

ARSENAL

Premier League: 12th   **FA Cup:** 3rd Round   **Coca-Cola Cup:** 5th Round   **ECWC Cup:** Finalists

M	DATE	COMP.	VEN	OPPONENTS	RESULT	H/T	LP	GOAL SCORERS/GOAL TIMES	ATT.
1	A 20	PL	H	Manchester City	W 3-0	2-0		Campbell 2, 36(og), Wright 76	38,368
2	23	PL	A	Leeds United	L 0-1	0-0			(34,218)
3	28	PL	A	Liverpool	L 0-3	0-3	13		(30,017)
4	31	PL	H	Blackburn Rovers	D 0-0	0-0	13		37,629
5	S 10	PL	A	Norwich City	D 0-0	0-0	12		(17,768)
6	15	ECWC1/1	A	Omonia Nicosia	W 3-1	1-0		Merson 37, 80, Wright 49	(20,000)
7	18	PL	H	Newcastle United	L 2-3	1-2	15	Adams 10, Wright 88	36,819
8	21	CC 2/1	A	Hartlepool United	W 5-0	2-0		Adams 32, Smith 37, Wright 54, 85, Merson 75	(4,421)
9	25	PL	A	West Ham United	W 2-0	1-0	14	Adams 18, Wright 54	(18,498)
10	29	ECWC1/2	H	Omonia Nicosia	W 3-0	2-0		Wright 9, 70, Schwarz 31	24,265
11	O 1	PL	H	Crystal Palace	L 1-2	0-2	14	Wright 72	34,136
12	5	CC 2/2	H	Hartlepool United	W 2-0	0-0		Campbell 79, Dickov 89	20,520
13	8	PL	A	Wimbledon	W 3-1	1-0	11	Wright 11, Smith 57, Campbell 65	(10,842)
14	15	PL	H	Chelsea	W 3-1	1-1	11	Wright 40, 63, Campbell 54	38,234
15	20	ECWC2/1	A	Brondby	W 2-1	2-0		Wright 16, Smith 18	(13,406)
16	23	PL	H	Coventry City	W 2-1	2-0	10	Wright 13, 32	31, 725
17	26	CC 3	A	Oldham Athletic	D 0-0	0-0			(9,303)
18	29	PL	A	Everton	D 1-1	1-1	10	Schwarz 24	(32,003)
19	N 3	ECWC2/2	H	Brondby	D 2-2	1-1		Wright 28 (pen), Selley 46	32,290
20	6	PL	H	Sheffield Wednesday	D 0-0	0-0	10		33,705
21	9	CC 3R	H	Oldham Athletic	W 2-0	2-0		Dickov 15, 40	22,746
22	19	PL	A	Southampton	L 0-1	0-0	11		(15,201)
23	23	PL	A	Leicester City	L 1-2	1-2	11	Wright 19 (pen)	(20,774)
24	26	PL	H	Manchester United	D 0-0	0-0	12		38,301
25	30	CC 4	H	Sheffield Wednesday	W 2-0	2-0		Morrow 29, Wright 34	27,390
26	D 3	PL	A	Nottingham Forest	D 2-2	2-1	12	Keown 59, Davis 76	(21,662)
27	12	PL	A	Manchester City	W 2-1	2-0	11	Smith 32, Schwarz 35	(20,580)
28	17	PL	H	Leeds United	L 1-3	0-1	12	Linighan 86	38,098
29	26	PL	A	Aston Villa	D 0-0	0-0	12		34,452
30	28	PL	A	Ipswich Town	W 2-0	1-0	9	Wright 16, Campbell 79	(22,054)
31	31	PL	H	Queens Park Rangers	L 1-3	0-1	13	Jensen 64	32,393
32	J 2	PL	A	Tottenham Hotspur	L 0-1	0-1	13		(28,747)
33	7	FAC 3	A	Millwall	D 0-0	0-0			(17,715)
34	11	CC 5	A	Liverpool	L 0-1	0-0			(35,026)
35	14	PL	H	Everton	D 1-1	1-1	13	Wright 4	34,743
36	18	FAC 3R	H	Millwall	L 0-2	0-1			32,319
37	21	PL	A	Coventry City	W 1-0	0-0	11	Hartson 78	(14,468)
38	24	PL	H	Southampton	D 1-1	1-1	11	Hartson 21	27,213
39	F 1	ESC 1/1	H	AC Milan	D 0-0	0-0			38,041
40	4	PL	A	Sheffield Wednesday	L 1-3	1-2	11	Linighan 3	(23,468)
41	8	ESC1/2	A	AC Milan	L 0-2	0-0			(23,953)
42	11	PL	H	Leicester City	D 1-1	0-0	12	Merson 52	31,373
43	21	PL	H	Nottingham Forest	W 1-0	0-0	10	Kiwomya 86	35,441
44	25	PL	A	Crystal Palace	W 3-0	2-0	8	Merson 24, Kiwomya 39, 78	(17,092)
45	M 2	ECWC3/1	H	Auxerre	D 1-1	0-0		Wright 59 (pen)	35,508
46	5	PL	H	West Ham United	L 0-1	0-1	11		36,295
47	8	PL	A	Blackburn Rovers	L 1-3	0-2	12	Morrow 49	(23,452)
48	16	ECWC3/2	A	Auxerre	W 1-0	1-0		Wright 15	(22,000)
49	19	PL	A	Newcastle United	L 0-1	0-0	13		(35,611)
50	22	PL	H	Manchester United	L 0-3	0-2	14		(43,623)
51	A 1	PL	H	Norwich City	W 5-1	3-1	10	Hartson 4, 13, Dixon 6, Merson 75, Newman 90 (og)	36,942
52	6	ECWC SF/1	H	Sampdoria	W 3-2	2-1		Bould 34, 36, Wright 69	38,089
53	8	PL	A	Queens Park Rangers	L 1-3	0-1	12	Adams 90	(16,341)
54	12	PL	H	Liverpool	L 0-1	0-0	12		38,036
55	15	PL	H	Ipswich Town	W 4-1	1-0	13	Merson 33, Wright 47, 50, 56	36,818
56	17	PL	A	Aston Villa	W 4-0	2-0	10	Hartson 31, 87, Wright 33, 72 (pen)	(32,005)
57	20	ECWC SF/2	A	Sampdoria	L 2-3	0-1		Wright 60, Schwarz 87, Won 3-2 on pens	(34,353)
58	29	PL	H	Tottenham Hotspur	D 1-1	0-0	10	Wright 61 (pen)	38,377
59	M 4	PL	H	Wimbledon	D 0-0	0-0	10		32,822
60	10	ECWC F	N	Real Zaragosa	L 1-2	0-0		Hartson 76	(42,424)
61	14	PL	A	Chelsea	L 1-2	1-1	12	Hartson 23	(29,542)

Best Home League Attendance: 38,377 v Tottenham Hotspur   **Smallest:** 27,213 v Southampton   **Av Home Att:** 35,330

Goal Scorers:

League (52): Wright 18 (3 pens), Hartson 7, Campbell 4, Merson 4, Adams 3, Kiwomya 3, Linighan 2, Schwarz 2, Smith 2, Opponents 2, Davis, Dixon, Jensen, Keown, Morrow
C/Cola Cup (11): Dickov 3, Wright 3, Adams, Campbell, Merson, Morrow, Smith
FA Cup (0):
ECW Cup (18): Wright 9 (2 pens), Bould 2. Merson 2, Schwarz 2, Hartson, Selley, Smith

Compared with 1993-94: +4,766

1	2	3	17	12	6	7	8	9	10	15	24	14	26	4	13	5	11	22	23	21	18	19	25	29	16	Referee	
Seaman	Dixon	Winterburn	Jensen	Bould	Adams	Campbell	Wright	Smith	Merson	Schwarz	Dickov	Keown	Harper	Davis	Bartram	Linighan	McGoldrick	Selley	Parlour	Morrow	Hillier	Carter	Flatts	Hughes	Hartson		
X	X	X	X		X2	X	X	X	X	X1	X			S1	S2	S										P. Durkin	1
X	X	X	X	X1	X	X	X	X	X	X1	X				S1		S	S								R. Dilkes	2
X	X	X	X1		X	X	X	X	X	X2	X			S2	S	S1										A. Wilkie	3
X	X	X	X		X2	X	X	X	X	X1	X				S	S2										K. Morton	4
X	X	X	X			X	X	X	S1	X					S	S	X1	X	X							R. Hart	5
X	X	X	X	S		X	X	X	X	X1	X			S	S	X	S	S1	X	S1						A. Marcal	6
X	X	X	X1		X	S2	X	X1	X	X	X				S			S1	X2							T. Holbron	7
X	X				X	X	X	X1	X	X			X	S	X	S1	X	X		S						D. Allison	8
X	X	X			X	S	X	X	X	X	X1			X	S	S1		X								K. Cooper	9
X	X	X	X1		X	S2	X	X	X2	X	S			S	S	X			X		S1					J. Ansuategui-Roca	10
X	X	X			X	S1	X	X	X	X	S			X1	S	X		X								M. Bodenham	11
X	X	X		X		X			X	X		X	X	X1	S		X	S	X	S	X					G. Poll	12
X	X	X	X	X		X	X	X	X1					S	S			X		S1						G. Ashby / S. Tomlin.	13
X	X	X	X1	X	X2	X	X	X	X			S2			S		S1	X								D. Gallagher	14
X	X	X	X	X	X	X	X	X	X						S	S	S	S	X							H. Muller	15
X	X	X	X		X	X	X	X	X1	X			X		S		S	X								A. Wilkie	16
X	X1	X		X	X	X2		X	X	X	S1				S		S2	X	X	S						P. Jones	17
X		X2	X	X			X	X	X1	X				X	S	S1	X	S2	X							K. Burge	18
X	X2	X	X	S2	X	S1	X1	X		X				X	S	S	S	X	X							S. Kusainov	19
X				X	X	S1		X1	X	X	X		X	X	S			X	S	S						R. Gifford	20
X		X	S1	X	X	X			S	X	X			S			X	X1	X							G. Ashby	21
X	X	X			X	X			X	X	X			S		X1			S		S1					R. Dilkes	22
X	X	X			X	S1	X			X	X			S	X1		X2		S2		X					D. Elleray	23
X	X	X	X2		X	X	X	X		S1	S2			S			X		X		X	X1				K. Morton	24
X1	X	X			X	X	X	X		S2	S3			S1		X2			X3							M. Bodenham	25
	X	X		X		X			X	X	S	X	X	X				X		X		X1				B. Hill	26
	X	X	X	X		X		X		X	X	S	X	S	X			X	X		S					G. Ashby	27
	X	X	X2	X		X		X1		X	X	S		X	S2			X	X			S1				G. Poll	28
	X	X			X	X			X	X	X	S	X	S			X	X			S1		X1			K. Morton	29
	X	X	X			X	X2	X1		X	S2	X†	S	X	S1			X								P. Danson	30
	X	X	X		X	X	X1		X	X	S		X	S1			X									G. Willard	31
X	X	X	X			X	X	S1		X		S	S	S			X	X1	X							M. Reed	32
X	X	X	X1			S2	X	X2		X	S1			S	X			X			X					D. Crick	33
X	X	X	X1			X	X			X	S2			S	X			X2	S1	X						P. Don	34
X	X	X	X2			X			X	X				S	X			X1	S2	X					X	R. Hart	35
X	X	X	X2		S1	X	X		X	X1				S	X			X	X			S2			X	D. Crick	36
X	X		X		X	X2		X		X				S	X			S1	X	X1					X	J. Worrall	37
X	X		X	X		X		X		X1				S	X			X2	X	S1					X	D. Gallagher	38
X	X	X	X2	X	X	X1	X		S1	X				S			S	S	X		S2			S	M. Van Der Ende	39
X	X	X	X1		X	X		X		X				S1	X			X2	S2						X*	K. Burge	40
X	X1	X	S	X	X	X2	X		X	X				S1	X		S	X	S2						X		41
X	X	X	X2		X	X		X		X				S1	X		X	X1	S2						X	G. Poll	42
X	X	X		X	X			X	X	S				S	X	X		S								P. Durkin	43
X	X	X1	X					X	X					S	X	X		S2		S1						K. Morton	44
X	X	X	X	X	X		X	X	X		S			S	S	X	1	S2							S1	L. Sundell	45
	X	X	X1	X			X	X	X				S		X			X	S1							B. Hill	46
	X	X		S2	X		S1	X	X				S		X	X2		X	S1	S					X1	A. Wilkie	47
X	X	X	X		X		X	X	X		X				S	S		X	S1	S					X1	N. Zhuk	48
X	X	X	X		X		X		X					S		S2		S1	S1	X					X2	G. Willard	49
	X	X			X		X		X					X	X		S		X1							K. Cooper	50
	X	X		X	X		X		X					S1	S	X			X1	X					X2	P. Jones	51
X	X	X		X	X		X1		X2	X				X		S	S	S	X	S2	X				X	J. Uilenberg	52
X	X	X		X	X		X		X					X		S			X	X1	S1				X2	P. Don	53
	X	X		X	X		X2	X	X					X		S			S2	X					S1	M. Bodenham	54
X	X	X1		X	X		X	X	X					X		S			S1						X	T. Holbrook	55
X	X	X		X	X		X2	X	X					X		S			X1	S1					X	K. Morton	56
X	X	X		X	X		X2	X	X					X		S	S	S1	S	X1					X	G. Grabher	57
X	X	X		X	X		X	X	X					X		S	S		S1						X	R. Hart	58
X	X	X	X		X		X	X	X					S		S	X	X	S						X1	R. Gifford	59
X	X2	X			X		X2	X	X					X1		S	X	S	S2	S1					X	P. Ceccarini	60
X	X		X	X		X		X		S2				S	S1			X							X	J. Worrall	61
31	39	39	24	30	27	19	30	17	24	34	4	24	3	11	13	9	10	22	11	5	2	1	1		14	League Appearances	
			1			4	1	2			5		7	1		2			4	1	2				1	League Sub Appearances	
6	5	5	1+1	5	4	5	3	3	2	4	2+2	3+2		2	+1	2	3+2	3	5	1+1	2					League Cup Appearances	
2	2	2	2	1		+1	1+1	2	1		1			1+1		2			2	1	2		+1			FA Cup Appearances	
9	9	9	5	6+1	8	1+2	9	4	8	8		5				3	1+1	1	7+1	+4	2+2				4+1	ECW Cup Appearances	

Also Played: Kiwomya S1(35,52,59),S2(37,38,46,51,53,55,56,57),S(60), Helder X(43,44,47,53,55,59),X2(46,61),X1(49,54,58),S2(57) Marshall S(26), Shaw S1(26), Clarke S1(31)McGowan 33(62)

† = Sent Off

ARSENAL

CLUB RECORDS

BIGGEST VICTORIES
League: 12-0 v Loughborough Town, Division 2, 12.3.1900.
F.A. Cup: 11-1 v Darwen, 3rd Round, 9.1.1932.
League Cup: 7-0 v Leeds United, 2nd Round, 4.9.1979.
Europe: (ECWC) 7-0 v Standard Liege, 2n Round 3.11.93.
(UEFA) 7-1 v Staevnet, 1st Round, 25.9.1963.
(Fairs Cup) 7-1 v Dinamo Bacau, Q/Final, 18.3.1970.

BIGGEST DEFEATS
League: 0-8 v Loughborough Town, Division 2, 12.12.1896.
F.A. Cup: 0-6 v Sunderland, 1st Round, 21.1.1893.
0-6 v Derby County, 1st Round, 28.1.1899.
0-6 v West Ham, 3rd Round, 5.1.1946.
League Cup: 2-6 v Manchester United, 4th Round,28.11.90.
0-3 v Liverpool, 4th Round, 8.12.1981.
Europe: (UEFA) 2-5 v Spartak Moscow, 1st Round, 29.9.82.

MOST POINTS
3 points a win: 83, 1990-91.
2 points a win: 66, 1930-31.

MOST GOALS SCORED
127, Division 1, 1930-31.
Lambert 38, Jack 31, Bastin 28, Hulme 14, James 5, Brain 4, John 2, Williams 2, Johnson 1, Roberts 1, Jones 1.

MOST GOALS CONCEDED
86, Division 1, 1926-27; Division 1, 1927-28.

MOST FIRST CLASS MATCHES IN A SEASON
70 - 1979-80 (League 42, FA Cup 11, League Cup 7, Charity Shield 1, ECWC 9).

MOST LEAGUE WINS
29, Division 1, 1970-71.

MOST LEAGUE DRAWS
18, Division 1, 1969-70.

MOST LEAGUE DEFEATS
23, Division 1, 1912-13; Division 1, 1924-25.

INDIVIDUAL CLUB RECORDS

MOST GOALS IN A SEASON
Ted Drake - 42, 1934-35.

MOST GOALS IN A MATCH
7. Ted Drake v Aston Villa, Division 1, 14.12.1935 (7-1).

OLDEST PLAYER
Jock Rutherford, 41 years 236 days v Manchester City, 20.3.1926.

YOUNGEST PLAYER
Gerry Ward, 16 years 321 days v Huddersfield, 22.8.1953.

MOST CAPPED PLAYER
Kenny Sansom (England) 77 1981-86.

BEST PERFORMANCES

League: 1930-31: Played 42, Won 29, Drawn 10, Lost 4, Goals for 127, Goals against 59, Points 66. First in Division 1.
Highest Position: Division 1 Champions.
F.A. Cup: Winners in 1929-30 v Huddersfield 2-0.
Winners in 1935-36 v Sheffield United 1-0.
Winners in 1949-50 v Liverpool 2-0.
Winners in 1970-71 v Liverpool 2-1.
Winners in 1978-79 v Manchester Utd 3-2.
Most Recent Success: 3rd Rnd, Yeovil Town (a) 3-1; 4th Rnd, Leeds United (h) 2-2, (a) 3-2 aet; 5th Rnd, Nottinghamshire Forest (h) 2-0; 6th Rnd Ipswich Town (a) 4-2; Semi-final Tottenham Hotspur 1-0; Final Sheffield Wednesday 1-1 aet, 2-1.
League Cup: Winners in 1986-87 v Liverpool 2-1.
Most Recent Success: 1992-93: 2nd Rnd Millwall (h) 1-1, (a) 1-1 (won 3-1 on pens.); 3rd Rnd, Derby County (a) 1-1, (h) 2-1; 4th Rnd, Scarborough (a) 1-0; 5th Rnd Nottingham Forest (h) 2-0; Semi-final, Crystal Palace (a) 3-1 (h) 2-0; Final Sheffield Wednesday 2-1.
Europe: (UEFA) 1969-70: 1st Rnd, Glentoran 5-0,0-1; 2nd Rnd Sp.ch.de Port 0-0,3-0; 3rd Rnd, Rouen 0-0,1-0; 4th Round Dinemo Bacau 2-0,7-1; Semi-final, Ajax 3-0,0-1; Final , Anderlect 1-3,3-0.
(ECWC) 1993-94: 1st Round Odense 2-1,1-1; 2nd Round Standard Leige 3-0,7-0; 2nd Round Torino 0-0,1-0; Semi-Final Paris St. Girman 1-1,1-0; Final Parma 1-0.

DIVISIONAL RECORD

	Played	Won	Drawn	Lost	For	Against	Points
Division 1/P	3,222	1,367	837	1018	5,165	4,292	3,831
Division 2	428	216	73	139	825	550	505
Total	3,650	1,583	910	1,157	5,990	4,842	4,336

ADDITIONAL INFORMATION
PREVIOUS NAME
None.

PREVIOUS LEAGUES
None.

Club Colours: Red with white sleeve shirts, white shorts, red and white stockings.
Change Colours: Blue with teal marked shirts, blue shorts, blue & teal stockings.

Reserve League: Football Combination.
Youth League: South Eastern Counties.

RECORDS AND STATISTICS

COMPETITIONS

Div 1/P	Div.2	Euro C	ECWC	UEFA
1904-13	1893-04	1971-72	1979-80	1963-64
1919-	1913-19	1991-92	1993-94	1969-70
			1994-95	1970-71
				1978-79
				1981-82
				1982-83

HONOURS

Div 1/P	FAC	Lge Cup	UEFA	ECWC	C/Sh'ld
1930-31	1929-30	1986-87	1969-70	1993-94	1930
1932-33	1935-36	1992-93			1931
1933-34	1949-50				1933
1934-35	1970-71				1934
1937-38	1978-79				1938
1947-48	1992-93				1948
1952-53					1953
1970-71					1992
1988-89					shared
1990-91					

MOST APPEARANCES

David O'Leary 682+40 (1975-93)
(Including 3 Charity Shield & 2 Others)

Year	League	FA Cup	Lge Cup	Europe
1975-76	27	1	2	
1976-77	33	3	4	
1977-78	41	6	6	
1978-79	37	11	1	5
1979-80	34	9	6	9
1980-81	24	1	2	
1981-82	40	1	5	4
1982-83	36	5	7	2
1983-84	36	1	4	
1984-85	36	3	3	
1985-86	35	5	7	
1986-87	39	4	9	
1987-88	23	4	6	
1988-89	26	2		
1989-90	28+6	3	4	
1990-91	11+10	5+1	0+1	
1991-92	11+14	1	0+1	1
1992-93	5+5	1+3	2	
	522+35	66+4	68+2	21

MOST GOALS IN A CAREER

Cliff Bastin - 178 (1929-37) includes 2 in Charity Shield

Year	League	FA Cup
1929-30	7	4
1930-31	28	1
1931-32	15	6
1932-33	33	
1933-34	13	2
1934-35	20	1
1935-36	11	6
1936-37	5	3
1937-38	15	2
1938-39	3	1
Total	150	26

Current top goalscorer: Ian Wright -121 (1991-1995)

MANAGERS

Name	Seasons	Best	Worst
T E Mitchell	1897-98	5(2)	5(2)
George Excoat	1898-99	7(2)	7(2)
Harry Bradshaw	1899-04	2(2)	8(2)
Phil Kelso	1904-08	6(1)	15(1)
George Morrell	1908-15	6(1)	15(1)
Leslie Knighton	1919-25	9(1)	20(1)
Herbert Chapman	1925-34	1(1)	14(1)
George Allison	1934-47	1(1)	6(1)
Tom Whittaker	1947-56	1(1)	6(1)
Jack Crayston	1956-58	5(1)	12(1)
George Swindin	1958-62	3(1)	15(1)
Billy Wright	1962-66	8(1)	17(1)
Bertie Mee	1966-76	1(1)	17(1)
Terry Neill	1976-83	3(1)	17(1)
Don Howe	1983-86	6(1)	7(1)
George Graham	1986-95	1(1)	6(1)
Bruce Rioch	1995		

RECORD TRANSFER FEE RECEIVED

Amount	Club	Player	Date
£2,000,000	Leeds United	David Rocastle	07/92
£1,500,000	Liverpool	Michael Thomas	12/91
£1,250,000	Crystal Palace	Clive Allen	08/80
£450,000	Liverpool	Ray Kennedy	07/74

RECORD TRANSFER FEE PAID

Amount	Club	Player	Date
£8,500,000	Inter Milan	Dennis Bergkamp	06/95
£2,500,000	Luton Town	Jon Hartson	01/95
£2,500,000	Crystal Palace	Ian Wright	09/91
£1,300,000	Queens Park R.	David Seaman	05/90

LONGEST LEAGUE RUNS

of undefeated matches:	26 (28.4.1990 - 19.1.1991)	of league matches w/out a win:	23 (28.9.1912 - 1.3.1913)
of undefeated home matches:	33 (1.10.1902-22.10.1904)	of undefeated away matches:	13 (5.51990 - 12.1.1991)
without home win:	16 (23.4.1912 - 1.3.1913)	without an away win:	15 (7.1.1928 - 6.10.1928)
of league wins:	10 (12.9.1987 - 14.11.1987)	of home wins:	15 (5.9.1903 - 4.4.1904)
of league defeats:	7 (12.21977 - 12.3.1977)	of away wins:	6 (22.10.1977 - 27.12.1977)

PLAYERS NAME / Honours	Ht	Wt	Birthdate	Birthplace / Transfers	Contract Date	Clubs	League	L/Cup	FA Cup	Other	Lge	L/C	FAC	Oth
G O A L K E E P E R S														
Vince Bartram	6.2	13.4	07.08.68	Birmingham	17.08.85	Wolverhampton (J)	5	2	3					
				Loan	27.10.89	Blackpool	9			2				
				£65,000	24.07.91	Bournemouth	132	10	14	6				
				£400,000	10.08.94	Arsenal	11	0+1						
Lee Harper	6.1	13.0	30.10.71	Chelsea		Sittingbourne								
				£150,000	16.06.94	Arsenal								
David Seaman E: 17, B.6, u21.10. Div.1'91. FAC'93. LC'93. FLgXI.1. ECWC'94.	6.2	13.0	10.09.63	Rotherham	22.09.81	Leeds United (A)								
				£4,000	13.08.82	Peterborough Utd	91	10	5					
				£100,000	05.10.84	Birmingham City	75	4	5					
				£225,000	07.08.86	Q.P.R.	141	13	17	4				
				£1,300,000	18.05.90	Arsenal	189	27	22	26				
D E F E N D E R S														
Tony Adams E: 35, B.4, u21.5, Y.5, S. CT'89. Div.1'89'91. LC'87'93. FAC'93. ECWC'94.	6.1	12.1	10.10.66	Romford	30.01.84	Arsenal (A)	343+3	48+1	29+1	28	23	3	5	3
Steve Bould E: 2, B.1. Div.1'89'91. CT'89. ECWC'94.	6.2	11.13	16.11.62	Stoke	15.11.80	Stoke City (A)	179+4	13	10	5	6	1		
				Loan	19.10.82	Torquay United	9		2					
				£390,000	13.06.88	Arsenal	184+8	22	17	13+3	5			2
Lee Dixon E: 21, B.4. Div.1'89'91. FLgXI.1. CT'89, FAC'93 ECWC'94.	5.9	10.12	17.03.64	Manchester	21.07.82	Burnley (J)	4	1						
				Free	16.02.84	Chester City	56+1	2	1	3	1			
				Free	15.07.85	Bury	45	4	8	1	6		1	
				£40,000	18.07.86	Stoke City	71	6	7	4	5			
				£400,000	29.01.88	Arsenal	251+3	32	26	28	16		1	
Martin Keown E: 11, B.1, u21.8, Y.4.	6.1	12.4	24.07.66	Oxford	02.02.84	Arsenal (A)	22		5					
				Loan	15.02.85	Brighton & H.A.	21+2	2		2	1	1		1
				£200,000	09.06.86	Aston Villa	109+3	12+1	6	2	3			
				£750,000	07.08.89	Everton	92+4	11	12+1	6				
				£2,000,000	04.02.93	Arsenal	62+18	6+2	3+2	9+5	1			
Andy Linighan E: B.4. LC'93. FAC'93. ECWC'94.	6.3	12.6	18.06.62	Hartlepool	19.09.80	Hartlepool United	110	7+1	8	1	4	1		1
				£200,000	15.05.84	Leeds United	66	6	2	2	3	1		
				£65,000	17.01.86	Oldham Athletic	87	8	3	4	6	2		
				£350,000	04.03.88	Norwich City	86	6	10	4	8			
				£1,250,000	04.07.90	Arsenal	74+15	11+1	12+1	7+1	4	1	1	1
Scott Marshall S: Y.S.	6.1	12.5	01.05.73	Islington	18.03.91	Arsenal (T)	2							
				Loan	03.12.93	Rotherham United	10		1		1			
				Loan	25.08.94	Sheffield United	17							
Nigel Winterburn E: 2, B.3, u21.1, Y.1. Div.1'89'91. CT'89, FLgXI.1 FAC'93. LC'93. ECWC'94.	5.10	10.7	11.12.63	Nuneaton	14.08.81	Birmingham City (A)								
				Free	22.09.83	Wimbledon	164+1	13	12	2	8			
				£407,000	26.05.87	Arsenal	271+1	35	30	30	5	3		
M I D F I E L D														
Mark Flatts E: Y.1, S.	5.6	9.8	14.10.72	Islington	28.12.90	Arsenal (T)	9+7	1	0+1					
				Loan	14.10.93	Cambridge United	5				1			
				Loan	31.12.93	Brighton & H.A.	9+1				1			
				Loan	23.03.95	Bristol City	4+2							
David Hillier E: u21.1. Div.1'91. FAYC'88.	5.10	11.6	18.12.69	Blackheath	11.02.88	Arsenal (T)	79+18	11+2	13+2	5+4	2			
Steve Hughes	6.0	12.12	18.09.76	Reading		Arsenal (T)	1							
John Jensen Danish Int. Euro'92. Danish Div.1, FAC. FAC'93.	5.11	12.4	03.05.65	Copenhagen		SV Hamburg								
						Brondby								
				£1,100,000	01.08.92	Arsenal	80+3	9+1	6+1	15	1			
Eddie McGoldrick Ei: 12, B.1. Div.4'87. FMC'91. ECWC'94	5.10	11.7	30.04.65	Islington		Kettering Town			2					
						Nuneaton Borough								
				£10,000	23.06.86	Northampton Town	97+10	9	6+1	7	9		1	1
				£200,000	10.01.89	Crystal Palace	139+8	21+1	5	13+2	11	2		3
				£1,000,000	18.06.93	Arsenal	32+5	7+2	1+1	4+4				1
Steve Morrow NI: 13, u23.1, Y, S. FAYC'88. LC'93. ECWC'94.	6.0	11.3	02.07.70	Belfast	05.05.88	Arsenal (T)	31+13	6+2	3+2	1+4	1	2		
				Loan	16.01.91	Reading	10							
				Loan	14.08.91	Watford	7+1		1					
				Loan	30.10.91	Reading	3							
				Loan	04.03.92	Barnet	1							
David Platt E: 55, B.3, u21.4.	5.10	11.12	10.06.66	Oldham		Chadderton								
					24.07.84	Manchester Utd (A)								
				Free	23.02.85	Crewe Alexandra	134	8	3	7	56	4	1	
				£200,000	02.02.88	Aston Villa	121	14	4	6	50	10	2	6
				£5,500,000	01.07.91	Bari	29				11			
				£6,500,000	01.06.92	Juventus	16				3			
						Sampdoria	55				17			
				£4,750,000	08.95	Arsenal								
Raymond Parlour E: u21.11. LC'93. ECWC'94.	5.10	11.12	07.03.73	Romford	06.03.91	Arsenal (T)	64+20	10+1	9	7+2	4		1	
Ian Selley E: u21.3, S. LC'93. FAC'93. ECWC'94.	5.9	10.1	14.06.74	Chertsey	06.05.92	Arsenal (T)	35+5	5+1	3	8+2				2

F O R W A R D S

Name	Ht	Wt	DOB	Birthplace / Fee	Date	Club								
Dennis Bergkamp	6.0	12.05	18.05.69	Amsterdam		Ajax	185				103			
Dutch Int.						Inter Milan	52				11			
				£7,500,000	08.95	Arsenal								
Adrian Clarke	5.10	11.0	28.09.74	Cambridge	06.07.93	Arsenal (T)	0+1							
E: Y.1.														
Paul Dickov	5.6	11.5	01.11.72	Livingston	28.12.90	Arsenal (T)	5+8	2+2			2	3		
S: u21.5, Y, S. ECWC'94.					Loan 08.10.93	Luton Town	8+7				1			
					Loan 23.03.94	Brighton & H.A.	8				5			
John Hartson	6.1	14.6	05.04.75	Swansea	19.12.92	Luton Town (T)	21+13	0+1	2+3	2	6		1	
W: u21.2.				£2,500,000	13.01.95	Arsenal	14+1			6+1	7			1
Glen Helder	5.11	11.7	28.10.68	Leiden (Hol)		Vitesse Arnhem								
				£2,300,000	14.02.95	Arsenal	12+1							
Chris Kiwomya	5.9	10.7	02.12.69	Huddersfield	31.03.87	Ipswich Town (T)	184+26	14	13	5+1	48	8	2	3
Div.2'92.				£1,550,000	13.01.95	Arsenal	5+9			1+2	3			
Paul Merson	5.10	11.9	20.03.68	Harlesden	01.12.85	Arsenal (A)	219+38	28+2	23+3	25+2	66	9	4	5
E: 14, B.3, u21.4, u19.3, Y. Div.1'89'91. CT'89.					Loan 22.01.87	Brentford	6+1			1+1				
LC'93. FAC'93. ECWC'94.														
Paul Shaw	5.11	12.4	04.09.73	Burnham	18.09.91	Arsenal (T)	0+1							
E: Y.1.					Loan 23.03.95	Burnley	8+1				4			
Ian Wright	5.10	11.0	03.11.63	Woolwich		Greenwich Boro								
E: 20, B.3. FMC'91. LC'93. FAC'93.				Free	02.08.85	Crystal Palace	206+19	19	9+2	19+3	90	9	3	16
				£2,500,000	24.09.91	Arsenal	129+2	18	12	18	80	16	11	15

TOP GOALSCORER 1994/95
Ian Wright

Premiership goals (games)	18 (30+1)
Coca-Cola Cup goals	3 (3)
F.A. Cup Goals	0 (2)
EUFA Cup Goals	9 (9)
Total for 1994/95	**30 (44+1)**
Total for Arsenal since 1991	121 (205+2)
Total for England (full caps only)	5 (10+10)
Career Total up to June 1995	244 (468+25)

MANAGER
BRUCE RIOCH

Date of Birth . . . . 6th September 1947
Place of Birth . . . . Aldershot
Date of Appointment . . . . June 1995

PREVIOUS CLUBS
As Manager . . . . Millwall, Middlesbrough, Bolton Wanderers
As Player/Manager . . . . Torquay United
As a Player . . . . Luton, Aston Villa, Derby, Everton, Derby, Torquay,
. . . . Birmingham (loan), Sheffield United.

HONOURS
As a Manager
Middlesbrough: Promotion to Div.2 1987, Promotion to Div.1 1988.
Bolton: Promotion to Div.1 1993. Promotion to Premiership 1995.

As a Player
Derby: Division 1 Championship 1974-75.
International: 24 full caps for Scotland.

Arsenal Stadium

Highbury, London N5 1BU
Tel: 0171 226 0304

Capacity ....39,000.
First game...v Leicester Fosse, Division 2, 6.9.1913.
First floodlit game...v Glasgow Rangers, 1951.

ATTENDANCES
Highest..73,295 v Sunderland, Div.1, 9.3.1935.
Lowest...600v Loughborough Town, Div.2, 12.3.1900.

OTHER GROUNDS ....Plumstead Common 1886-1887. Sportsman's Ground 1887-1888.
.................Manor Road 1888-1890/1893-1913. Invicta Ground 1890-1893. Highbury 1913 to date.

MATCHDAY TICKET PRICES

East & West Stand
Upper Tier Centre blocks £25
Upper Tier next to centre £18
Upper Tier wings £16
Lower Tier Centre blocks. £12.50
Lower Tier wings £11.50
North Bank Stand
Upper Tier Centre block £19
Upper Tier wings £15
Lower Tier Centre block £15
Lower Tier wings £12
Clock End Stand £11

Ticket Office Telephone No. 0171 354 5404

CLUBCALL
0898 20 20 20
Calls cost 39p per minute cheap rate and 49p per minute at all other times.
Call costings correct at time of going to press.

HOW TO GET TO THE GROUND

From the North
Leave Motorway M1 at junction 2 and follow signs to the City. In 6.2 miles pass Holloway Road Station and then take 3rd turning on left into Drayton Park Road. In 0.7 miles turn right into Avenell Road for Arsenal FC.

From the South
From London Bridge follow signs, to Bank of England, then follow signs to Angel (Islington). At traffic signals turn right (S.P. The North) and in 1 mile at Highbury roundabout forward into Holloway Road. Then take 3rd turning on right into Drayton Park Road. In 0.7 miles turn right into Avenell Road for Arsenal FC.

From the West
Leave motorway M4 at junction 1, Chiswick, and followed A315 (S.P. Chiswick). In 0.9 miles turn left A40 then follow signs to City to join motorway M41, then A40(M) at end forward into Ring Road A501. At Angel (Islington) turn left to Highbury roundabout, keep forward into Holloway Road. Then take 3rd turning on right into Drayton Park Road. In 0.7 miles turn right into Avenell Road for Arsenal FC.

Car Parking
Parking is permitted in adjacent streets with restrictions.
Nearest Railway Station
Finsbury Park and Highbury & Islington.

MATCHDAY PROGRAMME

Programme Editor . . . . Kevin Connolly.

Number of pages 48

Price £1.50

Subscriptions . . . . Subscription price on application to club shop.

Local Newspapers . . . . Islington Gazette.

Local Radio Stations . . . . Capital Radio, BBC Radio London.

ASTON VILLA
(The Villa)
F.A. CARLING PREMIERSHIP
SPONSORED BY: A.S.T. COMPUTER

Back Row (L-R): Trevor Berry, Scott Murray, Phil King, Paul Browne, Michael Oakes, Mark Bosnich, Nigel Spink, Riccardo Scimeca, Shaun Teal, Lee Hendrie, Stephen Cowe. **Middle Row:** Paul Barron, Bryan Small, Neil Davies, Paul McGrath, Gareth Southgate, Ian Taylor, Ugo Ehiogu, Gareth Farrelly, Gary Charles, David Farrell, Tommy Johnson, Jim Walker. **Front Row:** Graham Fenton, Steve Staunton, Franz Carr, Mark Draper, Allan Evans, Brian Little, John Gregory, Savo Milosevic, Dwight Yorke, Andy Townsend, Alan Wright.

**ASTON VILLA
FORMED IN 1874
TURNED PROFESSIONAL IN 1885
LTD COMPANY IN 1896**

PRESIDENT: Harold Musgrove
CHAIRMAN: Doug Ellis
DIRECTORS:
J A Alderson, Dr D H Targett,
P D Ellis, S Stride
SECRETARY: Steven Stride
(0121 327 2299)
COMMERCIAL MANAGER
Abdul Rashid (0121 327 5399)

MANAGER: Brian Little
ASSISTANT: Allan Evans

RESERVE TEAM MANAGER
John Gregory
YOUTH TEAM MANAGER
Tony McAndrew
PHYSIOTHERAPIST
Jim Walker

CLUB STATISTICIAN FOR THE DIRECTORY
Dave Hodges

10th in 1994; 18th in 1995. At first glance a season of considerable under-achievement which, in many respects, it was. But the bare facts certainly do not tell the whole story.

Under 'Big' Ron's Atkinson Villa began their championship well enough - five games without defeat (two wins and three draws) - seven goals scored and four conceded, with potential match winner Dean Saunders netting three times.

September 17th and Villa occupied a very reasonable position of 8th, and surly no-one, at this early stage,could have foreseen what traumas were to follow in the weeks and months to come.

Initially, their poor league form was more than compensated by some exciting Cup performances, none more so than in the dramatic UEFA Cup-tie with Inter Milan. 1-0 down after the first leg, Villa reversed the scoreline at home and then in a nail-biting penalty shoot-out upset the Italians 5-4. In the Coca-Cola League Cup, they easily disposed of Third Division opposition in the shape of Wigan Athletic in round Two, 8-0 on aggregate with Dwight Yorke notching four in the first encounter at Villa park.

However, in the FA Carling Premiership things were not so good. Only one in ten games between 17th September and 19th November was undoubtedly of crisis proportions. A second Round UEFA Cup reverse on the away goal rule at the hand of the unfancied Turkish outfit, Trabzonspor, hardly helped to boost the Villa men's confidence either, so it was no real surprise when Ron Atkinson left the Manager's seat, to be replaced by Jim Barron on a temporary basis and then Leicester City boss Brian Little.

With caretaker manager Barron in charge they gained a fine 4-3 away win at Tottenham, the winner coming in the 90th minute from saunders. New man Little began his reign with a 1-1 home draw with Sheffield Wednesday, but this was followed only three days later by a 4-2 4th Round Coca-Cola defeat by fellow strugglers Crystal Palace at Selhurst park. As holders of the League Cup this reverse was indeed a bitter pill to swallow.

A 3-0 home win over Chelsea during he Christmas period was just the shot-in-the-arm Brian little's troops so badly needed, and as it turned out it was the start of a seven match unbeaten run, which lifted Villa from 20th place to a much more respectable 12th place on 25th January.

A top ten position was reached towards the end of February, thanks to some notable victories, particularly the 7-1 drubbing of Wimbledon. Also Dean Saunders was beginning to find the net again - another big plus-point. In the FA Cup a Third Round dispatching of Barnsley, 2-0, kept Villa Park's hopes alive of a long Cup Run. But it was not to be with Manchester City coming out on top at Maine Road in Round Four, 1-0.

Villa's place in the premier League's top dozen lasted for less than a month, and by 16th April they were down to 16th place as in their final 13 games as a result of defeats by Chelsea (1-0) and Arsenal (4-0). In fact, in their final 13 games Villa managed two wins, but a final standing of 18th was just enough to keep them in football's top flight.

Their highest attending of over 40,000 against Liverpool was indeed proof of Villa's pulling power and it would indeed be a surprise if they were to struggle again during 1995-96. Certainly their thousands of loyal fans hope so anyway! **GREG TESSER.**

ASTON VILLA

Premier League: 18th   **FA Cup:** 4th Round   **Coca-Cola Cup:** 4th Round   **EUFA Cup:** 2nd Round

M	DATE	COMP.	VEN	OPPONENTS	RESULT	H/T	LP	GOAL SCORERS/GOAL TIMES	ATT.
1	A 20	PL	A	Everton	D 2-2	0-1	7	Fashanu 66, Saunders 75	(35,544)
2	24	PL	H	Southampton	D 1-1	1-0	12	Saunders 22	24,179
3	27	PL	H	Crystal Palace	D 1-1	1-0	12	Staunton 46	23,305
4	29	PL	A	Coventry City	W 1-0	1-0	9	Yorke 2	(12,218)
5	S 10	PL	H	Ipswich Town	W 2-0	1-0	9	Staunton 15, Saunders 85	22,241
6	15	UEFA 1/1	A	Internazionale	L 0-1	0-0	-		(22,639)
7	17	PL	A	West Ham United	L 0-1	0-0	8		(18,326)
8	21	CC 2/1	H	Wigan Athletic	W 5-0	2-0	-	Yorke 4, Atkinson 26, 85, Saunders 70, Lamptey 73	(12,433)
9	24	PL	A	Blackburn Rovers	L 1-3	0-1	9	Ehiogu 90	(22,694)
10	29	UEFA 1/2	H	Internazionale	W 1-0	1-0	-	Houghton 41, (AET) (won 5-4 on penalties)	30,533
11	O 1	PL	A	Newcastle United	L 0-2	0-0	12		29,960
12	5	CC 2/2	A	Wigan Athletic	W 3-0	1-0	-	Lamptey 43, 85, Whittingham 60	(2,633)
13	8	PL	H	Liverpool	L 2-3	1-2	14	Whittingham 37, Staunton 90	(32,158)
14	15	PL	A	Norwich City	D 1-1	0-0	15	Saunders 62	22,468
15	18	UEFA 2/1	A	Trabzonspor	L 0-1	0-0	-		(27,500)
16	22	PL	H	Nottingham Forest	L 0-2	0-1	16		29,217
17	26	CC 3	H	Middlesbrough	W 1-0	1-0	-	Townsend 30	19,254
18	29	PL	A	Queens Park Rangers	L 0-2	0-1	18		(16,073)
19	N 1	UEFA 2/2	H	Trabzonspor	W 2-1	0-0	-	Atkinson 76, Ehiogu 90, (lost on away goals)	(23,858)
20	6	PL	H	Manchester United	L 1-2	1-1	19	Atkinson 29	32,136
21	9	PL	A	Wimbledon	L 3-4	2-1	19	Parker 19, Saunders 38, 50	(6,221)
22	19	PL	A	Tottenham Hotspur	W 4-3	3-1	19	Atkinson 8, Fenton 20, 26, Saunders 90	(26,899)
23	27	PL	H	Sheffield Wednesday	D 1-1	1-0	19	Atkinson 15	25,082
24	30	CC 4	A	Crystal Palace	L 1-4	1-0	-	Atkinson 33	(12,653)
25	D 3	PL	A	Leicester City	D 1-1	0-1	19	Whittingham 61	(20,896)
26	10	PL	H	Everton	D 0-0	0-0	20		29,678
27	19	PL	A	Southampton	L 1-2	0-1	20	Houghton 80	(13,874)
28	26	PL	A	Arsenal	D 0-0	0-0	20		(34,452)
29	28	PL	H	Chelsea	W 3-0	2-0	19	Sinclair 9 (OG), Yorke 32, Taylor 82	32,901
30	31	PL	A	Manchester United	D 2-2	0-1	20	Brightwell 57 (OG), Saunders 60	(22,513)
31	J 2	PL	H	Leeds United	D 0-0	0-0	19		35,038
32	7	FAC 3	A	Barnsley	W 2-0	0-0	-	Yorke 48, Saunders 84	(11,469)
33	14	PL	H	Queens Park Rangers	W 2-1	1-0	18	Fashanu 6, Ehiogu 76	26,578
34	21	PL	A	Nottingham Forest	W 2-1	1-0	14	Fashanu 32, Saunders 67	(24,548)
35	25	PL	H	Tottenham Hotspur	W 1-0	1-0	12	Saunders 17	40,017
36	28	FAC 4	A	Manchester City	L 0-1	0-1	-		(21,177)
37	F 4	PL	A	Manchester United	L 0-1	0-1	14		(43,795)
38	11	PL	H	Wimbledon	W 7-1	4-1	13	Reeves 13 (OG), Johnson 22, 26, 38, Saunders 48, 67 (PEN), Yorke 83	(23,982)
39	18	PL	A	Sheffield Wednesday	W 2-1	2-0	9	Saunders 26,44	(24,063)
40	22	PL	H	Leicester City	D 4-4	2-0	9	Saunders 7, Staunton, 37, Yorke 59, Johnson 66	30,825
41	25	PL	A	Newcastle United	L 1-3	1-1	11	Townsend 41	(34,637)
42	M 4	PL	H	Blackburn Rovers	L 0-1	0-1	11		40,114
43	6	PL	A	Coventry City	D 0-0	0-0	10		26,186
44	18	PL	H	West Ham United	L 0-2	0-1	15		26,682
45	A 1	PL	A	Ipswich Town	W 1-0	0-0	13	Swailes 90 (OG)	(15,710)
46	4	PL	A	Crystal Palace	D 0-0	0-0	11		(12,606)
47	15	PL	A	Chelsea	L 0-1	0-1	16		(17,015)
48	17	PL	H	Arsenal	L 0-4	0-2	16		32,005
49	29	PL	A	Leeds United	L 0-1	0-0	17		(32,955)
50	M 3	PL	H	Manchester City	D 1-1	1-0	18	Ehiogu 9	30,133
51	6	PL	A	Liverpool	W 2-0	2-0	15	Yorke 25,35	40,154
52	13	PL	A	Norwich City	D 1-1	1-0	18	Staunton 7	(19,374)
53									
54									
55									
56									
57									
58									
59									
60									

Best Home League Attendance: 40,154 v Liverpool   **Smallest:** 22,241 v Ipswich Town   **Av Home Att:** 29,756

Goal Scorers:

Compared with 1993-94: +741

League (51): Saunders 15, Yorke 6, Staunton 5, Johnson 4, Opponents 4, Atkinson 3, Ehiogu 3, Fashanu 3, Fenton 2, Whittingham 2, Houghton, Parker, Taylor, Townsend
C/Cola Cup (10): Atkinson 3, Lamptey 3, Saunders, Townsend, Whittingham, Yorke
FA Cup (2): Saunders, Yorke
UEFA Cup: (3): Atkinson, Ehiogu, Houghton

1994-95

Bosnich M. (13)	Staunton S. (3)	McGrath P. (5)	Richardson K. (6)	Houghton R. (7)	Fashanu J. (8)	Saunders D. (9)	Townsend A. (11)	Parker G. (14)	Ehiogu U. (16)	Yorke D. (18)	Atkinson D. (10)	King P. (15)	Oakes M. (30)	Spink M. (1)	Barrett E. (2)	Lampey N. (12)	Teale S. (4)	Whittingham G. (22)	Fenton G. (19)	Farrell D. (21)	Boden C. (24)	Small B. (20)	Taylor I. (17)	Charles G. (22)	Johnson T. (25)	Referee	
X	X1	X	X	X	X	X	X	X	X	X	X	S	S1	S												K. Morton	1
X		X	X	X	X2	X	X	X1	X	X	S1	X		S	S1											P.Don	2
X	X	X	X	X1	X	X	X		X	S1	X	S		S	X											J. Worrall	3
X	X	X	X		X	X	X	S	X	X		X		S	X		S									P. Durkin	4
	X	X	X	X1	X	X	X	S	X	X		X		S	X											G. Willard	5
	X	X	X	S1	X1	X	X	S	X	X	X	S		X	X			S	S							P. Mikkelsen	6
X		X	X	X	X	X	X	S	X	X1	S1			S	X		X									S. Lodge	7
X	S					X	X1	X	X	X	X			S	X	X	X		S1							G. Ashby	8
X	X	X	X			X	X		X	X	X			S	X	S1•	X1		S2•							M. Bodenham	9
X		X	X2	X	S	X1	X	X		X2		X	X		S		S1									J. Quinion	10
	S2		X2			X	X	X	X			X		X	S1		X	X1								D. Gallagher	11
S	X	X					S	X		X		X	X		S	X	X	X	X	X						P. Jones	12
X	X	X			X2		X1	X	X			S1		S	X	S2	X									K. Burge	13
X	X1	X	X	S1	X			X	X	X	X2			S	X		S2									A. Wilkie	14
	X	X	X	X		X	X	S	X		S	X	S	X	X		S	X	S							M. Pirauo	15
	X	X		X		X	X	S1	X	X	X			S	X	S1	X1									K. Cooper	16
X	X	X	S	X		X	X	S	X	X	X			S	X	S1	X1									K. Morton	17
	X	X	X1	X		X	X	S1	X		X	X	S	X	X		S1									R. Hart	18
	X	X	X1	X		X	X	S1	X		X	X	S	X	X		S	S	S							J. Ullenberg	19
S	X1	X	X2		X	X	S2	X	S1		X	X		X	X											P. Don	20
X		X	S1	X1		X2	X†	X	X	X	X	X		S	X			S2								D. Elleray	21
X		X	X	X		X		X	X	X1	X	X		S	X		X		S			X				P. Durkin	22
X		X	X	X		X		X	X	X1	X	X		S	X		S1	X	S			S				G. Poll	23
X		X		X		X		X	X†	X	X1	X		S	X		S2	S1	X2							G. Willard	24
S		S2		X		X		X	X		X1			X	X		X	X	X2		S1	X				M. Bodenham	25
S		S	X	X				X	X		X1			X	X	S1	X	X	X2			X				R. Gifford	26
S		X	X	X	X	X		X		S1				X	X		X	S				X				S. Lodge	27
S	X	S1	X	X	X	X1	X†		X					X	X		X	S					X			K. Morton	28
S	X1	S1	X	X		X	X		X	X				X	X		X	S					X			K. Burge	29
	X2	S1	X	X	S2	X	X1		X	X			S	X	X		X	S					X			J. Worrall	30
	X	X	X1	S1		X		X	X		S			X	X		X	S					X			P. Danson	31
S	X	X	S	S	X	X	X		X	X				X	X		X	X					X			R. Dilkes	32
X	X	X		S1	X1	X		X	X			S			X		X	X					X	S	X	A. Wilkie	33
X	X	X		S1	X	X		X	X1					S	X		X						X	S2	X2	K. Cooper	34
X	X	X		S1	X	X		X	X2					S	X		X						X	S2	X1	R. Hart	35
X	X	X		S	X	X		X	X1					S	X		X						X		S1	J. Worrall	36
X	X	X		S2	X1	X		X	X2					S	X		X					X	X	X	S1	D. Elleray	37
X	X	X	S			X	X		X	X				S	X		X		S			X	X	X	X	B. Hill	38
X	X	X				X	X	X	X	X2	S1			S	X		X					X	X	X1		D. Gallagher	39
X	X	X				X	X	X	X	X				S	X		X					X	X	X		K. Morton	40
X	X	X		S		X	X	X	X	S1				S	X		X1					X	X	X		P. Don	41
X	X	X		S1		X	X1	X	X					S	X		X		S2			X	X	X2		R. Gifford	42
X	X	X		X2		X		X	X					S	X		X		S1			X	X	X1		G. Poll	43
X	X	X		S1		X		X	S2	X2				S	X		X					X	X	X1		M. Bodenham	44
X	X	X				X1	X		X	X	S1			S	X		X					X	X	X		J. Worrall	45
X	X1	X				X		X	X	X	X			S	X		X		S1			X	X	X		K. Cooper	46
X	X	X				X		X	X	X	X1			S	X		X		S2			X	X		S1	K. Burge	47
X	X	X				X		X	X	X	X			S	X		X		S			X	X	S	X	K. Morton	48
X†	X	X				X	X1		X	X2				S2			X		S1			X	X	S	X	D. Elleray	49
X	X	X				X		X	X	X				S			X		S			X	X	S	X	S. Lodge	50
X	X1	X				X		X	X	X				S			X		S1			X	X	S	X	R. Hart	51
	X	X				X1	X		X	X		S2	S	X			X		X2				X	S1		K. Cooper	52
																											53
																											54
																											55
																											56
																											57
																											58
																											59
																											60
30	34	36	18	19	11	39	32	12	38	33	11	13		12	24	1	28	4	7			5	22	14	11	League Appearances	
1	4		1	7	2			2	1	4	5	3		1	1	5		3	10	1				2	3	Substitute Appearances	
3	2	3		2		3	2	4	3	4	2	3	1		3	2+1	2	2+1	1+2	2						C/Cola Appearances	
1	2	2		2	2	2		2	2					1	2		2						2		0+1	FA Cup Appearances	
4	4	4	3+1	1	4	4	0+2	4		3	4			4	4		1+1									UEFA Cup Appearances	

Also Played: F. Carr, A. Wright

ASTON VILLA

CLUB RECORDS

BIGGEST VICTORIES
League: 12-2 v Accrington, Division 1, 12.3.1892.
11-1 v Charlton Athletic, Division 2, 24.11.1959.
10-0 v Sheffield Wednesday, Division 1, 5.10.1912.
10-0 v Burnley, Division 1, 29.8.1925.
7-1 v Wimbledon, Premier Division, 11.2.1995.
F.A. Cup: 13-0 v Wednesday Old Athletic, 3.10.1886
League Cup: 8-1 v Exeter City, Round 2 2nd leg, 7.10.1985.
Europe: 5-0 v Valur, Round 1, 16.9.1981.

BIGGEST DEFEATS
League: 0-7 v Blackburn Rovers, Division 1, 19.10.1989.
0-7 v Everton, Division 1, 4.1.1890.
0-7 v West Bromwich Albion, Division 1, 19.10.1935.
0-7 v Manchester United, Division 1, 8.3.1950.
0-7 v Manchester United, Division 1, 24.10.1964.
F.A. Cup: 1-8 v Blackburn Rovers, Round 3, 16.2.1889.
League Cup: 1-6 v West Bromwich Albion, Round 2, 14.9.1966.
Europe: (UEFA) 1-4 v Antwerp, Round 2, 17.9.1975.
0-3 v Inter Milan, Round 2, 17.11.1990.

MOST POINTS
3 points a win: 78, Division 2, 1987-88.
2 points a win: 70, Division 3, 1971-72. (Division 3 record)

MOST GOALS
128, 1930/31 (Division 1 record).
Waring 49, Houghton 30, Walker 15, Beresford 14, Mandley 8, Brown 5, Chester 3, Gibson 2, Talbot 1, Tate 1.

MOST LEAGUE GOALS CONCEDED
110, Division 1, 1935-36.

MOST FIRST CLASS MATCHES IN A SEASON
61 (42 League, 3FA Cup, 6 League Cup, 1 Charity Shield, 9 European Cup) 1981-82.

MOST LEAGUE WINS
32, Division 3, 1971-72.

MOST LEAGUE DRAWS
17, Division 1, 1975-76.

MOST LEAGUE DEFEATS
24, Division 1, 1966-67.

INDIVIDUAL CLUB RECORDS

MOST GOALS IN A SEASON
Tom 'Pongo' Waring, 50 (49 League, 1 FA Cup) 1930-31.

MOST GOALS IN A MATCH
5, Harry Hampton v Sheffield Wednesday 10-0, 5.10.1912.
5, Harold Halse v Derby County 5-1, 19.10.1912.
5, Len Capwell v Burnley 10-0, 29.8.1925.
5, George Brown v Leicester 8-3, 2.1.1932.
5, Gerry Hitchens v Charlton Athletic 11-1, 18.11.1959.

OLDEST PLAYER
Ernie Callaghan, 39 years 257 days v Grimsby Town, Division 1, 12.4.1947.

YOUNGEST PLAYER
Jimmy Brown, 15 years 349 days v Bolton (a), 17.9.1969.

MOST CAPPED PLAYER
Paul McGrath (Republic of Ireland) 34.
David Platt (England) 22.

BEST PERFORMANCES

League: Division 3 Champions 1971-72: Matches played 46, Won 32, Drawn 6, Lost 8, Goals for 88, Goals against 32, Points 70.
Highest: Division 1 Champions.

F.A. Cup: Winners in 1886-87 v West Bromwich Albion 2-0.
1894-95 v West Bromwich Albion 1-0.
1896-97 v Everton 3-2.
1904-05 v Newcastle United 2-0.
1912-13 v Sunderland 1-0.
1919-20 v Huddersfield Town 1-0.
Most recent success: 1956-57: 3rd Rnd. Luton Town 2-2, 2-0; 4th Rnd. Middlesbrough 3-2; 5th Rnd. Bristol City 2-1; 6th Rnd. Burnley 1-1, 2-0; Semi-Final West Bromwich Albion 2-2, 1-0; Final Manchester United 2-1.

League Cup: Winners in 1960-61 v Rotherham 0-2, 3-0.
1974-75 v Norwich City 1-0.
1976-77 v Everton 0-0, 1-1, 3-2.
Most recent success: 1993-94: 2nd Rnd. Birmingham City 1-0, 1-0; 3rd Rnd. Sunderland 4-1; 4th Rnd. Arsenal 1-0; 5th Rnd. Tottenham Hotspur 2-1; Semi-Final Tranmere 1-3, 3-1 (5-4 on pens.); Final Manchester United 3-1.

Europe: (EC) 1981-82: 1st Rnd. Valur 5-0, 2-0; 2nd Rnd. Dynamo Berlin 2-1, 0-1; 3rd Rnd. Dynamo Kiev 0-0, 2-0; Semi-Final Anderlecht 1-0, 0-0; Final Bayern Munich 1-0.

DIVISIONAL RECORD

	Played	Won	Drawn	Lost	For	Against	Points
Division 1/P	3,272	1,374	731	1,167	5,645	5,086	3,668
Division 2	422	179	111	132	617	487	491
Division 3	92	51	21	20	139	78	123
Total	3,786	1,604	863	1,319	6,401	5,651	4,282

ADDITIONAL INFORMATION
PREVIOUS NAME
None.

PREVIOUS LEAGUES
None

Club Colours: Claret shirts with light blue sleeves, light blue & yellow trim, white shorts claret & blue trim, claret socks light blue trim.
Change Colours: Navy blue shirts, light blue & red trim, light blue shorts, navy blue socks light blue trim.

Reserve League: Pontins Central League Division 2.
Youth League: Midland Purity Youth League.

RECORDS AND STATISTICS

COMPETITIONS

Div 1/P	Div.2	Div.3	Euro C.	UEFA	W.C.C.
1888-36	1936-38	1970-72	1981-82	1975-76	1982-83
1938-59	1959-60		1982-83	1977-78	
1960-67	1967-70			1983-84	
1975-87	1972-75		E S Cup	1990-91	
1988-	1987-88		1982-83		

HONOURS

Div 1/P	Div.2	Div.3	FAC	Lge Cup	Euro C.
1893-94	1937-38	1971-72	1887	1961	1981-82
1895-96	1959-60		1895	1975	
1896-97			1897	1977	E.S.C.
1898-99			1905	1994	1982-83
1899-00			1913		
1909-10			1920	C/Sh'ld	
1980-81			1957	1981	

MOST APPEARANCES

CHARLIE AITKEN 656+3 (1960-76)

Year	League	FA Cup	Lge Cup	Europe
1960-61	1			
1961-62	35	4	3	
1962-63	42	3	8	
1963-64	34	2	1	
1964-65	42	5	6	
1965-66	42	1	5	
1966-67	39	2	1	
1967-68	30+2	2	1	
1968-69	42	4	1	
1969-70	31	1	2	
1970-71	44	1	10	
1971-72	43	1	6	
1972-73	33	1	4	
1973-74	38	4	1	
1974-75	42	3	10	
1975-76	21	0+1	2	2
	559+2	34+1	61	2

MOST GOALS IN A CAREER

BILLY WALKER - 244 (1919-1934)

Year	League	FA Cup
1919-20	8	5
1920-21	27	4
1921-22	21	6
1922-23	23	0
1923-24	14	3
1924-25	19	6
1925-26	21	1
1926-27	15	0
1927-28	10	1
1928-29	19	0
1929-30	8	3
1930-31	15	1
1931-32	9	0
1932-33	5	0
1933-34	0	0
Total	214	30

Current top goalscorer: Dwight Yorke - 35 (1990-95)

RECORD TRANSFER FEE RECEIVED

Amount	Club	Player	Date
£5,500,000	Bari	David Platt	7/91
£1,750,000	Wolves	Andy Gray	9/79
£200,000	Derby County	Bruce Rioch	3/74
£100,000	Chelsea	Tony Hateley	10/66

RECORD TRANSFER FEE PAID

Amount	Club	Player	Date
£3,500,000	Partizen Belgrade	Savo Milosevic	7/95
£2,500,000	Crystal Palace	Gareth Southgate	7/95
£2,100,000	Chelsea	Andy Townsend	7/93
£2,100,000	Liverpool	Dean Saunders	9/92

MANAGERS

Name	Seasons	Best	Worst
Jim McMullen	1934-36	13(1)	21(1)
Jim Hogan	1936-39	12(1)	9(2)
Alex Massie	1945-50	6(1)	12(1)
George Martin	1950-53	6(1)	15(1)
Eric Houghton	1953-58	6(1)	20(1)
Joe Mercer	1958-64	7(1)	1(2)
Dick Taylor	1964-67	16(1)	21(1)
Tony Cummings	1967-68	16(2)	16(2)
Arthur Cox (CT)	1968		
Tommy Docherty	1968-70	18(2)	21(2)
Vic Crowe	1970-74	3(2)	4(3)
Ron Saunders	1974-82	1(1)	2(2)
Tony Barton	1982-84	6(1)	11(1)
Graham Turner	1984-86	10(1)	16(1)
Billy McNeil	1986-87		
Graham Taylor	1987-90	2(1)	2(2)
Jozef Venglos	1990-91	17(1)	17(1)
Ron Atkinson	1991-94	2(P)	10(P)
Brain LIttle	1994-	18(P)	18(P)

LONGEST LEAGUE RUNS

of undefeated matches:	15 (16.1.1897 - 18.9.1897)	of league matches w/out a win:	12 (10.11.73 - 2.2.74)
	(18.12.1890 - 26.3.1910. 12.3.1949 - 27.8.1949)		(27.12. 1986 - 25.3.1987)
of undefeated home matches:	37 (24.4.1909 - 22.4.1911)	of undefeated away matches:	13 (5.9.1987 - 23.1.1988)
without home win:	8 (11.12.1920 - 28.3.1921)	without an away win:	27 (21.9. 1963 - 26.12.1964)
of league wins:	9 (22.3. - 18.9.1897. 15.10. - 10.12.1910)	of home wins:	14 (10.1.1903 - 25.11.1903)
of league defeats:	11 (22.3. 1963 - 4.4. 1963)	of away wins:	6 (6.2.1897 - 11.9. 1897)

ASTON VILLA

PLAYERS NAME Honours	Ht	Wt	Birthdate	Birthplace Transfers	Contract Date	Clubs	APPEARANCES				GOALS			
							League	L/Cup	FA Cup	Other	Lge	L/C	FAC	Oth
G O A L K E E P E R S														
Mark Bosnich	6.2	13.7	13.01.72	Sydney (Aus)		Sydney Croatia								
Australian Int. LC'94.				Free	05.06.89	Manchester United	3							
						Sydney Croatia								
				Free	28.02.92	Aston Villa	76	10+1	5	2				
Michael Oakes	6.1	12.6	30.10.73	Northwich	16.07.91	Aston Villa (J)		1						
E: u21.5.				Loan	26.11.93	Scarborough	1			1				
Nigel Spink	6.2	14.6	08.08.58	Chelmsford		Chelmsford								
E: 1, B.2. EC'82. ESC'82. LC'94. FLgXI.				£4,000	01.01.77	Aston Villa	357+2	45	28	25+1				
D E F E N D E R S														
Paul Browne	6.1	12.0	17.02.75	Glasgow	07.07.93	Aston Villa (T)								
Gary Charles	5.9	11.2	13.04.70	Newham	07.11.87	Nottingham F. (T)	54+2	9	8+2	4+2	1		1	
E: 2, u21.6. FMC'92.				Loan	16.03.89	Leicester City	5+3							
				£750,000	29.07.93	Derby County	61	5+1	1	9	3			
				£1.450,000	06.01.95	Aston Villa	14+2							
Ugochuku Ehiogu	6.1	12.0	03.11.72	Hackney	13.07.89	West Brom. A. (T)	0+2							
E: u21.15.				£40,000	12.07.91	Aston Villa	57+11	4+1	2+2	5	3			1
Phillip King	5.8	11.9	28.12.67	Bristol	07.01.85	Exeter City (A)	24+3	1		1+2				
				£3,000	14.07.86	Torquay United	24	2	1	2	3			
				£155,000	06.02.87	Swindon Town	112+4	11	5	13	4			
				£400,000	30.11.89	Sheffield Wed.	124+5	17	9	4	2			
				Loan	22.10.93	Notts County	6			2				
				£250,000	01.08.94	Aston Villa	13+3	3		4				
Paul McGrath	6.0	14.0	04.12.59	Ealing		St Patricks								
Ei: 76. FAC'85. LC'94. FLgXI.				£30,000	30.04.82	Manchester United	159+4	13	15+2	9	12	2	2	
				£400,000	03.08.89	Aston Villa	219+4	24	20	15	7	1		
Riccardo Scimeca	6.1	12.09	13.06.75	Leamington	07.07.93	Aston Villa								
Steve Staunton	5.11	11.2	19.01.69	Dundalk		Dundalk								
Ei: 59, u21.4. Div.1'90. FAC'89. CS'89. LC'94.				£20,000	02.09.86	Liverpool	55+10	6+2	14+2	1		4	1	1
				Loan	13.11.87	Bradford City	7+1	2		1				
				£1,100,000	07.08.91	Aston Villa	137+1	14	14	6	13			
Alan Wright	5.4	9.4	28.09.71	Ashton-u-Lyne	13.04.89	Blackpool (T)	91+7	10+2	8	11+2				
E: u21.2, Y, S.				£400,000	25.10.91	Blackburn Rovers	67+7	8+1	5	3	1			
				£1,000,000	10.04.95	Aston Villa	8							
M I D F I E L D														
Mark Draper	5.10	11.0	11.11.70	Long Eaton	12.12.88	Notts County (T)	206+16	14+1	10	21+2	40	2	2	5
E: u21.3.				£1,250,000	22.07.94	Leicester City								
				£3,250,000	08.95	Aston Villa								
Gareth Farrelly	6.0	12.07	28.08.75	Dublin		Home Farm								
					21.09.92	Aston Villa								
				Loan	21.03.95	Rotherham United	9+1			2				
Gareth Southgate	5.10	12.03	03.09.70	Watford	17.01.89	Crystal Palace (T)	148+4	23+1	9	6	15	7		
Div.1'94.				£2.500,000	23.06.95	Aston Villa								
Ian k Taylor	6.1	12.4	04.06.68	Birmingham		Moor Green								
AGT'93.				£15,000	13.07.92	Port Vale	83	4	6	13	28	2	1	4
				£1,000,000	12.07.94	Sheffield Wed.								
				£1,000,000	21.12.94	Aston Villa	22		2		1			
Andy Townsend	5.11	12.7	27.07.63	Maidstone		Welling United								
Ei: 54. LC'94.				£13,500		Weymouth			1					
				£35,000	15.01.85	Southampton	77+6	7+1	2+3	3+2	5			
				£300,000	31.08.88	Norwich City	66+5	3+1	10	3	8		2	
				£1,200,000	05.07.90	Chelsea	110	17	7	4	12	7		
				£2,100,000	26.07.93	Aston Villa	64	10	5	8	4	1		1
F O R W A R D S														
Franz Carr	5.7	10.12	24.09.66	Preston	30.07.84	Blackburn Rov. (A)								
E: u21.9. Y.4, u19.1. LC'90. SC'89. Div.1'93.				£100,000	02.08.84	Nottingham Forest	122+9	16+2	4	5+2	17	5		1
				Loan	22.12.89	Sheffield Wed.	9+3	2						
				Loan	11.03.91	West Ham United	1+2							
				£250,000	13.06.91	Newcastle United	20+5	2+2		3+1	3			
				£120,000	12.01.93	Sheffield United	18		4	1	5			
				£100,000	08.10.94	Leicester City	12+1				1			
				£250,000	10.02.95	Aston Villa	0+2							

ASTON VILLA

PLAYERS NAME Honours	Ht	Wt	Birthdate	Birthplace Transfers	Contract Date	Clubs	League	L/Cup	FA Cup	Other	Lge	L/C	FAC	Oth
David Farrell	5.11	11.9	11.11.71	Birmingham		Redditch								
				£45,000	06.01.92	Aston Villa	5+1	2						
				Loan	25.01.93	Scunthorpe United	4+1			2	1			
Graham Fenton	5.10	11.9	22.05.74	Wallsend	13.02.92	Aston Villa (T)	16+13	2+3			3			
LC'94.				Loan	10.01.94	West Bromwich A.	7				3			
Tommy Johnson	5.10	10.6	15.01.71	Newcastle-u-T.	19.01.89	Notts County (T)	100+18	7+2	3+2	14+3	47	5	1	4
E: u21.7.				£1,300,000	12.03.92	Derby County	91+7	9+1	5	16	30	2	1	8
				£1,450,000	06.01.95	Aston Villa	11+3		0+1		4			
Savo Milosevic						Parison Belgrade								
				£3,500,000	08.95	Aston Villa								
Dwight Yorke	5.10	11.12	03.11.71	Canaan (Tobago)		Signal Hill (Tobago)								
T&T. 20.				£120,000	19.12.89	Aston Villa	92+36	9+2	13+2	1	27	1	7	1

Top Goalscorer 1994/95
Dean Saunders

Premiership goals (games)	15 (39)
Coca-Cola Cup goals	1 (3)
F.A. Cup Goals	1 (2)
EUFA Cup Goals	0 (4)
Total for 1994/95	**17 (48)**

Total for Aston Villa 1992-95 . . . . 50 (143+1)
Career Total up to June 1995 . . . . 202 (534+20)

THE MANAGER
BRIAN LITTLE

Date of Birth . . . . 25th November 1953
Place of Birth . . . . Newcastle upon Tyne
Date of Appointment . . . . November 1994

PREVIOUS CLUBS
As Manager . . . . Darlington, Wolverhampton Wanderers, Leicester City
As Coach . . . . Wolverhampton Wanderers
As a Player . . . . Aston Villa

HONOURS
As a Manager
Darlington: GM Vauxhall Conference Championship 1989-90.
Division Four Championship 1990-91
Leicester: Promotion to Premier League 1993-94.

As a Player
Promotion to Div. 1 1975, League Cup Winners 1975 & 1977, FA Youth Cup Winners 1972.
International: 1 Full Cap and Youth for England.

Villa Park

Trinity Road, Birmingham B6 6HE
Tel: 0121 327 2299

Capacity ....40,000.
First game..v Blackburn, Div.1, 17.4.1897 (3-0).
First floodlit game...v Portsmouth, Div.1, 25.8.1958 (3-2).
Internationals played at Villa Park...England v Scotland 8.4.1899, 3.5.1902, 8.4.1922.
v Wales 10.11.1948, 26.11.1958. v Ireland 14.11.1951. Argentina v Spain 13.7.1966. v W.Germany 16.7.1966.
....Spain v W.Germany 20.7.1966. Brazil v Sweden 4.6.95.

ATTENDANCES
Highest ....76,588 v Derby Co. FAC 6th Rnd, 2.3.1946.
Lowest ....2,900 v Bradford City, Div.1. 13.2.1915 (0-0).

OTHER GROUNDS...Aston Park 1874-96. Perry Bar 1876-1897.Villa Park 1897-

---

HOW TO GET TO THE GROUND

From North, East, South and West
Use Motorway, M6, junction 6.
Leave motorway and follow signs to Birmingham (NE).
Shortly at roundabout take fourth exit, A38 (Sign posted Aston).
In half a mile turn right into Aston Hall Road for Aston Villa FC.

Car Parking
Asda Park in Aston Hall Road, a Park & Ride. Street Parking also available.

Nearest Railway Station: Witton or Aston

CLUBCALL
0891 12 11 48
Calls cost 39p per minute cheap rate and 49p per minute at all other times.
Call costings correct at time of going to press.

MATCHDAY TICKET PRICES

North Stand £13
Juv/OAP £6.50

Holte End Upper £13
Juv/OAP £6.50
Lower £12
Juv/OAP £5

Trinity Road Upper. £15
Juv/OAP £8
Trinity Road Lower Tier £13
Juv/OAP £7

Doug Ellis Stand Upper £15
Juv/OAP £8
Doug Ellis Stand Lower £13
Juv/OAP £7

Ticket Office Telephone No. 0121 327 5353

Credit Card Ticket Sales 0121 327 7373

MATCHDAY PROGRAMME

Programme Editor . . . . Bernard Gallagher.

Number of pages. 32

Price £1.20

Subscriptions . . . . £43 within the UK.

Local Newspapers. . . . . Birmingham Post & Mail, Sports Argus,
. . . . Express & Star, Daily News, Sunday Mercury.

Local Radio Stations . . . . BRMB, BBC Radio W.M, Xtra. AM.

BLACKBURN ROVERS
(The Rovers)
F.A. CARLING PREMIERSHIP
SPONSORED BY: MCEWANS

Back Row (L-R): Paul Warhurst, Nick Marker, Paul Harford, Ian Pearce, Colin Hendry, Chris Sutton, Mike Newell, Robbie Slater (new West Ham). **Middle Row:** Steve Foster (Physio), Lee Makel, Stuart Ripley, Jason Wilcox, Bobbie Mimms, Tim Flowers, Shay Given, Richard Witschge, Jeff Kenna, Graeme Le Saux, Tony Parkes (Chief Coach). **Front Row:** Henning Berg, Kevin Gallacher, Alan Shearer, Ray Harford (Manager), Kenny Dalglish (Director of Football), Tim Sherwood, David Batty, Mark Atkins.

BLACKBURN ROVERS
FORMED IN 1875
TURNED PROFESSIONAL IN 1880
LTD COMPANY IN 1897

PRESIDENT: W H Bancroft
SENIOR VICE PRESIDENT: J Walker
CHAIRMAN: R D Coar, BSC

DIRECTORS
T W Ibbotson
(Vice Chairman & Managing Director)

SECRETARY
John Howath FAA

COMMERCIAL MANAGER
Ken Beamish

DIRECTOR OF FOOTBALL
Kenny Dalglish
MANAGER: Ray Harford

YOUTH TEAM MANAGER
Jim Furnell

STATISTICIAN FOR THE DIRECTORY
Harry Berry

Blackburn dramatically won their first championship for 81 years by a single point on the last day of the season. If the pressure eventually got to them, as seven points from the final six games would suggest, it is axiomatic that they had gained sufficient points by the start of April to weather the storm. Despite being on the wrong end of controversial refereeing decisions in both games against Manchester United, that produced a potential swing of nine points in Unitedís favour, the title eventually went to a team that prospered on hard work, an absence of ego and the capability to play efficiently and effectively on a regular basis.

The team was forced to change itís style due to the absence of the chief playmaker David Batty for most of the season, and due to the need to accommodate their five million pound signing Chris Sutton into the attack. Sutton possessed different qualities from Mike Newell, who he replaced, and who had bought width to their play by drifting wide to the wings. Changes being necessary the club opted for a more direct style, getting the ball forward earlier into the channels where Shearer and Sutton operated. The media criticised this simple style of football, overlooking the fact that the team were the Premiershipís top scorers. Ripley and Wilcox had to contribute significantly to succeed the wide players, but half way through the season injuries either hampered them or kept them out altogether. Natural replacements were on hand for neither and the only solution was hard work and application.

The club experienced a series of set backs which would have unhinged a lesser team. The defection of David May to Manchester United was first covered by the dramatic recycling of veteran Tony Gale, and after experiments involving Berg and the versatile Paul Warhurst, by the unexpected blossoming of Ian Pearce. Midfield without Batty was a more troublesome area. Initially Australian Robbie Slater did well but gave way to the varied talents of Warhurst. When he lost out Dalglish elected to go with the long serving Mark Atkins, underestimated by many he proved utterly reliable, played to the system, getting goal side of his man and defending the last third of the field and demonstrated his intelligence by making forward runs that contributed six goals. However, the creative force was sometimes lacking in mid-field and without the key widemen Ripley and Wilcox and supply of chances waned. To compensate Sutton willingly dropped back to assist in mid-field and this undoubtedly led to his goal starvation.

The team was hampered by injuries to key players, including Ripley, Wilcox, Warhurst, Gallacher, Newell who missed the early months of the season, and Batty who missed almost all of it. These injuries, the early defeats in the FA Cup to Newcastle and the UEFA Cup to Trelleborgs, the television proved injustice of refereeing decisions against Manchester United and late equalising goals conceded against Newcastle and Leeds (twice), and Alex Fergusonís psychological pressure in the form of taunts and jeers during the nervous final weeks of the season could have undermined moral. However, they emerged breathless but deserved champions looking out towards a future in Europe. Kenny Dalglish, already recognised as one of the gameís greatest influences, proved himself to be legendary by taking a Second Division team to the Premiership title in just four years. He has always acknowledged his reliance and debt to his right hand man Ray Harford, and it is nice to see that in the new all seater Ewood there is still a place for that great club man Tony Parkes.

Finally a word for the man whose money was rewarded with his dream, Jack Walker. Despite his immense wealth his commitment to the club has been staggering. No-one could have envisaged that even with the amount that he had invested he could bring back the title to his home-town. Unlike other entrepreneurs he makes no great pronouncements about the game nor does he attempt to control events. He chose a manager, granted him the funds and sat back. In doing so he wrote a page that history will not forget. **HARRY BERRY.**

BLACKBURN ROVERS

Premier Division: 1st   **FA Cup:** 3rd Round   **Coca-Cola Cup:** 4th Round

M	DATE	COMP.	VEN	OPPONENTS	RESULT	H/T	LP	GOAL SCORERS/GOAL TIMES	ATT.
1	A 20	PL	A	Southampton	D 1-1	0-1		Shearer 61	(14,209)
2	23	PL	H	Leicester	W 3-0	1-0		Sutton 18, Berg 59, Shearer 73	21,050
3	27	PL	H	Coventry	W 4-0	0-0		Sutton 67, 74, 88, Wilcox 77	21,657
4	31	PL	A	Arsenal	D 0-0	0-0	7		(37,629)
5	S 10	PL	H	Everton	W 3-0	2-0	3	Shearer 17, 60 (pen), Wilcox 43	26,538
6	18	PL	A	Chelsea	W 2-1	1-0	2	Johnsen 26 (OG), Sutton 65	(17,513)
7	20	CC 1/2	H	**Birmingham City**	W 2-0	0-0		**Wilcox 55, Sutton 68**	**14,517**
8	24	PL	H	Aston Villa	W 3-1	1-0	2	Shearer 17 (pen), 72, Sutton 56	22,694
9	O 1	Pl	A	Norwich	L 1-2	1-1	2	Sutton 4	(18,146)
10	4	CC 2/2	A	**Birmingham City**	D 1-1	0-1		**Sutton 71**	**(16,275)**
11	9	PL	A	Newcastle United	D 1-1	0-0	2	Shearer 59 (pen)	(34,344)
12	15	PL	H	Liverpool	W 3-2	0-1	2	Atkins 52, Sutton 57, 72,	30,263
13	23	PL	H	Manchester United	L 2-4	1-1	4	Warhurst 13, Hendry 51	30,260
14	27	CC 3	H	**Coventry City**	W 2-0	0-0		**Shearer 54, 63**	**14,538**
15	29	PL	A	Nottingham Forest	W 2-0	1-0	4	Sutton 7, 68	(22,131)
16	N 2	PL	A	Sheffield Wednesday	W 1-0	0-0	2	Shearer 53	(24,297)
17	5	PL	H	Tottenham Hotspur	W 2-0	0-0	2	Wilcox 8, Shearer 49 (pen)	26,933
18	19	PL	A	Ipswich	W 3-1	2-1	2	Sutton 8, Sherwood 30, Shearer 70	(17,329)
19	26	PL	H	Queens Park Rangers	W 4-0	1-0	1	Sutton 9, Shearer 56, 66 (pen), 89	21,302
20	30	CC 4	H	**Liverpool**	L 1-3	0-1		**Sutton 89**	**30,115**
21	D 3	PL	A	Wimbledon	W 3-0	0-0	1	Atkins 52, Wilcox 72, Shearer 74	(12,341)
22	10	PL	H	Southampton	W 3-2	2-0	1	Atkins 6, Shearer 13,74	23,372
23	17	PL	A	Leicester	D 0-0	0-0	1		(20,559)
24	26	PL	H	Manchester City	W 3-1	2-1	1	Shearer 9, Atkins 16, Le Saux 67	(23,397)
25	31	PL	A	Crystal Palace	W 1-0	0-0	1	Sherwood 66	(14,232)
26	J 2	PL	H	West Ham United	W 4-2	1-0	1	Shearer 14 (pen), 75, 79 (pen), Le Saux 61	25,503
27	8	FAC 3	A	**Newcastle United**	D 1-1	1-0	1	**Sutton 31**	**(31,721)**
28	14	PL	H	Nottingham Forest	W 3-0	0-0	1	Warhurst 54, Wilcox 78, Chettle 88 (OG)	27,510
29	18	FAC 3	H	**Newcastle**	L 1-2	0-0	1	**Sutton 75**	**22,658**
30	22	PL	A	Manchester United	L 0-1	0-0	1		(43,742)
31	28	PL	H	Ipswich	W 4-1	2-0	1	Shearer 3, 29, 90 (pen), Sherwood 49	21,325
32	F 1	PL	H	Leeds	D 1-1	1-0	1	Shearer 6 (pen)	28,561
33	5	PL	A	Tottenham Hotspur	L 1-3	0-2	1	Sherwood 47	(28,124)
34	12	PL	H	Sheffield Wednesday	W 3-1	2-1	1	Sherwood 28, Atkins 35, Shearer 66	22,223
35	22	PL	H	Wimbledon	W 2-1	2-1	1	Shearer 3, Atkins 25	20,586
36	25	PL	A	Norwich	D 0-0	0-0	1		25,579
37	M 4	PL	A	Aston Villa	W 1-0	1-0	1	Hendry 12	(40,114)
38	8	PL	H	Arsenal	W 3-1	2-0	1	Shearer 4, 48 (pen), Le Saux 18	23,452
39	11	PL	A	Coventry City	D 1-1	0-1	1	Shearer 87	(18,547)
40	18	PL	H	Chelsea	W 2-1	2-1	1	Shearer 16, Sherwood 37	25,490
41	A 1	PL	A	Everton	W 2-1	2-1	1	Sutton 1, Shearer 2	(37,900)
42	4	PL	A	Queens Park Rangers	W 1-0	0-0	1	Sutton 68	(16,508)
43	15	PL	A	Leeds	D 1-1	1-0	1	Hendry 44	(39,426)
44	17	PL	H	Manchester City	L 2-3	1-1	1	Shearer 7, Hendry 39	27,851
45	20	PL	H	Crystal Palace	W 2-1	0-0	1	Kenna 47, Gallagher 51	28,005
46	30	PL	A	West Ham United	L 0-2	0-0	1		(24,202)
47	M 8	PL	H	Newcastle	W 1-0	1-0	1	Shearer 29	30,545
48	14	PL	A	Liverpool	L 1-2	1-0	1	Shearer 17	(40,014)
49									
50									
51									
52									
53									
54									
55									
56									
57									
58									
59									
60									

Best Home League Attendance: 30,545 v Newcastle United   **Smallest:** 20,586 v Wimbledon   **Av Home Att:** 24,257

Goal Scorers: Compared with 1993-94: -6,925

League (80): Shearer 34, Sutton 15, Sherwood 6, Atkins 6, Wilcox 5, Hendry 4, Le Saux 3, Warhurst 2, Berg, Gallacher, Kenna, Opponent

C/Cola Cup (6): Sutton 3, Shearer 2, Wilcox

FA Cup (2): Sutton 2

T. Flowers	R. Mimms	S. Given	K. Berg	T. Gale	C. Hendry	G. Le Saux	P. Warhurst	J. Pearce	A. Wright	J. Kenna	T. Sherwood	R. Slater	M. Atkins	D. Batty	S. Ripley	A. Shearer	C. Sutton	M. Newell	J. Wilcox	L. Makel	A. Morrison	R. Witschge	N. Marker	K. Gallagher	Referee	#
X	S		X	X	X	X		S			X	X	S		X	X	X		X						K. Cooper	1
X	S		X	X	X	X	S1	S2			X	X				X	X	X2	X						K. Burge	2
X	S		X1	X	X	X	X	S1			X	X	S2			X2	X		X						G. Poll	3
X	S		X	X	X	X	S1				X	X				X1	X	X	X	X		S			K. Morton	4
X	S		X	X	X	X		S2			X	X	S1			X1	X	X2	X						R. Dilkes	5
X	S		X	X	X	X	S1	S			X	X1	X			X	X		X						P. Durkin	6
X	S		X		X	X		S1			X	X1				X	X		X	X	S				K. Cypton	7
X	S		X	X	X	X	S1	S			X		X			X1	X		X						M. Bodenham	8
X	S		X		X	X	X	S			X1	S1	X			X	X		X						P. Jones	9
X	S		X		X	X	X	S			X		X			X	X		X		S				R. Gifford	10
X	S		X		X	X	X	S			X	S	X			X	X		X						S. Lodge	11
X	S		X	X		X	X	S				S	X			X	X		X						B. Hill	12
X	S		X	X1	X	X	X	S2				S1	X1			X	X		X						G. Ashby	13
X	S		X	X	X	X	X	S					X			X	X		X		S				D. Gallagher	14
X	S		X		X	X	X	S1			X		X			X	X1	X	X						P. Danson	15
X	S		X	X	X	X	X				X		S			X	X	X	S	X					R. Hart	16
X	S		X	X	X	X	X				X		S			X	X	X	S	X					T. Holbrook	17
X	S			X		X	X	X	S			X	X	X		X	X	X	S						K. Burge	18
X	S		X			X	X	X	S2			X	X			X2	X	X1	S1						J. Worrall	19
X	S		X	X1		X	X	X	S			X		S		X	X	X	S1	X					R. Dicken	20
X	S		X		X	X	X	S			X		X			X	X	X	S1	X					P. Jones	21
X	S		X		X	X	X				X	S1	X			X1	X	X2	S2	X					A. Wilkie	22
X	S		X	X		X		X			X	S	X			X	X	X	S	X					P. Don	23
X	S		X	X	X	S					X		X			X	X	X	S	X					P. Danson	24
X	S		X		X	X	S	X			X		X			X	X1	X	S	X					D. Elleray	25
X	S		X	X	X	X	S1				X		X1			X	X1	X	S2	X					K. Morton	26
X	S		X		X	X	X	S1			X		X1			X	X	X	S1	X					D. Gallagher	27
X	S		X	S		X	X	X	X			X	X			X	X	S1	X1						J. Worrall	28
X	S		X		X	X	X	X	S1			X1	X2			X	X	S2	X						D. Gallagher	29
X	S		X		X	X	X	S2	X		X		X2			X	X	S1	X1						P. Durkin	30
X	S		X		X	X	X1	X			X	X	S1			X	X2	S2	X						G. Poll	31
X	S1		X		X	X	X	X	S			X	X1			X	X	S	X						R. Gifford	32
	X	S		X		X	X	X	X			X		S2		X1	X	X	X2						M. Bodenham	33
	X	S	X	S		X	X	X	X	X		X	X				X	X	X						P. Jones	34
	X	S		X		X	X	X	X	S		X	X1	X		S1		X		X					S. Lodge	35
X	S		X		X	X	S1	X	S			X		X1		X	X		X	X					M. Reed	36
X	S		X		X	X	S	X				X		X		X	X	X	S	X					R. Gifford	37
X	S		X		X	X	S1	X				X		X		X	X	X2	S2	X1					A. Wilkin	38
X	S		X		X	X	X	X				X	S1	X1		X	X	X2	S2						T. Holbrook	39
X	S		X		X	X		X		X	X	S			X	X	X	S							P. Danson	40
X	S		X		X	X		X		X	X				X	X	X	S			S				D. Gallagher	41
X	S		X		X	X	S		X		X	X			X	X	X				S				R. Hart	42
X	S		X		X	X		X		X	X		X	S	X	X	X							S	G. Poll	43
X	S		X		X	X		X		X	X	X1	S1	X		X	X							S	K. Cooper	44
X	S		X			X		X		X		S1	X	X	X	X	X	S						X1	B. Hill	45
X	S		X		X	X				X	X		S	X	X1	X	X	S1			X				K. Morton	46
X	S		X		X	X		X		X	X	S1			X	X1	X	X	S						P. Don	47
X	S		X		X	X		X		X	X	S			X	X1	X	X	S						D. Elleray	48
39	3		40	15	38	39	20	22	4	9	38	12	30	4	36	42	40	2	27			1		1	League Appearances	
	1						7	6	1			6	4	1	1			10							League Sub Appearances	
4			4	2	4	4	4	+1			3	1	3		4	3	4	+1	4						C/Cola Appearances	
2			2	2	2	2	1	+1			1	1	2		1	2	2	+2	2						FA Cup Appearances	

Players on Loan: Witschge

BLACKBURN ROVERS

CLUB RECORDS

BIGGEST VICTORIES
League: 9-0 v Middlesbrough, Division 2, 6.11.1954.
F.A. Cup: 11-0 v Rossendale, Round 1, 13.10.1884.
League Cup: 6-1 v Watford, Round 4, 9.12.1992.

BIGGEST DEFEATS
League: 0-8 v Arsenal, Division 1, 25.2.1933.
0-8 v Lincoln City, Division 2, 29.8.1953.
F.A. Cup: 0-6 v Nottingham Forest, Round 3, 1879-80.
1-6 v Manchester United, 1908-09.
1-6 v Luton Town, Round 3, 1952-53.
League Cup: 0-5 v Wimbledon, 24.9.1985.
1-6 v Nottingham Forest, 15.9.1979.
Europe: (UEFA) 0-1 v Trelleborgs, 27.9.1994.

MOST POINTS
3 points a win: 89, Premiership, 1994-95.
2 points a win: 60, Division 3, 1974-75.

MOST GOALS SCORED
114, 1954-55, Division 2.
Briggs 33, Quigley 28, Crossan 18, Mooney 16, Langton 13,
Clayton 2, Bell 1, og 3.

MOST GOALS CONCEDED
102, Division 1, 1932-33.

MOST FIRST CLASS MATCHES IN A SEASON
60 - 1979-80 (League 46, FA Cup 7, League Cup 4, Anglo-Scottish
Cup 3).
60 - 1988-89 (League 46, FA Cup 3, League Cup 4, Simod Cup 3,
League Play-offs 4).

MOST LEAGUE WINS
27, Premiership, 1994-95.

MOST LEAGUE DRAWS
18, Division 2, 1980-81.

MOST LEAGUE DEFEATS
30, Division 1, 1980-81.

INDIVIDUAL CLUB RECORDS

MOST GOALS IN A SEASON
Ted Harper - 45, 1925-26 (League 43, FAC 2).

MOST GOALS IN A MATCH
7, Tommy Briggs v Bristol Rovers, Division 2, 5.2.1953.

OLDEST PLAYER
Bob Crompton, 40 years 151 days, 23.2.1920.

YOUNGEST PLAYER
Harry Dennison, 16 years 155 days, 8.4.1911.

MOST CAPPED PLAYER
Bob Crompton (England) 41.

BEST PERFORMANCES

League: 1994-95: Played 42, Won 27, Drawn 8, Lost 7, Goals for
80, Goals against 39, Points 89. Premiership Champions.
Highest Position: 1994-95 Premiership Champions.
F.A. Cup: Winners in 1884 v Queens Park, 2-1.
Winners in 1885 v Queens Park, 2-0.
Winners in 1886 v West Bromwich 0-0,2-0.
Winners in 1890 v Sheffield Wednesday 6-1.
Winners in 1891 v Notts County 3-1.
Most Recent Success: (1928) 3rd Rnd. Newcastle United 4-1; 4th
Rnd. Exeter City 2-2,3-1; 5th Rnd. Port Vale 2-1; 6th Rnd.
Manchester United 2-0; Semi-Final Arsenal 1-0; Final Huddersfield
Town 3-1.
League Cup: Semi-Finalists in 1961-62 v Rochdale, 1-3.
Most Recent Success: (1992-93) 2nd Rnd. Huddersfield Town (a)
1-1, (h) 4-3 aet; 3rd Rnd. Norwich City 2-0; 4th Rnd. Watford (h) 6-
1; 5th Rnd. Cambridge United (h) 3-2; Semi-Final Sheffield
Wednesday (h) 2-4, (a) 1-2.
Europe: (UEFA) 1st Rnd. Trelleborg (h) 0-1, (a) 2-2.

ADDITIONAL INFORMATION
PREVIOUS NAME
Blackburn Grammar School Old Boys.
PREVIOUS LEAGUES
None.

Club Colours: Blue & white halves shirts, blue shorts and blue with
red and white topped socks.
Change Colours: Red & black striped shirts, red shorts, black
socks with red band halfway.

Reserve League: Pontins Central League Division 1.

DIVISIONAL RECORD

	Played	Won	Drawn	Lost	For	Against	Points
Division 1/P	2108	800	487	821	3510	3523	2132
Division 2	1446	583	364	499	2134	1981	1723
Division 3	230	104	59	67	299	249	267
Total	3784	1487	910	1387	5943	5753	4122

RECORDS AND STATISTICS

COMPETITIONS

Div 1/P	Div.2	Div.3	A/Scot
1888-1936	1936-39	1971-75	1975-76
1939-47	1947-57	1979-80	1976-77
1957-66	1966-71		1977-78
1992-	1975-79		1978-79
	1980-92		1979-80
			1980-81

HONOURS

Div 1/P	Div.2	Div.3	FAC	FMC	C/Sh'ld
1911-12	1938-39	1974-75	1884	1986-87	1912
1913-14			1885		
1994-95			1886		
			1890		
			1891		
			1928		

MOST APPEARANCES

D Fazakerley 689+3 (1970-87)

Year	League	FA Cup	Lge Cup	A/Scottish
1970-71	14			
1971-72	39	2	2	
1972-73	46	3	1	
1973-74	46	5	3	
1974-75	22+1	1	2	
1975-76	42	1	2	
1976-77	37+1	4	3	
1977-78	28	2	2	
1978-79	37	2	1	
1979-80	46	7	4	
1980-81	38	1	5	
1981-82	39	1	3	
1982-83	38	1	2	
1983-84	39	3	2	
1984-85	39	4	2	
1985-86	36+1	3	2	
1986-87	7		2	
	593+3	40	38	18

MOST GOALS IN A CAREER

Simon Garner - 192 (1978-92)

Year	League	FA Cup	Lge Cup	Others
1978-79	8			
1979-80	6			
1980-81	7		1	
1981-82	14	2	2	
1982-83	22	1		
1983-84	19	1	3	
1984-85	12		2	
1985-86	12			
1986-87	10		1	4
1987-88	14	1		
1988-89	20	1	2	
1989-90	18			2
1990-91	1	1		
1991-92	5			
Total	168	7	11	6

Current leading goalscorer: Alan Shearer - 93 (1992-95)

RECORD TRANSFER FEE RECEIVED

Amount	Club	Player	Date
£1,250,000	Manchester Utd	David May	5/94
£700,000	Manchester City	Colin Hendry	11/89
£400,000	Q.P.R.	Simon Barker	7/88
£357,000	Leeds United	Kevin Hird	2/79

RECORD TRANSFER FEE PAID

Amount	Club	Player	Date
£5,000,000	Norwich City	Chris Sutton	7/94
£3,300,000	Southampton	Alan Shearer	7/92
£1,300,000	Middlesbrough	Stuart Ripley	7/92
£1,200,000	Q.P.R.	Roy Wegerle	3/92

MANAGERS

Name	Seasons	Best	Worst
Eddie Hapgood	1946-48	17(1)	21(1)
Will Scott	1948-50	14(2)	16(2)
Jack Britton	1950-52	6(2)	14(2)
Jackie Bestall	1952-53	9(2)	9(2)
John Carey	1953-58	2(2)	9(2)
Dally Duncan	1958-61	8(1)	17(1)
Jack Marshall	1961-69	7(1)	19(2)
Eddie Quigley	1969-71	8(2)	21(2)
John Carey	1971-72	10(3)	10(3)
Ken Furphy	1972-74	3(3)	13(3)
Gordon Lee	1974-75	1(3)	1(3)
Jim Smith	1975-78	5(2)	11(2)
Jim Iley	1978-79	22(2)	22(2)
Howard Kendall	1979-81	4(2)	2(3)
Bobby Saxton	1981-86	6(2)	19(2)
Don Mackay	1986-91		
Kenny Dalglish	1991-95	1(P)	6(2/1)
Ray Harford	1995-		

LONGEST LEAGUE RUNS

of undefeated matches:	23 (30.9.1987-27.2.1988)	of league matches w/out a win:	16 (25.11.1978-28.3.1979)
of undefeated home matches:	30 (14.4.1911-21.12.1912)	of undefeated away matches:	11(15.2.1912-1.11.1913)
			(30.9.1987-27.2.1988)
without home win:	11 (16.9.1978 - 24.3.1979)	without an away win:	24 (12.2.1910 - 27.2.1988)
of league wins:	8 (1.3.1980 - 7.4.1980)	of home wins:	13 (12.2.1910 - 20.11.1954)
of league defeats:	7 (12.3.1966 - 16.4.1966)	of away wins:	7 (12.1.1980 - 12.4.1980)

BLACKBURN ROVERS

PLAYERS NAME / Honours	Ht	Wt	Birthdate	Birthplace / Transfers	Contract Date	Clubs	APPEARANCES League	L/Cup	FA Cup	Other	GOALS Lge	L/C	FAC	Oth
G O A L K E E P E R S														
Tim Flowers	6.2	14.0	03.02.67	Kenilworth	28.08.84	Wolverhampton (A)	63	5	2	2				
E: 7, u21.3, Y.1.				£70,000	13.06.86	Southampton	192	26	16	8				
				Loan	23.03.87	Swindon Town	2							
				Loan	13.11.87	Swindon Town	5							
				£2,400,000	04.11.93	Blackburn Rovers	68	4	6	3				
Bobby Mimms	6.2	12.10	12.10.63	York	05.08.81	Halifax Town (A)								
E: u21.3. Div.1'87. CS'86'87.				£15,000	06.11.81	Rotherham United	83	7	3	1				
				£150,000	30.05.85	Everton	29	2	2	4				
				Loan	13.03.86	Notts County	2			1				
Loan 11.12.86 Sunderland 4 Lge App.				Loan	23.01.87	Blackburn Rovers	6							
Loan 24.09.87 Manchester City 3 Lge App.				£325,000	25.02.88	Tottenham Hotspur	37	5	2					
				Loan	16.02.90	Aberdeen	6		2					
				£250,000	22.12.90	Blackburn Rovers	125+1	14	9	4				
D E F E N D E R S														
Mark Atkins	6.0	12.5	14.08.68	Doncaster	09.07.86	Scunthorpe Utd (J)	45+5	3+1	5	6+1	2			
E: S.				£45,000	16.06.88	Blackburn Rovers	224+29	20+4	11+3	16+1	34	4		1
Henning Berg	6.0	11.9	01.09.69	Norway		Lillestrom (Swe)								
				£400,000	26.01.93	Blackburn Rovers	80+5	9	6	3	2			
Colin Hendry	6.1	12.2	07.12.65	Keith		Dundee	17+24		2+3		2		1	
S: 11, B.1. FMC'87.				£30,000	11.03.87	Blackburn Rovers	99+3	4	3	13	22			1
				£700,000	16.11.89	Manchester City	57+6	4+1	5	4	5	1	2	2
				£700,000	08.11.91	Blackburn Rovers	127+5	16	9+1	6	9			
Jeff Kenna	5.11	11.7	27.08.70	Dublin	25.04.89	Southampton (T)	82+4	2	5+1	3	4			
Ei u21.8.				£1,500,000	15.03.95	Blackburn Rovers	9				1			
Adam M Reed	6.0	12.0	18.02.75	B. Auckland	16.07.93	Darlington (T)	34+4	1	1	2	1			
				£200,000	08.95	Blackburn Rovers								
Graeme Le Saux	5.10	11.2	17.10.68	Harrow		St. Pauls (Jersey)								
E: 10, B.2, u21.4. FLgXI.1.				Free	09.12.87	Chelsea	77+13	7+6	7+1	8+1	8	1		
					25.03.93	Blackburn Rovers	88+1	8	6	3	5			
Nick Marker	6.0	12.11	03.05.65	Budleigh Salt.	04.05.83	Exeter City (A)	196+6	11	8	8	3	1		3
				£95,000	31.10.87	Plymouth Argyle	201+1	15	9	7	13	3	1	1
				£500,000	23.09.92	Blackburn Rovers	28+10	3	4					
M I D F I E L D														
David Batty	5.7	10.7	02.12.68	Leeds	03.08.87	Leeds United (T)	201+10	17	12	17	4			
E: 15, B.5, u21.7, Y.2. Div.1'92. Div.2'90.				£2,750,000	26.10.93	Blackburn Rovers	30+1	2	4					
Lee Makel	5.10	9.10	11.01.73	Sunderland	11.02.91	Newcastle Utd (T)	6+6	1		0+1	1			
				£160,000	20.07.92	Blackburn Rovers	1+2	0+3		0+1				
Ian Pearce	6.1	12.4	07.05.74	Bury St.Ed.	01.08.91	Chelsea (J)	0+4			0+1				
E: Y.10.				£300,000	04.10.93	Blackburn Rovers	23+10	0+3	1+2	1+1		1	1	
Stewart Ripley	5.11	12.6	20.11.67	Middlesbrough	23.12.85	Middlesbrough (A)	210+39	21+2	17+1	20+1	26	3	1	1
E: 1, u21.8, Y.4.				Loan	18.02.86	Bolton Wanderers	5			0+1	1			
				£1,300,000	20.07.92	Blackburn Rovers	114+3	15	9	3	11		2	
Tim Sherwood	6.0	11.6	06.02.69	St. Albans	07.02.87	Watford (A)	23+9	4+1	9	4+1	2			
E: B.1, u21.4, u19.2.				£175,000	18.07.89	Norwich City	66+5	7	4	5+1	10	1		2
				£500,000	12.02.92	Blackburn Rovers	121+5	14	8+1	3	11		1	
F O R W A R D S														
Kevin Gallacher	5.8	10.10	23.11.66	Clydebank		Dundee United	118+13	13	20+3	15+6	27	5	5	3
S: 19, B.2, u21.7, Y.				£900,000	29.01.90	Coventry City	99+1	11	4	2	28	7		
				£1,500,000	23.03.93	Blackburn Rovers	37+3	4	4		13		1	
Paul Harford	6.3	14.0	21.10.74	Chelmsford		Arsenal (T)								
				Free	24.08.93	Blackburn Rovers								
				Loan	02.09.94	Wigan Athletic	3							
				Loan	15.12.94	Shrewsbury Town	3+3							
Matthew Holmes	5.7	10.7	01.08.69	Luton	22.08.88	Bournemouth (T)	105+9	7	8+2	5	8			
				Loan	23.03.89	Cardiff City	0+1							
				£40,000	19.08.92	West Ham United	63+13	4	6	3	5			1
				£1,200,000	08.95	Blackburn Rovers								
Mike Newell	6.0	11.0	27.01.65	Liverpool		Liverpool (J)								
E: B.2, u21.4. FRT'85.				Free	28.09.83	Crewe Alexandra	3							
				Free	31.10.83	Wigan Athletic	64+8	6	8	5+1	25	1	6	3
				£100,000	09.01.86	Luton Town	62+1		5		18		1	
				£350,000	16.09.87	Leicester City	81	9	2	4	21	5		
				£1,100,000	27.07.89	Everton	48+20	7+3	6+4	6	15	4		2
				£1,100,000	15.11.91	Blackburn Rovers	87+13	10+2	7+2	3	25	7	6	2

BLACKBURN ROVERS							APPEARANCES				GOALS			
PLAYERS NAME / Honours	Ht	Wt	Birthdate	Birthplace / Transfers	Contract Date	Clubs	League	L/Cup	FA Cup	Other	Lge	L/C	FAC	Oth
Alan Shearer	5.11	11.3	13.08.70	Newcastle	14.04.88	Southampton (T)	105+13	16+2	11+3	8	23	11	4	5
E: 17, B.1, u21.12, Y.5.				£3,600,000	24.07.92	Blackburn Rovers	97+6	12	6	2	81	9	2	1
Chris Sutton	6.3	12.1	10.03.73	Nottingham	02.07.91	Norwich City (T)	89+13	8+1	10	6	35	3	5	
E: B.1, u21.13.				£5,000,000	13.07.94	Blackburn Rovers	40	4	2	2	15	3	2	1
Paul Warhurst	6.1	12.10	26.09.69	Stockport	01.07.88	Manchester City (T)								
E: u21.8.				£10,000	27.10.88	Oldham Athletic	60+7	8	5+4	2	2			
				£750,000	17.07.91	Sheffield Wed.	60+6	9	7+1	5	6	4	5	3
				£2,700,000	17.08.93	Blackburn Rovers	24+12	5	2	0+1	2			
Jason Wilcox	5.10	11.6	15.07.71	Farnworth	13.06.89	Blackburn Rov (T)	138+12	13+1	11	5	19	1	1	

TOP GOALSCORER 1994/95
Alan Shearer

Premiership goals (games) . . . . *Top Premiership striker 94/95* - 34 (42)
Coca-Cola Cup goals. 2 (3)
F.A. Cup Goals 0 (2)
EUFA Cup Goals 1 (2)
International Goals (94/95). 2 (5)
Total for 1994/95. . . . . **39 (54)**

Total for Blackburn since 24.07.92 . . . . 92 (117+6)
Total for England 5 (14)
Career Total up to June 1995 . . . . 141 (271+24)

THE MANAGER
RAY HARFORD

Date of Birth. . . . . 1st June 1945.
Place of Birth. . . . . Halifax.
Date of Appointment . . . . July 1995.

PREVIOUS CLUBS
As Manager. . . . . Fulham, Luton Town, Wimbledon.
As Coach/Assistant. . . . . . . Fulham, Luton Town, Wimbledon, Blackburn Rovers.
As a Player. . . . . Charlton Athletic, Exeter City, LIncoln City, Mansfield Town,
. . . . Port Vale, Colchester United.

HONOURS
As a Manager
Luton Town: League Cup winners 1988, runners-up 1989. Simod Cup runners-up 1988.

As a Player
None.

Ewood Park

Blackburn, Lancashire BB2 4JF
Tel: 01254 554 32

Capacity . . . . .31,750.
First game . . . . .v Accrington, (Friendly), 13.9.1890.
First floodlit game . . . . .v Werder (Friendly), 1958-59.
Second set . . . . .v Aberdeen (Friendly), 7.12.1976.

Internationals played at Ewood . . . . .England v Scotland, 6.4.189. England v Wales, 3.3.1924.

ATTENDANCES
Highest . . . . .61,783 v Bolton Wanderers, FA Cup, 2.3.1929.
Lowest . . . . .1,200 v West Bromwich Albion, Div.1, 22.12.1894.

OTHER GROUNDS . . . . .Brookhouse Ground 1875-76. Alexandra Meadow 1876-81.
. . . . .Leamington Road 1881-1890. Ewood Park 1890 to date.

MATCHDAY TICKET PRICES

Jack Walker Stand
Upper Tier Central £17.50
Upper Tier Outer (Adult/Juv&OAP) . . . . . £16.50/£8
Lower Tier Central . . . . £16.50/£8
Lower Tier Outer . . . . £14/£7

Walker Steel Stand . . . . £14/£7

Darwen Stand Upper & Lower Tier . . . . £14/£7

Blackburn End Upper Family Stand & lower £14/£7
(Under 8 free. Minimum purchase 1 adult + 1 child)

Ticket Office Telephone No. 01254 696 767

CLUBCALL
0898 12 11 79

Calls cost 39p per minute cheap rate and 49p per
minute at all other times.
Call costings correct at time of going to press.

HOW TO GET TO THE GROUND

From the North and West
M6 to junction 31 or A666 into Blackburn. A666 into Bolton Road, left into Kidder Street for Ewood Park.

From the South
M6 to junction 31 as from North or A666 via Bolton. After Darwen turn right into Kidder Street for Ewood Park.

From the East
A679 or A677 to Blackburn then A666 toward Bolton into Bolton Road. Left into Kidder Street for Ewood Park.

Car Parking
Ewood car park within walking distance.

Nearest Railway Station
Blackburn Central (01254 662 537/8).

MATCHDAY PROGRAMME

Programme Editor . . . . Peter White.

Number of pages 32

Price £1.50

Subscriptions . . . . £75 home & away, £40 home.

Local Newspapers . . . . Lancashire Evening Telegraph.

Local Radio Stations . . . . . . Red Rose Radio, BBC Radio Lancashire.

BOLTON WANDERERS
(The Trotters)
F.A. CARLING PREMIERSHIP
SPONSORED BY: REEBOK

Back Row (L-R): Richard Sneekes, Jimmy Phillips, Scott Green, Chris Fairclough, Simon Coleman, Neil McDonald, Andy Todd, Nicky Spooner. **Middle Row:** Ewan Simpson, Jason McAteer, Fabian de Freitas, Gudni Bergsson, Keith Branagan, Gerry Taggart, Aidan Davison, Alan Thompson, Mark Patterson, Steve Carroll, Ian McNeil. **Front Row:** David Lee, Owen Coyle, Alan Stubbs, Colin Todd, Roy McFarland, Mixu Paatelainen, John McGinlay, Stewart Whittaker.

**BOLTON WANDERERS
FORMED IN** 1874
TURNED PROFESSIONAL IN 1880
LTD COMPANY IN 1895

PRESIDENT: Nat Lofthouse
CHAIRMAN: G Hargreaves
DIRECTORS
G Ball, G Seymour, G Warburton,
W B Warburton, P Gartside, B Scowcroft

SECRETARY/Chief Executive
D McBain (01204 389 200)
COMMERCIAL MANAGER
T Holland

MANAGER: Roy McFarland
ASSISTANT: Colin Todd
RESERVE TEAM MANAGER
Steve Carroll
YOUTH TEAM MANAGER
Dean Crombie
PHYSIOTHERAPIST
Ewan Simpson

CLUB STATISTICIAN FOR THE DIRECTORY
Simon Marland

Two Wembley appearances were a just reward for some exciting football played by the club throughout the season which culminated in a seven goal play-off thriller and a return to the top flight after fifteen years absence.

The Wanderers made their now traditional slow start and were as low as 15th place in the first division during September. The Coca-cola Cup proved to be a springboard to better results in the league and after November had been reached the team never fell out of the top six.

Defeat at Burnden in the opening home league fixture by Bristol City didn't augur well for the grounds centenary season, but after that the Wanderers were unbeaten in 26 consecutive league and cup games. Included in that run were superb performances against Charlton Athletic and promotion rivals Wolves who were both beaten 5-1. Eventual champions Middlesbrough also fell at Burnden Park, a Mixu Paatelainen goal separating the sides.

Form away from Burnden told a different story with only five league victories, eleven defeats being the highest suffered by any promotion winning Wanderers side. The final four away games of the term yielded only a single point and that was to deny the team any chance of automatic promotion.

In the play-offs the side appeared to gain a second wind. Wolves were beaten in the semi final thanks to a memorable performance in the second leg at Burnden to overcome a deficit from Molineux. No-one believed the Wanderers would lose at Wembley, but to give Reading a two goal start tested the nerves of the most ardent supporters.

Keith Branagan's penalty save before half-time proved to be a watershed. Slowly Reading began to wilt and, although the Wanderers two goals to level matters came later on, you sensed there was only going to be one winner in extra time.

In previous seasons the Wanderers had made a name for themselves in the FA Cup, but during 1994/95 it was to be the Coca-Cola Cup that earned the club more headlines.

Premiership sides Ipswich Town, West Ham United and Norwich City were all accounted for with perhaps the hardest tie being the two legged semi-final with Swindon Town. Trailing 2-1 from the first leg at the County Ground, Bolton again made things difficult by giving Swindon a goal start in the game at Burnden, only to hit back with three late goals to reach the final for the first time.

At Wembley Liverpool ran out winners, but the country saw how much progress Bolton Wanderers had made under the management team of Bruce Rioch and Colin Todd.

SIMON MARLAND.

BOLTON WANDERERS

Division One: 3rd   FA Cup: 3rd Round   Coca-Cola Cup: 5th Round

M	DATE	COMP.	VEN	OPPONENTS	RESULT	H/T	LP	GOAL SCORERS/GOAL TIMES	ATT.
1	A 13	EL	A	Grimsby Town	D 3-3	2-1		Paatelainen (2), McGinlay (pen)	(8,393)
2	20	EL	H	Bristol City	L 0-2	0-1			12,127
3	27	EL	A	Middlesbrough	L 0-1	0-1			(19,570)
4	30	EL	H	Millwall	W 1-0	0-0		Patterson	9,519
5	S 3	EL	H	Stoke City	W 4-0	1-0	9	McGinlay (pen), McAteer (2), Paatelainen	11,515
6	10	EL	A	Sheffield United	L 1-3	0-1	15	McGinlay	(14,116)
7	13	EL	A	Luton Town	W 3-0	0-0	5	McGinlay (2), Sneekes	(5,764)
8	17	EL	H	Portsmouth	D 1-1	1-1	10	McGinlay	11,284
9	21	CC 2/1	A	Ipswich Town	W 3-0	1-0		McAteer, McGinlay, Thompson	(7,787)
10	24	EL	A	Southend United	L 1-2	1-0	12	Sneekes	(4,507)
11	O 1	EL	H	Derby County	W 1-0	0-0	8	McGinlay	12,015
12	5	CC 2/2 1	H	Ipswich Town	W 1-0	0-0		Sneekes	8,212
13	8	EL	A	Burnley	D 2-2	1-0	9	McGinlay, Coleman	(16,687)
14	16	EL	H	Oldham Athletic	D 2-2	2-0	10	Paatelainen, Lee	11,106
15	22	EL	A	Port Vale	D 1-1	1-0	12	Green	(10,003
16	25	CC 3	A	Sheffield United	W 2-1	1-0		Paatelainen, Scott (og)	(6,939)
17	29	EL	H	Watford	W 3-0	1-0	7	Paatelainen, McGinlay 2(1pen)	10,483
18	N 1	EL	H	Swindon Town	W 3-0	1-0	5	Coleman, Thompson, de Freitas	10,046
19	5	EL	A	Charlton Athletic	W 2-1	1-0	5	Sneekes (2)	(9,793)
20	19	EL	H	Notts County	W 2-0	1-0	3	de Freitas, Paatelainen	11,698
21	23	EL	A	Wolverhampton Wand.	L 1-3	1-0	3	Paatelainen	(5,903)
22	26	EL	A	Barnsley	L 0-3	0-2	4		(8,507)
23	30	CC 4	A	West Ham United	W 3-1	1-0		McGinley 2 (1 pen) Lee	(18,190)
24	D 6	EL	H	Port Vale	W 1-0	0-0	4	Patterson	10,324
25	10	EL	A	Bristol City	W 1-0	1-0	4	Patterson	(6,144)
26	17	EL	H	Grimsby Town	D 3-3	1-2	3	Coyle (2), Lee	10,522
27	26	EL	A	Sunderland	D 1-1	0-0	5	Paatelainen	(19,758)
28	27	EL	H	Tranmere Rovers	W 1-0	1-0	2	Thompson	16,782
29	31	EL	A	West Brom Albion	L 0-1	0-1	6		(18,184)
30	J 2	EL	H	Reading	W 1-0	1-0	4	Coleman	14,705
31	7	FAC 3	A	Portsmouth	L 1-3	1-1		Sneekes	(9,721)
32	12	CC 5	H	Norwich City	W 1-0	0-0		Lee	17,029
33	14	EL	A	Watford	D 0-0	0-0	3		(9,113)
34	21	EL	H	Charlton Athletic	W 5-1	2-1	3	McGinlay (2), McAteer, Coyle, Paatelainen	10,516
35	F 4	EL	H	Wolverhampton Wand.	W 5-1	2-1	1	Sneekes, Coleman, Phillips, Coyle, Thompson	16,964
36	7	EL	A	Notts County	D 1-1	0-0	1	Coyle	(7,553)
37	12	CC S	A	Swindon Town	L 1-2	1-1		Stubbs	(15,341)
38	18	EL	H	Barnsley	W 2-1	2-0	1	Thompson, Sneekes	12,463
39	26	EL	A	Derby County	L 1-2	1-0	3	McAteer	(11,003)
40	M 4	EL	H	Southend United	W 3-0	1-0	3	Thompson, Lee, McAteer	10,766
41	8	CC SF	A	Swindon Town	W 3-1	0-0		McAteer, Paatelainen, McGinlay	19,851
42	11	EL	H	Middlesbrough	W 1-0	1-0	3	Paatelainen	18,370
43	19	EL	A	Millwall	W 1-0	0-0	2	McGinley	(6,103)
44	22	EL	H	Sheffield United	D 1-1	1-1	3	Stubbs	16,756
45	25	EL	A	Portsmouth	D 1-1	1-0	2	Paatelainen	(7,765)
46	A 2	CC F	N	Liverpool	L 1-2	0-1		Thompson	(75,595)
47	5	EL	A	Swindon Town	W 1-0	0-0	3	Thompson	(8,100)
48	8	EL	H	West Bromwich A.	W 1-0	0-0	3	Thompson (pen)	16,207
49	11	EL	H	Luton Town	D 0-0	0-0	2		13,619
50	14	EL	A	Tranmere Rovers	L 0-1	0-1	3		(15,595)
51	17	EL	H	Sunderland	W 1-0	0-0	2	McGinlay	15,030
52	21	EL	A	Reading	L 1-2	0-1	2	Lee	(13,223)
53	29	EL	A	Oldham Athletic	L 1-3	1-2	3	McGinlay	(11,901)
54	M 3	EL	A	Stoke City	D 1-1	1-1	2	McGinlay	(15,557)
55	7	EL	H	Burnley	D 1-1	0-0	3	Paatelainen	16,853
56	14	PO1	A	Wolverhampton Wand.	L 1-2	0-1		McAteer	(26,153)
57	17	PO2	H	Wolverhampton Wand.	W 2-0	1-0		McGinlay (2)	20,041
58	29	POF	N	Reading	L 4-3	0-2		de Freitas (2), Coyle, Paatelainen	64,107
59									
60									

Best Home League Attendance: 20,041 v Wolverhampton Wanderers   Smallest: 8,212 v Ipswich Town   Av Home Att: 13,511

Goal Scorers: Compared with 1993-94: + 3,013

League (74):   McGinlay 18, Paatelainen 13, Thompson 7, McAteer 6, Sneekes 6, Coyle 6, Coleman 4, de Freitas 4, Lee 4, Patterson 3, Green, Phillips, Stubbs

C/Cola Cup (15):   McGinlay 4, Paatelainen 2, Thompson 2, Lee 2, McAteer 2, Stubbs, Sneekes

FA Cup (1):   Sneekes   Play-offs (7):   de Freitas 2, McAteer (2), McGinlay 2, Coyle, Paatelainen

Appearance grid — shirt numbers worn by each player per match. Rightmost column "Referee" (blank) with match number.

Branagan K.	McDonald N.	Phillips J.	McAteer J.	Lydiate J.	Stubbs A.	Lee D.	Patterson M.	Paatelainen M.	McGinlay J.	Thompson A.	Coyle O.	Sneekes R.	Kernaghan A.	Fisher N.	De Freitas F.	Kelly A.	Spooner N.	Coleman S.	Green S.	Whitaker S.	Davison A.	Seagraves M.	Bergsson G.	Dreyer I.	Shilton P.	Referee
1	2	3	4	5	6	7	8	9	10	11	12	14														1
1	2	3	4		6	7	8	9	10	14	12	11	5													2
1		3	4	2	6		11	9	12			8	5	7	10											3
1		3	4	2	6		11	9	12			8	5	7	10											4
1		3	4	2	6			9	10			8	5	7		11										5
1		3	4	2	6			9	10	14	12	8	5	7		11										6
1		3	4	2	6			9	10			8	5	7		11										7
1		3	4	2	6	12		9	10			8	5	7		11										8
1		3	4	2	6	11		9	10	5		8	14	7	12											9
1		3	4	2	6	11		9	10	5		8	12	7	14											10
1		3	4	2		11		9	10	5		8	6	7												11
1		3	4	2		11	12	9	10	5		8		7	14		6									12
1		3	4	2		11		9	10	5		8	12	14			6		7							13
1		3	4	2		11		9	10	5		8	12	7				6								14
1		3	4		11			9	10	5	14	8		2	7	12			14							15
1		3	4	2		11		9	10	5	14	8			12		7									16
1		3		2		11	4	9	10	5		8					6	7								17
1		3	12	2		11	4	9		5	14	8			10		7	6								18
1		3	12	2		11	4	9		5	14	8			10		7	6								19
1		3		2	12	11	4	9		5	14	8			10		7	6								20
1		3		2	12	11	4	9		5	14	8			10		7	6								21
1		3	11	2	4	12		9	10	5	14	8					7	6								22
1		3	4		6	7	14	9	10	11	12	8					5	6								23
1		3	4		6	7	11	9	10			8					5	2								24
1		3	4		6	7	11	9	10		12	8					5	2								25
1		3	4		6	7	11	9		12	10	8					5	2								26
1		3	4		6	7		9		11	10	8					5	2								27
1		3	4		6	7	8	9	10	11	12						5	2								28
1		3	4		6	7	12	9	10	11		8					5	2								29
1		3	4		6	7	9	12	10		11	8					5	2	14							30
1		3	4		6	12	11	7	10	14	9	8					5	2								31
1		3	4	14	6	7		9	10	11	12	8					5	2								32
1			4			7		9	10	11		8					5	2								33
1		3	4	14	6	7		9	10	11	12	8					5	2								34
1		3	4		6	7		9		11	10	8					5	2								35
1		3	4		6	7		9		11		8			12		5	2		15						36
1		3	4	14	6	7		9		11	10	14					5	2								37
1		3	4		6	7		9	10	11		8			14		5	2		1						38
		3	4		6	7	12	9	10	11		8					5	2								39
1		3	4		6	7	8		10	11	9							2			5					40
1		3	4		6	7	8	12	10	11	9	8						2			5					41
1		3	4		6	12	8	9	10	11		7						2			5					42
1		3	4		6			9	10	11		7						2			5					43
1		3	4		6	7		9	10	11		8						2			5					44
1		3	4		6	12		9		11	10	7						2			5					45
1		3	4		6	7	12	9	10	11								2			5	14				46
1		3	4		6	7	8	9	10	11								12			5	2				47
1		3	4		6	7	8	9	10	11					14			12			5	2				48
1		3	4		6			9	12	11		8			10			7			5	2				49
1		3	4		6	7	12	9	10	11		8									5	2				50
1		3	4		6	7	11	9	10			8			12						5	2	14			51
1		3	4		6	7	8		10	11	9										5	2				52
1		3	4		6	7	8	9	10	11											5	2				53
		3	4		6	7	8	9	10	11								12		1	5	2		15		54
		3	4		6	7	8	9	10	11								2		1	5					55
	7	3	4		6	12		9	10	11	14							2			5	8	1			56
1		3	4		6	7		9	10	11	8				12			2			5	14				57
1	7	3	4		6			9	10	11	8				12			2			5	14				58
43	4	46	41	17	37	35	23	43	34	34	8	37	9	10	7	4	1	22	26		3	13	8	1		League Appearances
	2						2	1	2	4	3	1	3	3	11	1	2	1	6				5	1	1	1	League Sub Appearances
8		8	7	3	6	8	2+2	7+1	8		2+1	7+1			2			0+3		1	4	6			2	0+1	C/Cola Cup Appearances
1		1	1		1	0+1	1	1	1	0+1	1	1								1	1					FA Cup Appearances
2	2	3	3		3	1+1		3	3	3	2+1				0+2				3				3	1+2	1	Play-off Appearances

BOLTON WANDERERS

BIGGEST VICTORIES
League: 8-0 v Barnsley, Division 2, 6.10.1934.
F.A. Cup: 13-0 v Sheffield United, Round 2, 1.2.1890.
League Cup: 6-2 v Grimsby Town, Round 2, 26.10.1960.

BIGGEST DEFEATS
League: 0-7 v Burnley, Division 1, 1.3.1890.
0-7 v Sheffield Wednesday, Division 1, 1.3.1915.
0-7 v Manchester City, Division 1, 21.3.1936.
F.A. Cup: 1-9 v Preston North End, Round 2, 10.12.1887.
League Cup: 0-6 v Chelsea, Round 4 Replay, 8.11.1971.

MOST POINTS
3 points a win: 90, Division 3/2, 1992-93.
2 points a win: 61, Division 3, 1972-73.

MOST GOALS SCORED
96, 1934-35, Division 2.
Milsom 31, Westwood 30, Taylor 8, Cook 6, Eastham 6, Rimmer 4,
Gosling 2, Atkinson 2, Cameron, Chambers, Walton 1 each,
Opponents 4.

MOST GOALS CONCEDED
92, Division 1, 1932-33.

MOST FIRST CLASS MATCHES IN A SEASON
64 - (league 46, FA Cup 8, League Cup 4, Anglo Italian 6)

MOST LEAGUE WINS
27, Division 2, 1904-05, 1992-93.

MOST LEAGUE DRAWS
17, Division 3, 1991-92.

MOST LEAGUE DEFEATS
25, Division 2, 1970-71.

MOST GOALS IN A SEASON
Joe Smith - 38, 1920-21 (League 38).

MOST GOALS IN A MATCH
5, J.Cassidy v Sheffield United, 13-0, FA Cup, 1.2.1890.
5, T.Caldwell v Walsall, 8-1, Division 3, 10.9.1983.

OLDEST PLAYER
Peter Shilton, 45 years 239 days v Wolves, 14.5.1995.

YOUNGEST PLAYER
Ray Parry, 15 years 267 days v Wolverhampton Wanderers,
13.10.1951.

MOST CAPPED PLAYER
Nat Lofthouse (England) 33.

League: Second in Division 2,1899-00: Matches played 34, Won
22, Drawn 8, Lost 4, Goals for 79, Goals against 25, Points 52.
Highest Position: 3rd Division 1, 1891-92, 1920-21, 1924-25.

F.A. Cup: Winners in 1922-23 v West Ham United, 2-0.
Winners in 1925-26 v Manchester City, 1-0.
Winners in 1928-29 v Portsmouth, 2-0.
Most Recent Success: (1957-58) 3rd Rnd. Preston North End (a)
3-0; 4th Rnd. York City (a) 0-0, (h) 3-0; 5th Rnd. Stoke City (h) 3-1;
6th Rnd. Wolverhampton W. (h) 2-1; Semi-Final Blackburn Rovers
2-1; Final Manchester United 2-0.

League Cup: (1994-95) 2nd Round Ipswich (A) 3-0, (H) 1-0,
3rd Round Sheffield Utd (A) 2-1, 4th Round West Ham (A) 3-1,
5th Round Norwich (H) 1-0, Semi-Final Swindon (A) 1-2, (H) 3-1,
Final Liverpool 1-2.

ADDITIONAL INFORMATION
PREVIOUS NAME
Christ Church FC 1874-1877.
PREVIOUS LEAGUES
None.

Club Colours: White shirts with red & blue trim, navy blue shorts,
red socks.
Change Colours: Two tone blue shirts, blue shorts, blue socks.

Reserves League: Pontins Central League Division 1.
'A' Team: Lancashire League Division 2.

DIVISIONAL RECORD

	Played	Won	Drawn	Lost	For	Against	Points
Division 1/P	2,308	868	513	927	3,581	3,722	2,249
Division 2/1	987	417	241	329	1,508	1,217	1,131
Division 3/2	513	201	137	175	672	598	692
Division 4	46	22	12	12	66	42	78
Total	**3,854**	**1,508**	**903**	**1,443**	**5,827**	**5,579**	**4,150**

RECORDS AND STATISTICS

COMPETITIONS

DIV 1/P	DIV.2/1	DIV.3/2	DIV.4
1888-99	1899-1900	1971-73	1987-88
1900-03	1903-05	1983-87	
1905-08	1908-09	1988-93	
1909-10	1910-11		
1911-33	1933-35		
1935-64	1964-71		
1978-80	1973-78		
1995-	1980-83		
	1993-95		

HONOURS

DIV.2	DIV.3	FA CUP	AMC (SVT)
1908-09	1972-73	1922-23	1988-89
1977-78		1925-26	
		1928-29	
		1957-58	

MOST APPEARANCES

EDIE HOPKINSON 578 (1956-70)

YEAR	LEAGUE	FA CUP	LGE CUP
1956-57	42	1	
1957-58	33	7	
1958-59	39	6	
1959-60	26	3	
1960-61	42	3	5
1961-62	42	1	2
1962-63	39	1	1
1963-64	31	4	1
1964-65	40	3	1
1965-66	42	3	2
1966-67	41	3	1
1967-68	40	1	3
1968-69	42	2	1
1969-70	20		4
	519	**38**	**21**

MOST GOALS IN A CAREER

NAT LOFTHOUSE - 290 (1945-61)

YEAR	LEAGUE	FA CUP	LGE CUP	OTHERS
1945-46		2		
1946-47	18	3		
1947-48	18			
1948-49	7	1		
1949-50	10	3		
1950-51	21	1		
1951-52	18			
1952-53	22	8		
1953-54	17	1		
1954-55	15			
1955-56	32	1		
1956-57	28			
1957-58	17	3		
1958-59	29	4		
1959-60				
1960-61	3		3	
Total	**255**	**27**	**3**	**5**

Current leading goalscorer: John McGinlay 77 (1992-95)

RECORD TRANSFER FEE RECEIVED

AMOUNT	CLUB	PLAYER	DATE
£550,000	Celtic	Andy Walker	6/94
£340,000	Birmingham City	Neil Whatmore	8/81

RECORD TRANSFER FEE PAID

AMOUNT	CLUB	PLAYER	DATE
£450,000	Leeds United	Chris Fairclough	07/95
£400,000	FC Volendam	Fabien Defreitas	8/94
£350,000	Aberdeen	Mixu Paatelainen	8/94
£350,000	West Brom Albion	Len Cantello	5/79

MANAGERS

NAME	SEASONS	BEST	WORST
John Somerville	1908-10	19(1)	1(2)
Will Settle	1910-15	4(1)	2(2)
Tom Mather	1915-19		
Charles Foweraker	1919-44	3(1)	3(2)
Walter Rowley	1944-50	14(1)	18(1)
Bill Ridding	1951-68	4(1)	12(2)
Nat Lofthouse (x3)	1968-71	12(2)	22(2)
Jimmy McIlroy	1970		
Jimmy Meadows	1971		
Jimmy Armfield	1971-74	11(2)	7(3)
Ian Greaves	1974-80	17(1)	10(2)
Stan Anderson	1980-81	18(2)	18(2)
George Mulhall	1981-82	19(2)	19(2)
John McGovern	1982-85	22(2)	19(3)
Charles Wright	1985	17(3)	17(3)
Phil Neal	1985-92	4(3)	3(4)
Bruce Rioch	1992-95	3(2/1)	2(3/2)
Roy McFarland	1995-		

LONGEST LEAGUE RUNS

of undefeated matches:	23 (13.10.1990 - 9.3.1991)	of league matches w/out a win:	26 (7.4.1902 - 10.1.1903)
of undefeated home matches:	27 (24.4.1920 - 24.9.1921)	of undefeated away matches:	11 (10.12.1904 - 21.4.1905)
without home win:	11 (19.4.1902 - 10.1.1903)	without an away win:	36 (25.9.1948 - 2.9.1950)
of league wins:	11 (5.11.1904 - 2.1.1905)	of home wins:	17 (11.10.1924 - 25.4.1925)
of league defeats:	11 (7.4.1902 - 18.10.1902)	of away wins:	5 (10.12.1904 - 18.3.1905)

BOLTON WANDERERS

PLAYERS NAME / Honours	Ht	Wt	Birthdate	Birthplace / Transfers	Contract Date	Clubs	APPEARANCES League	L/Cup	FA Cup	Other	GOALS Lge	L/C	FAC	Oth
G O A L K E E P E R S														
Keith Branagan	6.0	11.0	10.07.66	Fulham	04.08.83	Cambridge Utd (J)	110	12	6	6				
				£100,000	25.03.88	Millwall	46	1	5	1				
				Loan	24.11.89	Brentford	2			1				
				Loan	01.10.91	Gillingham	1							
				Free	03.07.92	Bolton Wanderers	99	16	7	7				
Aidan Davison	6.1	13.2	11.05.68	Sedgefield		Spennymoor Utd			1					
						Billingham Synth.			1					
					25.03.88	Notts County	1							
				£6,000	07.10.89	Bury								
				Free	14.08.91	Millwall	34	3	3	2				
				£25,000	26.07.93	Bolton Wanderers	33+2		8	4				
D E F E N D E R S														
Simon Coleman	6.0	10.8	13.03.68	Worksop	29.07.85	Mansfield Town (J)	96	9	7	7	7			1
				£400,000	26.09.89	Middlesbrough	51+4		5	10	2			1
				£300,000	15.08.91	Derby County	62+8	5+1	5	12	2			
				£250,000	20.01.94	Sheffield Wed.	10+5	3	2		1			
				£350,000	05.10.94	Bolton Wanderers	22	4	1		4			
Chris Fairclough E: B1, u21.7; Div1'92; Div2'90	5.11	11.2	12.04.64	Nottingham	12.10.81	Nottingham F. (A)	102+5	9+1	6	9+2	1	1		
				£387,000	03.07.87	Tottenham Hotspur	60	7	3		5			
				£500,000	23.03.89	Leeds United	189+6	17+2	14+1	14	21	2		
				£500,000	08.95	Bolton Wanderers								
Neil McDonald E: u21.5, Y.7, S.	5.11	11.4	02.11.65	Wallsend	19.02.83	Newcastle Utd (A)	163+17	12	10+1	3	24	3	1	
				£525,000	03.08.88	Everton	76+14	7	17	10+1	4	3		
				£500,000	01.10.91	Oldham Athletic	19+5	3	2		1			
				Free		Bolton Wanderers	4			2				
James Phillips	6.0	12.0	08.02.66	Bolton	01.08.83	Bolton W. (A)	103+5	8	7	14	2			
				£95,000		Glasgow Rangers	19+6	4		4				
				£110,000	26.08.88	Oxford United	79	3	4	2	6			1
				£250,000	15.03.90	Middlesbrough	139	16	10	5	6			2
				£250,000	20.07.93	Bolton Wanderers	87+1	12	8	9	1			2
Nicky Spooner	5.10	11.0	05.06.71	Manchester	12.07.89	Bolton W. (T)	22+1	2	3	0+1	2			
Greg Strong E: Y,S.	6.2	11.12	05.09.75	Bolton	01.10.92	Wigan Athletic (T)	28+7	5	1	3+1	3			
					08.95	Bolton Wanderers								
Alan Stubbs E: B.	6.2	12.12	06.10.71	Liverpool	24.07.90	Bolton W. (T)	157+20	20	14+3	12+1	5	4	2	
Gerald Taggart NI: 28, u23.1.	6.1	13.4	18.10.70	Belfast	01.07.89	Manchester City (T)	10+2			1	1			
				£75,000	10.01.90	Barnsley	168+3	11	14	6	13		2	1
				£1,500,000	08.95	Bolton Wanderers								
Andrew J J Todd	5.9	10.6	21.09.74	Derby	06.03.92	Middlesbrough (T)	7+1	1+1		5				
				Loan	27.02.95	Swindon Town	13							
				£250,000	08.95	Bolton Wanderers								
M I D F I E L D														
Gudni Bergsson Icelandic Int.CS'91.	5.10	10.7	21.07.65	Reyjkavik		Valur (Iceland)								
				£100,000	15.12.88	Tottenham Hotspur	51+20	4+2	2+2	5+1	3			
				£65,000	21.05.95	Bolton Wanderers	8	0+1		3				
Scott Green	5.10	11.12	15.01.70	Walsall	20.07.88	Derby County (T)								
				£50,000	17.03.90	Bolton Wanderers	133+44	16+1	16+2	16+4	20	1	2	
David Lee	5.7	10.0	05.11.67	Blackburn	08.08.86	Bury (T)	203+5	15	6	19+1	35	1		4
				£350,000	27.08.91	Southampton	11+9		0+1	1+1				
				£300,000	02.11.92	Bolton Wanderers	102+10	12	11+1	8+1	14	2		
Jason McAteer Ei: 9	5.10	10.5	18.06.71	Birkenhead		Marine								
					22.01.92	Bolton Wanderers	105+5	11	11	8+1	8	2	3	2
Mark Patterson FMC'87.	5.6	10.10	24.05.65	Darwen	01.05.83	Blackburn Rov. (A)	89+12	4	3+1	2+4	20	1		1
				£20,000	15.06.88	Preston North End	54+1	4+1	4	7	19			2
				£80,000+PE	01.02.90	Bury	42	2	1	4	10			
				£65,000	10.01.91	Bolton Wanderers	146+7	11+3	17	9	10	1	1	
Richard Sneekes via Volendam, Fortuna Sittard to	5.11	12.02	30.10.68	Amsterdam		Ajax								
				£200,000	12.08.94	Bolton Wanderers	37+1	7+1	1		6	1	1	
Alan Thompson E: Y.11.	6.0	12.5	22.12.73	Newcastle	11.03.91	Newcastle Utd (T)	13+3		1	3				
				£250,000	22.07.93	Bolton Wanderers	53+11	11+1	3+1	7+1	13	2	1	1
F O R W A R D S														
Owen Coyle Ei: 1, B, u21.2.	5.9	10.5	14.07.66	Glasgow		Dumbarton	85+18	4	2		36			
					01.08.88	Clydebank	63	2	3		33		1	
				£175,000	01.02.90	Airdrie	116+7	6	9+1	4	50	2	1	
				£250,000	30.06.93	Bolton Wanderers	33+16	5+2	8	7+1	12	1	5	5
Fabian De Freitas	6.1	12.9	28.07.72	Paramaribo		Vollendam								
				£400,000	19.08.94	Bolton Wanderers	7+6	0+3		0+2	2			2

BOLTON WANDERERS

PLAYERS NAME / Honours	Ht	Wt	Birthdate	Birthplace / Transfers	Contract Date	Clubs	League	L/Cup	FA Cup	Other	Lge	L/C	FAC	Oth
							APPEARANCES				GOALS			
John McGinlay	5.9	11.6	08.04.64	Inverness		Yeovil Town			5				2	
S: 9, B. Isth Lge Prem'88.						Elgin			1				1	
					22.02.89	Shrewsbury Town	58+2	4	1	3	27	2	2	
				£175,000	11.07.90	Bury	16+9	1	1	1+1	9			
				£80,000	21.01.91	Millwall	27+7	2+1	2	2	10			1
				£125,000	30.09.92	Bolton Wanderers	104+6	10+1	14	11	57	5	8	7
Mixu Paatelainen	6.0	13.11	03.02.67	Helsinki		Valkeakosken Haka								
						Dundee United	101+32	8+2	20+1	2+1	34	5	2	1
						Aberdeen	53+22	6	7+1	3	23	3	1	1
				£300,000	29.07.94	Bolton Wanderers	43+1	7+1	1	3	12	2		1
Stuart Whittaker	5.7	8.11	02.01.75	Liverpool		Liverpool (T)								
				Free	14.05.93	Bolton Wanderers	2+1							

TOP GOALSCORER 1994/95
John McGinlay

Division One goals (games)	16 (36)
Coca-Cola Cup Goals	4 (7+1)
F.A. Cup goals	0 (1)
Total	**20 (36)**
Total goals for Bolton since 30.09.92	75 (130+3)
Total for Country (full caps only)	
Career total as at June 1st 1995	129 (254+23)

THE MANAGER
ROY McFARLAND

Date of Birth . . . . 5th April 1948.
Place of Birth . . . . Liverpool.
Date of Appointment . . . . June 1995.

PREVIOUS CLUBS
As Manager . . . . Derby County.
As Coach . . . . Derby County.
As a Player . . . . Tranmere Rovers, Derby County, Bradford, Derby County.

HONOURS
As a Manager
None.

As a Player
Derby County: Division 1 championship 1972, 1975. Division 2 championship 1969.
International: 28 full caps and 5 u23 for England.

Burnden Park

Manchester Road, Bolton, Lancs BL3 2QR
Tel: 01204 389 200

Capacity . . . . .21,258.
First game . . . . .v P.N.E., Dai Jones Benefit, 11.9.1895.
First floodlit game . . . . .v Heart of Midlothian, 14.10.1957.

ATTENDANCES
Highest . . . . .69,912 v Manchester City, FA Cup 5th Round, 18.2.1933.
Lowest . . . . .1,507 v Rochdale, Autoglass Trophy, 10.12.1991.

OTHER GROUNDS . . . . .Pikes Lane.

MATCHDAY TICKET PRICES

Manchester Road Stand . . . . £15/£9

Burnden Stand . . . . £15/£9

Great Lever Stand. . . . . £11/£8

Terrace . . . . £11/£8

Ticket Office Telephone No. 01204 21101

CLUBCALL
0898 12 11 64
Calls cost 39p per minute cheap rate and 49p per
minute at all other times.
Call costings correct at time of going to press.

HOW TO GET TO THE GROUND

From the North:
Leave M61 at junction 5 or enter Bolton via A666 or A676. Then follow signs for Farnworth B653 into Manchester Road. In 0.6 miles
turn left into Croft Lane to Bolton Wanderers FC.

From South, East and West:
Use M62 until junction 14 then join M61. In 2.1 miles leave Motorway
and at roundabout take first exit B6536. In 2.1 miles turn right into
Croft Lane for Bolton Wanderers FC.

Car Parking:
Private car parking only in forecourt. Large car park 200 yards from
ground. Limited street parking nearby. Multi-storey car parks are in
town centre.

Nearest Railway Station:
Bolton (01204 28216).

MATCHDAY PROGRAMME

Programme Editor. . . . . Simon Marland.

Number of pages . . . . 44.

Price . . . . £1.50.

Subscriptions. . . . . £40 (All home matches).

Local Newspapers. . . . . Bolton Evening News.

Local Radio Stations . . . . Piccadilly Radio, G.M.R.

CHELSEA
(The Blues)
F.A. CARLING PREMIERSHIP
SPONSORED BY: COORS EXTRA GOLD

Back Row (L-R): Dave Collyer (Yth Dev. Officer), Terry Byrne (Asst. Physio), Robert Fleck, Gareth Hall, Michael Duberry, Nigel Spackman, Paul Furlong, Jakob Kjeldbjerg, Erland Johnsen, Paul Hughes, Mussie Izzet, Mark Nicholls, Junior Mendes, Christian McCann, Bernie Dixson (Yth Dev. Officer), Ian Oliver (Reflexologist). **Middle Row:** George Price (Res. Team Physio), Mike Banks (Physio), Scott Minto, Anthony Barness, Zeke Rowe, Andy Myers, Russell Kelly, Dmitri Kharine, Kevin Hitchcock, Steve Clarke, Craig Burley, David Lee, Terry Skiverton, Darren Barnard, Gwyn Williams (Scout/Admin Manager), Bob Orsborn (Kit Manager). **Front Row:** Eddie Niedzwiecki (res. Manager), Eddie Newton, Mark Stein, Andy Dow, Ruud Gullit, Dennis Wise, Glenn Hoddle (Manager), Peter Shreeves (Asst. Manager), Gavin Peacock, Mark Hughes, David Rocastle, Frank Sinclair, John Spencer, Graham Rix (Yth Manager).

CHELSEA
FORMED IN 1905
TURNED PROFESSIONAL IN 1905
LTD COMPANY IN 1905

PRESIDENT: G M Thomson
CHAIRMAN: K W Bates

DIRECTORS
C Hutchinson (Managing), Y Todd, M Harding.
SECRETARY
Keith Lacy
COMMERCIAL MANAGER
Samantha Parfitt/Carole Phair

MANAGER: Glenn Hoddle
ASSISTANT MANAGER: Peter Shreeves

RESERVE TEAM MANAGER
Eddie Niedzwiecki
YOUTH TEAM MANAGER
Graham Rix
PHYSIOTHERAPIST
Mike Banks

STATISTICIAN FOR THE DIRECTORY
Ron Hockings

Once again, and depressingly, the pattern of Chelsea's season followed an all-too-familiar trail. A promising start was not maintained and the failure to win a single home fixture in the Premiership between October 23rd and April 15th brought relegation clouds hovering menacingly over Stamford Bridge as the final weeks of the season approached.

Happily, a victory against Aston Villa, chiselled out from an ill-tempered and physical contest, then proved a turning point and more impressive performances against F.A. Cup finalists Manchester United and Everton, in Lancashire, and home wins at the expense of Queens Park Rangers and Arsenal contributed to a sequence of seven unbeaten games to end the season on a happier note, and make the earlier, largely self-inflicted, troubles seem all the more unnecessary and futile.

Early exits from both domestic cup competitions were balanced by reaching the semi-final of the European Cup Winners' Cup, marking Chelsea's first appearance in Europe since winning that trophy in 1971.

Unfortunately, an indifferent display against Zaragoza in Spain made a 3-goal leeway too large a deficit to reclaim, although the ensuing 3-1 victory in the second 'leg' provided the highlight of the season and produced a wonderfully tense and passionate night of skill and commitment at Stamford Bridge, too rarely enjoyed in recent years.

Admittedly, an ongoing catalogue of injuries constantly disrupted Glen Hoddle's team-building plans and fully tested the depth of his large squad of players, several of whom would appear to have little future at the club. Most certainly, Dennis Wise played no football during the final two months of the season and the loss of his influence and inventive skills proved a severe handicap.

Just before the curtain came down, Hoddle announced his retirement as a player. For more than an hour in the closing fixture against Arsenal he captivated an audience of almost 30,000 with his own inimitable repertoire of passing, skills with the ball, and tactical genius, before leaving the scene to a standing ovation from home and visiting fans alike.

Chelsea can only hope that some of his talents can be transmitted to his team from his, sadly, now permanent post in the dug-out. Certainly it is a matter of urgency that the progress being in the re-development of the facilities of the stadium are accompanied by a similar improvement on the pitch.

SCOTT CHESHIRE

CHELSEA

Premier League: 11th   **FA Cup:** 4th Round   **Coca-Cola Cup:** 3rd Round   **Cup Winners Cup:** Semi-Final

M	DATE	COMP.	VEN	OPPONENTS	RESULT	H/T	LP	GOAL SCORERS/GOAL TIMES	ATT.
1	A 20	PL	H	Norwich City	W 2-0	1-0		Sinclair 43, Furlong 75	23,098
2	27	PL	A	Leeds United	W 3-2	2-0	6	Spencer 37, 87, Wise 37 (pen)	(32,212)
3	31	PL	H	Manchester City	W 3-0	1-0	5	Peacock 3, Wise 73, Vonk 83 (og)	21,740
4	S 10	PL	A	Newcastle United	L 2-4	2-2	6	Peacock 15, Furlong 27	(34,435)
5	15	ECWC1/1	H	**Viktoria Zizkov**	W 4-2	2-2		**Sinclair 4, Rocastle 54, Wise 69, Furlong 3**	22,036
6	18	PL	A	Blackburn Rovers	L 1-2	0-1	7	Spencer 55	17,513
7	22	CC2/1	H	**Bournemouth & B**	W 1-0	1-0		**Rocastle 27**	8,974
8	24	PL	A	Crystal Palace	W 1-0	0-0	5	Furlong 51	(16,030)
9	29	ECWC1/2	A	**Viktoria Zizkov**	D 0-0	0-0			(6,000)
10	O 2	PL	H	West Ham United	L 1-2	0-0	7	Furlong 62	18,696
11	4	CC 2/2	A	**Bournemouth & B**	W 1-0	0-0		**Peacock 83**	(9,784)
12	8	PL	H	Leicester City	W 4-0	2-0	6	Peacock 4, Spencer 1, 48, Shipperley 76	18,397
13	15	PL	A	Arsenal	L 1-3	1-1	7	Wise 34	(38,234)
14	20	ECWC 2/1	H	**FK Austria**	D 0-0				22,560
15	23	PL	A	Ipswich Town	W 2-0	0-0	7	Wise 74, Shipperley 83	15,068
16	26	CC 3	A	**West Ham United**	L 0-1	0-1			(18,815)
17	29	PL	A	Sheffield Wednesday	D 1-1	1-0	7	Wise 40	(25,450)
18	N 3	ECWC 2/2	A	**FK Austria**	D 1-1	1-0		**Spencer 42**	(25,000)
19	6	PL	H	Coventry City	D 2-2	0-1	8	Kjeldbjerg 70, Spencer 47	17,090
20	9	PL	A	Liverpool	L 1-3	1-3	8	Spencer 1	(32,855)
21	19	PL	A	Nottingham Forest	W 1-0	0-0	7	Spencer 27	(22,092)
22	23	PL	A	Tottenham Hotspur	D 0-0	0-0	6		(27,037)
23	26	PL	H	Everton	L 0-1	0-0	8		28,115
24	D 3	PL	A	Southampton	W 1-0	0-0	7	Furlong 89	(14,404)
25	10	PL	A	Norwich City	L 0-3	0-2	8		(18,246)
26	18	PL	H	Liverpool	D 0-0	0-0	8		27,050
27	26	PL	H	Manchester United	L 2-3	0-1	9	Spencer 58 (pen), Newton 77	31,161
28	28	PL	A	Aston Villa	L 0-3	0-2	10		(32,901)
29	31	PL	H	Wimbledon	D 1-1	0-0	10	Furlong 57	16,105
30	J 7	FAC 3	H	**Charlton Athletic**	W 3-0	2-0		**Sinclair 41, Peacock 9, Spencer 89**	24,485
31	14	PL	H	Sheffield Wednesday	D 1-1	1-0	12	Spencer 34	17,285
32	21	PL	A	Ipswich Town	D 2-2	0-0	12	Stein 67, Burley 87	(17,296)
33	25	PL	A	Nottingham Forest	L 0-2	0-1	13		17,890
34	28	FAC 4	A	**Millwall**	D 0-0	0-0			(18,573)
35	F 4	PL	A	Coventry City	D 2-2	2-2	12	Stein 14, Spencer 32 (pen)	(13,429)
36	8	FAC 4R	H	**Millwall**	L 1-1	0-0	4-5	**Stein7**	I25,515
37	11	PL	H	Tottenham Hotspur	D 1-1	0-1	13	Wise 75	30,812
38	25	PL	A	West Ham United	W 2-1	0-1	13	Burley 67, Stein 75	(21,500)
39	28	ECWC 3/1	A	**Club Brugge**	L 0-1	0-0			(18,000)
40	M 5	PL	H	Crystal Palace	D 0-0	0-0	13		14,130
41	8	PL	A	Manchester City	W 2-1	1-1	10	Stein 5,81	(21,800)
42	11	PL	A	Leeds United	L 0-3	0-2	11		20,174
43	14	ECWC 3/2	H	**Club Brugge**	W 2-0	2-0		**Stein 16, Furlong 38**	28,661
44	18	PL	A	Blackburn Rovers	L 1-2	1-2	14	Stein 2	(25,490)
45	22	PL	A	Queens Park Rangers	L 0-1	0-0	15		(15,103)
46	A 1	PL	A	Newcastle United	D 1-1	1-0	15	Peacock 38	22,987
47	6	ECWC SF/1	A	**Real Zaragoza**	L 0-3	0-2			(35,000)
48	10	PL	A	Wimbledon	D 1-1	1-1	14	Sinclair 36	(7,022)
49	12	PL	H	Southampton	L 0-2	0-2	15		16,738
50	15	PL	H	Aston Villa	W 1-0	0-0	14	Stein 41	17,015
51	17	PL	A	Manchester United	D 0-0	0-0	14		(43,728)
52	20	ECWC SF/2	H	**Real Zaragoza**	W 3-1	1-0		**Furlong 30, Sinclair 62, Stein 86**	26,456
53	29	PL	H	Queens Park Rangers	W 1-0	0-0	12	Sinclair 64	21,704
54	M 3	PL	A	Everton	D 3-3	1-1	12	Furlong 29, 83, Hopkin 51	(33,180)
55	6	PL	A	Leicester City	D 1-1	1-1	12	Furlong 15	(18,140)
56	14	PL	H	Arsenal	W 2-1	1-1	11	Furlong 21, Stein 53	29,542
57									
58									
59									
60									

Best Home League Attendance: 31,161 v Manchester United   **Smallest:** 8,974 v Bournemouth   **Av Home Att:** 21,062

Goal Scorers:
League (50): Spencer 11 (2 pens), Furlong 10, Stein 8, Wise 6 (1 pen), Peacock 4, Sinclair 3, Burley 2, Shipperley 2, Hopkin, Kjeldbjerg, Newton, Opponent
C/Cola Cup (2): Rocastle, Peacock
FA Cup (4): Peacock, Sinclair, Spencer, Stein
ECWC (10): Furlong 3, Sinclair 2, Stein 2, Rocastle, Wise, Spencer

Compared with 1993-94: + 1,680

Kharin D.	Clarke S.	Kjeldbjerg J.	Johnsen E.	Sinclair F.	Rocastle D.	Spackman N.	Peacock G.	Wise D.	Shipperley N.	Furlong P.	Hoddle G.	Newton E.	Hitchcock K.	Minto S.	Spencer J.	Colgan N.	Rix G.	Fleck R.	Lee D.	Barness A.	Hall G.	Hopkin D.	Myers A.	Birley C.	Stein M.	Referee	
	X	X	X	X2	X	X	X	X	X	X1	X	S1	S2	S												T. Holbrook	1
X	X	X	X	X	X1	X	X	X		X	S	S1	S		X											G. Ashby	2
X	X	X	X	X	X	X	X	X		X	S2	S1	S		X1	S										M . Reed	3
X	X	X	X	X	X2	X1	X	X		X	S2	S1			X	S										P. Jones	4
X			X	X	X1	X	X	X		X		X		X	X		S1									C. Fallstrom	4
X	X	X	X	X	X1	X	X	X		X		S1			X	S	S									P. Durkin	5
X	X	X	X	X	X	X	S	X	S1	X		X			X1	S										P. Vanes	6
X	X	X	X	X	X	X	X		S	X		X			X	S				S						R. Dilkes	8
X	X		X	X		X	X			X		X					X			X						G. Beschilin	9
X	X	X	X	X	X2		X			S1		X	S		X				S2	X1						P. Don	10
X	X	X	X	X	X	X1	X	X	X	X2		S1	S						S2							P. Durkin	11
X	X	X	X	X	X1	X	X	X	X2	S1	X		S2	S		X1										J. Worrall	12
X	X	X	X	X1	X	X	X	X	X	X		X	S				S									D. Gallagher	13
X		X	X	X1	X	X	X	X	X	X		X2					S1			S2						A. Ouzounov	14
X	X2	X		X		X	X	X	X1	X		X	S				S2	X	X	S1						B. Hill	15
X	X	X		X	X	X1	X	X	X	X		X	S				S2	X	X2	S1						K. Cooper	16
X	X	X		X1	X	X	X	X	X	X		X	S				S	X	X	X	S1					M. Reed	17
X	X		X2	X	X	X	X	S2	X	X	S1	X					X	X1	X							F. Vanden Wungaert	18
X	X	X1	X			X	X	X	X	X		X				S	X	X	X	S1						S. Lodge	19
X	X	X1	X	X2	X	X	X	X	X		X					X	S1	X	S2							G. Poll	20
X	X	X		X	X2	X	S2	X	X		S	X	X1	X		X			S1							T. Holbrook	21
X		X	X1	X	X	X	X2	X	X		S	X		S2	X		X			S1						G. Willard	22
X		X	X	X	X	S1	S2	X1	S	X	X		X				X				X2					R. Hart	23
X	X	X	X	X	X	S1	X	S	X	X2	X		X1		S2	X										R. Gifford	24
X		X	X1	X	X	X	X	X	X	S	X		X1	S		S1										J. Worrall	25
X	X	X1	X	X	X	X	X2	X	X	S			S2							S1						D. Gallagher	26
X	X	X	X	X	X	X	X2	S2	S	X			X								X	X1	S1			M. Reed	27
X	X	X	X	X	X	X	X	X	X	S	X									X	X1	S1	X			K. Burge	28
X	X	X	X	X1	X	X	X	S1	X	S	X		S								X					K. Morton	29
X	X	X	X	X	X	X	X	S	S1	X	X									X1						T. Holbrook	30
X	X	X	X	X1	X	X	X	S	S1	X	X									X1						G. Willard	31
X	X	X	X	X	X1	X	X	X	S	X									S2			S1	X			P. Don	32
X	S	X	X	X1	X	S1	X	S	X	X												S1	X			M. Bodenham	33
X	X1	X	X	X	X	X	S	S	X	X											S1	X				R. Dilkes	34
X	X1	X	X	S1	X	X	X	S2	S	X	X										X	X2	X			R. Hart	35
X	X	X	X1	X2	X	S2	S1	S	X								X				X	X				M. Bodenham	36
X	X2	X1	X	S1	S2	X	S	X					X				X				X					P. Durkin	37
X2	X	X1	X	S1	X	S2	X	X					X				X			S	X	X				G. Ashby	38
X	X	S1	X	X	X1	X	X	X1	X				X				S						X	X			S. Mohmentaler	39
X	X	X	X1	S	X	X	X	X	X1	S							S	S2	S1	X	X2	X	X			D. Ellery	40
X	X	X	X	X	X1	X	X	X1	X				S				S2	S1	X	X	X					P. Jones	41
X	X	X2	X	X1	X	X	X	X	X1				S2	S1	X	X										P. Pairetto	43
X	X	X1	X2	X	X	X	X	S					S2	S1	X	X1	X									P. Danson	44
S	X	X	X	X	S1	X	X	X					X							S1	S2	X				B. Hill	45
S	X	X2	X	X	X	X	S1	X	X1	X2									S1		S2	X				M. Bodenham	46
X1	X	X	X	X	X	X	S1	X	X2											X		S2				L. Sundell	47
S		X	X	X	X	X	X	X1					S1		S	X			X	X	X1	X				K. Morton	48
X	X	X2	X	S1	X	X	X	X1					S2				X			X	X1	X2				A.Wilkie	49
X	X1	X	X	X	X	S	S2	X	S1								X			X						K. Burge	50
X	X	X1	X	X2	S	S2	S1	X									X	X			S1	X				S. Lodge	51
X	X2	X1	X	X	X	S2	S1	X					S				X					X				J. Coroada	52
X	X2	X1	X	X	S2	X	S	X				S				X	S1				X					G. Ashby	53
X	X	X	X	X	S1	X	X	X				S				X	S	X	X1	X						B. Hill	54
X	X	X	X	X	X	S2	X	X1				X					X	S	S	X1	X					G. Willard	55
X	X	X	X2	X																						J. Worrall	56
31	29	23	33	35	26	36	38	18	6	30	3	22	11	19	26				9	10	4	7	9	16	21	League Appearances	
					2		1	4	6	9	8	1		3		1	5	2	2	8	1	9	3			League Sub Appearances	
3	2	3	3	2	3	2	3	3	2+1	2+1		2+1			1			0+2	1	1	0+1					C/Cola Appearances	
3	3	2	2	3		3	3	2	1	0+2	3	3						1		1	2+1	1+1		1+1	3	FA Cup Appearances	
4	5	1	8	7	7+1	7	7	5	2	7	0+3	5	4	5+1	4+1		1+2	1+1	2+1	1+1		2	1	2+1		ECWC Appearances	

Also Played: A. Judge S (19,20)

CHELSEA

CLUB RECORDS

BIGGEST VICTORIES
League: 7-0 v Lincoln City, Division 2, 29.10.1910.
7-0 v Port Vale, Division 2, 3.3.1906.
9-2 v Glossop N.E., Division 2, 1.9.1906.
7-0 v Portsmouth, Division 2, 21.5.1963.
7-0 v Walsall (a), Division 2, 4.2.1989.
F.A. Cup: 9-1 v Worksop, 1st Round, 31.1.1908.
League Cup: 7-0 v Doncaster Rovers, 3rd Round, 16.11.1960.
Europe: 13-0 v Jeunesse Hautcharge, ECWC, 29.9.1971.

BIGGEST DEFEATS
League: 1-8 v Wolverhampton W., Division 1, 26.9.1923.
0-7 v Leeds United, Division 1, 7.10.1967.
0-7 v Nottingham Forest, Division 1, 20.4.1991
F.A. Cup: 0-6 v Sheffield Wednesday, 2nd Round replay, 5.2.1913.
1-7 v Crystal Palace, 3rd Round, 16.11.1960.
League Cup: 2-6 v Stoke City, 3rd Round, 22.10.1974.
Europe: 0-5 v Barcelona, Semi-Final EUFA, 25.5.1966.

MOST POINTS
3 points a win: 99, Division 2, 1988-89 (Division 2 record, 46 games).
2 points a win: 57, Division 2, 1906-07.

MOST GOALS SCORED
98, Division 1, 1960-61.
Greaves 41, Tindall 16, Tambling 9, Brabrook 8, Livesey 8, Blunstone 5, Silett 2, Anderton 1, Bradbury 1, Bridges 1, Brooks 1, Gibbs 1, Mortimore 1, Harrison 1, opponents 2.

MOST GOALS CONCEDED
100, Division 1, 1960-61.

MOST FIRST CLASS MATCHES IN A SEASON
60 - 1965-66 (League 42, FA Cup 6, Fairs Cup 12).
60 - 1970-71 (League 42, FA Cup 3, League Cup 3, Charity Shield 1, ECWC 10).

MOST LEAGUE WINS
29, Division 2, 1988-89.

MOST LEAGUE DRAWS
18, Division 1, 1922-23.

MOST LEAGUE DEFEATS
27, Division 1, 1978-79.

INDIVIDUAL CLUB RECORDS

MOST GOALS IN A SEASON
Jimmy Greaves: 43 goals in 1960-61 (League 41, League Cup 2).

MOST GOALS IN A MATCH
6. George Hilsdon v Worksop, FA Cup (9-1), 11.1.1908.

OLDEST PLAYER
Dick Spence, 39 years 1 month, 1947-48.
Graham Rix made his Chelsea debut on 15.09.1994 (ECWC) aged 37 years 11 months, he made his League debut on 14.05.1995.
YOUNGEST PLAYER
Ian Hamilton, 16 years 4 months, 1966-67.

MOST CAPPED PLAYER
Glen Hoddle (England) 53.

BEST PERFORMANCES

League: 1988-89: Matches Played 46, Won 29, Drawn 12, Lost 3, Goals for 96, Goals against 50. Points 99. First in Division 2.
Highest Position: 1954-55, 1st in Division 1.
F.A. Cup: 1969-70: 3rd Round Birmingham City 3-0; 4th Round Burnley 2-2,3-1; 5th Round Crystal Palace 4-1; 6th Round Queens Park Rangers 4-2; Semi-Final Watford 5-1; Final Leeds United 2-2,2-1.
League Cup: 1964-65: 2nd Round Birmingham City 3-0; 3rd Round Notts County 4-0; 4th Round Swansea 3-2; 5th Round Workington 2-2,2-0; Semi-Final Aston Villa 3-2,1-1; Final Leicester City 0-0,3-2.
Europe: ECWC - 1970-71: 1st Round Aris Salonica 1-1,5-1; 2nd Round CSKA Sofia 1-0,1-0; 3rd Round Bruges 0-2,4-0; Semi-Final Manchester City 1-0,1-0; Final Real Madrid 1-1,2-1.
EUFA - 1965-66: 1st Round A.S.Roma 0-0,4-1; 2nd Round Wiener S.H. 0-1,2-0; 3rd Round A.C.Milan 2-1,1-2,1-1 (Chelsea won on toss of a coin); Semi-Final Barcelona 2-0,0-2, 0-5.

ADDITIONAL INFORMATION

PREVIOUS NAMES
None.
PREVIOUS LEAGUES
None.

Club colours: Royal blue shirts with white trim, blue shorts & socks.
Change colours: Grey shirts with orange trim, orange shorts, grey socks.

Reserve League: Avon Insurance Combination.

DIVISIONAL RECORD

	Played	Won	Drawn	Lost	For	Against	Points
Division 1/P	2,486	868	660	958	4,089	3,916	2,538
Division 2	786	383	202	201	1,323	887	1,018
Total	**3,272**	**1,251**	**862**	**1,159**	**4,912**	**4,803**	**3,556**

RECORDS AND STATISTICS

COMPETITIONS

Div 1/P	Div.2	ECWC	EUFA	A/Scot
1907-10	1905-07	1970-71	1965-66	1975-76
1912-24	1910-12	1971-72	1968-69	1976-77
1930-62	1924-30	1994-95		1977-78
1963-75	1962-63			
1977-79	1975-77			
1984-87	1979-84			
1989-	1988-89			

HONOURS

Div 1	Div.2	FA Cup	Lge Cup	ECWC	C/shld
1954-55	1983-84	1970	1965	1971	1955
	1988-89				FMC
					1986
					1990

MOST APPEARANCES

Ron Harris 791+12 (1961-80)

Year	League	FA Cup	Lge Cup	ECWC	EUFA	A/Scott
1961-62	3					
1962-63	7					
1963-64	41	3	1			
1964-65	42	5	6			
1965-66	36	6		10		
1966-67	42	7	3			
1967-68	40	5	1			
1968-69	40	5	3		4	
1969-70	30	8	3			
1970-71	38	3	4	9		
1971-72	41	3	9	4		
1972-73	36	3	7			
1973-74	36	2	1			
1974-75	42	2	4			
1975-76	38+2	4	1			3
1976-77	15+4	2	0+1			2
1977-78	37	4	1			2+1
1978-79	38+2	1	1			
1979-80	38+1	1	1+1			
	646+9	64	46+2	13	14	7+1

MOST GOALS IN A CAREER

Bobby Tambling - 202 (1958-69

Year	League	FA Cup	Lge Cup	EUFA
1958-59	1	-	-	-
1959-60	1	-	-	-
1960-61	9	-	3	-
1961-62	20	2	-	-
1962-63	35	2	-	-
1963-64	17	2	-	-
1964-65	15	4	6	-
1965-66	16	5	-	2
1966-67	21	6	1	-
1967-68	12	3	-	-
1968-69	17	1	-	2
Total	164	25	10	3

Current leading goalscorer: Dennis Wise - 44 (1990-95)

RECORD TRANSFER FEE RECEIVED

Amount	Club	Player	Date
£2,200,000	Tottenham H.	Gordon Durie	8/91
£1,700,000	Leeds United	Tony Dorigo	6/91
£925,000	Everton	Pat Nevin	7/88
£825,000	Manchester Utd	Ray Wilkins	8/79

RECORD TRANSFER FEE PAID

Amount	Club	Player	Date
£2,300,000	Watford	Paul Furlong	5/94
£2,100,000	Norwich City	Robert Fleck	8/92
£1,800,000	Wimbledon	Dennis Wise	7/90
£1,200,000	Norwich City	Andy Townsend	7/90

MANAGERS

Name	Seasons	Best	Worst
J T Robertson	1905-06	3(2)	3(2)
David Calderhead	1907-33	8(1)	9(2)
Leslie Knighton	1933-39	8(1)	20(1)
Billy Birrell	1939-52	13(1)	19(1)
Ted Drake	1952-62	1(1)	22(1)
Tommy Docherty	1962-67	3(1)	2(2)
Dave Sexton	1967-74	3(1)	17(1)
Ron Stuart	1974-75	21(1)	21(1)
Eddie McCreadie	1975-77	2(2)	11(2)
Ken Shellitto	1977-78	16(1)	16(1)
Danny Blanchflower	1978-79	22(1)	22(1)
Geoff Hurst	1979-81	4(2)	12(2)
John Neal	1981-85	1(2)	18(2)
John Hollins	1985-88	6(1)	18(1)
Bobby Campbell	1988-91	5(1)	1(2)
Ian Porterfield	1991-93		
David Webb (Trail)	1993	11(P)	11(P)
Glenn Hoddle	1993-	11(P)	11(P)

LONGEST LEAGUE RUNS

of undefeated matches:	27 (29.10.1988 - 15.4.1989)	of league matches w/out a win:	21 (3.11.1987 - 2.4.1988)
of undefeated home matches:	34 (28.4.1910 - 24.2.1912)	of undefeated away matches:	13 (5.11.1988 - 8.4.1989)
without home win:	11 (30.3.1974 - 28.9.1974)	without an away win:	22 (1.3.1952 - 14.3.1953)
of league wins:	8 (5.2.27 - 21.3.27 & 15.3.89 - 8.4.89)	of home wins:	13 (12.11.1910 - 2.9.1911)
of league defeats:	7 (1.11.1952 - 20.12.1952)	of away wins:	7 (4.2.1989 - 8.4.1989)

CHELSEA

PLAYERS NAME Honours	Ht	Wt	Birthdate	Birthplace Transfers	Contract Date	Clubs	League	L/Cup	FA Cup	Other	Lge	L/C	FAC	Oth
G O A L K E E P E R S														
Kevin Hitchcock	6.1	12.2	05.10.62	Canning Town		Barking			3					
FRT'87.				£15,000	04.08.83	Nottingham Forest								
					01.02.84	Mansfield Town	182	12	10	20				
				£250,000	25.03.88	Chelsea	68+1	8	5	13				
Dmitri Kharine	6.2	12.4	16.08.68	Moscow		CSKA Moscow								
CIS. USSR. Russan Int. Olympic G.Medal'88.				£200,000	22.12.92	Chelsea	76	6	11	4				
D E F E N D E R S														
Anthony Barness	5.10	10.12	25.03.73	Lewisham	06.03.91	Charlton Ath. (T)	21+6	2	3	1+1	1		1	
				£350,000	08.09.92	Chelsea	12+2	1		2+1				
				Loan	12.08.93	Middlesbrough				1				
Steve Clarke	5.9	11.10	29.08.63	Saltcoats		St. Mirren	151	21	19	6	6		1	
S: 6, B.2, u21.8, Y. SLge.1. Div.2'89.				£422,000	19.01.87	Chelsea	247+4	16	20	21	6	1	1 1	
Andrew Dow	5.9	10.7	07.02.73	Dundee		Dundee	8+10		1		1			
S: u21.3				£250,000	15.07.93	Chelsea	13+1	2	1					
Gareth Hall	5.10	12.0	20.03.69	Croydon	25.04.86	Chelsea (A)	115+16	12+1	6	10+4	3			1
W: 9, u21.1. Div.2'89. ZDC'90.														
Ruud Gullit	6.0	13.0	01.09.62	Surinam		DWS Amsterdam								
Dutch Int.					1979-80	Haalem	91				32			
					1982-83	Feyenoord	85				30			
					1985-86	PSV Eindhoven	68				46			
					1987-88	AC Milan	117				35			
					1993-94	Sampdoria	31				15			
					1994-95	AC Milan	8				3			
					1994-95	Sampdoria	22				9			
				Free	08.95	Chelsea								
Erland Johnsen	6.1	13.5	05.04.67	Frederikstad, Norway		Bayern Munich								
Norweigan Int.				£306,000	06.12.89	Chelsea	103+2	4	14	12	1			
Jakob Kjeldbjerg				Silkeborg										
Norweigan Int.				£400,000	13.08.93	Chelsea	52	6	6+1	1	2			
David Lee	6.3	13.12	26.11.69	Kingswood	01.07.88	Chelsea (T)	88+30	12+4	3+4	6+2	9	1		1
E: u21.10, Y.1. Div.2'89				Loan	30.01.92	Reading	5				5			
				Loan	12.08.94	Portsmouth	4+1							
Scott Minto	5.9	10.7	06.08.71	Heswall	02.02.89	Charlton Ath. (T)	171+9	8	8+2	7	6	2		1
E: u21.6, Y.8.				£775,000	28.05.94	Chelsea	19		3	5+1				
Andrew Myers	5.8	9.10	03.11.73	Hounslow	25.07.91	Chelsea (T)	27+6	1+1	6	3	1			
E: Y.12, S.3.														
Frank Sinclair	5.8	11.2	03.12.71	Lambeth	17.05.90	Chelsea (T)	114	11	12	7	4	1	1	2
				Loan	12.12.91	West Bromwich A.	6				1			
M I D F I E L D														
Darren S Barnard	5.10	11.0	30.11.71	Rintein (Germany)		Wokingham Town								
E: u18.4				£50,000	25.07.90	Chelsea	18+11	1+1	1+1		2			
Craig Burley	6.1	11.7	24.09.71	Irvine	01.09.89	Chelsea (T)	43+17		9+2	3	5		3	
Edward Newton	5.11	11.2	13.12.71	Hammersmith	17.05.90	Chelsea (T)	87+14	11+1	7+2	5	7	1		
E: u21.2.				Loan	23.01.92	Cardiff City	18				4			
Gavin Peacock	5.8	11.5	18.11.67	Eltham	19.11.84	Q.P.R. (A)	7+10		0+1		1			
E: Y.3, S, u19.3. Div.1'93.				£40,000	05.10.87	Gillingham	69+1	4	2	5	11			1
				£250,000	16.08.89	Bournemouth	56	6	2	2	8			
				£150,000	30.11.90	Newcastle United	102+3	6	6	3	35	5	2	4
				£1,250,000	12.08.93	Chelsea	75	5	11	7	12	1	7	
David Rocastle	5.9	11.1	02.05.67	Lewisham	31.12.84	Arsenal (A)	204+14	32+1	18+2	9	24	6	4	
E: 14, B.2, u21.14. LC'87. Div.1'89'91. CT'89.				£2,000,000	04.08.92	Leeds United	17+8	0+3	0+3	2+1	2			
				£2,000,000	22.12.93	Manchester City	21		2		2			
				£1,250,000	.08.95	Chelsea	26+2	3		7+1		1		1
Nigel Spackman	6.1	12.4	02.12.60	Romsey		Andover								
Div.1'88, Div.2'84, FMC'86, SPD'90'91'92				Free	08.05.80	Bournemouth	118+1	5	7		10			
SCL'91, SFAC'92				£40,000	20.06.83	Chelsea	139+2	22+1	8	7	12		1	1
				£400,000	24.02.87	Liverpool	39+12	6+1	5					
				£500,000	02.02.89	QPR	27+2	2		2	1	1		
				£500,000	30.11.89	Glasgow Rangers	100	10	9	5	1	1	1	
				£487,000	08.09.92	Chelsea	47+4	4	6	7				
F O R W A R D S														
Robert Fleck	5.7	10.8	11.08.65	Glasgow		Glasgow Rangers	61+24	3+5	1+1	3+4	29	2		3
S: 4, u21.7, Y. SPD'87. SLC'87'88.				Loan		Partick Thistle	1+1				1			
				£580,000	17.12.87	Norwich City	130+13	13	16+2	7	40	11	11	4
				£2,100,000	13.08.92	Chelsea	35+5	7	1		3	1		
				Loan	17.12.93	Bolton Wanderers	6+1			1	1			
				Loan	12.01.95	Bristol City	10				1			
Paul A Furlong	6.0	11.8	01.10.68	Wood Green		Enfield			4					1
E: S-P5; FAT'88				£130,000	31.07.91	Coventry City	27+10	4	1+1	1	4	1		
				£250,000	24.07.92	Watford	79	7	2	2	3	37	4	
				£2,300,000	26.05.94	Chelsea	30+6	2	1	7	10			3

CHELSEA

PLAYERS NAME Honours	Ht	Wt	Birthdate	Birthplace Transfers	Contract Date	Clubs	APPEARANCES League	L/Cup	FA Cup	Other	GOALS Lge	L/C	FAC	Oth
Mark Hughes	5.9	11.2	01.11.63	Wrexham	05.11.80	Manchester Utd (A)	85+4	5+1	10	14+2	37	4	4	2
W: 57, u21.5, Y. FAC'85'90'94. ECWC'91.				£2,500,000	01.07.86	Barcelona	28				4			
ESC'91. LC'92. Prem'93'94. CS'93.				Loan		Bayern Munich	18				6			
				£1,500,000	20.07.88	Manchester United	251+5	32	34+1	27+1	82	12	13	8
				£1,500,000	08.95	Chelsea								
John Spencer	5.7	9.10	11.09.70	Glasgow		Glasgow Rangers	7+6	2		1+1	2			1
S: u21.3				Loan	04.03.89	Morton	4				1			
				£450,000	01.08.92	Chelsea	52+19	1+4	8+4	4+1	23		3	1
Mark E S Stein	5.6	10.0	28.01.66	South Africa	31.01.84	Luton Town (J)	41+13	4+1	9	3	19		3	1
E: u19.2, Y1; LC'88; AGT'92; Div2'93				Loan	29.01.86	Aldershot	2				1			
				£300,000	26.08.88	Q.P.R.	20+13	4	2+1	4	4	2	1	
					15.09.89	Oxford United	72+10	4	2+1	3	18			
				£100,000	15.09.91	Stoke City	94	8	4	17	50	8		10
				£1,500,000	28.10.93	Chelsea	37+3		9	2+1	16		2	2
Dennis F Wise	5.6	9.5	15.12.66	Kensington		Southampton (A)								
E: 6, B3, u21.1; FAC'88				Free	28.03.85	Wimbledon	127+8	14	11	5	26		3	
				£1,600,000	03.07.90	Chelsea	150+2	14	11	10	27	6	2	3

TOP GOALSCORER 1994/95
John Spencer

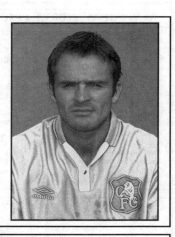

Premiership goals (games)	11 (26+3)
Coca-Cola Cup Goals	0 (1)
F.A. Cup goals	1 (3)
ECWC	1 (4+1)
Total	**13 (34+4)**

Total goals for Chelsea since 01.08.92 . . . . 27 (65+28)

Career total as at June 1st 1995 . . . . 31 (79+35)

THE MANAGER
GLENN HODDLE

Date of Birth . . . . 27th November 1957.
Place of Birth . . . . Hayes.
Date of Appointment . . . . June 1993.

PREVIOUS CLUBS
As Manager . . . . Swindon Town.
As Coach . . . . None.
As a Player . . . . Tottenham Hotspur, Monaco, Swindon Town, Chelsea.

HONOURS
As a Manager
Swindon Town: Promotion to Premier League via the play-offs 1992-93.
Chelsea: FA Cup runners-up 1993-94.
As a Player
Tottenham Hotspur: UEFA Cup Winners. FA Cup Winner.
International
33 full caps, Youth, U21 & 'B' caps for England.

STAMFORD BRIDGE
Fulham Road, London SW6 1HS
Tel: 0171 385 5545

Capacity 31,544

First game..v Liverpool (friendly) 4-0, 4.9.1905.
First floodlit game..v Sparta, 19.3.1951.
Internationals...England v Scotland, 1913. v Wales, 1929. v Austria, 1932.

ATTENDANCES
Highest...82,905 v Arsenal, Division 1, 12.10.1935.
Lowest...4,767 v Plymouth, Simod Cup, 9.11.1988.

OTHER GROUNDS..None.

MATCHDAY TICKET PRICES

Categories	A	B
North Stand		
Upper Tier (Members only)	£20	£15
Lower Tier	£20	£15
(Members only until one week prior to match)		
East Stand		
Upper Tier	£25	£16
Middle Tier	£35	£22
Lower Tier	£20	£17
Family Section		
1+1	£18	£14
Add. Juv/Unaccompanied Juv	£6	£4
Add. Qualifying Adult	£18	£14
West Stand	£25	£16
Western Enclosure	£12	£10
Concessions	£6	£5
Ticket Sales.	0898 12 10 11	

CLUBCALL 0898 12 11 59
Calls cost 39p per minute cheap rate and 49p per minute at all other times.
Call costings correct at time of going to press.

HOW TO GET TO THE GROUND

From the North
From motorway (M1) and A1. Follow signs to Central London to Hyde Park Corner, then follow signs to Guildford (A3) into Knightsbridge (A4). In 1 mile turn left (A308) into Fulham Road for Chelsea FC.

From the East
Via Hyde Park Corner as above or via Embankment and Cheyne Walk (A3212). Follow signs to Chelsea (A3220) then at crossroads turn left (A308) into Fulham Road for Chelsea FC.

From the South
Use A13 or A24 then A219 to cross Putney Bridge. Follow signs to the West End (A304), then join A308 into Fulham Road for Chelsea FC.

From the West
From motorway (M4). Follow signs to Central London, then Westminster (A3220). In 0.8 miles, at crossroads, turn right (A308) into Fulham Road for Chelsea FC.

Car Parking: Street parking only, very limited.

Nearest Tube Station: Fulham Broadway (District Line).

MATCHDAY PROGRAMME

Programme Editor . . . . Neil Barnett.

Number of pages . . . . 64.

Price . . . . £2.

Subscriptions . . . . £42 (UK postage).
. . . . All League and any FA Cup and Coca-Cola Cup.

Local Newspapers . . . . Fulham Chronicle, West London Observer,
. . . . Chelsea News.

Local Radio Stations . . . . LBC (away games only) 261 MW.

COVENTRY CITY
(The Sky Blues)
F.A. CARLING PREMIERSHIP
SPONSORED BY: PEUGEOT

Back Row (L-R): Isaias, David Burrows, Iyseden Christie, John Filan, Steve Ogrizovic, Jonathan Gould, Peter Shilton, Gary Gillespie, Leigh Jenkinson, Carlita. **Middle Row:** Trevor Gould (Yth Manager), Jim Blythe (GK Coach), George Dalton (Physio), Paul Williams, Marcus Hall, John Williams, David Busst, Steve Morgan, Paul Cook, David Rennie, Willie Boland, Gary Pendry (Coach), Brian Roberts (Res. Manager). **Front Row:** Julian Darby, Brian Borrows, Kevin Richardson, Dion Dublin, Ron Atkinson (Manager), Gordon Strachan (Asst. Manager), John Salako, Peter Ndlovu, Paul Telfer, Ally Pickering.

COVENTRY CITY
FORMED IN 1883
TURNED PROFESSIONAL IN 1893
LTD COMPANY IN 1907

PRESIDENT: Eric Grove
CHAIRMAN: Bryan A Richardson
DEPUTY CHAIRMAN: Mike McGinnity
DIRECTORS
J F W Reason, A M Jepson,
P D H Robins
SECRETARY
Graham Hover (01203 223 535)
DIRECTOR OF SALES & MARKETING
Mark Jones (01203 633 823)

MANAGER: Ron Atkinson
ASSISTANT MANAGER: Gordon Strachan
COACH: Gary Pendry
RESERVE TEAM MANAGER
Brian Roberts
YOUTH TEAM MANAGER
Trevor Gould
PHYSIOTHERAPIST
George Dalton

STATISTICIAN FOR THE DIRECTORY
Jim Brown

The turbulent history of Coventry City continued with another change of manager in mid season, Ron Atkinson taking over from Phil Neal in February and becoming the sixth manager in five years. Neal's fate was sealed after eleven League games without a win in the mid winter which saw City fall from 10th to 20th place. With four down relegation was looking a certainty, but 'Big Ron's' influence saw an immediate improvement and a six game unbeaten run culminated in a superb 3-2 win at Anfield, with Peter Ndlovu scoring the first hat-rick by a visiting player for 33 years.

Despite a late scare relegation was never a serious threat but mathematical safety was guaranteed with another superb away win at Tottenham with the new 38-year-old player/assistant manager Gordon Strachan creating three goals.

Long term injuries to Lee Hurst and Stewart Robson, and short term injuries to Busst, Flynn, Wegerle, Ndlovu and Ogrizovic didn't help team selection, but gave opportunities to Youth products Boland and Hall and long term investments such as Filan, Pickering and Pressley.

After an outstanding World Cup Babb was sold to Liverpool for a record fee for a defender, £3.75 million and Neal invested over half of the proceeds on Dion Dublin. Dublin kicked City's season into action with ten goals in his first thirteen games and made his price tag look cheap. Neal's other signings Cook, Jones, Pressley and Marsh had mixed fortunes. 'Big Ron' also stepped into the market with good effect, buying the experienced Richardson and Burrows.

With the club being run on solid lines and gates up to almost 16,000 expectations are higher than at any time since the Sillett days, but competition gets hotter in the Premier League every season. City can't compete with the big clubs in the transfer market and will have to increasingly rely on 'Big Ron's' eye for a bargain, his motivational skills and the burgeoning Youth policy to ensure a Premier League future.

JIM BROWN.

COVENTRY CITY

PREMIER LEAGUE: 16th   FA Cup: 4th Round   Coca-Cola Cup: 3rd Round

M	DATE	COMP.	VEN	OPPONENTS	RESULT	H/T	LP	GOAL SCORERS/GOAL TIMES	ATT.
1	A 20	PL	H	Wimbledon	D 1-1	0-0		Busst 70	11,005
2	24	PL	A	Newcastle United	L 0-4	0-3			(34,163)
3	27	PL	A	Blackburn Rovers	L 0-4	0-4	20		(21,657)
4	29	PL	H	Aston Villa	L 0-1	0-1	22		12,218
5	S 10	PL	A	Queens Park Rangers	D 2-2	1-2	20	Cook 27, Dublin 84	(11,398)
6	17	PL	H	Leeds United	W 2-1	0-0	18	Dublin 50, Cook 83(pen)	15,383
7	20	CC 2/1	A	**Wrexham**	W 2-1	1-1		**Darby 37, Flynn 77**	(5,286)
8	24	PL	H	Southampton	L 1-3	1-1	10	Dublin 2	11,798
9	O 3	PL	A	Leicester City	D 2-2	1-1	21	Wegerle 11, Dublin 73	(19,372)
10	5	CC 2/2	H	**Wrexham**	W 3-2	1-0		**Dublin 17, 59, Wegerle 63**	8,615
11	10	PL	H	Ipswich	W 2-0	1-0	17	Wark 45 (og), Cook 75 (pen)	9,509
12	15	PL	A	Everton	W 2-0	2-0	14	Dublin 8, Wegerle 17	(28,223)
13	23	PL	A	Arsenal	L 1-2	0-2	15	Wegerle 81 (pen)	(3,1725)
14	26	CC 3	A	**Blackburn Rovers**	L 0-2	0-0			(14,538)
15	29	PL	H	Manchester City	W 1-0	0-0	13	Dublin 85	15,802
16	N 2	PL	H	Crystal Palace	L 1-4	1-2	14	Dublin 23	10,729
17	6	PL	A	Chelsea	D 2-2	1-0	15	Dublin 45, Ndlovu 77	(17,090)
18	19	PL	H	Norwich City	W 1-0	0-0	13	Jones 62	11,891
19	26	PL	A	West Ham United	W 1-0	0-0	10	Busst 58	(17,251)
20	D 3	PL	H	Liverpool	D 1-1	0-1	10	Flynn 58	21,032
21	10	PL	A	Wimbledon	L 0-2	0-2	12		(7,349)
22	17	PL	A	Newcastle United	D 0-0	0-0	12		17,237
23	26	PL	H	Nottingham Forest	D 0-0	0-0	12		19,116
24	28	PL	A	Sheffield Wednesday	L 1-5	1-2	16	Ndlovu 17 (pen)	(26,056)
25	31	PL	H	Tottenham Hotspur	L 0-4	0-1	17		19,965
26	J 3	PL	A	Manchester United	L 0-2	0-1	17		(43,130)
27	7	FAC 3	H	**West Bromwich A.**	D 1-1	0-0		**Wegerle 52 (pen)**	16,563
28	14	PL	A	Manchester City	D 0-0	0-0	17		(20,632)
29	18	FAC 3R	A	**West Bromwich A.**	W 2-0	0-0		**Dublin 82, Ndlovu 84**	(23,230)
30	21	PL	H	Arsenal	L 0-1	0-0	19		14,557
31	25	PL	A	Norwich City	D 2-2	1-1	19	Dublin 22, Jenkinson 76	(14,024)
32	28	FAC 4	H	**Norwich City**	D 0-0	0-0			15,122
33	F 4	PL	H	Chelsea	D 2-2	2-2	20	Flynn 26, Burley 36 (og)	13,423
34	8	FAC 4R	A	**Norwich City**	L 1-3	1-1		**Ndlovu 32**	(14,673)
35	11	PL	A	Crystal Palace	W 2-0	0-0	17	Jones 75, Dublin 85	(11,871)
36	18	PL	H	West Ham United	W 2-0	1-0	14	Ndlovu 25, Marsh 67	(17,563)
37	25	PL	H	Leicester City	W 4-2	2-0	12	Flynn 18, 76, Marsh 27, Ndlovu 87	20,650
38	M 4	PL	A	Southampton	D 0-0	0-0	12		(14,505)
39	6	PL	A	Aston Villa	D 0-0	0-0	12		(26,186)
40	11	PL	H	Blackburn Rovers	D 1-1	1-0	12	Dublin 30	18,556
41	14	PL	A	Liverpool	W 3-2	2-0	9	Ndlovu 20, 35 (pen), 85	(27,183)
42	18	PL	A	Leeds United	L 0-3	0-1	10		(29,179)
43	A 1	PL	H	Queens Park Rangers	L 0-1	0-0	12		15,751
44	15	PL	H	Sheffield Wednesday	W 2-0	1-0	12	Dublin 3, Ndlovu 88	15,753
45	17	PL	A	Nottingham Forest	L 0-2	0-2	15		(26,253)
46	M 1	PL	H	Manchester United	L 2-3	1-1	15	Ndlovu 39, Pressley 72	21,858
47	6	PL	A	Ipswich Town	L 0-2	0-0	18		(12,893)
48	9	PL	A	Tottenham Hotspur	W 3-1	1-0	15	Ndlovu 32, 62 (pen) Dublin 67	(24,124)
49	14	PL	H	Everton	D 0-0	0-0	16		21,787
50									
51									
52									
53									
54									
55									
56									
57									
58									
59									
60									

Best Home League Attendance: 21,858 v Manchester United	Smallest: 9,509 v Ipswich	Av Home Att: 15,980

Goal Scorers:

Compared with 1993-94: + 2,622

League (44): Dublin 13, Ndlovu 11 (3 pens), Flynn 4, Cook 3 (2 pens), Wegerle 3 (1 pen), Busst 2, Jones 2, Marsh 2, Opponents 2 Jenkinson, Pressley,

C/Cola Cup (5): Dublin 2, Darby 1, Flynn, Wegerle

FA Cup (4): Ndlovu 2, Wegerle (pen), Dublin

64

1994-95

Ogrizovic	Burrows	Busst	Babb	Morgan	Boland	Darby	Rennie	Jenkinson	Quinn	Flynn	Cook	Wegerle	Gould	Pickering	Williams J.	Dublin	Jones	Gillespie	Davies	Ndlovu	Pressley	Sheridan	Marsh	Williams P.	Hall	Referee	#
X	X	X	X	X	X2	X	X	X1	X	X	S1	S2	S													R. Gifford	1
X	X	X		X	S2	X	X	X2	X	X1	X	X	S	S1												P. Danson	2
X	X	X	X	X	S	X	X		Xt	X1	X	X	S		S1											G. Poll	3
X	X	X	X	X		X	X		X1	X	X		S	S	S1											P. Durkin	4
X		X		X	S1	X	X		X2		X	X1	X		S2	X										J. Worrall	5
X		X		X	X	X	X				X	X	S	S		X	X	S								B. Hill	6
X		X		X	X	X	X				X	X	S	S		X	X	S								E. Lomas	7
X		X		X	X2	X	X1				X	X	S2			X	X	S1	S							K. Morton	8
X	S1	X		X		X		S			X	X	X1	S		X	X	Xt								K. Cooper	9
X	S	X		X		X		S			X	Xt	X	X		X	X	X								K. Burge	10
X	S	X		X		X	X				X	X	S			X	X1			S1						R. Hart	11
X	S	X		X		X	X		S		X	X	X			X	X									D. Ellery	12
X	S2	X		X2		X	X				X	X	S			X	X1			S1	X					A. Wilkie	13
X	X	X		S		X	X				X1	X	S			X	S1			X						D. Gallagher	14
X	X	X				X	X		S		X	X	S			X	S			X						M. Bodenham	15
X	X	X		S1	X	X			X2		X		S	X1		X	S2			X						P. Jones	16
X	X	X		X		X	S				S	X	X	S		X	X			X	X					S. Lodge	17
X	X	X		X		X			S1		X	X	S	S		X1	X			X	X					G. Willard	18
X	X	X		X		X	S1		X		X	X	S	S			X			X	X	S				K. Burge	19
X	X	X1		X		X	X				X	X	X1	S	S	S1	X			X	X					R. Dilkes	20
X	X	X		X			X				X	X	X1	S	S	S1	X			X	X					R. Danson	21
X	X	X1		X	S1	X					X	X	X1	S	S1		X			X	X					A. Wilkie	22
X	X1	X		X		S2					X	X	X2	S	S1		X			X2	X					K. Morton	23
X	X	X		X			S1		X	X2	X1	X	S	X			X	X		X2	X			S2		G. Ashby	24
X		X		X	S1		X		X2	X	X1	X	S	X		X	S2			Xt	X	X	X	S2		G. Willard	25
X	X	X		X	S1		X			X	X	X1	S			X	S			X	X	X	X			P. Durkin	26
X	X	X		X		X	X	X1			X	X				X	S			X	X	X	X			D. Gallagher	27
X	X	X		X	X	X1				Xt	S1	S				X	S			X	X	X	X			P. Durkin	28
X	X			X1	X	X			S	X	X					X	S1				X	X	X			J. Worrall	29
X	X			X1	X	X			S	X	S1	X				X				X	X	X	X			P. Don	30
X	X	X1		X		X	X				X	S1	S			X	S			X	X	X				G. Willard	31
X	X	X		X		X	X1		X			S1	X	S		X	X			X	X	X				R. Hart	32
X	X	X		X	S2	X	X1		X			S1	X	X2	S1	X	X			X	X	X	S			G. Willard	33
X	X	X		X	S1	X		X1			S	X	X			X	X			X	X	X	S			M. Bodenham	34
X	X	X		X	S	X				X	X	S	X			X				X	X	X	S			R. Dilkes	35
X	X	X		X		X				X	X	S	X			X	S			X	X	X	S			R. Gifford	36
	X	X		S	X	X		S		X	X	X				X				X		S	X			K. Morton	37
	X			S	X	X	S		X	X		X				X				X	S1		X	X1		G. Poll	38
	X			X	X	S		X		X	X	X			S	X				X	S		X			T. Holbrook	39
S	X			X	X2	X			X	X		X	X	S	X					X			X			M. Reed	40
S	X			S1	X2	X			X	X		X	X	S2		X				X			X			R. Hart	41
X				S		X			X1	X		X	X		X					X	X		X			P. Danson	42
X	X			X	X1	S	X	S1	X			X			X	X				X	X			S2		G. Willard	43
X	X			X1	S2	S	X	X		X		X			X	X				X	X	X2		S1		P. Durkin	44
X				S		X	X		X	X	S	X			X					X	S		X		X	P. Don	45
X				X		X		X		X	S	X			X	S1				X	X1		X			M. Reed	46
X				X1	X	X				X1	S	X			X	S1				X	S					A. Wilkie	47
X				X	X	X				S	X	X			X	S				X			S			P. Jones	48
																											50
33	**33**	**20**	**3**	**26**	**9**	**27**	**28**	**10**	**3**	**32**	**33**	**21**	**7**	**27**	**1**	**31**	**16**	**2**		**28**	**18**		**15**	**5**	**2**	League Appearances	
	2			2	3	2		1	3		1	5		4	6		5	1		2	1			3		League Sub Appearances	
3	1	3		2	1	3	2				3	3	2	3		3	2+1			1						C/Cola Cup Appearances	
4	4			4	1+2	3	3				2	3	2+2	2		4	0+1			3	3		4	2		FA Cup Appearances	

Also Played: Richardson (36,37,38,39,40,41,42,43,44,45,46,47,48,49), Burrows (38,39,40,41,42,43,44,45,47,48,49), Filan S(38,39,40,46,47)(48,49), Robertson S(43), Strachan (44,46,47,48,49)

COVENTRY CITY

CLUB RECORDS

BIGGEST VICTORIES
League: 9-0 v Bristol City, Division 3(S), 28.4.1934.
F.A. Cup: 7-0 v Scunthorpe United, 1st Round, 24.11.1934.
League Cup: 7-2 v Chester City, 2nd Round, 9.10.1985.
5-0 v Watford, 5th Round replay, 9.12.1980.
5-0 v Sunderland 5th Round replay, 24.1.1990.
Europe: 4-1 v Trakia Plovdiv, 1st Round (UEFA) 16.9.1970.

BIGGEST DEFEATS
League: 2-10 v Norwich, Division 3(S), 15.3.1930.
1-9 v Millwall, Division 3(S), 19.11.1927.
F.A. Cup: 2-11 v Berwick Rangers, 2.11.1901. (Qualifying Round)
League Cup: 1-8 v Leicester City (h), 1.12.1964.
Europe: (UEFA) 1-6 v Bayern Munich, 20.10.1970.

MOST POINTS
3 points a win: 63, Division 1, 1986-87.
2 points a win: 60, Division 4, 1958-59, Division 3, 1963-64.

MOST GOALS SCORED
108, Division 3(S), 1931-32.
Bourton 49, Lauderdale 19, Lake 14, Shepperd 7, White 6, Holmes
5, Cull 3, Baker, Bowden, Heinmann, Johnson, Opponents.

MOST GOALS CONCEDED
97, Division 3(S) 1935-36; Division 4, 1958-59.

MOST FIRST CLASS MATCHES IN A SEASON
57, 1962-63 (League 46, FA Cup 9, League Cup 2).

MOST LEAGUE WINS
24, Division 3(S), 1935-36; Division 4, 1958-59.

MOST LEAGUE DRAWS
17, Division 3, 1962-63.

MOST LEAGUE DEFEATS
22, Division 2, 1919-20; Division 2, 1924-25; Division 3(S), 1927-28;
Division 2, 1951-52; Division 1, 1984-85.

INDIVIDUAL CLUB RECORDS

MOST GOALS IN A SEASON
Clarrie Bourton: 50 goals in 1931-32 (League 49, FAC 1).
Previous holder: F.Herbert 27 (1926-27).

MOST GOALS IN A MATCH
5. C Bourton v Bournemouth, 6-1 (h), Division 3(S), 17.10.1931.
5. A Bacon v Gillingham, 7-3 (a), Division 3(S), 30.12.1933.
5. C Regis v Chester City, 7-2 (h), League Cup, 9.10.1985.

OLDEST PLAYER
Alf Wood, 44 years 207 days v Plymouth, FAC 2nd Rnd, 7.12.1958.

YOUNGEST PLAYER
Brian Hill, 16 years 281 days v Gillingham, Div.3 (S), 30.4.58.

MOST CAPPED PLAYER
Peter Ndlovu (Zimbabwe) 25.

BEST PERFORMANCES

League: 1966-67: Matches Played 42, Won 23, Drawn 13, Lost 6,
Goals for 74, Goals against 43, Points 59. First in Division 2.
Highest Position: 1969-70: 6th Division 1.

F.A. Cup: 1986-87: 3rd Round Bolton Wanderers 3-0 (h); 4th Round
Manchester United 1-0 (a); 5th Stoke City 1-0 (a); 6th Round
Sheffield Wednesday 3-1 (a); Semi-Final Leeds United 3-2;
Final Tottenham Hotspur 3-2.

League Cup: Semi-finalists in 1980-81.
Most recent success: 1989-90: 2nd Round Grimsby Town 1-3,3-0;
3rd round QPR 1-0; 4th Round Manchester City 1-0; 5th Round
Sunderland 0-0,5-0; Semi-Final Nottingham Forest 1-2,0-0.

Europe: (UEFA) 1970-71: 1st Round Trakia Plovdiv 4-1,2-0; 2nd
Round Bayern Munich 1-6,2-1.

DIVISIONAL RECORD

	Played	Won	Drawn	Lost	For	Against	Points
Division 1/P	1,162	370	325	467	1,356	1,629	1,249
Division 2	756	279	186	291	1,050	1,099	744
Division 3	230	93	66	71	403	347	252
Division 3(S)	696	282	158	256	1,278	1,102	722
Division 3(N)	42	16	6	20	73	82	38
Division 4	46	24	12	10	84	47	60
Total	2,932	1,064	753	1,115	4,244	4,306	3,065

ADDITIONAL INFORMATION
PREVIOUS NAMES
Singers FC, 1883-98.

PREVIOUS LEAGUES
Southern League, Birmingham & District League.

Club Colours: All Sky blue with white & navy trim.
Change colours: Purple & mauve stripes with gold trimmed shirts,
purple with gold trimmed shorts, yellow socks.
Green & black striped shirts, green shorts, green with black trim
socks.

Reserves League: Pontins Central League Division 2.

RECORDS AND STATISTICS

COMPETITIONS

Div 1/P	Div.2	Div.3	Div.3(S)	Div.4	Texaco
1967-	1919-25	1959-64	1926-36	1958-59	1971-72
	1936-52		1952-58		1972-73
	1964-67				1973-74
			Div.3(N)		**UEFA**
			1925-26		1970-71

HONOURS

Div.2	Div.3	Div.3(S)	FA Cup
1966-67	1963-64	1935-36	1987

MOST APPEARANCES

George Curtis - 534+4 (1955-70)

Year	League	FA Cup	League Cup
1955-56	3		
1956-57	19		
1957-58	15	1	
1958-59	43	2	
1959-60	45	2	
1960-61	46	3	2
1961-62	46	2	1
1962-63	45	9	2
1963-64	46	2	2
1964-65	41	1	4
1965-66	42	4	4
1966-67	42	1	3
1967-68	3+1		
1968-69	28+2	2	3
1969-70	19+1		1
	483+4	29	22

MOST GOALS IN A CAREER

C Bourton - 181 (1931-37)

Year	League	FA Cup
1931-32	49	1
1932-33	40	3
1933-34	25	
1934-35	26	3
1935-36	23	2
1936-37	9	
Total	**172**	**9**

Current leading goalscorer - Peter Ndlovu 34 (1991-95)

MANAGERS

Name	Seasons	Best	Worst
H Pollitt	1920-21	20(2)	20(2)
A Evans	1921-25	18(2)	22(2)
J Kerr	1926-28	15(3S)	20(3S)
J McIntyre	1928-31	6(3S)	14(3S)
H Storer	1931-45	4(2)	12(3S)
R Bayliss	1946-47	8(2)	8(2)
W Frith	1947-49	10(2)	16(2)
H Storer	1949-54	7(2)	14(3S)
J Fairbrother	1954-55	9(3S)	14(3S)
C Elliott		9(3S)	9(3S)
J Carver	1955-56	9(3S)	9(3S)
G Rayner			
H Warren	1957-58	8(3S)	19(3S)
W Frith	1958-62	4(3)	2(4)
J Hill	1962-68	20(1)	14(3)
N Cantwell	1968-72	6(1)	20(1)
R Dennison	1972		
J Mercer	1972-74	16(1)	19(1)
G Milne	1974-81	7(1)	19(1)
D Sexton	1981-83	14(1)	19(1)
R Gould	1983-84	18(1)	19(1)
D Mackay	1984-86	17(1)	18(1)
G Curtis/J Sillett	1986-87	10(1)	18(1)
J Sillett	1987-90	7(1)	12(1)
T Butcher	1990-92	16(1)	16(1)
D Howe	1992	19(1)	19(1)
R Gould	1992-93	16(1/P)	16(1/P)
P Neal	1993-95	11(P)	11(P)
R Atkinson	1995-	16(P)	16(P)

RECORD TRANSFER FEE RECEIVED

Amount	Club	Player	Date
£3,750,000	Liverpool	Phil Babb	8/94
£1,500,000	Blackburn Rovers	Kevin Gallacher	3/93
£365,000	Portland Timbers	Gary Collier	3/80
£200,000	Arsenal	Jeoff Blockley	10/72

RECORD TRANSFER FEE PAID

Amount	Club	Player	Date
£1,950,000	Manchester Utd	Dion Dublin	9/94
£900,000	Dundee United	Keith Gallacher	2/90
£800,000	Glasgow Rangers	Kevin Drinkell	10/89
£780,000	Chelsea	David Speedie	07/87

LONGEST LEAGUE RUNS

of undefeated matches:	25 (26.11.1966 - 13.5.1967)	of league matches w/out a win:	19 (30.8.1919 - 20.12.1919)
of undefeated home matches:	19 (11.4.1925 - 13.3.1926)	of undefeated away matches:	12 (19.11.1966 - 19.8.1967)
without home win:	10 (30.8.1919 - 20.12.1919 & 1.1.92 - 18.4.92)	without an away win:	28 (5.1.1924 - 4.4.1925)
of league wins:	6 (20.4.1954 - 28.8.1954 & 24.4.1964 - 1.9.1964)	of home wins:	11 (18.10.1952 - 28.2.1953)
of league defeats:	9 (30.8.1919 - 4.10.1919)	of away wins:	4 (24.5.1963 - 14.9.1963 & 19.8.1992 - 5.9.1992)

COVENTRY CITY

PLAYERS NAME / Honours	Ht	Wt	Birthdate	Birthplace / Transfers	Contract Date	Clubs	League	L/Cup	FA Cup	Other	Lge	L/C	FAC	Oth
							APPEARANCES				GOALS			
G O A L K E E P E R S														
John Filan	5.11	12.10	08.02.70	Sydney (Aus)		Sydney B'pest								
				£40,000	12.03.93	Cambridge United	52	4	3	1				
Loan 23.12.94 Nottingham Forest				Loan	02.03.95	Coventry City								
				£350,000	17.03.95	Coventry City	2							
Jonathan Gould	6.1	12.6	18.07.68	Paddington		Clevedon Town								
				Free	18.07.90	Halifax Town	32	2	5	5				
				Free	30.01.92	W.B.A.								
				£17,500	15.07.92	Coventry City	25							
Steve Ogrizovic	6.3	14.7	12.09.57	Mansfield	28.07.77	Chesterfield	16	2						
FAC'87; FLgXI.1				£70,000	18.11.77	Liverpool	4			1				
				£70,000	11.08.82	Shrewsbury Town	84	7	5					
				£82,000	22.06.84	Coventry City	415	40	25	11	1			
D E F E N D E R S														
Brian Borrows	5.10	10.12	20.12.60	Liverpool	23.04.80	Everton (J)	27	2						
E: B.1				£10,000	24.03.83	Bolton Wanderers	95	7	4	4				
				£82,000	06.06.85	Coventry City	359+6	35	22	10+1	11	1	1	
David Burrows	5.8	11.0	25.10.68	Dudley	08.11.86	W.B.A (A)	37+9	3+1	2	1	1			
E:u21.7, B.3. CS'89'90. Div.1'90. FAC'92. FLg XI				£550,000	20.10.88	Liverpool	135+11	16	16+1	14	3			
					17.09.93	West Ham United	25	3	3		1	1		
				P.E.	06.09.94	Everton	19	2	2					
				£1,100,000	02.03.95	Coventry City	11							
David Busst	6.1	12.7	30.06.67	Birmingham		Moor Green								
				Free	14.01.92	Coventry City	32+1	3+1	0+1		2			
Julian Darby	6.0	11.4	03.10.67	Bolton	22.07.86	Bolton Wanderers(T)	258+12	25	19	31+1	36	8	3	5
E: S. SVT'89.				£150,000	28.10.93	Coventry City	25+1		1		5			
Gary Gillespie	6.2	12.1	05.07.60	Stirling		Falkirk	22	2	1					
S: 12, u21.8, S.3. Div 1'86'88'90. CS'88				£75,000	10.03.78	Coventry City	171+1	16	13					
				£325,000	08.07.93	Liverpool	152+4	22	21+2	8+2	14	2		
				£900,000		Celtic								
				Free	23.11.94	Coventry City	2+1	1						
Marcus Hall	6.1	12.02	24.04.76	Coventry	01.07.94	Coventry City (T)	2+3							
Steve Morgan	5.11	12.0	19.09.68	Oldham	12.08.86	Blackpool (A)	135+9	13	16	10+1	10	2	1	1
E: u19.2.				£115,000	16.07.90	Plymouth Argyle	120+1	7	6	5	6			
				£150,000	14.07.93	Coventry City	65+3	5	5		2	3		
Ally Pickering	5.9	10.8	22.06.67	Manchester		Buxton								
				£18,500	02.02.90	Rotherham United	87+1	6	9	7	2			
				£110,000	27.10.93	Coventry City	28+7	3	2					
David Rennie	6.0	12.0	29.08.64	Edinburgh	18.05.82	Leicester City (A)	21	2			1			
S: Y.				£50,000	17.01.86	Leeds United	95+6	7	7	4	5		1	1
				£175,000	31.07.89	Bristol City	101+3	8	9	5	8			
				£120,000	20.02.92	Birmingham City	32+3	1		1	4			
				£100,000	11.03.93	Coventry City	71	5	3+1		1			
Paul D Williams	5.11	12.0	26.03.71	Burton	13.07.89	Derby County (T)	153+7	10+2	8	14+1	25	2	3	2
E: u21.6.				Loan	09.11.89	Lincoln City	3		2	1				
				£1,000,000	06.08.95	Coventry City								
M I D F I E L D														
Carlita	5.9	11.2	20.12.72	Angola		Farense (Portugal)								
				£500,000	07.06.95	Coventry City								
Willie Boland	5.9	10.9	06.08.75	Ennis (Eire)	04.11.92	Coventry City (J)	42+7	4						
Eire: u21.1.														
Paul Cook	5.11	10.10	22.02.67	Liverpool		Marine								
					20.07.84	Wigan Athletic	77+6	4	6+1	5+1	14			1
				£73,000	23.05.88	Norwich City	3+3			1+1				
				£250,000	01.11.89	Wolverhampton W.	191+2	7	5+2	6+1	19	1		1
				£500,000	18.08.94	Coventry City (T)	33+1	3	3		3			
Iyseden Christie	6.0	12.2	14.11.76	Coventry		Coventry City (T)								
Kevin Richardson	5.9	10.12	04.12.62	Newcastle	08.12.80	Everton (A)	95+14	10+3	13	7+2	16	3	1	
E: 1. Div.1'85'89. FAC'84. CS'84'86. ECWC'85.				£225,000	04.09.86	Watford	39	3	7	1	2			
LC'94				£200,000	26.08.87	Arsenal	88+8	13+3	9	3	5	2	1	
via Real Sociedad, £750,000, 01.07.90 to				£450,000	06.08.91	Aston Villa	142+1	15	12	10	13	3		
				£300,000	16.02.95	Coventry City	14							
Isaias	5.10	12.10				Benfica								
				£500,000	17.07.95	Coventry City								
Paul Telfer	5.9	10.2	21.10.71	Edinburgh	07.11.88	Luton Town (T)	91+7	3	10	2	10		2	1
S: u21.3, B.1.				£1,150,000	26.06.95	Coventry City								
F O R W A R D S														
J. Barnwell-Edinboro	5.10	11.06	26.12.75	Hull	1994-95	Coventry City (T)								
Dion Dublin	6.0	12.4	22.04.69	Leicester	24.03.88	Norwich City (T)								
Div.3'91.				Free	02.08.88	Cambridge United	133+23	8+2	21	14+1	53	5	11	5
				£1,000,000	07.08.92	Manchester United	4+8	1+1	1+1	0+1	2	1		
				£1,950,000	09.09.94	Coventry City	31	3	4		13	2	1	
Leigh Jenkinson	6.0	12.5	09.07.69	Thorne	15.06.87	Hull City (T)	95+35	7+2	6+1	9+2	13			1
				Loan	13.09.90	Rotherham United	5+2							
				£200,000	12.03.93	Coventry City	22+10	0+1	3		1			
				Loan	01.11.93	Birmingham City	2+1							
Peter Ndlovu	5.8	10.2	25.02.73	Zimbabwe		H'landers								
Zim: 25.				£20,000	16.08.91	Coventry City	104+21	6	5	0+1	31	1	2	

John Salako	5.10	11.0	11.02.69	Nigeria	03.11.86	Crystal Palace (A)	172+43	19+5	20		11+3	23	5	4	2
E: 5. FMC'91. Div.1'94.				Loan	14.08.89	Swansea City	13			2	3				1
				£1,500,000	08.95	Coventry City									
John Williams	6.2	12.4	11.05.68	Birmingham		Cradley Town									
				£5,000	19.08.91	Swansea City	36+3	2+1	3		1	11			
				£250,000	01.07.92	Coventry City	66+14	4	2			11			
Loan 07.09.94 Notts County 3+2 Lge App. 2 gls.				Loan	23.12.94	Stoke City	1+3								
				Loan	03.02.95	Swansea City	6+1					2			
A D D I T I O N A L C O N T R A C T P L A Y E R S															
Gordon Strachan	5.6	10.8	09.02.57	Edinburgh		Dundee	56+13	10+1	7			13	1	1	
S: 50, u21.1, Y. SPD'80'84. SC'82'83'84.				£50,000	01.11.87	Aberdeen	165+6	43+3	25	30+4		53	20	7	7
ECWC'83. ESC'83. FAC'85. Div.2'90. Div.1'92.				£500,000	13.08.84	Manchester United	155+5	12+1	22	10+2		33	1	2	3
				£300,000	23.03.89	Leeds United	188+9	19	14	14+1		37	3	2	3
				Free	22.03.95	Coventry City	5								
Peter Shilton	6.0	14.02	18.09.49	Leicester	01.09.66	Leicester City (A)	286	20	30			1			
E: 125, u23.3, Y, S. Div.1'78. Div.2'71. EC'79'80.				£300,000	01.11.74	Stoke City	110	4	7						
ESC'79. CS'78. LC'79.				£270,000	15.09.77	Nottingham Forest	202	26	18	26					
				£325,000	28.08.82	Southampton	188	28	17	8					
				£90,000	07.07.87	Derby County	175	18	10	8					
				Free	05.03.92	Plymouth Argyle	34	6	1	2					
Free 10.02.95 Wimbledon				Free	11.03.95	Bolton Wanderers	0+1			1					
				Free	08.95	Coventry City									

TOP GOALSCORER 1994/95
Dion Dublin

Premiership goals (games) 13 (31)
Coca-Cola Cup Goals 2 (3)
F.A. Cup goals 1 (4)

Total . . . . **16 (38)**

Total goals for Coventry City since September 1994 . . . . 16 (38)

Career total as at June 1st 1995 . . . . 93 (220 + 37)

THE MANAGER
RON ATKINSON

Date of Birth . . . . 18th March 1939.
Place of Birth . . . . Liverpool.
Date of Appointment . . . . February 1995.

PREVIOUS CLUBS
As Manager . . . . Kettering Town, Cambridge Utd, West Bromwich Albion,
. . . . . . Manchester United, Athletico Madrid, Sheffield Wednesday, Aston Villa.
As a Player . . . . Aston Villa (A), Oxford United.

HONOURS
As a Manager
Cambridge United: Promotion to Division 3, 1977. Promotion to Division 2, 1978.
Manchester United: FA Cup Winners 1983.
Sheffield Wednesday: Promotion to Division 1 and League Cup winners, 1991.
Aston Villa: Premier League runners-up., 1992-93. League Cup winners 1993-94.

As a Player
Oxford United: Promotion to Division 3, 1965. Division 3 Champions 1968.

HIGHFIELD ROAD

King Richard Street, Coventry CV2 4FW
Tel: 01203 223 535

Capacity..24,003.

First game ....v Shrewsbury Town 9.9.1899
First floodlit game...........................v Queen of the South, Friendly, 21.10.1953.
ATTENDANCES
Highest ....51,455 v Wolves, Div 2, 29.4.1967.
Lowest...1,086 v Millwall, FMC, 15.10.1985.

OTHER GROUNDS ....Binley Road 1883-87, Stoke Road 1887-99, Highfield Road since 1899.

MATCHDAY TICKET PRICES

Main Stand . . . Adults - A Grade £20, B Grade £17.
.... Juv & OAP - A £10*, B £8.50*.
M&B Stand............. Adults - A £18, B £15.
.... Juv & OAP - A £9, B £7.50.
East Stand.............. Adults - A £18, B £15.
.... Juv & OAP - A £9, B £7.50.
Co-Op Bank Family Stand . . Adults - A £15, B £12.
.... Juv & OAP - A £7.50, £6.
West Terrace .... Adults - A £15, B £12.
.... Juv & OAP - A £7.50, B £6.
J.S.B.................... All Matches - £4.
Visitors............... Adults - A £18, B - £15.
.... Juv & OAP - A £10, B £8.
*J.S.B. & Senior Citizen members only.
Student discount - £3 (West Stand only)
Ticket Office Telephone No. . . . . . 01203 225 545.

CLUBCALL
0891 12 11 66
Calls cost 39p per minute cheap rate and 49p per minute at all other times.
Call costings correct at time of going to press.

HOW TO GET TO THE GROUND

From the North and South
Exit the M6 at junction 2, take the A4600 and follow the signs for the City Centre. Cross the roundabout keeping along Ansty Road (A4600). It bears left, and you come to another roundabout. Take right exit and continue for a quarter-of-a-mile. Turn right into Swan Lane. Coventry F.C. is directly ahead of you.

From the East
Exit the M69 at its junction with the M6 and then follow the directions given above.

From the West
Exit the M40 at junction 15 and proceed along the A46 (dual carriageway) for approximately 10 miles until you reach the island, cross the island and continue until you reach the next island. At this point turn first left onto the B4110 sign-posted "Stoke", follow this road across all sets of traffic lights to a T-junction, then turn left into Walsgrave Road and immediately right into Swan Lane.

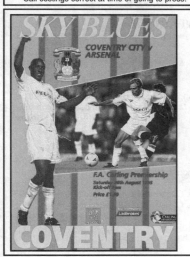

MATCHDAY PROGRAMME

Programme Co-ordinator........................ Mike Williams.

Number of pages .... 48.

Price .... £1.50.

Subscriptions .... Please apply to the club.

Local Newspapers .... Coventry Evening Telegraph.

Local Radio Stations................. Mercia Sound, BBC CWR.

EVERTON
(The Toffeemen)
F.A. CARLING PREMIERSHIP
SPONSORED BY: DANKA

Back Row (L-R): Graham Stuart, John Ebbrell, Paul Holmes, Jason Kearton, Craig Short, Neville Southall, Joe Parkinson, Paul Rideout, Andy Hinchcliffe. **Middle Row:** Jim Martin(Kit Manager), Jim Gabriel (Res. Team Coach), Matthew Jackson, Vinny Samways, Neil Moore, Tony Grant, Earl Barrett, Andrei Kanchelskis, Willie Donachie (1st Team Coach), Les Helm (Physio). **Front Row:** David Unsworth, Stuart Barlow, Gary Ablett, Barry Horne, Joe Royle (Manager), Dave Watson (Capt), Duncan Ferguson, Daniel Amokachi, Anders Limpar.

EVERTON
FORMED IN 1878
TURNED PROFESSIONAL IN 1885
LTD COMPANY IN 1892

CHAIRMAN: Dr D M Marsh
DIRECTORS
Sir Desmond Pitcher (Vice-Chairman),
A W Waterworth, K M Tamlin, D A B Newton,
Sir Phillip Carter, CBE, W Kenwright
SECRETARY
J Greenwood
COMMERCIAL MANAGER
D Johnston

MANAGER: Joe Royle
ASSISTANT MANAGER: Willie Donachie

RESERVE TEAM MANAGER
Jimmy Gabriel

PHYSIOTHERAPIST
Jim Helm

STATISTICIAN FOR THE DIRECTORY
Richard Swift

Following a relegation fight for much of 1993/94 it appeared rather surprising when few personnel changes were deemed necessary during the summer break. The new season began in earnest with a familiar pattern emerging, that of unfortunate injuries and inconsistency. A combination of these factors meant a treacherous position in the lower reaches of the division prevailed. Furthermore a continually changing line-up created obvious problem resulting in the team not functioning as a unit. In response Mike Walker invested heavily in stars such as Daniel Amokachi, but when instant results were not forthcoming Walker's future appeared questionable. The board's answer was to sack the manager and, after much speculation, installed Joe Royle as his successor.

As with many managerial switches, Everton's fortunes took a turn. A victory over arch rivals Liverpool, in his first match in charge, endeared him to the supporters. Whilst the season drew to a climax the Toffees found themselves languishing at the foot of the table but progressing well in the FA Cup. Consistency remained a problem, although in cup fixtures they played like a different team. For the Semi-Final, a meeting with Spurs proved to be a typical cup tie. Daniel Amokachi emerged as the unlikely hero by coming off the bench to score a hat-trick and land the club a place in the final.

Everton lined up against Manchester United at Wembley where both teams were evenly matched and for much of the game cancelled out each other's advances. Following Neville Southall's incredible goalkeeping, Paul Rideout will be the name listed in footballing history after scoring the winning goal. The sight of Dave Watson raising the trophy aloft is something Toffees supporters will want to get used to again.

RICHARD SWIFT.

EVERTON

Premier League: 15th **FA Cup:** Winners **Coca-Cola Cup:** 2nd Round

M	DATE	COMP.	VEN	OPPONENTS	RESULT	H/T	LP	GOAL SCORERS/GOAL TIMES	ATT.
1	A 20	PL	H	Aston Villa	D 2-2	1-0	8	Stuart 22, Rideout 70	35,544
2	24	PL	A	Tottenham Hotspur	L 1-2	0-2		Rideout 46	(24,553)
3	27	PL	A	Manchester City	L 0-4	0-0	19		(19,867)
4	30	PL	H	Nottingham Forest	L 1-2	0-1	19	Rideout 68	26,689
5	S 10	PL	A	Blackburn Rovers	L 0-3	0-2	22		(26,538)
6	17	PL	H	Queens Park Rangers	D 2-2	2-1	22	Amokachi 10, Rideout 24	27,285
7	20	CC 2/1	H	Portsmouth	L 2-3	0-2		Samways 57, Stuart 72 (pen)	14,043
8	24	PL	H	Leicester City	D 1-1	0-0	22	Ablett 50	28,003
9	O 1	PL	A	Manchester United	L 0-2	0-1	22		(43,803)
10	5	CC 2/2	A	Portsmouth	D 1-1	1-0		Watson 17	(13,605)
11	8	PL	A	Southampton	L 0-2	0-1	22		(15,163)
12	15	PL	H	Coventry City	L 0-2	0-2	22		28,233
13	22	PL	A	Crystal Palace	L 0-1	0-0	22		(14,505)
14	29	PL	H	Arsenal	D 1-1	1-1	22	Unsworth 14	32,003
15	N 1	PL	H	West Ham United	W 1-0	0-0	22	Ablett 54	28,338
16	5	PL	A	Norwich City	D 0-0	0-0	22		(18,377)
17	21	PL	H	Liverpool	W 2-0	0-0		Ferguson 56, Rideout 89	39,866
18	26	PL	A	Chelsea	W 1-0	1-0	19	Rideout 39	(21,302)
19	D 5	PL	H	Leeds United	W 3-0	1-0		Rideout 7, Ferguson 58, Unsworth 66	25,897
20	10	PL	A	Aston Villa	D 0-0	0-0	18		(29,678)
21	17	PL	H	Tottenham Hotspur	D 0-0	0-0	19		32,809
22	26	PL	H	Sheffield Wednesday	L 1-4	1-2		Ferguson 36	37,080
23	31	PL	H	Ipswich Town	W 4-1	1-0		Ferguson 27, Rideout 70, 73, Watson 89	25,659
24	J 2	PL	A	Wimbledon	L 1-2	1-2	20	Rideout 16	(9,506)
25	7	FAC 3	H	Derby County	W 1-0	0-0		Hinchcliffe 76	29,406
26	14	PL	A	Arsenal	D 1-1	1-1	20	Watson 13	(34,743)
27	21	PL	H	Crystal Palace	W 3-1	1-0	18	Ferguson 2, 87, Rideout 53	23,733
28	24	PL	A	Liverpool	D 0-0	0-0			(39,505)
29	29	FAC 4	A	Bristol City	W 1-0	0-0		Jackson 78	(19,816)
30	F 1	PL	A	Newcastle United	L 0-2	0-0			(34,465)
31	4	PL	H	Norwich City	W 2-1	1-0	18	Stuart 42, Rideout 65	23,293
32	13	PL	A	West Ham United	D 2-2	1-1	17	Rideout 43, Limpar 79	(21,081)
33	18	FAC 5	H	Norwich City	W 5-0	2-0		Limpar 6, Parkinson 23, Rideout 56, Ferguson 63, Stuart 88	31,616
34	22	PL	A	Leeds United	L 0-1	0-0			(30,793)
35	25	PL	H	Manchester United	W 1-0	0-0	16	Ferguson 58	40,011
36	M 4	PL	A	Leicester City	D 2-2	2-0	17	Limpar 5, Samways 45	(20,447)
37	8	PL	A	Nottingham Forest	L 1-2	1-1		Barlow 45	(24,526)
38	12	FAC 6	H	Newcastle United	W 1-0	0-0		Watson 65	35,203
39	15	PL	H	Manchester City	D 1-1	0-1		Unsworth 80 (pen)	28,485
40	18	PL	A	Queens Park Rangers	W 3-2	0-1	17	Barlow 58, McDonald 69 (og), Hinchcliffe 90	(14,488)
41	A 1	PL	A	Blackburn Rovers	L 1-2	1-2	17	Stuart 23	37,905
42	9	FAC S/F	N	Tottenham Hotspur	W 4-1	1-0		Jackson 35, Stuart 55, Amokachi 82, 90	(38,226)
43	14	PL	H	Newcastle United	W 2-0	1-0		Amokachi 23, 49	34,811
44	17	PL	A	Sheffield Wednesday	D 0-0	0-0	17		(27,880)
45	29	PL	H	Wimbledon	D 0-0	0-0	16		33,063
46	M 3	PL	H	Chelsea	D 3-3	1-1		Hinchcliffe 39, Ablett 50, Amokachi 70	33,180
47	6	PL	H	Southampton	D 0-0	0-0	17		36,840
48	9	PL	A	Ipswich Town	W 1-0	0-0		Rideout 49	(14,951)
49	14	PL	A	Coventry City	D 0-0	0-0	15		(21,814)
50	20	FAC F	N	Manchester United	W 1-0	1-0		Rideout 30	(79,592)
51									
52									
53									
54									
55									
56									
57									
58									
59									
60									
61									

Best Home League Attendance: 40,011 v Manchester United **Smallest:** 23,293 v Norwich City **Av Home Att:** 31,367

Goal Scorers:

Compared with 1993-94: +8,491

League (44): Rideout 14, Ferguson 7, Amokachi 6, Ablett 3, Stuart 3, Unsworth 3, Barlow 2, Hinchcliffe 2, Limpar 2, Watson 2, Samways, Opponent
C/Cola Cup (3): Samways, Stuart, Watson
FA Cup (13): Amokachi 2, Tackson 2, Rideout 2, Ferguson, Hinchcliffe, Limpar, Parkinson, Watson

Southall	Jackson	Watson	Unsworth	Ablett	Stuart	Samways	Ebrell	Limpar	Cottee	Rideout	Angell	Parkinson	Kearton	Hinchcliffe	Barlow	Amokachi	Burrows	Snodin	Holmes	Rowett	Ferguson	Durrant	Horne	Reeves	Barrett	Referee	
X	X	X1	X	X	X	X	X	X	X	X	S	S1	S													K. Morton	1
X	X	X	X	X	X	X	X		X	X2	S2	X1	S	S1												G. Willard	2
X	X	X	X	X	X	X	X	S1	X1	X		X	S	S												P. Don	3
X	X	X	X		X	X	X	X		X	X	S	S	X	S											G. Ashby	4
X	X	X	X		X	X	X	X		X	S	S	S			X	X									R. Dilkes	5
X	X	X	X		X	X	X	X1		X		S				X	X	S1								R. Gifford	6
X	X1	X	X		X	X				X2	S2	S				X	X	S1								M. Reed	7
X		X	X	X	X					X		S	S		S	X	X	X	X							T. Holbrook	8
X	S	X	X			X1	X					X	S	X	S1	X	X	X		X						G. Poll	9
X		X	X		X	X				S1		X	S	X1		X	X	X			X	S				K. Cooper	10
X	X1	X2	X		S1	X				X		X	X	X		X	X		X			S2				B. Hill	11
X	X		X	X	S1	X				S		X1	S			X	X				X	X	X			D. Ellery	12
X	X		X	X	X	X1						S1	S			X	X		S	X	X	X	X			S. Lodge	13
X	X		X1	X	X			S2		S1		X	S			X	X				X	X2	X			K. Burge	14
X	X	X		X	X1			S1		S2		X	S			X2	X				X	X	X			M Bodenham	15
X	X	X	X1	X	X			S1		X		X	S		S		X				X		X			P. Danson	16
X	X1	X	X		X			S2		S1		X	S	X		X2					X		X			D. Gallagher	17
X	X	X	X	X	S			X		X		X	S	X		S			X		X					R. Hart	18
X	X	X	X	X1	S1	X				X		X	S	X	S						X		X			P. Durkin	19
	X	X	X		S			X		X		X	X	X	S		X				X					R. Gifford	20
X	X	X	X		S			X	S1	X		X1	S	X	X		X						X			K. Cooper	21
X	X	X	X		S1			X		X			S	S		X1					X		X			T. Holbrook	22
X	X	X	X			X	S			X		X	S	X	S1		X1				X		X			R. Dilkes	23
X	X	X	X			X	S			X		X	S	S			X1				X		X			K. Burge	24
X	X	X	X			X	S1			X		X	S	X	S		X1				X		X			G. Ashby	25
X	X	X	X			X	S			X		X	S	X	S		X				X†		X			R. Hart	26
X	X	X	X			X	S			X		X	S	X			X				X		X	S		P. Jones	27
X	X	X	X			X	S			X		X	S	X			X				X		X	S		B. Hill	28
X	X	X	X		S1		S	X		X		X	X1	X			X						X	S		T. Holbrook	29
X		X	X	X		X	S2	X				X					X2					X†	S	X†		D. Ellery	30
X		X	X	X	X	S1	X			X	S	X1		X								X	S	X'		A. Wilkie	31
X	S	X	X	X1	X		X	S1		X		X									X	X	X	X		M. Reed	32
X	S	X		X	X		X	X		X1		X				X	S1				X		S			M Bodenham	33
X	S	X		X	S1		X	X		X1		X									X	X	S	X		D. Gallagher	34
X		X	X			S1	X1	X				X		X	X	S					X	X	S	X		T. Worrall	35
X	S2	X	X		S1	X†		X1				X		X	X2						X†	X	S	X		P. Durkin	36
X	S	X	X	X	X		X	X				X		X							X	X	S	X		R. Dilkes	37
X	X	X	X	S1	S	X	X1		X			X		X							X	X	S			K. Cooper	38
X		X	S2	X1	S1		X	X			X2	S	X								X	X		X		G. Willard	39
X	S1	X		X			X	X			X2	S	X	X							X	X		X		K. Morton	40
X	X	X		X	X			X				X	S	X	X1	X		S			X	X		X		D. Gallagher	41
X	X	X	X	X	X		X			X1		X	S	X		S1					X			X		R. Hart	42
X	S1	X	X	X	X		X					X	S	X		X1					X			X		R. Gifford	43
X	S1	X	X	X			X1			S1		X	S	X1							X2	X		X		M. Reed	44
X	S	X	X	X	X		X1			S1		X	S	X							X	X		X		P. Danson	45
X		X	X	X	X1	S	X					X	S	X	S1	X					X	X		X		B. Hill	46
X		X	X	X	S1	X1	S2	X		X		X	S	X2		X					X	X		X		T. Holbrook	47
X		X	X	X	S1	X	X1	X				X	S	S2†	X2						X	X		X		R. Hart	48
X	X	X	X	X	X	X1	X					X	S	S	X	S					S1			X		P. Jones	49
X	X	X	X	X	X			X2		X1		X	S	X		S2					S1	X				G. Ashby	50
41	25	38	37	26	20	14	26	18	3	25	3	32	1	28	7	17	19	2	2	2	22	4	30		17	League Appearances	
	3		1		8	5		8		4		2		1	4		1				1					League Sub Appearances	
2	1	2	2		2	2				1+1	0+1	2		2		2	2	1+1			1					C/Cola Cup Appearances	
6	6	6	5	4			3	5+1		5		6		5	2+1		2				3+1		4			FA Cup Appearances	

Also Played: Grant S1(30),S(33),X1(40),S1(41),S(42),S1(43),S2(44), Spear S(20)

† = Sent Off

EVERTON

CLUB RECORDS

BIGGEST VICTORIES
League: 8-0 v Stoke City, Division 1, 2.11.1889.
9-1 v Manchester City, Division 1, 3.9.1906.
9-1 v Plymouth Argyle, Division 2, 27.12.1930.
8-0 v Southampton, Division 1, 20.11.1971.
F.A. Cup: 11-2 v Derby County, 1st Round, 18.1.1890.
League Cup: 8-0 v Wimbledon, 2nd Round, 24.8.1978.
Europe: (UEFA) 5-0 v Finn Harps, 1st Round 1st leg, 12.9.1978.
5-0 v Finn Harps, 1st Round 2nd leg, 26.9.1978.

BIGGEST DEFEATS
League: 0-7 v Sunderland, Division 1, 26.12.1934.
0-7 v Wolverhampton Wndrs., Division 1, 22.2.1939.
0-7 v Portsmouth, Division 1, 10.9.1949.
F.A. Cup: 0-6 v Crystal Palace (h), 1st Round, 7.1.1922.
League Cup: No more than 3 goal difference.
Europe: (UEFA) 0-3 v Ujpest Dozsa, 2nd Round 1st leg, 3.11.1965.

MOST POINTS
3 points a win: 90, Division 1, 1984-85 (Division 1 record)
2 points a win: 66, Division 1, 1969-70.

MOST GOALS SCORED
121, Division 1, 1930-31.
Dean 39, Down 14, Critchley 13, Johnson 13, Stein 11, White 10, Martin 7, Rigby 4, Griffith 3, Gee 2, Wilkinson 2, McPherson 1, McLure 1, Opponents 1.

MOST GOALS CONCEDED
92, Division 1, 1929-30.

MOST FIRST CLASS MATCHES IN A SEASON
63 - 1984-85 (League 42, FA Cup 7, League Cup 4, Charity Shield 1, ECWC 9).
63 - 1985-86 (League 42, FA Cup 7, League Cup 5, Charity Shield 1, Screen Super Cup 8).

MOST LEAGUE WINS
29, Division 1, 1969-70.

MOST LEAGUE DRAWS
18, Division 1, 1925-26, 1971-72, 1974-75.

MOST LEAGUE DEFEATS
22, Division 1, 1950-51, 1993-94.

INDIVIDUAL CLUB RECORDS

MOST GOALS IN A SEASON
William 'Dixie' Dean: 63 goals in 1927-28 (League 60, FAC 3).
Previous holder: B Freeman 38 (1908-09).

MOST GOALS IN A MATCH
6. Jack Southwork v West Bromwich Albion, 7-1, Division 1, 30.12.1893.

OLDEST PLAYER
Ted Sager, 42 years, 1953.

YOUNGEST PLAYER
Joe Royle, 16 years, 1966.

MOST CAPPED PLAYER
Neville Southall (Wales) 85.

BEST PERFORMANCES

League: 1969-70: Matches played 42, Won 29, Drawn 8, Lost 5, Goals for 72, Goals against 34, Points 72. 1st Division 1.
Highest Position: Division 1 Champions nine times.
F.A. Cup: Winners in 1905-06, 1932-33, 1965-66, 1983-84.
Most Recent success: 1994-95: 3rd Round Derby County 1-0; 4th Round Bristol City 1-0; 5th Round Norwich City 5-0; 6th Round Newcastle United 1-0; Semi-Final Tottenham Hotspur 4-1; Final Manchester United 1-0.
League Cup: 1976-77: 2nd Round Cambridge United 3-0; 3rd Round Stockport County 1-0; 4th Round Coventry City 3-0; 5th Round Manchester United 3-0; Semi-Final Bolton Wanderers 1-1,1-0; Final Aston Villa 1-1,2-3.
Europe: (ECWC) 1984-85: 1st Round University of Dublin 0-0,1-0; 2nd Round Inter Bratislav 1-0,3-0; 3rd Round Fortuna S 3-0,2-0; Semi-Final Bayern Munich 0-0,3-1; Final Rapid Vienna 3-1.

ADDITIONAL INFORMATION
Previous Names
None.
Previous Leagues
None.

Club colours: Blue & white trim shirts, white shorts, blue socks.
Change colours: White & blue trimmed shirts, blue shorts, white socks.

Reserves League: Pontins Central League Division 1.

DIVISIONAL RECORD

	Played	Won	Drawn	Lost	For	Against	Points
Division 1/P	3,606	1,498	872	1,236	5,809	5,113	4,113
Division 2	168	77	45	46	348	257	199
Total	**3,774**	**1,575**	**917**	**1,282**	**6,157**	**5,370**	**4,312**

RECORDS AND STATISTICS

COMPETITIONS

Div 1/P	Div.2	Euro C	ECWC	UEFA	Texaco
1888-30	1930-31	1963-64	1966-67	1962-63	1973-74
1931-51	1951-54	1970-71	1984-85	1964-65	
1954-				1965-66	
				1975-76	
				1978-79	
				1979-80	

HONOURS

Div 1/P	Div.2	FA Cup	ECWC	C/Sh'ld
1890-91	1930-31	1906	1984-85	1928
1914-15		1933		1932
1927-28		1966		1963
1931-32		1984		1970
1938-39		1995		1984
1962-63				1985
1969-70				1986
1984-85				1987
1986-87				

MOST APPEARANCES

Neville Southall 649 (1981-95)

Year	League	FA Cup	Lge Cup	Europe	FMC	CT	CS
1981-82	26	1					
1982-83	17		2				
1983-84	35	8	11				
1984-85	42	7	4	9			1
1985-86	32	5	5		6		1
1986-87	31	3	3		2		
1987-88	32	8	7		1		
1988-89	38	8	5		3	1	
1989-90	38	7	4				
1990-91	38	6	3		6		
1991-92	42	2	4		2		
1992-93	40	1	6				
1993-94	42	2	3				
1994-95	41	6	2				
	494	**64**	**59**	**9**	**20**	**1**	**2**

MOST GOALS IN A CAREER

William Dean - 377 (1924-38)

Year	League	FA Cup
1924-25	2	
1925-26	32	1
1926-27	21	3
1927-28	60	3
1928-29	26	
1929-30	23	2
1930-31	39	9
1931-32	45	1
1932-33	24	5
1933-34	9	
1934-35	26	1
1935-36	17	
1936-37	24	3
1937-38	1	
Total	**349**	**28**

Current leading goalscorer: Dave Watson - 34 (1986-95)

RECORD TRANSFER FEE RECEIVED

Amount	Club	Player	Date
£2,800,000	Barcelona	Gary Lineker	6/86
£2,500,000	Arsenal	Martin Keown	1/93
£1,500,000	Glasgow Rangers	Trevor Steven	6/89
£1,250,000	Glasgow Rangers	Stuart McCall	8/91

MANAGERS

Name	Seasons	Best	Worst
Theo Kelly	1939-48	1(1)	14(1)
Cliff Britton	1948-56	11(1)	16(2)
Ian Buchan	1956-58	15(1)	16(1)
John Carey	1958-61	5(1)	16(1)
Harry Catterick	1961-73	1(1)	17(1)
Billy Bingham	1973-77	4(1)	11(1)
Steve Burtenshaw	1977		
Gordon Lee	1977-81	3(1)	19(1)
Howard Kendall	1981-87	1(1)	8(1)
Colin Harvey	1987-90	4(1)	8(1)
Howard Kendall	1990-94	9(1)	13(1/P)
Mike Walker	1994	22(P)	22(P)
Joe Royle	1994-	15(P)	15(P)

RECORD TRANSFER FEE PAID

Amount	Club	Player	Date
£5,000,000	Manchester Utd	Andrei Kanchelskis	08/95
£4,000,000	Glasgow Rangers	Duncan Ferguson	12/94
£3,000,000	Anderlecht	Daniel Amokachi	08/94
£2,300,000	West Ham Utd	Tony Cottee	8/88

LONGEST LEAGUE RUNS

of undefeated matches:	20 (29.4.1978 - 16.12.1978)	of league matches w/out a win:	14 (6.3.1937 - 4.9.1937)
of undefeated home matches:	39 (6.9.1961 - 7.9.1963)	of undefeated away matches:	11 (21.4.1908 - 27.9.1909)
without home win:	12 (14.9.1957 - 22.3.1958)	without an away win:	35 (19.9.1970 - 8.4.1972)
of league wins:	12 (27.3.1894 - 6.10.1894)	of home wins:	15 (4.10.1930 - 4.4.1931)
of league defeats: 6 (5.3.30-12.4.30, 29.3.58-19.4.58, 4.11.72-9.12.72)		of away wins:	6 (2.9.1908 - 14.11.1908)

EVERTON

PLAYERS NAME / Honours	Ht	Wt	Birthdate	Birthplace / Transfers	Contract Date	Clubs	League	L/Cup	FA Cup	Other	Lge	L/C	FAC	Oth
G O A L K E E P E R S														
Jason B Kearton	6.1	11.10	09.07.69	Australia		Brisbane Lions								
				Free	31.10.88	Everton	3+3	1	1					
				Loan	13.08.91	Stoke City	16			1				
				Loan	09.01.92	Blackpool	14							
				Loan	20.01.95	Notts County	10			2				
Neville Southall	6.1	12.2	16.09.58	Llandudno		Bangor City								
W: 74; Div1'85'87; FAC'84'95; CS'84'85;				Winsford United										
CS'84'85'95; ECWC'85				£6,000	14.06.80	Bury	39		5					
				£150,000	13.07.81	Everton	494	60	64	32				
				Loan	27.01.83	Port Vale	9							
D E F E N D E R S														
Gary Ablett	6.0	11.4	19.11.65	Liverpool	19.11.83	Liverpool (A)	103+6	10+1	16+2	9	1			
E:B1, u21.1; Div1'88'90; CS'88'90; FAC'89'95.				Loan	25.01.85	Derby County	3+3			2				
				Loan	10.09.86	Hull City	5							
				£750,000	14.01.92	Everton	115	11	9		5			
Graham Allen	6.1	12.00	08.04.77	Bolton	1994-95	Everton								
Earl D Barrett	5.10	11.2	28.04.67	Rochdale	26.04.85	Manchester C. (T)	2+1	1						
E: 3, B.4, u21.4. Div.2'91. FLgXI.1. LC'94.				Loan	01.03.86	Chester City	12							
				£35,000	24.11.87	Oldham Athletic	181+2	20	14	4	7	1	1	
				£1,700,000	25.02.92	Aston Villa	118+1	15	9	7	1	1		
				£1,700,000	30.01.95	Everton	17							
Andrew G Hinchcliffe	5.10	12.10	05.02.69	Manchester	17.06.86	Manchester city (A)	107+5	11	12	4	8	1	1	1
E: u21.1, Y7. FAC'95.				£800,000	17.07.90	Everton	114+5	14+2	11	4	4		1	
Paul Holmes	5.10	11.0	18.02.68	Stocksbridge	24.02.66	Doncaster Rovers (A)	42+5		3+1	1	1		1	
				£6,000	12.08.88	Torquay united	127+11	9	9+2	13+3	4			
				£40,000	05.06.92	Birmingham City	12		1					
				£100,000	19.03.93	Everton	20	4	1					
Mattew A Jackson	6.0	12.12	19.10.71	Leeds	04.07.90	Luton Town (J)	7+2	2		0+1				
E: u21.10, u19.5, S. FAC'95				Loan	27.03.91	Preston North End	3+1			1				
				£600,000	18.10.93	Everton	118+6	8	12	1	6			
Neil Moore	6.0	12.3	21.09.72	Liverpool	04.06.91	Everton (T)	4+1	0+1						
				Loan	09.09.94	Blackpool	7			1				
				Loan	16.02.95	Oldham Athletic	5							
Craig J Short	6.0	11.4	25.06.68	Bridlington		Pickering Town								
E: S.				Free	15.10.87	Scarborough	61+2	6	2	7	7			1
				£100,000	27.07.89	Notts County	128	6	8	16	6	1	1	2
				£2,500,000	18.09.92	Derby County	118	11	7	7	9		4	
				£2,400,000	08.95	Everton								
Alexander P Smith	5.7	9.0	15.02.76	Liverpool	01.07.94	Everton (T)								
David G Unsworth	6.0	13.0	16.10.73	Chorley	25.06.92	Everton (T)	48+2	5+1	2		5			
E: Y.14. FAC'95.														
David Watson	5.11	11.12	20.11.61	Liverpool	25.05.79	Liverpool (J)								
E: 12, u21.7; CS'87; Div1'87; Div2'86; MC'85;				£100,000	29.11.80	Norwich City	212	21	18		11	3	1	
UEFAu21'84. FAC'95.				£900,000	22.08.86	Everton	304+2	34	38	14	20	6	5	3
M I D F I E L D														
John K Ebbrell	5.7	9.12	01.10.69	Bromborough	07.11.86	Everton (T)	176+9	16	16	6+2	9	1	2	1
E: B1, u21.14, Y4, S; GMAFS. FAC'95.														
Anthony J Grant	5.10	10.2	14.11.74	Liverpool	08.07.93	Everton (T)	1+4							
Mark A Grugel	5.8	10.0	09.03.76	Liverpool	05.11.93	Everton(T)								
Peter I Holcroft	5.8	10.0	03.11.76	Liverpool	01.07.94	Everton (T)								
Barry Horne	5.10	12.3	18.05.62	St Asaph		Rhyl								
W:44; WFAC'86. FAC'95.				Free	26.06.84	Wrexham	136	10	7	15	17	1	2	3
				£60,000	17.07.87	Potysmouth	66+4	3	6		7			
				£700,000	22.03.89	Southampton	111+1	15+2	15	7	6	3	3	1
				£675,000	01.07.92	Everton	93+4	10+1	7+1		2			
Jonathan O'Connor	5.10	11.03	29.10.76	Darlington	28.10.93	Everton(T)								
E: Y.14, S														
Joseph S Parkinson	5.8	12.2	11.06.71	Eccles	01.04.89	Wigan Athletic (T)	115+4	11	9	8	6	1		
FAC'95.				£35,000	01.07.93	Bournemouth	30	4	4	1	1	1		
				£250,000	24.03.94	Everton	32+2	2	6		1			
Christopher Price	5.9	11.09	24.10.75	Liverpool	01.07.94	Everton (T)								
Gary Rowett	6.0	12.0	06.03.74	Bromsgrove	10.09.91	Cambridge United (T)	51+12	7	5+2	5	9	1		3
				£200,000	21.05.94	Everton	2+2							
Vincent Samways	5.8	9.0	27.10.68	Bethnal Green	09.11.85	Tottenham H. (A)	165+28	27+4	15+1	7+1	11	4	2	
E: u21.5, u19.3, Y6; FAC'91; CS'91.				£2,200,000	02.08.94	Everton	14+5	2			1	1		
FORWARDS														
Daniel O Amokachi	5.10	13.0	30.12.72	Groko, Nigeria		FC Bruges								
Nigerian Int. FAC'95.				£3,000,000	27.08.94	Everton	17+1	2	0+2		4		2	
Stuart Barlow	5.10	11.0	16.07.68	Liverpool	06.06.90	Everton	24+44	3+4	4+3		10	1	2	
				Loan	10.01.92	Rotheram United				0+1				

Player				Previous Club	Date	From/To		App				App			
Duncan Ferguson	6.4	14.6	27.12.71	Stirling	01.02.90	Dundee United	75+2	2+1	8		28	2	6	
S: 4, B, u21.7. SL'94. SLC'94. FAC'95.				£4,000,000	20.07.94	Glasgow Rangers	35	1+1	0+3	1	5			
				£4,400,000	04.10.94	Everton	22+1	1	3+1		7		1	
Andrei Kanchelskis	5.10	12.4	23.01.69	Kirowograd (USSR)		Shakhtor Donetsk								
USSR: ; Russia: ; ESC'92; LC'92;				£650,000	26.03.91	Manchester United	96+27	15+1	11+1	·10	28	3	4	1
Prem'93'94; FAC'94; CS'93				£4,500,000	08.95	Everton								
Anders Limpar	5.8	11.5	24.08.75	Soina (Sweden)		Cremonese								
Swe: Div1'91; FLgXl. FAC'95.				£1,000,000	06.08.90	Arsenal	76+20	9	7	4	17		2	1
				£1,600,000	24.03.94	Everton	28+8		5+1		2		1	
Paul D Rideout	5.11	12.2	14.08.64	Bournemouth	15.08.81	Swindon Town (A)	90+5	3	7		38	2	1	
E:u 21.5, Y9, S. FAC'95.				£200,000	01.06.83	Aston Villa	50+4	4+2	1+1	1	19	3		
				£400,000	01.07.85	Bari	80				24			
				£430,000	05.07.91	Swindon Town	9				1			
				£250,000	16.09.91	Notts County	9+2	2	1	2	3			
				£500,000	10.01.92	Glasgow Rangers	7+5	0+1	1+1		1			
				£500,000	14.08.92	Everton	63+14	8+1	7		23		8	1
Graham C Stuart	5.8	11.6	24.10.70	Tooting	15.06.89	Chelsea (T)	70+17	11	5+2	3+2	14	2	1	1
E: u21.5, Y5, S. FAC'95.				£850,000	19.08.93	Everton	26+4	2	1+1		3			

ADDITIONAL CONTRACT PLAYERS

Gerard Hennigan	08.95	Everton (T)
James Speare	08.95	Everton (T)
Andrew Weathers	08.95	Everton (T)
Matthew Woods	08.95	Everton (T)

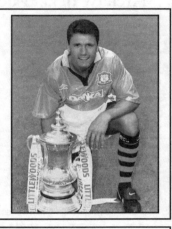

TOP GOALSCORER 1994/95
Paul Rideout

Premiership goals (games) . . . . 14 (25+4)
Coca-Cola Cup Goals. . . . . 0 (1+1)
F.A. Cup goals 2 (5)

Total . . . . **16 (31+5)**

Total goals for Everton since 14.08.92 . . . . 34 (78+15)

Career total as at June 1st 1995 . . . . 147 (432+44)

THE MANAGER
JOE ROYLE

Date of Birth . . . . 8th April 1949.
Place of Birth . . . . Liverpool.
Date of Appointment . . . . November 1994.

PREVIOUS CLUBS
As Manager . . . . Oldham Athletic.
As Coach. . . . . None.
As a Player . . . . Everton, Manchester City, Bristol City, Norwich City.

HONOURS
As a Manager
Oldham Athletic: League Cup finalists 1990. Division 2 champions 1990-91.
Everton: FA Cup winners 1994-95.

As a Player
Everton: League Championship 1970.
Manchester City: League Cup winners 1976.
International: 6 full caps and 10 U23 for England. Football League XI.

GOODISON PARK

Liverpool L4 4EL
Tel: 0151 330 2200

Capacity ....38,500.
First game ....v Bolton Wanderers, Division 1, 2.9.1892.
First floodlit game ....v Liverpool, 9.10.1957.
ATTENDANCES
Highest ....78,299 v Liverpool, Division 1, 18.9.1948.
Lowest ....2,079 v WBA, 23.2.1899.
Internationals.........................England v Scotland 1895, 1911.v Ireland 1907, 1924, 1928, 1935, 1947, 1953, 1973.
....v Eire 1949, v Portugal 1951, Poland 1966.
.Brazil v Bulgaria 1966, v Hungary 1966, Portugal 1966. Portugal v North Korea 1966. W.Germany v Russia 1966.
....Ireland v Wales 1973.

OTHER GROUNDS ....Stanley Park 1878-82, Priory Road 1882-84,
....Anfield Road 1884-92, Goodison Park 1892-

MATCHDAY TICKET PRICES

Categories	A	B
Main Stand		
Main Section	£17	£14
Top Balcony	£14	£12
Concessions	£6	£6
Family Enclosure	£14	£12
Concessions	£6	£6
Bullens Road Stand		
Upper Tier	£16	£14
Lower Tier	£14	£12
Concessions	£6	£6
Paddock	£14	£12
Park Stand	£15	£13
Gwladys Stand		
Stand	£14	£12
Terrace	£12	£10
Concessions	£6	£6
Visitors		
Upper & Lower	£16	£16
Concessions	£10	£10

Ticket Office Telephone no. 0151 330 2300

HOW TO GET TO THE GROUND

From the North
Use motorway M6 until junction 28 then follow signs Liverpool on A58 then A580 and forward into Walton Hall Avenue for Everton FC.

From the East, and South
Use motorway M6 then M62 until end of motorway then turn right A5058 into Queens Drive. In 3.7 miles turn left A580 into Walton Hall Avenue for Everton FC.

From the West
Use Mersey Tunnel into Liverpool City Centre, then follow signs to Preston (A580) into Walton Hall Avenue for Everton FC.

Car Parking
Extensive parking is available on site at the corner of Prior and Utting Avenue.

Nearest Railway Station
Liverpool (Lime Street) 0151 709 9696.

CLUBCALL 0898 12 11 99
Calls cost 39p per minute cheap rate and 49p per minute at all other times.
Call costings correct at time of going to press.

MATCHDAY PROGRAMME

Programme Editor . . . . Mike Beddow.

Number of pages . . . . 32.

Price . . . . £1.50.

Subscriptions . . . . £45 UK. (For overseas apply to club).

Local Newspapers . . . . Liverpool Daily Post, Liverpool Echo.

Local Radio Stations . . . . Radio Merseyside, Radio City.

LEEDS UNITED
(The Whites)
F.A. CARLING PREMIERSHIP
SPONSORED BY: THISTLE HOTELS

Back Row (L-R): David White, Brian Deane, Carlton Palmer, John Lukic, David Wetherall, Mark Beeney, Philemon Masinga, Lucas Radebe, Paul Beesley. **Middle Row:** Mike Hennigan (Asst. Manager), Matthew Smithard, Mark Ford, Noel Whelan, Robert Bowman, Mark Tinkler, Andy Couzens, Kevin Sharp, Tony Dorigo, Nigel Worthington, David O'Leary, David Williams (Coach), Geoff Ladley (Physio). **Front Row:** Rod Wallace, Anthony Yeboah, Gary McAllister, Howard Wilkinson (Manager), John Pemberton, Gary Speed, Gary Kelly.

LEEDS UNITED
FORMED IN 1919 (As United)
TURNED PROFESSIONAL IN 1919
LTD COMPANY IN 1920
PRESIDENT: Rt Hon Earl of Harewood
CHAIRMAN: L Silver OBE
MANAGING DIRECTOR: W J Fotherby
VICE-CHAIRMAN: P J Gilman
DIRECTORS
R Barker MCIT, MBIM,
J W G Marjason (Dep. Chairman)
M J Bedford, E Carlile, A Hudson, R Feldman,
P Ridsdale, K Woolmer
SECRETARY
Nigel Pleasants (01532 716 037)
COMMERCIAL MANAGER
Bob Baldwin (01532 716 037)
MANAGER: Howard Wilkinson
ASSISTANT MANAGER: Michael Hennigan
RESERVE TEAM COACHES
Peter Gunby, Robin Wray & David Williams
DIRECTOR OF YOUTH COACHING
Paul Hart
PHYSIOTHERAPIST
Geoff Ladley & Alan Sutton

STATISTICIAN FOR THE DIRECTORY
Mark Evans

Frustration could be the term to describe the club's season. Some impressive and long overdue results were achieved only to be offset by defeats to lowly opposition where points were expected to be picked up. Indeed the side finished the season in true championship form.

Four players joined the club pre-season, the main acquisition being England International, Carlton Palmer from Sheffield Wednesday; originally he was signed to play in central defence, a position he kept until the turn of the year before moving back to midfield. Also joining were the ever dependable and versatile Nigel Worthington and the unknown South Africans, Philomen Masinga and Lucas Radebe.

The main departure, was to be the premature retirement of Gordon Strachan, who eventually joined Coventry City as Ron Atkinson's Assistant. He left behind many marvellous memories.

On the playing pitch, youngsters Kelly, Wetherall and Whelan went from strength to strength, maturing into fine players, with Noel Whelan gaining International recognition.. John Lukic had a good consistent season, producing many fine saves, and when Palmer reverted to midfield John Pemberton came into central defence and was a real unsung hero.

But the side again struggled to score goals and Howard Wilkinson's desire to sign a proven World class striker was one of the worst kept secret of the season, being rejected on more than one occasion by prospective foreign imports. Alas, while the side was never out of the top ten, lack of goals was proving a major problem and the reason the side never challenged the championship leaders.

But, "cometh the hour, cometh the man" and enter Tony Yeboah. The search for a striker ended in January and what a signing it turned out to be. Yeboah scored twelve goals in sixteen games and a place in the UEFA Cup was becoming a real possibility as the season neared it's end. The Chairman's threat of participation in the Inter Toto Cup and nine victories in the last twelve games saw a final position of fifth place being gained along with the desired European qualification.

The Coca-Cola Cup brought a major disappointment and defeat in the second round to Third Division, Mansfield Town. A defeat which looked like being repeated in the FA Cup third round at Walsall until Wetherall's equaliser three minutes from time earned a deserved replay. The fifth round was reached for the first time in Wilkinson's reign, only for an inept first half performance to bring defeat at Old Trafford.

The club can look forward to a return to European Football next season. The Chairman, Directors and Management have the club on a sound footing, and as the summer began, was being linked with a number of International players. Once again success could be just around the corner.

MARK EVANS.

LEEDS UNITED

Premier League: 5th **FA Cup:** 5th Round **Coca-Cola Cup:** 2nd Round

M	DATE	COMP.	VEN	OPPONENTS	RESULT		H/T	LP	GOAL SCORERS/GOAL TIMES	ATT.
1	A 20	PL	A	West Ham United	D	0-0	0-0			(18,610)
2	23	PL	H	Arsenal	W	1-0	0-0		Whelan 89	34,218
3	27	PL	H	Chelsea	L	2-3	2-1	10	Masinga 4, Whelan 19	32,212
4	30	PL	A	Crystal Palace	W	2-1	1-0	6	White 15, Whelan 62	(13,654)
5	S 11	PL	H	Manchester United	W	2-1	1-0	6	Wetheralll 13, Deane 49	39,396
6	17	PL	A	Coventry City	L	1-2	0-0	6	Speed 85	(15,389)
7	21	CC 2/1	H	**Mansfield Town**	L	0-1	0-1			7,844
8	26	PL	A	Sheffield Wednesday	D	1-1	1-1	8	McAllister 13	(23,227)
9	O 1	PL	H	Manchester City	W	2-0	1-0	6	Whelan 27,90	30,938
10	4	CC 2/2	A	**Mansfield Town**	D	0-0	0-0		(Lost 0-1 on agg)	(17,390)
11	8	PL	A	Norwich City	L	1-2	0-1	9	Wallace 89	(17,390)
12	15	PL	H	Tottenham Hotspur	D	1-1	0-1	9	Deane 62	39,224
13	24	PL	H	Leicester City	W	2-1	1-0	9	McAllister 35, Whelan 67	28,547
14	29	PL	A	Southampton	W	3-1	0-1	6	Maddison 53 (og), Wallace 83,89	(15,202)
15	N 1	PL	A	Ipswich Town	L	0-2	0-1	6		(15,546)
16	5	PL	H	Wimbledon	W	3-1	3-1	6	Wetherall 13, Speed 38, White 45	27,284
17	19	PL	A	Queens Park Rangers	L	2-3	0-2	6	McDonald 55(og), Deane 72	(17,416)
18	26	PL	H	Nottingham Forest	W	1-0	0-0	6	Whelan 60	38,191
19	D 5	PL	A	Everton	L	0-3	0-1	8		(25,897)
20	10	PL	H	West Ham United	D	2-2	2-1	7	Worthington 3, Deane 25	28,897
21	17	PL	A	Arsenal	W	3-1	1-0	6	Masinga 24,85, Deane 88	(38,098)
22	26	PL	H	Newcastle Utd	D	0-0	0-0	6		39,387
23	31	PL	H	Liverpool	L	0-2	0-1	8		38,563
24	J 2	PL	A	Aston Villa	D	0-0	0-0	7		(35,038)
25	7	FAC 3	A	**Walsall**	D	1-1	0-1		**Wetherall 87**	(8,619)
26	14	PL	H	Southampton	D	0-0	0-0	8		28,953
27	17	FAC 3R	H	**Walsall**	W	5-2	2-1		**Deane 8, Wetherall 37, Masinga 105, 107, 114, (A.E.T.)**	17,881
28	24	PL	H	Queens Park Rangers	W	4-0	2-0	7	Masinga 31, 65, White 33, Deane 84	28,780
29	28	FAC 4	H	**Oldham Athletic**	W	3-2	2-0		**White 8, Palmer 45, Masinga 57**	25,010
30	F 1	PL	A	Blackburn Rovers	D	1-1	0-1	7	McAllister 84 (pen)	(25,561)
31	4	PL	A	Wimbledon	D	0-0	0-0	6		(10,211)
32	19	FAC 5	A	**Manchester United**	L	1-3	0-2		**Yeboah 53**	(42,744)
33	22	PL	H	Everton	W	1-0	0-0	6	Yeboah 81	30,793
34	25	PL	A	Manchester City	D	0-0	0-0	6		(22,892)
35	M 4	PL	H	Sheffield Wednesday	L	0-1	0-1	7		33,750
36	11	PL	A	Chelsea	W	3-0	2-0	7	Yeboah 25, 53, McAllister 29	(20,174)
37	15	PL	A	Leicester City	W	3-1	1-1	6	Yeboah 32, 60, Palmer 78	(20,068)
38	18	PL	H	Coventry City	W	3-0	1-0	6	Yeboah 39, Gould 51 (og), Wallace 56	29,179
39	22	PL	A	Nottingham Forest	L	0-3	0-3	6		(26,299)
40	A 2	PL	A	Manchester United	D	0-0	0-0	6		(43,712)
41	5	PL	H	Ipswich Town	W	4-0	4-0	6	Yeboah 4,35,45, Speed 31	28,600
42	9	PL	A	Liverpool	W	1-0	1-0	6	Deane 29	(37,454)
43	15	PL	H	Blackburn Rovers	D	1-1	0-1	6	Deane 90	39,426
44	17	PL	A	Newcastle United	W	2-1	2-1	6	McAllister 25 (pen), Yeboah 31	(39,426)
45	29	PL	H	Aston Villa	W	1-0	0-0	6	Palmer 90	32,955
46	M 6	PL	H	Norwich City	W	2-1	0-1	6	McAllister 80 (pen), Palmer 90	31,982
47	9	PL	H	Crystal Palace	W	3-1	2-0	4	Yeboah 6, 59, Wetherall 41	30,942
48	14	PL	A	Tottenham Hotspur	D	1-1	0-1	5	Deane 67	(33,040)
49										
50										
51										
52										
53										
54										
55										
56										
57										
58										
59										
60										

Best Home League Attendance: 39,426 v Blackburn Rovers   **Smallest:** 27,284 v Wimbledon   **Av Home Att:** 32,965

Goal Scorers: Compared with 1993-94: -1,561

League (59):   Yeboah 12, Dean 9, Whelan 7, McAllister 6, (3 pens), Masinga 5, Wallace 4, White 3, Weatherall 3, Speed 3, Palmer 3,
Opponents 3, Worthington
C/Cola Cup (0):
FA Cup (10):   Masinga 4, Weatherall 2, Deane, White, Palmer, Yeboah 1

1994-95

1 Luric J.	2 Kelly G.	15 Worthington N.	14 White D.	4 Palmer C.	6 Wetherall D.	7 Strachan G.	8 Wallace R.	9 Deane B.	10 McAllister G.	11 Speed G.	13 Benney M.	5 Fairclough C.	26 Masinga P.	12 Pemberton J.	19 Whelan N.	17 Tinkler M.	27 Radebe L.	3 Dorigo T.	21 Yeboah A.	23 Couzens A.	20 Sharp K.	Referee	
X	X	X	X	X	X	X	X1	X	X	X	S	S	S1									Burge K.	1
X	X	X	X	X	X	X1	X	X	X	X	S		X	S	S1							Dilkes R.	2
X	X	X	X	X	X		X		X	X	S		X	S	X	S						Ashby G.	3
X	X	X	X1	X	X	S	X		X	X	S	S1	X1		X							Gallagher D.	4
X	X	X	X1	X	X		X	S1	X	X	S		S2	X2	X							Elleray D.	5
X	X	X		X	X1	X	X		X	X	S	S1	X2	S2	X							Hill B.	6
X	X	X		X	X	X2	X	S1	X	X	S	X	X1		X		S2					Worrall J.	7
X	X	X		X	X		X	X1	X	X	S	X1		S1	X2	S2						Wilkie A.	8
X	X	X		X	X		X	X1	X	X	S	X		S1	X		S					Holbrook T.	9
X	X	X		X	X		X2	X	X	X	S	X1		S2	X				S1			Danson P.	10
X	X	X2		X	X		X2	X	X	X	S	S2		S1	X1		X					Don P.	11
X	X1	X		X	X		X	X	X	X	S			S1	X	S		X				Cooper K.	12
X	X	X	S	X	X		X	X	X	X	S		S	S	X		S1	X1				Burge K.	13
X	X	X	X1	X	X		X	X	X	X	S		S1	X		S	X					Gifford R.	14
X	X	X	X1	X	X		X	X	X	X	S	S1		X		S2						Gallagher D.	15
X	X	X	X2	X	X		X	X1	X	X	S	S1		X		S2						Hill B.	16
X	X	X	S1	X	X		X	X	X	X	S		S	X	X1							Bodenham M.	17
X	X		X	X	X		X1	X	X	X	S	S1	S2	X2		X						Jones P.	18
X	X		X	X	X		X	X	X	X	S	S		X		S	X					Durkin J.	19
X	X	X1	S1	X	X	X		X	X		S			X	X	S	X					Hart R.	20
X	X	S	S1	X	X			X		X	S	X	X	X1	X	X						Poll G.	21
X	X	S2	X		X	X2	S1		X	X	S	X1	X	X		X	X1					Worrall J.	22
X	X	S1	S2		X	X2		X	X	S	X	X	X		X	X1						Wilkie A.	23
X	X	X	X		X		S1	X	X	X	S	X1	X		S	X						Danson P.	24
X	X	X2	X		X		S2	X	X	X	S	S1	X		X1							Winter J.	25
X	X	X2	X		X		S2	X	X	X	S	S1	X		X1							Don P.	26
X	X	X		X2	X		X1	X	X	X	S	S1	X	X	S2		S1					Winter J.	27
X	X	X	X		X			X	X	X	S	X1	X		S		S1					Morton K.	28
X	X	X	X		X			X	X	X	S	X1	X		S		S2					Lodge S.	29
X	X	S1	X	X				X	X	X	S	X2	X		X1	X	S					Gifford R.	30
X	X	X	X			X	X	X		S	X	X	S		X	X	S2					Ashby G.	31
X	X	S1	X		X		X1		X	X	S	X2	X	X		X	X					Reed M.	32
X	X	S1	X		X			X	X	X	S	X	X	S		X1	X	X1				Gallagher D.	33
X	X	X	X		X	X	S1	X	X	X	S	X			S	X	X					Holbrook T.	34
X	X		X	X		X1	X	X	X	S	S1	X		S	X	X						Cooper K.	35
X	X		X	X		X	X	X	X	S	S	X		S	S	X	X					Jones P.	36
X	X		X	X		X	X	X	X	S		X		S	S	X	X					Gallagher D.	37
X	X	S	X	X			X	X	X	S			X	X1	X	X	S1					Hart R.	38
X	X1	S	S1	X			X	X	X	S		X			X	X	X					Reed M.	39
X	X	S2		X	X		X2	X1	X		S		X	S1		X	X	S1				Gifford R.	40
X	X1		X	X		X	X	X	X	S		X	S		X	X	S1					Willard G.	41
X	X	S		X	X		X	X1	X	X	S		X	S1		X	X					Burge K.	42
X	X	S		X	X		X	X	X	X	S		X	S		X	X					Poll G.	43
X	X	S1	X1	X	X			X	X	X	S	S2	X			X	X2					Danson P.	44
X	X	S		X	X		X	X	X	X	S		X	S		X	X					Elleray D.	45
X	X		X	X		X1	X	X	X	S		X	S2		X	X2	S1					Wilkie A.	46
X	X		X	X		X	X	X	X	S		X			X	X	S	S				Worrall J.	47
X	X		X	X		X1	X	X	X	S	S		X			X	X	S1				Durkin P.	48
42	42	21	18	39	38	5	30	33	41	39		1	15	22	18	3	9	28	16	2		League Appearances	
	6	5				1	2	2				4	7	5	5		3		2	2	2	League Sub Appearances	
2	2	2		2	1		2	1+1	2	2			2	1					0+1	0+1		C/Cola Cup Appearances	
4	4	3+1	3	3	4		2+1	3	4	4			2+2	4	2			1+1	1	0+2		FA Cup Appearances	

† = Sent Off

LEEDS UNITED

BIGGEST VICTORIES:
League: 8-0 v Leicester City, Division 1, 7.4.1934.
F.A. Cup: 8-1 v Crystal Palace, 3rd Round, 11.1.1930.
7-0 v Leeds Steelworks, Preliminary Round, 25.9.1920.
League Cup: 5-1 v Mansfield Town, 2nd Round, 26.9.1963.
4-0 v Chesterfield, 2nd Round, 23.11.1960.
4-0 v Burnley, 2nd Round, 6.9.1972.
4-0 v Colchester, 3rd Round, 26.11.1977.
4-0 v York City, 2nd Round, 6.10.1987.
Europe: 10-0 v Lyn Oslo, European Cup 1st Round 1st leg, 17.9.1969.

BIGGEST DEFEATS
League: 1-8 v Stoke City, Division 1, 27.8.1934.
F.A. Cup: 2-7 v Middlesbrough, 3rd Round 2nd leg, 4.9.1979.
League Cup: 0-7 v Arsenal, 2nd Round 2nd leg, 4.9.1979.
0-7 v West Ham United, 4th Round, 7.11.1966.
Europe: 0-4 v Lierse, 1st Round, 2nd leg UEFA, 29.9.1971.

MOST POINTS
3 points a win: 85, Division 2, 1989-90.
2 points a win: 67, Division 1, 1968-69.

MOST GOALS SCORED
98, Division 2, 1927-28.
Jennings 21, White 21, Keetley 18, Wainscoat 18, Mitchell 8, Turnbull 8, Armand 2, Hart 1, Townsley 1.

MOST GOALS CONCEDED
92, Division 1, 1959-60.

MOST FIRST CLASS MATCHES IN A SEASON
66- 1967-68 (League 42, FA Cup 5, League Cup 7, UEFA 12).

MOST LEAGUE WINS
27, Division 1, 1968-69, Division 1, 1970-71.

MOST LEAGUE DRAWS
21, Division 2, 1982-83.

MOST LEAGUE DEFEATS
30, Division 1, 1946-47.

MOST GOALS IN A SEASON
John Charles: 43 goals in 1953-54 (League 42, FA Cup 1).

MOST GOALS IN A MATCH
5. Gordon Hodgson v Leicester City, 8-2, Division 1, 1.10.1938.

OLDEST PLAYER
Peter Lorimer, 38 years 317 days v Barnsley, 27.10.1985.

YOUNGEST PLAYER
Peter Lorimer, 15 years 289 days v Southampton, 29.9.1962.

MOST CAPPED PLAYER
Billy Bremner (Scotland) 54.

League: 1968-69: Matches played 42, Won 27, Drawn 13, Lost 2, Goals for 66, Goals against 27, Points 67, 1st in Division 1. Highest Position: Division 1 Champions 1968-69, 1973-74, 1991-92.
F.A. Cup: 1971-72: 3rd Round Bristol Rovers 4-1; 4th Round Liverpool 0-0,2-0; 5th Round Cardiff City 2-0; 6th Round Tottenham Hotspur 2-1; Semi-Final Birmingham City 3-0; Final Arsenal 1-0.
League Cup: 1967-68: 2nd Round Luton 3-1; 3rd Round Bury 3-0; 4th Round Sunderland 2-0; 5th Round Stoke City 2-0; Semi-Final Derby County 1-0, 3-2; Final Arsenal 1-0.
Europe: UEFA Cup winners in 1967-68.
Most recent success: 1970-71: 1st Round Sarpsborg 1-0,5-0; 2nd Round Dynamo Dresden 1-0,1-2; 3rd Round Sparta Prague 6-0,3-2; 4th Round Vitoria Setubal 2-1,1-1; Semi-Final Liverpool 1-0,0-0; Final Juventus 2-2,1-1 (Leeds won on away goals).

ADDITIONAL INFORMATION
PREVIOUS NAMES
Leeds United were formed in October 1919 after Leeds City (formed 1904) had been suspended 'sine die' by the F.A. earlier that same month.

PREVIOUS LEAGUES
Leeds City: West Yorkshire League 1904-05 prior to becoming a Football League club.
Leeds United: Gained admission to the Midland League in November 1919 and the first team competed in this League prior to gaining Football League status in the summer of 1920.

DIVISIONAL RECORD

	Played	Won	Drawn	Lost	For	Against	Points
Division 1/P	1,718	707	442	569	2,619	2,350	1,957
Division 2	1,144	483	309	1,731	1,731	1,451	1,369
Total	3,142	1,190	751	921	4,350	3,801	3,326

Club colours: All white with blue logos.

Change colours: Blue & green stripes, blue shorts, green & blue socks.

Reserves League: Pontins Central League Division 1.

RECORDS AND STATISTICS

COMPETITIONS

Div 1/P	Div.2	Euro C	ECWC	UEFA
1924-27	1920-24	1969-70	1972-73	1965-66
1928-31	1927-28	1974-75		1966-67
1932-47	1931-32	1992-93		1967-68
1956-60	1947-56			1968-69
1964-82	1960-64			1970-71
1990-				1971-72
				1973-74
				1979-80

HONOURS

Div.1	Div.2	FA Cup	Lge Cup	UEFA	C/S'Ld
1968-69	1923-24	1972	1967-68	1967-68	1969
1973-74	1963-64			1970-71	1974
1991-92	1989-90				1992

MOST APPEARANCES

JACK CHARLTON 772 (1952-73)

Year	League	FA Cup	Lge Cup	Europe
1952-53	1			
1953-54				
1954-55	1			
1955-56	34	1		
1956-57	21	1		
1957-58	40	1		
1958-59	39	1		
1959-60	41	1		
1960-61	41	1	4	
1961-62	34	2	3	
1962-63	38	3	1	
1963-64	25		2	
1964-65	39	8	2	
1965-66	40	2	1	11
1966-67	29	6	4	7
1967-68	34	4	5	11
1968-69	41	2	2	7
1969-70	32	9	2	7
1970-71	40	4	1	10
1971-72	41	5	4	
1972-73	18	1	4	2
	629	52	35	55

Includes 1 Charity Shield appearance 1969-70.

MOST GOALS IN A CAREER

PETER LORIMER - 238 (1962-79 & 1983-85)

Year	League	FA Cup	Lge Cup	Europe
1965-66	13	3		3
1966-67	9	2	2	1
1967-68	17	2	4	8
1968-69	8	1		3
1969-70	14	2		3
1970-71	12	2		5
1971-72	23	3	2	1
1972-73	15	3	3	2
1973-74	12	2		
1974-75	9		3	4
1975-76	10		1	
1976-77	3			
1977-78	6		3	
1983-84	4			
1984-85	9		1	
1985-86	4			
Total	168	20	19	30

(plus 1 in the Charity Shield 1985-86)

Current leading goalscorer - Gary Speed - 50 (1988-95)

RECORD TRANSFER FEE RECEIVED

Amount	Club	Player	Date
£2,700,000	Blackburn Rovers	David Batty	10/93
£1,200,000	Manchester Utd	Eric Cantona	11/92
£1,000,000	Norwich City	Jon Newsome	6/94
£850,000	Everton	Ian Snodin	1/87

RECORD TRANSFER FEE PAID

Amount	Club	Player	Date
£3,400,000	Eintracht Frankfurt	Tony Yeboah	1/95
£2,700,000	Sheffield United	Brian Deane	7/93
£2,600,000	Sheffield Wed.	Carlton Palmer	6/94
£2,000,000	Arsenal	David Rocastle	7/92

MANAGERS

Name	Seasons	Best	Worst
Arthur Fairclough	1920-27	18(1)	14(2)
Dick Ray	1927-35	5(1)	2(2)
Billy Hampson	1935-47	9(1)	22(1)
Willis Edwards	1947-48	18(2)	18(2)
Frank Buckley	1948-53	5(2)	15(2)
Raich Carter	1953-58	8(1)	10(2)
Bill Lambton	1958-59	15(1)	15(1)
Jack Taylor	1959-61	21(1)	14(2)
Don Revie	1961-74	1(1)	19(2)
Brian Clough	1974		
Jimmy Armfield	1974-78	5(1)	10(1)
Jock Stein	1978		
Jimmy Adamson	1978-80	5(1)	11(1)
Allan Clarke	1980-82	9(1)	20(1)
Eddie Gray	1982-85	7(2)	10(2)
Billy Bremner	1985-88	4(2)	14(2)
Howard Wilkinson	1988-	1(1)	10(2)

LONGEST LEAGUE RUNS

of undefeated matches:	34 (26.10.1968 - 26.8.1969)	of league matches w/out a win:	17 (1.2.1947 - 26.5.1947)
of undefeated home matches:	39 (14.8.1968 - 28.2.1970)	of undefeated away matches:	17 (2.11.1968 - 26.8.1969)
without home win:	10 (6.2.1982 - 12.5.1982)	without an away win:	27 (29.4.1938 - 30.8.1947)
of league wins:	9 (26.9.1931 - 21.11.1931)	of home wins:	13 (23.11.1968 - 9.8.1969)
of league defeats:	6 (26.4.1947 - 26.5.1947)	of away wins:	8 (1.10.1963 - 21.12.1963)

LEEDS UNITED

PLAYERS NAME Honours	Ht	Wt	Birthdate	Birthplace Transfers	Contract Date	Clubs	League	L/Cup	FA Cup	Other	Lge	L/C	FAC	Oth
G O A L K E E P E R S														
Mark R Beeney	6.4	14.7	30.12.67	Tunbridge W.	17.08.85	Gillingham (J)	2	1						
E: S-P 1; GMVC'89				Free	31.01.87	Maidstone United	50	3	11	6				
Loan Aldershot (22.03.90), 7 Lg Apps.				£30,000	28.03.91	Brighton & H.A.	68+1	6	7	6				
				£350,000	20.04.93	Leeds United	23	2	3					
John Lukic	6.4	13.7	11.12.60	Chesterfield	16.12.78	Leeds united (A)	146	7	9	3				
E: B1, u21.7, Y10; Div1'89'92; LC'87; CT'89				£50,000	25.07.83	Arsenal	223	32	21	4				
				£1,000,000	14.06.90	Leeds United	181	16	14	11				
Paul A Pettinger	6.1	13.4	01.10.75	Sheffield	16.10.92	Leeds United(T)								
E: Y5; S; FAYC'93				Loan	23.12.94	Torquay United	3							
D E F E N D E R S														
Paul Beesley	6.1	11.5	21.07.65	Liverpool		Marine								
				Free	22.09.84	Wigan Athletic	153+2	13	6	11	3			
				£175,000	20.10.89	Leyton Orient	32		1	2	1			1
				£300,000	10.07.90	Sheffield United	162+6	12+1	9+2	3	5		1	1
				£250,000	08.95	Leeds United								
Robert A Bowman			06.08.75	Durham City	20.11.92	Leeds United (T)	3+1							
Andrew J Couzens	5.10	11.11	04.06.75	Shipley	05.03.93	Leeds United (T)	2+2							
FAYC'93														
Anthony R Dorigo	5.8	10.7	31.12.65	Australia	19.07.83	Aston Villa (A)	106+5	14+1	7	2	1			
E: 15, B7, u21.11; Div1'92; Div2'89; ZDC'90				£475,000	03.07.87	Chelsea	146	14	4	16	11	1		
				£1,300,000	06.06.91	Leeds United	136	8+1	9	7	4			
Anthony Grant	5.10	11.08	20.08.76	Louth	1994-95	Leeds United (T)								
Stephen D Heath			15.11.77	Hull	1994-95	Leeds United (T)								
Garry Kelly	5.9	10.0	09.07.74	Drogheda		Home Farm								
Ei: 7, u21.4, Y					24.09.91	Leeds United	84+2	4+1	7					
Jamie Marks	5.9	10.13	18.03.77	Belfast	1994-95	Leeds United (T)								
David A O'Leary	5.11	11.3	02.05.58	Stoke Newington	01.07.75	Arsenal (A)	525+35	68+2	66+3	26	11	2	3	
Ei: 67; FAC'79'93; LC'87'93; Div1'89'91				Free	16.07.93	Leeds United	10							
Alan O'Shea	5.10	10.12	21.07.77	Dublin	1994-95	Leeds United (T)								
John M Pemberton	5.11	11.9	18.11.64	Oldham		Chadderton								
Rochdale, Free, 26.9.84, 1Lg App.				Free	29.03.85	Crewe Alexandra	116+5	7	3	7	1	1		
				£80,000	24.03.88	Crystal Palace	76+2	6+1	8	12	2			
				£300,000	27.07.90	Sheffield United	67+1	4	4	1				
				£250,000	12.11.93	Leeds United	28+8	0+1	4					
Lucas Radebe	6.0	11.8	12.04.69	Johannesberg, S. A.		Kaizer Chiefs								
				£250,000	05.09.94	Leeds United	9+3	0+1	1+1					
Kevin P Sharpe	5.9	10.7	19.09.74	Canada		Auxerre								
E: S, Y; UEFA Youth'93; FAYC'93				£60,000	20.10.92	Leeds United	11+5							
David Wetherall	6.2	13.8	14.03.71	Sheffield	01.07.89	Sheffield Wed. (T)								
E: S; Su19.3				£125,000	15.07.91	Leeds United	82+2	5	8+2		5		3	
M I D F I E L D														
Jason Blunt	5.8	10.10	16.08.77	Penzance	1994-95	Leeds United (T)								
Mark Ford	5.7	9.3	10.10.75	Pontefract	05.03.93	Leeds United (T)	0+1							
E: Y5; FAYC'93														
Martin Foster	5.5	9.10	29.10.77	Sheffield	1994-95	Leeds United (T)								
Gary McAllister	6.1	11.5	25.12.64	Motherwell		Motherwell	52+7	3+1	7		6		2	
S: 28, B2, u21.1; SDiv1'85; Div1'92				£125,000	15.08.85	Leicester City	199+2	14+1	5	4	46	3	2	
				£1,000,000	02.07.90	Leeds United	194+1	18	18	10	26	3	3	3
Carlton L Palmer	6.2	11.10	05.12.65	Rowley Regis	21.12.84	West Brom. A. (T)	114+7	7+1	4	6	4	1		
E:18, B5, u21.4				£750,000	23.02.89	Sheffield Wed.	204+1	31	18	8+1	14	3		1
				£2,800,000	30.06.94	Leeds United	39	2	3		3		1	
Matthew Smithard	5.9	9.10	13.06.75	Leeds	05.03.93	Leeds United(T)								
Gary A Speed	5.11	10.12	08.09.69	Mancot	13.06.88	Leeds United (T)	202+17	18+1	17	10+3	37	8	4 1	
W: 25, u21.3, Y; Div2'90; Div1'92														
Mark Tinkler	6.0	11.4	24.10.74	Bishop Auckland	29.11.91	Leeds United (T)	8+5							
E: S, Y7; UEFA Yth'93; FAYC'93														
Nigel Worthington	5.10	12.6	04.11.61	Ballymena		Ballymena	67							
NI: 50, Y1; UC'81; IC' 81; LC'91				£100,000	01.07.81	Notts County	67	11	4		4			
				£125,000	06.02.84	Sheffield Wed.	334+4	41	29	9	12	1		1
				£2,225,000	04.07.94	Leeds United	21+6	2	3+1		1			
F O R W A R D S														
Andrew S Brown	6.3	13.0	11.10.76	Edinburgh	1994-95	Leeds United (T)								

APPEARANCES | GOALS

Player	Ht	Wt	DOB	Birthplace / Signed	Date	Club								
Brian C Deane	6.3	12.7	07.02.88	Leeds	14,12,85	Doncaster R. (J)	59+7	3	2+1	2+2	12		1	
E: 3, B3				£30,000	19.07.88	Sheffield United	197	16	23+1	2	83	11	11	2
				£2,900,000	14.07.93	Leeds United	74+2	3+1	6		20		2	
Jamie Forrester	5.6	10.4	01.11.74	Bradford		Auxerre								
E: S, Y3; UEFA Yth'93; FAYC'93				£60,000	20.10.92	Leeds United	7+2		1+1				2	
				Loan	01.09.94	Southend United	3+2							
				Loan	10.03.95	Grimsby Town	7+2				1			
Nathan P Lowndes	5.11	10.04	02.06.77	Salford	1994-95	Leeds United (T)								
Philemon R Masinga	6.2	12.0	28.06.69	South Africa		Marneldodi Sundown								
				£275,000	0.3.08.94	Leeds United	15+7	1	2+2		5		4	
Rodney S Wallace	5.7	10.1	02.10.69	Greenwich	19.04.88	Southampton (T)	11+17	18+1	10	3+1	44	6	3	2
E: B2, u21.11; Div1'92				£1,600,000	07.06.91	Leeds United	129+5	8	5+4	1+3	39	3		1
Noel Whelan	6.2	11.3	30.12.74	Leeds	05.03.74	Leeds United (T)	25+15	3	2		7	1		
E: Y2; UEFA Yth'93; FAYC'93														
David White	6.1	12.9	30.10.67	Manchester	07.11.85	Manchester City (A)	273+12	24+2	22	9	81	11	4	2
E:1, Y1, u21.6, B2				£2,000,000	22.12.93	Leeds United	27+11		6		8	2		
Anthony Yeboah	5.10	13.11	06.06.66	Ghana		Saarsruken								
						Eintracht Frankfurt								
				£3,400,000	05.01.95	Leeds United	16+2		0+2		13		1	

Top Goalscorer 1994/95
Tony Yeboah

Premiership goals (games) . . . . 12 (16+2)
Coca-Cola Cup Goals 0 (0)
F.A. Cup goals . . . . 1 (0+2)

Total . . . . **13 (16+4)**

Total goals for Leeds United since 01.95 . . . . 13 (16+4)

Career total as at June 1st 1995 . . . . 102 (190+4)
(Career total includes 28 (65) for Saarsruken & 61 (109) for Eintracht Frankfurt)

The Manager
Howard Wilkinson

Date of Birth . . . . 13th November 1943.
Place of Birth . . . . Sheffield.
Date of Appointment . . . . October 1988.

Previous Clubs
As Manager . . . . Boston United (Player/Manager), England Semi-Pro,
. . . . Notts County, Sheffield Wednesday.
As Assistant . . . . Notts County, England Under-21 Team.
As a Player . . . . Sheffield Wednesday, Brighton & H.A. Boston United.

Honours
As a Manager
Notts County: Promotion to Division 1, 1981. Sheffield Wednesday: Division 2 Runners-up, 1984.
Leeds United: Division 2 Champions 1989-90. Division 1 Champions 1991-92.
As a Player
International: England youth.

ELLAND ROAD
Leeds, West Yorkshire LS11 0ES
Tel: 01532 716 037

Capacity 38,950

First game ....1920.
First floodlit game ....v Hibernian, 9.11.1953.

ATTENDANCES
Highest...57,892 v Sunderland FA Cup 5th Round replay, 15.3.1967.
Lowest ....2,274 v Sheffield United, AMC, 16.10.1985.

OTHER GROUNDS..None.

MATCHDAY TICKET PRICES

Categories	A+	A	B	C
West Stand				
Upper Tier & Paddock . . . £25	£22	£21	£20
Stand B £19	£16	£15	£14
Revie Stand. £19	£16	£15	£14
East Stand				
Upper Tier £23	£20	£19	£18
Family Stand £21	£18	£17	£16
South Stand				
Upper & Lower Tiers. . . . £19	£16	£15	£14
North East &				
North West Stands £21	£18	£17	£16

Concessions available - contact club.
Ticket Office Telephone no. 01532 710 710

CLUBCALL
0891 12 11 80
Calls cost 39p per minute cheap rate and 49p per minute at all other times.
Call costings correct at time of going to press.

HOW TO GET TO THE GROUND

From the North
Use A58 or A61 into Leeds City Centre, then follow signs to motorway (M621) to join motorway. In 1.6 miles leave motorway and at roundabout join A643 into Elland Road for Leeds United FC.

From the East
Use A63 or A64 into Leeds city centre, then follow signs to motorway (M621) to join motorway. Then as above.

From the South
Use motorway (M1) then M621 until junction with A643, leave motorway and at roundabout join A643 into Elland Road for Leeds United FC.

From the West
Use motorway (M62) then M621 until junction with A643. Leave motorway and at roundabout join A643 into Elland Road for Leeds United FC.

Car Parking
Wesley Street Corner has park for 1,000 cars (approx), one minute walk from ground.

Nearest Railway Station
Leeds City (01532 448 133)

MATCHDAY PROGRAMME

Programme Editor . . . . Mike Beddow & John Curtis.

Number of pages . . . . 40.

Price . . . . £1.50.

Subscriptions . . . . £46 UK.

Local Newspapers . . . . Yorkshire Post, Yorkshire Evening Post, ... Bradford Telegraph & Argus.

Local Radio Stations . . . . BBC Radio Leeds, Radio Aire (Leeds), ... Pennie Radio (Bradford).

LIVERPOOL
(The Reds or Pool)
F.A. Carling Premiership
Sponsored by: Carlsberg

Back Row (L-R): Doug Livermore, Lee Jones, Rob Jones, John Scales, David James, Michael Stensgaard, Tony Warner, Mark Wright, Mark Walters, Domini Matteo, Sammy Lee.
Middle Row: Joe Corrigan, Ronnie Moran, Michael Thomas, Stig Bjornebye, Stan Collymore, Phil Babb, John Barnes, Jan Molby, Mark Leather.
Front Row: Mark Kennedy, Robbie Fowler, Steve Harkness, Neil Ruddock, Roy Evans, Ian Rush, Jamie Redknapp, Steve McManaman, Nigel Clough.

LIVERPOOL
FORMED IN 1892
TURNED PROFESSIONAL IN 1892
LTD COMPANY IN 1892

HON VICE-PRESIDENT
C J Hill, H E Roberts, W D Corkish FCA,
R Paisley, OBE, Hon Msc
CHAIRMAN: D R Moores
DIRECTORS
J T Cross, N White, FSCA, T D Smith,
P B Robinson, T W Saunders
CHIEF EXECUTIVE/SECRETARY
P B Robinson (0151 263 2361)
COMMERCIAL MANAGER
M L Turner

MANAGER: Roy Evans
ASSISTANT MANAGER: Doug Livermore
RESERVE TEAM MANAGER
Sammy Lee
YOUTH TEAM MANAGER
H McAuley
PHYSIOTHERAPIST
Mark Leather
STATISTICIAN FOR THE DIRECTORY
Brian Pead (0181 302 6446)

With Roy Evans at the helm, the Liverpool ship was steadied on to a more positive course and piloted into calmer waters after the rough seas that Souness had led the ship into. The more genial approach of Roy Evans - one of the 'backroom boys' - was able to bring the best out of his players, and Liverpool finished a creditable fourth in the League. By their own high standards past, fourth was not acceptable, but after the turmoil of the previous few years, the final position was remarkable when fans were talking of simple consolidation at the start of the season.

Liverpool, however, had begun in sensational fashion, winning 6-1 on the opening day of the season at Crystal Palace. They followed this with a 3-0 thrashing of Arsenal (a Robbie Fowler hat-trick), but fell away after a defeat at Old Trafford. The defence was still a little too generous on occasions, with Babb played out of position, but Scales and Ruddock settled down and goals were not conceded so frequently. At the end of November, Liverpool beat Blackburn 3-1 at Ewood Park in the Coca-Cola Cup, Ian Rush scoring a hat-trick. It was a brilliant performance against the top side in the country, and gave Liverpool fans an insight to what could be achieved with more time.

Scoring sensation Robbie Fowler just could not stop finding the back of the net, but overall, Liverpool relied on him just a little too much, and their 65 goals in the Premiership was somewhat disappointing.

In January, Liverpool's FA Cup run began inauspiciously with a goalless draw at Birmingham, and the Reds were fortunate to go through eventually on penalties. Then came a marvellous 1-0 Coca-Cola Cup win against Arsenal at Highbury, and Liverpool's season was gathering momentum on three fronts, though, in truth, the League was never a real possibility at this stage. As the season wore on into early March, a place in the Coca-Cola Cup final was assured after a two-leg victory over Crystal Palace, who offered sterner resistance than they had done earlier in the season.

Burnley and Wimbledon (away!) were beaten in the FA Cup, but Liverpool's luck ran out against Tottenham and Jurgen Klinsmann at Anfield. The Coca-Cola Cup was won in early April against First Division Bolton Wanderers with two goals from in-form Steve McManaman. Useful victories in the League were offset with some unnecessary defeats, but on the final day of the season, Liverpool finished their season with a 2-1 defeat of champions-elect Blackburn Rovers, managed by Kenny Dalglish. It was fitting that Liverpool won the match and that Rovers won the championship to prevent Manchester United from claiming the title for a third year in succession.

Liverpool's buys and their youngsters performed extremely well, getting back into Europe. The days of the long knives and the furious tempers are over. Calmness has been restored, but let no-one underestimate the depth of passion Roy Evans has for the club. He will stand no nonsense as he makes it his task to bring the glory days back to Liverpool FC. One gets the feeling that they are just around the corner...

BRIAN PEAD.

LIVERPOOL

Premier League: 4th   **FA Cup:** 6th Round   **Coca-Cola Cup:** Winners

M	DATE	COMP.	VEN	OPPONENTS	RESULT	H/T	LP	GOAL SCORERS/GOAL TIMES	ATT.
1	A 20	PL	A	Crystal Palace	W 6-1	3-0		Molby 12 (pen), McManaman 14, 70, Fowler 45, Rush 60, 74	(18,084)
2	28	PL	H	Arsenal	W 3-0	3-0		Fowler 26, 28, 31	30,017
3	31	PL	A	Southampton	W 2-0	1-0	4	Fowler 21, Barnes 78	(15,190)
4	S 10	PL	H	West Ham United	D 0-0	0-0	4		30,907
5	17	PL	A	Manchester United	L 0-2	0-0	5		(43,740)
6	21	CC 2	A	Burnley	W 2-0	1-0		Scales 42, Fowler 84	(23,359)
7	24	PL	A	Newcastle United	D 1-1	0-0	6	Rush 70	(34,435)
8	O 1	PL	H	Sheffield Wednesday	W 4-1	0-1	5	Rush 51, McManaman 54, 66, 86	31,493
9	5	CC 2	A	Burnley	W 4-1	1-0		Redknapp 14, 67, Fowler 50, Clough 75	(19,032)
10	8	PL	A	Aston Villa	W 3-2	2-1	4	Fowler 2, Ruddock	32,158
11	15	PL	A	Blackburn Rovers	L 2-3	1-0	5	Fowler 29, Barnes 60	(30,263)
12	22	PL	H	Wimbledon	W 3-0	2-0	5	McManaman 20, Fowler 35, Barnes 63	31,139
13	25	CC 3	H	Stoke City	W 2-1	1-1		Rush 4, 55	32,060
14	29	PL	A	Ipswich Town	W 3-1	1-0	5	Barnes 39, Fowler 56, 60	(22,513)
15	31	PL	A	Queens Park Rangers	L 1-2	1-0		Barnes 66	(18,295)
16	N 5	PL	H	Nottingham Forest	W 1-0	1-0	5	Fowler 14	33,329
17	9	PL	H	Chelsea	W 3-1	3-1		Fowler 8, 9, Ruddock 24	32,855
18	21	PL	A	Everton	L 0-2	0-0			(39,866)
19	26	PL	H	Tottenham Hotspur	D 1-1	1-0	4	Fowler 39	35,007
20	30	CC 4	A	Blackburn Rovers	W 3-1	1-0		Rush 19, 57, 73	(30,116)
21	D 3	PL	A	Coventry City	D 1-1	1-0	4	Rush 2	(21,029)
22	11	PL	H	Crystal Palace	D 0-0	0-0	4		30,972
23	18	PL	A	Chelsea	D 0-0	0-0	5		(27,000)
24	26	PL	A	Leicester City	W 2-1	0-0	4	Fowler 67 (pen), Rush 78	(21,393)
25	28	PL	H	Manchester City	W 2-0	0-0	3	Phelan 55 (og), Fowler 82	38,122
26	31	PL	H	Leeds United	W 2-0	1-0	3	Redknapp 18, Fowler 76	(38,563)
27	J 2	PL	H	Norwich City	W 4-0	2-0	3	Scales 13, Fowler 38, 46, Rush 83	34,709
28	7	FAC 3	A	Birmingham City	D 0-0	0-0			(25,326)
29	11	CC 5	H	Arsenal	W 1-0	0-0		Rush 59	35,026
30	14	PL	H	Ipswich Town	L 0-1	0-1	3		32,733
31	18	FAC 3R	H	Birmingham City	D 1-1	1-0		Redknapp 21	36,275
32	24	PL	H	Everton	D 0-0	0-0			39,505
33	28	FAC 4	A	Burnley	D 0-0	0-0			(20,551)
34	F 4	PL	A	Nottingham Forest	D 1-1	0-1	4	Fowler 90	25,480
35	7	FAC 4R	H	Burnley	W 1-0	0-0		Barnes 44	32,109
36	11	PL	H	Queens Park Rangers	D 1-1	1-1		Scales 71	35,996
37	15	CC SF	H	Crystal Palace	W 1-0	0-0		Fowler 90	25,480
38	19	FAC 5	H	Wimbledon	D 1-1	1-1		Fowler 33	25,124
39	25	PL	A	Sheffield Wednesday	W 2-1	1-1		Barnes 41, McManaman	(31,964)
40	28	FAC 5R	A	Wimbledon	W 2-0	2-0		Barnes 9, Rush 38	(12,553)
41	M 4	PL	H	Newcastle United	W 2-0	0-0	4	Fowler 57, Rush 62	39,300
42	8	CC SF	A	Crystal Palace	W 1-0	1-0		Fowler 27	(18,224)
43	11	FAC 6	H	Tottenham Hotspur	L 1-2	1-1		Fowler 38	38,592
44	14	PL	H	Coventry City	L 2-3	0-2		Molby 77 (pen), 90 (og)	27,183
45	19	PL	H	Manchester United	W 2-0	1-0	4	Redknapp 25, 86 (og)	38,906
46	22	PL	A	Tottenham Hotspur	D 0-0	0-0			(31,988)
47	A 2	CC F	N	Bolton Wanderers	W 2-1	1-0		McManaman 37, 68	75,595
48	5	PL	H	Southampton	W 3-1	1-1		Rush 28, 50, Fowler 71 (pen)	29,881
49	9	PL	A	Leeds United	L 0-1	0-1	5		37,454
50	12	PL	A	Arsenal	W 1-0	0-0		Fowler 90	(38,036)
51	14	PL	H	Manchester City	L 1-2	1-1		McManaman 21	(27,055)
52	17	PL	H	Leicester City	W 2-0	0-0	4	Fowler 74, Rush 80	36,012
53	29	PL	A	Norwich City	W 2-1	1-1	4	Harkness 7, Rush 84	(21,843)
54	M 2	PL	A	Wimbledon	D 0-0	0-0			(12,041)
55	6	PL	A	Aston Villa	L 0-2	0-2	4		(40,154)
56	10	PL	A	West Ham United	L 0-3	0-1			(22,446)
57	14	PL	H	Blackburn Rovers	W 2-1	0-1	4	Barnes 64, Redknapp 90	40,014
58									
59									
60									

Best Home League Attendance: 40,014 v Blackburn Rovers   **Smallest:** 27,183 v Coventry   **Av Home Att:** 31,629

Goal Scorers:

League (62): Fowler 25, Rush 12, McManaman 8, Barnes 7, Redknapp 3, Scales 2, Molby 2, Ruddock 2, Harkness 1
C/Cola Cup (16): Rush 6, Fowler 4, McManaman 2, Redknapp 2, Clough 1, Scales 1
FA Cup (6): Fowler 2, Barnes 2, Redknapp, Rush 1

Compared with 1993-94: - 6,876

1 James D.	2 Jones R.	4 Nicol S	5 Wright M.	6 Babb P.	7 Clough N.	8 Stewart P.	9 Rush I.	10 Barnes J.	11 Walters M.	12 Scales J.	13 Stensgaard M.	14 Molby J.	15 Redknapp J.	16 Thomas M.	17 McManaman S.	18 Charnock P.	19 Kennedy M.	20 Bjørnebye S.	21 Matteo D.	22 Harkness S.	23 Fowler R.	24 Jones L	25 Ruddock N.	28 Chamberlain A.	30 Warner A.	Referee	#
X	X	X					X	X			S	X	X	S	X			X		S	X		X			R. Hart	1
X	X	X					X	X			S	X1	X	S1	X			X	S		X		X			A. Wilkie	2
X	X	X			S		X	X			S	X	X		X			X		S	X		X			M. Bodenham	3
X	X		S	S			X	X		X	S	X	X		X			X			X		X			P. Danson	4
X	X		S1	S			X	X		X	S	X1	X		X			X			X		X			K. Morton	5
X	X		S	S			X	X		X	S	X	X		X			X			X		X			R. Dilks	6
X	X		X	S1			X1	X		X	S	X	S		X			X			X		X			P. Don	7
X	X	X	X	X			X	X			S	S	S		X			X			X		X			G. Willard	8
X	X	X	X	X						S	X1	X	S1	X2				X			X	S2	X			J. Worrall	9
X	X		X	S			X1	X		X	S	X	S1		X			X			X		X			K. Burge	10
X	X		X	S			X	X		X	S	X	S1		X			X			X		X			B. Hill	11
X	X		X	S1			X1	X		X	S	X			X			X			X	S1	X			P. Jones	12
X	X		X	S1			X1	X		X	S	X			X			X			X	S	X			R. Hart	13
X	X		X	S			X	X		X	S			S1	X			X			X		X			P. Durkin	14
X	X		X	S			X	X		X	S	S1			X			X			X		X			T. Holbrook	15
X	X		X	S			X	X	X1		S	S1			X			X			X		X			J. Worrall	16
X	X		X	S			X	X		X	S				X			X			X	S	X			G. Poll	17
X	X		X	S			X	X		X	S	X	S1		X			X			X		X			D. Gallagher	18
X	X		X	X			X	X1		X			X	S1	X			X			X	S	X			S. Lodge	19
X	X		X	S			X	X		X			X	X	X			X			X	S	X			R. Dilks	20
X			X	S			X			S1	X			X	X	X		X1			X		X			K. Burge	21
X			X	X			X		S1	X			X	X				X2		S	X		X			K. Morton	22
X		S		X	S		X		S1	X	X		X	X				X			X		X			D. Gallagher	23
X	X			X			X	X	S	X			S1	X	X			X			X		X			G. Ashby	24
X	X			X			X	X	S	X			X	S	X			X			X		X			R. Hart	25
X	X			X			X	X	S	X			X	S	X			X			X		X			A. Wilkie	26
X	X			X			X	X	S	X			X	S	X			X			X		X			K. Cooper	27
X	X			X			X	X	S	X			X	S	X			X			X		X			J. Parker	28
X	X			X			X	X1	S	X	S		X	S1	X			X			X		X			P. Don	29
X	X	S		X			X		S1	X	S		X	X	X			X1			X		X			R. Gifford	30
X	X	S		X			X		S	X	S		X	X	X			X			X		X			J. Parker	31
X	X			X			X	X	S	X	S		X	S	X			X			X		X			B. Hill	32
X	X			X			X	X	S2	X	S		X	S	X				X		X		X			K. Morton	33
X	X			X			X	X	S	X			X1	S1	X				X2		X		X			G. Willard	34
X	X			X	S		X	X	S1	X			X		X			X1			X		X			K. Morton	35
X	X			X			X	X	S1	X	S	S2	X2	X	X			X1			X		X			D. Gallagher	36
X	X			X			X	X	X	X	S		X	S	X			S			X		X			R. Hart	37
X	X			X	S		X	X		X			X	S	X			X			X		X			A. Wilkie	38
X	X			X	S			X	X1	X			X	X	X			X	S1		X		X			D. Ellerey	39
X	X			X			X	X	X1	X			X	X	X			X			X		X			A. Wilkie	40
X	X			X			X	X	X1	X	S		X	S1	X						X		X			P. Jones	41
X	X			X			X	X	S	X			X	S	X			X			X		X			K. Burge	42
X	X			X			X	X1	X	X			X	S1	X			S1			X		X			M. Bodenham	43
X	X	S		X			X		S1	X		X	X	X	X			X1			X		X			M. Reed	44
X		X	X				X2	X1	S2	X			X	S1	X			X			X		X			G. Ashby	45
X	X	S	S	X			X		X1	X			X	S	X			X			X		X			P. Danson	46
X	X			X			X	X	S1	X			X	S	X			X1			X		X			P. Don	47
X	X			X			X	X	S1	X			X	S	X			X			X		X			S. Lodge	48
X	X			X			X	X	X1	X			X	X	X					S1	X		X			K. Burge	49
X	X	S1		X				X	S2	X2			X	X	X				X		X		X			M. Bodenham	50
X		X	X	S2			X	X				X	X	X1				X		S2	X		X			J. Worrall	51
X		X		S1			X	X				X	X	X1				X1			X	X2	X			G. Poll	52
X		X		X	S1		X	X1	S2	X			X	X	X					S1	X	X2	X			B. Hill	53
X		X		S			X	X	X	X			X	X	X					S1	X	X	X1			T. Holbrook	54
X		X		S1			X	X1	X2	X			X	X	X					S2	X	X	X			R. Hart	55
X			X	X			X	S2	X	X			X	X	X		S1			X1	X	X2				P. Durkin	56
X			X	X			X	S	X1	X			X	X	X		X			S1	X	X				D. Ellerey	57
42	32	4	6	33	3	0	36	38	7	35	0	12	35	16	40	0	4	31	2	6	42	0	37	0	0	League Appearances	
0	0	2	3	3	27	0	0	0	25	0	28	4	5	23	0	0	2	2	6	3	0	6	0	0	0	League Sub Appearances	
8	8	1	0	7	1	0	7	6	1	7	0	2	8	1	8	0	0	7	0	0	8	0	8	0	0	C/Cola Cup Appearances	
7	7	0	0	6	0	0	7	6	2	7	0	0	6	2	7	0	0	5	1	0	7	0	7	0	0	FA Cup Appearances	

† = Sent Off

LIVERPOOL

CLUB RECORDS

BIGGEST VICTORIES
League: 10-1 v Rotherham United, Division 2, 18.2.1896.
9-0 v Crystal Palace, Division 1, 12.9.1989.
6-1 v Crystal Palace, Premiership, 20.8.1994.
F.A. Cup: 8-0 v Swansea City, 3rd Round replay, 9.1.1990.
League Cup: 10-0 v Fulham, 2nd Round 1st leg, 23.9.1986.
Europe: 11-0 v Stromsgodset Gwc, ECWC, 17.9.1974.

BIGGEST DEFEATS
League: 1-9 v Birmingham City, Division 2, 11.12.1954.
0-8 v Huddersfield Town, Division 1, 10.11.1934.
F.A. Cup: 0-5 v Bolton Wanderers, 4th Round, 1945-46.
League Cup: 1-4 v West Ham, 4th Round, 30.11.1988.
Europe: (UEFA) 1-5 v Ajax, 2nd Round, 7.12.1966.

MOST POINTS
3 points a win: 90, Division 1, 1987-88 (equalled record).
2 points a win: 68, Division 1, 1978-79 (Division 1 record).

MOST GOALS SCORED
106, 1895-96.
Allan 25, Ross 23, Becton 17, Bradshaw 12, Geary 11, McVean 7, McQue 5, Hannah 3, Wilkie 1, Bull 1, McCartney 1.

MOST GOALS CONCEDED
97, Division 1, 1953-54.

MOST FIRST CLASS MATCHES IN A SEASON
67 - 1983-84 (League 42, FA Cup 2, League Cup 13, Charity Shield 1, European Cup 9).

MOST LEAGUE WINS
30, Division 1, 1978-79.

MOST LEAGUE DRAWS
19, Division 1, 1951-52.

MOST LEAGUE DEFEATS
23, Division 1, 1953-54.

INDIVIDUAL CLUB RECORDS

MOST GOALS IN A SEASON
Ian Rush: 47 goals in 1983-84 (League 32, FA Cup 2, League Cup 8, European Cup 5).

MOST GOALS IN A MATCH
5. Andy McGuigan v Stoke City (h) 7-0, Division 1, 4.1.1902.
5. John Evans v Bristol Rovers (h) 5-3, Division 2, 15.9.1954.
5. Ian Rush v Luton Town (h) 6-0, Division 1, 29.10.1983.
5. Robbie Fowler v Fulham (h) 5-0, League Cup 2nd Rnd, 5.10.93.

OLDEST PLAYER
Kenny Dalglish, 39 years 58 days v Derby County, 1.5.1990.

YOUNGEST PLAYER
Phil Charnock, ECWC, 16.09.92.

MOST CAPPED PLAYER
Ian Rush (Wales) 59.
Emlyn Hughes (England) 59.

BEST PERFORMANCES

League: 1978-79: Matches played 42, Won 30, Drawn 8, Lost 4, Goals for 85, Goals against 16, Points 68. First in Division 1.
Highest Position: Division 1 champions 18 times.
F.A. Cup: Winners in 1964-65, 1973-74, 1985-86, 1988-89.
Most recent success: 1991-92: 3rd Round Crewe Alexandra 4-0; 4th Round Bristol Rovers 1-1,2-1; 5th Round Ipswich Town 0-0,3-2; 6th Round Aston Villa 1-0; Semi-Final Portsmouth 1-1,0-0 (won 3-1 on penalties); Final Sunderland 2-0.
League Cup: Winners in 1980-81, 1981-82, 1982-83, 1983-84.
Most recent success: 1994-95: 2nd Round Burnley 2-0,4-1; 3rd Round Stoke City 2-1; 4th Round Blackburn Rovers 3-1; 5th Round Arsenal 1-0; Semi-Final Crystal Palace 1-0,1-0; Final Bolton Wanderers 2-1.
Europe: European Cup winners in 1976-77, 1977-78, 1980-81.
Most recent success: 1983-84: 1st Round Odense 1-0,5-0; 2nd Round Athletico Bilbao 0-0,1-0; 3rd round Benfica 1-0,4-1; Semi-Final Dynamo Bucharest 1-0,2-1; Final Roma 1-1 (Won on pens).
UEFA Cup winners in 1972-73.
Most recent success: 1975-76: 1st round Hibernian 0-1,3-1; 2nd Round Real Sociedad 3-1,6-0; 3rd Round Slask Wroclaw 2-1,3-0; 4th Round Dynamo Dresden 0-0,2-1; Semi-Final Barcelona 1-0,1-1; Final Bruges 3-2,1-1.

DIVISIONAL RECORD

	Played	Won	Drawn	Lost	For	Against	Points
Division 1/P	3,222	1,461	800	961	5,280	4,103	4,029
Division 2	428	243	82	103	977	571	568
Total	**3,650**	**1,704**	**882**	**1,064**	**6,257**	**4,674**	**4,597**

ADDITIONAL INFORMATION
PREVIOUS NAMES
None.
PREVIOUS LEAGUES
Lancashire League.

Club Colours: All red with white trim.
Change Colours: White and dark green quarters, dark green shorts with white trim, white socks with dark green trim.

Reserves League: Pontins Central League Division 1.

RECORDS AND STATISTICS

COMPETITIONS

Div 1/P	Div.2	Euro C	ECWC	UEFA	Sup.C	WCC
1894-95	1893-94	1964-65	1965-66	1967-68	1977	1981
1894-04	1895-96	1966-67	1971-72	1968-69	1978	1984
1905-54	1904-05	1973-74	1974-75	1969-70		
1962-	1954-62	1976-77	1992-93	1970-71		Sc Sp
		1977-78		1972-73		Sup C
		1978-79		1975-76		1986
		1979-80		1991-92		
		1980-81				
		1981-82				
		1982-83				
		1983-84				
		1984-85				

HONOURS

Div 1	Div.2	FAC	Lge C	Euro C	UEFA	C/Sh'd
1900-01	1893-94	1964-65	1980-81	1976-77	1972-73	1964
1905-06	1895-96	1973-74	1981-82	1977-78	1975-76	1965
1921-22	1904-05	1985-86	1982-83	1980-81		1966
1922-23	1961-62	1988-89	1983-84	1983-84		1974
1946-47		1991-92	1994-95		ESC	1976
1963-64					1977	1977
1965-66			Sc Sp			1979
1972-73			Sup C			1980
1975-76			1986			1982
1976-77						1986
1978-79						1988
1979-80						1989
1981-82						
1982-83						
1983-84						
1985-86						
1987-88						
1989-90						

MOST APPEARANCES

Ian Callaghan 839+7 (1959-78)

Year	League	FA Cup	Lge Cup	Europe
1959-60	4			
1960-61	3		2	
1961-62	24	5		
1962-63	37	6		
1963-64	42	5		
1964-65	37	8		9
1965-66	42	1		9
1966-67	40	4		5
1967-68	41	9	2	6
1968-69	42	4	3	2
1969-70	41	6	2	3+1
1970-71	21+1	4	1	5
1971-72	41	3	3	4
1972-73	42	4	8	12
1973-74	42	9	6	4
1974-75	41	2	3	4
1975-76	40	2	3	12
1976-77	32+1	4+1	2	7
1977-78	25+1	1	7	5
	637+3	77+1	42	87+1

MOST GOALS IN A CAREER

Ian Rush - 337 (1980-1995)

Year	League	FA Cup	Lge Cup	Europe	Other
1980-81					
1981-82	17	3	8	2	
1982-83	24	2	2	2	1
1983-84	32	2	8	5	
1984-85	14	7		5	
1985-86	22	6	3		2
1986-87	30		4		6
1988-89	7	3	1		
1989-90	18	6	2		
1990-91	16	5	5		
1991-92	3	1	3	1	
1992-93	14	1	1	5	1
1993-94	14	1	4		
1994-95	12	1	5		
Total	223	38	46	20	10

Previous Holder: Roger Hunt - 285 (1959-70)
(Lge 245, FAC 18, Lge C 5, Europe 17)

RECORD TRANSFER FEE RECEIVED

Amount	Club	Player	Date
£3,200,000	Juventus	Ian Rush	6/87
£650,000	Sampdoria	Graham Souness	6/84
£500,000	S V Hamburg	Kevin Keegan	6/77
£240,000	Coventry City	Larry Lloyd	8/74

RECORD TRANSFER FEE PAID

Amount	Club	Player	Date
£8,500,000	Nottingham Forest	Stan Collymore	07/95
£3,600,000	Coventry City	Phil Babb	09/94
£2,900,000	Derby County	Dean Saunders	7/91
£2,800,000	Juventus	Ian Rush	8/88

MANAGERS

Name	Seasons	Best	Worst
John McKenna	1892-96	16(1)	1(2)
Tom Watson	1896-15	1(1)	1(2)
Dave Ashworth	1920-23	1(1)	4(1)
Matt McQueen	1923-28	4(1)	16(1)
George Patterson	1928-36	7(1)	18(1)
George Kay	1936-51	1(1)	19(1)
Don Welsh	1951-56	9(1)	11(1)
Phil Taylor	1956-59	3(2)	4(2)
Bill Shankly	1959-74	1(1)	3(2)
Bob Paisley	1974-83	1(1)	5(1)
Joe Fagan	1983-85	1(1)	2(1)
Kenny Dalglish	1985-91	1(1)	2(1)
Graeme Souness	1991-94	6(P)	6(P)
Roy Evans	1994-	4(P)	4(P)

LONGEST LEAGUE RUNS

of undefeated matches:	31 (4.5.1987 - 16.3.1988)	of league matches w/out a win:	14 (5.12.1953 - 3.4.1954)
of undefeated home matches:	63 (25.2.1978 - 31.1.1981)	of undefeated away matches:	16 (2.9.1893-3.9.94, 9.5.87-16.3.88)
without home win:	10 (13.10.1951 - 22.3.1952)	without an away win:	24 (21.2.1953 - 7.4.1954)
of league wins:	12 (21.4.1990 - 6.10.1990)	of home wins:	21 (29.1.1972 - 30.12.1972)
of league defeats:	9 (29.4.1899 - 14.10.1899)	away wins:	6 (24.9.1904-19.11.1904, 31.12.04-11.3.05, 27.2.82-24.4.82)

LIVERPOOL

PLAYERS NAME / Honours	Ht	Wt	Birthdate	Birthplace / Transfers	Contract Date	Clubs	APPEARANCES League	L/Cup	FA Cup	Other	GOALS Lge	L/C	FAC	Oth
GOALKEEPERS														
David B James	6.5	15.0	01.08.70	Welwyn Gard.	01.07.88	Watford (T)	89	6	2	1				
E: u21.10; FAYC'89. LC'95.				£1,000,000	06.07.92	Liverpool	84+1	9	7	1				
Stephen Pears	6.0	12.0	22.01.62	Brandon	25.01.79	Manchester Utd (A)	4	1						
Loan 01.11.83 Middlesbrough 12 Lge, 2 Oth App.				£80,000	09.07.85	Middlesbrough	322	30	23	27				
				Free	08.95	Liverpool								
Michael Stensgaard	6.2	13.04	01.09.74	Denmark	21.05.92	HVI Donvere								
Danish u21.				£400,000	31.05.94	Liverpool								
Anthony R Warner	6.4	13.9	11.05.74		01.01.94	Liverpool								
DEFENDERS														
Philip A Babb	6.0	11.7	30.11.70	Lambeth	25.04.89	Millwall (T)								
Ei: 9; FLC'95. LC'95.				Free	10.08.90	Bradford City	73+7	5+1	3	3+1	14			
				£500,000	21.07.92	Coventry City	70+7	5	2		3	1		
				£3,600,000	01.09.94	Liverpool	33+1	7	6					
Iain R Brunskill	5.10	12.5	05.11.76	Ormskirk	21.05.74	Liverpool (T)								
E: S														
Lee Brydon	6.0	11.4	15.11.74	Stockton	24.06.92	Liverpool (T)								
E: S														
Stig I Bjorneby	5.10	11.9	11.12.69	Rosenborg (Norway)		Rosenborg								
Norweigen Int. LC'95.				£600,000	18.12.92	Liverpool	48+3	7	7+2					
Steven Harkness	5.10	10.11	27.08.71	Carlisle	23.03.89	Carlisle United (T)	12+1							
E: Y13				£75,000	17.07.89	Liverpool	34+6	4+2	2	4+2	2			
				Loan	24.09.93	Huddersfield Town	5		1					
				Loan	03.02.95	Southend United	6							
Andrew D D Harris			26.02.77	Springs	24.03.94	Liverpool (T)								
Robert M Jones	5.11	11.0	05.11.71	Wrexham	20.12.88	Crewe A. (T)	59+16	9	0+3	3	2			
W: S; E: 4, Y2, u21.2; FAC'92. LC'95.				£300,000	04.10.91	Liverpool	127	15+1	20	4				
Dominic Matteo	6.1	11.8	28.04.74	Dumfries	27.05.92	Liverpool (T)	13+5	2	1					
E: Y1, u21.3														
Ashley J Neal	5.11	13.6	16.12.74	Northampton	27.04.93	Liverpool (T)								
Neil Ruddock	6.2	12.0	09.05.68	Wandsworth	03.03.86	Millwall (A)				3+1				1
E: , Y6, u21.4, u19.5. LC'95.				£50,000	14.04.86	Tottenham Hotspur	7+2		1+1				1	
£300k Millwall (29.6.88) + 2Lg1Gl, 1+1Oth				£250,000	13.02.89	Southampton	100+7	14+1	10	6	9	1	3	
				£750,000	29.07.92	Tottenham Hotspur	38	4	5		3			
				£2,500,000	22.07.93	Liverpool	76	13	9		5	1		
John R Scales	6.2	12.7	04.07.66	Harrogate		Leeds United (T)								
E: , B1: FAC'88; FLC'95. LC'95.				Free	11.07.85	Bristol Rovers	68+4	3	6	3+1	2			
				£70,000	16.07.87	Wimbledon	235+5	18+1	20+1	7+1	11			
				£3,500,000	02.09.94	Liverpool	35	7	7		2	2		
Mark Wright	6.3	12.11	01.08.63	Dorchester, Ox.	26.08.80	Oxford United (J)	8+2		1					
E: 43, u21.4; FAC'92; FLgXI.1				£80,000	25.03.82	Southampton	170	25	17	10	7	2	1	1
				£760,000	27.08.87	Derby County	144	15	5	7	10			
				£2,200,000	15.07.91	Liverpool	89+2	8+2	9	8	3	1		
MIDFIELD														
Jamie Cassidy	5.9	10.07	21.11.77	Liverpool	1994-95	Liverpool (T)								
Philip A Charnock	5.10	11.3	14.02.75	Southport	27.05.92	Liverpool (T)		1		0+1				
David L Clegg			23.10.76	Liverpool	1994-95	Liverpool (T)								
Jan Molby	6.1	13.8	04.07.63	Kolding, Jutland		Ajax, Amsterdam								
Den: ; Div1'86'90; FAC'86'92; CS'86				£575,000	24.08.84	Liverpool	195+23	25+3	24+4	16+2	44	9	4	4
Jamie F Redkanpp	5.11	11.8	25.06.73	Barton	27.06.90	Bournemouth (T)	6+7	3	3	2				
E: Y2, u21.16, S. LC'95.				£350,000	15.01.91	Liverpool	97+14	18	11	5+1	10	3	1	
Paul A Stewart	5.11	11.10	07.10.64	Manchester	13.10.81	Blackpool (A)	188+13	11	7	6	56	3	2	1
E: 3, B5, u21.1, Y2; FAC'91; CS'91; Div1'94				£200,000	19.03.87	Manchester City	51	6	4	2	6	2	1	1
				£1,700,000	21.06.88	Tottenham hotspur	126+5	23	9	9	28	7	2	
				£2,300,000	29.07.92	Liverpool	28+4	6	1	3	1			2
Loan 24.01.94 Crystal Palace 18 Lge App. 3gls.				Loan	02.09.94	Wolverhampton W.	5+3			2	2			
Michael L Thomas	5.10	12.4	24.08.67	Lambeth	31.13.84	Arsenal (A)	149+14	21+2	14+3	5+2	24	5	1 1	
E: 2, B5, u21.12, u19.6, Y14, S; LC'87'95				Loan	30.12.86	Portsmouth	3							
Div1'89'91; FAC'92; CT'89; CS'91; FLgXI.1				£1,500,000	16.12.91	Liverpool	39+16	2+2	9+1	2	4		2	
David A Thompson	5.7	10.0	12.09.77	Berkenhead	1994-95	Liverpool (T)								
FORWARDS														
John C B Barnes	5.11	11.10	07.09.63	Jamaica		Sudbury Court								
E: 73, u21.3; FAYC'82; Div1'88'90; CS'88'89'90;				Free	14.07.81	Watford	232+1	21	31	7	65	7	11	
FAC'89; PoY'88; FoY'88; FLgXI.1. LC'95.				£900,000	19.06.87	Liverpool	240+3	20	42	5	77	3	16	2
Nigel H Clough	5.9	11.8	19.03.66	Sunderland		Heanor Town								
E: 14, B3, u21.15; LC'89'90; FMC'89'92; FLgXI.1				Free	15.09.84	Nottingham Forest	307+4	46	28	11+3	101	22	6	1
				£2,275,000	07.06.93	Liverpool	28+9	3	2		7	2		
Stanley V Collymore	6.2	12.2	22.01.71	Stone	13.07.89	Wolverhampton (T)								
E: 1.						Stafford Rangers								
				£100,000		Crystal Palace	4+16	2+3			1	1		
				£100,000	20.11.92	Southend United	30		3		15		3	
				£2,000,000	05.07.93	Nottingham Forest	64+1	9	2	2	41	7	2	
				£8,500,000	08.95	Liverpool								

Player				From / Fee	Date	Club								
Robert B Fowler	5.8	10.3	09.04.75	Liverpool	23.04.92	Liverpool (T)	69+1	8	8		37	10	2	
E: Y7, u21.4; EUFA Yth'93. LC'95.														
Phillip L Jones	5.9	10.5	29.05.73	Wrexham	05.07.91	Wrexham (T)	24+15	2	1+2	4+1	9		1	2
W: u21.8 (6Gls, record scorer for Wales u21)				£300,000	12.03.92	Liverpool	0+1	0+1						
				Loan	03.09.93	Crewe Alexandra	4+4				1			
Mark Kennedy	5.11	11.9	15.05.76	Dublin	06.05.92	Millwall (T)	37+6	6+1	3+1		9	2	1	
Ei: Y5, u21				£1,500,000	21.03.95	Liverpool	4+2							
Steven McManaman	5.11	10.2	11.02.72	Bootle	19.02.90	Liverpool (T)	122+11	19+1	18+1	11	18	7	3	1
E: , Y2, u21.7; FAC'92. LC'95.														
Ian J Rush	6.0	12.6	20.10.61	St. Asaph	25.09.79	Chester City (A)	33+1		5		14		3	
W: 66 (24Gls Record Scorer), u21.2, S:				£300,000	01.05.80	Liverpool	182	38	22	31+1	109	21	20	17
Div1'82'83'84'86'90;LC'81'82'83'84'95;				£3,200,000	01.07.86	Juventus								
FAC'86'89'92; EC'84				Loan	01.07.86	Liverpool	42	9	3	3	30	4		6
				£2,800,000	23.08.88	Liverpool	213+12	29	30+2	14	85	22	18	7
Mark E Walters	5.9	11.5	02.06.64	Birmingham	18.05.82	Aston Villa (A)	168+13	20+1	11+1	7+3	39	6	1	2
E: 1, B1, Y10, u21.9, S; FAYC'80, ESC'82				£500,000	31.12.87	Glasgow Rangers	101+5	13	14	10	32	11	6	2
SPD'89'90'91; SLC'89'91; FAC'92. LC'95.				£1,250,000	13.08.91	Liverpool	58+36	10+2	6+3	8+1	14	4		1
				Loan	24.03.94	Stoke City	9				2			
				Loan	09.09.95	Wolverhampton W.	11				3			

ADDITIONAL CONTRACT PLAYER: Michael S Jensen

TOP GOALSCORER 1994/95
Robbie Fowler

Premiership goals (games)	25 (42)
Coca-Cola Cup Goals	4 (8)
F.A. Cup goals	2 (7)
Total	31 (57)
Total goals for Liverpool since 23.04.92	49 (90+1)
Career total as at June 1st 1995	49 (90+1)

THE MANAGER
ROY EVANS

Date of Birth	5th June 1948.
Place of Birth	Bootle.
Date of Appointment	January 1994.

PREVIOUS CLUBS

As Manager	None.
As Coach	Liverpool.
As a Player	Liverpool.

HONOURS
As a Manager
League Cup 1994/95.

As a Player
England Schools.

ANFIELD
Anfield Road, Liverpool L4 0TH
Tel: 0151 263 9199

Capacity 44,000

First game ....v Rotherham, 1.9.1892.
First floodlit game ....v Everton, 30.10.1957.
Internationals...England v Ireland 1899, 1926. v Wales 1905, 1922, 1931.
.... Wales v Scotland 1977.

ATTENDANCES
Highest ....61,905 v Wolves, FA Cup 4th Round, 2.2.1952.
Lowest ....1,000 v Loughborough, Division 2, 7.12.1895.

OTHER GROUNDS...None.

MATCHDAY TICKET PRICES

Premium £16
Kop Grandstand. £13
Family (1+1) - Andfield Rd Stand £24
Family (1+1) - Kop Grandstand £19.50

Standard. £15
Kop Grandstand. £12
Family (1+1) - Andfield Rd Stand. £22.50
Family (1+1) - Kop Grandstand £18

Ticket Office Telephone no. . . . . 0151 260 8680.

CLUBCALL
0891 12 11 84
Calls cost 39p per minute cheap rate and 49p per
minute at all other times.
Call costings correct at time of going to press.

HOW TO GET TO THE GROUND

From the North
Use motorway (M6) until junction 28, then follow signs to Liverpool on A58 and
forward into Walton Hall Avenue past Stanley Park and turn left into Anfield Road
for Liverpool FC.

From the East and South
Use motorway M6 then M62 until end of motorway, then turn right (A5058 into
Queens Drive. In 3 miles turn left into Utting Avenue. In 1 mile turn right into
Anfield Road for Liverpool FC.

From the West
Use Mersey tunnel into Liverpool City Centre, then follow signs to Preston
(A580) into Walton Hall Avenue, then on nearside of Stanley Park turn right into
Anfield Road for Liverpool FC.

Car Parking
Limited street parking. Mainly privately-owned car park in Priory Road (5 minutes
walk from ground).

Nearest Railway Station
Kirkdale or Lime Street (0151 709 9696)

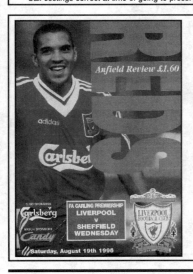

MATCHDAY PROGRAMME

Programme Editor . . . . Vince Wilson.

Number of pages . . . . 40.

Price . . . . £1.50.

Subscriptions. . . . . £44 inc. postage UK/Ireland,
. . . . £50 inc. postage overseas.

Local Newspapers . . . . Liverpool Daily Post, Liverpool Echo.

Local Radio Stations . . . . Radio Merseyside, Radio City.

MANCHESTER CITY
(City or The Blues)
F.A. Carling Premiership
Sponsored by: Brother

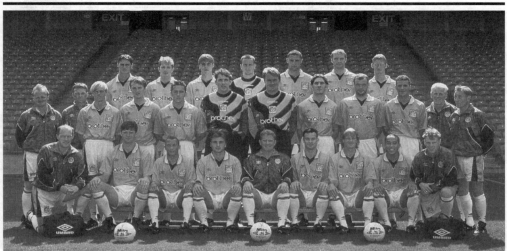

Back Row (L-R): Rae Ingram, Ian Brightwell, Garry Flitcroft, Martyn Margetson, Michael Vonk, Alan Kernaghan, Steve Lomas.
Middle Row: Neil McNab (Yth Coach), Les Chapman (Res. Coach), Scott Thomas, Nick Summerbee, John Foster, Tony Coton, Andy Dibble, Paul Lake, Uwe Rosler, Keith Curle, Tony Book (First Team Coach), Asa Hartford (Asst. Manager). **Front Row:** Roy Bailey (Physio), Niall Quinn, Terry Phelan, Georgiou Kinkladze, Alan Ball (Manager), Peter Beagrie, Paul Walsh, Richard Edghill, Ronnie Evans (Coach).

MANCHESTER CITY
FORMED IN 1887
TURNED PROFESSIONAL IN 1887
LTD COMPANY IN 1894

CHAIRMAN: Francis Lee
VICE-CHAIRMAN: Freddie Pye
DIRECTORS
I L G Niven FNII, A Thomas, G Doyle MBI.I
W A Miles, B Turnbull, J Greibach, D Holt,
J Dunkerley, A Lewis
SECRETARY
Bernard Halford (0161 226 1191/2/3)
COMMERCIAL MANAGER
Geoff Durbin, Mike Summerbee,
Joanne Parker
MANAGER: Alan Ball
ASSISTANT MANAGER: Asa Hartford
FIRST TEAM COACH: Tony Book
RESERVE TEAM MANAGER
Les Chapman
YOUTH COACH
Neil McNab
PHYSIOTHERAPIST
Eamonn Salmon

STATISTICIAN FOR THE DIRECTORY
Dennis Chapman

The beginning of the season, with two emphatic home wins aggregating seven goals to nil, was a tremendous fillip as to what should have been in store for an exciting season. This certainly dispelled the turmoil and unrest that was encountered the previous season with changes in the boardroom and at management level.

The playing staff was strengthened with the signing of Nicky Summerbee, the settling in permanently of Uwe Rosler, and the return of Niall Quinn to full fitness. Other younger players who are now recognised as Premiership material such as Edghill, Flitcroft and Foster have progressed well and in this department the quality of players is sustained for the future; Edghill and Flitcroft have already attended England work outs which is encouraging for themselves and the club.

Other than a hiccup in the Coca-Cola Cup at Barnet and a heavy defeat in November against Manchester United in the league, the season up until mid December was one of the best for many a season establishing sixth in the league; in the quarter-final of the Coca-Cola Cup, and with the FA Cup to come.

Yet for some unaccountable reason it all went down hill during January and February, when City gained only four points in ten league games and were dumped out of the Coca-Cola Cup at Crystal Palace.

In the FA Cup a brief flirtation with success was stopped at Newcastle United in the 5th round.

In the league, concern continued as the next nine matches gathered only a further nine points. It was then realised that the run in to the end of the season was on with only two points above a relegation spot.

An inspired effort over Easter brought City two magnificent wins over Liverpool and Blackburn Rovers. This, coupled with other strugglers dropping points enabled the team to steer clear of relegation, but it was very close.

This being the second season in succession where the club had marginally escaped relegation, feelings and unrest were voiced from within the club and supporters alike. It was expected therefore that sooner than later Brian Horton would leave the club. One must state however that Brian has had a very difficult 21 months, what with guiding the playing side back onto a settled plain after Peter Reid left and the change of Chairman last season. The disruption of good results by exceptionally serious injuries to key players throughout the season just finished genuinely had a bearing as to the inconsistency of results. **Dennis Chapman.**

MANCHESTER CITY

Premier League: 17th   **FA Cup:** 5th Round   **Coca-Cola Cup:** 5th Round

M	DATE	COMP.	VEN	OPPONENTS	RESULT	H/T	LP	GOAL SCORERS/GOAL TIMES	ATT.
1	A 20	PL	A	Arsenal	L 0-3	0-2			(38,368)
2	24	PL	H	West Ham United	W 3-0	2-0	10	Walsh 14, Beagrie 42, Rosler 56	19,150
3	27	PL	H	Everton	W 4-0	0-0	5	Rosler 56,80, Walsh 61,63	19,867
4	31	PL	A	Chelsea	L 0-3	0-1	9		(21,740)
5	S 10	PL	H	Crystal Palace	D 1-1	1-1	9	Walsh 18	19,971
6	17	PL	H	Sheffield Wednesday	D 1-1	1-1	10	Walsh 44	(26,776)
7	20	CC 2/1	A	Barnet	L 0-1	0-1			(3,120)
8	24	PL	H	Norwich City	W 2-0	0-0	7	Quinn 53, Rosler 62	21,,031
9	O 1	PL	A	Leeds United	L 0-2	0-1	11		(30,938)
10	5	CC 2/2	H	Barnet	W 4-1	0-0		Quinn 56, 88, Walsh 67, Summerbee 77	11,545
11	8	PL	H	Nottingham Forrest	D 3-3	1-1	11	Quinn 41, 54, Lomas 70	23,150
12	15	PL	A	Queens Park Rangers	W 2-1	0-0	8	Flitcroft 56, Walsh 58	(13,361)
13	22	PL	H	Tottenham Hotspur	W 5-2	3-1	7	Walsh 15, 44, Quinn 41, Lomas 52, Flitcroft 79	25,473
14	25	CC 3	A	Queens Park Rangers	W 4-3	1-2		Summerbee 37, Curle 47 (pen), Beagrie 54, Lomas 59	(11,701)
15	29	PL	A	Coventry City	L 0-1	0-0	9		(15,804)
16	N 5	PL	H	Southampton	D 3-3	0-1	9	Walsh 50, 61, Beagrie 79	21,589
17	10	PL	A	Manchester United	L 0-5	0-2	9		(43,738)
18	20	PL	A	Leicester City	W 1-0	1-0	8	Quinn 16	(19,006)
19	26	PL	H	Wimbledon	W 2-0	1-0	7	Flitcroft 7, Rosler 88	21,131
20	30	CC 4	H	Newcastle United	D 1-1	0-1		Rosler 69	25,162
21	D 3	PL	A	Ipswich Town	W 2-1	2-0	6	Flitcroft 20, Rosler 42	(13,504)
22	12	PL	H	Arsenal	L 1-2	0-2	6	Simpson 79	20,580
23	17	Pl	A	West Ham United	L 0-3	0-2	8		(17,286)
24	21	CC 4R	A	Newcasltle United	W 2-0	1-0		Rosler 11, Walsh 80	(30,156)
25	26	PL	H	Blackburn Rovers	L 1-3	1-2	10	Quinn 21	23,387
26	28	PL	A	Liverpool	L 0-2	0-0	11		(38,122)
27	31	PL	H	Aston Villa	D 2-2	1-0	11	Rosler 14, 52	22,513
28	J 2	PL	A	Newcastle United	D 0-0	0-0	11		(34,437)
29	8	FAC 3	A	Notts County	D 2-2	1-2		Beagrie 27, Brightwell D 68	(12,376)
30	11	CC 5	A	Crystal Palace	L 0-4	0-0			(16,668)
31	14	PL	H	Coventry City	D 0-0	0-0	11		20,632
32	18	FAC 3R	H	Notts County	W 5-2	3-1		Rosler 7, 37, 57, 81, Gaudino 44	14,261
33	25	PL	H	Leicester City	L 0-1	0-0	14		21,007
34	28	FAC 4	H	Aston Villa	W 1-0	1-0		Walsh 7	21,177
35	F 4	PL	A	Southampton	D 2-2	1-1	13	Kernaghan 30, Flitcroft 88	(14,902)
36	11	PL	H	Manchester United	L 0-3	0-0	14		26,368
37	19	FAC 5	A	Newcastle United	L 1-3	1-2		Rosler 29	(33,219)
38	22	PL	H	Ipswich Town	W 2-0	0-0	14	Quinn 68, Rosler 71	21,430
39	25	PL	H	Leeds United	D 0-0	0-0	15		22,892
40	M 4	PL	A	Norwich City	D 1-1	0-0	15	Simpson 86	(16,266)
41	8	PL	H	Chelsea	L 1-3	1-1	16	Gaudino 4	21,880
42	15	PL	A	Everton	D 1-1	1-0	16	Gaudino 26	(28,485)
43	18	PL	H	Sheffield Wednesday	W 3-2	1-2	12	Rosler 37, 83 Walsh 52	23,355
44	21	PL	H	Wimbledon	I 0-2	0-0	13		(5,2690)
45	A 1	PL	A	Crystal Palace	L 1-2	0-1	16	Rosler 57,	(13,312)
46	11	PL	A	Tottenham Hotspur	L 1-2	0-0	16	Rosler 49	(27,410)
47	14	PL	H	Liverpool	W 2-1	1-1	12	Summerbee 18, Gaudino 73	27,055
48	17	PL	A	Blackbutrn Rovers	W 3-2	1-2	12	Curle 32 (pen), Rosler 57, Walsh 71	(27,857)
49	29	PL	H	Newcaslte United	D 0-0	0-0	13		27,389
50	M 3	PL	A	Aston Villa	D 1-1	0-1	13	Rosler 63	(30,133)
51	6	PL	A	Nottingham Forrest	L 0-1	0-1	13		(28,882)
52	14	PL	H	Queens Park Rangers	L 2-3	1-1	17	Quinn 26, Curle 80 (pen)	27,850
53									
54									
55									
56									
57									
58									
59									
60									

Best Home League Attendance: 27,850 v Queens Park Rangers   **Smallest:** 19,150 v West Ham United   **Av Home Att:** 22,748

Goal Scorers: Compared with 1993-94: -3,961

League (53): Rosler 15, Walsh 12, Quinn 8, Flitcroft 5, Gaudino 3, Beagrie 2, Curle 2, Lomas 2, Simpson 2, Kernaghan, Summerbee

C/Cola Cup (11): Quinn 2, Rosler 2, Summerbee 2, Walsh 2, Beagrie, Curle, Lomas

FA Cup (9): Rosler 5, Beagrie, Brightwell D, Gaudino , Walsh

1994-95

Coton T.	Hill A.	Phelan T.	McMahon S.	Curle K.	Vonk M.	Summerbee N.	Walsh P.	Rosler U.	Flitcroft G.	Beagrie P.	Brightwell I.	Quinn N.	Dibble A.	Lomas S.	Brightwell D.	Mike A.	Edghill R.	Foster J.	Griffiths C.	Margetson M.	Tracey S.	Burridge J.	Kernaghan A.	Simpson F.	Kerr D.	Referee	
X	X	X	X	X	X	X	X2	X†	X	S1	S2	S														Durkin P.	1
X		X1	X	X	X	X	X2	X	X	S2	S	S1														Hart R.	2
X		X		X	X	X	X	X	X1	X	S1	S	S	X	S											Don P.	3
X		X1	X	X	X	X	X	X	X	S1	S	S	X	S												Reed M.	4.
X		X	X	X	X	X		X	X	X	S	S	S		S											Burge K.	5
X	X		X		X	X	X	X1		X	X	S1	S	X			X	S								Gallagher D.	6
X	X		X		X2	X	X	X1		X	X	S1	S	X			X	S2								Dunn S.	7
X	S2	X		X2	X	X	X1		X	X	X	S1		X			X									Poll G.	8
X	X1	X	S1		X	X		X	X	X	X	S	X	X2				S1								Holbrook T.	9
S	X	X		S	X	X1		X	X	X	X	X	X				X	S2								Lodge S.	10
S	X	X	S		X	X		X	X	X	X	X	X			S	X									Durkin P.	11
S3	S1	X		X		X3	X1		X	X	X	X	X†	X			S	X†								Willard G.	12
	S	X	X	X		X	X	X	X	X	X	X	S	X			S	X			S					Elleray D.	13
	S	X	X		X	X	X	X	X	X	X	X	S	X			S	X			S					Danson P.	14
	X	X		X	X	X	X	X	X	X	X	S	S			X					S					Bodenham M.	15
	X1	X		X	X	X	X	X	X	X		X	S1	S			X	S								Reed M.	16
	X		X	X	X	X	X	X	X	X	S	S			X	S										Cooper K.	17
X		X		X	S1	X	X	X	X1	X	X	X					S	S								Morton K.	18
X2		X		X	S1	X	X	X1	X	X	X	X					S	S2								Wilkie A.	19
X1		X		X	S1	X	X	X	X	X	X	S			X			S								Worrall J.	20
	X		X	X2	X	X	X1	X	X	X	X		X		X		S					S1	S2			Lodge S.	21
	X		X	X	X2	X	X	X	X		S		S	S1	S2			X	X1							Ashby G.	22
		S1	X	X	X	X		X	X	X2		S2	S		X			X1	Holbrook T.	23
		S2	X	X	X	X		S1	X	X		X	S		X2											Reed M.	24
	S1		S	X	X	X	X	X	X	X		X1	S		X			S								Danson P.	25
		X		S	X	X	X	X	X	X		X			X			S	X	S						Hart R.	26
		X		X	X	X	X	X	X	X		X			X			S	S	X						Worrall J.	27
		X	X1	X	X	X	X	X	X			X			X			S	S	X	S1					Wilkie A.	28
		X		X	X	X	X	X	X1	S2	X	X	S1		X2	S				S	X					Reed M.	29
		X	X	X	X	X	X	X	X	X1	X	X2	S2							S	X					Bodenham M.	30
		X	X	X	X	X	X	X	X		X1	S						S	S	X	S1					Gallagher D.	31
		X	X	X	X	X2	X1	X	X	S2	X	X			S			S1	S	S						Reed M.	32
		X	X	X	X	X1	S1	X	X	X1	S1	X		X				S	S							Lodge S.	33
X		X	X	X	X1	X	X	X	X	S1	X		X			S										Worrall J.	34
X1		X	X2	X	X	X	X	X	X	S1		X								X						Durkin P.	35
	S	X		X	X	X	X	X1	X	S1	X		X						S	X						Don P.	36
		X		X	X	X	X	X2	X		X1	S2	S1					S	X							Ashby G.	37
X	X2	X		X	X	X	X1	X	X	S1	S								X	S2						Cooper K.	38
X	X	X		X	X	X		X	X	S	S	X				S					X	X				Holbrook T.	39
X	S1	X		X	X2	X		X	X	S			S2								X	X				Gallagher D.	40
X		X		X1	X	X		X	X	S1	S				S						X					Elleray D.	41
X	X†	X	X	X	S	X	X1	X	X	X	S			S1							X					Willard G.	42
X		X	X	X	X	X	X	X		S	S			S							X					Burge K.	43
X		X	X	X	X	S1	X	X	X	S2	S			X							X	X1				Gifford R.	44
X	S		X	X1	S1	X	X	X	X		X			X							S	X				Holbrook T.	45
X	X	X		X	X	X	X	S1	X		X			X	X						S	S				Wilkie A.	46
X		X1	X		X2	X	X	S2	X			X		X	X						S	S1				Worrall J.	47
X		X		X	X1	X	X	S1	X		S			X	X						S	X	X			Cooper K.	48
X3		X		X	X2	X	X	S2	X		X							53	X	X1						Poll G.	49
	X1	X		X	X	X2	X	S1	X		X				X			S	X	X						Lodge S.	50
	S	X	X	X	X	X	X	X		S				X			S	X	X	X						Jones P.	51
		X	X2	X	X	X	X	X		X				X	X		S	X	X	S1						Reed M.	52
21	10	26	6	31	19	39	39	29	37	33	29	24	15	18	9	1	14	9			3	3	18	10	2	League Appearances	
1	3	1	1		2	2		4		11	1	2		1	2							1	4	5		League Sub Appearances	
1	3	3	1	3	1+1	6	6	3+1	5	6	5	4+2	5	6	1+1		3	1+1	0+1				3			League Cup Appearances	
1		1		3	1	4	3	4	4	4	4	1+3	3	1	3+1	0+1		1+1					3	0+1		FA Cup Appearances	

Also Played: Gaudino X1(24,26,40,46,51,52),X(25,31,32,33,34,36,37,38,39,41,42,4345,47),S(27),S1(30,49),S2(35,50), Thomas S1(51),S2(52)

Players on Loan: Tracey (Sheffield United), Gaudino (Eintracht Frankfurt), Burridge

† = Sent Off

MANCHESTER CITY

CLUB RECORDS

BIGGEST VICTORIES
League: 10-0 v Darwen, Division 2, 18.2.1899.
F.A. Cup: 10-1 v Swindon Town, 4th Round (Replay), 29.1.1930.
9-0 v Gateshead, 3rd Round (Replay), 18.1.1933.
League Cup: 6-0 v Scunthorpe United, 2nd Round, 10.9.1974.
6-0 v Torquay United, 2nd Round, 25.10.1983.
Europe: 5-0 v S K Lierse, 2nd Round, 26.11.1969.

BIGGEST DEFEATS
League: 0-8 v Burton Wanderers, Division 2, 26.12.1894.
1-9 v Everton, Division 1, 3.9.1906.
0-8 v Wolverhampton Wndrs, Division 1, 23.12.1933.
F.A. Cup: 0-6 v Preston North End, 30.1.1897.
2-8 v Bradford Park Avenue (h), 4th Round, 30.1.1946.
League Cup: 0-6 v Birmingham City, 5th Round, 11.12.1962.
Europe: No more than two goals. (4 games)

MOST POINTS
3 points a win: 82, Division 2, 1988-89.
2 points a win: 62, Division 2, 1946-47.

MOST GOALS SCORED
108, Division 2, 1926-27.
Johnson 25, Hicks 21, Roberts 14, W Cowan 11, Austin 10, Barrass 7, Broadhurst 7, Bell 4, McMullan 3, S Cowan 2, Gibson 2, Pringle 1, Opponents 1.

MOST GOALS CONCEDED
102, Division 1, 1962-63.

MOST FIRST CLASS MATCHES IN A SEASON
62 - 1969-70 (League 42, FA Cup 2, League Cup 7, Charity Shield 1, ECWC 10).

MOST LEAGUE WINS
26, Division 2, 1946-47, Division 1, 1967-68.

MOST LEAGUE DRAWS
18, Premiership, 1993-94.

MOST LEAGUE DEFEATS
22, Division 1, 1958-59, Division 1, 1959-60.

INDIVIDUAL CLUB RECORDS

MOST GOALS IN A SEASON
Tom Johnson: 38 goals in 1928-29 (Division 1).
Previous holder: F Roberts 31.

MOST GOALS IN A MATCH
5. Tom Johnson v Everton (a), 6-2, Division 1, 15.9.1928.
5. R.S. Marshall v Swindon Town, 10-1, FA Cup 4th Rnd (replay), 29.1.1930.
5. George Smith v Newport, 5-1, Division 2, 14.6.1947.

OLDEST PLAYER
Billy Meredith, 49 years 245 days v Newcastle United, FA Cup semi-final, 29.3.1924.

YOUNGEST PLAYER
Glyn Pardoe, 15 years 314 days v Birmingham City, Division 1, 11.4.1961.

MOST CAPPED PLAYER
Colin Bell (England) 48.

BEST PERFORMANCES

League: 1902-03: Matches played 34, Won 25, Drawn 4, Lost 5, Goals for 95, Goals against 29, Points 54. First in Division 2.
Highest Position: Champions of Division 1, 1936-37, 1967-68.
F.A. Cup: 1968-69: 3rd Round Luton Town 1-0; 4th Round Newcastle United 0-0,2-0; 5th Round Blackburn Rovers 4-1; 6th Round Tottenham Hotspur 1-0; Semi-final Everton 1-0; Final Leicester City 1-0.
League Cup: Winners in 1969-70.
Most recent success: 1975-76: 2nd Round Norwich City 1-1,2-2,6-1; 3rd Round Nottingham Forest 2-1; 4th Round Manchester United 4-0; 5th Round Mansfield Town 4-2; Semi-final Middlesbrough 0-1,4-0; Final Newcastle United 2-1.
Europe: ECWC 1969-70: 1st Round Athletico Bilbao 3-3,3-0; 2nd Round Lierse 3-0,5-0; 3rd Round Academica Colmbra 0-0,1-0; Semi-final Schalke 04 0-1,5-1; Final Gornick Zagrze 2-1.

DIVISIONAL RECORD

	Played	Won	Drawn	Lost	For	Against	Points
Division 1/P	2,898	1,097	720	1,081	4,424	4,406	3,046
Division 2	786	402	173	211	1,652	1,072	1,060
Total	**3,684**	**1,499**	**893**	**1,292**	**6,076**	**5,478**	**4,106**

ADDITIONAL INFORMATION
PREVIOUS NAMES
Ardwock F.C. 1887-95 (an amalgamation of West Gorton and Gorton Athletic).

PREVIOUS LEAGUES
Football Alliance.

Club colours: Sky blue shirts, white shorts, sky blue socks.
Change colours: Red/black small squared shirts, black/red trim shorts, black socks.

Reserves League: Pontins Central League Division 2.

RECORDS AND STATISTICS

COMPETITIONS

Div 1/P	Div.2	Euro C	ECWC	UEFA	Texaco
1899-02	1892-99	1968-69	1969-70	1972-73	1971-72
1903-09	1902-03		1970-71	1976-77	1974-75
1910-26	1909-10	**FMC**		1977-78	
1928-38	1926-28	1985-86		1978-79	A/Ital
1947-50	1938-47	1986-87			1970-71
1951-63	1950-51	1987-88			
1966-83	1963-66	1988-89			A/Scot
1985-87	1983-85	1989-90			1975-76
1989-	1987-89	1990-91			
		1991-93			

HONOURS

Div.1	Div.2	FA Cup	Lge Cup	ECWC
1936-37	1898-99	1903-04	1969-70	1969-70
1967-68	1902-03	1933-34	1975-76	
	1909-10	1955-56		**C/Sh'd**
	1927-28	1968-69		1937
	1946-47			1968
	1965-66			1972

MOST APPEARANCES

Alan Oakes 672+4 (1959-76)

Year	League	FA Cup	Lge Cup	Europe
1959-60	18	1		
1960-61	22			
1961-62	25			
1962-63	34	2	4	
1963-64	41	1	6	
1964-65	41	2	1	
1965-66	41	8	2	
1966-67	39	6	2	
1967-68	41	4	4	
1968-69	39	7	3	2
1969-70	40	2	7	9
1970-71	30	3	1	4
1971-72	31+1	2		
1972-73	13+1		0+1	2
1973-74	28		5	
1974-75	40	1	2	
1975-76	38+1	2	9	
	561+3	**41**	**46+1**	**17**

Also: 2 A/Ital Cup 70-71; 3 Texaco 74-75; 3 A/Scot 75-76.

MOST GOALS IN A CAREER

Eric Brook - 177 (1927-39)

Year	League	FA Cup
1927-28	2	
1928-29	14	
1929-30	16	1
1930-31	16	
1931-32	10	3
1932-33	15	6
1933-34	8	3
1934-35	17	
1935-36	13	3
1936-37	20	2
1937-38	16	1
1938-39	11	
Total	**158**	**19**

Current leading goalscorer: Niall Quinn - 67 (1990-95)

MANAGERS

Name	Seasons	Best	Worst
L Furniss	1892-93	5(2)	5(2)
J Parlby	1893-95	9(2)	13(2)
S Ormrod	1895-02	7(1)	6(2)
T Maley	1902-06	2(1)	1(2)
H W Newbould	1906-12	3(1)	1(2)
E Magnell	1912-24	2(1)	13(1)
D Ashworth	1924-25	10(1)	21(1)
P Hodge	1926-32	3(1)	3(2)
W Wild	1932-46	1(1)	5(2)
S Cowan	1946-47	1(2)	1(2)
J Thompson	1947-50	7(1)	21(1)
L McDowell	1950-63	4(1)	2(2)
G Poyser	1963-65	6(2)	11(2)
J Mercer OBE	1965-71	1(1)	1(2)
M Allison	1971-73	4(1)	11(1)
J Hart	1973		
R Saunders	1973-74	14(1)	14(1)
T Book	1974-79	2(1)	15(1)
M Allison	1979-80	17(1)	17(1)
J Bond	1980-83	10(1)	20(1)
J Benson	1983		
W McNeill MBE	1983-86	15(1)	4(2)
J Frizzell	1986-87	21(1)	21(1)
M Machin	1987-89	2(2)	9(2)
H Kendall	1989-90	14(1)	14(1)
P Reid	1990-93	5(1)	9(1/P)
B Horton	1993-95	16(P)	17(P)
A Ball	1995		

RECORD TRANSFER FEE RECEIVED

Amount	Club	Player	Date
£2,000,000	Leeds United	David White*	01/94
£1,700,000	Tottenham	Paul Stewart	6/88
£900,000	Everton	Mark Ward	6/91
£800,000	Sampdoria	Trevor Francis	7/82

*- Deal included David Rocastle joining Manchester City.

RECORD TRANSFER FEE PAID

Amount	Club	Player	Date
£2,500,000	Wimbledon	Keith Curle	8/91
£1,150,000	Wolves	Steve Daley	9/79
£350,000	Luton Town	Paul Futcher	6/78
£275,000	Sunderland	Denis Tueart	3/74

LONGEST LEAGUE RUNS

of undefeated matches:	22 (16.11.46-9.4.47, 26.12.36-1.5.37)	of league matches w/out a win:	17 (26.12.1979 - 7.4.1980)
of undefeated home matches:	41 (25.12.1919 - 19.11.1921)	of undefeated away matches:	12 (23.11.1946 - 14.5.1947)
without home win:	9 (26.12.1979 - 7.4.1980)	without an away win:	34 (11.2.1986 - 17.10.1987)
of league wins:	9 (8.4.1912 - 28.9.1912)	of home wins:	16 (13.11.1920 - 27.8.1921)
of league defeats:	6 (10.9.1910 - 8.10.1910)	of away wins:	6 (7.3.1903 - 26.9.1903)

PLAYERS NAME / Honours	Ht	Wt	Birthdate	Birthplace / Transfers	Contract Date	Clubs	League	L/Cup	FA Cup	Other	Lge	L/C	FAC	Oth
G O A L K E E P E R S														
Tony Coton	6.2	13.7	19.05.81	Tamworth		Mile Oak Rovers								
E: B.1.				Free	13.10.78	Birmingham City	94	10	10					
				£300,000	27.09.84	Watford	233	18	32	8				
				£1,000,000	20.07.90	Manchester City	162+1	16	12	3				
Andy Dibble	6.2	13.7	08.05.65	Cwmbran	27.08.82	Cardiff City (A)	62	4	4					
W: 3, u21.3, Y, S. LC'88.				£125,000	16.07.84	Luton Town	30	4	1	1				
				Loan	21.02.86	Sunderland	12							
Loan Huddersfield T., 26.03.87, 5 Lge App.				£240,000	01.07.88	Manchester City	101+2	12	8+1	2				
Loan Aberdeen, 12.10.90, 5 Lge App.				Loan	20.02.91	Middlesbrough	19		2					
Loan Bolton W., 06.09.91, 13 Lge, 1 Oth. App.				Loan	27.02.92	West Bromwich A.	9							
Eike Immel						VfB Stuttgart								
				£400,000	08.95	Manchester City								
Martyn Margetson	6.0	13.10	08.09.71	Neath	05.07.90	Manchester City (T)	6	0+1		1				
W: B.2, u21.7, Y, S.				Loan	08.12.93	Bristol Rovers	2+1							
				Loan	23.03.95	Luton Town								
D E F E N D E R S														
David Brightwell	6.2	12.7	07.01.71	Lutterworth	11.04.88	Manchester City (J)	35+8	2+1	5+2		1		1	
				Loan	22.03.91	Chester City	6							
Keith Curle	6.0	12.0	14.11.63	Bristol	20.11.81	Bristol Rovers (A)	21+11	3	1		4			
E: 3, B.4. FRT'86. SC'88. FLgXl.1				£5,000	04.11.83	Torquay United	16		1	1	5		1	
				£10,000	03.03.84	Bristol City	113+8	7+1	5	14+1	1			
				£150,000	23.10.87	Reading	40	8		5				
				£500,000	21.10.88	Wimbledon	91+2	7	5	6	3			1
				£2,500,000	14.08.91	Manchester City	139	15	9	1	11	1		
Richard Edghill	5.8	10.6	23.09.74	Oldham	15.07.92	Manchester City (T)	36	7	1					
E: B.1, u21.2.														
John Foster	5.11	11.2	19.09.73	Manchester	15.07.92	Manchester City (T)	1		1					
Andy Hill	5.11	12.0	20.01.65	Maltby	26.01.83	Manchester Utd (A)								
E: Y.2.				Free	04.07.84	Bury	264	22	212	19	10	1		1
				£200,000	21.12.90	Manchester City	91+7	11	2+1	1	6			
Rae Ingram	5.11	11.7	06.12.74	Manchester	09.07.93	Manchester City (T)								
Alan Kernaghan	6.1	12.13	25.04.67	Otley	08.03.85	Middlesbrough (A)	172+40	22+7	7+4	14+2	16	1	3 2	
Ei: 11				Loan	17.01.91	Charlton Athletic	13							
				£1,600,000	20.09.93	Manchester City	41+5	7	5		1		1	
				Loan	18.09.94	Bolton Wanderers	9+2							
Terry Phelan	5.8	10.0	16.03.67	Manchester	03.08.84	Leeds United (T)	12+2	3		2				
Ei: 25, B.1, u23.1, u21.1, Y. FAC'88.				Free	30.07.86	Swansea City	45	4	5	3				
				£100,000	29.07.87	Wimbledon	155+4	13+2	16	8	1		2	
				£2,500,000	25.08.92	Manchester City	93+1	10	8	1			1	
Nicholas Summerbee	5.8	11.8	26.08.71	Altrincham	20.07.89	Swindon Town (A)	89+23	9+1	2+4	7	6	3		1
E: B.1, u21.3.				£1,500,000	24.06.94	Manchester City	39+2	6	4		1	2		
Kit Symons	6.1	10.10	08.03.71	Basingstoke	30.12.88	Portsmouth (T)	160	19	10	13+1	10			1
W: 13, u21.2, Y.				£1,600,000	08.95	Manchester City								
Michael Vonk	6.2	12.2	28.10.68	Holland		SW Dordrecht								
				£500,000	11.03.92	Manchester City	87+4	3+2	6+1		4	1	1	
M I D F I E L D														
Ian Brightwell	5.10	11.7	09.04.68	Lutterworth	07.05.86	Manchester City (J)	204+30	24+2	13+4	4+3	16		1	
E: u21.4, S, Y.3.														
Michael Brown	5.7	10.06	25.01.77	Hartlepool	1994-95	Manchester City (T)								
Gary Flitcroft	5.10	11.0	06.11.72	Bolton	02.07.91	Manchester City (T)	84+6	10+1	10		13		1	
E: u21.10, Y.1, S.				Loan	05.03.92	Bury	12							
Kaare Inbrigsten	5.9	11.0	11.11.65	Trondheim		Rosenberg Trondheim								
Norweigen International				£600,000	25.01.93	Manchester City	4+11		2				3	
David W Kerr	5.11	11.2	06.09.74	Dumfries	10.09.91	Manchester City (T)	2+1							
Paul Lake	6.0	12.2	28.10.68	Penton	02.06.87	Manchester City (T)	106+4	10	9	5	7	1	2	1
E: B.1, u21.5														
Stephen Lomas	6.0	11.10	18.01.74	Hanover (Ger)	22.01.91	Manchester City (T)	35+8	11	2+1		2	1		
NI: 4, B.1, Y.														
F O R W A R D S														
Peter Beagrie	5.8	9.10	28.11.65	Middlesbrough	10.09.83	Middlesbrough (J)	24+8	1		1+1	2			
E: B.2, u21.2.				£35,000	16.08.86	Sheffield United	81+3	5	5	4	11			
				£210,000	29.06.88	Stoke City	54	4	3		7		1	
				£750,000	02.11.89	Everton	88+26	7+2	7+2	5+1	12	3		1
Loan Sunderland, 26.09.91, 5 Lge App, 1 gl.				£1,000,000	24.03.94	Manchester City	42+4	6	4		3	1	1	

Name	Ht	Wt	DOB	Birthplace	Date	Club								
Carl Griffiths	5.9	10.6	16.07.71	Welshpool	26.09.88	Shrewsbury T (T)	110+33	7+4	6	7+3	54	3	2 3	
W: B.1, u21.2, Y. FLge u18.1.					£500,000	29.10.93	Manchester City	11+7	0+1	2		4		
Georgiou Kinkladze							Dinamo Tbilisi							
					£2,000,000	08.95	Manchester City							
Niall Quinn	6.4	12.4	06.10.66	Dublin	30.11.83	Arsenal (J)	59+8	14+2	8+2	0+1	14	4	2	
Ei: 42, B.1, u23.1, u21.5, Y. LC'87.					£800,000	21.03.90	Manchester City	159+12	17+2	9+3	3	57	5	2	1
Ulve Rossler	6.0	12.4	15.11.68	Attenburg			D . Dresden							
E.Germany: 5. Germany: B.1.					£750,000	02.03.94	Manchester City	41+2	3+1	4		20	2	5	
E.Ger. Div.1. FAC'90														
Fitzroy Simpson	5.6	10.4	26.02.70	B'ford-on-Avon	06.07.88	Swindon Town (T)	78+27	15+2	2+1	3+2	9	1		
					£500,000	06.03.92	Manchester City	58+13	5+1	4+1		5			
Scott L Thomas	5.11	11.4	30.10.74	Bury	26.03.92	Manchester City (T)								
Paul Walsh	5.8	10.4	01.10.62	Plumstead	02.10.79	Charlton Athletic (A)	85+2	9	4		24	6	1	
E: 5, u21.7, Y.10. Div.1'86. SC'86.					£400,000	26.07.82	Luton Town	80	5	4		24	1	3	
FAC'91. CS'91.					£700,000	21.05.84	Liverpool	63+14	10+2	6+2	13+2	25	4	3	5
					£500,000	16.02.88	Tottenham Hotspur	84+44	9+6	4+4	1+3	19	2		
Loan Q.P.R, 16.09.91, 2 Lge App.					£400,000	03.06.92	Portsmouth	67+6	7+1	3	6+1	13	4		3
					£750,000	10.03.94	Manchester City	50	6	3		16	2	1	

TOP GOALSCORER 1994/95
Ulve Rossler

Premiership goals (games)	15 (29+2)
Coca-Cola Cup Goals.	2 (3+1)
F.A. Cup goals	5 (4)
Total	**22 (36+3)**
Total goals for Manchester City since 02.03.94	27 (48+3)

THE MANAGER
ALAN BALL

Date of Birth	12th May 1945.
Place of Birth	Farnworth.
Date of Appointment	14th July 1995.

PREVIOUS CLUBS
As Manager . . . . Blackpool, Vancouvr Whitecaps (as player/manager),
. . . . Portsmouth, Stoke City, Exeter City, Southampton.
As Coach . . . . Bristol Rovers, Portsmouth.
As a Player . . . . Blackpool, Everton, Arsenal, Southampton (twice),
. . . . Bristol Rovers.

HONOURS
As a Manager
Portsmouth: Promotion to Division 1, 1987.

As a Player
Everton: Division 1 Championship 1970.
International: 72 full caps and 8 u23. World Cup Winner 1966.

MAINE ROAD

Moss Side, Manchester M14 7WN
Tel: 0161 226 1191

Capacity ....31,000.

First game ....v Sheffield Utd, 2-1, 25.8.1923.
First floodlit game ....v Hearts, 14.10.1953.

ATTENDANCES
Highest ....84,569 v Stoke City, FA Cup 6th Round, 3.3.1934 (record outside London).
Lowest ....4,029 v Leeds United, FMC, 14.10.1985.

OTHER GROUNDS ....Clowes Street 1880-81; Kirkmanshulme C.C. 1881-82; Queens Road 1882-84;
..............................Pink Bank Lane 1884-85; Bulls Head Ground, Reddish Lane 1885-87; Hyde Road 1887-1923;
.... Maine Road 1923-

MATCHDAY TICKET PRICES

Main Stand
Blocks B, C £16
Other Blocks £15
Block G (OAP only) £5
North Stand £10
Juv/OAP £7
Blocks K,L (Juv/OAP). £5
Umbro Stand
Main Section £11
JD Sports Family Enclosure £8
Juv/OAP £5
Kippax Stand
Upper Tier £14
Lower Tier £11

Ticket Office telephone no. 0161 226 2224

CLUBCALL 0898 12 11 91

Calls cost 39p per minute cheap rate and 49p per
minute at all other times.
Call costings correct at time of going to press.

HOW TO GET TO THE GROUND

From the North
Use motorway M61 then M63 until junction 9. Leave motorway and follow signs
Manchester A5103. In 2.8 miles at crossroads turn right in Claremont Road. In
0.4 miles turn right into Maine Road for Manchester City FC.

From the East
Use motorway M61 until junction 17 then A56 into Manchester. Follow signs to
Manchester Airport then turn left to join motorway A57(M). Follow signs to
Birmingham to join A5103. Then in 1.3 miles turn left into Claremont Road. In
0.4 miles turn right into Maine Road for Manchester City.

From the South
Use motorway M6 until junction 19 then A556 and M56 until junction 3. Keep for-
ward A5103 sign posted Manchester. In 2.8 miles at crossroads turn right into
Claremont Road. In 0.4 miles turn right into Maine Road for Manchester City FC.

From the West
Use motorway M62 then M63 and route as from north. Or use M56 route as
from south.

Car Parking: Kippax Street car park holds 400 vehicles (approx). Some street
parking is permitted, parking at local schools.
Nearest Railway Station: Manchester Piccadilly (0161 832 8353).

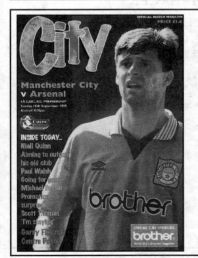

MATCHDAY PROGRAMME

Programme Editor . . . . Mike Beddow.

Number of pages . . . . 32.

Price . . . . £1.50.

Subscriptions . . . . £40 (£6 extra abroad and Eire).

Local Newspapers. . . . . Manchester Evening News, Football Pink.

Local Radio Stations . . . . . . BBC Radio Manchester, Piccadilly Radio.

MANCHESTER UNITED
(The Red Devils)
F.A. CARLING PREMIERSHIP
SPONSORED BY: SHARP

Back Row (L-R): Norman Davies (Kit Manager), Ryan Giggs, Roy Keane, Nicky Butt, David May, John O'Kane, Phil Neville, Gary Neville, Andy Cole, David Fevre (Physio). **Middle Row:** David Beckham, Patrick McGibbon, Eric Cantona, Gary Walsh, Peter Schmeichel, Kevin Pilkington, Gary Pallister, Lee Sharpe, Chris Casper. **Front Row:** Paul Parker, Brian McClair, Steve Bruce, Alex Ferguson (Manager), Brian Kidd (Asst. Manager), Denis Irwin, Ben Thornley, Paul Scholes.

MANCHESTER UNITED
FORMED IN 1878
TURNED PROFESSIONAL IN 1885
LTD COMPANY IN 1907

CHAIRMAN: C M Edwards

DIRECTORS
J M Edelson, Sir Bobby Charlton CBE,
E M Watkins, A M Midani, R L Olive,
R P Launders
SECRETARY
Kenneth R Merrett (0161 872 1661/2)
COMMERCIAL MANAGER
D A McGregor (0161 872 3488)

MANAGER: Alex Furguson
ASSISTANT MANAGER: Brian Kidd

RESERVE TEAM MANAGER
Jimmy Ryan
YOUTH TEAM MANAGER
E Harrison
PHYSIOTHERAPIST
David Fevre

STATISTICIAN FOR THE DIRECTORY
Richard Facer

So close and yet so far ! United were only two games away from completing the double - however a draw at West Ham handed Blackburn the title, and Everton were the victors in the FA Cup Final which was enough to prevent United winning any major silverware in the season.

The season began with United retaining the Charity Shield, beating Blackburn 2-0. However, league form was slightly indifferent. An impeccable 100% home record was kept up until December when Notts Forest defeated United (2-1). Notable results from this impressive run included the 5-0 mauling of nearest rivals Man City and victories over both Newcastle and Liverpool.

Away form though was United's main problem, and the reason why at the end of October they were only 4th in the league. A 4-2 victory at Blackburn was overshadowed by defeats at Ipswich (3-2), Sheffield Wednesday (1-0) and Leeds (2-1). By Christmas, United now 2nd in the league, had exited from two cup competitions - United youngsters were beaten by an experienced Newcastle side to end Alex Ferguson's interest in the Coca-cola Cup. A far more disappointing blow was United's failure to progress through the league stage of the European Cup with defeats away to both Gothenburg and Barcelona.

January saw the unexpected signing of £7 million goal king Andy Cole from arch rivals Newcastle. Cole's debut saw United reduce the gap at the top of the table, beating Blackburn 1-0 - courtesy of a brilliant Eric Cantona header. However, 3 days later, the football world saw the other side of the temperamental frenchman. Following a sending off at Crystal Palace, Cantona leapt at an abusive member of the crowd with a kung-fu style kick that earnt him an 8 months suspension.

Meanwhile, United safely progressed to the Fifth Round of the FA Cup with victories over Sheffield Utd (2-0) and Wrexham (5-2). Back in the league, United, without Cantona, gained 12 points from a possible 15 with results including the brilliant display that crushed Ipswich by a record 9-0 margin.

However, United then faltered losing to Liverpool and drawing against Leeds and Chelsea to leave Blackburn clear favourites for the title. But it was now Blackburn's turn to stumble and United won their next 3 games to leave the title on a knife edge for the final game of the season - Blackburn needed to draw or lose and United needed to win at West Ham for the title to be retained in Manchester.

Blackburn duly lost, but United, despite a plethora of late chances could only draw 1-1 and the title was Blackburn's.

United also reached the Cup Final - beating Leeds (3-1), QPR (2-0) and Crystal Palace (2-2, 2-0). However, the final against Everton saw a repeat of the league score at Goodison Park and the Merseysiders ran out 1-0 victors. The close season has, as well, bought disappointment for the fans with the sale of favourites Paul Ince, Mark Hughes and Andrei Kanchelskis - but it would still take a foolish man to bet against United bringing the league trophy back to Manchester in 1996.

RICHARD FACER.

MANCHESTER UNITED

Premier League: 2nd   **FA Cup:** Runners-Up   **Coca-Cola Cup:** 3rd Round

M	DATE	COMP.	VEN	OPPONENTS	RESULT	H/T	LP	GOAL SCORERS/GOAL TIMES	ATT.
1	A 14	C/S	N	Blackburn Rovers	W 2-0	1-0		Cantona 22, Ince 81	(60,402)
2	20	PL	H	Queens Park Rangers	W 2-0	0-0	4	Hughes 47, McClair 68	43,214
3	22	PL	A	Nottingham Forest	D 1-1	1-1		Kanchelskis 22	(22,072)
4	27	PL	A	Tottenham Hotspur	W 1-0	0-0	3	Bruce 48	(24,502)
5	31	PL	H	Wimbledon	W 3-0	1-0	2	Cantona 40, McClair 81, Giggs 85	43,440
6	S 11	PL	A	Leeds United	L 1-2	0-1		Cantona 73 (pen)	(39,396)
7	14	EC	H	Gothenburg	W 4-2	1-1		Giggs 34, 66, Kanchelskis 47, Sharpe 71	33,625
8	17	PL	H	Liverpool	W 2-0	0-0	3	Kanchelskis 72, McClair 73	43,740
9	21	CC 2/1	A	Port Vale	W 2-1	1-1		Scholes 36, 53	(18,605)
10	24	PL	A	Ipswich Town	L 2-3	0-2		Cantona 70, Scholes 73	(22,551)
11	28	EC	A	Galatasaray	D 0-0	0-0			(34,000)
12	O 1	PL	H	Everton	W 2-0	1-0	4	Kanchelskis 41, Sharpe 88	43,803
13	5	CC 2/2	H	Port Vale	W 2-0	1-0		McClair 34, May 61	31,615
14	8	PL	A	Sheffield Wednesday	L 0-1	0-1	5		(33,441)
15	15	PL	H	West Ham	W 1-0	1-0	4	Cantona 45	43,795
16	19	EC	H	Barcelona	D 2-2	1-0		Hughes 20, Sharpe 80	40,064
17	O 23	PL	A	Blackburn Rovers	W 4-2	1-1		Cantona 45 (pen), Kanchelskis 52, 82, Hughes 67	(30,260)
18	26	CC 3	A	Newcastle United	L 0-2	0-0			(34,178)
19	29	PL	H	Newcastle United	W 2-0	1-0	3	Pallister 12, Gillespie 76	43,795
20	N 2	EC	A	Barcelona	L 0-4	0-2			(120,000)
21	6	PL	A	Aston Villa	W 2-1	1-1		Ince 44, Kanchelskis 49	(32,136)
22	10	PL	H	Manchester City	W 5-0	2-0	4	Cantona 24, Kanchelskis 43, 47, 89, Hughes 70	43,738
23	19	PL	H	Crystal Palace	W 3-0	2-0	1	Irwin 8, Cantona 33, Kanchelskis 50	43,788
24	23	EC	A	Gothenburg	L 1-3	0-1		Hughes 64	(36,350)
25	26	PL	A	Arsenal	D 0-0	0-0	2		(38,301)
26	D 3	PL	H	Norwich City	W 1-0	1-0	2	Cantona 36	43,789
27	7	EC	H	Galatasaray	W 4-0	2-0		Davies 2, Beckham 37, Keane 48, Rulent 87 (og)	39,220
28	10	PL	A	Queens Park Rangers	W 2-3	1-2	2	Scholes 32, 47, Keane 38	(18,948)
29	17	PL	H	Nottingham Forest	L 1-2	0-1	2	Cantona 68	43,744
30	26	PL	A	Chelsea	W 3-2	0-1		Hughes 21, Cantona 45, McClair 78	(31,161)
31	28	PL	H	Leicester City	D 1-1	0-0		Kanchelskis 61	43,789
32	31	PL	A	Southampton	D 2-2	0-1		Butt 50, Pallister 79	(15,204)
33	J 3	PL	H	Coventry City	W 2-0	1-0	2	Scholes 27, Cantona 50 (pen)	43,130
34	9	FAC 3	A	Sheffield United	W 2-0	0-0		Hughes 80, Cantona 82	(22,322)
35	15	PL	A	Newcastle United	D 1-1	1-0	2	Hughes 12	(34,471)
36	22	PL	H	Blackburn Rovers	W 1-0	0-0	2	Cantona 80	43,742
37	25	PL	A	Crystal Palace	D 1-1	0-0	2	May 56	(18,224)
38	28	FAC 4	H	Wrexham	W 5-2	2-1		Irwin 16, 73 (pen), McClair 66, Humes 89 (og)	43,222
39	F 4	PL	H	Aston Villa	W 1-0	1-0	2	Cole 17	43,795
40	11	PL	A	Manchester City	W 3-0	0-0	2	Ince 58, Kanchelskis 74, Cole 77	(26,368)
41	19	FAC 5	H	Leeds United	W 3-1	2-0		Bruce 1, McClair 4, Hughes 71	42,744
42	22	PL	A	Norwich City	W 2-0	2-0	2	Ince 2, Kanchelskis 16	(21,824)
43	25	PL	A	Everton	L 0-1	0-0	2		(40,011)
44	M 4	PL	H	Ipswich Town	W 9-0	3-0	2	Keane 15, Cole 23, 36, 52, 64, Hughes 54, 58, Ince 72	43,804
45	7	PL	A	Wimbledon	W 1-0	0-0		Bruce 84	(18,224)
46	12	FAC 6	H	Queens Park Rangers	W 2-0	1-0		Sharpe 22, Irwin 53	42,830
47	15	PL	H	Tottenham Hotspur	D 0-0	0-0	2		43,802
48	19	PL	A	Liverpool	L 0-2	0-1	2		(38,906)
49	22	PL	H	Arsenal	W 3-0	2-0	2	Hughes 27, Sharpe 32, Kanchelskis 79	43,623
50	A 2	PL	H	Leeds United	D 0-0	0-0	2		43,712
51	9	FAC SF	N	Crystal Palace	D 2-2	0-1		Irwin 70, Pallister 96	(38,526)
52	12	FAC SFR	N	Crystal Palace	W 2-0	2-0		Bruce 29, Pallister 40	(17,987)
53	15	PL	A	Leicester City	W 4-0	2-0	2	Sharpe 33, Cole 45, 52, Ince 90	(21,281)
54	17	PL	H	Chelsea	D 0-0	0-0	2		(43,728)
55	M 1	PL	A	Coventry City	W 3-2	1-1	2	Scholes 32, Cole 55, 79	(21,885)
56									
57									
58									
59									
60									

Best Home League Attendance: 43,868 v Sheffield Wednesday   **Smallest:** 43,130 v Coventry City   **Av Home Att:** 43,681

Goal Scorers: Compared with 1993-94: -563

League (77): Kanchelkis 14, Cantona 12, Cole 12, Hughes 8, Ince 5, McClair 5, Scholes 5, Sharpe 3, Bruce 2, Irwin 2, Keane 2, May 2, Pallister 2, Butt, Giggs, Gillespie

C/Cola Cup (4): Scholes 2, May, McClair

FA Cup (15): Irwin 4, Bruce 2, Hughes 2, McClair 2, Pallister 2, Cantona, Sharpe, Opponent

European Cup (11): Giggs 2, Hughes 2, Sharpe 2, Beckham, Davies, Kanchelkis, Keane, Opponent

1994-95

Schmeichel	Bruce	Sharpe	Pallister	May	Ince	McClair	Cantona	Kanchelskis	Hughes	Giggs	Parker	Irwin	Keane	Pilkington	Butt	Dublin	Walsh	Neville G.	Scoles	Beckham	Davies	O'Kane	Gillespie	Tomlinson	Johnson	Referee	
X	X	X	X	X	X	X	X	X	X	X					S	S										Don P.	1
X	X	X2	X	X1	X	X		X	X	X	S1†	X	S2	S												Gallagher D.	2
X	X	X	X	X	X	X		X	X	X1	S	X	S1	S												Wilkie A.	3
X	X	X	X	X	X	X		X	X	X		X			S	S	S									Burge K.	4
X	X	X	X	X	X			X	X	X	X	X			S	S	S									Holbrook T.	5
X	X	S1	X	X	X	X1		X	X	X2		X			S2		S									Elleray D.	6
X	X	X	X	X	X			X	X	X		X		S	X			S	S	S	S					Goethlas G.	7
X	X	X	X	X	X	S1	X	X	X1	X		X		S	S	S										Morton K.	8
		S2		X		X				X		X	X	S	X2		X	X1	X	X		S1	X			Lloyd J.	9
	X	X1	X		X	X2	X	X		X		X	X	S	S2		X		S1							Jones P.	10
X	X	X	X	X	X			X	X	X1	S1	X	X		X											Van Der Ende M.	11
X	X	X	X	X	X	S1	X	X	X1			X	X				S		S							Poll G.	12
			X	X		X			X	X1	X	X		S	X		X	S2	X	X2	X	X1	S1			Wilkie A.	13
X	X	X	X	S1	X		X	X1	X	X		X			S			S2	S2			X2				Danson P.	14
X	X	X	X	X1	X	S	X	X	X	X		X		S1	S		S									Gifford R.	15
X	S1	X	X1	X			X	X	X	X		X	X2		S	S	S2		S							Cracinesch E.	16
	X	X	X		X	S1	X	X				X	X		X1		S				S					Ashby G.	17
	X	S12	X		X			X	X		X1		S	X		X	X		X	X		X	S2			Holbrook T.	18
X	X		X		X	X	X	X	X1	X		X	X		S		S		S1			S1				Worrell J.	19
	X		X		X	S1	X	X		X		X	X	S	X1		X		X2			S2				Don P.	20
	X		X		X			X	X	X1	X	X	X	X		X		X	S1							Quiniou J.	21
X	X		X		X	X	X	X	X1	X		X	X			S	S	S1								Cooper K.	22
X1	X		X	X	X	X	X3	X				X	S1			X	S2		X2		S3					Hill R.	23
	X		X	X1	X	X	X	X	X			X		S2	X	S1		X2								Trentalange A.	24
	X	X	X	X	X	X	X1	X†		X			S	S1	X	X		S2	X2						Morton K.	25
	X	X	X	X	X	X	X1	X		X			S	S1	X	X		X2	S2						Holbrook T.	26
	X		X	S		X	X			X	X	S	X	X	X	S	X	X	S			S	Wojeik R.	27
	X		X		X	X			X	X	S	X	S2		X1	X		X2		S1					Poll G.	28
	X		X1	X	X	X1	X	X2		X		X	S	S2	X	S1							Burge K.	29
	X		X1	X	X	S2	X	X		X		X	S	X2	X	S1							Reed M.	30
	X		S	X	X	X	X1	X		X		X	S		X	S							Gallagher D.	31
	X		X	X1	X		X	X		X		X	S	X	X	X	S			S1			Bodenham M.	32
	X		S	S1	X		X			X	X1	S	X	X	X	X			X				Willard G.	33
X	X	S2	X		X1	X		X	X			X	S	X	X		S1			X2			Hart R.	34
X	X	X	X	S1	X	X		X2		X	X	X1		S	S2							Lodge S.	35
X	X	X1	X	S	X	X	X	S1		X	X			S								Durkin P.	36
X	X2	X	X	X	X	X†	S1		X	X		S	S								Wilkie A.	37
X		X	X	X2		S1	X	X1		X		S	X	S2								Bodenham M.	38
X	X	X	S1	X	X	S2	X2		X		S	X1	X								Elleray D.	39
X	X	X	S1	X	X	X1	X		X		S	S2									Don P.	40
X	X	X	X	X	X	X	X		X	X		S	S	S							Reed M.	41
X	X	X	X	X	X	X	S	X	S	S											Holbrook T.	42
X		X	X	X1	S1	X	X	X		S	S										Worrall J.	43
X	X2	S1	X	X	X	X	X1	S2		S											Poll G.	44
X	X	X	X	X	X	X	X		S	X		S									Hart R.	45
X	X	X	X	X1	X	X1	X	S1		S	S										Gallagher D.	46
X	X	X	X	X1	X	X	X		S1	S	S										Morton K.	47
X	X	X1	X	X	X	X	X2	S2													Ashby G.	48
X	X	X	X	S	X	X	X	X	S	S											Cooper K.	49
X		X	X	X	X	X	X		S	S	X	S	X								Gifford R.	50
X	X	X	X	X	X	X	S1		S	X	X	S	X1								Ellerey D.	51
X	X		X	X†																	Ellerey D.	52
X	X	X1	X	X	X2		X	X	S	X	S2	S1									Bodenham M.	53
X	X		X	X	X		X	X	S	X	S2	X1	S12								Lodge S.	54
X		X	X	X	X	X	X		S	X	X1	S1									Don P.	55

30	33	26	40	18	33	34	18	26	34	32	3	37	23	2	9	2	9	14	4	2	3	0	3	0	0	League Appearances	
0	1	2	0	7	0	5	1	5	0	0	3	1	2	16	18	3	20	8	15	2	10	0	6	0	0	League Sub Appearances	
0	1	0+2	2	2	0	0	0	0	2	1	0+3	3	0	3	2+1	2	3	2	1+1	3	0+2	0				League Cup Appearances	
6	4	5	6	1	4	5	1	3	5	5	0	5	1	3	3	0	4	2	4	2	0	1	0	0	0	FA Cup Appearances	

Also Played: Cole X(36,37,39,40,42,43,44,45,47,49,50,53.54,55),S1(48), Neville X(38),X2(40),S(46), Casper S1(45),X(13), McGibbon

† = Sent Off

MANCHESTER UNITED

CLUB RECORDS

BIGGEST VICTORIES
League: 10-1 v Wolverhampton Wanderers, Division 2, 15.10.1892.
9-0 v Walsall, Division 2, 3.4.1895.
9-0 v Darwen, Division 2, 24.12.1898.
9-0 v Ipswich Town, Premiership, 4.3.95.
F.A. Cup: 8-0 v Yeovil Town, 5th Round, 12.2.1949.
League Cup: 7-2 v Newcastle United, 4th Round, 1976-77.
5-0 v Tranmere Rovers, 2nd Round, 1976-77.
5-0 v Rotherham United, 2nd Round, 12.10.1988.
5-0 v Hull City, 2nd Round, 23.9.1987.
Europe: 10-0 v Anderlecht, European Cup, 26.9.1956.
BIGGEST DEFEATS
League: 0-7 v Wolverhampton Wanderers, Division 2, 26.12.1931.
0-7 v Aston Villa, Division 1, 27.12.1930.
0-7 v Blackburn Rovers, Division 1, 10.4.1926.
F.A. Cup: 1-7 v Burnley, 1st Round, 1901
0-6 v Sheffield Wednesday, 2nd Round, 1904.
League Cup: 1-5 v Blackpool, 2nd Round, 1966-67.
0-4 v Manchester City, 4th Round, 12.11.1975.
Europe: (ECWC) 0-5 v Sporting Lisbon, Quarter-final, 18.3.1964.

MOST POINTS
3 points a win: 92, Premiership, 1993-94 (Divisional record).
2 points a win: 64, Division 1, 1956-57.
MOST GOALS SCORED
103, Division 1, 1956-57, 1958-59.
Whelen 26, Taylor 22, Violett 16, Charlton 10, Berry 8, Pegg 6, Edwards 5, Webster 3, Dawson 3, Scanlon 2, Coleman 1, Opponents 1.
(58-59) Charlton 29, Violet 21, Scanlon 16, Bradley 12, Goodwin 6, Webster 5, Dawson 4, Quixhall 4, Cope 2, McGuinness 1, Pearson 1, Opponents 1.
MOST GOALS CONCEDED
115, Division 1, 1930-31.

MOST FIRST CLASS MATCHES IN A SEASON
63 - 1993-94 (League 42, FA Cup 7, League Cup 9, European Cup 4, Charity Shield 1).

MOST LEAGUE WINS
28, Division 2, 1905-06, Division 1, 1956-57.

MOST LEAGUE DRAWS
18, Division 1, 1980-81.

MOST LEAGUE DEFEATS
27, Division 1, 1930-31.

INDIVIDUAL CLUB RECORDS

INDIVIDUAL CLUB RECORDS
MOST GOALS IN A SEASON
Dennis Law: 46 goals in 1963-64 (League 30, FA Cup 10, ECWC 6).

MOST GOALS IN A MATCH
6. Joe Cassidy v Walsall Town Swifts, 9-0, Division 2, 3.4.1895.
6. Harold Halse v Swindon Town, 8-4, Charity Shield, 1911.
6. George Best v Northampton Town (a), 8-2, FA Cup 5th Round, 7.2.1970.

OLDEST PLAYER
Billy Meredith, 46 years 285 days v Derby County, 7.5.1921.

YOUNGEST PLAYER
Duncan Edwards, 16 years 182 days v Cardiff City, 4.4.1953.

MOST CAPPED PLAYER
Bobby Charlton (England) 106.
(England's top goal scorer with 49).

BEST PERFORMANCES

League: 1956-57: Matches played 42, Won 28, Drawn 8, Lost 6, Goals for 103, Goals against 54, Points 64. First in Division 1.
Highest Position: Division 1/Premiership champions on 9 occasions.
F.A. Cup: Winners in 1908-09,1947-48, 1962-63, 1976-77, 1982-83, 1984-85, 1989-90.
1993-94: 3rd Round Sheffield United 1-0; 4th Round Norwich City 2-0; 5th Round Wimbledon 3-0; 6th Round Charlton Athletic 3-1; Semi-final Oldham Athletic 1-1,4-1; Final Chelsea 4-0.
League Cup: 1991-92: 2nd Round Cambridge United 3-0,1-1, 3rd round Portsmouth 3-1; 4th Round Oldham Athletic 2-0; 5th Round Leeds United 3-1; Semi-Final Middlesbrough 0-0,2-1; Final Nottingham Forest 1-0.
Europe: (European Cup) 1967-68: 1st Round Hibernians Valletta 4-0,0-0; 2nd Round Sarajevo 0-0,2-1; 3rd Round Gornik Zabrze 2-0,0-1; Semi-final Real Madrid 1-0,3-3; Final Benfica 4-1 aet.
(ECWC) 1990-91: 1st Round Pecsi Munkas 2-1,1-0; 2nd Round Wrexham 3-0,2-0; 3rd Round Montpellier 1-1,2-0; Semi-final Legia Warsaw 3-1,1-1; Final Barcelona 2-1.

DIVISIONAL RECORD

	Played	Won	Drawn	Lost	For	Against	Points
Division 1/P	2,866	1,239	737	890	4,747	3,972	3,497
Division 2	816	406	168	242	1,433	966	980
Total	**3,682**	**1,645**	**905**	**1,134**	**6,180**	**4,938**	**4,477**

ADDITIONAL INFORMATION
PREVIOUS NAMES
Newton Heath 1878-1902.

PREVIOUS LEAGUES
Football Alliance.

Club colours: Red shirts with black collar, white shorts, black socks.
Change colours: All black with gold trim.

Reserves League: Pontins Central League Division 1.

106

RECORDS AND STATISTICS

COMPETITIONS

Div.1/P	Div.2	Euro C	ECWC	UEFA	C/Shield	
1892-94	1894-06	1956-57	1963-64	1964-65	1908	1985
1906-22	1922-25	1957-58	1977-78	1976-77	1911	1990
1925-31	1931-36	1965-66	1983-84	1980-81	1952	1993
1936-37	1937-38	1967-68	1990-91	1982-83	1956	1994
1938-74	1974-75	1968-69	1991-92	1984-85	1957	
1975-		1993-94		1992-93	1965	Wat C
		1994-95			1967	1970
					1977	1971
					1983	

HONOURS

Div.1/P	Div.2	FA Cup	Lge Cup	Euro C	C/Shield
1907-08	1935-36	1908-09	1991-92	1967-68	1908
1910-11	1974-75	1947-48			1911
1951-52		1962-63			1952
1955-56		1976-77		ECWC	1956
1956-57		1982-83		1991	1957
1964-65		1984-85			1965*
1966-67		1989-90			1977*
1992-93		1993-94		ESC	1983
1993-94				1991	1990*
					1993
					1994
					*shared

MOST APPEARANCES

Bobby Charlton 756 (1956-73)

Year	League	FA Cup	Lge Cup	Europe
1956-57	14	2		1
1957-58	21	8		2
1958-59	38	1		
1959-60	37	3		
1960-61	39	3		
1961-62	37	7		
1962-63	28	6		
1963-64	40	7		6
1964-65	41	7		11
1965-66	38	7		8
1966-67	42	2		
1967-68	41	2		9
1968-69	32	6		8
1969-70	40	9	8	
1970-71	42	2	6	
1971-72	40	7	6	
1972-73	34+2	1	4	
	604+2	80	24	45

Includes 3 Charity Shield (1963-64, 1965-66 & 1967-68)

MOST GOALS IN A CAREER

Bobby Charlton - 248 (1956-73)

Year	League	FA Cup	Lge Cup	Europe
1956-57	10	1		1
1957-58	8	5		3
1958-59	29			
1959-60	17	3		
1960-61	21			
1961-62	8	2		
1962-63	7	2		
1963-64	9	2		4
1964-65	10			8
1965-66	16			2
1966-67	12			
1967-68	15	1		2
1968-69	5			2
1969-70	12	1	1	
1970-71	5		3	
1971-72	8	2	2	
1972-73	6		1	
Total	198	19	7	22

Includes 2 goals in the Charity Shield.

Current leading goalscorer: Brian McClair - 125 (1987-95)

RECORD TRANSFER FEE RECEIVED

Amount	Club	Player	Date
£7,000,000	Inter Milan	Paul Ince	07/95
£2,500,000	Barcelona	Mark Hughes	6/86
£1,500,000	AC Milan	Ray Wilkins	6/84
£800,000	Norwich City	Mark Robins	8/92

RECORD TRANSFER FEE PAID

Amount	Club	Player	Date
£7,000,000	Newcastle Utd	Andy Cole	01/95
£3,750,000	Nott'm Forest	Roy Keane	7/93
£2,300,000	Middlesbrough	Gary Pallister	8/89
£2,000,000	Q.P.R.	Paul Parker	8/91

MANAGERS

Name	Seasons	Best	Worst
E Magnall	1903-12	1(1)	3(2)
J R Robson	1914-21	12(1)	18(1)
J Chapman	1921-26	9(1)	14(2)
C Hilditch	1926-27	15(1)	15(1)
H Barnlett	1927-31	12(1)	22(1)
W Crickner	1931-32	12(1)	12(1)
A Scott Duncan	1932-37	21(1)	20(2)
M Busby	1945-69	1(1)	19(1)
J Murphy	1958		
W McGuiness	1969-70	8(1)	8(1)
M Busby	1970-71	8(1)	8(1)
F O'Farrell	1971-72	8(1)	8(1)
T Docherty	1972-77	3(1)	1(2)
D Sexton	1977-81	2(1)	10(1)
R Atkinson	1981-86	3(1)	8(1)
A. Ferguson	1986-	1(P)	13(1)

LONGEST LEAGUE RUNS

of undefeated matches:	26 (21.1.1956 - 20.10.1956)	of league matches w/out a win:	16 (19.3.1930 - 25.10.1930)
of undefeated home matches:	37 (27.4.1966 - 27.3.1968)	of undefeated away matches:	14 (21.1.1956 - 20.10.1956)
without home win:	7 (30.3.1920 - 6.9.1920, 19.4.1930 - 1.10.1930)		
(9.12.1933 - 3.3.1934, 22.2.1958 - 21.4.1958, 5.2.1978 - 29.3.1978)		without an away win:	26 (15.2.1930 - 3.4.1931)
of league wins:	14 (8.10.1904 - 1.2.1905)	of home wins:	18 (15.10.1904 - 30.4.1905)
of league defeats:	14 (26.4.1930 - 25.10.1930)	of away wins:	7 (5.4.1993 - 28.8.1993)

MANCHESTER UNITED — APPEARANCES — GOALS

PLAYERS NAME / Honours	Ht	Wt	Birthdate	Birthplace / Transfers	Contract Date	Clubs	League	L/Cup	FA Cup	Other	Lge	L/C	FAC	Oth
G O A L K E E P E R S														
Kevin W Pilkington	6.0	12.0	08.03.74	Hitchin	06.07.92	Manchester Utd (T)	0+1							
ESFAu18.1; FAYC'92														
Peter B Schmeichel	6.4	13.6	18.11.68	Glodstone (Denmark)		Brondby								
Den: ; Den: FAC'89; Div1'87'88'89				£550,000	12.08.91	Manchester United	154	16	20	14				
ESC'91; EuroC'92; E: LC'92, Prem'93'94; FAC'94														
D E F E N D E R S														
Stephen R Bruce	6.0	12.6	31.12.60	Corbridge	27.10.78	Gillingham (A)	203+2	15	14		29	6	1	
E: B1, Y8; Prem'93'94; Div2'86; LC'85'92; FAC'90				£125,000	24.08.84	Norwich City	141	20	9	10	14	5	1	
ECWC'91; CS'90'93; ESC'91; FLgXl.1; FAC'94				£800,000	18.12.87	Manchester United	279	31+1	36	30+2	35	6	3	7
Christopher M Casper	6.0	10.7	28.04.75	Burnley	03.02.93	Manchester Utd (T)	1							
E: Y8; FAYC'92; EUFA Yth'93														
David Hilton			10.11.77	Barnsley	1994-95	Manchester Utd (T)								
E: Yth.														
Joseph Dennis Irwin	5.8	10.10	31.10.65	Cork	03.11.83	Leeds United (A)	72	5	3	2	1			
Ei: 28, B1, u21.3, Y, S; ECWC'91; ESC'91				Free	22.05.86	Oldham Athletic	166+1	19	13	5	4	3		
LC'92; CS'90'93; Prem'93'94; FAC'94				£625,000	20.06.90	Manchester United	192+2	27+2	23	21	13		6	
David May	6.0	11.4	24.06.70	Oldham	16.06.88	Blackburn R. (T)	123	12+1	10	5	3	2	1	
				£1,400,000	01.07.94	Manchester United	15+4	2	1	5	2	1		
Patrick C G McGibbon	6.2	12.12	06.09.73	Lurgan		Portadown								
NI: B1, u21.1, S						Manchester Utd (T)								
Colin J Murdoch	6.1	12.0	02.07.75	Ballymena	21.07.92	Manchester United								
NI: Y4, S														
Gary A Neville	5.10	11.7	18.02.75	Bury	29.01.93	Manchester Utd (T)	17+2	2+1	4	1+3				
E: Y8; FAYC'92; EUFA Yth'93														
Philip J Neville	5.11	12.0	21.01.77	Bury	01.06.94	Manchester Utd (T)	1+1		1					
FAYC'95.														
John A O'Kane	5.10	11.5	15.11.74	Nottingham	29.01.93	MAnchester Utd (T)		1+1	1					
FAYC'92														
Gary Pallister	6.4	13.0	30.06.65	Ramsgate		Billingham								
E: 13, B9; FLgXl.1; FAC'90; CS'90'93; ECWC'91				Free	07.11.84	Middlesbrough	156	10	10	13	5		1	
ESC'91; LC'92; Prem'93'94; FAC'94				Loan	18.10.85	Darlington	7							
				£2,300,000	29.08.89	Manchester United	233+3	34	31	27+1	8		1	1
Paul A Parker	5.7	10.8	04.04.64	West Ham	15.04.82	Fulham (A)	140+13	16	11	2	2	1		
E:19, B3, u21.8, Y3; LC'92; Prem'93'94; FAC'94				£300,000	18.06.87	Q.P.R.	121+4	14	16	5	1			
CS'93				£2,000,000	08.08.91	Manchester United	95+4	14	13	8+2	1			
Ronald Wallwork			10.09.77	Manchester	1994-95	Manchester Utd (T)								
E: Yth.														
Ashley M Westwood	6.0	11.03	31.08.76	Bridgnorth	1994-95	Manchester Utd (T)								
Philip R Whittam	5.8	9.08	12.08.76	Bolton	1994-95	Manchester Utd (T)								
M I D F I E L D														
Michael A Appleton	5.9	11.13	04.12.75	Salford	1994-95	Manchester Utd (T)								
David R J Beckham	5.11	10.7	02.05.75	Leytonstone	29.01.93	Manchester Utd (T)	2+2	3+1	1+1	1				1
E: Y4; FAYC'92				Loan	28.02.95	Preston North End	4+1				2			
Grant I Brebner			06.12.77	Edinburgh	1994-95	Manchester Utd (T)								
Simon I Davies	5.11	11.8	23.04.74	Winsford	06.07.92	Manchester Utd (T)	3+2	3		2				1
FAYC'92				Loan	17.12.93	Exeter City	5+1		1		1			
Roy M Keane	5.10	11.3	10.08.71	Cork		Cobh Ramblers								
Ei: 26, u21.4, Y; FMC'92; Prem'94; FAC'94; CS'93				£10,000	12.08.90	Nottingham Forest	114	37	18	5	22	6	3	2
				£3,750,000	22.07.93	Manchester United	57+5	7+1	12+1	8	7		1	3
Paul Scholes	5.6	10.8	16.11.74	Salford	29.01.93	Manchester Utd (T)	6+11	3	1+2	0+2	5	2		
E: Y4; EUFA Yth'93														
Thomas E Smith			25.11.77	Northampton	1994-95	Manchester Utd (T)								
Benjamin L Thornley	5.9	10.9	21.04.75	Bury	29.01.93	Manchester Utd (T)	0+1							
E: S; ESFAu15; FAYC'92														
F O R W A R D S														
Desmond L Baker	5.9	10.12	25.08.77	Dublin	1994-95	Manchester Utd (T)								
Nicholas Butt	5.9	10.10	21.01.75	Manchester	29.01.93	Manchester Utd (T)	11+13	3	3+2	5+1	1			
E: Y7; ESAu.15; FAYC'92; EUFA Yth'93														
Eric Cantona	6.0	11.6	24.05.66	Paris		Auxerre (France)								
Fra: 21,Fra.Div1'89-90; Fra.FAC'89'90				£2,200,000		Marseille (France)								
Div'92; Prem'93'94; FAC'94; CS'93				Loan		Bordeaux (France)								
Loan Montpellier (France)				£1,000,000		Nimes (France)								
				£900,000	06.02.92	Leeds United	18+10	1		6	9			4
				£1,200,000	27.11.92	Manchester United	76+1	5	7	8	39	1	5	3

Player / Details	Fee	Date	Club								
Andrew Cole 5.10 11.2 15.10.71		Nottingham	18.10.89	Arsenal (T)	0+1			0+1			
E: 1, B.1, u21.8, Y.20, S. Div.1'93.	Loan	05.09.91	Fulham	13			2	3		1
	Loan	12.03.92	Bristol City	12				8		
	£500,000	21.07.92	Bristol City	29	3	1	4	12	4		1
	£1,750,000	12.03.93	Newcastle United	69+1	7	4	3	55	8	1	4
	£7,000,000	12.01.95	Manchester United	17+1				12			
Terence J Cooke 5.7 9.09 05.08.76		Marston Green	1994-95	Manchester Utd (T)							
Ryan J Giggs 5.11 10.9 29.11.73		Cardiff	01.12.90	Manchester Utd (T)	134+14	14+4	17+2	11+1	28	6	4	2
W:11, u21.1,Y; ESAu.15; ESC'91; LC'92; FAYC'92; Prem'93'94; FAC'94											
Richard J Irving 5.7 10.6 10.09.75		Halifax		Manchester Utd (T)							
E: Y4, S											
Brian J McClair 5.10 12.13 08.12.63		Belshill		Aston Villa (A)							
S:30, B1, u21.8: SPD'86; SC'85; Prem'93'94	Free	01.08.81	Motherwell	33+7	9+1	2		15	4	1	
FAC'90'94; CS'90'93; ECWC'91; ESC'91; LC'92	£100,000	01.07.83	Celtic	129+16	19+1	14+4	13+2	99	9	11	3
	£850,000	30.07.87	Manchester United	278+23	40+1	35+4	23	85	19	14	7
Lee S Sharpe 5.11 11.4 27.05.71		Halesowen	31.05.88	Torquay United (T)	9+5			2+3	3		
E: 8, B1, u21.8; ECWC'91; LC'92; Prem'93'94; FC'94	£185,000	10.06.88	Manchester United	139+23	13+8	18+5	16+2	17	9	1	3
Graeme Tomlinson 5.9 11.7 10.12.75		Keighley		Bradford City (T)	12+5		0+1		6		
	£100,000	12.07.94	Manchester United		0+2						

ADDITIONAL TRAINEES: Leslie M Hughes, Philip P Mulryne, Paul Teacher

---

TOP GOALSCORER 1994/95
Andrei Kanchelskis

Premiership goals (games) . . . . 14 (25+5)
Coca-Cola Cup Goals 0 (0)
F.A. Cup goals . . . . 0 (2+1)
European Cup 1 (5)
Total . . . . **15 (32+6)**

Total goals for Manchester United since 26.03.91 . . . . 36 (131+29)

MANAGER
ALEX FURGUSON

Date of Birth . . . . 31st December 1941.
Place of Birth . . . . Govan, Glasgow.
Date of Appointment . . . . 5th November 1986.

PREVIOUS CLUBS
As Manager . . . . East Sterling, St Mirren, Aberdeen.
Alex was appointed caretaker manager of Scotland in 1985 on the death of Jock
   Stein until Andy Roxburgh was made manager in July 1986.
As Coach . . . . None.
As a Player . . . . Rangers, Queens Park, Dunfermline.

HONOURS
As a Manager
Aberdeen: Scottish Champions 1980, 1984, 1985. Scottish Cup Winners 1982, 1983, 1984, 1986.
Scottish League Cup 1986. ECWC 1983.
Manchester United: FA Cup 1990,1994. ECWC 1991. League Cup 1992.
Premier League Champions 1992-93, 1993-94. Charity Shield 1994, 1994. Super Cup 1991.
As a Player
None.

OLD TRAFFORD
Manchester M16 0RA
Tel: 0161 872 1661

Capacity ....32,500 (Approx).
(Ground development has reduced the capacity this season, on completion the new capacity will be 55,300)

First game ....v Liverpool, 19.2.1910.
First floodlit game...v Bolton Wanderers, 25.03.1957.

ATTENDANCES
Highest..76,962 Wolves v Grimsby, FA Cup, 25.3.1939.
Lowest...Not Known.

OTHER GROUNDS ....North Road, Monsall Road 1880-1893,Bank Street 1883-1910,
.... Old Trafford 1910-1941, Maine Road 1941-49, Old Trafford 1949-

---

MATCHDAY TICKET PRICES

Contact club to check availability, due to re-development there will be no matchday tickets on sale until the completion of the North Stand.

Ticket Office Telephone no. . . . . . . 0161 872 0199.

HOW TO GET TO THE GROUND

From the North
Use motorway M61 then M63 until junction 4. Leave motorway and follow signs to Manchester A5081. In 2.5 miles turn right into Sir Matt Busby Way, then turn right into United Road for Manchester United FC.

From the East
Use motorway M62 until junction 17 then A56 into Manchester. Follow signs South then Chester into Chester Road. In 2 miles turn right into Sir Matt Busby Way, then turn left into United Road for Manchester United FC.

From the South
Use motorway M6 until junction 19 then follow signs to Stockport A556 then Altrincham A56. From Altrincham follow signs to Manchester. In 6 miles turn left into Sir Matt Busby Way, then turn left into United Road for Manchester United FC.

From the West
Use motorway M62 then M63 and route from north or as route from south.

Car Parking: Several large parks. Lancashire County Cricket Ground, Talbot Road and Great Stone Road (1,200).

Nearest Railway Station: Manchester Piccadilly (0161 832 8353).

CLUBCALL
0891 12 11 61
Calls cost 39p per minute cheap rate and 49p per minute at all other times.
Call costings correct at time of going to press.

MATCHDAY PROGRAMME

Programme Editor . . . . Cliff Butler.

Number of pages . . . . 48.

Price . . . . £1.50.

Subscriptions . . . . UK £39, Eire £39, Europe £49, Overseas £85.

Local Newspapers . . . . Manchester Evening News, Sunday Pink.

Local Radio Stations . . . . . . BBC Radio Manchester, Piccadilly Radio.
. . . . Manchester Utd Radio (Match Days only) 1413 AM.

MIDDLESBROUGH
(The Boro)
F.A. CARLING PREMIERSHIP
SPONSORED BY: CELLNET

Back Row (L-R): John Hendrie, Jamie Moreno, Michael Barron, Craig Liddle, Phil Stamp, Craig Hignett, Jamie Pollock, Derek Whyte, Alan Moore, Keith O'Halloran. **Middle Row:** Gordon McQueen (Res. Coach), David Geddis (Yth Coach), Jan Fjortoft, Steve Vickers, Phil Whelan, Alan Miller, Ben Roberts, Paul Wilkinson, Robbie Mustoe, Curtis Fleming, Tommy Johnson (Physio), Mike Kelly (GK Coach). **Front Row:** Bob Ward (Chief physio), Chris Morris, Graham Kavanagh, Bryan Robson (Player-manager), Nigel Pearson (Capt), Viv Anderson (Player-Asst. Manager), Clayton Blackmore, Neil Cox, John Pickering (First team coach).

MIDDLESBROUGH
FORMED IN 1876
TURNED PROFESSIONAL IN 1899
LTD COMPANY IN 1899 (Amateur 1876-99)

CHAIRMAN: S Gibson

DIRECTOR
G Cook
CHIEF EXECUTIVE/SECRETARY
K Lamb, F.C.A.
COMMERCIAL MANAGER
G Fordy

MANAGER: Bryan Robson
ASSISTANT MANAGER: Viv Anderson
FIRST TEAM COACH: John Pickering
RESERVE TEAM MANAGER
G McQueen
YOUTH TEAM MANAGER
David Geddis
PHYSIOTHERAPIST
M Nile/T Johnson

STATISTICIAN FOR THE DIRECTORY
David Grey

A season which began with high expectation for Middlesbrough eventually brought triumph for Bryan Robson in his first season of management.

During the close-season, Robson had secured several new signings, and the whole atmosphere was one of a club that finally meant business. The club had spent previous years with little apparent ambition; was this now about to change?

A good start to the season seemed to justify the summer optimism - it was the middle of September before the team lost a match, and by this time they were well in contention with the leaders. Although the team slipped a little during the autumn, the early season form was soon regained, and by Christmas, 'Boro had a healthy lead at the top of the table. This lead was needed as the usual New Year slump was encountered with no wins at all during January (including yet another rather embarrassing early FA Cup exit). However, they turned the corner once again, and held first position from the middle of March right through to the end of the season. In the end, the run-in was a very tense affair, with all clubs involved unexpectedly dropping points. For a long time, it looked as if the final game of the season at Tranmere was going to be the decider, but it turned out to be a celebration of the championship win secured as a result of games held earlier in the final week.

It was fortunate that such success was gained in the league, because the cup competitions brought nothing to cheer about. Apart from the FA Cup defeat mentioned earlier, 'Boro only progressed as far as the Third Round of the Coca-Cola Cup, and the Anglo Italian Cup was used simply as a means of giving younger players the opportunity for first team experience.

The feeling of ambition was maintained throughout the season; loan signing Uwe Fuchs soon gained the adulation of the crowd (9 goals in 13 games helped to achieve that) but he was soon to be replaced by Jan-Aage Fjortoft, signed just before the transfer deadline to break Middlesbrough's transfer record for the second time in less than a year.

In one way, the season ended on a rather sad note, as the team played their last ever match at Ayresome Park. However, this emotional farewell should be viewed as the prelude to a new era as the club begins life at the Cellnet Riverside Stadium.

So what of the future? Will relegation follow as quickly as it has done in recent previous encounters with the "Big Boys"? Only time will tell, though one or two big signings will be needed to bolster the present squad. In particular, someone will be required to take over Robson's own position in midfield. If this happens, Middlesbrough may be able to begin their season in the Premiership with continued optimism, now that the club as a whole seems to have regained the ambition that has been missing for many years.

DAVID GREY/NIGEL BALL.

MIDDLESBROUGH

Division One: 1st   **FA Cup:** 3rd Round   **Coca-Cola Cup:** 3rd Round   **Anglo Italian Cup:** Group Stage

M	DATE	COMP.	VEN	OPPONENTS	RESULT	H/T	LP	GOAL SCORERS/GOAL TIMES	ATT.
1	A 13	EL	H	Burnley	W 2-0	2-0		Hendrie 28, 35	23,343
2	20	EL	A	Southend Utd	W 2-0	1-0	1	Hendrie 30, 49	(5,722)
3	24	AIC	H	**Placenza**	D 0-0	0-0			5,348
4	27	EL	H	Bolton Wanderers	W 1-0	1-0	1	Wilkinson 9	19,570
5	31	EL	A	Derby County	W 1-0	1-0	1	Blackmore 19	(14,659)
6	S 3	EL	A	Watford	D 1-1	1-0	1	Blackmore34	(9,478)
7	10	EL	H	Sunderland	D 2-2	0-1	1	Moore 79, Pearson 81	19,578
8	13	EL	H	West Brom Albion	W 2-1	1-1	1	Mustoe 42, Hignett 90 (pen.)	14,878
9	17	EL	A	Port Vale	L 1-2	1-0	2	Pollock 38	(10,313)
10	20	CC 2./1	A	**Scarborough**	W 4-1	4-1		**Hendrie 7, Pollock 23, Moore 33, Mustoe 41**	(4,751)
11	24	EL	A	Bristol City	W 1-0	0-0	2	Hendrie 70	(8,642)
12	27	CC 2/2	H	**Scarborough**	W 4-1	1-1		**Wilkinson 41, 61, 65, Hignett 68**	7,739
13	O 1	EL	H	Millwall	W 3-0	0-0	2	Hendrie 46, Wilkinson 53, Beard 74 (og)	17,229
14	5	AIC	H	**Cesena**	D 1-1	0-0		**Moreno 56**	(3,273)
15	8	EL	H	Tranmere Rovers	L 0-1	0-0	2		18,497
16	15	EL	A	Luton Town	L 1-5	0-3	4	Whyte 83	(8,412)
17	18	AIC	A	**Udinese**	D 0-0	0-0			(300)
18	22	EL	A	Portsmouth	D 0-0	0-0	3		(7,281)
19	26	CC 3	A	**Aston Villa**	L 0-1	0-1			(19,254)
20	29	EL	H	Swindon Town	W 3-1	1-0	2	Cox 2, Hendrie 63, Wilkinson 65 (pen.)	17,328
21	N 1	EL	H	Oldham Athletic	W 2-1	0-1	2	Moore 53, Hignett 73	15,929
22	5	EL	A	Grimsby Town	L 1-2	0-2	2	Hignett 73 (pen.)	(8,488)
23	16	AIC	A	**Ancona**	L 1-3	1-0		**Morris 9**	(1,500)
24	20	EL	H	Wolverhampton Wand.	W 1-0	0-0	1	Hendrie 67	19,953
25	26	EL	A	Charlton Athletic	W 2-0	1-0	1	Hendrie 4, Pollock 54	(10,019)
26	D 3	EL	H	Portsmouth	W 4-0	2-0	1	Wilkinson 26, 75, Hignett 28,59	17,185
27	6	EL	A	Reading	D 1-1	0-0	1	Wilkinson 70 (pen.)	(10,301)
28	10	EL	H	Southend United	L 1-2	0-1	1	Hendrie 79	16,843
29	18	EL	A	Burnley	W 3-0	1-0	1	Hendrie 14, 64, 90	(12,049)
30	26	EL	A	Sheffield United	D 1-1	0-0	1	Hignett 73	(20,693)
31	28	EL	H	Notts County	W 2-1	2-1	1	Hignett 30, Pearson 36	21,558
32	31	EL	A	Stoke City	D 1-1	1-1	1	Vickers 9	(15,914)
33	J 7	FAC 3	A	**Swansea City**	D 1-1	0-1		**Moore 62**	(8,407)
34	15	EL	A	Swindon town	L 1-2	1-1	1	Hignett 13	(8,888)
35	17	FAC 3R	H	**Swansea City**	L 1-2	0-1		**Hendrie 79**	13,940
36	21	EL	H	Grimsby Town	D 1-1	0-0	1	Mustoe 85	15,360
37	F 4	EL	H	Reading	L 0-1	0-0	3		17,982
38	18	EL	H	Charlton Athletic	W 1-0	1-0	3	Fuchs 15	16,301
39	21	EL	A	Wolverhampton Wand.	W 2-0	0-0	2	Vickers 51, Fuchs 81	(27,611)
40	26	EL	A	Millwall	D 0-0	0-0	2		(7,247)
41	M 4	EL	H	Bristol City	W 3-0	1-0	2	Fuchs 9, 48, 65	17,371
42	7	EL	H	Watford	W 2-0	1-0	2	Mustoe 31, Fuchs 61	16,630
43	11	EL	A	Bolton Wanderers	L 0-1	0-1	2		(18,370)
44	14	EL	H	Barnsley	D 1-1	1-0	2	Moreno 36	19,655
45	18	EL	H	Derby County	L 2-4	0-3	2	Fuchs 52, Pollock 55	18,168
46	21	EL	A	Sunderland	W 1-0	0-0	1	Pollock 65	(16,501)
47	26	EL	H	Port Vale	W 3-0	2-0	1	Robson 14, Vickers 18, Fuchs 78	17,401
48	A 1	EL	A	West Bromwich A.	W 3-1	0-1	1	Pollock 57, Raven 61 (og), Moore 66	(20,256)
49	5	EL	A	Oldham Athletic	L 0-1	0-0	1		(11,024)
50	8	EL	H	Stoke City	W 2-1	1-1	1	Pearson 13, Moore 70	20,867
51	15	EL	A	Notts County	D 1-1	0-0	1	Fuchs 83	(9,377)
52	17	EL	H	Sheffield United	D 1-1	1-1	1	Fjortoft 7	23,225
53	22	EL	A	Barnsley	D 1-1	1-0	1	Fjortoft 38	(11,711)
54	M 1	EL	H	Luton Town	W 2-1	1-0	1	Hendrie 45, 72	23,903
55	8	EL	A	Tranmere Rovers	D 1-1	0-1	1	Fjortoft 51	(16,377)
56									
57									
58									
59									
60									

Best Home League Attendance: 23,903 v Luton Town   **Smallest:** 14,878 v West Bromich Albion   **Av Home Att:** 18,641

Goal Scorers: Compared with 1993-94: +8,241

League (67): Hendrie 15, Fuchs 9, Hignett 8, (2 pens.), Wilkinson 6 (2 pens.), Pollock 5, Moore 4, Fjortoft 3, Mustoe 3, Pearson 3, Vickers 3, Balckmore 2, Opponents 2, Cox, Moreno, Robson, Whyte
Coca Cola Cup (8): Wilkinson 3, Hendrie, Hignett, Moore, Mustoe, Pollock
FA Cup (2): Moore, Hendrie
Anglo/Ital Cup (6): Moreno, Morris

1994-95

Miller A.	Cox N.	Fleming C.	Vickers C.	Pearson N.	Blackmore C.	Robson B.	Pollock J.	Wilkinson P.	Hendrie J.	Moore A.	Whyte D.	Hignett C.	Roberts B.	Mustoe R.	Morris C.	Taylor M.	Todd A.	Stamp P.	Wright T.	Pears S.	Kavanagh G.	Moreno J	O'Halloran K.	Fuchs U.	Anderson V.	Referee	
1	2	3	4	5	6	7	8	9	10	11	S	S	S													R. Poulain	1
1	2	3	4	5	6	7	8	9	10	11	S	S	S	S												R. Bigger	2
1	12	S	4			S	8•	17			6	9		10	2	3	5	7*	11							G. Rosica	3
1	2	3	4	5	6	7	8*	9	10	11		S	S	12												J. Kirby	4
1	2	3	4	5	6*	7	8	9	10	11		S	S	12												E. Wolstenholme	5
1	2	3		5	6	7	8	9	10	11	4	S	S	S												C Wilkes	6
1	2	3	4	5	6•	7	8	9	10	11			14	S	S											A. Flood	7
1	2	3	4	5•	14	7*	8	9	10	11		6	S	12												E. Parker	8
	2	3	4				8	9	10	11	5	6	S	7	S					1						A. Flood	9
	2	3	4				8	9	10	11•	5	6	S	7	S				14	1						S. Lodge	10
	2	3	4				8	9	10	11	5	6	S	7	S					1						J. Lloyd	11
	12	3	4*				8	9	S		5	6	S	7	2				11	1		10				T. West	12
	2	3	4				8	9	10		5	11•	S	7						1		14				P. Harrison	13
		S			10		S				5	5			2	3	6	7	11	1	8	9				G. Borriello	14
	2	3	4		6•		8	9	10		5	11	S	7						1		14	S			W. Burns	15
S	2	3	4		6		8	9	10		5	7							11*	1	12	S				K. Cooper	16
1	4•	2	5		S							S	S			3	10†		7	11	S	8	9			K. Breen	17
1	2	3	4		6		8	9	10		5	14	S				7			S	11•					P. Foakes	18
1	2	3	4		6		8	9	10	11	5		S	12			7*		S							K. Morton	19
1	2	3	4		6		8	9	10	11*	5	12					7			S	S					E. Lomas	20
1	2	3	4		6*		8	9	10	11	5	12					7			S	S					R. Poulain	21
1	2		4		3		8	9	10	11	5	7					6			S	S					D. Allison	22
														1	10*	2			7	11		9•	8			J. Rushton	23
1	2		4		14		8	9•	10	11	5	7	S	6	3		S				S					A. Flood	24
1	2		4	6			8	9	10	11	5	7	3							S						M. Pierce	25
1	2		4			S	8	9	10•	11	5	7		6	3					S		14				E. Parker	26
1	2		4	6			8	9	10	12	5	7*		11†	3					S						J. Brandwood	27
1	7		4	5	12			9	10	11	3		6	2			8•					14*				E. Wolstenholme	28
1	2	3	4	6	S	7		9	10	11	5		S	8						S		S				P. Wright	29
1	2	3	4	6	S	7		9	10*	11	5	12	S								8					J. Rushton	30
1	2•	3		6				9	10	11	5	7	S	4						S						J. Kirby	31
1		3	4	5		7		S	8	9	10	S	11	S	6	2				S						U. Rennie	32
1		3	4	5		S	8	9	10	14	6•	11	S	7	2					S						K. Morton	33
1	3†	4	5		S		8		10	11•	S	7	2							14						G. Pooley	34
1	3	4	5			8		10	11•	S	7	6	2							14						K. Morton	35
1		3	4	5•	7		8		10	14		11	S	6	2					S						A. Dawson	36
1			4	5	6	7	8*	9	10	11	3	7•	S	6	2								14			J. Lloyd	37
1			4	5	6	7	8		11	3			S	10	2					S		9				G. Cain	38
1			4	5	6	7	8		11	3			S	10	2					S		9	S			K. Breen	39
1	12		4	5	6	7•	8*	14	11	3			S	10	2					S		9				C. Wilkes	40
1	2		4*	5	6			14	11	3	12		10				S		8		9•					E. Parker	41
1	2		4	5	6		7	S		11	3	S		10				S		8		9				T. West	42
1	2		4	5	6*	7•	8		11	3			10				12	S		14		9				P. Vanes	43
1	2		4	5			8	14	12	11	3	7*		6				S		10		9•				P. Harrison	44
1	2		4	5			7	8		10	11		6				S		12	3*	9	5				P. Wright	45
1	2		4	5		S	7	8		10	11		6				S		S		12		9			E. Wolstenholme	46
1	2		4	5	6	7	8	S		10	11*	3					S					9				G. Singh	47
1	2		4	5	6	7	8	S		10	11*	3					S					9	5			A. D'Urso	48
1	2		4	5•	6	7*	8	14		10	11	3	12				S					9				D. Allison	49
1	2•		4	5	14			8		10	11*	3	7				S	6	12							M. Riley	50
1	2		4	5			8		11	3	7•			14			S	6	10*		12					J. Holbrook	51
1	2		4	5	6		8		14	11•	3						S	7	S		9/					W. Burns	52
1	2	S	4		6		8		10	11	3						S	7		S	S	5				G. Cain	53
1	2		4	5	6	7	8		10	11	3						S		S		S					P. Vanes	54
1	2		4	5				10*		6	S	3		7			S		11							A. Flood	55
41	39	21	44	33	26	21	41	27	37	35	36	19		24	14		5	1	1	5	5	6	1	13	2	League Appearances	
	1			4	1		4	2	2					7	3	1			2		2	8		2		League Sub Appearances	
1	2+1	3	3		1		3	3	2	2	3	2		2+1	1		1		1+1	2						C/Cola Cup Appearances	
2	2	2	2		2		1+1		2		2	2		2	2		3	3	3	4	4	0+1	1	2	3	1	FA Cup Appearances	
2	1+1	1	2		1		2	1	1		2	1	1	2	2		3	3	3	4	4	1	2	3	1	Anglo/Ital Appearances	

Also Played: Fjortoft 10(48,49,52),9(50,51,53,54,55), Liddle 6(17),4(23),8(55), Freestone 12(55), Barron 4(14),5(23),15(17), Byrne 3(23), White 6(23), Norton 12(23), Richardson 14(23), Whittaker S(3,23), Johnson S(14), Collett S(14), Ward S(23)   Players on Loan: Fuchs (Kaiserslautern)

† = Sent Off

MIDDLESBROUGH

CLUB RECORDS

BIGGEST VICTORIES
League: 9-0 v Brighton & H.A., Division 2, 23.8.1958.
F.A. Cup: 11-0 v Scarborough, Qual. Round, 1890-91.
9-3 v Goole Town, 3rd Round, 1914-15.
League Cup: 5-0 v Brighton & H.A., 2nd Round, 21.9.93.

BIGGEST DEFEATS
League: 0-9 v Blackburn Rovers, Division 2, 6.11.1954.
F.A. Cup: 1-6 v Southampton, 3rd Round, 1905-06.
1-6 v Sheffield Wednesday, 2nd Round, 1894-95.
1-6 v Wolverhampton Wanderers, 3rd Round, 1936-37.
League Cup: 0-4 v Manchester City, Semi-final, 21.1.1976.

MOST POINTS
3 points a win: 94, division 3, 1986-87.
2 points a win: 65, Division 2, 1973-74.

MOST GOALS SCORED
122, Division 2, 1926-27.
Camsell 59, Pease 23, Birrell 16, Williams 9, Carr 6, McClelland 5, McKay 1, Ashman 1, J.Williams 1, Opponents 1.

MOST GOALS CONCEDED
91, Division 1, 1953-54.

MOST FIRST CLASS MATCHES IN A SEASON
60 - 1991-92 (League 46, FA Cup 4, League Cup 8, Zenith Data Cup 2).

MOST LEAGUE WINS
28, Division 3, 1986-87.

MOST LEAGUE DRAWS
19, Division 2, 1924-25.

MOST LEAGUE DEFEATS
27, Division 1, 1923-24.

INDIVIDUAL CLUB RECORDS

MOST GOALS IN A SEASON
George Camsell: 64 goals in 1926-27 (League 59, FA Cup 5).
(English record and League goals (59) is a Division 2 record)

MOST GOALS IN A MATCH
5. Andy Wilson v Nottingham Forest, 6.10.1923.
5. George Camsell v Manchester City 5-3 (a), 25.12.1926.
5. George Camsell v Aston Villa 7-2 (a), 9.9.1935.
5. Brian Clough v Brighton & H.A. 9-0, Division 2, 22.8.1958.

OLDEST PLAYER
Viv Anderson, 38 years 236 days v Barnsley, Division 1, 22.4.1995.

YOUNGEST PLAYER
Sam Lawrie, 16 years 323 days v Arsenal, Division 1, 3.11.51.
Stephen Bell, 16 years 323 days v Southampton, Division 1, 30.1.1982.

MOST CAPPED PLAYER
Wilf Mannion (England) 26, 1946-51.

BEST PERFORMANCES

League: 1986-87: Matches played 46, Won 28, Drawn 11, Lost 8, Goals for 67, Goals against 30, Points 94. Second in Division 3.
Highest Position: Third in Division 1, 1913-14.
F.A. Cup: 6th round in 1935-36, 1946-47, 1969-70, 1976-77.
Most recent success: 1980-81: 3rd Round Swansea City 5-0; 4th Round West Bromwich Albion 1-0; 5th Round Barnsley 2-1; 6th Round Wolverhampton Wanderers 1-1,1-3.
League Cup: Semi-final in 1975-76.
Most recent success: 1991-92: 2nd Round Bournemouth 1-1,2-1; 3rd Round Barnsley 1-0; 4th Round Manchester City 2-1; 5th Round Peterborough Utd 0-0,1-0; Semi-final Manchester United 0-0,1-2.

ADDITIONAL INFORMATION
PREVIOUS NAMES
None.

PREVIOUS LEAGUES
Northern League 1889-1899.

Club colours: Red shirts/white trim, white shorts/red trim, white socks.
Change colours: Blue/black shirts, blue shorts, blue/black socks.

Reserves League: Pontins Central League Division 2.

DIVISIONAL RECORD

	Played	Won	Drawn	Lost	For	Against	Points
Division 1/P	1,906	664	456	786	2,832	3,047	1,812
Division 2/1	1,510	624	367	519	2,389	2,053	1,779
Division 3	92	51	19	22	154	94	149
Total	3,508	1,439	842	1,327	5,375	6,194	3,740

RECORDS AND STATISTICS

COMPETITIONS

DIVISION 1/P	DIVISION 2/1	DIVISION 3
1902-24	1899-02	1966-67
1927-28	1924-27	1986-87
1929-54	1928-29	
1974-82	1954-66	
1988-89	1967-74	
1992-93	1982-86	
1995-	1987-88	
	1989-92	
	1993-95	

HONOURS

DIVISION 2/1	ANGLO/SCOT	AMATEUR CUP
1926-27	1975-76	1895
1928-29		1898
1973-74		
1994-95		

MOST GOALS IN A CAREER

GEORGE CAMSELL - 345 (1925-39)

YEAR	LEAGUE	FA CUP
1925-26	3	
1926-27	59	4
1927-28	33	4
1928-29	30	3
1929-30	29	2
1930-31	32	
1931-32	20	
1932-33	17	1
1933-34	23	1
1934-35	14	
1935-36	28	4
1936-37	18	
1937-38	9	1
1938-39	10	
Total	**325**	**20**

Current leading goalscorer: Paul Wilkinson - 67 (1991-95)

MOST APPEARANCES

TIM WILLIAMSON 602 (1902-23)

YEAR	LEAGUE	FA CUP
1901-02	2	
1902-03	16	
1903-04	34	4
1904-05	33	2
1905-06	34	5
1906-07	38	2
1907-08	37	1
1908-09	38	1
1909-10	38	2
1910-11	36	4
1911-12	36	4
1912-13	37	4
1913-14	29	1
1914-15	20	2
1919-20	37	2
1920-21	42	1
1921-22	26	1
1922-23	30	3
	563	**39**

MANAGERS

NAME	SEASONS	BEST	WORST
Peter McWilliam	1927-34	7(1)	1(2)
Wilf Gillow	1934-44	4(1)	20(1)
David Jack	1944-52	6(1)	19(1)
Walter Rowley	1952-54	13(1)	21(1)
Bob Dennison	1954-63	4(2)	14(2)
Raich Carter	1963-66	10(2)	21(2)
Stan Anderson	1966-73	4(2)	2(3)
Jack Charlton	1973-77	7(1)	1(2)
John Neal	1977-81	9(1)	14(1)
Bobby Murdoch	1981-82	22(1)	22(1)
Malcolm Allison	1982-84	16(2)	17(2)
Willie Maddren	1984-86	19(2)	21(2)
Bruce Rioch	1986-90	18(1)	2(3)
Colin Todd	1990-91	7(2)	21(2)
Lennie Lawrence	1991-94	21(1/P)	9(2/1)
Bryan Robson	1994-	1(2/1)	1(2/1)

RECORD TRANSFER FEE RECEIVED

AMOUNT	CLUB	PLAYER	DATE
£2,300,000	Manchester Utd	Gary Pallister	8/89
£600,000	Southampton	David Armstrong	8/81
£575,000	Liverpool	Craig Johnston	4/81
£482,322	W.B.A.	David Mills	1/79

RECORD TRANSFER FEE PAID

AMOUNT	CLUB	PLAYER	DATE
£5,250,000	Tottenham H.	Nick Barmby	8/95
£1,300,000	Swindon Town	Jan-Aage Fjortoft	03/95
£1,000,000	Aston Villa	Neil Cox	7/94
£900,000	Celtic	Derek Whyte	8/92

LONGEST LEAGUE RUNS

of undefeated matches:	24 (8.9.1973 - 9.1.1974)	of league matches w/out a win:	19 (3.10.1981 - 6.3.1982)
of undefeated home matches:	27 (8.2.1935 - 10.4.1937)	of undefeated away matches:	14 (14.4.1973 - 12.1.1974)
without home win:	10 (10.11.1984 - 2.3.1985)	without an away win:	33 (7.3.1903 - 7.9.1907)
of league wins:	9 (16.2.1974 - 6.4.1974)	of home wins:	11 (22.11.1913 - 22.4.1914)
of league defeats:	8 (25.8.1954 - 2.10.1954)	of away wins:	5 (18.2.1974 - 30.3.1974, 21.3.1987 - 9.5.1987)

MIDDLESBROUGH

PLAYERS NAME Honours	Ht	Wt	Birthdate	Birthplace Transfers	Contract Date	Clubs	League	L/Cup	FA Cup	Other	Lge	L/C	FAC	Oth
G O A L K E E P E R S														
Alan J Miller	6.2	13.8	29.03.70	Epping	05.05.88	Arsenal (T)	6+2							
E: u21.4, S; GMFAS; FAYC'88; ECWC'94				Loan	24.11.88	Plymouth Argyle	13		2]					
				Loan	15.08.91	West Bromwich A.	3							
				Loan	19.12.91	Birmingham City	15			1				
				£500,000	12.08.94	Middlesbrough	41	1	2	2				
Ben J Roberts	6.0	12.6	22.06.75	Bishop Auck.	24.03.93	Middlesbrough (T)				1				
Gary Walsh	6.3	14.0	21.03.68	Wigan	25.04.85	Manchester Utd (J)	49+1	7		6				
E: u21.2; ECWC'91; ESC'91; FAC'94				Loan	11.08.88	Airdrie	3	1						
				Loan	19.11.93	Oldham Athletic	6							
				£250,000	08.95	Middlesbrough								
D E F E N D E R S														
Vivian A Anderson	6.0	11.1	29.08.56	Nottingham	01.08.74	Nottingham F. (A)	323+5	39	23+1	33	15	5	1	
E: 50, u21.1, B.7; ASC'77; Div1'78;				£250,000	03.08.84	Arsenal	120	18	12		9	3	3	
EC'79'80; ESC'79; LC'78; CS'78				£250,000	09.07.87	Manchester United	50+4	6+1	7	2	2	1	1	
				Free	10.01.91	Sheffield Wed.	60+10	9	8+2	5	8	1	2	2
				Free	01.07.93	Barnsley	20	2			3			
				Free	23.07.93	Middlesbrough	2							
Michael J Barron	5.10	11.3	22.12.74	Salford	02.02.93	Middlesbrough (T)	1+1	1		3+3				
Clayton G Blackmore	5.9	11.3	23.09.64	Neath	28.09.82	Manchester Utd (A)	150+36	23+2	15+6	19	19	3	1	4
W: 38, u21.3, Y; FAC'90; CS'90;				Free	11.07.94	Middlesbrough	26+4	1		1	2			
ECWC'91; ESC'91; Prem'93														
Wesley J Byrne	5.10	11.6	09.02.77	Dublin	24.02.94	Middlesbrough (T)				1				
Neil J Cox	6.0	12.10	08.10.71	Scunthorpe	20.03.90	Scunthorpe Utd (T)	17		4	4+1	1			
E: u21.6; LC'94				£400,000	12.02.91	Aston Villa	26+16	5+2	4+2	2	3		1	
				£1,000,000	19.07.94	Middlesbrough	39+1	2+1		2	1			
Curtis Fleming	5.8	11.4	08.10.68	Manchester		St. Patricks								
Ei: Y, u21.5, u23.1; EiDiv1'90				£50,000	16.08.91	Middlesbrough	101+12	7+2	7	7+1				
Keith J O'Halloran	5.9	12.3	10.11.75	Dublin		Cherry Orchard								
					06.09.94	Middlesbrough	1		1					
Christopher B Morris	5.10	11.6	24.12.63	Newquay	01.10.92	Sheffield Wed.	61+13	5+5	7+5		1	1		
E:S, Ei:35; SPD'88; SFAC'88'89				£125,000		Celtic	154+16	16+1	22	9	8		1	
					01.08.92	Middlesbrough	50+5	6	4	4	1			1
Nigel G Pearson	6.1	12.6	21.08.63	Nottingham		Heanor Town								
LC'91				£5,000	12.11.81	Shrewsbury Town	153	19	6	3	5			
				£250,000	16.10.87	Sheffield Wed.	176+4	17+2	15	10	14	5	1	
				£750,000	19.07.94	Middlesbrough	33		2		3			
Stephen Vickers	6.3	12.0	13.10.67	Bishops Auckland		Spennymoor United								
LDC'90					11.09.85	Tranmere Rovers	310+1	20+1	19	36	11	5	3	1
				£700,000	03.12.93	Middlesbrough	69+1	3	4	2	6			
Richard T Ward			17.11.73	Scarborough	01.02.94	Middlesbrough (T)								
Phil Whelan	6.4	14.1	07.03.72	Stockport	02.07.90	Ipswich Town (J)	64+5	6+1	2+1	1	2			
E: u21.3.				£300,000	12.04.95	Middlesbrough								
Alan White	6.1	13.0	22.03.76	Darlington	08.07.94	Middlesbrough (T)				1				
Derek Whyte	5.11	11.5	31.08.68	Glasgow		Celtic	211+5	18+1	26	15	7			1
S: 6, u21.9, B2, Y; SPD'88; SFAC'88'89					01.08.92	Middlesbrough	112+1	8	1+1	6	2			
M I D F I E L D														
Craig Hignett	5.10	11.0	12.01.70	Prescot		Liverpool (T)								
				Free	11.05.88	Crewe Alexandra	108+13	9+1	11+1	6+1	42	4	8 3	
				£500,000	27.11.92	Middlesbrough	62+14	6+1	2	5+1	17	6		
Graham A Kavanagh	5.9	11.5	02.12.73	Dublin		Home Farm								
Ei: Y, u21.5					16.08.91	Middlesbrough	16+12	1	3+1	7	2		1	
				Loan	25.02.94	Darlington	5							
Craig Liddle	5.11	12.0	21.10.71	Chester Le Street		Blyth Spartans								
				Free	12.07.94	Middlesbrough	1			2				
Stephen McGargle			24.10.75	Gateshead	01.04.94	Middlesbrough (T)								
Robbie Mustoe	5.11	11.6	28.08.68	Witney	02.07.86	Oxford United (J)	78+13	2	2	3	10			
				£375,000	05.07.90	Middlesbrough	150+9	21+1	10	12+1	12	6		1
Jamie Pollock	6.0	11.2	16.02.74	Stockton	18.12.91	Middlesbrough (T)	113+11	11+2	10+1	4+1	17	1		
E: Y8														
Bryan Robson	5.10	12.12	11.01.57	Witton Gilbert	01.08.74	West Brom. A. (A)	193+4	17+1	10+2	12	39	2	2	3
E: 90, u21.7; B.3; Y; Flg.3, CS'83'93				£1,500,000	05.10.81	Manchester United	326+19	50+1	33+2	32+2	74	5 10	11	
FAC'83'85'90; ECWC'91; Prem'93'94				Free	01.05.94	Middlesbrough	21+1				1			
Philip L Stamp	5.9	11.9	12.12.75	Middlesboro'	04.02.93	Middlesbrough (T)	9+4	2	1	5+1				
E: u18.4														
F O R W A R D S														
Nick Barmby	5.6	11.0	11.02.74	Hull	09.04.91	Tottenham H. (T)	81+6	7+1	12+1		20	2	5	
E: u21.1, S, Y.8.				£5,250,000	08.95	Middlesbrough								

Player				Fee	Date	Club								
Jan A Fjortoft	6.0	12.8	10.01.67			Aaesund, Norway	Rapid Vienna							
				£500,000	29.07.93	Swindon Town	62+10	9	3+1	1+1	27	9	2	
				£1,300,000	31.03.95	Middlesbrough	8				3			
Christopher Freestone	5.11	11.7	04.09.71			Nottingham	Arnold Town							
				£10,000	02.12.94	Middlesbrough	0+1							
John G Hendrie	5.7	11.12	24.10.63			Lennoxtown	18.05.81 Coventry City (A)	15+8	2			2			
S: Y; Div 3'85; Div2'90				Loan	10.01.84	Hereford United	6							
				Free	02.07.84	Bradford City	173	17	11	11	46	3	6	4
				£500,000	17.06.88	Newcastle United	34	2	4	3	4	1		
				£600,000	20.06.89	Leeds United	22+5	1	1	2	5			
				£550,000	05.07.90	Middlesbrough	174+5	20	10+2	6	43	6	2	4
Alan Moore	5.10	10.7	25.11.74			Dublin	05.12.91 Middlesbrough (T)	77+4	6	1+1	3+1	14	1	2	
Ei: Y														
Jaime Moreno	5.9	11.09	19.01.74			Bolivia	Blooming							
Bolivian Int.				£250,000	20.09.94	Middlesbrough	6+8	1		3	2			1
Paul Wilkinson	6.0	11.9	30.10.69			Louth	08.11.82 Grimsby Town (A)	69+2	10	4+2		27	5	1	
E: u21.4; CS'86; Div'87				£250,000	28.03.85	Everton	19+12	3+1	3	6+2	6	7	1	1
				£200,000	26.03.87	Nottingham Forest	32+2	3	4+1	1	5	1	2	
				£300,000	16.08.88	Watford	133+1	4	8+1	8	52	1		3
				£550,000	16.08.91	Middlesbrough	159+4	16	11	5+1	53	8	5	4

TOP GOALSCORER 1994/95
John Hendrie

Division One goals (games) . . . . 15 (27+4)
Coca-Cola Cup Goals 1 (3)
F.A. Cup goals 1 (2)
Anglo Italian Cup . . . . 0 (0+1)
Total . . . . 17 (32+5)

Total goals for Middlesbrough since 05.07.90 . . . . 56 (201+10)

Career total as at June 1st 1995 . . . . 127 (505+21)

THE MANAGER
BRYAN ROBSON

Date of Birth . . . . 11th January 1957.
Place of Birth . . . . Witton Gilbert.
Date of Appointment . . . . May 1994.

PREVIOUS CLUBS
As Manager. . . . . None.
As Coach. . . . . None.
As a Player. . . . . West Bromwich Albion, Manchester United.

HONOURS
As a Manager
Middlesbrough: Division 1 championship 1994-95.

As a Player
Manchester United: Premiership championship 1992-93, 1993-94. FA Cup 1983, 1985, 1990.
ECWC 1991.
Charity Shield 1983. Flg. XI.3.
International: 90 full caps, 7 U21, 3 'B' and Youth for England. (Currently England first team Coach).

CELLNET RIVERSIDE STADIUM
Middlesbrough, Cleveland, TS3 6RS
Tel: 01642 227 227

Capacity..30,000.

First game...v Chelsea (2-1), Premier League, 26.08.1995.
First floodlit game ....v Southampton (0-0), Premier League, 12.09.1995.
ATTENDANCES
Highest ....Not yet known.
Lowest ....Not yet known.

OTHER GROUNDS....................................Old Archery Ground 1876-79. Breckon HIll Road 1879-80.
....Linthorpe Road 1880-1903. Ayresome Park 1903-1995.

MATCHDAY TICKET PRICES

Adults . . . . £10.00 - £15.00

Juniors/OAP . . . . £6.00 - £10.00

CLUBCALL
0891 12 11 81
Calls cost 39p per minute cheap rate and 49p per
minute at all other times.
Call costings correct at time of going to press.

HOW TO GET TO THE GROUND
From the North & South
Use A19 (sign posted Middlesbrough) until it's junction with A66.
Continue only A66 through Middlesbrough. At the first roundabout
turn left. Cross the railway for Middlesbrough FC.

From the West
Use A66 trhough Middlesbrough. At the first roundabout turn left.
Cross the railway for MIddlesbrough FC.

MATCHDAY PROGRAMME

Programme Editor . . . . Dave Allan.

Number of pages . . . . 40.

Price . . . . £1.30.

Subscriptions . . . . £28 home, £62 home & away (League only).

Local Newspapers . . . . Evening Gazette, Northern Echo,
. . . . Hartlepool Mail.

Local Radio Stations . . . . BBC Radio Cleveland, TFM.

NEWCASTLE UNITED
(The Magpies)
F.A. CARLING PREMIERSHIP
SPONSORED BY: NEWCASTLE BREWERIES LTD

Back row L-R: Chris Holland, Nicos Papavasiliou, Alan Neilson, Nathan Murray,Stephen Harper, Mike Jeffrey, Alex Mathie, Jason Drysdale, Malcolm Allen. **Middle Row:** Paul Ferros (assistant physio), Derek Fazakerley (first team coach),Scott Sellers, Lee Clark, Steve Howey, Mike Hooper, Steve Watson, PavelSrnicek, Philippe Albert, Marc Hottiger, Steve Guppy, Bob elliott, Jeff Clark(reserve team coach), Derek Wright (physio). **Front Row:** Barry Venison, JohnBeresford, Andy Cole, Peter Beardsley, Terry McDermott (asst.manager), KevinKeegan (manager), Arthur Cox (coach), Paul Bracewell, Ruel Fox, Robert Lee,Darren Peacock.

NEWCASTLE UNITED
FORMED IN 1892
TURNED PROFESSIONAL IN 1892
LTD COMPANY IN 1895

PRESIDENT: Trevor Bennett
CHAIRMAN: Sir John Hall

DIRECTORS
Douglas Hall, R S Jones
Freddie Shepherd (Vice-chairman)
CHIEF EXECUTIVE
Freddie Fletcher
GENERAL MANAGER/SECRETARY
Russell Cushing
COMMERCIAL MANAGER
Trevor Garwood (0191 232 0406)

MANAGER: Kevin Keegan
ASSISTANT MANAGER: Terry McDermott

PHYSIOTHERAPIST
Derek Wright/Paul Ferris

STATISTICIAN FOR THE DIRECTORY
Dave Graham & David Stewart

The season approached with the expectations high, with the side hoping to improve on the previous season's third placing. The manager had also strengthened the squad with the signing of Internationals Philippe Albert and Marc Hottiger.

The side got off to a magnificent start with nine wins and two draws in the first eleven league matches. Progress was also made in the UEFA Cup with a 10-2 aggregate victory over Royal Antwerp of Belgium and in the Coca-cola Cup where Barnsley and a much weakened Manchester United were overcome.

The first defeat of the season came in the league at Manchester United, closely followed by elimination from the UEFA Cup, where after building up a three goal lead at home to Atletico Bilbao they allowed the visitors to snatch two late goals, then lost the away leg 1-0 to go out on the away goals rule.

The strength of the squad was also being severely tested, with Beardsley, Venison, Bracewell, Clark, Elliot, Cole and Sellars all missing games, in fact Sellars was ruled out for the season with a knee problem. The injuries were undoubtedly affecting performances with only one victory in eight league games leading up to the new year, although the side was still in fourth place in the league.

Elimination from the Coca-cola Cup followed when after a much weakened side managed a magnificent draw at Manchester City, the replay was disappointingly lost 2-0 at St James Park.

On New Year's Eve the injury jinx struck again when Philippe Albert was ruled out for the rest of the season after injuring his knee in training. The new year was only two weeks old when the transfer that was to rock football unfolded, Andy Cole was sensationally sold to Manchester United with the talented Keith Gillespie joining the club in a package deal worth £7M. Manager Kevin Keegan was convinced that the deal would prove to be the right one for the future benefit of the club.

The side made progress in the FAC starting with prized scalp of Blackburn Rovers who were defeated in a replay at Ewood Park by 2-1 after a 1-1 draw at St James' Park. Home victories in the competition followed over Swansea City 3-0 and Manchester City 3-1, before losing 1-0 to Everton in the Quarter Final.

The club still had high hopes of qualifying for Europe, and third place in the league was held mainly due to six successive home victories over Wimbledon, Everton, Nottingham Forest, Aston Villa, Arsenal and Norwich City, but Leeds United gained a crucial Easter victory at St James' Park by 2-1. The side eventually finished in sixth place, so losing out on a European spot.

Kevin Keegan is determined to bring a major trophy to the club and has spent £14M on new players in the close season, with Les Ferdinand, David Ginola, Warren Barton and Shaka Hislop arriving at the club. A new sponsorship deal has also been agreed with sports giants Adidas.

These are exciting times at Newcastle with management and fans alike eagerly looking to the new season.

NEWCASTLE UNITED

Premier League: 6th   **FA Cup:** 6th Round   **Coca-Cola Cup:** 4th Round

M	DATE	COMP.	VEN	OPPONENTS	RESULT	H/T	LP	GOAL SCORERS/GOAL TIMES	ATT.
1	A 21	PL	A	Leicester City	W 3-1	0-0		Cole 51, Beardsley 58, Elliott 74	(20,048)
2	24	PL	H	Coventry City	W 4-0	3-0	1	Lee 21, 34, Watson 26, Cole 73	34,163
3	27	PL	H	Southampton	W 5-1	3-0	1	Watson 30, 37, Cole 40, 70, Lee 85	34,181
4	31	PL	A	West Ham United	W 3-1	2-0	1	Potts 32 (og), Lee 35, Mathie 88	(18,580)
5	S 10	PL	H	Chelsea	W 4-2	2-2	1	Cole 7, 66, Fox 21, Lee 53	34,435
6	13	UEFA 1/1	A	Royal Antwerp	W 5-0	3-0		Lee 1, 9, 51, Sellars 39, Watson 78	(19,700)
7	18	PL	A	Arsenal	W 3-2	2-1		Beardsley 7, 45 (pen), Fox 74	(36,819)
8	21	CC2/1	H	Barnsley	W 2-1	1-1		Cole 25, Fox 85	27,208
9	24	PL	H	Liverpool	D 1-1	0-0	1	Lee 50	34,435
10	27	UEFA 1/2	H	Royal Antwerp	W 5-2	4-0		Lee 11, Cole 26, 39, 88 Beardsley 36 (pen)	31,383
11	O 1	PL	A	Aston Villa	W 2-0	0-0	1	Lee 66, Cole 83	(29,960)
12	5	CC 2/2	A	Barnsley	W 1-0	1-0		Cole 41	(10,992)
13	9	PL	H	Blackburn Rovers	D 1-1	0-0	1	Flowers 88 (og)	34,344
14	15	PL	A	Crystal Palace	W 1-0	0-0	1	Beardsley 89	(17,760)
15	18	UEFA 2/1	H	Athletic Bilbao	W 3-2	2-0		Fox 9, Beardsley 33 (pen) Cole 56	32,440
16	22	PL	H	Sheffield Wednesday	W 2-1	2-0	1	Watson 35, Cole 37	34,408
17	26	CC3	H	Manchester United	W 2-0	0-0		Albert 82, Kitson 87	34,178
18	29	PL	A	Manchester United	L 0-2	0-1	1		(43,795)
19	N 1	UEFA 2/2	A	Athletic Bilbao	L 0-1	0-0			(47,000)
20	5	PL	H	Queens Park Rangers	W 2-1	2-0	1	Kitson 20, Beardsley 42	34,278
21	7	PL	A	Nottingham Forest	D 0-0	0-0	1		(22,110)
22	19	PL	A	Wimbledon	L 2-3	2-3	3	Beardsley 30, Kitson 32	(14,203)
23	26	PL	H	Ipswich Town	D 1-1	0-0	3	Cole 86	34,459
24	30	CC 4	A	Manchester City	D 1-1	1-0		Jeffrey 11	(25,162)
25	D 3	PL	A	Tottenham Hotspur	L 2-4	2-2	3	Fox 30, 42	(28,002)
26	10	PL	H	Leicester City	W 3-1	1-0	3	Albert 32, 70, Howey 50	34,400
27	17	PL	A	Coventry City	D 0-0	0-0	3		(17,233)
28	21	CC 4R	H	Manchester City	L 0-2	0-1			31,056
29	26	PL	A	Leeds United	D 0-0	0-0	3		(39,337)
30	31	PL	A	Norwich City	L 1-2	1-2	4	Fox 40 (pen)	(22,172)
31	J 2	PL	H	Manchester City	D 0-0	0-0	5		34,437
32	8	FAC3	H	Blackburn Rovers	D 1-1	0-1		Lee 57	31,721
33	15	PL	H	Manchester City	D 1-1	0-1	5	Kitson 68	34,471
34	18	FAC 3R	A	Blackburn Rovers	W 2-0	0-0		Hottiger 57, Clark 85	(22,658)
35	21	PL	A	Sheffield Wednesday	D 0-0	0-0	4		(31,215)
36	25	PL	H	Wimbledon	W 2-1	1-0	4	Fox 34, Kitson 51	34,374
37	28	FAC 4	H	Swansea City	W 3-0	1-0		Kitson 41, 46, 72	34,372
38	F 1	PL	H	Everton	W 2-0	0-0	3	Fox 74, Beardsley 80 (pen)	34,465
39	4	PL	A	Queens Park Rangers	L 0-3	0-3	3		(16,576)
40	11	PL	H	Nottingham Forest	W 2-1	0-0	3	Fox 47, Lee 73	34,471
41	19	FAC 5	H	Manchester City	W 3-1	2-1		Gillespie 18, 64, Beresford 35	33,219
42	25	PL	H	Aston Villa	W 3-1	1-1	3	Venison 31, Beardsley 55, 66	34,687
43	28	PL	A	Ipswich Town	W 2-0	2-0	3	Fox 12, Kitson 38	(18,639)
44	M 4	PL	A	Liverpool	L 0-2	0-0	3		(39,300)
45	8	PL	H	West Ham United	W 2-0	1-0	3	Clark 17, Kitson 52	(34,595)
46	12	FAC 6	A	Everton	L 0-1	0-0			(35,203)
47	19	PL	H	Arsenal	W 1-0	0-0	3	Beardsley 89	35,611
48	22	PL	H	Southampton	L 1-3	1-0	3	Kitson 10	(14,676)
49	A 1	PL	A	Chelsea	D 1-1	0-1	3	Hottiger 88	(22,987)
50	8	PL	H	Norwich City	W 3-0	2-0	3	Beardsley 8 (pen), 42, Kitson 74	35,518
51	14	PL	A	Everton	L 0-2	0-1	4		(34,811)
52	17	PL	H	Leeds United	L 1-2	1-2	5	Elliott 30	35,626
53	29	PL	A	Manchester City	D 0-0	0-0	5		(27,389)
54	M 3	PL	A	Tottenham Hotspur	D 3-3	2-3	5	Gillespie 7, Peacock 10, Beardsley 70	35,603
55	8	PL	A	Blackburn Rovers	L 0-1	0-1	5		(30,545)
56	14	PL	H	Crystal Palace	W 3-2	3-0	6	Fox 6, Lee 26, Gillespie 28	35,626
57									
58									
59									
60									

Best Home League Attendance: 35,626 v Leeds United   **Smallest:** 34,163 v Coventry City   **Av Home Att:** 34,692

Goal Scorers: Compared with 1993-94: +1,013

League (67): Beardsley 13 (3 pens), Fox 10 (1 pen), Lee 9, Cole 9, Kitson 8, Watson 4, Gillespie 2, Albert 2, Elliott 2, Opponents 2, Peacock, Hottiger, Clark, Venison, Howey, Mathie
C/Cola Cup (6): Cole 2, Fox, Albert, Kitson, Jeffrey
FA Cup (9): Kitson 3, Gillespie 2, Lee, Hottiger, Clark, Beresford
UEFA Cup (13): Lee 4, Cole 4, Beardsley 2 (2 pens), Fox, Watson, Sellars

1	2	3	4	5	6	7	8	10	12	15	18	19	26	28	11	27	30	18	21	23	16	31	20	9	14	Referee	
Srnicek	Venison	Beresford	Bracewell	Fox	Howey	Lee	Beardsley	Clark	Hottiger	Peacock	Gillespie	Watson	Elliott	Kitson	Sellars	Albert	Hooper	Guppy	Allen	Holland	Drysdale	Jeffrey	Neilson	Cole	Mathie		
X†	X	X		X		X	X2		X	X			S1		X1	X	S3							X	S2	Reed M.	1
X	X	X		X		X			X	X		X2	S1		X1	X	S							X	S2	Danson P.	2
X	X	X	X1			X			X	X		X	S2		X2	X	S							X	S1	Elleray D.	3
X	X	X			S	X1			X	X		X	S1		X	X	S							X	X	Hill B.	4
	X	X		S	S	X			X	X		X			X	X	X							X	S	Jones P.	5
X	X		X	S	S	X	X2		X	X		S2	S		X	X	S					S1		X1		Wojckik R.	6
X		X		X	X	X	X		X	X		S			X	X	S							X	S	Holbrook T.	7
X		X		X	X	X	X		X	X		S1			X1	X2	S							X	S2	Hart R.	8
X	X1	X		X	S1	X	X		X	X		S2			X2	X†	S							X		Don P.	9
X		X		X	X	X2	X1	S1	X	X		S2			X	X	S	S		S				X		Pederson R.	10
X		X		X	X	X	X1		X	X		S		S1	X	X	S							X		Gallagher D.	11
X		X		X		X		X	X	X		S			X1	X	X	S						X	S1	Lynch K.	12
X		X		X	X	X1	X		X	S	X		X	S1		X1	X	S						X		Lodge S.	13
X		X		X	X		X	S		X		X		X	X	X	S				S		X		S2	Morton K.	14
X		X		X	X		X	S		X		X		X1	X	X	S	S1						X		Krug H.	15
X		X		X		X		X	S	X	X		X		X	X	S							X	S	Poll G.	16
X		X			X		X	S	X	X		X		X	X	X	S	S1						X1		Holbrook T.	17
X		X	X1	X		X	X	S2	X2	X		X			X	X	S							S1		Worrall J.	18
X		X	X2	X	X	X	S1	X	X			X			X1	X	S	S			S	S2				Amendolia A.	19
X		X		X	X	X	X	X	X			X			X		X	S					S			Ashby G.	20
X	X	X		X	X	X	X	X	S2	X	X2	S1		X1		X	S						S		S	Burge K.	21
X	X	X		X	X	X2		S1	X			X			X1		S									Don P.	22
X	X	X		X	X		X	X	X			X					S			S	S	X	X	X	S2	Cooper K.	23
X	X	X		X			X	S	X	X		X					S			S	S	X	X	X	X	Worrall J.	24
X	X	X		X		X		X	S	X	X		X			X	S						X	X	S	Gallagher D.	25
X	X	X	S	X	X		X	X1	S1	X	X		X			X	S							X		Willard G.	26
X	X	X	S1	X			X	X1	S1	X	X		X		X		S					S	X			Danson P.	27
X	X	X	X	X		X		S		S		X		X		X	S							X		Reed M.	28
X	X	X	X	X	X	X	X		S1	S	X	X1			X		S							X		Worrall J.	29
X	X	X	X	X	X	X	X		S1	S	X	X		S	X1		S							X		Hill B.	30
	X	X	X	X	X	X	X			X			S	X1	S1		S							X		Wilkie A.	31
X	X	X		X	X	X		X	X			S	X	X		X	S									Gallagher D.	32
X	X	X	S	X	X	X		X	X			S	X	X		X	S							S		Lodge S.	33
X	X	X	S	X	X			X	X			S	X	X		X	S									Gallagher D.	34
X	X		S	X	X	X1	X	X	X	S1			X	X			S									Gifford R.	35
X	X		X	X	X		X	S	X	X	X	S	X	X		X	S									Reed M.	36
X	X		X	X	X		X		X	X	X	S	X	X		X	S							S		Hill B.	37
	X		X	X		X	X	S1	X		X	S	X1			X						X		X		Elleray D.	38
	X			X	X	X		X	X	X	X1		X	X		X				S		X		S1		Cooper K.	39
X	X	X	S1	X	X	X	X		X	X	X1	S		X		X	S									Morton K.	40
X	X	X	S	X	X	X	X		X	X	X	S		X		X	S									Ashby G.	41
X	X	X	S	X	X	X	X		X	X	X	S		X		X	S									Don P.	42
X	X	X	S	X	X	X	X		X	X	X	S		X		X	S									Ashby G.	43
X	X	X	S2	X2	X	X	X1		X	X	X	S1		X		X	S									Jones P.	44
X	X	X	S2	X	X2		X		X	X	X	S1		X1		X	S									Holbrook T.	45
X	X	X1	X	X		X		X	X2	X	X	S2	S1	X		X	S									Cooper K.	46
X	X		X	X		X1	X	S1	X	X		S	X	X	X			S								Willard G.	47
X	X		S	X	X	X	X		X	X	X	S	X	X			S									Worrall J.	48
X	X		X	X	X	X2	X	S2	X	X		S1	X	X1			S						S			Bodenham M.	49
X	X		X	X	X	X		X	X			S	X	X			S						S			Reed M.	50
	X		X	X1	X	X†	X	S2	X2	X	S1		X	X			X							S1		Gifford R.	51
X		X	X	X	X	X	X	X	X	X	X		X1	X			S		S					S		Danson P.	52
X		X	X	X	X	X	X	X	X	X	X	X					S		S					X		Poll G.	53
X†		X	X1	X2	X	X	X	X	X	X	X	X					S2		S1							Gallagher D.	54
X		X		X	X	X	X	X	X	X	X						S		S				S			Don P.	55
X		X		X	X	X	X	X	X	X	X	X					S		S				S			Ashby G.	56
38	28	33	13	40	29	35	34	9	38	35	15	22	10	24	12	17	4						5	18	3	League Appearances	
			3		1			10			2	5	4	2		2							1		6	League Sub Appearances	
5	2	5	0+1	2	3	2	3	3	5	4		3+1		3	3	4		0+1				1	1	5	1+2	C/Cola Cup Appearances	
5	5	4	3	5	4	4	3	2	4	5	3	0+1	3+1	4+1										1		FA Cup Appearances	
4	1	4		4	3	3	4	1+2	4	4		1+2		4	4						0+2		3			UEFACup Appearances	

Also Played: Burridge S(5), Harper S(38,39,51)   † = Sent Off

NEWCASTLE UNITED

CLUB RECORDS

BIGGEST VICTORIES
League: 13-0 v Newport County, Division 2, 5.10.1946 (joint record).
F.A. Cup: 9-0 v Southport, 4th Round, 1.2.1932.
League Cup: 7-1 v Notts County (A), 2nd Round, 5.10.1993.
Europe: 5-0 v Antwerp (h), (UEFA) 1st Round 1st leg, 13.9.1994.
(2nd leg United won 5-2, 27.9.1994)
5-1 v Vittoria Setubal (UEFA) 12.3.1969.
4-0 v Bohemians (UEFA) 28.9.1977.
4-0 v Feyenoord (UEFA) 1st Round, 11.9.1968.

BIGGEST DEFEATS
League: 0-9 v Burton Wanderers, Division 2, 15.4.1895.
F.A. Cup: 1-7 v Aston Villa, 2nd Round, 16.2.1895.
League Cup: 2-7 v Manchester United, 4th Round, 27.10.1976.
Europe: No more than 2 goals difference.

MOST POINTS
3 points a win: 96, Division 1, 1992-93 (46 games).
2 points a win: 57, Division 2, 1964-65.

MOST GOALS SCORED
98, Division 1, 1951-52.
G.Robledo 33, Milburn 25, Mitchell 9, Foulkes 6, Davies 5, Hannah 5, Duncan 3, Keeble 3, Prior 2, Walker 2, Brennan 1, Crowe 1, Harvey 1, Taylor 1, Opponents 1.

MOST GOALS CONCEDED
109, Division 1, 1960-61.

MOST FIRST CLASS MATCHES IN A SEASON
63 - 1973-74 (League 42, FA Cup 10, League Cup 3, Texaco Cup 8).

MOST LEAGUE WINS
29, Division 1, 1992-93.

MOST LEAGUE DRAWS
17, Division 2, 1990-91.

MOST LEAGUE DEFEATS
26, Division 1, 1977-78.

INDIVIDUAL CLUB RECORDS

MOST GOALS IN A SEASON
Andy Cole: 41 goals in 1993-94 (League 34, FA Cup 1, League Cup 6).

MOST GOALS IN A MATCH
6. L Shackleton v Newport, Division 2, 13-0, 5.10.1946.

OLDEST PLAYER
William Hampson, 44 years 225 days v Birmingham City, Division 1, 9.4.1927.

YOUNGEST PLAYER
Stephen Watson, 16 years 223 days v Wolverhampton Wders., Division 2, 10.11.1990.

MOST CAPPED PLAYER
Alf McMichael (Northern Ireland) 40.

BEST PERFORMANCES

League: 1992-93: Matches played 46, Won 29, Drawn 9, LOst 8, Goals for 92, Goals against 38, Points 96. First in Division 2/1.
Highest Position: Division 1 champions four times.
F.A. Cup: Winners in 1909-10, 1923-24, 1931-32, 1950-51, 1951-52.
Most recent success: 1954-55: 3rd Round Plymouth 1-0; 4th Round Brentford 3-2; 5th Round Nottingham Forest 1-1,2-2,2-1; 6th Round Huddersfield 1-1,2-0; Semi-final York City 1-1,2-0; Final Manchester City 3-1.
League Cup: 1975-76: 2nd Round Southport 6-0; 3rd Round Bristol Rovers 1-1,2-0; 4th Round Queens Park Rangers 3-1; 5th Round Notts County 1-0; Semi-final Tottenham 0-1,3-1; Final Manchester City 1-2.
Europe: (UEFA) 1968-69: 1st Round Feyenoord 4-0,0-2; 2nd Round Sporting Lisbon 1-1,1-0; 3rd Round Real Zaragossa 2-3,2-1; 4th Round Vittoria Setubal 5-1,1-3; Semi-final Rangers 0-0,2-0; Final Ujpest Dozsa 3-0,3-2.

DIVISIONAL RECORD

	Played	Won	Drawn	Lost	For	Against	Points
Division 1/P	2,628	1,034	626	968	4,104	3,862	2,800
Division 2/1	1,046	481	218	347	1,798	1,438	1,318
Total	3,674	1,515	844	1,315	5,902	5,300	4,118

ADDITIONAL INFORMATION
PREVIOUS NAMES
Newcastle East End 1882-92.

PREVIOUS LEAGUES
Northern League.

Club colours: Black/white striped shirts, black shorts, black socks/white tops.

Change colours: Red/blue hoops, white shorts, red with blue hooped shorts.

Reserves League: Pontins Central League Division 1.

RECORDS AND STATISTICS

COMPETITIONS

Div 1/P	Div.2/1	UEFA	A/Ital	A/Scot	Texaco
1898-1934	1893-98	1968-69	1972-73	1975-76	1971-72
1948-61	1934-48	1969-70		1976-77	1972-73
1965-78	1961-65	1970-71			1973-74
1984-89	1978-84	1977-78			1974-75
1993-	1989-93	1994-95			

HONOURS

Div.1	Div 2/1	FAC	UEFA	A/Ital	C/Shield
1904-05	1964-65	1909-10	1968-69	1972-73	1907
1906-07	1992-93	1923-24			1909
1908-09		1931-32		Texaco	
1926-27		1950-51		1973-74	
		1951-52		1974-75	
		1954-55			

MOST APPEARANCES

JIM LAWRENCE 496 (1904-22)

Year	League	FA Cup
1904-05	29	8
1905-06	33	8
1906-07	33	1
1907-08	38	6
1908-09	38	7
1909-10	34	8
1910-11	36	8
1911-12	27	
1912-13	34	8
1913-14	21	
1914-15	31	5
1919-20	20	1
1920-21	42	4
1921-22	16	
	432	64

MOST GOALS IN A CAREER

JACKIE MILBURN - 200 (1946-57)

Year	League	FA Cup
1945-46		2
1946-47	7	1
1947-48	20	
1948-49	19	
1949-50	18	3
1950-51	17	8
1951-52	25	3
1952-53	5	
1953-54	16	2
1954-55	19	2
1955-56	19	2
1956-57	12	
Total	177	23

Current leading goalscorer: Peter Beardsley - 100 (1983-87, 1993-95)

RECORD TRANSFER FEE RECEIVED

Amount	Club	Player	Date
£7,000,000*	Manchester Utd	Andy Cole	1/95
£2,300,000	Tottenham	Paul Gascoigne	7/88
£1,900,000	Liverpool	Peter Beardsley	7/87
£1,250,000	Chelsea	Gavin Peacock	7/93

*Included Keith Gillespie signing for Newcastle (valued at £1m)

RECORD TRANSFER FEE PAID

Amount	Club	Player	Date
£6,000,000	Q.P.R.	Les Ferdinand	06/95
£4,000,000	Wimbledon	Warren Barton	06/95
£2,700,000	Q.P.R.	Darren Peacock	3/94
£2,250,000	Norwich City	Ruel Fox	2/94

MANAGERS

Name	Seasons	Best	Worst
A Cunningham	1930-35	5(1)	6(2)
T Mather	1935-39	4(2)	19(2)
S Seymour	1939-47	5(2)	5(2)
G Martin	1947-50	*3(1)	2(2)
S Seymour	1950-54	4(1)	16(1)
D Livingstone	1954-56	*5(1)	8(1)
C Mitten	1958-61	8(1)	21(1)
N Smith	1961-62	11(2)	11(2)
J Harvey	1962-75	7(1)	8(2)
G Lee	1975-77	*7(1)	15(1)
R Dinnis	1977	5(1)	*22(1)
W McGarry	1977-80	21(1)	*22(2)
A Cox	1980-84	*3(2)	11(2)
J Charlton	1984-85	14(1)	14(1)
W McFaul	1985-88	11(1)	*19(1)
J Smith	1988-91	20(1)	*11(2)
O Ardiles	1991-92	11(2)	*23(2)
K Keegan	1992-	6(P)	20(2)

*Indicates position when manager left club.

LONGEST LEAGUE RUNS

of undefeated matches:	14 (22.4.1950 - 30.9.1950)	of league matches w/out a win:	21 (14.1.1978 - 23.8.1978)
of undefeated home matches:	31 (9.12.1905 - 12.10.1907)	of undefeated away matches:	10 (16.11.1907 - 23.3.1908)
without home win:	12 (28.12.1977 - 26.8.1978)	without an away win:	18 (4.9.1984 - 20.4.1985)
of league wins:	13 (25.4.1992 - 18.10.1992)	of home wins:	20 (24.4.1906 - 1.4.1907)
of league defeats:	10 (23.8.1977 - 15.10.1977)	of away wins:	6 (2.5.1922 - 18.10.1992)

NEWCASTLE UNITED

PLAYERS NAME / Honours	Ht	Wt	Birthdate	Birthplace / Transfers	Contract Date	Clubs	League	L/Cup	FA Cup	Other	Lge	L/C	FAC	Oth
G O A L K E E P E R S														
Stephen Harper	6.2	13.0	14.03.75	Easington		Seaham Red Star								
				Free	05.07.93	Newcastle United								
Shaka Hislop	6.6	12.0	22.02.69	London	09.09.92	Reading	104	10	3	9				
Div.2'94.				£1,575,000	08.95	Newcastle United								
Michael D Hooper	6.3	13.0	10.02.64	Bristol		Mangotsfield								
CS'86; SC'88				Free	08.11.83	Bristol City	1		1	1				
				Free	08.02.85	Wrexham	34	4						
Loan Leicester C., 21.9.90, 14Lg + 1 Oth App				£40,000	25.10.85	Liverpool	50+1	10	5	6+1				
				£550,000	23.09.93	Newcastle United	23+2	2	3					
Pavel Srnicek	6.4	14.9	10.03.68	Ostrava (Czech)		Banik Ostrava								
Czech: . Div1'93				£350,000	05.02.91	Newcastle United	111	8	9	10				
D E F E N D E R S														
Philippe Albert	6.3	13.7	10.08.67	Bouillon (Belgium)		Anderlecht								
Belgian International				£2,650,000	12.08.94	Newcastle United	17	4		4	2	1		
Warren Barton	6.0	11.0	19.03.69	Stoke Newington		Leyton Orient (T)								
E: 2,B.2.				Free		Leytonstone & I								
				£10,000	28.07.89	Maidstone United	41+1	0+2	3	7			1	
				£300,000	07.06.90	Wimbledon	178+2	16	11	2	10	1		
				£4,000,000	08.95	Newcastle United								
Robert J Elliot	5.10	11.6	25.12.73	Newcastle	03.04.91	Newcastle Utd (T)	37+7	1	5+1	1	2			
E: Y1														
Marc Hottiger	5.10	11.7	07.11.67	Lausanne (Switzerland)		Sion F.C.								
Swiss International				£600,000	04.08.94	Newcastle United	38	5	4	4	1		1	
Stephen N Howey	6.2	10.9	26.10.71	Sunderland	11.12.89	Newcastle Utd (T)	99+19	9+2	10+2	8	4	1		
E: 1. Div1'93														
Darren Peacock	6.2	12.6	03.02.68	Bristol	11.02.86	Newport C. (T)	24+4	2	1	1	1+1			
WFAC'90				Free	23.03.89	Hereford United	56+3	6	6	6	4		1	
				£200,000	22.12.90	Q.P.R.	123+3	12	3	2	6	1		
				£2,700,000	24.03.94	Newcastle United	44	4	5	4	1			
Stephen C Watson	6.0	12.7	01.04.74	North Shields	06.04.91	Newcastle Ud (T)	77+16	6+1	7+2	4+3	7			1
E: u21. 4, u19.11, u18.4														
M I D F I E L D														
Richard D Appleby	5.8	10.6	18.09.75	Middlesboro'	12.08.93	Newcastle Ud (T)				2				
E: Y.1				Loan	01.09.94	Darlington								
John Beresford	5.6	10.12	04.09.66	Sheffield	16.09.83	Manchester City (A)								
E: B.1, Y.10, u19.3, S; Div1'93				Free	04.08.86	Barnsley	79+9	5+2	5		5	2	1	
				£300,000	23.03.89	Portsmouth	102+5	12	11	2	8	2		
				£650,000	02.07.92	Newcastle United	109	12	11	6	1		1	
Lee Clark	5.8	11.7	27.10.72	Wallsend	09.12.89	Newcastle Ud (T)	122+20	13	11	5+2	19		2	1
E: u21.11, Y6; Div1'93														
James Crawford	5.11	11.06	01.05.73	USA		Bohemians								
					08.94	Newcaslte United								
Christopher J Holland	5.9	11.5	11.09.75	Whalley		Preston N. E. (T)	0+1			1				
E: Y.5, S				£100,000	20.01.94	Newcastle United	2+1							
Scott Sellars	5.8	10.0	27.11.65	Sheffield	25.07.83	Leeds United (A)	72+4	4	4	2	12	1		1
E: u21.3; FMC'87; Div1'87				£20,000	28.07.86	Blackburn Rovers	194+8	12	11	20	35	3	1	2
				£800,000	01.07.92	Leeds United	6+1	1+1		1				
				£700,000	09.03.93	Newcastle United	54+1	4+1	3	4	5	1		1
F O R W A R D S														
Malcolm Allen	5.8	11.2	21.03.67	Caernarfon	23.03.85	Watford (A)	27+12	4+1	6+8		5	2	6	
W: 14, B.1, Y				Loan	03.09.87	Aston Villa	4							
				£175,000	12.08.88	Norwich City	24+11	0+3	5	2+1	8		7	
				£400,000	20.03.90	Millwall	64+17	7	0+1	1	24	2		
				£300,000	13.08.93	Newcastle United	9+1	3			5	2		
Peter A Beardsley	5.8	11.7	18.01.61	Newcastle	09.08.79	Carlisle United	93+11	6+1	15		22		7	
E:52, B2; FLg.1; Div1'88'90; FAC'89;				£275,000	01.04.82	Vancouver Wh'caps								
CS'88'89'90'				£300,000	09.09.82	Manchester United		1						
				Free	01.03.83	Vancouver Wh'caps								
				£150,000	23.09.83	Newcastle United	146+1	10	6	1	61			
				£1,900,000	24.07.87	Liverpool	120+11	13+1	22+3	5	46	1	11	1
				£1,000,000	05.08.91	Everton	81	8	4	2	25	5	1	1
				£1,400,000	16.07.93	Newcastle United	69	6	6	4	34	1	2	2

	Ht	Wt	DOB					App				Gls			
Les Ferdinand	5.11	13.5	18.12.66	Acton			Hayes								
E: 6. Turkish FAC'89.				£15,000	12.03.87	Q.P.R.		152+11	11+2	6+1	1	80	7	3	
				Loan	24.03.88	Brentford		3							
				Loan		Besiktas (Turk)									
				£6,000,000	08.95	Newcastle United									
Ruel A Fox	5.6	10.0	14.01.68	Ipswich	20.01.86	Norwich City (A)		148+4	13+3		11+4	12+4	22	3	
E: B.1				£2,250,000	02.02.94	Newcastel United		54	2	5	1	12	1		1
Keith R Gillespie	5.10	10.11	18.02.75	Bangor	03.02.93	Manchester Utd (T)		3+6	3			1			
				£1,000,000	10.01.95	Newcaslte United		15+2		3		2		2	
David Ginola	6.0	13.0	25.01.67	Gossin		Toulon									
	via Racing Paris, Brest					Paris St Germain									
				£2,500,000	08.95	Newcastle United									
Paul Kitson	5.11	10.12	09.01.71	Peterlee	15.12.88	Leicester City (T)		39+11	5	1+1	5	6	3	1	1
E: u21.7. FLg u18.1.				£1,300,000	11.03.92	Derby County		105	7	5	13+1	36	3	1	9
				£2,250,000	24.09.94	Newcastle United		24+2	3	4+1		8	1	3	
Robert M Lee	5.10	11.6	01.02.66	West Ham		Hornchurch									
E: 2,B.1, u21.2; Div1'93				Free	12.07.83	Charlton Athletic		274+24	16+3	14	10+2	59	1	2	3
				£700,000	22.09.92	Newcastle United		112	8	11	3	26	2	3	4

TOP GOALSCORER 1994/95
Peter Beardsley

Premiership goals (games)	13 (34)
Coca-Cola Cup Goals	0 (3)
F.A. Cup goals	0 (3)
UEFA Cup goals	2 (4)
Total	**15 (44)**

Total goals for Newcastle since 23.9.83 until 1987 & 16.07.93 . . 100 (248+1)
Total for England (full caps only) . . . . 9 (46+11)

Career total as at June 1st 1995 . . . . 200 (549+27)

MANAGER
KEVIN KEEGAN

Date of Birth . . . . 14th February 1951.
Place of Birth . . . . Armthorpe.
Date of Appointment . . . . February 1992.

PREVIOUS CLUBS
As Manager . . . . None.
As Coach . . . . None.
As a Player . . . . Scunthorpe, Liverpool, SV Hamburg, Southampton,
. . . . Newcastle United.

HONOURS
As a Manager
Division 1 championship 1992-93.

As a Player
Liverpool: Division 1 championship (3 times). FA Cup, European Cup (twice). UEFA (twice).
International: 63 full caps and 5 U23 for England.

ST. JAMES PARK

Newcastle-upon-Tyne NE1 4ST
Tel: 0191 232 8361 (Fax: 0191 232 9875)

Capacity 34,390

First game...v Celtic, 3.9.1892.
First floodlit game ....v Celtic, 25.2.1953.

ATTENDANCES
Highest..68,386 v Chelsea, Division 1, 3.9.1930.
Lowest ....1,000 v Walsall T S, Div.2, 10.3.1894.

OTHER GROUNDS..................................Chillingham Road, Heaton 1882-1892. St. James Park 1892-

---

HOW TO GET TO THE GROUND

From the North
Use A1 into Newcastle then follow sign Hexham into Percy Street, then turn right into Leazes Park Road (or turn left then right into St James' Street) for Newcastle United FC.

MATCHDAY TICKET PRICES

Not known at the time of going to press.

Apply to club for prices.

Ticket Office Telephone no. 0191 261 1571

From the South
Use A1, A68 and then A6127, cross River Tyne and at roundabout take 1st exit into Mosley Street. One-way keep to left hand lane into Neville Street. At end turn right into Clayton Street for Newgate Street. Then turn left into Leazes Park Road (one-way) turn left then right into St James' Street for Newcastle United FC.

From the West
Use A69 (sign posted Newcastle) enter city centre then turn left into Clayton Street for Newgate Street. Then turn into Leazes Park Road (one-way) turn left then right into St James' Street for Newcastle United FC.

CLUBCALL
0891 12 11 90

Calls cost 39p per minute cheap rate and 49p per minute at all other times.
Call costings correct at time of going to press.

Car Parking
Parking on the north side of the ground. Also street parking is permitted.

Nearest Railway Station
Central Station (0191 232 6262).

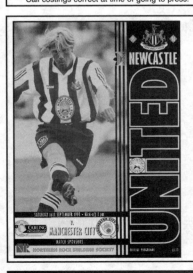

MATCHDAY PROGRAMME

Programme Editor . . . . Bernard Gallagher.

Number of pages . . . . 40.

Price . . . . £1.50.

Subscriptions . . . . Telephone: 0121 643 2729.

Local Newspapers . . . . Newcastle Chronicle, Newcastle Journal,
. . . . Sunday Sun, Northern Echo, South Shields Gazette.

Local Radio Stations . . . . Metro Radio, Radio Newcastle, Radio Tees.

NOTTINGHAM FOREST

(The Reds)

F.A. CARLING PREMIERSHIP

SPONSORED BY: LABATTS/SHIPSTONES (JOINT SPONSORS)

Back Row (R-L): Scot Gemmill, Paul McGregor, Lars Bohinen, Alf Haaland, Chris Bart-Williams, Kingsley Black, Neil Webb.
Middle Row: Richard Money (Res. Coach), Liam O'Kane (Coach), Andrea Silenzi, Jason Lee, Carl Tiler, Mark Crossley, Tommy Wright, Robert Rosario, Stephen Chettle, Kevin Campbell, John Haseldon (Physio), Peter Edwards (Fitness Consultant). **Front Row:** Des Lyttle, Stephen Stone, Bryan Roy, Frank Clark (Manager), Stuart Pearce (Capt), Alan Hill (Asst. Manager), Ian Woan, David Phillips, Colin Cooper.

**NOTTINGHAM FOREST
FORMED IN** 1865
TURNED PROFESSIONAL IN 1889
LTD COMPANY IN 1982

CHAIRMAN: F Reacher

DIRECTORS
G E McPherson JP, J F Hickling,
I I Korn (Vice-Chairman), J M Smith,
C Wootton, G W Waterhouse
SECRETARY
Paul White (01602 526 000)
COMMERCIAL MANAGER
Dave Pullan (01602 820 444)

MANAGER: Frank Clark
ASSISTANT MANAGER: Alan Hill

PHYSIOTHERAPIST
Graham Lyas

STATISTICIAN FOR THE DIRECTORY
Vacant

It was often said during the 1993-94 season that Forest were far too good to go down, but go down they did. The fact they regained their top flight status at the first attempt was evidence indeed of their pedigree. This pedigree was confirmed last season in the Premiership and, but for a sticky patch in November - four defeats in five games - they could well have seriously challenged for the title.

Stan Collymore (now a Liverpool player following his £8.5 million move) and Dutch international Brian Roy shared 40 goals between them in all competitions, but it was essentially a team effort.

Manager Frank Clark's men began the season like an express train, going fourteen games without defeat (League and Coca-Cola Cup), before suffering their first set-back at home to eventual champions Blackburn Rovers (2-0) on 29th October. Then came November's traumas which included a 2-0 4th Round Coca-Cola defeat by Millwall at the City ground. December dawned, and Forest were once more in the groove moving up one place in the table to 4th, although they had in fact occupied the number two spot in September and October.

1994 became 1995 and Forest began the New Year with a 2-0 success over Plymouth Argyle in Round Three of the FA Cup. Seven days later Blackburn turned on the style and walloped Forest 3-0. Another defeat, 2-1, at home to Aston Villa on 14th January sent out a few alarms, bur they were still in 5th position and well on course for a UEFA Cup place.

Their FA Cup ambitions were thwarted in Round Four by those knock-out experts from South London, Crystal Palace, who won by the odd goal in three at the City ground.

Out of both cups, Forest became even more determined to consolidate their high Premiership position, and this was borne out by their really impressive record from the end of February until the final day of the season, 13th May: Played 13 Won 9 Drawn 4. This gave them a final placing of 3rd and a passport to the lucrative world of European football.

Undoubtedly their most exhilarating performance was against Sheffield Wednesday at Hillsborough on April Fools' Day. Leading 2-0 at half-time, the Forest boys ran riot in the second period netting five more with just one reply from a shell-shocked Wednesday. Both Collymore and Roy bagged a brace on that memorable afternoon, and even though manager Clark will be without the predatory Stan for this campaign, he should still view the future with extreme optimism.
GREG TESSER.

NOTTINGHAM FOREST

Premier League: 3rd   FA Cup: 4th Round   Coca-Cola Cup: 4th Round

M	DATE	COMP.	VEN	OPPONENTS	RESULT	H/T	LP	GOAL SCORERS/GOAL TIMES	ATT.
1	A 20	PL	A	Ipswich Town	W 1-0	1-0	6	Roy 40	(18,882)
2	22	PL	H	Manchester United	D 1-1	1-1		Collymore 26	22,072
3	27	PL	H	Leicester City	W 1-0	1-0	4	Collymore 38	21,601
4	30	PL	A	Everton	W 2-1	1-0	3	Hinchcliffe 24 (og), Cooper 60	(26,689)
5	S 10	PL	H	Sheffield Wednesday	W 4-1	1-0	2	Black 34, Rohinen 52, Pearce 63 (pen), Roy 82	22,022
6	17	PL	A	Southampton	D 1-1	0-0	2	Collymore 43	(14,185)
7	21	CC 2/1	H	Hereford United	W 2-1	0-1		Collymore 48, 53	10,076
8	24	PL	A	Tottenham Hotspur	W 4-1	1-1		Stone 9, Roy 52, 64, Rominen 79	(24,558)
9	O 2	PL	H	Queens Park Rangers	W 3-2	0-0	2	Black 51, Roy 63, Collymore 88	21,449
10	4	CC 2/2	A	Hereford United	D 0-0	0-0			(9,865)
11	8	PL	A	Manchester City	D 3-3	1-1	2	Collymore 22, 51, Woan 92	(23,150)
12	17	PL	H	Wimbledon	W 3-1	1-0	2	Bohinen 40, Collymore 66, Woan 75	20,287
13	22	PL	A	Aston Villa	W 2-0	1-0	2	Pearce 1 (pen), Stone 70	(29,217)
14	26	CC 3	A	Wolverhampton Wand.	W 3-2	2-1		Pearce 5, 87, Roy 21	(23,369)
15	29	PL	H	Blackburn Rovers	L 0-2	0-1	2		22,131
16	N 5	PL	A	Liverpool	L 0-1	0-1			(33,329)
17	7	PL	H	Newcastle United	D 0-0	0-0	5		22,102
18	19	PL	H	Chelsea	L 0-1	0-1	5		22,092
19	26	PL	A	Leeds United	L 0-1	0-0	5		(38,191)
20	30	CC 4	H	Millwall	L 0-2	0-2			12,393
21	D 3	PL	H	Arsenal	D 2-2	1-1	5	Pearce 36 (pen), Roy 60	21,662
22	10	PL	H	Ipswich Town	W 4-1	4-1	4	Collymore 4, Gemmill 11, Haarland 26, Pearce 42	21,340
23	17	PL	A	Manchester United	W 2-1	1-0	4	Collymore 35, Pearce 62	(43,744)
24	26	PL	A	Coventry City	D 0-0	0-0			(19,224)
25	D 27	PL	H	Norwich City	W 1-0	0-0		Bohinen 51	21,010
26	31	PL	A	West Ham United	L 1-3	0-3		McGregor 89	(20,644)
27	J 2	PL	H	Crystal Palace	W 1-0	0-0	4	Bull 76	21,326
28	7	FAC 3	H	Plymouth Argyle	W 2-0	2-0		Collymore 7, Gemmill 16	19,821
29	14	PL	A	Blackburn Rovers	L 0-3	0-0	4		(27,510)
30	21	PL	H	Aston Villa	L 1-2	0-1	5	Collymore 53	24,598
31	25	PL	A	Chelsea	W 2-0	1-0		Collymore 33,54	(17,890)
32	28	FAC 4	H	Crystal Palace	L 1-2	1-1	5	Bominen 32	16,790
33	F 4	PL	H	Liverpool	D 1-1	1-0	5	Collymore 10	25,418
34	11	PL	A	Newcastle United	L 1-2	0-0	5	Lee 74	(34,471)
35	21	PL	A	Arsenal	L 0-1	0-0	5		(35,441)
36	26	PL	A	Queens Park Rangers	D 1-1	0-0		Stone 57	(13,363)
37	M 4	PL	H	Tottenham Hotspur	D 2-2	0-0		Bohinen 84, Lee 85	28,711
38	8	PL	H	Everton	W 2-1	1-1		Collymore 19, Pearce 54	24,526
39	11	PL	A	Leicester City	W 4-2	1-1	5	Pearce 8 (pen), Collymore 64, Woan 68, Lee 90	(20,423)
40	18	PL	H	Nottingham Forest	W 3-0	1-0	5	Roy 38, 81, Collymore 63	24,146
41	22	PL	H	Leeds United	W 3-0	3-0	4	Roy 9, 35, Collymore 44	26,299
42	A 1	PL	A	Sheffield Wednesday	W 7-1	2-0	4	Pearce 17, Woan 20, Roy 48, 64, Collymore 78, 80, Bohinen 85	(30,060)
43	8	PL	H	West Ham United	D 1-1	0-0	4	Collymore 78	28,361
44	12	PL	A	Norwich City	W 1-0	0-0	3	Stone 85	(19,005)
45	17	PL	H	Coventry City	W 2-0	2-0	3	Woan 9, Collymore 42	26,253
46	29	PL	A	Crystal Palace	W 2-1	1-0	3	Roy 14, Collymore 67	(15,886)
47	M 6	PL	H	Manchester City	W 1-0	1-0	3	Collymore 18	28,882
48	13	PL	A	Wimbledon	D 2-2	1-2	3	Phillips 13, Stone 75	(15,341)
49									
50									
51									
52									
53									
54									
55									
56									
57									
58									
59									
60									

Best Home League Attendance: 28,882 v Manchester City   Smallest: 20,287 v Wimbledon   Av Home Att: 22,632

Goal Scorers: Compared with 1993-94: -551

League (72): Collymore 23, Roy 13, Pearce 8, Bohinen 6, Stone 5, Woan 5, Lee 3, Black 2, Bull, Cooper, Gemmill, Haaland, McGregor, Phillips, Opponent

C/Cola Cup (5): Collymore 2, Pearce 2, Roy

FA Cup (3): Bohinen, Collymore, Gemmill

128

Crossley	Lyttle	Chettle	Cooper	Pearce	Woan	Gemmill	Stone	Phillips	Lee	Roy	Bohinen	Rosario	Rigby	Collymore	Black	Webb	Haaland	Wright	McGregor	Filan	Warner	Bull	Tyler	Warren	Mercer	Referee	
X	X	X	X	X	X	X	X1	X	X	X2	S1	S2	S	S												Lodge S.	1
X	X	X	X	X	X	X	X1	X	S	X1	S1		S	X	X											Wilkie A.	2
X	X	X	X	X	X	X	X	X	S	X	S			S	X											Willard G.	3
X	X	X†	X	X	X	X1	X	X	S	X	S1			S	X											Ashby G.	4
X	X	X	X	X		X	X	X	S	X	X		S	X	X	S										Don P.	5
X	X	X	X	X	S	X	X	X	S	X	X			X	X		X		S							Reed M.	6
X	X	X	X	X	S1	X	X	X	X1	X	S			X	X		S		S							Wolstenholme E.	7
X	X	X	X	X	X	X	X	X		X	X1			X	X		S1		S							Hart R.	8
X	X	X	X	X	S	X	X	X	S	X	X			X	X		S		S							Morton K.	9
X	X	X	X	X		X	X	X	S	X	X			X	X2		S		S							Reed M.	10
X		X	X	X	S2	X1	X	X	S1		X			X	X2		X									Durkin P.	11
X		X	X	X	X	S	X	X	S	X	X			X	X		X									Hart R.	12
X		X	X	X	X	X	X	X	S1	X	X			X	S		X									Cooper K.	13
X		X	X	X	X	S	X	X	S1	X	X			X1					S							Don P.	14
X	X	X	X	X	X1	X	X	X	X	X	X				S1		S		S							Danson P.	15
X	X	X	X	X	X	S	X	X	X	X	X				S				S							Worrall J.	16
X	X	X	X	X	X1	X	X	X	S	X	X			X	S1				S							Burge K.	17
X	X	X	X	X	X	X	X	S	X	X	X			X	S				S							Holbrook T.	18
X	X	X	X	X	X	S	X	X	X	X	X			X					S							Jones P.	19
X	X	X	X1	X	X	X	X	X	S2	X	X2		S	X			S1									Wilkie A.	20
X	X	X		X	X	X	X	X	S	X	X1		S	X	S1		X									Hill B.	21
X	X	X		X	X	X	X	X	S2	X2	X		S	X			X									Reed M.	22
X	X	X		X	X	X	X	X	X1	S1				X			X	S	S							Burge K.	23
X	X	X	X	X	X	X2	X	X1		X				X			S1	S2	S							Wilkie A.	24
X	X	X	X	X	X1	X		X		X	X			X		S1	X	S	S							Lodge S.	25
X	X	X	X1	X	X		X		X	X2				X	S2		X	S1	S							Gallagher D.	26
X	X	X		X	X	X	X1	X		X				X		S	X	S1	S1	S	X	X				Ashby G.	27
X	X	X		X	X	X	X	X		X1				X		S1	X			S		S				Elleray D.	28
X	X	X		X	X	X1	X	X		X1				X		S	X	S1	S				X			Worrall J.	29
X	X	X			X	S	X	X		X	X			X			X			S		S	X			Cooper K.	30
X	X	X	X		X	X	X	X		X1	X			X			X	S1	S			S	X			Bodenham M.	31
X	X	X	X		X1	X	X		X	X		S		X			S			S1			X			Hart R.	32
X	X	X	X		X	X	X	S1	X1				X		X		S	S								Willard G.	33
X	X	X	X	X	X	X	X	S1				X		X1	S	S										Morton K.	34
X	X	X	X	X	X1	X	X	X		X		S		X		S	S1									Durkin P.	35
X	X	X	X		X1	X	X	S	X	X		S		X		X									S1	Danson P.	36
X	X	X	X	X		X	X	S1	X1	X		S		X		X	S									Ashby G.	37
X	X	X	X	X	X	X	X	S1	X1	X		S		X		S										Dilkes R.	38
X	X	X	X	X	X	X	X	S1	X1	X		S		X		X	S									Donn P.	39
X	X	X	X	X	X	X	X	S1	X1	X		S		X		X	S									Cooper K.	40
X	X1	X	X	X		X	X	S2	X	X		X2		S1											S	Reed M.	41
X	X	X	X	X		X	X	S	X	X		X		S2											S	Wilkie A.	42
X	X	X	X	X	X2	X	X	S1	X	X1		X		S											S	Poll G.	43
X	X	X	X	X	X1	X	X	S1	X1	X		X		S					S1						S	Morton K.	44
X	X	X	X	X	X1	X	X	S2	X2	X		X		S1											S	Durkin P.	45
X	X	X	X	X	X	X	X	S1	X1			X		S			S								S	Burge K.	46
X	X	X	X	X	X	X	X	S1	X1			X		S			S								S	Jones P.	47
X	X	X	X	X	X	X	X	X				X	S	S											S	Lodge S.	48
42	38	41	35	36	34	19	41	38	4	37	31			37	5		18				1	1	3			League Appearances	
						1			17		4	1			5		2		10							League Sub Appearances	
4	4	4	4	3	2+1	1	4	0+2	4	4		4		2			0+1									C/Cola Cup Appearances	
2	2	2	1	1	1	2	2	2	2		1			2			0+1					0+1	1			FA Cup Appearances	

† = Sent Off

NOTTINGHAM FOREST

CLUB RECORDS

BIGGEST VICTORIES
League: 12-0 v Leicester City, Division 1, 12.4.1909 (Joint Division 1 record).
F.A. Cup: 14-0 v Clapton, 1st round, 17.1.1891 (a).
League Cup: 7-0 v Bury, 3rd Round 23.9.1980.
Europe: 5-1 v AEK Athens 2nd Round (Euro Cup), 15.11.1978.
4-0 v Eintracht Frankfurt, 1st Round (UEFA), 17.10.1967.

BIGGEST DEFEATS
League: 1-9 v Blackburn Rovers, Division 2, 10.4.1937.
0-8 v West Bromwich Albion, Division 1, 16.4.1900.
0-8 v Leeds City, Division 2, 29.11.1913.
0-8 v Birmingham City, Division 2, 10.3.1920.
0-8 v Burnley, Division 1, 21.11.1959.
F.A. Cup: 0-5 v Southampton, 6th Round, 1962-63.
League Cup: 0-4 v Manchester United, 5th Round, 19.1.1983.
Europe: 1-5 v Valencia, 1st Round, 14.10.1961.

MOST POINTS
3 points a win: 83, Division 1, 1993-94.
2 points a win: 70, Division 3(S), 1950-51 (Division 3(S) record).

MOST GOALS SCORED
110, Division 3(S), 1950-51.
Ardon 36, Capel 23, Collindridge 16, Johnson 15, Scott 9, Leverton 6, Gager 2, Love 1, Burkitt 1, Opponents 1.

MOST GOALS CONCEDED
90, Division 2, 1936-37.

MOST FIRST CLASS MATCHES IN A SEASON
65 - 1979-80 (League 42, FA Cup 2, League Cup 10, European Cup 9, European Super Cup 2).

MOST LEAGUE WINS
30, Division 3(S), 1950-51.

MOST LEAGUE DRAWS
18, Division 1, 1969-70 & 1978-79.

MOST LEAGUE DEFEATS
25, Division 1, 1971-72.

INDIVIDUAL CLUB RECORDS

MOST GOALS IN A SEASON
Wally Ardron: 36 goals in 1950-51 (All League).

MOST GOALS IN A MATCH
5. A Higgins v Clapton (a) 14-0, FA Cup 1st Round, 17.1.1891.

OLDEST PLAYER
Sam Hardy, 41 v Newcastle United, 4.10.1924.

YOUNGEST PLAYER
S J Burke, 16 years 22 days v Ayr United, Anglo-Scot Cup.

MOST CAPPED PLAYER
Stuart Pearce (England) 53.

BEST PERFORMANCES

League: 1950-51: Matches played 46, Won 30, Drawn 10, Lost 6, Goals for 110, Goals against 40, Points 70. First in Division 3(S).
Highest Position: Champions of Division 1, 1977-78.

F.A. Cup: Winners in 1897-98.
Most recent success: 1958-59: 3rd Round 2-2,3-0; 4th Round Grimsby Town 4-1; 5th Round Birmingham 1-1 (2); 6th Round Bolton Wanderers 2-1; Semi-final Aston Villa 1-0; Final Luton Town 2-1.

League Cup: Winners in 1977-78, 1978-79, 1988-89.
Most recent success: 1989-90: 2nd Round Huddersfield Town 1-1,3-3; 3rd Round Crystal Palace 0-0,5-0; 4th Round Everton 1-0; 5th Round Spurs 2-2,3-2; Semi-final Coventry City 2-1,0-0; Final Oldham Athletic 1-0.

Europe: (European Cup) Winners in 1978-79.
Most recent success: 1979-80: 1st Round Oester Vakjo 2-0,1-0; 2nd Round Agres Pitesti 2-1,2-0; 3rd Round Dynamo Berlin 0-1,3-1; Semi-final Real Madrid 2-0,0-1; Final S V Hamburg 1-0.

DIVISIONAL RECORD							
	Played	Won	Drawn	Lost	For	Against	Points
Division 1/P	2,064	772	511	780	2,953	2,991	2,282
Division 2/1	1,538	571	384	592	2,332	2,311	1,549
Division 3(S)	88	50	19	19	177	79	119
Total	3,690	1,393	914	1,383	5,462	5,381	3,950

ADDITIONAL INFORMATION
PREVIOUS NAMES
None.

PREVIOUS LEAGUES
Football Alliance.

Club colours: Red shirts, white shorts, red socks.

Change colours: Yellow shirts with blue & red trim, blue shorts with red & yellow trim.

Reserves League: Pontins Central League Division 1.

RECORDS AND STATISTICS

COMPETITIONS

Div 1/P	Div.2/1	Div. 3(S)	Euro C	UEFA	Sup C
1892-06	1906-07	1949-51	1978-79	1961-62	1970-80
1907-11	1911-22		1979-80	1967-68	1980-81
1922-25	1925-49		1980-81	1983-84	
1957-72	1951-57			1984-85	**Texaco**
1977-93	1972-77	**W.C.C.**			1970-71
1994-	1993-94	1982			
					A/Scot
					1976-77

HONOURS

Div.1	Div.2	Div.3(S)	FAC	Lge C	Euro C	A/Scot
1977-78	1906-07	1950-51	1898	1977-78	1978-79	1976-77
	1921-22		1959	1978-79	1979-80	
				1988-89		**Sup C**
			C/S'ld	1989-90	**Sim. C.**	1979-80
			1978		1988-89	
					1991-92	

MOST APPEARANCES

BOBBY McKINLAY 681+3 (1951-70)

Year	League	FA Cup	Lge Cup	Europe
1951-52	1	1		
1952-53	3			
1953-54	1			
1954-55	37	6		
1955-56	39	1		
1956-57	39	5		
1957-58	40	3		
1958-59	39	9		
1959-60	42	2		
1960-61	42	1	3	
1961-62	42	2	3	2
1962-63	42	7		
1963-64	42	2		
1964-65	42	3		
1965-66	41	1		
1966-67	42	7	2	
1967-68	42	2	2	4
1968-69	30+2	1	1	
1969-70	5+1			
	611+3	**53**	**11**	**6**

MOST GOALS IN A CAREER

GRENVILLE MORRIS - 225 (1898-1913)

Year	League	FA Cup
1898-99	7	8
1899-1900	8	3
1900-01	14	1
1901-02	7	2
1902-03	24	2
1903-04	12	2
1904-05	12	1
1905-06	19	3
1906-07	21	1
1907-08	7	
1908-09	12	
1909-10	19	1
1910-11	11	1
1911-12	10	
1912-13	16	1
Total	**199**	**26**

Current leading goalscorer: Stuart Pearce - 77 (1985-95)

RECORD TRANSFER FEE RECEIVED

Amount	Club	Player	Date
£8,500,000	Liverpool	Stan Collymore	07/95
£2,100,000	Tottenham H	Teddy Sheringham	9/92
£1,500,000	Sampdoria	Des Walker	5/92
£1,500,000	Manchester Utd	Neil Webb	7/89

RECORD TRANSFER FEE PAID

Amount	Club	Player	Date
£2,200,000	Southend United	Stan Collymore	7/93
£2,000,000	Millwall	Teddy Sheringham	7/91
£1,400,000	Barnsley	Carl Tiler	5/91
£1,250,000	Coventry City	Ian Wallace	7/80

MANAGERS

Name	Seasons	Best	Worst
Harry Radford	1889-97	7(1)	13(1)
Harry Haslam	1897-09	4(1)	1(2)
F W Earp	1909-12	14(1)	15(2)
Bob Masters	1912-25	20(1)	20(2)
Jack Baynes	1925-29	5(2)	17(2)
Stan Hardy	1930-31	17(2)	17(2)
Noel Watson	1931-36	5(2)	19(2)
Harold Wightman	1936-39	18(2)	20(2)
Billy Walker	1939-60	10(1)	4(3S)
Andy Beattie	1960-63	9(1)	19(1)
John Carey	1963-68	2(1)	18(1)
Matt Gillies	1969-72	15(1)	21(1)
Dave Mackay	1972-73	14(2)	14(1)
Allan Brown	1973-75	7(2)	16(2)
Brian Clough	1975-93	1(1)	8(2)
Frank Clark	1993-	3(P)	2(1)

LONGEST LEAGUE RUNS

of undefeated matches:	42 (26.11.1977 - 25.11.1978)	of league matches w/out a win:	16 (8.2.1913 - 18.10.1913)
of undefeated home matches:	51 (27.4.1977 - 17.11.1979)	of undefeated away matches:	21 (3.12.1977 - 9.12.1978)
without home win:	10 (20.11.1909 - 9.4.1910)	without an away win:	37 (25.1.1913 - 23.1.1915)
of league wins:	7 (24.12.1892 - 25.2.1893, 29.8.1921 - 1.10.1921)	of home wins:	12 (23.2.1980 - 20.9.1980)
of league defeats:	14 (8.2.1913 - 18.11.1913)	of away wins:	5 (5.4.1983 - 29.8.1983, 31.12.1988 - 25.3.1989)
			(21.11.1993 - 16.01.1994)

NOTTINGHAM FOREST

PLAYERS NAME Honours	Ht	Wt	Birthdate	Birthplace Transfers	Contract Date	Clubs	League	L/Cup	FA Cup	Other	Lge	L/C	FAC	Oth
G O A L K E E P E R S														
Richard Clark	5.11	12.4	06.04.77	Nuneaton	12.04.94	Nottingham F. (T)								
Mark G Crossley E: u21.3	6.0	15.0	16.06.69	Barnsley	02.07.87	Nottingham F. (T)	199+1	29	22	10				
Malcom R Rigby			13.03.76	Nottingham £50,000	.08.94	Notts County (T) Nottingham Forest								
Thomas J Wright NI: 22, u21.1; Div3'93 Loan 14.02.91 Hull City 6 Lge App.	6.1	13.5	29.08.63	Belfast £30,000 £450,000	27.01.88 24.09.93	Linfield Newcastle United Nottingham Forest	72+1 10	6 2	4	1				
D E F E N D E R S														
Stephen Chettle E: u21.12; LC'90; FMC'89'92	6.1	13.3	27.09.68	Nottingham	28.08.86	Nottingham F. (A)	243+13	36+3	24+1	13+2	7	1	1	
Colin T Cooper E: u21.8	5.8	9.4	28.02.67	Sedgefield £300,000 £1,700,000	17.07.84 25.07.91 21.06.93	Middlesbrough (J) Millwall Nottingham Forest	183+5 77 71+1	18 6 8	13 2 3	19+1 2	6 6 8	1	1	2
Danny Hinshelwood E: Yth.	5.9	10.11	04.12.75	Bromley	1992-93	Nottingham F. (T)								
Desmond Lyttle	5.9	12.0	24.09.71	Wolverhampton £12,500 £375,000	09.01.90 09.07.92 27.07.93	Leicester City (T) Worcester City Swansea City Nottingham Forest	46 75	2 10	5 4	5 1	1 1			
Ian Morgan	6.2	12.10	11.10.77	Birmingham	1994-95	Nottingham F. (T)								
Stuart Pearce E:56, u21.1; LC'89'90;FMC'89'92	5.10	13.0	24.04.62	Hammersmith £25,000 £200,000	20.10.83 03.06.85	Wealdstone Coventry City Nottingham Forest	52 337	57	2 2 31	16	4 55	9	7	6
Carl Tiler E: u21.13	6.2	13.0	11.02.70	Sheffield £1,400,000 Loan	02.08.88 30.05.91 18.10.94	Barnsley (T) Nottingham Forest Swindon Town	67+4 67+2 2	4 10+1	4+1 6	3+1 1	3 1		1	
Stuart Thom	6.2	11.8	27.12.76	Dewsbury	11.01.94	Nottingham F. (T)								
Vance Warner	6.0	11.12	03.09.74	Leeds	03.09.74	Nottingham F. (T)	2	1						
M I D F I E L D														
Paul Archer	5.7	9.04	25.04.78	Leicester	1994-95	Nottingham F. (T)								
Craig Armstrong	5.11	12.04	23.05.75	South Shields Loan	02.06.92 29.12.94	Nottingham F. (T) Burnley	4							
Craig Atkinson E: Yth.	6.0	11.02	29.09.77	Rotherham	1994-95	Nottingham F. (T)								
Chris Bart-Williams E: B.1, Y.12, u21.8.	5.8	11.0	16.06.74	Sierra Leone £275,000 £2,500,000	18.07.91 21.11.91 08.95	Leyton Orient (T) Sheffield Wed. Nottingham Forest	34+2 95+25	4 14+2	8+5	2 4	2 4	3	1	1
Lars Bohinen Norweigen Int.	5.11	12.2	08.09.66	Norway £450,000	05.11.93	Young Boys of Berne Nottingham Forest	52+5	6+1	2		7		1	
John Burns	5.8	10.08	04.12.77	Dublin	1994-95	Nottingham F. (T)								
Tony Carbone	5.10	11.06	13.10.74	Perth	1994-95	Perth Italia Nottingham Forest								
Lee Cowling	5.8	9.04	22.09.77	Doncaster	1994-95	Nottingham F. (T)								
John Finnigan	5.8	10.05	29.03.76	Wakefield	1992-93	Nottingham F. (T)								
Scot Gemmill S: B1, u21.4; FMC'92	5.10	11.0	02.01.71	Paisley	05.01.90	Nottingham F. (T)	123+3	21+1	10	7	18	3	1	4
Alf I R Haaland	5.10	12.0	23.11.72	Norway	25.01.94	Young Boys of Berne Nottingham Forest	21+2	0+4	1		1			
Stephen Howe	5.7	10.04	06.11.73	Annitsford	08.92	Nottingham F. (T)								
David O Phillips W: 52, u21.4, Y4; FAC'87	5.10	11.2	29.07.63	Wegburg (G) £65,000 £150,000 £525,000	03.08.81 23.08.84 05.06.86 31.07.89 20.08.93	Plymouth Albion (A) Manchester City Coventry City Norwich City Nottingham Forest	65+8 81 93+7 152 78+3	2+1 8 8 12 11	12+1 5 9 14 4	4 5 5+1 8 1	15 13 8 17 5	1	1 1 1	3 2 1
Paul A Smith	5.11	11.03	25.01.76	Hastings	1994-95	Nottingham F. (T)								
Steven B Stone	5.9	11.3	20.08.91	Gateshead	20.05.89	Nottingham Forest	97+2	9+1	4	2	11			
Lee Stratford	5.10	10.08	11.11.75	Barnsley	1992-93	Nottingham F. (T)								
Darren Turner	5.3	8.0	23.12.77	Derby	1994-95	Nottingham F. (T)								
Justin Walker E: Yth	5.10	11.08	06.09.75	Nottingham	1992-93	Nottingham F. (T)								
Neil J Webb E: 26, B4, u21.3, Y10; Div3'83; LC'89'92; SC'89; FAC'91; ECWC'91; ESC'91	6.1	13.7	30.07.63	Reading (A) £83,000 £250,000 £1,500,000 £800,000	14.11.80 29.07.82 03.06.85 24.07.89 23.11.92	Reading (A) Portsmouth Nottingham Forest Manchester United Nottingham Forest	65+7 123 146 70+5 26+4	2+2 9 21 14 2+3	2 6 13 9 6+1	6 12 1	22 34 47 8 3	3 4 1 1	1 2 1 1 2	4 1
F O R W A R D S														
Kingsley Black NI:30, u21.n, B, S; LC'88; FMC'92	5.8	10.11	22.06.68	Luton £1,500,000 Loan	07.07.86 02.09.91 02.03.95	Luton Town (J) Nottingham Forest Sheffield United	123+4 79+17 8+3	16+2 19+1	5+1 4	3+2 4+2	25 14 2	1 5	2	1
Gary W Bull GMVC'91	5.9	11.7	12.06.66	Tipton £2,000 Free	15.10.86 29.03.88 01.03.89 21.07.93	Paget Rangers Southampton Cambridge United Barnet Nottingham Forest	13+6 83 4+8	0+1 2	11 0+3	0+2 8	4 37 1	4	3	2
Kevin Campbell E: B.1, u21.4. Div.1'91. FAYC'88. LC'93. FAC'93. ECWC'94.	6.0	13.1	04.02.70	Lambeth Loan Loan £2,500,000	11.02.88 16.01.89 08.11.89 08.95	Arsenal (T) Leyton Orient Leicester City Nottingham Forest	105+38 16 11	9+10	12+5 1	12+2	42 9 5	5	2	5 1

132

Player				From / Fee	Date	Club								
Matthew Hurst	5.7	10.03	03.11.77	Farnborough	1994-95	Nottingham F. (T)								
Jason Lee	6.3	13.8	09.05.71	Forest Gate	02.06.89	Charlton Athletic (T)	0+1			0+2				
				Loan	06.02.91	Stockport County	2							
				£35,000	01.03.91	Lincoln City	86+7	6	2+1	4	21		1	
					06.08.93	Southend United	18+6	1	1	5+3	3			3
				£200,000	04.03.94	Nottingham Forest	15+20	0+2			5			
Paul A McGregor	5.10	10.4	17.12.74	Liverpool	13.12.91	Nottingham F. (T)	0+11				1			
Stephen Orr	5.7	10.0	19.01.78	Belper	1994-95	Nottingham F. (T)								
Darren Poole	5.8	10.03	09.11.77	Northampton	1994-95	Nottingham F. (T)								
Robert M Rosario	6.3	13.12	04.03.66	Hammersmith		Hillingdon Borough								
E: u21.4, Y3				Free	23.12.83	Norwich City	115+11	11	13+1	8+1	18	3	3 5	
				Loan	13.12.85	Wolverhampton W.	2		2	1				
				£600,000	27.03.91	Coventry City	54+5	3+1	3	1	8	2		
				£400,000	02.03.93	Nottingham Forest	25+2	1		2	3			
Brian E S Roy	5.10	10.08	12.02.70	Amsterdam		Foggia								
				£2,500,000	04.08.94	Nottingham Forest	37	4	2		13	1		
Andrea Silenzi	6.3	11.13	10.02.66	Sierra Leone		Reggiana								
Italy: 5, u21.8.	via Napoli, Roma, Inter Milan,					Torino								
				£1,800,000	08.95	Nottingham Forest								
Mark Walley	5.10	10.6	17.09.76	Barnsley	27.09.93	Nottingham F. (T)								
Ian S Woan	5.10	12.4	14.12.67	Heswall		Runcorn								
				£80,000	14.03.90	Nottingham Forest	114+8	10+2	10+1	5	21	1	1	1

Top Goalscorer 1994/95
Stan Collymore

Premiership goals (games) 23 (37)
Coca-Cola Cup Goals 2 (4)
F.A. Cup goals 1 (2)

Total . . . . **26 (43)**

Total goals for Nottingham Forest (05.07.1993-13.05.95) . . . . . . 50 (77+1)
Total for England (full caps only) . . . . 0 (0+2)

Career total as at June 1st 1995 . . . . 70 (116+20)

Signed for Liverpool July 1995 . . . . £8,500,000

The Manager
Frank Clark

Date of Birth . . . . 9th October 1943.
Place of Birth . . . . Rowlands Gill.
Date of Appointment . . . . May 1993.

Previous Clubs
As Manager . . . . Leyton Orient.
As Coach . . . . Sunderland, Nottingham Forest, Leyton Orient.
As a Player. . . . . Crook Town, Newcastle United, Nottingham Forest.

Honours
As a Manager
Promotion to Division 3 1988-89. Promotion to the Premiership 1993-94.

As a Player
Crook Town: FA Amateur Cup 1961.
Newcastle: UEFA 1969. Division 2 1965.
Nottingham Forest: ECWC 1979. Division 1 1978. League Cup 1978, 1979.
International: England youth.

CITY GROUND
City Road, Nottingham NG2 5FJ
Tel: 01602 526 000

Capacity ....30,602.

First game ....v Blackburn Rovers, 0-1, 3.9.1898.
First floodlit game ....v Gillingham, 11.9.1961.
Internationals ....England v Wales, 1909.

ATTENDANCES
Highest ....44,946 v Manchester Utd, Div.1, 28.10.1967.
Lowest ....2,624 v WBA, 30.3.1904.

OTHER GROUNDS ....Forest Racecourse 1865-79. The Meadows 1879-80. Trent Bridge 1880-82.
... Parkside Lenton 1882-85. Gregory Lenton 1885-90. Town Ground 1890-98. City Ground 1898-

MATCHDAY TICKET PRICES

Bridgford Stand
Upper Tier £17
Lower Tier (Visitors) £16

Main Stand £18

Trent End
Upper Tier £17
Lower Tier (Family) Adult £16
Lower Tier (Family) Junior £8

Executive Stand
Upper Tier £17
Lower Tier £16

Ticket Office Telephone no. 01602 813 801

CLUBCALL 0898 12 11 74

Calls cost 39p per minute cheap rate and 49p per
minute at all other times.
Call costings correct at time of going to press.

HOW TO GET TO THE GROUND

From the North
Use motorway (M1) until junction 26, leave motorway and follow signs into
Nottingham A610. Follow signs to Melton Mowbray, Trent Bridge A606. Cross
river and turn left into Radcliffe Road, then turn left into Colwick Road for
Nottingham Forest FC.

From the East
Use A52 sign posted Nottingham, into West Bridgeford, then turn left into
Colwick Road for Nottingham Forest FC.

From the South
Use motorway (M1) until junction 24, leave motorway and follow signs to
Nottingham (South) to Trent Bridge, turn right into Radcliffe Road, then turn left
into Colwick Road for Nottingham Forest FC.

From the West
USe A52 into Nottingham, then follow signs to Melton Mowbray, Trent Bridge
A606, cross river and turn left into Radcliffe Road, then turn left into Colwick
Road for Nottingham Forest FC.

Car Parking: Space for 300 cars in east Stand car park plus street parking off
Loughborough and Radcliffe Roads.
Nearest Railway Station: Nottingham Midland (01602 461 51).

MATCHDAY PROGRAMME

Programme Editor . . . . John Lawson.

Number of pages . . . . 32.

Price . . . . £1.50.

Subscriptions . . . . Contact 'Temple Printers' 01602 868 304.

Local Newspapers . . . . . . Nottingham Evening Post, Derby Telegraph.

Local Radio Stations . . . . Radio Nottingham, Radio Trent.

QUEENS PARK RANGERS
(The Rangers or The R's)
F.A. CARLING PREMIERSHIP
SPONSORED BY: COMPAQ

Back Row (L-R): John Cross, Danny Maddix, Karl Ready, Chris Plummer, Daniele Dichio, Tony Roberts, Richard Hurst, Alan McDonald, Alan McCarthy, Kevin Gallen, Simon Osborn, Steven Parmenter. **Middle Row:** Brian Morris (Physio), Terry Warren (Asst. Physio), Les Boyle (Kit Manager), Matthew Lockwood, David Bardsley, Michael Mahoney-Johnson, Trevor Sinclair, Sieb Dykstra, Steve Yates, Denis Bailey, Graeme Power, Nigel Quashie, Phil Parks (GK coach), Billy Bonds (Yth Manager), John Nolan (Asst. Kit Man.), John Hollins (Res. Manager). **Front Row:** Andrew McDermott, Mark Graham, Bradley Allen, Matthew Brazier, Steve Hodges, Andrew Impey, Ray Wilkins (Manager), Frank Sibley (Coach), Simon Barker, Gary Penrice, Trevor Challis, Rufus Brevett, Ian Holloway, Lee Charles.

QUEENS PARK RANGERS
FORMED IN 1885
TURNED PROFESSIONAL IN 1898
LTD COMPANY IN 1899

CHAIRMAN: P D Ellis
CORPORATE DIRECTOR: R B Copus
DIRECTORS
A Ellis, R C Thompson, A Ingham,
R Copus
SECRETARY
Miss S F Marson
COMMERCIAL MANAGER
Paul Marsden (0181 740 8737)

MANAGER: Ray Wilkins MBE
ASSISTANT MANAGER: Frank Sibley

RESERVE TEAM MANAGER
John Hollins MBE
YOUTH TEAM MANAGER
Billy Bonds MBE
PHYSIOTHERAPIST
Brian Morris

STATISTICIAN FOR THE DIRECTORY
Andy Shute

The league campaign started with defeat at Manchester United, followed by a home victory over Sheffield Wednesday, the only win in their first 11 league games. This poor run of results left Rangers in the bottom three, before two home wins in three days was followed by the shock news that manager Gerry Francis had resigned following an altercation with the chairman. Former Ranger Ray Wilkins, who had only left the club in the summer, was appointed as the new manager and the results and form began to improve almost immediately. By the end of the year QPR had climbed to 13th after a superb 3-1 win at Arsenal on New Years Eve. Rangers dropped back into the bottom part of the table after two away defeats in January, but then six wins and two draws from the next nine games took them to the fringes of the European places. Although Rangers only won two of their last six games, an impressive win against Tottenham and a first ever win at Manchester City, they again finished the season a respectable 8th in the Premier League.

The Coca-Cola League Cup campaign was short-lived, for following wins home and away against Third Division Champions Carlisle United, Rangers suffered a 3-4 defeat at home to Manchester City in the 3rd round.

In the FA Cup Rangers beat non-League Aylesbury United 4-0 in an 'away' tie at Loftus Road. In the 4th Round an Andy Impey goal was enough to beat West Ham 1-0, the reward of which was another home tie against London opposition, this time Millwall. A last minute penalty by Clive Wilson earned QPR another 1-0 win, and an away tie at FA Cup holders Manchester United. Screened live on Sky TV, Rangers fought bravely but went down 0-2, along with the Rangers fans' Wembley dreams.

As with last season, speculation continued surrounding the future of Les Ferdinand, though fortunately he stayed at QPR, and finished the season with 26 goals, the 3rd consecutive year as leading scorer at the club. The find of the season was ex-youth team player Kevin Gallen, who made his debut on the opening day of the season, forming a formidable partnership with 'Sir Les', and was rewarded with a call-up to the England U21s. Simon Barker and Andy Impey had their best seasons yet in the Rangers' colours, Impey unanimously voted as Player of the Year. Daniele Dichio progressed to the first team and deputised well for Ferdinand. Ex-England international Steve Hodge was signed from Leeds for £300,000 just prior to Gerry Francis' departure.

The 1995/96 season should see Rangers pushing for honours if they can continue their form from the latter part of the 94/95 season, and a European place is well within their grasp.

ANDY SHUTE.

QUEENS PARK RANGERS

Premier League: 8th   **FA Cup:** 6th Round   **Coca-Cola Cup:** 3rd Round

M	DATE	COMP.	VEN	OPPONENTS	RESULT	H/T	LP	GOAL SCORERS/GOAL TIMES	ATT.
1	A 20	PL	A	Manchester United	L 0-2	0-0			(43,214)
2	24	PL	H	Sheffield Wednesday	W 3-2	1-1		Ferdinand 22, Sinclair 57, Gallen 78	12,788
3	27	PL	H	Ipswich Town	L 1-2	0-1	15	Ferdinand 90	12,456
4	31	PL	A	Leicester City	D 1-1	1-0	14	Willis 41 (og)	(18,695)
5	S 10	PL	H	Coventry City	D 2-2	2-1	13	Penrice (35,37)	11,398
6	17	PL	A	Everton	D 2-2	1-2	12	Ferdinand 5, 48	(27,285)
7	20	CC 2/1	A	**Carlisle United**	W 1-0	1-0		**Ferdinand 17**	(9,580)
8	24	PL	H	Wimbledon	L 0-1	0-0	16		11,059
9	O 2	PL	A	Nottingham Forest	L 2-3	0-0	18	Ferdinand 54, Allen 84	(21,449)
10	5	CC 2/2	H	**Carlisle United**	W 2-0	2-0		**Allen 7, Wilson 39 (pen)**	6,561
11	8	PL	A	Tottenham Hotspur	D 1-1	1-0	17	Impey 43	(25,799)
12	15	PL	H	Manchester City	L 1-2	0-0	19	Wilson 63	13,631
13	22	PL	A	Norwich City	L 2-4	1-0	20	Barker 24, Gallen 62	(19,431)
14	25	CC 3	H	**Manchester City**	L 3-4	2-1		**Gallen 14, Sinclair 38, Penrice 87**	11,701
15	29	PL	H	Aston Villa	W 2-0	1-0	17	Dichio 36, Penrice 90	16,073
16	31	PL	H	Liverpool	W 2-1	1-0	15	Sinclair 29, Ferdinand 84	18,295
17	N 5	PL	A	Newcastle United	L 1-2	0-2	16	Dichio 60	(34,278)
18	19	PL	H	Leeds United	W 3-2	2-1	18	Ferdinand 20, 39, Gallen 67	17,416
19	26	PL	A	Blackburn Rovers	L 0-4	0-1	18		(21,302)
20	D 4	PL	H	West Ham United	W 2-1	2-0	16	Ferdinand 2, Sinclair 37	12,780
21	10	PL	H	Manchester United	L 2-3	1-2	17	Ferdinand 23,64	18,948
22	17	PL	A	Sheffield Wednesday	W 2-0	0-0	13	Maddix 60, Ferdinand 85	(22,766)
23	26	PL	A	Crystal Palace	D 0-0	0-0	17		(16,372)
24	28	PL	H	Southampton	D 2-2	1-1	16	Barker 7, Gallen 49	16,078
25	31	PL	A	Arsenal	W 3-1	1-0	13	Gallen 3, Allen 76, Impey 77	(32,393)
26	J 7	FAC 3	A	**Aylesbury United**	W 4-0	3-0		**Maddix 10, Ferdinand 25, Gallen 39, Meaker 78**	(15,417)
27	14	PL	A	Aston Villa	L 1-2	0-1	15	Yates 87	(26,578)
28	24	PL	A	Leeds United	L 0-4	0-2	17		(28,780)
29	28	FAC 4	H	**West Ham United**	W 1-0	1-0		**Impey 20**	17,549
30	F 4	PL	H	Newcastle United	W 3-0	3-0	17	Ferdinand 4, 8, Barker 18	16,576
31	11	PL	A	Liverpool	D 1-1	1-0	16	Gallen 5	(35,996)
32	18	FAC 5	H	**Millwall**	W 1-0	0-0		**Wilson 90 (pen)**	16,457
33	26	PL	H	Nottingham Forest	D 1-1	0-0	17	Barker 87	13,363
34	M 4	PL	A	Wimbledon	W 3-1	1-1	16	Ferdinand 24, 57, Holloway 47	(9,176)
35	8	PL	H	Leicester City	W 2-0	0-0	14	McDonald 72, Wilson 74	10,189
36	12	FAC 6	A	**Manchester United**	L 0-2	0-1			(42,830)
37	15	PL	H	Norwich City	W 2-0	0-0	11	Ferdinand 65, Gallen 86	10,519
38	18	PL	H	Everton	L 2-3	1-0	11	Ferdinand 35, Gallen 60	14,488
39	22	PL	H	Chelsea	W 1-0	0-0	9	Gallen 62	15,103
40	A 1	PL	A	Coventry City	W 1-0	0-0	9	Sinclair 85	(45,740)
41	4	PL	H	Blackburn Rovers	L 0-1	0-0	9		16,508
42	8	PL	H	Arsenal	W 3-1	1-0	9	Impey 27, Gallen 59, Ready 82	16,341
43	11	PL	A	Ipswich Town	W 1-0	0-0	8	Ferdinand 68	(11,767)
44	15	PL	A	Southampton	L 1-2	0-0	8	Ferdinand 63	(15,201)
45	17	PL	H	Crystal Palace	L 0-1	0-0	8		14,227
46	29	PL	A	Chelsea	L 0-1	0-0	8		(21,407)
47	M 3	PL	A	West Ham United	D 0-0	0-0	8		(22,923)
48	6	PL	H	Tottenham Hotspur	W 2-1	0-1	8	Ferdinand 64, 75	18,367
49	14	PL	A	Manchester City	W 3-2	1-1	8	Ferdinand 13, 89, Dichio 77	(27,850)
50									
51									
52									
53									
54									
55									
56									
57									
58									
59									
60									

Best Home League Attendance: 18,948 v Manchester United   **Smallest:** 10,189 v Leicester City   **Av Home Att:** 14,600

Goal Scorers:

Compared with 1993-94: -1,187

League (61): Ferdinand 24, Gallen 10, Barker 4, Sinclair 4, Dichio 3, Impey 3, Penrice 3, Allen 2, Wilson 2, Holloway, Maddix, McDonald, Ready, Yates, Opponent

C/Cola Cup (6): Ferdinand, Allen, Wilson (pen), Gallen, Sinclair, Penrice

FA Cup (6): Ferdinand, Gallen, Impey, Maddix, Meaker, Wilson (pen)

Roberts T.	Bardsley D.	Wilson C.	Yates S.	McDonald A.	Impey A.	Holloway I.	Sinclair T.	Barker S.	Ferdinand L.	Gallen K.	Penrice G.	Maddix D.	Dykstra S.	Ready K.	Brevett R.	Meaker M.	Allen B.	White D.	Dichio D.	Hodge S.	McCarthy A.	Wilkins R.	Referee	
X	X	X†	X	X	X	X	X	X	X1	X2	S1	S2	S										Gallagher D.	1
X	X	X	X	X	X1	X	X	X	X	X1	S	S1	S										Jones P.	2
X	X	X	X	X	X1	X	X	X	X	X	S1	S	S										Danson P.	3
X	X	X	X	X	X	X	X†	X	X	S1	X1	S	S										Lodge S.	4
X	X		X	X	X	X	X†	X	X	S1	X1		S	S	X								Worrall J.	5
X	X	X		X	X	X	X		X	X1	S	X		S	S1	X							Gifford R.	6
X	X	X		X	X		X	X	X	X	S1	X		S	S	X							Winter J.	7
X	X	X1	X	X	X			X	X	S1	X		S	S	X	X							Burge K.	8
X	X		X	X1	X	X	X	X			X			S	S	X		S1					Morton K.	9
X	X	X	X	X	X	X	X	X	X	X1	S1		S	S		X							Hill B.	10
X	X	X	X	X	X	X	X	X	X1	X†	S		X1	S			X						Jones P.	11
X	X	X	X1	X	X	X	X	X	X	X	S1		S	S		X							Willard G.	12
S	X	X	X	X		X	X	X		X		S	X		X1	S1	X						Reed M.	13
S	X	X	X	X		X	X	X1		X	S1		X	S		X							Danson P.	14
S	X	X	X	X		X2	X	X		X1	S1	S2	X					X	X				Hart R.	15
S	X	X	X	X	X		X	X	X	X		S	X					S	X				Holbrook T.	16
S	X	X	X	X	X		X	X	X	X		S	X					S1	X1				Ashby G.	17
S		X	X	X	X	S1	X	X	X	X	S		X	X					X1				Bodenham M.	18
S		X	X	X	X		X	X	X	X		X	X	S					X				Worrall J.	19
S		X	X	X	X		X	X1	X	X		X				S			X				Don P.	20
	X	X		X	X		X	X	X	X		X				S			X				Poll G.	21
S	X	X	S	X	X		X1	X	X	X		X							X				Durkin P.	22
S		X	X	X	X		X1	X	X	X		X		S	S1				X				Hill B.	23
S		X	X	X	X1		X	X	X	X		X		S1	X	S			X				Cooper K.	24
X	X	X		S	X	X		X		X1	X		X	S		X	S1		X				Willard G.	25
X	X	X		X		X	S2		X2	X	X1		X	S		X	S1		X				Jones P.	26
X	X	X1	X		X	X			X	X		X	S		X				X	S1			Wilkie A.	27
X	X		X		X	X	S1		X	X2		X	S		X	X			X	S2			Morton K.	28
X	X		X	X	X	X	X		X			X	S	S		S		X					Ellerey D.	29
X	X		S	X	X	X	X	X1	X			X	S		X				S1				Cooper K.	30
X	X	X	S	X	X	X	X	S	X			X	S		X								Gallagher D.	31
X	X	X	S	X	X	X	X		X			X	S			X			S				Don P.	32
X		X	X1	X	X		X	X	X	X	S1	X	S2		X								Danson P.	33
X		X		X	X	X	X	X	X1	X	S	X	S					X					Willard G.	34
X		X		X	X	X	X	X		X1	S1	S	S						X				Reed M.	35
X	X	X		X	X	X	X	X	X	S1	S	S	S										Gallagher D.	36
X	X	X		X	X	X	X	X	X	S	S	S	S										Ashby G.	37
X	X	X		X	X	X	X	X	X1	X	S1	S	S										Morton K.	38
X	X	X		X	X	X	X	X	X	S		S	X					X			S		Hill B.	39
X		X		X	X	X†	X	X	X	S		S	X	X				X			S		Danson P.	40
X		X		X	X	X	X	X	X1	S		S	X	X				S1	S1				Hart R.	41
X		X		X	X	X	X	X	X1	S1	S	S	X	X									Don P.	42
X		X		X	X	X	X	X	X1	S1	S	S	X	X									Gifford R.	43
X	X	X			X		X		X	X1	S1		S	X	X2				X		S2		Jones P.	44
X	X	X		X	X	X	X		X	X		S1	S	X1	X2				S2				Wilkie A.	45
X	X	X		X	X				X	S1	X		X	S		X			X	S	X1		Ashby G.	46
X	X	X1		X	X	X	X	X	X	S2	X2	X	S		S1								Willard G.	47
X	X		S	X	X	X	X	X	X	S	X	X	S		X								Poll G.	48
X	X		S1	X	X		X1	X	X	X2	X	X	S		X				S2				Reed M.	49
31	30	36	22	39	40	30	32	37	37	32	8	21	11	11	18	8	2	1	4	15		1	League Appearances	
					3				1		6	10	5		2	2		1	3	5	2	1	League Sub Appearances	
2	3	3	3	3	2	2	3	3	2	1+2	1+1	1						1		1			League Cup Appearances + Subs	
4	4	3	1	4	4	3+1	1	4	3	4	0+1	4			1	2	0+1		1	1			FA Cup Appearances + Subs	

Also Played: Caldwell S(9,21)

† = Sent Off

QUEENS PARK RANGERS

CLUB RECORDS

BIGGEST VICTORIES
League: 8-0 v Merthyr, Division 3S, 9.3.1929
F.A. Cup: 8-1 v Bristol Rovers (a), Round 1, 27.11.1937
7-0 v Barry Town, Round 1, 1961-62
League Cup: 8-1 Crewe, Round 2, 3.10.1983
Europe (UEFA): 7-0 v Brann Bergen, Round 1, 29-9-1976

BIGGEST DEFEATS
League: 1-8 v Mansfield, Division 3, 15.3.1965
1-8 v Manchester United, Division 1, 19.3.1969
0-7 v Southend United, Division 3S, 7.4.1928
0-7 v Coventry City, Division 3S, 4.3.1933
0-7 v Torquay United, Division 3S, 22.4.1935
0-7 v Barnsley, Division 2, 4.11.1950
F.A. Cup: 0-5 v Huddersfield, Round 4, 23.1.1932
0-5 v Derby County, Round 6, 12.3.1948
0-5 v Huddersfield (h), Round 3, 1948-49
1-6 v Burnley, Round 3, 1961-62
1-6 v Hereford, Round 2, 1957-58
League Cup: 0-4 v Reading, Round 2, 23.9.1964
0-4 v Newcastle, Round 2, 8.10.1974
Europe (UEFA): 0-4 v Partizan Belgrade, 7.11.1984

MOST POINTS
3 points a win: 85, Division 2, 1982-83
2 points a win: 67, Division 3, 1966-67

MOST GOALS
111, Division 3, 1961-62.
Bedford 36, Evans 19, Lazarus 12, Towers 12, McClelland 11,
Angell 6, Collins 6, Barber 4, Keen 2, Francis 1, og 2.

MOST LEAGUE GOALS CONCEDED
95, Division 1, 1968-69

MOST FIRST CLASS MATCHES IN A SEASON
59 (42 League, 2 FA Cup, 7 League Cup, 8 UEFA Cup) 1976-77

MOST LEAGUE WINS
26, Div 3S, 1947-48; Div 3, 1966-67; Div 2, 1982-83

MOST LEAGUE DRAWS
18, Division 1, 1991-92

MOST LEAGUE DEFEATS
28, Division 1, 1968-69

INDIVIDUAL CLUB RECORDS

MOST GOALS IN A SEASON
Rodney Marsh, 44 (League 30, FAC 3, League Cup 11) 1966-67.
(League Only) George Goddard, 37, Div 3S, 1929-30

MOST GOALS IN A MATCH
5. Alan Wilks v Oxford, Round 3, League Cup, 10.10.1967.

OLDEST PLAYER
Jimmy Langley, 38 years 96 days.

YOUNGEST PLAYER
Frank Sibley, 15 years 274 days.

MOST CAPPED PLAYER
Alan McDonald (Northern Ireland) 43

BEST PERFORMANCES

League: 1966-67: Matches played 46, Won 26, Drawn 15, Lost 5,
Goals for 103,Goals against 38, Points 67. First in Division 3

Highest: 1975-76: 2nd in Division 1.

F.A. Cup: 1981-82: 3rd rnd. Middlesbrough 1-1, 3-2; 4th rnd.
Blackpool 0-0, 5-1; 5th rnd. Grimsby 3-1; 6th rnd. Crystal Palace 1-
0; Semi-final West Bromwich Albion 1-0; Final Tottenham 1-1, 0-1.

League Cup: 1966-67: 1st rnd. Colchester 5-0; 2nd rnd. Aldershot
1-1, 2-0; 3rnd. Swansea 2-1; 4th rnd. Leicester 4-2; 5th rnd. Carlisle
2-1; Semi-final Birmingham 4-1, 3-1; Final West Bromwich Albion 3-
2.

UEFA Cup: 1976-77: 1st rnd. Brana Bergen 4-0, 7-0; 2nd rnd.
Slovan Bratislava 3-2, 5-2; 3rd rnd FC Cologne 3-0, 1-4; 4th rnd.
AEK Athens 3-0, 0-3.

ADDITIONAL INFORMATION
Previous Name: St. Judes 1885-87

Previous League: Southern League

Club colours: Blue and white shirts, white shorts, white with 3 blue
hoop socks.

Change colours: Navy blue with thin white hoops.

Reserves League: Avon Insurance Football Combination.

DIVISIONAL RECORD

	Played	Won	Drawn	Lost	For	Against	Points
Division 1/P	784	268	217	299	990	1,054	936
Division 2	546	233	141	172	809	671	654
Division 3	414	188	98	128	782	601	474
Division 3(S)	1,158	466	276	416	1,781	1,692	1,208
Total	**2,902**	**1,155**	**732**	**1,015**	**4,362**	**4,018**	**3,172**

RECORDS AND STATISTICS

COMPETITIONS

Div 1/P	Div.2	Div.3	Div.3(S)	UEFA
1968-69	1948-52	1958-67	1920-48	1976-77
1973-79	1967-68		1952-58	1984-85
1983-	1969-73			
	1979-83			

HONOURS

Div.2	Div.3	Div.3(S)	League Cup
1982-83	1966-67	1947-48	1966-67

MOST APPEARANCES

Tony Ingham 548 (1950-63)

Year	League	FA Cup	Lge Cup
1950-51	24		
1951-52	17		
1952-53	43	3	
1953-54	40	4	
1954-55	38	3	
1955-56	41	1	
1956-57	46	3	
1957-58	46	3	
1958-59	46	2	
1959-60	46	3	
1960-61	46	2	2
1961-62	40	4	2
1962-63	41	2	
	514	30	4

MOST GOALS IN A CAREER

George Goddard - 186 (1926-33)

Year	League	FA Cup
1926-27	22	
1927-28	26	
1928-29	36	1
1929-30	37	2
1930-31	24	4
1931-32	17	2
1932-33	12	3
Total	174	12

Current leading goalscorer: Bradley Allen - 31 (1988-95)

RECORD TRANSFER FEE RECEIVED

Amount	Club	Player	Date
£6,000,000	Newcastle Utd	Les Ferdinand	6/95
£2,700,000	Newcastle Utd	Darren Peacock	3/94
£2,700,000	Sheffield Wed.	Andy Sinton	8/93
£1,700,000	Manchester Utd	Paul Parker	7/91

RECORD TRANSFER FEE PAID

Amount	Club	Player	Date
£1,250,000	Borussia Dortmund	Ned Zelic	7/95
£1,100,000*	Reading	Simon Osborn	7/95
£1,000,000	Luton Town	Roy Wegerle	12/89
£800,000	Southampton	Colin Clarke	3/89

*Included Michael Meaker going to Reading.

MANAGERS

Name	Seasons	Best	Worst
James Cowan	1907-13		
James Howie	1919-20		
Ned Liddell	1920-25	3(3S)	22(3S)
Bob Hewison	1925-31	3(3S)	22(3S)
John Browman	1931		
Archie Mitchell	1931-33	13(3S)	16(3S)
Mitchell O'Brien	1933-35	4(3S)	13(3S)
Billy Birrell	1935-39	3(3S)	9(3S)
Ted Vizard	1939-44		
Dave Mangall	1944-52	13(2)	3(3S)
Jack Taylor	1952-59	10(3)	21(3S)
Alex Stock	1959-68	2(2)	15(3)
Tommy Docherty	1968		
Les Allen	1969-71	22(1)	11(2)
Gordon Jago	1971-74	4(1)	8(2)
Dave Sexton	1974-77	2(1)	14(1)
Frank Sibley	1977-78	19(1)	19(1)
Steve Burtenshaw	1978-79	20(1)	20(1)
Tommy Docherty	1979-80	5(2)	5(2)
Terry Venables	1980-84	5(1)	8(2)
Alan Mullery	1984		
Frank Sibley	1984-85	19(1)	19(1)
Jim Smith	1985-88	5(1)	16(1)
P Shreeve (Caretaker)	1988-89		
Trevor Francis	1989-90	9(1)	9(1)
Don Howe	1990-91	12(1)	12(1)
Gerry Francis	1991-94	5(1/P)	11(1)
Ray Wilkins	1994-	8(P)	8(P)

LONGEST LEAGUE RUNS

of undefeated matches:	20 (19.11.1966 - 11.4.1967)	of league matches w/out a win:	20 (23.11.1968 - 12.4.1969)
of undefeated home matches:	25 (18.11.1972 - 5.2.1974)	of undefeated away matches:	17 (27.8.1966 - 11.4.1967)
without home win:	10 (23.11.1968 - 10.4.1969)	without an away win:	22 (27.12.1954-26.12.1955, 11.5.69-13.9.70)
of league wins:	8 (7.11.1931 - 28.12.1931)	of home wins:	11 (26.12.1972 - 28.4.1973)
of league defeats:	9 (15.2.1969 - 12.4.1969)	of away wins:	7 (2.4.1927 - 4.9.1927)

QUEENS PARK RANGERS

PLAYERS NAME Honours	Ht	Wt	Birthdate	Birthplace Transfers	Contract Date	Clubs	League	L/Cup	FA Cup	Other	Lge	L/C	FAC	Oth
GOALKEEPERS														
Sieb Dykstra	6.5	14.7	20.10.66	Kerkrade		Roda JC								
						Motherwell	80	3	4					
				£250,000	22.07.94	Q.P.R.	11	1						
Richard Hurst	6.0	12.0	23.12.76	Hammersmith	1994-95	Q.P.R. (T)								
Anthony Roberts	6.1	12.4	04.08.69	Holyhead	24.07.87	Q.P.R. (T)	94	7	6+1	2				
W: 1, B.2, u21.2, Y.														
D E F E N D E R S														
David Bardsley	5.10	10.0	11.09.64	Manchester	05.11.82	Blackpool (A)	45	2	2			1		
E: 2, Y.2.				£150,000	23.11.83	Watford	97+3	6	13+1	1	7	1	1	
				£265,000	18.09.87	Oxford United	74	12	5	3	7			
				£500,000	15.09.89	Q.P.R.	212	18	18	3	4	1		1
Matthew Brazier	5.8	10.07	02.07.76	Leytonstone	01.07.94	Q.P.R. (T)								
Rufus Brevett	5.8	11.0	24.09.69	Derby	08.07.88	Doncaster Rov (T)	106+3	5	4	10+1	3			
				£250,000	15.02.91	Q.P.R.	50+8	2+1	2					
Trevor Challis	5.7	10.0	23.10.75	Paddington	01.07.94	Q.P.R. (T)								
E: Y.2, S.														
Daniel Maddix	5.10	11.7	11.10.67	Ashford	25.07.85	Tottenham H. (A)								
				Loan	01.11.86	Southend United	2							
				Free	23.07.87	Q.P.R.	143+23	15	18	2+3	7	2	2	
Alan McCarthy	5.11	12.10	11.01.72	Wandsworth	08.12.89	Q.P.R. (T)	8+3		0+1	1				
E: Y.1.				Loan	26.11.93	Watford	8+1							
				Loan	11.02.94	Plymouth Argyle	1+1							
Alan McDonald	6.2	12.7	12.10.63	Belfast	12.08.81	Q.P.R. (A)	332+5	39	28	5	10	2	1	
NI: 43, Y,S.				Loan	24.03.83	Charlton Athletic	9							
Chris Plummer	6.3	11.06	12.10.76	Hounslow	01.07.94	Q.P.R. (T)								
E: S.														
Karl Ready	6.1	12.2	14.08.72	Neath	13.08.90	Q.P.R.	33+6	0+2			2			
W: B.2, u21.5.														
Steve Yates	5.11	11.0	29.01.70	Bristol	01.07.88	Bristol Rovers (T)	196+1	9	11	21				
Div.3'90.				£650,000	16.08.93	Q.P.R.	49+3	3	2		1			
M I D F I E L D														
Simon Barker	5.9	11.0	04.11.64	Farnworth	06.11.82	Blackburn Rov. (A)	180+2	11	12	8	35	4		2
E: u21.4. FMC'87.				£400,000	20.07.88	Q.P.R.	200+21	21+2	20+1	7	17	5	3	
John Cross	5.8	10.10	01.07.94	Barking	01.07.94	Q.P.R. (T)								
Stephen Hodge	5.8	10.3	25.10.62	Nottingham	25.10.80	Nottingham F. (A)	122+1	10	6	11	30	2		4
E: 24, u21.8, B.2. UEFA u21'84. LC'89'90.				£450,000	27.08.85	Aston Villa	53	12	4	1	12	3	1	
SC'89. Div.1'92.				£650,000	23.12.86	Tottenham Hotspur	44+1	2	7		7		2	
				£550,000	17.08.88	Nottingham Forest	79+3	20+1	11+1	9	20	6	2	2
				£900,000	25.07.91	Leeds United	28+26	4+3	2+1	0+3	10			
				Loan	20.08.94	Derby County	10		1		2			2
				£300,000	28.10.94	Q.P.R.	15		1					
Ian Holloway	5.7	9.12	12.03.63	Kingswood	18.03.81	Bristol Rovers (A)	104+7	10	8	5	14	1	2	
Div.3'90.				£35,000	18.07.85	Wimbledon	19	3	1		2			
				£25,000	12.03.86	Brentford	27+3	2	3	0+1	2			
Loan Torquay U., 30.01.87, 5 Lge App.				£10,000	21.08.87	Bristol Rovers	179	5	10	20	26		1	3
				£230,000	12.08.91	Q.P.R.	104+16	10+1	6+1	1+1	3		1	
Andrew Impey	5.8	10.6	30.09.71	Hammersmith		Yeading								
FAV'90. E: u21.1.				£35,000	14.06.90	Q.P.R.	123+3	9+1	4+2	0+2	8	1	1	1
Matthew Lockwood	5.9	10.07	17.10.76	Rochford	1994-95	Q.P.R. (T)								
Simon Osborn	5.10	11.4	19.01.72	Croydon	03.01.90	Crystal Palace (T)	47+8	11	2	1+3	4	1		
				£90,000		Reading	31+1	4		3	5			
				£1,100,000	08.95	Q.P.R.								
Steven Parmenter	5.9	10.07	22.01.77	Chelmsford	1994-95	Q.P.R. (T)								
Trevor Sinclair	5.10	11.2	02.03.73	Dulwich	21.08.90	Blackpool (T)	84+28	8	6+1	8+5	15			1
E: u21.8, Y.1, S.				£600,000	12.08.93	Q.P.R.	62+3	6	2		8	2		
Ray Wilkins	5.8	11.2	14.09.56	Hillingdon	01.10.73	Chelsea (A)	176+3	6+1	10+1		30	2	2	
E: 84, u23.2, u21.1, Y, S. FAC'83. SPD'90.				£825,000	01.08.79	Manchester United	158+2	14+1	10	9	7	1	1	1
				£1,500,000	01.07.84	A.C. Milan								
						Paris St Germain								
				£250,000	01.11.87	Glasgow Rangers	69+1	10	8+1	7	2	1		
				Free	30.11.89	Q.P.R.	153+1	13	13	2	7		2	1
				Free	26.05.94	Crystal Palace	1							
				Free	17.11.94	Q.P.R.	1+1							
F O R W A R D S														
Bradley Allen	5.7	10.0	13.09.71	Romford	30.09.88	Q.P.R. (J)	51+22	5+2	1+2	1	26	5		
E: u21.8, Y.8.														
Dennis Bailey	5.10	11.6	13.11.65	Lambeth		Barking								
AMC'91.				Free	08.11.86	Fulham								
via Farnborough T., 1 FAC App, 1 gl.				£10,000	02.12.87	Crystal Palace	0+5		1					
				Loan	27.02.89	Bristol Rovers	17		1+1		9		1	
				£80,000	03.08.89	Birmingham City	65+10	6	6	3+3	23	2		
				Loan	28.03.91	Bristol Rovers	6				1			
				£175,000	02.07.91	Q.P.R.	32+7	5	1+1	1	10	3		
				Loan	29.10.93	Charlton Athletic	0+4		2				1	
				Loan	24.03.94	Watford	2+6				4			
Marvin Bryan	6.0	12.7	02.08.75	Paddington	17.08.92	Q.P.R. (T)								
				Loan	08.12.94	Doncaster Rovers	5				1			

Name			DOB	From	Date	Club								
Lee Charles				Chertsey										
				£67,500	08.95	Q.P.R.								
Daniel Dichio	6.2	11.0	19.10.74	Hammersmith	17.05.93	Q.P.R. (T)	4+5	1	1		3			
E: Y, S.				Loan	18.02.94	Welling United								
				Loan	24.03.94	Barnet	9				2			
Kevin Gallen	6.0	12.0	21.09.75	Chiswick	22.09.92	Q.P.R. (T)	31+6	1+1	4		10	1	1	
E: Y.11, S. UEFA Yth'93.														
Greg Goodridge	5.6	10.0	10.02.75	Barbados		Lambada, WI								
Barbados Int.				Free	24.03.94	Torquay United	32+6	4	2+1	3+1	4	1		1
				£100,000	08.95	Q.P.R.								
Mark Graham	5.7	10.0	24.10.74	Newry	26.05.93	Q.P.R. (T)								
NI: Y, S.														
M. Mahoney-Johnson	5.10	11.0	06.11.76	Paddington	1994-95	Q.P.R. (T)								
Gary Penrice	5.8	11.1	23.03.64	Bristol		Mangotsfield								
				Free	06.11.84	Bristol Rovers	186+2	11	11	13+2	53	3	7	2
				£500,000	14.11.89	Watford	41+2		4	1	17		1	1
				£1,000,000	08.03.91	Aston Villa	14+6				1			
				£625,000	29.10.91	Q.P.R.	46+14	4+1	2+1	1	17	1	1	
ADDITIONAL CONTRACT PLAYERS														
Andrew McDermott						Australia								
					08.95	Q.P.R.								
Ned Zelic						Borussia Dortmund								
				£1,500,000	08.95	Q.P.R.								

TOP GOALSCORER 1994/95
Les Ferdinand

Premiership goals (games) 24 (37)
Coca-Cola Cup Goals 1 (2)
F.A. Cup goals 1 (3)

Total . . . . **26 (42)**

Total goals for Q.P.R. from 12.03.87-14.05.95 . . . . 90 (170+14)
Total for England (full caps only) . . . . 3 (6+1)

Career total as at June 1st 1995 . . . . 93 (176+15)

Signed for Newcastle United 07.06.95 . . . . £6,000,000

THE MANAGER
RAY WILKINS

Date of Birth . . . . 14th September 1956.
Place of Birth . . . . Hillingdon.
Date of Appointment . . . . November 1994.

PREVIOUS CLUBS
As Manager . . . . None.
As Coach . . . . None.
As a Player . . . . Chelsea, Manchester Utd, A.C. Milan, Paris St Germain,
. . . . Glasgow Rangers, Q.P.R., Crystal Palace.

HONOURS
As a Manager
None.

As a Player
Manchester United: FA Cup 1983.
Glasgow Rangers: Scottish Premier Division Championship.
International: 84 full caps, 2 U23, 1 U21, Yth & S for England.

RANGERS STADIUM
South Africa Road, London W12 7PA
Tel: 0181 743 0262

Capacity 19,000
First game...v West Ham Utd, FA Cup, 8.9.1917.
First floodlit game...v Arsenal, 5.10.1953.
2nd Set...v Colchester, 23.8.1966.

ATTENDANCES
Highest ....35,353 v Leeds Utd, Div.1, 12.1.1974.
Lowest ....3,245 v Coventry City, Div 3, 22.5.1963.

OTHER GROUNDS .... Welfords Field 1885-89. London Scottish Ground, Brondesbury Home Farm,
.......Kensall Rise Green Gun Club, Wormwood Scrubs, Kilburn C.C. 1889-99, Kensal Rise 1899-1901, Latimer Rd,
....Knotting Hill 1901-04, Agriculture Soc, Park Royal 1904-07, Park Royal Ground 1907-17.
..... Loftus Road 1917-31, White City 1931-33, Loftus Road 1933-62. White City 1962-63. South Africa Road 1963-

MATCHDAY TICKET PRICES

'A' GAMES
South Africa Road £20
Ellerside Road £16
Juveniles. £8
'B' GAMES
South Africa Road £15
Ellerside Road £13
Juveniles. £6.50

Loftus Road Upper Level (Members only) £10
Juv/OAP £5
Lower Level ((Members). £10
Juv/OAP £5
Non-Members £12
Juv/OAP £6
East & West Paddocks (Members). £8
Juv/OAP £4
Non-Members £10
Juv/OAP £5
Ticket Office Telephone no.. . . . . . 0181 749 7798.

CLUBCALL 0891 12 11 62

Calls cost 39p per minute cheap rate and 49p per
minute at all other times.
Call costings correct at time of going to press.

HOW TO GET TO THE GROUND

From the North
Use motorway (M1) and A406 North Circular Road as for Neasden. In 0.7 miles
turn left then join A404, sign posted Harlesden, then follow signs Hammersmith
and turn right in to White City Road then turn left into South Africa Road for
Queens Park Rangers.
From the East
Use A12, A406 then A503 then join Ring Road and follow signs Oxford to join
A40 (M). In 2 miles branch left (sign posted The West) to join M41. At round-
about take 3rd exit (A40) then join A4020, sign posted Acton. In 0.3 miles turn
right into Loftus Road for Queens Park Rangers FC.
From the South
Use A206, A3 to cross Putney Bridge and follow signs Hammersmith. Follow
signs Oxford (A219) to Shepherds Bush then join A4020, sign posted Acton. In
0.3 miles turn right into Loftus Road for Queens Park Rangers FC.
From the West
Use motorway (M4) to Chiswick then A315 and A402 to Shepherds Bush, then
join A4020 sign posted Acton. In 0.3 miles turn right into Loftus Road for Queens
Park Rangers FC.

Car Parking
Limited side-street parking available.
Nearest Railway Station
Shepherds Bush (Tube), White City (Central Line)

MATCHDAY PROGRAMME

Programme Editor . . . . Sheila Marson.

Number of pages . . . . 36.

Price . . . . £1.50.

Subscriptions . . . . . . Full season £38 (Oversea, please apply to club).

Local Newspapers . . . . Shepherds Bush Gazette, Acton Gazette.

Local Radio Stations . . . . Capital Radio.

SHEFFIELD WEDNESDAY
(The Owls)
F.A. CARLING PREMIERSHIP
SPONSORED BY: SANDERSON ELECTRONICS PLC

Back Row (L-R): Andy Pearce, Mark Bright, Kevin Pressman, Julian Watts, Klas Ingesson, Chris Woods, Ryan Jones, Chris Waddle.
Middle Row: Danny Bergara (First Team Coach), Mark Pembridge, Peter Atherton, John Sheridan, Michael Williams, Lee Briscoe, Ian Nolan, Guy Whittingham, Dave Galley (Physio). **Front Row:** David Pleat (Manager), Graham Hyde, Marc Degryse, Dan Petrescu, Des Walker, Andy Sinton, David Hirst, Richie Barker (Football Devlopment/Manager's Assistant).

SHEFFIELD WEDNESDAY
FORMED IN 1867
TURNED PROFESSIONAL IN 1887
LTD COMPANY IN 1899

CHAIRMAN: D G Richards
DIRECTORS
K T Addy (Vice-Chairman), C Woodward,
E Barron, G K Hulley, R M Grierson FCA,
J Ashton MP, G Thorpe
SECRETARY
Graham Mackrell (01742 343 122)
COMMERCIAL MANAGER
Sean O'Toole

MANAGER: David Pleat
ASSISTANT MANAGER: Danny Bergara

RESERVE TEAM MANAGER
Frank Barlow
YOUTH TEAM MANAGER
Richie Barker
PHYSIOTHERAPIST
Dave Galley

STATISTICIAN FOR THE DIRECTORY
Michael Renshaw

Day one, and a woeful defensive display against Tottenham set the die for the rest of the season. It was a struggle to win the odd game and unrest appeared to be rife behind the scenes between the players and the management. Too many good players had been allowed to leave in the summer, and David Hirst's continuing absence for most of the season was again a big factor in the team's decline.

A period, midway through the season, of steadier results helped to lift the Owls and ease the pressure on the management team, and a win at Leeds in March had the more optimistic fans talking of a place in Europe. Sadly, it was to be only a temporary improvement. The continued lack of goals from all round the team held them back and although relegation seemed unlikely they came too close for comfort.

Only a last day win at home to already relegated Ipswich confirmed the Owl's Premier League status, although other results that day made them safe anyway.

Shortly after this last game the board parted company with manager Trevor Francis, "by mutual consent", and the guessing game about who was to take over began.

It is a most vital time for the Owls and they must make a good choice. The club seems to have, temporally I hope, lost its desire to join the elite clubs in chasing for trophies, something that two or three years ago seemed a possibility. The fans expect results but also flair football and the new manager must deliver both. So an important time lies ahead for the Owls.

MICHAEL RENSHAW.

SHEFFIELD WEDNESDAY

Premier League: 13th   **FA Cup:** 4th Round   **Coca-Cola Cup:** 4th Round

M	DATE	COMP.	VEN	OPPONENTS	RESULT	H/T	LP	GOAL SCORERS/GOAL TIMES	ATT.
1	A 20	PL	H	Tottenham Hotspur	L 3-4	0-2		Petrescu 54, Calderwood 66 (og), Hirst 83	34,051
2	24	PL	A	Queens Park Rangers	L 2-3	1-1		Sheridan 39, Hyde 75	(12,788)
3	27	PL	A	Wimbledon	W 1-0	1-0	14	Watson 76	(7,453)
4	31	PL	H	Norwich City	D 0-0	0-0	12		25,072
5	S 10	PL	A	Nottingham Forest	L 1-4	0-1	15	Hyde 56	(22,022)
6	17	PL	H	Manchester City	D 1-1	0-1	15	Watson 77	26,766
7	21	CC 2/1	H	Bradford City	W 2-1	0-0		Taylor 71, Hyde 81	15,705
8	26	PL	H	Leeds United	D 1-1	1-1	17	Bright 15	23,227
9	O 1	PL	A	Liverpool	L 1-4	1-0	19	Nolan 34	(31,493)
10	4	CC 2/2	A	Bradford City	D 1-1	1-0		Bart-Williams 30	(13,092)
11	8	PL	H	Manchester United	W 1-0	1-0	16	Hirst 44	33,441
12	16	PL	A	Ipswich Town	W 2-1	1-0	13	Bright 9, Hirst 89	(13,073)
13	22	PL	A	Newcastle United	L 1-2	0-2	14	Taylor 56	(34,408)
14	26	CC 3	H	Southampton	W 1-0	0-0		Bart-Williams 50	16,715
15	29	PL	H	Chelsea	D 1-1	0-1	15	Bright 67	25,450
16	N 2	PL	H	Blackburn Rovers	L 0-1	0-0	16		24,207
17	6	PL	A	Arsenal	D 0-0	0-0	16		(33,705)
18	19	PL	H	West Ham United	W 1-0	1-0	16	Petrescu 29	25,300
19	27	PL	A	Aston Villa	D 1-1	0-1	15	Atherton 58	(25,082)
20	30	CC 4	A	Arsenal	L 0-2	0-2			(27,390)
21	D 3	PL	H	Crystal Palace	W 1-0	1-0	14	Bart-Williams 19	21,930
22	10	PL	A	Tottenham Hotspur	L 1-3	1-0	15	Nolan 38	(25,912)
23	17	PL	H	Queens Park Rangers	L 0-2	0-0	18		22,766
24	26	PL	A	Everton	W 4-1	2-1	15	Bright 39, Whittingham 43, 79, Ingesson 48	(37,080)
25	28	PL	H	Coventry City	W 5-1	3-1	13	Bright 13, 44, Waddle 38, Whittingham 57, 64	26,056
26	31	PL	A	Leicester City	W 1-0	1-0	9	Hyde 40	(20,624)
27	J 2	PL	H	Southampton	D 1-1	1-0	10	Hyde 19	28,424
28	7	FAC 3	A	Gillingham	W 2-1	2-1		Waddle 31, Bright 32	(10,250)
29	14	PL	A	Chelsea	D 1-1	0-1	10	Nolan 89	(17,285)
30	21	PL	H	Newcastle United	D 0-0	0-0	9		31,215
31	23	PL	A	West Ham United	W 2-0	1-0	7	Waddle 33, Bright 83	(14,554)
32	30	FAC 4	H	Wolverhampton Wand.	D 0-0	0-0			21,757
33	F 4	PL	A	Arsenal	W 3-1	2-1	8	Petrescu 7, Ingesson 25, Bright 89	23,468
34	8	FAC 4R	A	Wolverhampton Wand.	D †1-1	0-1		Bright 56 (Lost 3-4 on penalties)	(28,136)
35	12	PL	A	Blackburn Rovers	L 1-3	1-2	8	Waddle 33	(22,223)
36	18	PL	H	Aston Villa	L 1-2	0-2	9	Bright 70	24,063
37	25	PL	H	Liverpool	L 1-2	1-1	9	Bart-Williams 14	31,964
38	M 4	PL	A	Leeds United	W 1-0	1-0	8	Waddle 11	(33,750)
39	8	PL	A	Norwich City	D 0-0	0-0	8		(13,530)
40	11	PL	H	Wimbledon	L 0-1	0-0	8		20,395
41	14	PL	A	Crystal Palace	L 1-2	1-0	8	Whittingham 31	(10,422)
42	18	PL	A	Manchester City	L 2-3	2-1	9	Whittingham 14, Hyde 22	(23,355)
43	A 1	PL	H	Nottingham Forest	L 1-7	0-2	11	Bright 53 (penalty)	30,060
44	8	PL	H	Leicester City	W 1-0	1-0	10	Whittingham 38	22,551
45	15	PL	A	Coventry City	L 0-2	0-1	11		(15,710)
46	17	PL	H	Everton	D 0-0	0-0	13		27,880
47	29	PL	A	Southampton	D 0-0	0-0	14		(15,189)
48	M 7	PL	A	Manchester United	L 0-1	0-1	14		(43,868)
49	14	PL	H	Ipswich Town	W 4-1	1-0	13	Whittingham 7, 59, Williams 55, Bright 89	30,213
50									
51									
52									
53									
54									
55									
56									
57									
58									
59									
60									

Best Home League Attendance: 34,051 v Tottenham Hotspur   **Smallest:** 20,395 v Wimbledon   **Av Home Att:** 26,595

Goal Scorers: **Compared with 1993-94:** -588

League (49): Bright 11 (1 pen), Whittingham 9, Hyde 5, Waddle 4, Nolan 3, Petrescu 3, Hirst 3, Bart-Williams 2, Ingleson 2, Watson 2, Sheridan, Taylor, Williams, Atherton, Opponent

C/Cola Cup (4): Bart-Williams 2, Hyde, Taylor

FA Cup (3): Bright 2, Waddle

1994-95

13 Pressman K.	5 Petrescu D.	3 Nocan I.	17 Wacker D.	2 Atherton P.	15 Sinton A.	11 Sheridan J.	4 Taylor I.	14 Bart-Williams C.	9 Hirst D.	10 Bright M.	20 Watson G.	28 Coleman S.	23 Key L.	16 Hyde G.	21 Jones R.	12 Pearce A.	18 Ingesson K.	29 Briscoe L.	Hardwick M.	7 Poric A.	24 Watts J.	8 Waddle C.	19 Wittingham G.	1 Woods C.	25 Williams M.	Referee	
X	X	X	X	X	X	X	X	X	X	X1	S1	S	S													Hill B.	1
X	X	X	X	X1	X	X	X	S2	X		X		S	X2	S1											Jones P.	2
X	X1	X	X	X		X	X	X2	X		S2		S	S1	X	X										Hart R.	3
X	X	X	X	X	X	X	X1	S1	X	X2	S2		S			X										Cooper K.	4
X	X1	X		X	X	X2		S2	X		S1	X	S	X		X	X									Don P.	5
X	X	X		X	X1	X		X	X	X2	S2		S	X		X	S1									Gallagher D.	6
X	X	X		X		X	S1	X	X	X2	S2		S	X		X	X1									Holbrook T.	7
X	X	X	X	X	X1	X		X	S2	X2	X		S	X												Wickie A.	8
X	X	X		X	X	X		X	S1	X	X1		S	X		S										Willard G.	9
X		X	X	X	X1	X		S1	X	S2	X2	X	S	X		X										Dickes L.R.	10
X		X	X	X		X		S1	X1	X	X2	S2	S	X		X		X								Danson P.S.	11
X		X	X	S1		X		S2	X2	X	X		S	X		X		X1								Reed M.	12
X	S2	X	X2	X	X	X	X	S1	X1	X			S	X		X			S							Poll G.	13
X	S	X	X	X	X	X	X	X					S	X		X										Hill B.	14
X	S2	X	X	X	X	X1	X	X2		X	S1		S	X		X										Reed M.	15
X	S1	X	X1	X	X	X	X	X2		X	S2		S	X		X										Hart R.	16
X	S2	X	X2	X	X1	X	X	X		X	S2		S	X		X										Gifford R.	17
X	X1	X	X	X	X	X	S1	X2		X	S2		S	X		X										Ashby G.	18
X	X	X	X	X	X	X	S1	X		X1			S	X		X					S					Poll G.	19
X	X	X		X	X	X	X	X		X1			S	X	S1	X						S				Bodenham M.	20
X	X	X		X	X	X	X1	X		X			S	X		X						S	S1			Cooper K.	21
X	X	X	X	X		X	X	S	X				S	X		X		X				S	X			Bodenham M.	22
X	S2	X	X	X2		X		X	X1				S	X	X	X	S1					X				Durkin P.	23
X		X	X	X	X1	X		X	X				S	X		X	X			S1		S	X			Holbrook T.	24
X		X	X	X		X		X	X2	S2			S	X		X	X1					S1	X			Morton K.	25
X	S1	X	X	X		X		X	X	S2			S	X		X						X1	X2			Reed M.	26
	X	S1	X	X	X		X		X	X	S2		S	X		X						X1	X2			Dickes R.	27
X	S2	X	X	X		X		X		X	S		S1	X		X						X2	X1			Bodenham M.	28
X	S2	X	X	X		X		X		X1	S1		S			X	X2					X	X			Willard G.	29
	X	X	X	X		X		X		S1	X1		S			X						X	X	X	S	Gifford R.	30
X	S2	X	X	X		X		X		X	S1			X		X	X					X2	X1	S		Danson P.	31
X	S2	X	X	X		X2		X		X	S1			X		X	X					X	X1	S		Wilkie A.	32
X	X	X	X1	X		X		S1		X2				X		X	X					X	S2	S		Burge K.	33
X		X	X	X	X2	S1		X		X				X		X	X1					X	S3	S1	S2	Wilkie A.	34
X	X2	X	X	X	X1	X3		X		X				X		X						X	S3	S1	S2	Jones P.	35
X	X	X	X	X	X2	X		S2		X				X		X		X1				X	S1	S		Gallagher D.	36
X	X2	X	X	X	X	S1		X		X	S2			X		X						X1	X	S		Ellerey D.	37
	X1	X	X	X	S1			X		X	S		S	X		X						X		X	X	Cooper K.	38
		X	X	X	S		X		X	S1		S	X		X		X					X1		X	X	Danson P.	39
X	X1	X	X	X				X		X				X2		X					S1	X	S2	S	X	Worrall J.	40
X		X	X	X	X1			X		X	S2		S	X2	X2	X						S1	X	S		Don P.	41
X	X2	X	X		X		X		X					X1		X						X	X	S	S1	Burge K.	42
X	X	X	X		X	X1		X		X				X		X					S	X	S1	S		Wilkie A.	43
S		X	X	X	S1	X		X2	S2					X		X	X1					X	X	X	X	Ashby G.	44
S	X1	X	X	X		X		S2	X					X		X	X2					S1	X	X		Willard G.	45
X		X	X	X		X		X2	S2					X1		X	S1					X	X	S		Reed M.	46
S		X	X	X				X		X					S1	X	S2			X1		X2	X	X	X	Worrall J.	47
S		X	X	X		X		X		X				X1		X				S2		S1	X2	X	X	Durkin P.	48
S		X	X	X	X1			X2	S2					S1		X						X	X	X	X	Poll G.	49
34	20	42	38	41	22	34	9	32	13	33	5	1		33	3	34	9	6		1		20	16	8	8	League Appearances	
4	2	4	2	4	3	4	2+2	4	1+1	3				2+1		4	0+1	4		1						C/Cola Cup Appearances	
3	0+2	3	3	3	1	2+1		3		3	0+1		0+1	3		3	1					3	2+1			FA Cup Appearances	

Also Played: Donaldson S2(42)

† = Sent Off

145

SHEFFIELD WEDNESDAY

CLUB RECORDS

BIGGEST VICTORIES
League: 9-1 v Birmingham, Division 1, 13.12.1930
8-0 v Sunderland, Division 1, 26.12.1911
F.A. Cup: 12-0 v Halliwell, Round 1, 17.1.1891
League Cup: 8-0 v Aldershot (a), Round 2, 3.10.1989
Europe: 8-1 v Spora Luxembourg, UEFA Cup Rnd 1 1st leg, 16.9.1992

BIGGEST DEFEATS
League: 0-10 v Aston Villa, Division 1, 5.10.1912
F.A. Cup: 0-5 v Wolves, Round 3, 2.3.1889
1-6 v Blackburn Rovers, Final, 29.3.1890
0-5 v Everton (h), Round 3 replay, 27.1.1988
League Cup: 2-8 v Queens Park R., Round 2, 1973-74
Europe: No more than 2 goals

MOST POINTS
3 points a win: 88, Division 2, 1983-84
2 points a win: 62, Division 2, 1958-59

MOST GOALS
106, 1958-59 (Division 2).
Shiner 28, Froggatt 26, Fantham 12, Wilkinson 12, Finney 11, Curtis 5, JMcAnearney 3, Kay 3, Quixall 2, Ellis 1, T McAnearney 1, Young 1, og 1.

MOST LEAGUE GOALS CONCEDED
100, Division 1, 1954-55

MOST FIRST CLASS MATCHES IN A SEASON
61 (46 League, 4 FA Cup, 10 League Cup, 1 ZDS) 1990-91

MOST LEAGUE WINS
28, Division 2, 1958-59

MOST LEAGUE DRAWS
19, Division 3, 1978-79

MOST LEAGUE DEFEATS
26, Division 1, 1919-20; Division 2, 1974-75

INDIVIDUAL CLUB RECORDS

MOST GOALS IN A MATCH
6. Douglas Hunt v Norwich, Division 2, 19.11.1938 (7-0)

MOST GOALS IN A SEASON
Derek Dooley 47, (46 League, 1 FAC) 1951-52.
5 goals once=5; 4 goals twice=8; 3 goals 3 times=9; 2 goals 9 times=18; 1 goal 7 times=7
Previous holder: J Trotter, 37 League (1925-26 & 1926-27).

OLDEST PLAYER
Tom Brittleton 41 years v Oldham, 1.5.1920.

YOUNGEST PLAYER
Peter Fox 15 years 269 days, 31.3.1973

MOST CAPPED PLAYER
Nigel Worthington (N. Ireland) 48

BEST PERFORMANCES

League: 1958-59: Matches played 42, Won 28, Drawn 6, Lost 8, Goals for 106, Goals against 48, Points 62. 1st in Division 2

Highest: 1st in Division 1

F.A. Cup: 1895-96: 1st rnd. Southampton 3-2; 2nd rnd. Sunderland 2-1; 3rd rnd. Everton 4-0; Semi-Final Bolton 3-1; Final Wolves 2-1.
1906-07: 3rd rnd. Wolves 3-2; 4th rnd. Southampton 1-1, 3-1; 5th rnd. Sunderland 0-0, 1-0; 5th rnd. Liverpool 1-0; Semi-Final Arsenal 1-0; FinalEverton 2-1.
1934-35: 3rd rnd. Oldham 3-1; 4th rnd. Wolves 2-1; 5th rnd. Norwich City 1-0;6th rnd. Arsenal 2-1; Semi-Final Burnley 3-0; Final West Bromwich A. 4-2.

League Cup: 1990-91: 2nd rnd. Brentford 2-1, 2-1; 3rd rnd. Swindon 0-0, 1-0; 4th rnd. Derby Co. 1-1, 2-1; 5th rnd. Coventry City 1-0; Semi-Final Chelsea 2-0, 3-1; Final Manchester Utd 1-0

EUFA: 1963-64: 1st rnd. Olympique Lyonnais 2-4, 5-2; 2nd rnd. AS Roma 4-0, 0-1;Q/Final Barcelona 3-2, 0-2.

DIVISIONAL RECORD

	Played	Won	Drawn	Lost	For	Against	Points
Division 1/P	2,392	923	565	898	3,739	3,729	2,563
Division 2	1,088	460	281	347	1,693	1,401	1,285
Division 3	230	83	76	71	297	266	242
Total	3,712	1,466	922	1,322	5,737	5,396	4,090

ADDITIONAL INFORMATION
Previous Name
The Wednesday 1867-1929

Previous League
Football Alliance

Club colours: Blue & white striped shirts, black shorts, blue socks.
Change colours: Black shirts with yellow pinstripe, black shorts and socks with yellow trim.

Reserves League: Pontins Central League Division 2.

RECORDS AND STATISTICS

COMPETITIONS

Div 1/P	Div.2	Div.3	EUFA
1892-99	1899-1900	1975-80	1961-62
1900-20	1920-26		1963-64
1926-37	1937-50		
1950-51	1951-52		
1952-55	1955-56		
1956-58	1958-59		
1959-70	1970-75		
1984-90	1980-84		
1991-	1990-91		

HONOURS

Div 1/P	Div.2	FA Cup	League Cup
1902-03	1899-1900	1896	1991
1903-04	1925-26	1907	
1928-29	1951-52	1935	**C/Shield**
1929-30	1955-56		1935
	1958-59		

MOST GOALS IN A CAREER
ANDREW WILSON - 216 (1900-20)

Year	League	FA Cup
1900-01	13	
1901-02	9	
1902-03	12	
1903-04	10	2
1904-05	15	2
1905-06	16	2
1906-07	17	4
1907-08	19	
1908-09	18	3
1909-10	12	
1910-11	9	1
1911-12	12	
1912-13	9	2
1913-14	15	
1914-15	13	1
Total	**199**	**17**

Current leading goalscorer: David Hirst 108 (1986-95)

MOST APPEARANCES
ANDREW WILSON 546 (1900-20)

Year	League	FA Cup
1900-01	31	1
1901-02	25	1
1902-03	34	2
1903-04	29	3
1904-05	30	3
1905-06	35	5
1906-07	35	7
1907-08	34	1
1908-09	37	4
1909-10	30	2
1910-11	38	1
1911-12	37	2
1912-13	37	4
1913-14	31	5
1914-15	38	3
1919-20	1	
	502	**44**

MANAGERS

Name	Seasons	Best	Worst
Rob Brown	1920-23	1(1)	14(2)
Bill Walker	1933-37	3(2)	22(2)
Jim McMullen	1937-42	3(2)	17(2)
Eric Taylor	1942-58	14(1)	20(2)
Harry Catterick	1958-61	2(1)	5(1)
Vic Buckingham	1961-64	6(1)	6(1)
Alan Brown	1964-67	8(1)	17(1)
Jack Marshall	1967-68	19(1)	19(1)
Tom McAnearney	1968-69	15(1)	15(1)
Danny Williams	1969-71	22(1)	15(1)
Derek Dooley	1971-74	10(2)	19(2)
Steve Burtenshaw	1974-75	22(2)	20(3)
Len Ashurst	1975-77	8(3)	14(3)
Jack Charlton	1977-83	4(2)	18(3)
Howard Wilkinson	1983-88	5(1)	2(2)
Peter Eustace	1989		
Ron Atkinson	1989-91	18(1)	3(2)
Trevor Francis	1991-95	3(1)	7(1/P)
David Pleat	1995-		

RECORD TRANSFER FEE RECEIVED

Amount	Club	Player	Date
£2,750,000	Blackburn Rov.	Paul Warhurst	8/93
£1,700,000	Real Sociedad	Dalian Atkinson	8/90
£800,000	Glasgow Rangers	Mel Sterland	3/89
£600,000	Arsenal	Brain Marwood	3/88

RECORD TRANSFER FEE PAID

Amount	Club	Player	Date
£2,750,000	Q.P.R.	Andy Sinton	8/93
£1,200,000	Glasgow Rangers	Chris Woods	8/91
£750,000	West Brom	Carlton Palmer	3/89
£475,000	Ipswich Town	Ian Cranson	3/88

LONGEST LEAGUE RUNS

of undefeated matches:	19 (3.12.1960 - 17.4.1961)	of league matches w/out a win:	20 (7.1.54-17.3.55, 11.1.75-6.9.75)
of undefeated home matches:	31 (13.12.1902 - 29.10.1904)	of undefeated away matches:	11 (6.11.1979 - 12.4.1980)
without home win:	13 (7.2.1974 - 6.9.1975)	without an away win:	35 (28.12.1974 - 16.10.1976)
of league wins:	9 (14.11.1903 - 16.1.1904)	of home wins:	19 (2.9.1899 - 6.10.1900)
of league defeats:	7 (7.1.1893 - 25.3.1893)	of away wins:	6 (28.4.1990 - 6.10.1990)

SHEFFIELD WEDNESDAY

PLAYERS NAME / Honours	Ht	Wt	Birthdate	Birthplace / Transfers	Contract Date	Clubs	League	L/Cup	FA Cup	Other	Lge	L/C	FAC	Oth
G O A L K E E P E R S														
Kevin Pressman	6.1	14.2	06.11.67	Fareham	07.11.85	Sheffield Wed. (A)	128	21	7	4				
E: B.1, u21.1, u19.3, Y.6, S.				Loan	10.03.92	Stoke City	4			2				
Chris Woods	6.2	13.5	14.11.59	Boston	01.12.76	Nottm. Forest (A)		7						
E: 43, u21.6, Y. Div'2'86. LC'78'85.				£250,000	04.07.79	Q.P.R.	63	8	1					
SPD'87'89'90'91 SLC'87'89'91.				£225,000	12.03.81	Norwich City	216	26	19	6				
				£600,000	02.07.86	Glasgow Rangers	173	21	15	21				
				£1,200,000	15.08.91	Sheffield Wed.	98+1	13	10	5				
D E F E N D E R S														
Peter Atherton	5.11	12.3	06.04.70	Orrell	12.02.88	Wigan Athletic (T)	145+4	8	7	12+1	1			
E: u21.1, S.				£300,000	23.08.91	Coventry City	113+1	4	2					
				£800,000	01.06.94	Sheffield Wed.	31	4	3		1			
Marc Burrows	5.9	10.05	20.12.75	Sheffield	22.05.94	Sheffield Wed (T)								
David Faulkner	6.2	11.0	08.10.75	Sheffield	23.12.92	Sheffield Wed (T)								
E: Y.1, S.														
Bryan Linighan	6.0	10.3	02.11.73	Hartlepool	16.07.92	Sheffield Wed (T)	1	1	1					
Ian Nolan	6.0	11.10	09.07.70	Liverpool	31.08.88	Preston N.E. (T)								
				Free		Northwich Victoria			2					
						Marine								
				£100,000	02.08.91	Tranmere Rovers	87+1	10	7	9	1	1		
				£1,500,000	.08.94	Sheffield Wed.	42	4	3	3				
Andy Pearce	6.6	14.6	20.04.66	Bradford-on-Avon		Halesowen Town								
				£15,000	14.05.90	Coventry City	68+3	6	3	1	4			
				£500,000	24.06.93	Sheffield Wed.	63+3	10+1	6+1		3		1	
Dan Petrescou	5.8	11.0	22.12.67	Romania		Steau Bucharest								
Romanian Int. Romanian Div.1'85'86'87'88						Foggia								
Romanian FAC'85'87'88.						Genoa								
				£1,250,000	06.08.94	Sheffield Wed.	20+9	2	0+2		3			
Simon A Stewart	6.1	11.0	01.11.73	Leeds	16.07.92	Sheffield Wed (T)	6	0+1						
Des Walker	5.11	11.9	26.11.65	Hackney	02.12.83	Nottm. Forest (A)	259+5	40	27	14	1			
E: 59, u21.7. LC'89'90. FMC'89'92.				£1,500,000	01.08.92	Sampdoria								
				£2,700,000	22.07.93	Sheffield Wed.	80	10	7					
Julian Watts	6.3	12.1	17.03.71	Sheffield	10.07.90	Rotherham Utd (T)	17+3	1	4	2	1			
				£80,000	13.03.92	Sheffield Wed.	3+2			1				
				Loan	18.12.92	Shrewsbury Town	9			1				
M I D F I E L D														
Darren Holmes	5.9	10.7	30.01.75	Sheffield	05.07.93	Sheffield Wed (T)								
Graham Hyde	5.7	11.7	10.11.70	Doncaster	17.05.88	Sheffield Wed (T)	83+21	14+2	8+5	4	7	2	1	1
Klas Ingesson	6.3	14.0	20.08.68	Odeshog		IFK Gothenburg								
						Mechelen								
						PSV Eindhoven								
				£2,000,000	01.09.94	Sheffield Wed.	9+4	1	1		2			
Ryan Jones	5.8	11.4	23.07.73	Sheffield		Sheffield Wed (T)	36+5	4+1	3		6	1		
W: 1, B.1, u21.1.														
Mark Pembridge	5.7	11.1	29.11.70	Merthyr Tydfil	01.07.89	Luton Town (T)	60	2	4	4	6			
W: 8, B.1, u21.1.				£1,250,000	02.06.92	Derby County	108+2	9	6	15	28	1	3	5
				£900,000	08.95	Sheffield Wed.								
Adam Poric	5.9	11.13	22.04.73	Australia		St George (Aust)								
Australian Int.				£60,000	01.10.93	Sheffield Wed.	3+7	0+2						
John Sheridan	5.9	10.8	01.10.64	Stretford		Manchester City (J)								
Ei: 24, u23.1, u21.2, Y. LC'91.				Free	02.03.82	Leeds United	225+5	14	11+1	11	47	3	1	1
				£650,000	03.08.89	Nottm. Forest		1						
				£500,000	03.11.89	Sheffield Wed.	174+4	24	17+1	4	25	3	3	2
Andy Sinton	5.7	10.7	19.03.66	Newcastle	13.04.83	Cambridge Utd (A)	90+3	6	3	2	13	1		1
E: 12, B.3, S. FLgXI.1.				£25,000	13.12.85	Brentford	149	8	11	14	28	3	1	2
				£350,000	23.03.89	Q.P.R.	160	14	13	3	22		2	1
				£2,750,000	19.08.93	Sheffield Wed.	47+3	10	4		3			
Michael A Williams	5.10	11.6	21.11.69	Bradford		Maltby MW								
				Free	13.02.91	Sheffield Wed.	14+3	1+1		1	1			
				Loan	18.12.92	Halifax Town	9			1	1			
F O R W A R D S														
Richard Barker	6.0	11.8	30.05.75	Sheffield	27.07.93	Sheffield Wed (T)								
Mark Bright	6.0	11.0	06.06.62	Stoke		Leek Town								
FMC'91.				Free	15.10.81	Port Vale	18+11	1+1	0+1	2	10		1	
				£33,000	19.07.84	Leicester City	26+16	3+1	1		6			
				£75,000	13.11.86	Crystal Palace	224+3	22	13+1	23	90	11	2	9
				£1,375,000	11.09.92	Sheffield Wed.	97+10	17	13		41	8	7	
Lee Briscoe	5.10	10.9	30.09.75	Pontefract	22.05.94	Sheffield Wed (T)	6+1							

O'Neill Donaldson 6.0 11.4 24.11.69 Birmingham		Hinckley Town								
	13.11.91	Shrewsbury Town	15+13			1	4			
Free	10.08.94	Doncaster Rovers	7+2	2		0+1	2			
Loan	23.12.94	Mansfield Town	4		1		6		1	
£50,000	09.01.95	Sheffield Wed.	0+1							
Marc Degryse 5.8 10.9 04.09.65 Roeselare (Belg)		Anderlecht								
£1,500,000	08.95	Sheffield Wed.								
Mark Guest 5.7 10.0 21.01.76 Mexborough	22.05.94	Sheffield Wed (T)								
David Hirst 5.11 12.5 07.12.67 Cudworth	08.11.85	Barnsley (A)	26+2	1			9			
E: 3, B.3, u21.7, u19.3, Y.8. LC'91. £200,000	11.08.86	Sheffield Wed.	209+24	23+8	11+5	8	87	10	6	5
Chris Waddle 6.0 11.5 14.12.60 Felling		Tow Law								
E: 62, u21.1. FLg.2. Fra: Div.1'90'91'92. FFAC'92. £1,000	28.07.80	Newcastle United	169+1	8	12		46	2	4	
£590,000	01.07.85	Tottenham Hotspur	137+1	21	14	4	33	4	5	
£4,250,000	01.07.89	Marseille								
£1,000,000	01.07.92	Sheffield Wed.	71+6	15	11+1	3+1	8		3	1
Guy Whittingham 5.10 11.12 10.11.64 Evesham		Oxford City								
LC'94.		Waterlooville								
		Yeovil Town								
Free	09.06.89	Portsmouth	149+11	7+2	7+3	9	88	3	10	3
£1,200,000	01.08.93	Aston Villa	13+5	2		1	3			
Loan	28.02.94	Wolverhampton W.	13		1		8			
£700,000	21.12.94	Sheffield Wed.	16+5		2+1		9			

TOP GOALSCORER 1994/95
Mark Bright

Premiership goals (games) . . . . 11 (33+4)
Coca-Cola Cup Goals 0 (3)
F.A. Cup goals 2 (3)

Total . . . . **13 (39+4)**

Total goals for Sheffield Wednesday since 11.09.92 . . . . 56 (127+10)

Career total as at June 1st 1995 . . . . 185 (460+44)

THE MANAGER
DAVID PLEAT

Date of Birth . . . . 15th January 1945.
Place of Birth . . . . Nottingham.
Date of Appointment . . . . June 1995.

PREVIOUS CLUBS
As Manager. . . . Nuneaton, Luton Town, Tottenham, Leicester City, Luton Town.
As Coach. . . . . Luton Town.
As a Player . . . . Nott'm Forest, Luton Town, Shrewsbury, Exeter, Peterborough.

HONOURS
As a Manager
Div. 2 championship 1981-82.

As a Player
None.
International: England schoolboy 1961, Youth 1962, 1963, 1964.

HILLSBOROUGH

Sheffield S6 1SW
Tel: 01142 343 122

Capacity 36,000

First game .... v Chesterfield, Div 2, 5-1, 2.9.1899.
First floodlit game .... v International XI, 9.3.1955.
Internationals .... England v Scotland 1920, v France 1962.
.... W.Germany v Switzerland & v Uruguay 1966. Switzerland v Spain & v Argentina 1966.
.... N.Ireland v Bulgaria 1974.

ATTENDANCES
Highest .... 72,841 v Man. City, FAC 5th Rnd, 17.2.1934.
Lowest .... 2,500 v Everton, 5.4.1902.
OTHER GROUNDS: .... Highfields 1867-69. Myrtle Rd 1869-77.
.... Sheaf Close 1877-87. Olive Grove 1887-99. Owlerton (changed to Hillsborough 1912) 1899-

MATCHDAY TICKET PRICES

.... Premier Category/Standard
North & South Centre .... £17/£12.50
Concession .... £11.50/£8.50

Kop & West Lower .... £11.50/£8.50
Concession .... £6.50/£5

West Upper .... £12.50/£12.50
Concession .... £8.50/£8.50

Family Enclosure .... £10/£10
Concession .... £6/£6

Ticket Office Telephone no. 01142 337 233

CLUBCALL
0898 12 11 86
Calls cost 39p per minute cheap rate and 49p per
minute at all other times.
Call costings correct at time of going to press.

HOW TO GET TO THE GROUND

From the North
Use motorway (M1) until junction 34, leave motorway and follow signs to
Sheffield (A6109). in 1.5 miles at roundabout take 3rd exit (A6102). In 3.2 miles
turn left into Harries Road South for Sheffield Wednesday FC.

From East and South
Use A57 from motorway M1 (junction 31 or 33) then at roundabout junction with
Rign Road take 3rd exit A610 into Prince of Wales Road. In 5.8 miles turn left
into Herries Road South for Sheffield Wednesday FC.

From the West
Use A57 (sign posted Sheffield) then turn left A6101. In 3.8 miles at 'T' junction
turn left A61 into Penistone Road for Sheffield Wednesday FC.

Car Parking
Street parking is available.

Nearest Railway Station
Sheffield (01142 726 411).

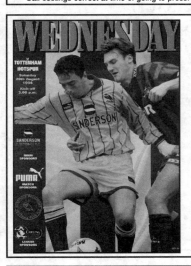

MATCHDAY PROGRAMME

Programme Editor .... Roger Oldfield.

Number of pages .... 24.

Price .... £1.50.

Subscriptions . . 1st Class £56.78, 2nd Class £46.70, surface mail £57.

Local Newspapers .... Sheffield Newspapers Ltd. (The Star).

Local Radio Stations .... BBC Radio Sheffield, Radio Hallam.

SOUTHAMPTON
(The Saints)
F.A. CARLING PREMIERSHIP
SPONSORED BY: SANDERSON ELECTRONICS

Back Row (L-R): Frankie Bennett, Alan Neilson, Neil Shipperley, Dave Beasant, Ken Monkou, Richard Hall, Peter Whiston, Neil Heaney.
Middle Row: Paul McDonald, Craig Maskell, Gordon Watson, Simon Charlton, Jason Dodd, Tommy Widdrington, David Hughes, Paul Tisdale, Paul Allen.
Front Row: Lew Chatterley (Asst. Manager), Neil Maddison, Matthew Le Tissier, Lawrie McMenemy (Director of Football), Dave Merrington (Manager), Francis Benali, Jim Magilton, Jim Joyce (Physio).

SOUTHAMPTON
FORMED IN 1885
TURNED PROFESSIONAL IN 1894
LTD COMPANY IN 1897

PRESIDENT: John Corbett
VICE-PRESIDENT: E T Bates
CHAIRMAN: F G Askham FCA
DIRECTORS
F St J Wiseman (Vice-Chairman),
I L Gordon, B D H Hunt, M R Richards FCA
Lawrie McMenemy
SECRETARY
Brian Truscott (01703 220 505)
COMMERCIAL MANAGER
John O'Sullivan

MANAGER: Dave Merrington
ASSISTANT MANAGERS
Lew Chatterley, John Mortimore
RESERVE TEAM MANAGER
Ray Graydon
YOUTH TEAM MANAGER
Dennis Rofe
PHYSIOTHERAPIST
Jim Joyce
STATISTICIAN FOR THE DIRECTORY
John Mason

Welcome to the world of 'Fantasy Football' where many have enjoyed the challenge of team ownership in various 'Dream Leagues' up and down the country. But imagine the dilemma facing the owner who has selected a team only costing a combined total of £1.6 million whilst fully aware that a figure of £20 million worth of talent is available to almost every other competitor. wake up to the realities of the management of Southampton Football Club entering, not an imaginary league, but the first day of the Premiership season just completed. Seven players field that afternoon commanded no transfer fee at all and the opponents were non other than Blackburn Rovers, the champions elect. However, to return to pure fantasy again, a point is obtained to immediately open the team's account.

The key to the opportunity of success, whether as a fantasy owner or in real life, is shuffling the pack within your means so that, subsequently to cost Saints a club record outlay; then Keena was transferred to cover the record equaling Watson's signature. A clever hire purchase arrangement with Barcelona enabled Ekelund delight the fans briefly before turning to Spain. The management currently has to set its sights a little lower than perhaps many would wish, and view their highest position finish for five years as a successful outcome to the season.

The problem the club has is not a lack of enthusiasm from the public locally, they filled the ground to an average 96% of capacity, but the size of their stadium and where the site provides no room to expand. They are desperate to re-locate to a community stadium complex for which they have planning consent, but are currently being blocked by the refusal of the county council to release their portion of the land even though it was identified as surplus to their requirements. It is hoped that when the opportunity to reconsider that decision is presented, a more enlightened approach is displayed.

The Saints are a family club, strongest when they and the community are one unit and pulling together. After the shock departure of Alan Ball, the appointment of the popular Dave Merrington as Manager is very much intended to maintain this spirit of unity.

JOHN MASON.

SOUTHAMPTON

Premier League: 10th   **FA Cup:** 5th Round   **Coca-Cola Cup:** 3rd Round

M	DATE	COMP.	VEN	OPPONENTS	RESULT	H/T	LP	GOAL SCORERS/GOAL TIMES	ATT.
1	A 20	PL	H	Blackburn Rovers	D 1-1	1-0		Banger 15	14,209
2	24	PL	A	Aston Villa	D 1-1	0-1		Le Tissier 89	(24,279)
3	27	PL	A	Newcastle United	L 1-5	0-3	16	Banger 52	(34,181)
4	31	PL	H	Liverpool	L 0-2	0-1	18		15,190
5	S 12	PL	A	Tottenham Hotspur	W 2-1	0-1	15	Le Tissier 75(pen), 88	(22,387)
6	17	PL	H	Nottingham Forest	D 1-0	0-0	14	Le Tissier 54 (pen)	14,185
7	20	CC 2/1	A	Huddersfield Town	W 1-0	0-0		Le Tissier 90	(13,814)
8	24	PL	A	Coventry City	W 3-1	1-1	13	Dowie 19, 55, Ekelund 82	(11,784)
9	O 1	PL	H	Ipswich Town	W 3-1	0-0	8	Maddison 53, Ekelund 65, Dowie 89	13,246
10	5	CC 2/2	H	Huddersfield Town	W 4-0	1-0		Le Tissier 41,66,69,84	12,032
11	8	PL	H	Everton	W 2-0	1-0	7	Ekelund 19, Le Tissier 72	15,163
12	15	PL	A	Leicester City	L 3-4	0-2	10	Dowie 78, 90, Le Tissier	(20,020)
13	22	PL	A	West Ham United	L 0-2	0-0	10		(18,853)
14	26	CC 3	A	Sheffield United	L 1-3	1-0	12		(16,715)
15	29	PL	H	Leeds United	L 1-3	1-0	12	Maddison 44	15,202
16	N 2	PL	H	Norwich City	D 1-1	0-0	13	Le Tissier 89 (pen)	12,976
17	5	PL	A	Manchester City	D 3-3	1-0	12	Hall 26, Ekelund 62, 66	(21,589)
18	19	PL	H	Arsenal	W 1-0	0-0	9	Magilton 60	15,201
19	26	PL	A	Crystal Palace	D 0-0	0-0	11		(14,007)
20	D 3	PL	H	Chelsea	L 0-1	0-0	13		14,404
21	10	PL	A	Blackburn Rovers	L 2-3	0-0	13	Le Tissier 65, 78	(23,372)
22	19	PL	H	Aston Villa	W 2-1	1-0	12	Hall 9, Le Tissier 90	13,874
23	26	PL	H	Wimbledon	L 2-3	2-2	14	Dodd 10, Le Tissier 42	14,603
24	28	PL	A	Queens Park Rangers	L 1-2	1-1	14	Dodd 15, Hughes 71	(16,078)
25	31	PL	H	Manchester United	D 2-2	1-0	15	Magilton 44, Hughes 74	15,204
26	J 2	PL	A	Sheffield Wednesday	D 1-1	0-1	15	Le Tissier 68	(28,424)
27	7	FAC 3	H	Southend United	W 2-0	2-0		Heaney 1, Le Tissier 42	13,003
28	14	PL	A	Leeds United	D 0-0	0-0	14		(28,953)
29	24	PL	A	Arsenal	D 1-1	0-1	14	Magilton 74	(27,213)
30	28	FAC 4	A	Luton Town	D 1-1	0-0		Shipperley 53	(9,938)
31	F 4	PL	H	Manchester City	D 2-2	1-1	15	Coton 24 (og), Le Tissier 60	14,902
32	8	FAC 4R	H	Luton Town	W 6-0	4-0		Le Tissier 6,36 (pen), Magilton 32, Heaney 40, Monkou 50, Hughes 67	15,075
33	11	PL	A	Norwich City	D 2-2	2-1	16	Hall 33, Magilton 36	(18,361)
34	18	FAC 5	A	Tottenham Hotspur	D 1-1	1-1		Le Tissier 22 (pen)	(28,091)
35	25	PL	H	Ipswich Town	L 1-2	1-0	18	Maddison 38	(16,076)
36	M 1	FAC 5R	H	Totenham Hotspur	L †2-6	2-0		Shipperley 5, Le Tissier 39 (pen)	15,172
37	4	PL	H	Coventry City	D 0-0	0-0	18		14,505
38	15	PL	H	West Ham United	D 1-1	0-1		Shipperley 48	15,178
39	18	PL	A	Nottingham Forest	A 0-3	0-1	20		(24,146)
40	22	PL	H	Newcastle United	W 3-1	0-1	19	Heaney 86, Watson 90, Shipperley 90	14,676
41	A 2	PL	H	Tottenham Hotspur	W 4-3	2-2	17	Heaney 12, Le Tissier 44, 57, Magilton 62	15,105
42	5	PL	A	Liverpool	L 1-3	1-1	17	Hall 13	(19,881)
43	12	PL	A	Chelsea	W 2-0	2-0	14	Shipperley 10, Le Tissier 33	(16,738)
44	15	PL	H	Queens Park Rangers	W 2-1	0-0	13	Shipperley 49, Watson 67	15,210
45	17	PL	A	Wimbledon	W 2-0	2-0	11	Le Tissier 9, Magilton 32	(10,521)
46	29	PL	H	Sheffield Wednesday	D 0-0	0-0	11		15,189
47	M 3	PL	H	Crystal Palace	W 3-1	2-1	10	Le Tissier 1, 86, Watson 9	15,151
48	6	PL	A	Everton	D 0-0	0-0	10		(36,840)
49	10	PL	A	Manchester United	L 1-2	1-1	10	Charlton 5	(43,479)
50	14	PL	H	Leicester City	D 2-2	1-0	10	Monkou 21, Le Tissier 56	15,101
51									
52									
53									
54									
55									
56									
57									
58									
59									
60									

Best Home League Attendance: 15,210 v Queens Park Rangers   **Smallest:** 12,976 v Norwich City   **Av Home Att:** 14,689

Goal Scorers: **Compared with 1993-94:**-75

League (61):   Le Tissier 20, Magilton 6, Dowie 5, Ekelund 5, Hall 4, Shipperley 4, Maddison 3, Watson 3, Banger 2, Dodd 2, Hughes 2, Heaney 2, Charlton, Monkou, Opponent

C/Cola Cup (5):   Le Tissier 5

FA Cup (12):   Le Tissier 5, Heaney 2, Shipperely 2, Magilton, Monkou, Hughes

1 Grobbelaar B.	2 Kenna J.	5 Hall R.	21 Widdrington T.	3 Benali F.	14 Charlton S.	11 Allen P.	4 Magilton J.	10 Maddison N.	7 Le Tissier M.	16 Banger N.	12 Heaney N.	20 Whiston P.	13 Beasant D.	6 Monkou K.	9 Dowie I.	24 Ekelund R.	15 Dodd J.	28 Tisdale P.	Bennett F.	23 Hopper N.	18 Hughes D.	19 McDonald P.	8 Maskell C.	9 Shipperley N.	16 Watson G.	Referee	
X	X	X	X	X	X	X1	X	X	X	X	S1	S	S													K. Cooper	1
X	X	X	X1	X	X	X	X	X	X	X	S1	S	S													P. Don	2
X	X	X2	X1	X	X	X	X	X	X	X	S1	S2	S													D. Elleray	3
X	X	S1	S	X	X	X	X	X	X	X	X		S		X1											M. Bodenham	4
X	X	X	S	X	X	X	X	X	X	X	S			X	X											A. Wilkie	5
X	X	X		X	X	X	X1	X	S	X			S		X	S1										M. Reed	6
X	X	X		X	X	X	X1	X	S	X			S		X		S1									P. Jones	7
X	X		S	X	X	X	X	X	X		S		S	X	X	X										K. Morton	8
X		X	S	X	X	X1	X	X			S1		S	X	X	X	X									G. Ashby	9
X		X1	X		X		X		X		X		S	X	X2	X	X	S1	S2							M. Pierce	10
X1	X	S	X		X		X		X		X		S1	X	X	X	S									B. Hill	11
	X	X		X	X	X1	X				S12		X	X	X	X	S2			S						B. Hart	12
	X	X		S1	X1	X	X2						X	X	X	X				S	S2					J. Worrall	13
X	X	X		X2	S2	X	X				S1		X	X	X	X1										B. Hill	14
X	X	X		S1	X1	X	X2	X	X		S2		X	X	X	X										R. Gifford	15
X	X	X	S	X1		X	X	X	X		X		S	X	X	X						S1				P. Durkin	16
X	X	X	X1	X		X	X	X			S1		S	X2	X	X	S2									M. Reed	17
X	X	X	X	X		X	X	X		X	S	S	S		X	X					S					R. Dilkes	18
X	X	X	X	X		X	X	X		X	S	S	S		X	X								S		P. Danson	19
X	X	X	X	X	S	X	X	X		X			S		X	X								S		R. Gifford	20
X	X	X	X	X	X	X	X				S		X			X1					S2			S1		A. Wilkie	21
X	X	X	X			X	X				X1		S	X	X		X				S1		X			S. Lodge	22
X	X	X1	X			X	X				X		S	X	X	X	X				X2	S2	S1			G. Poll	23
X	X	X1				X	X				X		S	X	X	X2	X				S2		S1			K. Cooper	24
X	X	X1				X	X				S1		S	X	X	X1	X				X		S			M. Bodenham	25
X	X1	X		X		X	X				S2		S	X	X		X	S1			X2					R. Dilkes	26
X	X	X		X		X	X				X		S	X			X1				S1		X			B. Hill	27
X	X	X	X1	X		X	X	X			X		S				X				S1		X			P. Don	28
X	X2	S2		X		X	X				X1		S				X				S2		X			D. Gallagher	29
X	X	X	X		X1	X	X	X			X		S	X			X				S1	S	X			G. Ashby	30
X	X	X	S	X	X	X	X				X		S	X			X				S		X			P. Durkin	31
X	X	X	X			X	X2	X1			X		S				X	S2			S1		X			G. Ashby	32
X	X	X	X			X	X1				X		S				X	S			S1		X			R. Hart	33
X	X	X	X	X		X	X				X		S				S				S1		X			D. Elleray	34
X		X1	X			X	X				X2		X				X	S2			S1		X			P. Jones	35
X		X1	X			X	X				X		S				X	S			S1		X			J. Worrall	36
X	X	X	S			X	X	X			X1		S				X				S1		X			K. Morton	37
	X	X	X			X	X2	X1			X	X	S2	X						S	S1		X			K. Burge	38
S		X1	X			X	X2	X			S1		X	X							S2		X		X	K. Cooper	39
X		X	S	X1		X	X	X			S1		X	X								S	X	X1		J. Worrall	40
X		X	S1		X	X	X	X			X1		X	X							S		X	X		G. Willard	41
S		X	X			X	X	X			X1		X	X				S1					X	X	X	S. Lodge	42
S		X	X		X	X	X1	X			X		X	X			S						X	X	X	A. Wilkie	43
S		X	X	S1		X	X	X			X		X	S			S1						X	X	X1	P. Jones	44
S		X	X			X	X	X1			X		X	S1			S1						X	X	X	G. Ashby	45
S		X		X	X2	X	X1				X		X	X			S1						X2	X	X	J. Worrall	46
S		X	S1	X1		X	X				X		X	X			S2						X	X	X	G. Poll	47
S		X	X	X1		X	X				X		X	X			S						X	X	X	T. Holbrook	48
S		X	S2	X1	X	X	X	X2		S1	X		X	X									X	X	X	P. Danson	49
S		X	S2	X	X	X	X1			S1	X		X	X									X2	X	X	K. Burge	50
30	28	36	23	32	25	11	42	35	41	4	21		12	31	17	15	2				2		2	19	12	**League Appearances**	
	1	5	3								13	1	1			2	2	7			10	2	4			**League Sub Appearances**	
3	2	2	1	3	2+1	2	3	2	3		2+1			2	3	2+1	1	0+1	0+1							**C/Cola Cup Appearances**	
5	5	4	5	4	1		5	4	5		5			4			3	0+1		0+4		1	4			**FA Cup Appearances**	

Also Played: Robinson S2(46), Oakley S1(48), Allan S(42,45)

† = Sent Off

SOUTHAMPTON

CLUB RECORDS

BIGGEST VICTORIES
League: 8-0 v Northampton, Division 3S, 24.12.1921.
F.A. Cup: 7-1 v Ipswich Town, Round 3, 7.1.1961
6-0 v Luton Town, Round 4, 8.2.1995
League Cup: 5-0 v Derby County, Round 3, 8.10.1974
5-0 v Wrexham, Round 2, 28.8.1979
5-0 v Rochdale, Round 2, 25.9.1990
Europe (UEFA): 5-1 v Vittoria G, Round 2, 12.11.1969
(ECWC): 4-0 v Marseilles, Round 1, 15.9.1976

BIGGEST DEFEATS
League: 0-8 v Tottenham Hotspur, Division 2, 28.3.1936.
0-8 v Everton, Division 1, 20.11.1971.
F.A. Cup: 0-5 v Manchester City, Round 2, 5.2.1910.
League Cup: 1-7 v Watford, Round 2, 2.9.1980.
Europe: No more than 2 goal defeat.

MOST POINTS
3 points a win: 77, Division 1, 1983-84.
2 points a win: 61, Division 3S, 1921-22, Division 3 1959-60.

MOST GOALS
112, 1957-58 (Division 3S).
Reeves 31, Roper 18, Hoskins 18, Raine 12, Clifton 7, Mulgrew 8, Sydenham 4,Page 4, Walker 3, McGowan 2, Traynor 2, McLaughlin 1, og 2.

MOST FIRST CLASS MATCHES IN A SEASON
61 (42 League, 7 FA Cup, 6 League Cup, 6 ZDS) 1991-92

MOST LEAGUE GOALS CONCEDED
92, Division 1, 1966-67

MOST LEAGUE WINS
26, Division 3, 1959-60

MOST LEAGUE DRAWS
18, Division 2, 1924-25; Division 1/P, 1972-73, 1994-95.

MOST LEAGUE DEFEATS
23, Division 1, 1971-72,1993-94

INDIVIDUAL CLUB RECORDS

MOST GOALS IN A SEASON
Derek Reeves 45 (League 39, FAC 6) 1959-60.
4 goals twice=8; 3 goals twice=6; 2 goals 3 times=6; 1 goal 25 times=25.
Previous holder: C Wayman 32 (1948-49).

MOST GOALS IN A MATCH
5. Charlie Wayman v Leicester, Div 2, 23.10.1948 (6-0)
5. Derek Reeves v Leeds (LC4) 5.12.1960 (5-4)

OLDEST PLAYER
Peter Shilton, 37 years 233 days v Coventry (Div 1) 9.5.1987.

YOUNGEST PLAYER
Danny Wallace 16 years 313 days v Manchester Utd (Div 1) 29.11.1980.

MOST CAPPED PLAYER
Peter Shilton (England) 49

BEST PERFORMANCES

League: 1921-22: Matches played 42, Won 23, Drawn 15, Lost 4, Goals for 68,Goals against 21, Points 61. 1st in Division 3S.
Highest: 1983-84: 2nd in Division 1.

F.A. Cup: 1975-76 (Div 2): 3rd rnd. Aston Villa 1-1, 2-1; 4th rnd. Blackpool 3-1; 5th rnd. West Bromwich Albion 1-1, 4-0; 6th rnd. Bradford City 1-0; Semi-final Crystal Palace 2-0; Final Manchester United 1-0.

League Cup: 1978-79 (Div 1): 2nd rnd. Birmingham City 5-2; 3rd rnd. DerbyCounty 1-0; 4th rnd. Reading 0-0 2-0; 5th rnd. Manchester City 2-1; Semi-finalLeeds United 2-2, 1-0; Final Nottingham Forest 2-3.

Europe (ECWC): 1976-77 (Div 2): 1st rnd. Marseille 4-0, 1-2; 2nd rnd Carrick R.5-2, 4-1; 3rd rnd. Anderlecht 0-2, 2-1.
(UEFA): 1969-70: 1st rnd. Rosenburg 0-1, 2-0; 2nd rnd. Vittoria Guimariers 3-3,5-1; 3rd rnd. Newcastle 0-0, 1-1.

DIVISIONAL RECORD

	Played	Won	Drawn	Lost	For	Against	Points
Division 1/P	1.036	351	290	395	1,434	1,532	1,193
Division 2	1,428	559	353	516	2,221	2,140	1,471
Division 3	92	43	20	29	194	155	106
Division 3(S)	314	150	77	87	562	368	377
Total	2,870	1,103	740	1,027	4,411	4,195	3,147

ADDITIONAL INFORMATION
Previous Name
Southampton St. Mary's

Previous League
Southern League

Club colours: Red & white striped shirts, black shorts, red & white socks.
Change colours: Yellow & royal blue striped shirts, blue shorts, yellow & blue socks.

Reserves League: Avon Insurance Football Combination.

RECORDS AND STATISTICS

COMPETITIONS

Div 1/P	Div.2	Div.3	Div.3(S)	UEFA	ECWC
1966-74	1922-53	1920-21	1921-22	1969-70	1976-77
1978-	1960-66	1958-60	1953-58	1971-72	
	1974-78			1981-82	
				1982-83	Texaco
				1984-85	1974-75

HONOURS

Division 3	Division 3(S)	FA Cup
1959-60	1921-22	1975-76

MOST APPEARANCES

Terry Paine 805+4 (1956-74)

Year	League	FA Cup	Lge Cup	Europe
1956-57	9			
1957-58	44	2		
1958-59	46	3		
1959-60	46	6		
1960-61	42	2	7	
1961-62	41	2	2	
1962-63	42	7	3	
1963-64	41	1	1	
1964-65	42	2	2	
1965-66	40	1	2	
1966-67	42	3	3	
1967-68	41	4	1	
1968-69	42	4	4	
1969-70	36	3	2	6
1970-71	41	4	1	
1971-72	37+3	2	2	2
1972-73	36+1	1	4	
1973-74	41	4	3	
	709+4	51	37	8

MOST GOALS IN A CAREER

Mike Channon - 227 (19966-77 & 1979-82)

Year	League	FA Cup	Lge Cup	Europe
1965-66	1			
1966-67				
1967-68	7	1		
1968-69	8	1	3	
1969-70	15	2	1	3
1970-71	18	1	1	
1971-72	14	1		1
1972-73	16		2	
1973-74	21	1	1	
1974-75	20	1	3	
1975-76	20	5		
1976-77	17	2	1	4
1979-80	10	1		
1980-81	10			
1981-82	8			1
Total	185	16	12	9

(Plus 5 in the Texaco Cup - 1974-75)

Current leading goalscorer: Matthew Le Tissier 158 (1986-95)

RECORD TRANSFER FEE RECEIVED

Amount	Club	Player	Date
£3,600,000	Blackburn Rov.	Alan Shearer	7/92
£1,600,000	Leeds United	Rodney Wallace	7/91
£1,200,000	Manchester Utd	Danny Wallace	9/89
£800,000	Q.P.R.	Colin Clarke	3/89

RECORD TRANSFER FEE PAID

Amount	Club	Player	Date
£1,200,000	Chelsea	Neil Shipperley	1/95
£1,000,000	Swindon Town	Alan McLoughlin	12/90
£750,000	Portsmouth	Barry Horne	3/89
£600,000	Middlesbrough	David Armstrong	8/81

MANAGERS

Name	Seasons	Best	Worst
George Swift	1911-12		
James McIntyre	1919-24	5(2)	2(3S)
Arthur Chadwick	1925-31	4(2)	17(2)
G Kay	1931-36	12(2)	19(2)
George Coss	1936-37	19(2)	19(2)
T Parker	1937-War	15(2)	18(2)
W Dodgin (Snr)	War-1949	3(2)	14(2)
Sid Cann	1949-51	13(2)	21(2)
George Roughton	1952-55	3(2)	6(3)
Ted Bates	1955-73	7(1)	14(3)
Lawrie McMenemy	1973-85	2(1)	13(2)
Chris Nicholl	1985-91	7(1)	14(1)
Ian Branfoot	1991-94	16(1)	18(1/P)
Alan Ball	1994-95	10(P)	18(P)
Dave Merrington	1995-		

LONGEST LEAGUE RUNS

of undefeated matches:	19 (5.9.1921 - 14.1.1922)	of league matches w/out a win:	20 (30.8.1969 - 17.1.1970)
of undefeated home matches:	31 (22.1.1921 - 28.8.1922)	of undefeated away matches:	9 (19.11.77-29.3.78, 17.9.49-21.1.50)
without home win:	10 (6.9.1969 - 17.1.1970)	without an away win:	33 (22.4.1933 - 25.12.1934)
of league wins:	6 (5.9.1964 - 13.10.1964, 3.3.1992 - 8.4.1992)	of home wins:	11 (10.10.1959 - 19.3.1960)
of league defeats:	5 (7.5.1927 - 10.9.1927, 12.1.1957 - 25.2.1957)	of away wins:	3 (On 10 different occasions)

(30.12.1967 - 10.2.1968, 31.12.1988 - 11.2.1989, Twice in 1993)

SOUTHAMPTON

PLAYERS NAME Honours	Ht	Wt	Birthdate	Birthplace Transfers	Contract Date	Clubs	APPEARANCES				GOALS			
							League	L/Cup	FA Cup	Other	Lge	L/C	FAC	Oth
G O A L K E E P E R S														
Dave Beasant	6.3	13.0	20.03.59	Willesden		Edgware Town								
E: 2, B.7. Div.4'83. Div.2'89. FAC'88. ZDC'90.				£1,000	07.08.79	Wimbledon	340	21	27	3				
				£800,000	13.06.88	Newcaslte United	20	2	2	1				
				£735,000	14.01.89	Chelsea	133	11	5	8				
Loan Grimsby Town, 24.10.92, 6 Lge App.				Loan	12.01.93	Wolverhampton W.	4		1					
				£300,000	04.11.93	Southampton	37+1		2					
Bruce Grobbelaar	6.1	12.0	06.10.57	Zimbabwe		Vancouver Wh'caps								
Zim. Div.1'82'83'84'86'88'90. LC'82'83'84.				Free	18.12.79	Crewe Alexandra	24				1			
FAC'86'89'92. CS'82'86'88'89'90. EC'84. SC'86.				Free		Vacouver Wh'caps								
Loan Stoek City, 17.03.93, 4 Lge App.				£250,000	12.03.81	Liverpool	440	70	62	56				
				Free	.08.94	Southampton	30	3	5					
D E F E N D E R S														
Derek Allan	6.0	10.13	24.12.74	Irvine		Ayr United	5							
				£70,000	16.03.93	Southampton	0+1							
Francis Benali	5.9	11.0	30.12.68	Southampton	05.01.87	Southampton (A)	151+22	13+6	17	3+1				
Simon Charlton	5.7	11.1	25.10.71	Huddersfield	01.07.89	Huddersfield T. (T)	121+3	9	10	14	1	1		
E: S.				£250,000	08.06.93	Southampton	54+4	3+1	2		2			
Jason Dodd	5.10	11.10	02.11.70	Bath		Bath City				0+1				
E: u21.8.				£50,000	15.03.89	Southampton	118+16	18+1	16	5	3			
Richard Hall	6.1	12.8	14.03.72	Ipswich	20.03.90	Scunthorpe Utd (T)	22	2	3	4	3			
E: u21.11.				£200,000	13.02.91	Southampton	89+7	7+1	10	3	11		2	
Kenneth Monkou	6.0	12.9	29.11.64	Surinam		Feyenoord								
Holland: u21. ZDC'90.				£100,000	02.03.89	Chelsea	92+2	12	3	10	2			
				£750,000	21.08.92	Southampton	99	6	7		6	1		
Alan B Neilson	5.11	12.4	26.09.72	Wegburg (Ger)	11.02.91	Newcastle Utd (T)	35+7	4		4	1			
W: 3, B.2, u21.7				£500,000	08.95	Southampton								
Peter Whiston	6.0	11.6	04.01.68	Widnes	17.12.87	Plymouth Argyle	4+6		1	1				
				Free	21.03.90	Torquay United	39+1	5	1	6	1	1		
				£25,000	13.09.91	Exeter City	85	7	10	10	7			1
				£30,000	.08.94	Southampton	0+1							
M I D F I E L D														
Paul Allen	5.7	9.12	28.08.62	Aveley	29.08.79	West Ham U. (A)	149+3	20+4	15+3	2+1	6	2	3	
E: u21.3, Y.27. FAC'80'91. UEFAY'80. CS'91.				£400,000	19.06.85	Tottenham Hotspur	276+16	42+2	26+1	12+2	23	4	1	
				£550,000	16.09.93	Southampton	40+3	4	2		1			
				Loan	23.12.94	Luton Town	4							
				Loan	20.01.95	Stoke City	17			2	1			
David Hughes	5.9	11.0	30.12.72	St. Albans	02.07.91	Southampton (J)	2+12		0+4		2		1	
W: u21.1. E: u19.4, S.														
Neil Maddison	5.9	11.8	02.10.69	Darlington	14.04.88	Southampton (T)	117+13	5+2	7+3	1	16			
Jim Magilton	5.10	12.7	06.05.69	Belfast	14.05.86	Liverpool (A)								
NI: 22, u21.1, u23.1.				£100,000	03.10.90	Oxford United	150	9	8	6	34	1	4	3
				£600,000	11.02.94	Southampton	57	3	5		6		1	
Matt Robinson	5.10	10.8	23.12.74	Exeter	01.07.93	Southampton (T)	0+1							
Paul Tisdale	5.9	10.9	14.01.73	Malta	05.06.91	Southampton (J)	0+7	0+1	0+1					
E: u18.3, SFA.				Loan	12.03.92	Northampton Town	5							
Christer Warren			10.10.74	Bournemouth		Cheltenham								
				£40,000	08.95	Southampton								
Tommy Widdrington	5.8	11.1	01.10.71	Newcastle	10.05.90	Southampton (T)	47+7	1+1	7		1			
				Loan	12.09.91	Wigan Athletic	5+1	2						
F O R W A R D S														
Frank Bennett	5.7	11.8	03.01.69	Birmingham		Halesowen Town								
				£7,500	24.02.93	Southampton	0+8	1+1	0+1		1			
Neil Heaney	5.9	11.1	03.11.71	Middlesbrough	14.11.89	Arsenal (T)	4+3	0+1						
E: u21.6, Y.3. FAYC'88				Loan	03.01.91	Hartlepool United	2+1							
				Loan	09.01.92	Cambridge United	9+4		1		2			
				£300,000	22.03.94	Southampton	23+13	2+1	5		2		2	
Paul McDonald	5.7	9.5	20.04.68	Motherwell		Hamilton Accies	187+28		8+2	8+1	8	26	2	3
SDiv.1'88. CC'92'93.				£75,000	08.06.93	Southampton	0+2							
Craig Maskell	5.10	11.4	10.04.68	Aldershot	15.04.86	Southampton (A)	2+4				1			
				£20,000	31.05.88	Huddersfield Town	86+1	6	8	7	43	4	3	4
				£250,000	07.08.90	Reading	60+12	2	5+1	1	26			

SOUTHAMPTON

PLAYERS NAME Honours	Ht	Wt	Birthdate	Birthplace Transfers	Contract Date	Clubs	APPEARANCES				GOALS			
							League	L/Cup	FA Cup	Other	Lge	L/C	FAC	Oth
Craig Maskell continued.				£225,000	09.07.92	Swindon Town	40+7	3+1	2+1	4+1	21	1		4
				£250,000	07.02.94	Southampton	8+8			1	1			
Neil Shipperley	5.11	13.2	30.10.74	Chatham	24.09.92	Chelsea (T)	20+7	2+1	3		5	1	1	
u21.1				£1,250,000	06.01.95	Southampton	19		4		4		2	
Paul Sheerin	5.10	11.1	28.08.74	Edinburgh		Alloa	7+2	1						
S: Y.				£60,000	23.10.92	Southampton								
Matthew Le Tissier	6.0	11.10	14.10.68	Guernsey	17.10.86	Southampton (A)	262+30	26+6	23+1	11+1	120	18	11	9
E: 3, B.5, u19.2, Y.1. FLgXl.1.														
Gordon Watson	6.0	12.9	20.03.71	Sidcup	05.04.89	Charlton Ath (T)	20+11	2	0+1	1+1	7	1		
E: u21.2.				£250,000	20.02.91	Sheffield Wed.	29+27	6+5	5+2	2+2	15	3	2	1
				£1,200,000	17.03.95	Southampton	12				3			

TOP GOALSCORER 1994/95
Matthew Le Tissier

Premiership goals (games) 20 (41)
Coca-Cola Cup Goals 5 (3)
F.A. Cup goals 5 (5)

Total . . . . **30 (49)**

Total goals for Southampton since 17.10.86 . . . . 158 (322+38)
Total for England (full caps only) . . . . 0 (2+4)

Career total as at June 1st 1995 . . . . 158 (324+42)

THE MANAGER
DAVE MERRINGTON

Date of Birth . . . . 26th January 1945.
Place of Birth . . . . Newcastle.
Date of Appointment . . . . 14th July 1995.

PREVIOUS CLUBS
As Manager . . . . None.
As Coach . . . . Bristol City, Burnley, Sunderland, Leeds United.
As a Player . . . . Burnley, Birstol City.

HONOURS
As a Manager
None.

As a Player
None.

THE DELL
Milton Road, Southampton SO9 4XX
Tel: 01703 220 505

Capacity 15,200

First game...v Brighton, Sth League, 3.9.1898.
First floodlit game..v Bournemouth, 31.10.1950.

ATTENDANCES
Highest ....31,044 v Manchester Utd, Div.1., 08.10.1969.
Lowest ....1,875 v Port Vale, Division 2, 30.3.1936.

OTHER GROUNDS.......Antelope Ground 1885-1897. County Cricket Ground 1897-98. The Dell 1898-

MATCHDAY TICKET PRICES

East/West Centre . . . . £18 (GG), £15 (SG)

Wings . . . . £17 (GG), £14 (SG)

Lower Tier. . . . . £15 (GG), £12 (SG)
Juv/OAP £6, £5

Milton Road. . . . . £17 (GG), £14 (SG)

Archers Road . . . . £17 (GG), £14 (SG)

GG- Gold Games. SG- Silver Games.

Ticket Office Telephone no. 01703 337 171

CLUBCALL
0891 12 11 78
Calls cost 39p per minute cheap rate and 49p per minute at all other times.
Call costings correct at time of going to press.

HOW TO GET TO THE GROUND

From the North
Use A33, sign posted Southampton, via The Avenue, then turn right into Northlands Road and at the end turn right into Archers Road for Southampton FC.

From the East
Use motorway M27 then A334 and follow signs to Southampton A3024. The follow signs to The West into Commercial Road then turn right into Hill Lane and take first turning right into Milton Road for Southampton FC.

From the West
Use M27 then A35 and follow signs to Southampton city centre A3024. Turn left over central station bridge, right into Fourpost Hill, then turn left into Hill Lane and take first turning right into Milton Road for Southampton FC.

Car Parking
Street parking and nearby municipal parks.

Nearest Railway Station
Southampton Central (01703 229 393).

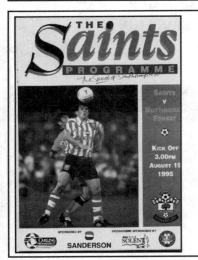

MATCHDAY PROGRAMME

Programme Editor . . . . Mr J Hughes.

Number of pages . . . . 48.

Price . . . . £1.50.

Subscriptions. . . . . £58 for all home games.

Local Newspapers . . . . . . Southern Evening Echo, Portsmouth News,
. . . . Hampshire Chronicle.

Local Radio Stations. . . . . Radio Solent, Power FM.

TOTTENHAM HOTSPUR
(The Spurs)
F.A. CARLING PREMIERSHIP
SPONSORED BY: HEWLETT PACKARD

Back Row (L-R): Andy Turner, Jason Cundy, Ronny Rosenthal, Darren Anderton, Erik Thorstvedt, Ian Walker, Kevin Scott, Colin Calderwood, Jason Dozzell, Stuart Nethercott. **Middle Row:** Tony Lenaghan (Physio), Danny Hill, Gerry McMahon, Clive Wilson, Ilie Dumitrescu, Chris Day, David Howells, Paul Mahorn, Kevin Watson, Steve Carr, Roy Reyland (Kit Manager). **Front Row:** Pat Jennings (Goalkeeping Coach), David Kerslake, Chris Armstrong, Justin Edinburgh, Gary Mabbutt, Gerry Francis (Manager), Roger Cross (Asst. Manager), Teddy Sheringham, Dean Austin, Sol Campbell, Darren Caskey, Chris Hughton (Reserve Team Manager).

TOTTENHAM HOTSPUR
FORMED IN 1882
TURNED PROFESSIONAL IN 1895
LTD COMPANY IN 1898

PRESIDENT: W E Nicholson
VICE-CHAIRMAN: F P Sinclair
CHAIRMAN: Alan M Sugar
DIRECTORS
A G Berry (Vice-Chairman), D A Alexiou, I Yawetz, C T Sandy, J Crystal
SECRETARY
Peter Barnes (0181 808 6666)
COMMERCIAL MANAGER
Mike Rollo (0181 808 0281)

MANAGER: Gerry Francis
ASSISTANT MANAGER: Roger Cross

RESERVE TEAM MANAGER
Chris Hughton
YOUTH TEAM MANAGER
Des Bulpin
PHYSIOTHERAPIST
Tony Lenaghan

STATISTICIAN FOR THE DIRECTORY
Andy Shute

A dramatic season for Tottenham, both on and off the pitch, started with Spurs on minus six points, and banned from the FA Cup. However, the surprise signing of German World Cup star Jurgen Klinsmann was a great boost to Spurs and three wins from their opening four games lifted spirits at the club, as did the attacking brand of football used by manager Ossie Ardiles. The defensive inadequacies though were soon highlighted as Spurs only won two of their next twelve games and languished in the relegation zone.

Ossie Ardiles paid the price with his job, and ex-QPR manager Gerry Francis was brought in, making an immediate impact and sealing up the leaky defence. Although Mr Francis' first game in charge was a 3-4 defeat to Aston Villa, Spurs recorded their first clean sheet of the season in the following home game, winning six and drawing four of their next ten games. One other major influence of this unbeaten run was that the FA lifted the six point handicap. Tottenham's resurgence in the league lifted them to sixth place, and the opportunity of European football beckoned. Tottenham's good form continued until mid-March, but just two wins in their final ten games ensured 7th place and therefore out of European places. Tottenham recorded their 1000th league victory in the top division with a 4-0 win at Coventry on New Years' Eve.

In the League Cup Tottenham beat Watford 8-6 on aggregate, with Jurgen Klinsmann scoring his first hat-trick in English football, in the away leg. In the 3rd round Spurs suffered a humiliating defeat at Notts County 0-3.

When the draw for the 3rd round of the FA Cup was made, Tottenham's chance to face non-League Altrincham rested with the outcome of a court case. The outcome favoured Tottenham, and Altrincham were beaten 3-0 at White Hart Lane. In the 4th round Spurs travelled to '93 finalists Sunderland, and in front of the TV cameras ran out 4-1 winners. Southampton held out for a 1-1 draw in the 5th round, but in the replay at the Dell Spurs came back from 0-2 down to win 6-2, thanks largely to substitute Ronny Rosenthal's hat-trick. Another superb performance in the 6th round saw Tottenham win 2-1 at Anfield. Unfortunately a poor performance in the Semi-final denied Spurs of a Wembley date as they lost 1-4 against Everton.

Klinsmann, 29 goals, and Teddy Sheringham, 24 goals, formed a superb partnership in the Spurs attack. However, the PFA Player of the Year, Klinsmann stunned Tottenham by leaving for Bayern Munich at the end of the season, and his replacement will have a tough act to follow. Gary Mabbutt won back his place after recovering from his injury and formed a solid central defensive partnership with Sol Campbell. Campbell had an outstanding season, brought to an unfortunate end by injury in March. David Howells had an excellent season, once Gerry Francis arrived, providing the link between defence and midfield. There were England squad call-ups for Anderton, Barmby, Campbell, Sheringham and Walker.

Now that Gerry Francis has settled in and agreed a new one year contract, the expectations for next season are high. If Spurs can carry on their form from the latter half of the 94/95 season then they have a real chance of honours next time round. **ANDY SHUTE.**

TOTTENHAM HOTSPUR

Premier League: 7th   **FA Cup:** Semi-Final   **Coca-Cola Cup:** 3rd Round

M	DATE	COMP.	VEN	OPPONENTS	RESULT	H/T	LP	GOAL SCORERS/GOAL TIMES	ATT.
1	A 20	PL	A	Sheffield Wednesday	W 4-3	2-0		Sheringham 19, Anderton 30, Barmby 71, Klinsmann 82	(34,051)
2	24	PL	H	Everton	W 2-1	2-0		Klinsmann 21, 34	24,553
3	27	PL	H	Manchester United	L 0-1	0-0	8		24,502
4	30	PL	A	Ipswich Town	W 3-1	3-0	6	Klinsmann 14, 38, Dumitrescu	(22,559)
5	S 12	PL	H	Southampton	L 1-2	1-0	8	Klinsmann 6	22,387
6	17	PL	A	Leicester City	L 1-3	0-1	9	Klinsmann 88	(21,300)
7	21	CC 2/1	A	Watford	W 6-3	4-1		Anderton 4, Klinsmann 15, 35, 45, Sheringham 75, Dumitrescu 87	(13,659)
8	24	PL	H	Nottingham Forest	L 1-4	1-1	10	Dumitrescu 32	24,558
9	O 1	PL	A	Wimbledon	W 2-1	1-1	10	Sheringham 28, Popescu 63	(16,802)
10	4	CC 2.2	H	Watford	L 2-3	1-1		Barmby 31, Klinsmann 63	17,798
11	8	PL	H	Queens Park Rangers	D 1-1	0-1	10	Barmby 80	25,799
12	15	PL	A	Leeds United	D 1-1	1-0	12	Sheringham 27	(39,224)
13	22	PL	A	Manchester City	L 2-5	1-3	13	Dumitrescu 29 (pen), 46	(25,473)
14	26	CC 3	A	Notts County	L 0-3	0-2			(16,952)
15	29	PL	H	West Ham United	W 3-1	1-1	12	Klinsmann 18, Sheringham 49, Barmby 63	26,271
16	N 5	PL	A	Blackburn Rovers	L 0-2	0-1	13		(26,933)
17	19	PL	H	Aston Villa	L 3-4	1-3	15	Sheringham, Klinsmann (pen)	26,899
18	23	PL	H	Chelsea	D 0-0	0-0	14		27,037
19	26	PL	A	Liverpool	D 1-1	0-1	13	Ruddock (og)	(35,007)
20	D 3	PL	H	Newcastle United	W 4-2	2-2	11	Sheringham 14, 39, 68, Popescu 79	28,002
21	10	PL	H	Sheffield Wednesday	W 3-1	0-1	10	Barmby 61, Klinsmann 72, Calderwood 80	25,912
22	17	PL	A	Everton	D 0-0	0-0	11		(32,809)
23	26	PL	A	Norwich City	W 2-0	1-0	9	Barmby 11, Sheringham 90	(21,814)
24	27	PL	H	Crystal Palace	D 0-0	0-0	9		27,730
25	31	PL	A	Coventry City	W 4-0	1-0	6	Darby 7 (og), Barmby 67, Anderton 77, Sheringham 81	(19,951)
26	J 2	PL	A	Arsenal	W 1-0	1-0	6	Popescu 22	28,747
27	7	FAC 3	H	Altrincham	W 3-0	2-0		Sheringham 9, Rosenthal 34, Nethercott 82	25,057
28	14	PL	A	West Ham United	W 2-1	0-1	6	Sheringham 58, Klinsmann	(24,573)
29	25	PL	A	Aston Villa	L 0-1	0-1	6		(40,017)
30	29	FAC 4	A	Sunderland	W 4-1	0-0		Klinsmann 50 (pen), 86, Sheringham 56, Mabbutt 63	(21,135)
31	F 5	PL	H	Blackburn Rovers	W 3-1	2-0	6	Klinsmann 18, Anderton 30, Barmby 79	28,124
32	11	PL	A	Chelsea	D 1-1	1-0	6	Sheringham 8	(30,812)
33	18	FAC 5	H	Southampton	D 1-1	1-1		Klinsmann 20	28,091
34	25	PL	H	Wimbledon	L 1-2	0-1	6	Klinsmann 49	27,258
35	M 1	FAC 5R	A	Southampton	W †6-2	0-2		Rosenthal 56, 58, 101, Sheringham 112, Barmby 114, Anderton 120	(15,172)
36	4	PL	A	Nottingham Forest	D 2-2	0-0	6	Sheringham 79, Calderwood 87	(28,717)
37	8	PL	H	Ipswich Town	W 3-0	2-0	6	Klinsmann 1, Barmby 14, Youds 82 (og)	24,930
38	11	FAC 6	A	Liverpool	W 2-1	1-1		Sheringham 45, Klinsmann 88	(39,592)
39	15	PL	A	Manchester United	D 0-0	0-0	7		(43,802)
40	18	PL	H	Leicester City	W 1-0	0-0	7	Klinsmann 82	30,851
41	22	PL	A	Liverpool	D 0-0	0-0	7		31,988
42	A 2	PL	A	Southampton	L 3-4	2-2	7	Sheringham 16, 58, Klinsmann 34	(15,105)
43	9	FAC SF	N	Everton	L 1-4	0-1		Klinsmann 64 (pen)	(38,226)
44	11	PL	H	Manchester City	W 2-1	0-0	7	Howells 53, Klinsmann 86	27,410
45	14	PL	A	Crystal Place	D 1-1	0-1	7	Klinsmann 87	(18,149)
46	17	PL	H	Norwich City	W 1-0	1-0	7	Sheringham 36	32,304
47	29	PL	A	Arsenal	D 1-1	0-0	7	Klinsmann 74	(39,377)
48	M 3	PL	A	Newcastle United	D 3-3	3-2	7	Barmby 22, Klinsmann 24, Anderton 26	(35,603)
49	6	PL	A	Queens Park Rangers	L 1-2	1-0	7	Sheringham 45	(18,367)
50	9	PL	H	Coventry City	L 1-3	0-1	7	Anderton 83	24,134
51	14	PL	H	Leeds United	D 1-1	1-0	7	Sheringham 30	33,040
52									
53									
54									
55									
56									
57									
58									
59									
60									

Best Home League Attendance: 33,040 v Leeds United   **Smallest:** 22,387 v Southampton   **Av Home Att:** 26,752

Goal Scorers: **Compared with 1993-94:-** 569

League (66): Klinsmann 20, Sheringham 19, Barmby 9, Anderton 5, Dumitrescu 4, Popescu 3, Opponents 3, Calderwood, Howells
C/Cola Cup (8): Klinsmann 4, Anderton, Barmby, Dumitrescu, Sheringham
FA Cup (17): Klinsmann 5, Rosenthal 4 Sheringham 4, Anderton, Barmby, Mabbutt, Nethercott

Walker I	Kerslake D	Edinburgh J	Calderwood C	Nethercott S	Dumitrescu I	Anderton D	Campbell S	Barmby N	Sheringham T	Klinsmann J	Mabbutt G	Hazard M	Day C	Popescu G	Hill D	Howells D	Scott K	Austin D	Dozzell J	Thorstvedt E	Rosenthal R	Caskey D	McMahon G	Turner A	Referee	
	X		X		X2		X1		X		S1		S												B. Hill	1
	X		X1		X1		X		X				S												G. Willard	2
	X		X1		X		X		X		S		S												K. Burge	3
	X		X		X		X		X		S1		S												R. Gifford	4
	X		X		X†		X		X		S		S												A. Wilkie	5
	X1		X		X		X		X		S		S												G. Ashby	6
	X		X		X		X		X				S		S1										J. Brandwood	7
	S		X		X		X		X				S		S1										R. Hart	8
	X		X1				X		X								X		X	S					M. Reed	9
	X						X		X						S1		X		X	S	X				D. Gallagher	10
	X2						X		X						X		X†		X	S	S1				P. Jones	11
	S1		X1				X										X		X	S					K. Cooper	12
	X		X				X										X		X1	S					D. Elleray	13
	X1				Xt		X		X		S								X	X					K. Burge	14
X					X		X		S1		X				S2				X						K. Morton	15
X	X1				X		X		X		X1		S						X2		S2				T. Holbrook	16
X1	X						X		X		X		S									X2			P. Durkin	17
	X			S1			X		X		X		S												G. Willard	18
	X			S1			X		X		X		S												S. Lodge	19
	X			S			X		X		X		S												D. Gallagher	20
	X						X		X		X		S							X	S				M. Bodenham	21
	X						X		X		X		S							X					K. Cooper	22
	X						X		X		X		S								S				R. Dilkes	23
	X						X		X		X		S								S2				G. Willard	24
	X						X		X		X		S								S2				G. Ashby	25
	X						X		X		X		S								X				M. Reed	26
	X						X		X		X		S								X1				B. Burns	27
	X						X		X		X		S												B. Hill	28
	X						X		X		X		S									S1			R. Hart	29
	X						X		X		X		S									S			M. Reed	30
	X						X		X		X											S			M. Bodenham	31
	X						X		X		X									S					P. Durkin	32
	X						X2		X		X									S					D. Elleray	33
	X								X		X									S	S1	S2			D. Gallagher	34
	X								X		X									S	S1	S2			J. Worrall	35
	X								X		X									S	X	S			G. Ashby	36
	X								X		X									S	X	S1			B. Hill	37
	X								X		X									S	X	S			M. Bodenham	38
	X								X		X									S	X	S			K. Morton	39
S1									X		X								S	X	S			S. Lodge	40
X	X								X		X								S	X				P. Danson	41
	X								X		X								S	X				G. Willard	42
	X								X		X								S	S1		S		R. Hart	43
	X								X		X								S	S1				A. Wilkie	44
	X								X		X								S	X	S			P. Don	45
	X1				S1				X		X								S	X	S1			R. Gifford	46
S1	X				X				X		X								S	X				R. Hart	47
	X				X				X		X								S	X1				D. Gallagher	48
	X								X		X								S	X				G. Poll	49
X	X								X		X					S			S			X	S	A. Wilkie	50
	S																	S1	S			X1	X	P. Durkin	51
16	35		11		29		41		33						1			4	6	1	14	1		2	1	League Appearances	
2	1		2		1		1		3						2						6	3				League Sub Appearances	
2	1		2		3		2		2						0+2				2	1	1					C/Cola Cup Appearances	
	6				3		6		6												2+2	0+1				FA Cup Appearances	

† = Sent Off

TOTTENHAM HOTSPUR

CLUB RECORDS

BIGGEST VICTORIES
League: 9-0 v Bristol Rovers, Division 2, 22.10.1977
F.A. Cup: 13-2 v Crewe Alexandra, Round 4, 3.2.1960
League Cup: 5-0 v West Brom. Alb, Round 3, 28.10.1970
7-2 v Doncaster Rovers, Round 5, 3.12.1975
5-0 v Birmingham City, Round 3, 1986-87
5-0 v West Ham United, Round 5, 2.2.1987
5-0 v Hartlepool Utd, Round 1, 26.9.1990
Europe (UEFA): 9-0 v Keflavic, Round 1, 28.9.1971
BIGGEST DEFEATS
League: 0-7 v Liverpool, Division 1, 2.9.1979
F.A. Cup: 0-5 v Stoke City, Round 1, 1.2.1896
1-6 v Huddersfield, Round 6, 3.3.1928
League Cup: 0-4 v Middlesbrough (h), Round 2, 1974-75
Europe 0(UEFA): 1-4 v Bayern Munich, Round 2, 3.11.1982
1-4 v Manchester Utd, Cup Winners Cup Round 2, 10.12.1963

MOST POINTS
3 points a win: 77, Division 1, 1984-85
2 points a win: 70, Division 2, 1919-1920 (Div 2 record)

MOST GOALS
115, 1960-61 (Division 1)
Smith 28, Allen 22, Jones 15, White 13, Dyson 12, Blanchflower 6,
Medwin 5,Norman 4, Mackay 4, Saul 3, Baker 1, og 2

MOST FIRST CLASS MATCHES IN A SEASON
68 (42 League, 5 FA Cup, 7 League Cup, 12 UEFA Cup, 2 Anglos-
Ital. Cup WinnersCup) 1971-72

MOST LEAGUE GOALS CONCEDED
95, Division 1958-59

MOST LEAGUE WINS
32, Division 2, 1919-20
MOST LEAGUE DRAWS
17, Division 1, 1968-69
MOST LEAGUE DEFEATS
22, Division 1, 1934-35

INDIVIDUAL CLUB RECORDS

MOST GOALS IN A MATCH
5. Ted Harper v Reading, Division 2, 30.8.1930 (7-1)
5. Alf Stokes v Birmingham, Division 1, 18.9.1957 (7-1)
5. Les Allen v Crewe Alex., FAC Round 4, 3.2.1960 (13-2)
5. Bobby Smith v Aston Villa, Division 1, 29.3.1958 (6-2)
5. V Woodwood v West Ham Utd, 1904-05
Jack Rowley netted 7 in war-time games
MOST GOALS IN A SEASON
Clive Allen 49 (League 33, League Cup 12, FAC 4) 1986-87
3 goals 3 times=9; 2 goals 9 times=18; 1 goal 22 times=22
League Goals Only: Jimmy Greaves 37, Div 1, 1962-63

OLDEST PLAYER
Jimmy Cantrell, 40 years 349 days v Birmingham, 24.4.1923
YOUNGEST PLAYER
Ally Dick, 16 years 301 days v Manchester City, 20.2.1982
MOST CAPPED PLAYER
Pat Jennings (Northern Ireland) 74

BEST PERFORMANCES

League: 1919-20: Matches played 42, Won 32, Drawn 6, Lost 4,
Goals for 102,against 32, Points 70. Division 2 Champions.
Highest: 1950-51, 1960-61: Division 1 Champions.

F.A. Cup: 1900-01: 1st rnd. Preston North End 1-1, 4-2; 2nd rnd.
Bury 2-1; 3rd rnd. Reading 1-1, 3-0; Semi-final West Bromwich
Albion 4-0; Final SheffieldUnited 2-2, 3-1
1920-21: 1st rnd. Bristol Rov. 6-2; 2nd rnd. Bradford City 4-0; 3rd
rnd.Southend 4-1; Semi-final Preston N E 2-1; Final Wolverhampton
Wndrs 1-0
1960-61: 3rd rnd. Charlton Athletic 3-2; 4th rnd. Crewe Alexandra 5-
1; 5th rnd.Aston Villa 2-0; 6th rnd. Sunderland 1-1, 5-0; Semi-final
Burnley 3-0; Final Leicester 2-0
1961-62: 3rd rnd. Birmingham City 3-3, 4-2; 4th rnd. Plymouth 5-1;
5th rnd.West Brom. Alb 4-2; 6th rnd. Aston Villa 2-0; Semi-final
Manchester United 3-1;Final Burnley 3-1
1966-67: 3rd rnd. Millwall 0-0, 1-0; 4th rnd. Portsmouth 3-1; 5th rnd.
Bristol City 2-0; 6th rnd. Birmingham City 0-0, 6-0; Semi-final
Nottingham Forest 2-1;Final Chelsea 2-1
1980-81: 3rd rnd. Queens Park Rangers 0-0, 3-1; 4th rnd. Hull City
2-0; 5th rnd. Coventry City 3-1; 6th rnd. Exeter City 2-0; Semi-final
Wolverhampton W.2-2, 3-0; Final Manchester City 1-1, 3-2
1981-82: 3rd rnd. Arsenal 1-0; 4th rnd. Leeds United 1-0; 5th rnd.
Aston Villa1-0; 6th rnd. Chelsea 3-2; Semi-final Leicester City 2-0;
Final Queens Park Rangers 1-1, 1-0
1990-91: 3rd rnd. Blackpool 1-0; 4th rnd. Oxford Utd 4-2; 5th rnd.
Portsmouth2-1; 6-1 rnd. Notts County 2-1; Semi-Final Arsenal 3-1;
Final Nottingham Forest2-1

League Cup: 1970-71: 2nd rnd. Swansea City 3-0; 3rd rnd.
Sheffield United 2-1;4th rnd. West Bromwich Albion 5-0; 5th rnd.
Coventry 4-1; Semi-final BristolCity 1-1, 2-0; Final Aston Villa 2-0
1972-73: 2nd rnd. Huddersfield 2-1; 3rd rnd Middlesbrough 1-1, 0-0,
2-1; 4thrnd Millwall 2-0; 5th rnd. Liverpool 1-1, 3-1; Semi-final
Wolverhampton W. 2-1,2-2; Final Norwich 1-0

ECWC: 1962-63: 2nd rnd. Rangers 3-2, 5-2; 3rd rnd Slovan
Bratisl., 2-0, 6-0;Semi-final OFK Belgrade 2-1, 3-1; Final Athletico
Madrid 5-1
UEFA: 1971-72: 1st rnd. Keflavic 6-1, 9-0; 2nd rnd. Nantes 0-0, 1-
0; 3rd rnd.Rapid Bucharest 3-0, 2-0; 4th rnd. UT Arad 2-0,
1-1; Semi-final AC Milan 2-1, 1-1; Final Wolverhampton W. 2-1, 1-1
1983-84: 1st rnd. Drogheda 6-0, 8-0; 2nd rnd. Feyenoord 4-2, 2-0;
3rd rnd.Bayern Munich 0-1, 2-0; 4th rnd. FK Austria 2-0, 2-2; Semi-
final Hadj. Split 1-2, 1-0; Final Anderlecht 1-1, 1-1, won on pens

DIVISIONAL RECORD

	Played	Won	Drawn	Lost	For	Against	Points
Division 1/P	2,482	1,007	600	875	3,992	3,624	2,849
Division 2	668	311	172	185	1,253	851	794
Total	3,150	1,318	772	1,060	5,245	4,475	3,643

ADDITIONAL INFORMATION
Previous Name
Hotspur F.C. 1882-84

Previous League
None.

Club colours: White shirts, blue shorts, white socks.
Change colours: All yellow.

Reserves League: Avon Insurance Football Combination.

RECORDS AND STATISTICS

COMPETITIONS

Div 1/P	Div.2	Euro C	ECWC	UEFA	Texaco
1909-15	1908-09	1961-62	1962-63	1971-72	1970-71
1920-28	1915-20		1963-64	1972-73	
1933-35	1928-33		1967-68	1973-74	
1950-77	1935-50		1981-82	1983-84	
1978-	1977-78		1982-83	1984-85	
			1991-92		

HONOURS

Div 1/P	Div.2	FAC	ECWC	Lge C	C/S'Ld
1950-51	1919-20	1900-01	1962-63	1970-71	1920
1960-61	1949-50	1920-21	1972-73		1951
		1960-61			1961
		1961-62	UEFA		1962
		1966-67	1971-72		1967
		1980-81	1983-84		1981
		1981-82			1992
		1990-91			shared

MOST APPEARANCES

Steve Perryman 860+4 (1969-86)

Year	League	FA Cup	Lge Cup	Europe
1969-70	21	4		
1970-71	42	5	6	
1971-72	40	5	6	12
1972-73	41	3	10	10
1973-74	40	1	1	12
1974-75	42	2	1	
1975-76	40	2	6	
1976-77	42	1	2	
1977-78	42	2	2	
1978-79	42	7	2	
1979-80	40	6	2	
1980-81	42	9	6	
1981-82	42	7	8	8
1982-83	32+1	3	2	2+1
1983-84	41	4	3	9
1984-85	42	3	5	8
1985-86	22+1	5	4	
	653+2	69	66	61+1

Including 1+1 Charity Shield, 10 Others.

MOST GOALS IN A CAREER

Jimmy Greaves - 266 (161-70)

Year	League	FA Cup	Lge Cup	Europe
1961-62	21	9		
1962-63	37			5
1963-64	35			1
1964-65	29	4		
1965-66	15	3		
1966-67	25	6		
1967-68	23	3		3
1968-69	27	4	5	
1969-70	8	3		
Total	220	32	5	9

Current leading goalscorer: Teddy Sheringham - 65 (1992-95)

RECORD TRANSFER FEE RECEIVED

Amount	Club	Player	Date
£5,500,000	Lazio	Paul Gascoigne	7/91
£4,500,000	Marseille	Chris Waddle	6/89
£1,500,000	Rangers	Richard Gough	9/87
£1,500,000	Barcelona	Steve Archibald	7/84

RECORD TRANSFER FEE PAID

Amount	Club	Player	Date
£4,500,000	Crystal Palace	Chris Armstrong	6/95
£2,600,000	Steaua Bucharest	Ilie Dumetrescu	8/94
£2,200,000	Chelsea	Gordon Durie	8/91
£2,000,000	Newcastle United	Paul Gascoigne	7/88

MANAGERS

Name	Seasons	Best	Worst
Frank Brettall	1895-88		
John Cameron	1898		
Fred Kirkham	1898-07		
Pete McWilliam	1907-08		
Billy Minter	1927-30	21(2)	12(2)
Percy Smith	1930-35	3(1)	8(2)
Jack Tresadern	1935-38	5(2)	10(2)
Pete McWilliam	1938-45	8(2)	8(2)
Joe Hulme	1945-49	5(2)	8(2)
Arthur Rowe	1949-55	1(1)	1(2)
Jim Anderson	1955-58	2(1)	18(1)
Bill Nicholson	1958-74	1(1)	11(1)
Terry Neill	1974-76	9(1)	19(1)
Keith Burkinshaw	1976-84	4(1)	3(2)
Peter Shreeves	1984-86	3(1)	10(1)
David Pleat	1986-87	3(1)	3(1)
Terry Venables	1987-91	3(1)	13(1)
Peter Shreeve	1991-92	15(1)	15(1)
Doug Livermore	1992-93	8(1/P)	8(1/P)
Ossie Ardiles	1993-94	15(P)	15(P)
Gerry Francis	1994-	7(P)	7(P)

LONGEST LEAGUE RUNS

of undefeated matches:	22 (31.8.1949 - 31.12.1949)	of league matches w/out a win:	16 (29.12.1934 - 13.4.1935)
of undefeated home matches:	33 (2.1.1932 - 23.9.1933)	of undefeated away matches:	16 (10.11.1984 - 21.8.1985)
without home win:	14 (23.10.1993 - 4.4.1994)	without an away win:	22 (25.2.1928 - 16.3.1929)
of league wins:	13 (23.4.1960 - 1.10.1960)	of home wins:	14)24.1.1987 - 3.10.1987)
of league defeats:	7 (1.1.94-27.2.94, 1.10.55-29.10.55)	of away wins:	10 (15.4.1960 - 29.10.1960)
	(18.2.75-22.3.75)		

TOTTENHAM HOTSPUR

PLAYERS NAME / Honours	Ht	Wt	Birthdate	Birthplace / Transfers	Contract Date	Clubs	APPEARANCES League	L/Cup	FA Cup	Other	GOALS Lge	L/C	FAC	Oth
G O A L K E E P E R S														
Chris Day E: Y. EUFA Yth'93.	6.2	12.4	28.07.75	Waltham Cross	16.04.93	Tottenham H. (T)								
Erik Thorstvedt Norwegen Int. FAC'91. CS'91. via Borusia M.	6.3	12.1	28.10.62	Stavanger		Viking Stavanger IFK Gothenburg								
				£400,000	22.12.88	Tottenham Hotspur	171+2	25	14	7				
Ian Walker E: u21.9, Y.17. FAYC'90. CS'91.	6.1	11.9	31.10.71	Watford	04.12.89	Tottenham H. (T)	87+1	6	8	2				
				Loan	31.08.90	Oxford United	2	1						
D E F E N D E R S														
Dean Austin	5.11	11.11	26.04.70	Hemel Hempstead		St. Albans								
				£12,000	22.03.90	Southend United	96	4	2	7	2	1		
				£375,000	04.06.92	Tottenham Hotspur	76+5	4+2	11+1					
Colin Calderwood Div.4'86.	6.0	12.0	20.01.65	Stranraer	19.03.82	Mansfield Town	97+3	3+4	6	7	1		1	
				£30,000	01.07.85	Swindon Town	328+2	35	17	32	20		1	
				£1,250,000	22.07.93	Tottenham Hotspur	61+1	6	9		2			
Sulzeer Campbell E: u21.6, S, Y. EUFA Yth'93.	6.1	12.10	18.09.74	Newham	23.09.92	Tottenham H. (T)	56+9	8	4+2		1	1		
Steve Carr Ei: u21.	5.9	12.02	29.08.76	Dublin	08.93	Tottenham H. (T)	1							
Jason Cundy E: u21.3.	6.1	13.7	12.11.69	Wandsworth	01.08.88	Chelsea (T)	40+1	6	64	2				
				£750,000	26.03.92	Tottenham Hotspur	23+2	2						
Justin Edinburgh FAC'91. CS'91.	5.9	11.6	18.12.69	Brentwood	05.08.88	Southend United (T)	36+1	2+1	2	4+1				1
				£150,000	30.07.90	Tottenham Hotspur	120+7	14+3	17	3	1			
Gary Mabbutt E: 16, B.9, u21.7, Y.11. UEFA'84. FAC'91. CS'91.	5.10	10.6	23.08.61	Bristol	09.01.79	Bristol Rovers (A)	122+9	10	5+1		10	1	1	
				£105,000	11.08.82	Tottenham Hotspur	417+16	56+2	39+2	29+4	27	2	3	4
Paul Mahorn	5.8	10.10	13.08.73	Whipps Cross	31.01.92	Tottenham H. (T)	1							
				Loan	23.09.93	Fulham	1+2			1				
Stuart Nethercott Loan 05.09.91 Maidstone 13 Lge 1gl 1 Oth App.	5.9	12.4	21.03.73	Ilford	17.08.91	Tottenham H. (T)	20+12		3+2				1	
				Loan	13.02.92	Barnet	3							
Kevin Scott FAYC'85. Div.1'93.	6.2	11.6	17.12.66	Easington	19.12.84	Newcastle United (A	227	18	15+1	12+1	8		1	2
				£850,000	01.02.94	Tottenham Hotspur	16				1			
M I D F I E L D														
Darren Caskey E: S, Y.15. UEFA Yth'93.	5.8	10.7	21.08.74	Basildon	06.03.92	Tottenham H. (T)	17+12	3+1	3+1		4	1		
Jason Dozzell E: u21.9, Y.5. Div.2'92.	6.2	12.0	09.12.87	Ipswich	20.12.84	Ipswich Town (A)	312+20	29+1	22	22	52	3	12 4	
				£1,900,000	01.08.93	Tottenham Hotspur	34+5	6	2		9	1		
Ilie Dumitrescu Romanian Int.	5.9	10.07	06.01.69	Bucharest		Steaua Bucharest								
				£2,600,000	03.08.94	Tottenham Athletic	11+2	2			4	1		
Mike Hazard FAC'82. UEFA'84.	5.7	10.5	05.02.60	Sunderland	02.02.78	Tottenham H. (A)	73+18	11+3	7+3	23	13	5	2	3
				£310,000	19.09.85	Chelsea	78+3	7+3	4+2	5+1	9	1	1	2
				£100,000	11.01.90	Portsmouth	8				1			
				£130,000	01.09.90	Swindon Town	112+7	12	7	3+2	17	1		
				£50,000	03.11.93	Tottenham Hotspur	15+13	1+1	2		2			
Danny Hill E: S.	5.9	11.03	01.10.74	Enfield	09.09.92	Tottenham T. (T)	4+6	0+2						
David Howells E: u19.2, Y.8. FLgXI.1. FAC'91. CS'91.	5.11	11.1	15.12.67	Guildford	28.01.85	Tottenham H. (T)	163+33	19+5	15+3	7	17	3	1	
David Kerslake E: u21.1, u19.4, Y.27, S.	5.8	11.0	19.06.66	Stepney	01.06.83	Q.P.R. (A)	38+20	6+2	2+2	2+2	6	4		
				£110,000	24.11.89	Swindon Town	133+2	12	8	10	1			
				£500,000	11.03.93	Leeds United	8							
				£450,000	24.09.93	Tottenham Hotspur	32+3	5	1+1					
Gerry McMahon NI: B, u21.1.	5.11	11.6	29.12.73	Belfast		Glenavon								
				£100,000	31.07.92	Tottenham Hotspur	2							
				Loan	20.09.94	Barnet	10		2	1	2		1	
Clive Wilson Div.2'89.	5.7	9.10	13.11.61	Manchester	08.12.79	Manchester City (J)	107+2	10	2	5	9	2		
				Loan	16.09.82	Chester City	21				2			
				£250,000	19.03.87	Chelsea	68+13	3+3	4	10+2	5			
				£450,000	04.07.90	Q.P.R.	170+2	16	8	2+1	12	1	1	
				Free	08.95	Tottenham Hotspur								
F O R W A R D S														
Chris Armstrong E: B.1. Div.1'94.	6.0	11.0	19.06.71	Newcastle		Llay Welfare								
				Free	03.03.89	Wrexham	40+20	2+1	0+1	5+1	13			3
				£50,000	16.08.91	Millwall	11+17	3+1	0+1	0+1	5	2		
				£1,000,000	01.09.92	Crystal Palace	118	8	8	2	46	6	5	1
				£4,500,000	08.95	Tottenham Hotspur								
Darren Anderton E: 3, Y.1, u21.12	6.0	11.7	03.03.72	Southampton	05.02.90	Portsmouth (T)	53+9	3+2	7+1	2	7	1	5	
				£1,750,000	03.06.92	Tottenham Hotspur	104+4	9	13+1		17	2	2	

TOTTENHAM HOTSPUR

PLAYERS NAME / Honours	Ht	Wt	Birthdate	Birthplace / Transfers	Contract Date	Clubs	League	L/Cup	FA Cup	Other	Lge	L/C	FAC	Oth
John Hendry	5.11	10.4	06.01.70	Glasgow		Dundee	0+2							
				Loan	01.02.90	Forfar	10				6			
				£50,000	31.07.90	Tottenham Hotspur	5+12	0+2	0+1		5			
				Loan	27.02.92	Charlton Athletic	1+4				1			
Ronny Rosenthal	5.11	12.0	11.10.63	Haifa (Israel)		Maccabi Haifa								
Israel. CS'90.			via FC Bruges to			Standard Liege								
				Loan	22.03.90	Liverpool	5+3							
				£1,000,000	29.06.90	Liverpool	27+39	2+7	5+3	2+4	21	1		
				£250,000	26.01.94	Tottenham Hotspur	25+10	1	2+2		6			
Teddy Sheringham	5.11	10.9	29.10.61	Walthamstow	19.01.84	Millwall (A)	205+15	16+1	12	11+2	93	8	5	5
E: 2, u21.1, Y.11. Div.2'88. FMC'92.				Loan	01.02.85	Aldershot	4+1			1				
				£2,000,000	23.07.91	Nottingham Forest	42	10	4	6	14	5	2	2
				£2,100,000	28.08.92	Tottenham Hotspur	96+3	8	11		53	6	8	
Andrew Turner	5.9	10.4	28.03.75	Woolwich	08.04.92	Tottenham H. (A)	8+12	0+2	0+1		3	1		
Ei: u21.2.				Loan	26.08.94	Wycombe W.	3+1							

TOP GOALSCORER 1994/95
Jurgen Klinsmann

Premiership goals (games) 20 (41)
Coca-Cola Cup Goals 4 (3)
F.A. Cup goals 5 (6)

Total . . . . **29 (50)**

Signed for Bayern Munich June 1995 . . . . £2,000,000.

THE MANAGER
GERRY FRANCIS

Date of Birth . . . . 6th December 1951.
Place of Birth . . . . Chiswick.
Date of Appointment . . . . November 1994.

PREVIOUS CLUBS
As Manager . . . . Bristol Rovers, Queens Park Rangers.
As Coach. . . . . None.
As a Player . . . . . QPR, C.Palace, QPR, Coventry City, Exeter City, Cardiff City,
. . . . Swansea City, Portsmouth, Bristol Rovers.

HONOURS
As a Manager
Bristol Rovers: Division 3 champions 1990.

As a Player
International: 12 full caps and U23 level for England.

WHITE HART LANE

748 High Road, Tottenham, London N17 0AP
Tel: 0181 808 6666

Capacity 32,786

First game...v Notts County (Friendly), 4-1, 4.9.1899.
Internationals ....England v France 1935, Germany 1935,
....Czechoslovakia 1937, v Italy 1949.

ATTENDANCES
Highest...75,038 v Sunderland, FAC 6th Rnd, 5.3.1938.
Lowest ....5,000 v Sunderland, Division 1, 19.12.1914.

OTHER GROUNDS ....Tottenham Marshes, 1882-1885. Northumberland Park 1885-1898. White Hart Lane 1898-

---

MATCHDAY TICKET PRICES

North Members Stand
Upper Tier - Standard/Premier . . . . £16*/£19*
Lower Tier . . . . £14*/£17*
West Stand
Upper Tier. . . . . £27/£32
Lower Tier. . . . . £20/£25
East Stand
Upper Tier Members. . . . . £20*/£23*
Upper Tier Non-Members . . . . £22/£27
Lower Tier Members. . . . . £18*/£21*
Lower Tier Non-Members . . . . £18/£21
South Stand
Upper Tier. . . . . £18/£21
Lower Tier. . . . . £15/£18
*for concessions halve the full price.

CLUBCALL
0891 100 300
Calls cost 39p per minute cheap rate and 49p per
minute at all other times.
Call costings correct at time of going to press.

HOW TO GET TO THE GROUND

From all directions
Use A406 North Circular Road to Edmonton then at traffic
signals follow signs to Tottenham A1010 into Fore Street for
Tottenham Hotspur FC.

Car Parking
No street parking within a quarter-of-a-mile radius of the
ground.

Nearest Railway Station
White Hart Lane (from Liverpool Street, Central London).
Northumberland Park (Liverpool Street).

MATCHDAY PROGRAMME

Programme Editor. . . . . John Fennelly.

Number of pages . . . . 48.

Price . . . . £1.50.

Subscriptions . . . . . UK/BFPO £45, Overseas please contact the club.

Local Newspapers . . . . . Tottenham Herald, Waltham Forest Guardian,
. . . . North London News.

Local Radio Stations . . . . Radio London, Hospital Broadcasts,
. . . . WNK Radio, Capital Radio.

WEST HAM UNITED
(The Hammers)
F.A. CARLING PREMIERSHIP
SPONSORED BY: DAGENHAM MOTORS

Back Row (L-R): Simon Webster, Ian Feuer, Marc Rieper, Ludek Miklosko, Jeroen Boere, Les Sealey, Alvin Martin.
Middle Row: Eddie Gillam (Kit Manager), Marco Boogers, Adrian Whitbread, Kenny Brown, Tim Breacker, Dale Gorden, John Moncur, Mark Watson, Matthew Rush, Danny Williamson, Martin Allen, John Green (Physio).
Front Row: Keith Rowland, Tony Cottee, Don Hutchison, Harry Redknapp (Manager), Steve Potts, Frank Lampard (Asst. Manager), Julian Dicks, Ian Bishop, Matt Holmes (Now with Blackburn).

WEST HAM UNITED
FORMED IN 1900
TURNED PROFESSIONAL IN 1900
LTD COMPANY IN 1900

CHAIRMAN: Terence W Brown
VICE-CHAIRMAN: Martin W Cearns
DIRECTORS
Charles Warner, P Storrie (Managing Director)
SECRETARY
Richard Skirrow (0181 548 2748)
COMMERCIAL MANAGER
Kate Bouchard (0181 548 2722)

MANAGER: Harry Redknapp
ASSISTANT MANAGER: Frank Lampard

RESERVE TEAM MANAGER
Paul Hilton
YOUTH TEAM MANAGER
Tony Carr
PHYSIOTHERAPIST
John Green, BSC (Hons), MCSP, SRP

STATISTICIAN FOR THE DIRECTORY
John Northcutt

After a poor pre-season the Hammers found it tough in the early league games. They found themselves in 19th place after five games without a win and only one goal scored.

Midfielder, Don Hutchison, was signed from Liverpool for a club record fee of £1.5 million, but it was a goalscorer that was needed most. The fans were therefore pleased when former striker Tony Cottee came back from Everton in a swap deal which took David Burrows to Goodison. Cottee scored the winner against Aston Villa on his home debut which inspired further victories in the London derbies against Chelsea and Crystal Palace. There was further joy when it was announced that Julian Dicks had been resigned from Liverpool. Julian was the fans favourite and they looked forward to his strong tackling and ferocious shooting.

In the Coca-Cola cup, Third Division Walsall were narrowly beaten 3-2 on aggregate, whilst in the next round it was the brilliance of goalkeeper Miklosko who helped West Ham to a 1-0 win against Chelsea. November was a poor month with defeats at lowly Spurs and Everton and dreadful home displays in losing to Coventry and to Bolton in the Coca-Coal cup.

The big Dutchman Jeroen Boere was brought in to partner Cottee and his first two goals at Leeds earned a 2-2 draw. An excellent hat-trick from Cottee gave West Ham a 3-0 home win over Manchester City , which was followed by another good home win by 3-1 against Nottingham Forest.

Potts and Martin were playing well in defence but in 16th place there was still cause for concern. Manager Harry Redknapp then went abroad to capture two players on loan, Irish winger Michael Hughes came from Strasbourg, whilst Danish centre-back Marc Rieper joined from Bromby. Midfielder Mike Marsh was then released to Coventry.

The difficult FA Cup tie at Wycombe was won by 2-0, but after this the gloom returned. Sheffield Wednesday won at Upton Park where Alvin Martin was sent-off - video evidence latter reduced the penalty to a booking. West Ham went out of the FA Cup in the 4th round losing 0-1 away to Queens Park Rangers. Cottee scored twice against his former Everton team mates but this was not enough to win the match which finished 2-2.

By earl y March the Hammers were in 19th place and were one of the relegation candidates. However in a marvellous end of season run they were only beaten twice in the last thirteen games. There was a 1-0 victory at Highbury, two Cottee goals in the last five minutes against Norwich and a superb goal from Dicks at Nottingham Forest which earnt a 1-1 draw. Champions elect, Blackburn, were beaten 2-0 in a terrific tussle where the Dane, Marc Rieper, was outstanding. Next came Liverpool, where Don Hutchison was delighted with his two goals against his old club mates, in the 3-0 win. Finally a super display from Ludek Miklosko ended the championship hopes of Manchester United in the 1-1 draw.

Congratulations to Steve Potts the 'Hammer of the Year" who was ever present and ever brilliant throughout the campaign. If Harry Redknapp can sign a partner for Cottee and the end of season form continues then the bubbles will be flying high again over Upton Park.

JOHN NORTHCUTT.

WEST HAM UNITED

Premier League: 14th   **FA Cup:** 4th Round   **Coca-Cola Cup:** 4th Round

M	DATE	COMP.	VEN	OPPONENTS	RESULT	H/T	LP	GOAL SCORERS/GOAL TIMES	ATT.
1	A 20	PL	H	Leeds United	D 0-0	0-0			18,610
2	24	PL	A	Manchester City	L 0-3	0-2	17		(19,150)
3	27	PL	A	Norwich City	L 0-1	0-0	18		(19,110)
4	31	PL	H	Newcastle United	L 1-3	0-2	21	Hutchison 87 (pen)	18,580
5	S 10	PL	A	Liverpool	D 0-0	0-0	19		(30,907)
6	17	PL	H	Aston Villa	W 1-0	0-0	17	Cottee 86	18,326
7	20	CC 2/1	A	**Walsall**	L 1-2	1-1		**Ntamark (og)**	**(5,994)**
8	25	PL	H	Arsenal	L 0-2	0-1	19		18,498
9	O 2	PL	A	Chelsea	W 2-1	0-0	15	Allen 53, Moncur 66	(18,696)
10	5	CC 2/2	H	**Walsall**	W 2-0	0-0		**Hutchison 62, Moncur 94**	**13,553**
11	8	PL	H	Crystal Palace	W 1-0	0-0	13	Hutchison 72	16,959
12	15	PL	A	Manchester United	L 0-1	0-1	14		(43,795)
13	22	PL	H	Southampton	W 2-0	0-0	12	Allen 49, Rush 61	18,853
14	26	CC 3	H	**Chelsea**	W 1-0	1-0		**Hutchison 2**	**18,815**
15	29	PL	A	Tottenham Hotspur	L 1-3	1-1	13	Rush 42	(24,271)
16	N 1	PL	A	Everton	L 0-1	0-0	13		(28,338)
17	5	PL	H	Leicester City	W 1-0	0-0	14	Dicks (pen)	18,780
18	19	PL	A	Sheffield Wednesday	L 0-1	0-1	17		(25,300)
19	26	PL	H	Coventry City	L 0-1	0-0	17		17,251
20	30	CC 4	H	**Bolton Wanderers**	L 1-3	0-1		**Cottee 83**	**18,190**
21	D 4	PL	A	Queens Park Rangers	L 1-2	0-2	18	Boere 89	(12,780)
22	10	PL	A	Leeds United	D 2-2	1-2	19	Boere 45, 79	(28,987)
23	17	PL	H	Manchester City	W 3-0	2-0	17	Cottee 6, 9, 57	17,286
24	26	PL	H	Ipswich Town	D 1-1	1-0	18	Cottee 16	20,562
25	28	PL	A	Wimbledon	L 0-1	0-1	18		(11,212)
26	31	PL	H	Nottingham Forest	W 3-1	3-0	16	Cottee 24, Bishop 26, Hughes 44	20,644
27	J 2	PL	A	Blackburn Rovers	L 2-4	1-1	16	Cottee 32, Dicks 58	(25,503)
28	7	FAC 3	A	**Wycombe Wanderers**	W 2-0	0-0		**Cottee 47, Brown 78**	**(9,007)**
29	14	PL	H	Tottenham Hotspur	L 1-2	0-1	19	Boere 10	24,573
30	23	PL	H	Sheffield Wednesday	L 0-2	0-1	19		14,554
31	28	FAC 4	A	**Queens Park Rangers**	L 0-1	0-1			**(17,694)**
32	F 4	PL	A	Leicester City	W 2-1	2-1	20	Cottee 29, Dicks (pen)	(20,375)
33	13	PL	H	Everton	D 2-2	1-1	20	Cottee 22, 40	21,081
34	18	PL	A	Coventry City	L 0-2	0-1	20		(17,554)
35	25	PL	H	Chelsea	L 1-2	1-0	20	Hutchison 11	21,500
36	M 5	PL	A	Arsenal	W 1-0	1-0	19	Hutchison 20	(34,295)
37	8	PL	A	Newcastle United	L 0-2	0-1	19		(34,595)
38	11	PL	H	Norwich City	D 2-2	0-1	18	Cottee 82, 88	21,464
39	15	PL	A	Southampton	D 1-1	1-0	19	Hutchison 39	(15,178)
40	18	PL	A	Aston Villa	W 2-0	1-0	18	Moncur 11, Hutchison 49	(28,682)
41	A 8	PL	A	Nottingham Forest	D 1-1		19	Dicks 65	(28,361)
42	13	PL	H	Wimbledon	W 3-0	1-0	17	Dicks 41 (pen), Boere 76, Cottee 78	21,084
43	17	PL	A	Ipswich	D 1-1		18	Boere 90	(19,099)
44	30	PL	H	Blackburn Rovers	W 2-0		16	Reiper 50, Hutchison 83	24,202
45	M 3	PL	H	Queens Park Rangers	D 0-0	0-0	15		22,923
46	6	PL	A	Crystal Palace	L 0-1	0-0	16		(18,224)
47	10	PL	H	Liverpool	W 3-0	1-0	13	Holmes 29, Hutchison 60, 61	22,446
48	14	PL	H	Manchester United	D 1-1	1-0	14	Hughes 31	24,783
49									
50									
51									
52									
53									
54									
55									
56									
57									
58									
59									
60									

Best Home League Attendance: 24,783 v Manchester United   **Smallest:** 14,554 v Sheffield United   **Av Home Att:** 19,730

Goal Scorers:

Compared with 1993-94: - 844

League (44): Cottee 13, Hutchison 9, Boere 6, Dicks 5, Allen 2, Hughes 2, Moncur 2, Rush 2, Bishop, Holmes, Rieper
C/Cola Cup (5): Hutchison 2, Cottee, Moncur, Opponent
FA Cup (2): Brown, Cottee

1994-95

#	1	2	3	4	8	6	17	27	25	11	7	26	5	10	14	15	33	8	16	17	19	9	12	22	20	18	Referee	
	Miklosko	Breacker	Dicks	Potts	Rieper	Allen	Hughes	Cottee	Boere	Holmes	Bishop	Hutchison	Martin	Moncur	Rush	Brown	Burrows	Butler	Chapman	Jones	Marsh	Morley	Rowland	Whitbread	Williamson	Webster	Referee	
	X	X		X1		X				X2	X		X					X	X			S2	X		S1		K. Burge	1
	X	X		X		X					X	X		X			X	X2	X1		S1	X		S2			R. Hart	2
	X	X		X		X					X		X	X			X		S1	X	X2		X1	S2			P. Jones	3
	X	X		X		X1				X		X	X			X	X			S1	X			S			B. Hill	4
	X	X		X		X		X				X	X	X			X		S		X		X		S		P. Danson	5
	X	X		X		X		X				X	X	X			X1	S1			X		X		S		S. Lodge	6
	X	X		X		X2		X				X	X	X	X1				S2		X		X		S2		P. Harrison	7
	X	X		X		X				X1		X	X	X	S1				X		X		X		S		K. Cooper	8
	X	X		X		X				S		X	X	X	X				X		X		X		S		P. Don	9
	X	X		X		X				X		X1				S1		X	X1		X		X		X		J. Holbrook	10
	X	X		X		X		X				X	X	X	S1				X1		X		X		S		G. Poll	11
	X	X		X		X		X			S	X	X	X	X				X		X		X		S		R. Gifford	12
	X	X	X	X		X		X				X		X					X		X		S		S		J. Worray	13
	X	X	X	X		X		X				X	X				X			S1	X		X		S2		K. Cooper	14
	X		X	X		X2						X	X1	X			X			S1	X		X		S	X	K. Morton	15
	X		X	X				X		S		X	X	X			X			X	X		S		X		K. Bodenham	16
	X		X	X		X1						X	X	X	X	X	S1			S	X		X		X		L. Dilkes	17
	X		X	X		X1		X				X		X	X	X	X			S1	X	S					G. Ashby	18
	X		X	X				X	X	X1				X	S1	X				X	X	S	X				M. Reed	19
	X		X	X				X	X	X	X			X	X	X				S1	S	X					P. Durkin	20
	X		X	X	X			X	X					X	X	X				X	S	X		S			P. Don	21
	X		X	X	X		S1	X	X	X	X			X	X						S	X1					R. Hart	22
	X	X	X	X	S		X	X	X	X	X		X		X					S							T. Holbrook	23
	X	X	X	X1	S1		X	X	X	X	X		X		X					S							P. Durkin	24
	X	X	X	X1			X	X	X	X	X			S1											S		P. Don	25
	X	X	X	X	S2		X	X	X1	X	X		X	X2	S1												D. Gallagher	26
	X	X	X	X	X		X	X	X	X1	X			X	S1	S											K. Morton	27
	X	X		X																							G. Willard	28
	X	X		X	S1	X1	X	X	X2	X		X	X		X						S2						B. Hill	29
	X	X		X	S1	S2	X1	X	X	X2	X		X	X		X											P. Danson	30
	X	X		X																							D. Ellery	31
	X	X	X	X	S	X	X	X	S1			X1	X	X											X		J. Worray	32
	X		X	X	S	X	X1	X	S1			X	X	X		X									X		M. Reed	33
	X	X	X	X	S1	X		X	S2	X2		X	X1	X											X		R. Dilkes	34
	X	X	X	X	X	X		X			X	X		X	S	S					X						G. Ashby	35
	X	X	X	X	X	X		X			X	X		X	S1						X1	S					B. Hill	36
	X	X	X	X	X	X	X	X			X	X		X1							S1	S					T. Holbrook	37
	X	X	X	X	X		S1	X			X	X		X1							X	S		X			A. Wilkie	38
	X	X	X	X	X	X		X	S1	X	X		X	X1								S					K. Burge	39
	X	X	X	X	X	X		X	S2	X1	X	X2	X								S1						M. Bodenham	40
	X		X	X	X	X	X	X	X	X1	X				X									S1	S		G. Poll	41
	X	X	X	X	X	X	X	X	X	X	X		S			S											M. Reed	42
	X	X	X	X	X1		X	X	X	X	S1		X		S												M. Bodenham	43
	X	X	X	X	X		X1	X	X	X2	X	S1											S1			S2	K. Morton	44
	X	X	X	X	X		X1	X	X	X2	X											S1				S2	G. Willard	45
	X	X	X	X	X2			X	X	X	X1											S1				S2	S. Lodge	46
	X	X	X1	X	X	S	X			X	X	X	X								X					S1	P. Durkin	47
	X	X		X	X	S1	X2			X	X	X1	X								X	X				S2	A. Wilkie	48
League Appearances	42	33	29	42	17	26	15	31	15	24	31	22	24	30	15	8	4	5	7	1	13	10	11	3	4		League Appearances	
League Sub Appearances					4		3		2												3	4		1		5	League Sub Appearances	
C/Cola Cup Appearances	4	3	2	4		3		3	1	1	3		3	2	3	3	1+1				3	4	3	0+1	2	2+1	C/Cola Cup Appearances	
FA Cup Appearances	2	2	2	2		1	2	2	2	2	1	2	0+1	2	2		0+1					0+1					FA Cup Appearances	

Also Played: Feuer S(1,2,3,4,5,6,7,8,9,10,11,12,13,14,15,16,17,18,19,20), Sealey S(21,22,23,24,25,26,27,28,29,30,31,32,33,34,35,36,37,38,39,40,41,42,43,44,45,46,47,48)

WEST HAM UNITED

CLUB RECORDS

BIGGEST VICTORIES
League: 8-0 v Rotherham United, Division 2, 8.3.1958
8-0 v Sunderland, Division 1, 19.10.1968
F.A. Cup: 6-0 v Bury, Round 2, 1919-20
6-0 v Arsenal, Round 3, 1945-46
League Cup: 10-0 v Bury, Round 2, 25.10.1984
Europe: No more than 4 goals

BIGGEST DEFEATS
League: 0-7 v Sheffield Wednesday, Division 1, 28.11.1959
0-7 v Everton, Division 1, 22.10.1927
0-7 v Barnsley, Division 2, 1.9.1919
F.A. Cup: 0-5 v Aston Villa, Round 2, 1912-13
0-5 v Tottenham Hotspur, Round 3, 1925-26
1-6 v Queens Park Rangers, Round 4 replay, 28.1.1978
League Cup: 0-6 v Oldham Athletic, Semi-Final, 14.2.1990
Europe 0(ECWC): No more than 3 goals

MOST POINTS
3 points a win: 88, Division 1, 1992-93
2 points a win: 66, Division 2, 1980-81

MOST GOALS
101, 1957-58, Division 2.
Dick 21, Keeble 19, Dare 14, Smith 11, Musgrove 9, Bond 8, Cantwell 4, Malcolm3, Lewis 3, Newman 2, Grice 2, Landsowne 2, Allison 2, og 2.

MOST LEAGUE GOALS CONCEDED
107 Division 1, 1931-32

MOST FIRST CLASS MATCHES IN A SEASON
62 (42 League, 4 FA Cup, 10 League Cup, 6 European Cup Winners Cup) 1965-66

MOST LEAGUE WINS
28, Division 2, 1980-81

MOST LEAGUE DRAWS
18, Division 1, 1968-69

MOST LEAGUE DEFEATS
23, Division 1, 1931-32

INDIVIDUAL CLUB RECORDS

MOST GOALS IN A MATCH
6. Geoff Hurst v Sunderland, 8-0, Division 1, 19.10.1968
6. Vic Watson v Leeds United, 8-2, Division 1, 9.2.1929

MOST GOALS IN A SEASON
Vic Watson 50 (League 42, FAC 8) 1929-30.
4 goals once=4; 3 goals 3 times=9; 2 goals 8 times=16; 1 goal 21 times=21.
Previous holder: Vic Watson 34, 1926-27

OLDEST PLAYER
Billy Bonds 41 years 225 days v Southampton (Div 1), 30.4.1988

YOUNGEST PLAYER
Paul Allen, 17 years 32 days v Burnley, Div. 2, 29.9.1979

MOST CAPPED PLAYER
Bobby Moore (England) 108

BEST PERFORMANCES

League: 1980-81: Matches played 42, Won 28, Drawn 10, Lost 4, Goals for 79.Goals against 29, Points 66. First in Division 2.

Highest: 1985-86: Third in Division 1.

F.A. Cup: 1963-64: 3rd rnd. Charlton Athletic 3-0; 4th rnd. Orient 1-1, 3-0;5th rnd. Swindon Town 3-1; 6th rnd. Burnley 3-2; Semi-final Manchester United3-1; Final Preston North End 3-2.
1974-75: 3rd rnd. Southampton 2-1; 4th rnd. Swindon Town 1-1, 2-1; 5th rnd.Queens Park Rangers 2-1; 6th rnd. Arsenal 2-0; Semi-final Ipswich Town 0-0, 2-1; Final Fulham 2-0.
1979-80: 3rd rnd. West Bromwich Albion 1-1, 2-1; 4th rnd. Orient 3-2; 5th rnd.Swansea City 2-0; 6th rnd. Aston Villa 1-0; Semi-final Everton 1-1, 2-1; Final Arsenal 1-0.

League Cup: 1965-66: 2nd rnd. Bristol Rovers 3-3, 3-2; 3rd rnd. Mansfield Town4-0; 4th rnd. Rotherham United 2-1; 5th rnd. Grimsby Town 2-2, 1-0; Semi-final Cardiff City 5-2, 5-1; Final West Bromwich Albion 2-1, 1-4.

Europe (ECWC): 1964-65: 1st rnd. La Gantoise 1-0, 1-1; 2nd rnd. Sparta Prague2-0, 1-2; 3rd rnd. Lausanne 2-1, 4-3; Semi-final Real Zaragoza 2-1, 1-1; Final Munich 1860 2-0.

DIVISIONAL RECORD

	Played	Won	Drawn	Lost	For	Against	Points
Division 1/P	1,674	575	412	687	2,518	2,720	1,720
Division 2/1	1,230	537	300	393	1,958	1,622	1,444
Total	**2,904**	**1,112**	**712**	**1,080**	**4,476**	**4,342**	**3,164**

ADDITIONAL INFORMATION
Previous Name
Thames Ironworks 1895-1900

Previous League
Southern League

Club colours: Claret shirts with sky blue side panels & trim, white shorts & socks with blue trim.
Change colours: White shirts, shorts & socks with claret & blue piping.

Reserves League: Avon Insurance Football Combination.

RECORDS AND STATISTICS

COMPETITIONS

Div 1/P	Div.2/1	ECWC	Watney	A/Ital
1923-32	1919-23	1964-65	1973	1975
1958-78	1932-58	1965-66		1992-93
1981-89	1978-81	1975-76	Texaco	
1919-92	1989-91	1980-81	1974-75	
1993-	1992-93			

HONOURS

Div.2	FA Cup	C/Shield	ECWC
1957-58	1963-64	1964	1964-65
	1974-75		
	1979-80		

MOST APPEARANCES

Billy Bonds 781+12 (1967-88)

Year	League	FA Cup	Lge Cup	ECWC
1967-68	37	3	2	
1968-69	42	3	2	
1969-70	42	1	2	
1970-71	37	1	2	
1971-72	42	4	10	
1972-73	39	2	2	
1973-74	40	2	1	
1974-75	31	8	3	
1975-76	17+1		5	9
1976-77	41	2	3	
1977-78	29	3		
1978-79	39	1	1	
1979-80	34	5	9	
1980-81	41	3	8	6
1981-82	29	2	4	
1982-83	34	1	4	
1983-84	27	0+1	2	
1984-85	19+3		4	
1985-86				
1986-87	13+4	3+1	1+2	
1987-88	22	2		
	655+8	46+2	65+2	15

MOST GOALS IN A CAREER

Vic Watson - 326 (1920-35)

Year	League	FA Cup
1920-21	2	
1921-22	12	1
1922-23	22	5
1923-24	3	
1924-25	22	1
1925-26	20	
1926-27	34	3
1927-28	16	
1928-29	29	1
1929-30	42	8
1930-31	14	
1931-32	23	2
1932-33	23	4
1933-34	26	3
1934-35	10	
Total	**298**	**28**

Current leading goalscorer: Tony Cottee - 133 (1982-95 - 2 spells)

RECORD TRANSFER FEE RECEIVED

Amount	Club	Player	Date
£2,000,000	Everton	Tony Cottee	7/88
£850,000	Celtic	Frank McAvennie	10/87
£800,000	Manchester Utd	Paul Ince	9/89
£400,000	Newcastle Utd	Paul Goddard	10/86
£400,000	Tottenham H.	Paul Allen	6/85

RECORD TRANSFER FEE PAID

Amount	Club	Player	Date
£1,500,000	Liverpool	Don Hutchison	8/94
£1,250,000	Celtic	Frank McAvennie	3/89
£800,000	Q.P.R.	Paul Goddard	8/79
£527,000	Q.P.R.	Phil Parkes	2/79

MANAGERS

Name	Seasons	Best	Worst
Syd King	1902-32	7(1)	7(2)
Charlie Paynter	1932-50	4(2)	20(2)
Ted Fenton	1950-61	6(1)	16(1)
Ron Greenwood	1961-77	6(1)	20(1)
John Lyall	1977-89	3(1)	7(2)
Lou Macari	1989-90		
Billy Bonds	1990-94	13(P)	7(2)
Harry Redknapp	1994-	14(P)	14(P)

LONGEST LEAGUE RUNS

of undefeated matches:	27 (27.12.1980 - 10.10.1981)	of league matches w/out a win:	17 (31.1.1976 - 21.8.1976)
of undefeated home matches:	27 (30.8.1980 - 21.11.1981)	of undefeated away matches:	13 (10.1.1981 - 3.10.1981)
without home win:	13 (29.10.1988 - 15.4.1989)	without an away win:	31 (12.12.1931 - 14.3.1933)
of league wins:	9 (19.10.1985 - 14.12.1985)	of home wins:	16 (30.8.1980 - 7.3.1981)
of league defeats:	9 (28.3.1932 - 29.8.1932)	of away wins:	5 (16.12.22-15.2.23, 26.12.35-15.3.36, 5.10.85-7.12.85)

WEST HAM UNITED

PLAYERS NAME / Honours	Ht	Wt	Birthdate	Birthplace / Transfers	Contract Date	Clubs	APPEARANCES League	L/Cup	FA Cup	Other	GOALS Lge	L/C	FAC	Oth
G O A L K E E P E R S														
Les Sealey	6.0	11.6	29.09.57	Bethnal Green	01.03.76	Coventry City (A)	158	11	9					
FAC'90. ECWC'91. CS'90				£100,000	03.08.83	Luton Town	207	21	28	3				
				Loan	05.10.84	Plymouth Argyle	6							
				Loan	21.03.90	Manchester United	2		1					
				Free	06.06.90	Manchester united	31	8	3	9				
				Free	19.07.91	Aston Villa	18		4	2				
				Loan	25.03.92	Coventry City	2							
				Loan	02.10.92	Birmingham City	12		3					
				Free	06.01.93	Manchester United		1	0+1					
				Free	18.07.94	Blackpool	7	2						
				Free	28.11.94	West Ham United								
Ludek Miklosko	6.5	14.0	09.12.61	Ostrava		Banik Ostrava								
				£300,000	19.02.90	West Ham United	230	17	20	8				
D E F E N D E R S														
Tim Breaker	6.0	12.6	02.07.65	Bicester	15.05.83	Luton Town (A)	204+6	22+2	21	7	3			
E: u21.2. LC'88.				£600,000	12.10.90	West Ham United	168+2	11	22	7	8			
Kenny Brown	5.8	11.6	11.07.67	Upminster	10.07.85	Norwich City (J)	24+1			3				
				Free	10.08.88	Plymouth Argyle	126	9	6	3	4			
				£175,000	02.08.91	West Ham United	52+8	1+1	7+2	2+2	5		1	
Julian Dicks	5.7	11.7	11.12.68	Bristol	12.04.86	Birmingham City (A)	83+6	5+1	5	2	1			
E: u21.4. B.2.				£300,000	25.03.88	West Ham United	159	19	14	11	29	5	2	4
				£1,500,000	17.09.93	Liverpool	24	3	1		3			
				£1,000,000	20.10.94	West Ham United	29	2	2		5			
Alvin Martin	6.1	13.9	29.07.58	Bootle	01.07.76	West Ham Utd (A)	452+3	69	39	16	27	6		1
E: 17, B.2, Y. FAC'80, Div.2'81.														
Steve Potts	5.8	10.5	07.05.67	Hartford (USA)	11.05.84	West Ham Utd (A)	268+10	27+1	31	14+1	1			
E: Y.11.														
Marc Rieper	6.4	14.2	05.06.68	Rodoure		Brondby								
				Loan	08.12.94	West Ham United	17+4				1			
				£500,000	08.95	West Ham United								
Simon Webster	6.0	11.7	20.01.64	Hinckley	01.12.81	Tottenham H. (A)	2+1							
Loan Exeter City, 10.11.83, 26 Lge + 3 Oth apps.				£15,000	21.02.85	Huddersfield Town	118	7	7	2	4			
				£35,000	18.03.88	Sheffield United	26+11	5	5+1	3+1	3			
				£50,000	16.08.90	Charlton Athletic	127	7	6	3	7			
				£525,000	30.06.93	West Ham United	0+5							
				Loan	23.03.95	Oldham Athletic	7							
Adrian Whitbread	6.2	11.8	22.10.71	Epping	13.11.89	Leyton Orient (T)	125	10+1	11	8	2		1	
				£500,000	29.07.93	Swindon Town	34+1		2		1			
				£650,000	17.08.94	West Ham United	3+5	2+1						
M I D F I E L D														
Martin Allen	5.10	11.0	14.08.65	Reading	27.05.83	Q.P.R. (A)	128+8	15+3	9	2	16	1	1	1
E: u21.2, u19.3, Y.				£675,000	24.08.89	West Ham United	160+27	15+3	14	10	25	5	4	
Ian Bishop	5.9	10.12	29.05.65	Liverpool		Everton (A)	0+1							
E: B.1.				Loan	22.03.84	Crewe Alexandra	4							
				£15,000	11.10.84	Carlisle United	131+1	8	5	4	14	1	1	
				£35,000	14.07.88	Bournemouth	44	4	5	1	2			
				£465,000	02.08.89	Manchester City	18+1	4		1	2	1		
				£500,000	28.12.89	West Ham United	176+1	13	17+1	4+1	10		3	1
Dale Gordon	5.10	11.8	09.01.67	Gt Yarmouth	17.01.84	Norwich City (A)	194+12	21	19	14+2	31	3	6	3
E: B.2, u21.4,Y.1,S. SPD'92'93. SFAC'92. SLC'93				£1,200,000	08.11.91	Glasgow Rangers	41+4	1+1	6+1	1	6	1	1	
				£750,000	20.07.93	West Ham United	8	1			1			
				Loan	23.03.95	Peterborough Utd	6				1			
Stan Lazaridis						West Adelaide								
				£300,000	08.95	West Ham United								
John Moncur	5.7	9.10	22.09.66	Stepney	22.08.84	Tottenham H. (A)	10+11	1+2			1			
Loan Doncaster Rov., 25.9.86, 4 Lge App.				Loan	27.03.87	Cambridge United	3+1							
Loan Portsmouth, 22.3.89, 7 Lge App.				Loan	11.08.89	Brentford	5			1	1			
Loan Ipswich T., 24.10.91, 5+1 Lge App.				£80,000	30.03.92	Swindon Town	53+5	4	1	4	5			1
				£900,000	24.08.94	West Ham United	30	3	2		2	1		
Keith Rowland	5.10	10.0	01.09.71	Portadown	02.10.89	Bournemouth (T)	65+7	5	8	3	2			
NI: Y. SLP'91. Flg u18.1.				Loan	01.08.90	Farnborough Town			1					
Loan Coventry C., 8.1.93, 0+2 Lge App.				£110,000	06.08.93	West Ham United	27+8	3	4					
Matthew Rush	5.11	12.10	06.08.71	Hackney	24.03.90	West Ham Utd (T)	29+19	4		2+1	5			
Ei: u21.3.				Loan	12.03.93	Cambridge United	4+6							
				Loan	10.01.94	Swansea City	13			4				
Robbie Slater	5.11	13.0	22.11.64	Skelmersdale		Lens								
Australian Int.				£300,000	04.08.94	Blackburn Rovers	12+6	1	1	2				
				£600,000+PE	08.95	West Ham United								
Daniel Williamson	5.11	12.3	05.12.73	Newham	03.07.92	West Ham Utd (T)	6+1				1			
				Loan	04.02.93	Farnborough Town								
				Loan	08.10.93	Doncaster Rovers	10+3		2	1	1		2	

WEST HAM UNITED

PLAYERS NAME Honours	Ht	Wt	Birthdate	Birthplace Transfers	Contract Date	Clubs	APPEARANCES League	L/Cup	FA Cup	Other	GOALS Lge	L/C	FAC	Oth
F O R W A R D S														
Jeroen Boere	6.3	13.5	18.11.67	Arnhem		Go Ahead								
Netherlands: u21.				£250,000	22.09.93	West Ham United	15+9	1+1	2		7	1		
				Loan	24.03.94	Portsmouth	4+1							
				Loan	08.09.94	West Bromwich A.	5							
Marco Boogers						Sparta Rotterdam								
				£1,000,000	08.95	West Ham United								
Tony Cottee	5.8	11.5	11.07.65	West Ham	01.09.82	West Ham Utd (A)	203+9	19	24	1	92	14	11	1
E: 7, u21.8, Y.3.				£2,300,000	02.08.88	Everton	158+23	19+4	15+6	11+2	72	11	4	12
				£300,000+PE	07.09.94	West Ham United	31	3	2		12	1	1	
Don Hutchison	6.2	11.04	09.05.71	Gateshead	20.03.90	Hartlepool Utd (T)	19+5	1+1	2	1	3			
S: B.1.				£175,000	27.11.90	Liverpool	33+12	7+1	1+2	3+1	7	2		1
				£1,500,000	30.08.94	West Ham United	22+1	3	0+1		9	2		

TOP GOALSCORER 1994/95
Tony Cottee

Premiership goals (games)................................ 13 (31)
Coca-Cola Cup Goals 1 (3)
F.A. Cup goals 1 (2)

Total .... **15 (36)**

Total goals for West Ham since 01.09.82 (2 spells) .... 133 (283+9)
Total for England (full caps only)........................... 0 (7)

Career total as at June 1st 1995...................... 239 (486+44)

THE MANAGER
HARRY REDKNAPP

Date of Birth .... 2nd March 1947.
Place of Birth .... Poplar.
Date of Appointment .... 10th August 1994.

PREVIOUS CLUBS
As Manager... Bournemouth.
As Coach.. None.
As a Player .... West Ham United, Bournemouth, Brentford.

HONOURS
As a Manager
Bournemouth: Division 3 champions 1987.

As a Player
None.

UPTON PARK

Green Street, London E13 9AZ
Tel: 0181 548 2700

Capacity 26,014

First game...v Millwall, Sth Lge, 1.9.1904.
First floodlit game ....v Tottenham Hotspur, 16.4.1953.

ATTENDANCES
Highest...42,322 v Tottenham, Div.1, 17.10.1970.
Lowest ....4,500 v Doncaster, Div.2, 24.2.1955.

OTHER GROUNDS ....Memorial Recreation Ground, Canning Town 1900-04. Upton Park 1904-

---

MATCHDAY TICKET PRICES

West Stand . . . . £17-£25
Juv/OAP £10

East Stand Upper Tier . . . . £17-£25
Juv/OAP £10

Bobby Moore Stand . . . . £14-£21
Juv/OAP £10

Centenary Stand (North) £15
JUv/OAP £8
Reductions are available to members.
Ticket Office Telephone no. 0181 548 2700

CLUBCALL
0891 12 11 65
Calls cost 39p per minute cheap rate and 49p per
minute at all other times.
Call costings correct at time of going to press.

HOW TO GET TO THE GROUND

From the North and West
Take North Circular (A406) to A124 (East Ham), then on Barking Road for
approx 1.5 miles until you approach traffic lights on crossroads. Turn right into
Green Street, ground is on right hand side.

From the East
Use A13, sign posted London, then at crossroads turn right (A117). In 0.9 miles
at crossroads turn left (A124). In 0.6 miles turn right into Green Street for West
Ham United FC.

From the South
Use Blackwall Tunnel and A13 to Canning Town, then follow signs East Ham
(A124). In 1.7 miles turn left into Green Street for West Ham United FC.

Car Parking
Ample side-street parking available.

Nearest Railway Station
Upton Park (District Line Tube).

MATCHDAY PROGRAMME

Programme Editor . . . . Peter Stewart.

Number of pages . . . . 48.

Price . . . . £1.50.

Subscriptions . . . . £63.50 for all 1st team home matches.

Local Newspapers . . . . Stratford Express, Ilford Recorder.

Local Radio Stations. . . . . Essex Radio.

WIMBLEDON
(The Dons)
F.A. CARLING PREMIERSHIP
SPONSORED BY: ELONEX

Back Row (L-R): Alan Reeves, Brian McAllister, Paul Heald, Neil Sullivan, Andy Thorn, Gary Elkins, Mick Harford.
Middle Row: Efan Ekoku, Neal Ardley, Grant Payne, Scott Fitzgerald, Aidan Newhouse, Vinny Jones, Marcus Gayle, Stewart Castledine, Jon Goodman, Robbie Earle. **Front Row:** Joe Kinnear, Steve Talboys, Alan Kimble, Chris Perry, Peter Fear, Mark Thomas.

WIMBLEDON
FORMED IN 1889
TURNED PROFESSIONAL IN 1964
LTD COMPANY IN 1964

CHAIRMAN: S G Reed
DEPUTY-CHAIRMAN: J H Lelliott

DIRECTORS
P E Cork, PR Lloyd Cooper,
S G N Hammam (Managing Director),
P. Miller
SECRETARY
Steve Rooke (0181 771 2233)
COMMERCIAL MANAGER
Reg Davis

MANAGER: Joe Kinnear
ASSISTANT MANAGER: Terry Burton

YOUTH TEAM MANAGER
Ernie Tippett
PHYSIOTHERAPIST
Steve Allen

STATISTICIAN FOR THE DIRECTORY
Simon Case

It was another very satisfactory season for Wimbledon. They made their usual slow start to the season, failing to get a win from their opening four games and obtained only two victories in the league up to late October.

The Don's season began to gain momentum around November with impressive wins over Aston Villa in a 4-3 thriller and a great win over Newcastle. Their form continued to become better and more consistent and by mid-January a 2-1 win at Norwich saw them reach seventh place, their highest league position of the season.

With a possible place in Europe in sight Wimbledon tried determinedly to crack the top five or six which, come the season's end, was just beyond them and they finished a very credible ninth.

Wimbledon's best performance in the season's cup competitions came in the FA Cup, where they reached the firth round before succumbing to Liverpool after a replay.

Injuries throughout the year robbed the Don's of vital players, including the talented Robbie Earle who missed most of the campaign. With the early season record £3.5 million sale of John Scales to Liverpool, Wimbledon spent more during a season than in recent times. Buys included the returning Andy Thorn (from Crystal Palace), Alan Reeves (from Rochdale), Ken Cunningham and Jon Goodman (from Millwall), club record buy Efan Ekoku for £900,000 (from Norwich) and Norweigan World Cup player Oyvind Leonhardsen on loan.

All settled in well and had relatively good seasons, in particular the consistent Cunningham and Reeves at the back, and the lively Leonhardsen. Ekoku finished top scorer with nine league goals and he and Goodman provided extra options up-front. Others having good personal season's were again, Vinny Jones, who made his international debut for Wales, the versatile Gary Elkins, much sought after Warren Barton, who made his deserved England debut and was excellent all season, impressive youngster Chris Perry and goal-keeper Neil Sullivan who came in late on for Hans Segers and took his chance well with some good performances. The veteran striker Mick Harford also played well and proved a bargain buy in his first season at Wimbledon with eight goals overall, including league match winners against Newcastle and Everton. **SIMON CASE.**

WIMBLEDON

Premier League: 9th | **FA Cup:** 5th Round | **Coca-Cola Cup:** 3rd Round

M	DATE	COMP.	VEN	OPPONENTS	RESULT	H/T	LP	GOAL SCORERS/GOAL TIMES	ATT.
1	A 20	PL	A	Coventry City	D 1-1	0-0		Castledine 55	(10,962)
2	23	PL	H	Ipswich Town	D 1-1	1-0		Holdsworth 19	5,853
3	27	PL	H	Sheffield Wednesday	L 0-1	0-0	16		7,453
4	31	PL	A	Manchester United	L 0-3	0-1			(43,440)
5	S 10	PL	H	Leicester City	W 2-1	2-1		Harford 29, Willis 45 (og)	7,683
6	17	PL	A	Crystal Palace	D 0-0	0-0	12		(12,100)
7	20	CC 2/1	H	**Torquay United**	W 2-0	2-0		**Gayle 35, Harford 43**	**2,451**
8	24	PL	A	Queens Park Rangers	W 1-0	0-0	10	Reeves 48	(11,059)
9	O 1	PL	H	Tottenham Hotspur	L 1-2	1-1	13	Talboys 29	16,802
10	5	CC 2/2	A	Torquay United	W 1-0	1-0		Holdsworth 38	(4,244)
11	8	PL	H	Arsenal	L 1-3	0-1	15	Jones 82	10,842
12	17	PL	A	Nottingham Forest	L 1-3	0-1		Gayle 82	(20,287)
13	22	PL	A	Liverpool	L 0-3	0-2	20		(31,139)
14	25	CC 3	H	**Crystal Palace**	L 0-1	0-0			**9,394**
15	30	PL	H	Norwich City	W 1-0	0-0		Ekoku 63	8,242
16	N 5	PL	A	Leeds United	L 1-3	1-3	18	Ekoku 25	(27,284)
17	9	PL	H	Aston Villa	W 4-3	1-2	16	Barton 8 (pen), Ardley 65, Jones 83, Leonhardsen 90	6,221
18	19	PL	H	Newcastle United	W 3-2	3-2	14	Clarke 1, Ekoku 27, Harford 36	14,203
19	26	PL	A	Manchester City	L 0-2	0-1	15		(21,131)
20	D 3	PL	H	Blackburn Rovers	L 0-3	0-0	16		12,341
21	10	PL	A	Coventry City	W 2-0	2-0	15	Leonhardsen 4, Harford 17	7,349
22	16	PL	A	Ipswich Town	D 2-2	1-1	14	Holdsworth 2, Goodman 62	(11,367)
23	26	PL	A	Southampton	W 3-2	2-2		Holdsworth 20, 72 (pen), Harford 38	(14,603)
24	28	PL	H	West Ham United	W 1-0	0-0		Fear 55	11,212
25	31	PL	A	Chelsea	D 1-1	0-0		Ekoku 68	(16,105)
26	J 2	PL	H	Everton	W 2-1	2-1	9	Harford 4, 8	9,506
27	7	FAC 3	H	**Colchester United**	W 1-0	1-0		**Harford 8**	**6,903**
28	14	PL	A	Norwich City	W 2-1	1-1	7	Reeves 44, Ekoku 50	(18,261)
29	25	PL	A	Newcastle United	L 1-2	0-1	9	Ekoku 78	(34,374)
30	29	FAC 4	A	**Tranmere Rovers**	W 2-0	1-0		**Leonhardsen 32, Earle 52**	**(11,637)**
31	F 4	PL	H	Leeds United	D 0-0	0-0	9		10,211
32	11	PL	A	Aston Villa	L 1-7	1-4	9	Barton 11	(23,982)
33	19	FAC 5	A	**Liverpool**	D 1-1	1-1		**Clarke 2**	**(25,124)**
34	22	PL	A	Blackburn Rovers	L 1-2	1-2	10	Ekoku 39	(20,586)
35	25	PL	H	Tottenham Hotspur	W 2-1	1-0	10	Ekoku 37, 63	(27,258)
36	28	FAC 5R	H	**Liverpool**	L 0-2	0-2			**12,553**
37	M 4	PL	H	Queens Park Rangers	L 1-3	1-1	10	Holdsworth 12	9,176
38	7	PL	H	Manchester United	L 0-1	0-0	13		18,224
39	11	PL	A	Sheffield Wednesday	W 1-0	0-0	9	Reeves 63	(20,395)
40	18	PL	H	Crystal Palace	W 2-0	1-0	8	Jones 36, Gayle 60	8,835
41	21	PL	H	Manchester City	W 2-0	0-0	8	Thorn 59, Elkins 76	5,268
42	A 1	PL	A	Leicester City	W 4-3	0-1	8	Goodman 63, 89, Leonhardsen 65, 85	(15,489)
43	10	PL	H	Chelsea	D 1-1	0-1	9	Goodman 56	7,022
44	13	PL	A	West Ham United	L 0-3	0-1	9		(21,804)
45	17	PL	H	Southampton	L 0-2	0-2	9		10,521
46	29	PL	A	Everton	D 0-0	0-0	9		(33,063)
47	M 2	PL	H	Liverpool	D 0-0	0-0	9		12,041
48	4	PL	A	Arsenal	D 0-0	0-0	9		(32,822)
49	13	PL	H	Nottingham Forest	D 2-2	2-1	9	Holdsworth 35, 40 (pen)	15,341
50									
51									
52									
53									
54									
55									
56									
57									
58									
59									
60									

Best Home League Attendance: 18,224 v Manchester United | **Smallest:** 5,268 v Manchester City | **Av Home Att:** 9,826

Goal Scorers:

Compared with 1993-94: - 616

League (48): Ekoku 9, Holdsworth 7 (2 pens), Harford 6, Goodman 4, Leonhardsen 4, Jones 3, Reeves 3, Barton 2 (1 pen), Gayle 2, Ardley, Castledine, Clarke, Elkins, Fear, Talboys, Opponent

C/Cola Cup (3): Gayle, Harford, Holdsworth

FA Cup (4): Harford, Leonhardsen, Earle, Clarke

1	2	6	12	15	4	19	20	18	25	10	26	11	23	7	16	21	15	24	17	28	9		35	36	37		1994-95
Segers H.	Barton W.	Fitzgerald S.	Elkins G.	Scales J.	Jones V.	Castledine S.	Gayle M.	Talboys S.	Harford M.	Holdsworth D.	Ardley N.	Blissett G.	Sullivan N.	Clarke A.	Kimble A.	Perry C.	Reeves A.	Fear P.	Joseph R.	Thom A.	Ekoku E.	Murphy	Leonhardsen O.	Goodman J.	Cunningham K.	Referee	
X	X	X	X	X	X	X	X	X1	X2	X	S1	S2	S													R. Gifford	1
X	X	X	X	X	X	X	X	S	X	X	X1	S		S1												J. Worrall	2
X	X	X	X	X	X	X	X	S	X		X	X1	S	S1												R. Hart	3
X	X	X	X		X	X1	X	X	X			S		S1	X		S									T. Holbrook	4
X	X	X	X1		Xt		X		X2	X			S	S2	X		X	S1								G. Poll	5
X	X	X	X		X		X		X	X			S	S	X		X	S								K. Cooper	6
X	X	X	X		X		X		X2	X	X1		S	S2	X		X	S1								P. Foakes	7
X	X	X	X				X1	X	X			S1		S	X	X	S2	X	X2							K. Burge	8
X	X	X	X				X	X	X	X	X2			S	S2	X	S1	X1	X							M. Reed	9
X	X	X	X				X1		X	X			S	X2	X	X		X	S2							M. Bodenham	10
X	X	X	X		X		X2		X1	X	S1		S		X		X	X	S2							G. Ashby/S. Tomlin	11
X	X	X	X		X	X	X		S			S1		S		X	X1	X	X							R. Hart	12
X	X	X	X		X		S2	X2				X	S1			X1	X	X	X		X	S				P. Jones	13
X	X	X2	X		X		X1		S2		X	X	S	X			S1	X	X		X					R. Gifford	14
X	X	S	X		X		X1	X			X	S	S1			X		X	X	X						D. Gallagher	15
X	X	S	X		X		X	X			X	S	S1			X		X	X	X1						B. Hill	16
X	X	S2	X		X			X1	S1		X		S	X2			X		X	X	X					D. Elleray	17
X	X2	S2	X		Xt			S1					S	X			X		X	X	X		X	X1	X	P. Don	18
X	X	S1	X		X				X1	S			S	X		Xt	X		X	X	X		X		X	A. Wilkie	19
X	X	X	X		X			S1	X	S			S	X			X1		X	X	X		X	S2	X	P. Jones	20
X	X	X	X		X			X2	X1				S	S1	X		X		X	X	X		X	S2	X	R. Dilkes	21
X	X	X	S1		X			S2	X2				S		X		X		X	X	X1	X	X	D. Elleray	22
X	X		X					X	X1	S1			S	S	X	X			Xt	X					X	G. Poll	23
X	X		X1		X2			X	X				S	S1	X	X		S2		X	X				X	P. Don	24
X	X		X		X			X	X1				S	S1	X	X		S		X	X				X	K. Morton	25
X	X		X		X			X	X			S		S	X	X	X	X	S1		X1				X	K. Burge	26
X			X		X			X	X			S		S	S	X	X	S	X	X					X	P. Danson	27
X	X	S2	X		X				X1				S	S1	X	X	X			X	X			X2	X	M. Bodenham	28
X	X	S1	X		X							S2		S	X2	X1	X			X	X			X	X	M. Reed	29
X	X		X		X			X2				S1		S			X			X	X1	X	S2	X	P. Durkin	30
X	X		X		X			X2				S1		S			X			X	X1	X	S2	X	G. Ashby	31
X	X		X		X			X2	X1				S				S2	X		X	X	X	S1	X	B. Hill	32
X	X							S1	S2	X		X		X	X	X				X1	X			X	A. Wilkie	33
X	X							S1	S2	X		S	X1	X	X	X				X2	X			X	S. Lodge	34
X	X					X		S	S			S		X	X	X	X		X	X				X	D. Gallagher	35
X	X							S2	S1	X		S		X	X	X			X2	X1	X			X	A. Wilkie	36
X	X				X			X	X			S		S1	X	X	X			X2	S2		X	P. Willard	37
X	X		X		X			X1	S	X	S1		S		Xt	X	X			X			X	R. Hart	38
S	X		X		X			X1	S1	X2			X			X	X				S2	X	X	J. Worrall	39
S	X		X		X1			X2	S1	X			X			X	X				S2	X	X	D. Gallagher	40
S			X		X			X	S	X			X		X	X	S		X			X	X	R. Gifford	41
S	X2		X		X1			S1	X			X		X	S2	X		X		X	X2	X	D. Elleray	42
S	X		X		X			S2	S1	X			X		X1	X		X		X		X	K. Morton	43
S	X		X		X1			X	X			X	S1		S	X		X		X		X	M Reed	44
S	X		X		X				X			X	S1		S	X		X	X	X1	X*	X	S2	X	G. Ashby	45
S			X		X				X			X		X	S1	X	X	X1	X*	X	S2	X	P. Danson	46
S	X		X		X	X2			X			X	S1	X	X	X	S2		X1	X	T. Holbrook	47
S	X		X		X			X2				X	S2	X	X	X	S1		X1	X	S3	X	R. Gifford	48
S2			X3		X			X1				X	X2	S1	X	X	X			X	S3	X	S. Lodge	49
31	39	14	33	3	33	5	22	7	17	27	9	4	11	8	26	17	31	8	3	22	24		18	13	28	League Appearances	
1		3	3			1	1		9	1	5	5		17		5		5		1			2	6		League Sub Appearances	
3	3	3	3		2		2	1	2+1	2	2+1	1		2+1	2	2		1+2	1+1	1						C/Cola Cup Appearances	
4	3		1		2				2+2	1+2	2	0+1		3	3	3	2	1					3	0+1	4	FA Cup Appearances	

Also Played: Earle (23,25,26,27,28,29,30,31,33,34,35,36,37), Shilton (33)   Players on Loan: Leonhardsen (Rosenborg)   † = Sent Off

WIMBLEDON

CLUB RECORDS

BIGGEST VICTORIES
League: 6-0 v Newport County, Division 3, 3.9.19830
F.A. Cup: 7-2 v Windsor & Eton, Rnd 1, 22.11.1980
League Cup: 5-0 v Blackburn, Round 1, 24.9.1985

BIGGEST DEFEATS
League: 1-7 v Aston Villa (A), Premier League, 112.95.
1-6 v Carlisle Utd., Division 2, 23.3.1985
1-6 v Gillingham, Division 2, 13.2.1982
F.A. Cup: 0-6 v Fulham, Rnd 1 replay, 1930-31
League Cup: 0-8 v Everton, Round 2, 29.8.1978

MOST POINTS
3 points a win: 98, Division 4, 1982-83.
2 points a win: 61, Division 4, 1978-79.

MOST GOALS
97, 1983-84, Division 3
Cork 28, Hodges 16, Evans 12, Fishender 8, Ketteridge 7, Downes 4, Park 4, Morris 3, Peters 3, Smith 3, Thomas 3, Hatter 2, Galliers 1, Winterburn 1, og2.

MOST LEAGUE GOALS CONCEDED
81, Division 3, 1979-80

MOST FIRST CLASS MATCHES IN A SEASON
56 (46 League, 2 FA Cup, 2 League Cup, 6 Football League Group Cup) 1981-82

MOST LEAGUE WINS
29, Division 4, 1982-83

MOST LEAGUE DRAWS
16, Division 1, 1977-78, 1989-90

MOST LEAGUE DEFEATS
22, Division 3, 1979-80

INDIVIDUAL CLUB RECORDS

MOST GOALS IN A MATCH
4. Alan Cork v Torquay United, Division 4, 28.2.1979 (4-1).

MOST GOALS IN A SEASON
Alan Cork 33, (League 29, FAC 2, Lge C 2) 1983-84
3 goals once=3; 2 goals 6 times=12; 1 goal 17 times=17

OLDEST PLAYER
Dave Donaldson, 37 years 4 months. v Hartlepool (Div 4) 9.2.1979.

YOUNGEST PLAYER
Kevin Gage 17 years 15 days v Bury (Div 4), 2.5.1981.

MOST CAPPED PLAYER
Terry Phelan (Eire) 8

BEST PERFORMANCES

League: 1982-83: Matches played 46, Won 29, Drawn 11, Lost 6, Goals for 95, Goals against 45, Points 98. First in Division 4.

Highest: 1986-87, 1993-94: 6th in Division 1.

F.A. Cup: 1987-88: 3rd rnd. West Bromwich Albion 4-1 (h); 4th rnd. Mansfield Town 2-1 (a); 5th rnd. Newcastle United 3-1 (a); 6th rnd. Watford 2-1 (a); Semi-final Luton Town 2-1; Final Liverpool 1-0.

League Cup: 1993-94: 5th Round

ADDITIONAL INFORMATION
Previous Name
Wimbledon Old Centrals 1887-1905

Previous Leagues
Isthmian League, Southern League

Club colours: Dark blue with yellow.

Change colours: All red.

DIVISIONAL RECORD

	Played	Won	Drawn	Lost	For	Against	Points
Division 1/P	364	134	111	119	478	455	513
Division 2	84	37	23	24	129	113	134
Division 3	138	50	34	54	210	232	174
Division 4	184	91	47	46	304	204	258
Total	**770**	**312**	**215**	**243**	**1,121**	**1,004**	**1,079**

RECORDS AND STATISTICS

COMPETITIONS

Div.1/P	Div.2	Div.3	Div.4
1986-	1984-86	1979-80	1977-79
		1981-82	1980-81
		1983-84	1982-83

HONOURS

Division 4	FA Cup
1982-83	1988

MOST APPEARANCES

Alan Cork 414+96 (1977-92)

Year	League	FA Cup	Lge Cup	Others
1977-78	17			
1978-79	45	5	3	
1979-80	41+1	5	5	
1980-81	41	5	4	
1981-82	6		2	
1982-83	7			
1983-84	41+1	2	5	1
1984-85	26+2	5	1	
1985-86	36+2	1	3	
1986-87	22+8	0+3	1	
1987-88	28+6	5+1	2+1	0+1
1988-89	9+16	1+1	2+2	0+1
1989-90	12+19	0+1	0+1	1+1
1990-91	9+16	1+1	1+1	1+0
1991-92	12+7		0+2	0+1
	352+78	30+7	29+7	3+4

MOST GOALS IN A CAREER

Alan Cork - 167 (1977-92)

Year	League	FA Cup	Lge Cup
1977-78	4		
1978-79	22	2	1
1979-80	12		1
1980-81	23	2	1
1981-82			
1982-83	5		
1983-84	29	2	2
1984-85	11		
1985-86	11		4
1986-87	5		2
1987-88	9	1	2
1988-89	2		
1989-90	5		
1990-91	5	1	
1991-92	2		
Total	**145**	**8**	**14**

Current leading goalscorer: Dean Holdsworth - 51 (1992-95)

RECORD TRANSFER FEE RECEIVED

Amount	Club	Player	Date
£4,000,000	Newcastle Utd	Warren Barton	06/95
£3,500,000	Liverpool	John Scales	08/94
£2,500,000	Manchester City	Keith Curle	8/91
£2,500,000	Manchester City	Terry Phelan	9/92

MANAGERS

Name	Seasons	Best	Worst
Allen Batsford	1977-78	13(4)	13(3)
Dario Gradi	1978-81	22(3)	4(4)
Dave Bassett	1981-87	6(1)	1(4)
Bobby Gould	1987-90	7(1)	12(1)
Ray Harford	1990-91	7(1)	7(1)
Peter Withe	1991-92		
Joe Kinnear	1992-	6(P)	13(1)

RECORD TRANSFER FEE PAID

Amount	Club	Player	Date
£775,000	Port Vale	Robbie Earle	7/91
£720,000*	Brentford	Dean Holdsworth	7/92
£700,000	Chelsea	Vinnie Jones	8/92
£500,000	Reading	Keith Curle	10/88

*Transfer included Kruszynski & Bennett in exchange.

LONGEST LEAGUE RUNS

of undefeated matches:	22 (15.1.1983 - 14.5.1983)	of league matches w/out a win:	14 (23.2.1980 - 15.4.1980)
of undefeated home matches:	21 (22.1.1983 - 3.12.1983)	of undefeated away matches:	12 (22.1.1983 - 27.8.1983)
without home win:7 (26.2.80-15.4.80, 4.4.88-24.9.88, 2.5.90-3.11.90)		without an away win:11 (5.4.1989-30.9.1989, 14.9.1991-25.2.1992)	
of league wins:	7 (9.4.1983 - 7.5.1983)	of home wins:	8 (9.4.1983 - 17.9.1983, 8.4.1978 - 14.10.1978)
of league defeats:	4 (3.4.1982 - 14.4.1982)	of away wins: 3 (23.12.78-28.2.79, 31.3.84-14.4.84, 10.4.91-20.4.91)	

PLAYERS NAME / Honours	Ht	Wt	Birthdate	Birthplace / Transfers	Contract Date	Clubs	League	L/Cup	FA Cup	Other	Lge	L/C	FAC	Oth
G O A L K E E P E R S														
Paul A Heald	6.2	12.5	20.09.68	Wath on Dearne	30.06.87	Sheffield United (T)								
					02.12.88	Leyton Orient	176	13	9	21				
Loan 10.03.92 Coventry City 2 Lge App.				Loan	24.03.94	Swindon Town	1+1							
				£125,000	08.95	Wimbledon								
Brendan Murphy	5.11	11.12	19.08.75	Wexford		Bradford City (T)								
				Free	26.09.94	Wimbledon								
Hans Segers	5.11	12.7	30.10.61	Eindhoven (H)		PSV Eindhoven								
				£50,000	14.08.84	Nottm. Forest	58	4	5					
Loan Stoke C., 13.2.87, 1 Lge App.				Loan	19.11.87	Sheffield United	10			1				
Loan Dunfermline, 1.3.88, 4 Lge App.				£180,000	28.09.88	Wimbledon	262+1	26	22	7				
Neil Sullivan	6.0	12.1	24.02.70	Sutton	26.07.88	Wimbledon (T)	15+1							
				Loan	01.05.92	Crystal Palace	1							
D E F E N D E R S														
Dean Blackwell	6.1	12.10	05.12.69	Camden	07.07.88	Wimbledon (T)	67+17	3	7+1	1	1			
E: u21.6.				Loan	15.03.90	Plymouth Argyle	5+2							
Ken Cunningham	5.11	11.2	28.06.71	Dublin		Tolka Rov								
Ei: u21.4, B.1.					18.09.89	Millwall	132+4	10	1	5+1	1			1
				£650,000	09.11.94	Wimbledon	28		4					
Gerald Dobbs	5.8	11.7	24.01.71	Lambeth	21.07.89	Wimbledon (T)	21+12	2	1+1		1		1	
Gary Elkins	5.9	11.13	04.05.66	Wallingford	03.12.83	Fulham (A)	100+4	6	2+2	7+1	2			
E: Y.11.				Loan	23.12.89	Exeter City	5							
				£20,000	20.08.90	Wimbledon	93+7	7	7	1+1	3		1	
Scott Fitzgerald	6.0	12.2	13.08.69	Westminster	13.07.89	Wimbledon (T)	93+9	13	5	1	1			
EI: B.1, u21.2.														
Andrew Futcher	5.7	10.07	10.02.78	Enfield	1994-95	Wimbledon (T)								
Roger Joseph	5.11	11.10	24.12.65	Paddington		Southall								
E: B2.				Free	04.10.84	Brentford	103+1	7	1	8	2			
				£150,000	25.08.88	Wimbledon	155+7	17+2	11+1	6				
				Loan	02.03.95	Millwall	5							
Alan Kimble	5.10	12.4	06.08.66	Dagenham	08.08.84	Charlton Ath. (J)	6							
Div.3'91.				Loan	23.08.85	Exeter City	1	1						
				Free	22.08.86	Cambridge United	295+4	23+1	29	22	24		1	
				£175,000	27.07.93	Wimbledon	40	5	3					
Brian McAllister	5.11	12.5	30.11.70	Glasgow	01.03.89	Wimbledon (T)	49+4	5	3	1				
				Loan	05.12.90	Plymouth Argyle	7+1							
Chris Perry	5.8	10.8	20.04.75	Surrey	02.07.91	Wimbledon (T)	17+7	2	3					
Alan Reeves	6.0	12.0	19.11.67	Birkenhead		Heswall								
					20.09.88	Norwich City								
Loan 09.02.89 Gillingham 18 Lge App.				£10,000	18.08.89	Chester City	31+9	1+1	3	3	2			
				Free	02.07.91	Rochdale	114+2	10	6	5	9	1		
				£300,000	06.09.94	Wimbledon	31		2		3			
Justin Skinner	5.8	10.12	17.09.72	Dorking	02.07.91	Wimbledon (T)	1							
				Loan	07.03.94	Bournemouth	16							
Mark Thomas	5.9	10.10	22.11.74	Tooting	12.07.93	Wimbledon (T)								
				Loan	17.12.93	Bromley								
Andrew Thorn	6.0	11.5	12.11.66	Carshalton	13.11.84	Wimbledon (T)	106+1	7	9	1	2			
E: u21.5. FAC'88.				£850,000	01.08.88	Newcastle United	36	4		3	2	1		
				£650,000	05.12.89	Crystal Palace	128	19	10	11	3	4		
				Free	05.10.94	Wimbledon	22+1	1	3		1			
M I D F I E L D														
Stewart Castledine	6.1	12.13	22.01.73	Wandsworth	02.07.91	Wimbledon (T)	8+3				2			
Robbie Earle	5.9	10.10	27.01.65	N'castle-U-Lyn.	05.07.82	Port Vale (J)	284+10	21+2	20+1	18+1	77	4	4	5
				£775,000	19.07.91	Wimbledon	133	12	14	1	30	3	2	1
Peter Fear	5.10	11.7	10.09.73	Sutton	02.07.92	Wimbledon (T)	33+8	3+2	2		1			
E: u21.3.														
Vinny Jones	6.0	11.12	05.01.65	Watford		Wealdstone			0+1					
FAC'88. Div.2'90.				£10,000	20.11.86	Wimbledon	77	6+2	11+2	3	9		1	
				£650,000	20.06.89	Leeds United	44+2	2	1	4	5			
				£700,000	13.09.90	Sheffield United	35	4	1	1	2			
				£575,000	30.08.91	Chelsea	42	1	4	5	4		1	2
				£700,000	10.09.92	Wimbledon	93	11	8		6	2		
Oyvind Leonhardsen	5.10	11.02	17.08.70	Norway		Rosenborg								
Norweigan Int.				Loan	10.94	Wimbledon	18+2		3		4		1	
				£660,000	08.95	Wimbledon								
Steven Talboys	5.10	11.6	18.09.66	Bristol		Gloucester City			3				2	
				£10,000	10.01.92	Wimbledon	16+5	1+1	0+1		1			
F O R W A R D S														
Neal Ardley	5.11	11.9	01.09.72	Epsom	29.07.91	Wimbledon (T)	55+10	8+2	8		6	2		
E: u21.10.														
Gary Blissett	6.0	12.7	29.06.64	Manchester		Altrincham								
Div.3'92.					23.08.83	Crewe Alexandra	112+10	9	4	6+1	39	3		4
				£60,000	26.03.87	Brentford	220+13	16+3	14	23+2	79	9	7	10
				£350,000	23.07.93	Wimbledon	10+17	1+2	1+2		3			
Andrew Clarke	5.10	11.7	22.07.67	Islington		Barnet			5+1				1	
E: S-P.2. GMVC'91.				£250,000	21.02.91	Wimbledon	60+67	9+5	7+1		14	2	1	
Efangwu Ekoku	6.1	12.0	08.06.67	Manchester		Sutton United			1					
				£100,000	11.05.90	Bournemouth	43+19	0+2	5+2	3+1	21		2	2
				£500,000	26.03.93	Norwich City	21+10	2	1+1	3	15	1		1
				£900,000	14.10.94	Wimbledon	24		3		9			
Marcus Gayle	6.1	12.9	27.09.70	Hammersmith	06.07.89	Brentford (T)	118+38	6+3	6+2	14+6	22		2	2
E: Y.1. Div.3'92.				£250,000	24.03.94	Wimbledon	32+1	2			2	1		
Jon Goodman	6.0	12.3	02.08.71	Walthamstow		West Ham U. (T)								
Free to Bromley				£50,000	20.08.90	Millwall	97+20	5+4	5+1	3	27			
				£650,000	09.11.94	Wimbledon	13+6		0+1		4			

	Ht	Wt	DOB	Birthplace/Fee	Date	Club								
Mick Harford	6.2	12.9	12.02.59	Sunderland	06.07.77	Lincoln City	109+6	8	3		41	5		
E: 2, B.1. LC'88.				£180,000	24.12.80	NewcastleUnited	18+1				4			
				£160,000	24.08.81	Bristol City	30	5	5		11	1	2	
				£100,000	26.03.82	Birmingham City	92	10	7		25	6	2	
				£250,000	13.12.84	Luton Town	135+4	16	27	4	57	10	11	3
				£450,000	18.01.90	Derby County	58	7	1	2	15	3		
				£325,000	12.09.91	Luton Town	29	1		1	12			
				£300,000	13.08.92	Chelsea	27+1	5	1		9	2		
				£250,000	18.03.93	Sunderland	10+1				2			
				£200,000	12.07.93	Coventry City	0+1				1			
				£70,000	18.08.94	Wimbledon	17+10	2+1	2+2		6	1	1	
Dean Holdsworth	5.11	11.13	08.11.68	Walthamstow	12.11.86	Watford (A)	2+14			0+4	3			
E: B.1. Div.3'92.				Loan	11.02.88	Carlisle United	4				1			
Loan Port Vale, 18.3.88, 6 Lge App + 2gls.				Loan	25.08.88	Swansea City	4+1				1			
Loan Brentford, 13.10.88, 2+5 Lge App + 1gls.				£125,000	29.09.89	Brentford	106+4	7+1	6	12+2	53	6	7	9
				£720,000	20.07.92	Wimbledon	103+3	10+1	6+3		43	5	3	
Aidan Newhouse	6.1	13.5	23.05.72	Wallasey	01.07.89	Chester City (T)	29+15	5+1	0+2	2+3	6			1
E: Y.13.				£100,000	22.02.90	Wimbledon	7+16	1+1	2	0+1	2			
				Loan	21.01.94	Port Vale	0+2		0+1					
				Loan	02.12.94	Portsmouth	6				1			
Grant Payne	5.9	10.6	25.12.75	Woking	02.07.92	Wimbledon (T)								

TOP GOALSCORER 1994/95
Efan Ekoku

Premiership goals (games) . . . . 9 (29+1)
Coca-Cola Cup Goals 0 (1)
F.A. Cup goals 0 (3)

Total . . . . **9 (33+1)**

Total goals for Wimbledon since 17.9.94 . . . . 9 (27)

Career total as at June 1st 1995 . . . . 51 (111+36)

THE MANAGER
JOE KINNEAR

Date of Birth . . . . 27th December 1946.
Place of Birth . . . . Dublin.
Date of Appointment . . . . January 1991.

PREVIOUS CLUBS
As Manager. . . . . None.
As Reserve Team Manager. . . . . Wimbledon.
As a Player . . . . Tottenham Hotspur, Brighton & Hove Albion.

HONOURS
As a Manager
None.

As a Player
None.
International: 26 full caps for Eire.

SELHURST PARK

London SE25 6PU
Tel: 0181 653 1000

Capacity 26,500

First game...v Sheffield Wed., Division 2, 30.8.1924.
First floodlit game ....v Chelsea, 28.9.1953.
ATTENDANCES
Highest...30,115 v Manchester Utd, Prem, 9.5.1993.
Lowest..2,151 v Hereford, Lge Cup, 5.9.1993.

OTHER GROUNDS ....Plough Lane

HOW TO GET TO THE GROUND

From the North
From motorway (M1) or A1, use A406 North Circular Road to Chiswick. Follow signs South Circular Road (A205) to Wandsworth. Then use A3 to A214 and follow signs to Streatham. Join A23. In 1 mile turn left (B273). At the end turn left into High Street then forward into Whitehorse Lane for Crystal Palace FC.

From the East
Use A232 (sign posted Croydon) to Shirley then join A215 (sign posted Norwood). In 2.2 miles turn left (B266) into Whitehouse Lane.

From the South
Use A23 (sign posted London) then follow signs Crystal Palace (B266) via Thornton Heath into Whitehorse Lane.

From the West
Use motorway (M4) to Chiswick then route from North or A232 (sign posted Croydon) to Beddington, then follow signs London A23. After, follow signs Crystal Palace (B266) via Thornton Heath into Whitehorse Lane.

Car Parking: Club car park (468 spaces) on first come first served basis. Street parking is also available.

Nearest Railway Station: Thornton Heath/Norwood Junction/Selhurst.

MATCHDAY PROGRAMME

Programme Editor . . . . Reg Davis.

Number of pages . . . . 40.

Price . . . . £1.50.

Subscriptions . . . . Home matches £50 including postage.
. . . . Home & away £84 including postage.

Local Newspapers . . . . Wimbledon Guardian, South London Press
. . . . Wimbledon News, Surrey Comet.

Local Radio Stations . . . . Capital Radio.

Division 1

FOOTBALL LEAGUE CHAMPIONSHIP

Endsleigh League

Endsleigh
Insurance League

1995-96

ENDSLEIGH LEAGUE
DIVISION ONE

FINAL LEAGUE TABLE

			HOME					AWAY					
		P	W	D	L	F	A	W	D	L	F	A	Pts
1	MIDDLESBROUGH	46	15	4	4	41	19	8	9	6	26	21	82
PLAY-OFFS													
2	READING	46	12	7	4	34	21	11	3	9	24	23	79
3	**BOLTON WANDERERS**	46	16	6	1	43	13	5	8	10	24	32	77
4	WOLVERHAMPTON W.	46	15	5	3	39	18	6	8	9	38	43	76
5	TRANMERE ROVERS	46	17	4	2	51	23	5	6	12	16	35	76
6	BARNSLEY	46	15	6	2	42	19	5	6	12	21	33	72
7	WATFORD	46	14	6	3	33	17	5	7	11	19	29	70
8	SHEFFIELD UNITED	46	12	9	2	41	21	5	8	10	33	34	68
9	DERBY COUNTY	46	12	6	5	44	23	6	6	11	22	28	66
10	GRIMSBY TOWN	46	12	7	4	36	19	5	7	11	26	37	65
11	STOKE CITY	46	10	7	6	31	21	6	8	9	19	32	63
12	MILLWALL	46	11	8	4	36	22	5	6	12	24	38	62
13	SOUTHEND	46	13	2	8	33	25	5	6	12	21	48	62
14	OLDHAM ATHLETIC	46	12	7	4	34	21	4	6	13	26	39	61
15	CHARLTON ATHLETIC	46	11	6	6	33	25	5	5	13	25	41	59
16	LUTON TOWN	46	8	6	9	35	30	7	7	9	26	34	58
17	PORT VALE	46	11	5	7	30	24	4	8	11	28	40	58
18	PORTSMOUTH	46	9	8	6	31	28	6	5	12	22	35	58
19	WEST BROMWICH A.	46	13	3	7	33	24	3	7	13	18	33	58
20	SUNDERLAND	46	5	12	6	22	22	7	6	10	19	23	54
RELEGATED													
21	SWINDON TOWN	46	9	6	8	28	27	3	6	14	26	46	48
22	BURNLEY	46	8	7	8	36	33	3	6	14	13	41	46
23	BRISTOL CITY	46	8	8	7	26	28	3	4	16	16	35	45
24	NOTTS COUNTY	46	7	8	8	26	28	2	5	16	19	38	40

ENDSLEIGH LEAGUE DIVISION ONE - 1995-96

BARNSLEY
(The Tykes)
ENDSLEIGH LEAGUE DIVISION 1
SPONSORED BY: T. HAYSELDEN LTD

Back Row (L-R): Scott Jones, Robert Hanby, Chris Jackson, Russell Harmer, Brendon O'Connell, Glynn Hurst, Steve Davies, Troy Bennett, Charlie Bishop, Dean Fearon, Luke Bennett. **2nd Row:** Paul Smith (Physio), Eric Winstanley (Coach), Darren Clyde, David Brooke, Andy Rammell, Adam Solite, Lee Butler, David Watson, Gerry Taggart (now Bolton), Andy Liddell, Mark Burton, Colin Walker (Yth Coach), Malcolm Shotton (Res. Coach). **3rd Row:** Shane Hulson, Chris Morgan, Mark Feeney, Jonathan Perry, Andrew Gregory, Neil Redfearn, Nicky Eaden, Gary Fleming, Danny Wilson (Manager), Andy Payton, Owen Archdeacon, Martin Bullock, Darren Sheridan, Adrian Moses, Simon Bochenski, Sean McClare, Richard Cannon. **Front Row:** Sean Hayes, Mark Hume, Craig Deacon, Dean Jones, Steven Clayton, Glynn Clyde, Rudi Coleano, Ian Shaw, Duanne Beckett, Carl Rose, Paul Bashaw, Daniel Shenton, Chris Harris.

BARNSLEY
FORMED IN 1887
TURNED PROFESSIONAL IN 1888
LTD COMPANY IN 1899

PRESIDENT: Arthur Raynor
CHAIRMAN: John Dennis
VICE-CHAIRMAN: Barry Taylor
DIRECTORS:
Christopher Harrison,
Michael Hayselden, Stuart Manley,
John Kelly, Ian Potter.
GENERAL MANAGER/SECRETARY:
Michael Spinks
COMMERCIAL MANAGER
Ian Davies (01226 286 718)

MANAGER: Danny Wilson
ASSISTANT: Malcolm Shotton

YOUTH TEAM MANAGER
Colin Walker

PHYSIOTHERAPIST
Steve Stafford

CLUB STATISTICIAN FOR THE DIRECTORY
Ian Sawyer

Nothing to write home about in Barnsley's cup season, but in the League The Tykes kept their hopes of achieving a play-off place alive until the penultimate week-end of the season.

Mind you, they hardly had an auspicious start. A 2-1 home win over Derby County on the opening day of the season was definitely the party before the big hangover, as just one victory was gained in the next eleven games. Their position on 24th September was a precariously-placed 21st, hardly the basis with which to mount a serious promotion challenge.

But, come the onset of winter, and the Yorkshire lads really picked up the pace. Yet, unbelievably, on the first day of November they were at the wrong end of a 6-1 thrashing at high-flying Tranmere Rovers. Thankfully, three wins on the trot quickly put matters to rights and lifted The Tykes to 6th.

A 4-1 home Boxing Day success over Grimsby Town brought much festive cheer to the Oakwell crew and, as such, a top three position was attained - the season's best. However, what followed were five reverses in seven games and a drop to 10th place and the world of the also-rans.

Consistency, never Barnsley's strong point during the season, returned in March with an impressive points tally of 13 out of a possible 18, and by 15th April they were very much back in contention for a play-off place. Unfortunately, however, away reverses at Grimsby and Southend put paid to any dreams of the Twin Towers and the Division One Play-Off Final.

In the Coca-Cola Cup, a First Round success over Darlington on the away goals rule certainly did not augur well for a good showing in the competition. Round Two paired them with in-form Newcastle United, and although losing the first leg 2-1 at St. James's Park, the tie was still very much up for grabs. In front of nearly 11,000 fans at Oakwell, the Geordies clinched a place in Round Three with a hard fought 1-0 victory. In the FA Cup they fell at the first hurdle at home to Aston Villa.

It will be interesting to see if Barnsley are able to go one better this season and do the impossible by getting into the Premiership. One thing is for certain, in strikers Andy Payton and Andrew Liddell, they had one of the most potent goal scoring duos in the division last term.

GREG TESSER.

BARNSLEY

Division One: 6th   **FA Cup:** 3rd Round   **Coca-Cola Cup:** 2nd Round

M	DATE	COMP.	VEN	OPPONENTS	RESULT	H/T	LP	GOAL SCORERS/GOAL TIMES	ATT.
1	A 13	EL	H	Derby County	W 2-1	2-1	5	Rammell 10, 22	
2	17	CC 1/1	A	**Darlington**	D 2-2	2-0		**Taggart 28, Redfearn 37**	(2,207)
3	20	EL	A	Charlton Athletic	D 2-2	0-0	3	Payton 72, Davis 90	(8,171)
4	22	CC 1/2	H	**Darlington**	D 0-0†	0-0		**(Barnsley go through on Away Goals)**	3,263
5	27	EL	H	Reading	L 0-2	0-1	10		4,771
6	30	EL	A	Port Vale	L 1-2	0-1		O'Connell 70	(7,228)
7	S 3	EL	A	Burnley	W 1-0	0-0	11		(7,228)
8	10	EL	H	Watford	D 0-0	0-0	11		4,251
9	13	EL	H	Notts County	D 1-1	0-0		Rammell 47	3,298
10	17	EL	A	Sunderland	L 0-2	0-0	18		(16,145)
11	21	CC 2/1	A	**Newcastle United**	L 1-2	1-1		**Redfearn 20**	(27,208)
12	24	EL	A	Oldham Athletic	L 0-1	0-0			(7,941)
13	O 1	EL	H	Swindon Town	W 2-1	1-0	18	Redfearn 39, 80	3,911
14	5	CC 2/2	H	**Newcastle United**	L 0-1	0-1			10,992
15	8	EL	H	Southend United	D 0-0	0-0	18		3,659
16	16	EL	A	Sheffield United	D 0-0	0-0			(12,317)
17	22	EL	H	West Bromwich Albion	W 2-0	1-0	15	O'Connell 39, Redfearn 72	5,082
18	29	EL	A	Luton Town	W 1-0	0-0	9	Rammell 67	(5,592)
20	5	EL	H	Stoke City	W 2-1	1-0	7	O'Connell 45, Sheridan 77	5,117
21	19	EL	A	Millwall	W 3-0	2-0	6	Eaden 8, Davis 24, Redfearn 73	8,507
22	26	EL	H	Bolton Wanderers	W 2-1	1-1		Liddell 32, Archdeacon 84	4,305
25	10	EL	H	Charlton Athletic	W 2-1	1-0	5	Redfearn 25, Liddell 81	5,465
26	17	EL	A	Derby County	L 0-1	0-0	5		(13,205)
27	26	EL	H	Grimsby Town	W 4-1	2-1	3	Payton 2, 45, 58, Liddell 79	8,669
28	27	EL	A	Portsmouth	L 0-3	0-3			(6,751)
29	31	EL	H	Wolverhampton Wand.	L 1-3	1-2	7	Redfearn 20	9,207
30	J 7	FAC 3	H	**Aston Villa**	L 0-2	0-0			11,469
31	14	EL	H	Luton Town	W 3-0	0-0	6	Redfearn 67, Liddell 72, 79	4,808
32	F 4	EL	A	Bristol City	L 2-3	0-0	9	Rammell 47, Wilson 86	(6,408)
33	11	EL	H	Tranmere Rovers	D 2-2	1-1	9	Rammell 6, Redfearn 49	5,506
34	18	EL	A	Bolton Wanderers	L 1-2	0-1	10	Liddell 73	(12,463)
35	21	EL	H	Millwall	W 4-1	1-0		Redfearn 12,61, Payton 53, 65	4,733
36	25	EL	A	Swindon Town	D 0-0	0-0	9		(8,158)
37	M 7	EL	H	Burnley	W 2-0	1-0		Taggart 41, Payton 88	5,537
38	11	EL	A	Reading	W 3-0	1-0	7	O'Connell 45, Taggart 63, Payton 84	(7,556)
39	14	EL	A	Middlesbrough	D 1-1	1-0		Payton 60	(19,645)
40	18	EL	H	Port Vale	W 3-1	2-0	7	Liddell 18, 35, Sheridan 89	6,878
41	21	EL	A	Watford	L 2-3	0-1		Liddell 56, 66	(6,883)
42	24	EL	H	Sunderland	W 2-0	0-0	7	Shotton 65, Payton 85	7,803
43	A 1	EL	A	Notts County	W 3-1	1-1	7	O'Connell 11, Wilson 47, Liddell 60	(6,834)
44	8	EL	A	Wolverhampton Wand.	D 0-0	0-0	6		(26,385)
45	12	EL	A	Stoke City	D 0-0	0-0	5		(10,752)
46	15	EL	H	Portsmouth	W 1-0	0-0	5	Payton 65	6,825
47	17	EL	A	Grimsby Town	L 0-1	0-1			(7,277)
48	22	EL	H	Middlesbrough	D 1-1	0-1	6	Liddell 51	11,711
49	29	EL	H	Sheffield United	W 2-1	1-1	6	O'Connell 16, 48	10,844
50	M 2	EL	H	Oldham Athletic	D 1-1	1-1	6	Taggart 18	9,383
51	7	EL	A	Southend United	L 1-3	0-1		Redfearn 72	(6,426)
52									
53									
54									
55									
56									
57									
58									
59									
60									

Best Home League Attendance: 11,711 v Middlesbrough   **Smallest:** 3,928 v Notts County   **Av Home Att:** 3,253

Goal Scorers:

Compared with 1993-94: -4,338

League (63): Liddell 13, Payton 12, Refearn 11, O'Connell 7, Rammell 7, Taggart 3, Davis 2, Sheridan 2, Wilson 2, Archdeacon, Eaden, Jackson, Shotton
C/Cola Cup (3): Redfearn 2, Taggart
FA Cup (0):

186

Watson	Eaden	Fleming	Wilson	Taggart	Bishop	O'Connell	Redfern	Rammell	Payton	Snodin	Liddell	Bullock	Butler	Davis	Jones	Jackson	Sheridan	Archdeacon	Sollitt	Moses	Shotton	Clyde	Hurst	Referee	#
1	2	3	4	5	6	7	8	9	10	11	S	S	S											I. Cruickshank	1
1	2	3	4	5	6	7	8	9	10	11	S	S	S											D. Allison	2
1	2	3	4	5	6	7*	8	9	10	11		S	S	12										I. Hemley	3
1	2*	3	4	5	6	7*	8	9	10	11	12	14	S											E. Wolstenhome	4
1	2*	3	4	5		7*	8	9	10	11	12	13	14	5	6									B. Burns	5
1	2	3*	4	5	6	7	8	9	10	11*		12	S	14										J. Parker	6
1	2	3	4	5		7	8	9	10	11	S	S	S	6	S									J. Watson (R. Sutton)	7
1	2	3	4	5	S	7	8	9	10*	11	12		S	6										T. Lunt	8
1	2	3	4	5	S	7	8	9	10*	11	12		S	6										J. Rushton	9
1	S	3*	4	5	2	7	8	9	10	11	12		S	6										P. Harrison	10
1	S	3	4	5	2	7	8	9*	10	11	12		S	6										R. Hart	11
1	12	3	4	5	2*	7	8	9•	10	11	14		S	6										T. Meilbron	12
1	2	3	4	5	6		8		10*	11	7	12	S	S	S	9								K. Lupton	13
1	2	3*	4	5	11	7	8	12	10		12		S	6		9•								K. Lynch	14
1	2	3	4	4		7*	8	14	10		12		S	6		9•	11							G. Cain	15
1	2	3	4	5		7	8	9	10		S		S	6			11	S						J. Winter	16
1	2	3	4	5		7	8	9	10		S		S	6			11	S						I. Cruishanks	17
1	2	3	4	5		7	8	9	10		S		S	6			11	S						M. Pierce	18
1	2	3	4	5		7	8	9	10*		14		S	6			11•	12						J. Brandwood	19
1	2	3	4	5		7	8		10		S		S	6		9	11	S						P. Wright	20
	2	3	4*	5		7	8	14					1	6		9*	11	12	S					T. West	21
	2	3		5		7	8	12	10		S		1	6		9*	11	4	S					J. Brandwood	22
	2	3		5		7	8	S	10		S		1	6		9	11	4	S					K. Breen	23
	2	3		5		7*	8	14	10		12		1	6		9*	11	4	S					E. Wolstenhome	24
	2	3		5		7	8	9	10		S		1	6		S	11	4	S					J. Lloyd	25
	2	3		5		7	8	9	10		12		1	6		S	11	4*	S					T. Heilbron	26
5	2	3		5	S	7	8	S	9		10	4	1	6			11							I. Cruishanks	27
5	2	3		5*	12	7	8	14	9•		10	4	1	6			11							G. Singh	28
5	2	3		5		7	8	12	9	5	10	4	1	6			11*							S. Mathieson	29
1	2	3*	4•			7	8	12	9	10		14	S	6			11			5				L. Dilkes	30
1	2	3	4			7	8	9	S	10		S	S	6			11			5				N. Barry	31
1	2	3	4			7*	8	9	10		12		S				11			5	6	S		G. Singh	32
1	2	3*	4	5		7•	8	9	10•		12		S	6			11				6			A. Butler	33
1	2	3*	4	5		7•	8	9	12	10	14		S	6			11							J. Watson	34
1	2	3	4*	5		7	8	9	10		12		S	6			11			S				T. West	35
1	2	3	4*	5		7	8*	9	12	10	14		S	6			11•							M. Pierce	36
1	2	3	4	5		7		9	10	8			S	6			11			S		S		K. Lynch	37
1	2	3	4	5		7		9	10	8	5		6*					11			S		S		P. Alcock	38
1	2	3	4	5		7		9	10	8	5		6*					11			S		S		P. Harrison	39
1	2	3	4	5		7	14	9	10•	8		S					11	6*		12				M. Bailey	40
1	2	3*	4	5		7	12	9	10	8		S					11	6		S				P. Vanes	41
1	2	3	4	5		7	S	S	9	10	8		S				11	6						D. Allison	42
1	2	3	4	5		7	S	12	9	10	8		S				11	6						P. Richards	43
1	2	3	4†	5		7	12	S	9†	10*	8		S				11	6						P. Harrison	44
1	2	3	4	5		7	S	12	9	10*	8		S				11	6						K. Cooper	45
1	2	3	4*	5		7	12	S	9	11	10	8	5	6										J. Lloyd	46
1	2	3		5		7	14	12	9	S	10*	8	5	6			11							J. Winter	47
1	2	3		7	4		9	10*	8	5	6	S					11				5		12	G. Cain	48
1	2	3		7	4		9	10	8	5	6	S					11				5	S		J. Watson	49
1	2	3*		5	7	4		9	10*	8		S	6				12	11					14	W. Burns	50
1	2	3*	4•	5		14	7	10	9	12	8		S	6			11							P. Alcock	51
																									52
																									53
																									54
																									55
																									56
																									57
																									58
																									59
																									60
37	44	46	34	41	7	44	37	17	38	11	30	17	9	34		7	35	6		3	8			League Appearances	
	1				1		2	7	4	3	8	11	2		1		3	1			2			League Sub Appearances	
4	3	4	4	4	4	4	3+1	4	3	0+3	0+1	2		1										C/Cola Appearances	
1	1	1	1		1	1	0+1	1		1	0+1		1			1								FA Cup Appearances	

BARNSLEY

CLUB RECORDS

BIGGEST VICTORIES
League: 9-0 v Loughborough Town, Division 2, 28.1.1899.
9-0 v Accrington Stanley, Division 3N, 3.2.1934 (a).
F.A. Cup: 8-0 v Leeds City, Qualifying Rnd, 3.11.1894.
League Cup: 6-0 v Peterborough, Round 1, 15.9.1981.

BIGGEST DEFEATS
League: 0-9 v Notts County, Division 2, 19.11.1927.
F.A. Cup: 1-8 v Derby County, Round 1, 30.1.1897.
League Cup: No defeat by more than 3 goals.

MOST POINTS
3 points a win: 74, Division 2, 1988-89.
2 points a win: 67, Division 3N, 1938-39.

MOST GOALS SCORED
118 Division 3(N), 1933-34.

MOST GOALS CONCEDED
108, Division 2, 1952-53.

MOST FIRST CLASS MATCHES IN A SEASON
58 - 1960-61 (46 League, 10 FA Cup, 2 League Cup).

MOST LEAGUE WINS
30, Division 3(N), 1938-39.
30, Division 3(N), 1954-55.

MOST LEAGUE DRAWS
18, Division 3, 1971-72.

MOST LEAGUE DEFEATS
29, Division 2, 1952-53.

INDIVIDUAL CLUB RECORDS

MOST GOALS IN A SEASON
Cecil McCormack: 34 - 1950-51 (League 33, FAC 1).

MOST GOALS IN A MATCH
5, F.Eaton v South Shields, 6-1, Division 3(N), 9.4.1927.
5, P.Cunningham v Darlington, 6-2, Division 3(N), 4.2.1933.
5, B.Asquith v Darlington, 7-1, Division 3(N), 12.11.1938.
5, C.McCormack v Luton, 6-1, Division 2, 9.9.1950.

OLDEST PLAYER
Beaumont Asquith, 37 years 3 months v Coventry City, 19.11.1927.

YOUNGEST PLAYER
Glyn Riley, 16 years 171 days v Torquay United, 11.1.1975.

MOST CAPPED PLAYER
Gerry Taggart (Northern Ireland) 19 caps.

BEST PERFORMANCES

League: 1938-39: Matches played 42, Won 30, Drawn 7, Lost 5, Goals for 94, Goals against 34, Points 67. First in Division 3(N).
Highest Position: 1914-15, 1921-22, Third Division 2.
F.A. Cup: 1911-12: 3rd Rnd. Birmingham City 0-0,3-1; 4th Rnd. Leicester City 1-0; 6th Rnd. Bradford City 0-0,0-0,0-3,0; Semi-Final Swindon Town 0-0, 1-0; Final West Bromwich Albion 0-0,1-0.
League Cup: 1981-82: 1st Rnd. Peterborough United 3-2,6-0; 2nd Rnd. Swansea City 2-0,2-3; 3rd Rnd. Brighton & Hove Albion 4-1; 4th Rnd. Manchester City 1-0; 5th Rnd. Liverpool 0-0,1-3.

ADDITIONAL INFORMATION
PREVIOUS NAMES
Barnsley St.Peters.
PREVIOUS LEAGUES
Midland.

Club Colours: Red shirts, white shorts, red stockings.
Change Colours: White shirts, red shorts, white stockings.

Reserves League: Pontins Central League Division 1.
Youth League: Northern League.

DIVISIONAL RECORD

	Played	Won	Drawn	Lost	For	Against	Points
Division 2/1	2,412	835	590	987	3,335	3,784	2,489
Division 3	552	183	159	210	736	838	525
Division 3N	218	130	38	50	467	278	298
Division 4	460	177	127	156	628	555	481
Total	3,642	1,325	914	1,403	5,166	5,455	3,793

RECORDS AND STATISTICS

COMPETITIONS

Div.2/1	Div.3	Div.3(N)	Div.4
1898-32	1959-65	1932-34	1965-68
1934-38	1968-72	1938-39	1972-79
1939-53	1979-81	1953-55	
1955-59			
1981-			

HONOURS

Div.3(N)	FA Cup
1933-34	1911-12
1938-39	
1954-55	

MOST APPEARANCES

BARRY MURPHY 564 (1962-78)

Year	League	FA Cup	Lge Cup
1962-63	21		2
1963-64	4		1
1964-65	22	1	1
1965-66	7+3		2
1966-67	14		
1967-68	46	1	1
1968-69	46	6	3
1969-70	46	4	1
1970-71	45	4	1
1971-72	46	3	3
1972-73	42	2	2
1973-74	10+1		2
1974-75	35	1	1
1975-76	36+1		2
1976-77	46	2	4
1977-78	43	2	3
	509+5	26	29

MOST GOALS IN A CAREER

ERNIE HINE - 130 (1921-26 & 1934-38)

Year	League	FA Cup
1921-22	12	1
1922-23	23	1
1923-24	19	
1924-25	15	
1925-26	12	
1934-35	9	
1935-36	14	5
1936-37	13	
1937-38	6	
Total	123	7

Current top goalscorer: Andy Rammell 45 (1990-95)

RECORD TRANSFER FEE RECEIVED

Amount	Club	Player	Date
£1,400,000	Nott'm Forest	Carl Tiler	5/91
£750,000	Nott'm Forest	David Currie	1/90
£300,000	Portsmouth	John Beresford	3/89
£200,000	Manchester City	Mick McCarthy	12/83

RECORD TRANSFER FEE PAID

Amount	Club	Player	Date
£250,000	Oldham Athletic	David Currie	9/91
£200,000	Aston Villa	Gareth Williams	8/91
£180,000	Burnley	Steve Davies	7/91
£175,000	Barnet	Phil Gridelet	9/90

MANAGERS

Name	Seasons	Best	Worst
John McCartney	1901-04	8(2)	11(2)
Arthur Fairclough	1904-12	6(2)	19(2)
John Hastie	1912-14	4(2)	5(2)
Harry Lewis	1914-19	3(2)	13(2)
Peter Sant	1919-26	3(2)	16(2)
John Commins	1926-29	11(2)	16(2)
Arthur Fairclough	1929-30	17(2)	17(2)
Brough Fletcher	1930-37	14(2)	8(3N)
Angus Seed	1937-53	9(2)	1(3N)
Tim Ward	1953-60	16(2)	17(3N)
John Steel	1960-71	7(3)	18(4)
John McSeventy	1971-72	22(3)	22(3)
John Steel	1972-73	14(4)	14(4)
Jim Iley	1973-78	6(4)	13(4)
Allan Clarke	1978-80	11(3)	4(4)
Norman Hunter	1980-84	6(2)	2(3)
Bobby Collins	1984-85	11(2)	11(2)
Alan Clarke	1985-89	7(2)	14(2)
Mel Machin	1989-93	8(2)	19(2)
Viv Anderson (P)	1993-94	18(1/2)	18(1/2)
Danny Wilson (P)	1994-	6(1)	6(1)

LONGEST LEAGUE RUNS

of undefeated matches:	21 (1.10.1933 - 5.5.1934)	**of league matches w/out a win:**	26 (13.12.52 - 29.8.53)
of undefeated home matches:	36 (6.2.1933 - 24.11.1934)	**of undefeated away matches:**	10 (27.12.1938 - 15.4.1939)
without home win:	11 (6.12.1952 - 24.9.1953)	**without an away win:**	29 (14.3.1908 - 19.11.1910)
of league wins:	10 (5.2.1955 - 23.4.1955)	**of home wins:**	12 (3.10.1914 - 8.3.1915)
of league defeats:	9 (14.3.1953 - 25.4.1953)	**of away wins:**	5 (27.12.1938 - 25.2.1939)

BARNSLEY

PLAYERS NAME / Honours	Ht	Wt	Birthdate	Birthplace / Transfers	Contract Date	Clubs	League	L/Cup	FA Cup	Other	Lge	L/C	FAC	Oth
G O A L K E E P E R S														
Lee Butler	6.2	13.0	30.06.66	Sheffield		Haworth CW								
				Free	16.06.86	Lincoln City	30	1	1					
				£100,000	21.08.87	Aston Villa	8			2				
				Loan	18.03.91	Hull City	4							
				£165,000	22.07.91	Barnsley	117	5	9	4				
David N Watson E: u21.2, Y.8.	6.0	12.0	10.11.73	Barnsley	04.07.92	Barnsley (T)	51	6	1	1				
D E F E N D E R S														
Charlie Bishop via Free 17.04.86 Watford	6.0	12.11	16.02.68	Nottingham		Stoke City (A)								
				Free	10.08.87	Bury	104+10	5	4	12+1	6		1	
				£50,000	24.07.91	Barnsley	112+5	8+1	9	5	1			
Darran Clyde	6.4	13.0	26.03.76	N. Ireland	28.03.95	Barnsley (T)								
Steven Davis E: Y.1.	6.0	12.7	26.07.65	Birmingham		Stoke City (A)								
				Free	17.08.83	Crewe Alexandra	140+5	10	3	7+1	1			
				£15,000	03.10.87	Burnley	147	7	9	19	11			1
				£180,000	26.07.91	Barnsley	52+4	2	1	2				
Nicholas Eaden	5.10	11.3	12.12.72	Sheffield	04.06.91	Barnsley	81+3	3+1	5	2	3			
Dean Fearon	6.1	13.12	09.01.76	Barnsley	06.07.94	Barnsley (T)								
Gary Fleming NI: 28.	5.9	11.1	17.02.67	Londonderry	19.11.84	Nottingham F. (A)	71+3	5+1	2+1	0+1				
				£150,000	17.08.89	Manchester City	13+1	4		1				
				Loan	08.03.90	Notts County	3			1				
				£85,000	23.03.90	Barnsley	234+2	14	12	6				
Darren Hanby	5.10	11.8	24.12.74	Pontefract	06.07.93	Barnsley (T)								
Glyn Hurst	5.10	11.06	17.01.76	Barnsley		Tottenham H. (T)								
				Free	13.07.94	Barnsley	0+2							
Scott Jones	5.10	11.06	01.05.75	Sheffield	01.02.94	Barnsley (T)								
Adrian Moses	6.1	12.5	04.05.75	Doncaster	02.07.93	Barnsley	3+1		1					
M I D F I E L D														
Tory Bennett E: Y.1.	5.4	11.08	25.12.75	Barnsley		Barnsley (T)	2							
David Brooke	5.10	11.5	23.11.75	Barnsley	07.07.93	Barnsley (T)								
Martin Bullock	5.5	10.07	05.03.75	Derby		Eastwood Town								
				£15,000	04.09.93	Barnsley	17+12		0+1	1				
Marc Burton	5.9	10.6	07.05.73	Barnsley	06.07.91	Barnsley (T)	5			2				
Mark Feeney	5.7	11.0	26.07.74	Derry N.I.	06.07.93	Barnsley (T)	0+2							
Neil Redfern Div.2'91.	5.10	12.4	20.06.65	Dewsbury		Nottingham F. (A)								
				Free	23.06.82	Bolton Wanderers	35	2	4		1			
				£8,250	23.03.84	Lincoln City	96+4	4	3	7	13		1	
					22.08.86	Doncaster Rovers	46	2	3	2	14		1	
				£100,000	31.07.87	Crystal Palace	57	6	1	1	10			
				£150,000	21.11.88	Watford	22+2	1	1	6	3		3	1
				£150,000	12.01.90	Oldham Athletic	56+6	3	7+1	1	16	1	3	
				£150,000	05.09.91	Barnsley	164+3	11	10	5	30	3	2	
Darren Sheridan	5.6	10.12	08.12.67	Manchester		Winsford United				1				
				£10,000		Barnsley	37+1		1	1+1	2			
Danny Wilson NI: 24. ASC'81. LC'88'91.	5.7	10.3	01.01.60	Wigan		Wigan Athletic				1				
				Free	21.09.77	Bury	87+3	4	11		8		2	
				£100,000	22.07.80	Chesterfield	100	8	9		13	1	1	
				£50,000	24.01.83	Nottingham Forest	9+1			0+1	1			
				Loan	07.10.83	Scunthorpe United	6				3			
				£100,000	30.11.83	Brighton & H.A.	132+3	7	10	3	33	3	1	2
				£150,000	16.07.87	Luton Town	110	20	8	4	24	3	2	
				£200,000	08.08.90	Sheffield Wed.	91+7	22	9+1	5+2	11	2		1
				£200,000	01.07.93	Barnsley	77	6	5	1	2			
F O R W A R D S														
Owen Archdeacon S: u21.1, Y. SPD'86.	5.7	11.0	04.03.66	Greenock		Gourock United								
						Celtic	38+38	1+4	3+1	1+3	8	1		
				£80,000	07.07.89	Barnsley	186+9	12+1	12+1	9+1	20	2	2	4
Simon Bochenski	5.8	11.13	06.12.75	Worksop	06.07.94	Barnsley (T)								
Chris D Jackson E: Y.2, SFA u15.	6.0	12.0	16.01.76	Barnsley	19.01.93	Barnsley (T)	10+5	1+1		0+1	2			
Andrew Liddell S: u21.1.	5.8	10.5	28.06.73	Leeds	06.07.91	Barnsley (T)	58+25	3+1	2+1	2+1	16	1		

BARNSLEY

PLAYERS NAME Honours	Ht	Wt	Birthdate	Birthplace Transfers	Contract Date	Clubs	APPEARANCES				GOALS			
							League	L/Cup	FA Cup	Other	Lge	L/C	FAC	Oth
Brendan O'Connell	5.10	10.9	12.11.66	Lambeth	01.07.85	Portsmouth (T)								
				Free	04.08.86	Exeter City	73+8	3+1	3	4	19	2		
				Free	01.07.88	Burnley	62+2	6	3	5	17	3	1	2
				Loan	30.11.89	Huddersfield Town	11				1			
				£50,000	23.03.90	Barnsley	192+23	10+1	12	7+1	34	1	1	2
Andy Payton	5.9	10.6	03.10.67	Whalley	29.07.85	Hull City (T)	116+28	9+2	8	3	55	2		
				£750,000	22.11.91	Middlesbrough	8+11		1+3		3			
				P.E.	14.08.92	Celtic	20+18	3+2	1+1	3	15	5		
				£100,000+PE	25.11.93	Barnsley	63+5	4	5		24		1	
Andrew Rammell	5.10	11.7	10.02.67	Nuneaton		Atherstone			0+1					
				£40,000	26.09.89	Manchester United								
				£100,000	14.09.90	Barnsley	138+27	10+2	11+1	8	40		4	1

TOP GOALSCORER 1994/95
Andy Liddell

Division One goals (games)	13 (30+8)
Coca-Cola Cup goals	0 (0+3)
F.A. Cup Goals	0 (1)
Total for 1994/95	**13 (31+11)**
Total for Barnsley since 06.07.91	17 (64+30)
Career Total up to June 1995	17 (64+30)

(Neil Redfearn also scored 13 in total, but the 'Top Goalscorer' is based
on the amount of League goals scored, Redfearn scored 11 Lge, 2 Lge Cup.)

THE MANAGER
DANNY WILSON (PLAYER MANAGER)

Date of Birth . . . . 1st January 1960.
Place of Birth . . . . Wigan.
Date of Appointment . . . . July 1994.

PREVIOUS CLUBS
As Manager. . . . . None.
As Coach. . . . . Barnet.
As a Player . . . . Wigan Athletic, Bury, Chesterfield, Nottingham Forest,
. . . . Brighton & H.A., Luton Town and Sheffield Wednesday.

HONOURS
As a Manager
None.

As a Player

Luton Town: League Cup runner-up 1988.
Sheffield Wednesday: League Cup winner 1991
International: 25 full caps for Northern Ireland.

Oakwell Ground

Grove Street, Barnsley, Yorkshire S71 1ET
Tel: 01226 295 353

Capacity . . . . .27,310.
Covered Standing . . . . .17,767.
Seating . . . . .9,543.
First game . . . . .v Gawber (Friendly) 15.10.1887 (0-0).
First floodlit game . . . . .v Bolton W. (Friendly) 23.1.1962.

ATTENDANCES
Highest . . . . .40,255 v Stoke City, FA Cup 5th Rnd, 15.2.1936.
Lowest . . . . .1,627 v Grimsby Town, Anglo Italian Cup, 14.9.93.

MATCHDAY TICKET PRICES

East Stand Upper Tier £12
OAP/Juveniles £6
East Stand Lower Tier £10
OAP/Juveniles £5.50
The Ora Stand £10
OAP/Juveniles £5.50

Visiting Supporters
West Stand Upper Tier £12
West Stand Lower Tier £10
Spion Kop £10

Ticket Office Telephone No. . . . . 01226 295 353.

CLUBCALL
0898 12 11 52
Calls cost 39p per minute cheap rate and 49p per
minute at all other times.
Call costings correct at time of going to press.

HOW TO GET TO THE GROUND

From The North
M1 to J37. Take A628 towards Barnsley and follow signs for Football Ground.

From The South
M1 to J37. Proceed as above.

From The East
A635 towards Barnsley and follow signs for Football Ground.

From The West
A628 towards Barnsley and shortly after crossing M1 Jnt 37 follow signs for Football Ground.

Car Parking: Official car parks for 1,200 vehicles adjacent to ground. Cost £1. Visitors use Queens Ground car park.

Railway Station: Barnsley 01742 26411.

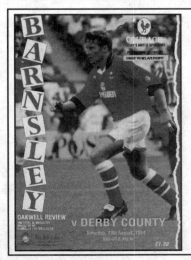

MATCHDAY PROGRAMME

Programme Editor . . . . Keith Lodge

Number of pages 32

Price . . . . £1.40.

Subscriptions. . . . . . . £34.50 for 23 home fixtures (inc post & packing)

Local Newspapers . Barnsley Chronicle (weekly), Barnsley Star (Daily) . . . . Yorkshire Post, Yorkshire on Sunday.

Local Radio Stations . . . . Radio Sheffield, Hallam FM.

BIRMINGHAM CITY
(The Blues)
ENDSLEIGH LEAGUE DIVISION 1
SPONSORED BY: AUTO-WINDSCREENS

Back Row (L-R): Lil Fuccillo (Chief Scout), Kenny Lowe, Ken Charlery, Peter Shearer, Dave Barnett, Simon Black, Ryan Price, Liam Daish (Team Capt), Andy Edwards, Chris Whyte, Steve Castle, John Frain (Club Capt), Neil McDairmid (Physio). **Middle Row:** David Howell (Res. Manager), Ian Muir, John Bass, Paul Challinor, Steve Claridge, Paul Harding, Ian Bennett, Gary Poole, Ben Sedgemore, Neil Doherty, Steve Finnan, Paul Tait, Edwin Stein (Asst. Manager). **Front Row:** Richard Forsyth, Ricky Otto, Jason Bowen, Steve Robinson, Jae Martin, Barry Fry (Manager), Jonathon Hunt, Louie Donowa, Mark Ward (Player coach), Scott Hiley, Gary Cooper.

BIRMINGHAM CITY
FORMED IN 1875
TURNED PROFESSIONAL IN 1885
LTD COMPANY IN 1888

CHAIRMAN: J F Wiseman
Managing Director: Karren Brady
Assistant M.D.: Peter Day

DIRECTORS:
D Sullivan & A Hones
SECRETARY: Alan G Jones, BA, MBA
COMMERCIAL MANAGER
Mark Bowler

MANAGER: Barry Fry
ASSISTANT:

RESERVE TEAM MANAGER

YOUTH TEAM MANAGER
Tony Taylor

PHYSIOTHERAPIST
Paul Heath

CLUB STATISTICIAN FOR THE DIRECTORY
Dave Drage

In last year's review I said that the injustice of Blues relegation to Division 2 would be corrected. Even so not even the most committed supporter could have imagined just what a fantastic season it would turn out to be.

Not only was the Second Division deservedly won in style but also the Auto Windscreen Final at Wembley on a day that 48,000 'Blue noses' will always remember. Success was also enjoyed in both the Coca-Cola Cup and the FA Cup, when only teams of the calibre of Blackburn and Liverpool halted Blues progress.

Barry Fry and the players, deserve tremendous credit for their achievements this season particularly in view of the demanding schedule and the appaling injury crisis which resulted in 17 major operations, and particular gratitude must to David Sullivan and the Gold brothers for the tremendous enthusiasm and financial backing. The rebuilt St Andrews is proof of this.

Many records were set up during the season. Most points in a season (89), longest unbeaten record - 25 matches including 20 in the LEague. Most games played in a season (63) including 33 home games (also a record). Nine successive clean sheets by Ian Bennett (a record). Record attendance for every round of the Auto Windscreen Shield and most League goals (84) since 1967/68.

Truly a memorable season and no doubt that this particular sleeping giant is awake and on the move at last.

DAVE DRAGE.

193

BIRMINGHAM CITY

Division One: 1st   **FA Cup:** 3rd Round   **Coca-Cola Cup:** 2nd Round   **Auto Windscreen Shield:** Winners

M	DATE	COMP.	VEN	OPPONENTS	RESULT	H/T	LP	GOAL SCORERS/GOAL TIMES	ATT.
1	A 13	EL	A	Leyton Orient	L 1-2	1-1		Claridge 18	(7,578)
2	16	CC 1/1	A	Shrewsbury Town	L 1-2			Daish 83	(5,049)
3	20	EL	H	Chester City	W 1-0	1-0	14	Donowa 20	12,188
4	23	CC 1/2	H	Shrewsbury Town	W 2-0	2-0		Saville 11, Claridge 33 (Pen)	9,847
5	27	EL	A	Swansea City	W 2-0	0-0	10	Claridge 76,80	(5,797)
6	30	EL	H	Wycombe Wanderers	L 0-1	0-0			14,305
7	S 3	EL	H	Plymouth Argyle	W 4-2	2-0	8	Regis 40,89, Patterson 44 (og), Tait 47	13,202
8	10	EL	A	Oxford United	D 1-1	0-0	11	Claridge 79	(8,077)
9	13	EL	A	Rotherham United	D 1-1	0-1		Bull 54	(3,799)
10	18	EL	H	Peterborough United	W 4-0	3-0	6	Bull 19,33, Tait 22, Dominguez 70	10,600
11	20	CC 2/1	A	Blackburn Rovers	L 0-2				(14,517)
12	24	EL	H	Hull City	D 2-2	1-1	9	Claridge 29 (Pen), Dominguez 53	12,192
13	27	AWS P	A	Peterborough United	W 5-3			Bull 10, Dominguez 30, Hunt 44,65,72	(2,044)
14	O 1	EL	A	Wrexham	D 1-1	0-1	9	Claridge 88	(6,002)
15	4	CC 2/2	H	Blackburn Rovers	D 1-1			McGavin 10	16,275
16	8	EL	H	Huddersfield Town	D 1-1	1-1	9	Bull 45	15,265
17	15	EL	A	Brighton & H.A.	W 1-0	0-0	9	Donowa 86	(11,004)
18	18	AWS P	H	Walsall	W 3-0	1-0		Shearer 38, 46, Donowa 79	10,089
19	22	EL	A	Brentford	W 2-1	1-0	9	Shearer 40, Ward 70	(7,779)
20	29	EL	H	Bristol Rovers	W 2-0	2-0	6	Bull 28, Claridge 42	15,886
21	N 1	EL	H	Crewe Alexandra	W 5-0	3-0		Hunt 25,31,90, Donowa 40, Claridge 84	14,212
22	5	EL	A	Shrewsbury Town	W 2-0	1-0	3	Bull 4, Hunt 64	(5,942)
23	12	FAC 1	A	Slough Town	W 4-0	4-0		Shearer 9,36, McGavin 34,41 (Played at Birmingham)	(13,394)
24	19	EL	H	Bournemouth	D 0-0	0-0	3		15,477
25	26	EL	A	Stockport County	W 1-0	0-0	3	Hunt 83	(5,577)
26	29	AWS 2	H	Gillingham	W 3-0	2-0		McGavin 38, Poole 43, Tait 68	17,028
27	D 2	FAC 2	H	Scunthorpe United	D 0-0	0-0			13,832
28	10	EL	A	Chester City	W 4-0	2-0	2	Daish 24, Claridge 45, McGavin 66, Lowe 76	(3,946)
29	14	FAC 2R	A	Scunthorpe United	W 2-1	0-0		McGavin 63, Cooper 66	(6,280)
30	17	EL	H	Leyton Orient	W 2-0	1-0	2	Donowa 2, 86	20,022
31	26	EL	H	Cambridge United	D 1-1	1-1	2	Otto 20	20,098
32	28	EL	A	Cardiff City	W 1-0	0-0		Otto 59	(7,420)
33	31	EL	H	Blackpool	W 7-1	3-1		Bradshaw 12 (og), Donowa 25,64, Clarridge 37,73, Lowe 53, Parris 86	18,025
34	J 2	EL	A	Bradford City	D 1-1	0-1	1	Cooper 89	(10,539)
35	7	FAC 3	H	Liverpool	D 0-0	0-0			25,326
36	10	AWS 3	H	Hereford United	W 3-1			Claridge 6, Ward 68 (pen), Otto 72	22,352
37	14	EL	A	York City	L 0-2	0-1	1		(6,828)
38	18	FAC 3R	A	Liverpool	D 1-1	0-1		Otto 69 (Lost 0-2 on penalties)	(36,275)
39	31	AWS SF	H	Swansea City	W 3-2			Claridge 13, Francis 65, Tait 97	20,326
40	F 4	EL	H	Stockport County	W 1-0	0-0	1	Dinning 80 (og)	17,160
41	11	EL	A	Crewe Alexandra	L 1-2	0-1	1	Donowa 90	(6,359)
42	18	EL	H	York City	W 4-2	2-0	3	Francis 9,10, Otto 62, Shearer 77	14,846
43	21	EL	A	Bournemouth	L 1-2	0-1		Francis 66	(6,024)
44	25	EL	H	Wrexham	W 5-2	1-2	2	Francis 24,49, Shearer 46, Otto 51, Donowa 80	18,884
45	28	AWS AF	H	Leyton Orient	W 1-0	1-0		Shearer 4	24,002
46	M 4	EL	A	Hull City	D 0-0	0-0	3		(9,854)
47	11	EL	H	Swansea City	L 0-1	0-1	4		16,191
48	14	AWS AF	A	Leyton Orient	W 3-2			Claridge 42,47, Williams 57	(10,830)
49	18	EL	A	Wycombe Wanderers	W 3-0	2-0	4	Shearer 33, Claridge 45, Poole 90	(7,289)
50	21	EL	H	Oxford United	W 3-0	1-0		Francis 19, Claridge 57, Daish 61	19,781
51	25	EL	A	Peterborough United	D 1-1	0-0	3	Shearer 64	(8,796)
52	29	EL	A	Bristol Rovers	D 1-1	0-1		Claridge 72	(8,010)
53	A 1	EL	H	Rotherham United	W 2-1	0-1	3	Francis 56, Shearer 68	16,077
54	4	EL	A	Blackpool	D 1-1	1-1		Claridge 17	(4,494)
55	11	EL	H	Shrewsbury Town	W 2-0	1-0		Claridge 42,70	18,366
56	15	EL	H	Cardiff City	W 2-1	1-1	2	Tait 20, Ward 88 (Pen)	17,455
57	17	EL	A	Cambridge United	L 0-1	0-0	3		(5,317)
58	19	EL	A	Plymouth Argyle	W 3-1	0-0		Whyte 50, Claridge 74,85	(8,550)
59	23	AWS F	N	Carlisle United	W 1-0	0-0		Tait 103	(76,663)
60	26	EL	H	Brentford	W 2-0	0-0		Francis 56, Daish 64	25,581
61	29	EL	H	Brighton & H.A.	D 3-3	2-1	1	Dominguez 9, Shearer 25, Ward 80	19,006
62	M 2	EL	H	Bradford City	D 0-0	0-0			25,139
63	6	EL	A	Huddersfield Town	W 2-1	0-0	1	Claridge 73, Tait 85	(18,775)

Best Home League Attendance: 25,581 v Brentford   **Smallest:** 10,600 v Peterborough United   **Av Home Att:** 17,071

Goal Scorers:

Compared with 1993-94: +2,693

League (84): Claridge 20 (1 pen), Donowa 9, Francis 8, Shearer 7, Bull 6, Hunt 5, Otto 4, Tait 4, Daish 3, Dominguez 3, Ward 3 (1 pen), Lowe 2, Regis 2, Cooper 1, McGavin 1, Parris 1, Wallace 1, Whyte 1, Opponents 3.

C/Cola Cup (4): Claridge 1 (pen), Daish 1, McGavin 1, Saville 1.   **FA Cup (7):** McGavin 3, Shearer 2, Cooper 1, Otto 1.

AWS (22): Claridge 4, Hunt 3, Shearer 3, Tait 3, Bull 1, Dominguez 1, Donowa 1, Francis 1, McGavin 1, Otto 1, Poole 1, Ward 1 (Pen), Williams 1.

Bennett	Hiley	Ward	Shearer	Whyte	Claridge	Saville	Donowa	Regis	Dominguez	Frain	Daish	Harding	Scott	De Souza	Tait	Bull	Poole	Hunt	McGavin	Barnett	Cooper	Otto	Francis	Robinson	Williams	Referee	
1	2	4	5	6	8	9	11	12	14																	T West	1
1	2		4	6	8		7	9	14		5	10	3													A Butler	2
1	2	4		5	8	9	7		12	3	6	10														M Bailey	3
1	2	4		6	8	9	7				5	10	3	11												W Flood	4
1	2	4	5		8	9	11	12	14		6	10	3	7												S Dunn	5
1	2	4	5		8	12	14	9	11		6		3	7	10											D Allison	6
1	2	4	5		8		12	9	14		6	7	3		10											E Parker	7
1		4	5		8			9	14		6	7	2		10											J Lloyd	8
1			5		8			9	14	3		7	2		10	6										T Hellbron	9
1		4	6		8				14			12			10	9	2	7								R Poulain	10
1		4	6		8				12	3		10	2		7				14		9					K Lupton	11
1		4	5		8				11		6				10	9	2	7	14							P Richards	12
		4			8				11	3	6		2			9	10	7	14	5						I Hemley	13
1		4			8				11	3	6			12	10	9	2	7		5						K Breen	14
1		4	8						11									9		5						R Gifford	15
1		4	11		8				12			10				9	2	7		5	3					K Lynch	16
1		4	11		8				12			10				9	2	7		5						G Barber	17
1		4	11		8				3		6				10	9	2	7	14	5						G Singh	18
1		4	11	3	8				10		12	6				9	2	7		5						C Wilkes	19
1		4	11	3	8				10		12	6				9	2	7	14	5						P Harrison	20
1		4	11	3	8				10		12	6				9	2	7	14	5						G Cain	21
1		4	11	3	8				10		12	6				9	2	7	14	5						E Lomas	22
1		4	11	3	8				10			6		14	12		2	7	9	5						P Jones	23
1		4	11	3	8				12			6		14			2	7	9	5						R Furnandiz	24
1		4	11	3	8				10		12	6		14			2	7	9	5						K Lupton	25
1		4		3	8				7		10	6			11		2		9	5	12					A D'Urso	26
1		4		3	8				7		10	6			11		2		9	5	14					L Dilkes	27
1				3	8				7		10	6			11		2		9	5	4					J Brandwood	28
1		4		3	8				7		10	6			11		2		9	5	4					L Dilkes	29
1		4		3	8	14	7					6					2		9	5	10	10				K Breen	30
1		4		3	8	14	7										2		9	5	11	10				S Matthieson	31
1		4		3	8									9			2			5	11	10				C Wilkes	32
1		4		3	8		7				6						2	12	5	11						J Rushton	33
1		4			8		7				6			12			2	9	5	3						T West	34
1		4	11		8		7				6						2		5	3	10					E Parker	35
1			11		8		7				6						2		5	3	10					R Harris	36
1		4			8		7				6			14			2	9	5	3	10					U Rennie	37
1		4			8		7				6						2	12	5	11	10					E Parker	38
1		4		6	8		7				12			2					5	3	10	9				W Flood	39
1		4		2	8		7		12					11					5	3	10	9				E Parker	40
1		4	12	3			7		14		6			11		2			5	8	10	9				J Winter	41
1		4	12			14	7							11	2		8		5	3	10	9				E Wolstenholme	42
1		4	12			14	7							11	2		8		5	3	14	9				G Pooley	43
1		4	11	3		12	7		10						2				5	8	10	9				A Butler	44
1				12	8		7				6				2		14		5	3	10	9				J Kirkby	45
1			11	3	8	12	7				6			4	2				5		10	9	14			R Furnandiz	46
1		4		3	8						6			11	2		9		5		12		7			U Cruickshanks	47
1		4		3		8	7				6				2				5		10		7	9		C Wilkes	48
1		4	11		8						6				2		3		5		14	9	7	10		T West	49
1		4	11		8						6				2		3		5		10	9	7	10		N Barry	50
1		4	11		8						6			14	2		3		5		10	9		7		P Foakes	51
1			11	3	8			14						6	2				4		10	9	7	8		P Alcock	52
1	2	4	11	3	8				12		6					7					10	9		14		K Lupton	53
1		4	11		8				12		6			4	7			5		3	14	9		10		J Lloyd	54
1	2	4	11		8				7		6			12				5		3	10	9		14		P Harrison	55
1		4			8	12	7				6			11		2		5		3	10		9			K Lynch	56
1	2	4			8	12	7				6					11	14	5		3	10			9		M Pierce	57
1		4	5		8				12		6				2	7			10	14	9	11				R Harris	58
1		4	11		8		7				6				2			5		3	10	9				P Foakes	59
1		4	11		8				12		6			14	2	7		5		3	10	9				M Riley	60
1	2	4	11	5	8				12	9	6			14		7				3	10					U Rennie	61
1		4		5	8		9		10		6			11	2	7				3	12		14			E Parker	62
1		4		5	8				12	3	6			14	2	7					11			10		J Winter	63
46	9	41	20	30	41	3	21	4	12	6	37	5	5	4	18	10	34	18	27	10	31	18	15	5	8	**League Appearances**	
			3		1	7			1		1		4	7			2				4		6		1	**League Sub Appearances**	3
4	2	3	2	3	3	1	3	1	1+2	2	1	3	3	3	2	1				1+1	1	1				**League Cup Appearances**	
5		4	2	3	5		5		2+1	1	5			0+1	2+1			5	3+1	5	3+1	2				**FA Cup Appearances**	
7		7	4	3+1	7	1	5		2+2	1	7			2	1	2+3	2	7	3	1+3	8	4+1	5	3	1 1 1	**Auto Windscreen Shield**	

Also Played: Dryden, Lowe, Willis, Doherty, Wallace, Small, Howell, Parris, Bodley, Hendon

BIRMINGHAM CITY

CLUB RECORDS

BIGGEST VICTORIES

League: 12-0 v Walsall Town Swifts, Division 2, 17.12.1892.
12-0 v Doncaster Rovers, Division 2, 1.4.1903.
F.A. Cup: 10-0 v Druids, 9.11.1889.
League Cup: 6-0 v Manchester City, 11.12.1962.
Europe: 5-0 v Boldklub Copenhag, 7.12.1960.

BIGGEST DEFEATS

League: 1-9 v Sheffield Wednesday, Division 1, 13.12.1930.
1-9 v Blackburn Rovers, Division 1, 5.1.1895.
0-8 v Derby County, Division 1, 30.11.1895.
0-8 v Newcastle United, Division 1, 23.11.1907.
0-8 v Preston North End, Division 1, 1.2.1958.
F.A. Cup: 0-6 v Wednesbury O.B., Qualifying Rnd., 17.10.1881.
0-6 v Tottenham Hotspur, 6th Rnd., 12.4.1967.
League Cup: 0-5 v Tottenham Hotspur, 3rd Rnd., 29.10.1986.
Europe: (Fairs) 1-4 v Barcelona, Final, 4.5.1960.

MOST POINTS

3 points a win: 89, Division 2, 1994-95.
2 points a win: 59, Division 2, 1947-48.

MOST GOALS SCORED

103, Division 2, 1893-94.
Mobley 24, Wheldon 22, Walton 16, Hands 14, Hallam 9, Jenkyns 6, Izon 4, Lee 3, Jolley 2, Pumfrey, Devey, Jackson 1 each.

MOST GOALS CONCEDED

96, Division 1, 1964-65.

MOST FIRST CLASS MATCHES IN A SEASON

63 - 1994-95 (46 League, 5 FA Cup, 4 League Cup, 8 AMC)

MOST LEAGUE WINS

27, Division 2, 1979-80.

MOST LEAGUE DRAWS

18, Division 1, 1937-38 & Division 2, 1971-72.

MOST LEAGUE DEFEATS

29, Division 1, 1985-86.

INDIVIDUAL CLUB RECORDS

MOST GOALS IN A SEASON

Walter Abbott 42 - 1898-99 (League 34, FAC 8).
5 goals once; 3 goals 5 times; 2 goals 7 times, 1 goal 8 times.

MOST GOALS IN A MATCH

5, Walter Abbott v Darwen (h), 8-0, Division 2, 26.11.1898.
5, John McMillan & R McRoberts v Blackpool (h), 10-1, Division 2, 2.3.1901.
5, Ben Green v Middlesbrough (h), 7-0, Division 1, 26.12.1905.
5, Jimmy Windridge v Glossop (h), 11-1, Division 2, 23.1.1915.

OLDEST PLAYER

Dennis Jennings, 40 years 190 days, 6.5.1950.

YOUNGEST PLAYER

Trevor Francis, 16 years 7 months v Cardiff City, 5.9.1970.

MOST CAPPED PLAYER

Malcolm Page (Wales) 28, 1971-79.
Harry Hibbs (For England), 25, 1951-54.

BEST PERFORMANCES

League: First in Division 2 - 1947-48: Matches played 42, Won 22, Drawn 15, Lost 5, Goals for 55, Goals against 24, Points 59.
Highest Position: 6th in Division 1, 1955-56.

F.A. Cup: Winners in 1930-31 v West Bromwich Albion, 1-2.
Most Recent Success: (1955-56) 3rd Rnd. Torquay United 7-1 (a); 4th Rnd. Leyton Orient 4-0 (a); 5th Rnd. West Bromwich Albion 1-0 (a); 6th Rnd. Arsenal 3-1 (a); Semi Final Sunderland 3-0 (n); Final Manchester City 1-3.
League Cup: (1962-63) 2nd Rnd. Doncaster Rovers 5-0; 3rd Rnd. Barrow 1-1 (a), 5-1 (h); 4th Rnd. Notts County 3-2 (h); 5th Rnd. Manchester City 6-0 (h); Semi-Final Bury 1-1 (a), 3-2(h); Final Aston Villa 0-0(a),3-1(h).
Europe: (Fairs Cup) Runners-up in 1958-60 v Barcelona, 0-0(h),1-4(a).
Most Recent Success: (1960-61) 1st Rnd. Ujpest Dozsa 3-2(h),2-1(a); 2nd Rnd. Boldklub Copenhagen 4-4(a),5-0(h); Semi-Final Inter Milan 2-1(a),2-1(h); Final A.S.Roma 2-2(h),0-2(a).
Auto Windscreen Shield: Winners 1994-95.

DIVISIONAL RECORD

	Played	Won	Drawn	Lost	For	Against	Points
Division 1	2,040	651	501	888	2,776	3,296	1,845
Division 2/1	1,492	658	348	486	2,448	1,959	1,745
Division 3/2	184	82	55	47	258	197	310
Total	3,716	1,391	904	1,421	5,482	5,452	3,900

ADDITIONAL INFORMATION

Previous Names: Small Heath Alliance (1875-88); Small Heath (1888-1905).
Previous League: Football Alliance.

Club Colours: Royal blue/white & red trim shirts, white with blue trim shorts, red stockings.
Change colours:

Reserves League: Midland Intermediate.

RECORDS AND STATISTICS

COMPETITIONS

Div 1/P	Div.2	Euro C
1894-96	1892-94	1989-92
1901-02	1896-1901	1994-95
1903-08	1902-03	
1921-39	1908-21	
1948-50	1939-48	
1955-65	1950-55	
1972-79	1965-72	
1980-84	1979-80	
1985-86	1984-85	
	1992-94	
	1995-	

HONOURS

Div.2	Div.3/2	League Cup	A.M. Cup
1892-93	1994-95	1962-63	1990-91
1920-21			1994-95
1947-48			
1954-55			

MOST GOALS IN A CAREER

JOE BRADFORD - 267 (1920-35)

Year	League	FA Cup
1920-21	1	
1921-22	10	
1922-23	18	1
1923-24	24	
1924-25	11	
1925-26	26	1
1926-27	22	1
1927-28	29	3
1928-29	22	2
1929-30	23	
1930-31	14	8
1931-32	26	2
1932-33	14	
1933-34	5	
1934-35	4	
Total	249	18

Current Top goalscorer - Steve Claridge - 32 (1994-95)

MOST APPEARANCES

GIL MERICK 551 (1945-60)

Year	League	FA Cup	Europe
1945-46		8	
1946-47	41	4	
1947-48	36		
1948-49	41	2	
1949-50	42	1	
1950-51	42	6	
1951-52	41	2	
1952-53	35	7	
1953-54	38	2	
1954-55	27	4	
1955-56	38	6	2
1956-57	40	7	2
1957-58	28	1	3
1958-59	34	6	2
1959-60	2		1
	485	56	10

MANAGERS

Name	Seasons	Best	Worst
Bob McRoberts	1910-15	3(2)	20(2)
Bill Beer	1923-27	8(1)	17(1)
Les Knighton	1928-33	9(1)	15(1)
George Liddell	1933-39	12(1)	20(1)
Willie Camkin	1939-45		
Ted Goodier	1945		
Harry Storer	1945-48	1(2)	3(2)
Bob Brocklebank	1949-54	17(1)	6(2)
Arthur Turner	1954-58	6(1)	1(2)
Albert Beasley	1958-60	9(2)	19(2)
Gil Merrick	1960-64	17(2)	20(2)
Joe Mallett	1964-65	22(2)	22(2)
Stan Cullis	1965-70	4(2)	18(2)
Fred Goodwin	1970-75	10(1)	9(2)
Willie Bell	1975-77	13(2)	19(2)
Sir Alf Ramsey	1977-78	11(1)	11(1)
Jim Smith	1978-82	13(1)	3(2)
Ron Saunders	1982-86	17(1)	2(2)
John Bond	1986-87	19(2)	19(2)
Gary Pendry	1987-89	19(2)	12(3)
Dave Mackay	1989-90	7(3)	7(3)
Lou Macari	1991		
Terry Cooper	1991-94	19(2/1)	2(3)
Barry Fry	1994-	22(1)	22(1)

RECORD TRANSFER FEE RECEIVED

Amount	Club	Player	Date
£1,180,000	Nottingham Forest	Trevor Francis	2/79
£350,000	Everton	B Latchford + PE	2/74
£100,000	Stoke City	Jimmy Greenhoff	8/69

RECORD TRANSFER FEE PAID

Amount	Club	Player	Date
£800,000	Stockport County	Kevin Francis	01/95
£800,000	Southend Utd	Ricky Otto	12/94
£350,000	Derby County	David Langan	6/80
£300,000	Everton	Colin Toss	7/79

LONGEST LEAGUE RUNS

of undefeated matches:	20 (1994-95)	of league matches w/out a win:	17 (1985-86)
of undefeated home matches:	36 (1970-72)	of undefeated away matches:	15 (1947-48)
without home win:	11 (1962-63)	without an away win:	32 (1980-82)
of league wins:	13 (1892-93)	of home wins:	17 (1902-03)
of league defeats:	8 (1978-79, 1985)	of away wins:	9 (1897)

BIRMINGHAM CITY							APPEARANCES				GOALS			
PLAYERS NAME Honours	Ht	Wt	Birthdate	Birthplace Transfers	Contract Date	Clubs	League	L/Cup	FA Cup	Other	Lge	L/C	FAC	Oth
G O A L K E E P E R S														
David Bennett	6.0	12.0	10.10.70	Worksop		Q.P.R. (T)								
Div.2'95. AWS'95 Free 20.03.91 Newcastle United				Free		Peterborough Utd	72	10	3	4				
				£325,000	22.03.91									
					17.12.93	Birmingham City	68	4	6	7				
Ryan Price	6.4	14.0	13.03.70	Stafford		Bolton W. (T)								
E: SP.3.				via Stafford Rangers		Birmingham City				1				
				£20,000	09.08.94									
D E F E N D E R S														
David K Barnett	6.1	12.8	16.04.67	Birmingham		Windsor								
Div.2'95. AWS'95					25.08.88	Colchester United	19+1	2	3+2	3				
via Edmonton O. (Canada)				Free	13.10.89	West Bromwich A.								
				Free	17.07.90	Walsall	4+1	2						
Free 01.10.90Kidderminster H. 3 FAC App.				£10,000	29.02.92	Barnet	58+1	5	3	5	2			
				£150,000	20.12.93	Birmingham City	39+1	1	5	8				
Jon Bass	6.0	12.02	01.07.76	Weston-S-M.	27.06.94	Birmingham City (J)								
Paul Challinor	6.1	12.02	06.04.76	Newcastle	27.06.94	Birmingham City (J)	1							
Gary Cooper	5.8	11.3	20.11.65	Hammersmith	02.06.83	Q.P.R. (A)	1	1+1		0+1				
E; Y.11, S. Sth Prem'87. Div.2'95. AWS'95.				Loan	01.09.85	Brentford	9+1							
via Fisher Athletic 0+1 FAC app.					01.03.89	Maidstone United	53+7	3	3+1	10	7			1
				£20,000	28.03.91	Peterborough Utd	83+5	12	5	9	10	1	2	1
				Free	17.12.93	Birmingham City	42+1	1	4+1	4+1	2		1	
Liam Daish	6.2	13.5	23.09.68	Portsmouth	29.09.86	Portsmouth (A)	1		1+1					
Ei: 1, u21.5. Div.3'91. Div.2'95. AWS'95				Free	11.07.88	Cambridge United	138+1	11	17	15	5			3
				£50,000	01.94	Birmingham City	56	3	5	7	3	1		
Scott Hiley	5.9	10.4	27.09.68	Plymouth	04.08.86	Exeter City (T)	205+5	17	14	16+2	12			
Div.4'90. Div.2'95.				£100,000	12.03.93	Birmingham City	44	6	1	1				
Gary Poole	6.0	11.0	11.09.67	Stratford	15.07.85	Tottenham H. (J)								
GMVC'91. Div.2'95. AWS'95				Free	14.08.87	Cambridge United	42+1	2	2	3				
				£3,000	01.03.89	Barnet	39+1	2	7	6	2			1
				Free	05.06.92	Plymouth Argyle	39	6	2	0+1	5	2		
				£350,000	09.07.93	Southend United	38		1	6	2			
				£50,000+PE	16.09.94	Watford	34		5	7	1			1
Simon Rea	6.1	13.0	20.09.76	Coventry	1994-95	Birmingham City (T)								
Chris Whyte	6.1	13.0	02.09.61	Islington	24.12.79	Arsenal (A)	86+4	14	5	3+1	8			
E: u21.4. Div.1'92. Div.2'95.				Loan	23.08.84	Crystal Palace	13	4						
via L.A. Lazers to				Free	25.08.88	West Bromwich A.	83+1	5	5	2	7	2		
				£400,000	18.06.90	Leeds United	113	14+1	8	11	5	1		
				£250,000	12.08.93	Birmingham City	64	7	4	4+1	1			
M I D F I E L D														
Simon Black	6.1	12.0	09.11.75	Marston Green	27.06.94	Birmingham City (T)	2			1+1				
				Loan	01.02.95	Sutton United								
Jason Bowen	5.6	8.11	24.08.72	Merthyr Tydfil	01.07.90	Swansea City (T)	93+31	6+1	9+2	15+3	26	2	1	8
W: 1, u21.5, Y. AGT'94.				£275,000	08.95	Birmingham City								
Steve Castle	5.11	12.5	17.05.66	Barkingside	18.05.84	Leyton Orient (A)	232+11	15+1	23+1	18+2	55	5	6	
				£195,000	30.06.92	Plymouth Argyle	98+3	5	8	6	35	1	1	
				£275,000	08.95	Birmingham City								
Andrew Edwards	6.2	12.7	17.09.71	Epping	14.12.89	Southend United (T)	41+6	5	4	9	2			2
				£400,000	08.95	Birmingham City								
Steve Finnan				Kent		Woking (T)								
				£100,000	08.95	Birmingham City								
Richard Forsyth			03.10.70	Dudley		Kidderminster								
GMVC. FAXI.				£50,000	08.95	Birmingham City								
John Frain	5.9	11.9	08.10.68	Birmingham	10.10.86	Birmingham City (A)	242+8	22	10	20	23	1		2
AMC'91.														
Kenny Lowe	6.1	11.4	06.11.61	Sedgefield		Hartlepool (A)	50+4	1+1	2	1	3			
via Gateshead, Spearwood (Aust), Morcambe, Barrow Free					15.01.88	Scarborough	4							
NPL'86'89. FAT'90 via Barrow				£40,000	01.03.91	Barnet	55+17	2+1	5	4	5			
APL'91. E: SP.2. Div.2'95.				Free	05.08.93	Stoke City	3+6	2		2				
				£75,000	17.12.93	Birmingham City	14+5	0+1	3+1	2+1	3			
				Loan	01.02.95	Carlisle United	1+1							
Steven Robinson	5.4	10.11	17.01.75	Nottingham	09.06.93	Birmingham City (T)	5+1			1				
Ben Sedgemore	5.10	13.11	05.08.75	W'hampton	17.05.93	Birmingham City (T)								
				Loan	22.12.94	Northampton Town	1							
Peter Shearer	6.0	11.6	04.02.67	Coventry	05.02.85	Birmingham City (A)	2+2	1			1			
ESP.1. Div.2'95. AWS'95.				Free	04.08.86	Rochdale	1	1			2			
Free Nuneaton Borough 1 FAC app.				£7,000		Cheltenham Town								
				£18,000	09.03.89	Bournemouth	76+9	6	5	2+1	10	1	1	1
				£75,000	05.01.94	Birmingham City	22+3	2	2	4	7		2	3
Paul Tait Div.2'95.AWS'95	6.1	10.0	31.07.71	Sutton C'dfield	02.08.88	Birmingham City (T)	95+22	9	5+2	12+4	11			4
Mark Ward	5.5	10.0	10.10.62	Huyton	05.09.80	Everton (A)								
E: SP.1. Div.2'95. AWS'95.				Free		Northwich Victoria			3				2	
				£10,000	19.07.83	Oldham Athletic	84	5	3		12			
				£250,000	15.08.85	West Ham United	163+2	20+1	17	6	12	2		
				£1,000,000	29.12.89	Manchester City	55	3	6	3	14			2
				£1,100,000	12.08.91	Everton	82+1	6	4	1	6	1		
Loan 24.03.94 Birmingham C. 9 Lge App. 1gl.				£500,000	04.08.94	Birmingham City	41	3	4	7	3			1
F O R W A R D S														
Ken Charlery	6.1	12.7	28.11.64	Stepney		Beckton								
via Basildon & Fisher Ath. (1 FAC App) £35,000					01.03.89	Maidstone United	41+18	1+3	0+3	5+4	11	1		
				£20,000	28.03.91	Peterborough United	45+6	10	3	11	19	5	1	7
				£350,000	16.10.92	Watford	45+3	3	1	0+1	13			
				£150,000	16.12.93	Peterborough United	70	2	2+1	2	24		3	1
				£350,000	08.95	Birmingham City								
Steve Claridge	5.11	11.8	10.04.66	Portsmouth		Portsmouth (A)								
Div.3'91. Div.2'95. AWS'95				via Fareham to	30.11.84	Bournemouth	3+4			1	1			
				£10,000		Weymouth			1					
				£14,000	13.10.88	Aldershot	2+4	2+1	6	5	19		1	2
via Crystal Palace (11.10.88)				£75,000	08.02.90	Cambridge United	56+23	2+4	1	6+3	28	2		1
				£160,000	17.07.92	Luton Town	15+1	2		2	2	3		1
				£195,000	20.11.92	Cambridge United	53	4	4	3	18	3		
				£350,000	07.01.94	Birmingham City	58+2	3	5	7	20	1		4

Player	Ht	Wt	DOB	Fee	Date	Club								
Neil Doherty NPL'89. FAT'90.	5.9	10.09	21.02.89	Barrow	05.03.87	Watford (T)								
				Free		Barrow								
				£40,000	09.02.94	Birmingham City	15+6	1	0+1	0+2	1			
Louie Donowa E: u21.3. FAYC'83. MC'85. Div.2'95. AWS'95. via Real Deportivo 01.02.86 £40,000 & Willem II (Hol) Loan 15.01.93 Burnley 4 Lge App. 2gls.	5.9	12.2	24.09.64	Ipswich	28.09.82	Norwich City (A)	56+6	13+2	1+2		11	3	1	
				Loan	23.12.85	Stoke City	4		0+1		1			
				Free	14.08.89	Ipswich Town	17+8	0+2	2	2+1	1			1
				£55,000	10.08.90	Bristol City	11+13	1	0+1		3			
				£60,000	30.08.91	Birmingham City	73+26	12+2	7	8+3	18		1	1
				Loan	27.01.94	Shrewsbury Town	4							
Kevin Francis Div.2'95. AWS'95.	6.7	15.08	06.12.67	Birmingham		Mile Oak Rovers								
				Free	02.02.89	Derby County	0+10	1+2	1+2	0+1			1	
				£45,000	21.02.91	Stockport County	131+4	8	9	25	76	4	6	18
				£800,000	20.01.95	Birmingham City	15			3	8			1
Jonathan Hunt Div.2'95. AWS'95.	5.10	12.3	02.11.71	Camden		Barnet	12+21	1	0+1	6+2				1
				Free	20.07.93	Southend United	36+6	0+2	1	6+1	6			
				£50,000+PE	16.09.94	Birmingham City	18+2		1	3	5			3
Jae Martin	5.11	11.0	05.02.76	London	07.05.93	Southend United (T)	1+3			0+1				
				Free	09.95	Birmingham City								
Ian Muir E: Y1.1, S. LCD'90. Free 27.08.83 Birmingham City 1 Lge, 1 Oth App. Loan 28.01.85 Swindon Town 2 Lge, 1 Oth App.	5.8	11.0	05.05.63	Coventry	03.09.80	Q.P.R. (A)	2				2			
				Loan	08.10.82	Burnley	1+1				1			
				Free	15.02.84	Brighton & H.A.	3+1							
				Free	26.07.85	Tranmere Rovers	283+31	22+3	17+1	29+7	140	6	14	
				£125,000	08.95	Birmingham City								
Ricky Otto Div.2'95. AWS'95.	5.10	10.10	09.11.67	Hackney		Haringey Borough								
				Free	07.11.90	Leyton Orient	41+15	3	2+1	5+1	13			2
				£100,000	09.07.93	Southend United	44+1	2	1	8	13			2
				£800,000	19.12.94	Birmingham City	18+6			2	5	4	1	1

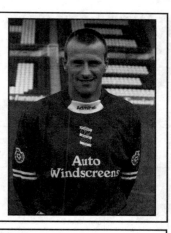

Top Goalscorer 1994/95
Steve Claridge

First Division Goals (games)	20 (41+1)
Coca-Cola Cup goals	1 (3)
F.A. Cup Goals	0 (5)
Auto Windscreen Shield	4 (7)
Total for 1994/95	**25 (56+1)**

Total for Birmingham since 07.01.94	32 (73+2)
Career Total up to June 1995	113 (297+46)

Manager
Barry Fry

Date of Birth	7th April 1945.
Place of Birth	Bedford.
Date of Appointment	December 1993.

PREVIOUS CLUBS
As Manager . . . . Dunstable, Hillingdon, Bedford T., Maidstone, Barnet, ... Southend United.
As Coach . . . . None.
As a Player . . . . Manchester Utd, Bolton W., Luton, Leyton Orient, ... Gravesend & Northfleet, Dunstable.

HONOURS
As a Manager
Barnet: GM Vauxhall Conference 1990-91.
Birmingham: Division 2 & FMC 1994-95.

As a Player
England Schoolboys.

St. Andrews

Birmingham B9 4NH
Tel: 0121 772 0101

Capacity...28,235.
Covered Standing..9,400.
Seating...5,500.
First game..
First floodlit game ....

ATTENDANCES
Highest...66,844 v Everton ,FA Cup 5th Round, 11.2.1939.
Lowest ....1,500 v Chesterfield, Division 2, 17.4.1909.

MATCHDAY TICKET PRICES

Seats £11
Juveniles/OAP £5.50

Terraces. £9
Juveniles/OAP £4.50

Ticket Office Telephone No. . . . . 0121 766 8274.

HOW TO GET TO THE GROUND

From North and East: M6 to J6, A38 (M). Branch left, first exit from round-abouts. A45 along Dartmouth Middleway. Left into St. Andrews Road for ground.

From South: M5 to J4, or A435 or A41 into Birmingham. A45 to Coventry Road then left into St. Andrews Road for ground.

From West: A456, A41 then A45 into Coventry Road, left into St. Andrews Road for ground.

Car Parking
Car parks in Coventry Road and Cattell Road. £2 per car on match days.

Nearest Railway Station
Buses from Birmingham New Street or Snow Hill, or walk from Bordesley Station from Birmingham Moor Street.

CLUBCALL
0898 88 86 82
Calls cost 39p per minute cheap rate and 49p per minute at all other times.
Call costings correct at time of going to press.

MATCHDAY PROGRAMME

Programme Editor . . . . Ben Hallam

Number of pages. 40

Price £1.20

Subscriptions . . . . £40 for first 26 issues.

Local Newspapers . . . . Birmingham Post & Evening Mail, Sports Argus.

Local Radio Stations . . . . BBC Radio W.M. & BRMB.

CHARLTON ATHLETIC
(The Addicks)
ENDSLEIGH LEAGUE DIVISION 1
SPONSORED BY: VIGLEN

Back Row (L-R): Stuart Reynolds, Steve Brown, Richard Rufus, Mike Ammann, Mike Salmon, Andy Petterson, Carl Leaburn, Dean Chandler, Jamie Stuart. **Middle Row:** Jimmy Hendry (Physio), Gary Moss (Asst. Physio), Keith Dowson, Shaun Newton, Lee Bowyer, Paul Mortimer, Phil Chapple, Andy Larkin, Kim Grant, Peter Garland, Paul Linger, Steve Watts (Yth Dev. Officer). **Front Row:** John Humphrey, Paul Sturgess, David Whyte, Garry Nelson, Alan Curbishley (Manager), Keith Jones, Les Reed (First team coach), Stuart Blamer, Colin Walsh, John Robinson, Mark Robson.

CHARLTON ATHLETIC
FORMED IN 1905
TURNED PROFESSIONAL IN 1920
LTD COMPANY IN 1919

CHAIRMAN: M A Simons
VICE- CHAIRMAN & MANAGING DIRECTOR
R A Murray
DIRECTORS
R N Alwen, G P Bone, R D Collins, C Norris,
M C Stevens, D G Ufton
SECRETARY
Chris Parkes
COMMERCIAL MANAGER
Steve Dixon

MANAGER: Alan Curbishley

RESERVE TEAM MANAGER
Keith Peacock
YOUTH TEAM MANAGER
Neil Banford
PHYSIOTHERAPIST
Jimmy Hendry

STATISTICIAN FOR THE DIRECTORY
Paul Clayton

A disappointing season for The Addicks with most of the campaign spent in mid-table. Relegation never looked a serious threat, whilst the play-offs never looked very likely. The season started with a 5-2 defeat at Oldham, but only one further defeat in the first ten games. Consistency was the problem, emphasised by the fact that no more than two consecutive wins were achieved throughout the season. Only two wins were secured in the last nine matches, resulting in a final placing of 15th.

It was a similar story in the Cup competitions. A fine 3-1 away win at Swindon in the Coca-Cola Cup, left the second leg looking a mere formality. However Charlton lost 1-4 after extra-time to go out. A 3-0 defeat at Chelsea, also saw an early exit from the FA Cup in the 3rd round.

Five new players joined the club in the Summer months, including two goalkeepers Andy Petterson from Luton Town and American Mike Ammann. Also signed were striker Scott McGleish from Edgware Town, and Crystal Palace pair David Whyte and Paul Mortimer, the latter for his second spell at the club. Whyte and Mortimer were part of the exchange deal that took Darren Pitcher to Crystal Palace, and it was a tremendous deal for Charlton with Whyte scoring 21 goals during the season, the highest figure by a Charlton player for fourteen years. Keith Jones was then signed from Southend United for £150,00 in September to bolster the midfield.

Charlton used a total of 28 players during the season, giving debuts to several youngsters. Lee Bowyer, Dean Chandler and Jamie Stuart all broke into the first team, Stuart making the left-back position his own. The pick of the bunch however was central defender Richard Rufus, who had a splendid season, picking up the Supporters Player of the Year award. He formed a solid defensive partnership with Stuart Balmer, and finished the season being called up for the England Under-21 squad. Other players who consistently performed well were Steve Brown and Mark Robson. Special mention must be given to Garry Nelson, who was having one of his best ever seasons at the club, when an injury finished his season in early March. He still ended up second top scorer with nine goals.

Gates were once again up, with the average league gate topping the 10,000 mark. New faces are certainly needed for next season, and a striking partner for David Whyte would seem a priority, if a return to the elite is to become a reality.

PAUL CLAYTON.

CHARLTON ATHLETIC

Division One: 15th   **FA Cup:** 3rd Round   **Coca-Cola Cup:** 2nd Round

M	DATE	COMP.	VEN	OPPONENTS	RESULT	H/T	LP	GOAL SCORERS/GOAL TIMES	ATT.
1	A 13	EL	A	Oldham Athletic	L 2-5	2-2	23	Whyte 24, Robinson 27	(8,924)
2	20	EL	H	Barnsley	D 2-2	0-0	16	Whyte 80, chapple 90	8,167
3	27	EL	A	Portsmouth	D 1-1	1-1	18	Nelson 8	(10,566)
4	30	EL	H	Sheffield United	D 1-1	1-1	19	Brown 25 (pen)	8,708
5	S 3	EL	H	Bristol City	W 3-2	1-0	14	Mortimer 25, Whyte 63, 70	9,019
6	10	EL	A	Grimsby Town	W 1-0	0-0	8	Robson 58	(3,970)
7	14	EL	A	Stoke City	L 2-3	0-2	12	Nelson 72, Whyte 76	(10,643)
8	17	EL	H	Swindon Town	W 1-0	1-0	8	Whyte 13	9,420
9	**21**	**CC 2/1**	**A**	**Swindon Town**	**W 3-1**	**0-0**		**Nelson 59, 81 Whyte 85**	**(4,932)**
10	24	EL	A	Notts County	D 3-3	1-2	6	Whyte 24, Nelson 84, 86	(5,726)
11	**27**	**CC 2/2**	**H**	**Swindon Town**	**L 1-4**	**0-3**		**Whyte 85**	**5,370**
12	O 1	EL	H	Watford	W 3-0	0-0	5	Nelson 47, Grant 56, Whyte 86	8,417
13	8	EL	H	Reading	L 1-2	0-1	6	Robson 56	10,602
14	15	EL	A	Port Vale	W 2-0	0-0	6	Chapple 48, Whyte 71	(7,707)
15	22	EL	H	Burnley	L 1-2	0-0	6	Whyte 81	9,488
16	29	EL	A	Derby County	D 2-2	1-1	6	Grant 8, 77	(12,588)
17	N 1	EL	A	Sunderland	D 1-1	0-1	7	Grant 72	(14,085)
18	5	EL	H	Bolton Wanderers	L 1-2	0-1	10	Brown 88 (pen)	9,816
19	13	EL	H	West Bromich A.	D 1-1	1-0	11	Grant 14	10,921
20	19	EL	A	Tranmere Rovers	D 1-1	1-0	11	Nelson 45	(7,567)
21	26	EL	H	Middlesbrough	L 0-2	0-1	15		10,019
22	D 10	EL	A	Barnsley	L 1-2	0-1	19	Mortimer 83	(5,465)
23	19	EL	H	Oldham Athletic	W 2-0	0-0	17	Whyte 58, Jones 76	8,970
24	26	EL	H	Southend United	W 3-1	0-1	16	Whyte 50, Leaburn 83, 86	9,525
25	28	EL	A	Wolverhampton Wand.	L 0-2	0-2	16		(27,500)
26	J 1	EL	H	Millwall	D 1-1	0-1	16	Robinson 52	10,652
27	2	EL	A	Luton Town	W 1-0	1-0	15	Whyte 19	(7,642)
28	**7**	**FAC 3**	**A**	**Chelsea**	**L 0-3**	**0-2**			**(24,485)**
29	14	EL	H	Derby County	L 3-4	3-1	17	Whyte 23, Pardew 38 Robson 43	9,412
30	21	EL	A	Bolton Wanderers	L 1-5	1-2	17	Whyte 32	(10,516)
31	F 5	EL	A	West Bromich A.	W 1-0	0-0	14	Nelson 58	(12,084)
32	11	EL	H	Sunderland	W 1-0	0-0	14	Whyte 57	12,380
33	18	EL	A	Middlesbrough	L 0-1	0-1	12		(16,301)
34	21	EL	H	Tranmere Rovers	L 0-1	0-0	13		(11,893)
35	M 4	EL	H	Notts County	W 1-0	1-0	14	Mortimer 31	13,638
36	7	EL	A	Bristol City	L 1-2	0-1	14		(6,118)
37	11	EL	H	Portsmouth	W 1-0	1-0	13	Leaburn 4	9,475
38	18	EL	A	Sheffield United	L 1-2	0-0	13	Pardew 89	(11,862)
39	21	EL	H	Grimsby Town	W 2-1	1-1	12	Robinson 45, Balmer 86	9,551
40	25	EL	A	Swindon Town	W 1-0	0-0	12	Grant 67	(9,106)
41	A 1	EL	H	Stoke City	D 0-0	0-0	12		10,002
42	4	EL	A	Burnley	L 0-2	0-1	13		(10,045)
43	8	EL	A	Millwall	L 1-3	1-2	14	Balmer 7	(9,506)
44	15	EL	H	Wolverhampton Wand.	W 3-2	1-1	14	Whyte 12, Walsh 55, Mortimer 61	11,017
45	18	EL	A	Southend United	L 1-2	0-0	15	Whyte 48	(6,397)
46	22	EL	H	Luton Town	W 1-0	0-0	13	Whyte 72	10,876
47	29	EL	H	Port Vale	D 1-1	1-1	13	Brown 43	12,596
48	M 2	EL	A	Watford	L 0-2	0-0	13		(6,024)
49	7	EL	A	Reading	L 1-2	0-1	15	Chandler 73	(12,137)
50									
51									
52									
53									
54									
55									
56									
57									
58									
59									
60									

Best Home League Attendance: 13,638 v Notts County   **Smallest:** 8,167 v Barnsley   **Av Home Att:** 10,198

Goal Scorers:

League (58): Whyte 19, Nelson 7, Grant 6, Mortimer 4, Brown 3 (2 pens), Leaburn 3, Pardew 3, Robinson 3, Robson 3, Balmer 2, Chapple 2, Chandler, Jones, Walsh

C/Cola Cup (4): Nelson 2, Whyte 2
FA Cup (0):

Compared with 1993-94: +1,795

Salmon M.	Brown S.	Sturgess P.	Mortimer P.	Chapple P.	McLeary M.	Robinson J.	Neson G.	Pardew A.	Whyte D.	Walsh C.	Balmer S.	Grant K.	Pettersen A.	Robson M.	Garland P.	Linger P.	Ammann M.	Newton S.	Jones K.	Leaburn C.	Bowyer L.	McGleish S.	Bennett M.	Rufus R.	Stuart J.	Referee	
1	2	3	4	5	6	7	8	9	10*	11	S	12	S													J Lloyd	1
1†	2	3	4	5	6	7*	8	9	10					11•	12	14	13									I. Hemley	2
	2	3•	4	5	6	7	8		10			14	S	11*	9		1	12								C. Wilkes	3
	2	3	4*	5	6	7•	8		10		12	14	S	11	9		1									P. Foakes	4
	2	3	4	5	6		8		10	12		14	S	11*	9•		1	7								T. West	5
	2	3	4	5	6		8		10•	12		14	S	11*	9		1	7								K. Lupton	6
	2	3		5	6		8	12	10	4		14	S	11	9•		1	7*								K. Breen	7
	2	3		5		8	14	10*	9	6			1	11*			S	7	4	12						S. Dunn	8
	2	3		5		8		10	9	6	S	1	11	4			S	7		S						D. Gallagher	9
	2	3		S		8		10	9*	6	14	1	11	12			S	7•	4		12					N. Barry	10
	2	3		5		8		10	9	6	14	1	11	4*			S	7•	4		12					G. Pooley	11
	2	3		5		8*		10	9	6	12	1	11				S	14			7					K. Cooper	12
	2	3		5		8*		10	9•	6	12	1	11				S	14	4		7					G. Singh	13
	2	3		5	S			10*	9	6	8	1	11				S		4		7	12				D. Allison	14
	2	3		5	S			10*	9	6	8	1	11				S		4		7*	12				M. Bailey	15
	2	3		5	6	11•		10*	9		8	S					1	12	4				7	14		B. Burns	16
	2	3		5	6	11		10	9		8•	S				14	1	12				7*	4			W. Flood	17
	2	3		9	6*	11•		10			8	S	7			1	14	4	12					5		G.Singh	18
	2*	3			6		10	4		11		8	S	7			1	12	4	9		S		5		K. Cooper	19
S	2	3			6		10	S		11		8*		7			1	12	4	9				5		I. Cruikshank	20
S	2	3			6		10			14	11*	8•		7			1	12	4	9				5		M. Pierce	21
S	2	3	11		6		12	S		10		8					1	7	4	9*				5		J. Lloyd	22
1	2	3	11*		6		S			10	12	8		7			S		4	9				5		P. Foakes	23
1	2	3*	11		6			14		10	12	8•		7			S		4	9				5		G. Pooley	24
1	2*		3	5	6			12		10	11	8		7•			S		4	9			14			P. Harrison	25
1			3	5	6	8•		14		10	11*			7			S	12		9			2			K. Leach	26
1	3		4	5	6	8		12	11	10				7*			S			9			3		S	P. Alcock	27
1	2		3	5	6	8•		12	14	10	11			7			S			9			4*			T. Holbrook	28
1	2		3•	5	6			12	8	10	11			7			S			9*			4			P. Vanes	39
	2	3			6			8*	9	10	11	12	S	7•			1						4	5		J. Rushton	30
1	2		11					8	9	10•		6		S	7*				4			14	12	5	3	P. Wright	31
1	2						12	8•	9	10		6		S	7				4			14	11•	5	3	G. Singh	32
1	2						12	8	9	10		6		S	7*				4			14	11•	5	3	G. Cain	33
1	2						12	8•	9	10		6		S	7				4	14		11*	5	3		S. Dunn	34
1	2		11•				12	8	9	10		6		S	7*				4	14			5	3		C. Wilkes	35
1	2		11				14	8	9	10		6		S	7*				4	12			5	3*		J. Holbrook	36
1	2		3					11		9	10	6		S	7*		S		12	4	8			5		D. Orr	37
1			3	2		11			9	10*	4	6	12	S	7				S		8			5		J. Watson	38
1	2		3			11			9			6	10•	S	7*		14		12	4	8			5		M. Pierce	39
1	2•		3			11			9			6	10	S	7•		12			14	4	8*		5		K. Leach	40
1	2		3			11		9•	12			6	10•	S	7•					14	4	8		5		G. Barber	41
1†	2		3			11*		9				6	10•	S	7				12	4	8		14	5		K. Lupton	42
		3•	7		2*	11		9		14	6	10	1			4	S			8			12	5		J. Brandwood	43
	2		11					9	10	4	6		S	7*		S	1	12		8				5	3	A. D'Urso	44
	2								10	11	6	8	S	7*	12	9	1	5	4					3		G. Pooley	45
	2		11						10	9	6		S	7*			1	S	4	8*		12		5	3	P. Alcock	46
	2								10	9	6		S	7*	12		11*	12	1	7	4	8	S	5	3	C. Wilkes	47
	2								10	9	6		S		11*	12	1	7	4	8	9		S	5	3	S. Dunn	48
									10•			14	1	7		11*		2	4	8	9		12	5	3	P. Foakes	49
20	42	23	26	21	22	16	21	22	36	23	28	14	8	40	6	3	18	10	31	22	5		9	27	12	League Appearances	
						5	6	2	2	5	1								16		5	1	6	5	1	League Sub Appearances	
2	2		2		2		2	2	2	0+1	2	2	2			2			2			0+1				C/Cola Appearances	
1	1		1	1	1	0+1	0+1	1	1					1				1				1		1		FA Cup Appearances	

Also Played: T. Hovi 14 (29,30), S. Gritt S (45), D. Chandler 6 (49), D. Lee S (49)   Loan Players: Hovi (Hamarkameratene)   † = Sent Off

CHARLTON ATHLETIC

CLUB RECORDS

BIGGEST VICTORIES
League: 8-1 v Middlesbrough, Division 1, 12.9.1953.
F.A. Cup: 7-0 v Burton Albion, Round 3, 7.1.1956.
League Cup: 5-0 v Brentford, Round 1, 12.8.1980.

BIGGEST DEFEATS
League: 1-11 v Aston Villa, Division 2, 14.11.1959.
F.A. Cup: 0-6 v Wrexham, Round 3, 5.1.1980.
League Cup: 1-7 v Blackpool, Round 2, 25.9.1963.

MOST POINTS
3 points a win: 77, Division 2, 1985-86.
2 points a win: 61, Division 3(S), 1934-35.

MOST GOALS SCORED
107, Division 2, 1957-58.
Summers 28, Leary 17, Ayre 11, Ryan 10, Kierman 8, Hewie 6,
Werge 6, Lucas 6, White 2, Firmani 2, Lawrie 2, Jago 1, Allen 1,
Opponents 7.

MOST GOALS CONCEDED
120, Division 1, 1956-57.

MOST FIRST CLASS MATCHES IN A SEASON
60 - 1993-94 (League 46, FA Cup 6, League Cup 2, Anglo-Italian
Cup 6).

MOST LEAGUE WINS
27, Division 3(S), 1934-35.

MOST LEAGUE DRAWS
17, Division 2, 1969-70, 1990-91.

MOST LEAGUE DEFEATS
29, Division 1, 1956-57.

INDIVIDUAL CLUB RECORDS

MOST GOALS IN A SEASON
Ralph Allen: 33 goals in 1934-35 (League 32, FA Cup 1).

MOST GOALS IN A MATCH
5. Wilson Lennox v Exeter (a), Division 3(S), 2.2.1929 (5-2).
5. Eddie Firmani v Aston Villa, Division 1, 5.2.1955 (6-1).
5. John Summers v Huddersfield, Division 2, 21.12.1957 (7-6).
5. John Summers v Portsmouth, Division 2, 1.10.1960 (7-4).

OLDEST PLAYER
Sam Bartram, 42 years 48 days v Arsenal, Division 1, 10.3.1956.

YOUNGEST PLAYER
Mark Penfold, 16 years 258 days v York City, Division 3, 25.8.1973.

MOST CAPPED PLAYER
John Hewie (Scotland) 19.

BEST PERFORMANCES

League: 1934-35: Matches Played 42, Won 27, Drawn 7, Lost 8,
Goals for 103, Goals against 52, Points 61. First in Division 3(S).
Highest Position: 2nd in Division 1, 1936-37.
F.A. Cup: 1946-47: 3rd Round Rochdale 3-1; 4th round West
Bromwich Albion 2-1; 5th round Blackburn Rovers 1-0; 6th Round
Preston North End 2-1; Semi-Final Newcastle United 4-0; Final
Burnley 1-0.
League Cup: 4th round in 1962-63, 1964-65, 1978-79.
Most Recent Success: 1986-87: 2nd Round Lincoln City 3-1,1-0;
3rd Round Queens Park Rangers 1-0; 4th Round Arsenal 0-2.
Full Members Cup: 1986-87: 2nd Round Birmingham City 3-2; 3rd
round Bradford City 2-0; 4th Round Everton 2-2 aet (won 6-5 on
penalties); Semi-Final Norwich City 2-1 aet, Final Blackburn Rovers
0-1.

ADDITIONAL INFORMATION
PREVIOUS NAMES
None.
PREVIOUS LEAGUES
Southern League.

Club colours: Red shirts, white shorts, red socks.
Change colours: White shirts, black shorts, white socks.
Third strip: Green & purple striped shirts, purple shorts, green socks.

Reserves League: Avon Insurance Football Combination.

DIVISIONAL RECORD

	Played	Won	Drawn	Lost	For	Against	Points
Division 1	746	262	171	313	1,082	1,209	732
Division 2/1	1,490	517	384	589	2,206	2,423	1,577
Division 3	184	83	39	62	274	245	205
Division 3(S)	420	165	109	146	622	567	439
Total	2,840	1,027	703	1,110	4,184	4,444	2,953

RECORDS AND STATISTICS

COMPETITIONS

Div 1/P	Div.2/1	Div.3	Div 3(S)
1936-57	1929-33	1972-75	1921-29
1986-90	1935-36	1980-81	1933-35
	1957-72		
	1975-80		
	1981-86		
	1990-		

HONOURS

FA Cup	Div 3(S)
1947	1928-29
	1934-35

MOST APPEARANCES

Sam Bartram 623 (1934-56)

Year	League	FA Cup
1934-35	18	
1935-36	39	1
1936-37	42	1
1937-38	41	5
1938-39	42	1
1945-46	-	10
1946-47	41	6
1947-48	42	3
1948-49	41	1
1949-50	42	4
1950-51	37	2
1951-52	41	1
1952-53	38	1
1953-54	40	2
1954-55	42	3
1955-56	33	3
	579	44

MOST GOALS IN A CAREER

Derek Hales - 168 (1973-76 & 1978-85)

Year	League	FA Cup	Lge Cup
1973-74	8	-	-
1974-75	20	-	1
1975-76	28	-	3
1976-77	16	-	2
1978-79	8	-	1
1979-80	8	-	1
1980-81	17	4	2
1981-82	11	-	2
1982-83	14	1	2
1983-84	10	-	1
1984-85	8	-	-
Total	**148**	**5**	**15**

Current leading goalscorer: Carl Leaburn - 43 (1987-95)

Stuart Leary scored most League goals (153) 1951-62.
(League 153, FA Cup 8, League Cup 2) Total 163.

RECORD TRANSFER FEE RECEIVED

Amount	Club	Player	Date
£775,000	Chelsea	Scott Minto	5/94
£700,000	Newcastle Utd	Robert Lee	9/92
£650,000	Crystal Palace	Mike Flanagan	8/79
£600,000	Sheffield Wed.	Paul Williams	8/90

RECORD TRANSFER FEE PAID

Amount	Club	Player	Date
£600,000	Chelsea	Joe McLaughlin	8/89
£430,000	Chelsea	Colin Pates	10/88
£350,000	Port Vale	Andy Jones	9/87
£324,000	Barcelona	Allan Simonsen	10/82

MANAGERS

Name	Seasons	Best	Worst
Walter Rayner	1920-25	12(3S)	16(3S)
Alex McFarlane	1925-28	13(3S)	21(3S)
Albert Lindon	1928	11(3S)	11(3S)
Alex McFarlane	1928-32	10(2)	1(3S)
Albert Lindon	1932-33	22(2)	22(2)
Jimmy Seed	1933-56	2(1)	5(3S)
Jimmy Trotter	1956-61	22(1)	10(2)
Frank Hill	1961-65	4(2)	20(2)
Bob Stokoe	1965-67	16(2)	19(2)
Eddie Firmani	1967-70	3(2)	20(2)
Theo Foley	1970-74	20(2)	14(3)
Andy Nelson	1974-80	7(2)	3(3)
Mike Bailey	1980-81	3(3)	3(3)
Alan Mullery	1981-82	13(2)	13(2)
Ken Craggs	1982	17(2)	17(2)
Lennie Lawrence	1982-91	5(1)	17(2)
A Curbishley/ S Gritt	1991-95	7(2)	15 (2/1)
A Curbishley	1995-		

LONGEST LEAGUE RUNS

of undefeated matches:	15 (4.10.80 - 20.12.80)	of league matches w/out a win:	16 (26.2.1955 - 22.8.1955)
of undefeated home matches:	28 (13.4.1935 - 3.10.1936)	of undefeated away matches:	7 (4.10.80-6.12.80 & 29.12.90- 1.4.91)
without home win:	9 (5.3.1955 - 20.8.1955)	without an away win:	33 (29.3.1969 - 14.11.1970)
of league wins:	7 (7.10.1980 - 1.11.1980)	of home wins:	11 (4.12.1937 - 18.4.1938)
of league defeats:	10 (11.4.1990 - 15.9.1990)	of away wins:	5 (26.1.1935 - 23.3.1935)

CHARLTON ATHLETIC

PLAYERS NAME / Honours	Ht	Wt	Birthdate	Birthplace / Transfers	Contract Date	Clubs	League	L/Cup	FA Cup	Other	Lge	L/C	FAC	Oth
G O A L K E E P E R S														
Michael A Ammann	6.2	13.2	08.02.71	California		LA Cobras								
USA: B				Free	20.07.94	Charlton Athletic	18+1							
Andrew Petterson	6.2	14.2	26.09.69	Freemantle	30.12.88	Luton Town	16+3	2		2				
				Loan	26.03.93	Ipswich Town	1							
				£85,000	15.07.94	Charlton Athletic	8+1	2						
				Loan	08.12.94	Bradford City	3							
Michael Salmon	6.2	12.12	14.07.64	Leyland	16.10.81	Blackburn Rov (J)	1							
				Loan	18.10.92	Chester City	16		2					
				Free	03.08.83	Stockport County	118	10	3	3				
				Free	31.07.86	Bolton Wanderers	26	2	4	4				
				£18,000	07.03.87	Wrexham	100	4	4	9				
				£100,000	06.07.89	Charlton Athletic	87	3	5	6				
D E F E N D E R S														
Stuart Balmer	6.1	12.4	20.06.69	Falkirk		Celtic								
				£120,000	24.08.90	Charlton Athletic	130+17	6	6	9	5		1	
Steven B Brown	6.1	12.0	13.05.72	Brighton	03.07.90	Charlton Athletic (T)	60+2	2	7	2	3			
Dean A R Chandler	6.2	11.10	06.05.76	London	13.04.94	Charlton Athletic (T)	1				1			
Philip Chapple	6.2	12.7	26.11.66	Norwich	10.07.85	Norwich City (T)								
Div3'91					29.03.88	Cambridge United	183+4	11	23	17	18	2	1	
				£100,000	13.08.94	Charlton Athletic	61+4	4	4	5	7			
John Humphrey	5.10	10.13	31.01.61	Paddington	14.02.79	W'hampton W.(A)	149	8	7		3			
FMC'91; Div1'94				£60,000	22.07.85	Charlton Athletic	194	13	9	15	3			1
				£400,000	18.06.90	Crystal Palace	135+5	19+2	5	8+1	2			
				Loan	09.12.93	Reading	8		1					
				Free	.08.95	Charlton Athletic								
Andrew Larkin	6.1	11.09	24.09.77	Kent		Charlton Ath. (T)								
Richard R Rufus	6.1	11.2	12.01.75	Lewisham	01.07.93	Charlton Athletic (T)	27+1							
Jamie C Stuart	5.10	10.7	15.10.76	Southwark	18.01.95	Charlton Athletic (T)	12							
E: Y														
Paul C Sturgess	5.11	12.5	04.08.75	Dartford	01.07.93	Charlton Athletic (T)	52+6	4		5				
M I D F I E L D														
Lee D Bowyer	5.9	9.11	03.01.77	London	13.04.94	Charlton Athletic	5	0+1						
E: Y														
Alan Curbishley	5.10	11.7	08.11.57	Forest Gate	14.08.75	West Ham Utd (A)	78+7	3	5		5			
E: u21.1, Y, S				£275,000	11.07.79	Birmingham City	128+2	12	10		11	3	1	
				£100,000	25.03.83	Aston Villa	34+2	5		2	1			
				£40,000	24.12.84	Charlton Athletic	62+1	1	3	2+1	6			
				£32,000	21.08.87	Brighton& H. A.	111+5	4	6	6	13		2	
				Free	03.07.90	Charlton Athletic	22+6		1					
Peter Garland	5.10	12.0	20.01.71	Croydon	01.07.89	Tottenham H. (T)	0+1							
E: Y6				£35,000	24.03.92	Newcastle United	0+2			0+2				
				18.12.92	Charlton Athletic	37+13	3	2	4+1	2			1
Keith Jones	5.9	10.11	14.10.65	Dulwich	16.08.83	Chelsea (A)	43+9	9+2	1	4+1	7	3		
E: Y2, S				£40,000	03.09.87	Brentford	167+12	15	13	16	13	2	4	1
				£175,000	21.10.91	Southend United	81+2	2	5	9	11			1
				£150,000	16.09.94	Charlton Athletic	31				1			
Jamie Kyte	5.7	10.0	17.09.77	Erith	19.10.94	Charlton Ath. (T)								
Paul H Mortimer	5.11	11.3	08.05.68	Kensington		Fulham (A)								
E: u21.2				Free		Farnborough Town								
				Free	22.09.87	Charlton Athletic	108+5	4+1	8	3+1	17			
				£350,000	24.07.91	Aston Villa	10+2	2			1			
				£500,000	18.10.91	Crystal Palace	18+4	1	1	3	2			
				Loan	22.01.93	Brentford	6			2				
				P.E.	05.07.94	Charlton Athletic	26		1		4			
Shaun Newton	5.8	10.4	20.08.75	Camberwell	01.07.93	Charlton Athletic (T)	33+40	6	0+1	2+1	2			
John R Robinson	5.10	11.2	29.08.71	Bulawayo	21.04.89	Brighton & H. A. (T)	57+5	5	2+1	1+1	6	1		2
W: u21.2				£75,000	15.09.92	Charlton Athletic	58+5	1+1	4+1	2	6			
Colin Walsh	5.9	11.0	22.07.62	Hamilton	16.08.79	Nottingham F. (A)	115+24	8+5	9+2	12	32		2 3	
S: u21.5, Y				£125,000	11.09.86	Charlton Athletic	218+18	16	11+2	17	21	4	5	
				Loan	02.02.89	Peterborough Utd	5				1			
				Loan	17.01.91	Middlesbrough	10+3		1		1			
F O R W A R D S														
Kim Grant	5.10	10.12	25.09.72	Ghana	06.03.91	Charlton Athletic (T)	54+39	2+5	6+4	5+2	11		3	1

CHARLTON ATHLETIC

PLAYERS NAME / Honours	Ht	Wt	Birthdate	Birthplace / Transfers	Contract Date	Clubs	League	L/Cup	FA Cup	Other	Lge	L/C	FAC	Oth
Carl Leaburn	6.3	13.0	30.03.69	Lewisham	22.04.87	Charlton Athletic (A)	185+39	11	13+2	7+5	33	3	3 4	
E: Y1, u19				Loan	22.03.90	Northampton Town	9							
Paul Linger	5.6	9.5	20.12.74	Stepney	01.07.93	Charlton Athletic (T)	3+12							
Garry Nelson	5.10	11.10	16.01.61	Braintree	09.07.79	Southend United (J)	106+23	3+1	6+2		17	1		
Div4'81				£10,000	17.08.83	Swindon Town	78+1	4	5	5	7	1		1
				£15,000	12.07.85	Plymouth Argyle	71+3	4	7	3	20		2	
				£80,000	17.07.87	Brighton & H. A.	132+12	7	7	8	45		6 6	
Loan 08.11.90 Notts County	0+2 Lge App.			£50,000	16.08.91	Charlton Athletic	135+20	8	9+2	8	35	2	1	
Mark A Robson	5.7	10.2	22.05.69	Newham	17.12.86	Exeter City (A)	26		2	2	7			
				£50,000	17.07.87	Tottenham Hotspur	3+5	1						
Loan Reading (24.03.88) 5+2Lge				Loan	05.10.89	Watford	1							
Loan Plymouth Argyle (22.12.89) 7Lge				Loan	03.01.92	Exeter City	7+1			3	1			1
				Free	14.08.92	West Ham United	42+5	2	2	4+1	8		1	
				£125,000	17.11.93	Charlton Athletic	60+3	2	7	1	5		1	
David Whyte	5.8	10.7	03.10.71	Greenwich		Greenwich Borough								
Div1'94				Free	15.02.89	Crystal Palace	17+10	5+2	0+1	0+3	4	2		1
				Loan	26.03.92	Charlton Athletic	7+1				2			
				£450,000	05.07.94	Charlton Athletic	36+2	2	1		19	2		

TOP GOALSCORER 1994/95
David Whyte

Division One (games) . . . . 19 (36+2)
Coca-Cola Cup Goals 2 (2)
F.A. Cup goals 0 (1)

Total . . . . 21 (39+2)

Total goals for Charlton Athletic since 26.03.92 (Loan) . . . . 23 (46+3)

Career total as at June 1st 1995 . . . . 30 (68+19)

THE MANAGER
ALAN CURBISHLEY

Date of Birth . . . . 8th November 1957.
Place of Birth . . . . Forest Gate.
Date of Appointment . . . . . 20th July 1991 as joint manager, June 1995 as sole.

PREVIOUS CLUBS
As Manager . . . . None.
As Coach . . . . None.
As a Player . . . West Ham, Aston Villa, Brighton, Birmingham, Charlton Athletic.

HONOURS
As a Manager
None.

As a Player
None.

THE VALLEY
Floyd Road, Charlton, London SE7 8BL
Tel: 0181 293 4567

Capacity 15,000

First game ....v Summerstown (Sth Suburban Lge) 13.9.19.
First Lge game..v Exeter City (Div 3(S) 27.8.21.
First floodlit game ....Rotherham Utd (Div 2) 20.9.61.

ATTENDANCES
Highest..75,031 v Aston Villa, FA Cup, 12.2.1938.
Lowest...1,452 v Pisa, Anglo Italian Cup, 22.12.93)
OTHER GROUNDS......Siemens Meadow 1906-07. Woolwich Common1907-08. Pound Park 1908-13.
.... Horn Lane 1913-19. The Valley 1919-23. The Mount 1923-24. The Valley 1924-85.
....Selhurst Park 1985-91. Upton Park 1991-92. The Valley 1992-

MATCHDAY TICKET PRICES

North Stand
Adult/Adult non-member . . . . £8/£12
Senior/Young member £4
Concession £6
Junior £3
West Stand
Adult/Adult non-member . . . . £10/£12
Senior/Young member £5
Concession £6
Junior £3
Junior Red (Family Stand only) £1
East Stand & Family Stand
Adult/Adult non-member . . . . £10/£12
Senior/Young member £5
Concession £6
Junior/Junior Red . . . . £3/£1
Ticket Office Telephone no. 0181 858 5888

CLUBCALL 0891 12 11 46
Calls cost 39p per minute cheap rate and 49p per
minute at all other times.
Call costings correct at time of going to press.

HOW TO GET TO THE GROUND

By Road
From M25 take junction 2 (A2 London bound) and follow until road becomes
A102 (M). Take the turning marked 'Woolwich Ferry' and turn right along A206
Woolwich Road. This route takes you into Charlton.

Visitors Parking
Visiting coaches located in Anchor and Hope LAne, five minutes walk from
ground. Also street parking.

By Rail
Charlton Station (British Rail main line) can be reached from Charing Cross,
Waterloo (East) or London Bridge and is two minutes from the ground.

Nearest Railway Station
Charlton.

MATCHDAY PROGRAMME

Programme Editor . . . . Peter Burrows.

Number of pages 40

Price . . . . £1.50.

Subscriptions . . . . £50 home, £50 away, £90 home & away.

Local Newspapers . . . . . . Kentish Times, South East London Mercury,
. . . . . South London Press, News Shopper, Greenwich Comet Leader,
. . . . Kent Messenger, Kent Today.

Local Radio Stations . . . . RTM, Capital Gold.

CRYSTAL PALACE
(The Eagles)
ENDSLEIGH LEAGUE DIVISION 1
SPONSORED BY: TDK

Back Row (L-R): Danny Boxall, Bjorn Enqvist, Rory Ginty, Jason Harris, Robert Quinn, Paul Sparrow. **3rd Row:** Richard Shaw, George Ndah, Brian Launders, Andy Roberts, Jimmy Glass, Damian Matthew, Marc Edworthy, Jamie Vincent. **2nd Row:** Brian Sparrow, Peter McClean (Physio), Simon Rodger, Ian Cox, David Hopkin, Steve Taylor, Nigel Martyn, Rhys Wilmot, Bruce Dyer, Anthony Scully, Gareth Davies, Vic Bettonelli (Kit Manager), Steve Kember (Res. Manager). **Front Row:** Darren Patterson, Dean Gordon, Ray Houghton, Ray Lewington (First Team Coach), Steve Coppell (Technical Director), Peter Nicholas (First Team Coach), Iain Dowie, Darren Pitcher, Chris Coleman.

CRYSTAL PALACE
FORMED IN 1905
TURNED PROFESSIONAL IN 1905
LTD COMPANY IN 1905

CHAIRMAN: R G Noades
DIRECTORS
B Coleman OBE, A S C De'Souza,
G Geraghty, M C Lee, S Hume-Kendall,
P H N Norman, R Anderson,
V E Murphy, C L Noades
SECRETARY
Mike Hurst
COMMERCIAL MANAGER
Tony Shaw

DIRECTOR OF FOOTBALL: Steve Coppell
ASSISTANT MANAGERS
Ray Lewington/Peter Nicholas
RESERVE TEAM MANAGER
Steve Kember
YOUTH TEAM MANAGER
Brian Sparrow & John Acteson
PHYSIOTHERAPIST
Peter McClean

STATISTICIAN FOR THE DIRECTORY
Mike Purkiss

An amazing return to the Premiership saw a long term struggle to score and win matches, form that saw them finish in the fourth relegation spot. Yet, in cup competition, Palace were within a game from each final, Liverpool halted them in the two legged Coca-Cola semi-final and in the FA Cup it took a replay before Manchester United booked their place in the final.

Liverpool started the league season with a 1-6 win at Selhurst, our new signings, Pitcher, Preece, Wilkins and substitute 'keeper Wilmot all making their debuts (the latter only on the bench). For Wilkins this was the only game he appeared in, an injury and then the appointment of manager at Q.P.R. saw to that.

Manager Smith gave his young players a chance, leaving Young, Humphreys, Williams and Thorn in the reserves, he also gave Patterson his first team debut after two years in the reserves.

After seven games without a win we went to Highbury, a ground at which we had never won a League game, and came away with three points, Salako scoring two goals. A spell of very erratic form followed. Four consecutive wins and nine goals were recorded, followed by nine league games without scoring - a new club record - during which time 13 goals were netted in cup competitions. Newman was the hero to break the league run with a brilliant volley verses Leicester City.

Our defence was one of the best, even after the six on the first day. Shaw and Coleman enjoyed an outstanding partnership, and it was no coincidence when Coleman picked up an injury 13 goals were conceded in the last six games.

The problems were at the other end. The £4 million rated Armstrong had only scored three in the league by March, and coupled with his ban from the FA, he was finding it hard to settle in the Premiership. However, his total of eight league goals (10 in cup competitions) saw him finish up as top goalscorer, underlining the point that Palace had found it hard to score goals. The signings of Dowie and Houghton had come to late, Palace managed to score only 16 goals at home thus creating a new record, their previous record being 18. In fact their total of 34 goals in 42 league games was almost bettered by their cup tally of 27 in 15 games.

Our captain, Gareth Southgate, added to his ever-present total, the only player this season.

Congratulations to Richard Shaw for the Player of the Year Award and to our Juniors, who again won the South East Counties Championship under the management of Peter Nicholas.

Unfortunately Alan Smith paid the price of relegation with his dismissal/resignation but Palace are hopeful of a quick return to the top flight, as they did in 1993-94.

MIKE PURKISS.

CRYSTAL PALACE

Premier League: **FA Cup:** Semi-Finalists   **Coca-Cola Cup:** Semi-Finalists

M	DATE	COMP.	VEN	OPPONENTS	RESULT	H/T	LP	GOAL SCORERS/GOAL TIMES	ATT.
1	A 20	PL	H	Liverpool	L 1-6	0-3		Armstrong 49	18,084
2	24	PL	A	Norwich City	D 0-0	0-0	20		(19,015)
3	27	PL	A	Aston Villa	D 1-1	0-0	18	Southgate 86	(23,305)
4	30	PL	H	Leeds United	L 1-2	0-1	17	Gorden 55	14,453
5	S 10	PL	A	Manchester City	D 1-1	1-1	17	Dyer	(19,971)
6	17	PL	H	Wimbledon	D 0-0	0-0	21		12,366
7	20	CC 2/1	A	Lincoln City	L 0-1	0-0			(4,310)
8	24	PL	H	Chelsea	L 0-1	0-0			16,064
9	O 1	PL	A	Arsenal	W 2-1	2-0	16	Salako19, 41	(34,136)
10	4	CC 2/2	H	Lincoln City	W 3-0	0-0		Gordon 90, Armstrong 101, Dyer 110	7,041
11	8	PL	A	West Ham United	L 0-1	0-0	18		(16,959)
12	15	PL	A	Newcastle United	L 0-1	0-0	21		17,739
13	22	PL	H	Everton	W 1-0	0-0	19	Preece 53	15,026
14	25	CC 3	A	Wimbledon	W 1-0	0-0		Armstrong 72	(9,394)
15	29	PL	A	Leicester City	W 1-0	1-0	16	Preece 36	(20,022)
16	N 2	PL	A	Coventry City	W 4-1	2-1	12	Preece 18, 49 Sawako 20, Newman 80	(10,732)
17	5	PL	H	Ipswich Town	W 3-0	1-0	10	Newman 19, Armstrong 83, Salako 87	13,450
18	19	PL	A	Manchester United	L 0-3	0-2	12		(43,788)
19	26	PL	H	Sothampton	D 0-0	0-0	13		14,186
20	30	CC 4	H	Aston Villa	W 4-1	0-1		Armstrong 48, 88 Southgate 59, 75	12,807
21	D 3	PL	A	Sheffield Wednesday	L 0-1	0-1	15		(21,930)
22	11	PL	A	Liverpool	D 0-0	0-0	13		(30,972)
23	17	PL	H	Norwich City	L 0-1	0-0	16		12,252
24	26	PL	H	Queens Park Rangers	D 0-0	0-0	17		16,372
25	27	PL	A	Tottenham Hotspur	D 0-0	0-0	16		(27,730)
26	31	PL	A	Blackburn Rovers	L 0-1	0-0	18		14,232
27	J 2	PL	A	Nottingham Forest	L 0-1	0-0	18		(21,326)
28	8	FAC 3	H	Lincoln City	W 5-1	3-0		Coleman 7, Armstrong 24, Gorden 33 (pen), Salako 62, 87	6,541
29	11	CC 5	H	Manchester City	W 4-0	0-0		Pitcher 60, Salako 80, Armstrong 84, Preece 87	16,668
30	14	PL	H	Leicester City	W 2-0	2-0	16	Newman 23, Noah 44	12,707
31	21	PL	A	Everton	L 1-3	0-1	17	Coleman 79	(23,733)
32	25	PL	H	Manchester United	D 1-1	0-0	16	Southgate 80	18,224
33	28	FAC 4	A	Nottingham Forest	W 2-1	1-1		Armstrong 5, Dowie 53	(16,790)
34	F 4	PL	A	Ipswich Town	W 2-0	0-0	16	Dowie 55, Gorden 86 (pen)	(15,570)
35	11	PL	H	Coventry City	L 0-2	0-0	18		11,891
36	15	CC SF 1	A	Liverpool	L 0-1	0-0			(25,480)
37	18	FAC 5	A	Watford	D 0-0	0-0			(13,814)
38	25	PL	A	Arsenal	L 0-3	0-2	19		17,092
39	M 1	FAC 5	H	Watford	W †1-0	0-0		Noah 118	10,321
40	5	PL	A	Chelsea	D 0-0	0-0	20		(14,130)
41	8	CC SF 2	H	Liverpool	L 0-1	0-0			18,224
42	11	FAC 6	H	Wolverhamton Wand.	D 1-1	0-0		Dowie 53	14,604
43	14	PL	H	Sheffield Wednesday	W 2-1	0-1	18	Armstrong 55, Dowie 65	10,422
44	18	PL	A	Wimbledon	L 0-2	0-1	19		(8,835)
45	22	FAC 6	A	Wolverhampton Wand.	W 4-1	3-1		Armstrong 32, 67, Dowie 37, Pitcher 45	(27,548)
46	A 1	PL	H	Manchester City	W 2-1	1-0	18	Armstrong 33, Patterson 64	13,312
47	4	PL	H	Aston Villa	D 0-0	0-0	19		12,606
48	9	FAC SF	N	Manchester United	D †2-2	1-0		Dowie 33, Armstrong 92	(38,256)
49	12	FAC SFR	N	Manchester United	L 0-2	0-2			(17,987)
50	14	PL	H	Tottenham Hotspur	D 1-1	1-0	20	Armstrong 41	18,149
51	17	PL	A	Queens Park Rangers	W 1-0	0-0	19	Dowie 56	(14,227)
52	20	PL	A	Blackburn Rovers	L 1-2	0-0	19	Houghton 71,	(28,005)
53	29	PL	H	Nottingham Forest	L 1-2	0-1	19	Dowie 76	15,886
54	M 3	PL	A	Southampton	L 1-3	1-2		Southgate 26	(15,151)
55	6	PL	H	West Ham United	W 1-0	0-0	19	Armstrong 50	18,234
56	9	PL	A	Leeds United	L 1-3	0-2	19	Armstrong 67	(30,942)
57	14	PL	A	Newcastle United	L 2-3	0-3	19	Armstrong 51, Houghton 81	(35,626)
58									
59									
60									

Best Home League Attendance: 18,224 v Manchester United   **Smallest:** 10,422 v Sheffield Wednesday   **Av Home Att:** 14892

Goal Scorers:

Compared with 1993-94: -467

League (34): Armstrong 8, Dowie 4, Preece 4, Salako 4, Newman 3, Southgate 3, Gorden 2, Houghton 2, Coleman, Dyer, Noah, Patterson

C/Cola Cup (12): Armstrong 5, Southgate 2, Dyer, Gorden, Noah, Pitcher

FA Cup (15): Armstrong 5, Dowie 4, Salako 2, Coleman, Gorden, Noah, Pitcher

1994-95

Martin	Pitcher	Gorden	Southgate	Young	Coleman	Rodger	Wilkins	Armstrong	Preece	Salako	Dyer	Bowey	Wilmot	Patterson	Newman	Cox	Shaw	Matthew	Ndah	Launders	Humphrey	Williams	Dowie	Houghton	Glass	Referee
1	2	3	4	5	6	7	8*	9	10+	11	12+	14*	S													R. Hart 1
1		3	4		6+	7		9		11	10*	S8	S	2	12+	14*	5									B. Hill 2
1	12+	3	4		6	7+		9		11	10		S	2	8	14*	5									J. Worrall 3
1	12+	3	4		6	7+		9	10	11		8	S	2	12+	S	5									D. Gallagher 4
1	S	3	4		6			9		11	10		S		8		5	7	S							K. Burge 5
1	S	3	4		6			9		11	10		S		8		5	7+	12							K.Cooper 6
1		3	4		6			9	12	11	10+		S	2	8		5		7							W. Burns 7
1		3	4		6			9		11	12	S	S	2	8		5		7		10+					L. Dilkes 8
1		3	4		6			9		11	S	7		2	8		5		S		10					M. Bodesham 9
1		3	4		6			9		11	12+	7	S	2+	8		5				10	14*				G. Willard 10
1		3	4		6			9		11	12	7	S	2+	8		5				10	14				G. Poll 11
1	S	3	4		6			9	10	11	S	7	S		8		5				2					K. Morton 12
1	12	3	4		6			9	10	11	S	7+	S		8		5				2					S. Lodge 13
1	S	3	4		6			9	10	11	S	7	S		8		5				2					R. Gifford 14
1	12	3	4		6			9	10	11	S	7+	S		8		5				2					P. Don 15
1		3	4		6			9	10	11	S	7			8		5				2					P. Jones 16
1	S	3	4		6			9	10	11		7			8		5	S			2					A. Wilkie 17
1	S	3	4		6			9	10	11	12	S	7*		8		5				2					B. Hill 18
1	S	3	4		6			9	10+	11	12	7	S		8		5				2					P. Danson 19
1	S	3	4		6			9	10	11	7+	S			8		5	S			2					G. Willard 20
1	S	3	4		6			9	10	11	7+	S			8		5	S			2					K. Cooper 21
1	6	3	4					9	10	11	S	7	S		8		5	S			2					K. Morton 22
1	12+	3	4		6			9	10	11	14*	7*	S		8		5+				2	12				R. Hart 23
1	S	3	4		6			9	10	11		S			8	7+	5				2	12				B. Hill 24
1	10	3	4		6			9		11+	7		S	2	8		5		S		2	12+				G. Willard 25
1	S	3	4		6			9	10		S	11+	8				5	12			2	7				D. Ellery 26
1*	7+	3	4		6			9		S	12*	11	8				5	14			2	10				G. Ashby 27
1	7	3	4		6			9	12	11	S	S	8				5	10			2					P. Wright 28
1	7	3	4		6			9	12	11	S	S	8				5	10			2					M. Bodenham 29
1	7	3	4		6			9	12	11	S	S	8				5	10			2					P. Durkin 30
1	7	3	4		6			9		11	S	S	8				5	12			2		10+			P. Jones 31
1	7	3	4		6			9	12	11	S	S	2		8		5						10+			A. Wilkie 32
1	7	3	4		6			9	12	11	S	S	2		8		5						10			R. Hart 33
1	7	3	4		6			9+	S	11	12	S	2		8		5						10			S. Lodge 34
1	7	3	4		6				12	11	8+	S	2				5	S	10				9			M. Bodenham 35
1	7	3	4		6			9		11	S	S			5	8					2					R. Hart 36
1	7	3	4		6			9	10	11	S	S			8	S	5	S			2					B. Hill 37
1	7	3	4		6			9		11	12	S	10*		8+		5	14			2					K. Morton 38
1	7	3	4		14			10*	11	S	6				8		5	12			2+		9			B. Hill 39
1	7	3	4	6+				10*	11	S	2				8		5	14+			12		9			M. Reed 40
1	7	3	4		6			9	10+	11	12	S	2		S		5	8			9*					K. Burge 41
1	7	3	4		6				10	11	14*	S	8		5		2+	12+			9*					G. Willard 42
1	7	12	4		6	3		9	10+	11	S		2		5		S	8								P. Don 43
1	7	12	4		6	3		9	10+	11	S		2*		5		14	8								D. Gallagher 44
1	7		4		6	3		9*		11	S		2		12+	8+	5						10			G. Willard 45
1	7		4		6	3		9		11	10	S	2		14		5	12						8		T. Holbrook 46
1	7	12+	4		6	3		9		11	10*	S	2		14*		5							8		K. Cooper 47
1	7	12+	4		6	3+		9		11	S		2		S		5	10						8		D. Elleray 48
	7+	3	4		6			9		11			1	2	12	14	5						10	8	S	D. Elleray 49
	7+	3	4		6		5		8	11*			1	12+	14*	2							10	8	S	P. Don 50
		3	4		6	5		9	11+		14		1	7	12+*	2							10	8	S	A. Wilkie 51
		3	4		6+	5		9		11	7		1	11	7	14*	2		12+*				10	8	S	B. Hill 52
		3	4		6*			9		11	14+		1	7+	12*	5		2					10	8	S	K. Burge 53
S	7	3	4		6			9		11	12+		1	S	S		5	2+					10	8		G. Toll 54
1	7	3	4		6			9		11	S		S	S			5	2					10	8		S. Lodge 55
1	7	3	4		6			9		11*	12*		S	2			14	5					10	8+		J. Worrall 56
1	7	3	4		6			9		11*	12		S	2		S	5						10	8		G. Ashby 57
																										58
																										59
																										60
37	21	38	42	13	35	4	1	40	17	39	7	13	5	22	32	1	41	2	5	1	19	2	15	10		League Appearances
	4				3				3	9	5	1			2	7		1	2		2					League Sub Appearances
7	3	7	7	1	7			5	4	7	1	3		4	5		7	1	4		4					C/Cola Appearances
										2		2								1						
7	8	5	8	4	6			6	2	8	1		1	6	4	1	8	1	1		3		6	2		FA Cup Appearances

CRYSTAL PALACE

CLUB RECORDS

BIGGEST VICTORIES
League: 9-0 v Barrow, Division 4, 10.10.1959.
F.A. Cup: 7-0 v Luton Town, 3rd Round, 16.1.1929.
League Cup: 8-0 v Southend, 2nd Round, 25.9.1990.

BIGGEST DEFEATS
League: 0-9 v Liverpool, Division 1, 12.9.1989.
F.A. Cup: 0-9 v Burnley, 2nd Round replay, 1908-09.
League Cup: 0-5 v Nottingham Forest, 3rd Round replay, 1.11.89.

MOST POINTS
3 points a win: 90, Division 1, 1993-94.
2 points a win: 64, Division 4, 1960-61.

MOST GOALS SCORED
110, Division 4, 1960-61.
Byrne 30, Summersby 25, Heckman 14, Woan 13, Gavin 8,
Petchley 7, Uphill 6, Barnett 2, Lunnis 1, McNicholl 1, Noakes 1,
Opponents 2.

MOST GOALS CONCEDED
86, Division 3(S), 1953-54.

MOST FIRST CLASS MATCHES IN A SEASON
59 - 1988-89 (League 46, FA Cup 1, League Cup 3, Simod Cup 5,
Play-offs 4).

MOST LEAGUE WINS
29, Division 4, 1960-61.

MOST LEAGUE DRAWS
19, Division 2, 1978-79.

MOST LEAGUE DEFEATS
29, Division 1, 1980-81.

INDIVIDUAL CLUB RECORDS

MOST GOALS IN A SEASON
Peter Simpson: 54 goals in 1930-31 (League 46, FA Cup 8).
Previous holder: P.A.Cherrett, 32 goals in 1926-27.

MOST GOALS IN A MATCH
6. Peter Simpson v Exeter, 7-2, Division 3(S), 4.10.1930.

OLDEST PLAYER
Wally Betteridge, 41 (Debut - Player/coach), 27.10.1928 (0-8).

YOUNGEST PLAYER
Phil Hoadley, 16 years 3 months, 27.4.1968.

MOST CAPPED PLAYER
Eric Young (Wales) 19.

BEST PERFORMANCES

League: 1960-61: Matches played 46, Won 29, Drawn 6, Lost 11,
Goals for 110, Goals against 69, Points 64. 2nd in Division 4.
Highest Position: 1990-91, 3rd in Division 1.
F.A. Cup: 1989-90: 3rd Round Portsmouth 2-1; 4th Round
Huddersfield Town 4-0; 5th Round Rochdale 1-0; 6th Round
Cambridge 1-0; Semi-Final Liverpool 4-3; Final Manchester United
3-3 aet, replay 0-1.
League Cup: 1992-93: 2nd Round Lincoln City (a) 3-1, (h) 1-1; 3rd
Round Southampton (a) 2-0; 4th Round Liverpool (a) 1-1, (h) 2-1
aet; 5th Round Chelsea (h) 3-1; Semi-Final Arsenal (h) 1-3, (a) 0-2.

ADDITIONAL INFORMATION
PREVIOUS NAMES
None.

PREVIOUS LEAGUES
Southern League.

Club colours: Red and blue wide-striped shirt, red shorts, red
socks.
Change colours: White shirts, white shorts, white socks with claret
and blue trim.

Reserves League: Neville Ovenden Football Combination.

DIVISIONAL RECORD

	Played	Won	Drawn	Lost	For	Against	Points
Division 1/P	454	122	135	197	468	659	448
Division 2/1	892	338	240	314	1,126	1,093	1,075
Division 3	276	113	86	77	419	332	312
Division 3(S)	1,166	438	292	436	1,831	1,853	1,168
Division 4	138	68	30	40	284	204	166
Total	2,926	1,079	783	1,064	4,128	4,141	3,169

RECORDS AND STATISTICS

COMPETITIONS

Div .1/P	Div.2/1	Div.3	Div.3(S)	Div.4
1969-73	1921-25	1920-21	1925-58	1958-61
1979-81	1964-69			
1989-93	1973-74			Texaco
1994-95	1976-79			1972-73
	1981-89			
	1993-94			

HONOURS

Div. 2/1	Div. 3	FMC
1978-79	1920-21	1991
1993-94		

MOST APPEARANCES

Jim Cannon 665 + 4 (1972-86)

Year	League	FA Cup	Lge Cup	Others
1972-73	3			
1973-74	13+1		1	
1974-75	34+2	2	0+1	
1975-76	40	8	2	
1976-77	46	6	3	
1977-78	39	1	4	
1978-79	41	4	4	
1979-80	42	3	3	
1980-81	33	1	4	
1981-82	42	5	4	
1982-83	41	4	5	
1983-84	30	2	2	
1984-85	40	2	2	
1985-86	42	1	4	1
1986-87	42	2	4	1
1987-88	40	1	1	1
	568+3	42	43+1	3

MOST GOALS IN A CAREER

Peter Simpson - 166 (1929-34)

Year	League	FA Cup
1929-30	36	1
1930-31	46	8
1931-32	24	1
1932-33	14	1
1933-34	20	1
1934-35	14	
Total	154	12

Current leading goalscorer: Eric Young - 17 (1990-95)

RECORD TRANSFER FEE RECEIVED

Amount	Club	Player	Date
£4,500,000	Tottenham H.	Chris Armstrong	06/95
£2,500,000	Arsenal	Ian Wright	9/91
£1,350,000	Arsenal	Kenny Sansom	8/80
£400,000	Derby County	Dave Swindlehurst	4/80

RECORD TRANSFER FEE PAID

Amount	Club	Player	Date
£2,300,000	Millwall	Andy Roberts	7/95
£1,800,000	Sunderland	Marco Gabbiadini	9/91
£1,350,000	Bristol Rovers	Nigel Martin	11/89
£1,000,000	Arsenal	Clive Allen	8/80

MANAGERS

Name	Seasons	Best	Worst
John Robson	1905-07	1(2)	19(1)
Eddie Goodman	1907-25	14(2)	1(3S)
Alec Maley	1925-27	6(3S)	13(3S)
Fred Maven	1927-30	2(3S)	9(3S)
Jack Tresadern	1930-35	2(3S)	12(3S)
Tom Bromilow	1935-36	6(3S)	6(3S)
R.S. Moyse	1936	14(3S)	14(3S)
Tom Bromilow	1937-39	2(3S)	7(3S)
George Irwin	1939-47	13(3S)	22(3S)
Jack Butler	1947-49	3(3S)	3(3S)
Ron Rooke	1949-50	3(3S)	3(3S)
F Dawes/C Slade	1950-51	24(3S)	24(3S)
Laurie Scott	1951-54	13(3S)	22(3S)
Cyril Spiers	1954-58	14(3S)	23(3S)
George Smith	1958-60	7(4)	8(4)
Arthur Rowe	1960-63	11(3)	2(4)
Dick Graham	1963-66	7(2)	2(3)
Arthur Rowe (Acting)	1966		
Bert Head	1966-72	18(1)	11(2)
Malcolm Allison	1972-76	21(1)	5(3)
Terry Venables	1976-80	13(1)	3(3)
Ernie Walley	1980	20(1)	22(1)
Malcolm Allison	1980-81	22(10	22(1)
Dario Gradi	1981	22(1)	15(2)
Steve Kember	1981-82	15(2)	15(2)
Alan Mullery	1982-84	15(2)	18(2)
Steve Coppell	1984-93	3(1)	15(2)
Alan Smith	1993-95	1(1)	1(1)
Steve Coppell	1995-		

LONGEST LEAGUE RUNS

of undefeated matches:	18 (1.3.1969 - 16.8.1969)	of league matches w/out a win:	20 (24.2.1962 - 13.10.1962)
of undefeated home matches:	32 (28.2.1930 - 8.10.1932)	of undefeated away matches:	10 (22.12.1928 -1.4.1929,
			26.12.1968 - 10.8.1969, 16.8.1975 - 6.12.1975, 18.11.78 - 3.4.79).
without home win:	11 (14.4.1973 - 17.11.1973)	without an away win:	31 (15.3.1980 - 3.10.1981).
of league wins:	8 (9.2.1991 - 26.3.1921)	of home wins:	12 (19.12.1925 - 28.8.1926).
of league defeats:	8 (18.41925 - 19.9.1925)	of away wins:	4 (1931-32, 1932-33 & 1975-76)

CRYSTAL PALACE

PLAYERS NAME Honours	Ht	Wt	Birthdate	Birthplace Transfers	Contract Date	Clubs	League	L/Cup	FA Cup	Other	Lge	L/C	FAC	Oth
GOALKEEPERS														
James R Glass	6.1	11.10	01.08.73	Epsom	04.07.91	Crystal Palace (T)								
Anthony Nigel Martyn	6.2	13.10	11.08.66	St Austell		St. Blazey								
E:3, B6, u21.11; Div3'90; FMC'91; Div1'94				Free	06.08.87	Bristol Rovers	101	6	6	11				
				£1,000,000	21.11.89	Crystal Palace	226	32	20	16				
Rhys Wilmot	6.1	12.0	21.02.62	Newport	08.02.80	Arsenal (A)	8	1						
W: u21.6, S				Loan	18.03.83	Hereford United	9							
				Loan	27.05.84	Leyton Orient	46	4	4	3				
Loan Swansea City, 26.8.88, 16 Lg Apps.				Loan	23.02.89	Plymouth Argyle	17							
				£100,000	20.07.89	Plymouth Argyle	116	8	2	4				
				£87,500	01.07.92	Grimsby Town	33	4	4	2				
				£80,000	09.08.94	Crystal Palace	5+1		1					
DEFENDERS														
Danile J Boxall	5.8	10.05	24.08.77	Croydon	1994-95	Crystal Palace (T)								
Christopher Coleman	6.2	12.10	10.06.70	Swansea		Manchester City (J)								
W: 4, u21.3,Y, S; WFAC'89'91; Div1'94				Free	01.09.87	Swansea City	159+1	8	13	15	2		1	
				£275,000	19.07.91	Crystal Palace	126+11	20+2	8	2	13	2	1	
Gareth M Davies	5.10	11.3	11.12.73	Hereford	10.04.92	Hereford United (T)	91+4	5+2	4	5	2			
W: u21.2				£120,000	08.95	Crystal Palace								
Marc Edworthy	5.7	9.6	24.12.72	Barnstaple	30.03.91	Plymouth A. (T)	52+17	5+2	5+2	2+2	1			
				£350,000	08.95	Crystal Palace								
Darren J Patterson	6.2	11.10	15.10.69	Belfast	05.07.88	West Brom. A. (T)								
NI: 2, B1, u21.1, Y				Free	17.04.89	Wigan Athletic	69+28	7+1	5+4	7	6	3	1	
				£225,000	01.07.92	Crystal Palace	22	4	6		1			
Darren E J Pitcher	5.9	12.2	12.10.69	Stephney	12.01.88	Charlton Athletic (T)	170+3	11	12	8	9		3	
E: S				£40,000 + P.E	01.07.94	Crystal Palace	21+4	3	8			1	1	
Robert Quinn	5.11	11.02	08.11.76	Sidcup	1994-95	Crystal Palace (T)								
Simon L Rodger	5.9	10.13	03.10.71	Shoreham		Bognor Regis Town								
Div1'94				£1,000	02.07.90	Crystal Palace	83+8	14	2+1	2+1	5			
Richard E Shaw	5.9	11.5	11.09.68	Brentford	04.09.86	Crystal Palace (A)	178+14	24+2	18	12+1	3			
FMC'91; Div1'94				Loan	14.12.89	Hull City	4							
Paul Sparrow	6.1	11.0	24.03.75	London	13.07.93	Crystal Palace(T)								
Jamie R Vincent	5.10	11.6	18.06.75	London	13.07.93	Crystal Palace (T)								
Eric Young	6.3	12.6	25.03.60	Singapore		Staines Town								
W: 20; FAC'88; IsthPL'81; FMC'91; Div1'94						Slough Town			2					
				£10,000	01.11.82	Brighton & H.A.	126	8	11	2	10		1	
				£70,000	29.07.87	Wimbledon	96+3	12	6+1	7	9		1	
				£850,000	15.08.90	Crystal Palace	161	25	10	8	15	1		1
MIDFIELD														
Bruce A Dyer	6.0	10.9	13.04.75	Ilford	19.04.93	Watford (T)	29+2	4	1	2	6	2		1
E: u21.5; Div1'94				£1,100,000	10.03.94	Crystal Palace	9+10	1+2	1+2		1	1		
Bjorn Enquist	5.10	10.09	12.10.77	Lund		Malmo								
					1994-95	Crystal Palace								
Dean D Gordon	6.0	11.5	10.02.73	Croydon	04.07.91	Crystal Palace (T)	85+15	10+3	6+1	2+1	7	2	1	
E: u21.5; Div1'94														
David Hopkin	6.0	13.0	21.08.70	Greenock		Morton	33+15	2	2					
				£300,000	25.09.92	Chelsea	14+11		3+2					
				£800,000	08.95	Crystal Palace								
Raymond J Houghton	5.7	10.10	09.01.62	Glasgow	05.07.79	West Ham U (J)	0+1							
Ei: 62. LC'86'94. Div.1'88'90. CS'88'90. FAC'89'92.				Free	07.07.82	Fulham	129	12	4		16	2	3	
				£147,000	13.09.85	Oxford United	83	13	3	6	10	3		1
				£825,000	19.10.87	Liverpool	147+6	14	26+1	8	28	3	4	3
				£900,000	28.07.92	Aston Villa	83+12	11+2	7	4+2	6	2	2	1
				£300,000	23.03.95	Crystal Palace	10		2		2			
Damian Matthew	5.11	10.10	23.09.70	Islington	13.06.89	Cheslsea (T)	13+8	5		1				
E;u21.9; Div1'94				Loan	25.09.92	Luton Town	3+2			1				
				£150,000	11.02.94	Crystal Palace	13+3	1	1		1			
Andrew J Roberts	5.10	11.5	20.03.74	Dartford	29.10.91	Millwall (T)	132+6	12	7	4	5	2		1
				£2,520,000	08.95	Crystal Palace								
FORWARDS														
Ian G Cox	6.0	12.2	25.03.71	Croydon		Crystal Palace (J)								
						Whyteleaf								
						Carsholton Athletic			0+1					
				£35,000	08.03.94	Crystal Palace	1+10		1+1					
Iain Dowie	6.1	12.12	09.01.65	Hatfield		Hendon								
NI: 25, u21.1.				£30,000	14.12.88	Luton Town	53+13	3+1	1+2	5	15			4
Loan Fulham, 13.09.89, 5 Lge App. 1 gl.				£480,000	22.03.91	West Ham United	12				4			
				£500,000	03.09.91	Southampton	115+7	8+3	6	4	30	1	1	
				£400,000	13.01.95	Crystal Palace	15		6		4		4	
Rory V Ginty	5.9	10.02	23.01.77	Galway	1994-95	Crystal Palace (T)								

CRYSTAL PALACE

PLAYERS NAME Honours	Ht	Wt	Birthdate	Birthplace Transfers	Contract Date	Clubs	APPEARANCES				GOALS			
							League	L/Cup	FA Cup	Other	Lge	L/C	FAC	Oth
Brian T Launders	5.10	11.12	08.01.76	Dublin	02.09.93	Crystal Palace	1+1	0+1						
George E Ndah E: Y3	6.1	10.0	23.12.74	Dulwich	10.08.92	Crystal Palace (T)	4+10	2+3		1+1		1		
Anthony D T Scully	5.7	11.12	12.06.76	Dublin	02.12.93	Crystal Palace (T)								
Steve Taylor				Birmingham		Bromsgrove Rovers								
				£90,000	08.95	Crystal Palace								
Paul A Williams E: u21.4; LC'91; Div1'94	5.7	10.3	16.08.65	Stratford		Woodford Town				1				
				£12,000	23.02.87	Charlton Athletic	74+8	6	6+1		23	3	3	
				Loan	20.10.87	Brentford	7			1	3			3
				£700,000	15.08.90	Sheffield Wed.	78+15	10+3	3+2	3	25	3		
				£625,000	11.09.92	Crystal Palace	38+10	4+1		2	7			2
				Loan	19.01.95	Sunderland	3							
				Loan	13.03.95	Birmingham	8+3			1				1

TOP GOALSCORER 1994/95
Chris Armstrong

Premiership goals (games) 8 (40)
Coca-Cola Cup Goals 5 (5)
F.A. Cup goals 5 (6)

Total 18 (51)

Total goals for Crystal Palace from 01.09.92 - 1995 . . . . 58 (136)

Career total as at June 1st 1995 . . . . 81 (197+43)

DIRECTOR OF FOOTBALL (MANAGER)
STEVE COPPELL

Date of Birth . . . . 9th July 1955.
Place of Birth . . . . Liverpool.
Date of Appointment . . . . June 1995.

PREVIOUS CLUBS
As Manager . . . . Crystal Palace.
As Coach . . . . None.
As a Player . . . . Tranmere Rovers, Manchester United.

HONOURS
As a Manager
Promotion to Division 1. FA Cup finalists 1989-90. Zenith Data Winners 1991.

As a Player
Manchester United: FA Cup Winners 1977. FA Cup runners-up 1976, 1979. Milk Cup Finalists 1983.

SELHURST PARK

London SE25 6PU
Tel: 0181 653 1000

Capacity...26,500

First game...v Sheffield Wed., Division 2, 30.8.1924.
First floodlit game ....v Chelsea, 28.9.1953.
ATTENDANCES
Highest...51,482 v Burnley, Division 2, 5.5.1979.
Lowest ....2,207 v Brighton, FMC, 16.10.1985.

OTHER GROUNDS ....Crystal Palace 1905-15. Herne Hill 1915-18. The Nest 1918-24.
.... Selhurst Park 1924-

MATCHDAY TICKET PRICES

Directors Box	£25
Juv/OAP	£16
Main Stand	£18
Juv/OAP	£12
Family Enclosure	£10
Juv/OAP	£5
Arthur Wait Stand.	£14
Juv/OAP	£10
Whitehorse Lane	£12
New Holmesdale Stand Upper	£14
Lower	£10
Juv/OAP	£5
Family Ticket Lower	£10
Juv/OAP	£5
Ticket Office Telephone no.	0181 771 8841.

CLUBCALL
0891 400 333

Calls cost 39p per minute cheap rate and 49p per
minute at all other times.
Call costings correct at time of going to press.

HOW TO GET TO THE GROUND

From the North
From motorway (M1) or A1, use A406 North Circular Road to Chiswick. Follow signs South Circular Road (A205) to Wandsworth. Then use A3 to A214 and follow signs to Streatham. Join A23. In 1 mile turn left (B273). At the end turn left into High Street then forward into Whitehorse Lane for Crystal Palace FC.

From the East
Use A232 (sign posted Croydon) to Shirley then join A215 (sign posted Norwood). In 2.2 miles turn left (B266) into Whitehouse Lane.

From the South
Use A23 (sign posted London) then follow signs Crystal Palace (B266) via Thornton Heath into Whitehorse Lane.

From the West
Use motorway (M4) to Chiswick then route from North or A232 (sign posted Croydon) to Beddington, then follow signs London A23. After, follow signs Crystal Palace (B266) via Thornton Heath into Whitehorse Lane.

Car Parking: Club car park (468 spaces) on first come first served basis. Street parking is also available.

Nearest Railway Station: Thornton Heath/Norwood Junction/Selhurst.

MATCHDAY PROGRAMME

Programme Editor . . . . Pete King & James Coome.

Number of pages . . . . 48.

Price . . . . £1.50.

Subscriptions . . . . £54 (inland) Home only.

Local Newspapers . . . . Croydon Advertiser, South London Press.

Local Radio Stations . . . . G.L.R., Capital Gold.

DERBY COUNTY
(The Rams)
ENDSLEIGH LEAGUE DIVISION 1
SPONSORED BY: PUMA

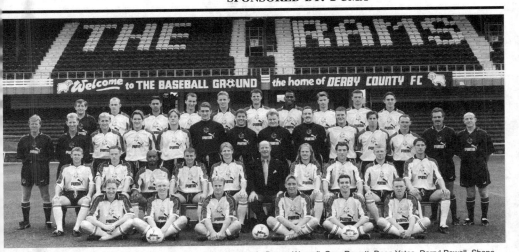

Back Row (L-R): Peter Melville (Physio), Lee Carsley, Jason Kavanagh, Darren Wassall, Gary Rowett, Dean Yates, Darryl Powell, Shane Nicholson, Andrew Tretton, Mark Stallard. **3rd Row:** Steve McLaren (Asst. Manager), Billy McEwan (Coach), Paul Trollope, Matt Warren, Ian Ashbee, Russell Hoult, Andy Quy, Martin Taylor, Steve Sutton, Craig Smith, John Harkes, Sean Flynn, Eric Steele (Goalkeeping coach), Gordon Guthrie (Asst. Physio). **2nd Row:** Steve Round, Wayne Sutton, Dean Sturridge, Paul Simpson, Marco Gabbiadini, Jim Smith (Manager), Robin van der Laan, Ron Willems, Chris Boden, Will Davies. **Front Row:** Nick Wright, Darren Wrack, Carl Cunningham, Matt Green, Steve Powell, Kevin Cooper.

DERBY COUNTY
FORMED IN 1884
TURNED PROFESSIONAL IN 1884
LTD COMPANY IN 1896

CHAIRMAN: B E Fearn
VICE-CHAIRMAN: L V Pickering

DIRECTORS
J N Kirkland BSc, CEng, MICE,
W Hart, C W McKerrow, A Cox, M Mills,
M Horton
SECRETARY
Michael Dunford (01332 40105)
COMMERCIAL MANAGER
Colin Tunnicliffe (01332 40105)

MANAGER: Jim Smith
ASSISTANT MANAGER: Steve McLaren

YOUTH TEAM MANAGER
Richie Williams
PHYSIOTHERAPIST
Peter Melville

STATISTICIAN FOR THE DIRECTORY
Steve McGhee

Once again Derby started the season as expected promotion candidates, but after 4 weeks and lying at the foot of the table the players were clearly under-achieving. Experienced players such as Gordon Cowans and Martin Kuhl were sold as well as Paul Kitson, whose on-off transfer to Newcastle had everyone confused. The desire for top level football saw Villa sign Tommy Johnson and Gary Charles and allowed some of the clubís highly rated youngsters to force their way into the first team. Of these, Lee Carsley perhaps made thebiggest impression.

By Christmas and with a much-changed side, the club lay in mid-table and a promotion bid looked unlikely. After the FA Cup exit at Everton, however, Roy MacFarland entered the transfer market to sign Lee Mills from Wolves and Paul Trollope from Torquay and from then on a series of results, based on a sound defensive record, saw Derby rapidly climb to the edge of the play-off zone. At the last, however, they ran out of steam and had to be content with a place just inside the top 10.

It was perhaps unsurprising that the manager Roy MacFarland, given the level of investment in the team over the past 2 years, should lose his job after another failed promotion attempt. New boss Jim Smith inherits a squad without both Mark Pembridge and Paul Williams, both gone to the Premier Division, but has brought in players perhaps more suited to the style of play necessary in Division 1.

The current players are quite capable of sustaining a serious promotion attempt, but with rivals investing heavily in players and 4 down from the Premier, perhaps a play-off place is a more realistic proposition.Whatever the season holds, once again the level of support, especially away from home, indicates the wish to return to the top flight.

STEVE McGHEE.

DERBY COUNTY

Division One: 9th   **FA Cup:** 3rd Round   **Coca-Cola Cup:** 4th Round

M	DATE	COMP.	VEN	OPPONENTS	RESULT	H/T	LP	GOAL SCORERS/GOAL TIMES	ATT.
1	A 13	EL	A	Barnsley	L 1-2	1-2	1	Pembridge 29	(8,737)
2	20	EL	H	Luton Town	D 0-0	0-0	19		13,060
3	23	AIC	A	Ancona	L 1-2	1-2		Pembridge 24	(8,500)
4	27	EL	A	Millwall	L 1-4	0-1	21	Sturridge 67	(8,809)
5	30	EL	H	Middlesbrough	L 0-1	0-1			14,659
6	S 3	EL	H	Grimsby Town	W 2-1	1-0	21	Charles 1, Pembridge 46	12,027
7	6	AIC	H	Cesena	W 6-1	5-0		Hodge 8, 38, Kitson 16, 29,31,73	2,101
8	11	EL	A	Swindon Town	D 1-1	1-1		Kitson 17	(9,054)
9	13	EL	A	Bristol City	W 2-0	1-0		Kitson 22, Carsley 53	(8,029)
10	17	EL	H	Oldham Athletic	W 2-1	1-0	11	Carsley 10, Short 81	13,746
11	20	CC 2/2	A	Reading	L 1-3	1-1		Gabbiadini 45	(6,056)
12	25	EL	H	Stoke City	W 3-0	2-0		Hodge 28, Gabbiadini 38, Charles 83	11,782
13	28	CC 2/2	H	Reading	W 2-0	1-0		Gabbiadini 10, Williams 82	9,476
14	O 1	EL	A	Bolton Wanderers	L 0-1	0-0	9		(12,015)
15	5	AIC	A	Piacenza	D 1-1	0-0		Williams 77	(6,000)
16	8	EL	H	Watford	D 1-1	0-1	11	Hodge 72	13,413
17	16	EL	A	Southend United	L 0-1	0-1	19		(4,218)
18	23	EL	A	Notts County	D 0-0	0-0			(6,389)
19	26	CC 3	A	Portsmouth	W 1-0	0-0		Simpson 46	(8,568)
20	29	EL	H	Charlton Athletic	D 2-2	1-1	16	Short 30, Johnson 60	12,588
21	N 2	EL	H	Reading	L 1-2	0-1	19	Gabbiadini 76	10,585
22	12	EL	A	Sheffield United	L 1-2	0-0	19	Simpson 66 (pen)	(15,001)
23	15	AIC	H	Uninese	W 3-1	2-0		Johnson 19, 72, Stallard 20	
24	19	EL	H	Port Vale	W 2-0	1-0	14	Johnson 24, 72	13,357
25	27	EL	A	Wolverhampton Wand.	W 2-0	1-0		Johnson 14, Stallard 63	(22,768)
26	30	CC 4	A	Swindon Town	L 1-2	1-1		Stallard 35	(8,920)
27	D 3	EL	H	Notts County	D 0-0	0-0	12		14,278
28	11	EL	A	Luton Town	D 0-0	0-0			(6,400)
29	17	EL	H	Barnsley	W 1-0	0-0	10	Johnson 68	13,205
30	26	EL	A	Tranmere Rovers	L 1-3	0-1		Johnson 74	(11,581)
31	31	EL	A	Sunderland	D 1-1	0-0		Johnson 61	(13,979)
32	J 2	EL	H	West Brom Albion	D 1-1	0-1	16	Trollope 57	16,035
33	7	FAC 3	A	Everton	L 0-1	0-0			(29,406)
34	14	EL	A	Charlton Athletic	W 4-3	1-3	13	Short 28, Gabbiadini 50, 87, Stallard 74	(9,389)
35	22	EL	H	Portsmouth	W 3-0	0-0	9	Simpson 47, 76, 89	11,143
36	F 4	EL	H	Sheffield United	L 2-3	1-1		Williams 22, Kauanagh 61	15,882
37	11	EL	A	Reading	L 0-1	0-1	13		(8,834)
38	21	EL	A	Port Vale	L 0-1	0-0	16		(9,387)
39	26	EL	H	Bolton Wanderers	W 2-1	0-1		Yates 82, Mills 85	11,003
40	M 4	EL	A	Stoke City	D 0-0	0-0	13		(13,462)
41	7	EL	A	Grimsby Town	W 1-0	0-0		Pembridge 88	(5,310)
42	11	EL	H	Millwall	W 3-2	1-1	10	Pembridge 11, Trollope 52, Gabbiadini 69	12,490
43	15	EL	H	Burnley	W 4-0	1-0		Mills 28, Trollope 51, Simpson 54, Gabbiadini 90	13,922
44	18	EL	A	Middlesbrough	W 4-2	3-0	8	Lee 18,29, Pembridge 44, Gabbiadini 65	(18,168)
45	25	EL	A	Oldham Athletic	L 0-1	0-1			(7,696)
46	A 1	EL	H	Bristol City	W 3-1	2-1	8	Gabbiadini 6, Williams 15, Wrack 61	14,555
47	8	EL	H	Sunderland	L 0-1	0-1	8		15,442
48	12	EL	H	Wolverhampton Wand.	D 3-3	1-1		Simpson 35 (pen), 63, Gabbiadini 52	16,040
49	15	EL	A	Burnley	L 1-3	0-2	8	Trollope 68	(11,534)
50	17	EL	H	Tranmere Rovers	W 5-0	2-0		Pembridge 32, 57, Mills 45, Williams 53, Gabbiadini 62	13,957
51	22	EL	A	West Brom Albion	D 0-0	0-0	7		(15,265)
52	29	EL	H	Southend United	L 1-2	0-2	7	Mills 63	12,528
53	M 7	EL	A	Watford	L 1-2	0-1	9	Pembridge 71	(8,492)
54									
55									
56									
57									
58									
59									
60									

Best Home League Attendance: 16,035 v West Bromwich Albion   **Smallest:** 11,003 v Bolton Wanderers   **Av Home Att:** 13,520

Goal Scorers:

Compared with 1993-94: - 2,417

League (66): Gabbiadini 9, Pembridge 8, Johnson 7, Simpson 7, Trollope 4, Mills 3, Short 3, Williams 3, Charles 2, Carsley 2, Kitson 2, Hodge 2, Stallard, Kavanagh, Yates, Wrack
C/Cola Cup (5): Gabbiadini 2, Simpson, Stallard, Williams
FA Cup (0):
Anglo/Ital Cup (11): Kitson 4, Hodge 2, Johnson 2, Pembridge, Stallard, Williams

1994-95

Taylor	Charles	Forsyth	Hayward	Short	Williams	Cowans	Gabbiadini	Kitson	Pembridge	Simpson	Harkes	Wassall	Sutton	Johnson	Kuhl	Nicholson	Kavanagh	Sturridge	Hodge	Stallard	Carsley	Guy	Trollope	Wrack	Sutton W.	Referee	
1	2	3*	4	5	6	7	8	9	10	11	12	14	S													I. Cruikshanks	1
1	2	3	4	5		7	12	9	10	11		6	S	8*	S											K. Breen	2
																											3
1	2	5	8			7*		9•	10	11		6	S			4	3	12	14							M. Pierce	4
1	2	3		5		7•		9	10	11		6	S					12	8	4*	14					E. Wolstenholme	5
1	2	3		5		7		9	10	12	11*	6	S					S	8	4						A. Flood	6
																											7
1	2	3		5	6	7	8	9	10	S		S	S							4	11					G. Singh	8
1	2	3		5	6	7	8	9*	10	12		S	S							4	11					P. Vanes	9
1	2	3		5	6	7	8*	9	10	12	14	S								4	11•					N. Barry	10
1	2	3		5	6	7	8		10	S	4	S	S	9							11					P. Alcock	11
1	2	3		5	6	7	8		10	12	14	S	9*						4		11•					J. Winter	12
1	2	3		5	6	7	8		10	14	4*	11	S	9•							12					K. Cooper	13
1	2	3		5	6	7*			10	9	11•	12	S						8	4	14					M. Brandwood	14
																											15
1	2	3			6	7			10	S		5	S					S	8	4						J. Holbrook	16
1*	2	3		5	6	7			10*	12•	11	14	G					8	4		9					G. Pooley	17
	2	3		5	6	7				11•		S	1	10				9	4	12	8	S				D. Allison	18
	2	3		5	6	7	10			11•		4	1*	9*		14		S		12	8	G				S. Dunn	19
	2	3		5	6	7	10			11		4	1	9		S		S		8	S					W. Burns	20
	2	3		5	6	7	10			11		4	1	9		S		S		8	S					E. Lomas	21
	2	3*			6	7	10			11		5	1	9	4•	14		12		8	S					K. Lupton	22
																											23
				5	6					11	7	S	1	9	4	3	2	S	10		8	S				P. Harrison	24
				5	6					11	7	S	1	9	4	3	2	S	10		8	S				J. Lloyd	25
				5	6					11	7*	S	1	9	4	3	2	12	10		8	S				J. Kirkby	26
				5	6					11	7	S	1	9	4	3	2	S	10		8	S				P. Wright	27
				5	6	S				11	7	S	1	9	4	2	3		10		8	S				K. Cooper	28
		3			6	S				11*	7	5	1	9	4		2		10		8	S	12			T. Heilbron	29
	2				6	12				11*	7	5	1	9	4		3		10		8	S	S			A. Flood	30
		3*		5	6					7	14	1	9		11		2		10		8	S	4	12•		J. Winter	31
				5	6					11	7*	S	1		3		2		10		8	S	4	9		R. Poulain	32
	12			5	6				10	11	7		1		3		2	9•			8	S		12	4*	G. Ashby	33
	6			5					10	11	7		1		3		2	9			8	S	S	14	S	P. Vanes	34
	6			5*					10	11	7		1		3		2	9			S	2	12	8		I. Cruikshanks	35
	12			5	6				10	11	7		1		3*		2	9	7*		S	4	14	8*		T. Heilbron	36
				5	6				10	11	12		1		3		3	9•			8	S	4	14		P. Rejer	37
				5	6				10	11	12	2*	1		3			9•			8	S	4	14		J. Watson	38
				5					10	11	7		1		3		2				8*	S	4	12		M. Bailey	39
				5					10	8	11	7	12		3		2*				S	4	S		E. Lomas	40
				5					10	8	11	7	2		3			S			S	4	14		J. Rushton	41
				5	6				10	8•	11	7	12								S	4	14		W. Burns	42
				5•					10	8	11	7	3								S	4	14		G. Cain	43
				5	6				10	8	11	7	3*				12				S	4	12	S	P. Wright	44
				5					10	8	11	7	3		12						S	4	14		K. Lupton	45
					6				10	8	11•	7	3	S			5	14				4	12		J. Kirkby	46
			4						10	7	9•	5	3	S	2	12						8	6*		V. Rennie	47
				5	6				10	8	11•	7	3	S	2						S	4	S	S	J. Holbrook	48
				5	6				10	8	11•	7	3	S	2*							4	14		A. Butler	49
				5	6				10	8	11	7	3	S							S	4	S	S	K. Leach	50
				5	6				10	8	11	7	3	S								4	12	S	T. Heilbron	51
					6				10	8•	11	7		S			5	14				4		12	J. Parker	52
					6				10•	8	7	2	1				5	14			S	4		3*	R. Harris	53
12	17	21	3	35	35	16	30	8	26	40	31	31	19	12	8	15	24	12	10	16	22	0	23	15	4	League Appearances	
0	0	0	0	0	0	1	1	0	0	2	0	6	11	0	1	0	4	4	0	2	0	24	1	5	5	League Sub Appearances	
2	3	3	0	4	4	3	3	0	2	3+1	2	2+2	2+2	4	1	1	2	1	0	2	4	1+1	0	1	1	C/Cola Cup Appearances	
0	0	1	0	1	0	1	0	0	1	0	1	1	0	0	1	0	0	1	0	0	1	0+1	0	1	1	FA Cup Appearances	

Also Played: Yates 2(37,42,43*,44,45,46*),4(38),6(39), Mills 9(39,30,41,42,43,44*,45•,46,48,49,50,51,52,53), Davies 9(16), 12(32,35), Parkes 11(16), Hoult S(38),1(39,40,41,42,43,44,45,46,47,48,49,50,51,52), Cooper S(28,39)12(53), Ashbee 3(52*), Boden 14(47),12(49),2(50,51*,52),11(53)

219

DERBY COUNTY

CLUB RECORDS

BIGGEST VICTORIES
League: 9-0 v Wolverhampton Wanderers, 10.1.1891.
9-0 v Sheffield Wednesday, Division 1, 2.1.1899.
F.A. Cup: 8-1 v Barnsley, 1st Round, 30.1.1897.
League Cup: 7-0 v Southend, 2nd Round 2nd leg, 7.10.1992.
Europe: (UEFA) 12-0 v Finns Harps, 3rd Round, 15.9.1976.

BIGGEST DEFEATS
League: 0-8 v Blackburn Rovers, Division 1, 3.1.1891.
0-8 v Sunderland, Division 1, 1.9.1894.
F.A. Cup: 2-11 v Everton, 1st Round, 18.1.1890.
League Cup: 0-5 v Southampton, 8.10.1974.
0-5 v West Ham United, 3rd Round, 1.11.1988.
Europe: (UEFA) 1-5 v Real Madrid, 2nd Round, 5.11.1975.

MOST POINTS
3 points a win: 84, Division 3, 1985-86. Division 2, 1986-87.
2 points a win: 63, Division 3(N) 1955-56 & 1956-57, Division 2 1968-69.

MOST GOALS SCORED
111, Division 3(N), 1956-57.
Straw 37, Woodhead 14, Ryan 12, Brown 9, Parry 7, Crowshaw 5, Buchanan 5, Barrowcliffe 4, Ackerman 4, Mays 4, Powell 1, Pye 1, Davies 1, Wyer 1, Opponents 5.

MOST GOALS CONCEDED
90, Division 1, 1936-37.

MOST FIRST CLASS MATCHES IN A SEASON
64 - 1992-93 (League 46, FA Cup 5, League Cup 4, Anglo-Italian 9).

MOST LEAGUE WINS
28, Division 3(N), 1955-56.

MOST LEAGUE DRAWS
19, Division 1, 1976-77. Division 2, 1982-83.

MOST LEAGUE DEFEATS
26, Division 2, 1954-55.

INDIVIDUAL CLUB RECORDS

MOST GOALS IN A SEASON
Jack Bowers: 39 goals in 1930-31 (League 37, FAC 2).

MOST GOALS IN A MATCH
6. Steve Bloomer v Sheffield Wednesday, Division 1, 2.1.1899.

OLDEST PLAYER
Peter Shilton, 42 years 164 days v Watford, Division 2, 29.2.1992.

YOUNGEST PLAYER
Steve Powell, 16 years 33 days v Arsenal, Division 1, 23.10.1971.

MOST CAPPED PLAYER
Peter Shilton (England) 34.

BEST PERFORMANCES

League: 1956-57: Matches played 46, Won 26, Drawn 11, Lost 9, Goals for 111, Goals against 53, Points 63. First in Division 3(N).
Highest Position: Division 1 Champions 1971-72, 1974-75.
F.A. Cup: 1945-46: 3rd Round Luton Town 6-0,3-0; 4th Round West Bromwich Albion 1-0,3-1; 5th Round Brighton & H.A. 4-1,6-0; 6th Round Aston Villa 4-3,1-1; Semi-Final Birmingham City 1-1,4-0; Final Charlton 4-1.
League Cup: 1967-68: 2nd Round Hartlepool United 4-0; 3rd Round Birmingham City 3-1; 4th Round Lincoln City 1-1,3-1; 5th Round Darlington 5-4; Semi-Final Leeds United 0-1,2-3.
Europe: (European Cup) 1972-73: 1st Round Zelj Znicars 2-0,2-1; 2nd Round Benefica 3-0,0-0; 3rd Round Spartak Trnava 0-1,2-0; Semi-Final Juventus 1-3,0-0.

ADDITIONAL INFORMATION
PREVIOUS NAMES
None.

PREVIOUS LEAGUES
None.

Club colours: White shirts with black sleeves, gold piping, black shorts, white socks.
Change colours: Blue shirts & shorts, gold piping, black socks.

Reserves League: Pontins Central League Division 1.

DIVISIONAL RECORD

	Played	Won	Drawn	Lost	For	Against	Points
Division 1	2,202	838	515	849	3,493	3,490	2,236
Division 2/1	1,420	576	346	497	2,230	2,033	1,635
Division 3	92	42	28	22	145	95	154
Division 3(N)	92	54	18	20	221	108	126
Total	3,806	1,510	907	1,389	6,089	5,708	4,151

RECORDS AND STATISTICS

COMPETITIONS

Div.1	Div.2/1	Div.3	Div.3(N)	Euro C	Texaco
1889-07	1907-12	1984-86	1955-57	1972-73	1971-72
1912-14	1914-15			1975-76	
1919-21	1921-26				Wat C
1926-53	1953-54			UEFA	1970
1969-80	1957-69			1974-75	
1987-91	1980-84			1976-77	
	1986-87				
	1991-				

HONOURS

Div.1	Div.2	Div 3(N)	FAC	Texaco
1971-72	1911-12	1956-57	1945-46	1971-72
1974-75	1914-15			
	1968-69		Wat C	C/S'ld
	1986-87		1970	1975

MOST APPEARANCES

Kevin Hector 581+8 (1966-82)

Year	League	FA Cup	Lge Cup	Other
1966-67	30	1		
1967-68	41	1	7	
1968-69	41	1	8	
1969-70	41	4	6	
1970-71	42	3	3	
1971-72	42	5	2	6
1972-73	41	5	3	8
1973-74	42	4	3	
1974-75	38	2	2	6
1975-76	29+3	2	2	4
1976-77	28+1	4	2	3
1977-78	11		2	
1980-81	25	2		
1981-82	27+4		2	
	478+8	34	42	27

MOST GOALS IN A CAREER

Steve Bloomer - 331 (1892-1914)

Year	League	FA Cup
1892-93	11	
1893-94	19	
1894-95	10	
1895-96	22	5
1896-97	24	7
1897-98	15	5
1898-99	24	6
1899-1900	19	
1900-01	24	
1901-02	15	3
1902-03	12	1
1903-04	20	5
1904-05	13	
1905-06	12	
1910-11	20	4
1911-12	18	1
1912-13	13	1
1913-14	2	
Total	293	38

Current leading goalscorer: Marco Gabbiadini - 41 (1992-95)

RECORD TRANSFER FEE RECEIVED

Amount	Club	Player	Date
£2,900,000	Liverpool	Dean Saunders	7/91
£2,200,000	Liverpool	Mark Wright	6/91
£800,000	Millwall	Paul Goddard	12/89
£525,000	Aston Villa	Nigel Callaghan	2/89

RECORD TRANSFER FEE PAID

Amount	Club	Player	Date
£2,500,000	Notts County	Craig Short	9/92
£1,300,000	Notts County	Tommy Johnson	3/92
£1,200,000	Crystal Palace	Marco Gabbiadini	1/92
£1,000,000	Oxford United	Dean Saunders	10/88

MANAGERS

Name	Seasons	Best	Worst
Harry Newbould	1896-06	3(1)	15(1)
Jimmy Methvan	1906-22	7(1)	14(2)
Cecil Potter	1922-25	3(2)	14(2)
George Jobey	1925-41	2(1)	3(2)
Ted Magner	1941-46		
Stuart McMillan	1946-53	3(1)	22(1)
Jack Barker	1953-55	18(2)	22(2)
Harry Storer	1955-62	7(2)	2(3S)
Tim Ward	1962-67	8(2)	18(2)
Brian Clough	1967-73	1(1)	18(2)
Dave Mackay	1973-76	1(1)	4(1)
Colin Murphy	1976-77	15(1)	15(1)
Tommy Docherty	1977-79	12(1)	19(1)
Colin Addison	1979-81	19(1)	6(2)
John Newman	1981-83	13(2)	16(2)
Peter Taylor	1982-84	20(2)	20(2)
Arthur Cox	1984-93	5(1)	7(2)
Roy McFarland	1993-95	6(2/1)	6(2/1)
Jim Smith	1995-		

LONGEST LEAGUE RUNS

of undefeated matches:	22 (8.3.1969 - 25.10.1969)	of league matches w/out a win:	20 (1.12.1990 - 4.5.1991)
of undefeated home matches:	23 (5.10.1929 - 11.10.1930)	of undefeated away matches:	13 (18.1.1969 - 27.9.1969)
without home win:	9 (24.11.1990 - 4.5.1991)	without an away win:	33 (1.9.1919 - 2.4.1921)
of league wins:	9 (15.3.1969 - 9.8.1969)	of home wins:	12 (23.10.1971 - 1.4.1972)
of league defeats:	8 (3.4.1965 - 15.9.1965 & 12.12.87 - 10.2.88)	of away wins:	7 (3.10.1992 - 20.12.1992)

DERBY COUNTY

PLAYERS NAME Honours	Ht	Wt	Birthdate	Birthplace Transfers	Contract Date	Clubs	League	L/Cup	FA Cup	Other	Lge	L/C	FAC	Oth
G O A L K E E P E R S														
Russell Hoult	6.4	13.2	22.11.72	Leicester	28.03.91	Leicester City (T)	10	3		1				
				Loan	27.08.91	Lincoln City	2	1						
				Loan	22.07.93	Kettering Town								
				Loan	03.11.93	Bolton Wanderers	3+1							
				£200,000	.08.95	Derby County	15							
Andrew Quy	6.0	13.01	04.07.76	Harlow	12.07.94	Derby County								
Stephen J Sutton LC'89'90; SC'89	6.1	14.0	16.04.61	Hartington	16.04.79	Nottingham F. (A)	199	33	14	11				
				Loan	10.03.81	Mansfield Town	8							
				Loan	25.01.85	Derby County	14							
				Loan	01.02.91	Coventry	1							
				Loan	28.11.91	Luton Town	14							
				£300,000	06.03.92	Derby County	54+1	6	3	11				
Martin J Taylor	5.11	12.4	09.12.66	Tamworth		Mile Oak Rovers								
					02.07.86	Derby County	94	7	4	11				
				Loan	23.09.87	Carlisle United	10	1	1	2				
				Loan	17.12.87	Scunthorpe United	8							
D E F E N D E R S														
Ian Asbee	6.1	12.10	06.09.76	Birmingham	09.11.94	Derby County (T)	1							
Christopher D Boden	5.9	11.0	13.10.73	Wolverh'ton	03.12.91	Aston Villa (T)	0+1							
				Loan	15.10.93	Barnsley	4							
				£150,000	23.03.95	Derby County	4+2							
Lee K Carsley	5.11	11.11	28.04.74	Birmingham	31.05.94	Derby County (T)	22+1	3+1	1	3	2			
Jason C Kavanagh E: Y14, S	5.9	11.0	23.11.71	Meriden	09.12.88	Derby County (T)	66+24	2+2	6	8+8	1			
Shane M Nicholson APL (GMVC)'88	5.10	11.0	03.03.70	Newark	19.07.88	Lincoln City (T)	122+11	8+3	6	7+1	7		1	
				£100,000	22.04.92	Derby County	44	1	3	5	1		1	
Stephen Round FLg u18.1	5.10	11.0	09.11.70	Burton	13.07.89	Derby County (T)	8+1							
Wayne F Sutton	6.0	13.02	01.10.75	Derby	31.05.94	Derby County (T)								
Andrew T Tretton	6.1	12.07	09.10.76	Derby	31.05.94	Derby Coutny (T)								
Darren P Wassall FMC'92	5.11	12.3	27.06.68	Birmingham	01.06.86	Nottingham F. (A)	17+10	6+2	3+1	4+2				1
				Loan	23.10.87	Hereford United	5		1	1				
				Loan	02.03.89	Bury	7				1			
				£600,000	15.06.92	Derby County	74+7	8	4	11				
Dean Yates E: u21.5	6.1	11.0	26.10.67	Leicester	14.06.85	Notts County (A)	291+2	20	20	32	33			4
				£350,000	26.01.95	Derby County	11			1	1			
M I D F I E L D														
Kevin L Cooper	5.6	10.7	08.02.75	Derby	31.05.94	Derby County (T)	0+1			0+1				
Sean M Flynn	5.7	11.2	13.03.68	Birmingham		Halesowen Town			5				2	
				£20,000	03.12.91	Coventry City	90+7	5	3		9	1		
				£225,000	.08.95	Derby County								
Matthew R Green	5.8	11.04	22.10.75	Northampton	12.07.94	Derby County (T)								
John A Harkes USA: ; LC'91	5.10	11.10	08.03.67	New Jersey (USA)		North Carolina Uni								
				£70,000	03.10.90	Sheffield Wed	59+22	17	12+1	7	7	3	1	
					17.08.93	Derby County	60+6	5		6	2			1
Stephen R Powell	5.9	11.05	14.05.76	Derby	31.05.94	Derby COunty (T)								
Gary Rowett	6.0	12.0	06.03.74	Bromsgrove	10.09.91	Cambridge Utd (T)	51+12	7	5+2	5	9	1		2
				£200,000	21.05.94	Everton	0+2							
				£300,000	.08.95	Derby County								
Paul D Simpson E: u21.5, Y2	5.6	11.3	26.07.66	Carlisle	04.08.83	Manchester City (A)	99+22	10+1	10+2	8+3	18	2	4	
				£200,000	31.10.88	Oxford United	138+6	10	9	5	43	3	2	2
				£500,000	02.02.92	Derby County	112+15	8+1	3+1	14+2	36	4		2
Paul J Trollope	6.0	12.2	03.06.72	Swindon	23.12.89	Swindon Town (T)								
				Free	26.03.92	Torquay United	85+3	5+1	3	6+1	12	1		
				Loan	16.12.94	Derby County	4+1				1			
				£100,000	19.01.95	Derby County	19				3			
Robin Van der Laan AGT'93	5.10	12.0	05.09.68	Sceidam		Wageningen								
				£80,000	21.02.91	Port Vale	111+21	8	7+1	11+1	19	1	1	1
				£475,000	.08.95	Derby County								
F O R W A R D S														
William Davies	6.2	13.4	27.09.75	Derby	12.07.94	Derby County (T)	1+1			1+1				

DERBY COUNTY

PLAYERS NAME / Honours	Ht	Wt	Birthdate	Birthplace Transfers	Contract Date	Clubs	League	L/Cup	FA Cup	Other	Lge	L/C	FAC	Oth
Marco Gabbiadini	5.10	12.4	20.01.68	Nottingham	05.09.85	York City (A)	42+18	4+3		4	14	1		3
E: B1, u21.2, Y; FLgXl.2; Div3'88				£80,000	23.09.87	Sunderland	155+2	14	5	9	75	9		4
				£1,800,000	01.10.91	Crystal Palace	15	6	1	3	5	1		1
				£1,000,000	31.01.92	Derby County	125+10	9	7	16+1	39	6	2	8
Darryl Powell	6.0	12.3	15.11.71	Lambeth	22.12.88	Portsmouth (T)	49+49	6+3	8	9+5	11			4
				£750,000	.08.95	Derby County								
Mark Stallard	6.0	12.6	24.10.74	Derby County	06.11.91	Derby County (T)	16+8	1+1	2+2	3	2	1		1
				Loan	23.09.94	Fulham								
Dean C Sturridge	5.7	10.10	26.07.73	Birmingham	01.07.91	Derby County (T)	16+7	0+1		2+1	1			
Darren Wrack	5.9	11.10	05.05.74	Cleethorpe	12.07.94	Derby County (T)								
Nicholas J Wright	5.11	11.02	15.10.75	Derby	12.07.94	Derby County (T)								

ADDITIONAL CONTRACT PLAYER

Ron Willems						Grasshoppers -Zurich								
				£300,000	.08.95	Derby County								

TOP GOALSCORER 1994/95
Marco Gabbiadini

Division One Goals (games) . . . . 9 (28+2)
Coca-Cola Cup Goals 2 (3)
F.A. Cup goals 0 (1)

Total . . . . **11 (32+2)**

Total goals for Derby since 31.01.92 . . . . 52 (153+11)

Career total as at June 1st 1995 . . . . 165 (411+34)

THE MANAGER
JIM SMITH

Date of Birth . . . . 17th November 1940.
Place of Birth . . . . Sheffield.
Date of Appointment . . . . August 1995.

PREVIOUS CLUBS
As Manager . . . . Boston Utd, Colchester Utd, Blackburn Rovers,
. . . . Birmingham City, Oxford Utd, Q.P.R., Newcaslte Utd, Portsmouth.
As Coach . . . . Middlesbrough.
As a Player . . . . Sheffield Utd, Aldershot, Halifax Town, Lincoln City,
. . . . Boston Utd, Colchester Utd.

HONOURS
As a Manager
Colchester Utd: Promotion to Division 3, 1974.
Birmingham City: Promotion to Division 1, 1980.
Oxford United: Division 3 Championship, 1984. Division 2 Championship, 1983.

As a Player
None.

BASEBALL GROUND

Shaftesbury Crescent, Derby DE3 8NB
Tel: 01332 40105

Capacity...17,300 (while rebuilding work continues).
Should be 25,000 for 1996-97.

First game ....v Sunderland, 2-0, 14.9.1885.
First floodlit game...
Internationals ....England v Ireland, 9.3.1895.

ATTENDANCES
Highest ....41,826 v Tottenham, Div. 1, 20.9.1969.
Lowest...1,990 v W.B.A., 27.10.1894.

OTHER GROUNDS ....Race Course Ground 1884-95. Baseball Ground since 1895.

MATCHDAY TICKET PRICES

Adults . . . . £12 & £11
Concessions £6

Normanton Lower Tier £7
Concessions £4

Ticket Office Telephone no. 01332 40105

CLUBCALL
0891 12 11 87

Calls cost 39p per minute cheap rate and 49p per
minute at all other times.
Call costings correct at time of going to press.

HOW TO GET TO THE GROUND

From the North
Follow signs to Derby (A38) into Town Centre, then follow signs to Melbourne
(A514). Then on nearside of Railway Bridge turn right into Shaftesbury Street for
Derby County FC.

From East, South and West
Use Derby Ring Road, from East and South (sign posted Burton) and from West
(sign posted Nottingham), as far as junction with A514, then follow signs to Town
Centre into Osmaston Road. In 1.3 miles turn left into Shaftesbury Street for
Derby County FC.

Car Parking
Eight parks within half-a-mile of the ground run by club in co-operation with local
corporation. Street parking within same distance.

Nearest Railway Station
Derby Midland (-1332 32051)
Ramsline Halt (Specials only)

MATCHDAY PROGRAMME

Programme Editor . . . . I. Guildford.

Number of pages . . . . 40.

Price . . . . £1.50.

Subscriptions. . . . . £49.99 per season.

Local Newspapers. . . . . Derby Evening Telegraph.

Local Radio Stations . . . BBC Radio Derby, Radio Trent (Commercial).

GRIMSBY TOWN
(The Mariners)
ENDSLEIGH LEAGUE DIVISION 1
SPONSORED BY: 'EUROPES FOOD TOWN'

Back Row (L-R): Simon Buckley, Neil Woods, Jimmy Neil, Peter Handyside, Paul Crichton, Jason Pearcey, Graham Rodger, Stewart Petchley, Mark Lever, Joby Gowshall, Mark Brookes.
Middle Row: Mike Bielby (Kit Manager), Nicky Southall, Tommy Watson, Craig Shakespeare, Jack Lester, Steve Livingstone, Ashley Fickling, Jim Dobbin, Paul Groves, Gerry Delahunt (Physio).
Front Row: Kevin Jobling, Clive Mendonca, Gary Childs, Kenny Swain (Asst. Manager), Brian Laws (Manager), John Cockerill (Yth Manager), John McDermott, Gary Croft.

GRIMSBY TOWN
FORMED IN 1878
TURNED PROFESSIONAL IN 1890
LTD COMPANY IN 1890

LIFE PRESIDENT
T J Lindley, T Wilkinson
CHAIRMAN: W H Carr
VICE-CHAIRMAN: T Aspinall
DIRECTORS
P W Furneaux, J Teanbyl, G Lamming,
J Mager
SECRETARY
Ian Fleming (01472 697 111)
COMMERCIAL MANAGER
Tony Richardson

MANAGER: Brian Laws
ASSISTANT MANAGER: Kenny Swain
RESERVE TEAM MANAGER
Kenny Swain
YOUTH TEAM MANAGER
John Cockerill
PHYSIOTHERAPIST
Gerry Deldholt

STATISTICIAN FOR THE DIRECTORY
Les Triggs

There is little doubt that this season was dominated as much by events off the field as those on. The long expected departure of manager Alan Buckley came at the end of October, when he took over at West Bromwich Albion, the circumstances being exacerbated by the fact that he took his entire management team with him and that all this occurred whilst the club chairman was out of the country.

Former player and 'Football in the Community' officer John Cockerill was given temporary charge of the side who proceeded to have one of their best spells of the season, rising to fourth position in the first division table. It was to great surprise and chagrin of supporters, therefore, that both Cockerill and veteran Paul Futcher were passed over and Nottingham Forest pair Brian Laws and Kenny Swain were imported to take over the team.

Almost immediately Futcher left the club in circumstances which remain shrouded in mystery. His notable lack of success in charge of Darlington seems to indicate that he was not yet ready for management.

All this seemed to be too much for chairman Peter Furneaux, who very soon afterwards relinquished this office. In these circumstances the new team of Laws and Swain had some difficulty in winning over the fans. That they have done so is great tribute to them.

On the field it has been the season of the sucker punch. Ten league goals have been conceded in the last five minutes of matches, lapses that undoubtedly cost the side a place in the divisional play-offs. Following a somewhat uncertain start to the season, apart from a slight lapse following the installation of the new management team the Mariners maintained a position on the fringe of the play-offs for most of the season. However, a spell in March and early April saw both key strikers, Clive Mendonca and Neil Woods, out of action which killed off any lingering hopes of promotion. The final League position of tenth just failed to equal the ninth position of two seasons ago, which was the best of the Buckley era; although in terms of performance this season was slightly better in comparison of both goals scored and points gained.

In both major Cup competitions the Mariners fell at the first fence.

The bright light remains the performance of young defenders Peter Handyside and Gary Croft. Handyside again appeared at U21 level for Scotland and Croft made his debut at under-21 level in the Toulon Tournament, Croft indeed went on to receive both Player of the Year and Young Player of the Year awards.

The consistent failure of the club to draw spectators in spite of playing attractive football remains a cloud on the horizon. The attendance of 3,216 who turned up for the home game against Port Vale in September was the poorest for any club in the first division throughout the season.

With a million pounds having to be spent merely to update the ground on a temporary basis, pending possible re-location, and with ground capacity reduced to 8,607 with the elimination of standing areas, it seems that any prospect of strengthening the side is faint. Indeed the probability of having to sell the clubs rising stars in order to survive cannot be ignored. **LES TRIGGS**

GRIMSBY TOWN

Division One: 10th   **FA Cup:** 3rd Round   **Coca-Cola Cup:** 1st Round

M	DATE	COMP.	VEN	OPPONENTS	RESULT	H/T	LP	GOAL SCORERS/GOAL TIMES	ATT.
1	A 13	EL	H	Bolton Wanderers	D 3-3	1-2		Mendonca 9, 55, 70 (pen)	8,393
2	16	CC 1/1	A	**Bradford City**	L 1-2	0-0		**Gilbert 48**	(5,986)
3	20	EL	A	Watford	D 0-0	0-0	13		(6,324)
4	23	CC 1/2	H	**Bradford City**	L 1-2	1-2		**Groves 43**	3,498
5	27	EL	H	Tranmere Rovers	W 3-1	2-0	5	Livingstone 5, 41, Groves 74	4,087
6	30	EL	A	Sunderland	D 2-2	1-1		Childs 45, Mendonca 90 (pen)	15,788
7	S 3	EL	A	Derby County	L 1-2	0-1	13	Mendonca 60	12,027
8	10	EL	H	Charlton Athletic	L 0-1	0-0	17		3,970
9	13	EL	H	Port Vale	W 4-1	1-0	8	Woods 30, Mendonca 54, 79, Gilbert 86	14,496
10	17	EL	A	W.B.A.	D 1-1	0-1	12	Shakespeare 66	14,496
11	24	EL	A	Swindon Town	L 2-3	1-1	14	Woods 38, Groves 77	(8,219)
12	O 1	EL	H	Portsmouth	W 2-0	1-0	10	Mendonca 17 (pen), Woods 90	4,172
13	8	EL	H	Sheffield United	D 0-0	0-0	14		8,930
14	15	EL	A	Woverhampton Wand.	L 1-2	1-1	17	Groves 43	(24,447)
15	22	EL	H	Bristol City	W 1-0	0-0	11	Childs 61	4,024
16	29	EL	A	Southend United	D 0-0	0-0	13		(5,086)
17	N 1	EL	A	Luton Town	W 2-1	0-0	8	Gilbert 71, 90	(5,839)
18	5	EL	H	Middlesbrough	W 2-1	2-0	6	Woods 4, Dobbin 11	8,488
19	12	EL	H	Millwall	W 1-0	0-0	5	Woods 47	5,261
20	19	EL	A	Stoke city	L 0-3	0-2	6		(12,055)
21	26	EL	H	Burnley	D 2-2	1-0	7	Woods 43, Gilbert 67	7,084
22	D 3	EL	A	Bristol City	W 2-1	0-0	4	Gilbert 47, Childs 73	(6,060)
23	10	EL	H	Watford	D 0-0	0-0	8		6,288
24	17	EL	A	Bolton W	D 3-3	2-1	8	Woods 5, Jubling 8, Groves 90	(10,552)
25	26	EL	A	Barnsley	L 1-4	1-2	9	Woods 7	(8,669)
26	27	EL	H	Oldham Athletic	L 1-3	0-2	13	Woods 90	6,958
27	31	EL	A	Reading	D 1-1	1-0	12	Shakespeare 27	(8,526)
28	J 7	FAC 3	H	**Norwich City**	L 0-1	0-0			11,198
29	14	EL	H	Southend	W 4-1	1-0	8	Shakespeare 42, Groves 54, Woods 56, Croft 63	3,915
30	21	EL	A	Middlesbrough	D 1-1	0-0	8	Woods 69	(15,360)
31	28	EL	H	Notts County	W 2-1	1-0	7	Woods 43, Mondonca 81	5,161
32	F 4	EL	A	Millwall	L 0-2	0-1	8		(7,373)
33	11	EL	H	Luton Town	W 5-0	2-0	8	Dubbin 8, Gilbert 27, Woods 72, Watson 77, 85	4,615
34	18	EL	A	Burnley	W 2-0	1-0	7	Mendonca 25, 81	(10,511)
35	21	EL	H	Stoke City	D 0-0	0-0	7		6,384
36	25	EL	A	Portsmouth	L 1-2	1-1	7	Rudger 45	(8,274)
37	M 4	EL	H	Swindon Town	D 1-1	1-0	7	Watson 23	4,934
38	7	EL	H	Derby County	L 0-1	0-0	7		5,310
39	11	EL	A	Tranmere Rovers	L 0-2	0-2	9		(15,810)
40	19	EL	H	Sunderland	W 3-1	1-0	9	Livingstone 29, 68, Forrester 90	5,697
41	21	EL	A	Charlton Athletic	L 1-2	1-1	10	Childs 15	(5,601)
42	25	EL	H	W.B.A.	L 0-2	0-1	10		7,393
43	A 1	EL	A	Port Vale	W 2-1	2-0	9	Livingstone 13, Laws 31	(7,150)
44	8	EL	H	Reading	W 1-0	0-0	9	Livingstone 63	4,519
45	15	EL	A	Oldham Athletic	L 0-1	0-1	10		(6,757)
46	17	EL	H	Barnsley	W 1-0	1-0	9	Woods 3	7,277
47	11	EL	A	Notts County	W 2-0	1-0	9	Livingstone 2, Reece (og) 58	(5,286)
48	29	EL	H	Wolverhampton Wand	D 0-0	0-0	9		10,112
49	M 6	EL	A	Sheffield United	L 1-3	1-2	10	Livingstone 45	(14,323)
50									
51									
52									
53									
54									
55									
56									
57									
58									
59									
60									

Best Home League Attendance: 10,115 v Wolverhampton Wanderers   **Smallest:** 3,216 v Port Vale   **Av Home Att:** 5,965

Goal Scorers:

League (62): Woods 14, Mendonca 11, Livingstone 8, Gilbert 6, Groves 5, Childs 4, Shakespeare 3, Watson 3, Dubbin 2, Jobling , Croft, Rodger, Forrester, Laws, Opponent

C/Cola Cup (2): Gilbert, Groves

FA Cup (0):

Compared with 1993-94: -169

Crichton	Jobling	Croft	Futcher	Lever	Shakespeare	Watson	Gilbert	Livingstone	Mendonca	Groves	Agnew	Lester	Woods	Handyside	Childs	Dobbin	McDermott	Rodger	Laws	Forrester	Fickling	Pearcey	Referee	
1	2	3	4	5	6	7*	8	9	10	11	12	S											T. Winter	1
1	2	3	4	5	6	7	8	9*	10	11	S		12										P. Richards	2
1		2	4	5	6	S	8	9	10	11	3		12	7									J. Lloyd	3
1		2	4	5*	6		8	9	10	11	3	12	14	7.									E. Parker	4
1		2	4	5	6		8	9	10	11	3	12	S	7*									P. Harrison	5
1	3	2	4	5*	6		8	9.	10	11			14		12	7							R. Burns	6
1	3	2	4	5	6		8	9.	10	11	12		14			7*							A. Flood	7
1		2	S	5	6		8*		10	11	3		9	4		7	12						K. Lupton	8
1		2		5	6		8	12	10	11	3		9*	4		7	S						J. Kirkby	9
1		2		5	6		8	14	10	11	3		9.	4		7*	12						K. Lynch	10
1		2	S	5	6		8	12	10	11	3		9*	4		7							T. Lunt	11
1	12	2		5	6		8		10	11	3	S	9	4		7*							I. Cruikshanks	12
1	3	2	S	5	6		8		10	11	12		9	4		7							K. Breen	13
1	3	2	14	5	6		8		10	11			9	4	12	7							K. Breen	14
1	3	2	S	5		7	11	9		6			10	4	12	8							M. Pierce	15
1	3	2		5		7	11	9		6	S		10	4	S	8							A. Dawson	16
1	3	2	S			7	11	9		6	12		10	4	S	8							G. Singh	17
1	3	2		5		7	11	9		6			10	4	S	8							P. Alcock	18
1	3	2		5		7	11	9		6			10	4	S	8							D. Allison	19
1	3	2		5		7*	11	9.		6			10	4	12	8	14						G. Cain	20
1	3	2		5		S	11	9.		6			10	4	7	8						S	J. Lloyd	21
1	3	2		5*			11	9.		6	14		10	4	7	8	12					S	R. Poulain	22
1	3	2					11	9		6	S		10	4	7	8	12	5				S	K. Cooper	23
1	3	2					11*	9^		6	S		10	4	7	8	12	5				S	E. Lomas	24
1	3			5		14	11	9*		6		12	10	4	7.	8		2				S	J. Winter	25
1	3			5	12	7	11	9.	14	6			10	4		8*		2				S	I. Cruikshanks	26
1	3					7	11*	9		6	12		10	4	S	8		5	2			S	P. Wright	27
1	14	3					11*	9		6		12	10	4	7.	8		5	2			S	A. D'Urso	28
1	2	3				7	11	9		6	S	S	10	4		8		5				S	G. Poll	29
1	2*	3		5		7.	11	9		6			10	4		8	12					S	W. Flood	30
1	2	3		5*		7	11	9		6			10	4	S	8						S	A. Dawson	31
1	2	3		5		7	11.	9		6			10	4	14	8	12					S	J. Brandwood	32
1		3		5*		7	11.	9		6			10	4	14	8	12	2				S	S. Dunn	33
1		3				7*	11	9		6			10	4	S	8	12	2	5			S	R. Furnandiz	34
1	3	2				7	11	9		6			10	4	S	8*	12	5				S	K. Leach	35
1	3					7.	11	9		6			10	4		8	12	2*	52			S	D. Babsk	36
1	3					7	11	9		6			10	4		8	12	2	5			S	D. Foulkes	37
1	3					14	11	9		6			10	4	7.	8*		2	5		S	S	T. Heilbron	38
1	3	2	S				11	9		6				4	7	8	12	52				S	J. Rushton	39
1	3	2	S				11	9		6				4	7	8		5	S			S	D. Allison	40
1	3	2	S				11	9		6				4	7	8		5	S	10		S	J. Kirkby	41
1	3	2	4		12		11.	9		6					7	8*	12	5		10		S	M. Pierce	42
1	3		4				11	9		6					7	8	14	5		10		S	J. Watson	43
1	3		4			7	11	9		6	12					8		5	2	10		S	A. Butler	44
1	3					7	11	9*		6	12					8		5	2	10*	S		K. Breen	45
1	3		4			7	11.	9*		6			10	4	14	8		5	2	10		S	G. Cain	46
S	3		4			7	11	9		6			10		S	8	12	5	2			S	J. Winter	47
S	3		4^			7	11	9		6			10			8	12	5	2		S	1	G. Singh	48
S	3	2	4		8		11.	9		6			10*		7		14	5	2		S	1	J. Poulain	49
																			12			1		50
																								51
																								52
																								53
																								54
																								55
																								56
																								57
																								58
																								59
																								60
43	37	44	6	31	16	20	46	29	21	46	7	1	33	34	18	35	8	20	6	7	1	3	League Appearances	
	1		1		3	1		5	1		3	5	4	1		7	3	4	1	10	2		League Sub Appearances	
2	1	2	2	2	1	2	2	2	2	2	1+1	0+1	0+1	1	1	1		1	1				C/Cola Appearances	
1		1			1		1		1	1		0+1	1	1		1			1	1			FA Cup Appearances	

Loan Players: D. (Blackburn), N. Colgan (Chelsea), J. Pearce (Mansfield), J. Forrester (Leeds)

GRIMSBY TOWN

CLUB RECORDS

BIGGEST VICTORIES
League: 9-2 v Darwen, Division 2, 15.4.1899.
7-0 v v Bristol Rovers (a), Division 2, 1957-58.
F.A. Cup: 10-0 v Boston, 2nd Round, 24.10.1981.
League Cup: 6-1 v Rotherham United, 2nd Round, 6.11.1984.

BIGGEST DEFEATS
League: 1-9 v Arsenal, Division 1, 28.1.1931.
F.A. Cup: 1-9 v Phoenix Bessemer, 2nd Round, 25.11.1982.
League Cup: 0-6 v Burnley, 2nd Round, 10.9.1968.

MOST POINTS
3 points a win: 83, Division 3, 1990-91.
2 points a win: 68, Division 3(N), 1955-56.

MOST GOALS SCORED
103, Division 2, 1933-34.
Glover 42, Craven 18, jennings 13, Bestall 11, Holmes 7, Kelly 3, Dyson 3, Ponting 2, Moralee 2, Dodds 1, Lewis 1.

MOST GOALS CONCEDED
111, Division 1, 1947-48.

MOST FIRST CLASS MATCHES IN A SEASON
59 - 1979-80 (League 46, FA Cup 4, League Cup 9).

MOST LEAGUE WINS
31, Division 3(N), 1955-56.

MOST LEAGUE DRAWS
20, Division 1, 1993-94.

MOST LEAGUE DEFEATS
28, Division 1, 1947-48.

INDIVIDUAL CLUB RECORDS

MOST GOALS IN A SEASON
Pat Glover: 43 goals in 1933-34 (League 42, FA Cup 1).

MOST GOALS IN A MATCH
6. Tommy McCairns v Leicester Fosse, Division 2, 11.4.1896.

OLDEST PLAYER
George Tweedy, 40 years 84 days v York City, 3.4.1953.

YOUNGEST PLAYER
Tony Ford, 16 years 143 days (Sub) v Walsall, 4.10.1975.

MOST CAPPED PLAYER
Pat Glover (Wales) 7.

BEST PERFORMANCES

League: 1925-26: Matches Played 42, Won 26, Drawn 9, Lost 7, Goals for 93, Goals against 40, Points 61. First in Division 3(N).
Highest Position: 5th Division 1, 1934-35.
F.A. Cup: Semi-finalists 1935-36.
Most recent success: 1938-39: 3rd Round Tranmere Rovers (h) 6-0; 4th round Millwall (a) 2-2, (h) 3-2; 5th Round Sheffield United (a) 0-0, (h) 1-0; 6th Round, Chelsea (a) 1-0; Semi-Final Wolverhampton Wndrs. 0-5.
League Cup: 5th Round 1979-80.
Most Recent success: 1984-85: 2nd Round Barnsley (h) 3-0, (a) 1-1; 3rd Round Rotherham United (a) 0-0, (h) 6-1; 4th Round Everton (a) 1-0; 5th Round Norwich City (h) 0-1.

ADDITIONAL INFORMATION
PREVIOUS NAMES
Grimsby Pelham.

PREVIOUS LEAGUES
Football Alliance; Midland League (1910).

Club colours: Black & white striped shirts, black shorts and white socks.
Change colours: Red & blue striped shirts, blue shorts and red socks.

Reserves League: Pontins Central League.
Youth: Midland Purity League.

DIVISIONAL RECORD

	Played	Won	Drawn	Lost	For	Against	Points
Division 1	488	167	97	224	756	940	431
Division 2/1	1,748	651	386	711	2,648	2,783	1,832
Division 3	690	272	170	248	976	913	750
Division 3(S)	42	15	9	18	49	59	39
Division 3(N)	432	200	85	147	672	534	485
Division 4	368	155	92	121	520	460	441
Total	3,768	1,460	839	1,469	5,621	5,689	3,978

RECORDS AND STATISTICS

COMPETITIONS

Div.1	Div.2/1	Div.3	Div.3(N)	Div.4
1901-03	1892-01	1920-21	1921-26	1968-72
1929-32	1903-10	1959-62	1951-56	1977-79
1934-48	1911-20	1964-68		1988-90
	1926-29	1972-77		
	1932-34	1979-80		
	1948-51	1987-88		
	1956-59	1990-91		
	1962-64			
	1980-87			
	1991-			

HONOURS

Div.2	Div.3(N)	Div.3	Div.4
1900-01	1925-26	1979-80	1971-72
1933-34	1955-56		

MOST GOALS IN A CAREER

Pat Glover - 197 (1930-39)

Year	League	FA Cup
1930-31	2	
1931-32	12	4
1932-33	22	2
1933-34	42	1
1934-35	34	2
1935-36	31	4
1936-37	29	4
1937-38	4	
1938-39	4	
Total	180	17

MOST APPEARANCES

Keith Jobling 493 (1953-66)

Year	League	FA Cup	Lge Cup
1953-54	9		
1954-55	6	1	
1956-57	6		
1957-58	13		
1958-59	42	3	
1959-60	42	2	
1960-61	36	1	1
1961-62	46	1	1
1962-63	41	1	1
1963-64	41	1	1
1964-65	46	4	2
1965-66	42	6	5
1966-67	21	2	4
1967-68	18	1	
1968-69	41	1	4
	450	24	19

RECORD TRANSFER FEE RECEIVED

Amount	Club	Player	Date
£650,000	Sunderland	Shaun Cunnington	7/92
£500,000	Q.P.R.	Andy Tillson	12/90
£300,000	Everton	Paul Wilkinson	8/85
£125,000	Aston Villa	Terry Donovan	7/79

RECORD TRANSFER FEE PAID

Amount	Club	Player	Date
£140,000	Chelsea	Steve Livingstone	10/93
£135,000	Luton Town	Graham Rodger	1/92
£115,000	W.B.A.	Craig Shakespeare	7/93
£110,000	Watford	Jimmy Gilligan	7/85

MANAGERS

Name	Seasons	Best	Worst
Hayden Price	1920		
George Fraser	1921-24	3(3N)	14(3N)
Wilf Gillow	1924-32	13(1)	12(3N)
Frank Womack	1932-36	5(1)	13(2)
Charles Spencer	1937-51	16(1)	22(2)
Bill Shankly	1951-54	2(3N)	17(3N)
Bill Walsh	1954-55	17(3N)	23(3N)
Allenby Chilton	1955-59	13(2)	23(3N)
Tim Ward	1960-62	2(3)	6(3)
Tom Johnston	1962-64	19(2)	21(2)
Jimmy McGuigan	1964-67	10(3)	17(3)
Don McEvoy	1967-68	22(3)	22(3)
Bill Harvey	1968-69	22(3)	23(4)
Bobby Kennedy	1969-71	16(4)	23(4)
Lawrie McMenemy	1971-73	9(3)	19(4)
Ron Ashman	1973-75	6(3)	16(3)
Tommy Casey	1975-76	16(3)	18(3)
John Newman	1977-79	2(4)	6(4)
George Kerr	1979-82	7(2)	1(3)
Dave Booth	1982-85	5(2)	19(2)
Mick Lyons	1985-87	15(2)	21(2)
Bobby Roberts	1987-88	22(3)	22(3)
Alan Buckley	1988-94	9(2/1)	9(4)
Brain Laws	1994-	10(1)	10(1)

LONGEST LEAGUE RUNS

of undefeated matches:	19 (16.2.1980 - 30.8.1980)	of league matches w/out a win:	18 (10.10.1981 - 16.3.1982)
of undefeated home matches:	33 (8.10.1974 - 28.2.1976)	of undefeated away matches:	9 (23.2.80-30.8.80, 19.11.83-10.3.84)
without home win:	12 (27.9.1947 - 17.3.1948)	without an away win:	23 (2.10.1982 - 28.10.1983)
of league wins:	11 (19.1.1952 - 29.3.1952)	of home wins:	17 (9.3.1894 - 28.3.1895)
of league defeats:	9 (30.11.1907 - 18.1.1908)	of away wins:	5 (26.1.1952 - 22.3.1952)

GRIMSBY TOWN

PLAYERS NAME / Honours	Ht	Wt	Birthdate	Birthplace / Transfers	Contract Date	Clubs	League	L/Cup	FA Cup	Other	Lge	L/C	FAC	Oth
G O A L K E E P E R S														
Paul A Crichton	6.0	12.1	03.10.68	Pontefract	23.05.86	Nottingham Forest								
Loan Notts County, (19.9.86), 5Lg Apps.				Loan	30.01.87	Darlington	5							
Loan Peterborough, (27.03.87), 4 Lg Apps.				Loan	28.09.87	Darlington	3	1		1				
Loan Swindon Town, (24.12.87), 4Lg Apps.				Loan	09.03.88	Rotherham United	6							
				Loan	25.08.88	Torquay United	13	2						
					03.11.88	Peterborough Utd	47		5	3				
				Free	25.08.90	Doncaster Rovers	77	5	3	5				
				Free	09.07.93	Grimsby Town	89	5	3	2				
Jason Pearcey	6.1	13.5	23.07.71	Leamington	18.07.89	Mansfield Town (T)	74	5	2	6				
				Loan	03.11.94	Grimsby Town								
					16.12.94	Grimsby Town	3							
D E F E N D E R S														
Gary Croft	5.9	1.8	17.02.74	Burton-on-Trent	07.07.92	Grimsby Town (T)	103+10	5	3+2	3	2	1		
Ashley Fickling	5.10	11.0	15.11.72	Sheffield	26.07.91	Sheffield United		1						
E: u18.8				Loan	26.11.92	Darlington	14			1				
				Loan	12.08.93	Darlington	1	1						
				Free	23.03.95	Grimsby Town	1							
Joby Gowshall			07.08.75	Peterlee	13.07.94	Grimsby Town (T)								
Peter D Handyside	6.1	12.3	31.07.74	Dumfries	21.11.92	Grimsby Town (T)	56+3	3	3	4				
S: u21.4														
Mark Lever	6.3	12.8	29.03.70	Beverley	09.08.88	Grimsby Town (T)	213+6	15+1	10+1	9	7			
John McDermott	5.7	10.0	03.02.69	Middlesbrough	01.06.87	Grimsby Town (T)	263+13	17+1	16+1	11	4			
James D Neil	5.8	10.05	28.02.76	Bury St Ed.	13.07.94	Grimsby Town (T)								
Graham Rodger	6.2	11.13	01.04.67	Glasgow		Wolves (A)	1							
E: u21.4; FAC'87				Free	18.02.85	Coventry City	31+5	3+1	1+1	0+1	2			
				£150,000	01.08.89	Luton Town	27+1	2		3	2			
				£135,000	08.01.92	Grimsby Town	83+8	3	5	2	9			
M I D F I E L D														
Mark Brookes	5.9	10.06	19.09.75	Nottingham	23.02.95	Grimsby Town (T)								
Simon J Buckley	5.10	11.0	29.02.76	Stafford	12.07.94	Grimsby Town (T)								
James Dobbin	5.9	10.7	17.09.63	Dunfermline		Celtic	1+1	4					1	
S: Y				Loan	01.02.84	Motherwell	1+1							
				£25,000	19.03.84	Doncaster Rovers	56+8	5	2	3	13	1		
				£35,000	19.09.86	Barnsley	116+13	3+1	11	4	12		1	
				£200,000	15.07.91	Grimsby Town	133+5	11	6	5	18	3	1 1	
Paul Groves	5.11	11.5	28.02.66	Derby	01.10.86	Burton Albion			2				1	
				£12,000	18.04.88	Leicester City	7+9	1	0+1	0+1	1	1		
				Loan	20.08.89	Lincoln city	8	2			1			
				£60,000	25.01.90	Blackpool	106+1	6	9	13	21	1	4 3	
				£125,000	12.08.92	Grimsby Town	137+1	8+1	7	4	28	2	1	1
Kevin A Jobling	5.9	10.11	01.01.68	Sunderland	09.01.86	Leicester City (A)	4+5		0+1	3				2
					19.02.88	Grimsby Town	207+17	12+1	4+3	5+4	9		1	
				Loan	10.01.94	Scunthorpe United				1				
Craig R Shakespeare	5.10	12.5	26.10.63	Birmingham	05.11.81	Walsall (A)	276+8	31	22	18	45	6	6	2
				£300,000	19.06.89	Sheffield Wed.	15+2	3		0+1	1			
				£275,000	08.02.90	West Bromwich A.	104+8	6	5	5	12	1	2	1
				£115,000	14.07.93	Grimsby Town	37+15	4+1	1+2	0+1	6			
Thomas R Watson	5.8	10.10	29.09.69	Liverpool	12.07.88	Grimsby Town (A)	134+36	9+5	4	8+2	24	2		
F O R W A R D S														
Gary P C Childs	5.7	10.8	19.04.64	Birmingham	13.02.82	West Brom. A. (A)	2+1							
E: Y4				£15,000	07.10.83	Walsall	120+11	14+2	9+1	7	17	2	2 2	
				£50,000	08.07.87	Birmingham City	39+16	0+2	3	2	2			
				Free	20.07.89	Grimsby Town	152+19	13	9	7+2	22	1		
Jack W Lester	5.10	11.2	08.10.75	Sheffield	08.07.94	Grimsby Town (J)	1+6	0+1	0+1					
Stephen Livingstone	6.1	12.7	08.09.69	Middlesbrough	16.07.86	Coventry City (A)	17+14	8+2		0+	5	10		
				£450,000	17.01.91	Blackburn Rovers	25+5	2	1		10		1	
				£350,000	23.03.93	Chelsea	0+1							
				Loan	03.09.93	Port Vale	4+1							
				£140,000	29.10.93	Grimsby Town	56+5	2	1		11			
Clive P Mendoca	5.10	10.7	09.09.68	Islington	10.09.86	Sheffield United (A)	8+5	0+1		1	4			
Loan Doncaster Rovers, (26.02.88), 2 Lg Apps.				£35,000	25.03.88	Rotherham United	71+13	5+2	4+1	4+2	27	1	2	1
				£110,000	01.08.91	Sheffield United	4+6	0+2		0+1	1			
Loan Grimsby, (09.01.92), 10Lg Apps + 3 Gl				£85,000	13.08.92	Grimsby Town	98+5	8+1	7	2	35	4	2	1

GRIMSBY TOWN

PLAYERS NAME Honours	Ht	Wt	Birthdate	Birthplace Transfers	Contract Date	Clubs	APPEARANCES				GOALS			
							League	L/Cup	FA Cup	Other	Lge	L/C	FAC	Oth
Nicholas Southall	5.10	11.4	28.01.72	Stockton		Darlington (T)								
				£40,000	.08.95	Grimsby Town								
Neil S Woods	6.0	12.11	30.07.66	Bradford	31.08.83	Doncaster R. (A)	55+10	4	5	5+2	16	1	2	3
				£120,000	22.12.86	Glasgow Rangers	0+3							
				£120,000	03.08.87	Ipswich Town	15+12			4	5			1
					01.03.90	Bradford City	13+1				2			
				£82,000	23.08.90	Grimsby Town	129+30	9+1	3	7	38	1		1

TOP GOALSCORER 1994/95
Neil Woods

First Division goals (games) . . . . 14 (33+4)
Coca-Cola Cup Goals. . . . . 0 (0+1)
F.A. Cup goals 0 (1)

Total . . . . 14 (34+5)

Total goals for Grimsby Town since 23.08.90. . . . . 40 (148+31)

Career total as at June 1st 1995 . . . . 70 (245+59)

THE MANAGER
BRIAN LAWS

Date of Birth . . . . 14th October 1961.
Place of Birth . . . . Wallsend.
Date of Appointment . . . . November 1995.

PREVIOUS CLUBS
As Manager. . . . . None.
As Coach. . . . . None.
As a Player . . . Burnley, Huddersfield Town, Middlesbrough, Nottingham Forest.

HONOURS
As a Manager
None.

As a Player
Football League XI.
England 'B' cap.

BLUNDELL PARK

Cleethorpe, South Humberside DN35 7PY
Tel: 01472 697 111

Capacity 8,607
....(Away seating 1,778)

First game ....v Luton Town, 3-3, 2.9.1899.
First floodlit game ....v Gainsborough T, 9.3.1953.

ATTENDANCES
Highest ....31,657 v Wolves, FA Cup 5th Rnd, 20.2.1937.
Lowest ....970 v Scunthorpe Utd, AMC, 15.12.1987.

OTHER GROUNDS...None.

MATCHDAY TICKET PRICES

Upper Stones Stand & Main Stand
Adults £12
Children - all seats £5
OAP's - all seats £6

Pontoon End & Lower Stones
Adults . . . . £10 (with Mariners Discount Card)
. . . . . . £12 without Card (Apply to club for Card)

Ticket Office Telephone no. 01472 697 111

HOW TO GET TO THE GROUND

From the North and West
Use motorway (M18) then A180, sign posted Grimsby, then follow signs to Cleethorpes A1098.

From the South
Use A1 then A16 and follow signs to Cleethorpes and at roundabout take first exit into Grimsby Road A1098 for Grimsby Town FC.

Car Parking
Street parking available.

Nearest Railway Station
Cleethorpes, Grimsby (01472 353 556).

CLUBCALL
0898 12 15 76
Calls cost 39p per minute cheap rate and 49p per minute at all other times.
Call costings correct at time of going to press.

MATCHDAY PROGRAMME

Programme Editor . . . . Paul Cope.

Number of pages . . . . 32.

Price . . . . £1.20.

Subscriptions . . . . £40 per season.

Local Newspapers . . . . Grimsby Evening Telegraph,
. . . . Sports Telegraph, Grimsby Target.

Local Radio Stations . . . . Radio Humberside, Viking Radio.

HUDDERSFIELD TOWN
(The Terriers)
ENDSLEIGH LEAGUE DIVISION 1
SPONSORED BY: PANASONIC

Back Row (L-R): Simon Baldry, Iain Dunn, Chris Billy, Jon Whitney, Ronnie Jepson, Andrew Booth, Simon Collins, Kevin Gray.
Middle Row: Dennis Booth (Coach), David Moss (Yth Coach), Craig Whittington, Simon Trevitt, Richard Logan, Tony Norman, Steve Francis, Jonathan Dyson, Patrick Scully, Dave Wilson (Physio).
Front Row: Rodney Rowe, Tom Cowan, Darren Bullock, Lee Sinnott, Brian Horton (Manager), Paul Reid, Lee Duxbury, Gary Crosby, Gary Clayton.

HUDDERSFIELD TOWN
FORMED IN 1908
TURNED PROFESSIONAL IN 1908
LTD COMPANY IN 1908

CHAIRMAN: D G Headey

DIRECTORS
M Asquith, D A Taylor, E R Whiteley,
T Fisher,
C Senior (Vice-President)
SECRETARY
A D Sykes (01484 420 335/6)
COMMERCIAL MANAGER
Alan Stevenson

MANAGER: Brian Horton
COACH: Dennis Booth

RESERVE TEAM MANAGER
David Moss
YOUTH TEAM MANAGER
Gerry Murphy
PHYSIOTHERAPIST
Dave Wilson

STATISTICIAN FOR THE DIRECTORY
Richard Stead

The roller coaster ride that marked Neil Warnock's mangership has finally come to an abrupt end, but not before he had achieved consecutive appearances at Wembley and promotion to Division One.

As the Second Division's joint longest tenants, promotion was long overdue and everything was put into place before the season started to ensure Town were in the best possible position to attain it.

The major feeling before the start of the season was that the squad was good enough to achieve promotion, and the only major pre season strengthening was the purchase of Tom Cowan from Sheffield United, who made a major impression whilst on loan at the end of the previous season, and, like Andrew Booth was selected for the PFA Second Division team of the season.

This season also saw the move to the magnificent, all-seater £15 million Alfred McAlpine Stadium which captured the imagination of the supporters and, coupled with success on the pitch, saw average attendances rise by an incredible 83% to 11,666. Indeed, only four home league crowds dipped below the 10,000 mark.

On the pitch, the season got off to the best possible start, and despite losing the first league game played in the new stadium, results went from strength to strength. As the season progressed, the race for the one automatic promotion soon turned in to a three horse race with Brentford and Birmingham, characterised by some great team performances but if anything, driven by the free scoring exploits of Ronnie Jepson and particularly Andrew Booth. Booth, rated at over £2 million by the club is hotly tipped for Premier League stardom and is already a regular in the England under-21s, continuing his scoring prowess in an England shirt.

As the season headed to a close the squad was strengthened prior to the transfer deadline with Lee Sinnott and Lee Duxbury being purchased from local rivals Bradford City , and becoming ever pre-sents in the side in the run in to the end of the season. The former becoming a very able captain in the absence of Paul Reid.

Only at the end of the season did the team run out of steam and secured a play-off place in fifth place, one of the lowest positions of the season. This, however didn't prevent Town beating Brentford by the narrowest of margins and overcoming Bristol Rovers in front of nearly 60,000 at Wembley. The result was made even more significant by the fact that both goals were scored by players born in Huddersfield and who cost the club nothing in transfer fees.

What would appear to be a recipe for continued future success however was soon followed by the sacking of Chairman Terry Fisher by the rest of the board. Warnock's replacement is Brian Horton who will need all his Premier League experience to ensure he continues the progress of Huddersfield Town A.F.C.

RICHARD STEAD.

HUDDERSFIELD TOWN

Division Three: 5th **FA Cup:** 2nd Round **Coca-Cola Cup:** 2nd Round **Auto Windscreens Trophy:** 2nd Round

M	DATE	COMP.	VEN	OPPONENTS	RESULT	H/T	LP	GOAL SCORERS/GOAL TIMES	ATT.
1	A 13	EL	A	Blackpool	W 4-1	2-0	5	Reid 31, 84, Jepson 43, 71	(8,343)
2	16	CC 1/1	A	Scunthorpe	L 1-2	0-1		Scully 90	(2,841)
3	20	EL	H	Wycombe Wanderers	L 0-1	0-1	12		13,334
4	23	CC 1/2	H	Scunthorpe	W 3-0	3-0		Jepson 10, 21, Reid 35	6,455
5	27	EL	A	Chester City	W 2-1	1-0	8	Booth 10, Dunn 74	(2,895)
6	30	EL	H	Leyton Orient	W 2-1	0-1	6	Booth 49, Reid 90	8,528
7	S 3	EL	A	Oxford United	D 3-3	1-2	5	Booth 39, Starbuck 51 (pen) Bullock 58	10,122
8	10	EL	A	Plymouth Argyle	W 3-0	2-0	4	Booth 7, 9, 89	(5,464)
9	13	EL	A	Peterborough United	D 2-2	1-2	4	Dunn 44, 51	(5,316)
10	17	EL	H	Stockport County	W 2-1	1-1	2	Booth 1, 78	9,552
11	20	CC 2/1	H	Southampton	L 0-1	0-0			13,814
12	24	EL	A	Bradford City	W 4-3	1-0	2	Reid 40, Jepson 70, Booth 81,84	(11,300)
13	O 1	EL	H	Brighton	W 3-0	1-0	1	Booth 43, Reid 62, Logan 63	10,321
14	5	CC 2/2	A	Southampton	L 0-4	0-1			(12,032)
15	8	EL	A	Birmingham City	D 1-1	1-1	1	Bullock 13	(15,261)
16	11	AWS 1	A	Bradford City	W 2-1	0-1		Baldry 58, Booth 74	(3,772)
17	15	EL	A	Cambridge United	W 3-1	0-1	1	Jepson 52, 79 (pen) Dunn 73	10,742
18	18	AWS 1	H	York City	L 3-0	1-0		Mitchell 14, Clayton 76, Starbuck 82 (pen)	4,183
19	22	EL	A	Crewe Alexandra	D 3-3	2-3	1	Jepson 1, Billy 22, Booth 59	(5,352)
20	29	EL	H	A.F.C. Bournemouth	W 3-1	2-0	1	Booth 4, Jepson 26, Scully 63	11,251
21	N 1	EL	H	Wrexham	W 2-1	1-0	1	Bullock 6, Billy 73	9,639
22	5	EL	A	York City	L 0-3	0-2	1		(6,3450)
23	12	FAC 1	A	Doncaster Rovers	W 4-1	2-0		Bullock 8, Booth 12, Jepson 77, Dunn 88	6,626
24	19	EL	H	Brentford	W 1-0	0-0	1	Jepson 50	10,889
25	26	EL	A	Bristol Rovers	D 1-1	1-1	2	Jepson 45 (pen)	(5,679)
26	30	AWS 2	H	Lincoln City	W 3-2	0-2		Crosby 85, Jepson 88 (pen), Dunn 107	5,738
27	D 3	FAC 2	A	Lincoln City	L 0-1	0-0			(4,143)
28	10	EL	A	Wycombe Wanderers	L 1-2	0-1	4	Jepson 12	(6,790)
29	17	EL	H	Blackpool	D 1-1	0-0	4	Booth 63	11,536
30	26	EL	A	Hull City	L 0-1	0-0	4		(10,220)
31	27	EL	H	Rotherham United	W 1-0	1-0	4	Booth 11	15,557
32	31	EL	A	Swansea City	D 1-1	0-0	4	Booth 72	(5,438)
33	J 2	EL	H	Shrewsbury Town	W 2-1	1-1	2	Jepson 33, Duxbury 90	12,748
34	7	EL	A	Crewe Alexandra	L 1-2	1-1	2	Booth 18	11,466
35	14	EL	A	Cardiff City	D 0-0	0-0	2		(3,808)
36	24	AWS QF	A	Bury	L 1-2	0-1		Clayton 61	(3,311)
37	28	EL	A	A.F.C. Bournemouth	W 2-0	0-0	2	Jepson 57, Duxbury 90	12,748
38	F 4	EL	H	Bristol Rovers	D 1-1	0-1	3	Booth 46	10,389
39	11	EL	A	Wrexham	W 2-1	0-1	2	Booth 56, Jepson 63	(5,894)
40	18	EL	A	Cardiff City	W 5-1	4-0	2	Booth 2, Cowan 22, Jepson 33, Reid 37, Crosby 74	10,035
41	21	EL	A	Brentford	D 0-0	0-0	2		(9,562)
42	25	EL	A	Brighton	D 0-0	0-0	3		(7,751)
43	28	EL	H	York City	W 3-0	1-0	1	Jepson 3, Bullock 61, Crosby 75	10,495
44	M 4	EL	H	Bradford City	D 0-0	0-0	1		17,404
45	7	EL	A	Oxford United	L 1-3	0-0	2	Dyson 77	(7,160)
46	11	EL	A	Chester City	W 5-1	3-1	2	Cowan 9, Jepson 16, Booth 30,65,68	9,606
47	18	EL	A	Leyton Orient	W 2-0	0-0	2	Dunn 67, Jepson 76 (pen)	(3,177)
48	21	EL	H	Plymouth Argyle	W 2-0	1-0	1	Dyson 1, Booth 48	12,099
49	25	EL	A	Stockport County	W 2-1	1-0	1	Jepson 33 (pen) Gannon 71 (og)	(5,383)
50	A 1	EL	H	Peterborough United	L 1-2	0-1	2	Bullock 79	11,324
51	8	EL	H	Swansea City	W 2-0	1-0	1	Crosby 40,81	10,105
52	15	EL	A	Rotherham United	D 1-1	0-0	1	Booth 58	(6687)
53	17	EL	H	Hull City	D 1-1	0-0	2	Sinnott 72	12,402
54	22	EL	A	Shrewsbury Town	L 1-2	0-2	3	Jepson 83 (pen)	(4758)
55	29	EL	A	Cambridge United	D 1-1	1-1	3	Booth 26	(5188)
56	M 6	EL	H	Birmingham City	L 1-2	0-0	5	Bullock 87	18,775
57	14	PO SF/1	H	Brentford	D 1-1	1-1		Billy 9	14,160
58	17	PO SF/2	A	Brentford	W †1-1	1-1		Booth (Won 4-3 on penalties)	(11,161)
59	28	PO F		Bristol Rovers	W 2-1	1-1		Booth 45, Billy 81	(59,175)
60									

Best Home League Attendance: 18,775 v Birmingham City   **Smallest:** 8,528 v Leyton Orient   **Av Home Att:** 11,666

Goal Scorers:

League (79): Booth 26, Jepson 19, Bullock 6, Reid 6, Dunn 5, Crosby 4, Billy, 2 Cowan 2, Dyson 2, Duxbury 2 Logan, Scully, Sinnott, Starbuck, Opponent

C/Cola Cup (4): Jepson 2, Reid, Scully

FA Cup (4): Booth, Bullock, Dunn, Jepson

AWS: (9): Clayton 2, Baldry, Booth, Crosby, Dunn, Jepson, Mitchel1, Starbuck

Compared with 1993-94: +5,301

Francis	Billy	Cowan	Starbuck	Scully	Mitchell	Baldry	Bullock	Booth	Jepson	Reid	Dunn	Dyson	Blackwell	Trevitt	Short	Williams	Logan	Crosby	Gray	Sinnott	Clayton	Duxbury	Collins	Whittington	O'Connor	Referee	
1	2	3	4	5	6•	7*	8	9	10	11	12	14	GK													P. Wright	1
1	2	3	4	5		7*	8	9	10	11	12	6	GK				14									G. Cain	2
1	2	3	4	5†	6	7*	8	9	10	11	12	14	GK													T. Lunt	3
1	2	3		5		7	8	9	10	11	12	6	GK	14			4								14	A. Dawson	4
1	2	3	10•	5		7*	8	9		11	12	6	GK	14			4									J. Parker	5
1	2	3		5		7	8	9		11	12	6	GK	14			4							10*		J. Watson	6
1	2	3	7	12	14		8	9	10•	11		6	GK				4	5*								B. Burns	7
1	2	3		5	6	7	8*	9	14	11	10•	12	GK				4									J. Holbrook	8
1	2	3		5	6*	7	8	9	14	11	10	12	GK				4									K. Cooper	9
1	2	3	12	5		7•	8*	9	14	11	10	6	GK				4									K. Lupton	10
1	2•	3	8	5				9	14	11	10	6	GK	7			4						12			P. Jones	11
1	2	3	12	5			8	9	14	11	10*	6	GK	7			4•									R. Furnandiz	12
1		3	14	5			8	9•	10	11	12	6	GK	2			4	7								A. Flood	13
1•	14	3	11	5			8	9*	10		12	6	GK	2			4	7•								M. Pierce	14
1•		3	14	5			8	9	10	11	12	6	GK	2			4	7								K. Lynch	15
	2	3	11•		6	14		9		10			1				4	7*	5		8		12		GK	J. Kirkby	16
		3	14	5			8	9	10	11	12	6	1	2			4•	7*							GK	P. Richards	17
	3		11	5*	4	14			10			9•	12	1	2		7	6		8						T. West	18
GK	7	3*	14	5			8	9	10	11•	12	6	1	2			4									P. Vanes	19
1	7•	3		5	6		8	9	10*	11	12		GK	2			4	14								S. Mathieson	20
1	7	3		5	6		8	9	10	11	12	14	GK	2			4									J. Watson	21
1	7	3†		5	6*		8	9	10•	11	12	4	GK	2			14									M. Riley	22
1	7	3		5	6		8	9	10*	11	12		GK	2			4•						14			J. Parker	23
1	7			5	6		8	9*		11	12		GK	3			4						14			A. Dawson	24
	7			5†	6		8	9	10	11	12			1	2	3	4	14	5				14		GK	J. Rushton	25
GK	7*				6			12	10		9		1	2		3	4	14	5		8*			11•	GK	E. Lomas	26
GK	7*	3		5	6		8	9	10	11	12			1	2		14	4								J. Rushton	27
1	7*	3			6		8	9	10	11	12		GK	2			14	4•	5							I. Hemley/P. Taylor	28
1	7•	3			6		8	9	10	11*	12		GK	2			4	14	5							G. Singh	29
1	12	3		5*			8	9	10	11	14				2		4			6				7•		U. Rennie	30
1	7	3				14		9	10	11	12	5	GK		2		4			6		8*				I. Cruikshanks	31
1	7*	3						9	14	11	10	5	GK		2		4			6•		8	12			J. Brandwood	32
1	7*	3						9	10	11	12	5	GK		2		4			6		8	14			T. Heilbron	33
1		3				7*	4	9	10	11•	12	5	GK		2					6		8				K. Lupton	34
1	14	3		5				12	10*	11*	9		GK		2		4	7		6		8				P. Wright	35
1	12	3		5				9	10	11	7	6	GK		2*		4	14				8•				G. Singh	36
1	7*	3		5				9	10		12		GK	2			4•	11		6		14	8			P. Vanes	37
1	7*	3		5				9	10		12		GK	2			4	11		6		14	8			J. Watson	38
1	12	3		5			4	9	10	11			GK	2				7		6		14	8			J. Parker	39
1	14	3		5			4	9	10*	11•	12		GK	2				7		6			8			B. Burns	40
1		3		5			4	9	10	11•	12		GK					7		6		14	8			G. Barber	41
1	14	3		5			4	9	10*	11•	12		GK	2				7*		6			8			B. Harris	42
1	2	3		5			4•	9	10*	11	12	14	GK					7		6			8			P. Richards	43
1	2	3†		5			4	9	10*	11	12	14	GK					7*		6		14	8			K. Lupton	44
1	2	3		5			4	9	10*	11	12	14	GK					7*		6			8			M. Pierce	45
1	7•	3		5			14	4	9	10*	11	12	2	GK						6			8			P. Rejer	46
1				5			14	4	9	10	11	7	2	GK		3				6		12	8			P. Alcock	47
1	12			5				4	9	10	11	7•	2	GK		3				6			8			G. Cain	48
1	14			5				4	9•	10	11	7	2	GK		3			6			12	8			T. West	49
1	12			5				4	9	10	11*	7•	2	GK		3				6			8			E. Wolstenholme	50
1	7							4	9	14	11	12	2	GK		3		10	5	6			8•			K. Lynch	51
1	7			5				4	9		11	12•	2	GK		3	14	10*		6†			8			R. Furnandiz	52
1	7•			5				4	9	10	11*	12	2	GK		3				6			8	14		I. Cruikshanks	53
1	7•	3		5				4	9	10	11*	12	2	GK				4		6			8	14		D. Allison	54
1		3		5				4	9	10		11	GK	2			12			6		14	8	7		P. Foakes	55
1	12	3		5				4	9	10		11*	GK	2						6			8	7•		J. Winter	56
1	7	3		5				4	9	10	12	14	GK	2			11*			6			8			S. Dunn	57
1	7	3		5				4	9	10	12		GK	2			11*			6		14	8			P. Foakes	58
1	7	3		5				4	9	10	12	14	GK	2•			11*			6			8			C. Wilkes	59

Francis	Billy	Cowan	Starbuck	Scully	Mitchell	Baldry	Bullock	Booth	Jepson	Reid	Dunn	Dyson	Blackwell	Trevitt	Short	Williams	Logan	Crosby	Gray	Sinnott	Clayton	Duxbury	Collins	Whittington	O'Connor	
43	30	37	4	38	11	8	39	45	36	42	13	23	3	20	6	9	24	16	5	25	0	26	2	1	0	League Appearances
0	7	0	5	0	1	3	0	1	5	0	26	5	1	1	0	0	3	3	0	2	0	2	0	0	0	League Sub Appearances
4	3+1	4	3	4	0	2	3	4	3	3	1+2	4	0+1	2	0	0	3	1	0	0	0	0	0	0	0	C/Cola Cup Appearances
1	2	2	0	2	2	0	2	2	2	2	0+2	0	1	2	0	1	1	0	0+1	0	0	0	0	0	0	FA Cup Appearances
1	3+1	2	2	2	3	0+2	2	2+1	3	1	4	1+1	3	2	1	1	3	2+2	3	0	0	0	1+1	0	0	AWT Cup Appearances
3	3	3		3			3	3	3		0+3	0+2	3				3		3			3				Play-off Appearances

Also Played: Moulden 14 (50, 56), Robinson GK (18)

† = sent off

HUDDERSFIELD TOWN

CLUB RECORDS

BIGGEST VICTORIES
League: 10-1 v Blackpool, Division 1, 13.12.1930.
F.A. Cup: 7-0 v Lincoln City, 1st Round, 16.11.1991.
7-1 v Chesterfield (a), 3rd Round, 12.1.1929.

BIGGEST DEFEATS
League: 1-10 v Manchester City, Division 2, 7.11.1987.
F.A. Cup: 0-6 v Sunderland, 3rd Round, 1949-50.

MOST POINTS
3 points a win: 82, Division 3, 1982-83.
2 points a win: 66, Division 4, 1979-80.

MOST GOALS SCORED
101, Division 4, 1979-80.

MOST GOALS CONCEDED
100, Division 2, 1987-88.

MOST FIRST CLASS MATCHES IN A SEASON
61 - 1993-94 (League 46, Lge Cup 4, AMC 8, FA Cup 3)
61 - 1992-93 (League 46, Lge Cup 4, AMC 5, FA Cup 6)
61 - 1991-92 (League 46, Lge Cup 5, AMC 5, FA Cup 3, P/Off 2)

MOST LEAGUE WINS
28, Division 2, 1919-20.

MOST LEAGUE DRAWS
17, Division 1, 1926-27. Division 2, 1972-73.

MOST LEAGUE DEFEATS
28, Division 2, 1987-88.

INDIVIDUAL CLUB RECORDS

MOST GOALS IN A SEASON
Dave Mangnall: 42 goals in 1931-32 (League 33, FA Cup 9).

MOST GOALS IN A MATCH
5. D Mangnall v Derby County (h), 6-0, Division 1, 21.11.1931.
5. A P Lythgoe v Blackburn Rovers (h), 6-0, Division 1, 13.4.1935.

OLDEST PLAYER
W H Smith, 39 years, 1934.

YOUNGEST PLAYER
Dennis Law, 15 years 10 months, 1956.

MOST CAPPED PLAYER
Jimmy Nicholson (Northern Ireland) 31.
Ray Wilson (England) 30.

BEST PERFORMANCES

League: Champions of Division 1 (3).

F.A. Cup: Winners (1).
League Cup: Semi-Final 1967-68.

PREVIOUS NAMES
None.

PREVIOUS LEAGUES
Midland League.

Club colours: Blue & white striped shirts, white shorts, blue & white hoop on turnover socks.
Change colours: White shirts with black sleeves, black shorts, white socks with black turnovers.

Reserves League: Pontins Central League.
Youth League: Northern Intermediate League.

DIVISIONAL RECORD

	Played	Won	Drawn	Lost	For	Against	Points
Division 1	1,260	480	317	463	1,874	1,854	1,277
Division 2/1	1,116	433	283	400	1,607	1,493	1,211
Division 3/2	552	217	148	187	753	674	750
Division 4	230	100	64	66	337	246	264
Total	3,158	1,230	812	1,116	4,571	4,267	3,502

RECORDS AND STATISTICS

COMPETITIONS

Div.1	Div.2/1	Div.3/2	Div.4
1919-51	1910-19	1972-74	1974-79
1952-55	1951-52	1979-82	
1969-71	1955-69	1987-88	
	1971-72	1987-95	
	1995-		

HONOURS

Div.1	Div.2	Div.4	FA Cup
1923-24	1969-70	1979-80	1922
1924-25			
1925-26			

Huddersfield were the first, of only three clubs, to win the Championship three years in succession.

MOST APPEARANCES

W H Smith 574 (1913-34)

Year	League	FA Cup
1913-14	4	
1914-15	24	1
1915-16		
1916-17		
1917-18		
1918-19		
1919-20	39	5
1920-21	33	2
1921-22	40	9
1922-23	35	5
1923-24	39	3
1924-25	41	1
1925-26	28	2
1926-27	39	1
1927-28	38	8
1928-29	32	6
1929-30	33	5
1930-31	30	
1931-32	31	4
1932-33	17	
1933-34	18	1
1934-35		
	521	53

MOST GOALS IN A CAREER

George Brown - 159 (1921-29)

Year	League	FA Cup
1921-22	4	
1922-23	6	
1923-24	8	
1924-25	20	
1925-26	35	
1926-27	27	1
1927-28	27	8
1928-29	15	8
Total	142	17

Current top goalscorer: Andrew Booth - 40 (1992-95)

RECORD TRANSFER FEE RECEIVED

Amount	Club	Player	Date
£300,000	Leicester City	Iwan Roberts	10/93
£275,000	Southampton	Simon Charlton	6/93
£250,000	Reading	Craig Maskell	8/90
£250,000	Swindon	Duncan Shearer	6/88

RECORD TRANSFER FEE PAID

Amount	Club	Player	Date
£300,000	Bradford City	Lee Duxbury	12/94
£275,000	Watford	Iwan Roberts	8/90

MANAGERS

Name	Seasons	Best	Worst
F Walker	1908-10	5(ML)	16 (NEL)
D Pudan	1910-12	13(2)	17(2)
A Fairclough	1912-19	8(2)	13(2)
A Langley	1919-21	17(1)	2(2)
H Chapman	1921-25	1(1)	14(1)
C Potter	1925-26	1(1)	1(1)
J Chaplin	1926-29	2(1)	16(1)
C Stephenson	1929-42	2(1)	19(1)
T Magner	1942-43	5(FLNRS)	8(FLNRS)
D Steele	1943-47	15(1)	20(1)
G Stephenson	1947-52	15(1)	21(1)
A Beatie	1952-56	3(1)	12(2)
W Shankly	1956-60	6(2)	14(2)
E Boot	1960-64	6(2)	12(2)
T Johnston	1964-68	6(2)	14(2)
I Greaves	1968-74	15(1)	10(3)
R Collins	1974-75	24(3)	24(3)
T Johnston	1975-77	5(4)	9(4)
J Haselden	1977-78	11(4)	11(4)
M Buxton	1978-86	12(2)	9(4)
S Smith	1986-87	17(2)	17(2)
M MacDonald	1987-88	23(2)	23(2)
E Hand	1988-92	8(3)	14(3)
I Ross	1992-93	3(3)	15(3)
Neil Warnock	1993-95	1(2)	11(2)
Brian Horton	1995-		

ML= Midland League.   NEL= North Eastern League.
FLNRS= Football League, North Regional Section.

LONGEST LEAGUE RUNS

of undefeated matches:	27 (1924-25)	of league matches w/out a win:	22 (1971-72)
of undefeated home matches:	28 (1982-83)	of undefeated away matches:	18 (1924-25)
without home win:	11 (1971-72)	without an away win:	31 (1936-37)
of league wins:	11 (1919-21)	of home wins:	11 (1925-26)
of league defeats:	7 (1913-14, 1955-56)	of away wins:	5 (1924-25)

HUDDERSFIELD TOWN

PLAYERS NAME Honours	Ht	Wt	Birthdate	Birthplace Transfers	Contract Date	Clubs	League	L/Cup	FA Cup	Other	Lge	L/C	FAC	Oth
G O A L K E E P E R S														
Stephen S Francis	5.11	11.5	29.05.64	Billericay	24.08.82	Chelsea (A)	71	6	10	1				
E: Y2; FMC'86'88				£20,000	27.02.87	Reading	216	15	15	13				
				£150,000	01.08.93	Huddersfield Town	89	8	4	12				
Tony Norman	6.2	12.8	24.02.58	Deeside	01.08.76	Burnley (J)								
W: 5, B.1.				£30,000	14.02.80	Hull City	372	22	26	13				
				£200,000+PE	29.12.88	Sunderland	198	8	14	7				
				Free	08.95	Huddersfield Town								
D E F E N D E R S														
Simon Collins	5.9	10.5	16.12.73	Pontefract	01.07.92	Huddersfield T. (T)	3+3	0+1		1+3				
				Loan	14.01.94	Halifax Town								
Thomas Cowan	5.8	10.8	28.08.69	Bellshill		Clyde	16		2			2		
						Glasgow Rangers	8+4		0+1	2				
				£350,000	01.08.91	Sheffield United	45	5	2	1				
				Loan	01.10.93	Stoke City	14	1		3				
				£150,000	24.03.94	Huddersfield Town	47	4	2	6	2			
Jonathan P Dyson	6.1	12.0	23.03.72	Mirfield	29.12.90	Huddersfield T. (J)	57+8	9	3	7+4	2			
Patrick J Scully	6.1	12.7	23.06.70	Dublin	16.09.87	Arsenal(T)								
Ei: 1, B2, u23.1, u21.9				Loan	07.09.89	Preston North End	13		1	1	1			
				Loan	23.08.90	Northampton Town	15		1					
				£100,000	08.01.91	Southend United	114+1	3	4	5	6			
				Free	24.03.94	Huddersfield Town	49	4	2	6	1	1		
Simon Trevitt	5.11	11.10	20.12.67	Dewsbury	16.06.86	Huddersfield T. (T)	212+13	21	13	19+1	3	1		
Jonathan D Whitney	5.10	12.3	23.12.70	Nantwich		Wigan Athletic (T)								
via Skelmersdale U. (F) & Winsford, 1 FAC App.				£10,000	21.10.93	Huddersfield Town	14			4				
				Loan	17.03.95	Wigan Athletic	12							
M I D F I E L D														
Darren J Bullock	5.8	12.4	12.02.69	Worcester		Nuneaton Borough								
				£55,000	19.11.93	Huddersfield Town	59	3	2	9	9		1	1
Paul Dalton	5.11	12.0	25.04.67	Middlesbrough		Brandon United								
FLgXl.1.				£35,000	03.05.88	Manchester United								
				£20,000	04.03.89	Hartlepool United	140+11	10	7	9	37	2	1	3
				£275,000	11.06.92	Plymouth Argyle	93+5	5	7	6	25	2	5	
				£125,000+PE	08.95	Huddersfield Town								
Kevin J Gray	6.0	13.0	07.01.72	Sheffield	01.07.90	Mansfield Town (T)	129+12	8	6+1	12+2	3	1		2
				£20,000	18.07.94	Huddersfield Town	5			3				
Richard A Logan	6.1	13.3	24.05.69	Barnsley		Belper Town								
via Gainsborough Trinity to				Free	15.11.93	Huddersfield Town	33+10	3	1	9	1			1
Paul R Reid	5.9	10.8	19.01.68	Oldbury	09.01.86	Leicester City (A)	140+22	13	5+1	6+2	21	4		
Loan Bradford City, (19.03.92), 7 Lg Apps.				£25,000	27.07.92	Bradford City	80+2	3	3	5	15	2		1
				£70,000	20.05.94	Huddersfield Town	42	3	2	1	6	1		
F O R W A R D S														
Simon Baldry	5.10	11.0	12.02.76	Huddersfield	14.07.94	Huddersfield T. (T)	18+3	2		1+2	2			1
Andrew D Booth	6.0	10.8	17.03.73	Huddersfield	01.07.92	Huddersfield T. (T)	66+14	6+1	4	12+1	38		1	4
Iain G W Dunn	5.10	11.7	01.04.70	Howden	07.07.88	York City (J)	46+31	3+1	3+1	1+3	11			
E: u19.4				Free	14.08.91	Chesterfield	8+5			1				
via Scarborough (F) to				Free	29.09.92	Peterborough United				0+1				
via Scarborough (F) & Goole Town (F) to				Free	04.12.92	Huddersfield Town	58+43	5+2	5+2	11+7	14	3	3	9
Ronald F Jepson	6.1	13.2	12.05.63	Stoke		Nantwich Town								
				Free	23.03.89	Port Vale	12+10	1+1	1+1					
Loan P'borough, (25.01.90), 18 Lg App. + 5 Gls				£80,000	12.02.91	Preston North End	36+2	2		3	8			4
				£60,000	29.07.92	Exeter City	50+3	6	3	4	21	2	1	1
				£80,000	07.12.93	Huddersfield Town	55+9	3+1	2	6	19	2	1	1
Rodney C Rowe	5.8	12.8	30.07.75	Huddersfield	12.07.93	Huddersfield T. (T)	7+6		3	3	1		1	1
				Loan	11.08.94	Scarborough	10+4	4			1	1		
				Loan	20.03.95	Bury	1+2							
Sam J Collins	6.2	13.05	05.06.77	Pontefract	06.07.94	Huddersfield T (T)								
Gary Crosby	5.7	9.13	08.05.64	Sleaford		Lincoln United								
LC'90. FMC'92.				Free	23.08.86	Lincoln City	6+1	2						
			via Grantham to	£20,000	21.12.87	Nottingham Forest	139+13	29+1	18+3	10+1	12	6	3	4
				Loan	23.08.93	Grimsby Town	2+1							
				Free	27.08.94	Huddersfield Town	16+3	1	1	5+2	4			1
Lee E Duxbury	5.8	11.0	07.10.69	Keighley	04.07.88	Bradford City (T)	204+5	18+1	11	13	25	1		
				Loan	18.01.90	Rochdale	9+1		1					
				£250,000	23.12.94	Huddersfield Town	26			3	2			
Ian J Lawson	5.11	10.05	04.11.71	Huddersfield	27.01.95	Huddersfield T. (T)								
Stephen Murphy			05.04.78	Dublin	16.05.95	Huddersfield T. (T)								

HUDDERSFIELD TOWN

PLAYERS NAME / Honours	Ht	Wt	Birthdate	Birthplace / Transfers	Contract Date	Clubs	APPEARANCES League	L/Cup	FA Cup	Other	GOALS Lge	L/C	FAC	Oth
Derek P O' Connor			09.03.78	Dublin		Crumplin Utd (Eire)								
					16.05.95	Huddersfield Town								
Robert P Ryan			16.05.77	Dublin		Belvedere								
				Free	26.07.94	Huddersfield Town								
Lee Sinnott	6.1	11.9	12.07.65	Pelsall	16.11.82	Walsall (A)	40	3	4		2			
E: u21.1, Y.4.				£100,000	15.09.83	Watford	71+7	6	11		2			
				£130,000	23.07.87	Bradford City	173	19	9	12	6		1	
				£300,000	08.08.91	Crystal Palace	53+2	9+1	1	2				
					09.12.93	Bradford City	34	2	2	2	1			
				£105,000	23.12.94	Huddersfield Town	25			3	1			
Craig Whittington	5.11	12.4	03.09.70			Crawley								
				£50,000	19.11.93	Scarborough	26+1		1		10			
						Huddersfield Town	1							
				Loan	25.11.94	Rochdale	1							

TOP GOALSCORER 1994/95
Andrew Booth

Division Two goals (games) . . . . 26 (45+1)
Coca-Cola Cup Goals 0 (4)
F.A. Cup goals 1 (2)
Other goals . . . . 1 (2+1)
Total . . . . 28 (53+2)

Total goals for Huddersfield since 01.07.92 . . . . 40 (85+6)
Career total as at June 1st 1995 . . . . 40 (85+6)

THE MANAGER
BRIAN HORTON

Date of Birth . . . . 4th February 1949.
Place of Birth . . . . Hednesford.
Date of Appointment . . . . June 1995.

PREVIOUS CLUBS
As Manager . . . . Hull City, Manchester City.
As Coach . . . . Oxford United.
As a Player . . . . Walsall, Hednesford T., Port Vale, Brighton & H.A.,
. . . . Luton Town, Hull City.

HONOURS
As a Manager
Hull: Promotion to Division 2.

As a Player
Brighton: Promotion to 2nd & 1st Divisions.
Luton: Promotion to1st Division.

THE ALFRED MCALPINE STADIUM

Huddersfield, West Yorkshire
Tel: 01484 420 335

Capacity 20,000

First game ....v Wycombe W., Div 2. 8/94.
First floodlit game ....As above.

ATTENDANCES
Highest...18,775 v Birmingham City, Division 2, 06.05.95, (1-2).
Lowest..4,183 v York City, AMC, 18.10.94, (3-0).

OTHER GROUNDS...Leeds Road

MATCHDAY TICKET PRICES

Kilner Bank & South. £9
Juv/OAP £5

Riverside Upper £13
Juv/OAP £7

Riverside Lower £11
Juv/OAP £6

Match & Ticket Information
Advance reservations only for special matches,
otherwise admission to ground and stands on day of
matches.

Ticket Office Telephone no. 01484 420 335

CLUBCALL
0891 12 16 35
Calls cost 39p per minute cheap rate and 49p per
minute at all other times.
Call costings correct at time of going to press.

HOW TO GET TO THE GROUND

From the East and M1 (Junction 38)
Use A642, sign posted Huddersfield, into town centre, then follow signs Leeds
(A62) into Leeds Road, turn right down Bradley Mills Road for Huddersfield
Town FC.

From the South
Use A616 (sign posted Huddersfield) into town centre, then follow signs Leeds
(A62) into Leeds Road, turn right down Bradley Mills Road for Huddersfield
Town FC.

From the West
Use motorway M62 until junction 23 then A640 or A62 into Leeds Road, turn
right down Bradley Mills Road for Huddersfield Town FC.

Car Parking
Parking for 1,400 cars.

Nearest Railway Station
Huddersfield (01484 531 226).

MATCHDAY PROGRAMME

Programme Editor . . . . Alan Stevenson & Will Venters.

Number of pages . . . . 40.

Price . . . . £1.50.

Subscriptions . . . . Inland £40, Abroad £45.

Local Newspapers. . . . . Huddersfield Examiner.

Local Radio Stations . . . . Radio Leeds, Pennine Radio,
 . . . . Radio Aire, The Pulse.

IPSWICH TOWN
(The Blues or The Town)
ENDSLEIGH LEAGUE DIVISION 1
SPONSORED BY: GREENE KING

Back Row (L-R): Leo Cotterell, Steve Palmer, Simon Portrey, Lee Chapman, Claus Thomsen, James Scowcroft, Kevin Ellis, Frank Yallop.
Middle Row: Bryan Klug (Coach), Geraint Williams, Simon Milton, David Linighan, Steve Sedgley, Richard Wright, Craig Forrest, Clive Baker, Richard Naylor, Chris Swailes, Tony Vaughan, Adam Tanner, Dale Roberts (Coach).
Front Row: Mauricio Taricco, Stuart Slater, Ian Marshall, Paul Mason, Alex Mathie, George Burley (Manager), John Wark, Neil Gregory, Mick Stockwell, Neil Thompson, Lee Norfolk, Lee Durrent.

IPSWICH TOWN
FORMED IN 1887
TURNED PROFESSIONAL IN 1936
LTD COMPANY IN 1936

CHAIRMAN: David R Sheepshanks
DIRECTORS
John Kerridge,
Richard Moore, Philip Hope-Cobbold,
John Kerr MBE
SECRETARY
David Rose (01473 219 211)
COMMERCIAL MANAGER
Clive Turner (01473 212 202)

MANAGER: George Burley
ASSISTANT MANAGER: Dale Roberts

RESERVE TEAM COACH
Bryan Klug
YOUTH TEAM COACH
Phil Goddard
PHYSIOTHERAPIST
David Bingham

STATISTICIAN FOR THE DIRECTORY
Paul Voller

Ipswich began their third F.A. Premiership campaign with a home defeat at the hands of newly promoted Forest, without either of their summer signings, who were both injured. Sedgley had a shin problem while Thomsen was recovering from a hernia operation. Little did we know it but the opening day summed up the whole season - a very poor home record coupled with more than a fair share of injuries proved to be a recipe for disaster. John Lyall had assembled the biggest first team squad in the club's history but it proved to be a case of quantity rather than quality.

An away win at Q.P.R. briefly hoisted them to eighth in the table during August but they then proceeded to lose ten out of their next eleven games and found themselves in the bottom two by mid October, where they stayed for the rest of the season. The only win in this eleven game sequence was, unbelievably, a 3-2 home defeat of champions Manchester United where Town's midfield were able to hustle their more illustrious counterparts out of their stride and create some goalscoring opportunities. The game marked the debut of Paz, a much heralded import from Uruguay, who arrived in September, along with Taricco.

They were knocked out of the Coca-Cola Cup in the second round by Bolton and their only other success before Christmas was a 2-0 defeat of Leeds, during which Williams scored his first goal for the club.

Lyall resigned on the 5th December after another home defeat, and Goddard took over as caretaker manager while the board decided upon the successor, but he had and better success in the four games that he was in charge.

George Burley took over as manager after Christmas and immediately began introducing some of the younger players into the side. Tanner scored on his debut against Leicester as they started the New Year with a convincing win but then became giantkilling victims at Wrexham in the FA Cup before recording their first ever win at Anfield with Tanner again the marksman.

Mathie arrived from Newcastle and Chapman joined from West Ham but nobody proved able to stem the slide into the Endsleigh League and they were officially relegated on Good Friday without even playing.

It was indeed a strange season - how could the same players that played so well against Manchester United and Liverpool perform so poorly against everybody else? Unless Mr. Burley can find an answer to that question the Endsleigh League will not be an easy ride for him.

PAUL VOLLER.

IPSWICH TOWN

Premier League: 22nd   **FA Cup:** 3rd Round   **Coca-Cola Cup:** 2nd Round

M	DATE	COMP.	VEN	OPPONENTS	RESULT	H/T	LP	GOAL SCORERS/GOAL TIMES	ATT.
1	A 20	PL	H	Nottingham Forest	L 0-1	0-1	18		18,882
2	23	PL	A	Wimbledon	D 1-1	0-1		Milton 60	(5,853)
3	27	PL	A	Queens Park Rangers	W 2-1	1-0	8	Yates 19 (og), Guentchev 49	(12,456)
4	30	PL	H	Tottenham Hotspur	L 1-3	0-3	15	Kiwomya 86	22,559
5	S 10	PL	A	Aston Villa	L 0-2	0-1	16		(22,241)
6	19	PL	H	Norwich City	L 1-2	1-1		Ward 45 (pen)	17,447
7	21	CC 2/1	H	**Bolton Wanderers**	**L 0-3**	**0-1**			**7,787**
8	24	PL	H	Manchester United	W 3-2	2-0	14	Mason 15, 43, Sedgley 80	22,559
9	O 1	PL	A	Southampton	L 1-3	0-1	16	Marshall 77	(13,246)
10	5	CC 2/2	A	**Bolton Wanderers**	**L 0-1**	**0-0**			**(8,212)**
11	10	PL	A	Coventry City	L 0-2	0-1	19		(9,526)
12	16	PL	H	Sheffield Wednesday	L 1-2	0-1	21	Wark 50	13,073
13	23	PL	A	Chelsea	L 0-2	0-0	21		(15,068)
14	29	PL	H	Liverpool	L 1-3	0-1	21	Paz 64	22,519
15	N 1	PL	H	Leeds United	W 2-0	1-0	20	Sedgley 7, Williams 64	15,956
16	5	PL	A	Crystal Palace	L 0-3	0-1	20		(13,349)
17	19	PL	H	Blackburn Rovers	L 1-3	1-2	20	Thomson 29	17,329
18	26	PL	A	Newcastle United	D 1-1	0-0	22	Thomson 89	(34,459)
19	D 3	PL	H	Manchester City	L 1-2	0-2	22	Mason 74	13,504
20	10	PL	A	Nottingham Forest	L 1-4	1-4	22	Thomson 44	(21,340)
21	16	PL	H	Wimbledon	D 2-2	1-1	22	Milton 7, Sedgley 84	11,367
22	26	PL	A	West Ham United	D 1-1	0-0	22	Thomson 71	(20,562)
23	28	PL	H	Arsenal	L 0-2	0-1	22		22,054
24	31	PL	A	Everton	L 1-4	1-1	22	Sedgley 9	(25,659)
25	J 2	PL	H	Leicester City	W 4-1	1-0	21	Kiwomya 34, 62, Tanner 54, Yallop 73	15,803
26	7	FAC 3	A	**Wrexham**	**L 1-2**	**0-0**		Linigham 84	**(8,324)**
27	14	PL	A	Liverpool	W 1-0	1-0	21	Tanner 30	(32,733)
28	21	PL	H	Chelsea	D 2-2	0-0	21	Slater 74, Wark 81 (pen)	17,296
29	28	PL	A	Blackburn Rovers	L 1-4	0-2	21	Wark 76 (pen)	(21,325)
30	F 4	PL	H	Crystal Palace	L 0-2	0-0	21		15,570
31	22	PL	A	Manchester City	L 0-2	0-0	21		(21,430)
32	25	PL	H	Southampton	W 2-1	0-1	21	Mathie 70, Chapman 77	16,076
33	28	PL	H	Newcastle United	L 0-2	0-2	21		18,639
34	M 4	PL	A	Manchester United	L 0-9	0-3	21		(43,804)
35	8	PL	A	Tottenham Hotspur	L 0-3	0-2	21		(24,930)
36	20	PL	A	Norwich City	L 0-3	0-0	21		(17,510)
37	A 1	PL	H	Aston Villa	L 0-1	0-1	21		15,710
38	5	PL	A	Leeds United	L 0-4	0-4	22		(28,600)
39	11	PL	H	Queens Park Rangers	L 0-1	0-0	22		22,767
40	15	PL	A	Arsenal	L 1-4	0-1	22	Marshall 71	(36,818)
41	17	PL	H	West Ham United	D 1-1	1-0	22	Thomson 11	19,099
42	29	PL	A	Leicester City	L 0-2	0-0	22		(15,248)
43	M 6	PL	H	Coventry City	W 2-0	0-0	22	Marshall 53, Presley 63 (og)	12,893
44	9	PL	H	Everton	L 0-1	0-0	22		14,951
45	14	PL	A	Sheffield Wednesday	L 1-4	0-1	22	Mathie 50	(30,213)
46									
47									
48									
49									
50									
51									
52									
53									
54									
55									
56									
57									
58									
59									
60									

Best Home League Attendance: 22,559 v Manchester United   **Smallest:** 11,367 v Wimbledon   **Av Home Att:** 16,907

Goal Scorers:

League (36): Thomsey 5, Sedgley 4, Wark 4 (3 pens), Kiwomya 3, Marshall 3, Mason 3, Mathie 2, Milton 2, Tanner 2, Opponents 2, Chapman, Guentchev, Paz, Slater, Williams, Yallop

C/Cola Cup (0):

FA Cup (1): Linigham

Compared with 1993-94: +496

242

1	2	19	8	5	16	7	17	10	11	21	9	18	13	6	8	14	24	12	23	26	27	20	28	15	30	
Forrest	Stockwell	Yallop	Mason	Wark	Youds	Williams	Milton	Marshall	Kiwomya	Slater	Guentchev	Palmer	Baker	Linighan	Johnson	Sedgley	Taricco	Thomsen	Morgan	Paz	Cotterell	Gregory D.	Vaughan	Whelan	Gregory N.	Referee
X	X	X	X	X	X	X	X	X	X	X1	X	S1	S	S												Lodge S. 1
X	X	X	X	X	S	X	X	X	X			S	S	X												Worrall J. 2
X	X	X	X	X	S	X			X	X	X	S	S	X												Danson P. 3
X	X	X	X			X	X	S	X	X	X	S	S	X												Clifford R. 4
X	X	X	X			X	X	S	X	X	X	S	S	X												Willard G. 5
X		X		X		X	X	X1	X	S1	X			S	X	X	X	S								Dilkes R. 6
X		X				X	X	S2	X2	X				S1	X	X	X	X	X1	S						Poll G. 7
X		X	X	X2		X	S2					S1	X	S	X	X		X		X1						Jones P. 8
X		X	X1	X2		X		S1				X	X	S	X	X		X			S2					Ashby G. 9
X		X		X1		X			X	X	X	X1	X	S	X	X		X			S1	S				Heilbron T. 10
X		X		X		X		X	X1			X	X	S	X	X		X			S1	S				Hart R. 11
X		X		X1	S1	X	X					X	X	S		X		X		X		S				Reed M. 12
X	S1	X			X	X2	X					X	X	S		X		X		X1		S2	X			Hill B. 13
X	X	S			X	X						X	X1	S	S1	X		X		X			X			Durkin P. 14
X		X				X	X1	S1		S2	X2				X	X		X	S	X				X		Gallagher D. 15
X	X	X				X	X	S1		S2	X2				X	X		X	S	X				X1		Wilkie A. 16
X		X	X			X	X	S1	X		S				X	X		X	S	X				X1		Burge K. 17
X		X	X			X	X		X1	S1					X	S		X	S	X				X		Cooper K. 18
X		X	X			X		S2	X	S1					X1	S1		X2	S	X				X		Lodge S. 19
X		X	X			X	S2		X	S1					S	X		X	S	X1				X		Reed M. 20
X		X	X	X		X	X		X	S1				S		X1		X		X	S1	X	X		X1	Elleray D. 21
X		X	X	X		X	X		X	S1			S		X1	X		X				X	X	X†	S	Durkin P. 22
X		X	X2	X		X1	X		X			S1	S2	S	X	X		X				X	X	X1		Danson P. 23
X		X	X2	X1					X	X	X	S1	S	X		X		X		3		X	X	S1		Dilkes R. 24
X		X	X2						X	X	X	S1	S	X		X		X		2		X	X	S2		Holbrook T. 25
		X	X1						X	X2	X			X	X	S1		X	S	S2		X	X			Rushton J. 26
X		X	S	X	S	X						X	S	X	X	X	31	X		X						Gifford R. 27
X		X	S	X		X		33	X			S		X	X	X		X		X1						Don P. 28
X		X	X	X		X			X			S		S1	X			X1	S			X	X			Poll G. 29
X		X	X	X2		X			X			X1		X		S2	S	S1	S	X2						Lodge S. 30
X		X	X	X		X			X1			X		X	X	S1		S	S2	X						Cooper K. 31
X		X	X	X			X1	X				X		X	X	X	S1		S	S2	X					Jones P. 32
X		X	S1	X		X		S	X	X1	X	X	X	X		X			S	X						Ashby G. 33
X		X	S	X		X		S1	X	X	X	X		X		X			S	X						Poll G. 34
X		X		X	X	X	X1	S2				X		X		X		S1	S	X2	X					Hill B. 35
X		X	X†			X	X	X	X	X1			S		S			X		X			X			Durkin P. 36
X		X	X			X	X	X	X	X1			S		S			X		X						Worrall J. 37
X		X				X	X	X1	X	S1	S	S	S	X				X		X						Willard G. 38
	X	X				X	S	X	X1	X		X	S	X				X		X						Gifford R. 39
	X	X				X	S2	X	X1	X		X	X	X				X	S							Holbrook T. 40
	X	X	S1	X		X	X2	X2	X	X		X	X	X				X	S							Bodenham M. 41
	X	S		X		X	X	X	X	X	X			X		X		X	X							Wilkie A. 42
X	X	X				X		X	X			X2						X	S	X						Reed M. 43
X	X2	X				X		X	X1	X		X	S2					X	S							Hart R. 44
X	X	X				X		X		X		X2						X1	S							Poll G. 45
36	14	41	19	26	9	38	19	14	13	22	11	10	2	31	14	26	1	31	1	13	9	0	10	12	1	League Appearances
	1			2	1		6	3				5	5	2			1	3		2	2		4	1	1		League Sub Appearances
2		2	2			2	1			2	2	1	1+1	2	2			2		2			0+1	1	1	C/Cola Cup Appearances
1	1		1			1	1	0+1	1			1	1	1				1		0+1			1	1		FA Cup Appearances

Also Played: Tanner (25, 26, 27, 28, 29, 30, 32, 33, 35, 43, 45), Chapman (28, 29, 30, 31, 32, 33, 34, 35, 36, 37, 38, 39, 40, 41, 42, 43, 44, 45), Swailes (37, 44, 45), Ellis (40), Wright (42, 43, 44, 45)
† = Sent Off

IPSWICH TOWN

CLUB RECORDS

BIGGEST VICTORIES
League: 7-0 v Portsmouth, Division 2, 7.11.1964.
7-0 v Southampton, Division 1, 2.2.1974.
7-0 v West Bromwich Albion, Division 1, 6.11.1976.
F.A. Cup: 11-0 v Cromer, 3rd Qualifying Round, 31.10.1936.
League Cup: 5-0 v Northampton, 2nd Round, 30.8.1977
6-1 v Swindon, 4th Round, 26.11.1985.
Europe: 10-0 v Floriana, 25.9.1962.

BIGGEST DEFEATS
League: 0-9 v Manchester Utd, 4.3.95.
1-10 v Fulham, Division 1, 16.12.1963.
F.A. Cup: 1-7 v Southampton, 3rd Round, 2.2.1974.
League Cup: 0-4 v Arsenal, 2nd Round, 9.9.1971.
2-6 v Aston Villa, 4th Round, 30.11.1988.
Europe: 0-4 v Bruges, 2nd Round, 5.11.1975.

MOST POINTS
3 points a win: 84, Division 2, 1991-92.
2 points a win: 64, Division 3(S), 1953-54, 1955-56.

MOST GOALS SCORED
106, Division 3(S), 1955-56.
Parker 30, Garneys 19, Grant 16, Reed 12, Blackman 8, McLuckie 6, Elsworthy 3, Leadbetter 4, Acres 2, Brown 2, Myles 1, Snell 1, Opponents 2.

MOST GOALS CONCEDED
121, Division 1, 1963-64.

MOST FIRST CLASS MATCHES IN A SEASON
66 - 1980-81 (League 42, FA Cup 7, League Cup 5, UEFA Cup 12).

MOST LEAGUE WINS
27, Division 3(S), 1953-54.

MOST LEAGUE DRAWS
18, Division 2, 1990-91.

MOST LEAGUE DEFEATS
29, Premiership 1994-95.

INDIVIDUAL CLUB RECORDS

MOST GOALS IN A SEASON
Ted Phillips: 46 goals in 1956-57 (League 41, FA Cup 5).

MOST GOALS IN A MATCH
5. Ray Crawford v Florina, 10-0, European Cup, 25.9.1962.
5. Alan Brazil v Southampton, 5-2, Division 1, 16.2.1982.

OLDEST PLAYER
Mick Burns, 43 years 219 days v Gateshead, FA Cup, 12.1.1952.

YOUNGEST PLAYER
Jason Dozzell, 16 years 56 days v Coventry, 4.2.1984.

MOST CAPPED PLAYER
Allan Hunter (Northern Ireland) 47.

BEST PERFORMANCES

League: 1955-56: Matches played 46, Won 25, Drawn 14, Lost 7, Goals for 106, Goals against 64, Points 64. Third in Division 3(S).
Highest Position: First in Division 1, 1961-62.
F.A. Cup: 1977-78: 3rd Round Cardiff City 2-0; 4th Round Hartlepool United 4-1; 5th Round Bristol Rovers 2-2,3-0; 6th Round Millwall 6-1; Semi-final W.B.A. 3-1; Final Arsenal 1-0.
League Cup: Semi-finalists in 1981-82.
Most recent success: 1984-85: 2nd Round Derby County 4-2,1-1; 3rd Round Newcastle United 1-1,2-1; 4th Round Oxford United 2-1; 5th Round Q.P.R. 0-0,2-1; Semi-final Norwich City 1-0,0-2.
Europe: (UEFA) 1980-81: 1st Round Aris Salonika 5-1,1-3; 2nd Round Bohemians 0-2,3-0; 3rd Round Widzew Lodz 5-0,0-1; 4th Round St. Ettiene 4-1,3-1; Semi-final Cologne 1-0,1-0; Final AZ67 Alkmaar 3-0,2-4.

DIVISIONAL RECORD

	Played	Won	Drawn	Lost	For	Against	Points
Division 1/P	1,008	373	250	385	1,344	1,392	1,104
Division 2	648	272	175	211	1,034	932	823
Division 3(S)	486	214	112	160	806	695	540
Total	2,142	859	527	756	3,184	3,019	2,467

ADDITIONAL INFORMATION
PREVIOUS NAMES
None.

PREVIOUS LEAGUES
Southern League.

Club colours: Royal blue shirts fading into white, royal blue shorts fading into white, white socks with blue tops.
Change colours: Jade shirts with maroon sleaves and mustard trim, maroon shorts with jade side panels, maroon socks with jade tops.

Reserves League
Avon Insurance Football Combination.

RECORDS AND STATISTICS

COMPETITIONS

Div 1/P	Div.2/1	Div.3(S)	Euro C	UEFA	ECWC
1961-64	1954-55	1938-54	1962-63	1973-74	1978-79
1968-86	1957-61	1955-57		1974-75	
1992-95	1964-68			1975-76	Texaco
	1986-92			1977-78	1972-73
	1995-			1979-80	
				1980-81	
				1981-82	
				1982-83	

HONOURS

Div.1	Div.2	Div.3(S)	FA Cup	UEFA
1961-62	1960-61	1953-54	1977-78	1980-81
	1967-68	1956-57		Texaco
	1991-92			1972-73

MOST GOALS IN A CAREER
Ray Crawford - 227 (1958-69)

Year	League	FA Cup	Lge Cup	Europe
1958-59	25	1		
1959-60	18			
1960-61	40			
1961-62	33	1	3	
1962-63	25			8
1963-64	2			
1965-66	8			
1966-67	21	3	1	
1967-68	16		5	
1968-69	16		1	
Total	204	5	10	8

Current top goalscorer - John Wark 177 (1974-1995 - 3 spells)

MOST APPEARANCES
Mick Mills 737+4 (1966-82)

Year	League	FA Cup	Lge Cup	Europe
1965-66	2			
1966-67	21+1	1	2	
1967-68	9+1	1	1+1	
1968-69	35+1	1		
1969-70	40	1	3	
1970-71	42	6	2	
1971-72	35	2	1	
1972-73	42	2	2	
1973-74	42	3	4	8
1974-75	42	9	5	
1975-76	42	3	1	4
1976-77	37	3	2	
1977-78	34	7	2	5
1978-79	42	5	1	6
1979-80	37	4	2	3
1980-81	33	6	5	10
1981-82	42	3	8	2
1982-83	11		2	2
	588+3	57	43+1	40

Plus 8 Texaco Cup 1972-73 & 1 Charity Shield 1978-79.

MANAGERS

Name	Seasons	Best	Worst
Michael O'Brien	1936-37		
Adam Scott Duncan	1937-55	1(1)	3(3S)
Alf Ramsey	1955-63	1(1)	3(3S)
Jackie Milburn	1963-64	22(1)	22(1)
Bill McGarry	1964-68	1(2)	15(2)
Bobby Robson	1968-82	2(1)	19(1)
Bobby Ferguson	1982-87	9(1)	5(2)
John Duncan	1987-90	8(2)	9(2)
John Lyall	1990-95	1(2)	14(2)
George Burnley	1995-	20(P)	20(P)

RECORD TRANSFER FEE RECEIVED

Amount	Club	Player	Date
£1,750,000	Tottenham H	Jason Dozzell	8/93
£800,000	Sheffield Utd	Brian Gayle	9/91
£750,000	Glasgow Rangers	Terry Butcher	8/86
£500,000	Tottenham H	Alan Brazil	3/83

RECORD TRANSFER FEE PAID

Amount	Club	Player	Date
£1,000,000	Tottenham Hotspur	Steve Sedgley	6/94
£750,000	Oldham Athletic	Ian Marshall	8/93
£650,000	Derby County	Geriant Williams	5/92
£400,000	Aberdeen	Paul Mason	6/93

LONGEST LEAGUE RUNS

of undefeated matches:	23 (8.12.1979 - 26.4.1980)	**of league matches w/out a win:**	21 (28.8.1963 - 20.12.1963)
of undefeated home matches:	33 (27.10.1979 - 28.3.1981)	**of undefeated away matches:**	11 (15.12.1979 - 18.4.1980)
without home win:	9 (24.8.1963 - 28.12.1963)	**without an away win:**	27 (10.5.1963 - 29.9.1964)
of league wins:	8 (19.8.1953 - 16.9.1953)	**of home wins:**	14 (19.9.1956 - 9.3.1957)
of league defeats:	10 (9.9.1954 - 16.10.1954)	**of away wins:**	5 (10.9.1976 - 27.12.1976)

IPSWICH TOWN

PLAYERS NAME / Honours	Ht	Wt	Birthdate	Birthplace / Transfers	Contract Date	Clubs	League	L/Cup	FA Cup	Other	Lge	L/C	FAC	Oth
GOALKEEPERS														
Clive E Baker	5.9	11.0	14.03.59	North Walsham	29.07.77	Norwich City (J)	14		2					
				Free	07.07.84	Barnsley	291	15	23	8				
				Free	23.09.91	Coventry City		1						
				Free	20.08.92	Ipswich Town	47+1	5	5					
Craig L Forrest	6.4	14.4	20.09.67	Vancouver	31.08.85	Ipswich Town (A)	236	18	13	11				
Can: ; Div2'92				Loan	01.03.88	Cochester United	11							
Richard I Wright	6.2	13.0	05.11.77	Ipswich	02.01.95	Ipswich Town (T)	3							
E: S.														
DEFENDERS														
Leo S Cotterell	5.9	10.0	02.09.74	Cambridge	01.07.93	Ipswich Town (T)	0+2	0+1						
E: S														
Kevin Ellis	5.10	11.5	12.05.77	Gt Yarmouth	08.94	Ipswich Town (T)	1							
David S Gregory	5.11	11.6	23.01.70	Sudbury	31.03.87	Ipswich Town (T)	16+16	3+2	1	3+2	2			4
David Linighan	6.2	12.6	09.01.65	Hartlepool	03.03.82	Hartlepool Utd(J)	84+7	3+1	4	3	5	1		
FLgXl.1; Dlv2'92				£25,000	11.08.86	Derby County								
				£30,000	04.12.86	Shrewsbury Town	65	5	3	1	1			
				£300,000	23.06.88	Ipswich Town	273+3	20	18	10	12		1	
Christopher W Swailes	6.1	12.11	11.10.70	Gateshead	23.05.89	Ipswich Town (T)								
FA Vase'93.				£10,000	28.03.91	Peterborough Utd								
				£8,000	01.09.91	Boston United								
via Kettering Town, Bridlington				Free	27.10.93	Doncaster Rovers	49	2	1	2		1		
				£150,000	23.03.95	Ipswich Town	4							
Mauricio R Taricco	5.9	11.7	10.03.73	Buenos Aires		Argentinos Jnrs.								
				£175,000	09.09.94	Ipswich Town		1						
Neil Thompson	6.0	13.7	02.10.63	Beverley		Nottingham F. (A)								
E: S-P4; BLT'84; GMVC'87; Div2'92				Free	28.11.81	Hull City	29+2							
				Free	01.08.93	Scarborough	87	8	4	9	15	1		1
				£100,000	09.06.89	Ipswich Town	24+17	14+1	17	8	18	1	2	1
Anthony J Vaughan	6.1	11.02	11.10.75	Manchester	01.07.94	Ipswich Town (T)	10		1					
E: S														
Frank W Yallop	5.10	10.3	04.04.64	Watford	05.01.82	Ipswich Town (A)	286+23	22+2	14+3	21+2	7	1		
Can: ; E:Y5; Div2'92														
MIDFIELD														
Lee R Durrant	5.10	11.7	18.12.72	GtYarmouth	13.07.92	IpswichTown (T)	3+4							
E: S														
Paul D Mason	5.8	12.1	03.09.63	Liverpool		Everton (A)								
SLC'90; SFAC'90				Free		F.C. Groningen								
				£200,000	01.08.88	Aberdeen	138+20	13+2	11+1	7	27	8	1	1
				£400,000	18.06.93	Ipswich Town	37+6	3	2+2		6	1		
Simon C Milton	5.10	11.0	23.08.63	Fulham		Bury Town								
Div2'92				£5,500	17.07.87	Ipswich Town (A)	168+33	11+3	8	10+1	39	2	1	3
				Loan	01.11.87	Exeter City	2		1		3			
				Loan	01.03.88	Torquay United	4			1				
Lee R Norfolk	5.10	11.3	17.10.75	Dunedin, NZ	01.07.94	Ipswich Town (T)	1+2							
Stephen L Palmer	6.1	12.7	31.03.68	Brighton		Cambridge United								
Div2;92				Free	01.08.89	Ipswich Town	82+24	3	8+3	3+2	2		1	
Stephen P Sedgley	6.1	12.6	26.05.68	Enfield	02.06.86	Coventry City (A)	81+3	9	2+2	5+1	3	2		
E: u21.11; FAC'91; CS'91				£750,000	28.07.89	Tottenham Hotspur	147+17	24+3	12+1	5+3	8	1	1	
				£1,000,000	15.06.94	Ipswich Town	26	2	1		4			
Michael T Stockwell	5.6	10.3	14.02.65	Chelmsford	17.12.82	Ipswich Town (A)	299+16	23+3	18+3	16+2	20	2	1	1
Div2'92														
Adam D Tanner	6.0	12.1	25.10.73	Maldon	13.07.92	Ipswich Town (T)	9+1		1		2			
Claus Thomsen	6.3	11.6	31.05.70	Aarhus, Denmark		Arhus								
Den:				£250,000	15.06.94	Ipswich Town	31+2	2	1		5			
John Wark	5.10	12.10	04.08.57	Glasgow	01.08.74	Ipswich Town (A)	295+1	24+1	36+1	25	94	12	10	18
S: 29, u21.9, UEFA'81; FAC'78; SC'86; Div2'92				£450,000	10.03.84	Liverpool	64+6	6+4	11+2	13+2	28	3	6	5
				£100,000	04.01.88	Ipswich Town	87+2	4	3	9	23			2
				£50,000	23.08.90	Middlesbrough	31+1	5	2	1	3			
				Free	21.09.91	Ipswich Town	136+2	12+1	14	3	16		2	
David Geraint Williams	5.7	10.6	05.01.62	Treorchy	12.01.80	Bristol Rovers (A)	138+3	14	9+2	5	8		2	
W: 12, u21.2, Y: Div2'92				£40,000	29.03.85	Derby County	276+1	26+1	17	11	9	1		
				£650,000	01.07.92	Ipswich Town	109	9+1	9		1			
FORWARDS														
Lee R Chapman	6.2	13.0	05.02.59	Lincoln	22.06.78	Stoke City (J)	95+4	5	3		34	3	1	
E: B.1, u21.1. LC'89. SC'90. Div.2'90. Div.1'92.				Loan	05.12.78	Plymouth Argyle	3+1							
				£500,000	25.08.82	Arsenal	15+8	0+2	0+1	2	4			2
				£200,000	29.12.83	Sunderland	14+1		2		3		1	
				£100,000	24.08.84	Sheffield Wed.	147+2	17	17+1	2+1	63	6	10	
via Niort (Fra), £350,000, 01.06.88 to				£350,000	17.10.88	Nottingham Forest	48	12	5	6	15	6	3	3
				£400,000	11.01.90	Leeds United	133+4	15	11	10	63	10	4	4
				£250,000	16.09.93	Portsmouth	5			1	2			
				£250,000	16.09.93	West Ham United	33+7	4+1	6		7	2	2	
				Loan	13.01.95	Southend United	1				1			
				£70,000	19.01.95	Ipswich Town	9+7				1			

IPSWICH TOWN

PLAYERS NAME / Honours	Ht	Wt	Birthdate	Birthplace / Transfers	Contract Date	Clubs	APPEARANCES				GOALS			
							League	L/Cup	FA Cup	Other	Lge	L/C	FAC	Oth
Neil R Gregory	6.0	11.10	07.10.72	Ndola (Zambia)	21.02.92	Ipswich Town (T)	1+2							
				Loan	03.02.94	Chesterfield	2+1				1			
				Loan	03.03.95	Scunthorpe United	10				7			
an P Marshall	6.1	12.12	20.03.66	Liverpool	23.03.84	Everton (A)	9+6	1+1		7	1	1		
Div2'91; CS'86				£100,000	24.03.86	Oldham Athletic	165+5	17	14	2+1	36		3	1
				£750,000	09.08.93	Ipswich Town	42+5	3	5		13	2	3	
Alexander Mathie	5.10	10.7	20.12.68	Bathgate		Celtic	7+4		1	0+1				
				£100,000	01.08.91	Morton	73+1	2	5	7	31	1	3	9
				Loan	30.03.93	Port Vale	0+3							
				£285,000	30.07.93	Newcaslte United	3+22	2+2			4			
				£500,000	24.02.95	Ipswich Town	13				2			
ames B Scowcroft	6.1	12.2	25.10.73	Bury St Ed.	01.07.94	Ipswich Town (T)								
Stuart I Slater	5.7	10.5	27.03.69	Sudbury	02.04.87	West Ham Utd (T)	134+7	16+1	16	5	11	2	3	2
E: B2, u21.3				£1,500,000	14.08.92	Celtic	40+4	3+2	3	4	3			
				£750,000	30.09.93	Ipswich Town	22+5	2	1		1			
Russ Uhlenbeek	5.9	12.5		Holland		Tops SV								
				£100,000	08.95	Ipswich Town								

ADDITIONAL CONTRACT PLAYERS: (F) Richard Naylor - Ipswich (T). (M/F) Simon Portey - Ipswich (Y).

TOP GOALSCORER 1994/95
Claus Thomsen

Premiership goals (games). . . . . 5 (31+2)
Coca-Cola Cup Goals 0 (2)
F.A. Cup goals 0 (1)

Total . . . . 5 (34+2)

Total goals for Ipswich since 08.94 . . . . 5 (34+2)

THE MANAGER
GEORGE BURLEY

Date of Birth . . . . 3rd June 1956.
Place of Birth. . . . . Cumnock.
Date of Appointment . . . . December 1994.

PREVIOUS CLUBS
As Manager. . . . . Aye United, Colchester United.
As Coach . . . . Motherwell, twice.
As a Player . . . . Ipswich Town, Sunderland, Gillingham.

HONOURS
As a Manager
None.

As a Player
Ipswich Town: FA Cup 1978, UEFA 1981.
International: 11 full caps, 2 U23, 5 U21, Y, S for Scotland.

PORTMAN ROAD

Ipswich, Suffolk IP1 2DA
Tel: 01473 219 211

Capacity 22,500

First game ....v V Beccles Caxton,
....Suffolk Challenge Cup, 7-1, 2.3.1889.
First floodlit game...v Arsenal, Friendly, 16.2.1960.

ATTENDANCES
Highest ....38,010 v Leeds Utd, FAC 6th Rnd, 8.3.1975.
Lowest ....3,116 v Leyton Orient, 25.3.1953.

OTHER GROUNDS..None.

MATCHDAY TICKET PRICES

Portman Stand A Block -	£16/£10
B Block -	£14/£9
Portman Lower	£9/£5
Pioneer Stand H, N, O Blocks	£16/£10
G, I M, P Blocks	£14/£9
F, J, R Blocks	£11.50/£8.50
Q Block	£14/£9
Pioneer Lower	£9/£5
Pioneer Family F, K, L Blocks	£10.50/£6
Churchmans Stand	£9/£5
North Stand	£9

Ticket Office Telephone no. 01473 221 133

HOW TO GET TO THE GROUND

From the North and West
Use A45 sign posted to Ipswich West.
Proceed straight through Post House traffic lights.
At the second set of traffic lights turn right into West End Road.
The ground is 400 metres along on the left.

From the South
Follow signs for Ipswich West, then proceed as above.

Car Parking
Large parks in Portman Road, Portman's Walk & West End Road.

Nearest Railway Station
Ipswich (01473 57373)

CLUBCALL
0839 66 44 88
Calls cost 39p per minute cheap rate and 49p per minute at all other times.
Call costings correct at time of going to press.

MATCHDAY PROGRAMME

Programme Controller .... Mike Noye.

Number of pages .... 40.

Price .... £1.50.

Subscriptions .... Apply to club.

Local Newspapers .... East Anglian Daily Times, Evening Star.

Local Radio Stations..... SGR FM, Saxon Radio, BBC Radio Suffolk.

LEICESTER CITY
(The Foxes)
ENDSLEIGH LEAGUE DIVISION 1
SPONSORED BY: WALKERS CRISPS

Back Row (L-R): Jamie Lawrence, Lee Philpott, Garry Parker, Simon Grayson, Colin Hill, Mark Blake, Phil Gee, Craig Hallam.
Middle Row: Mark McGhee (Manager), Colin Lee (Asst. Manager), Richard Smith, Jimmy Willis, Iwan Roberts, Kevin Poole, Steve Walsh, Brian Carey, Mike Whitlow, Mike Hickman (1st Team Coach), Alan Smith (Physio). **Front Row:** Taff Davies (Kit Manager), Julian Joachim, Sam McMahon, Neil Lewis, David Lowe, Scott Taylor, Mark Robins, Paul Bedder, Mick Yoeman (Physio).

LEICESTER CITY
FORMED IN 1884
TURNED PROFESSIONAL IN 1888
LTD COMPANY IN 1897

PRESIDENT: K R Brigstock
CHAIRMAN: Martin George
CHEIF EXECUTIVE: Barrie Pierpoint
DIRECTORS
T Smeaton, J M Elsom FCA, R W Parker,
J E Sharp, T W Shipman, W K Shooter FCA
FOOTBALL SECRETARY
Ian Silvester
HEAD OF PUBLICITY
Paul Mace

MANAGER: Mark McGhee
ASSISTANT MANAGER: Colin Lee
COACH: Mike Hickman

YOUTH DEVELOPMENT OFFICER
David Nish

PHYSIOTHERAPIST
Alan Smith & Mick Yoeman

STATISTICIAN FOR THE DIRECTORY
Dave Smith

It was always going to be a difficult season, the first in the Premiership after a seven year absence from the top flight. Most pundits were agreed that the squad needed strengthening by at least four quality players to be able to compete. Season ticket sales reached record levels to generate cash during the summer of 1994. Yet only one player of Premiership quality, Mark Draper, was signed. In addition, the three players most likely to adapt readily to the demands at the highest level - Steve Walsh, David Speedie and Julian Joachim - all saw their personal season virtually obliterated by injury.

Consequently, City struggled throughout, although there were a couple of early season highs that offered a smattering of false hope: spectacular home victories over Tottenham and Southampton. However, an ignominious League Cup exit to lowly Brighton was more indicative of the long winter to follow.

By November the focus had undoubtedly shifted to events off the field. The manner of Brian Little's departure and his subsequent association with Aston Villa was an unsavoury chapter throughout, badly handled by all relevant parties, leaving a groundswell of ill will on the terraces that poured out in December when Villa visited Filbert Street. It was in no way an appropriate manner in which to treat the man who had lifted the club off the floor and taken them to Wembley in three successive seasons.

His successor, Mark McGhee, arrived just before Christmas and soon realised the enormity of the task before him. By early in the new year, relegation was already all but a mathematical certainty and McGhee set about rebuilding his battle weary squad for the future. He almost had the bonus of an unexpected cup run to savour. City scrambled past non-League Enfield, then accounted for Portsmouth in the mud to reach the last 16 for the first time since 1985. Dreams of another "relegation and Wembley" double, as the club achieved in 1969, were dashed at Molineux by former Fox David Kelly and fans were left to contemplate a long run in to the season with little to play for, for the first time in several years.

On an individual front, Draper impressed until the relegation battle was lost and then rejoined his former mentor, Brian Little, during the summer, thus simultaneously becoming the club's record incoming and outgoing signing. More consistent throughout was Player of the Season, Kevin Poole, who certainly had plenty of practice between the sticks. Others flattered briefly to deceive but failed to produce the goods regularly at Premiership level. Overall it was a season best forgotten where the only mystery remaining was how on earth City did not actually manage to finish bottom of the table - things must have been really dire at Portman Road! **DAVE SMITH.**

LEICESTER CITY

Premier League: 21st   **FA Cup:** 5th Round   **Coca-Cola Cup:** 2nd Round

M	DATE	COMP.	VEN	OPPONENTS	RESULT	H/T	LP	GOAL SCORERS/GOAL TIMES	ATT.
1	A 21	PL	H	Newcastle United	L 1-3	0-0		Joachim 90	20,048
2	23	PL	A	Blackburn Rovers	L 0-3	0-1			(21,050)
3	27	PL	A	Nottingham Forest	L 0-1	0-1	22		(21,601)
4	31	PL	H	Queens Park Rangers	D 1-1	0-1	20	Gee 89	18,695
5	S 10	PL	A	Wimbledon	L 1-2	1-2	21	Lowe 27	(7,683)
6	17	PL	H	Tottenham Hotspur	W 3-1	1-0	20	Joachim 45, 90, Lowe 87	21,300
7	21	CCC 2/1	A	Brighton & H.A.	L 0-1	0-0			(11,041)
8	24	PL	A	Everton	D 1-1	0-0	18	Draper 81	(28,003)
9	O 3	PL	H	Coventry City	D 2-2	1-1	19	Roberts 45, 85	19,372
10	5	CCC 2/2	H	Brighton & H.A.	L 0-2	0-1			14,258
11	8	PL	A	Chelsea	L 0-4	0-2	20		(18,397)
12	15	PL	H	Southampton	W 4-3	2-0	18	Blake 3, 53, Roberts 21, Carr 82	20,020
13	24	PL	A	Leeds United	L 1-2	0-1	18	Blake 53	(28,547)
14	29	PL	H	Crystal Palace	L 0-1	0-1	19		20,022
15	N 5	PL	A	West Ham United	L 0-1	0-0	21		(18,780)
16	20	PL	H	Manchester City	L 0-1	0-1	21		19,006
17	23	PL	H	Arsenal	W 2-1	2-1	20	Seaman 16 (og), Lowe 28	20,774
18	26	PL	A	Norwich City	L 1-2	1-0	21	Draper 23	(20,657)
19	D 3	PL	H	Aston Villa	D 1-1	1-0	21	Gee 5	20,896
20	10	PL	A	Newcastle United	L 1-3	0-1	21	Oldfield 48	(34,400)
21	17	PL	H	Blackburn Rovers	D 0-0	0-0	21		20,559
22	26	PL	H	Liverpool	L 1-2	0-0	21	Roberts 87	21,393
23	28	PL	A	Manchester United	D 1-1	0-1	21	Whitlow 63	(43,789)
24	31	PL	H	Sheffield Wednesday	L 0-1	0-1	21		20,624
25	J 2	PL	A	Ipswich Town	L 1-4	0-1	22	Roberts 52	(15,803)
26	7	FAC 3	H	Enfield	W 2-0	1-0		Oldfield 9, Roberts 67	17,351
27	14	PL	A	Crystal Palace	L 0-2	0-2	22		(12,707)
28	25	PL	A	Manchester City	W 1-0	0-0	22	Roberts 68	(21,007)
29	28	FAC 4	A	Portsmouth	W 1-0	1-0		Roberts 44	(14,928)
30	F 4	PL	H	West Ham United	L 1-2	1-2	22	Roberts 45	20,375
31	11	PL	A	Arsenal	D 1-1	0-0	22	Draper 78	(31,373)
32	18	FAC 5	A	Wolverhampton Wand.	L 0-1	0-1			(28,544)
33	22	PL	A	Aston Villa	D 4-4	0-2	21	Robins 60, Roberts 77, Lowe 80,90	(30,825)
34	25	PL	A	Coventry City	L 2-4	0-2	22	Lowe 63, Roberts 73	(20,633)
35	M 4	PL	H	Everton	D 2-2	0-2	22	Draper 59, Roberts 82	20,447
36	8	PL	A	Queens Park Rangers	L 0-2	0-0	22		(10,189)
37	11	PL	H	Nottingham Forest	L 2-4	1-1	22	Lowe 16, Draper 71	20,423
38	15	PL	H	Leeds United	L 1-3	1-1	22	Roberts 21	20,068
39	18	PL	A	Tottenham Hotspur	L 0-1	0-0	22		(30,851)
40	A 1	PL	H	Wimbledon	L 3-4	1-1	22	Robins 13, Willis 79, Lawrence 84	15,489
41	5	PL	H	Norwich City	W 1-0	0-0	21	Parker 48	15,992
42	8	PL	A	Sheffield Wednesday	L 0-1	0-1	21		(22,551)
43	15	PL	H	Manchester United	L 0-4	0-2	21		21,281
44	17	PL	A	Liverpool	L 0-2	0-0	21		(36,012)
45	29	PL	H	Ipswich Town	W 2-0	0-0	21	Whitlow 67, Lowe 90	15,248
46	M 6	PL	H	Chelsea	D 1-1	1-1	21	Willis 24	18,140
47	14	PL	A	Southampton	D 2-2	0-1	21	Parker 59, Robins 88	(15,101)
48									
49									
50									
52									
52									
53									
54									
55									
56									
57									
58									
59									
60									

Best Home League Attendance: 21,393 v Liverpool   **Smallest:** 15,248 v Ipswich Town   **Av Home Att:** 19,532

Goal Scorers:

Compared with 1993-94: +3,527

League (45): Roberts 9, Lowe 8, Draper 5, Robins 5, Blake 3, Joachim 3, Whitlow 2, Willis 2, Gee 2, Parker 2, Carr, Oldfield, Lawrence, Opponent

C/Cola Cup (0):

FA Cup (3): Roberts 2, Oldfield

1 Ward	2 Grayson	3 Whitlow	12 Smith	19 Hill	14 Mohan	6 Agnew	8 Blake	10 Draper	18 Parker	7 Joachim	17 Thompson	9 Roberts	33 Poole	4 Willis	21 Philiott	34 Galloway	25 Lowe	26 Gee	24 Lewis	15 Carey	16 Carr	20 Oldfield	11 Ormandroyd	22 Lawrence	6 Robins	Referee	
X	X2	X	X	X	X	X	X1	X		X	S1	S2	S													M. Reed	1
X	X	X		X1	X	X	X	X		X2	S1	S2	S	X												P. Burge	2
S	X	X2	X		X	X	X	X1		X	S1	X	X	X	S2											G. Willard	3
S		X	X1		X	X	S				X	X	X	X	X											S. Lodge	4
S	X					S1	X	X			S2	X	X	X	X		X		X1	X	X2					G. Poll	5
S	X				X	S1	X	X		X		X	X	X	X1		S2		X		X2					G. Ashby	6
S	X				X	X	X	X		X		X1	X	X	X		S1		X		S					P. Durkin	7
S	X		S		X	S	X	X		X		X	X	X	X				X		X					T. Holbrook	8
S	X		S1		X	S2	X	X		X		X	X	X	X				X2		X1					K. Cooper	9
S	X	X			X	S1	X1	X2		X		X	X	X	X				X			S2				J. Rushton	10
S	X1	X	S1		X		X	X		X		X	X	X	X2		S2			X						J. Worrall	11
X	X	X					X1	X		X		X	S	X	X		X2	S2	X		X		S1			R. Hart	12
X	X	X			X		X1	X		X		X	S		X2		S2		X		X		S1			K. Burge	13
X	X	X			X		X	X		X1		X	S		X		S1		X		X2	S2				P. Don	14
X	X	X	S		X		X	X		X		X	X	X			X		X		X	S				R. Dilkes	15
S	X	X	X		X			X			X	S2	X	X			X2		X			S1	X1			K. Moreton	16
S		X			X		X	X			X	S	X	X			X	S				X	X			D. Elleray	17
S		X			X		X	X			X	S	X	X			X1	S1				X	X			R. Gifford	18
S		X	X		X		X		S1	X	S2	X			X2				X			X	X1			M. Bodenham	19
S	X2	X		X	X		X	X		S1	X		X		X		X1		S2	X						G. Willard	20
S	X	X		X		S	X	X		S1	X		X		X		X1			X						P. Don	21
S	X	X		X			S2	X		X2	S1	X	X	X						X1	X					G. Ashby	22
S	X	X		X			X	S2	X		X	X	X	X	X2		S1						X1			D. Gallagher	23
S	X	X		X			X2	S2	X		X	X	X	X			X2						X1			M. Reed	24
S	X	X		X			X			X1	X	X	X	X	S1		X2		X				S2			T. Holbrook	25
S	X	X		X	S	X1					X	X	X	X	X		S1		X				X			J. Worrall	26
S			X	X	X		X	X			X	X	X		X		S1					S2	X2		X	P. Durkin	27
S	X		X	X	X		X	X			X	X	X		X		S							X	X	S. Lodge	28
S	X	X	X	X	X			X			X	X	X		X		S		S						X	D. Gallagher	29
S	X	X1	X		X			X			X	X	X	X	X									S1	X	J. Worrall	30
S	X	X	X1	X				X			X	X	X	X	X2	S1		S2						X	X	G. Poll	31
S1	X2	X		X				X	X		X	X	X1	X	S2	X	S								X	R. Hart	32
S	X	X1		X				X	X		X	X	X		X	S2		X	S12						X	K. Martin	33
S	X			X			S		X	X		X	X	X		X	X	S	X						S	R. Gifford	34
S		X		X1				X	X		X	X	X		X	X	S	X						S1	X	P. Durkin	35
S			X		X	X	X				X	X	X		X		S1								X	M. Reed	36
S			X		X	X	X				X	X		S1	X		X		X	X				X1	X	P. Don	37
S	X			X		X	X1	X			X2	X			X		X		X	X				S1	X	D. Gallagher	38
S	X	X		X		X	X1	X			X2	X			X		X	S1	X					S2	X	S. Lodge	39
S	X	X		X1	X2			X				X	X		X		X		X			X		S1	X	D. Elleray	40
S	X	X		X				X				X	X		X		X		X			S		X	X	T. Holbrook	41
S	X2	X		X			S2	X	X			X	X		X		X		X1					S1	X	G. Ashby	42
S	X1	X		X			S1	X	X			X	X		X2				S2					X	X	M. Bodenham	43
S	X	X		X			X	X	X			X	X		S				X					S1	X	G. Poll	44
S		X		X			X1	X	X			X	X		X				X					S1	X	A. Wilkie	45
	X			X	S			X	X	X		X	X	X					S1					X	X1	G. Willard	46
	X1	X		X				X	X	X		X	X	X					X2					X	S2	K. Burge	47
6	34	28	10	24	23	7	26	39	14	11	16	32	36	29	19	4	19	3	13	11	12	8	6	9	16	League Appearances	
		2				4	4			4	3	5		4			10	4	3	1	1			8	1	League Sub Appearances	
	2	1			2	1+1	2	2		2		2	2	2	2		0+1		2				0+1			C/Cola Cup Appearances	
0+1	3	3	1	3	1	1		2	1		3	3	3	2	2+1	1	0+1		1				1		2	FA Cup Appearances	

Also Played: Mills X(4), Walsh X(1,2,16,17,18), Heskey (X1(36),S(37)), McMahon S(36,41,45),S2(40), Hoult S(46,47)   Players on Loan: Galloway (Celtic)   † = Sent Off

LEICESTER CITY

BIGGEST VICTORIES
League: 10-0 v Portsmouth (h) Division 1, 20.10.1928.
F.A. Cup: 13-0 v Notts Olympic (h), 1st Qual. Round, 13.10.1894.
7-0 v Crook Town (h) 3rd Round, 9.1.1932.
League Cup: 8-1 v Coventry City (a) 5th Round, 1.12.1964.
Europe: 4-1 v Glenavon (a) 1st Round, 13.9.1961.

BIGGEST DEFEATS
League: 0-12 v Nottingham Forest (a) Division 1, 21.4.1909.
F.A. Cup: No more than 4 clear goals (7 instances).
League Cup: 1-7 v Sheffield Wednesday (a) 3rd Round,
27.10.1992.
Europe: 0-2 v Atletico Madrid (a) 2nd Round, 15.11.1961.

MOST POINTS
3 points a win: 77, Division 2, 1991-92.
2 points a win: 61, Division 2, 1956-57.

MOST GOALS SCORED
109, Division 2, 1956-57.

MOST GOALS CONCEDED
112, Division 1, 1957-58.

MOST FIRST CLASS MATCHES IN A SEASON
61 - 1991-92 (League 46, FA Cup 2, League Cup 4, Zenith Data 6,
Play-offs 3).

MOST LEAGUE WINS
25, Division 2, 1956-57.

MOST LEAGUE DRAWS
19, Division 1, 1975-76.

MOST LEAGUE DEFEATS
25, Division 1/Premiership, 1977-78, 1994-95.

MOST GOALS IN A SEASON
Arthur Rowley: 44 goals in 1956-57 (League 44, 5 pens).

MOST GOALS IN A MATCH
6. John Duncan v Port Vale, 7-0, Division 2, 25.12.1924.
6. Arthur Chandler v Portsmouth, 10-0, Division 1, 20.10.1928.

OLDEST PLAYER
Joe Calvert, 40 years 313 days, 13.12.1947.

YOUNGEST PLAYER
Dave Buchanan, 16 years 192 days, 1.1.1979.

MOST CAPPED PLAYER
John O'Neill (Northern Ireland) 39.

League: 1956-57: Matches played 42, Won 25, Drawn 11, Lost 6,
Goals for 109, Goals against 67, Points 61. First in Division 2.
Highest Position: 1928-29: 2nd in Division 1.
F.A. Cup: Runners-up in 1948-49, 1960-61, 1962-63, 1968-69.
Most recent success: 1968-69: 3rd Round Barnsley 1-1,2-1; 4th
Round Millwall 1-0; 5th Round Liverpool 0-0,1-0; 6th Round
Mansfield Town 1-0; Semi-Final West Bromwich Albion 1-0; Final
Manchester City 0-1.
League Cup: 1963-64: 2nd Round Aldershot 2-0; 3rd Round
Tranmere Rovers 2-1; 4th Round Gillingham 3-1; 5th Round
Norwich City 1-1,2-1; Semi-Final West Ham United 4-3,2-0; Final
Stoke City 1-1,3-2.
Europe: (ECWC) 1961-62: 1st Round Glenavon 4-1,3-1; Atletico
Madrid 1-1,0-2.

ADDITIONAL INFORMATION
PREVIOUS NAMES
Leicester Fosse 1884-1919.

PREVIOUS LEAGUES
Midland League.

Club colours: All royal blue.
Change colours: All gold

Reserves League: Pontins Central League Division 2.

DIVISIONAL RECORD

	Played	Won	Drawn	Lost	For	Against	Points
Division 1/P	1,634	525	421	688	2,487	2,871	1,526
Division 2/1	2,028	835	500	693	3,246	2,873	2,330
Total	3,662	1,360	921	1,381	5,733	5,744	3,856

RECORDS AND STATISTICS

COMPETITIONS

Div 1/P	Div.2/1	ECWC	Texaco	A/Scot
1908-09	1894-08	1961-62	1972-73	1975-76
1925-35	1909-25		1973-74	
1937-39	1935-37			**A/Italian**
1954-55	1939-54			1971-72
1957-69	1955-57			1992-93
1971-78	1969-71			1993-94
1980-81	1978-80			
1983-87	1981-83			
1994-95	1987-94			
	1995-			

HONOURS

Div.2	League Cup	C/Shield
1924-25	1963-64	1971
1936-37		
1953-54		
1956-57		
1970-71		
1979-80		

MOST APPEARANCES

GRAHAM CROSS 596+3

Year	League	FA Cup	Lge Cup	Europe
1960-61	1			
1961-62	6			2
1962-63	29	6	2	
1963-64	39	1	6	
1964-65	35	5	9	
1965-66	38	4	1	
1966-67	41	1	3	
1967-68	29	6	1	
1968-69	37	8	2	
1969-70	42	5	6	
1970-71	42	6	5	
1971-72	39	3	1	
1972-73	38	2	1	
1973-74	40	7	1	
1974-75	38+2	5	2	
1975-76	1+1			
	495+3	**59**	**40**	**2**

MOST GOALS IN A CAREER

ARTHUR CHANDLER - 273 (1923-34)

Year	League	FA Cup
1923-24	24	
1924-25	32	6
1925-26	26	
1926-27	28	1
1927-28	34	
1928-29	34	
1929-30	32	
1930-31	18	
1931-32	12	2
1932-33	4	
1933-34	6	5
1934-35	9	
Total	**259**	**14**

Current leading goalscorer: Steve Walsh - 48 (1986-95)

RECORD TRANSFER FEE RECEIVED

Amount	Club	Player	Date
£3,250,000	Aston Villa	Mark Draper	07/95
£1,350,000	Derby County	Paul Kitson	3/92
£0.8+0.25m	Everton	Gary Lineker	7/85+7/86
£1,000,000	Leeds United	Gary McAllister	7/90

RECORD TRANSFER FEE PAID

Amount	Club	Player	Date
£1.25m+£0.5m	Notts County	Mark Draper	7/94+7/95
£360,000	Portsmouth	Mark Blake	3/94
£350,000	Luton Town	Mike Newell	9/87
£350,000	Derby County	Ian Ormondroyd	3/92

MANAGERS

Name	Seasons	Best	Worst
Peter Hodge	1919-26	17(1)	14(2)
Willie Orr	1926-32	2(1)	19(1)
Peter Hodge	1932-34	17(1)	19(1)
Arthur Lochhead	1934-36	21(1)	6(2)
Frank Womack	1936-39	16(1)	1(2)
Tom Bromilow	1939-45		
Tom Mather	1945-46		
John Duncan	1946-49	9(2)	19(2)
Norman Bullock	1949-55	21(1)	15(2)
David Halliday	1955-58	18(1)	5(2)
Matt Gillies	1959-68	4(1)	14(1)
Frank O'Farrell	1968-71	21(1)	3(2)
Jimmy Bloomfield	1971-77	7(1)	18(1)
Frank McLintock	1977-78	22(1)	22(1)
Jock Wallace	1978-82	21(1)	17(2)
Gordon Milne	1982-86	15(1)	3(2)
Bryan Hamilton	1986-87	20(1)	13(2)
David Pleat	1987-91	13(2)	22(2)
Gordon Lee	1991	22(2)	22(2)
Brian Little	1991-94	4(2/1)	6(2/1)
Mark McGhee	1994-	21(P)	21(P)

LONGEST LEAGUE RUNS

of undefeated matches:	19 (6.2.1971 - 18.8.1971)	of league matches w/out a win:	18 (12.4.1975 - 1.11.1975)
of undefeated home matches:	40 (12.2.1898 - 17.4.1900)	of undefeated away matches:	10 (27.2.1971 - 14.8.1971)
without home win:	9 (3.12.1994 - 1.4.1995)	without an away win:	23 (19.11.1988 - 4.11.1989)
of league wins:	7 (15.2.08-28.3.08, 24.1.25-17.3.25)	of home wins:	13 (3.9.1906 - 29.12.1906)
	(26.12.62-9.3.1963, 28.2.93-27.3.93)		
of league defeats: 7 (28.11.1931 - 16.1.1932, 28.8.1990 - 29.9.1990)		of away wins:	4 (13.3.1971 - 12.4.1971)

LEICESTER CITY

PLAYERS NAME Honours	Ht	Wt	Birthdate	Birthplace Transfers	Contract Date	Clubs	League	L/Cup	FA Cup	Other	Lge	L/C	FAC	Oth
GOALKEEPERS														
Russell Hoult	6.4	13.2	22.11.72	Leicester	28.03.91	Leicester City (T)	10	3		1				
				Loan	27.08.91	Lincoln City	2	2						
				Loan	22.07.93	Kettering Town								
				Loan	03.11.93	Bolton Wanderers	3+1			1				
Zeljko Kalac						Sydney United								
				£760,000	08.95	Leicester City								
Kevin Poole	5.10	11.11	21.07.63	Bromsgrove	26.06.81	Aston Villa (A)	28	2	1	1				
				Loan	08.11.84	Northampton Town	3							
					27.08.87	Middlesbrough	34	4	2	2				
				Loan	27.03.91	Hartlepool United	12							
				£40,000	30.07.91	Leicester City	111	6	6	9				
DEFENDERS														
Mark A Blake E: Y4, u21.9, S	5.11	12.7	16.12.70	Nottingham	01.07.89	Aston Villa (T)	26+5	1+1	2	2	2			
				Loan	17.01.91	Wolverhampton W.	2							
				£400,000	05.08.93	Portsmouth	15			4+1				
				£360,000	24.03.94	Leicester City	36+5	2		3	4			
Brian P Carey Ei: 3, u21.1	6.3	13.9	31.05.68	Cork		Cork City								
				£100,000	02.09.89	Manchester United								
				Loan	17.01.91	Wrexham	3							
				Loan	24.12.91	Wrexham	13	3	3	1				
				£250,000	16.07.93	Leicester City	35+4	1	0+1	4				
Colin F Hill NI: 6	5.11	11.11	12.11.63	Uxbridge	07.08.81	Arsenal (A)	46	4	1		1			
				Free		Maritime (Portugal)								
				Free	30.10.87	Colchester United	64+5	2	7	3+1		2		
				£85,000	01.08.89	Sheffield United	77+5	5	10+2	3	3			
				Loan	26.03.92	Leicester City	10			3				
				£220,000	31.07.92	Leicester City	100+1	6	6	6		1		
Richard G Smith	5.11	12.4	03.10.70	Lutterworth	15.12.88	Leicester City (T)	81+16	4	5	12	2		1	
				Loan	06.09.89	Cambridge United	4	1						
Steven Walsh FRT'85	6.2	11.10	03.11.64	Preston	11.09.82	Wigan Athletic	123+3	7	6	10+2	4			
				£100,000	24.06.86	Leicester City	248+2	21	7	19	40	3		4
James A Willis GMVC'90; Div4'91	6.2	12.4	12.07.68	Liverpool		Blackburn R. (T)								
				Free	21.08.86	Halifax town								
				Free	30.12.87	Stockport County	10							
				£12,000	24.03.88	Darlington	90	5	5	6	6			1
				£100,000	20.12.91	Leicester City	47+1	3	4	5+1	3			
				Loan	26.03.92	Bradford City	9				1			
MIDFIELD														
Gary Coatsworth Div.4'91.	6.1	11.6	07.10.68	Sunderland	19.02.87	Barnsley (J)	3+3							
				Free	01.07.89	Darlington	15+7	1+1		2+1	2			
				£15,000	31.10.91	Leicester City	27+5		1	3+2	4			
Simon N Grayson	5.11	10.7	16.12.69	Ripon	13.06.88	Leeds United (T)	2			1+1				
				£50,000	13.03.92	Leicester City	100+11	6+1	13+1	2				
Sam K McMahon	5.7	11.5	09.02.76	Newark	10.07.94	Leicester City (T)	0+1							
Garry S Parker E: B, u21.6, u19.3,Y1; LC'89'90'94; SC'89	5.8	11.0	07.09.65	Oxford	05.05.83	Luton Town (A)	31+11	1+3	6+2		3	1		
				£72,000	21.02.86	Hull City	82+2	5	4	2	8			
				£260,000	24.03.88	Nottingham Forest	93+4	22+1	16	9	17	4	5	3
				£650,000	29.11.91	Aston Villa	79+2	8	10		11		1	
				£550,000	10.02.95	Leicester City	14		1		2			
Lee Philpott Div3'91	5.9	11.8	21.02.70	Barnet	17.07.86	Peterborough Utd (T)	1+3		0+1	0+2				
				Free	31.05.89	Cambridge United	118+16	10	19	15	17		3 2	
				£350,000	24.11.92	Leicester City	56+13	2+1	4+1	4+1	3			
Scott D Taylor	5.10	10.0	28.11.70	Portsmouth	22.06.89	Reading (T)	164+43	7+5	11+2	12+4	24	1	3	1
				£500,000	08.95	Leicester City								
Michael W Whitlow Div2'90; Div1'92	6.1	11.6	13.01.68	Northwich		Witton Albion								
				£10,000	11.11.88	Leeds United	62+15	4+1	1+49	4				
				£250,000	27.03.92	Leicester City	86+2	4	5	13	3	1		
FORWARDS														
Philip J Gee Div2'87	5.9	10.0	19.12.64	Pelsall		Gresley Rovers								
				£5,000	02.09.85	Derby County	107+17	11+2	6+1	7+1	26	3	2	
					11.03.92	Leicester City	34+17	2+3		5+1	9			4
				Loan	27.01.95	Plymouth Argyle	6							
Emile Heskey	6.1	13.0	11.01.78	Leicester		Leicester City (T)	1							
Paul Holsgrove	6.1	11.10	26.08.69	Telford	09.02.87	Aldershot (T)	0+3			1				
				Loan		Farnborough Town			1					
via Wokingham to				£25,000	01.01.91	Luton Town	1+1							
via Heracles to				Free	13.08.92	Millwall	3+8	0+1	0+1	2				
				Free	10.08.94	Reading	23+1	2+2	1		3	1		
					08.95	Leicester City								

Name	Ht	Wt	DOB	From	Date	Club	Lge	Sub	FLC	FAC	Other	Goals			
Julian K Joachim	5.6	11.10	12.09.74	Peterborough	15.09.92	Leicester City (T)	63+14	5+1	3	4+2	24	2	1	2	
E: Y8, u21.6; UEFA Yth'93															
James H Lawrence	5.10	12.3	08.03.70	Balham		Cowes									
					15.10.93	Sunderland	2+2	0+1							
				£20,000	17.03.94	Doncaster Rovers	16+9	2	1	3	3				
				£175,000	06.01.95	Leicester City	9+8				1				
Neil A Lewis	5.7	10.9	28.06.74	Wolverhampton	09.07.92	Leicester City (T)	26+5	2	1	2					
David A Lowe	5.10	11.4	30.08.65	Liverpool	01.06.83	Wigan Athletic (A)	179+9	8	16+1	18	40		4	9	
E: u21.2, Y7; FRT'85; Div2'92				£80,000	26.06.87	Ipswich Town	121+13	10	3	10+2	37	2	6		
Loan 19.03.92 Port Vale 8+1 Lge App. 2gls				£250,000	13.07.92	Leicester City	47+19	0+3	1+2	3	19	1			
				Loan	18.02.94	Port Vale	18+1				5				
Iwan W Roberts	6.3	12.6	26.06.68	Bangor	04.07.86	Watford (T)	40+23	6+2	1+6	5	9	3			
W: 4, Y				£275,000	02.08.90	Huddersfield Town	141+1	13+1	12	14	51	6	4	8	
				£100,000	25.11.93	Leicester City	58+5	15	3		9		2		
Mark G Robins	5.7	10.1	22.12.69	Ashton-u-Lyne	23.12.86	Manchester Utd (T)	19+29	0+7	4+4	4+3	11	2	3	1	
E: u21.6; FAC'90; ECWC'91; ESC'91				£800,000	14.06.92	Norwich City	57+10	6+3		1+1	20	1			
				£1,000,000	16.01.95	Leicester City	16+1	2			5				

A D D I T I O N A L   C O N T R A C T   P L A Y E R

Name				From	Date	Club
Steve Corica						Marconi
				£100,000	08.95	Leicester City

TOP GOALSCORER 1994/95
Iwan Roberts

Premiership goals (games) . . . . 9 (32+5)
Coca-Cola Cup Goals 0
F.A. Cup goals 2

Total **11**

Total goals for Leicester since 25.11.93 24

Career total as at June 1st 1995 . . . . 105 (296+38)

THE MANAGER
MARK McGHEE

Date of Birth . . . . 25th May 1957.
Place of Birth . . . . Glasgow.
Date of Appointment . . . . December 1994.

PREVIOUS CLUBS
As Manager . . . . Reading.
As Coach. . . . . None.
As a Player. . . Bristol City (A), Morton, Newcastle Utd, Aberdeen, SV Hamburg,
. . . . Celtic, Newcastle Utd, Reading (player-manager).

HONOURS
As a Manager
Division 2 Champions 1993-94.

As a Player
Scottish League Champions 1980'84'86'88. Scottish Cup 1982'83'84'88'89. ECWC 1983.
International: 4 full caps and 1 U21 cap for Scotland.

FILBERT STREET
Leicester LE2 7EL
Tel: 01162 555 000

Capacity 22,517

First game ....v Nottingham Forest 'A' (F) 7.11.1891.
First floodlit game ....v Borussia Dortmund (F) 23.10.1957.

ATTENDANCES
Highest ....47,298 v Spurs, FAC 5th Rnd, 18.2.1928.
Lowest ....3,440 v Huddersfield, Simod 1st Rnd, 10.11.1987. (Post WW1)

OTHER GROUNDS ....Fosse Road/Racecourse 1884-85. Victoria Park 1885-87.
....Belgrave Road 1887-88. Victoria Park 1888-89. Mill Lane 1889-91.
.... Aylestone Road 1891. Filbert Street 1891-

MATCHDAY TICKET PRICES

Stand
Carling Centre (O-F). . . Adult £15/£7. Juvenile £8/9
Carling Wing (A-C, G-J) . . . . £13/£15. £7/8
Carling Members (WM 1-4) £10
Carling Family (WF1 -4) £10. £5
North Family (X). £10. £5
South Upper (M-S) £13. £7
South Lower. £10. £5
East (V) £10. £5

Visitors
East (U) £13. £7
East (T) £10. £5
Ticket Office Telephone no. 0116 291 5232

CLUBCALL
0891 12 11 85
Calls cost 39p per minute cheap rate and 49p per minute at all other times.
Call costings correct at time of going to press.

HOW TO GET TO THE GROUND

From the North
Use motorway (M1) until junction 22 or A46/A607 into Leicester city centre. Follow signs to Rugby into Almond Road, then at end turn right into Aylestone Road. Shortly turn left into Walnut Street, then turn left into Filbert Street for Leicester City FC.
From the East
Use A47 into Leicester city centre. Follow signs to Rugby into Almond Road, then at end turn right into Aylestone Road. Shortly turn left into Walnut Street, then turn left into Filbert Street for Leicester City FC.
From the South
Use M1 or M69 until junction 21, then A46 (sign posted Leicester). Under railway bridge and in 0.2 miles turn right into Upperton Road, then turn right into Filbert Street for Leicester City FC.
From the West
Use motorway M69 or A50 into Leicester City centre and follow signs to Rugby into Almond Road, then at end turn into Aylestone Road. Shortly turn left into Walnut Street, then left into Filbert Street for Leicester City FC.

Car Parking: Parking adjacent to stadium for season ticket holders only. Street parking is available and there is also a public car park five minutes walk from the ground.

Nearest Railway Station: Leicester (0116 248 1000)

MATCHDAY PROGRAMME
(Voted top programme of 1994/95)

Programme Editor . . . . Paul Mace.

Number of pages . . . . 48 (full colour).

Price . . . . £1.50.

Local Newspapers . . . . . . Leicester Mercury, Leicester Herald & Post, ... Melton Times, Coalville Times.

Local Radio Stations . . . . Leicester Sound, BBC Radio Leicester.

LUTON TOWN
(The Hatters)
ENDSLEIGH LEAGUE DIVISION 1
SPONSORED BY: UNIVERSAL SALVAGE AUCTIONS

Back Row (L-R): Ben Chenery, Danny Power, Gary Simpson, Fred Barber, Paul McLaren, Rob Matthews, Gavin Johnson, David Greene, Steve Davis, Kelvin Davis, John Taylor, Trevor Peake, Julian James. **Middle Row:** Chris Green (Director), Cliff Bassett (Director), Clive Goodyear (Physio), Paul Lowe (Yth Dev. Officer), Richard Harvey, Aaron Skelton, David Oldfield, Mitchell Thomas, Des Linton, Marvin Johnson, Bontcho Guentchev, Matthew Woolgar, Wayne Turner (Res coach), John moore (Yth coach), Les Shannon (Scout), Nigel Terry (Director). **Front Row:** Jamie Woodsford, Gary Waddock, Tony Thorpe, Ceri Hughes, Mick McGiven (Asst. Manager), David Kohler (Chairman), Terry Westley (Manager), Scott Oakes, Nathan Jones, Graham Alexander, Dwight Marshall.

LUTON TOWN
FORMED IN 1885
TURNED PROFESSIONAL IN 1890
LTD COMPANY IN 1897

PRESIDENT: Ed Pearson
CHAIRMAN: D A Kohler B.Sc(Hons) ARICS

DIRECTORS
C Chris, C Bassett, N Terry
SECRETARY
Cherry Newbury
COMMERCIAL MANAGER
Kathy Leather

MANAGER: Terry Westley
ASSISTANT MANAGER: Mick McGiven

RESERVE TEAM MANAGER
Wayne Turner
YOUTH TEAM MANAGER
John Moore
PHYSIOTHERAPIST
Clive Goodyear

STATISTICIAN FOR THE DIRECTORY
Vacant

Pre-season optimism that David Pleat's side could mount a promotion challenge was rapidly dispelled as the Luton faithful waited until October 5th for a home win and , in the meantime, suffered a first round exit from the Coca-Cola Cup at Fulham.

The first home win was Luton's best performance of the season. League leaders Middlesborough were brushed aside 5-1. Thereafter only Portsmouth left Kenilworth Road without reward as the run of poor home form continued until Christmas when the biggest league crowd of the season was given a festive treat by a 3-0 victory over Sunderland.

Bristol Rovers were the visitors for the start of the F.A. Cup campaign in January. Hartson's last goal before his departure to Arsenal earned a replay at Twerton Park. Top scorer Marshall scored the only goal to secure a home tie against Southampton in the Fourth Round.

Pleat moved quickly to fill the gap created by Hartson's transfer. The much-traveled striker, Biggins, scored on his debut as just under ten thousand fans saw the Saints held to a 1-1 draw. The replay at the Dell was the heaviest defeat of the season, Luton could find no answer to the genius of Le Tissier who led the Premiership team to an emphatic 6-0 win.

Left to concentrate on the League, Luton at last found form at home and enjoyed a six match unbeaten run on their own turf. Frustratingly the strong away form which had sustained faint hopes of the play-offs lapsed. Just three points were gained from the last ten away fixtures.

This was a season in which expectancy exceeded achievement. The mood of disappointment with all the last four matches lost was prolonged by the departure of David Pleat to manage Sheffield Wednesday. However, the side performed well enough on occasions to raise hopes that, if Pleat's successor can instill some consistency, better times are not far away.

LUTON TOWN

Division One: 16th   **FA Cup:** 4th Round   **Coca-Cola Cup:** 1st Round

M	DATE	COMP.	VEN	OPPONENTS	RESULT	H/T	LP	GOAL SCORERS/GOAL TIMES	ATT.
1	A 13	EL	H	West Bromwich Albion	D 1-1	0-1	11	Oakes 49	8,640
2	16	CC 1/1	H	**Fulham**	**D 1-1**	**0-0**		**Oakes 81**	**3,287**
3	20	EL	A	Derby County	D 0-0	0-0	14		(13,060)
4	22	CC 1/2	A	**Fulham**	**D †1-1**	**0-1**		**Marshall 74 (Fulham won 4-3 on Pens)**	**(2,320)**
5	27	EL	H	Southend United	D 2-2	1-0	17	Hartson 44, Hughes 70	5,918
6	30	EL	A	Tranmere Rovers	L 2-4	0-0		Hughes 54, Hartson 86	(5,480)
7	S 3	EL	A	Port Vale	W 1-0	0-0	15	Marshall 69	(8,541)
8	10	EL	H	Burnley	L 0-1	0-1	18		6,911
9	13	EL	H	Bolton Wanderers	L 0-3	0-0			5,764
10	17	EL	A	Watford	W 4-2	3-2	16	Oakes 28, Dixon 31, Telfer 41,55	(8,880)
11	14	EL	A	Millwall	D 0-0	0-0	16		(7,150)
12	O 1	EL	H	Bristol City	L 0-1	0-0	20		6,633
13	9	EL	A	Stoke City	W 2-1	1-0		Marshall 22, Preece 82	(11,712)
14	15	EL	H	Middlesbrough	W 5-1	3-0	8	Wilkinson 21 (og), Marshall 35, 58, Preece 40, Hartson 63	8,412
15	22	EL	A	Sheffield United	W 3-1	1-1	7	Gayle 33 (og), James 72, Dixon 79	(13,317)
16	29	EL	H	Barnsley	L 0-1	0-0	10		7,212
17	N 1	EL	H	Grimsby Town	L 1-2	0-0	13	Oakes 82	5,839
18	5	EL	A	Wolverhampton Wand.	W 3-2	1-0		Preece 37, Marshall 47, Dixon 54	(26,749)
19	12	EL	A	Oldham Athletic	D 0-0	0-0	7		(7,907)
20	19	EL	H	Portsmouth	W 2-0	1-0	8	Dixon 2, Preece 55	8,214
21	26	EL	A	Swindon Town	W 2-1	1-1	5	Dixon 44, Oakes 61	(9,455)
22	D 3	EL	H	Sheffield United	L 3-6	0-2	8	Harson 67, Gayle 71 (og), Johnson 73 (pen)	6,400
23	11	EL	H	Derby County	D 0-0	0-0	12		6,400
24	18	EL	A	West Bromwich A.	L 0-1	0-1			(14,392)
25	26	EL	A	Reading	D 0-0	0-0			(11,623)
26	27	EL	H	Sunderland	W 3-0	2-0		Oakes 22,26, Hartson 49	8,953
27	31	EL	A	Notts County	W 1-0	0-0		Telfer 71	(6,249)
28	J 2	EL	H	Charlton Athletic	L 0-1	0-1	9		7,642
29	7	FAC 3	H	**Bristol Rovers**	**D 1-1**	**1-1**		**Hartson 37**	**7,571**
30	14	EL	A	Barnsley	L 1-3	0-0	11	Dixon 47	(4,808)
31	18	FAC 3R	A	**Bristol Rovers**	**W 1-0**	**0-0**		**Marshall 62**	**(8,218)**
32	28	FAC 4	H	**Southampton**	**D 1-1**	**0-0**		**Biggins 81**	**9,938**
33	F 4	EL	H	Oldham Athletic	W 2-1	1-0	10	Marshall 1, 18	6,903
34	8	FAC 4R	A	**Southampton**	**L 0-6**	**0-4**			**(15,075)**
35	11	EL	A	Grimsby Town	L 0-5	0-2	10		(4,615)
36	18	EL	H	Swindon Town	W 3-0	1-0	9	Horlock 19 (og), Marshall 50, 63	6,595
37	21	EL	A	Portsmouth	L 2-3	1-0		Telfer 10, James 73	(7,363)
38	25	EL	A	Bristol City	D 2-2	1-0	10	Oakes 29, 54	(7,939)
39	M 4	EL	H	Millwall	D 1-1	1-0	10	Marshall 32	6,864
40	7	EL	H	Port Vale	W 2-1	0-0		Telfer 50, Dixon 82	5,947
41	11	EL	A	Southend United	L 0-3	0-1	11		(4,558)
42	18	EL	H	Tranmere Rovers	W 2-0	1-0	9	James 15, Biggins 67	6,660
43	21	EL	A	Burnley	L 1-2	0-0		Marshall 61	(9,551)
44	26	EL	H	Watford	D 1-1	1-0		Telfer 4	7,984
45	A 4	EL	H	Wolverhampton Wand.	D 3-3	2-0		Telfer 6, 11, Taylor 51	9,651
46	8	EL	H	Notts County	W 2-0	1-0	12	Telfer 3, Oakes 68 (pen)	6,428
47	11	EL	A	Bolton Wanderers	D 0-0	0-0			(13,619)
48	15	EL	A	Sunderland	D 1-1	1-0	11	Taylor 9	(17,292)
49	17	EL	H	Reading	L 0-1	0-1			8,717
50	22	EL	A	Charlton Athletic	L 0-1	0-0	12		(10,867)
51	30	EL	A	Middlesbrough	L 1-2	0-1	16	Taylor 62	(23,903)
52	M 7	EL	H	Stoke City	L 2-3	1-0	16	Harvey 43, Waddock 83	8,252
53									
54									
55									
56									
57									
58									
59									
60									

Best Home League Attendance: 9,938 v Southampton   **Smallest:** 5,764 v Bolton Wanderers   **Av Home Att:** 7,350

Goal Scorers: **Compared with 1993-94:** -527

League (61): Marshall 1, Oakes 9, Telfer 9, Dixon 7, Hartson 5, Opponents 4, Preece 4, James 4, Taylor 3, Hughes 2, Biggins, Harvey, Johnson, Waddock

C/Cola Cup (2): Marshall, Oakes

FA Cup (3): Biggins, Hartson, Marshall

258

Sommer	James	Johnson	Skelton	Greene	Peake	Telfer	Oakes	Dixon	Preece	Houghton	Linton	Marshall	Barber	Hughes	Thomas	Hartson	Waddock	Williams	Thorpe	Jones	Allen	Davis	Adcock	Harvey	Chenery	Referee	
1	2	3	4*	5	6	7	8	9	10	11•	12	14	S													Pooley G.	1
1	2	3		5	6	7	8	9	10	11•	14	12		4*												Bigger R.	2
1	2	3	S	5	6	7		9	10	S	4	8	S	11												Breen K.	3
1	2	3	12	5•		7	14	9	10		4*	8	S	11†												Pierce M.	4
1	2*	3		5	6	7	4	12	10			8•	S	11	14	9										Brandwood J.	5
1	2	3	4*	5	6	7	8		10			12	S	11	S	9										Poulain R.	6
1	2*	3	4	5	6	7	11	9	10•			8	S			12										Winter J.	7
1	2	3	5•		6	7	11	12	10			8			14	9	4*									Dunn S.	8
1	2	3			6	7	8	9	10		12	14	S		5*	11•	4									Leach K.	9
1	2	3			6	7	8	9	10		S	11	S		5	S	4									Railey M.	10
1	2	3	S		6	7	8	9*	10			11	S		5	12	4									Orr D.	11
1	2	3			6	7	8	9•	10			11	S	12	5*	14	4									Foakes P.	12
1	2	3			6	7	12		10*			11	S	8	5	9	4	S								Heilbron T.	13
1	2	3			6	7	12	S	10*			11	S	8	5	9	4									Cooper K.	14
1	2	3			6	7	12	9	10*			11	S		5		4	S	S							Parker J.	15
1	2	3			6	7	14	12	10			11•	S	8	5	9	4*									Pierce M.	16
1	2	3			6	7	12	S	10			11	S	8*	5	9	4									Alcock P.	17
1		3			6	7	8	9*	10			11	S		5	12	4		S	2						Wolstenholme E.	18
1	2	3			6	7	8	9	10			11*	S		5	12	4									Lynch K.	19
1	2	3			6	7	8	9	10			11*	S		5	S	4									Kirkby J.	20
1	2	3			6	7	8	9	10			11	S		5	12	4									Wilkes C.	21
1	2	3			6	7	8	9*	10		12	11•	S		5	12	4†									Foakes P.	22
1	2	3			6	7	8	9*	10		12		S		5	14	4				11•					Cooper K.	23
1	2*	3			6	7	8	9	10			11	S		5	12	4									Brandwood M.	24
1	2	3			6	7	12	9•	10			11	S		5	12	4			8*	S					Singh G.	25
1	2	3	12		6	7	8		10*			11•			5	9	4	14			S					Holbrook J.	26
1	2	3	S		6	7	8		10			11*			5	9	4				S	12				Harris R.	27
1	2*	3	5		6	7	8					11			5	9	4		10		S	12				Alcock P.	28
1	2	3			6	7	8		10			11*			5	9	4	5			S	12				Rejer P.	29
1	2	3	12		6	7	8	9				11			5		4				S			10*		Barry N.	30
1		3	5		6	7	8	9	10			11			5		4				S			2		Rejer P.	31
1		3	5		6	7	8	9*	10			11			5		4	12			S					Ashby G.	32
1	2	3			6	7	8	9*				11			5		4		12		S	S				Vanes P.	33
1	2*	3			6	7	8	12	10			11			5		4		14		S					Ashby G.	34
1	2	3			6	14	8	9*	10			11			5		4				S					Furnandiz R.	35
1	2	3			6	7	8	12	10•			11			5		4				S					Kirkby J.	36
1	2	3			6	7	8•	9	10*			11			5		4*				S			14		Leach K.	37
1	2	3			6	7	8	9	10*			11			5		4				S					Flood W.	38
1	2	3			6	7	8	14	10			11			5		4*				S					Lloyd J.	39
1	2	3			6	7	8	14	10			11			5		4*				S	S				Foakes P.	40
1	2	3			6	7	8	9*				11			5		4				S					Holbrook J.	41
1	2	3			6	7	8	S	10			11			5		4				S					Pooley G.	42
1	2	3			6	7		9	10•			11			5*		4				S			12		Poulain R.	43
	2	3			6	7			10			11					4		12		S	1		5		Breen K.	44
S	2	3			6	7	8		10			11*					4					1		5		Pooley G.	45
S	2*	3			6	7	8		10		12	11•					4					1		5		Pierce M.	46
S	2*	3			6	7	8		10		14	12					4					1		5		Rennie D.	47
S		3	12		6	7	8		10		2*	14					4					1		5		Richards P.	48
S	2*	3			6	7	8		10		12	11					4•					1		5		Kirkby J.	49
S		3	2		6	7	8		10			12			5*		4					1		14		Alcock P.	50
S		3			6	7	8*		10		2	11	S				4		12			1		5		Vanes P.	51
S		3			6	7	8		10			12			2		4					1		5		Pooley G.	52
37	41	46	3	7	46	45	37	23	42	1	5	36		5	33	11	40			1	4	9		9		League Appearances	
	2		1	1				6	6		5	9		1	3	9					2			3		League Sub Appearances	
2	2	0+1		2	2	2	1+1	2	2	1	1+1	1+1		2												C/Cola Cup Appearances	
4	2	4			4	4	4	2+1	4			4													1	FA Cup Appearances	

Also Played: Biggins 2(32),10(33),9•(34,39,40),9*(36,42),S(38),12(41), Matthews 12(39,40,42),10(41), 8(43),8*(44)S(45),14(46,49),11•(47,48,50), Woodsford 14(7,38,43),S(21,30,31),12(35,37,45),11(52*), Margetson S(44,51), Taylor 9(44,45,46,47,48,49,50,51,52), McLaren S(52)

† = Sent Off

LUTON TOWN

CLUB RECORDS

BIGGEST VICTORIES
League: 12-0 v Bristol Rovers, Division 3 (S), 13.4.1936 (Divisional record).
F.A. Cup: 9-0 v Clapton, 1st Round, 30.11.1927.
League Cup: 7-2 v Mansfield, 2nd Round, 3.10.1989.

BIGGEST DEFEATS
League: 0-9 v Birmingham City, Division 2, 12.11.1898.
F.A. Cup: 0-7 v Crystal Palace, 1st Round, 16.1.1929.
League Cup: 1-5 v Everton, 3rd Round, 1968-69.

MOST POINTS
3 points a win: 88, Division 2, 1981-82.
2 points a win: 66, Division 4, 1967-68.

MOST GOALS SCORED
103, 1936-37.
Payne 55, Stephenson 17, Ball 8, Dawes 8, Roberts 8, Rich 2, Finlayson 2, Fellowes 1, Hancock 1, Hodge 1.

MOST GOALS CONCEDED
95, Division 2, 1898-99.

MOST FIRST CLASS MATCHES IN A SEASON
58 - 1987-88 (League 40, FA Cup 6, League Cup 8, Simod Cup 4).

MOST LEAGUE WINS
27, Division 3(S), 1936-37, Division 4, 1967-68.

MOST LEAGUE DRAWS
21, Division 2/1, 1992-93.

MOST LEAGUE DEFEATS
24, Division 2, 1962-63, Division 3, 1964-65.

INDIVIDUAL CLUB RECORDS

MOST GOALS IN A SEASON
Joe Payne: 58 goals in 1936-37 (League 55, FA Cup 3).

MOST GOALS IN A MATCH
10. Joe Payne v Bristol Rovers, 12-0, Division 3(S), 13.4.1936 (League record).

OLDEST PLAYER
Dally Duncan, 39 years, 11 days, 25.10.1947.

YOUNGEST PLAYER
Mike O'Hara, 16 years, 32 days, 1.10.1960.

MOST CAPPED PLAYER
Mal Donaghy (Northern Ireland) 58.

BEST PERFORMANCES

League: 1981-82: Matches played 42, Won 25, Drawn 13, Lost 4, Goals for 86, Goals against 46, Points 88. First in Division 2.
Highest Position: 7th in Division 1, 1986-87.
F.A. Cup: 1958-59: 3rd Round Leeds United 5-1; 4th Round Leicester City 1-1,4-1; 5th Round Ipswich Town 5-2; 6th Round Blackpool 1-1,1-0; Semi-final Norwich City 1-1,1-0; Final Nottingham Forest 1-2.
League Cup: 1987-88: 2nd Round Wigan 1-0,4-2; 3rd Round Coventry City 3-1; 4th Round Ipswich Town 1-0; 5th Round Bradford City 2-0; Semi-final Oxford United 1-1,2-0; Final Arsenal 3-2.

ADDITIONAL INFORMATION
PREVIOUS NAMES
None.

PREVIOUS LEAGUES
United League, Southern League.

Club colours: White with navy/orange trim, navy blue shorts, white stockings with orange/blue trim.
Change colours: Navy blue/white trim, navy blue shorts, orange stockings/white and navy trim.

Reserves League: Neville Ovenden Football Combination.

DIVISIONAL RECORD

	Played	Won	Drawn	Lost	For	Against	Points
Division 1	658	213	168	277	863	1,011	725
Division 2/1	1,240	463	320	457	1,901	1,821	1,296
Division 3	184	75	46	63	266	255	196
Division 3(S)	714	308	175	231	1,295	1,038	791
Division 4	138	67	29	42	236	187	163
Total	**2,934**	**1,126**	**738**	**1,070**	**4,561**	**4,312**	**3,171**

RECORDS AND STATISTICS

COMPETITIONS

Div.1	Div.2/1	Div.3	Div.3(S)	Div.4	Texaco
1955-60	1897-1900	1920-21	1921-37	1965-68	1974-75
1974-75	1937-55	1963-65			
1982-92	1960-63	1968-70			Wat Cup
	1970-74				1971
	1975-82				
	1992-				

HONOURS

Div.2	Div.3(S)	Div.4	Leagues Cup
1981-82	1936-37	1967-68	1987-88

MOST APPEARANCES

Bib Morton 550 (1948-64)

Year	League	FA Cup	Lge Cup
1948-49	17	3	
1949-50	10	0	
1950-51	24	2	
1951-52	28	6	
1952-53	42	4	
1953-54	40	4	
1954-55	39	3	
1955-56	39	1	
1956-57	40	2	
1957-58	27	1	
1958-59	35	9	
1959-60	33	3	
1960-61	27	3	
1961-62	27	3	3
1962-63	34	1	3
1963-64	33	3	1
	495	48	7

MOST GOALS IN A CAREER

Gordon Turner - 265 (1949-64)

Year	League	FA Cup	Lge Cup
1951-52	4	2	
1952-53	13	3	
1953-54	16		
1954-55	32	5	
1955-56	19		
1956-57	30	1	
1957-58	33		
1958-59	14		
1959-60	6	3	
1960-61	26	2	1
1961-62	20		1
1962-63	14		2
1963-64	16	2	
Total	243	18	4

Current leading goalscorer: David Preece - 27 (1984-95)

RECORD TRANSFER FEE RECEIVED

Amount	Club	Player	Date
£2,500,000	Arsenal	John Hartson	01/95
£1,500,000	Nottingham Forest	Kingsley Black	8/91
£1,300,000	Derby County	Mark Pembridge	5/92
£1,000,000	Q.P.R.	Roy Wegerle	12/89

RECORD TRANSFER FEE PAID

Amount	Club	Player	Date
£650,000	Odense	Lars Elstrup	8/89
£300,000	Arsenal	Steve Williams	8/88
£250,000	Birmingham City	Mike Harford	12/84
£200,000	Bristol Rovers	Steve White	12/79

MANAGERS

Name	Seasons	Best	Worst
George Thomson	1925-27	7(3S)	8(3S)
John McCartney	1927-29	7(3S)	13(3S)
George Kay	1929-31	7(3S)	13(3S)
Harold Wightman	1931-35	4(3S)	14(3S)
Edwin Liddell	1935-38	12(2)	2(3S)
Neil McBain	1938-39	7(2)	7(2)
George Martin	1939-47	13(2)	13(2)
Dally Duncan	1947-58	8(1)	19(2)
Syd Owen	1959-60	22(1)	22(1)
Sam Bartram	1960-62	13(2)	13(2)
Jack Crompton	1962		
Bill Harvey	1962-64	22(2)	18(3)
George Martin	1964-66	21(3)	6(2)
Allan Brown	1966-68	1(4)	17(4)
Alec Stock	1968-72	6(2)	3(3)
Harry Haslam	1972-78	20(1)	13(2)
David Pleat	1978-86	9(1)	18(2)
John Moore	1986-87	7(1)	7(1)
Ray Harford	1987-90	9(1)	16(1)
Jim Ryan	1990-91	17(1)	18(1)
David Pleat	1991-95	16(2/1)	20(2/1)
Terry Westley	1995-		

LONGEST LEAGUE RUNS

of undefeated matches:	19 (13.1.68-27.4.68, 7.4.69-11.10.69)	of league matches w/out a win:	16 (1964)
of undefeated home matches:	39 (24.1.1925 - 30.4.1927)	of undefeated away matches:	10 (20.4.1981 - 14.11.1981)
without home win:	10 (26.10.64-25.1.65, 16.9.72-6.1.73)	without an away win:	32 (26.11.1898 - 28.4.1900)
of league wins:	9 (22.1.1977 - 8.3.1977)	of home wins:	15 (1.4.1967 - 26.12.1967)
of league defeats:	8 (11.11.1899 - 6.1.1900)	of away wins:	5 (2.5.1981 - 3.10.1981)

LUTON TOWN

PLAYERS NAME / Honours	Ht	Wt	Birthdate	Birthplace / Transfers	Contract Date	Clubs	League	L/Cup	FA Cup	Other	Lge	L/C	FAC	Oth
G O A L K E E P E R S														
Frederick Barber	5.10	12.10	26.08.63	Ferryhill	27.08.91	Darlington (A)	135	9	12	7				
FLgXI.1				£50,000	08.04.86	Everton								
				£100,000	20.10.86	Walsall	153	912	15					
Loan, 16.10.89, Peterborough Utd 6 Lge App.				Loan	18.10.90	Chester City	3							
Loan, 29.11.90, Blackpool 2 Lge App.				Loan	28.03.91	Chester City	5							
				£25,000	15.08.91	Peterborough Utd	63	8	5	10				
Loan, 01.11.94, Kettering Town.				Loan	01.02.93	Chesterfield				2				
Loan, 19.03.93, Colchester United 10 Lge App.				£25,000	12.08.94	Luton Town								
				Loan	23.12.94	Peterborough Utd								
Kelvin G Davis	6.1	13.2	29.09.76	Bedford	01.07.94	Luton Town (T)	9							
				Loan	16.09.94	Torquay United	2	1		1				
Juergen Sommer	6.4	15.12	27.02.69	New York	05.09.91	Luton Town	80	4	11	2				
				Loan	13.11.91	Brighton & H.A.	1							
				Loan	31.10.92	Torquay United	10			1				
D E F E N D E R S														
Graham Alexander	5.10	11.10	10.10.71	Coventry	20.03.90	Scunthorpe Utd (T)	111+8	9+1	8	11+2	14	2		2
				£100,000	.08.95	Luton Town								
Benjamin R Chenery	6.1	11.5	28.01.77	Ipswich	07.03.95	Luton Town (T)		1						
Stephen M Davis	6.2	12.8	30.10.68	Hexham	06.07.87	Southampton (T)	5+1							
Div4'92				Loan	21.11.89	Burnley	7+2							
				Loan	28.03.91	Notts County	6+2							
				£60,000	17.08.91	Burnley	119	6	14	13	15	2	1	
				£750,000	.08.95	Luton Town								
David M Greene	6.2	11.10	26.10.73	Luton	03.09.91	Luton Town (J)	18+1	2	1	0+1				
E: u21.5														
Richard G Harvey	5.9	11.10	17.04.69	Letchworth	10.01.87	Luton Town (A)	100+17	6	6+2	5	3	1		
E: Y3, u19.3				Loan	30.10.92	Blackpool	4+1							
Julian C James	5.10	11.11	22.03.70	Tring	01.07.88	Luton Town (T)	172+15	8+1	16+1	8+1	12			
E: u21.2				Loan	12.09.91	Preston North End	6							
Gavin Johnson	5.11	11.7	10.10.70	Eye	01.03.89	Ipswich Town (T)	100+15	8+1	12	3+1	11	2	2 1	
Marvin A Johnson	5.11	11.6	29.10.68	Wembley	12.11.86	Luton Town (A)	155+11	8+2	8+1	8	4			
Nathan Jones				Cardiff City		Merthyr Tydfil								
				£10,000	.08.95	Luton Town								
Desmond M Linton	6.1	11.13	05.09.71	Birmingham	09.01.90	Leicester City (T)	6+5	0+1		1				
				P.E.	22.10.91	Luton Town	56+10	3+1	7	3	1			
Paul McLaren	6.0	12.06	17.11.76	Wycombe	31.05.94	Luton Town (T)	0+1							
Trevor Peake	6.0	12.9	10.02.57	Nuneaton		Nuneaton Borough								
E: S-P2; FAC'87				£27,750	15.06.79	Lincoln City	171	16	7		7	2		
				£100,000	06.06.83	Coventry City	277+1	30	17	10	6		1	
				£100,000	27.08.91	Luton Town	160	7	13	3				
Gary Simpson	6.2	14.0	14.02.76	Ashford	05.07.94	Luton Town (T)								
Mitchell A Thomas	6.0	12.0	02.10.64	Luton	27.08.92	Luton Town (A)	106+1	5	18		1			
E: B1, u21.3, Y3				£233,000	07.07.86	Tottenham Hotspur	136+21	28+1	12		6	1	1	
				£525,000	07.08.91	West Ham United	37+1	5	4	2	3			
				Free	12.11.93	Luton Town	50+6		4		1			
M I D F I E L D														
Ceri M Hughes	5.9	11.6	26.02.71	Pontypridd	01.07.89	Luton Town (T)	100+16	6	8	3	11		1	
W: 4, B2, Y														
David Oldfield	6.0	12.2	30.05.68	Perth (Aus)	16.05.86	Luton Town (A)	21+8	4+2	0+1	2+1	4	2		2
E: u21.1				£600,000	14.03.89	Manchester City	18+8	2+1		0+1	6	2		1
				£150,000	12.01.90	Leicester City	155+19	10+1	6	11+3	25	1	2 2	
				Loan	24.02.95	Millwall								
				£150,000	.08.95	Luton Town								
Aaron Skelton	5.10	11.05	22.11.74	Welwyn Gar.	31.05.94	Luton Town (T)	3+2	0+1						
Matthew Woolgar	5.10	11.10	05.01.76	Bedford	1994-95	Luton Town (T)								
F O R W A R D S														
Bontcho Guentchev	5.10	11.7	07.07.64	Tchoshevo (Bulgaria)		Sporting Lisbon								
Bul:				£250,000	29.12.92	Ipswich Town	28+17	4	6+2		5		5	
				Free	.08.95	Luton Town								
Dwight W Marshall	5.11	11.8	03.10.65	Jamaica		Grays Athletic								
				£35,000	09.08.91	Plymouth Argyle	93+8	8	7+2	7+1	26	1	4	4
				Loan	25.03.93	Middlesbrough	0+3							
				£150,000	15.07.94	Luton Town	36+9	1+1	4		11	1	1	

Player	Ht/Wt/DOB	From	Fee	Date	Club								
Robert Matthews	6.0 12.5 14.10.70	Slough			Loughborough Uni								
E: Su18.3			Free	26.03.92	Notts County	12+13		1+2	1+1	8			
			£80,000	03.03.95	Luton Town	6+5							
Scott J Oakes	5.10 9.12 05.08.72	Leicester		09.05.90	Leicester City (T)	1+2							
E: u21.1			P.E.	22.10.91	Luton Town	110+34	3+3	11+2	0+3	24	1	5	
John Taylor	6.1 12.2 24.10.64	Norwich		17.12.82	Colchester Utd (J)								
Div3'91	via Sudbury to			24.08.88	Cambridge United	139+21	9+2	21	12+2	46	2	10	2
				28.03.92	Bristol Rovers	91+4	4	3	5	44	1		
			£300,000	05.07.94	Bradford City								
			£200,000	23.03.95	Luton Town	9				3			
Anthony Thorpe	5.9 12.0 10.04.74	Leicester		18.08.92	Luton Town (T)	4+10		1+1		1		1	
Gary Waddock	5.10 11.12 17.03.62	Kingsbury		26.07.79	Q.P.R. (A)	191+12	21+1	14	1	8	2		
EI: 21, B, 1, u23.1, u21.1; Div2'83			Free		Charleroi (Belgium)								
			£130,000	16.08.89	Millwall	51+7	5+1	5	3	2			1
			Free	20.12.91	Q.P.R.								
			Loan	19.03.92	Swindon Rovers	5+1							
			£100,000	07.11.92	Bristol Rovers	70	2	2	2	1			
			Free	09.12.94	Luton Town	40		4		1			
Jamie Woodsford	5.9 11.0 09.11.76	Ipswich		07.03.95	Luton Town (T)	1+6							

Top Goalscorer 1994/95
Dwight Marshall

First Division goals (games)	11 (36+9)
Coca-Cola Cup Goals	1 (1+1)
F.A. Cup goals	1 (4)
Total	**13 (41+10)**
Total goals for Luton since 15.07.94	13 (41+10)
Career total as at June 1st 1995	48 (156+22)

The Manager
Terry Westley

Date of Birth . . . .
Place of Birth . . . .
Date of Appointment . . . . July 1995.

Previous Clubs
As Manager . . . .
As Coach . . . . Luton Town.
As a Player . . . .

Honours
As a Manager
None.

As a Player
None.

KENILWORTH ROAD

1 Maple Road, Luton, Beds LU4 8AW
Tel: 01582 411 622

Capacity 13,410
Covered Standing 4,350
Seating...8.956

First game ....v Plymouth, 4.9.1905.
First floodlit game ....v Fenerbahce, 7.10.1957.
ATTENDANCES
Highest...30,069 v Blackpool, FA Cup 6th Round replay, 4.3.1959.
Lowest ....1,823 v Southend, Anglo Italian Cup, 5.9.1993.

OTHER GROUNDS ....Excelsior Dallow Lane 1885-97, Dunstable Road 1897-05,
....Kenilworth Road 1905-

MATCHDAY TICKET PRICES

	14 days before match	less than 14 days
Main Stand A&E	£14.50	£15.50
Juv/OAP	£7.50	£8
Block F	£11.50	£12.50
Juv/OAP	£5.50	£6
Block G	£7.50	£8
Juv/OAP	£5	£5.50
Main Stand C&G	£11.50	£12.50
Juv/OAP	£5.50	£6
Restricted View B,H&J	£7.50	£8
Juv/OAP	£5	£5.50
Kenilworth Upper tier	£11.50	£12.50
Juv/OAP	£5.50	£6
Kenilworth Lower Tier	£11.50	£12.50
Juv/OAP	£5.50	£6
New Stand	£14.50	£15.50
Juv/OAP	£7.50	£8

Ticket Office Telephone no. 01582 416 976

CLUBCALL 0898 12 11 23

Calls cost 39p per minute cheap rate and 49p per
minute at all other times.
Call costings correct at time of going to press.

HOW TO GET TO THE GROUND

From the North and West
Use motorway (M1) until junction 11 then follow signs to Luton A505 into
Dunstable Road. Forward through one-way system and then turn right into
Kenilworth Road for Luton Town FC.

From the South and East
Use motorway (M1) until junction 10 or A6/A612 into Luton Town centre, then follow signs to Dunstable into Dunstable Road A505. Under railway bridge then
turn left into Kenilworth Road for Luton Town FC.

Car Parking
Street parking near ground only available.

Nearest Railway Station
Luton Midland Road (01582 27612).

MATCHDAY PROGRAMME

Programme Editor. . . . . Simon Oxley.

Number of pages . . . . 48.

Price . . . . £1.50.

Subscriptions . . . . Apply to club.

Local Newspapers . . . . Luton News, The Herald.

Local Radio Stations. . . . . Chiltern Radio, Three Counties Radio.

MILLWALL
(The Lions)
ENDSLEIGH LEAGUE DIVISION 1
SPONSORED BY: CAPTAIN MORGAN

Back Row (L-R): Mickey Bennett, Kerry Dixon, Tony Witter, Uwe Fuchs, Jason Van Blerk, Chris Malkin, Greg Berry, Anton Rogan, Damian Webber.
Middle Row: Keith Johnstone (Physio), Michael Harle, Keith Stevens, Ricky Newman, Dave Savage, Jimmy Nielsen, Kasey Keller, Dave Wietecha, Alistair Edwards, Bobby Bowry, Maurice Doyle, Richard Cadette, Ian McDonald (Coach).
Front Row: Phil O'Neil, Ben Thatcher, Scott Taylor, Alex Rae, Mick McCarthy (Manager), Ian Evans (First Team Coach), Steve Forbes, Lee McRobert, James Connor, Mark Beard.

MILLWALL
FORMED IN 1885
TURNED PROFESSIONAL IN 1893
LTD COMPANY IN 1894

PRESIDENT
Lord Melish of Bermondsey
CHAIRMAN: P Mead
DIRECTORS
B E Mitchell, J D Burnige,
Councillor D Sullivan, R Butt
CHIEF EXECUTIVE/SECRETARY
G I S Hortop (0171 232 1222)
COMMERCIAL MANAGER
Billy Neill (0171 231 4650)

MANAGER: Mick McCarthy
ASSISTANT MANAGER: Ian Evans
RESERVE TEAM MANAGER
Ian McDonald
YOUTH TEAM MANAGER
Tom Walley
PHYSIOTHERAPIST
Keith Johnstone

STATISTICIAN FOR THE DIRECTORY
Richard Lindsay

The highlight of a disappointing season's campaign in the Endsleigh League was the magnificent displays in reaching the fifth rounds in both the Coca-Cola and FA Cup. The brilliant third round replay victory at Highbury over Arsenal came via two great goals from two of the clubs most promising youth team graduates, Mark Beard and Mark Kennedy. Such was Kennedy's progress that Liverpool paid over £2 million for him in March 1995.

Another replay at Stamford Bridge in the fourth round, Dave Savage equalised to take the tie to a penalty shoot-out, a brilliant save by Kasey Keller saw the Lions through 5-4. This sparked off crowd disorder among the Chelsea fans who invaded the pitch and assaulted three Millwall players, this was somehow completely turned around by the ignorant media to become Millwall's fault, enquiry - what enquiry, one rule for one club etc etc. At Q.P.R. in the next round a last minute penalty saved Rangers's blushes.

The Coca-Cola cup witnessed an exceptional display at Nottingham Forest. Two goals from Greg Berry completing the job. This was after negotiating a tough two legged meeting with Sunderland and achieving a first ever win at Field Mill, Mansfield 2-0.

League form was severely disrupted by a string of injuries, 34 players were used equalling the club record of 1929/30 season. The return of captain Keith Stevens saw a steady climb to mid-table. Twenty-year-old Andy Roberts took over the leadership while Stevens was out and showed exceptional maturity on field, resulting in U21 appearances for England, Ben Thatcher was also a regular squad member. Savage and Kennedy won Eire U21 caps. Alex Rae Scotland 'B', John Kerr adding two more USA caps to his collection and scoring against Uraquay, Dave Mitchell with Australia.

Long serving Chairman Reg Burr handed over the reigns to Peter Mead after nine years in the hot seat.

Alex Rae was again the leading scorer from his attacking midfield role. The only hat-trick came from John Kerr who became the clubs first substitute to bag three goals, this was in the 4-1 demolition of Derby County. The transfer deadline signing of Kerry Dixon sparked some life into the team along with the introduction of promising youngsters McRobert, Taylor and earlier in the season Connor.

If Millwall can hang on to their young stars forthcoming seasons look very rosy indeed.

MILLWALL F.C. MUSEUM.

MILLWALL

Division One: 12th   FA Cup: 5th Round   Coca-Cola Cup: 5th Round

M	DATE	COMP.	VEN	OPPONENTS	RESULT	H/T	LP	GOAL SCORERS/GOAL TIMES	ATT.
1	A 13	EL	H	Southend United	W 3-1	1-0	3	Mitchell 22, Goodman 56, OG 90	8,283
2	20	EL	A	Sunderland	D 1-1	1-0	2	Rae 45	(17,296)
3	27	EL	H	Derby County	W 4-1	1-0	2	Rae 27, Kerr 47, 63, 80	8,809
4	30	EL	A	Bolton Wanderers	L 0-1	0-0	4		(9,519)
5	S 3	EL	A	Reading	D 0-0	0-0	5		(8,715)
6	10	EL	H	West Bromwich Albion	D 2-2	1-1	7	Goodman 17, 57	8,378
7	14	EL	H	Burnley	L 2-3	0-0	11	Savage 46, Rae 73 (pen)	7,375
8	17	EL	A	Tranmere Rovers	L 1-3	1-1	15	Roberts 25	(6,243)
9	21	CC 2/1	H	Burnley	L 2-3	0-0	11	Goodman 21, Kennedy 26	5,095
10	24	EL	H	Luton Town	D 0-0	0-0	15		7,150
11	O 1	EL	A	Middlesbrough	l 0-3	0-0	19		(17,229)
12	4	CC 2/2	A	Sunderland	D 1-1	0-0		Goodman 64	(9,698)
13	8	EL	A	Bristol City	L 0-1	0-0	20		(7,499)
14	15	EL	H	Stoke City	D 1-1	1-0	21	Goodman 13	7,856
15	22	EL	A	Wolverhampton	D 3-3	1-1	22	Goodman 39, 86, Cadette 84	(25,059)
16	25	CC 3	A	Mansfield Town	W 2-0	1-0		Cadette 22, Kennedy 90	(5,359)
17	29	EL	H	Sheffield United	W 2-1	0-0	22	Kennedy 61 (pen), Cadette 90	8,445
18	N 2	EL	H	Portsmouth	D 2-2	2-1	21	Goodman 3, Rae 39	7,108
19	5	EL	A	Swindon Town	W 2-1	0-0	17	Goodman 47, Kennedy 53	(9,311)
20	12	EL	A	Grimsby Town	L 0-1	0-0	19		(5,261)
21	19	EL	H	Barnsley	L 0-1	0-1	19		7,040
22	26	EL	A	Port Vale	l 1-2	0-0	20	Kennedy 69	(8,016)
23	30	CC 4	H	Nottingham Forest	W 2-0	2-0		Berry 18,41	12,393
24	D 4	EL	H	Wolverhampton	W 1-0	0-0	20	Mitchell 67	8,025
25	10	EL	A	Sunderland	W 2-0	0-0	15	Kennedy 54, Mitchell 76	7,698
26	17	EL	A	Southend United	W 1-0	1-0	15	Cadette 10	(5,833)
27	26	EL	A	Notts County	W 1-0	0-0	13	Mitchell 47	(6,758)
28	27	EL	H	Watford	W 2-1	0-0	10	Rae 51, (pen), Cadette 61	12,289
29	J 1	EL	A	Charlton Athletic	D 1-1	1-0	11	Rae 33	(10,655)
30	3	EL	H	Oldham Athletic	D 1-1	1-0	11	Rae 50 (pen)	7,438
31	7	FAC 3	H	Arsenal	D 0-0	0-0			17,715
32	11	CC 5	A	Swindon Town	L 1-3	0-2		Mitchell 85	(11,772)
33	14	EL	A	Sheffield United	D 1-1	1-0	12	Beard 18	(12,650)
34	18	FAC 3R	A	Arsenal	W 2-0	1-0		Beard 10, Kennedy 89	(32,319)
35	28	FAC 4	H	Chelsea	D 0-0	0-0			(18,573)
36	F 4	EL	H	Grimsby Town	W 2-0	1-0	11	Kennedy 13, Roberts 75	7,397
37	8	FAC 4R	A	Chelsea	D 1-1	0-0		Savage 79	(25,515)
38	18	FAC 5	A	QPR	L 0-1	0-0			(16,457)
39	21	EL	A	Barnsley	L 1-4	0-1	12	Webber 58	(4,733)
40	26	EL	H	Middlesbrough	D 0-0	0-0	13		7,247
41	M 1	EL	H	Swindon Town	W 3-1	0-0	11	Rae 49, 82, Van Blerk 53	5,950
42	4	EL	A	Luton Town	D 1-1	0-1	11	Mitchell 57	(6,864)
43	8	EL	H	Reading	W 2-0	1-0	10	Oldfield 10, Mitchell 90	7,546
44	11	EL	A	Derby County	L 2-3	1-1	12	Rae 45, Mitchell 90	(12,490)
45	15	EL	A	Portsmouth	L 2-3	1-1	12	Oldfield 35, Witter 89	(6,032)
46	19	EL	H	Bolton Wanderers	L 0-1	0-0	12		6,103
47	22	EL	A	West Bromwich Albion	L 0-3	0-1	13		(11,782)
48	25	EL	H	Tranmere Rovers	W 2-1	0-0	13	Dixon 72, Roberts 78	7,470
49	A 1	EL	A	Burnley	W 2-1	1-0	11	Oldfield 38,57	(10,454)
50	5	EL	A	Port Vale	L 1-3	0-2	11	Oldfield 76	5,260
51	8	EL	H	Charlton A	W 3-1	2-1	11	McRobert 3, Thatcher 33, Dixon 49	9,506
52	14	EL	A	Watford	L 0-1	0-1	12		(6,907)
53	19	EL	H	Notts County	D 0-0	0-0	12		5,471
54	22	EL	A	Oldham Athletic	W 1-0	0-0	11	Savage 76	(6,319)
55	29	EL	A	Stoke City	L 3-4	2-2	11	Dixon 22, Webber 45, Oldfield 50	(9,111)
56	M 7	EL	H	Bristol City	D 1-1	1-1	12	Dixon 21	8,805
57									
58									
59									
60									

Best Home League Attendance: 12,289 v Watford   **Smallest:** 5,260 v Port Vale   **Av Home Att:** 7,679

Goal Scorers: Compared with 1993-94: -2,132

League (60):   Rae 10, Goodman 8, Mitchell 7, Oldfield 6, Kennedy 5, Cadette 4, Dixon 4, Kerr 3, Roberts 3, Savage 2, Webber 2, Beard , McRobert, Thatcher, Van Blerk, Witter, Opponent

C/Cola Cup (8):   Berry 2, Goodman 2, Kennedy 2, Cadette, Mitchell

FA Cup (3):   Beard, Kennedy, Savage 1

Keller K.	Cunningham K.	Thatcher B.	May A.	McCarthy A.	Roberts A.	Savage D.	Rae A.	Mitchell D.	Goodman J.	Kennedy M.	Kerr J.	Beard M.	Chapman D.	Van Blerk J.	Witter A.	Cadette R.	Dawes I.	Stevens K.	Webber D.	Berry G.	Beckford J.	Edwards A.	Oldfield D.	McRobert L.	Joseph R.	Referee
	1	2	3	4	5	6	7*	8	9*	10	11	12	14													G. Singh 1
1	2	3	4	5	6	7	8	9*	10	11	12	5														K. Lynch 2
1	2	3	4	5	6	7	8	9*	10	11	12	14														M. Pierce 3
1	2	3		5	6	7	8		10	11	9	5	4													4
1	2	3		5	6	7*	8		10	11*	9	14	4													P. Vanes 5
1	2	3		5	6	7	8		10	11	9	5	4													P. Foakes 6
1	2	3		5	6	7	8	12	10	11*	9	14	4													7
1	2	3		5	6	7	8	9*	10	10	12				14											D. Allison 8
1†	2	3		5	6	7	8	9	10	11•	5				5											C. Wilkes 9
1	2	3		5	6	7	8	9	10*	11	12				14											D. Orr 10
1		3		5	6	7	8		10	11	9	2	12		14											P. Harrison 11
1		3		5	6	7	8		10	11	9	2	12		4*											R. Poulain 12
	2	3		5	6	14	8†	10		11	9	7	12		4											J. Rushton 13
1	2	3			6	7	8	12	10*	11						5	9	14								T. West 14
1	2	3			6	7	9*	10		11			14			5	12	8								J. Kirkby 15
1	2	3		5	6	7*		12	10	11			14				9	8								A. Dawson 16
1	2			4		7		12	10*	11			3	S		5	9	8	6							M. Bailey 17
1	2			4		7	3	12	10*	11			14			5	9	8	6							K. Leach 18
1	8			4		7	3	12	10*	11						5	9	14	6†							E. Parker 19
1	8			4			3	10		11			2*			5	9	7		S						20
1	8			4			3	10		11			2			5	9	5	12							21
1		3		4		7*	8	10		11			2			5	9	5	6		12					I. Cruikshanks 22
1		3		4		7*	8	10		11			2			5		14	6	12	9					A. Wilkie 23
1		3		4		S	8	10		11			2			5	12	7	6			9*				I. Hemley 24
1		3		4		14	8	10		11			2			5	12	7				9*				P. Vanes 25
1				4			8	10		11*			12	3		9	2	6		14	7					M. Bailey 26
1				4				10		11			12	3		5	9	2	6	14	7*					K. Breen 27
1		3		4		7	8	10					2	11		5	9		6	14						G. Pooley 28
1		3		4			8				14	12	11	5	9	2		6								K. Leach 29
1		3		4			8				14	10	12	11	5	9	2	6		7*						30
1		3		4		7	8	10					14		11	5	9	2	6	5						D. Crick 31
1		3		4		7	8	10		11			5		3		9	2	6	5		S				P. Foakes 32
1				4		14	8	10		11			7	12	3		2	6	5				9*			P. Harrison / K. Powell 33
1				4		7	8	10*		11			7		3	5	2	6	12				9*			D. Crick 34
1	6		5	4		S	8	10		11			7		3	5	2						9			R. Dilkes 35
1	6			4		12	8	10		11			7		3	5	2					14	9*			36
1		3		4		12	8	10					7		11	5	2	6					9*			M. Bodenham 37
1		3	8	S	4	7		10*		11			2		9	5		6				12				P. Don 38
1		3	8	11	4	7					12		2		10	5*		6				9		14		39
1		3		5	4	7	8						2		11	5		6			10		9		14	C. Wilkes 40
1		3		12	4	7*	8						2		11	5		6			10	14	9*			P. Foakes 41
1		3		4		7*	8	10	S						11	5		12			9				2	J. Lloyd 42
1		3		4		7	8	10		14					11	5		6			12	9*			2	D. Orr 43
	12	7*		4		14	8	10		11					3	5		6			9				2	W. Burns 44
	12	2		4		7	8*	10		11					3	5		6		5	9				2	R. Harris 45
1		3		14		7		10		11			2		8	5		6	5		9					46
1		3		5		4		10					7		11	14		6	5	9		8			2	T. Heilbron 47
1		3		10		4		12					7		11			6	5	14		8•			2*	M. Bailey 48
1		3		10		4		7*					2	12	11			6	5	S		8				49
1		3		10		4							2	12		6		5	11	7*		8				P. Alcock 50
1		3		10		4		7					2*		11			5	12			8		6		J. Brandwood 51
1		3	7		4		10						2		11			6	5*			8		12		P. Foakes 52
1		2		4		7	8						3		11			6	5	12		14	11			P. Rejer 53
1		3		4		7*	8						2		5			6	5	S		10				54
1		3		4		7*	8						2				12	6	5			10	11•			J. Kirkby 55
1		3		4			8						2		11	5		6				10	7*			T. West 56
44	15	38	14	12	44	31	38	23	15	28	7	24	4	24	26	12	12	20	19	4	6	3	16	4	5	League Appearances
	2	2			6		5			2	7	7	8		3	1	4	2		3	5	3	1	1	3	League Sub Appearances
5	2	4		3	5	4		3+1		5		1		2+1	-1	2	1	2	2+1	2		1+1	1			C/Cola Cup Appearances
5		4		1		5		2+2		4		5		3+1	5	1		4	3			3+1				FA Cup Appearances

Also Played: Dixon 9(48,49,50,51,52,53,54,55,56),Taylor 14(50,51,52,55,56),10(53*), Huxford 12(5), Connor 4(14), Kelly 12(20,6(21*), Wright S(12), Van Den Hauwe 4(8,9,10,11*,15,16), Barber S(54), Forbes 14(56), Carter 1(13,44), GK Sub 9 +S(1-12,14-43,45-54), Wietecha Sub GK (13,44,55,56)Gordon S(6), Allen S(28)

Players on Loan: Joseph (Wimbledon), Oldfield (Leicester), Power (Bradford City), Cadette (Falkirk), Witter (Queen's Park Rangers)

† = Sent Off

MILLWALL

CLUB RECORDS

BIGGEST VICTORIES
League: 9-1 v Torquay United, Division 3(S), 29.8.1927.
9-1 v Coventry City, Division 3(S) 19.11.1927.
F.A. Cup: 7-0 v Gateshead, 2nd Round, 12.12.1936.
League Cup: 5-1 v Northampton, 3rd Round replay, 16.10.1967.

BIGGEST DEFEATS
League: 1-8 v Plymouth, Division 2, 16.1.1932.
F.A. Cup: 1-9 v Aston Villa, 4th Round, 28.1.1946.
League Cup: 1-7 v Chelsea, 1st Round, 10.10.1960.

MOST POINTS
3 points a win: 90, Division 3, 1984-85.
2 points a win: 65, Division 3(S), 1927-28 & Division 3, 1965-66.

MOST GOALS SCORED
127, Division 3(S) (Record), 1927-28.

MOST GOALS CONCEDED
100, Division 3(S), 1955-56.

MOST FIRST CLASS MATCHES IN A SEASON
61 - 1984-85 (League 46, FA Cup 7, League Cup 4, Freight Rover Trophy 4).

MOST LEAGUE WINS
30, Division 3(S), 1927-28.

MOST LEAGUE DRAWS
18, Division 3(S), 1921-22; Division 3(S), 1922-23.

MOST LEAGUE DEFEATS
26, Division 3(S), 1957-58.

INDIVIDUAL CLUB RECORDS

MOST GOALS IN A SEASON
Richard Parker: 38 goals in 1926-27 (League 37, FA Cup 1).
Peter Burridge: 38 goals in 1960-61 (League 35, FA Cup 2, League Cup 1).
E.Sheringham: 38 goals in 1990-91 (League 33, FA Cup 2, league Cup 2, FMC 1).

MOST GOALS IN A MATCH
5. Richard Parker v Norwich City, 6-1, Division 3(S), 28.8.1926.

OLDEST PLAYER
Jack Fort, 41 years 8 months.

YOUNGEST PLAYER
David Mehmet, 16 years 5 months.

MOST CAPPED PLAYER
Eamonn Dunphy (Eire) 23.

BEST PERFORMANCES

League: 1927-28: Matches played 42, Won 30, Drawn 5, Lost 7, Goals for 127, Goals against 50, Points 65. First in Division 3(S). (Millwall are the only Football League club to be unbeaten at home in four different divisions: Division 3(S) 1927-28, Division 4 1964-65, Division 3 1965-66 & 1984-85, Division 2, 1971-72.
Highest Position: 10th in Division 1, 1988-89.
F.A. Cup: Semi-finals in 1899-00, 1902-03, 1936-37.
Most recent success: 1936-37: 1st Round Aldershot 6-1; 2nd Round Gateshead 7-0; 3rd Round Fulham 2-0; 4th Round Chelsea 3-0; 5th Round Derby County 2-1; 6th Round Manchester City 2-0; Semi-final Sunderland 1-2.
League Cup: 5th Round in 1973-74, 1976-77, 1994-95.
Most recent success: 2nd Round Sunderland 2-1, 1-1; 3rd Round Mansfield Town 2-0; 4th Round Nottingham Forest 2-0; 5th Round Swindon Town 1-3.

DIVISIONAL RECORD

	Played	Won	Drawn	Lost	For	Against	Points
Division 1	76	19	22	35	86	117	79
Division 2/1	1,240	451	335	454	1,659	1,703	1,383
Division 3	460	182	128	150	643	605	586
Division 3(S)	956	410	233	313	1,508	1,253	1,053
Division 4	228	105	61	62	422	323	271
Total	2,960	1,167	779	1,014	4,328	4,001	3,372

ADDITIONAL INFORMATION
PREVIOUS NAMES
Millwall Rovers 1885.
Millwall Athletic 1889.

PREVIOUS LEAGUES
United, London, Western Leagues.
Southern District Combination.
Southern League.

Club colours: Blue shirts, white shorts, blue socks.

Change colours: Green & white halved shirts, green shorts.

Reserves League: Avon Insurance Football Combination.

RECORDS AND STATISTICS

COMPETITIONS

Div.1/P	Div.2	Div.3	Div.3(S)	Div.4
1988-90	1928-34	1962-64	1920-28	1958-62
	1938-48	1965-66	1934-38	1964-65
	1966-75	1975-76	1948-58	
	1976-79	1979-85		
	1985-88			**FLT**
	1990-			1982-83

HONOURS

Div.2	Div.3(S)	Div 3(S) KO	Div.4	FLT
1987-88	1927-28	1936-37	1961-62	1982-83
	1937-38			

MOST APPEARANCES

Barry Kitchener 589+7 (1966-82)

Year	League	FA Cup	Lge Cup
1966-67	3+2		
1967-68	42	1	4
1968-69	42	3	2
1969-70	42	1	2
1970-71	42	1	3
1971-72	42	3	1
1972-73	40	3	3
1973-74	41		7
1974-75	39	3	1
1975-76	45	5	2
1976-77	38	1	9
1977-78	31	5	3
1978-79	40	1	3
1979-80	10+2	1+2	
1980-81	18+1	1	2
1981-82	3		
	518+5	**29+2**	**42**

MOST GOALS IN A CAREER

Teddy Sheringham - 111 (1983-91)

Year	League	FA Cup	Lge Cup	Am & FMC
1983-84	1			1
1984-85				
1985-86	4			
1986-87	13		2	1
1987-88	22			2
1988-89	11	1	3	
1989-90	9	2	1	
1990-91	33	2	2	1
Total	**93**	**5**	**8**	**5**

Current leading goalscorer: Alex Rae - 55 (1990-95)

MANAGERS

Name	Seasons	Best	Worst
F B Kidd	1894-99	1(SL)	9(SL)
E R Stopher	1899-1900	7(SL)	7(SL)
G A Saunders	1900-11	3(SL)	15(SL)
H Lipsham	1911-18	6(3S)	7(3S)
R Hunter	1918-33	7(2)	13(3S)
W McCracken	1933-36	21(2)	12(3S)
C Hewitt	1936-40	13(2)	8(3S)
W Voisey	1940-44		
J Cook	1944-48	18(2)	22(2)
C Hewitt	1948-56	2(3S)	22(3S)
R Gray	1956-58	23(3S)	23(3S)
J Seed	1958-59	9(3S)	9(3S)
J Smith	1959-61	5(4)	6(4)
R Gray	1961-63	16(3)	1(4)
W Gray	1963-66	2(3)	2(4)
B Fenton	1966-74	3(2)	12(2)
G Jago	1974-77	10(2)	3(3)
G Petchley	1978-80	21(2)	12(3)
P Anderson	1980-82	15(3)	16(3)
G Graham	1982-86	9(2)	17(3)
I Docherty	1986-90	10(1)	16(2)
B Rioch	1990-92	5(2)	5(2)
M McCarthy	1992-	3(2/1)	12(2/1)

RECORD TRANSFER FEE RECEIVED

Amount	Club	Player	Date
£2,300,000	Crystal Palace	Andy Roberts	7/95
£2,300,000	Liverpool	Mark Kennedy	3/95
£2,000,000	Nott'm Forest	Teddy Sheringham	7/91
£1,500,000	Aston Villa	Tony Cascarino	3/90

RECORD TRANSFER FEE PAID

Amount	Club	Player	Date
£800,000	Derby County	Paul Goddard	12/89
£300,000	Tottenham	Neil Ruddock	6/88
£225,000	Gillingham	Tony Cascarino	7/87
£150,000	Barnsley	Trevor Aylott	8/82

LONGEST LEAGUE RUNS

of undefeated matches:	19 (27.4.1959 - 7.11.1959)	of league matches w/out a win:	20 (26.12.1989 - 5.5.1990)
of undefeated home matches:	59 (20.4.1964 - 14.1.1967)	of undefeated away matches:	10 (5.3.21-7.9.21, 13.2.88-15.10.88)
without home win:	9 (1.1.1990 - 1.9.1990)	without an away win:	26 (7.11.1979 - 26.12.1980)
of league wins:	10 (10.3.1928 - 26.4.1928)	of home wins:	13 (15.12.1923 - 30.8.1924)
of league defeats:	11 (10.4.1929 - 21.9.1929)	of away wins:	5 (17.3.1928 - 25.4.1928)

MILLWALL							APPEARANCES				GOALS			
PLAYERS NAME Honours	Ht	Wt	Birthdate	Birthplace Transfers	Contract Date	Clubs	League	L/Cup	FA Cup	Other	Lge	L/C	FAC	Oth
G O A L K E E P E R S														
Kasey Keller USA:	5.11	11.13	27.11.69	Washington (USA) Free	20.02.92	Portland University Millwall	134	11	7	4				
Jimmy K Nielson	6.3	12.11	06.08.77	Denmark	08.12.94	Aalborg Millwall								
David M Wietecha	6.3	15.0	01.11.74	Colchester Loan	02.09.94	Millwall Chesham United								
D E F E N D E R S														
Mark Beard	5.10	10.12	08.10.74	Southwark	18.03.93	Millwall (T)	32+13	3+1	4		2		1	
Ian R Dawes E: S; Div2'83	5.8	10.2	22.02.63	Croydon £150,000	24.12.80 26.08.88	Q.P.R. (A) Millwall	229 219+6	28 17+1	8 16	5 8+1	3 5	1		
Michael J L Harle			31.10.72	Lewisham £50,000	01.07.89	Gillingham (T) Sittingbourne Millwall	1+1				1			
Michael McCarthy Ei: 57; SPD'88; SFA'88'89	6.2	13.7	07.02.59	Barnsley £200,000 £500,000 £500,000 £500,000	28.07.77 15.12.83 31.05.87 21.03.90	Barnsley (A) Manchester City Celtic Lyon (France) Millwall	272 14 48 43+4	27 10 3 5	16 7 8 1	 6 5 1+1	7 2 2	3 1	1	
Keith H Stevens Div2'88; FLT'83	6.0	12.5	21.06.64	Merton	23.06.81	Millwall (A)	403+7	31	28	24	7	1		
Ben D Thatcher	5.10	11.10	30.11.75	Swindon	08.06.92	Millwall (T)	46+2	4	5	1	1			
Jason C Van Blerk	6.1	13.0	16.03.68	Sydney £300,000	08.09.94	Go Ahead Eagles Millwall	24+3	2	5		1			
Damian J Webber	6.4	14.0	08.10.68	Rustington		Bognor Regis T. Millwall	19+3	1+1	1+2		2			
Anthony J Witter	6.2	13.2	12.08.65	London £10,000 £125,000 Loan Loan £100,000	24.10.90 19.08.91 09.01.92 11.02.94 14.12.94	Grays Athletic Crystal Palace Q.P.R. Plymouth Argyle Reading Millwall	1 3 4 26+1	1	1 5		1			
M I D F I E L D														
Michael R Bennett E: u19.2. Y.	5.11	11.3	27.07.69	Camberwell £250,000 £60,000 Free Free	27.04.87 09.01.90 14.07.92 24.03.94 16.05.95	Charlton Ath (A) Wimbledon Brentford Charlton Athletic Millwall	24+11 12+6 40+6 19+5	4 1+1 4+1	1 0+1 1 1	6+1 1+1 6+1	2 2 4 1			
Robert Bowry Div1'94	5.8	10.0	19.05.71	Hampstead Free £220,000	08.08.90 04.04.92 08.95	Q.P.R. Crystal Palace Millwall	23+9	7	1		1			
Maurice Doyle	5.8	10.7	17.10.69	Ellesmere Port £120,000 Loan	11.07.88 21.04.89 17.01.91 17.05.95	Crewe Alexandra (T) Q.P.R. Crewe Alexandra Millwall	6+2 6 6+1				2			
Steven D Forbes	6.2	12.6	24.12.75	London £45,000	11.07.94	Sittingbourne Millwall	0+1							
Lee McRobert	5.9	10.12	04.10.72	Bromley £35,000	17.02.95	Sittingbourne Millwall	4+3				1			
Gavin T Maguire W: 7, B.1 Loan Newcastle United(10.10.91) 3 Lge	5.10	11.8	24.11.67	Hammersmith £225,000 £115,000 Loan	08.10.85 04.01.89 25.03.93 24.03.94	Q.P.R. (A) Portsmouth Millwall Scarborough	33+7 87+4 12 2	1+2 9	5+1 3	4+1				
Richard A Newman Div1'94	5.9	10.7	05.08.70	Guildford Loan £500,000	22.01.88 28.02.92 08.95	Crystal Palace (J) Maidstone United Millwall	43+5 9+1	5	5+2	2	3 1			
Philip J O'Neil	5.9	11.10	22.10.77	Sidcup	12.07.94	Millwall (T)								
Alex Rae S: u21.9	5.8	11.8	30.09.69	Glasgow £100,000	20.08.90	Falkirk Millwall	71+12 168+13	5 11+2	2+1 11	10	20 50	1	4	1
F O R W A R D S														
Greg J Berry	5.11	12.0	05.03.71	Grays £2,000 £250,000 £200,000	03.07.89 17.08.92 24.03.94	East Thurrock Leyton Orient Wimbledon Millwall	68+12 6+1 9+10	6 1	8+2 0+1	5+3 1	14 1 1	3 2	2	1 1
Richard R Cadette B&QC'94. Loan 13.10.94 Falkirk	5.8	11.7	21.03.65	Hammersmith Free Free £130,000 £80,000 Loan £135,000	25.08.84 15.08.85 20.07.87 22.07.88 22.03.90 09.01.94 03.11.94	Wembley Leyton Orient Southend United Sheffield United Brentford Bournemouth Falkirk Millwall	19+2 90 26+2 67+20 4+4 74+10 12+4	4 5+1 1 10+3 3+1 2	1 4 2 9 5+1 1	2 5 2 14 4	4 49 7 20 1 29 4	1 6 4 1	1 5 1 1 1	1 4 6
Tony C Dolby	5.11	11.4	16.04.74	Greenwich Loan Loan	29.10.91 16.02.94 16.12.94	Millwall (T) Barnet Chesham United	17+18 13+3	4		1+1	1 2			
James R Connor	6.0	12.9	22.08.74	Twickenham	21.11.92	Millwall (T)	1							

							League App	Sub	FLC		FAC		Lge Gls	FLC	FAC	Oth
Kerry M Dixon 6.0 13.10 24.07.61			Luton	01.07.78	Tottenham H. (A)											
E: 8, u21.1. Div2'84'89. ZDC'90.			Free		Dunstable											
			£20,000	22.07.80	Reading	110+6	6+1	2+1		51					
			£175,000	04.08.83	Chelsea	331+4	40+1	18+2	25	147	24	8	12		
			£575,000	19.07.92	Southampton	8+1	2	1		2					
			Loan	19.02.93	Luton Town	16+1				3					
			Free	13.08.93	Luton Town	50+8	2	7+2	2	16			1		
			£5,000	23.03.95	Millwall	9				4					
Alistair M Edwards 6.1 12.6 21.06.68			Whyalia (Aus)		Sydney Olympic										
			Free	29.11.89	Brighton & H.A.	1									
					Selangor										
			Free	15.12.94	Millwall	3+1		3+1							
Uwe Fuchs 6.1 12 23.07.66			Kaiserslautern		Kaiserslautern										
Div.1'95.			Loan	27.01.95	Middlesbrough	13+2				9					
			£750,000	08.95	Millwall										
Chris Malkin 6.3 12.0 04.06.67			Hoylake		Stork AFC										
LCD'90.			Free	27.07.87	Tranmere Rovers	184+48	20+5	9+4	26+7	59	6	2	8		
			£400,000	08.95	Millwall										
David P T Savage 6.2 12.7 30.07.73			Dublin		Brighton & H.A.										
					Longford Town										
			£15,000	27.05.94	Millwall	31+6	5	2+2		2		1			
Scott J Taylor 5.10 11.4 05.05.76			Chertsey		Staines										
			£15,000	08.02.95	Millwall	1+5									

TOP GOALSCORER 1994/95
Alex Rae

Division One goals (games) 10 (38)
Coca-Cola Cup Goals 0 (4)
F.A. Cup goals 0 (4)

Total . . . . **10 (46)**

Total goals for Millwall since 20.08.90 . . . . 55 (200+15)

Career total as at June 1st 1995 . . . . 76 (278+28)

THE MANAGER
MICK McCARTHY

Date of Birth . . . . 7th February 1959.
Place of Birth . . . . Barnsley.
Date of Appointment . . . . March 1992.

PREVIOUS CLUBS
As Manager . . . . None.
As Coach . . . . None.
As a Player . . . . Barnsley, Manchester City, Celtic, Lyon (France), Millwall.

HONOURS
As a Manager
None.

As a Player
Celtic: Scottish League championship 1987-88. Scottish FA Cup 1987-88, 1988-89.
International: 57 full caps for Eire.

THE NEW DEN

London SE16 3LN
Tel: 0171 232 1222

Capacity 20,146

First game ....v Sporting LIsbon, 1-2, 4.8.1993.
First floodlit game ....As above.

ATTENDANCES
Highest..20,093 v Arsenal, FA Cup 3rd Round, 10.1.1994.
Lowest..4,003 v Charlton Athletic, Anglo Italian Cup, 1.9.1993.

OTHER GROUNDS ....Glengall Road 1885-86. Back of Lord Nelson 1886-90. East Ferry Road 1890-01.
.... North Greenwich 1901-10. The Den 1910-93. The New Den 1993-

MATCHDAY TICKET PRICES

West Stand Upper Tier. £20
Juv/OAP . . . . £5/£10

West Stand Lower Tier. £15
Juv/OAP. . . . . £5/£7.50

East Stand Upper Tier. £17.50
Juv/OAP. . . . . £5/£8.50

East Stand Lower Tier £12
Juv/OAP . . . . £5/£6

South Stand Upper & Lower. £10
Juv/OAP £5

Family Enclosure £11
Juv/OAP. . . . . £3/£4.50

Ticket Office Telephone no. 0171 231 9999

CLUBCALL 0891 40 03 00

Calls cost 39p per minute cheap rate and 49p per
minute at all other times.
Call costings correct at time of going to press.

HOW TO GET TO THE GROUND

From the North
From motorway M1 and A1 follow signs London A1 then City, then follow signs
to Shoreditch, Whitechapel. Then follow signs to Ring Road, Dover to cross
Tower Bridge. In 1.8 miles at roundabout turn left into Old Kent Road, turn left
before Railway Bridge (Ilderton Road). Take 7th right for new stadium.

From the East
Use A2 sign posted London. At New Cross follow signs, City, Westminster, into
Kendar Street and at end turn left. Turn right at next traffic lights (Ilderton Road)
and then take 7th right for new stadium.

From the South and West
Use A2 sign posted London. At New Cross follow signs, City, Westminster, into
Kendar Street and at end turn left. Turn right at next traffic lights (Ilderton Road)
and then take 7th right for new stadium.

Car Parking
Street parking. Car Park in Juro Way. Stadium Car Park - Officials & members
only.

Nearest Railway Station
New Cross Gate BR & tube, New Cross BR & Tube, South Bermondsey BR
(Away) and Surrey Quays tube.

MATCHDAY PROGRAMME

Programme Editor . . . . Deano Standing & Rob Bowden.

Number of pages . . . . 40.

Price . . . . £1.60.

Subscriptions . . . . Home League £44, All home games £59,
. . . . Every game home & away £105

Local Newspapers . South London Press, South East London Mercury,
. . . . Southwark News.

Local Radio Stations . . . . Capital Radio.

NORWICH CITY
(The Canaries)
ENDSLEIGH LEAGUE DIVISION 1
SPONSORED BY: NORWICH & PETERBOROUGH BUILDING S.

Back Row (L-R): Ade Akinbiyi, Daryl Sutch, Mike Sheron, Ashley Ward, Rob Newman, Lee Bray, Jon Newsome, Spencer Prior, Andy Johnson, Keith O'Neill, Danny Mills. **Middle Row:** Tim Sheppard (Physio), Stacey Kreft, Johnny Wright, Shaun Carey, Jeremy Goss, Andrew Brownrigg, Steve Walford (Res. Manager), Paul Franklin (Asst. Manager), John Faulkner (Coach), Carl Bradshaw, Mark Bowen, Robert Ullathorne, Ali Gibb, Justin Harrington, Keith Webb (Yth Manager). **Front Row:** Darren Eadie, Neil Adams, Karl Simpson, John Polston, Bryan Gunn, Martin O'Neill (Manager), Andy Marshall, Ian Crook, Mike Milligan, Jamie Cureton, Jamie Mitchell.

NORWICH CITY
FORMED IN 1902
TURNED PROFESSIONAL IN 1905
LTD COMPANY IN 1905

PRESIDENT: G C Watling
HON.SENIOR LIFE VICE-PRESIDENT
Sir Arthur South J.P.
CHAIRMAN: R T Chase, JP
VICE-CHAIRMAN: J A Jones
DIRECTORS
B W Lockwood, G A Paterson
SECRETARY
Andrew Neville (01603 760 760)
COMMERCIAL MANAGER
Ray Cossey
MANAGER: Martin O'Neill
ASSISTANT MANAGER: Paul Franklin

RESERVE TEAM MANAGER
Steve Walford
YOUTH TEAM MANAGER
Keith Webb
PHYSIOTHERAPIST
Tim Sheppard MCSP, SRP

STATISTICIAN FOR THE DIRECTORY
John Brock

Just eighteen months after the club's fine run in the UEFA Cup, Norwich City suffered the embarrassment of relegation from the Premier League. There is little doubt, after demonstrations at the last two home games, that the majority of supporters apportion most of the blame to chairman Robert Chase and his Board. The Board's policy of continually selling the best players has never gone down well. Indeed *The Sunday Times* summed up the situation by referring to the club as "betrayed by a chronic lack of ambition in the boardroom" and "selling their way into obscurity".

The club lost three important members of the previous season's successful team before the new season started. Chris Sutton was sold; captain Ian Butterworth suffered a serious injury and has sadly had to retire; and Ian Culverhouse was incredibly dropped (for not accepting a new contract) and was later sold to Swindon Town. Nevertheless manager John Deehan appeared to buy wisely: Jon Newsome (appointed captain), Carl Bradshaw, Mike Milligan and Mike Sheron.

After a slow start Norwich City picked up momentum, highlighted by home wins over Blackburn Rovers and Leeds United in October. It was in this month that Efan Ekoku was sold to Wimbledon. No reason was given for the sale. He did not want to go; nor did the supporters want him to go; but he was made to feel unwelcome by the Norwich City management. And then the same thing happened again in January, when the popular Mark Robins was first dropped and then sold to Leicester City.

With so many of the club's strikers on their way out, it was as well that John Deehan bought Ashley Ward from Crewe Alexandra in December. He was an instant hit, scoring two goals on his debut and the only goal in his next game. At Christmas there was no sign of the trouble ahead. Norwich City were seventh in the Premier League.

Just after Christmas goalkeeper Bryan Gunn was injured and out for the rest of the season. Andy Marshall performed well in his place; but John Deehan claimed the defence lacked the authority that Gunn gave to it. There were other injuries and suspensions. But it was probably the sale of experienced strikers and the consequent lack of goals that, more than anything, led to the club's relegation. Indeed Norwich City won only one league game between New Year's Day and the end of the season - a 3-0 defeat of hapless neighbours Ipswich Town, which completed the first double over them for forty-three years.

John Deehan resigned as manager on 9th April for the good of the club. The chairman, however, did not see his own position in the same light. He says he has "learnt a very bitter lesson" and will make millions of pounds available for team-strengthening to get the club back into the top flight at the first attempt (a feat achieved on each of the club's three previous relegations). A positive and popular move has been made by appointing Martin O'Neill as manager. Let us hope that the new manager gets the backing from his Board that his predecessors appear to have lacked.

JOHN BROCK.

NORWICH CITY

Premier League: 20th   **FA Cup:** 5th Round   **Coca-Cola Cup:** 5th Round

M	DATE	COMP.	VEN	OPPONENTS	RESULT	H/T	LP	GOAL SCORERS/GOAL TIMES	ATT.
1	A 20	PL	A	Chelsea	L 0-2	0-1			(23,098)
2	24	PL	H	Crystal Palace	D 0-0	0-0	17		19,015
3	27	PL	H	West Ham United	W 1-0	0-0	10	Robins 65	19,110
4	31	PL	A	Sheffield Wednesday	D 0-0	0-0	11		(25,072)
5	S 10	PL	H	Arsenal	D 0-0	0-0	11		17,768
6	19	PL	A	Ipswich Town	W 2-1	1-1	10	Newman 11, Bradshaw 53	(17,447)
7	21	CC 2/1	H	Swansea City	W 3-0	1-0		Sheron 36, Bradshaw 49 (pen), Adams 63	8,053
8	24	PL	A	Manchester City	L 0-2	0-0	11		(21,031)
9	O 1	PL	H	Blackburn Rovers	W 2-1	1-1	9	Bowen 29, Newsome 56	18,146
10	4	CC 2/2	A	Swansea City	L 0-1	0-0			(3,568)
11	8	PL	H	Leeds United	W 2-1	0-0	8	Robins 61, Adams 90	17,390
12	15	PL	A	Aston Villa	D 1-1	0-0	6	Milligan 49	(22,468)
13	22	PL	H	Queens Park Rangers	W 4-2	0-1	6	Robins 46, Bowen 54, Sheron 58, White 62 (og)	19,431
14	26	CC 3	A	Tranmere Rovers	D 1-1	1-0		Polston 45	(10,232)
15	30	PL	A	Wimbledon	L 0-1	0-0	8		(8,242)
16	N 2	PL	A	Southampton	D 1-1	0-0	7	Robins 48	(12,976)
17	5	PL	A	Everton	D 0-0	0-0	7		18,377
18	9	CC 3R	H	Tranmere Rovers	W 4-2	0-1		Prior 56, McGreal 61 (og), Polston 65, Newman 85	13,311
19	19	PL	A	Coventry City	L 0-1	0-0	8		(11,885)
20	26	PL	H	Leicester City	W 2-1	0-0	9	Newsome 57, Sutch 89	20,657
21	30	CC 4	H	Notts. County	W 1-0	1-0		Eadie 1	14,030
22	D 3	PL	A	Manchester United	L 0-1	0-1	9		(43,789)
23	10	PL	H	Chelsea	W 3-0	2-0	9	Ward 24, 45, Cureton 87	18,246
24	17	PL	A	Crystal Palace	W 1-0	0-0	7	Ward 47	(12,252)
25	26	PL	H	Tottenham Hotspur	L 0-2	0-1	7		21,814
26	27	PL	A	Nottingham Forest	L 0-1	0-0	7		(21,010)
27	31	PL	H	Newcastle United	W 2-1	2-1	7	Adams 2, Ward 11	21,172
28	J 2	PL	A	Liverpool	L 0-4	0-2	8		(34,709)
29	7	FAC 3	A	Grimsby Town	W 1-0	1-0		Crook 54	(11,198)
30	11	CC 5	A	Bolton Wanderers	L 0-1	0-0			(17,029)
31	14	PL	H	Wimbledon	L 1-2	1-1	9	Goss 23	18,261
32	25	PL	H	Coventry City	D 2-2	1-1	10	Adams 33 (pen), Ward 56	14,024
33	28	FAC 4	A	Coventry City	D 0-0	0-0			(15,101)
34	F 4	PL	A	Everton	L 1-2	0-1	10	Milligan 80	(23,293)
35	8	FAC 4R	H	Coventry City	W 3-1	1-1		Sheron 9, 108, Eadie 103	14,673
36	11	PL	H	Southampton	D 2-2	1-2	10	Newsome 38, Ward 89	18,361
37	18	FAC 5	A	Everton	L 0-5	0-2			(31,616)
38	22	PL	H	Manchester United	L 0-2	0-2	12		21,824
39	25	PL	A	Blackburn Rovers	D 0-0	0-0	14		(25,579)
40	M 4	PL	H	Manchester City	D 1-1	0-0	13	Cureton 82	16,266
41	8	PL	H	Sheffield Wednesday	D 0-0	0-0	15		13,530
42	11	PL	A	West Ham United	D 2-2	1-0	14	Eadie 22, Ullathorne 53	(21,464)
43	15	PL	A	Queens Park Rangers	L 0-2	0-0	15		(10,519)
44	20	PL	H	Ipswich Town	W 3-0	0-0	11	Cureton 54, Ward 58, Eadie 78	17,510
45	A 1	PL	A	Arsenal	L 1-5	1-3	14	Cureton 32	(36,942)
46	5	PL	A	Leicester City	L 0-1	0-0	14		(15,992)
47	8	PL	A	Newcastle United	L 0-3	0-2	14		(35,518)
48	12	PL	H	Nottingham Forest	L 0-1	0-0	16		19,005
49	17	PL	A	Tottenham Hotspur	L 0-1	0-1	20		(32,304)
50	29	PL	H	Liverpool	L 1-2	1-1	20	Ullathorne 17	21,843
51	M 6	PL	A	Leeds United	L 1-2	1-0	20	Ward 35	(31,982)
52	14	PL	H	Aston Villa	D 1-1	0-1	20	Goss 57	19,374
53									
54									
55									
56									
57									
58									
59									
60									

Best Home League Attendance: 21,843 v Liverpool   **Smallest:** 13,530 v Sheffield Wednesday   **Av Home Att:** 18,625

Goal Scorers:

Compared with 1993-94: +446

League (37): Ward 8, Cureton 4, Robins 4, Adams 3 (1 pen), Newsome 3, Bowen 2, Eadie 2, Goss 2, Milligan 2, Ullathorne 2, Bradshaw, Newman, Sheron, Sutch, Opponent

C/Cola Cup (9): Polsten 2, Adams, Bradshaw (pen), Eadie, Newman, Prior, Sheron, Opponent

FA Cup (4): Sheron 2, Crook, Eadie

274

1	16	2	3	4	5	10	7	9	11	18	6	15	13	20	26	24	22	8	19	14	32	21	25	33	7	Referee	
Gunn B.	Bradshaw C.	Bowen M.	Newman R.	Crook I.	Newsome J.	Polston J.	Ekoku E.	Robins M.	Goss J.	Ullathorne R.	Adams N.	Sutch D.	Howie S.	Eadie D.	Akinbiyi A.	Marshall A.	Sheron M	Milligan M.	Johnson A.	Prior S.	Wright J.	O'Neill K.	Cureton J.	Milk D.	Ward A.		
X	X	X	X1	X	X	X	X2	X	X	X	X	S1	S2	S												Holbrook T.	1
X	X	X	S	X	X	X	X	X1	X	X	X		S	S1												Hill B.	2
X	X	X	S2	X	X	X	X1	X2	X	X	X				S1	S										Jones P.	3
X	X	X	S2	X	X	X	X2	X	X	X	X				X1		S1									Cooper K.	4
X	X	X	X	X	X	X2	S2	X	X	X1	S1				S											Hart R.	5
X	X	X	X	X1	X	X	S2	X	X	X		S	S1				X2	X								Dilkes L.	6
X	X	S2	S1	X	X2		X	X	X	X		S	X				X	X1								West T.	7
X	X	X	X	X	X	S2	X	X2	X1		X					X	S1									Poll G.	8
X	X	X	X	X	X	X	X1	S1	S2	X2		X		S		X										Jones P.	9
X	X	X	X	S2	X	X1	S1	X	X		X		S		X2		X1	S2								Ashby G.	10
X	X	X	X	X2	X		X	S1	X		X		S	X		X1		S2								Don P.	11
X	X2	X	X	X1			X		X		X	S1	S	X	X		X	X		S2						Wilkie A.	12
X		X	S1	X	X		X	S2	X2		X		S	X	X		X	X1								Reed M.	13
X		X	X	X	X		S2	X	X	X1	S1	X2			S	X	X	X								Lodge S.	14
X		X	X	S1		X		X	X1	S2	X			X2	S	X	X	X								Gallagher D.	15
X		X2	X		X		X	X		X	S1			X1	S		X	X		S2						Durkin P.	16
X		X	X		X		X1	X		X	X			S		X	X	X		S1	S					Danson P.	17
X		X	X	X1		X		X	S1		X	X		X		S	X	X		S						Hill B.	18
X		X	X	X	X		X2	S1	X1	S2	X			S		X	X	X								Willard G.	19
X		X	X	X	X		S2		X	X		X		S	X1	X2				S1						Gifford R.	20
X		X	X	X	X			S2		X	X			X2		S	X1	X		S1						Morton K.	21
X	X	X	X1	X	X			X		X				X		S		S		S1					X	Holbrook T.	22
X	X		S2	X2	X	X		X1		X				X		S		X		S1					X	Worrall J.B.	23
X	X1	S1	S2	X2	X		X		X			X				S		X							X	Hart R.	24
X		X2	S2	X	X		X	X		X1		X					S	X							X	Dilkes L.	25
X1			X	X	X		X	X		X	S1	X			S1		X		S			X2			X	Lodge S.	26
		S2	X2	X	X		X	X		X		X				X	X1	X				S1			X	Hill B.	27
		X1	X		X		X2	X	S1	X		S2			X		X	X				S2			X	Cooper K.	28
		X	X		X		S1	X†	X1	X		X		S2		X	X2	X				S2			X	Poll G.	29
	X	X	X		X			X	S1	X2	X			X1	S2	X	X									Elleray D.	30
	X		X2	X		X		X	X	X1						S2	X	X							X	Bodenham M.	31
	X	X		X	X			X	X1		S1			X	S	S	X	X		X		S			X	Don P.	32
	X2			X	X			X	X		X			X	S2	S1	X3	X				S3			X	Willard G.	33
	X		X	X	X		S2	X	S1	X1		X			X	X2	X								X	Wilkie A.	34
	X		X1	X	X			S1	X	X2	X			X	X	S2	X									Willard G.	35
X	X		X	X				X	X1	S2	S1			X	X		X2								X	Hart R.	36
X	X	X		X+				X	X1	S	X			X	X	S	X		X1						X	Bodenham M.	37
X	X	S		X	X					X	S			X	X	X	X								X	Holbrook T.	38
X	X		X	X					X1	S1	X			X	X	X2	X			S2					X	Reed M.	39
X	X2	X		X				X		X				X	X	S1	X1	X		X					X	Gallagher D.	40
X1	X	S2	X2	X				X		X				X2	S2	X		S1		X					X	Danson P.	41
	X		X	X				X	S1	X				X2	S2	X		X†	X	X1					X	Wilkie A.	42
	X		X	X				X	S2	X				X	S1	X	X X2	X		X1					X	Ashby G.	43
	X	S2	X	X	X				X	X1	S1			X		X		X		X2					X	Durkin P.	44
X	X	X		X				X1	X	S1				X		X		X		X					X	Jones P.	45
X	S2	X		X				X2		X				X		X		S1		X					X	Holbrook T.	46
X	X		X	X	X2			X1		S1				X		X		X		S2					X	Reed M.	47
X	X		X	X				X		S2	X1	S2	X			S1	X1 X2	X		X2					X	Morton K.	48
X	X		X	X	X				S2					S1	S	X	X1 X2	X							X	Gifford R.	49
X1	X		X	X				X2	S2	X				X	X					S1					X	Hill B.	50
S2	X	X	X2	X	X		X	X		X				X1	X	S1									X	Wilkie A.	51
X	X		X	X	X		X	X		S	X			X1	X	S1									X	Cooper K.	52

21	25	34	23	33	35	38	5	14	19	27	23	20		22	6	20	17	25	6	12	1		9		25	League Appearances	
	1	2	9	1			1	3	6		10	10		4	7	1	4	1	1	5	1	1	8			League Sub Appearances	
5	2	5	5+1	4+2	4	5	1	3+1	3+3	1+1	6	3+1		6	0+1	1	4	4	1	3			0+1			C/Cola Cup Appearances	
	1	3	3	2	4	3			1+2	4	3	4		4	0+2	2+1	4	3	1	0+1			0+2			FA Cup Appearances	

Also Played: Crowfoot S(24,27,28,40,41,42,),Tracey S(29,30,31,34,35,36,38,39),X(32,37),X1(33), Rhodes S(43,44,45,46,47,48,49,50,51,52), Brownrigg S(45)   † = Sent Off

NORWICH CITY

BIGGEST VICTORIES
League: 10-2 v Coventry City, Division 3(S), 15.3.1930.
8-0 v Walsall, Division 3(S), 29.12.1951.
F.A. Cup: 8-0 v Sutton United, 4th Round, 28.1.1989.
League Cup: 7-1 v Halifax Town, 4th Round, 27.11.1963.

BIGGEST DEFEATS
League: 0-7 v Walsall, Division 3(S), 13.9.1930.
0-7 v Sheffield Wednesday, Division 2, 19.11.1938.
F.A. Cup: 0-6 v Luton Town, 2nd Round, 10.12.1927.
0-6 v Manchester City, 4th Round, 24.1.1981.
League Cup: 1-6 v Manchester City, 2nd Round 2nd replay,
29.9.1975.

MOST POINTS
3 points a win: 84, Division 2, 1985-86.
2 points a win: 64, Division 3(S), 1950-51.

MOST GOALS SCORED
99, Division 3(S), 1952-53.
Ackerman 20, Gavin 20, Johnston 15, Summers 10, Ashman 9,
Kinsey 7, McCrohan 7, Rattray 5, Adams 3, Coxon 2, Opponents 1.

MOST GOALS CONCEDED
100, Division 3(S), 1946-47.

MOST FIRST CLASS MATCHES IN A SEASON
60 - 1972-73 (League 42, FA Cup 3, League Cup 7, Texaco Cup 8).

MOST LEAGUE WINS
26, Division 3(S), 1951-52.

MOST LEAGUE DRAWS
23, Division 1, 1978-79.

MOST LEAGUE DEFEATS
24, Division 3(S), 1930-31 & 1946-47. Division 2, 1938-39.

MOST GOALS IN A SEASON
Ralph Hunt: 31 goals in 1955-56, Division 3(S).

MOST GOALS IN A MATCH
5. Roy Hollis v Walsall, Division 3(S), 29.12.1951.
5. T Hunt v Coventry City, 10-2, Division 3(S), 15.3.1930.

OLDEST PLAYER
Albert Sturgess, 42 years 249 days v Millwall Athletic, Division 3(S),
14.2.1925.

YOUNGEST PLAYER
Ian Davies, 17 years 29 days (sub) v Birmingham City, Division 1,
27.4.1974.

MOST CAPPED PLAYER
Mark Bowen (Wales) 30.

League: 1950-51: Matches played 46, Won 25, Drawn 14, Lost 7,
Goals for 82, Goals against 45, Points 64. Second in Division 3(S).
Highest Position: 3rd in Premier League, 1992-93.
F.A. Cup: Semi-finalists 1958-59, 1988-89.
Most recent success: 1991-92: 3rd Round Barnsley 1-0; 4th Round
Millwall 2-1; 5th Round Notts County 3-0, 6th Round Southampton
0-0,2-1 (aet); Semi-final Sunderland 0-1.
League Cup: Winners in 1961-62.
Most recent success: 1984-85: 2nd Round Preston North End 3-3
6-1; 3rd Round Aldershot 0-0, 4-0; 4th Round Notts County 3-0; 5th
Round Grimsby Town 1-0; Semi-final Ipswich Town 0-1,2-0; Final
Sunderland 1-0.
Europe: 1993-94: 1st Round Vitesse Arnhem 0-0,0-3; 2nd Round
Bayern Munich 1-2,1-1; 3rd Round Inter Milan 0-1,0-1.

ADDITIONAL INFORMATION
PREVIOUS NAMES
None.

PREVIOUS LEAGUES
Southern League.

Club colours: Yellow shirts with green trim, green shorts with yellow trim, yellow socks with green tops.
Change colours: Blue tartan shirts, dark blue shorts, black socks with green tops.
Reserves League: Neville Ovenden Football Combination.

DIVISIONAL RECORD

	Played	Won	Drawn	Lost	For	Against	Points
Division 1/P	826	257	251	318	970	1,177	930
Division 2	840	329	209	302	1,231	1,188	914
Division 3	92	46	24	22	171	116	116
Division 3(S)	1,124	423	291	410	1,779	1,725	1,137
Total	2,882	1,055	775	1,052	4,151	4,206	3,097

RECORDS AND STATISTICS

COMPETITIONS

Div 1/P	Div.2	Div.3	Div.3(S)	A/Scot	Texaco
1972-74	1934-39	1958-60	1920-34	1975-76	1972-73
1975-81	1960-72		1939-58	1976-77	1973-74
1982-85	1974-75			1977-78	1974-75
1986-95	1981-82	**UEFA**		1978-79	
	1985-86	1993-94			
	1995-				

HONOURS

Division 2	Division 3(S)	League Cup
1971-72	1933-34	1961-62
1985-86		1984-85

MOST APPEARANCES

Kevin Keeland 680 (1963-80)

Year	League	FA Cup	Lge Cup	Others
1963-64	16		1	
1964-65	23	1		
1965-66	42	4	1	
1966-67	39	3	1	
1967-68	30	3	3	
1968-69	32	1	3	
1969-70	33		1	
1970-71	38	1	4	
1971-72	42	1	5	
1972-73	42	3	7	7
1973-74	42	1	7	4
1974-75	38	1	9	3
1975-76	42	5	3	3
1976-77	38	1	2	3
1977-78	26	2	1	1
1978-79	22	1	3	
1979-80	26	3	6	
	571	31	57	21

MOST GOALS IN A CAREER

John Gavin - 132 (1949-58)

Year	League	FA Cup
1949-50	1	
1950-51	17	1
1951-52	19	1
1952-53	20	
1953-54	13	1
1954-55	6	
1955-56	13	2
1956-57	16	
1957-58	17	5
Total	**122**	**10**

Current leading goalscorer: Mark Bowen 25 (1987-95)

MANAGERS

Name	Seasons	Best	Worst
A Turner	1902-05		
J Bowman	1905-07		
J McEwen	1907-09		
A Turner	1909-10		
J Stansfield	1910-15		
F Buckley	1919-20		
C O'Hagan	1920		
A Gosnell	1921-26	11(3S)	18(3S)
J Stansfield	1926		
C Potter	1926-29	16(3S)	17(3S)
J Kerr	1929-33	3(3S)	22(3S)
T Parker	1933-37	11(2)	1(3S)
R Young	1937-39	14(2)	14(2)
A Jewell	1939	21(2)	21(2)
R Young	1939-45		
D Lochhead	1945-46		
C Spiers	1946-47	21(3S)	21(3S)
D Lochhead	1947-50	10(3S)	21(3S)
N Low	1950-55	2(3S)	11(3S)
T Parker	1955-57	7(3S)	24(3S)
A Macaulay	1957-61	4(2)	8(3S)
W Reid	1961-62	17(2)	17(2)
G Swindin	1962		
R Ashman	1962-66	6(2)	17(2)
L Morgan	1966-69	9(2)	13(2)
R Saunders	1969-73	20(1)	11(2)
J Bond	1973-80	10(1)	3(2)
K Brown	1980-87	5(1)	3(2)
D Stringer	1987-92	4(1)	18(1)
Mike Walker	1992-94	3(P)	3(P)
John Deehan	1994-95	12(P)	20(P)
Martin O'Neill	1995-		

RECORD TRANSFER FEE RECEIVED

Amount	Club	Player	Date
£5,000,000	Blackburn Rovers	Chris Sutton	7/94
£2,250,000	Newcastle Utd	Ruel Fox	2/94
£2,100,000	Chelsea	Robert Fleck	8/92
£1,200,000	Glasgow Rangers	Dale Gordon	11/91
£1,200,000	Chelsea	Andy Townsend	7/90
£1,200,000	Arsenal	Andy Linighan	7/90

RECORD TRANSFER FEE PAID

Amount	Club	Player	Date
£1,000,000	Leeds United	Jon Newsome	6/94
£925,000	Port Vale	Darren Beckford	6/91
£700,000	Derby County	Paul Blades	7/90
£580,000	Glasgow Rangers	Robert Fleck	12/87

LONGEST LEAGUE RUNS

of undefeated matches:	20 (31.8.1950 - 11.1.1951)
of undefeated home matches:	31 (21.8.1971 - 2.12.1972)
without home win:	12 (29.9.1956 - 2.3.1957)
of league wins:	10 (23.11.1985 - 1.2.1986)
of league defeats: 7 (4.9.1935 - 5.10.1935, 12.1.1957 - 2.3.1957)	
	(1.4.1995 - 14.5.1995)
of league matches w/out a win:	25 (22.9.1956 - 2.3.1957)
of undefeated away matches:	12 (14.9.1985 - 8.3.1986)
without an away win:	41 (3.9.1977 - 18.8.1979)
of home wins:	12 (15.3.1952 - 4.10.1952)
of away wins:	5 (3.9.1988 - 19.11.1988)

NORWICH CITY

PLAYERS NAME Honours	Ht	Wt	Birthdate	Birthplace Transfers	Contract Date	Clubs	League	L/Cup	FA Cup	Other	Lge	L/C	FAC	Oth
GOALKEEPERS														
Bryan Gunn	6.2	12.5	22.12.63	Thurso		Aberdeen	15	4	1	1				
S: 6, u21.9, Y, S, B.3				£150,000	23.10.86	Norwich City	304	25	24	22				
Andrew J Marshall	6.2	12.7	14.04.75	Bury St Ed.	06.07.93	Norwich City (T)	20+1	1	2+1					
DEFENDERS														
Mark R Bowen	5.8	11.6	07.12.63	Neath	01.12.81	Tottenham H. (A)	14+3		3	0+1	2			
W:26, u21.3,Y,S				£97,000	23.07.87	Norwich City	285+4	28	27	17	22	1	1	1
Andrew D Brownrigg	6.0	11.13	02.08.76	Sheffield	03.01.95	Hereford (T)	8		1					
S: Yth.				£100,000	09.03.95	Norwich City								
Ian Butterworth	6.1	12.6	25.01.64	Crewe	05.08.81	Coventry City (A)	80+10	5	5+1					
E: u21.8.				£250,000	03.06.85	Nottingham Forest	26+1	6	1					
				Loan	19.09.88	Norwich City	4							
				£160,000	05.12.86	Norwich City	226+5	17+1	25	14+1	4			
Stacey Kreft	5.9	11.0	02.02.76	Salisbury	01.07.94	Norwich City (T)								
Daniel Mills	5.11	11.09	18.05.77	Norwich		Norwich (T)								
Robert N Newman	6.2	12.0	13.12.63	B'ford-on-Avon	05.10.81	Bristol City (A)	382+12	29+1	27	33	52	2	2	5
FRT'86				£600,000	15.07.91	Norwich City	112+11	17+1	11	7	12	2	1	
Jon Newsome	6.2	13.11	06.09.70	Sheffield	01.07.89	Sheffield Wed. (T)	6+1	3						
Div1'92				£150,000	11.06.91	Leeds United	62+14	3	3+1	5	3			
				£1,000,000	30.06.94	Norwich City	35	4	4		3			
John D Polston	5.11	11.3	10.06.68	Walthamstow	16.07.85	Tottenham H. (T)	17+7	3+1						
E: Y6				£250,000	24.07.90	Norwich City	139+3	11+1	15+1	9	6	2		1
Spencer Prior	6.3	12.10	22.04.71	Southend	22.05.89	Southend Utd (T)	135	9	5	7	3			1
				£200,000	24.06.93	Norwich City	25+5	4	0+1	2		1		
Robert Ullathorne	5.8	10.7	11.10.71	Wakefield	06.07.90	Norwich City (T)	60+5	5+1	6+1	1	7			
E: Y1														
Jonathon Wright	5.8	11.04	24.11.75	Belfast	01.07.94	Norwich City (T)	1+1							
MIDFIELD														
Shaun P Carey	5.9	10.06	13.05.76	Kettering	01.07.94	Norwich City (T)								
Ian S Crook	5.8	10.6	18.01.63	Romford	01.08.80	Tottenham H. (A)	10+10	1	0+1	1+1	1			
E: B1				£80,000	13.06.88	Norwich City	254+22	25+5	18+4	16+1	1	14	1	1
Darren M Eadie	5.8	10.6	10.06.75	Chippenham	05.02.93	Norwich City (T)	31+10	9	4	1+1	5	1	1	
E: u21.2, Y2														
Jeremy Goss	5.9	10.9	11.0565	Cyprus	23.03.83	Norwich City (J)	146+26	14+3	13+5	15	13	3		6
W:6; FAYC'83														
Alistair S Gibb	5.9	10.08	17.02.76	Salisbury	01.07.94	Norwich City (T)								
Andrew J Johnson	6.0	11.6	02.05.74	Bristol	04.03.92	Norwich City (T)	9+4	2	1		1			
E: Y1														
Michael J Milligan	5.8	11.0	20.02.67	Manchester	02.03.85	Oldham Athletic (T)	161+1	19+1	12	4	17	1	1	
Ei:1, B1,u21.1				£1,000,000	24.08.90	Everton	16+1	0+1	1	4+1	1			1
				£600,000	17.07.91	Oldham Athletic	117	11	9	1	6	1		1
				£800,000	27.06.94	Norwich City	25+1	4	3		2			
Keith P O'Neil	6.1	11.0	16.02.76	Dublin	01.07.94	Norwich City (T)	0+1							
Michael N Sheron	5.9	11.3	11.01.72	Liverpool	05.07.90	Manchester City (T)	82+18	9+1	5+3	1	24	1	3	
E: u21.16.				Loan	28.03.91	Bury	1+4			2	1			
				£1,000,000	26.08.94	Norwich City	17+4	4	4		1	1	2	
Daryl Sutch	5.11	10.12	11.09.71	Beccles	06.07.90	Norwich City (T)	42+26	6+3	4+1	2+3	3			
E: u21.4, Y2														
FORWARDS														
Neil J Adams	5.8	10.8	23.11.65	Stoke	01.07.85	Stoke City	31+1	3	1	3	4			
E: u21.1; Div1'87; CS'86;Div2'91				£150,000	07.07.86	Everton	17+3	4+1		5+1		1		
Loan Oldham Athletic (11.1.89) 9 Lg				£100,000	21.06.89	Oldham Athletic	93+36	13+2	10+2	1+1	23	2	2	
				£250,000	17.02.94	Norwich City	34+13	6	3		3	1		
Adeola P Akinbiyi	6.1	12.0	10.10.74	Hackney	05.02.93	Norwich City (T)	6+9	0+1	1+2	0+1				
				Loan	21.01.94	Hereford United	3+1				2			
				Loan	24.11.94	Brighton & H.A.	7				4			
Carl Bradshaw	6.0	11.0	02.10.68	Sheffield	23.08.86	Sheffield Wed. (A)	16+16	2+2	6+1	1	4		3	
E: Y4				Loan	23.08.86	Barnsley	6							
				£50,000	30.09.88	Manchester City	1+4		0+1	0+1				
				£50,000	07.09.89	Sheffield United	122+25	10+1	12+1	4	8	2	3	
				£500,000	28.07.94	Norwich City	25+1	2	1		1	1		

PLAYERS NAME / Honours	Ht	Wt	Birthdate	Birthplace / Transfers	Contract Date	Clubs	APPEARANCES				GOALS			
							League	L/Cup	FA Cup	Other	Lge	L/C	FAC	Oth
Jamie Cureton	5.8	10.0	28.08.75	Bristol	05.02.93	Norwich City (T)	9+8	0+1	0+2		4			
?: Y4														
Justin D Harrington	5.9	10.09	18.09.75	Truro	01.07.94	Norwich City (T)								
Ashley S Ward	6.1	12.4	24.11.70	Manchester	05.08.89	Manchester City (T)	0+1		0+2		2			
				Loan	10.01.91	Wrexham	4			1	2			
				£80,000	30.07.91	Leicester City	2+8	2+1	0+1	0+1				
				Loan	21.11.92	Blackpool	2				1			
				£80,000	01.12.92	Crewe Alexandra	58+3	4	2	7	25	2	4	5
				£500,000	08.12.94	Norwich City	25				8			

TOP GOALSCORER 1994/95
Ashley Ward

Premiership goals (games). 8 (25)
Division Two goals (with Crewe). 8 (16)
Coca-Cola Cup Goals 1 (2)
F.A. Cup goals 4 (2)
Auto Windscreen Trophy 4 (3)
Total . . . . **25 (48)**

Total goals for Norwich since 8.12.1994 . . . . 8 (25)

Career total as at June 1st 1995. . . . . 47 (84+17)

THE MANAGER
MARTIN O'NEILL

Date of Birth. . . . . 1st March 1952.
Place of Birth . . . . Kilrea, Northern Ireland.
Date of Appointment . . . . June 1995.

PREVIOUS CLUBS
As Manager . . . . . . Grantham, Shepshed Charterhouse, Wycombe Wanderers.
As Coach. . . . . None.
As a Player . . . . . . Distillery, Nottingham Forest, Norwich City, Manchester City,
. . . . Norwich City, Notts. County.

HONOURS
As a Manager
Wycombe W.: FA Trophy 1991, 1993. Bob Lord Trophy 1992. GMVC champions and promoted to Endsleigh League 1993. Promotion to Endsleigh League Division Two 1994 (via the play-offs).

As a Player
Irish Cup 1971. Division 1 championship 1978. League Cup 1978, 1979. European Cup 1980. Promotion to Football League Division One 1977, 1982.

CARROW ROAD

Norwich NR1 1JE
Tel: 01603 760 760

Capacity 21,909

First game .... v West Ham, Div.2, 31.8.1935.
First floodlit game .... v Sunderland, 17.10.1956.

ATTENDANCES
Highest .... 43,984 v Leicester City, FAC 6th Rnd, 30.3.1963.
Lowest .... 1,801 v Northampton, FLT, 14.8.1982.

OTHER GROUNDS .... Newmarket Road 1902-08.The Nest, Rosary Road 1908-35.
.... Carrow Road 1935-

MATCHDAY TICKET PRICES

Category A
Lounges. £25
Reserved £15
Juv. £10

Category B
Lounges. £15
Reserved £10
Juv. £5

Match and Ticket Information
Applications to Box Office 28 days before match with
payment and SAE.

Ticket Office Telephone no. 01603 761 661

CITY LINE
0891 10 15 00

Calls cost 39p per minute cheap rate and 49p per
minute at all other times.
Call costings correct at time of going to press.

HOW TO GET TO THE GROUND

From the North
Use A140 to junction with Ring Road, then follow signs to Yarmouth (A47). In 3.5
miles at 'T' junction turn right. In half-a-mile turn left into Carrow Road for
Norwich City FC.

From the East
Use A47, sign posted Norwich, on entering city keep left into Ring Road for
Carrow Road for Norwich City FC.

From the South and West
Use A11, A140 into Norwich and follow signs to Yarmouth (A47) into Ring Road,
Carrow Road for Norwich City FC.

Car Parking
Numerous private parks nearby. Multistory parks in Malt House Road and St
Andrews Street. Street parking nearby in Rose Lane, Carrow Hill and side
streets of King Street. Coaches must park at Lower Clarence Road Car Park.

Nearest Railway Station
Norwich (01603 -1603 632 055)

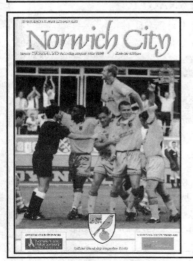

MATCHDAY PROGRAMME

Programme Editor . . . . Kevan Platt.

Number of pages . . . . 40.

Price . . . . £1.50.

Subscriptions . . . . £40 for all games (£47 Europe).

Local Newspapers . . . . Eastern Counties Newspapers.

Local Radio Stations . . . . Radio Norfolk, Radio Broadland.

OLDHAM ATHLETIC
(The Latics)
ENDSLEIGH LEAGUE DIVISION 1
SPONSORED BY: J D SPORTS

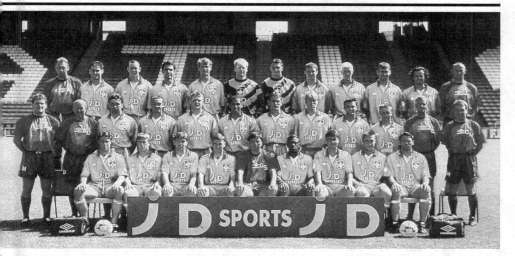

Back Row (L-R): Andy Holden (Res. Coach), Steve Redmond, Richard Graham, Craig Fleming, Richard Jobson, Jon Hallworth, Paul Gerrard, Simon Kay, Ian Olney, Ricky Evans, Lee Richardson, John Bowden (Kit Manager). **Middle Row:** Alexis Moreno (Physio), Billy Urmson (Yth Coach), Rick Holden, Carl Serrant, Darren Lonergan, Martin Pemberton, Paul Bernard, Gunnar Halle, Nicky Banger, David Beresford, Jim Cassell (Chief Scout), Colin Harvey (First Team Coach). **Front Row:** Sean McCarthy, Paul Rickers, Mark Brennan, Nick Henry, Graeme Sharp (Manager), Darren Beckford, Ian Snodin, Chris Makin, Neil Pointon.

OLDHAM ATHLETIC
FORMED IN 1895
TURNED PROFESSIONAL IN 1899
LTD COMPANY IN 1906

PRESIDENT: R Schofield
CHAIRMAN: I H Scott

DIRECTORS
D A Brierley (Vice-Chairman),
G T Butterworth, P Chadwick, J C Slevin,
D R Taylor, N Holden
SECRETARY
J T Cale (0161 624 4972)
COMMERCIAL MANAGER
A Hardy (0161 624 0966)

MANAGER: Graeme Sharp
ASSISTANT MANAGER: Colin Harvey
RESERVE TEAM MANAGER
Andy Holden
YOUTH TEAM MANAGER
Bill Urmson
PHYSIOTHERAPIST
Alexis Moreno

STATISTICIAN FOR THE DIRECTORY
Gordon A Lawton

The 1994/95 season was a season of change in many ways. Joe Royle, Latics' longest serving manager in their history, departed for Everton taking with him Willie Donachie as coach. Their replacements, as the management team, were funnily enough ex Evertonians, Graeme Sharp stepping up from player manager and Latics new coach and assistant to Sharp was Colin Harvey.

On the playing front, re-grouping was the key word after relegating from the Premier League the previous season.

New signings came in the form of Lee Richardson from Aberdeen, Nicky Banger from Southampton and Ian Snodin from Everton, but even these experienced players could not stop mid-season jitters that saw Latics lose five and draw three from 11 games.

Sean McCarthy was top scorer with 18 goals followed by veteran striker Andy Ritchie's 13, but 14th position in the First Division was not up to many supporters expectations. Then again 14th position was heaven if you were a Swindon supporter!

G A LAWTON.

OLDHAM ATHLETIC

Division One: 14th   **FA Cup:** 4th Round   **Coca-Cola Cup:** 3rd Round

M	DATE	COMP.	VEN	OPPONENTS	RESULT	H/T	LP	GOAL SCORERS/GOAL TIMES	ATT.
1	A 13	EL	H	Charlton Athletic	W 5-2	2-2		McCarthy (2), Richardson (2), Sharp	8,924
2	20	EL	A	Port Vale	L 1-3	0-0	7	Sharp	(10,051)
3	27	EL	H	Burnley	W 3-0	0-0	4	Ritchie, McCarthy (2) 1 pen	11,310
4	30	EL	A	Notts County	W 3-1	1-1		McCarthy (3)	(6,603)
5	S 3	EL	A	Southend United	L 0-1	0-0	3		(4,435)
6	10	El	H	Reading	L 1-3	1-1	6	Richardson	8,412
7	13	EL	H	Watford	L 0-2	0-1			7,243
8	17	EL	A	Derby County	L 1-2	0-1	14	McCarthy (Pen)	(13,746)
9	20	CC 2/1	A	**Oxford United**	D 1-1			Ritchie	(5,070)
10	24	EL	H	Barnsley	W 1-0	0-0	10	Halle	7,941
11	O 1	EL	A	Sheffield United	L 0-2	0-1	15		(14,223)
12	4	CC 2/2	H	**Oxford United**	W 1-0			**Richardson**	4,525
13	8	EL	H	Portsmouth	W 3-2	1-0	8	R Holden (2 pens), Graham	7,683
14	16	EL	A	Bolton Wanderers	D 2-2	0-2	9	Bernard, McCarthy	(11,106)
15	22	EL	A	Stoke City	D 0-0	0-0	13		8,954
16	26	CC 3	H	**Arsenal**	D 0-0	0-0			**9,364**
17	29	EL	A	Sunderland	D 0-0	0-0	14		(17,252)
18	N 1	EL	A	Middlesbrough	L 1-2	1-0		Graham	(15,929)
19	6	EL	H	Tranmere Rovers	D 0-0	0-0	19		6,475
20	9	CC 3R	A	**Arsenal**	L 0-2				**(22,746)**
21	12	EL	H	Luton Town	D 0-0	0-0			7,907
22	19	EL	A	West Bromwich Albion	L 1-3	0-2	18	Halle (pen)	(14,616)
23	26	EL	H	Bristol City	W 2-0	0-0	17	Richardson, McCarthy	7,277
24	D 4	EL	A	Stoke City	W 1-0	0-0	14	McCarthy	(12,558)
25	10	EL	H	Port Vale	W 3-2	1-1	12	Ritchie (3)	7,712
26	17	EL	A	Charlton Athletic	L 0-2	0-0	14		(8,970)
27	26	EL	H	Wolverhampton W.	W 4-1	1-0	11	Ritchie (3), McCarthy	11,962
28	27	EL	A	Grimsby Town	W 3-1	2-0	8	Ritchie, Henry, McCarthy	(6,958)
29	31	EL	H	Swindon Town	D 1-1	1-1	9	Halle	8,917
30	J 3	EL	A	Millwall	D 1-1	1-0		Richardson (pen)	(7,438)
31	7	FAC 3	A	**Reading**	W 3-1			**Halle, Richardson, Sharp**	**(8,886)**
32	14	EL	H	Sunderland	D 0-0	0-0	8		9,742
33	22	EL	A	Tranmere Rovers	L 1-3	1-1	10	Makin	(5,581)
34	28	FAC 4	A	**Leeds United**	L 2-3			**Halle, Opponents**	**(25,010**
35	F 4	EL	A	Luton Town	L 1-2	0-1	13	R Holden	(6,903)
36	18	EL	A	Bristol City	D 2-2	1-2	13	Halle, Ritchie	(7,851)
37	21	EL	H	West Bromwich Albion	W 1-0	1-0		Richardson	7,690
38	25	EL	H	Sheffield United	D 3-3	2-2	11	Banger (2), Ritchie	9,640
39	M 7	EL	H	Southend United	L 0-2	0-1			7,168
40	11	EL	A	Burnley	L 1-2	0-1	14	McCarthy	(11,620)
41	14	EL	H	Notts County	D 1-1	1-0		Henry	5,465
42	21	EL	A	Reading	L 1-2	1-0		Halle	(6,921)
43	25	EL	H	Derby County	W 1-0	1-0	15	Graham	7,696
44	A 1	EL	A	Watford	W 2-1	2-1	14	Banger, Brennan	(8,090)
45	5	EL	H	Middlesbrough	W 1-0	0-0		Ritchie	11,024
46	8	EL	A	Swindon Town	L 1-3	1-2	13	Ritchie	(7,488)
47	15	EL	H	Grimsby Town	W 1-0	1-0	13	McCarthy	6,757
48	17	EL	A	Wolverhampton W.	L 1-2	1-1	13	Bernard	(25,840)
49	22	EL	H	Millwall	L 0-1	0-0	15		6,319
50	29	EL	H	Bolton Wanderers	W 3-1	2-1	12	McCarthy (2), Rickers	11,901
51	M 2	EL	A	Barnsley	D 1-1	1-1		Eyre	(9,838)
52	7	EL	A	Portsmouth	D 1-1	1-0	14	McCarthy (pen)	(11,002)
53									
54									
55									
56									
57									
58									
59									
60									

Best Home League Attendance: 11,962 v Wolverhampton Wanderers   **Smallest:** 5,465 v Notts County   **Av Home Att:** 8,440

Goal Scorers: Compared with **1993-94:** -4,130

League (60:   McCarthy 18 (3 pens), Ritchie 12, Halle 5 (1 pen), Richardson 6 (1pen), Banger 3, Graham 3, R Holden 3 (2 pens), Henry 2, Sharp 2, Bernard 2, Brennan 1, Eyre 1, Makin 1, Rickers 1.

C/Cola Cup (2):   Richardson, Ritchie

FA Cup (5:   Halle 2, Richardson, Sharp, Opponents

Hallworth J.	Makin C.	Barlow A.	Kenny W.	Jobson R.	Fleming C.	Halle G.	Richardson L.	Sharp G.	McCarthy S.	Holden R.	Henry N.	Ritchie A.	Gerrard P.	Brennan M.	Redmond S.	Graham R.	Banger N.	Pointon N.	Rickers P.	Bernard P.	Eyre J.	Beckford D.	Snodin I.	Moore N.	Webster S.	Referee	
1	2	3	4	5	6	7	8	9	10	11																	1
1	2	3	4	5	6		8	9	10	11	12	14															2
	3			5	6	7	2	9	10	11	4	12	1	8	4												3
	3			5	6	7	2	9	10	11			1	8	4												4
15	3			5	6	7	2	9	10	11		12	1	8	6												5
15	3		4	5		7	2	9	10	11		12	1	8	6	5											6
1	3		4			7	2	9	10	11		12	1	8	6	9											7
	3			5		7	2		10	12	4	11	1	8	6	9											8
	3			5		7	2		10		4	11	1	8	6	9											9
1				5		7	2		10	12	4	11	1	8	6		14			7							10
				5			2	9	10	12	14	4		11	6	9	12										11
1	3			5		7	2		10	12	4	14	1	11	6	9				8							12
				5		7	2		10	11	4		1	14	6	9	12	8		7							13
				5		7	2		10	11	4		1		6	9	8	3		7		12					14
				5			2		10	11	4		1		6	9	8	3		7		14					15
				5			2		10	11	4		1		6	9	8	3		7							16
				5			2		10	11	4		1		6	9	8	3		7							17
				5			2		10	11	4		1	8	6	12		3									18
	3			5			2		10	11	4		1		6	9	8										19
	3			5			2		10	14	4	12	1	11	6	9		8		7							20
	2			5		7			10	11	4		1	12	6	9		8	3								21
	2					7		9	10	11	4		1	11	6	10	12	3									22
	2					7		9		11	4	8	1	14	6	10	12	3									23
	2					7		9		11	4	8	1	14	6	10	12	3									24
	2					7		9		11	4	8	1	14	6	10	12	3									25
	2							9	14		4	8	1	11	6	5	12	3		7							26
	2					7		9	10		4	8	1	11	6	5		3				12					27
	2					7		9	10		4	8	1	11	6	5		3				12					28
	2					7		9	10		14	4	8	1	11	6	5	12		3							29
	2					7		9	10			4	1	11	6	5	8	3				12					30
	2					7		9	10		4	8	1	11	6	5		3				12					31
	2					7		9	10		14	8	1	11	6	5	12	3					4				32
	2					7		10			12	8	1	11	6	5	9	3					4				33
	2					7		10			14	4	8	1	11	6	5	9	3			12					34
						7		10	12	14	4	8	1	11	6	9		3					2				35
						7		10	12	14	4	8	1	11	6	9		3					2	5			36
						7		10	12	14	4	8	1	11	6	9		3					2	5			37
						7		10	12		4	8	1	11	6	9		3					2	5			38
						7		10			4	8	1	11	6	9		3				12	2	5			39
						7		10			4	8	1	11	6		3		4	9			2	5			40
						7		9			12	4	1	11	6	5	10	3		8			2				41
						7		9			4	12	1	11	6	5	10	3		8			2				42
						7		9			12		1	11	6	4	10	3		8			2		5		43
						7		9			4		1	11	6	12	10	3		8			2		5		44
						7		9			4	12	1	11	6		10	3		8			2		5		45
						7		4			9		1	11	6	12	10	3		8			2		5		46
						7		9			4	10	1	11	6			3		8			2		5		47
						7		9			4	10	1	11	6	12	14	3		8			2		5		48
	2					7		9			4	8	1	11	6			3		12					5		49
	2							12	9		4		1	11	6	5	10	3	7	8		14					50
	2							4	9				1	11	6	5		3	7	8		10					51
	2							4	9				1	11	6			3	7	8		10	5				52
																											53
																											54
																											55
																											56
																											57
																											58
																											59
																											60
4	28	2	4	20	5	40	28	10	35	18	33	25	42	34	43	29	20	32	4	16	3		17	5	7	League Appearances	
2							2	2	4	13	1	8		6		3	8			1	5	3				Substitute Appearances	
1	3			4		4	2	0+1	4	0+2	4	2+1	3	3	4	4	2	1	1+2	2			0+2	2		C/Cola Appearances	
	2						2	2	1		0+1	2	2	2	2	2	2	1		2			0+2	2	0+1	FA Cup Appearances	

Also Played: A. Holden 5 (26), McNiven 2 (51), Beresford 12 (51,52)

OLDHAM ATHLETIC

CLUB RECORDS

BIGGEST VICTORIES
League: 11-0 v Southport, Division 4, 26.12.1962
F.A. Cup: 11-1 v Lytham, Round 1, 18.11.1925
League Cup: 7-0 v Scarborough, Round 3, 25.10.1989

BIGGEST DEFEATS
League: 4-13 v Tranmere Rovers, Division 3N, 26.12.1935
0-9 v Hull City, Division 3N, 5.4.1958
F.A. Cup: 0-6 v Huddersfield Town, Round 3, 13.1.1932
0-6 v Tottenham H, Round 3, 14.1.1933 (h)
League Cup: 1-7 v Sunderland, Round 2, 24.9.1962

MOST POINTS
3 points a win: 88, Division 2, 1990-91
2 points a win: 62, Division 3, 1973-74

MOST GOALS
95, 1962-63, Division 4.
Lister 30, Whittaker 17, Colquhoun 13, Ledger 8, Frizzell 5, Johnstone 5, Bowie5, Williams 5, McCall 4, og 3

MOST LEAGUE GOALS CONCEDED
95, Division 2, 1934-35

MOST FIRST CLASS MATCHES IN A SEASON
65 (46 League, 9 FA Cup, 9 League Cup, 1 Zenith Data) 1989-90

MOST LEAGUE WINS
25, Division 3, 1973-74
25, Division 2, 1990-91

MOST LEAGUE DRAWS
21, Division 2, 1988-89

MOST LEAGUE DEFEATS
26, Division 2, 1934-35; Division 4, 1958-59; Division 4, 1959-60

INDIVIDUAL CLUB RECORDS

MOST GOALS IN A SEASON
Tom Davis 35 (League 33, FAC 2) Div 3N, 1936-37
3 goals four times=12, 2 goals 3 times=6, 1 goal 17 times
Previous holder: W Walsh 32 (1935-36)

MOST GOALS IN A MATCH
7. Eric Gemmill v Chester, Division 3N, 19.1.1953 (11-2)
7. Bert Lister v Southport, Division 4, 20.12.1962
Frank Bunn scored 6 goals against Scarborough, Lge Cup, 25.10.1989, thus setting a record for the competition

OLDEST PLAYER
Bobby Collins, 42 years, 63 days v Rochdale 20.04.1973.

YOUNGEST PLAYER
Eddie Hopkinson, 16 years, 76 days v Crewe Alexandra 12.01.1952

MOST CAPPED PLAYER
Gunnar Halle 53 (Norway)

BEST PERFORMANCES

League: 1990-91: Matches played 46, Won 25, Drawn 13, Lost 8, Goals against 53, Points 88. First in Division 2
Highest: 1914-15: Second in Division 1
F.A. Cup: 1912-13: 3rd rnd. Bolton Wanderers 2-0, 4th rnd. Nottingham Forest 5-1; 5th rnd. Manchester City 0-0, 2-1; 6th rnd. Everton 1-0; Semi-final Aston Villa 0-1.
1989-90: 3rd rnd. Birmingham City 1-1, 1-0; 4th rnd. Brighton & H.A 2-1; 5th rnd. Everton 2-2, 1-1, 2-1; 6th rnd. Aston Villa 3-0; Semi-Final Manchester Utd3-3, 1-2
1993-94: 3rd rnd. Derby County 2-1; 4th rnd. Stoke City 0-0, 0-1; 5th rnd.Barnsley 1-0; 6th rnd. Bolton W. 0-1; Semi-Final Manchester Utd 1-1, 1-4
League Cup: 1989-90: 2nd rnd. Leeds Utd 2-1, 2-1; 3rd rnd. Scarborough 7-0; 4th rnd. Arsenal 3-1; 5th rnd. Southampton 2-2, 2 0; Semi-Final West Ham United 6-0, 0-3; Final Nott'm Forest 0-1

DIVISIONAL RECORD

	Played	Won	Drawn	Lost	For	Against	Points
Division 1/P	484	159	129	196	604	713	483
Division 2/1	1,434	537	369	528	2,055	2,079	1,628
Division 3	414	156	96	162	593	609	408
Division 3(N)	658	256	171	231	1,085	1,002	683
Division 4	320	121	70	129	499	513	312
Total	3,310	1,229	835	1,246	4,836	4,916	3,514

ADDITIONAL INFORMATION

PREVIOUS NAME
Pine Villa

PREVIOUS LEAGUE
Lancashire League

Club colours: Royal blue shirts, blue shorts, blue socks.

Change colours: Tangerine & blue shirts with white chest band, navy shorts with tangerine piping, tangerine socks with blue tops.

Reserves League: Pontins Central League Division 1.

RECORDS AND STATISTICS

COMPETITIONS

Div 1/P	Div.2/1	Div.3	Div.3(N)	Div.4	Texaco	A/Scot
1910-23	1907-10	1963-69	1935-53	1958-63	1974-75	1977-78
1991-94	1923-35	1971-74	1954-58	1969-71		1978-79
	1953-54					1979-80
	1974-91					1980-81
	1994-					

HONOURS

Division 2	Division 3	Division 3(N)
1990-91	1973-74	1952-53

MOST APPEARANCES

Ian T Wood 562+8 (1965-80)

Year	League	FA Cup	Lge Cup
1965-66	1		
1966-67	14		
1967-68	25+3	1+1	1
1968-69	40	1	
1969-70	46	3	1
1970-71	45	1	2
1971-72	46	1	2
1972-73	46	2	1
1973-74	44	6	2
1974-75	40	1	1
1975-76	35+2	1	2
1976-77	30+1	3	2
1977-78	33	2	2
1978-79	36	3	
1979-80	36+1	1	2
	517+7	27+1	18

MOST GOALS IN A CAREER

Roger Palmer - 157 (1980-92)

Year	League	FA Cup	Lge Cup	Other
1980-81	6			
1981-82	7	3		
1982-83	15			
1983-84	13	1		
1984-85	9			
1985-86	15		1	
1986-87	16	1		
1987-88	17	3		
1988-89	15			
1989-90	16	1	3	
1990-91	9			1
1991-92	3	1	1	
Total	141	10	5	1

Current leading goalscorer: Greame Sharpe - 39 (1991-95

RECORD TRANSFER FEE RECEIVED

Amount	Club	Player	Date
£1,700,000	Aston Villa	Earl Barrett	2/92
£850,000	Everton	Mike Milligan	8/90
£700,000	Manchester Utd	Dennis Irwin	7/90
£350,000	Leicester City	Tommy Wright	7/89

RECORD TRANSFER FEE PAID

Amount	Club	Player	Date
£700,000	Aston Villa	Ian Olney	5/92
£600,000	Everton	Mike Milligan	7/91
£500,000	Everton	Graeme Sharp	7/91
£480,000	Nott'm Forest	David Currie	7/90

MANAGERS

Name	Seasons	Best	Worst
David Ashworth	1906-14	4(1)	6(2)
Herbert Bamlett	1914-21	2(1)	19(1)
Charles Roberts	1921-22	19(1)	19(1)
David Ashworth	1923-24	7(2)	7(2)
Robert Mellor	1924-27	7(2)	18(2)
Andrew Wilson	1927-32	3(2)	18(2)
Robert Mellor	1932-33	16(2)	16(2)
Jim McMullen	1933-34	9(2)	9(2)
Robert Mellor	1934-35	21(2)	7(3)
Frank Womack	1945-47	6(3N)	19(3N)
Bill Wooton	1947-50	6(3N)	11(3N)
George Hardwick	1950-56	22(2)	15(3N)
Ted Goodier	1956-58	15(3N)	19(3N)
Norman Dodgin	1958-60	21(4)	23(3N)
Danny McLennan	1960		
Jack Rowley	1960-63	2(4)	12(4)
Les McDowell	1963-65	9(3)	20(3)
Gordon Hurst	1965-66	20(3)	20(3)
Jimmy McIlroy	1966-68	10(3)	16(3)
Jack Rowley	1968-69	24(3)	24(3)
Jimmy Frizzell	1970-82	8(2)	3(4)
Joe Royle	1982-94	17(1)	16(2)
Graham Sharpe	1994-	14(1)	14(1)

LONGEST LEAGUE RUNS

of undefeated matches:	20 (1.5.1990 - 10.11.1990)	of league matches w/out a win:	17 (4.9.1920 - 18.12.1920)
of undefeated home matches:	28 (3.2.23-18.4.24, 14.1.89-28.3.90)	of undefeated away matches:	11 (14.4.1973 - 10.11.1973)
without home win:	9 (4.9.1920 - 18.12.1920)	without an away win:	31 (24.4.1974 - 15.11.1975)
of league wins:	10 (12.1.1974 - 12.3.1974)	of home wins:	14 (11.1.1903 - 25.11.1903)
of league defeats:	8 (27.12.32-18.2.33, 15.12.34-2.2.35)	of away wins:	5 (12.1.1974 - 5.3.1974)

OLDHAM ATHLETIC

PLAYERS NAME Honours	Ht	Wt	Birthdate	Birthplace Transfers	Contract Date	Clubs	League	L/Cup	FA Cup	Other	Lge	L/C	FAC	Oth
G O A L K E E P E R S														
Paul W Gerrard	6.2	13.1	22.01.73	Heywood	02.11.91	Oldham Athletic (T)	82+1	5	4					
E: u21.11														
Jonathan G Hallworth	6.2	13.10	26.10.65	Stockport	26.05.83	Ipswich Town (A)	45	4	1	6				
Div2'91				Loan	01.01.85	Bristol Rovers	2			1				
				£75,000	03.02.89	Oldham Athletic	157+2	18	20	1				
D E F E N D E R S														
Craig Fleming	6.0	11.7	06.10.71	Halifax	21.03.90	Halifax Town (T)	56+1	4	3	3+2				
				£80,000	15.08.91	Oldham Athletic	93+5	7+1	10	1	1			
Gunner Halle	5.11	11.2	11.08.65	Oslo		Lillestrom (Sweden)								
Nor: ; Div2'91				£280,000	15.02.91	Oldham Athletic	130+5	9	4		11	1	2	
Richard I Jobson	6.1	12.10	09.05.63	Holderness		Burton Albion								
E:B2; Div2'91				£22,000	05.11.82	Watford	26+2	2	0+1	5+1	4			
				£40,000	07.02.85	Hull City	219+2	12	13	9	17		1	
				£460,000	30.08.90	Oldham Athletic	176+1	13	13	2	10	1		
Neil G Pointon	5.10	12.10	28.11.64	Warsop	10.08.82	Scunthorpe Utd (A)	159	13	13	4	2	1		
Div1'87; CS'87				£75,000	08.11.85	Everton	95+7	6+2	16+2	9+3	5			
				£600,000	17.07.90	Manchester City	74	8	4	4	2			
				£600,000	10.07.92	Oldham Athletic	57+2	4	5+1		3		2	
Stephen Redmond	5.10	11.2	02.11.67	Liverpool	03.12.84	Manchester City (A)	231+4	24	17	11	7			
E: u21.14,Y7; FAYC'86				£300,000	10.07.92	Oldham Athletic	102+5	12	4+2		1			
M I D F I E L D														
David Beresford			11.11.76	Middlesboro'	22.07.94	Oldham Athletic (T)	0+3							
E: 5														
Paul R J Bernard	5.11	11.8	30.12.72	Edinburgh	16.07.91	Oldham Athletic (T)	98+7	10+1	11	0+1	17	2	1	
S: u21.15														
Mark R Brennan	5.9	11.1	04.10.65	Rossendale	07.04.83	Ipswich Town (A)	165+3	21+1	12	11	19	2	3	1
E: Y4,u21.5				£375,000	27.07.88	Middlesbrough	61+4	6	4	8	6			
				£500,000	25.07.90	Manchester City	25+4	4	1	2	6	1		
				£200,000	24.11.92	Oldham Athletic	59+6	5+1	4	3	1			
Richard E Graham	6.2	12.1	28.11.74	Dewsbury	16.07.93	Oldham Athletic (T)	33+4	4	2		2			
Nicholas I Henry	5.6	10.8	21.2.69	Liverpool	06.07.87	Oldham Athletic (A)	229+8	25+3	20	4	18	3		
Div2'91														
William Kenny	5.8	11.0	19.09.73	Liverpool	18.06.92	Everton (T)	16+1	4	2		1			
E: u21.1.				Free	26.08.94	Oldham Athletic	4							
Christopher Makin	5.10	10.6	08.05.73	Manchester	02.11.91	Oldham Athletic (A)	54+1	5	9		2			
E: u21.5, Y1, S				Loan	28.08.92	Wigan Athletic	14+1				2			
Martin C Pemberton			01.02.76	Bradford	22.07.94	Oldham Athletic (T)								
Lee J Richardson	5.11	11.0	12.03.69	Halifax	06.07.87	Halifax Town (T)	43+13	4	4+2	6	2			
				£175,000	09.02.89	Watford	40+1	1+1	1		1			
				£250,000	15.08.90	Blackburn Rovers	50+12	1		2+2	3			
					16.09.92	Aberdeen	59+5	2+2	9	3	6	1	2	1
				£300,000	12.08.94	Oldham Athletic	28+2	2	2		6	1		
Paul S Rickers	5.10	11.0	09.05.75	Leeds	16.07.93	Oldham Athletic (T)	4				1			
Ian Snodin	5.7	9.0	15.08.63	Rotherham	18.08.80	Doncaster Rov. (A)	181+7	9	11+1	3	25	1	1	
E: B.2, u21.4, Y.4. Div.1'87.				£200,000	22.05.85	Leeds United	51	3	1		6	2		
				£840,000	16.01.87	Everton	142+6	19+4	26	3	3	2	2	
Loan 13.10.94 Sunderland 6 Lge App.				Free	09.01.95	Oldham Athletic	17							
F O R W A R D S														
Nicholas L Banger	5.8	10.6	25.02.71	Southampton	25.04.89	Southampton (T)	18+37	2+2	0+2	1	8	3		
				£250,000	04.10.94	Oldham Athletic	20+8	2	1		3			
Darren R Beckford	6.1	11.1	12.05.67	Manchester	21.08.94	Manchester City (A)	7+4	0+1						
E: Y3, S				Loan	10.10.85	Bury	12				5			
				£150,000	26.03.87	Port Vale	169+9	12	14	9+1	71	3	4	3
				£925,000	14.06.91	Norwich City	32+6	3+2	4+1	1	8	3	1	1
				£300,000	25.03.93	Oldham Athletic	19+13	2	5+3		9	1	3	
Andy Holden	6.1	13.2	14.09.62	Flint		Rhyl								
W: 1, u21.1.				£3,000	18.08.83	Chester City	100	8	2	4	17	1	2	2
				£45,000	30.10.86	Wigan Athletic	48+1	3	7	7	4			
				£130,000	12.01.89	Oldham Athletic	23		2		4			
Richard W Holden	5.11	12.0	09.09.64	Skipton	27.03.86	Burnley	0+1							
Div2'91				Free	24.09.86	Halifax Town	66+1	2	7	8	12			
				£125,000	24.03.88	Watford	42	2	6	3+1	8		1	1
				£165,000	18.08.89	Oldham Athletic	125+4	15+1	13	3	19	4	2	1
				£900,000	10.07.92	Manchester City	49+1	3	5		3	1	1	
				£450,000	11.10.93	Oldham Athletic	46+14	3+2	7+1		9		1	

OLDHAM ATHLETIC

PLAYERS NAME / Honours	Ht	Wt	Birthdate	Birthplace Transfers	Contract Date	Clubs	League	L/Cup	FA Cup	Other	Lge	L/C	FAC	Oth
Sean C McCarthy	6.1	11.7	12.09.67	Bridgend		Bridgend Town								
W: B1					22.10.85	Swansea City	76+15	4+1	5+2	9+1	25	3	4	6
				£50,000	18.08.88	Plymouth Albion	67+3	7	3	0+1	19	5	1	1
				£250,000	04.07.90	Bradford City	127+4	10+2	8	8+1	60	10	2	7
				£500,000	03.12.93	Oldham Athletic	54+5	4	1		22			
an D Olney	6.1	12.4	17.12.69	Luton	25.07.88	Aston Villa (T)	62+26	8+2	5+1	8+2	16	1	2	2
?: u21.10				£700,000	01.07.92	Oldham Athletic	42+2	4	2		13		1	
Graeme M Sharpe	6.1	11.8	16.10.60	Glasgow		Dumbarton	37+3	2	2		17		2	
S: 12, u21.1; CS'84'87; FAC'84;				£125,000	04.04.80	Everton	306+16	46+2	52+2	21+1	111	15	20	
Div1'85'87; ECWC'85				£500,000	17.07.91	Oldham Athletic	103+6	12+1	11+1	1	31	4	2	

ADDITIONAL CONTRACT PLAYERS

PLAYERS NAME	Ht	Wt	Birthdate	Birthplace Transfers	Contract Date	Clubs	League	L/Cup	FA Cup	Other	Lge	L/C	FAC	Oth
ee Darnborough					27.09.94	Oldham Athletic (T)								
D) Darren Lonergan			28.01.74	Cork		Waterford (Eire)								
					09.09.95	Oldham Athletic								
M) Lloyd M Richardson			07.10.77	Dewsbury	11.10.94	Oldham Athletic (T)								
D) Carl Serrant			12.09.75	Bradford	22.07.94	Oldham Athletic (T)								

TOP GOALSCORER 1994/95
Sean McCarthy

Division One Goals (games) . . . . 18 (35+4)
Coca-Cola Cup Goals 0 (4)
F.A. Cup goals 0 (1)

Total . . . . **18 (40 +4)**

Total goals for Oldham since 03.12.1993 . . . . 22 (59+5)

Career total as at June 1st 1995 . . . . 165 (383+35)

THE MANAGER
GRAEME SHARP

Date of Birth . . . . 16th October 1960.
Place of Birth . . . . Glasgow.
Date of Appointment . . . . November 1994.

PREVIOUS CLUBS
As Manager . . . . None.
As Coach . . . . None.
As a Player . . . . Dumbarton, Everton, Oldham Athletic.

HONOURS
As a Manager
None.

As a Player
Everton: FA Cup 1984. Charity Shield 1984, 1987. Division 1 championship 1985, 1987. ECWC 1985.
International: 12 full caps and 1 U21 cap for Scotland.

BOUNDARY PARK

Oldham, Lancashire OL1 2PA
Tel: 0161 624 4972

Capacity 13,599

First game..v Colne (Lancs. Comb), 1.9.1906.
First floodlit game ....v Burnley, 1961-62.

ATTENDANCES
Highest ....47,671 v Sheffield Wednesday, FA Cup 4th Round, 25.1.1930.
Lowest ....1,841 v WBA, Simod Cup, 10.11.1987.

OTHER GROUNDS ....Sheepfoot Lane 1895-1905. Boundary Park 1905-
.... (In 1986 En Tout Cas Sporturf laid an artificial surface, new grass was laid in 1991)

MATCHDAY TICKET PRICES

George Hill Stand. . . . . Matchday Members
Blue block £13
Grey block £12
Juv/OAP £8
White block £12
Green block £11
Juv/OAP £7.50
Existing S/T holders only.
Lookers Stand
Seats £12
Juv/OAP £8
Paddock or uncovered £7.50
Juv/OAP £5
Seton Stand
Seats £10.50
Juv/OAP £6.50
Rochdale Road Stand . . . . Non-Members
Visitors. £12
Juv/OAP £8
Home Supporters . . . . £12 (Members £10.50)
Juv/OAP . . . . £8 (Members £6.50)
Ticket Office Telephone no. 0161 624 4972

HOW TO GET TO THE GROUND

From North, East, South and West
Use motorway M62 until junction 20, then A627 to junction A664.
Leave motorway and at roundabout take 1st exit onto Broadway.
1st right off Broadway into Hilbre Avenue, which leads to car park.

Car Parking
Parking for 1,200 cars on site adjacent to ground.

Nearest Railway Station
Werneth.

CLUBCALL
0891 12 11 42
Calls cost 39p per minute cheap rate and 49p per minute at all other times.
Call costings correct at time of going to press.

MATCHDAY PROGRAMME

Programme Editor . . . . Alan Hardy.

Number of pages . . . . 44.

Price . . . . £1.50.

Subscriptions. . . . . £1.60 per programme (UK only).

Local Newspapers . . . . Oldham Chronicle,
. . . . . Manchester Evening News (Saturday Pink), Oldham Advertiser.

Local Radio Stations . . . . Radio Piccadilly, Radio Manchester,
. . . . . . Radio Cavell (Hospital), Key 103, Sunset Radio, Radio Latics.

PORT VALE
(The Valiants)
ENDSLEIGH LEAGUE DIVISION 1
SPONSORED BY: TUNSTALL ASSURANCE LTD.

Back Row (L-R): Martin Foyle, Allen Tankard, Stewart Talbot, Jermaine Holwyn, Paul Musselwhite, Gareth Griffiths, Arjan van Heusden, Lee Mills, Neil Aspin (Capt), Dean Glover, Steve Guppy. **Middle Row:** Mark Grew (Yth Coach), Stan Nicholls (Kit manager), John Jeffers, Ray Walker, Wayne Corden, Kevin Kent, Richard Eyre, Bradley Sandeman, Jim Cooper Community Officer), Rick Carter (Physio). **Back Row:** John Rudge (Manager), Ian Bogie, Craig Lawton, John McCarthy, Tony Naylor, Andy Porter, Dean Stokes, Dean Cunningham, Bill Dearden (First Team Coach).

PORT VALE
FORMED IN 1876
TURNED PROFESSIONAL IN 1885
LTD COMPANY IN 1911

PRESIDENT: J Burgess
CHAIRMAN: W T Bell, L.A.E., MIMI

DIRECTORS
D Bundy (Vice-Chairman), I McPherson, A Belfield
SECRETARY
R A Allan ((01782 814 134)
COMMERCIAL MANAGER
Margaret Moran-Smith (01782 835 524)

MANAGER: John Rudge
COACH: Bill Dearden

YOUTH TEAM MANAGER
Mark Grew
PHYSIOTHERAPIST
J Joyce

STATISTICIAN FOR THE DIRECTORY
Philip Sherwin

Port Vale achieved their main objective of avoiding relegation despite many ups and downs in their first season after promotion, to hopefully give a sound base for progression.

Five wins in their first ten games (one of which was against the previously unbeaten leaders Middlesbrough) bred even greater optimism at one stage but that preceded nine without a win including two Coca-Cola cup-ties against Manchester United. The euphoria that greeted that particular draw soon evaporated when it transpired that United were going to field a team of youngsters, but they still proved more than adequate.

Eleven goals in two home games, against Southend and Hartlepool (FAC 1st Round) promised better things but then the season's low point arrived in the Second Round of the FA Cup with a 1-0 defeat at bottom of the Third Division Scarborough.

The abandonment of a crucial game at Burnley when Vale were leading 2-1 helped to push the club into the bottom four at the turn of the year and to add to their woes central defenders Gareth Griffiths and Dean Glover were both injured. Tottenham's Kevin Scott filled the breach on loan, and he helped to stem the goals conceded alongside the excellent Neil Aspin allowing the club to climb the table.

The pitch became really heavy as a result of the rainy winter weather but crucial home wins over West Brom., Bristol City and Portsmouth helped to keep the club hovering in around 17th place. Alarm bells began to ring after three successive defeats at the end of March but a comprehensive 3-1 victory at Millwall and a 3-3 draw at eventual runners-up Reading, after being 0-3 down at one stage prevented any late season collapse.

Safety was mathematically achieved at Stoke City of all places, and the 1-0 victory savoured by the fans was the club's first league win on neighbouring territory for 68 years.

The goalscorer in that game, Martin Foyle, was a deserving winner of the Supporters Player of the Year award, not only for his 20 goals, but also for his general all round play and both Neil Aspin and Robin Van der Laan can look back on the campaign with satisfaction.

Goalkeeper Paul Musselwhite took his run of consecutive appearances to 161 before it was decided to blood the club's other Dutchman, Arjan Van Heusden for the last couple of games.

Off field activities during the close season included the building of a new all seater stand at the Caudwell End of the ground and the replacement of the top six inches of the pitch in a bid to solve the drainage problem.   PHIL SHERWIN.

PORT VALE

Division One: 17th   **FA Cup:** 2nd Round   **Coca-Cola Cup:** 2nd Round

M	DATE	COMP.	VEN	OPPONENTS	RESULT	H/T	LP	GOAL SCORERS/GOAL TIMES	ATT.
1	A 14	EL	A	Swindon Town	L 0-2	0-1	23		(10,431)
2	17	CC 1/1	A	**Bristol Rovers**	W 3-1	0-1		**Foyle 51, Naylor 53, L. Glover 56**	(3,307)
3	20	EL	H	Oldham Athletic	W 3-1	0-0	11	Kenny 49 (og), Foyle 70, Naylor 74	10,051
4	23	CC 1/2	H	**Bristol Rovers**	D 1-1	1-0		**L. Glover 6**	4,728
5	27	EL	A	Bristol City	D 0-0	0-0	12		(8,940)
6	30	EL	H	Barnsley	W 2-1	1-0	8	L. Glover 15, Burke 87	7,228
7	S 3	EL	H	Luton Town	L 0-1	0-0	12		8,541
8	10	EL	A	Portsmouth	W 2-0	1-0	5	L. Glover 44, Naylor 71	(8,989)
9	13	EL	A	Grimsby Town	L 1-4	0-1	8	Foyle 51	(3,216)
10	17	EL	H	Middlesbrough	W 2-1	0-1	7	Naylor 46, L. Glover 60	10,313
11	21	CC 2/1	H	**Manchester United**	L 1-2	1-1		**L. Glover 7**	18,605
12	24	EL	H	Sheffield United	L 0-2	0-0	9		9,324
13	O 1	EL	A	Wolves	L 1-2	0-0	12	Allon 83	(27,469)
14	5	CC 2/2	A	**Manchester United**	L 0-2	0-1			(31,615)
15	8	EL	A	Notts. County	D 2-2	0-1	15	Kelly 63, Foyle 66	(6,903)
16	15	EL	H	Charlton Athletic	L 0-2	0-0	19		7,707
17	22	EL	H	Bolton Wanderers	D 1-1	0-0	19	Allon 88	9,080
18	29	EL	A	Tranmere Rovers	D 1-1	0-0	20	Jeffers 64	(6,972)
19	N 2	EL	A	West Bromwich	D 0-0	0-0	20		(14,513)
20	5	EL	A	Southend United	W 5-0	2-0	14	Van Der Laan 5, Allon 26, Foyle 54, Walker 73, Porter 79	7,141
21	12	FAC 1	H	**Hartlepool United**	W 6-0	3-0		**Foyle 44, 68, 80, Griffiths 37, Allon 38, D. Glover 69**	6,199
22	19	EL	A	Derby County	L 0-2	0-1	19		(13,357)
23	26	EL	H	Millwall	W 2-1	0-0	18	Allon 52, Burke 90	8,016
24	29	EL	H	Sunderland	D 0-0	0-0	15		8,121
25	D 3	FAC 2	A	**Scarborough**	L 0-1	0-0			(2,382)
26	6	EL	A	Bolton Wanderers	L 0-1	0-0	16		(10,324)
27	10	EL	A	Oldham Athletic	L 2-3	1-1	17	Van Der Laan 32, Guppy 87	(7,712)
28	17	EL	H	Swindon Town	D 2-2	1-1	18	Foyle 11, 58	7,747
29	28	EL	H	Reading	L 0-2	0-1	21		7,891
30	31	EL	A	Watford	L 2-3	1-1	22	Foyle 16, 62	(7,794)
31	J 15	EL	H	Tranmere Rovers	W 2-0	1-0	21	Tankard 30, Foyle 58	7,944
32	28	EL	A	Southend United	W 2-1	1-1	18	Foyle 14, Van Der Laan 90	(3,619)
33	F 4	EL	A	Sunderland	D 1-1	1-1	20	Naylor 36	(13,377)
34	11	EL	H	West Bromwich	W 1-0	0-0	18	Guppy 83	10,751
35	21	EL	H	Derby County	W 1-0	0-0	15	Kent 58	9,387
36	25	EL	H	Wolves	L 2-4	1-3	18	Naylor 18, Kent 56	13,676
37	M 4	EL	A	Sheffield United	D 1-1	0-0	17	L. Glover 77	(13,647)
38	7	EL	A	Luton Town	L 1-2	0-0	18	Porter 85	(5,947)
39	11	EL	H	Bristol City	W 2-1	1-1	15	Scott 8, Naylor 75	7,646
40	14	EL	H	Stoke City	D 1-1	1-1	16	Naylor 3	19,510
41	18	EL	A	Barnsley	L 1-3	0-2	17	Allon 85	(6,878)
42	21	EL	H	Portsmouth	W 1-0	1-0	15	Allon 37	7,388
43	26	EL	A	Middlesbrough	L 0-3	0-2	17		(17,401)
44	28	EL	A	Burnley	L 3-4	1-1	17	Foyle 41, 82, Allon 68	(10,058)
45	A 1	EL	H	Grimsby Town	L 1-2	0-2	17	Naylor 59	7,150
46	5	EL	A	Millwall	W 3-1	2-0	16	Van Der Laan 2, Foyle 20, Bogie 46	(5,260)
47	8	EL	H	Watford	L 0-1	0-0	17		7,276
48	15	EL	A	Reading	D 3-3	0-3	17	Porter 63, Bogie 68 (pen), Naylor 81	(8,635)
49	17	EL	H	Burnley	W 1-0	1-0	16	Van Der Laan 39	9,663
50	22	EL	A	Stoke City	W 1-0	0-0	14	Foyle 68	(20,429)
51	29	EL	A	Charlton Athletic	D 1-1	1-1	17	Foyle 33	(12,596)
52	M 7	EL	H	Notts. County	D 1-1	1-0	17	Foyle 29	9,452
53									
54									
55									
56									
57									
58									
59									
60									

Best Home League Attendance: 19,510 V Stoke City   **Smallest:** 7,141 v Southend United   **Av Home Att:** 9,174

Goal Scorers:

League (58):   Foyle 16, Naylor 9, Allon 7, Van Der Laan 5, L. Glover 4, Porter 3, Burke 2, Guppy 2, Kent 2, Bogie 2 (1 pen),
Kelly, Jeffers, Walker, Tankard, Scott, Opponent

C/Cola Cup (5):   L. Glover 3, Foyle, Naylor

FA Cup (6):   Foyle 3, Griffiths, Allon, D. Glover

Compared with 1993-94: +851

Musselwhite P.	Sandeman B.	Tankard A.	Porter A.	Griffiths G.	Glover D.	Ken K.	Van Der Laan R.	Royle M.	Glover L.	Jeffers J.	Billing P.	Walker R.	Van Heusden A.	Naylor T.	Burke M.	Allon J.	Kelly T.	Aspin N.	Guppy S.	Lawton C.	Scott K.	Stokes D.	Bogie I.	Talbot S.	Bumdred J.	Referee M.	
1	2	3	4	5	6	7	8	9	10	11•	S	14	S													Pierce M.	1
1	2	3	4	5	6	7	8	9	10	S		S	S	11												Singh G.	2
1	2	3	4	5	6	7	8	9	10			S	S	11	S											Cooper K.	3
1	2	3	4•	5	6	7	8	9	10				14	11*	12											Lunt T.	4
1	2	3	4	5	6	7	8	9	10			S	S	11*	12											Pooley G.	5
1	2	3	4	5	6	7	8	9	10			S	S	11*	12											Parker J.	6
1	2	3	4•	5	6	7	8	9	10				14	11*	12											Winter J.	7
1	2	3	4	5	6	7	8•	9	10				14	11	S											Alcock P.	8
1	2	3	4	5	6	7*	8	9	10					S	11•	12	14									Kirkby J.	9
1	2	3	4	5	6	7	8	9	10					S	11	S										Flood A.	10
1	2	3	4	5	6	7	8	9	10					S	11*	12										Lloyd J.	11
1	2	3	4	5	6†	7•	8	9	10					S	S	11	14									Cain G.	12
1	2	3	4		6		14		10		5•			S	9	11*	12	7	8							Wolstenholme E.	13
1	2	3	4		6		8•	14	9	10				S	11*	12	7	5								Wilkie A.	14
1	2	3	4•					8•	9	10	5	6		S	11		S	7	5							Poulain R.	15
1	2	3	4•					8•	9	10	12	6		S	11	14		7	5							Allison D.	16
1		3	4	5		7	8	10		11•	6			S	9*	14	12		2							Breen K.	17
1		3	4	5	6	7*	8	10			12			11	S	S	9		2							Wright P.	18
1		3	4	5	6		8	10	S		7			11	S	S	9		2							Dunn S.	19
1		3	4	5	6		8	10*		12	7			11	S		14	9	2							Vanes P.	20
1		3	4•	5	6		8	10	12	7•				11	S		14	9*	2							Lodge S.	21
1		3	4	5	6		8	10	12					11	S		14	9*	2		7					Harrison P.	22
1		3	4	5	6		8•	10	12					11	S		14	9*	2		7					Cruikshanks I.	23
1		3	4	5	6		8	10		S				11•	S		14	9	2		7					Brandwood J.	24
1		3	4•	5	6		8	10	12					11	S		14	9*	2		7					Allison D.	25
1		3	12	5	6	11•	8	9	10					4•	S		14		2		7					West T.	26
1			4	5	6	7	8•	9*	10	3					S	12	14		2		11					Kirkby J.	27
1	3		4	5	6	S	8	9	10•					S	14	7			2		11					Wolstenholme E.	28
1	3		4	5	6	S	8	9	10					S	14	7			2		11•					Heilbron T.	29
1	3		4	6*	7	8	9	10			5		11	S	S				2	12						Barber G.	30
1	2	3	4			S	8	9				11	S	10			S	5	7		6					Wilkes C.	31
1	2	3	4			14	8	9				11•	S	10*		12		5	7•		6					West T.	32
1	2	3	4		14	11	8	9					S	10		S		5	7		6					Flood A.	33
1	2	3	4			11	8	9	S				S	10		S		5	7		6					Rennie U.	34
1	2	3				11	8	9*	S			4	S	10		12		5	7		6					Watson J.	35
1	2	3				11	8	9*	14			4•	S	10		12		5	7•		6					Lloyd J.	36
1	2	3	4				8	9	14			11	S	10		S		5	7•		6					Holbrook J.	37
1	2	3	4				8•	9	14			11	S	10*		12		5	7		6					Foakes P.	38
1	2	3	4				8	9*	12		S	11	S	10				5	7		6					Barry N.	39
1	2	3	4			14		9•		6		11•	S	10		12		5	7							Dawson A.	40
1	2•	3	4			14	8		9•			11	S	10		12		5	7		6					Bailey M.	41
1	2		4				8	12		14		11	S	10*		9•		5	7		6	3				Parker J.	42
1	2		4				8	12				11	S	10*		9		5	7		6	3	5			Singh G.	43
1	2	3	4				8	10				11•	S	S		9		5	7		6		14			Burns W.	44
1	2	3	4			11	8	9					S	12		10*		5	7•		6		14			Butler A.	45
1	2	3	4		11		8	9	S					S		10		5	5		6		7			Alcock P.	46
1	2	3•	4		11		8	9	12					S		10*		5	14		6•		7			Cooper K.	47
1	2	3	4		11		8	9	5					S		10		5	14		6		7			Pooley G.	48
1	2	3	4		6	14	8	9	S					S		10		5	11•				7			Harris R.	49
1	2	3	4		6		S	8	9	S				S		10		5	11				7			Dunn S.	50
S	2	3	4		6		S		9	10	S		1					5	11				7	8		Wilkes C.	51
S	2		4		6			9		12			1					5	11•			3	7	8		Poulain R.	52
44	37	39	43	20	28	19	43	40	21	6	6	20	2	29	4	10	3	37	25		17	3	7	2	1	League Appearances	
			1		1		4	1	2	7	4		3		4	1	9	1			2		2			League Sub Appearances	
4	4	4		3	4	4	3+1	4	4			3			4		3	1+2	0+1	1			1			C/Cola Cup Appearances	
2		2	2	2	2		2	2	0+2	1		2			0+2	2		2	4		0+1					FA Cup Appearances	

Also Played: Corden W 14(52)   Loan Players: Scott (Tottenham Hotspur)

PORT VALE

BIGGEST VICTORIES
League: 9-1 v Chesterfield, Division 2, 24.9.1932
8-0 v Gateshead, Division 4, 26.12.1958
F.A. Cup: 7-1 v Irthlingborough (a), Rnd 1, 12.1.1907
League Cup: 5-1 v Wrexham, Rnd 1, 13.9.1983

BIGGEST DEFEATS
League: 0-10 v Sheffield United, Division 2, 10.12.1892
0-10 v Notts County, Division 2, 26.2.1895
F.A. Cup: 0-7 v Small Heath, 5th Qual. Round, 10.12.1898
League Cup: 0-4 v Northampton Town, Rnd 1, 2.9.1987

MOST POINTS
3 points a win: 89, Division 2, 1992-93
2 points a win: 69, Division 3N, 1953-54

MOST GOALS
110, 1958-59 (Division 4)
Steele 23, Wilkinson 21, Barnett 20, Poole 17, Cunliffe 14, Jackson 8, Kinsey3, Hall 2, Sproson 1, og 1.

MOST LEAGUE GOALS CONCEDED
106, Division 2, 1935-36

MOST GOALS IN A SEASON
Wilf Kirkham (1926-27) 38 League, 3 FA Cup, Total 41

MOST FIRST CLASS MATCHES IN A SEASON
61 (46 League, 4 FA Cup, 2 League Cup, 6 Autoglass, 3 Play-offs) 1992-93

MOST LEAGUE WINS
30, Division 3N, 1929-30

MOST LEAGUE DRAWS
20, Division 3, 1977-78

MOST LEAGUE DEFEATS
28, Division 2, 1956-57

MOST GOALS IN A MATCH
6. Stewart Littlewood v Chesterfield, Division 2, 24.9.1932 (9-1)

OLDEST PLAYER
Tom Holford, 46 yrs 3 months, 5.4.1924

YOUNGEST PLAYER
Malcolm McKenzie, 15yrs 347 days, 12.4.1965

MOST CAPPED PLAYER
Sammy Morgan (Northern Ireland) 7

League: 1953-54: Matches played 46, Won 26, Drawn 17, Lost 3, Goals for 74,Goals against 21, Points 69. 1st in Division 3N.

Highest: 5th Division 2, 1930-31.

F.A. Cup: 1953-54: 1st rnd. Darlington 3-1; 2nd rnd. Southport 1-1, 2-0; 3rd rnd. Queens Park Rangers 1-0; 4th rnd. Cardiff City 2-0; 5th rnd. Blackpool 2-0; 6th rnd. Leyton Orient 1-0; Semi-Final West Bromwich Albion 1-2.

League Cup: 1991-92: 1st rnd. Bye, 2nd rnd. Notts County 2-1, 2-3, 3rd rnd.Liverpool 2-2, 1-4.
2nd rnd. 1960-61; 1962-63; 1963-64; 1967-68; 1972-73; 1981-82; 1983-84; 1984-85; 1985-86; 1986-87; 1988-89; 1989-90; 1990-91; 1994-95.

ADDITIONAL INFORMATION
Previous Leagues: Midland League
Previous Name: Burslem Port Vale 1884-1909

Club colours: White shirts, black shorts.
Change colours: All yellow.

Reserves League: Pontins Central League Division 2
Youth League: Midland Purity Youth League.

DIVISIONAL RECORD

	Played	Won	Drawn	Lost	For	Against	Points
Division 2/1	1,398	472	304	622	1,944	2,385	1,303
Division 3/2	920	336	255	329	1,240	1,237	1,047
Division 3(N)	218	105	66	47	367	230	276
Division 3(S)	348	122	89	137	458	460	333
Division 4	598	220	185	193	802	713	704
Total	**3,482**	**1,255**	**899**	**1,328**	**4,811**	**5,025**	**3,663**

(Excluding Leeds City results 1919-20)

RECORDS AND STATISTICS

COMPETITIONS

Div.2/1	Div.3(N)	Div.3(S)	Div.3/2	Div.4
1892-96	1929-30	1938-52	1959-65	1958-59
1898-07	1936-38	1957-58	1970-78	1965-70
1919-29	1952-54		1983-84	1978-83
1930-36			1986-89	1984-86
1954-57			1992-94	
1989-92				
1994-				

HONOURS

Division 3(N)	Division 4	AGT
1929-30	1958-59	1992-93
1953-54		

MOST APPEARANCES
Roy Sproson 831+5 (1950-72)

Year	League	FA Cup	Lge Cup
1950-51	10		
1951-52	28		
1952053	45	2	
1953-54	45	8	
1954-55	42	3	
1955-56	42	2	
1956-57	39	2	
1957-58	37	3	
1958-59	21	1	
1959-60	41	6	
1960-61	43	3	3
1961-62	46	7	1
1962-63	42	4	1
1963-64	46	5	1
1964-65	45	2	1
1965-66	28+2	4	
1966-67	30+1	2	1
1967-68	32	1	1
1968-69	41+1	5	
1969-70	46	5	1
1970-71	5+1		1
1971-72	1		
	755+5	**65**	**11**

MOST GOALS IN A CAREER
Wilf Kirkham - 164 (1923-29 & 1931-33)

Year	League	FA Cup
1923-24	7	
1924-25	26	7
1925-26	35	
1926-27	38	3
1927-28	13	1
1928-29	15	
1931-32	4	
1932-33	15	
Total	**153**	**11**

Current leading goalscorer: Martin Foyle - 67 (1991-95)

MANAGERS

Name	Seasons	Best	Worst
T Clare	1905-06	17(2)	17(2)
S Gleaves	1906-07	16(2)	16(2)
A Walker	1911-13		
H Myatt	1913-14		
T Holford	1914-17		
J Cameron	1918-19		
J Schofield	1919-29	8(2)	21(2)
T Morgan	1929-32	5(2)	1(3N)
T Holford	1932-36	8(2)	21(2)
W Cresswell	1936-37	11(3N)	11(3N)
T Morgan	1937-39	15(3N)	18(3S)
W Frith	1944-46		
G Hodgson	1946-51	8(3S)	13(3S)
I Powell	1951		
F Steele	1951-57	12(2)	13(3S)
N Low	1957-62	7(3)	15(3S)
F Steele	1962-65	3(3)	22(3)
J Mudie	1965-67	13(4)	19(4)
S Matthews	1967-68	18(4)	18(4)
G Lee	1968-74	6(3)	13(4)
R Sproson	1974-77	6(3)	19(3)
C Harper	1977		
R Smith	1977-78	21(3)	21(3)
D Butler	1978-79	16(4)	16(4)
A Bloor	1979		
J McGrath	1979-83	23(3)	20(4)
J Rudge	1983-	11(2)	12(4)

RECORD TRANSFER FEE RECEIVED

Amount	Club	Player	Date
£1,000,000	Sheffield Wed.	Ian Taylor	08/94
£925,000	Norwich City	Darren Beckford	6/91
£350,000	Charlton Athletic	Andy Jones	8/87
£135,000	Stoke City	Mark Chamberlain	8/82

RECORD TRANSFER FEE PAID

Amount	Club	Player	Date
£450,000	York City	Jon McCarthy	07/95
£375,000	Oxford United	Martin Foyle	6/91
£200,000	Middlesbrough	Dean Glover	2/89
£40,000	Leicester City	Gary Ford	12/87

LONGEST LEAGUE RUNS

of undefeated matches:	19 (16.8.1969 - 18.11.1969)	of league matches w/out a win:	17 (7.12.1991 - 21.03.1992)
of undefeated home matches:	43 (20.12.1952 - 18.9.1954)	of undefeated away matches:	12 (16.9.1953 - 9.1.1954)
without home win:	13 (28.3.1978 - 21.10.1978)	without an away win:	24 (2.12.1893 - 23.3.1895)
of league wins:	8 (8.4.1893 - 30.9.1893)	of home wins:	12 (9.2.1952 - 8.9.1952, 31.8.1953 - 25.12.1953)
of league defeats:	9 (9.3.1957 - 20.4.1957)	of away wins:	5 (20.3.1993 - 24.4.1993)

PLAYERS NAME / Honours	Ht	Wt	Birthdate	Birthplace / Transfers	Contract Date	Clubs	League	L/Cup	FA Cup	Other	Lge	L/C	FAC	Oth
G O A L K E E P E R S														
Paul Musselwhite	6.2	12.9	22.12.68	Portsmouth		Portsmouth (A)								
AGT'93.				Free	21.03.88	Scunthorpe United	132	11	7	13				
				£20,000	30.07.92	Port Vale	131	6	11	13				
Arjan Van Heusden	6.4	12.0	11.12.72	Holland		Noordwijk								
				£4,500	15.08.94	Port Vale	2							
D E F E N D E R S														
Neil Aspin	6.0	12.8	12.04.65	Gateshead	06.10.82	Leeds United (A)	203+4	9	17	11	5	1		
AGT'93.				£200,000	28.07.89	Port Vale	235+2	12	16	15	2			
Dean Glover	5.9	11.2	29.12.63	West Brom	30.12.81	Aston Villa (A)	25+3	7	3	1		1		
AGT'93.				Loan	17.10.86	Sheffield United	5							
					17.06.87	Middlesbrough	44+6	4	5	7	5			2
				£200,000	03.02.89	Port Vale	166+1	18	16	20	13			3
Gareth Griffiths	6.4	14.0	10.04.70	Winsford		Rhyl								
				£1,000	08.02.93	Port Vale	3+1				2			
Dean Stokes			23.05.70	Birmingham		Halesowen Town								
					15.01.93	Port Vale	24		3	1				
Alan Tankard	5.10	11.7	21.05.69	Fleet	27.05.87	Southampton (A)	5			2				
				Free	04.07.88	Wigan Athletic	205+4	15	13	20	4	1		
				£87,500	26.07.93	Port Vale	61+4	6	4	3	1		1	
M I D F I E L D														
Ian Bogie	5.7	10.2	06.12.67	Newcastle	18.12.85	Newcastle Utd (A)	7+7	0+1	1+2	3				1
				P.E.	09.02.89	Preston North End	67+12	3+1	3	4+1	12			
				£145,000	16.08.91	Millwall	44+7	1	2	3	1			
				£100,000	14.10.93	Leyton Orient	62+3	2	2	8+1	5			
				£50,000	23.03.95	Port Vale	7+2				2			
Wayne Corden			01.11.75	Leek	20.07.94	Port Vale (T)	0+1							
John Jeffers	5.10	10.10	05.10.68	Liverpool	13.10.86	Liverpool (A)								
				£30,000	11.12.88	Port Vale	147+33	8+1	13+2	13+2	10			1
				Loan	06.01.95	Shrewsbury Town	3		2	1				
Craig Lawton	5.8	10.3	05.01.72	Mancot	01.07.90	Manchester Utd (T)								
W: B.1, Y, S.				Free	02.08.94	Port Vale	0+1							
Jon McCarthy	5.9	11.5	18.07.70	Middlesbrough	07.11.87	Hartlepool Utd (J)	0+1							
				Free		Shepshed Albion								
				Free	22.03.90	York City	198+1	8	11	15	31	1	3	3
				£450,000	08.95									
Andy Porter	5.9	11.2	17.09.68	Macclesfield	29.06.87	Port Vale (T)	197+30	14	11+4	19+1	4		2	
AGT'93.														
Bradley Sandeman	5.10	10.8	24.02.70	Northampton	14.07.88	Northampton T (T)	28+30	2+3	2	6+1	2			
				£10,000	22.02.91	Maidstone United	55+2	1	2	2	7			
				Free	14.08.92	Port Vale	61+7	5+1	3+1	2	1			
Robin Van der Laan	5.10	12.0	05.09.68	Schiedam		Wageningen								
AGT'93.				£80,000	21.02.91	Port Vale	154+22	11+1	9+1	11+1	24	1	1	1
Ray Walker	5.10	12.0	28.09.63	North Shields	26.09.81	Aston Villa (A)	15+8	2+1	2					
E: Y.6. FAYC'80.				Loan	07.09.84	Port Vale	15				1			
				£12,000	05.08.86	Port Vale	292+7	16+1	22	19	32	1	3	3
				Loan	23.09.94	Cambridge United	5			2				
F O R W A R D S														
Martin Foyle	5.10	11.2	02.05.63	Salisbury	13.08.80	Southampton (A)	6+6	0+2			1	2		
AGT'93.				£10,000	03.08.84	Aldershot	98	10	8	6	35	5	5	
				£140,000	26.03.87	Oxford United	120+6	16	5	3+1	36	4	3	1
				£375,000	25.06.91	Port Vale	129+9	12	9+1	11+1	49	6	7	5
Edward Lee Glover	5.10	12.1	24.04.70	Kettering	02.05.87	Nottm. Forest (A)	61+15	6+5	8+2	4+1	9	2	1	1
S: u21.3, Y. FMC'92.				Loan	14.09.89	Leicester City	3+2				1			
				Loan	18.01.90	Barnsley	8		4					
				Loan	02.09.91	Luton Town	1							
				£200,000	02.08.94	Port Vale	21+7	4	0+2		4	3		
Stephen Guppy	5.11	10.10	29.03.69	Winchester		Wycombe Wands.	41	4	8	10	8		2	
E: S-P.1. GMVC'93. FAT'91'93.				£15,000	02.08.94	Newcastle United								
				£225,000	25.11.94	Port Vale	25+2		1		2			
Kevin Kent	5.8	11.0	19.03.65	Stoke	31.12.82	West Brom. A. (A)	1+1							
FRT'87. AGT'93.				Free	09.07.84	Newport County	23+10	2	0+1	3+1	1			1
				Free	15.08.85	Mansfield Town	223+6	10	13	21+2	36	2	4	4
				£80,000	22.03.91	Port Vale	87+27	9	2	7+5	7			

PORT VALE						APPEARANCES					GOALS			
PLAYERS NAME Honours	Ht	Wt	Birthdate	Birthplace Transfers	Contract Date	Clubs	League	L/Cup	FA Cup	Other	Lge	L/C	FAC	Oth
Lee Mills	6.1	12.11	10.07.70	Mexborough		Stocksbridge								
					09.12.92	Wolverhampton W.	12+13	1	3+1	3	2		1	1
				£400,000	24.02.95	Derby County	16				7			
				£200,000	.08.95	Port Vale								
Tony Naylor	5.5	9.0	29.03.67	Manchester		Droylsden								
				£20,000	22.03.90	Crewe Alexandra	104+18	7+2	9	12	45	5	6	9
				£150,000	18.07.94	Port Vale	29+4	3			9	1		
ADDITIONAL CONTRACT PLAYERS														
Stuart Talbot						Moor Green								
					02.08.94	Port Vale	2							
Jermaine Holwyn						Ajax								
				£5,000	.08.94	Port Vale								
Matthew Boswell (NC)			19.08.77	Shrewsbury	19.07.94	Port Vale (T)								

TOP GOALSCORER 1994/95
Martin Foyle

First Division goals (games) . . . . 16 (40+2)
Coca-Cola Cup Goals 1 (4)
F.A. Cup goals 3 (2)

Total . . . . **20 (46+2)**

Total goals for Port Vale since 25.06.91 . . . . 67 (161+11)

Career total as at June 1st 1995 . . . . 159 (433+26)

THE MANAGER
JOHN RUDGE

Date of Birth . . . . 21st October 1944.
Place of Birth . . . . Wolverhampton.
Date of Appointment . . . . December 1983.

PREVIOUS CLUBS
As Manager . . . . None.
As Coach . . . . Torquay United.
As a Player . . . . Huddersfield Town, Carlisle United, Torquay United,
. . . . Bristol Rovers, Bournemouth.

HONOURS
As a Manager
Port Vale: Promotion to Division 3, 1986. Promotion to Division 2, 1989. AGT Winners 1993. Promotion to Division 1, 1994.

As a Player
Bristol Rovers: Promotion to Division 2, 1974.

VALE PARK
Burslem, Stoke-on-Trent ST6 1AW
Tel: 01782 814 134

Capacity..23,000
Seating...17,042

First game...v Newport Co., Div.3(S), 24.8.1950.
First floodlit game...v WBA (Friendly), 24.9.1958.

ATTENDANCES
Highest.......................................49,768 v Aston Villa, FAc 5th Rnd, 20.2.1960.
Lowest...994 v Hereford Utd, AMC, 22.12.1986.

OTHER GROUNDS......................Limekiln Lane 1876-81. Westport 1881-84.Moorland Road 1884-86.
...................................Athletic Ground 1886-1913.Recreation Ground 1913-1950. Vale Park 1950-

MATCHDAY TICKET PRICES

Railway Stand......................... £10.50
Juv/OAP £8
Railway Paddock....................... £9
Juv/OAP £7
Sential Stand......................... £9
Juv/OAP £7
Family Stand.......................... £7.50
Juv/OAP £5
Terraces.................... Lome Street £8
Juv/OAP £5.50

Visiting Supporters........... Caudwell End £9

Ticket Office Telephone no....... 01782 814 134

CLUBCALL
0891 12 16 36

Calls cost 39p per minute cheap rate and 49p per
minute at all other times.
Call costings correct at time of going to press.

HOW TO GET TO THE GROUND

From the North
Use motorway (M6) until junction 16 then join A500, sign posted Stoke. In 5.9 miles branch left and at roundabout take 1st exit A527. In 0.4 miles turn right B5051 into Newcastle Street and at end over crossroads into Moorland Road. Shortly turn left into Hamil Road for Port Vale FC.

From the East
Use A50 or A52 into Stoke-on-Trent then follow signs to Burslem A50 into Waterloo Road. At Burslem crossroads turn right into Moorland Road. Shortly turn left into Hamil Road for Port Vale FC.

From the South and West
Use motorway (M6) until junction 15 then A5006 and A500. In 6.3 miles branch left and at roundabout take 3rd exit A527. In 0.4 miles turn right B5051 into Newcastle Street and at end over crossroads into Moorland Road. Shortly turn left into Hamil Road for Port Vale FC.

Car Parking
(Ample) behind the Railway Stand, on Hamil Road car park and streets.

Nearest Railway Station
Longport, Stoke-on-Trent (01782 411 411)

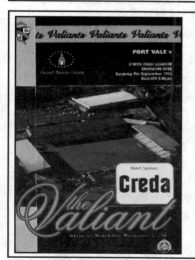

MATCHDAY PROGRAMME

Programme Editor........................... Chris Harper.

Number of pages .... 40.

Price .... £1.50.

Subscriptions..... £40 (home only), £75 (home & away) inc. postage.

Local Newspapers................. The Sentinel, The Green'Un.

Local Radio Stations .... Radio Stoke, Signal Radio.

PORTSMOUTH
(The Pompey)
ENDSLEIGH LEAGUE DIVISION 1
SPONSORED BY: THE NEWS

Back Row (L-R): Danny Hounsell, Alan McLoughlin, Mark Stimson, Kevin Braybrook, Aaron Flahavan, Tony Dobson, Jimmy Carter, Jimmy Frazer, Deon Burton, Alex Totten. **Middle Row:** Gordon Neave (Kit), Neil Sillett (Physio), Jason Rees, Lloyd McGrath, Mart Poom, Kieth Waldon (First Team Coach), Alan Knight, Guy Butters, Russell Perrett, Larry May (Youth Team Coach), Martin Hinshelwood (Res. Manager). **Front Row:** Sammy Igoe, Paul Hall, Andy Awford, Simon Barnard, David Waterman, Gerry Creaney, Terry Fenwick (Manager), Kit Symons, John Durnin, Paul Wood, Lee Russell, Robbie Pethick, Anthony Tilley.

PORTSMOUTH
FORMED IN 1898
TURNED PROFESSIONAL IN 1898
LTD COMPANY IN 1898

MANAGING DIRECTOR: M H Gregory

DIRECTORS
B A V Henson FCA, J S Hutchinson,
R G Smith, V J Jenner JP. MBA. FIMgt,
F E Dinenage

SECRETARY
P A Weld (01705 731 204)
COMMERCIAL MANAGER
Julie Baker

MANAGER: Terry Fenwick

YOUTH TEAM MANAGER
Martin Hinshelwood
PHYSIOTHERAPIST
N Sillett

STATISTICIAN FOR THE DIRECTORY
Peter Macey

For Pompey 1994/95 was a season of struggle and change, with a change in manager and a fight against relegation. They finished the season in 18th place avoiding the drop in the end by 10 points, but at times near the end of the season it was very close. The team failed to live up to their potential on to many occasions and improvement will be greatly needed next season if they are to push for the play-offs or more.

In January after an FA Cup defeat against Leicester Jim Smith was sacked and replaced by a management rookie in Terry Fenwick. Smith had picked up 30 points in his 28 league games, while Fenwick picked up 28 points in his 18 league games, a very obvious and needed improvement in the final third of the season. Pompey picked up 13 of the last 18 points available and this included wins away at both Swindon and Burnley, relegating both teams in the process. In the cups the highlight was a 3-2 win at Everton in the second round of the Coca-Cola Cup and a 3-1 home win against Bolton in the third round of the FA Cup.

The squad will need to be improved for 1995/96, and although Terry Fenwick thinks the team can challenge for promotion next season, I think the proof will be in the pudding. There were some bright performances during the season including Robbie Pethick at full-back and Gerry Creaney up front, the emergence of youngsters Deon Burton and Alex Totten, and the consistent performances of goalkeeper Alan Knight, who was rewarded with the Player of the Year award for the first time since 1981/82.

1995/96 should be a new start for Pompey with a new manager, and hopefully a play-off place is within the grasp of the team, but only time will tell.

PETER MACEY.

PORTSMOUTH

Division One: 18th   **FA Cup:** 4th Round   **Coca-Cola Cup:** 3rd Round

M	DATE	COMP.	VEN	OPPONENTS	RESULT	H/T	LP	GOAL SCORERS/GOAL TIMES	ATT.
1	A 13	EL	H	Notts County	W 2-1	1-0		Powell 5, Symons 89	10,487
2	17	CC 1/1	H	**Cambridge United**	**W 2-0**	**2-0**		**Stimson 35, Powell 44**	**3,854**
3	20	EL	A	Reading	D 0-0	0-0	5		(9,106)
4	23	CC 1/2	A	**Cambridge United**	**W 3-2**	**1-1**		**Creaney 6, Powell 51, 53**	**(2,571)**
5	27	EL	H	Charlton Athletic	D 1-1	1-1	6	Symons 11	10,566
6	30	EL	A	Southend United	W 2-1	1-1	3	Creaney 26, Powell 54	(4,333)
7	S 10	EL	H	Port Vale	L 0-2	0-1	12		8,989
8	14	EL	H	Tranmere Rovers	D 1-1	0-0	16	Hall 89	6,383
9	17	EL	A	Bolton Wanderers	D 1-1	1-0	13	Creaney 69	(11,284)
10	20	CC 2/1	A	**Everton**	**W 3-2**	**2-0**		**Creaney 2, 15, Kristensen 56**	**14,043**
11	24	EL	H	Wolverhampton Wand.	L 1-2	1-1	19	Creaney 11 (pen)	13,466
12	28	EL	A	West Bromwich A.	W 2-0	1-0	19	Pethick 7, Hall 49	(13,585)
13	O 1	EL	A	Grimsby Town	L 0-2	0-1	14		(4,172)
14	5	CC 2/2	H	**Everton**	**D 1-1**	**0-1**		**Hall 89**	**13,605**
15	8	EL	A	Oldham Athletic	L 2-3	0-1		Creaney 50, Hall 86	(7,683)
16	15	EL	H	Swindon Town	W 4-3	2-1	12	Mcloughlin 17, 19, Powell 51, Creaney 64 (pen)	10,610
17	23	EL	H	Middlesbrough	D 0-0	0-0	14		7,281
18	26	CC 3	H	**Derby County**	**L 0-1**	**0-0**			**8,568**
19	29	EL	A	Bristol City	D 1-1	0-1	14	Powell 81	(7,328)
20	N 2	EL	A	Millwall	D 2-2	1-2	14	Rees 30, Mcloughlin 90 (pen)	(7,108)
21	6	EL	H	Derby County	L 0-1	0-0	20		5,507
22	19	EL	A	Luton Town	L 0-2	0-1	20		(8,214)
23	26	EL	H	Sunderland	L 1-4	0-3	21	Powell 50	7,527
24	30	EL	H	Stoke City	L 0-1	0-0	22		5,272
25	D 3	EL	A	Middlesbrough	L 0-4	0-2	22		(17,185)
26	10	EL	H	Reading	D 1-1	1-0	22	Creaney 4	8,578
27	17	EL	A	Notts County	W 1-0	0-0	21	Wood 60	6,382
28	26	EL	A	Watford	L 0-2	0-0	22		(9,953)
29	27	EL	H	Barnsley	W 3-0	3-0	19	Newhouse 12, Creaney 20, 35	6,751
30	31	EL	A	Sheffield United	L 1-3	1-0	21	Creaney 33	(13,467)
31	J 2	EL	H	Burnley	W 2-0	1-0	19	Preki 25, Creaney 87	9,097
32	7	FAC 3	H	**Bolton Wanderers**	**W 3-1**	**1-1**		**Creaney 31, Preki 60, 84**	**9,721**
33	14	EL	H	Bristol City	D 0-0	0-0	19		8,809
34	22	EL	A	Derby County	L 0-3	0-0	19		(11,143)
35	28	FAC 4	H	**Leicester City**	**L 0-1**	**0-1**			**14,928**
36	F 4	EL	A	Stoke City	W 2-0	0-0	19	Preki 54, Creaney 90	(9,704)
37	18	EL	A	Sunderland	D 2-2	1-2	18	McLoughlin 43, Doling 79	(12,372)
38	21	EL	H	Luton Town	W 3-2	0-1	16	Mcloughlin 50, Preki 76, Creaney 79	7,363
39	25	EL	H	Grimsby	W 2-1	1-1	13	Creaney 43, Symons 89	8,274
40	M 5	EL	A	Wolverhampton Wand.	L 0-1	0-0	15		(23,284)
41	8	EL	H	West Bromwich A.	L 1-2	1-1	17	Creaney 37	7,160
42	11	EL	A	Charlton Athletic	L 0-1	0-1	20		(9,443)
43	15	EL	H	Millwall	W 3-2	1-1	17	Creaney 15, 49, Hall 80	6,032
44	18	EL	H	Southend United	D 1-1	1-0	17	McLoughlin 40	6,667
45	21	EL	A	Port Vale	L 0-1	0-1	17		(7,001)
46	25	EL	H	Bolton Wanderers	D 1-1	0-1	18	Creaney 52	7,765
47	A 1	EL	A	Tranmere Rovers	L 2-4	1-3	19	Preki 19, Irons 65(og)	(8,722)
48	8	EL	H	Sheffield United	W 1-0	0-0	19	Creaney 60	8,216
49	15	EL	A	Barnsley	L 0-1	0-0	20		(6,825)
50	17	EL	H	Watford	W 2-1	1-0	18	Durnin 27 (pen), Burton 82	8,396
51	22	EL	A	Burnley	W 2-1	1-0	17	Durnin 36 (pen), Symons 61	(10,666)
52	29	EL	A	Swindon Town	W 2-0	1-0	18	Preki 40, Burton 55	(9,220)
53	M 7	EL	H	Oldham Athletic	D 1-1	0-1	18	Hall 62	11,002
54									
55									
56									
57									
58									
59									
60									

Best Home League Attendance: 13,466 v Wolves   **Smallest:** 5,272 v Stoke   **Av Home Att:** 8,269

Goal Scorers: **Compared with 1993-94:** -3,421

League (53):   Creaney 18, McLoughlin 6, Hall 5, Powell 5, Preki 5, Symons 4, Burton 2, Durnin 2, Doling, Pethick, Wood, Newhouse, Rees, Opponents

C/Cola Cup (9):   Creaney 3, Powell 3, Hall, Kristensen, Stimson

FA Cup (3):   Preki 2, Creaney

Knight	Gitters	Stimson	McLoughlin	Symons	Dobson	Neill	Pethick	Powell	Creaney	Hall	Lee	Daniel	Poom	Rees	Doling	Burton	Awford	Kristensen	Preki	Flahaven	McGrath	Durnin	Russell	Totten	Butters	Referee	
1	2	3	4	5	6	7	8	9	10	11	12	14	S													Foakes P.	1
S	2	3	4	5	6	7	8	9		11		10	1	12	14											Orr D.	2
1	2	3	4	5	6	7	12	9	10	11	8	14	S													Dunn S.	3
S	2	3	4	5	6	7	8	9	10	11		14	1			12										Cooper K.	4
1	2	3	4	5	6	7	12	9	10	11	8	14	S													Wilkes C.	5
1	2	3	4	5	6	7	12	9	10	11	8	14	S													Hemley I.	6
1	2	3	4	5	6	7	12	9	10	11	8	14	S													Alcock P.	7
1	2	3	4	5		7	12	9	10	11		14	S					6	8							Pooley G.	8
1	2	3	4	5	6		14		10	11		9	S					7	8		12					Wright P.	9
1	2	3	4	5	7		14	9	10	11			S					6	8		12					Reed M.	10
1	2	3	4	5	7		14	9	10	11			S					6	8		12					Bailey M.	11
1	2	3	4	5	6*		9		10	12		7					14		8	RG	11					Rushton J.	12
1	2	3	4	5	6		9		10	11		7	S	12		14			8							Cruickshanks I.	13
1	2	3	4	5	6		11	9	10	14		12	S						8		7					Cooper K.	14
1	2	3	4	5			6	9	10	11		7		12					8	RG	14					Winter J.	15
1	2	3	4	5			7	9	10	11							12		8	RG	6	14				Vanes P.	16
1	2	3	4				7	9	10*	11				14			12		8	RG	6					Foakes P.	17
1	2	3	4				7	9	10	11							12		8	RG	6	14				Dunn S.	18
1	2	3					7	9	10	14				12			4		8	RG	6					Flood A.	19
1	2		4	5	11		7	9		12				10			3		8	RG	6		14			Leach K.	20
1		3	4	5	11		7	9	10					11			8		14	RG		12	6	2		Brondwood J.	21
1	2		4		3		7	9	10					14		11	8	5		RG			6	12		Kirkby J.	22
1	2		4		3	6	7	9	10	8						11		14	12	RG				5		Dunn S.	23
1	2		4	5	6		7	9	10	11		3				14		8	12	RG						Hemley I.	24
1	2			5	6		7	9	10	14							8	12	RG			4			3	Parker J.	25
1	2	14					7	9	10	12							8		RG	4			3		5	Pooley G.	26
1	2	14	5				7	9	10	12							8		RG	4					3	West T.	27
1	2		5				7	9	10	12	8						8		RG	4					3	Cooper K.	28
1	2		5				7	9	10	12		3					8		RG	4					6	Sig G.	29
1	2		5				7	9	10	14		3					8		RG	4					6	Rejer P.	30
1	2		5				7	9	10	14		3		12			8		RG	4					6	Holbrook T.	31
1	2		5				7	9	10	14		3		12			8		RG	4					6	Alcock P.	32
1			5				7	9	10	12		3					14	8	RG	4		2			6	Bailey M.	33
1							7	9	10	12		3		14			11	8	RG	5		2			6	Cruickshanks I.	34
1*	2*	12					7	9	10			3		14			11	8	RG	4					6	Gallagher D.	35
1	2		4	5			7	9	10	12		3		11			14	8	RG						6	Burns W.	36
			4	5			2		10	9		3		11	14		7	8	RG			12			6	Harrison P.	37
1			4	5			2		10	9		3		11	14			8			7	12			6	Leach K.	38
1	2		4	5			7		10	9		3		11				8		14		12			6	Foakes P.	39
1	2		4	5			7		10	9								8		11		12	3		6	Cain G.	40
1	2		4	5			7	11	10	9								8		14		12	3		6	Pooley G.	41
1	2		4	5			7	9	10	14								8		11		12	3		6	Orr D.	42
1	2		4	5			7	9	10	11								8		14		12	3		6	Harris R.	43
1	2		4	5			7	9	10	11				6				14	8			12	3			Dunn S.	44
S	2		4	5			7	9	10	11				3				14	8			12			6	Parker E.	45
S	2						7	9	10	11				3	12			5	8			4	6			Wilkes C.	46
1			4				7	9	10	11				12	14			5	8	RG		3	6		2	Furnandiz R.	47
1			4				7	9	10	11				12	14			5	8			3	6		2	Alcock P.	48
1	12		4	5			7			11			S	9	2			14	8			10	6		3	Lloyd J.	49
1	3		4	5			7			11			S	9	2	14		12	8			10	6		2	Bailey M.	50
1	3		4	5			7			11			S	9		8		12	14			10	6		2	Winter J.	51
1	3		4	5			7			11			S	9		8		12	14			10	6			Brandwood J.	52
1			4	5			2			11			S	9		8		12	7			10	6		3	Vanes P.	53
43	37	15	36	40	14	7	39	34	39	30	4	17		14	2	5	3	15	30		15	8	18	3	24	League Appearances	
	1		2				5		13	1		5		5	3	2	1	10	10		3	8	1	1		League Sub Appearances	
3	5	5	5	5	3	2	4+1	5	4	4+1		2+1	2				0+1	1	2+1	2+1		1	0+1		2	C/Cola Cup Appearances	
2	2		0+1	1			2	2	2			2					0+1		1	2	0+1	2		1	2	FA Cup Appearances	

Also Played: Wood 6(26,28), 6X(27), 14 (29), 11(31,32,33), Glass L, 1(37,45,46),RG(38,39,40,41,42,43,44,48), Newhouse 11(25,26,27,28,29,30) Waterman 14(46), Igoe(14(53)

Loan Players: David Lee (Chelsea), Aiden Newhouse (Wimbledon), Jimmy Glass (Crystal Palace)

PORTSMOUTH

CLUB RECORDS

BIGGEST VICTORIES
League: 9-1 v Notts County, Division 2, 9.4.1927
F.A. Cup: 7-0 v Stockport (h), Rnd 3, 8.1.1949
League Cup: 5-0 v Rotherham United Rnd 2, 5.10.1993

BIGGEST DEFEATS
League: 0-10 v Leicester City, Division 1, 20.10.1928
F.A. Cup: 0-5 v Everton, Round 1, 1902-03
0-5 v Tottenham H, Round 3, 16.1.1937
0-5 v Blackburn Rov, Rnd 1 2nd Replay, 1899-90
League Cup: 0-5 v Queens Park Rangers, Round 2, 6.10.1981

MOST POINTS
3 points a win: 91, Division 3, 1982-83
2 points a win: 65, Division 3, 1961-62

MOST GOALS
91, 1979-80 (Division 4)
Garwood 17, Laidlaw 16, Hemmerman 13, Brisley 12, Rogers 9, Gregory 5, Ashworth 4, Aizelwood 2, Bryant 2, Perrin 2, Davey 1, McLaughlin 1, Purdie 1, Todd 1, Showers 1, og 4

MOST LEAGUE GOALS CONCEDED
112, Division 1, 1958-59

MOST FIRST CLASS MATCHES IN A SEASON
61 (46 League, 2 FA Cup, 7 League Cup, 6 Anglo Italian) 1993-94

MOST LEAGUE WINS
27, Division 3, 1961-62; Division 3, 1982-83

MOST LEAGUE DRAWS
19, Division 3, 1981-82

MOST LEAGUE DEFEATS
27, Division 1, 1958-59

INDIVIDUAL CLUB RECORDS

MOST GOALS IN A MATCH
5. Alf Strange v Gillingham, Division 3, 27.1.1923 (6-1)
5. Peter Harris v Aston Villa, Division 1, 3.9.1958 (5-2)
(Peter Harris's 5th goal was his 200th league & cup goal for Portsmouth)

MOST GOALS IN A SEASON
Guy Whittingham 47 (Lge 42, Lg Cup 2, Anglo-Ital 3) 1992-93
4 goals once=4, 3 goals three times=9, 2 goals 6 times=12, 1 goal 22 times=22
Previous holder: Billy Haines 43 (Lg 40, FAC 3) 1926-27

OLDEST PLAYER
Jimmy Dickinson MBE, 40 exactly v Northampton, 24.4.1965

YOUNGEST PLAYER
Clive Green, 16 years 259 days v Wrexham, 21.8.1976
(also youngest goalscorer when 16 yrs 280 days v Lincoln City, 11.9.1976)

MOST CAPPED PLAYER
Jimmy Dickenson (England) 48

BEST PERFORMANCES

League: 1961-62: Matches played 46, Won 27, Drawn 11, Lost 8, Goals for 87, Goals against 47, Points 65. 1st in Division 3.
Highest: 1948-49, 1949-50: 1st in Division 1.

F.A. Cup: 1938-39: 3rd rnd. Lincoln 4-0; 4th rnd. West Bromwich Albion 2-0; 5th rnd. West Ham United 2-0; 6th rnd. Preston North End 1-0; Semi-final Huddersfield 2-1; Final Wolves 4-1.

League Cup: 1960-61: 2nd rnd. Coventry 2-0; 3rd rnd. Manchester City 2-0; 4th rnd. Chelsea 1-0; 5th rnd. Rotherham 0-3. 1993-94: 5th rnd.
1993-94: 2nd rnd. Rotherham 0-0, 5-0; 3rd rnd. Swindon 2-0; 4th rnd. Peterborough 0-0, 1-0; 5th rnd. Manchester Utd 2-2, 0-1.

ADDITIONAL INFORMATION
Previous League: Southern League.

Club colours: Royal blue shirts, white shorts, red socks.
Change colours: Red & black striped shirts, black shorts, red socks.

Reserves League: Avon Insurance Football Combination.

DIVISIONAL RECORD

	Played	Won	Drawn	Lost	For	Against	Points
Division 1	1,090	405	257	428	1,729	1,828	1,074
Division 2/1	1,288	454	342	492	1,825	1,871	1,446
Division 3	318	120	95	103	412	379	376
Division 3(S)	126	61	36	29	207	121	158
Division 4	92	44	24	24	153	97	112
Total	**2,914**	**1,084**	**754**	**1,076**	**4,326**	**4,296**	**3,166**

RECORDS AND STATISTICS

COMPETITIONS

Div.1	Div.2/1	Div.3	Div.3(S)	Div.4
1927-59	1924-27	1920-21	1921-24	1978-80
1987-88	1959-61	1961-62		
	1962-76	1976-78		
	1983-87	1980-83		
	1988-			

HONOURS

Div.1	Div.3	Div.3(S)	FA Cup	C/Shield
1948-49	1961-62	1923-24	1938-39	1949
1949-50	1982-83			

MOST APPEARANCES

Jimmy Dickinson 829 (1946-65)

Year	League	FA Cup	Lge Cup	C/Shield
1946-47	40	2		
1947-48	42	2		
1948-49	41	5		
1949-50	40	5		1
1950-51	41	1		
1951-52	40	4		
1952-53	40	2		
1953-54	40	7		
1954-55	25			
1955-56	39	2		
1956-57	42	2		
1957-58	42	2		
1958-59	39	4		
1959-60	42	1		
1960-61	40	1	4	
1961-62	46	1	4	
1962-63	42	5	3	
1963-64	42	1	2	
1964-65	41	2	2	
	764	49	15	1

MOST GOALS IN A CAREER

Peter Harris - 208 (1946-60)

Year	League	FA Cup
1946-47	1	
1947-48	13	1
1948-49	17	5
1949-50	16	1
1950-51	5	
1951-52	9	1
1952-53	23	
1953-54	20	4
1954-55	23	
1955-56	23	1
1956-57	12	2
1957-58	18	
1958-59	13	
1959-60	1	
Total	193	15

Current leading goalscorer: Gerry Creaney - 33 (1994-95)

MANAGERS

Name	Seasons	Best	Worst
Since joining the League			
John McCartney	1920-27	2(2)	12(3S)
John Tinn	1927-47	4(1)	20(1)
J R Jackson	1947-52	1(1)	8(1)
Eddie Lever	1952-58	3(1)	20(1)
Freddie Cox	1958-61	22(1)	21(2)
Bill Thompson	1961		
George Smith	1961-70	5(2)	1(3)
Ron Tindall	1970-73	16(2)	17(2)
John Mortimore	1973-74	15(2)	15(2)
Ron Tindall	1974		
Ian St John	1974-77	17(2)	20(3)
Jimmy Dickinson	1977-79	24(3)	7(4)
Frank Burrows	1979-82	6(3)	4(4)
Bobby Campbell	1982-84	16(2)	1(3)
Alan Ball	1984-89	20(1)	4(2)
John Gregory	1989-90		
Frank Burrows	1990-91		
Jim Smith	1991-95	3(2/1)	17(2/1)
Terry Fenwick	1995-		

RECORD TRANSFER FEE RECEIVED

Amount	Club	Player	Date
£1,700,000	Tottenham H.	Darren Anderton	6/92
£1,000,000	Inter Milan	Mark Hateley	6/84
£130,000	Brighton & H.A.	Steve Foster	6/79
£75,000	Carlisle United	David Kemp	3/78

RECORD TRANSFER FEE PAID

Amount	Club	Player	Date
£500,000	Celtic	Gerry Creaney	1/94
£450,000	Q.P.R.	Colin Clarke	5/90
£315,000	Aston Villa	Warren Aspinall	8/88
£300,000	Barnsley	John Beresford	3/89

LONGEST LEAGUE RUNS

of undefeated matches:	15 (18.4.1924 - 18.10.1924)	of league matches w/out a win:	25 (22.1.1958 - 17.10.1959)
of undefeated home matches:	32 (3.1.1948 - 27.8.1949)	of undefeated away matches:	14 (1.3.1924 - 18.10.1924)
without home win:	16 (6.2.1958 - 17.10.1959)	without an away win:	24 (26.1.1938 - 11.3.1939)
of league wins:	7 (19.4.1980-30.8.1980, 22.1.1983-1.4.1983)	of home wins:	14 (13.9.1986 - 28.2.1987)
of league defeats:	9 (22.11.1959-17.1.1960, 21.3.1959-29.8.1959)	of away wins:	6 (1.4.1980 - 30.8.1980)
	(3.11.1963 - 22.12.1963, 21.10.1975 - 6.12.1975)		

PORTSMOUTH

PLAYERS NAME Honours	Ht	Wt	Birthdate	Birthplace Transfers	Contract Date	Clubs	League	L/Cup	FA Cup	Other	Lge	L/C	FAC	Oth
G O A L K E E P E R S														
Aaron Flahavan	6.1	12.10	15.12.75	Southampton	15.02.94	Portsmouth (T)				0+1				
Alan Knight	6.1	13.1	03.07.61	Balham	12.03.79	Portsmouth (A)	578	48	34	21				
E: u21.2, Y.3. Div.3'83.														
Mart Poom				Switzerland		FC Will								
Estonian Int.				£200,000	.08.94	Portsmouth		2						
D E F E N D E R S														
Andrew Awford	5.9	11.9	14.07.72	Worcester	24.07.89	Portsmouth (T)	138+8	16+1	10	12				
E: u21.9, Y.13.														
Guy Butters	6.3	13.0	30.10.69	Hillingdon	05.08.88	Tottenham H. (T)	34+1	2+1	1		1			
E: u21.3.				Loan	13.01.90	Southend United	16			2	3			
				£375,000	28.09.90	Portsmouth	104+6	11+1	6	7+2	4	1		
				Loan	04.11.94	Oxford United	3			1	1			
Tony Dobson	6.1	12.10	05.02.69	Coventry	07.07.86	Coventry City (A)	51+3	5+3		0+1	1			
E: u21.4.				£300,000	17.01.91	Blackburn Rovers	36+5	5	2	1				
				£150,000	22.09.93	Portsmouth	37+1	5	1+1	4	2			1
				Loan	15.12.94	Oxford United	5							
Jon Gittens	5.11	12.6	22.01.64	Birmingham		Paget Rangers								
				£10,000	16.10.85	Southampton	18	4	1					
				£40,000	22.07.87	Swindon Town	124+2	15+1	9	13+1	6			1
				£400,000	28.03.91	Southampton	16+3	4		1				
Loan Middlesbrough, 19.02.92, 9+3 Lge App.				£200,000	27.07.92	Middlesbrough	13	0+1	1					
				Free	09.08.93	Portsmouth	67+1	10	2	3	1			
Robert Pethick	5.10	11.7	08.09.70	Tavistock		Plymouth Argyle (T)								
						Weymouth								
				£30,000	01.10.93	Portsmouth	53+9	5+2	2	3+1				
Lee Russell	5.10	11.4	03.09.69	Southampton	12.07.88	Portsmouth (T)	60+16	2+1	3+2	5+2	1			
				Loan	09.09.94	Bournemouth	3							
Mark Stimson	5.11	11.0	27.12.67	Plaistow	15.07.85	Tottenham H. (T)	1+1							
				Loan	15.03.88	Leyton Orient	10							
Loan Gillingham, 19.01.89, 18 Lge App.				£200,000	16.06.89	Newcastle United	82+4	5	7	6	2		1	
Loan Portsmouth, 10.12.92, 3+1 Lge App.				£100,000	23.07.93	Portsmouth	43+1	9	2	3	1	1		
M I D F I E L D														
Stuart Doling	5.6	10.6	28.10.72	Newport IOW	25.06.90	Portsmouth (T)	20+17	4+3	1	4+3	4			1
E: Y.														
Samuel Igoe			30.09.75	Spelthorne	15.02.94	Portsmouth (T)	0+1							
Lloyd McGrath	5.8	10.6	24.02.65	Birmingham	31.12.82	Coventry City (A)	200+14	22	16	6	4	1		
				Free	06.94	Hong Kong								
					17.10.94	Portsmouth	15+3	1	2					
Alan McLoughlin	5.8	10.0	20.04.67	Manchester	25.04.85	Manchester Utd (A)								
Ei: 16, B.2.				Free	15.08.86	Swindon Town	101+5	11+3	4+2	10	18	5		1
				Loan	13.03.87	Torquay United	21+3				4			
				£1,000,000	13.12.90	Southampton	22+2	0+1	4	1	1			
Loan Aston Villa, 30.09.91, 1 Oth. App.				£400,000	17.02.92	Portsmouth	133+3	14	6+1	9	23	3	5	1
Jason Rees	5.5	9.8	22.12.69	Aberdare	01.07.88	Luton Town (T)	58+23	3+2	2+1	5+1				2
W: 1, u21.3, B.1, Y.				Loan	23.12.93	Mansfield Town	15		1		1			
				Free	18.07.94	Portsmouth	14+5	0+1	0+1		1			
F O R W A R D S														
Deon Burton			25.10.76	Reading	15.02.94	Portsmouth (T)	6+3	0+1			2			
Jimmy Carter	5.10	10.4	09.11.65	Hammersmith	15.11.83	Crystal Palace (A)								
Div.2'88.				Free	30.09.85	Q.P.R.								
				£15,000	12.03.87	Millwall	99+11	6+1	6+1	5+1	11		2	
				£800,000	10.01.91	Liverpool	2+3		2	0+1				
				£500,000	08.10.91	Arsenal	18+7	1	2+1		2			
Loan 23.03.94 Oxford United 8+1 Lge App.				Free	08.95	Portsmouth								
Gerry Creaney	5.10	10.7	13.04.70	Coatbridge		Glasgow Rangers	85+28	9+1	9+1	7+3	36	7	8	3
S: u21.12.				£500,000	25.01.94	Portsmouth	57	5	2		29	3	1	
John Durnin	5.10	11.4	18.08.65	Bootle		Waterloo Dock								
				Free	29.03.86	Liverpool		1+1						
Loan W.B.A., 20.10.88, 5 Lge App., 2 gls.				£225,000	10.02.89	Oxford United	140+21	7	7	4+1	44	1	1	1
				£200,000	15.07.93	Portsmouth	31+13	7+1	1+1	4+2	8	2		1
Paul Hall	5.9	10.2	03.07.72	Manchester	09.07.90	Torquay Utd (T)	77+16	7	4+1	5+1	1		2	1

PLAYERS NAME Honours	Ht	Wt	Birthdate	Birthplace Transfers	Contract Date	Clubs	League	L/Cup	FA Cup	Other	Lge	L/C	FAC	Oth
					£70,000	25.03.93	Portsmouth	46+25	4+2	0+1	5+2	9	1		2
Darryl Powell	6.0	12.03	15.11.71	Lambeth	22.12.88	Portsmouth (T)	83+54	11+3	10	9+5	16	3		4
Predrag Radosalehjvic	5.11	12.10	24.06.63	Belgrade		St Louis Storms								
					£100,000	28.08.92	Everton	22+24	2+4	1		4			
					£100,000	27.07.94	Portsmouth	30+10	2+1	2		5		2	
Paul Wood	5.9	10.1	01.11.64	Saltburn	03.11.82	Portsmouth (A)	25+22	5+3	2	2+2	7	1		3
					£40,000	28.08.87	Brighton & H.A.	77+15	4	2+2	5	8			
					£90,000	09.02.90	Sheffield United	19+9	1		1	3			
Loan 31.01.91 Bournemouth 20+1 Lge App.					£40,000	03.10.91	Bournemouth	73+5	1+1	13	5	18		2	2
						18.02.94	Portsmouth	12+5		1		2			
A D D I T I O N A L C O N T R A C T P L A Y E R S														
Lee Bradbury							British Army & C.							
					Free	08.95	Portsmouth								
James Fraser							Swindon Town							
					Free	08.95	Portsmouth								
Alexander Totten	5.7	11.7	01.10.76	Southampton	23.11.94	Portsmouth (T)	3+1							

TOP GOALSCORER 1994/95
Gerry Creaney

Premiership goals (games) 18 (39)
Coca-Cola Cup Goals 3 (4)
F.A. Cup goals 1 (2)

Total . . . . **22 (45)**

Total goals for Portsmouth since 25.01.94 . . . . 33 (64)

Career total as at June 1st 1995 . . . . 87 (173+32)

THE MANAGER
TERRY FENWICK

Date of Birth . . . . 17th November 1959.
Place of Birth . . . . Seaham.
Date of Appointment . . . . February 1995.

PREVIOUS CLUBS
As Manager . . . . None.
As Coach . . . . None.
As a Player Crystal Palace, Queens Park Rangers, Tottenham, Leicester (Loan)

HONOURS
As a Manager
None.

As a Player
Crystal Palace: Division 2 championship 1979. FAYC 1977, 1978.
Queens Park Rangers: Division 2 championship 1983.
Tottenham Hotspur: FA Cup 1991.
International: 20 full caps and 11 U21 caps for England. UEFA U21 1982.

FRATTON ROAD
Frogmore Road, Portsmouth PO4 8RA
Tel: 01705 731 204

Capacity...26,452
Covered standing...2,700
Seating...6,652

First game...v Southampton (Friendly) 2-0, 6.9.1899.
First floodlit game..v Newcastle, 2.3.1953.
Second Set ....v Burnley, 10.10.1962.

ATTENDANCES
Highest....................................51,385 v Derby County, FAC 6th Rnd, 20.2.1949.
Lowest...............................2,499 v Wimbledon, Z.Data 1st Rnd, 5.12.1989.

OTHER GROUNDS..None.

MATCHDAY TICKET PRICES

South Stand
A Section (Adults/Concessions) . . . . £13/£9
B Section . . . . £15/£10
C Section . . . . £15/£10

North Stand
E Section. . . . . £11/£7
F Section . . . . £13/£8
G Section. . . . . £11/£5*
Terrace . . . . £8/£5
Family Section. £8/£3*
*Family Section passes must be produced to gain
access into these sections and Adults must be
accompanied by a Junior passholder.
Ticket office Telephone no. 01705 750 825

CLUBCALL
0898 12 11 82
Calls cost 39p per minute cheap rate and 49p per
minute at all other times.
Call costings correct at time of going to press.

HOW TO GET TO THE GROUND

From the North and West
Use motorway (M27) and (M275) and at end at roundabout take 2nd exit and in
0.2 miles, at 'T' junction turn right (A2047) into London Road.
In 1.3 miles over railway bridge and turn left into Goldsmith Avenue. In 0.6 miles
turn left into Frogmore Road for POrtsmouth FC.

From the East
Use A27 then follow signs to Southsea (A2030). In 3 miles at roundabout turn
left (A288). Then turn right into Priory Crescent then take next turning right into
Carisbrooke Road for Portsmouth FC.

Car Parking
Side-street parking only.

Nearest Railway Station
Fratton (by Fratton Park), Portsmouth 01705 825 711)

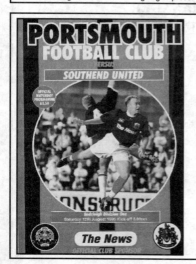

MATCHDAY PROGRAMME

Programme Editor . . . . Julie Baker.

Number of pages . . . . 40.

Price . . . . £1.50.

Subscriptions . . . . Available from Club.

Local Newspapers. . . . . Portsmouth Evening News.

Local Radio Stations. . . . . Ocean F.M., Radio Solent.

READING
(The Royals)
ENDSLEIGH LEAGUE DIVISION 1
SPONSORED BY: AUTOTRADER (SHIRTS)

Back Row (L-R): Trevor Morley, Jeff Hopkins, Michael Thorp, Matthew Stowell, Ron Grant (Kitman), Stuart Lovell, David Bass, Martin Williams, Alan Carey. **Middle Row:** Lee Nogan, Michael Murphy, Michael Gilkes, Andy Bernal, Stuart Jones, Phil Parkinson, Simon Sheppard, Keith McPherson, Michael Meaker, Paul Holsgrove, Dylan Kerr. **Front Row:** Phil Holder (Coach), Derek Simpson, James Lambert, Steven Swales, Jimmy Quinn (joint player/Manager), Adrian Williams (capt), Mick Gooding (joint player/Manager), Dariusz Wdowczyk, Tom Jones, Gareth Randell, Paul Turner (Physio).

READING
FORMED IN 1871
TURNED PROFESSIONAL IN 1895
LTD COMPANY IN 1895

CHAIRMAN: R J Madejski

DIRECTORS
G J Denton, I Wood-Smith
GENERAL MANAGER
Adrian Porter
SECRETARY
Andrea Barker
COMMERCIAL MANAGER
Kevin Girdler

PLAYER MANAGERS
Mick Gooding & Jimmy Quinn

YOUTH TEAM MANAGER
Phil Holder
PHYSIOTHERAPIST
P Turner

STATISTICIAN FOR THE DIRECTORY
David Downs

So near yet so far - Reading enjoyed what was, statistically, the best season in the club's 124-year long history, even if it ended in frustration and disappointment. The team finished as runners-up in Division One, a feat which in any previous campaign would have guaranteed automatic promotion to the Premiership. In 1994-95, it meant qualification for the play-offs, where Reading performed superbly to defeat Tranmere 3-1 on aggregate and earn the right to meet Bolton Wanderers at Wembley. There, in front of the largest crowd ever to watch the Royals play, Reading were within four minutes of the Premiership, when Bolton scored a late equaliser and went on to win the game in extra-time.

So Reading remain in Division One for another season. But an overall, dispassionate analysis shows that great progress was made during the twelve months, and hopes are high that Reading can go one better in 1995-96, especially if the club can hold on to its hugely talented young players such as Hislop, Lovell, Nogan, Osborn, Taylor and Williams. This group can be the backbone of the team for many years to come.

The achievement in reaching second place and a spot at Wembley was all the more creditable considering the mid-season upheaval which disrupted the club. Manager Mark McGhee left abruptly for Leicester City, taking his coaching staff with him. Chairman John Madejski made an in-house appointment to replace him, the experienced Mick Gooding and Jimmy Quinn taking over as joint player-managers. Those two did magnificently in leading by example, motivating the players, coaching, refining the playing system to cater for the heavy grounds of mid-winter, and then making an astute signing by bringing Lee Nogan from Watford.

Nogan's introduction to a striking partnership with Lovell provided the boost which saw Reading win seven of their last ten league games. But the quality of football played throughout the season was outstanding. The team spirit - and the squad included players from Australia, England, Germany, Malta, Northern Ireland, Poland, Trinidad & Tobago and Wales - was high, and the team carried its attacking policy into away games. Eleven matches, including a 1-0 victory at champions Middlesbrough, were won on their travels, as the players showed supreme confidence in their ability to score goals from all angles and areas of the field. They were a joy to watch, and several players were recognised at national level. In addition to his other duties, Quinn continued to play for Northern Ireland, Williams gained further caps for Wales, Nogan was recalled to the Welsh squad and Hislop was selected as the PFA Division One goalkeeper of the season.

Although the club had no reserve team, the fringe players had some success too, winning the Berks & Bucks Senior Cup for the first time since 1892, beating Slough Town 1-0 with a Quinn penalty in the final. The team also contained several youngsters, evidence of the continued commitment to a youth development policy. Half the first team squad joined Reading from school, and four more - Murphy, Randell, Simpson and Stowell - have signed as professionals for next season. Eight local schoolboys will be joining the Youth Training Scheme, and the club confirmed its reputation as a focal point for the community when forty thousand fans supported the Royals at Wembley.

Reading Football Club is a prime example of what can be achieved with slender resources, even if the potential is great. A new stadium is a must for the near future if the club is to hold on to its new-found support. Elm Park is an antiquated structure, terraced on three sides, and unable to hold the crowds needed to sustain the drive towards the Premiership. The team has almost outgrown the club, but if progress off the field can match that on it, then the promotion to the Premiership may only be delayed by a season.

Next year it may not just be a case of so near yet so far, rather so far so good. Up the Royals! DAVID DOWNS.

READING

Division One: 2nd   **FA Cup:** 3rd Round   **Coca-Cola Cup:** 2nd Round

M	DATE	COMP.	VEN	OPPONENTS	RESULT	H/T	LP	GOAL SCORERS/GOAL TIMES	ATT.
1	A 13	EL	A	Wolverhampton W.	L 0-1	0-1	18		(27,012)
2	16	CC 1/1	A	Gillingham	W 1-0	0-0		Hopkins 50	(2,556)
3	20	EL	H	Portsmouth	D 0-0	0-0	21		9,106
4	22	CC 1/2	H	Gillingham	W 3-0	0-0		Quinn 52,88, Lovell 64	3,436
5	27	EL	A	Barnsley	W 2-0	1-0	12	Osborn 21, Taylor 90	(4,771)
6	30	EL	H	Stoke City	W 4-0	0-0	5	Lovell 62, Kerr 72, Gilkes 86, Taylor 90	7,103
7	S 3	EL	H	Millwall	D 0-0	0-0	6		8,715
8	10	EL	A	Oldham Athletic	W 3-1	1-1	2	Lovell 30, 74, Osborn 54	(8,412)
9	14	EL	A	Swindon Town	L 0-1	0-0	4		(11,551)
10	17	EL	H	Sheffield United	W 1-0	0-0	3	Quinn 61	9,036
11	20	CC 2/1	H	Derby County	W 3-1	1-1		Quinn 8, 77, Holsgrove 52	6,056
12	24	EL	A	Watford	D 2-2	0-2	5	Osborn 52, Lovell 55	(8,015)
13	28	CC 2/2	A	Derby County	L 0-2	0-1			(9,476)
14	O 1	EL	H	Notts County	W 2-0	1-0	3	Lovell 37, Hartenberger 87	7,465
15	8	EL	A	Charlton Athletic	W 2-1	1-0	3	Osborn 5, Gilkes 60	(10,544)
16	15	EL	H	Bristol City	W 1-0	0-0	2	Gilkes 90	9,389
17	22	EL	H	Sunderland	L 0-2	0-1	2		10,757
18	29	EL	A	W. Bromwich Albion	L 0-2	0-0	4		(14,313)
19	N 2	EL	A	Derby County	W 2-1	1-0	4	Taylor 32, Gilkes 81	(10,585)
20	5	EL	H	Burnley	D 0-0	0-0	4		8,150
21	19	EL	A	Southend United	L 1-4	1-1	5	Quinn 14	(5,511)
22	26	EL	H	Tranmere Rovers	L 1-3	0-2	8	Jones 67	7,887
23	D 3	EL	A	Sunderland	W 1-0	0-0	5	Taylor 69	(14,021)
24	6	EL	H	Middlesbrough	D 1-1	0-0	5	Taylor 88	10,301
25	10	EL	A	Portsmouth	D 1-1	0-	6	Quinn 50 (pen)	(8,578)
26	18	EL	H	Wolverhampton W.	W 4-2	2-1	5	Osborn 24, Quinn 38, Gilkes 63, 89	10,136
27	26	EL	H	Luton Town	D 0-0	0-0	6		11,623
28	28	EL	A	Port Vale	W 2-0	1-0	4	Quinn 17 (pen), Taylor 80	(7,891)
29	31	EL	H	Grimsby Town	D 1-1	0-1	4	Lambert 86	8,526
30	J 2	EL	A	Bolton Wanderers	L 0-1	0-1	6		(14,705)
31	7	FAC 3	H	Oldham Athletic	L 1-3	1-2		Taylor 14	8,886
32	14	EL	H	W.Bromwich Albion	L 0-2	0-0	7		9,390
33	21	EL	A	Burnley	W 2-1	2-0	4	Nogan 5, Taylor 10	(9,841)
34	F 4	EL	A	Middlesbrough	W 1-0	0-0	5	Holsgrove 52	(17,982)
35	11	EL	H	Derby County	W 1-0	1-0	4	Kavanagh 31 (og)	8,834
36	18	EL	A	Tranmere Rovers	L 0-1	0-0	5		(8,744)
37	21	EL	H	Southend United	W 2-0	0-0	4	Holsgrove 57, Nogan 65	7,895
38	25	EL	A	Notts County	L 0-1	0-0	4		(7,183)
39	M 4	EL	H	Watford	W 4-1	1-0	4	Gilkes 44, 77, Holsgrove 80, Hartenberger 88	9,705
40	8	EL	A	Millwall	L 0-2	0-1	6		(7,546)
41	11	EL	H	Barnsley	L 0-3	0-1	6		7,556
42	18	EL	A	Stoke City	W 1-0	1-0	6	Taylor 37	(10,006)
43	21	EL	H	Oldham Athletic	W 2-1	0-1	4	Nogan 82, Lovell 90	6,921
44	25	EL	A	Sheffield United	D 1-1	0-0	2	Nogan 66	(19,241)
45	A 1	EL	H	Swindon Town	W 3-0	2-0	4	Lovell 29, 32 (pen), 89	12,565
46	8	EL	A	Grimsby Town	L 0-1	0-0	5		(4,519)
47	15	EL	H	Port Vale	D 3-3	3-0	6	Nogan 23, 35, 40	8,635
48	17	EL	A	Luton Town	W 1-0	1-0	5	Williams 43	(8,717)
49	22	EL	H	Bolton Wanderers	W 2-1	1-0	5	Lovell 14, Nogan 87	13,223
50	29	EL	A	Bristol City	W 2-1	1-0	2	Lovell 18, Nogan 58	(9,474)
51	M 7	EL	H	Charlton Athletic	W 2-1	1-0	2	Nogan 6, Williams 89	12,137
52	14	POSF1	A	Tranmere Rovers	W 3-1	1-1		Lovell 9, 82, Nogan 75	(12,207)
53	17	POSF2	H	Tranmere Rovers	D 0-0	0-0			13,245
54	29	POF	N	Bolton Wanderers	L 3-4	2-0		Nogan 4, Williams 12, Quinn 119	(64,107)
55									
56									
57									
58									
59									
60									

Best Home League Attendance: 13,245 v Tranmere Rovers   **Smallest:** 6,921 v Oldham Athletic   **Av Home Att:** 9,350

Goal Scorers:

League (58): Lovell 11 (1 pen), Nogan 10, Gilkes 8, Taylor 8, Osborn 5, Quinn 5 (2 pens), Holsgrove 3, Hartenberger 2, Williams 2, Jones, Kerr, Lambert, Opponent.

C/Cola Cup (7): Quinn 4, Holsgrove, Hopkins, Lovell

FA Cup (1): Taylor

Play-Offs (6): Lovell 2, Nogan 2, Quinn, Williams

Compared with 1993-94: +2,426

Hislop	Bernal	Kerr	Wdowczyk	Williams	Parkinson	Taylor	Gooding	Quinn	Lovell	Osborn	Gilkes	Hopkins	Holsgrove	Hartenberger	Jones	Sheppard	McPherson	Murphy	Lambert	Carey	Barnard	Nogan	Thorp	Viveash	Referee	
1	2	3	4•	5	6	7*	8	9	10	11	12	14													Parker J.	1
1	2	3		5	6*	7	8	9	10	11		4	12	5											Bailey M.	2
1	2	3	4	5	6	7*	8	9	10	11	12	S													Dunn S.	3
1		3	4	5	6*	S	8	9	10	11	7	2	12												Lloyd J.	4
1		3	4	5	6	12	8	9	10	11	7	2*	S												Burns B.	5
1		3	4	5	6	12	8	9	10	11•	7	2*	14												Pooley G.	6
1		3	4		6•	12	8*	9	10	11	7	2	5		14	S									Vanes P.	7
1	S	3	4	5		S	8	9	10	11	7	2	6			S									Wright P.	8
1	2	3	4†	5		S	12	8	9*	10	11	7		6		S									Brandwood J.	9
1	2*	3	4	5	12	14	8	9	10	11	7		6•			S									Wilkes C.	10
1	2*	3	4	5		14	8	9	10•	11	7	12	6			S									Alcock P.	11
1		14	4	5	3•	10*	8	9	12	11	7	2	6			S									Pierce M.	12
1	2•	3		5	7*	12	8	9	10	11	4	6				S	14								Cooper K.	13
1		3	4	5	8*	12		9•	10	11	2	6	14		S										Kirby J.	14
1	2	3	4	5	14	12	8	9		11	7•		6	10*		S									Singh G.	15
1	2	3	4	5	14		8	9		11	7		6•	10*		S		12							Leach K.	16
1	2	3	4	5	6•	10*	8	9		11	7						S	14	12						Wolstenholme E.	17
1		3	4	5	6•	12	8			11*	7†	2		9	10	S	14								Barry N.	18
1	2	3	4		6	9	8			11	7	5			10	S	S		S						Lomas E.	19
1	2†	3	4*		6	9	8			11	7	5			10	S	12		S						Foakes P.	20
1		3	4			7	8	9		11		2			6	S	5		S	12	10*				Pierce M.	21
1	2*	3	4			7	8	9		11		5*			6	S	12		14		10				Bailey M.	22
1	2	3	4			12	8	9	10•	11					6	S	5		14		7*				Poulain R.	23
1	2	3	4		5	12	8	9	10	11	7				6*	S	5†								Brandwood J.	24
1	2	3				6	4*	8	9	10	11	7				S	S	5		12					Pooley G.	25
1	2	3				6	4	8	9	10*	11	7			12	S	S	5							Alcock P.	26
1	2		5			6	4*	8	9	10	11	7			S	3	S		12						Singh G.	27
1	2		4			6	12	8	9*	10	11	7				3	S	5		S					Heilbron T.	28
1	2*		4			6	12	8•	9	10	11	7				3	S	5		14					D'Urso A.	29
1			4			6	3	8	9	10		7			12	2	S	5		S					Cain G.	30
1	5		4			6	3*	8	9	10•		7	12	11	14	2	S		11*						Kirkby J.	31
1	5					6	3	8	9*	12		7	4	11		2						10	S		Foakes P.	32
1	2					11	8	10*	12		7	5	4		3	S						9	S	6	Cain G.	33
1	2*		3			12	8	10	14		7	5	4		11	S						9•		6	Lloyd J.	34
1		3	4		14	8		10•			7*	2	6		11	S			12			9		5	Rejer P.	35
1		3	4			8	7	10•				2	6	14	11*	S			12			9		5	Lupton K.	36
1		3				8	11	12				4	6	10•	2	S			7*	14		9		5	Vanes P.	37
1		3		14†	8	7		12				5	4	10•	2	S			11*			9		6	Dawson A.	38
1	2	3		5	12	11	8*	S			7	4	6	10		S						9			Rushton J.	39
1	2	3	14	5		11	8†	12			7	6•	4	10*		S						9			Orr D.	40
1	2	3	4			11	8	9	12		7	6•				S	5		14			10*			Alcock P.	41
1	2	3	4		10	11*	8	9	S		7	6				S	5					12			Flood A.	42
1	2*	3	4		8	11	12	9•			7	6				S	5		S			14			Cooper K.	43
1	2	3	4		8	11			10*		7	6	12			S	5		S			9			Winter J.	44
1	2	3	4*		8	11			10	12	7•		6	14		S	5					9			Dunn S.	45
1	2	3	4	12		11	14			8•	7		6	10*		S	5					9			Breen K.	46
1	2	3		5		11	8	S		10*	6	7			12	S	4					9			Pooley G.	47
1	2	3	4	5		11	8	S		10*	7	12				S	6					9			Kirkby J.	48
1	2	5	4	5		11	8	S		10	3	7				S	6					9			Lloyd J.	49
1	2		4*	5	12	11	8	S		10	3	7				S	6					9			Wright P.	50
1	2*		4	5		11	8	14		10•	3	7			12	S	6					9			Foakes P.	51
1	2		4	5		11	8	S		10	3	7				S	6					9			Kirby J.	52
1	2		4	5*		11	8	14		10•	3	7	12			S	6					9			Alcock P.	53
1	2•		4	5		11	8	12		10	3	7	14			S	6					9*			Foakes P.	54
46	33	35	37	20	25	31	37	31	25	31	37	20	24	8	18		19		3		3	18		6	League Appearances	
	1	1	2	6	13	2	4	5	1	3	1		7	2			4	1	8	2	1	2			League Sub Appearances	
4	3	4	2	4	3	1+2	4	4	4	4	2	3+1	2+2				0+1								C/Cola Cup Appearances	
1	1		1		1	1	1	1	1	1	1	1	0+1	1	0+1	1									FA Cup Appearances	
3	3		3	3		3	3	0+2	3	3	3	0+2					3					3			Play-Off Appearances	

Players on Loan: Barnard (Chelsea), Viveash (Swindon Town)

† = Sent Off

READING

BIGGEST VICTORIES
League: 10-2 v Crystal Palace, Division 3S, 4.9.1946
F.A. Cup: 8-3 v Corinthians, Rnd.1, 1935-36
6-0 v Leyton, Round 2, 1925/26
League Cup: 4-0 v QPR, Round 2, 23.9.1964
5-1 v Southend United, Round 2, 1965/66
5-1 v Oxford United, Round 1, 1979/80

BIGGEST DEFEATS
League: 1-8 v Burnley, Division 2, 13.9.1930
F.A. Cup: 0-18 v Preston North End, Round 1, 27.1.1894
League Cup: 0-5 v Leicester City, Round 2, 1966/67
0-5 v Watford, Round 2, 1977/78

MOST POINTS
3 points a win: 94, Division 3, 1985-86
2 points a win: 65, Division 4, 1978-79

MOST GOALS
112, 1951-52 (Division 3S)
Blackman 39, Bainbridge 18, Lewis 15, Edelston 14, Henley 10, Simpson 8, Owens4, Brice 2, Brooks 1, 1og.

MOST FIRST CLASS MATCHES IN A SEASON
60 (46 league + 10 FA Cup + 4 Lge Cup) 1989-90

MOST LEAGUE GOALS CONCEDED
96, Division 2, 1930-31

MOST LEAGUE WINS
29, Division 3, 1985-86

MOST LEAGUE DRAWS
19, Division 4, 1973-74
Division 3, 1989-90

MOST LEAGUE DEFEATS
24, Division 2, 1930-31
Division 3, 1976-77

MOST GOALS IN A MATCH
6. Arthur Bacon v Stoke City, Division 2, 3.4.1931 (7-3)

MOST GOALS IN A SEASON
Trevor Senior, 36 League, 1 FA Cup, 4 Lge Cup, Total 41 (1983-84)
3 goals 2 times = 6, 2 goals 10 times = 20, 1 goal 15 times = 15.
Previous holder: Ronnie Blackman, 40 (39 league, 1 FA Cup) 1951-52.

OLDEST PLAYER
Beaumont Ratcliffe, 39 years 336 days v Northampton Town, 1947-48

YOUNGEST PLAYER
S Hetkze, 16 years 184 days v Darlington, 4.12.71

MOST CAPPED PLAYER
Jimmy Quinn (Northern Ireland) 15

League: 1985-86: Matches played 46, Won 29, Drawn 7, Lost 10, Goals for 67,Goals against 51, Points 94. 1st in Division 3.

Highest: 2nd, Division 1, 1994-95.

F.A. Cup: 1926-27: 1st rnd. Weymouth 4-4, 5-0; 2nd rnd. Southend, 3-2; 3rd rnd.Manchester United, 1-1,2-2,2-1; 4th rnd. Portsmouth, 3-1; 5th rnd. Brentford,1-0; 6th rnd, Swansea, 3-1; Semi-Final, Cardiff City, 0-3.

League Cup: 1965-66: 1st rnd, Port Vale, 2-2, 1-0; 2nd rnd, Southend, 5-1; 3rd rnd, Derby County, 1-1, 2-0; 4th rnd, Cardiff City 1-5.
1978-79: 1st rnd, Gillingham, 3-1, 2-1; 2nd rnd, Wolves, 1-0; 3rd rnd,Rotherham, 2-2, 1-0, 4th rnd, Southampton, 0-0, 0-2.

ADDITIONAL INFORMATION
Previous League: Southern League

Club colours: Blue & white hooped shirts, white shorts and socks.

Change colours: Red shirts, shorts and socks.

Reserves League: Capital League.

Youth League: S E Counties, Allied Counties Youth League.

DIVISIONAL RECORD

	Played	Won	Drawn	Lost	For	Against	Points
Division 2/1	342	113	83	146	469	565	332
Division 3/2	1,196	471	296	429	1,779	1,722	1,238
Division 3(S)	1,124	480	260	384	1,892	1,585	1,220
Division 4	368	161	110	97	513	392	432
Total	**3,030**	**1,225**	**749**	**1,056**	**4,653**	**4,264**	**3,222**

RECORDS AND STATISTICS

COMPETITIONS

Div.2/1	Div.3.2	Div.3(S)	Div.4	Watney C.
1926-31	1958-71	1920-26	1971-76	1970
1986-88	1976-77	1931-58	1977-79	
1994-	1979-83		1983-84	
	1984-86			
	1986-94			

HONOURS

Div.3/2	Div.3(S)	Div.4	Div.3(S) Cup
1985-86	1925-26	1978-79	1937-38
1993-94			
			Simod Cup
			1987-88

MOST APPEARANCES

Martin Hicks 601+2 (178-91)

Year	League	FA Cup	Lge Cup	Others
1977-78	19			
1978-79	46	4	7	
1979-80	1		2	
1980-81	27	1	1	
1981-82	43+1	1	2	3
1982-83	32		1	5
1983-84	46	3	2	
1984-85	40	2	2	2
1985-86	34	6	2	1+1
1986-87	34	1	4	
1987-88	44	1	5	6
1988-89	45	7	4	3
1989-90	44	10	4	3
1990-91	44	1	2	2
	499+1	39	38	25+1

MOST GOALS IN A CAREER

Trevor Senior - 154 (1983-92)

Year	League	FA Cup	Lge Cup	Others
1983-84	36	1	4	
1984-85	22	4	1	
1985-86	27	4		
1986-87	17	1	6	
1988-89	16	4		4
1989-90	14	4	3	
1990-91	15			
1991-92	7			
Total	154	18	14	4

Current leading goalscorer: Jimmy Quinn - 73 (1992-95)

RECORD TRANSFER FEE RECEIVED

Amount	Club	Player	Date
£1,575,000	Newcastle Utd	Shaka Hislop	08/95
£1,100,000*	Q.P.R.	Simon Osborn	07/95
£500,000	Wimbledon	Keith Curle	10/88
£320,000	Watford	Trevor Senior	7/87

*Included Michael Meaker coming from Q.P.R.

RECORD TRANSFER FEE PAID

Amount	Club	Player	Date
£250,000	Watford	Lee Nogan	8/95
£250,000	Huddersfield	Craig Maskell	8/90
£220,000	Leicester City	Steve Moran	11/87
£82,500	Brentford	Terry Hurlock	2/86

MANAGERS

Name	Seasons	Best	Worst
Harry Matthews	1902-22	13(3S)	20(3S)
Arthur Chadwick	1923-25	14(3S)	19(3S)
Angus Wylie	1926-31	14(2)	1(3S)
Joe Smith	1931-35	2(3S)	4(3S)
Billy Butler	1935-39	3(3S)	6(3S)
John Cochrane	1939		
Joe Edelston	1939-47	9(3S)	9(3S)
Ted Drake	1947-52	2(3S)	10(3S)
Jack Smith	1952-55	8(3S)	18(3S)
Harry Johnson	1955-63	4(3S)	20(3)
Roy Bentley	1963-69	4(3)	14(3)
Jack Mansell	1969-72	8(3)	16(4)
Charlie Hurley	1972-77	21(3)	6(4)
Maurice Evans	1977-84	7(3)	8(4)
Ian Branfoot	1984-89	13(2)	18(3)
Ian Porterfield	1989-91	10(3)	15(3)
Mark McGhee	1991-94	1(2/3)	15(3)
M Gooding & J Quinn	1994-	2(1)	2(1)

LONGEST LEAGUE RUNS

of undefeated matches:	19 (1973)	of league matches w/out a win:	14 (1927)
of undefeated home matches:	55 (1933-36)	of undefeated away matches:	11 (1985)
without home win:	8 (1954, 1991)	without an away win:	21 (1952-53)
of league wins:	13 (1985, record for start of a season)	of home wins:	19 (1931-32)
of league defeats:	6 (1971)	of away wins:	7 (1951-52, 1985)

READING

PLAYERS NAME Honours	Ht	Wt	Birthdate	Birthplace Transfers	Contract Date	Clubs	League	L/Cup	FA Cup	Other	Lge	L/C	FAC	Oth
G O A L K E E P E R S														
Simon Sheppard	6.4	14.13	07.08.73	Clevedon	30.04.91	Watford (T)	23	4	1	2				
E: Y.5, S.				Loan	17.03.94	Scarborough	9							
					02.09.94	Reading								
D E F E N D E R S														
David Bass	5.11	12.7	29.11.74	Frimley	14.07.93	Reading (T)	7+2							
Alan Carey	5.7	10.2	21.08.75	Greenwich		Reading (T)	0+3							
				Loan	06.03.95	Weymouth								
Jeff Hopkins	6.0	12.11	14.04.64	Swansea	10.09.81	Fulham (A)	213+6	26	12	3	4	2		
W: 16, u21.5, Y. Div.2'94.				£240,000	17.08.88	Crystal Palace	70	7	4	12	2	1	1	
				Loan	24.10.91	Plymouth Argyle	8			1				
				Free	05.03.92	Bristol Rovers	4+2							
				Free	13.07.92	Reading	96+3	8+1	6+1	6+2	3	1		
Dylan Kerr	5.9	11.4	14.01.67	Valetta (Malta)	01.09.84	Sheffield Wed (J)								
Div.2'94.				Free		Arcadia Shepherds								
				Free	08.02.89	Leeds United	6+7	2	1	0+4				
Loan 22.08.91 Doncaster Rovers 7 Lge App. 1gl.				Loan	31.12.91	Blackpool	12			1	1			
				£75,000	15.07.93	Reading	80+1	8	2	3+1	3			
Keith McPherson	5.11	11.0	11.09.63	Greenwich	12.09.81	West Ham U. (A)	1							
FAYC'81. Div.4'87. Div.2'94.				Loan	30.09.85	Cambridge United	11				1			
				£15,000	23.01.86	Northampton Town	182	9	12	13	8	1		
				P.E.	24.08.90	Reading	172+5	10+1	10+1	20+1	7			
Steve Swales	5.8	10.0	26.12.73	Whitby	03.08.92	Scarborough (T)	51+3		5	3				
				£70,000	08.95	Reading								
Dariusz Wdowczyk	5.11	11.11	21.09.62	Warsaw		Legia Warsaw								
Polish Int.				£450,000		Celtic	112+4	11	13	6+1	4		2	
				Free	.08.94	Reading	37+1	2	1	3				
Adrian Williams	6.2	12.6	16.08.71	Reading	04.03.89	Reading (T)	160+5	15	14	14	12	1	2	2
W: 1. Div.2'94.														
M I D F I E L D														
Andrew Bernal	5.10	12.5	16.07.66	Canberra		Sporting Giion								
					24.09.87	Ipswich Town	4+5			0+2				
via Sydney Olympic to				£30,000	26.07.9	Reading	33	3	1	3				
Mick Gooding	5.9	10.7	12.04.59	Newcastle		Bishop Auckland								
Div.3'81'89. Div.2'94.					18.07.79	Rotherham United	90+12	9	3		10	3		
					24.12.82	Chesterfield	12							
					09.09.83	Rotherham United	149+7	18	13	7	32	3	4	
				£18,000	13.08.87	Peterborough United	47	8	1	4	21	2	2	2
				£85,000	20.09.88	Wolverhampton W.	43+1	4		5+1	4			1
				£65,000	26.12.89	Reading	226+5	13	14+1	16	23		2	2
Tom Jones	5.10	11.7	07.10.64	Aldershot		Chelsea (A)								
E: S-P.1. Div.2'94.				Free		Farnborough Town			2					
						Weymouth								
				£30,000		Aberdeen	14+14		1+2		3			
					27.09.88	Swindon Town	162+6	14+4	10	11	12			
				£125,000	09.07.92	Reading	50+8	3	3	1	2			
Stuart Lovell	5.10	11.0	09.01.72	Sydney (Aus)	13.07.90	Reading (T)	124+27	9	5+5	7+3	45	3	2	2
Div.2'94.														
Michael Meaker	5.11	11.5	18.08.71	Greenford	07.02.90	Q.P.R. (T)	14+12	1	1	0+1	1	1		
W: u21.2.				Loan	20.11.91	Plymouth Argyle	4			1				
				£550,000	08.95	Reading								
Phil Parkinson	6.0	11.6	01.12.67	Chorley	07.12.85	Southampton (A)								
Div.2'94.				£12,000	08.03.88	Bury	133+12	6+1	4	13	5		1	1
				£37,500	10.07.92	Reading	105+7	9	6	4+2	6	1	1	
Martin Williams	5.9	11.12	12.07.73	Luton		Leicester City (T)								
				Free	13.09.91	Luton Town	12+28	1	0+1	2+1	2			
				Free	08.95	Reading								
F O R W A R D S														
Michael Gilkes	5.8	10.10	20.07.65	Hackney		Leicester City (J)								
FMC'88. FLgXI'88. Div.2'94.				Free	10.07.84	Reading	285+32	22+4	28+2	26+2	42	6	1	2
				Loan	28.01.92	Chelsea	0+1			0+1				
				Loan	04.03.92	Southampton	4+2							
Chris Jimmy Lambert	5.7	10.4	14.09.73	Henley	03.07.92	Reading (J)	13+31	0+1	4	2+3	4			1
Trevor Morley	5.11	12.1	20.03.61	Nottingham		Derby County (A)								
E: S-P.6. Sthrn Lge'82. Div.4'87.				Free		Corby Town								
				£10,000		Nuneaton Borough			3					
				£20,000	21.06.85	Northampton Town	107	10	6	7	39	4	2	
				£175,000	22.01.88	Manchester City	69+3	7	1	2	18	3		
				£500,000	28.12.89	West Ham United	159+19	10+1	14+5	5+1	57	5	7	1
				Free	08.95	Reading								

PLAYERS NAME / Honours	Ht	Wt	Birthdate	Birthplace Transfers	Contract Date	Clubs	League	L/Cup	FA Cup	Other	Lge	L/C	FAC	Oth
							APPEARANCES				GOALS			
Lee Nogan	5.10	11.0	21.05.69	Cardiff	25.03.87	Oxford United (T)	57+7	4+1	2+1	4+1	10		1	1
W: 1, B.1, u21.1.				Loan	25.03.87	Brentford	10+1				2			
				Loan	17.09.87	Southend United	6	2		1	1			1
				£350,000	12.12.91	Watford	97+8	5+2	2	1+2	26	3	1	
				Loan	17.03.94	Southend United	4+1							
				£250,000	13.01.95	Reading	18+2			3	10		2	
Jimmy Quinn	6.0	11.6	18.11.59	Belfast		Oswestry								
NI: 41. Div.2'94				£10,000	31.12.81	Swindon Town	34+15	1+1	5+3	1	10		6	2
				£32,000	15.08.84	Blackburn Rovers	58+13	6+1	4	2	17	2	3	1
				£50,000	19.12.86	Swindon Town	61+3	6	5	10+1	30	8		5
				£210,000	20.06.88	Leicester City	13+18	2+1	0+1	0+1	6			
					17.03.89	Bradford City	35	2		1	13	1		
				£320,000	30.12.89	West Ham United	34+13	3	4+2	1	19	1	2	
				£40,000	05.08.91	Bournemouth	43	4	5	2	19	2	2	1
				£55,000	27.07.92	Reading	119+4	9	7	6+3	57	7	3	6
Michael Murphy	5.10	10.6	05.05.77			Slough Town								
					07.10.94	Reading	0+1							
A D D I T I O N A L C O N T R A C T P L A Y E R S														
(D) Michael Thorp			05.12.75	Wallington		Reading (T)								

TOP GOALSCORER 1994/95
Stuart Lovell

Division One goals (games) . . . . 11 (25+5)
Coca-Cola Cup Goals 1 (4)
F.A. Cup goals 0 (1)
Play off goals 2 (3)
Total . . . . **14 (33+5)**

Total goals for Reading since 13.07.90 . . . . 52 (145+35)

Career total as at June 1st 1995 . . . . 52 (145+35)

PLAYER-MANAGERS
MICK GOODING AND JIMMY QUINN

Date of Birth . . . . 12th April 1959 (MG). 18th November 1959 (JQ).
Place of Birth . . . . Newcastle (MG). Belfast (JQ).
Date of Appointment . . . . January 1995.

PREVIOUS CLUBS
As Manager . . . . None.
As Coach . . . . None.
As a Player . . . . MG - Bishop Auckland, Rotherham (x2), Chesterfield, Peterborough, Wolves, Reading. JQ - Oswestry, Swindon, Blackburn, Leicester, ... Bradford, West Ham, Bournemouth, Reading.

HONOURS
As a Manager
None.
As a Player
MG - Rotherham: Division 3 championship 1983
 Reading: Division 3 championship 1989, Division 2 1994.
JQ - Reading: Division 2 championship 1994.
 International: 49 full caps and 1 B cap for Northern Ireland.

ELM PARK
Norfolk Road, Reading RG3 2EF
Tel: 01734 507 878

Capacity 14,058
Seating 2,242

First game .... v London XI, 05.09.1896.
First floodlit game .... v Racing Club de Paris, 06.10.1954.

ATTENDANCES
Highest .... 33,042 v Brentford, FAC, 19.2.1927.
Lowest .... 1,403 v Orient, FRT, 6.3.1986.

OTHER GROUNDS .... Reading Recreation Ground 1871. Reading CC 1882. Coley Park 1882-89.
.... Caversham CC 1889-96. Elm Park 1896-

MATCHDAY TICKET PRICES

B & D Stand £9.50

C Stand £11

E Stand (Family Area) £8

Terrace £7.50

Ticket Office Telephone no. 01734 507 878

HOW TO GET TO THE GROUND

From the North
From Oxford use A423, A4074 and A4155 and cross railway bridge into Reading, follow signs Newbury (A4) into Castle Hill, turn right into Tilehurst Road. In 0.7 miles turn right into Cranbury Road, turn left, then take 2nd left into Norfolk Road for Reading FC.
From the East
Use motorway (M4) until junction 10, leave motorway and use A329 and A4 into Reading. Follow signs to Newbury into Bath Road. Over railway bridge then take 3rd turning on right into Liebenrood Road. At end turn left then right into Waverley Road, turn right into Norfolk Road for Reading FC.
From the South
Use A33 into Reading then follow signs to Newbury (A4) into Bath Road. Over railway bridge then take third turning on right into Liebenrood Road. Then proceed as from the East.
From the West
Use motorway (M4) until junction 12, leave motorway and follow signs to Reading (A4). In 3.3 miles turn left into Liebenrood Road. Then proceed as from the East.

Car Parking: Space for 300 in Norfolk Road and Tilehurst Road. Only available on season ticket basis.
Nearest Railway Station: Reading (01734 595 911) and bus or Reading West (1o minutes walk).

CLUBCALL
0891 12 10 00

Calls cost 39p per minute cheap rate and 49p per minute at all other times.
Call costings correct at time of going to press.

MATCHDAY PROGRAMME

Programme Editor . . . . Maurice O'Brien.

Number of pages . . . . 48.

Price . . . . £1.50.

Subscriptions . . . . Contact supporters club.

Local Newspapers . . . . Reading Evening Post, Reading Chronicle.

Local Radio Stations . . . . Radio Berkshire, Radio 210.

SHEFFIELD UNITED

(The Blades)

ENDSLEIGH LEAGUE DIVISION 1

SPONSORED BY: S H WARD & CO LTD (WARDS BREWERY)

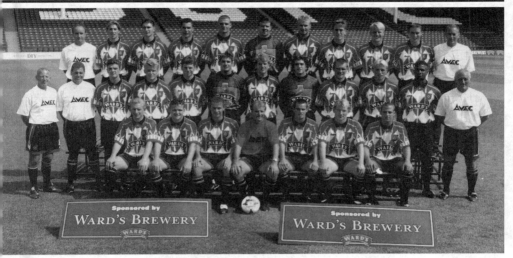

Back Row (L-R): Denis Circuit (Physio), Rob Scott, Doug Hodgson, Brian Gayle, Mark Foran, Alan Kelly, Jostein Flo, Dave Tuttle, Paul Rogers, Andy Scott, Brian Eastick (Coach). **Middle Row:** Derek French (Physio), John Greaves (Kitman), Mark Blount, Phil Starbuck, Carl Veart, Billy Mercer, Glyn Hodges, Salvatore Bibbo, Charlie Hartfield, Roger Nilsen, Nathan Blake, Geoff Taylor (Asst.Manager). **Front Row:** John Reed, Paul Holland, Dane, Whitehouse, Dave Bassett (Manager), Mitch Ward, Kevin Gage, Ross Davidson.

SHEFFIELD UNITED
FORMED IN 1889
TURNED PROFESSIONAL IN 1889
LTD COMPANY IN 1889

CHAIRMAN: R Brealey

DIRECTORS
A H Laver, B Proctor, D Dooley, J Plant, JP
SECRETARY
David Capper (0114 273 8956)
COMMERCIAL MANAGER
Andy Daykin

MANAGER: Dave Bassett
ASSISTANT MANAGER: Geoff Taylor

COACHES: Brian Eastick, Wally Downes

YOUTH TEAM MANAGER
Keith Mincher
PHYSIOTHERAPIST
Denis Circuit

STATISTICIAN FOR THE DIRECTORY
Andrew Treherne

Following relegation from the Premier League, hopes were high that United could make an immediate return to the Premier League. Carl Bradshaw had departed for Norwich City, and United signed the two Australians Carl Veart and Doug Hodgson, who had impressed on the club's summer tour.

The opening game saw a comfortable 3-0 win over Watford, and then a home defeat by Notts County. This was to be typical of the season ahead: good performances against the better teams in the division, but costly defeats against the strugglers. A slow start saw United mainly in the lower half of the table.

The end of October saw United in nineteenth place, and eliminated from the Coca-Cola Cup by a last minute own goal against Bolton Wanderers. (This after an excellent 6-1 aggregate win over Stockport County, where United scored three times in the final nine minutes of the first leg to seal the tie.) The League form suddenly showed a dramatic improvement, and a run of fourteen games without defeat saw United in a play-off spot. The highlight of this run was probably a 6-3 away win at Luton, including two goals from fullback and player of the season Kevin Gage. Not surprisingly, the run ended with a defeat at Bristol City.

With a 2-0 home victory over Tranmere Rovers on 7th March, United moved into third place and seemed certain to be in the play-offs. This position was maintained with a home victory over Charlton Athletic in mid March, but then they had a run of eight matches without a win, picking up only five points. The final match against Grimsby Town saw the play-offs out of reach, and so it was switched back to the Saturday. An improved performance saw a 3-1 victory, but all too late as the team finished in a disappointing eighth place.

The cup competitions were once again a disappointment. The last minute exit from the Coca-Cola Cup was followed by elimination in the Group section of the Anglo Italian Cup. Indeed the first match against Udinese saw three United players dismissed. A close defeat meant that qualification was unlikely, and the remaining games were used to blood some of the youngsters, who performed well.

Incredibly, in the FA Cup, United were once again paired with Manchester United in the third round. In a bruising encounter, Charlie Hartfield was sent off after thirteen minutes for cuffing Eric Cantona, who was lucky to remain on the pitch himself. The remaining ten men fought valiantly, but were sunk by late goals from Hughes and Cantona.

The players were undoubtedly hampered by the demolition of the John Street Stand, the return to a three sided ground at Bramall Lane leading to a lack of atmosphere. The coming season will once again be tough, as the new stand will not be finished until the New Year, and the team will face a fierce battle to return to the Premier League.   **ANDREW TREHERNE.**

SHEFFIELD UNITED

Division One: 8th   **FA Cup:** 3rd Round   **Coca-Cola Cup:** 3rd Round   **Anglo Italian Cup:** Group B

M	DATE	COMP.	VEN	OPPONENTS	RESULT	H/T	LP	GOAL SCORERS/GOAL TIMES	ATT.
1	A 13	EL	H	Watford	W 3-0	2-0	2	Flo 7, Ward 43,56	17,277
2	24	AIC	H	Udinese	L 1-2	1-1		Littlejohn 35	7,497
3	27	EL	H	Notts County	L 1-3	0-2	15	Whitehouse 63 (pen)	15,301
4	30	EL	A	Charlton Athletic	D 1-1	1-1	13	Rogers 16	(8,678)
5	S 3	EL	A	Tranmere Rovers	L 1-2	0-2	18	Hodges 64 (pen)	(7,253)
6	6	AIC	A	Piacenza	D 2-2	1-1		Carr 7, Gammon 84	(4,744)
7	10	EL	H	Bolton Wanderers	W 3-1	1-0	13	Veart 11, 49, Davison 89	14,904
8	13	EL	H	Sunderland	D 0-0	0-0	16		15,239
9	17	EL	A	Reading	L 0-1	0-0	20		(9,036)
10	20	CC 2/1	A	Stockport County	W 5-1	1-0		Whitehouse 31, 87 (pen), 90, Flo 5,681	(5,109)
11	24	EL	A	Port Vale	W 2-0	0-0	12	Whitehouse 68 (pen) Blake 77	(9,324)
12	27	CC 2/2	H	Stockport County	W 1-0	1-0		Ascott 33	5,065
13	O 1	EL	H	Oldham Athletic	W 2-0	1-0	8	Reed 4, Flo 48	14,223
14	5	AIC	H	Ancona	D 3-3	2-1		Ward 6 (pen), Battersby 24, A. Scott 80	1,827
15	8	EL	A	Grimsby Town	D 0-0	0-0	10		(8,930)
16	16	EL	H	Barnsley	D 0-0	0-0	14		12,317
17	18	EL	A	West Brom Albion	L 0-1	0-0	14		(12,715)
18	22	EL	H	Luton Town	L 1-3	1-1	17	Blake 17	13,317
19	25	CC 3	H	Bolton Wanderers	L 1-2	0-1		Blake 47	6,939
20	29	EL	A	Millwall	L 1-2	0-0	19	Blake 66	(8,445)
21	N 2	EL	A	Stoke City	D 1-1	1-0	18	Gage 15	(11,556)
22	5	EL	H	Bristol City	W 3-0	2-0	15	Hartfield 5, Gage 10, Veart 74	11,568
23	12	EL	H	Derby County	W 2-1	0-0	9	Blake 47, Whitehouse 59	15,001
24	15	AIC	A	Cesena	W 4-1	1-1		A. Scott 35,52, Hawthorne 66, Reed 69	(400)
25	20	EL	A	Burnley	L 2-4	1-1	12	Winstanley 44 (og), A.Scott 82	(11,475)
26	26	EL	H	Southend United	W 2-0	1-0	10	Whitehouse 41 (pen), Veart 64	13,405
27	D 3	EL	A	Luton Town	W 6-3	2-0	6	Gage 12, 24, Veart 52, 88, Hodges 69, A.Scott 82	(8,516)
28	10	EL	H	West Brom Albion	W 2-0	1-0	7	Veart 39, A.Scott 72	13,891
29	17	EL	A	Watford	D 0-0	0-0	6		(8,919)
30	26	EL	H	Middlesbrough	D 1-1	0-0	7	Hodges 67	20,693
31	27	EL	A	Swindon Town	W 3-1	1-0	6	Reed 11, Bodin 66 (og), Littlejohn 78	(11,007)
32	31	EL	H	Portsmouth	W 3-1	0-1	5	Blake 46, 47, A.Scott 80	13,467
33	J 2	EL	A	Wolverhampton Wand.	D 2-2	0-0	5	Blake 59, 69	(27,809)
34	9	FAC 3	H	Manchester United	L 0-2	0-0			22,322
35	14	EL	H	Millwall	D 1-1	0-1	5	Gage 47	12,650
36	21	EL	A	Bristol City	L 1-2	0-0	6	Gayle 65	(10,211)
37	F 4	EL	A	Derby County	W 3-2	1-1	6	Veart 8, 84, Whitehouse 54	(15,882)
38	11	EL	H	Stoke City	D 1-1	1-1	7	Starbuck 6	13,900
39	18	EL	A	Southend United	W 3-1	1-1	6	Blake 44, 47, Veart 85	(4,700)
40	21	EL	H	Burnley	W 2-0	1-0	5	Blake 44, 90	13,349
41	15	EL	A	Oldham Athletic	D 3-3	2-2	4	Rogers 7, Blake 11, Flo 82	(9,640)
42	M 4	EL	H	Port Vale	D 1-1	0-0	5	Veart 52	13,647
43	7	EL	H	Tranmere Rovers	W 2-0	1-0	3	Black 2, Blake 57	14,127
44	11	EL	A	Notts. County	L 1-2	0-1	5	Beesley 64	(11,102)
45	18	EL	H	Charlton Athletic	W 2-1	0-0	3	Glo 60, Beesley 74	11,862
46	22	EL	A	Bolton Wanderers	D 1-1	1-1	5	Blake 37	(16,756)
47	25	EL	H	Reading	D 1-1	0-0	6	Blake 52	19,241
48	A 1	EL	A	Sunderland	L 0-1	0-0	6		(17,259)
49	8	EL	A	Portsmouth	L 0-1	0-0	7		(8,216)
50	15	EL	H	Swindon Town	D 2-2	0-1	7	Rogers 47, Hodges 85	12,217
51	17	EL	A	Middlesbrough	D 1-1	1-1	9	Blake 17	(23,225)
52	22	EL	H	Wolverhampton Wand.	D 3-3	1-0	8	Whitehouse 15 (pen), Faran 72, Flo 90	16,714
53	29	EL	A	Barnsley	L 1-2	1-1	8	Rogers 41	(10,844)
54	M 6	EL	H	Grimsby Town	W 3-1	2-1	8	Whitehouse 38, Black 41, Flo 85	14,323
55									
56									
57									
58									
59									
60									

Best Home League Attendance: 20,693 v Middlesbrough   **Smallest:** 11,568 v Bristol City   **Av Home Att:** 14,462

Goal Scorers:

League (74): Blake 17, Veart 11, Whitehouse 7 (4 pens), Flo 6, Gage 5, A. Scott 4, Hodges 4 (1 pen), Rogers 4, Ward 4, Ward 2, Reed 2, Opponents 2, Beesley 2, Black 2, Davison, Harfield, Littlejohn, Gayle, Starbuck, Foran
C/Cola Cup (7): Whitehouse 3 (1 pen), Flo 2, A Scott, Blake
FA Cup (0): Saunders, Yorke
Anglo-Ital. (10): A Scott 3, Littlejohn, Carr, Gannon, Ward (pen), Battersby, Hawthorne, Reed

Compared with 1993-94: -5,099

Kelly A.	Gage K.	Nilsen R.	Rogers P.	Gayle B.	Beesley P.	Ward M.	Flo J.	Blake N.	Hodges G.	Whitehouse D.	Hartfield C.	Littlejohn A.	Bibbo S.	Tracey S.	Hoyland J.	Veart C.	Scott A.	Marshall S.	Blount M.	Davison R.	Reed J.	Gannon J.	Foran M	Mercer W.	Starbuck P.	Referee	
	4		6				8		10*		12		S													J. Rushton	1
2•	4								10†		8†				5		14									F. Arena	2
2	4						8†		10																	K. Lupton	3
2	4						8		10																	P. Foakes	4
2	4						12		10		8•									9*	14					K. Leach	5
															6		3	4		9	8					J. Parker	6
2	4								10								12			14	7•					T. West	7
2	4								10*								12			14	7•					J. Lloyd	8
2	4															14	12				7*	10				C. Wilkes	9
2	4								9						8					10•	12					T. Lunt	10
2	4								10			S				14					7	8				G. Cain	11
	4								9*			S			6		3				8	8	5			G. Singh	12
2	4								10			S					3			7*	8					A. Dawson	13
												1			7					11			14			E. Pellegrino	14
2	4								10			S					3			7*	8					K. Breen	15
2	4								10		14						3•			7*	8			S		J. Winter	16
2	4								10•								3				8			S		E. Wolstenholme	17
2	4•								10*								3			7	8			S		J. Parker	18
2					6						4		S				3			7						P. Vanes	19
2											4						S			7*				S	12	M. Bailey	20
2	7		5								4						12							S	9	K. Lynch	21
2	7										4						14							S	9	W. Burns	22
2	7									12	4						14						1	S	9•	K. Lupton	23
											4		S			1	3		5	7*	4						24
2	7						10*		12		4						14							S	9	P. Vanes	25
2	7		6						14	10•	4						12							S	9*	D. Allison	26
2	7		6						14	10	4						11•							S	9	P. Foakes	27
2	7		6						10	4*	4						11•							S	9	K. Lynch	28
2	7		6						10•		4						11							S	9	M. Pierce	29
2	7		6†				S		10		4						11							S	12	J. Rushton	30
2	7		6						9		4						3			11*		S		S	8	A. Flood	31
2	7						S		10		4						6							S	9*	P. Rejer	32
2	7						S		10		4						11*							S	9	P. Wright	33
2	7								14	10*	4†						11							S	12	R. Hart	34
2	7		6						10		4						11							S	9•	P. Harrison/K. Powell	35
2†	7		12						14	10*	4						11•						1		9	P. Alcock	36
	7		6						10			S					12			4			1		9*	T. Heilbron	37
	7		6						10								12			4				S	9	P. Richards	38
	7		6						10								12	3	S	4	5			S	9*	G. Singh	39
2	7		6						10								5	3		4*				S	14	J. Brandwood	40
2	7		6						10								14	3		4*				S		R. Poulain	41
2	7		6						12		4													S	9*	J. Holbrook	42
2	7		6						9		4								12					S		E. Wolstenholme	43
2	7		6						9		4							5						S		S. Dunn	44
2	7		6						9							12				8*				S		J. Watson	45
2	7		6						14								11•									D. Allison	46
2	7		6						9*		4						12								8•	J. Winter	47
2	7		6							14	4•						12									S. Mathieson	48
2	7		6						10	12	4*						14						7•			P. Alcock	49
2	7		6						9	10							12	4							8•	E. Lomas	50
2	7								9	10							12						6			W. Burns	51
	7					2			14	10					12		9						6			N. Barry	52
	7		6			S	4		10†								2				5					J. Watson	53
	4		6				8		10				S				12									K. Lupton	54

Kelly A.	Gage K.	Nilsen R.	Rogers P.	Gayle B.	Beesley P.	Ward M.	Flo J.	Blake N.	Hodges G.	Whitehouse D.	Hartfield C.	Littlejohn A.	Bibbo S.	Tracey S.	Hoyland J.	Veart C.	Scott A.	Marshall S.	Blount M.	Davison R.	Reed J.	Gannon J.	Foran M	Mercer W.	Starbuck P.		
40	44		26		25		20		23								18		4	1	11	12	4	3	20	League Appearances	
			1		7		5		2							2	19		1	2	1				3	League Sub Appearances	
2	2		1		2		1									2	2			1	1	1+1	1		0+1	C/Cola Cup Appearances	
1	1		0+1		1		1									1			2	2	1	2	0+1			FA Cup Appearances	
																		2	2	1	2	0+1			Anglo/Ital Appearances	

Also Played: Black 10(42,43,44,45•),11(47,48,49),14(50),S(51),12(52,53),7(54), Tuttle 5(47,48•,49,51,52,54) Davidson 3*(2),2*(14),2(54), Evans S(6,9,10,24), Foreman 2(6),12(2,24),S(4,14) Hodgson 6(2),6*(10)12(18)S(12), Johnston S(6) Anthony S(2,53),10(14),8(24),12(40) Zivkovic S(6) Carr 10(6), Fickling 5(6,14),2(12),12(19),6(24), Spooner S(14), Scott 7(6),12(14,31),14(9),11(24), Letts S(14,24), Hawthorne 6(4,14),10(24), Butterfield S(24), Battersby12(6),9(14,24), Pearson S(24) Players on Loan: Marshall (Arsenal) Black (Nottingham Forest)

SHEFFIELD UNITED

CLUB RECORDS

BIGGEST VICTORIES
League: 10-0 v Port Vale (a), Div 2, 10.12.1892 (The only time a club has scored 10 Lge goals away from home)
10-0 v Burnley, Division 1, 19.1.1929
(Most goals) 11-2 v Cardiff City, 1.1.1926
F.A. Cup: 5-0 v Corinthians, Round 1, 10.1.1925
5-0 v Newcastle, Round 1, 10.1.1914
5-0 v Barrow, Round 3, 7.1.1956
League Cup: 4-0 v Fulham, Round 1, 25.9.1961
5-1 v Grimsby, Round 2, 26.10.1982
5-1 v Rotherham United, Round 1, 3.9.1985

BIGGEST DEFEATS
League: 1-8 v Arsenal, Division 1, 12.4.1930
2-9 v Arsenal, Division 1, 24.12.1932
3-10 v Middlesbrough, Division 1, 18.11.1933
0-7 v Tottenham Hotspur, Division 2, 12.11.1949
F.A. Cup: 0-13 v Bolton Wanderers, Round 2, 1.2.1890
League Cup: 0-5 v West Ham United, Round 5, 17.11.1971

MOST POINTS
3 points a win: 96, Division 4, 1981-82
2 points a win: 60, Division 2, 1952-53

MOST GOALS
102, Division 1, 1925-26.
Johnson 23, Tunstall 20, Boyle 13, Gillespie 12, Menlove 12, Mercer 8,Partridge 6, Hoyland 3, Roxborough 1, Waugh 1, Longworth 1, Grew 1, og 1.

MOST FIRST CLASS MATCHES IN A SEASON
61 (46 League, 7 FA Cup, 5 League Cup, 3 Sherpa Van Trophy) 1988-89

MOST LEAGUE GOALS CONCEDED
101, Division 1, 1933-34

MOST LEAGUE WINS
27, Division 4, 1981-82

MOST LEAGUE DRAWS
18, Division 1, 1920-21, Premier Division 1993-94

MOST LEAGUE DEFEATS
26, Division 1, 1975-76

INDIVIDUAL CLUB RECORDS

MOST GOALS IN A SEASON
Jimmy Dunne 46 (League 41, FAC 5) 1930-31
4 goals once=4; 3 goals 5 times=15; 2 goals 4 times=8; 1 goal 19 times=19.
Previous holder: Jimmy Dunne 36, 1928-29.

MOST GOALS IN A MATCH
5. Harry Hammond v Bootle, 8-3, Division 2, 26.11.1892
5. Harry Johnson v West Ham Utd, 6-2, Division 1, 26.12.1927

OLDEST PLAYER
Jimmy Hagan, 39 years 236 days v Derby County, 14.9.1957

YOUNGEST PLAYER
Julian Broddle, 17 years 62 days v Halifax Town, 2.1.1982

MOST CAPPED PLAYER
Billy Gillespie (Northern Ireland) 25

BEST PERFORMANCES

League: 1981-82: Matches played 46, Won 27, Drawn 15, Lost 4, Goals for 94,Goals against 41, Points 96. First in Division 4.
Highest: Division 1 Champions.
F.A. Cup: 1898-99: 1st rnd. Burnley 2-2, 2-0; 2nd rnd. Preston North End 2-2,2-1; 3rd rnd. Notts County 1-0; Semi-final Liverpool 2-2, 4-4, 1-0; Final Derby 4-1.
1901-02: 1st rnd. Northampton 2-0; 2nd rnd. Bolton Wanderers 2-1; 3rd rnd. Newcastle Utd. 1-1, 2-1; Semi-final Derby County 1-1, 1-1, 1-0; Final Southampton 1-1, 2-1.
1914-15: 3rd rnd. Blackpool 2-1; 4th rnd. Liverpool 1-0; 5th rnd. Bradford 1-0; 6th rnd. Oldham 0-0, 3-0; Semi-final Bolton Wanderers 2-1; Final Chelsea 3-0.
1924-25: 3rd rnd. Corinthians 5-0; 4th rnd. Sheffield Wednesday 3-2; 5th rnd.Everton 1-0; 6th rnd. West Bromwich Albion 2-0; Semi-final Southampton 2-0;Final Cardiff 1-0.
League Cup: 1961-62: 1st rnd. Fulham 1-1, 4-0; 2nd rnd. Newcastle 2-2, 2-0; 3rd rnd. Portsmouth 1-0; 4th rnd. Bye; 5th rnd Blackpool 0-0, 0-2.
1966-67: 1st rnd. Bye; 2nd rnd. Sunderland 1-1, 1-0; 3rd rnd. Burnley 2-0; 4th rnd. Walsall 2-1; 5th rnd. Birmingham 2-3.
1971-72: 1st rnd. Bye; 2nd rnd. Fulham 3-0; 3rd rnd. York City 3-2; 4th rnd.Arsenal 0-0, 2-0; 5th rnd. West Ham United 0-5.

DIVISIONAL RECORD

	Played	Won	Drawn	Lost	For	Against	Points
Division 1/P	2,318	861	552	905	3,499	3,707	2,325
Division 2/1	1,124	494	278	352	1,888	1,505	1,300
Division 3	230	100	49	81	366	300	317
Division 4	46	27	15	4	94	41	96
Total	**3,718**	**1,482**	**894**	**1,342**	**5,847**	**5,553**	**4,100**

ADDITIONAL INFORMATION
Club colours: Red/white stripes with white diamonds shirts, black shorts, red/black socks.
Change colours: Yellow and purple halved shirts, yellow shorts, yellow/purple socks.

Reserves League
Pontins League Division 1.

RECORDS AND STATISTICS

COMPETITIONS

Div 1/P	Div.2/1	Div.3	Div.4	Texaco	Watney
1893-1934	1892-93	1979-81	1981-82	1972-73	1970
1945-49	1934-39	1982-84		1973-74	1972
1953-56	1949-53	1988-89		1974-75	
1961-68	1956-61				A/Scot
1971-76	1968-71			A/Ital	1975-76
1990-94	1976-79			1994-95	1977-78
	1984-88				1978-79
	1989-90				1979-80
	1994-				1980-81

HONOURS

Div.1	Div.2	Div.4	FA Cup
1897-98	1952-53	1981-82	1899
			1902
			1915
			1925

MOST APPEARANCES

JOE SHAW 689 (1948-66)

Year	League	FA Cup	Lge Cup
1948-49	19		
1949-50	37	3	
1950-51	36		
1951-52	39	5	
1952-53	42	3	
1953-54	35	2	
1954-55	41	1	
1955-56	19		
1956-57	30	1	
1957-58	41	4	
1958-59	41	6	
1959-60	39	3	
1960-61	42	7	1
1961-62	37	5	5
1962-63	40	3	1
1963-64	41	3	
1964-65	25	3	
1965-66	27	2	
	631	51	7

MOST GOALS IN A CAREER

J JOHNSON - 223 (1919-31)

Year	League	FA Cup
1919-20	12	1
1920-21	12	
1921-22	17	
1922-23	17	1
1923-24	15	
1924-25	16	5
1925-26	23	1
1926-27	23	1
1927-28	33	9
1928-29	33	
1929-30	3	
1930-31	1	
Total	205	18

Current leading goalscorer: Dane Whitehouse - 33 (1989-95)

MANAGERS

Name	Seasons	Best	Worst
J Wolstinholm	1898-99	16(1)	16(1)
J Nicholson	1899-32	2(1)	20(1)
J Davison	1932-52	6(1)	11(2)
R Freeman	1952-54	13(1)	1(2)
J Mercer	1954-59	22(1)	7(2)
J Harris	1959-68	5(1)	4(2)
A Rowley	1968-69	9(2)	9(2)
J Harris	1969-73	10(1)	6(2)
K Furphy	1973-76	6(1)	13(1)
J Sirrell	1976-78	22(1)	11(2)
C Coldwell	1978	12(2)	12(2)
H Haslam	1978-81	20(2)	12(3)
M Peters	1981	21(3)	21(3)
I Porterfield	1981-86	7(2)	1(4)
B McEwan	1986-88	9(2)	9(2)
D Bassett	1988-	9(1)	2(3)

RECORD TRANSFER FEE RECEIVED

Amount	Club	Player	Date
£2,700,000	Leeds United	Brian Deane	7/93
£750,000	Notts County	Tony Agana	11/91
£575,000	Chelsea	Vinny Jones	9/91
£400,000	Leeds United	Alex Sabella	7/80

RECORD TRANSFER FEE PAID

Amount	Club	Player	Date
£700,000	Ipswich Town	Brain Gayle	9/91
£650,000	Leeds United	Vinny Jones	9/90
£375,000	Leyton Orient	Paul Beesley	7/90
£250,000	Bury	Jamie Hoyland	6/90

LONGEST LEAGUE RUNS

of undefeated matches:	22 (2.9.1899 - 20.1.1900)	of league matches w/out a win:	19 (27.9.1975 - 14.2.1976)
of undefeated home matches:	27 (31.8.1936 - 6.11.1937)	of undefeated away matches:	11 (3.12.1892 - 30.10.1893)
without home win:	10 (26.3.1949 - 22.10.1949)	without an away win:	20 (19.4.1975 - 14.4.1976)
of league wins:	8 (6.2.1893-12.4.1893, 5.9.1903-31.10.1903)	of home wins:	11 (30.4.1960 - 3.12.1960)
	(1.2.1958 - 5.4.1958, 14.9.1960 - 22.10.1960)		
of league defeats:	7 (19.8.1975 - 23.9.1975)	of away wins:	6 (10.12.1891 - 12.4.1892)

SHEFFIELD UNITED

PLAYERS NAME Honours	Ht	Wt	Birthdate	Birthplace Transfers	Contract Date	Clubs	League	L/Cup	FA Cup	Other	Lge	L/C	FAC	Oth
G O A L K E E P E R S														
Salvatore Bibbo			24.08.74	Basingstoke		Bournemouth (T)								
via Fisher Ath. & Crawley T. to				Free	18.08.93	Sheffield United				2				
				Loan	10.02.95	Chesterfield	0+1							
Alan Kelly	6.2	12.5	11.08.68	Preston	25.09.85	Preston N.E. (T)	142	1	8	13				
Ei: 3, u23.1, u21.1, Y.				£150,000	24.07.92	Sheffield United	99+2	6	9					
Billy Mercer	6.1	11.0	22.05.69	Liverpool	21.08.87	Liverpool (T)								
					16.02.89	Rotherham United	104	12	12	10				
				£75,000	12.10.94	Sheffield United	3							
				Loan	21.03.95	Nottingham Forest								
Simon Tracey	6.0	12.0	09.12.67	Woolwich	03.02.86	Wimbledon (A)	1			1				
				£7,500	19.10.88	Sheffield United	141+2	7	10	7				
				Loan	28.10.94	Manchester City	3							
				Loan	03.01.95	Norwich City	1		2					
D E F E N D E R S														
Mark Blount			05.01.74	Derby		Derby County (T)								
via Gresley Rovers (Free) to				£12,500	11.02.94	Sheffield United	4+1			2				
Ross Davidson	5.10	11.6	13.11.73	Chertsey		Walton & Hersham								
					05.06.93	Sheffield United	1			2				
Mark Foran	6.4	13.12	30.10.73	Aldershot	03.11.90	Millwall (T)								
Loan Slough Town, 08.92, 1 FAC App.				£25,000	28.08.93	Sheffield United	4	1		0+1	1			
				Loan	26.08.94	Rotherham United	3							
Kevin Gage	5.9	12.8	21.04.64	Chiswick	04.01.82	Wimbledon (A)	135+33	7+2	8+3	0+1	15	1	1	
E: Y.5. Div.4'83.				£100,000	17.07.87	Aston Villa	113+2	13	9	8	8	3	1	
				£150,000	15.11.91	Sheffield United	105+5	6	10+2	1	7			
Brian Gayle	6.1	12.7	06.03.65	Kingston	31.10.84	Wimbledon (A)	76+7	7	8	2	3	1	1	
				£325,000	06.07.88	Manchester City	55	8	2	1	3			
				£330,000	19.01.90	Ipswich Town	58	3	0+1		4			
				£750,000	17.09.91	Sheffield United	112	9	10	1	10		1	1
Charles Hartfield	6.0	12.0	04.09.71	Lambeth	20.09.89	Arsenal (T)								
E: Y.4.				Free	06.08.91	Sheffield United	44+10	2+1	4	1	1			
Roger Nilsen	5.9	11.8	08.08.69	Norway		Viking Stavanger								
Norweigan Int.				£550,000	02.11.93	Sheffield United	54+1	1	1+1					
David Tuttle	6.1	12.0	06.02.72	Reading	08.02.90	Tottenham H. (T)	10+3	3+1		1				1
E: Y.12. FAYC'90.				Loan	21.01.93	Peterborough Utd	7							
				£350,000	01.08.93	Sheffield United	37	1	1					
M I D F I E L D														
Graham Anthony	5.7	9.7	09.08.75	South Shields	07.07.93	Sheffield Utd (T)	0+1			2				
John Gannon	5.8	10.10	18.12.66	Wimbledon	19.12.84	Wimbledon (A)	13+3	1+1		1	2			
Loan Crewe A. 19.12.86, 14+1 Lge, 1 Oth App.				Free	23.02.89	Sheffield United	150+12	13+1	13	6	6			1
				Loan	05.11.93	Middlesbrough	6+1			2				
Paul Holland	5.11	12.4	08.07.73	Lincoln	04.07.91	Mansfield Town (J)	149	11	7	9	25	3		
ESFAu18.4				£250,000	08.95	Sheffield United								
John Reed	5.6	8.11	27.08.72	Rotherham	03.07.90	Sheffield Utd (T)	11+2	1		1	2			1
Loan Scarborough, 10.01.94, 14 Lge App, 5 gls.				Loan	26.09.91	Scarborough	5+1	1						
Loan Darlington, 19.03.93, 8+2 Lge App., 2 gls.				Loan	23.09.93	Mansfield Town	12+1		1	3	2			2
Paul Rogers	6.0	11.9	21.03.65	Portsmouth		Sutton United			13				1	
E: S-P 6. ILP'85'86.				£35,000	29.01.92	Sheffield United	107+2	7	4	1	10	1		
Robert Scott	6.1	11.4	15.08.73	Epsom		Dorking								
via Sutton United to				£20,000	01.08.93	Sheffield United	0+1	0+1		2+1				
				Loan	22.03.95	Scarborough	8				3			
Mitchum Ward	5.8	10.7	19.06.71	Sheffield	01.07.89	Sheffield Utd (T)	59+13	3+3	4+2	2+1	5	1	2	1
				Loan	01.11.90	Crewe Alexandra	4		1	2	1		1	
Dane Whitehouse	5.9	10.12	14.10.70	Sheffield	01.07.89	Sheffield Utd (T)	121+25	9+1	11+3	3	25	4	1	2
FLge u18.1.														
F O R W A R D S														
Tony Battersby	6.0	12.7	30.08.75	Doncaster	05.07.93	Sheffield Utd (T)				2+1				1
				Loan	23.03.95	Southend United	6+2				1			
Nathan Blake	6.0	12.8	27.01.72	Cardiff		Chelsea (T)								
W: 2, B.1, u21.5. WFAC'92'93. Div.3'93.				Free	20.08.90	Cardiff City	113+18	6+2	10	13+2	35		4	1
				£300,000	17.02.94	Sheffield United	35+12	2+1	1	1	22	1		
Jostein Flo	6.4	13.12	03.10.64	Eid (Norway)		Sogndal (Nor.)								
Norweigen Int.				£400,000	10.08.93	Sheffield United	57+8	3	0+1		15	2		
Glyn Hodges	6.0	12.3	30.04.63	Streatham	03.02.81	Wimbledon (A)	200+32	14+2	13+2	0+1	49	3	2	
W: 16, B.1, u21.5, Y. Div'83.				£200,000	15.07.87	Newcastle United	7							
				£300,000	01.10.87	Watford	82+4	5	8	2+1	15	2	1	1
				£410,000	16.07.90	Crystal Palace	5+2	2+2					1	
				£450,000	17.01.91	Sheffield United	101+24	4+1	12+1	1	16		3	

SHEFFIELD UNITED							APPEARANCES				GOALS			
PLAYERS NAME Honours	Ht	Wt	Birthdate	Birthplace Transfers	Contract Date	Clubs	League	L/Cup	FA Cup	Other	Lge	L/C	FAC	Oth
Andrew Scott	6.1	12.0	02.08.72	Epsom		Sutton United				2				
				£50,000	01.12.92	Sheffield United	31+23	2	1+1	3+1	4	1		3
Phil Starbuck	5.11	12.4	24.11.68	Nottingham	19.08.86	Nottingham F. (A)	9+27	1+3	2+5	0+4	2			
				Loan	07.03.88	Birmingham City	3							
				Loan	19.02.90	Hereford United	6			1				
				Loan	06.09.90	Blackburn Rovers	5+1				1			
				Free	17.08.91	Huddersfield Town	116+12	10+2	5+1	14+3	35	4		6
				Loan	28.10.94	Sheffield United								
				£150,000	06.01.95	Sheffield United	20+3		0+1		1			
Carl Veart	5.11	12.8	21.05.70	Whyalla (Aust)		Adelaide C.								
Australian Int.				£250,000	22.07.94	Sheffield United	30+9	1	1	2	11			
A D D I T I O N A L C O N T R A C T P L A Y E R S														
Doug Hodgson	6.2	13.10	27.02.69	Frankston (Aust)		Heidelberg Alex								
				£30,000	22.07.94	Sheffield United	0+1	1		1				
Marvin Marston						Notts County								
					12.08.94	Sheffield United								
Wayne Quinn					06.12.94	Sheffield United (T)								

TOP GOALSCORER 1994/95
Nathan Blake

Division One goals (games)	17 (28+7)
Coca-Cola Cup Goals.	1 (2+1)
F.A. Cup goals	0 (1)
Anglo Italian Cup	0 (1)
Total	**18 (32+8)**

Total goals for Sheffield United since 17.02.94 . . . . 23 (39+13)
Total for Wales (full caps only). . . . . 0(2)

Career total as at June 1st 1995 . . . . 63 (183+35)

MANAGER
DAVE BASSETT

Date of Birth . . . . 4th September 1944.
Place of Birth . . . . Wembley.
Date of Appointment . . . . 21st January 1988.

PREVIOUS CLUBS
As Manager . . . . Wimbledon, Watford.
As Coach . . . . Wimbledon.
As a Player . . . . . . Walton & Hersham, Wimbledon, Hendon, Chelsea, Watford.

HONOURS
As a Manager
Wimbledon: Promotion to Div 3 1981. Division 4 Championship 1983. Promotion to Div 2 1984. Promotion to Div 1 1986.
Sheffield United: Promotion to Div 2 1989. Promotion to Div 1 1990.
As a Player
Amateur Cup Winners Medal 1973.

BRAMALL LANE GROUND
Sheffield S2 4SU
Tel: 0114 273 8955

Capacity 23,327

First game ....Sheffield Club v Hallam (Charity Match), 0-0, 28.12.1862.
As Sheffield Utd.. v Birmingham St Georges (friendly) 0-4, 28.9.1889.
First floodlit game...v Rotherham, 16.3.1954.

ATTENDANCES
Highest ....68,287 v Leeds United, FAC 5th Rnd, 15.1.1936.
Lowest ....1,500 v Bootle, Division 1, 10.9.1892.

OTHER GROUNDS...None.

MATCHDAY TICKET PRICES

South Stand. £14
Juv/OAP £7
Kop £9
Juv/OAP £6
Stone Best Bitter Stand £9
Juv/OAP £6
Family Enclosure £10
Juv/OAP £5
Visiting. £14
Juv/OAP £7
(in the Stones Best Bitter Upper Stand)

Ticket Office telephone no. 0114 276 6771

CLUBCALL
0891 888 650
Calls cost 39p per minute cheap rate and 49p per
minute at all other times.
Call costings correct at time of going to press.

HOW TO GET TO THE GROUND

From the North
Use motorway M1 until junction 34. Leave motorway and follow signs, Sheffield (A6109). In 3.4 miles turn left and shortly at roundabout take 4th exit into Sheaf Street. Then at 2nd roundabout take 5th exit into St Mary's Road (sign posted Bakewell). In half-a-mile left into Bramall Lane for Sheffield United FC.

From the East and South
Use (A57) from motorway M1 (junction 31 or 33) then at roundabout take 3rd exit into Sheaf Street. Then at 2nd roundabout take 5th exit in St Mary's Road and proceed as above.

From the West
Use A57, sign posted Sheffield, and at roundabout take 4th exit A6134 into Upper Hanover Street. Then at 2nd roundabout take 3rd exit into Bramall Lane.

Car Parking
The ground is five minutes away from car parks in the City Centre. Side-street parking is ample.

Nearest Railway Station
Sheffield Midland (0114 272 6411)

MATCHDAY PROGRAMME

Programme Editor . . . . Andy Pack

Number of pages . . . . 40.

Price . . . . £1.30.

Subscriptions . . . . £27.30 + £9.45 postage (homes).
. . . . Double price for aways also.

Local Newspapers. Sheffield Newspaper Ltd
. . . . (The Star, Sheffield Telegraph)

Local Radio Stations . . . . BBC Radio Sheffield, Radio Hallam.

SOUTHEND UNITED
(The Shrimpers)
ENDSLEIGH LEAGUE DIVISION 1
SPONSORED BY: UNITED ARTISTS

Back Row (L-R): Domonic Iorfa, Luke Morrish, Andy Sussex, Paul Sansome, Dave Regis, Simon Royce, Mark Hone, Danny Foot, Leo Roget. **Middle Row:** Danny Greaves, Ijah Anderson, Declan Perkins, Gary Jones, Roger Willis, Phil Gridlet, Steve Tilson, Keith Dublin, John Gowans. **Front Row:** Andy Ansah, Andy Thompson, Theo Foley, Mick Bodley, Ronnie Whelan, Julian Hails, Chris Powell.

SOUTHEND UNITED
FORMED IN 1906
TURNED PROFESSIONAL IN 1906
LTD COMPANY IN 1919

PRESIDENT: N J Woodcock
CHAIRMAN: V T Jobson
VICE-CHAIRMAN/CHIEF EXECUTIVE
J W Adams
DIRECTORS
J Bridge, B R Gunner, W R Kelleway,
D M Marksheffel, C Wooldridge
MARKETING DIRECTOR
C Wooldridge

PLAYER/MANAGER: Ronnie Whelan
ASSISTANT MANAGER: Theo Foley
COACH: Danny Greaves

SPORTS THERAPISTS
John Gowans and Spencer Barham

STATISTICIAN FOR THE DIRECTORY
Dave Goody

As has happened in two of the previous three seasons, Southend's on the field exploits were overshadowed by the managerial side of the club both during and after the end of the 1994/95 season.

The season started with Peter Taylor in charge of team affairs. He had taken over midway through the previous season when Barry Fry defected to Birmingham City. Taylor had asked that the fans did not judge him until he had been in charge for twelve months, and had had time to build his own team. The first win of the new season did not come until the fifth game and, by the time the club lost 1-4 and 0-5 in successive matches to Stoke City and Wolves in late September, they were languishing in 23rd position. However, these two games were the first played for the club by Ronnie Whelan who had joined for a one month loan spell, being unable to attract interest form a Premiership side.

Soon the club's fortunes changed and by the start of November an eight game unbeaten run had lifted the Blues into sixth place, and had seen Whelan sign a permanent contract. The New Year, and a narrow defeat against Southampton in the FA Cup in January seemed to signal yet another turnaround, and the loss through injury of Whelan saw the sides fortunes plummet. Just two points earned in eight games, and no foreseeable change in direction spelt the end of the road for Peter Taylor, who was relieved of his duties in favour of Steve Thompson, who was placed in charge in a caretaker's capacity. After defeats in his first two games, Thompson managed to instill a confidence and determination in the team which had been so badly missed in the previous two months. Players who had not been in the first team squad under Taylor, such as Mick Bodley and Andy Sussex, were brought in by Thompson and flourished in a run-in that saw them win eight and draw two of their final twelve matches, finishing in a very respectable thirteenth position.

Steve Thompson was crowned king of Roots Hall for his performance in saving a team which had already resigned themselves to relegation, and he was offered the manager's job on a permanent basis. Unfortunately, the contract was not written up quickly enough, and Colin Murphy another ex-Southend manager came in and persuaded Thompson to join newly relegated Notts County. There was much discontent amongst both club officials and fans alike, that yet again a manager had walked out on the Blues like Barry Fry and Dave Webb in previous seasons. Chairman Vic Jobson threatened legal action against County and Thompson, but nothing came of it.

Ronnie Whelan accepted Jobsoní offer to become manager of the Blues, and all the fans hope that he can bring some of his majestic skills to the field of play and encourage the other players to perform in a similar manner. The signing of Mike Lapper, the USA international centre-half, is likely to fill the gap left by Andy Edwards departure to Birmingham City, in what is likely to be Southend's toughest season since joining this division in 1991. **DAVE GOODY.**

SOUTHEND UNITED

Division One: 13th **FA Cup:** 3rd Round **Coca-Cola Cup:** 1st Round

M	DATE	COMP.	VEN	OPPONENTS	RESULT	H/T	LP	GOAL SCORERS/GOAL TIMES	ATT.
1	A 13	EL	A	Millwall	L 1-3	0-1	19	Iorfa 75	(8,283)
2	16	CC 1/1	H	Watford	D 0-0	0-0			2,859
3	20	EL	H	Middlesbrough	L 0-2	0-1	24		5,722
4	23	CC 1/2	A	Watford	L 0-1	0-1			(4,582)
5	27	EL	A	Luton Town	D 2-2	0-1	20	Dublin 51, Otto 75	(5,918)
6	30	EL	H	Portsmouth	L 1-2	1-1	22	Thomson 32	4,333
7	S 3	EL	H	Oldham Athletic	W 1-0	0-0	20	Otto 88	4,435
8	10	EL	A	Stoke City	L 1-4	0-2	22	Butler 67 (og)	(11,808)
9	13	EL	A	Wolverhampton Wand.	L 0-5	0-3	23		(23,608)
10	17	EL	H	Bristol City	W 2-1	1-0	22	Thompson 8, Whelan 60	3,663
11	24	EL	H	Bolton Wanderers	W 2-1	0-1	17	Otto 47, Thomson 59	4,507
12	O 1	EL	A	Sunderland	W 1-0	1-0	13	Thomson 16	(15,520)
13	8	EL	A	Barnsley	D 0-0	0-0	16		(3,659)
14	16	EL	H	Derby County	W 1-0	0-0	8	Regis 89	4,218
15	22	EL	A	Swindon Town	D 2-2	2-1	10	Thomson 8, Otto 18	(9,909)
16	29	EL	H	Grimsby Town	D 0-0	0-0	11		5,086
17	N 1	EL	H	Notts County	W 1-0	1-0	6	Thomson 25	4,302
18	5	EL	A	Port Vale	L 0-5	0-2	9		(7,141)
19	12	EL	A	Watford	L 0-1	0-0	11		(8,551)
20	19	EL	H	Reading	W 4-1	1-0	10	Bressington 6 (pen), G. Jones 54, 63, Thomson 90	5,511
21	26	EL	A	Sheffield United	L 0-2	0-1	11		(13,405)
22	D 3	EL	H	Swindon Town	W 2-0	1-0	11	Willis 2, Edwards 62	5,803
23	10	EL	A	Middlesbrough	W 2-1	1-0	9	Hails 44, Gridelet 67	(16,843)
24	17	EL	H	Millwall	L 0-1	0-1	11		5,833
25	26	EL	A	Charlton Athletic	L 1-3	1-0	15	Bressington 33 (pen)	(9,525)
26	27	EL	H	West Bromwich Albion	W 2-1	1-1	12	O'Regan 38 (og), Gridelet 57	6,886
27	31	EL	A	Burnley	L 1-5	0-2	14	Willis 71	(10,561)
28	J 2	EL	H	Tranmere Rovers	D 0-0	0-0	13		5,195
29	7	FAC 3	A	Southampton	L 0-2	0-2			(13,003)
30	14	EL	A	Grimsby Town	L 1-4	1-1	15	Chapman 2	(3,619)
31	28	EL	H	Port Vale	L 1-2	1-1	14	Thomson 39	3,619
32	F 4	EL	H	Watford	L 0-4	0-3	14		4,914
33	11	EL	A	Notts County	D 2-2	1-1	15	Edwards 33, Willis 90	(6,768)
34	18	EL	H	Sheffield United	L 1-3	1-1	16	Willis 13	4,700
35	21	EL	A	Reading	L 0-2	0-0	16		(7,895)
36	25	EL	H	Sunderland	L 0-1	0-1	20		4,686
37	M 4	EL	A	Bolton Wanderers	L 0-3	0-1	20		(10,766)
38	7	EL	A	Oldham Athletic	W 2-0	1-0	18	G. Jones 28, Thomson 60	(7,168)
39	11	EL	H	Luton Town	W 3-0	1-0	16	G. Jones 28, Thomson 76, Dublin 89	4,558
40	18	EL	A	Portsmouth	D 1-1	1-1	18	G. Jones 18	(6,667)
41	21	EL	H	Stoke City	W 4-2	2-0	17	G. Jones 17, Tilson 26, Edwards 57, Sussex 78 (pen)	4,240
42	25	EL	A	Bristol City	D 0-0	0-0	16		(6,159)
43	A 1	EL	H	Wolverhampton Wand.	L 0-1	0-0	16		8,522
44	8	EL	H	Burnley	W 3-1	2-0	15	G. Jones 5, Hails 6, Battersby 54	5,027
45	15	EL	A	West Bromwich A	L 0-2	0-1	18		(14,393)
46	18	EL	H	Charlton Athletic	W 2-1	0-0	17	G. Jones 59, Tilson 61	6,397
47	21	EL	A	Tranmere Rovers	W 2-0	2-0	14	McGreal 1 (og), G. Jones 34	(9,971)
48	29	EL	A	Derby County	W 2-1	2-0	14	Gridelet 22, G. Jones 39	(12,528)
49	M 7	EL	H	Barnsley	W 3-1	1-0	13	Gridelet 1, Thomson 73, G. Jones 74	6,425
50									
51									
52									
53									
54									
55									
56									
57									
58									
59									
60									

Best Home League Attendance: 8,522 v Wolverhampton Wanderers **Smallest:** 3,619 v Port Vale **Av Home Att:** 5,156

Goal Scorers:

Compared with 1993-94: -952

League (54): Jones 11, Thompson 11, Gridelet 4, Otto 4, Willis 4, Edwards 3, Opponents 3, Bressington 2 (2 pens), Dublin 2, Hails 2, Tilson 2, Battersby, Chapman, Iorfa, Regis, Susex (1pen), Whelan,

C/Cola Cup (0):
FA Cup (0):

1994-95

Sansome	Poole	Powell	Jones K.	Edwards	Dublin	Hunt	Tilson	Iorfa	Otto	Thomson	Hone	Martin	Royce	Bressington	Sussex	Davidson	Forrester	Whelan	Gridelet	Willis	Regis	Jones G.	Bodley	Hails	Ansah	Referee	
1	2	3	4	5	6	7*	8	9	10	11	12	S	S													G. Singh	1
S	2	3	4		6	7		9	10	11*	8	12	1	5	S											P. Foakes	2
S	2	3	4	11	6	7*		9	10		8	12	1	5	S											O. Bigger	3
S	2	3	4	5	6	12	7	9*			8	10*	1		11	14										S. Dunn	4
1	2	3	4	5	6	14		9*	10	11•	8	12	S		7											J. Brandwood	5
1	2	3	4	5		7	S		10	9	8*	12	S	6	11											I. Hernley	6
1	2*	3	4	5	6	12			10	9	8		S	6	11		7									M. Bailey	7
1	S	3	4	5	S	7			10	9	2		S	6			11	8								I. Cruikshanks	8
1	12	3	4	14	5	7			10	9	2		S	6•			11*	8								R. Poulain	9
1		3		5	6		14		10	11*	2		S				12	8	4•	7	9					M. Pierce	10
1		3		5	6		S		10	11*	2		S				12	8	4	7	9					P. Alcock	11
1		3		5	6		S		10	11	2		S			S		8	4	7	9					P. Wright	12
1		3		5	6		12		10	11	2		S	S				8	4	7	9*					G. Cain	13
1		3		5	6		S		10	11	2		S	S				8	4	7	9					G. Pooley	14
1		3		5	6		12		10	11	2		S	4				8	4•	7	9	9*	S			A. Flood	15
1		3		5	6		12		10	11	2		S	14				8	4•	7	9*					G. Singh	16
1		3		5	6		12		10	11	2		S	7*				8	4		9	S				P. Foakes	17
1		3		5	6		12		10	11	2*		S					8	4	7	9•	14				P. Vanes	18
1		3		5	6				10	11	2		S	8	S				4	7	9*	12				J. Rushton	19
1		3		5	6		12		10	11*	2		S	8	S				4	7	9					M. Pierce	20
1		3		5	6		12		10		2		S	8*	S			7	4	9		11				D. Allison	21
1		3		5	6		10			11	2		S		S			8	4	7*	9		12			S. Dunn	22
1		3		5	6					11	2		S	7	S			8	4		9		10			K. Breen	23
1		3		5	6		12	14		11	2		S	7				8	4*		9•		10			M. Bailey	24
1		3		5	6			14		12	2		S	7				8	4	9			11•	10*		E. Wolstenholme	25
1		3		5	6		S	S		11	2		S					8	4	9			7	10		M. Pierce	26
1		3		5			S			11	2		S	6	12			8	4	9			7	10*		R. Furnandiz	27
1		3		S	6	11				9	2		S	5				8	4	10		12	7*			C. Wilkes	28
1		3		S	6	11				9	2		S	5				8	4	10			S	7		B. Hill	29
1		3		5	6					11*	2		S					8*		10		14	4	7		W. Flood	30
1		3		5	6		8	12		9	2		S	4					7		10*		11•	14		T. West	31
1		3		5*	6			10•		9	2		S						7			11	12			K. Cooper	32
1				5	6					9*	2		S	3				4	7			11•	10			S. Mathieson	33
1		3		5	6		12			9*	2		11•				4	7			14	10				G. Singh	34
1				12	6					9•	2		7					4				11	10			P. Vanes	35
1		3		6						9•	2	14	S		8						12		7			D. Orr	36
1		3		6						9*	2		S		10		4					12	S	7		K. Lynch	37
S		3		6	11		10			9	2		1		8		4			7*	5	S				K. Breen	38
S		3		6	11		10*			9	2		1		8		4			7	5		14			J. Holbrook	39
S		3		6	11		10			9*	2		1		8		4	S		7	5		12			S. Dunn	40
S		3		6	11		10				2		1		8		4	12		7*	5		9			P. Alcock	41
S		3		6	11		10				2		1		8		4	S		7*	5		9			J. Brandwood	42
S		3		6	11		10				2*		1		8		4	14		7	5		9•			M. Pierce	43
S		3			6		10				1			8*			4	2		7	5		9			G. Barker	44
S		3		6	2		10			12			1		8•		4	14		7*	5		9			M. Bailey	45
S		3		6	2		10			9*			1		S		4	8		7	5		12			G. Pooley	46
S		3		6	2		10						1		9*		4	8		7	5		12			J. Winter	47
S		3		6	2		10			12			1				4	8		7	5		9*			J. Parker	48
S		3		6	2		10			12			1				4	8•		7	5		9			P. Alcock	49
33	5	45	7	42	40	5	17	4	19	35	39		13	19	14		3	33	26	21	9	18	12	20	7	League Appearances	
			1			2	9	4		4	1	4		1	1		2		3			6		6	2	League Sub Appearances	
2		2	2	1	2	1+1	1	2	1	1	2	1+1	2	1	1	0+1										C/Cola Cup Appearances	
1						1		1	1		1	1						1	1	1					1	FA Cup Appearances	

Also Played: Foot 12(30),3(35),4(36), Chapman 9(30), Harkness 8(32,33,34,35),10(36),11(37), Perkins 14(32,35,44),12(33,39),11*(36),S(38,41), Oliver S(34,35), Battersby 12(42,43), 11•(44,47,48), 11(45,46),11*(49) Players on Loan: Forrester (Leeds United), Chapman (West Ham United), Westley (Brentford), Harkness (Liverpool), Battersby (Sheffield United)

SOUTHEND UNITED

CLUB RECORDS

BIGGEST VICTORIES
League: 9-2 v Newport Co., Div 3S, 5.9.1936
7-0 v QPR, Div 3S, 7.4.1928
8-1 v Cardiff City, Div 3S, 20.2.1937
7-0 v Workington, Div 4, 29.3.1968
F.A. Cup: 10-1 v Golders Green, Round 1, 24.11.1934
9-0 v Kings Lynn, Round 1, 16.11.1968
10-1 v Brentwood, Round 2, 7.12.1968
League Cup: 6-1 v Bournemouth, 13.8.1968

BIGGEST DEFEATS
League: 0-8 v Northampton Town, Div 3S, 22.3.1924
1-9 v Brighton, Div 3, 27.11.1965
F.A. Cup: 0-6 v Burnley, Round 2, 30.1.1915
League Cup: 0-8 v Crystal Palace, Rnd 2, 25.9.1990

MOST POINTS
3 points a win: 85, Division 3, 1990-91
2 points a win: 67, Division 4, 1980-81

MOST GOALS
92, Division 3S, 1950-51
Stubbs 19, Wakefield 15, Davies 12, Tippett 12, Grant 12, French 5,
Sibley 5, Lawler 4, McAlinden 2, Anderson 1, Butler 1, Woods 1, og 3

MOST LEAGUE GOALS CONCEDED
85, Division 4, 1969-70

MOST FIRST CLASS MATCHES IN A SEASON
57 (46 League, 1 FA Cup, 2 League Cup, 8 Anglo Italian Cup)
1993-94

MOST LEAGUE WINS
30, Division 4, 1980-81

MOST LEAGUE DRAWS
19, Division 4, 1976-77

MOST LEAGUE DEFEATS
26, Division 3, 1965-66

INDIVIDUAL CLUB RECORDS

MOST GOALS IN A MATCH
5. Jim Shankly v Merthyr Tydfil, 6-0, Div 3S, 1.3.1930
5. H. Johnson v Golders Green, 10-1, FAC Rnd 1, 24.11.1934
5. Billy Best v Brentwood, 10-1, FAC Rnd 2, 7.12.1968

MOST GOALS IN A SEASON
Jim Shankly 35 (League 34, FAC 1) 1928-29
3 goals 2 times=6; 2 goals 6 times=12; 1 goal 17 times=17. Total 35

OLDEST PLAYER
Not known.

YOUNGEST PLAYER
Phil O'Connor, 16 years 76 days, 26.12.1969.

MOST CAPPED PLAYER
George McKenzie (Eire) 9

BEST PERFORMANCES

League: 1980-81: Matches Played 46, Won 30, Drawn 7, Lost 9,
Goals for 79, Goals against 31, Points 67. First in Division 4

Highest: 12th Division 2, 1991-92

F.A. Cup: 1920-21: Last sixteen
1925-26: 1st rnd. Dulwich (h) 5-1; 2nd rnd. Gillingham (h) 1-0; 3rd
rnd. Southport (h) 5-2; 4th rnd. Derby County (h) 4-1; 5th rnd.
Nottingham Forest (h) 0-1
1951-52: 1st rnd. Bournemouth (h) 6-1; 2nd rnd. Oldham Athletic (h)
5-0; 3rd rnd. Southampton (h) 3-0; 4th rnd. Bristol Rovers (h) 2-1;
5th rnd. Sheffield Utd (h) 1-2
1975-76: 1st rnd. Swansea City (h) 2-0; 2nd rnd. Dover (h) 4-1; 3rd
rnd. Brighton (h) 2-1; 4th rnd. Cardiff City (h) 2-1; 5th rnd Derby
County (a) 0-1
1992-93: 3rd rnd. Millwall (h) 1-0; 4th rnd. Huddersfield (a) 2-1; 5th
rnd. Sheffield Wednesday (a) 0-2

League Cup: Never past Round 3

DIVISIONAL RECORD

	Played	Won	Drawn	Lost	For	Against	Points
Division 2/1	184	65	40	79	234	267	235
Division 3	920	319	238	363	1,266	1,358	972
Division 3(S)	1,334	503	312	519	2,074	2,065	1,318
Division 4	598	262	144	192	871	742	746
Total	**3,036**	**1,149**	**734**	**1,153**	**4,445**	**4,432**	**3,271**

ADDITIONAL INFORMATION
Previous Names
None.

Previous League
Southern League

Club colours: Blue shirts with red collar & cuff, blue shorts, blue
socks.
Change colours: All red

Reserves League: Capital League.

RECORDS AND STATISTICS

COMPETITIONS

Div.2/1	Div.3(S)	Div.3	Div.4
1991-	1921-58	1920-21	1966-72
		1958-66	1976-78
		1972-76	1980-81
		1978-80	1984-87
		1981-84	1989-90
		1987-89	
		1990-91	

HONOURS

Division 4
1980-81

MOST APPEARANCES

A W (Sandy) Anderson 452 (1950-63)

Year	League
1950-51	30
1951-52	46
1952-53	23
1953-54	45
1954-55	45
1955-56	9
1956-57	27
1957-58	40
1958-59	41
1959-60	38
1960-61	43
1961-62	45
1962-63	20
	452

MOST GOALS IN A CAREER

Roy Hollis - 120 (1953-60)

Year	League
1953-54	10
1954-55	27
1955-56	23
1956-57	18
1957-58	18
1958-59	17
1959-60	7
Total	**120**

Current leading goalscorer: Andrew Ansah - 38 (1990-95)

RECORD TRANSFER FEE RECEIVED

Amount	Club	Player	Date
£2,200,000	Nott'm Forest	Stan Collymore	7/93
£375,000	Tottenham H.	Dean Austin	7/92
£150,000	Wolves	Shane Westley	6/89
£120,000	Crystal Palace	Peter Taylor	10/73

RECORD TRANSFER FEE PAID

Amount	Club	Player	Date
£350,000	Plymouth Argyle	Gary Poole	7/93
£175,000	Brentford	Keith Jones	10/91
£111,111	Blackpool	Derek Spence	12/79
£50,000	Tottenham H	Mike Stead	11/78
£50,000	Sheffield Wed	Dave Cusak	9/78

MANAGERS

Name	Seasons	Best	Worst
Tom Mather	1920-21	3(3S)	22(3S)
F L Birnie	1921-24	3(3S)	22(3S)
D B Jack	1924-39	10(3S)	21(3S)
Harry Warren	1946-56	3(3S)	18(3S)
Eddie Perry	1956-60	7(3S)	12(3)
Frank Broome	1960	20(3)	20(3)
Ted Fenton	1961-65	8(3)	16(2)
Alvin Williams	1965-67	21(3)	6(4)
Ernie Shepherd	1967-69	6(4)	7(4)
Geoff Hudson	1969-70	17(4)	17(4)
Arthur Rowley	1970-76	12(3)	18(4)
Dave Smith	1976-82	7(3)	10(4)
Peter Morris	1982-84	22(3)	22(3)
Bobby Moore	1984-86	9(3)	20(4)
David Webb	1986-87	7(3)	20(4)
Dick Bate	1987		
Paul Clark	1987-88	19(3)	19(3)
Dave Webb	1988-92	12(3)	3(4)
Colin Murphy	1992-93		
Barry Fry	1993-94	18(2/1)	18(2/1)
Peter Taylor	1993-95	15(2/1)	15(2/1)
Steve Thompson	1995		
Ronnie Whelan	1995-		

LONGEST LEAGUE RUNS

of undefeated matches:	16 (20.2.1932 - 29.8.1932)	of league matches w/out a win:	7 (31.12.1983 - 14.4.1984)
of undefeated home matches:	32 (16.2.1980 - 1.5.1981)	of undefeated away matches:	9 (4.3.1972 - 29.4.1972)
without home win:	8 (2.10.1948 - 22.1.1949)	without an away win:	27 (13.11.1920 - 4.2.1922)
of league wins:	7 (4.10.1924 - 6.11.1924, 24.4.1990 - 18.9.1990)	of home wins:	18 (4.4.1980 - 9.1.1981)
of league defeats:	6 (29.8.1987 - 19.9.1987)	of away wins:	5 (31.8.1931 - 3.10.1931, 9.4.1991 - 3.9.1991)

SOUTHEND UNITED

PLAYERS NAME / Honours	Ht	Wt	Birthdate	Birthplace / Transfers	Contract Date	Clubs	League	L/Cup	FA Cup	Other	Lge	L/C	FAC	Oth
G O A L K E E P E R S														
Simon Royce	6.1	12.0	09.09.71	Forest Gate		Heybridge Swifts								
				£10,000	15.10.91	Southend United	21+2	2	1	1				
Paul Sansome	6.0	13.8	06.10.61	New Addington		Crystal Palace (A)								
FLT'83.				Free	18.04.80	Millwall	156	12	13	9				
				£40,000	24.03.88	Southend United	305	18	8	22				
D E F E N D E R S														
Michael Bodley	5.11	12.0	14.09.67	Hayes	17.09.85	Chelsea (A)	6	1		1	1			
GMVC'91.				£50,000	12.01.89	Northampton Town	20			2				
				£15,000	01.10.89	Barnet	69	2	10	9	3			
				Free	15.07.93	Southend United	28	1	1	3	1			
				Loan	23.11.94	Gillingham	6+1			1				
				Loan	23.01.95	Birmingham City	3							
Keith Dublin	5.7	10.0	29.01.66	H. Wycombe	28.01.84	Chelsea (A)	50+1	6	5	5+1				
E: u19.4, Y.				£3,500	14.08.87	Brighton & H.A.	132	5	7	7	5		1	
				£275,000	17.07.90	Watford	165+3	12	4	6	2			
				P.E.	21.07.94	Southend United	40	2	1		2			
Daniel Foot	5.10	12.0	06.09.75	Edmonton		Tottenham H. (T)								
				Free	02.08.94	Southend United	2+1							
				Loan	18.11.94	Crawley Town								
Mark Hone	6.1	12.0	21.08.69	Croydon		Crystal Palace (T)	4	3+1						
				£5,000		Welling United			3				1	
				£5,000	11.08.94	Southend United	39+1	2	1					
Chris Powell	5.8	10.13	08.09.69	Lambeth	24.12.87	Crystal Palace (T)	2+1	0+1		0+1				
				Loan	11.01.90	Aldershot	11							
				Free	30.08.90	Southend United	219+2	11	7	17	3			
M I D F I E L D														
Phil Gridelet	5.11	12.0	30.04.67	Hendon		Hendon			1					
E: S-P.4.				£25,000	01.09.90	Barnet		0+1						
				£175,000	21.09.90	Barnsley	3+3		1	1				
				Loan	05.03.93	Rotherham United	9							
				Free	01.08.85	Southend United	47+11		1	4	4			1
Julian Hails	5.9	11.0	20.11.67	Lincoln		Hemel Hempstead								
					29.08.90	Fulham	99+13	5+1	2	9	12			
				Free	02.12.94	Southend United	20+6				2			
David Roche	5.11	12.1	13.12.70	Newcastle	30.08.88	Newcastle Utd (T)	23+13	2	1	1+2				
				Loan	08.01.93	Peterborough Utd	4							
					01.10.93	Doncaster Rovers	49+1		3	3	8			1
				£55,000	23.03.95	Southend United	0+4							
Ronnie Whelan	5.9	10.13	25.09.61	Dublin		Home Farm								
Ei: 45, u21.1. Div.1'82'83'84'86'88'90.				Free	01.10.79	Liverpool	351+11	46+4	40+1	38+2	46	14	7	6
FAC'86'89. EC'84. LC'82'83'84				Free	14.10.94	Southend United	33		1		1			
F O R W A R D S														
Andrew Ansah	5.10	11.1	19.03.69	Lewisham		Dorking								
				Free	21.03.89	Brentford	3+5	0+1			2			
				Free	29.03.90	Southend United	141+12	7+2	4	6+2	33		5	
				Loan	04.11.94	Brentford	2+1			2	1			1
Dominic Iorfa	6.1	12.12	01.10.68	Lagos (Nig.)		Royal Antwerp								
Nigerian Int.				£145,000	23.03.90	Q.P.R.	1+7	1						
					01.12.91	Galatasary								
					24.10.92	Peterborough Utd	27+33	2+1	2+2	1	9			1
				£15,000	03.08.94	Southend United	4+4	2			1			
Gary Jones	6.1	12.9	06.04.69	Huddersfield		Rossington Main								
				Free	26.01.89	Doncaster Rovers	10+10	1			2			
via Grantham, 01.11.89, £8,500 to				£17,500	01.01.90	Kettering								
				£3,000	01.08.91	Boston United								
				£25,000	03.06.93	Southend United	33+14	1	1	4+1	14			2
Loan16.08.93 Dag & Redbridge				Loan	17.09.93	Lincoln City	0+4			0+1	2			
David Regis	6.3	13.0	03.03.64	Paddington		Dunstable								
Clubcall Cup. Div.3'92.						Fisher Athletic								
			via Windsor & Eton	£8,000		Barnet								
				£25,000	28.09.90	Notts County	31+15	0+2		6	16			2
				£200,000	07.11.91	Plymouth Argyle	28+3	2	1		4	3		
				Loan	13.08.92	Bournemouth	6				2			
				£100,000	23.10.92	Stoke City	49+14	2	4+1	7+1	15	1	2	2
				£200,000	01.08.94	Birmingham City	4+2	1			2			
				£100,000+PE	16.09.94	Southend United	9				1			

SOUTHEND UNITED							APPEARANCES				GOALS			
PLAYERS NAME / Honours	Ht	Wt	Birthdate	Birthplace / Transfers	Contract Date	Clubs	League	L/Cup	FA Cup	Other	Lge	L/C	FAC	Oth
Andrew Sussex	6.0	11.6	23.11.64	Enfield	25.11.82	Leyton Orient (A)	126+18	7+1	8	5+3	17	2	1	
				£16,000	23.06.88	Crewe Alexandra	86+16	10	7+1	5	24	6	4	2
				£100,000	04.07.91	Southend United	48+11	5	2+1	3+1	13			1
Stephen Tilson	5.11	12.6	27.07.66	Wickford		Witham Town								
					07.02.89	Southend United	146+26	6+1	3	10+1	21			3
				Loan	16.09.93	Brentford	2							
Andy Thomson			01.04.71	Motherwell		Queen of the South								
				£250,000	04.07.94	Southend United	35+4	1	1		11			
Roger Willis	6.2	12.0	17.06.67	Sheffield	20.07.89	Grimsby Town	1+8	0+1						
GMVC'91.				£10,000	01.08.90	Barnet	39+5	2	5+1	1+4	13		3	1
				£175,000	06.10.92	Watford	30+6		1		2			
				£150,000	31.12.93	Birmingham City	11+5		0+1		5			
				£100,000+PE	16.09.94	Southend United	21				4			
ADDITIONAL CONTRACT PLAYERS														
Declan Perkins	5.11	12.4	17.10.75	Ilford	27.05.94	Southend United (T)	1+5							
Ei: u21.1.				Loan	23.12.94	Chelmsford City								

Top Goalscorer 1994/95
Gary Jones (Pictured) & Andy Thomson

Gary Jones
Division One Goals (games) . . . . 11 (18+6)
Did not play in the Coca-Cola Cup or FA Cup
Total . . . . **11 (18+6)**
Total goals for Southend Utd since 03.06.1993 . . . . 16 (38+15)
Career total as at June 1st 1995 . . . . 18 (49+25)
Andy Thomson
Division One Goals . . . . 11 (35+4)
Coca-Cola Cup Goals.....0(1) . . . . F.A. Cup goals.....0 (1)
Total . . . . **11 (37+4)**
Total goals for Southend Utd since 04.07.94 . . . . 11 (37+4)
Career total as at June 1st 1995 . . . . 11 (37+4)

The Manager (Player)
Ronnie Whelan

Date of Birth . . . . 25th September 1961.
Place of Birth . . . . Dublin.
Date of Appointment . . . . July 1995.

Previous Clubs
As Manager . . . . None.
As Coach . . . . None.
As a Player . . . . Home Farm, Liverpool, Southend United.

Honours
As a Manager
None.

As a Player
Liverpool: Division 1 championship 1982, 1983, 1984, 1986, 1988, 1990. FA Cup 1986, 1989.
League Cup 1982, 1983, 1984. European Cup 1984.
International: 45 full caps and 1 u21 cap for Eire.

ROOTS HALL

Victoria Avenue, Southend-on-Sea SS2 6NQ
Tel: 01702 340 707

Capacity..13,000
Covered Seating..2,465
Seating..5,100

First game...v Norwich City, Div. 3(S) (3-1, 20.08.55. Att: 17,700.
First floodlit game...Not Known.
ATTENDANCES
Highest..31,033 v Liverpool, FAC 3rd Rnd, 10.1.1979.
Lowest...653 v Northampton, AMC, 13.3.1986.
OTHER GROUNDS..Roots Hall 1909-1919. The Kursaal 1919-1934.
...Southend Stadium 1934-1955. Played at New Writtle Street,Chelmsford in 1940, during the war.

MATCHDAY TICKET PRICES

East Stand . . . . Blue Block £11
. . . . Yellow Block £13
. . . . Red Block £15
. . . . Black Block £12
. . . . Green Block £15
South Stand (Home) . . . . Lower Tier £8
. . . . Upper Tier £10
UB40 Members £4

Family Stand £9
Juv/OAP £4.50

North Stand (away supporters) £8, £10

Ticket Office Telephone no. 01702 435 602

CLUBCALL
0839 66 44 44

Calls cost 39p per minute cheap rate and 49p per
minute at all other times.
Call costings correct at time of going to press.

HOW TO GET TO THE GROUND

From the North and East
Use A127, sign posted Southend, and then at roundabout take 3rd
exit into Victoria Avenue for Southend United FC.

From the South
Use A13, sign posted Southend, and then turn left into West Road
and at end turn left into Victoria Avenue for Southend United FC.

Car Parking
Reserved car park on match days. Ample street parking is available.

Nearest Railway Station
Southend Central (01702 611 811) Prittlewell.

MATCHDAY PROGRAMME

Programme Editor . . . . Kevin O'Donnell.

Number of pages . . . . 40.

Price . . . . £1.50.

Subscriptions . . . . Apply to club.

Local Newspapers . . . . Evening Echo, Standard Recorder,
. . . . Yellow Advertiser.

Local Radio Stations . . . . Essex Radio, BBC Essex.

STOKE CITY
(The Potters)
ENDSLEIGH LEAGUE DIVISION 1
SPONSORED BY: CARLING

Back Row (L-R): Ian Clarkson, Keith Scott, Lee Sandford, Ian Cranson, Graham Potter, Vince Overson (Captain), John Dreyer, John Gayle Carl Beeston. **Middle Row:** Ashley Grimes, Lou Macari, Mohammed Gargo, Toddy Orlygsson, Ronnie Sinclair, Carl Muggleton, Mark Prudhoe, Nigel Gleghorn, Larus Sigurdsson, Ian Liversage (Physio), Chic Bates. **Front Row:** Kevin Keen, Simon Sturridge, Paul Peschisolido, Ray Wallace, Martin Carruthers.

STOKE CITY
FORMED IN 1868
TURNED PROFESSIONAL IN 1885
LTD COMPANY IN 1908

PRESIDENT: Sir Stanley Matthews
CHAIRMAN: P Coates

DIRECTORS
K A Humphreys (Vice-Chairman)
D J Edwards, M E Moors
SECRETARY
M J Potts (01782 413 511)
CHIEF EXECUTIVE
Jez Moxey

MANAGER: Lou Macari
ASSISTANT MANAGER: Chic Bates

RESERVE TEAM MANAGER
Ashley Grimes
YOUTH TEAM MANAGER
Tony Lacey
PHYSIOTHERAPIST
Ian Liversage

STATISTICIAN FOR THE DIRECTORY
Wade Martin

Despite the previous season's exploits that saw the club in with a chance of a play-off position until the death there was no great optimism within the supporters hearts as the campaign opened. This was all due to a Summer of signings that failed to spark any imagination and the presence of Joe Jordan in the manager's chair.

Jordan was undoubtedly an astute and deep thinking coach who was extremely professional in all he did however he had a thankless job in following the fans' hero Lou Macari and had singularly failed to open any level of communication up with the average Stoke fan. Perhaps clubs are fortunate who find a good communicator as well as a good coach but when things turn sour and the fans call for a managers' head a poor communicator has nowhere to go.

So it was when City Chairman Peter Coates decided a change was appropriate in September. He and the fans knew Lou Macari was fully available to return having parted company with Celtic during the Summer. After an appropriate period of haggling Macari made a hero's return. Later joined by Chic Bates he saw the side slip perilously close to the end of the season. A late recovery saw the side end the season in 11th place. It would be unique for a club's fan to say that their team's final League position flattered them and this is no time to start but this is as close as Stoke will get to such sacrilege.

On the pitch there were all too few highlights. The usual two victories over West Brom. - how we enjoy beating our Staffordshire rivals - a truly memorable game at Liverpool when we silenced the Anfield throng before losing 2-1 and an end of season game at home to Bolton Wanderers that had more incident than most club's see in a season.

Looking ahead Lou Macari has much to do to reshape a squad back into his preferred image. There will be a clear out in the Summer and hopes to strengthen the squad for a serious attempt at the Premier League. Like all supporters Stoke fans continue to dream of a higher League. Clearly their hopes have to be realistic but with decisions on the stadium to be taken the directors face the usual demands to show their commitment to the club and to get their cheque books out! If it were so simple.

WADE MARTIN.

STOKE CITY

Division One: 11th   **FA Cup:** 3rd Round   **Coca-Cola Cup:** 3rd Round   **Anglo Italian Cup:** Semi-Finalists

M	DATE	COMP.	VEN	OPPONENTS	RESULT	H/T	LP	GOAL SCORERS/GOAL TIMES	ATT.
1	A 13	EL	H	Tranmere Rovers	W 1-0	0-0		Gleghorn 48	15,915
2	20	EL	A	Burnley	D 1-1	0-1		Dreyer 90	(15,331)
3	24	AIC Gp B	A	Cesena	W 2-0	1-0		Clark 38, Carruthers 76	(1,139)
4	27	EL	H	Sunderland	L 0-1	0-1			15,159
5	30	EL	A	Reading	L 0-4	0-0			(7,103)
6	S 3	EL	A	Bolton Wanderers	L 0-4	0-1	22		(11,515)
7	6	AIC Gp B	H	Ancona	D 1-1	0-1		Biggins 50	3,330
8	10	EL	H	Southend United	W 4-1	2-0	16	Orlygsson 11, Williams 14 (og), Dreyer 47, Biggins 62	11,808
9	14	EL	H	Charlton Athletic	W 3-2	2-0		Gleghorn 18, Orlygsson 23, Peschisolido 57	10,643
10	17	EL	A	Notts County	W 2-0	1-0	6	Peschisolido 31, 70	(8,281)
11	20	CC 2/1	A	Fulham	L 2-3	0-0		Orlygsson 70 (pen), Gleghorn 71	(3,721)
12	25	EL	A	Derby County	L 0-3	0-2			(11,782)
13	28	CC 2/2	H	Fulham	W 1-0	1-0		Peschisolido 3	7,440
14	O 2	EL	H	West Bromwich Albion	W 4-1	2-1	7	Carruthers 25, 86, Wallace 36, Peschisolido 69	14,203
15	5	AIC Gp B	A	Udinese	W 3-1	0-1		Sandford 69, Biggins 73, Butler 74	(1,200)
16	9	EL	H	Luton Town	L 1-2	0-1	7	Carruthers 81	11,712
17	15	EL	A	Millwall	D 1-1	0-1	7	Peschisolido 54	(7,856)
18	22	EL	A	Oldham Athletic	D 0-0	0-0	9		(8,954)
19	25	CC 3	A	Liverpool	L 1-2	1-1		Peschisolido 41	(32,060)
20	30	EL	H	Wolverhampton Wand.	D 1-1	1-1		Keen 17	15,928
21	N 2	EL	H	Sheffield United	D 1-1	0-1		Gleghorn 78	11,556
22	5	EL	A	Barnsley	L 0-2	0-1	16		(5,117)
23	15	AIC Gp B	H	Piacenza	W 4-0	2-0		Butler 12, Carruthers 37, 50, Gleghorn 85	7,240
24	19	EL	A	Grimsby Town	W 3-0	2-0	12	Peschisolido 23, 44, Carruthers 60	12,055
25	26	EL	A	Watford	D 0-0	0-0	13		(9,126)
26	30	EL	A	Portsmouth	W 1-0	0-0		Beeston 75	(5,272)
27	D 4	EL	H	Oldham Athletic	L 0-1	0-0	12		12,558
28	10	EL	H	Burnley	W 2-0	0-0	10	Orlygsson 68 (pen), 83	13,040
29	17	EL	A	Tranmere Rovers	W 1-0	0-0	9	Carruthers 82	(7,615)
30	26	EL	H	Swindon Town	D 0-0	0-0	8		17,662
31	27	EL	A	Bristol City	L 1-3	0-0		Cranson 83	(8,500)
32	31	EL	H	Middlesbrough	D 1-1	1-1	11	Gleghorn 20	15,914
33	J 7	FAC 3	A	Bristol City	D 0-0	0-0			(9,683)
34	14	EL	A	Wolverhampton Wand.	L 0-2	0-1	14		(28,298)
35	18	FAC 3R	H	Bristol City	L 1-3	1-0		Scott 17	11,579
36	24	AIC SF1	A	Notts County	D 0-0	0-0			(5,135)
37	31	AIC SF2	H	Notts County	D †0-0	0-0		(Lost 2-3 on penalties)	10,741
38	F 4	EL	H	Portsmouth	L 0-2	0-0	15		9,764
39	11	EL	A	Sheffield United	D 1-1	1-1	16	Peschisolido 26	(13,900)
40	21	EL	A	Grimsby Town	D 0-0	0-0			(6,384)
41	25	EL	A	West Bromwich Albion	W 3-1	1-1	14	Scott 34, Peschisolido 65, 80	(16,591)
42	M 4	EL	H	Derby County	D 0-0	0-0			13,462
43	11	EL	A	Sunderland	L 0-1	0-0	18		(12,282)
44	14	EL	A	Port Vale	D 1-1	1-1	18	Sandford 33	(19,510)
45	18	EL	H	Reading	L 0-1	0-1	20		10,006
46	21	EL	A	Southend United	L 2-4	0-2	19	Allen 49, Biggins 60 (pen)	(4,240)
47	25	EL	H	Notts County	W 2-1	1-0	19	Gleghorn 13, Sturridge 77	10,204
48	A 1	EL	A	Charlton Athletic	D 0-0	0-0	18		(10,008)
49	4	EL	H	Watford	W 1-0	1-0	16	Sigurdsson 43	9,576
50	8	EL	A	Middlesbrough	L 1-2	1-1	18	Peschisolido 30	(20,867)
51	12	EL	H	Barnsley	D 0-0	0-0			10,752
52	15	EL	H	Bristol City	W 2-1	1-1		Zayangola 27, Peschisolido 89	10,172
53	17	EL	A	Swindon Town	W 1-0	1-0	14	Orlygsson 36	(10,549)
54	22	EL	H	Port Vale	L 0-1	0-0	15		20,429
55	29	EL	H	Millwall	W 4-3	2-2	15	Scott 16, Gleghorn 40, 65, Keen 90	9,111
56	M 3	EL	H	Bolton Wanderers	D 1-1	1-1	13	Orlygsson 12 (pen)	15,557
57	7	EL	A	Luton Town	W 3-2	0-1	11	Orlygsson 52, Peschisolido 79, Scott 87	(8,252)
58									
59									
60									

Best Home League Attendance: 20,867 v Port Vale   **Smallest:** 9,111 v Millwall   **Av Home Att:** 12,921

Goal Scorers: **Compared with 1993-94:** -3,044

League (50): Peschisolido 13, Gleghorn 7, Orlygsson 7 (2 pens), Carruthers 5, Scott 3, Dreyer 2, Biggins 2 (1 pen), Keen 2, Wallace, Beeston, Cranson, Sandford, Allen, Sturridge, Sigurdsson, Zay Angola, Opponents

C/Cola Cup (4): Peschisolido 2, Gleghorn, Orlygsson (pen)

FA Cup (1): Stott

Anglo/Ital Cup (10): Carruthers 3, Biggins 2, Butler 2, Clark, Gleghorn, Sandford

Muggleton C.	Clark J.	Sandford L.	Dreyer J.	Overson V.	Orlygsson T.	Carruthers M.	Wallace R.	Biggins W.	Peschisolido P.	Gleghorn N.	Beckford J.	Prudhoe M.	Butler J.	Sturridge S.	Shaw G.	Cranson I.	Downing K.	Clarkson I.	Sinclair R.	Keen K.	Potter G.	Beeston C.	Sigurdsson L.	Allen	Scott	Referee	
1	2	3	4	5	6	7	8	9	10*	11	12	S	S													J. Kirkby	1
1	2	3	4	5	6*	7*	8	9		11		S	14	10	12											W. Flood	2
1	2	3	4			16	8	9•		11		S	7	10	S	5	6*	15								D. Allison	3
1	2	3	4			12	8	9	7	11		S	S	10*		5	6									G. Lunt	4
1	2	3	4			12	8	9†	7*	11			S	10			6									G. Pooley	5
1	2•	3	4	5			8	9	7	11			14	10	S		6									A. Dawson	6
1		3	4	5		12	8	9*	7	11			10	S		2	S	S	6•							C. Bolognino	7
1		3	4	5	6	14	12	9•	10	11		7*	S	2			8									I. Cruickshanks	8
1		3	4		6	9	7	10	11				S	2		5	8	S								K. Lynch	9
1		3	4		6	9	7	10	11			S	S	2		5	8									E. Wolstenholme	10
1		3	4		6	9	7	10	11			S	2			5	8									M. Bailey	11
1		3	4		6	9•	7	14	10	11		S	2			5	8									N. Barry	12
1		3	4		6	7	9	10	11			S	S	2		5	8									J. Watson	13
1		3	4	12	6	9	2	14	10•	11		7*				5	8	S								I. Cruickshanks	14
1		3	4	7	6	9•	2*	10	14	11		12				5	8									T. Heilbron	15
1		3	4†	12	6	9	2*	10•	11	14		7				5	8	S								P. Alcock	16
1		3	4	2	6	9	12	10*	11	S		7				5	8	S								T. West	17
1		3		5	6	9	14	10•	11			2				4	S	7	12							R. Hart	18
1		3		5	6	9*	12	10	11•			2				4	8	S	7							J. Holbrook	19
1		3		5	6	9	14	10	11•			2				4	S	7	8	S						F. Stretton	20
1		3		5	6	9	S	10	11			2				4	S	7•	8							K. Lynch	21
1		3		5	6	9		10•	11			2				4	2	S	7	8						P. Wright	22
1		3		5		9•	7	14	10	11		2*	S	12		4	6	S	8							C. Dinelli	23
1		3	S	5	6	9	S	10	11			2				4	7		8							J. Lloyd	24
1		3	S	5	6	9	S	14	10	11		2				4	8	S	7							P. Foakes	25
1		3	S	5	6	9	S	10	11			2				4	S	7•	8	S						I. Hemley	26
1		3		5	6	9	14	10	11			2				4	2	S	7•	8	12					K. Leach	27
1		3		5	6	9•	14	10	11			7*				4	2	S	8	12						C. Wilkes	28
1G		3	12	5	6	9•	14	10	11			2				4	7	G	8*							R. Poulain	29
1		3	5		6	9		10	11			2				4	7	S	8*	S						D. Allison	30
8		3	5•		6	9*		12	11			2	14			4	8	1	7							P. Vanes	31
1G		3		5	6	9*		10	11			2				4	7	G	S	8						U. Rennie	32
		3		5	6			10*	11	S	2	12				4	8•	7	1	14		9				K. Cooper	33
		3	8*	5	6	12		10	11	S		7	2			4	2	1		9•						J. Winter	34
		3		5	6	12	8	S	10	11	S	7				4	2*	1		9						K. Cooper	35
		3	S	5		9	8		11•	S		7	S			4	14	2	1	S		6				P. Vanes	36
		3		5		9	7	8•	11			S	16			4	15	2	1	S		6				E. Parker	37
			3•		7			8	11	S		12				4	10	2*	1	5		6	9			W. Burns	38
			12		6			8	11	S		3				4	10*	2	1	5		7	9•			P. Richards	39
		3		5	6	12		9	11	S		10				4		1	S	2		7	8*			E. Parker	40
		3		5	6	9•		11*	S	7	14					4	1	12	2			8	10			E. Wolstenholme	41
S		3		5	6*	9•		12		7						4	1	14	11	2		8	10			E. Lomas	42
S		3		5				11*		7	14					4	1	12	6	2		8	10•			J. Lloyd	43
S		3		5	6*	9•		12					2			4	1		12	8		7	10			A. Dawson	44
S		3		5	6	9		12					2*	14		4	1		8	7		10	11•			A. Flood	45
S		3•		5	6	9†							2	12		4	1		10*	8		7				P. Alcock	46
				5	6	9		11		S			2	14		4	1	12	8	3		7*	10•			N. Barry	47
				5		14		9•		11			S	2		4	12	1	6	8*		3	7	10		G. Barber	48
				5				9*		11			S	2		4	8	12	1	6		3	7	10		I. Cruickshanks	49
						8	4	9		11			S	2			6	5	1			3	7			M. Riley	50
				6				9		11			S	2		4	7	3	1	S		5	8	10•		K. Cooper	51
				6	14	4		9		11			S	2			8*	1	12			3	7•			D. Allison	52
				5	6	9	14			11			S	2		4	1		8•			3	12			G. Singh	53
				5		10•	3	9		11			S	2		4†	1		8			6	S			S. Dunn	54
		S		5	6	S	7	9		11			S	2		4	1		8			3	10			J. Kirkby	55
		12		5*	6	14	7	9		11			S	2		4	1		8			3	10•			P. Wright	56
		4		5	6	7		9*		11			S	2		12	1		8			3	10			G. Pooley	57
24	5	34	16	33	38	26	16	8	39	44	2		38	2	1	37	16	15	22	15	1	15	22	17	16	League Appearances	
	1	2	2		6	4	9	1	2	2			3	6	2			3	2	6		1	1		1	League Sub Appearances	
3		3	2	1	3	3	1	1+1	3	3			3			3	2	1		0+1	1					C/Cola Cup Appearances	
		2			2	2	0+1	1	2	2			2	0+1		2	1	2	2				0+1		2	FA Cup Appearances	
4	1	6	3	5	1	4+2	6	3+1	3+1	6	1		4+1	1+1	0+1	5	3+2	3+1	2			1				Anglo/Ital Appearances	

Also Played: Wade 14 (21), Stokoe S (15,23,57), Williams 12(30,32),10(31), Leslie 14(38),S(3),16(7), Drury S(15), Macari S(15), Gayle 10(36),10*(37),10•(50), 14(39,46,54), Zay Angola S(49), 14(50,51),10(52),10*(53), Whittle S(50)   Players on Loan: Williams (Coventry City), Allen (Southampton), Zay Angola (Academico, Port.ugali)   † = Sent Off

STOKE CITY

CLUB RECORDS

BIGGEST VICTORIES
League: 9-0 v Plymouth Argyle, Division 2, 17.12.1960
F.A. Cup: 7-1 v Burnley, Round 2, 20.2.1896
League Cup: 6-2 v Chelsea, Round 2, 22.10.1974
Europe: 3-1 v Kaiserslautern, UEFA Cup, 1972-73

BIGGEST DEFEATS
League: 0-10 v Preston North End, Division 1, 4.2.1937
F.A. Cup: 0-7 v Leicester City, 14.11.1910
League Cup: No more than 3 goals
Europe: 0-4 v Kaiserslautern, UEFA Cup 1972-73

MOST POINTS
3 points a win: 93, Division 3/2, 1992-93
2 points a win: 63, Division 3N, 1926-27

MOST GOALS
92, Division 3N, 1926-27
Wilson 25, Davies 14, Eyres 12, Bussey 8, Williams 6, Archibald 6, Johnson 5, Armitage 5, Williams 5, Watkin 3, Cull 1, Beswick 1, Opponents 1

MOST LEAGUE GOALS CONCEDED
91, Division 1, 1984-85

MOST FIRST CLASS MATCHES IN A SEASON
67 (42 League, 9 FA Cup, 12 League Cup, 4 Texaco Cup) 1971-72

MOST LEAGUE WINS
27, Division 3(N), 1926-27
27, Division 3/2, 1992-93

MOST LEAGUE DRAWS
19, Division 2, 1989-90

MOST LEAGUE DEFEATS
31, Division 1, 1984-85

INDIVIDUAL CLUB RECORDS

MOST GOALS IN A MATCH
7. Neville Coleman v Lincoln, Div 2, 23.2.1957

MOST GOALS IN A SEASON
Charles Wilson, 38, (32 League, 6 FA Cup) 1927-28
3 goals twice=6, 2 goals seven times=14, 1 goal 18 times=18

OLDEST PLAYER
Sir Stanley Matthews, 50 years 5 days v Fulham, 6.2.1965

YOUNGEST PLAYER
Peter Bullock, 16 years 163 days v Swansea, 19.4.1958

MOST CAPPED PLAYER
Gordon Banks (England) 36

BEST PERFORMANCES

League: 1926-27: Matches played 42, Won 27, Drawn 9, Lost 6, Goals for 92, Goals against 40, Points 63. 1st in Division 3N

Highest: Fourth in Division 1, 1935-36 & 1946-47

F.A. Cup: 1898-99: 3rd rnd. Sheffield Wednesday (a) 2-2, (h) 2-0; 4th rnd. Birmingham City (h) 2-2, (a) 2-1; 5th rnd. Tottenham H (h) 4-1; Semi-final Derby County 1-3
1970-71: 3rd rnd. Millwall 2-1; 4th rnd. Huddersfield 3-3, 0-0, 1-0; 5th rnd. Ipswich Town 0-0 1-0; 6th rnd. Hull City 3-2; Semi-final Arsenal 2-2, 0-2
1971-72: 3rd rnd. Chesterfield 2-1; 4th rnd. Tranmere Rov 2-2, 2-0; 5th rnd. Hull City 4-1; 6th rnd. Manchester Utd 1-1, 2-1; Semi-final Arsenal 1-1, 1-2

League Cup: 1971-72: 2nd rnd. Southport 2-1; 3rd rnd. Oxford United 1-1, 1-0; 4th rnd. Manchester Utd 1-1, 0-0, 2-1; 5th rnd. Bristol Rov 4-2; Semi-final West Ham Utd, 1-2, 1-0, 0-0, 3-2; Final Chelsea 2-1.

DIVISIONAL RECORD

	Played	Won	Drawn	Lost	For	Against	Points
Division 1	1,992	662	474	856	2,447	3,137	1,842
Division 2/1	1,358	531	348	479	1,949	1,794	1,512
Division 3/2	138	64	38	36	197	142	230
Division 3(N)	42	27	9	6	92	40	63
Total	3,530	1,284	869	1,377	4,685	5,113	3,647

ADDITIONAL INFORMATION
Previous Name: Stoke Ramblers, Stoke-upon-Trent, Stoke.

Previous League: Southern League; Birmingham League; Football Alliance

Club colours: Red and white striped shirts, white shorts, red & white socks.
Change colours: Green & black striped shirts, black shorts, green & black socks.
Reserves League: Pontins Central League Division 1

RECORDS AND STATISTICS

COMPETITIONS

Div.1	Div.2/1	Div.3/2	Div.3(N)
1888-90	1890-91	1890-93	1926-27
1891-1907	1907-08		
1922-23	1919-22		
1933-53	1923-26		
1963-77	1927-33		
1979-86	1953-63		
	1977-79		
	1986-90		
	1993-		

HONOURS

Div.2	Div.3/2	Div.3(N)	Lge Cup	Watney
1932-33	1992-93	1926-27	1971-72	1973
1962-63				**AMC**
				1991-92

MOST APPEARANCES

Eric Skeels 591 (1959-76)

Year	League	FA Cup	Lge Cup	Europe
1959-60	2			
1960-61	37	6	1	
1961-62	42	3	1	
1962-63	38	1	2	
1964-64	39	5	10	
1964-65	42	3	5	
1965-66	41	1	5	
1966-67	40	1	1	
1967-68	34	3	4	
1968-69	35+1	4		
1969-70	34+1	0+1	1+1	
1970-71	27+2	9+1	1	
1971-72	13+6	4	1+1	
1972-73	30+1	1	2	1
1973-74	15	1	1	
1974-75	22+1		1	
1975-76	4			
	495+12	42+2	36+2	1

Including 1 appearance in the Texaco Cup.

MOST GOALS IN A CAREER

John Ritchie - 171 (1962-66 & 1969-75)

Year	League	FA Cup	Lge Cup	Others
1963-64	18	2	10	
1964-65	25	2	2	
1965-66	13			
1966-67	8		1	
1969-70	14	2		
1970-71	13	6		
1971-72	12	2	4	2
1972-73	14		1	1
1973-74	14	1		
1974-75	4			
Total	**135**	**15**	**18**	**3**

Current leading goalscorer: Nigel Gleghorn - 22 (1992-95)

MANAGERS

Name	Seasons	Best	Worst
Tom Slaney	1874-83		
Walt Cox	1883-84		
Harry Lockett	1884-90	12(1)	12(1)
Joe Bradshaw	1890-92	13(1)	13(1)
Arthur Reeves	1892-95	7(1)	14(1)
William Rowley	1895-97	6(1)	13(1)
H Austerberry	1897-08	6(1)	10(2)
A J Barker	1908-14		
Peter Hodge	1914-15		
Joe Schofield	1915-19		
Arthur Shallcross	1919-23	21(1)	20(2)
John Rutherford	1923		
Tom Mather	1923-25	6(2)	20(2)
Bob McGory	1935-52	4(1)	1(3N)
Frank Taylor	1952-60	21(1)	17(2)
Tony Waddington	1960-77	5(1)	18(2)
George Eastham	1977-78	7(2)	7(2)
Alan A'Court	1978		
Alan Durban	1978-81	11(1)	3(2)
Ritchie Barker	1981-83	13(1)	18(1)
Bill Asprey	1984-85	18(1)	22(1)
Mick Mills	1985-89	8(2)	13(2)
Alan Ball	1989-91	22(2)	14(3)
Lou Macari	1991-93	1(3/2)	4(3)
Joe Jordan	1993-94	10(2/1)	19(2/1)
Lou Macari	1994-		

RECORD TRANSFER FEE RECEIVED

Amount	Club	Player	Date
£1,500,000	Chelsea	Mark Stein	11/93
£750,000	Everton	Peter Beagrie	10/89
£700,000	Everton	Adrian Heath	1/82
£600,000	Tottenham H.	Garth Crooks	7/80

RECORD TRANSFER FEE PAID

Amount	Club	Player	Date
£450,000	Sheffield Wed	Ian Cranston	7/89
£350,000	Manchester Utd	Sammy McIlroy	2/82
£325,000	Leicester City	Peter Shilton	11/74
£240,000	Chelsea	Alan Hudson	1/74

LONGEST LEAGUE RUNS

of undefeated matches:	25 (5.9.1992 - 20.2.1993)	of league matches w/out a win:	7 (15.9.1984 - 22.12.1984)
of undefeated home matches:	23 (15.12.1973 - 21.12.1974)	of undefeated away matches:	12 (12.9.1992 - 30.1.1993)
without home win:	9 (15.4.1963 - 30.11.1963)	without an away win:	30 (16.1.1897 - 18.12.1899)
of league wins:	7 (2.9.1905 - 23.9.1905, 4.4.1947 - 26.5.1947)	of home wins:	11 (30.3.1895 - 21.12.1895)
of league defeats:	11 (6.4.1985 - 17.8.1985)	of away wins:	5 (14.1.1922 - 11.3.1922, 4.4.1947 - 26.5.1947)

STOKE CITY

PLAYERS NAME Honours	Ht	Wt	Birthdate	Birthplace Transfers	Contract Date	Clubs	APPEARANCES League	L/Cup	FA Cup	Other	GOALS Lge	L/C	FAC	Oth
G O A L K E E P E R S														
Phil Morgan	6.1	13.0	18.12.74	Stoke-on-Trent	01.07.93	Ipswich Town (T)								
E: S.				Free	08.95	Stoke City								
Carl Muggleton	6.0	11.13	13.09.68	Leicester	17.09.86	Leicester City (A)	46		3	5				
E: u21.1.				Loan	10.09.87	Chesterfield	17			2				
Loan Blackpool, 01.02.88, 2 Lge App.				Loan	28.10.88	Hartlepool United	8			2				
Loan Stockport Co., 01.03.90, 4 Lge App.				Loan	13.08.93	Stoke City	6	1		2				
				£150,000	11.01.94	Celtic	12		1					
				£200,000	21.07.94	Stoke City	24	3		4				
Mark Prudhoe	6.0	13.0	11.11.63	Washington	11.09.81	Sunderland (A)	7							
GMVC'90. Div.4'91. FLgXI.				Loan	04.11.83	Hartlepool United	3							
Loans from Walsall				£22,000	24.09.84	Birmingham City	1	4						
Loan Doncaster Rovers, 11.12.85, 5 Lge App.				£22,000	27.02.86	Walsall	26	4	1					
Loan Grimsby Town, 26.03.87, 8 Lge App.				£10,000	11.12.87	Carlisle United	34	2						
Loan Hartlepool United, 29.08.87, 13 Lge App.				Loan	16.03.89	Darlington	146	8	9	6				
Loan Bristol City, 6.11.87, 3 Lge, 2 Oth App.				£120,000	24.06.93	Stoke City	30	3	2	3				
Loan 30.09.94 Peterborough Utd 6 Lge App.				Loan	29.11.94	Liverpool								
Ronnie Sinclair	5.9	11.12	19.11.64	Stirling	30.10.82	Nottm. Forest (A)								
S: Y, S. Div.2'93.				Loan	01.03.84	Wrexham	11			1				
				£10,000	27.06.86	Leeds United	8	1						
Loan Halifax Town, 01.03.87, 4 Lge App.				Loan	23.12.88	Halifax Town	10			1				
				Free	01.09.89	Bristol City	44	3	5	3				
Loan Walsall, 05.09.91, 10 Lge, 1 Oth App.				£25,000	21.11.91	Stoke City	77+2	2	4	9				
				Loan	26.08.94	Bradford City								
D E F E N D E R S														
Carl Beeston	5.9	10.3	30.06.67	Stoke	01.07.85	Stoke City (A)	194+8	12	7+1	15	13	1	1	2
E: u21.1. Div.2'93														
Ian Clarkson	5.11	11.8	04.12.70	Solihull	15.12.88	Birmingham City (T)	125+11	12	5+1	17+1				
AMC'91.				£40,000	13.09.93	Stoke City	29+3	3	3	4+2				
Ian Cranson	5.11	12.4	02.07.64	Easington	05.07.82	Ipswich Town (A)	130+1	15	11+1	7	5			
E: u21.5. AGT'92. Div.2'93.				£450,000	24.03.88	Sheffield Wed.	29+1	2	2	1				
				£450,000	25.07.89	Stoke City	191+2	16	13	26	8	1	1	1
John Dreyer	6.0	11.6	11.06.63	Alnwick		Wallingford								
Loans from Oxford United					08.01.85	Oxford United	57+3	10+1	2	3	2			
Loan Torquay United, 13.12.85, 5 Lge App.				£140,000	27.06.88	Luton Town	212+2	13+1	14	8	14	1		
Loan Fulham, 27.03.88, 12 Lge App. 2 gls.				Free	15.07.94	Stoke City	16+2	2		3	2			
				Loan	23.03.95	Bolton Wanderers	1+1			1+1				
Vince Overson	6.0	13.0	15.05.62	Kettering	16.11.79	Burnley (A)	207+4	9	19	10	6	1		
Div.3'82. Div.2'93. AMC'91'92.				Free	11.06.86	Birmingham City	179+3	11+1	8	11	3		1	
				£55,000	29.08.91	Stoke City	149+3	10	10	21	6	1		
Graham Potter	5.11	11.0	20.05.75	Solihull	01.07.92	Birmingham City (T)	23+2		1	6	2			
E: Y.1.				Loan	17.09.93	Wycombe W.	2+1	1		1				
				£75,000	20.12.93	Stoke City	3+1	0+1	2					
Lee Sandford	6.1	12.2	22.04.68	Basingstoke	04.12.85	Portsmouth (A)	66+6	11	4	2+1	1			
E: Y, S. AGT'92. Div.2'93.				£140,000	22.12.89	Stoke City	209+3	16	14	27	8		2	4
Ray Wallace	5.6	10.2	02.10.69	Greenwich	21.04.88	Southampton (A)	33+2	8	2	2				
E: u21.4.				£100,000	08.07.91	Leeds United	5+2							
				Loan	20.03.92	Swansea City	2							
Loan11.03.94 Reading 3 Lge App.				Free	12.08.94	Stoke City	16+4	1	1	6	1			
				Loan	16.12.94	Hull City	7							
M I D F I E L D														
Mark Devlin	5.9	11.3	18.01.73	Irvine	06.04.91	Stoke City (T)	21+3	1+1			2			
Nigel Gleghorn	6.0	12.13	12.08.62	Seaham		Seaham Red Star								
AMC'91. Div.2'93.				Free	30.08.85	Ipswich Town	54+12	3+2	3+1	7+2	11		2	
				£47,500	04.08.88	Manchester City	27+7	2	0+1	1	7	2	1	1
				£175,000	09.09.89	Birmingham City	142	13	7	14	33	5	3	2
				£100,000	24.10.92	Stoke City	116+4	7	8	17	17	2	2	1
Kevin Keen	5.6	10.3	25.02.67	Amersham	08.03.84	West Ham U. (A)	187+32	21+1	15+7	14+2	21	5	1	3
E: Y.10, S.				£600,000	07.07.93	Wolverhampton W	37+5	2+1	5	4	7		1	1
				£300,000	19.10.94	Stoke City	15+6				2			
Thorvaldur Orlygsson	5.11	10.13	02.08.66	Odense (Iceland)		KA Akureyri								
Icelandic Int.				£175,000	09.12.89	Nottingham Forest	31+6	5+1	1	0+1	2	2		
				Free	05.08.93	Stoke City	80+3	7	6	6	16	1	1	1
Larus Sigurdsson	6.0	11.5	04.06.73	Iceland		Iceland								
Icelandic Int. u21, Yth.				£150,000	21.10.94	Stoke City	22+2		0+1		1			
F O R W A R D S														
Martin Carruthers	5.11	11.9	07.08.72	Nottingham	04.07.90	Aston Villa (T)	2+2		0+1	0+1				
				Loan	31.10.92	Hull City	13			3	6			
				£300,000	05.07.93	Stoke City	50+16	4+2	2+1	8+3	10	1	3	3
John Gayle	6.4	13.1	30.07.64	Bromsgrove		Burton Albion								
AMVC'91				£30,000	01.03.89	Wimbledon	17+3	3			2			
				£175,000	21.11.90	Birmingham City	39+5		2	8+1	10			4
				Loan	20.08.93	Walsall	4				1			
				£100,000	13.09.93	Coventry City	3	1+2						
					01.09.95	Burnley	7+7	1+1	1+1		3	1	1	
				£70,000	23.01.95	Stoke City	1+3			2				

STOKE CITY

PLAYERS NAME / Honours	Ht	Wt	Birthdate	Birthplace / Transfers	Contract Date	Clubs	APPEARANCES League	L/Cup	FA Cup	Other	GOALS Lge	L/C	FAC	Oth
Steven Leslie	5.4	10.7	06.02.70	Dumfries	20.03.93	Stoke City (T)	0+1			0+1				
Paolo Peschisolido	5.4	10.5	25.05.71	Scarboro' (Can.)		Toronto Bl (Can.)								
Candadian Int.				£25,000	11.11.92	Birmingham City	37+6	2	0+1	1+1	16	1		
				£400,000	.08.94	Stoke City	39+1	3	2	3+1	13	2		
Keith Scott	6.3	13.4	10.06.67	London		Hinckley United								
GMVC'93. FAT'91'93.				Free		Leicester United								
				Free	22.03.90	Lincoln City	7+9	0+1		1+1	2			
				£30,000	05.07.93	Wycombe Wands.	15	4	8	10	10	2	1	2
				£300,000	18.11.93	Swindon Town	43+8	5		3	12	3		1
				£300,000	30.12.94	Stoke City	16+2		2		3		1	
Simon Sturridge	5.5	10.7	09.12.69	Birmingham	08.07.88	Birmingham City (T)	129+21	10+4	8	14	30	125		
AMC'91.					24.09.93	Stoke City	7+14	1	1+3	3+3	1			
A D D I T I O N A L C O N T R A C T P L A Y E R S														
(M) Marl Bailey	5.8	10.12	12.08.76	Stoke	12.07.94	Stoke City (T)								
(D) Mark Holden	5.8	11.0	02.04.76	Dudley	12.07.94	Stoke City (T)								
				Loan	30.03.95	Telford United								
(M) Gary Holt	6.1	11.11	09.03.73	Irvine		Celtic								
						Stoke City								
Michael Macari			04.02.73	Kilwinning	31.07.91	Stoke City (T)								
Paul Macari					31.05.94	Stoke City (T)								
Justin Whittle						Celtic								
				Free	20.10.94	Stoke City								

TOP GOALSCORER 1994/95
Paolo Peschisolido

Division One goals (games) . . . . 13 (39+1)
Coca-Cola Cup Goals 2 (3)
F.A. Cup goals 0 (2)
Anglo Italian . . . . 0 (3+1)
Total . . . . **15 (47+2)**

Total goals for Stoke City since 08.94 . . . . 15 (47+2)

Career total as at June 1st 1995 . . . . 32 (87+10)

THE MANAGER
LOU MACARI

Date of Birth . . . . 7th June 1949.
Place of Birth . . . . Edinburgh.
Date of Appointment . . . . September 1994.

PREVIOUS CLUBS
As Manager . . . . Swindon, West Ham, Birmingham, Celtic.
As Coach . . . . None.
As a Player . . . . Celtic, Manchester United.

HONOURS
As a Manager
Swindon: Promotion to Div.3, 1985-86. Promotion to Div.2, 1986-87.
Birmingham: Leyland Daf Cup 1991.
Stoke: Promotion to Div.1, 1992-93.
As a Player
Celtic: League Championship 3 times. Scottish Cup twice.
Manchester United: FA Cup 1977.
International: 24 full caps for Scotland.

VICTORIA GROUND

Stoke-on-Trent, Staffordshire ST4 4EG
Tel: 01782 413 511

Capacity 25,409
Seating 9,650

First game..v Talke Rangers (Friendly) 25.3.1878.
First floodlit game ....v Port Vale, 10.10.1956.
Internationals..England v Wales 1889, 1893, v Ireland 1936.

ATTENDANCES
Highest ....51,380 v Arsenal, Division 1, 29.3.1937.
Lowest..3,516 v Coventry City, FMC, 18.9.1985.

OTHER GROUNDS ....Sweeting Fields 1875-78.   Victoria Ground 1878-

---

MATCHDAY TICKET PRICES

Boothen Stand Blocks B, C & D.
Adults £12
Juv/OAP £6
Butler Street Stand Block C.
Adults £12
Juv/OAP £6
Stoke End Stand £12
Family Ticket £10
Junior £5
Boothen End
Adult £8
Juv/OAP £5

Ticket Office Telephone no. 01782 413 961

CLUBCALL
0891 12 10 40

Calls cost 39p per minute cheap rate and 49p per
minute at all other times.
Call costings correct at time of going to press.

HOW TO GET TO THE GROUND

From the North, West and South
Use motorway M6 until junction 15, leave motorway and follow signs
to Stoke(A5006) then join A500. In 0.8 miles branch left and shortly
at roundabout take 2nd exit into Campbell Road for Stoke City FC.

From the East
Use A50 into Stoke town centre and at crossroads turn left into
Lonsdale Street for Campbell Road for Stoke City FC.

Car Parking
Whieldon Road Car Park - £1.
Also street parking.

Nearest Railway Station
Stoke (01782 411 411).

MATCHDAY PROGRAMME

Programme Editor . . . . Tony Tams.

Number of pages . . . . 48.

Price . . . . £1.50.

Subscriptions . . . . £36 UK, £42 Overseas.

Local Newspapers . . . . . . The Sentinel, North Staffordshire Advertiser.

Local Radio Stations . . . . BBC Radio Stoke, Signal Radio.

SUNDERLAND
(The Rokerites)
ENDSLEIGH LEAGUE DIVISION 1
SPONSORED BY: VAUX

Back Row (L-R): Martin Smith, Gary Bennett, Gordon Armstrong, Brett Angell, Richard Ord, Andy Melville, Lee Howey.
Middle Row: Mick Ferguson, Gordon Ellis, Paul Bracewell, Derek Furguson, Brain Atkinson, John Kay, Alec Chamberlain, David Preece, Michael Gray, Steve Agnew, Phil Gray, Martin Gray, Martin Scott, Steven Grant, Bobby Saxton, Pop Robson, Steve Smelt.
Front Row: Ricky Sbragia, Scott Coates, Christopher Lawless, Paul Heckingbottom, Dariusz Kubicki, Kevin Ball, Peter Reid, Craig Russell, David Mawson, Stephen Brodie, Sam Aiston, Joey McGiven, Stephen Pickering, John Cooke.

SUNDERLAND
FORMED IN 1879
TURNED PROFESSIONAL IN 1886
LTD COMPANY IN 1906

CHAIRMAN: J Featherstone
DIRECTORS
G S Wood (Vice-Chairman), J Wood,
R S Murray FCA, A E Ring, J M Ficking
SECRETARY
Paul Fiddaman
COMMERCIAL MANAGER
A King

MANAGER: Peter Reid
ASSISTANT MANAGER: Paul Bracewell
FIRST TEAM COACH: Bobby Saxton
RESERVE TEAM MANAGER
Bryan 'Pop' Robson
YOUTH TEAM MANAGER
Ricky Sbragia

PHYSIOTHERAPIST
S Smelt

STATISTICIAN FOR THE DIRECTORY
Eddie Brennan

For the second time in three years, Sunderland avoided relegation to Division Two by one point, after a season riddled with unrest as the long-suffering Roker fans' frustrations came to boiling point. With proposed boardroom takeovers amounting to nothing and the club's planned move to a new stadium very much in the balance, it is little wonder that many supporters are worried as to what the future holds for Sunderland.

On the field, a total of only forty one goals largely explains why this was a season of non-achievement. Despite the team suffering only one defeat in the first nine games, only two victories were recorded; indeed the Rokermen went on to equal a club record number of draws for a season. Manager Mick Buxton's defence-first policy may have saved the club the previous term but this time around it merely ensured that Sunderland were never going to be involved at the top end of the the division.

Admittedly, Buxton was not aided by the lack of money available for new signings and was forced to sell striker Don Goodman for £1.1 million. Three new faces were brought in; midfielder Steve Agnew from Leicester, defender Martin Scott from Bristol City and Everton striker Brett Angell, the latter signed on transfer deadline day in March. However, Angell was to feature in only one game for his new boss. A 0-2 reverse at Barnsley, a fourth consecutive defeat, signalled Buxton's demise with the club in 20th place and in real dire straits. To add extra farce, it was revealed afterwards that the on-loan Dominic Matteo had played for the Rokerites as an un-registered player at Oakwell and the club faced losing vital league points as a result. In the end the punishment was 'only' a £2,000 fine.

With the drop looking likely, the board turned to ex-Manchester City boss Peter Ried who was given seven games to stave off relegation. The former England midfielder soon brought a new enthusiasm to the club. A run of only one defeat in those seven games, that by a late strike at promotion-seeking Bolton, ensured that Sunderland were kept afloat for another year.

The fact that relegation battles seem to be the norm at Roker is nothing short of ridiculous and insulting for a club who can attract average gates of over 15,000 to watch a struggling side. It is hoped that the two year contract given to Peter Reid and the continued emergence of players like Richard Ord and Martin Smith, the latter making his England Under-21 debut last term, will signal better times on Wearside. They are certainly long overdue.
EDDIE BRENNAN.

SUNDERLAND

M	DATE	COMP.	VEN	OPPONENTS	RESULT	H/T	LP	GOAL SCORERS/GOAL TIMES	ATT.
1	A 13	EL	A	Bristol City	D 0-0	0-0			(11,127)
2	20	EL	H	Millwall	D 1-1	0-1	15	Goodman 53	17,296
3	27	EL	A	Stoke City	W 1-0	1-0	8	P. Gray 23	(15,159)
4	30	EL	H	Grimsby Town	D 2-2	1-1	11	Goodman 39 (pen), P. Gray 58	15,788
5	S 3	EL	H	Wolverhampton Wand.	D 1-1	1-1	11	P. Gray 22	15,111
6	11	EL	A	Middlesbrough	D 2-2	1-0	11	Russell 38, 54	(19,578)
7	13	EL	A	Sheffield United	D 0-0	0-0	12		(15,239)
8	17	EL	H	Barnsley	W 2-0	0-0	9	P. Gray 77, Goodman 85	16,145
9	20	CC 1/1	A	Millwall	L 1-2	0-2		Russell 53	(5,095)
10	24	EL	A	Tranmere Rovers	L 0-1	0-0	10		(7,500)
11	O 1	EL	A	Southend United	L 0-1	0-0	16		15,520
12	4	CC 1/2	H	Millwall	D 1-1	0-0		P. Gray 58	9,698
13	8	EL	A	West Bromwich Albion	W 3-1	2-0	12	M. Smith 27, P. Gray 35, 56	(13,717)
14	15	EL	H	Burnley	D 0-0	0-0	10		17,700
15	22	EL	A	Reading	W 2-0	1-0	8	Melville 11, P. Gray 48	(10,757)
16	29	EL	H	Oldham Athletic	D 0-0	0-0	8		17,252
17	N 1	EL	H	Charlton Athletic	D 1-1	1-0	10	M. Smith 18	14,085
18	5	EL	A	Notts County	L 2-3	0-2	12	P. Gray 62, Owers 66	(8,890)
19	19	EL	H	Watford	L 1-3	0-2	16	M. Smith 57	15,063
20	26	EL	A	Portsmouth	W 4-1	3-0	12	Russell 19, Melville 21, P. Gray 41 (pen), M. Smith 86	(7,527)
21	29	EL	A	Port Vale	D 0-0	0-0	12		(8,121)
22	D 3	EL	H	Reading	L 0-1	0-0	15		14,021
23	10	EL	A	Millwall	L 0-2	0-0	16		(7,698)
24	17	EL	H	Bristol City	W 2-0	0-0	16	Howey 54, 75	11,661
25	26	EL	H	Bolton Wanderers	D 1-1	0-0	16	M. Smith 49	19,758
26	27	EL	A	Luton Town	L 0-3	0-2	17		(8,953)
27	31	EL	H	Derby County	D 1-1	0-0	16	P. Gray 46	13,979
28	J 7	FAC 3	H	Carlisle United	D 1-1	0-0		Russell 47	15,523
29	14	EL	A	Oldham Athletic	D 0-0	0-0	18		(9,742)
30	17	FAC 3R	A	Carlisle United	W 3-1	2-0		Armstrong 6, 19, P. Gray 66	(12,201)
31	21	EL	H	Notts County	L 1-2	0-1	18	Armstrong 51	14,334
32	29	FAC 4	H	Tottenham Hotspur	L 1-4	0-0		P. Gray 75	21,135
33	F 4	EL	H	Port Vale	D 1-1	1-1	21	Ball 24	13,377
34	11	EL	A	Charlton Athletic	L 0-1	0-0	21		(12,380)
35	18	EL	H	Portsmouth	D 2-2	2-1	21	M. Smith 11, 30	12,372
36	21	EL	A	Watford	W 1-0	1-0	20	Russell 8	(8,189)
37	25	EL	A	Southend United	W 1-0	1-0	17	Agnew 44	(4,686)
38	M 5	EL	H	Tranmere Rovers	L 0-1	0-0	20		12,043
39	8	EL	A	Wolverhampton Wand.	L 0-1	0-0	20		(25,926)
40	11	EL	H	Stoke City	W 1-0	0-0	17	Melville 87	12,282
41	15	EL	A	Swindon Town	L 0-1	0-0	19		(8,233)
42	19	EL	A	Grimsby Town	L 1-3	0-1	19	Agnew 47	(5,697)
43	21	EL	H	Middlesbrough	L 0-1	0-0	20		16,501
44	24	EL	A	Barnsley	L 0-2	0-0	20		(7,803)
45	A 1	EL	H	Sheffield United	W 1-0	0-0	20	Russell 89	17,259
46	8	EL	A	Derby County	W 1-0	1-0	20	Ball 41	(15,442)
47	15	EL	H	Luton Town	D 1-1	1-0	19	P. Gray 59	17,292
48	17	EL	A	Bolton Wanderers	L 0-1	0-0	20		(15,030)
49	22	EL	H	Swindon Town	W 1-0	1-0	20	M. Smith 43	16,874
50	29	EL	A	Burnley	D 1-1	1-1	20	M. Smith 15	(15,121)
51	M 7	EL	H	West Bromwich Albion	D 2-2	1-0	20	M. Smith 16, P. Gray 90	18,232
53									
54									
55									
56									
57									
58									
59									
60									

Best Home League Attendance: 19,758 v Bolton Wanderers   **Smallest:** 11,661 v Bristol City   **Av Home Att:** 15,389

Goal Scorers: Compared with 1993-94: -1,608

League (41): P. Gray 12 (1 pen), M. Smith 10, Russell 5, Goodman 3 (1 pen), Melville 3, Agnew 2, Ball 2, Howey 2, Armstrong, Owers
C/Cola Cup (2): P. Gray, Russell
FA Cup (5): Armstrong 2, P Gray 2, Russell

13 Norman A.	16 Gray Ma.	26 Kubicki D.	4 Bennett G.	19 Melville A.	7 Owers G.	5 Ferguson D.	6 Ball K.	17 Gray M.	8 Goodman D.	10 Gray P.	15 Atkinson B.	18 Howey L.	1 Chamberlain A.	14 Cunnington S.	11 Russell C.	3 Ord R.	22 Smith M.	12 Rodgerson I.	30 Musgrave S.	25 Snodin I.	9 Armstrong G.	23 Brodie S.	5 Scott M.	8 Agnew S.	7 Williams P.	Referee	
X	X1	X	X	X	X	X	X	X	X	X	X	S1	S	S												P. Alcock	1
X		X	X	X	X1	X	X	X	X	X	X		S	S	S1											K. Lynch	2
X		X	X	X	X	X	X1	X	X	X			S	S1	S											T. Lunt	3
X		X	X1	X	X	X	X	X	X	X			S	S1	S											W. Burns	4
X		X		X	X	X	X	X	X	X		S	S	S	X	X										D. Allison	5
X		X		X	X	X	X	S2	X	X	X1		S	S1	X2	X										J. Rushton	6
X		X	S1	X	X	X	X	S	X	X			S		X1	X	X									J. Lloyd	7
X		X	X1	X	X	X	X	S	X	X					X	X	S1									P. Harrison	8
X		X	X	X	X	X1	X	S	X	X					X	X	S1									C. Wilkes	9
X	X	X	S	X	X†		X	S	X	X			S		X	X	X			X						E. Lomas	10
X2	X1	X		X	X		X	S	X	X				S2	X	X	X	S1								P. Wright	11
X	X1	X		X	X		X	S2	X	X		S1	S		X	X2	X									R. Poulain	12
	X	X	X	X			X		X	X		S	S		X1	X	X	S1		S						J. Kirkby	13
	X1	X		X			X	S	X	X		S1	X		X	X	X			S	X					M. Breen	14
	X	X		X			X		X	X		S	X		X1	X	X	S1		S	X					E. Wolstenholme	15
	X1	X		X	S1		X		X	X		S2	X		X	X	X			S	X2					K. Lupton	16
	S2	X		X	X		X		X	X			X		S1	X	X1	X		X2						W. Flood	17
	S	X		X	X		X		X	X			X		S1	X	X1	X	S	X						M. Bailey	18
S		X		X	X		X		X	X	X1		X		S2	X	X2	X			X	S1				J. Parker	19
S	X	X		X	X		X		S	X	X		X		X	X	X				S					S. Dunn	20
S	X	X		X	X		X	S1	X	X			X		X1	X	X				S					J. Brandwood	21
S	X	X		X	X1		X		X	X2	S2		X		X	X	X				S1					K. Poulain	22
S	X	X	X		X		X	S		X1		SQ	X		X	X	X				X					P. Vanes	23
S	X	X	X	X	X	X	X	S1		X			X		X		X				X1	S				D. Allison	24
S	S1	X	X†		X	X1		X		X			X	X1	X		X				S		X			N. Barry	25
S	X	X		X			X		X	X	S1	X1	X		X		X				S		X			J. Holbrook	26
S		X	X		X		S1		X	X1	X	S	X		X		X				X	S	X			J. Winter	27
S		X	X		X		S1		X	X1	X	S	X		X		X				X		X			W. Burns	28
S		X		X	X		S1		X		X		X		X	S	X				X1		X	X		J. Lloyd	29
S	S	X	X		X		X		X		X		X		X1		X				X		X			J. Worrall	30
S		X		X			S		X		S1		X		X		X				X	X	X1	X	W. Burns	31
S	S1	X	X†	X			S		X		X		X		X		X				X1		X			M. Reed	32
X		X		X	X		X		X		S	S	S		S1		X				X		X	X	X	E. Lomas	33
X		X	X			X2	X	S2	X		S1	S	X	X	X							X	X		X1	G. Singh	34
X		X		S	X	X	X		X1		X	S		S1	X	X						X	X			P. Harrison	35
X		X	X		X	X		X					S		X2	X	X1				S2	S1	X	X		C. Wilkes	36
X		X	X		X	X		X							X2	X	X1				S2	S1	X	X		D. Orr	37
X		X	X		X	X			X1		S1		S		X	X	X1				S		X	X		R. Poulain	38
X		X	X		X	X					X	S			X	X	X1				S	S1	X	X		P. Wright	39
X		X1		X	X	X	S				X	S			X	X1					X	S1	X	X		J. Lloyd	40
X		X	X1	X	X	X			X		X	S					X2				X1	S2	X	X		K. Breen	41
X		X		X	X	X			X		X	S	S2	X	X2						X1	S1	X	X		J. Kirkby	42
X		X		X	X				X			S2	S	X1	X2	X					X	S1	X	X		E. Wolstenholme	43
X	S12	X		X					X						S2	X	X				X1		X	X		D. Allison	44
X	S1	X	X		X1				X	X					S2	X	X						X	X		S. Mathieson	45
X	S1	X	X			X			X	X					X	X	X				S		X	X1		U,. Rennie	46
X	X	X	X1			X	S1		X	X					S2	X	S2						X			P. Richards	47
X	X	X		X			X	X		X	X2				S1	X	X						X			R. Furnandiz	48
X	X	X		X			X	X		X	X				S	X1	X						X			T. West	49
X	X	X		X			X	X		X1					S1	X	X					S	X			W. Flood	50
X	X	X		X			X	X		S1					S	X	X					X1	X			P. Wright	51
29	17	46	19	36	18	23	42	10	17	41	16	6	17	3	28	33	33	3		6	10	1	24	16	3	**League Appearances**	
	5		1		1			6	1	1	1	9	1	5	10		2	3		5	7					**League Sub Appearances**	
2	1	2	1	2	2	1	2	0+1	2		2	0+1			2	2	1+1									**League Cup Appearances**	
0+1	3	3	2		3	2	0+1		3	1	1+1	3			3	3	3				3		3			**FA Cup Appearances**	

Also Played: Angel X(44,46,49,50,51), X1(48), X2(45,47), Preece S(37,44,45,46,47,48,49,50,51), Matteo 20(44), Smith 21(S1,49)

Players on Loan: Snodin (Everton), Williams (Crystal Palace), Matteo (Liverpool)

† = Sent Off

SUNDERLAND

CLUB RECORDS

BIGGEST VICTORIES
League: 9-1 v Newcastle, Division 1, 5.12.1908
8-0 v Derby County, Division 1, 1.9.1894
F.A. Cup: 11-1 v Fairfield, Round 1, 2.2.1895
League Cup: 7-1 v Oldham Athletic, Round 2, 24.9.1962

BIGGEST DEFEATS
League: 0-8 v Sheffield Wednesday, Division 1, 26.12.1911
0-8 v West Ham Utd, Division 1, 19.10.1968
0-8 v Watford, Division 1, 25.9.1982
F.A. Cup: 2-7 v Aston Villa, Round 4, 27.1.1934
0-5 v Arsenal, Round 2, 1905-06
0-5 v Liverpool, Round 1 replay, 1921-22
0-5 v Tottenham Hotspur, Round 6 replay, 1960-61
League Cup: 0-6 v Derby County, Round 3, 31.10.1990

MOST POINTS
3 points a win: 93, Division 3, 1987-88
2 points a win: 61, Division 2, 1963-64

MOST GOALS
109, Division 1, 1935-36
Carter 31, Gurney 31, Gallagher 19, Davis 10, Conner 6, Duns 5, Goddard 2, Hornby 2, Thompson 1, McNab 1, og 1.

MOST LEAGUE GOALS CONCEDED
97, Division 1, 1957-58

MOST FIRST CLASS MATCHES IN A SEASON
59 (46 League, 1 FA Cup, 8 League Cup, 1 Zenith, 3 Play-Offs) 1989-90

MOST LEAGUE WINS
27, Division 3, 1987-88

MOST LEAGUE DRAWS
18, Division 1, 1954-55, Division 2/1 1994-95

MOST LEAGUE DEFEATS
22, Division 1, 1956-57; Division 1, 1969-70; Division 1, 1984-85; Division2/1 1992-93

INDIVIDUAL CLUB RECORDS

MOST GOALS IN A MATCH
5. C Buchan v Liverpool, 7.12.1919 (7-0)
5. R Gurney v Bolton W., 7.12.1935 (7-2)
5. D Sharkey v Norwich, 20.2.1962 (7-1)

MOST GOALS IN A SEASON
Dave Halliday 43, 1928-29
4 goals once=4, 3 goals twice=6, 2 goals ten times=20, 1 goal 13 times=13

OLDEST PLAYER
Bryan `Pop' Robson, 38 years 128 days v Leicester, 12.5.1984

YOUNGEST PLAYER
Derek Forster, 15 years 184 days v Leicester, 22.8.1964

MOST CAPPED PLAYER
Martin Harvey (Northern Ireland) 34

BEST PERFORMANCES

League: 1963-64: Matches played 42, Won 25, Drawn 11, Lost 6, Goals for 87, Goals against 37, Points 61. 2nd in Division 2.

Highest: First in Division 1.

F.A. Cup: 1936-37: 3rd rnd. Southampton (A) 3-2; 4th rnd. Luton Town (A) 2-2,(H) 3-1; 5th rnd. Swansea (H) 3-0; 6th rnd. Wolverhampton W. 1-1 (A), 2-2 (H),4-0 (N); Semi-final Millwall 2-1; Final Preston North End 3-1.
1972-73: 3rd rnd. Notts County 1-1 (A), 2-0 (H); 4th rnd. Reading 1-1 (H), 3-1(A); 5th rnd. Manchester City 2-2 (A), 3-1 (H); 6th rnd. Luton 2-0 (H); Semi-final Arsenal 2-1; Final Leeds 1-0.

League Cup: 1984-85: 2nd rnd. Crystal Palace 2-1 (H), 0-0 (A); 3rd rnd.Nottingham Forest 1-1 (A), 1-0 (H); 4th rnd. Tottenham Hotspur 0-0 (H), 2-1(A); 5th rnd. Watford 1-0; Semi-final Chelsea 2-0 (H), 3-2 (A); Final Norwich 0-1.

Europe (ECWC): 1973-74: 1st rnd. VASAS Budapest 2-0 (A), 1-0 (H); 2nd rnd. Sporting Lisbon 2-1 (H), 0-2 (A).

DIVISIONAL RECORD

	Played	Won	Drawn	Lost	For	Against	Points
Division 1	2,732	1,107	621	1,004	4,531	4,217	2,889
Division 2/1	990	399	274	317	1,447	1,237	1,192
Division 3	46	27	12	7	92	48	93
Total	3,768	1,533	907	1,328	6,070	5,502	4,174

ADDITIONAL INFORMATION
Previous Names
Sunderland & District Teachers' Association F.C. 1879-80.

Previous League
Northumberland & District Football Association 1880-90.

Club colours: Red and white striped shirts, black shorts, red socks with white band.
Change colours: Teal shirts with red trim, teal shorts with red trim, teal socks.

Reserves League: Pontins Central League Division 2

RECORDS AND STATISTICS

COMPETITIONS

Div.1	Div.2/1	Div.3	ECWC
1890-58	1958-64	1987-88	1973-74
1964-70	1970-76		
1976-77	1977-80		
1980-85	1985-87		
1990-91	1988-90		
	1991-		

HONOURS

Div.1	Div.2	Div.3	FA Cup
1891-92	1975-76	1987-88	1937
1892-93			1973
1894-95			
1901-02			
1912-13			
1935-36			

MOST APPEARANCES

JIM MONTGOMERY 611+12 (1961-77)

Year	League	FA Cup	Lge Cup	Others
1961-62	12		1	
1962-63	42	4	7	
1963-64	42	6	1	
1964-65	9			
1965-66	29	1	2	
1966-67	42	5	2	
1967-68	39	2	3	
1968-69	42	1	1	
1969-70	41	1	1	4
1970-71	42	1	1	
1971-72	31	3	1	4
1972-73	41	9	1	
1973-74	41	2	4	
1974-75	40	1	1	
1975-76	38	5	1	
1976-77	6		4	
	537	41	33	8

Includes 4 appearances in the ECWC 1973-74.

MOST GOALS IN A CAREER

R Gurney - 228 (1925-39)

Year	League	FA Cup
1925-26	4	
1926-27	7	
1927-28	4	
1929-30	15	2
1930-31	31	2
1931-32	16	
1932-33	15	7
1933-34	21	1
1934-35	30	4
1935-36	31	
1936-37	20	6
1937-38	9	1
1938-39	2	
Total	205	23

Current leading goalscorer: Gordon Armstrong - 61 (1985-95)

MANAGERS

Name	Seasons	Best	Worst
Tom Watson	1890-96	1(1)	7(1)
Robert Campbell	1896-99	2(1)	15(1)
Alex Mackie	1899-05	1(1)	6(1)
Robert Kyle	1905-28	1(1)	16(1)
Johnny Cochrane	1928-39	1(1)	16(1)
William Murray	1939-57	3(1)	20(1)
Alan Brown	1957-64	21(1)	16(2)
George Hardwick	1964-65	15(1)	15(1)
Ian McColl	1965-68	15(1)	19(1)
Alan Brown	1968-72	17(1)	16(2)
Bob Stokoe	1972-76	1(2)	6(2)
Jimmy Adamson	1976-78	20(1)	6(2)
Billy Elliott	1978-79	4(2)	4(2)
Ken Knighton	1979-81	17(1)	2(2)
Alan Durban	1981-84	13(1)	19(1)
Len Ashurst	1984-85	21(1)	21(1)
Lawrie McMenemy	1985-87	18(2)	20(2)
Denis Smith	1987-91	19(1)	1(3)
Malcolm Crosby	1991-93	18(2)	18(2)
Terry Butcher	1993	21(2/1)	21(2/1)
Mick Buxton	1993-95	12(1)	12(1)
Peter Reid	1995-	20(1)	20(1)

RECORD TRANSFER FEE RECEIVED

Amount	Club	Player	Date
£1,800,000	Crystal Palace	Marco Gabbiadini	9/91
£275,000	Sheffield Wed.	Mark Proctor	9/87
£275,000	Manchester Utd	Chris Turner	7/85
£275,000	Everton	Paul Bracewell	4/84

RECORD TRANSFER FEE PAID

Amount	Club	Player	Date
£900,000	West Brom	Don Goodman	12/91
£450,000	Oxford United	Andy Melville	9/91
£400,000	Hull City	Tony Norman	12/88
£355,000	St. Johnstone	Ally McCoist	8/81

LONGEST LEAGUE RUNS

of undefeated matches:	16 (11.11.1922 - 24.2.1923)	of league matches w/out a win:	14 (16.4.1985 - 14.9.1985)
of undefeated home matches:	44 (18.10.1890 - 6.12.1893)	of undefeated away matches:	14 25.11.1978 - 18.8.1979)
without home win:	12 (5.9.1981 - 27.2.1982)	without an away win:	28 (15.11.1952 - 2.1.1954)
of league wins:	13 (14.11.1891 - 22.4.1892)	of home wins:	19 (10.1.1891 - 16.4.1892)
of league defeats:	9 (23.11.1976 - 15.1.1977)	of away wins:	5 (1891-92, 1892, 1912-13, 1963)

SUNDERLAND

PLAYERS NAME / Honours	Ht	Wt	Birthdate	Birthplace / Transfers	Contract Date	Clubs	League	L/Cup	FA Cup	Other	Lge	L/C	FAC	Oth
							APPEARANCES				GOALS			
G O A L K E E P E R S														
Alec Chamberlain	6.2	11.11	20.06.64	March		Ramsey Town								
				Free	27.07.81	Ipswich Town								
				Free	03.08.82	Colchester United	188	11	10	12				
				£80,000	28.07.87	Everton								
Loan 01.11.87 Tranmere Rovers 15 Lge App.				£150,000	27.07.88	Luton Town	138	7	7	7				
				Free	08.07.93	Sunderland	60+1	5	6	1				
				Loan	23.03.95	Liverpool								
D E F E N D E R S														
Kevin Ball	5.9	11.6	12.11.64	Hastings		Coventry City (A)								
				Free	06.10.82	Portsmouth	96+9	8+1	8	6	4			
				£350,000	16.07.90	Sunderland	185+2	11	14	4	9	2		1
Gary E Bennett	6.1	12.1	04.12.61	Manchester		Ashton United								
Div.3'88.				Free	08.09.79	Manchester City								
				Free	16.09.81	Cardiff City	85+2	6	3		11	1		
				£65,000	26.07.84	Sunderland	362+7	34+1	17+1	21	23	1		1
Michael Gray	5.7	10.8	03.08.74	Sunderland	01.07.92	Sunderland (T)	49+16	2+3	1+1		3			
John Kay	5.10	11.6	29.01.64	Great Lumley	07.08.81	Arsenal (A)	13+1							
Div.3'88.				£25,000	20.07.84	Wimbledon	63	3	3	1	2			
				Loan	08.01.85	Middlesbrough	8							
				£22,500	22.07.87	Sunderland	196+3	19	12	6				
Darisz Kubicki	5.10	11.7	06.06.63	Warsaw		Legia Warsaw								
Polish Int.				£200,000	28.08.91	Aston Villa	24+1	3	4+1	1				
				£100,000	04.03.94	Sunderland	61	2	3					
Andrew Melville	6.1	12.6	29.11.68	Swansea	25.07.86	Swansea City (T)	165+10	10	14+1	13	22		5	2
W: 20, B.1, u21.2. WFAC'89.				£275,000	23.07.90	Oxford United	135	12	6	6	13	1		1
					09.08.93	Sunderland	80	7	5	2	5			
Richard Ord	6.2	12.8	03.03.70	Murton	14.07.87	Sunderland (T)	136+18	11+5	7+1	5+1	4		1	
E: u21.3.				Loan	22.02.90	York City	3							
Martin Scott	5.9	11.0	07.01.68	Sheffield	10.01.86	Rotherham Utd (A)	93+1	11	7+2	7	3	2		2
Div.4'89.				£200,000	05.12.90	Bristol City	171	10	10	8	14	1		1
				£750,000	23.12.94	Sunderland	24		3					
M I D F I E L D														
Steve Agnew	5.9	10.6	09.11.65	Shipley	10.11.83	Barnsley (A)	185+9	13	20	6+1	29	3	4	
				£700,000	25.06.91	Blackburn Rovers	2	2						
				Loan	21.11.92	Portsmouth	3+2							
				£250,000	09.02.93	Leicester City	52+4	4+1	2	2	4			
				£250,000	12.01.95	Sunderland	16				2			
Gordon Armstrong	6.0	11.10	15.07.67	Newcastle	10.07.85	Sunderland (A)	331+17	25+3	19	18+1	50	3	4	4
Brian Atkinson	5.10	11.6	19.01.71	Darlington	21.07.89	Sunderland (T)	114+20	5+2	13	2+3	4		2	
E: u21.6.														
Paul Bracewell	5.8	10.9	19.07.62	Heswall	06.02.80	Stoke City (A)	123+6	6	6		5		1	
E: 3, u21.13. CS'84'85. Div.1'85'93.				£250,000	01.07.83	Sunderland	38	4	2		4			
ECWC'85. UEFA u21'84.				£425,000	25.05.84	Everton	95	11	19+2	17+2	7	2		1
				£250,000	23.08.89	Sunderland	112+1	9	10	6	2			
				£250,000	16.06.92	Newcastle United	67+9	3+1	6+2	2	3	1		
				£100,000	08.95	Sunderland								
Derek Ferguson	5.8	10.11	31.07.67	Glasgow	01.08.83	Glasgow Rangers	92+19	6+4	8	11+2	7	1		1
S: 2, u21.5, Y, S. SPD'87'89. SLC'87'88'89.				Loan	01.01.90	Dundee	4							
					01.08.90	Hearts	99+4	8	11	3+2	4		1	
					29.07.93	Sunderland	64	3	6	2			1	
Martin D Gray	5.9	10.11	17.08.71	Stockton	01.02.90	Sunderland (T)	42+15	5+1	0+2	3+1	1			
				Loan	09.01.91	Aldershot	3+2			1				
F O R W A R D S														
Brett Angell	6.2	12.8	20.06.68	Marlborough	01.08.86	Portsmouth (T)								
				Free		Cheltenham Town			1				1	
				£40,000	19.02.88	Derby County								
				£33,000	20.10.88	Stockport County	60+10	3	3	8	28		1	4
				£100,000	02.08.90	Southend United	109+6	7+1	3	9+1	47	4	2	10
				£500,000	17.01.94	Everton	16+4	0+1			1			
				£600,000	23.03.95	Sunderland	8							
Stephen Brodie	5.10	10.6	14.01.73	Sunderland	01.07.91	Sunderland (T)	1+11							
Phil Gray	5.10	11.7	02.10.68	Belfast	21.08.86	Tottenham H. (A)	4+5		0+1					
NI: 9, u23.1, u21.1.				Loan	17.01.90	Barnsley	3		1					
				Loan	08.11.90	Fulham	3			2				1
				£275,000	16.08.91	Luton Town	54+5	4	2	2	22	3	1	
				£800,000	19.07.93	Sunderland	80+3	5	6	2	26	4	2	
Lee Howey	6.2	13.9	01.04.69	Sunderland		Ipswich Town (A)								
via Seaham Red Star & Bishop Auckland to				Free	25.03.93	Sunderland	13+17	0+4	2+2	0+1	5		1	
Chris Lawless			04.10.74	Dublin	21.01.94	Sunderland								

| SUNDERLAND | | | | | | | APPEARANCES | | | | GOALS | | | |
PLAYERS NAME Honours	Ht	Wt	Birthdate	Birthplace Transfers	Contract Date	Clubs	League	L/Cup	FA Cup	Other	Lge	L/C	FAC	Oth
John Mullin	6.0	11.5	11.08.75	Bury	18.08.92	Burnley (T)	7+11		2		2			
				£40,000	08.95	Sunderland								
Craig Russell	5.10	12.0	04.02.74	South Shields	01.07.92	Sunderland (T)	58+19	3	3+2	2	14	1	1	
Martin Smith E: S.	5.11	12.0	13.11.74	Sunderland	09.09.92	Sunderland (T)	60+4	1+1	6		18		1	
A D D I T I O N A L C O N T R A C T P L A Y E R S														
Sam Alston						Newcastle United								
				Free	08.95	Sunderland								
Stephen Grant						Athlone								
				Free	08.95	Sunderland								
Paul Heckingbottom						Manchester Utd (T)								
				Free	08.95	Sunderland								
Joe McGiven						Watford								
				Free	08.95	Sunderland								
David Preece			26.08.76	Sunderland	30.06.94	Sunderland (T)								

TOP GOALSCORER 1994/95
Phil Gray

Division One Goals (games) . . . . 12 (41+1)
Coca-Cola Cup Goals 1 (2)
F.A. Cup goals. . . . . 2(3)

Total . . . . **15 (46+1)**

Total goals for Sunderland since 19.07.93. . . . . 32 (93+3)
Total for Northern Ireland (full caps only). 3 (12)

Career total as at June 1st 1995 . . . . 59 (168+14)

THE MANAGER
PETER REID

Date of Birth. . . . . 20th June 1956.
Place of Birth . . . . Liverpool.
Date of Appointment . . . . March 1995.

PREVIOUS CLUBS
As Manager. . . . . Manchester City.
As Coach. . . . . None.
As a Player . . . . Bolton Wanderers, Everton, Q.P.R, Manchester City,
. . . . Southampton, Notts County, Bury.

HONOURS
As a Manager
None.

As a Player
Division 1 championship 1985, 1987. Division 2 championship 1978. FA Cup 1984. ECWC 1985.
P.F.A. Player of the Year 1985. CS 1984, 1985, 1987.
International: 13 full caps and 6 under-21 caps for England.

ROKER PARK

Sunderland, Tyne & Wear SR6 9SW
Tel: 0191 514 0332

Capacity..22,657
Covered Standing..9,000
Seating 7,765

First game..v Liverpool, 10.9.1898.
First floodlit game...v Dundee, 11.12.52.

ATTENDANCES
Highest ....75,118 v Derby County, FA Cup 6th Round replay, 8.3.1933.
Lowest...68,004 v Newcastle United, Div 1, 29.4.1935.

OTHER GROUNDS...................................Blue House Field, Groves Field, Horatio Street, ABBS Field.

MATCHDAY TICKET PRICES

Centre £15

Wings £13

Junior Family Enclosure. £9
Clock Stand Wings

Standing is by payment at the turnstiles on the day
of the match.

Members £10
Non-Members £11
Juniors. £6

Ticket Office Telephone no. 0191 514 0332

CLUBCALL
0898 12 11 40
Calls cost 39p per minute cheap rate and 49p per
minute at all other times.
Call costings correct at time of going to press.

HOW TO GET TO THE GROUND

From the North
Take A184 Newcastle - Sunderland road. After Boldon pass Greyhound Stadium
on left. Straight on at roundabout. After 150 yards bear left (signs for Fulwell,
Seaburn and Roker). At 'T' junction turn left to traffic lights at Blue Bell Public
House, then turn right. After about 0.5 miles ground is on the left up side street
(opposite Redby School) for Sunderland FC.

From the South
Use A1(M) North. Take A690 to Sunderland. Head for Town Centre. Follow signs
for Whitburn (A183) and South Shields (A1018). Pass over Wearmouth Bridge,
keep in right hand lane and take signs for Roker, Seafront and Whitburn. After
approximately 1 mile the ground is on the left up a side street.

From the West
Take A1231 towards Sunderland (north). Follow signs for Roker, Seafront and
Whitburn. After one mile ground is on left up side street.

Car Parking
Parking for 1,500 cars 200 yards from ground.

Nearest Railway Station
Seaburn.

MATCHDAY PROGRAMME

Programme Editor . . . . Clair Cogdon.

Number of pages . . . . 32.

Price . . . . £1.50.

Subscriptions . . . . Home, 1st class £16.50, 2nd class £15.50.
. . . . Home & away, 1st class £24.50. Overseas £27.00.

Local Newspapers. . Journal/Chronicle/Sunday Sun, Sunderland Echo,
. . . Northern Echo, Sunderland & Washington Times, Shields Gazette.

Local Radio Stations . . . . Metro Radio, Radio Tees,
. . . . Radio Newcastle, Wear FMs.

TRANMERE ROVERS
(The Rovers)
ENDSLEIGH LEAGUE DIVISION 1
SPONSORED BY: WIRRAL BOROUGH COUNCIL

Back Row (L-R): Alan Morgan, John McGreal, Dave Challinor, Graham Branch, Jamie Jardine, Shaun Garnett, Gary Jones, Gary Bennett, Kenny Irons, John Morrissey. **Middle Row:** Norman Wilson (Club Secretary), Warwick Rimmer (Youth Dev. Officer), Kenny Jones (trainer), Alan Rogers, Dave Higgins, Jamie Hughes. Martin Jones, Eric Nixon, Danny Coyne, Nick Edwards, Ian Moore, Phil Davies, Ronnie Moore (First Team Coach), Les Parry (Physio),Ray Marthias (Reserve Team Manager), **Front Row:** Alan Mahon, Ged Brannan, Tony Thomas, Gary Stevens, Steve Mungall, John King (Manager), John Aldridge, Pat Nevin, Jon Kenworthy, Liam O'Brien, Billy Woods. (Liverpool Senior Cup)

TRANMERE ROVERS
FORMED IN 1885
TURNED PROFESSIONAL IN 1912
LTD COMPANY IN 1912

PRESIDENT: H B Thomas
CHAIRMAN: Frank Corfe
DIRECTORS
N Wilson, F Williams, A J Adams,
J Holsgrove, H Jones, C N Wilson
SECRETARY
Norman Wilson (0151 652 2578
COMMERCIAL MANAGER
Janet Ratcliffe (0151 608 0371)

MANAGER: John King
COACH: Ronnie Moore

RESERVE TEAM MANAGER
Ray Mathias
YOUTH DEVELOPMENT OFFICER
Warwick Rimmer
PHYSIOTHERAPIST
Les Parry

STATISTICIAN FOR THE DIRECTORY
Peter Bishop

Sections of the national press had a field day when Tranmere's promotion challenge collapsed during the final weeks of the season. "Tranmere did a Devon Loch on the final furlong" and "Rovers are mounting their annual battle against promotion" were typical.

Though such comments were cruel, they were nevertheless understandable. For the third year in succession Tranmere had failed to reach the play-off finals at Wembley. But this time it was even harder to bear for the fans, for at one stage Tranmere had it in their own hands to go up as outright champions, only to fail to win any of their last five League matches, thereby handing the title on a plate to Middlesbrough. Given a second chance via the play-offs, Rovers produced a miserable performance in the first leg against Reading, going down 3-1 at home, and although some pride was salvaged in the no score return, the damage had been done.

Rovers may have had the best home from of the promotion contenders with 17 victories, but away form was their achilles heel. They picked up just five wins - the best at 'Boro in October - on their travels.

With some £1.5 million in the bank from the early season club record sale of Ian Nolan to Sheffield Wednesday, manager John King choose only to spend £350,000 of it on Rangers ex-England full-back Gary Stevens, but he proved to be another astute buy. Many Fans would argue the side should have been further strengthened for the title push, but John King drew a blank in his efforts to sign a top quality player or two before the deadline.

But with the departure of millionaire chairman Peter Johnson to Everton and gates falling short of expectations, money for players was tight, especially in view of the fact that Rovers rebuilt their Prenton Park ground into a splendid 16,789 all seater stadium inside nine months at a cost of over £3.2 million.

Additional revenue from Cup runs was not forthcoming either. Despite home ties against Norwich and Wimbledon in the Coca-Cola Cup and FA Cup respectively, Rovers were unable to make the advantage of 'Fortress Prenton' pay dividends and bowed out at comparatively early rounds.

While the Anglo Italian Cup provided a pleasant diversion, the cost of travel set against poor home gates proved a financial burden the club could have done without.

Despite missing a third of the season through injury, John Aldridge still finished as top League scorer (with 24) in the division to earn himself a 'Golden Boot'. Partner Chris Malkin netted 19- his best tally for five years - but only once away from Prenton Park.

However, with Aldo now approaching 37, and nine others in the squad over 30, manager John King may have to look to the clubs' excellent youth scheme to rebuild for the future and another assault on the Premiership prize that has eluded them during the past three seasons.

TRANMERE ROVERS

Division One: 5th **FA Cup:** 4th Round **Coca-Cola Cup:** 3rd Round **Anglo Italian Cup:** Group Stage

M	DATE	COMP.	VEN	OPPONENTS	RESULT		H/T	LP	GOAL SCORERS/GOAL TIMES	ATT.
1	A 13	EL	A	Stoke City	L	0-1	0-0			(15,915)
2	20	EL	H	Swindon Town	W	3-2	1-2		Aldridge 3, 63, Nevin 65	8,482
3	24	AIC Gp A	H	**Venezia**	D	2-2	2-0		**Aldridge 30, Malkin 45**	**3,012**
4	27	EL	A	Grimsby	L	1-3	0-2	16	Aldridge 80 (pen)	(4,087)
5	30	EL	H	Luton Town	W	4-2	0-0	9	Aldridge 52, 58, 61 (pen), Malkin 83	5,486
6	S 3	EL	H	Sheffield United	W	2-1	2-0	4	Malkin 23, Aldridge 41	7,253
7	6	AIC Gp A	A	**Atalanta**	L	0-2	0-2			**(4,000)**
8	10	EL	A	Wolverhampton Wand.	L	0-2	0-1	9		(27,030)
9	14	EL	A	Portsmouth	D	1-1	0-0	7	O'Brien 51	(6,383)
10	17	EL	H	Millwall	W	3-1	1-0	5	Malkin 13, 63, Aldridge 72	6,243
11	20	CC 2/1	H	**Brentford**	**W**	**1-0**	**1-0**		**Brannan 7**	**3,754**
12	24	EL	H	Sunderland	W	1-0	0-0	4	Malkin 72	7,500
13	27	CC 2/2	A	**Brentford**	D	0-0	0-0			**(4,076)**
14	O 1	EL	A	Burnley	D	1-1	1-0	4	Aldridge 25	(12,427)
15	4	AIC Gp A	H	**Ascoli**	L	0-1	0-1			**4,546**
16	8	EL	A	Middlesbrough	W	1-0	0-0	4	Aldridge 83	(18,497)
17	15	EL	H	West Bromwich Albion	W	3-1	2-1	3	Aldridge 5, 19, 48	7,397
18	22	EL	A	Watford	L	0-2	0-1	3		(6,987)
19	26	CC 3	H	**Norwich City**	D	1-1	0-1		**Aldridge 69**	**10,232**
20	29	EL	H	Port Vale	D	1-1	0-0	3	Morrissey 55	6,972
21	N 1	EL	H	Barnsley	W	6-1	2-0	3	Aldridge 25, 30, 58, 83, Malkin 49, 88	5,592
22	6	EL	A	Oldham Athletic	D	0-0	0-0	3		(6,475)
23	9	CC 3/2	A	**Norwich City**	L	2-4	1-0		**Irons 11, Nevin 51**	**(13,311)**
24	15	AIC Gp A	A	**Leece**	L	0-3	0-2			**(286)**
25	19	EL	H	Charlton Athletic	D	1-1	0-1	4	Malkin 69	7,567
26	26	EL	A	Reading	W	3-1	2-0	3	Brannan 10, Muir 19, 82	7,887
27	D 3	EL	H	Watford	W	2-1	0-0	2	Malkin 56, Irons 89	7,301
28	6	EL	A	Notts County	L	0-1	0-0	2		(4,703)
29	10	EL	A	Swindon Town	D	2-2	1-2	3	Mungall 10, Stevens 77	(8,608)
30	17	EL	H	Stoke City	L	0-1	0-0	4		7,615
31	26	EL	H	Derby County	W	3-1	1-0	2	Malkin 12, 81, G. Jones 86	11,581
32	27	EL	A	Bolton Wanderers	L	0-1	0-1	3		(16,782)
33	31	EL	H	Bristol City	W	2-0	2-0	3	G. Jones 8, Irons 42	7,439
34	J 2	EL	A	Southend United	D	0-0	0-0	3		(5,195)
35	7	FAC 3	A	**Bury**	D	2-2	0-2		**Muir 82, 89**	**(5,755)**
36	15	EL	A	Port Vale	L	0-2	0-1	4		(7,944)
37	18	FAC 3R	H	**Bury**	**W**	**3-0**	**3-0**		**O'Brien 13, Muir 16, Malkin 35**	**7,921**
38	22	EL	A	Oldham Athletic	W	3-1	1-1	4	Malkin 23, Muir 74, Brannan 88	5,581
39	29	FAC 4	H	**Wimbledon**	L	0-2	0-1			**11,637**
40	F 4	EL	H	Notts County	W	3-2	1-0	2	Malkin 24, 58, Morrissey 65	6,105
41	11	EL	A	Barnsley	D	2-2	1-1	3	G. Jones 13, Muir 62	(5,508)
42	18	EL	H	Reading	W	1-0	0-0	2	Muir 49	8,744
43	21	EL	A	Charlton Athletic	W	1-0	0-0	1	Nevin 81	(11,860)
44	25	EL	H	Burnley	W	4-1	1-0	1	Muir 16, 78, Nevin 48, Aldridge 90	9,909
45	M 5	EL	A	Sunderland	W	1-0	0-0	1	Garnett 82	(12,043)
46	7	EL	A	Sheffield United	L	0-2	0-1	1		(14,127)
47	11	EL	H	Grimsby Town	W	2-0	2-0	1	Morrissey 21, Aldridge 43 (pen)	15,810
48	18	EL	A	Luton Town	L	0-2	0-1	1		(6,660)
49	25	EL	A	Millwall	L	1-2	0-0	3	Malkin 83	(7,470)
50	A 1	EL	H	Portsmouth	W	4-2	3-1	2	Malkin 1, Aldridge 12, 34, Irons 72	8,722
51	8	EL	A	Bristol City	W	1-0	1-0	2	Aldridge 39 (pen)	(6,723)
52	14	EL	H	Bolton Wanderers	W	1-0	1-0	2	Nevin 34	14,959
53	17	EL	A	Derby County	L	0-5	0-2	3		(13,957)
54	21	EL	H	Southend United	L	0-2	0-2	3		9,971
55	30	EL	A	West Bromwich Albion	L	1-5	0-1	5	Aldridge 66 (pen)	(17,486)
56	M 3	EL	H	Wolverhampton Wand.	D	1-1	1-0	5	Adlridge 35	12,306
57	7	EL	H	Middlesbrough	D	1-1	1-0	5	Irons 45	16,377
58	14	PO SF1	H	**Reading**	L	1-3	1-1		**Malkin 15**	**12,307**
59	17	PO SF2	A	**Reading**	D	0-0	0-0			**(13,245)**
60										

Best Home League Attendance: 16,377 v Middlesbrough	Smallest: 5,486 v Luton Town	Av Home Att: 8,909

Goal Scorers:

Compared with 1993-94: +814

League (67): Aldridge 24 (5 pens), NMalkin 16, Muir 7, Irons 4, Nevin 4, G. Jones 3, Morrisey 3, Brannaw 2,
Garnett, Mungall, O'Brien, Malkin

C/Cola Cup (4): Nevin, Irons, Brannan, Aldridge
FA Cup (5): Muir 3, O'Brien, Malkin
Anglo/Ital Cup (2): Aldridge, Malkin
Play-Offs (1): Malkin

Coyna	Higgins	Mungall	Brannaw	Garnett	O'Brien	Morrissey	Aldridge	Irons	Nevin	Thomas	Muir	Proctor	Jones	Malkin	McGreal	Nixon	Kenworthy	Jones G.	Edwards	Branch	Johnson	Moore	Stevens	Referee	
1	2	3	4	5*	6	7	8	9	10	11	12		S											J. Kirkby	1
1	2*	14	3	5	6	7	8	4	10	11•	12		S	9										A. Dawson	2
1•	2•	11	3	5	6	7	8	4	10		12			9*	14	15								G. Lana	3
1	2	11	3	5*	6	7	8	4	10*		12		S	9	14									P. Harrison	4
1	2	S	3		6	7	8	4	10	11	S		S	9	5									R. Poulain	5
1		12	3	5*	6	7•	8	4		11				9	2	S	10	14						K. Leach	6
	2	6	3	5*				4		11			S	8	1		9	7	10	5	12			P. Vanes	7
S		S	3	5	6	7*	8	4	10	11	12			9	2	1								I. Hemley	8
S		12	3	5	6	S	8	4	10	11				9	2	1		7						G. Pooley	9
S		14	3	5	6	7	8	4	10	11•				9	2	1		12						D. Allison	10
S	2*	11	3	5	6	7	8	4•	10					9		1		12	14					E. Parker	11
S		3	10	5	6	7	8		11					9	4	1	S		S				2	E. Lomas	12
S		3	10	5	6	7	8		11*					9	4	1	S	12	S				2	G. Poll	13
S		3	10	5	6	7	8		11					9	4	1	S		S				2	K. Lynch	14
S	S	3		5	6	7	8		11					9	4	1	S		10				2	R. Bettin	15
S		3	10	5	6	7	8		11					9	4	1	S		S				2	W. Burns	16
S		3	10	5	6	7	8		11					9	4	1	S		S				2	J. Lloyd	17
S	S	3		5	6	12	8		11					9	4	1			7*				2	P. Alcock	18
S		3	10	5	6*	7	8		12	11				9	4	1	S						2	S. Lodge	19
S		3	10			7	8	6		11				9	4	1	S		S				2	P. Wright	20
	5	3	10			7	8	6		11			S	9	4	1	S		S				2	J. Brandwood	21
S		3	10			7		6		11	8*			9	4	1	S	12	S				2	J. Rushton	22
S		3	10			7	8	6		11	S			9	4	1	S		S				2	B. Hill	23
	6	3*		5		7			10•		8	14	S	9	4	1	12		11				2	P. Harrison	24
S		3	10			7		6		11	8			9	4	1	S		S				2	I. Cruikshanks	25
S		3	10			7	8	6		11	S			9	4	1	S			S			2	M. Bailey	26
S		3	10			7		6		11	S			9	4	1	S		S				2	E. Wolstenholme	27
S	7	3•	10					6		11	14			9*	4	1		12					2	J. Winter	28
S	4	3	10					6		11	12			9*		1		S					2	P. Harrison	29
S	5	S	3*		10	7	8	6		11				9	4	1			12				2	R. Poulain	30
S	5*	12			6	7		3	10	11				9	4	1	S	8					2	A. Flood	31
S	5				6	7		3	10	11				9	4	1	S	8	S				2	W. Burns	32
S	5	S			6	7		3	10	11				9	4	1	S	8					2	P. Richards	33
S	5	12	3		6	7			10	11				9	4*	1	S	8					2	C. Wilkes	34
S	11*	3			6	7			10		12			9	4	1	S	8					2	A. Wilkie	35
S	5	12			6	7		10	11	3	8			9	4	1			S				2	C. Wilkes	36
S	5	S			6	7		10	11	3	8			9	4	1			12				2*	A. Wilkie	37
S	2	12	5		6*	7		10	11	3	8			9	4	1			S				2	E. Parker	38
S		14	5		6•	7	12	10	11	3	8*			9	4	1			S				2	P. Durkin	39
S		10	5		6	7		S	7*	11	3			9	4	1	S		12				2	K. Lynch	40
S		10	5†		6	S			7*	11	3			9	4	1	S		12				2	A. Butler	41
S		10	5		6	7			7*	11	3			9	4	1	S		S				2	K. Lupton	42
S		10	5		6	12			7*	11	3			9•	4	1			14				2	S. Dunn	43
S		10	5		6	7	12		S	11	3			9*	4	1							2	T. West	44
S		10*	5		6	7	14	12		11	3			9•	4	1							2	R. Poulain	45
S		3	5		6	7	8*			11•	10			12	4	1			14				2	E. Wolstenholme	46
S		3	5		6	7*	8		10	11	12			9	4	1			S				2	D. Allison	47
S		10•	5		6		8	7	11	3				9*	4	1	14	12					2	G. Pooley	48
S	5	3			6		8	10	11*					9	4	1	7	12				S	2	M. Bailey	49
S	5	3			6	7•	8	10	11					9*	4	1	14	12				S	2	R. Furnandiz	50
S		3			6		8	10	11						4	1	S	9				S	2	P. Vanes	51
S		14	5		6	7*	8	10	11	3				9	4	1		12					2	T. Heilbron	52
S		7	5		6	S	8	10	11	3				9*	4	1		12					2	K. Leach	53
S		14	5		6•	7	8	10	11	3				9*	4	1		12					2	J. Winter	54
S	5†	14			6		8	10	11*	3					4	1	7•	9				12	2	K. Cooper	55
S		7	5		6		8	10	11	3				9	4	1	S	S					2	J. Lloyd	56
S		7	5*		6		8	10	11	3•				9	4	1	14	12					2	A. Flood	57
S		14	5		6	7	8	10	11	3*				9	4	1		S					2	J. Kirkby	58
1		5	6		14	7	8	10	11•	3†				9*	4	S		12					2	P. Alcock	59

Coyna	Higgins	Mungall	Brannaw	Garnett	O'Brien	Morrissey	Aldridge	Irons	Nevin	Thomas	Muir	Proctor	Jones	Malkin	McGreal	Nixon	Kenworthy	Jones G.	Edwards	Branch	Johnson	Moore	Stevens	
5	16	19	37	34	38	34	31	37	44	26	12			42	42	41	3	6	2				37	League Appearances
	7	4			2	2	1			7				1	1		3	13	1	0+1		0+1		League Sub Appearances
	1	4	4		4	3	4	4	2+1	4				4	3	4		0+1	0+2				3	C/Cola Cup Appearances
		1	2+1	2		3	3	0+1	3	2	3	2+1			3	2	3		1+1				3	FA Cup Appearances
1	3	4	2	4	2	3	2	3	2	1	1+1	0+1		3	3+1	3+1	0+1	1	3	1		0+1	2	Anglo/ Ital Cup Appearances
1		1	1+1	1		1+1	2	2	2	2	2			2	2	1		0+1					2	Play-Offs Appearances

† = sent off

TRANMERE ROVERS

CLUB RECORDS

BIGGEST VICTORIES
League: 11-1 v Durham City, Div 3N, 7.1.1928
13-4 v Oldham, Div 3N, 26.12.1935
F.A. Cup: 13-0 v Oswestry, 10.10.1914
League Cup: 5-1 v Oxford Utd, Rnd 2, 21.9.1993

BIGGEST DEFEATS
League: 2-9 v Q.P.R., Div 3, 3.12.1960
0-8 v Grimsby Town, Div 3N, 14.9.1925
0-8 v Bradford City, Div 3N, 6.3.1929
0-8 v Lincoln City, Div 3N, 21.4.1930
0-8 v Bury, Div 3, 10.1.1970
F.A. Cup: 1-9 v Tottenham, Rnd 3 replay, 14.1.1953
League Cup: 0-6 v Q.P.R., Rnd 3, 23.9.1969
0-6 v West Ham Utd, Rnd 2, 11.9.1974

MOST POINTS
3 points a win: 80, Division 4, 1988-89, Div 3, 1989-90
2 points a win: 60, Division 4, 1964-65

MOST GOALS
111, Division 3N, 1930-31
J Kennedy 34, Dixon 32, Watts 27, Meston 8, Urmson 7, Barton 1, Lewis 1, og 1

MOST LEAGUE GOALS CONCEDED
115, Division 3, 1960-61

MOST FIRST CLASS MATCHES IN A SEASON
65 (46 League, 1 FA Cup, 7 League Cup, 8 Leyland Daf, 3 Play-Offs) 1989-90

MOST LEAGUE WINS
27, Division 4, 1964-65

MOST LEAGUE DRAWS
22, Division 3, 1970-71

MOST LEAGUE DEFEATS
31, Division 2, 1938-39

INDIVIDUAL CLUB RECORDS

MOST GOALS IN A MATCH
9. Robert `Bunny' Bell v Oldham Athletic, 26.12.1935

MOST GOALS IN A SEASON
Robert `Bunny' Bell 40 (League 35, FA Cup 5,) 1933-34
4 goals twice=8; 3 goals 4 times=12; 1 goal 12 times=12. Total 40
John Aldridge 40 (League 22, Lge Cup 8, FA Cup 3, AMC 7) 1991-92
3 goals 4 times=12; 2 goals 5 times=10, 1 goal 18 times=18. Total 40

OLDEST PLAYER
George Payne, 39 years 202 days, Div 3, 11.3.1961

YOUNGEST PLAYER
William `Dixie' Dean, 16 years 355 days, Div 3N, 12.1.1924

MOST CAPPED PLAYER
John Aldridge (Eire) 24

BEST PERFORMANCES

League: 1992-93: Matches Played 46, Won 23, Drawn 10, Lost 13, Goals for 72, Goals against 56, Points 79.
Fourth in Division 1

Highest: 4th Division 1, 1992-93

F.A. Cup: 1967-68: 1st rnd. Rochdale (h) 5-1; 2nd rnd. Bradford P.A. (a) 3-2;3rd rnd. Huddersfield (h) 2-1; 4th rnd. Coventry City 1-1 2-0; 5th rnd.Everton (a) 0-2

League Cup: 1993-94: 2nd Rnd. Oxford United 5-1,1-1; 3rd Rnd. Grimsby 4-1; 4th Rnd. Oldham Ath. 3-0; 5th Rnd. Nottingham F. 1-1,2-0; Semi-Final Aston Villa 3-1,1-3 (lost 5-4 on pens).

DIVISIONAL RECORD

	Played	Won	Drawn	Lost	For	Against	Points
Division 2/1	226	86	53	87	303	322	305
Division 3	736	242	213	281	980	1,028	743
Division 3(N)	1,240	506	255	479	2,073	1,987	1,267
Division 4	780	318	185	277	1,179	1,057	955
Total	**2,982**	**1,152**	**706**	**1,124**	**4,535**	**4,394**	**3,270**

ADDITIONAL INFORMATION
Previous Name
Belmont 1884-85

Previous League
Central League 1919-21

Club colours: All white with green & blue trim.
Change colours: Old gold & black stripes, black shorts and socks.

Reserves League: Pontins Central League Division 1.
Youth League: Lancashire League Divisions 1 & 2.

RECORDS AND STATISTICS

COMPETITIONS

Div.2/1	Div.3(N)	Div.3	Div.4
1938-39	1921-38	1958-61	1961-67
1991-	1939-58	1967-75	1975-76
		1976-79	1979-89
		1989-91	

HONOURS

Division 3(N)	Leyland Daf	Welsh Cup
1937-38	1990	1934-35

MOST APPEARANCES

Ray Mathias 626+10 (1967-84)

Year	League	FA Cup	Lge Cup	Others
1967-68	13			
1968-69	26	1	5	
1969-70	20+4			
1970-71	46	3	3	
1971-72	46	7	3	
1972-73	45	2	1	
1973-74	38+1	2	3	
1974-75	40	1	3	
1975-76	46	1	2	
1976-77	46	1	3	
1977-78	46	2	2	
1978-79	45	3	2	
1979-80	38+4	3	4	
1980-81	37	3	4	
1981-82	1		1	
1982-83	16		3	1+1
1983-84	6+1	1		
1984-85	2			
	557+10	29+1	40	1+1

MOST GOALS IN A CAREER

Ian Muir -180 (1985-95)

Year	League	FA Cup	Lge Cup	Others
1985-86	14	1		
1986-87	20	3		2
1987-88	27	2		
1988-89	21	5	2	1
1989-90	23		4	8
1990-91	13			8
1991-92	5			
1992-93	2			
1993-94	9			
1994-95	7	3		
Total	141	14	6	19

Current leading goalscorer: John Aldridge - 120 (1991-95)

RECORD TRANSFER FEE RECEIVED

Amount	Club	Player	Date
£1,500,000	Sheffield Wed.	Ian Nolan	08/94
£750,000	Middlesbrough	Steve Vickers	11/93
£120,000	Cardiff City	Ronnie Moore	2/79
£60,000	Manchester Utd	Steve Coppell	3/75

RECORD TRANSFER FEE PAID

Amount	Club	Player	Date
£350,000	Glasgow Rangers	Gary Stevens	10/94
£350,000	Glasgow Celtic	Tommy Coyne	3/93
£300,000	Everton	Pat Nevin	8/92
£250,000	Real Sociedad	John Aldridge	6/91

MANAGERS

Name	Seasons	Best	Worst
Bert Cooke	1912-35	4(3N)	21(3N)
Jack Carr	1935-36	3(3N)	3(3N)
Jim Knowles	1936-39	22(2)	19(3N)
Bill Ridding	1939-45		
Ernie Blackburn	1946-55	4(3N)	19(3N)
Noel Kelly	1955-57	16(3N)	23(3N)
Peter Farrall	1957-60	7(3)	20(3)
Walter Galbraith	1961	21(3)	21(3)
Dave Russell	1961-69	7(3)	15(4)
Jackie Wright	1969-72	16(3)	20(3)
Ron Yeats	1972-75	10(3)	22(3)
John King	1975-80	12(3)	15(4)
Bryan Hamilton	1980-85	6(4)	21(4)
Frank Worthington	1985-87	19(4)	20(4)
Ronnie Moore	1987		
John King	1987-	4(2/1)	20(4)

LONGEST LEAGUE RUNS

of undefeated matches:	18 (16.3.1970 - 4.9.1970)	of league matches w/out a win:	15 (19.2.1979 - 18.4.1979)
of undefeated home matches:	26 (24.10.1988 - 10.11.1989)	of undefeated away matches:	10 (27.12.1983 - 21.4.1984)
without home win:	11 (19.2.1979 - 9.5.1979)	without an away win:	35 (19.11.1977 - 14.4.1979)
of league wins:	9 (9.2.1990 - 19.3.1990)	of home wins:	18 (22.8.1964 - 28.3.1965)
of league defeats:	8 (29.10.1938 - 17.12.1938)	of away wins:	4 (17.2.1990 - 17.3.1990)

TRANMERE ROVERS							APPEARANCES				GOALS			
PLAYERS NAME Honours	Ht	Wt	Birthdate	Birthplace Transfers	Contract Date	Clubs	League	L/Cup	FA Cup	Other	Lge	L/C	FAC	Oth
G O A L K E E P E R S														
Daniel Coyne W: u21.2, S, Y.	6.0	12.7	27.08.73	Prestatyn	08.05.92	Tranmere Rov. (T)	10+1			2				
Martin Jones	6.1	12.0	27.03.75	Liverpool	14.07.93	Tranmere Rov. (T)				0+1				
Eric Nixon LDC'90.	6.4	14.3	04.10.62	Manchester		Cuzon Ashton								
				£1,000	10.12.83	Manchester City	58	8	10	8				
				Loan	29.08.86	Wolverhampton W.	16							
				Loan	28.11.86	Bradford City	3							
				Loan	23.12.86	Southampton	4							
				Loan	23.01.87	Carlisle United	18							
				£60,000	24.03.88	Tranmere Rovers	316	34	18	45+1				
D E F E N D E R S														
Gerald Brannan	6.0	13.3	15.01.72	Prescot	03.07.90	Tranmere Rov. (T)	152+8	19	8+1	26+1	14	3		1
David Challinor	6.1	12.0	02.10.75	Chester	18.07.94	Tranmere Rov. (T)								
Shaun Garnett LDC'90.	6.2	11.0	22.11.69	Wallasey	15.06.88	Tranmere Rov. (T)	93+1	12	3	15+2	5	1		
				Loan	01.10.92	Chester City	9							
				Loan	11.12.92	Preston North End	10		1		2			
				Loan	26.02.93	Wigan Athletic	13			1				
Dave Higgins	6.0	11.0	19.08.61	Liverpool		Eagle								
				Free	22.08.83	Tranmere Rovers	27+1		2	5				
				Free		South Liverpool			1					
Free Carnarfon					20.07.87	Tranmere Rovers	278+2	25	17	34	10			
John McGreal	5.11	10.11	02.08.72	Liverpool	03.07.90	Tranmere Rov. (T)	59+2	5	2	5+1	1			
Steve Mungall LDC'90.	5.8	11.5	22.05.58	Belishill		Motherwell	14+6	11+2						
				Free	03.07.79	Tranmere Rovers	476+30	32+3	30+1	43+2	14	2	1	
Alan Rogers	5.10	11.8	03.01.77	Liverpool		Tranmere Rov. (T)								
Michael (Gary) Stevens E: 46, B.1, u21.1. Div.1'85'87. FAC'84, CS'84'85. ECWC'85.	5.11	10.12	27.03.63	Barrow-in-Furness		Everton (A)	207+1	30	39	10	9	1	3	
				£1,000,000	19.07.88	Glasgow Rangers	186+1	22	22	14	8		1	
				£350,000	14.10.94	Tranmere Rovers	37	3	3	4	1			
Shaun Teale E: SP.1. LC'94.	6.0	13.7	10.03.64	Southport		Weymouth								
				£50,000	22.01.89	Bournemouth	99+1	8	5	3	4		1	
				£300,000	25.07.91	Aston Villa	118+11	13	11	6	2	3		
				£500,000	08.95	Tranmere Rovers								
Tony Thomas LDC'90.	5.11	12.5	12.07.71	Liverpool	01.02.89	Tranmere Rov. (T)	195+1	18+1	5	26	12	1		1
M I D F I E L D														
Phil Davies W: u18.	5.11	12.0		Bangor		Tranmere Rov. (T)								
Michael Edwards	5.11	11.5	11.09.74	Bebington	05.07.93	Tranmere Rov. (T)	2+1	0+2		3				
				Loan	04.02.94	Stalybridge Celtic								
Kenneth Irons	5.9	11.0	04.11.70	Liverpool	09.11.89	Tranmere Rov. (T)	175+17	13+3	11+1	28+3	27	4	3	3
Alan Mahon Ei: S.	5.10	11.5		Dublin	19.04.95	Tranmere Rov. (T)								
Alan Morgan	5.10	11.0	02.11.73	Aberystwyth	08.05.92	Tranmere Rov. (T)								
Liam O'Brien Ei: 11, Y. Ei Lge'84'85'86. Ei Cup'85'86. Div.1'93.	6.1	11.10	05.09.64	Dublin		Shamrock Rovers								
				£60,000	14.10.86	Manchester United	16+15	1+2	0+2		2			
				£250,000	15.11.88	Newcastle United	131+20	9	12+2	9+2	19	1	1	1
				£300,000	21.01.94	Tranmere Rovers	55	7	3	5+1	2		1	
Billy Woods Ei: u21.	6.0	12.0	24.10.73	Cork		Cork City								
				£30,000		Tranmere Rovers								
F O R W A R D S														
John Aldridge Ei 63. Div.1'88. Div.2'85. LC'86. WFAC'80. CS'88. FAC'89.	5.11	10.4	18.09.58	Liverpool		South Liverpool								
				£3,500	02.05.79	Newport County	159+11	11	12+1	4	69	5	7	2
				£78,000	21.03.84	Oxford United	111+3	17	5	5	72	14	2	2
				£750,000	27.01.87	Liverpool	69+14	7+1	12	1	50	3	8	2
				£1,100,000	01.09.89	Real Sociedad								
				£250,000	11.07.91	Tranmere Rovers	137+3	18	6+1	18	88	18	4	10
Gary Bennett FRT'85.	6.1	12.6	20.09.63	Liverpool		Kirby Town								
				Free	09.10.84	Wigan Athletic	10+10		1	3+1	3			1
				Free	22.08.85	Chester City	109+17	6+4	8+1	10	36	1	5	5
					11.11.88	Southend United	36+6	4	1	2+1	6	4		
				£20,000	01.03.90	Chester City	71+9	8	5	4+1	15	2	1	1
				Free	12.08.92	Wrexham	120+1	9	7	17	77	7	3	11
				£300,000	08.95	Tranmere Rovers								
Graham Branch	6.2	13.0	12.02.72	Liverpool		Heswell								
				Free	02.07.91	Tranmere Rovers	6+15	0+2	0+1	2+1				
				Loan	20.11.92	Bury	3+1		1		1			
Gary S Jones	6.3	14.0	11.05.75	Chester	05.07.93	Tranmere Rov. (T)	2+4				2			

TRANMERE ROVERS							APPEARANCES				GOALS			
PLAYERS NAME / Honours	Ht	Wt	Birthdate	Birthplace / Transfers	Contract Date	Clubs	League	L/Cup	FA Cup	Other	Lge	L/C	FAC	Oth
Kenworthy / W: u21.3, Yth.	5.7	10.6	18.08.74	St Asaph Flint	14.07.93	Tranmere Rov. (T)	14+8	3		1+2	2			
an Moore			26.08.76	Liverpool	06.07.94	Tranmere Rov. (T)								
John Morrissey / E: Y.2.	5.8	11.9	08.03.65	Liverpool	10.03.83	Everton (A)	1			0+1				
				Free	02.08.85	Wolverhampton W.	5+5	1			1			
				£8,000	02.10.85	Tranmere Rovers	335+27	29+2	25+1	39+3	47		5	6
Pat Nevin / S: 22, B.3, u21.5, Y. SDic.2'82. Div.2'84. FMC'86.	5.6	11.9	06.09.63	Glasgow		Clyde	60+13	5+3	10		17		3	
				£95,000	14.07.83	Chelsea	190+3	25+1	8+1	13	36	5	1	4
				£925,000	13.07.88	Everton	81+28	10+1	12+6	9+3	16	2	2	1
				Loan	04.03.92	Tranmere Rovers	8							
				£300,000	18.08.92	Tranmere Rovers	132	13	6	14	25	5	2	2

TOP GOALSCORER 1994/95
John Aldridge

Division One Goals (games) . . . . 24 (31+2)
Coca-Cola Cup Goals 1 (4)
F.A. Cup goals . . . . 0 (0+1)
Anglo Italian 1 (2)
Play-offs 0 (2)
Total . . . . **26 (39+3)**

Total goals for Tranmere since 11.07.91 . . . . 120 (179+4)
Total for Eire (full caps only) 63

Career total as at June 1st 1995 . . . . 356(592+34)
(The above total does not include goals scored for Real Sociedad)

THE MANAGER
JOHN KING

Date of Birth . . . . 15th April 1938.
Place of Birth . . . . London.
Date of Appointment . . . . 13th April 1987.

PREVIOUS CLUBS
As Manager . . . . Tranmere Rovers, Northwich Victoria, Caernarvon Town.
As Coach . . . . Rochdale, Tranmere.
As a Player . . . . Everton, Bournemouth, Tranmere Rovers, Port Vale.

HONOURS
As a Manager
Tranmere: Promotion to Division 3 1976, 1989. AMC 1990. Promotion to Division 2 1991.

As a Player
Promotion with Tranmere 1967. Promotion with Port Vale 1970.

PRENTON PARK
Prenton Road West, Birkenhead,
Merseyside L42 9PN
Tel: 0151 608 3677

Capacity 16,789

First game ....v Lancaster, 8-0, 9.3.1912.
First floodlit game ....v Rochdale, 2-1, 29.9.1958.

ATTENDANCES
Highest ....24,424 v Stoke City, FAC 4th Rnd, 5.2.1972.
Lowest...937 v Halifax, AMC, 20.2.1984.

OTHER GROUNDS..Steeles Field 1884-87. Ravenshaws Field (later renamed Prenton Park) 1887-1912.

MATCHDAY TICKET PRICES

Main Stand . . . . £10 - £10.50.
Juniors/OAP. . . . . £6.50/£8

Cow Shed, Borough Rd, Kop Stand £8
Juniors/OAP . . . . £3/£6

Family Area Seating. £8
Juniors. £3

Ticket Office Telephone no. 0151 609 0137

CLUBCALL
0891 12 16 46
Calls cost 39p per minute cheap rate and 49p per
minute at all other times.
Call costings correct at time of going to press.

HOW TO GET TO THE GROUND

From the North
Use Mersey Tunnel and motorway M53 until junction 3. Leave motorway and at roundabout take 1st exit (A552). In 1.3 miles at Half-way House crossroads turn right (B5151) then turn left into Prenton Road West for Tranmere Rovers FC.

From the South
Use motorway M53 until junction 4, leave motorway and at roundabout take 4th exit B5151. In 2.5 miles turn right into Prenton Road West for Tranmere Rovers FC.
Away supporters should use the Kop end of the ground. Entrance from main car park.

Car Parking
No car parking available at ground on match days, except for visiting coaches. Car park tickets cost £50 for season.

Nearest Railway Station
Hamilton Square, Rock Ferry (1 mile).
Liverpool Lime Street (Main Line).

MATCHDAY PROGRAMME

Programme Editor . . . . Peter Bishop.

Number of pages . . . . 40.

Price . . . . £1.40.

Subscriptions . . . . Details available from Club.

Local Newspapers . . . . Liverpool Daily Post & Echo, Wirral News,
. . . . Wirral Globe.

Local Radio Stations. . . . . BBC Radio Merseyside,
. . . . City Gold and City FM (Radio City), MFM (Marcher Sound).

WATFORD
(The Hornets)
ENDSLEIGH LEAGUE DIVISION 1
SPONSORED BY: BLAUPUNKT

Back Row (L-R): John McDermott (Yth Dev. Officer), David Barnes, Gary Fitzgerald, Robert Page, Colin Simpson, Peter Beadle, Colin Foster, Keith Millen, Robert Calderhead, Richard Johnson, Jamie Moralee, Billy Hails (Physio). **Middle Row:** Len Cheesewright (Chief scout), Ken Brooks (Kit manager), Dominic Ludden, Kevin Phillips, Darren Bazeley, Steve Cherry, Kevin Miller, Paul Wilkerson, David Holdsworth, Craig Ramage, Gerard Lavin, Stuart Murdoch (Reserves Manager), Robert Marshall (Football in Comm. Asst.). **Front Row:** Kenny Sansom (Player/coach), Geoff Pitcher, John White, Gary Porter, Nigel Gibbs (club captain), Glenn Roeder (Manager), Andy Hessenthaler (Capt), Tommy Mooney, David Connolly, Derek Payne, Kenny Jackett (Yth Manager). **Seated:** Paul Robinson, Colin Pluck, Clint Easton, Craig Pearl, Vincent Cave, Mark Rooney, Wayne Andrews, Mark Jones, Chris Johnson, Daniel Grieves, Kevin Belgrave, Andrew Johnson, Darren Ward.

WATFORD
FORMED IN 1891
TURNED PROFESSIONAL IN 1897
LTD COMPANY IN 1909

LIFE PRESIDENT: Elton John
CHAIRMAN: Dr Stuart R Timperley PhD
VICE-CHAIRMAN: Geoff Smith
DIRECTORS
Mervyn Winwood, Stuart L Rogers,
Jack Petchey, Charles Lissack, Eddie Plumley
SECRETARY
John Alexander
COMMERCIAL MANAGER
Paul Biffen

MANAGER: Glenn Roeder
ASSISTANT MANAGER: Kenny Sansom

RESERVE TEAM MANAGER
Stuart Murdoch
YOUTH TEAM MANAGER
Kenny Jackett
PHYSIOTHERAPIST
Billy Hails

STATISTICIAN FOR THE DIRECTORY
Audrey Adams

Watford started the 1994-95 season as favourites for relegation and ended up narrowly missing a place in the play-offs: their best performance for six seasons. The term remains short of Premiership class, but is clearly developing in the right direction and manager Glenn Roeder, abetted by an enlightened chairman in Stuart Timperley, deserves great credit.

Roeder's major achievement of the season was to tighten up the defence. Kevin Miller, a £250,000 signing from Birmingham, became the latest in a long line of distinguished Watford goalkeepers: by keeping nine successive clean sheets between 2nd January and 18th February he broke a club record that had stood since 1949 and was deservedly voted Watford's Player of the Year. The Foster-Millen-Holdsworth axis proved a formidable obstacle to most opposing attacks and Lavin consolidated his place at right back, while the return of Nigel Gibbs after a two-year battle with a knee injury was a welcome bonus. The only problem, never satisfactorily resolved, was at left back.

The midfield also did well, with Andy Hessenthaler, an inspiring captain, and Derek Payne providing bite and energy, and Gary Porter and Craig Ramage, skill and vision. That left the attack, seriously denuded after the departure of Furlong and Dyer. Their replacements, Moralee and Mooney, failed to last the pace, and the search for a new strike force became a familiar Roeder refrain throughout the season. Lee Nogan sparkled briefly with nine goals in 15 matches before deciding he would be happier with Reading; Darren Bazeley reverted to striker during an injury crisis and weighed in with a hat-trick at Southend; and 17-year-old David Connolly gave notice of promise to come as he too was pressed into service.

Possible salvation finally arrived in the unlikely form of Kevin Phillips, a 21-year-old storeman recruited from Baldock Town, who scored nine goals in 16 matches. Next season will show whether or not he can sustain his promise, but he has already demonstrated an ability to be in the right place at the right time, calmness under pressure and a priceless knack of scoring late goals.

Both cups provided welcome diversion and entertainment. The FA Cup run, the best since 1988, lasted until the 118th minute of a 5th round replay against Crystal Palace. The League Cup brought Tottenham, Jurgen and all, to Vicarage Road: an extraordinary match ensued, Spurs winning 6-3, though both teams could have doubled their tally. Watford had the consolation of winning the away leg 3-2.

Vicarage Road is now all-seater following the opening of a smart new £1.5 million stand at the Rookery end. A new purpose and optimism is running through the club, and there seems every reason to look forward to further progress and success next season.

AUDREY ADAMS.

WATFORD

Division One: 7th   **FA Cup:** 5th Round   **Coca-Cola Cup:** 2nd Round

M	DATE	COMP.	VEN	OPPONENTS	RESULT	H/T	LP	GOAL SCORERS/GOAL TIMES	ATT.
1	A 13	EL	A	Sheffield United	L 0-3	0-2			(16,820)
2	16	CC 1/1	A	Southend United	D 0-0	0-0			(2,859)
3	20	EL	H	Grimsby Town	D 0-0	0-0			6,324
4	23	CC 1/2	H	Southend United	W 1-0	1-0		Ramage 24	4,582
5	27	EL	A	Swindon Town	L 0-1	0-1			(9,781)
6	30	EL	H	Wolverhampton Wand.	W 2-1	1-0	17	Foster 15, Johnson 87	10,108
7	S 3	EL	H	Middlesbrough	D 1-1	0-1	17	Johnson 57	9,478
8	10	EL	A	Barnsley	D 0-0	0-0	19		(4,251)
9	13	EL	A	Oldham Athletic	W 2-0	1-0	15	Holdsworth 25, Porter 84 (pen)	(7,243)
10	17	EL	H	Luton Town	L 2-4	2-3	19	Moralee 21, Mooney 44	8,880
11	21	CC 2/1	H	Tottenham Hotspur	L 3-6	1-4		Ramage 1, Mooney 65, Mabbutt 88 (og)	13,659
12	24	EL	A	Reading	D 2-2	2-0	18	Johnson 5, Moralee 28	8,015
13	O 1	EL	A	Charlton Athletic	L 0-3	0-0	21		(8,169)
14	4	CC 2/2	A	Tottenham Hotspur	W 3-2	1-1		Foster 15, Nogan 48, 75	(17,798)
15	8	EL	A	Derby County	D 1-1	1-0	19	Nogan 35	(13,413)
16	15	EL	H	Notts County	W 3-1	2-0	17	Nogan 3, Moralee 13, Ramage 47	7,008
17	22	EL	H	Tranmere Rovers	W 2-0	1-0	14	Nogan 25, 75	6,987
18	29	EL	A	Bolton Wanderers	L 0-3	0-1	17		(10,483)
19	N 1	EL	A	Burnley	D 1-1	1-0	16	Nogan 38	(11,739)
20	5	EL	H	West Bromwich A.	W 1-0	1-0	13	Mooney 20	8,419
21	12	EL	H	Southend United	W 1-0	0-0	7	Nogan 90	8,551
22	19	EL	A	Sunderland	W 3-1	2-1	7	Hessenthaler 1, Nogan 36, Mooney 71 (pen)	(15,063)
23	26	EL	H	Stoke City	D 0-0	0-0	9		9,126
24	D 3	EL	A	Tranmere Rovers	L 1-2	0-0	10	Moralee 58	(7,301)
25	10	EL	A	Grimsby Town	D 0-0	0-0	13		(6,288)
26	17	EL	H	Sheffield United	D 0-0	0-0	13		8,919
27	26	EL	A	Portsmouth	W 2-0	0-0	10	Ramage 63, Shipperley 85	9,953
28	27	EL	A	Millwall	L 1-2	0-0	14	Ramage 73	(12,289)
29	31	EL	H	Port Vale	W 3-2	1-1	10	Foster 31, Musselwhite 56 (og), Ramage 90	7,794
30	J 2	EL	A	Bristol City	D 0-0	0-0	9		(9,423)
31	7	FAC 3	A	Scarborough	D 0-0	0-0			(3,544)
32	14	EL	H	Bolton Wanderers	D 0-0	0-0	9		9,113
33	17	FAC 3R	H	Scarborough	W 2-0	0-0		Hessenthaler 50, Holdsworth 72	7,047
34	28	FAC 4	H	Swindon Town	W 1-0	1-0		Hessenthaler 45	11,202
35	F 1	EL	A	West Bromwich A.	W 1-0	0-0	9	Phillips 77 (pen)	(15,754)
36	4	EL	A	Southend United	W 4-0	3-0	7	Bazeley 15, 30, 35, Ramage 88 (pen)	(4,914)
37	11	EL	H	Burnley	W 2-0	0-0	6	Ramage 52, Bazeley 71	9,297
38	18	FAC 5	H	Crystal Palace	D 0-0	0-0			13,814
39	21	EL	H	Sunderland	L 0-1	0-1	8		8,189
40	M 1	FAC 5R	A	Crystal Palace	L †0-1	0-0			(10,321)
41	4	EL	A	Reading	L 1-4	0-1	8	Phillips 90	(9,705)
42	7	EL	A	Middlesbrough	L 0-2	0-1	10		(16,630)
43	11	EL	H	Swindon Town	W 2-0	0-0	8	Hessenthaler 67, Phillips 89	7,123
44	18	EL	A	Wolverhampton Wand.	D 1-1	0-1	10	Phillips 90	(24,380)
45	21	EL	H	Barnsley	W 3-2	1-0	9	Millen 43, Porter 50, Phillips 81	6,883
46	26	EL	A	Luton Town	D 1-1	0-1	9	Phillips 63	(7,984)
47	A 1	EL	H	Oldham Athletic	L 1-2	1-2	10	Ramage 45	8,090
48	4	EL	A	Stoke City	L 0-1	0-1	10		(9,576)
49	8	EL	A	Port Vale	W 1-0	0-0	10	Porter 88	(7,276)
50	14	EL	H	Millwall	W 1-0	1-0	9	Pitcher 41	6,907
51	17	EL	H	Portsmouth	L 1-2	0-1	10	Phillips 89	(8,396)
52	22	EL	H	Bristol City	W 1-0	0-0	10	Phillips 62	7,190
53	29	EL	A	Notts County	L 0-1	0-1	10		(5,083)
54	M 2	EL	A	Charlton Athletic	W 2-0	0-0	7	Beadle 66, Phillips 72	6,024
55	7	EL	H	Derby County	W 2-1	1-0	7	Phillips 1, Ramage 73 (pen)	8,492
56									
57									
58									
59									
60									

Best Home League Attendance: 10,108 v Wolves   **Smallest:** 6,024 v Charlton   **Av Home Att:** 8,124

Goal Scorers:

League (52): Ramage 9 (3 pens), Phillips 9, Nogan 7, Moralee 4, Bazeley 4, Mooney 3 (1 pen), Johnson 3, Porter 3, (1 pen), Hessenthaler 2, Foster 2, Holdsworth, Shipperley, Millen, Pitcher, Beadle, Opponent

C/Cola Cup (7): Ramage 2, Nogan 2, Mooney, Foster, Opponent

FA Cup (3): Hessenthaler 2, Holdsworth

Compared with 1993-94: +123

354

Miller	Bazeley	Watson	Foster	Holdsworth	Ramage	Hessenthaler	Payne	Moralee	Porter	Mooney	Soloman	Nogan	Digweed	Johnson	Ludden	Millen	Sansom	Fitzgerald	Wilkerson	Page	Lavin	Beadle	Shipperley	Gibbs	Jemson	Referee	
1	2	3	4	5	6*	7	8	9	10	11	12	S	S													J. Rushton	1
1	2		4	5	6	7	8	9	10	11	S	S	S	3												P. Foakes	2
1	2		4	5	6	7	8	9	10	11	S	S	S	3												J. Lloyd	3
1	2		4	5	6	7	8	9	10	11	S	S	S	3												S. Dunn	4
1	2		4	5	6	7	8	9	10	11		S	S	3	S											P. Vanes	5
1	2		4	5	6	7	8	9	10	11		S	S	3		S										J. Kirby	6
1†	2		4	5	6	7		9	10		S	S*	3	8*		S										C. Wilkes	7
1	2		4	5	6	7		9		11	S	S	3	8	10											T. Lunt	8
1	2		4	5	6	7	8	9	10	11•		14	S	3	S											W. Burns	9
	2			5	6	7	8	9	10	11	12	S	1	3				4*	SG							M. Bailey	10
	2			5	6	7	8	9	10	11		S	1	3			4		SG	S						J. Brandwood	11
	2		4	5	6	7	8*	9				11	1	3					SG	S	10	12				M. Pierce	12
1	3		4	5	6	7		9	10	11	S	S		8		S					2					K. Cooper	13
1	3*		4	5	6	7		9	10	11	12	S		8		S					2					D. Gallagher	14
1			4		6	7		9	10	11		8	S	3	S	5				S	2					J. Holbrook	15
1			4		6	7		9	10	11		8*	S	3		5				S	2	14				A. Flood	16
1	S		4		6	7		9	10	11		8	S	3		5					2	S				P. Alcock	17
1	14		4		6	7			10	11		8	S	3		5					2	9•				J. Poulain	18
1	14		4		6	7		9	10	11		8*	S	3		5					2	12				J. Winter	19
1	S		4		6	7		9	10	11		8	S	3		5					2	S				G. Pooley	20
1			4	5	6	7		9	10	11		8	S	3		S					2	S				J. Rushton	21
1	S		4	5	6	7		S	10	11		8	S	3		9					2					J. Parker	22
1	S		4*	5	6	7		S	12	11		8	S	3		9					2					P. Foakes	23
1	S			5	6	7		9	10	11		8		3		4			SG		2	S				E. Wolstenholme	24
1	S			5	6	7		9*	10	11		8		3		4					2	12				E. Lomas	25
1	S		4	5	6	7		S	10	11		8		3		5					2	9				M. Pierce	26
1	S		4	5	6	7		9*	10	11		S		3		5					2	12	8			K. Cooper	27
1	14		4	5	6	7		9*	10	11		S		3•		5					2	12	8			G. Pooley	28
1	3		4	5	6	7		8*	10	11		S				5					2	12•	9	14		G. Barber	29
1	3		4	5	6	7			10	11		S	S			5					2	9	8			J. Kirkby	30
1	3		4	5	6	7	S						1			9			SG	S	2		S	9		G. Singh	31
1	3		4	5	6	7		S	10					S		11					2		S	9		S. Dunn	32
1	3	14	4	5*	6	7			10					S		11				12	2		S	8		G. Singh	33
1	3		4		6	7		9•	10					S		5				S	2		11			P. Dawson	34
1	3		4	12	6	7	8		10*					S		5					2		11	9•		D. Allison	35
1	3		4	5	6	7	8		10					S		5					2		11	9		K. Cooper	36
1	3		4	7	6		8	9•	10					S	S	5					2		11		14	A. D'Urso	37
1	3	14	4	7	6		8	9•	10					S	S	5					2		11			B. Hill	38
1	3		4	7	6		8		10					S	12	5					2		11*			C. Wilkes	39
1	3		4	7	6			9*	10	12				S	8	5					2		2			B. Hill	40
1	3		4*	8	6	7			10•	9				S	12	5					2	2				J. Rushton	41
1	2		4		6	7	8		10	11				S		3		5*		14		12		9•		T. West	42
1	2*		4		6	7	8		10	11•				S	12	5									3*	P. Harrison	43
1			4		6	7	8		10					S	12	5					2	14			3*	K. Lupton	44
1		7	4		6				10	11				3	S	5			SG		2	12				P. Vanes	45
1			4		6	7	8		10	S				3	S	5					2	12				K. Breen	46
1			4		6	7	8		10				S	3	S	5					2	12				P. Rejer	47
1	3		4		6*		8							S	12	5					2	9			10	I. Cruikshanks	48
1			4		6•		8		10					S				3		2	9*	S				K. Cooper	49
1			4			7	8		10				S	14		5				3	2	9*				P. Foakes	50
1	14		4			7	8		10					S	12	5				3	2	9•				M. Bailey	53
1	12		4			7	8		10					S		5				3	2	9•				S. Mathieson	52
1	12	3	4		6	7	8		10•					S		5					2	9•				E. Wolstenholme	53
1	10	3	4		6	7	8							S		5					2	9				S. Dunn	54
1	10	3	4		6	7	8							S	12	5					2	9*				R. Harris	55
44	22	1	34	38	44	43	24	23	41	29		13	2	27	1	31	1	1		4	35	9	5	9	3	League Appearances	
	6			1			1				2	1	8					1				11	1	2	1	League Sub Appearances	
3	4		3	4	4	4	3	4	4	4		0+1	1	4		1										C/Cola Cup Appearances	
4	5	0+2	5	4	5	3	2	3	5	1+1		1		1		5				0+1	4				5	FA Cup Appearances + Subs	

Also Played: Phillips S(32),9(39,42.,43),14(41),11(44,46,47,48,49,50,51,52,53,54*,55), Connolly 9.(33),14(34,35),S(36),12(54), Pitcher S(39,40,52,54,55),14(49,53),6(50.,51*), Barnes 11(40,41), Quinn (9(44,.45*,46*,47*), S(48), 12(50)) Players on Loan: Shipperley (Chelsea), Jemson (Notts County), Quinn (Coventry City)

† = Sent Off

WATFORD

CLUB RECORDS

BIGGEST VICTORIES
League: 8-0 v Sunderland, Division 1, 25.9.1982
F.A. Cup: 10-1 v Lowestoft, Round 1, 27.11.1927
League Cup: 8-0 v Darlington, Round 2, 6.10.1987
Europe: 3-0 v Kaiserslauten, Round 1, 28.9.1983

BIGGEST DEFEATS
League: 1-8 v Crystal Palace, Division 4, 23.9.1959
1-8 v Aberdare, Division 3S, 2.1.1926
0-7 v Port Vale, Division 3S, 15.9.1947
F.A. Cup: 0-10 v Wolverhampton W., Round 1, 13.12.1912
League Cup: 0-5 v Coventry City, Round 1, 9.12.1980
1-6 v Blackburn Rovers, Round 4, 9.12.1992
Europe: 0-4 v Sparta Prague, UEFA 3, 1983-84

MOST POINTS
3 points a win: 80, Division 2, 1981-82
2 points a win: 71, Division 4, 1977-78

MOST GOALS
92, 1959-60 (Division 4).
Holton 42, Uphill 29, Hartle 6, Benning 5, Gregory 3, Bunce 3, Walter 2, Chung1, og 1.

MOST LEAGUE GOALS CONCEDED
89, Division 3S, 1925-26

MOST FIRST CLASS MATCHES IN A SEASON
60 (46 League, 6 FA Cup, 2 League Cup, 4 Simod Cup, 2 Play-Offs) 1988-89

MOST LEAGUE WINS
30, Division 4, 1977-78

MOST LEAGUE DRAWS
18, Division 3S, 1921-22

MOST LEAGUE DEFEATS
28, Division 2, 1971-72

INDIVIDUAL CLUB RECORDS

MOST GOALS IN A MATCH
5, Eddie Mummery v Newport County (8-2), Div 3(S), 5.1.1924

MOST GOALS IN A SEASON
Cliff Holton, 48 (42 League, 6 FA Cup), 1959-60

OLDEST PLAYER
Joe Calvert 42 years 25 days

YOUNGEST PLAYER
Keith Mercer 16 years 125 days.

MOST CAPPED PLAYER
John Barnes (England) 31 & Kenny Jackett (Wales) 31

BEST PERFORMANCES

League: 1977-78: Matches played 46, Won 30, Drawn 11, Lost 5, Goals for 85,Goals against 38, Points 71. First in Division 4.
Highest: 1982-83: Second in Division 1.

F.A. Cup: 1983-84: 3rd rnd. Luton Town 2-2, 4-3; 4th rnd. Charlton Athletic 2-0; 5th rnd. Brighton & HA 3-1; 6th rnd. Rotherham 3-1; Semi-final Plymouth 1-0;Final Everton 0-2.

League Cup: 1978-79: 1st rnd. Brentford 4-0, 3-1; 2nd rnd. Newcastle 2-1; 3rd rnd. Manchester United 2-1; 4th rnd. Exeter City 2-0; 5th rnd. Stoke City 0-0,3-1; Semi-Final Notts' Forest 0-0, 1-3.

Europe (UEFA): 1983-84: 1st rnd. Kaiserslautern 1-3, 3-0; 2nd rnd. Levski Spartak 1-1, 3-1; 3rd rnd. Sparta Prague 2-3, 0-4.

DIVISIONAL RECORD

	Played	Won	Drawn	Lost	For	Against	Points
Division 1	250	93	58	99	386	372	337
Division 2/1	574	189	158	227	674	737	674
Division 3	598	241	164	193	886	766	646
Division 3(S)	1,334	488	333	513	1,972	2,029	1,309
Division 4	230	110	51	69	387	296	271
Total	2,986	1,121	764	1,101	4,305	4,200	3,237

ADDITIONAL INFORMATION
Previous Names
Watford Rovers until 1891 or amalgamation of West Herts & Watford St. Marys in1898
Previous Leagues
Southern League

Club colours: Yellow shirts with black/red trim, black shorts with red and yellow trim, black socks with red & yellow tops.
Change colours: Blue/white shirts, white shorts with dark blue trim, white socks, with dark blue tops.

Reserves League: Avon Insurance Football Combination.

RECORDS AND STATISTICS

COMPETITIONS

Div.1	Div.2/1	Div.3	Div.3(S)	Div.4	UEFA
1982-88	1969-72	1920-21	1921-58	1958-60	1983-84
	1979-82	1960-69		1975-78	
	1988-	1972-75			
		1978-79			

HONOURS

Division 3	Division 4	Division 3(S) Cup
1968-69	1977-78	1936-37
		(shared)

MOST APPEARANCES

Luther Blissett 443+52 (1975-92 - 3 spells)

Year	League	FA Cup	Lge Cup	FMC
1975-76	1+2			
1976-77	1+3			
1977-78	17+16			
1978-79	40+1	1	6+1	
1979-80	40+2	4	2	
1980-81	42	3	8	
1981-82	40	3	6	
1982-83	41	4	3	
1984-85	38+3	5	5	
1985-86	20+3		3	
1986-87	35	5	1	1
1987-88	17+8	4+2	1+2	
1988-89	3		1	
1991-92	34+8	1	4	0+1
	369+46	32+2	41+3	1+1

MOST GOALS IN A CAREER

Luther Blissett - 180 (1975-92 - 3 spells)

Year	League	FA Cup	Lge Cup
1975-76	1		
1976-77			
1977-78	6		
1978-79	21		7
1979-80	10	1	
1980-81	11		2
1981-82	19		3
1982-83	27	2	1
1984-85	21	6	1
1985-86	7		1
1986-87	11	4	
1987-88	4		
1988-89	1		
1991-92	9	2	1
Total	148	15	17

Current leading goalscorer: Gary Porter - 55 (1984-95)

RECORD TRANSFER FEE RECEIVED

Amount	Club	Player	Date
£2,300,000	Chelsea	Paul Furlong	05/94
£1,250,000	Crystal Palace	Bruce Dyer	3/94
£1,000,000	Liverpool	David James	6/92
£1,000,000	Aston Villa	Gary Penrice	3/91
£1,000,000	Manchester City	Tony Coton	7/90

RECORD TRANSFER FEE PAID

Amount	Club	Player	Date
£550,000	A C Milan	Luther Blissett	8/84
£500,000	Bristol Rovers	Gary Penrice	11/89
£425,000	Millwall	Jamie Moralee	7/94
£300,000	Charlton Athletic	Joe McLaughlin	8/90

MANAGERS

Name	Seasons	Best	Worst
John Goodhall	1903-10		
Harry Kent	1910-26	6(3S)	20(3S)
Fred Pagnam	1926-29	8(3S)	21(3S)
Neil McBain	1929-37	4(3S)	16(3S)
Bill Findlay	1937-47		
Jack Bray	1947-48	15(3S)	15(3S)
Eddie Hapgood	1948-50	6(3S)	17(3S)
Ron Gray	1950-51	23(3S)	23(3S)
Haydn Green	1951-52	21(3S)	21(3S)
Len Goulden	1952-55	4(3S)	10(3S)
John Paton	1955-56	21(3S)	21(3S)
Len Goulden	1956		
Neil McBain	1956-59	11(3S)	15(4)
Ron Burgess	1959-63	4(3)	4(4)
Bill McGarry	1963-64	3(3)	3(3)
Ken Furphy	1964-71	18(2)	12(3)
George Kirby	1971-73	22(2)	19(3)
Mike Keen	1973-77	7(3)	8(4)
Graham Taylor	1977-87	2(1)	1(4)
Dave Bassett	1987-88		
Steve Harrison	1988-90	20(1)	4(2)
Colin Lee	1990	15(2)	15(2)
Steve Perryman	1990-93	10(2)	20(2)
Glenn Roeder	1993-	7(1)	7(1)

LONGEST LEAGUE RUNS

of undefeated matches: 15 (27.1.34-2.2.35, 11.11.78-10.3.79)	of league matches w/out a win: 19 (27.11.1971 - 8.4.1972)
of undefeated home matches: 27 (15.10.1963 - 19.12.1964)	of undefeated away matches: 12 (17.3.1977 - 16.9.1978)
without home win: 9 (14.12.1971-15.4.1972, 25.8.1990-1.12.1990)	without an away win: 32 (17.4.1971 - 25.11.1972)
of league wins: 7 (17.11.34-29.12.34, 26.12.77-28.1.78)	of home wins: 8 (29.8.31-21.11.31, 3.11.34-2.2.35, 6.9.77-12.11.77)
of league defeats: 9 (26.12.1972 - 27.2.1973)	of away wins: 5 (25.4.1981 - 22.9.1981)

WATFORD

PLAYERS NAME Honours	Ht	Wt	Birthdate	Birthplace Transfers	Contract Date	Clubs	League	L/Cup	FA Cup	Other	Lge	L/C	FAC	Oth
G O A L K E E P E R S														
Steve Cherry	5.11	11.0	05.08.60	Nottingham	22.03.78	Derby County (A)	77	5	8					
E: Y.4.				Loan	26.11.80	Port Vale	4		4					
				£25,000	10.08.84	Walsall	71	10	7	6				
				£17,000	23.10.86	Plymouth Argyle	73	4	5	1				
				Loan	01.12.88	Chesterfield	10			3				
				£70,000	16.02.89	Notts County	266	17	14	31				
				Free	08.95	Watford								
Kevin Miller	6.1	13.0	15.03.69	Falmouth		Newquay								
Div.4'90.				Free	09.03.89	Exeter City	163	7	12	18				
				£250,000	14.05.93	Birmingham City	24	4		2				
				£250,000	.08.94	Watford	44	3	4					
Geoffrey Pitcher	5.6	10.13	15.08.75	Sutton	18.03.93	Millwall (T)								
					13.07.94	Watford	2+2				1			
Paul Wilkerson	6.3	13.11	11.12.74	Hertford	18.06.93	Watford								
				Loan	04.02.94	Stevenage Borough								
D E F E N D E R S														
David Barnes	5.10	11.4	16.11.61	Paddington	31.05.79	Coventry City (A)	9		4					
E: Y.7. UEFA.Y'80.				Free	12.04.82	Ipswich Town	16+1							
				£35,000	03.10.84	Wolverhampton W.	86+2	7	6	6	4			
				£25,000	22.08.87	Aldershot	68+1	2	2+2	4	1			
				£50,000	11.07.89	Sheffield United	82	6	14	4	1			
				£50,000	14.01.94	Watford	6		1					
Gary Fitzgerald	6.1	12.4	27.10.76	Hampstead	14.11.94	Watford	1							
Colin Foster	6.4	14.1	16.07.64	Chislehurst	04.02.82	Leyton Orient (A)	173+1	12	19	5	10		5	1
					04.03.87	Nottingham Forest	68+4	8	5	2	5	1		
					22.09.89	West Ham United	88+5	5	9	2+2	5		2	
				Loan	10.01.94	Notts County	9			2				
				£100,000	23.03.94	Watford	40	3	5		3	1		
Nigel Gibbs	5.7	11.11	20.11.65	St. Albans	23.11.83	Watford (A)	277+5	15	30+1	13	3	2		
E: u21.5, u19.3, Y.6. FAYC'82.														
David Holdsworth	6.1	12.4	08.11.68	Walthamstow	08.11.86	Watford (A)	223+8	18	12+1	8+2	9	2	1	
E: u21.1, Y.6.														
Dominic Ludden	5.8	11.0	30.03.74	Basildon	06.07.92	Leyton Orient (T)	50+8	1	0+1	6	1			1
ESFA u18.4.				£100,000	.08.94	Watford	1							
Keith Millen	6.1	12.0	26.09.66	Croydon	07.08.84	Brentford (A)	301+4	26	18	30+1	17	2	1	
Div.3'92.					22.03.94	Watford	41	1	5		1			
Robert Page	6.0	11.8	03.09.74	Llwynipia	19.04.93	Watford (T)	8+1		0+1					
M I D F I E L D														
Andrew Hessenthaler	5.7	11.0	17.08.65	Dartford		Dartford			5				1	
E: S-P.1. ILP'91.				Redbridge Forest										
				£65,000	12.09.91	Watford	165	13	5	4	12	1	2	
Richard Johnson	5.10	11.4	27.04.74	Newcastle (Aus)	11.05.92	Watford (T)	50+15	4+1	2	0+1	3			
Gerard Lavin	5.8	10.8	05.02.74	Corby	11.05.92	Watford (T)	105+5	9	6	2+1	3	1		
S: u21.7.														
Derek Payne	5.6	10.8	26.04.67	Edgware		Hayes			2					
				£12,000	22.07.91	Barnet	50+1	2	2	3+1	6			
				Free	15.07.93	32+3	2	1	8				1	
				P.E.	21.07.94	Watford	24	3	2					
Gary Porter	5.6	10.6	06.03.66	Sunderland	06.03.84	Watford (A)	328+37	26+2	25+2	12+1	46	4	3 2	
E: u21.12, Y.13. FAYC'82.														
Craig Ramage	5.9	11.8	30.03.70	Derby	20.07.88	Derby County (T)	33+9	6+1	3+1	0+3	4	2	1	
E: u21.2.				Loan	16.02.89	Wigan Athletic	10			0+1	2			
				£90,000	21.02.94	Watford	55+2	4	5		9	2		
John White	5.8	11.3	09.09.74	Honiton	09.04.93	Watford (T)								
F O R W A R D S														
Darren Bazeley	5.10	10.9	05.10.72	Northampton	06.05.91	Watford (T)	66+38	7+3	5+1	3+1	12	1		
Peter Beadle	6.1	11.12	13.05.72	Lambeth	05.05.90	Gillingham (T)	42+25	2+4	1+1	1	14	2		
				£300,000	04.06.92	Tottenham Hotspur								
				Loan	25.03.93	Bournemouth	9				2			
				Loan	04.03.94	Southend United	8				1			
					12.09.94	Watford	9+11				1			
David Connolly	5.8	11.4	06.06.77	London	14.11.94	Watford (T)	0+2		1+1					
Kevin Phillips	5.7	11.0	25.07.73	Hitchin		Baldock Town								
				£10,000	19.12.94	Watford	15+1				9			

WATFORD							APPEARANCES				GOALS			
PLAYERS NAME Honours	Ht	Wt	Birthdate	Birthplace Transfers	Contract Date	Clubs	League	L/Cup	FA Cup	Other	Lge	L/C	FAC	Oth
Thomas Mooney Flg u18.1.	5.11	12.6	11.08.71	Middlesbrough	23.11.89	Aston Villa (T)								
				Free	01.08.90	Scarborough	96+11	11+2	3	6	29	8		2
				£100,000	12.07.93	Southend United	9+5	1+1		2+3	5			
				Loan	17.03.94	Watford	10				2			
				P.E.	21.07.94	Watford	29	4	1+1		3	1		
Jamie Moralee	5.11	11.0	02.12.71	Wandsworth	03.07.90	Crystal Palace (T)	25+5	4	3		4			
Colin Simpson	6.1	11.05	30.04.76	P.E.	03.09.92	Millwall	56+11	3+1	1	3+1	19	1		
				£450,000	13.07.94	Watford								

TOP GOALSCORER 1994/95
Craig Ramage

Division One Goals (games) 9 (44)
Coca-Cola Cup Goals 2 (4)
F.A. Cup goals 0 (5)

Total . . . . **11 (53)**

Total goals for Watford since 21.02.94. . . . . 11 (64+2)

Career total as at June 1st 1995 . . . . 20 (116+17)

THE MANAGER
GLENN ROEDER

Date of Birth . . . . 13th December 1955.
Place of Birth . . . . Woodford.
Date of Appointment . . . . 9th July 1993.

PREVIOUS CLUBS
As Manager . . . . Gillingham.
As Coach . . . . None.
As a Player . . . . Leyton Orient, Queens Park Rangers, Newcastle Utd,
. . . . Watford, Gillingham.

HONOURS
As a Manager
None.

As a Player
England 'B' international.

VICARAGE ROAD STADIUM
Watford WD1 8ER
Tel: 01923 230 933

Capacity 22,000

First game...v Millwall, Div 3(S), 0-0, 30.8.1922.
First floodlit game ....v Luton Town, Friendly, October 1953.

ATTENDANCES
Highest ....34,099 v Manchester Utd, FAC, 3.2.1969.
Lowest ....1,700 v Southend, ZDS Cup, 2.10.1991.

OTHER GROUNDS ....Cassio Road 1899-1922. Vicarage Road 1922-

MATCHDAY TICKET PRICES

North & South Stand - Adults/Concess . . . £11/£8
East Stand (Blocks C, D & E) . . . . £11/£8
Rous Stand (Upper Tier) £13/N/A
Family Areas (Including Blocks A & B in East Stand)
Adult £11
12 & Under £1
Under-16 . . . . £5
2nd Parent £8
Wheelchair Areas (Chairbound/Helper) . . . £6/£11
Visitors (Rous Stand Lower Tier) . . . . £11/£8*
*Concessionary tickets for visitors must be purchased in advance from the visiting club.

Ticket Office Telephone no. 01923 496 010

CLUBCALL
0891 12 10 30

Calls cost 39p per minute cheap rate and 49p per minute at all other times.
Call costings correct at time of going to press.

HOW TO GET TO THE GROUND

From the North
Use motorway M1 until junction 6. Leave motorway and follow signs to Watford A405/A41 and A411. Follow signs to Slough (A412) and in 0.7 miles turn left into Harwoods Road. At end of 'T' junction turn left into Vicarage Road for Watford FC.

From the East and South
Use motorway M1 until junction 5. Leave motorway and follow signs for Watford (A41) and A412. Then follow signs to Slough (A412) and in 0.7 miles turn left into Harwoods Road. At end of 'T' junction turn left into Vicarage Road for Watford FC.

From the West
Use A412, sign posted Watford, and pass Croxley Green Station, then in 0.9 miles turn right into Harwoods Road. At end of 'T' junction turn left into Vicarage Road for Watford FC.

Car Parking
No public parking available at ground. There are several multi-story parks nearby and street parking.

Nearest Railway Station
Watford Junction or Watford High Street (01923 245 001) or Watford Halt.

MATCHDAY PROGRAMME

Programme Editor . . . . Ed Coan & Gabriela Lyons.

Number of pages . . . . 32.

Price . . . . £1.50.

Subscriptions . . . . £35 all home games,
. . . . plus £13 postage, packing and handling.

Local Newspapers . . . . Watford Observer, Watford Review,
. . . . St Albans Herald and Post, Watford Free Observer,
. . . . London Evening Standard.

Local Radio Stations . . . Chiltern Radio, Radio London, Capital Radio,
. . . . BBC Three Counties Radio.

WEST BROMWICH ALBION
(The Throstles, 'Baggies' or 'Albion')
ENDSLEIGH LEAGUE DIVISION 1
SPONSORED BY: GUEST MOTORS

Back Row (L-R): Tony Brien, Daryl Burgess, Andy Hunt, Paul Raven, Bob Taylor, Mike Phelan, Paul Agnew. **Middle Row:** Richard O'Kelly (Yth Coach), Paul Michell (Physio), Ian Hamilton, Stuart Naylor, Gary Germaine, Chris Hargreaves, Ronnie Allen (Coach), John Trewick (Res. Coach). **Front Row:** Tony Rees, Stacy Coldicott, Lee Ashcroft, Arthur Mann (Asst. Manager), Paul Mardon, Alan Buckley (Manager), Paul Edwards, Kevin Donovan, David Smith.

WEST BROMWICH ALBION
FORMED IN 1878-79
TURNED PROFESSIONAL IN 1885
LTD COMPANY IN 1892

PRESIDENT: Sir F A Millichip
VICE-PRESIDENT: J Silk
CHAIRMAN: A B Hale
DIRECTORS
J W Brandiwck, T Guy, T J Summers,
C M Stapleton, B Hurst
SECRETARY
Dr. John Evans (0121 525 8888)
COMMERCIAL EXECUTIVE
Tom Cardall

MANAGER: Alan Buckley
ASSISTANT MANAGER: Arthur Mann

RESERVE TEAM MANAGER
Richard O'Kelly
YOUTH TEAM MANAGER
John Trewick
PHYSIOTHERAPIST
Paul Mitchell

STATISTICIAN FOR THE DIRECTORY
Tony Matthews

Like it had been in season 1993-94, Albion were again involved in a battle to stave off relegation - and once more they just managed to hold on to their First Division status, avoiding the drop with two games remaining following a 0-0 home draw v. Derby.

For a long time during a mediocre campaign, Albion were lingering far too near the trap-door for comfort, inconsistency being their problem, and if it hadn't been for their reasonably good home form (they recorded 13 wins including a terrific 2-0 victory over arch neighbours Wolves, a 5-1 drubbing of promotion-chasing Tranmere, a 2-0 defeat of Reading and a 1-0 triumph over in-form Bolton) then the fans would be watching Second Division football at The Hawthorns this coming season.

Indeed, until Alan Buckley took over as manager from Keith Burkenshaw in mid-October, the Baggies had struggled desperately and were bedded down at the foot of the table. But things started to improve within a matter of weeks once Buckley had taken charge and at the turn of the year Albion had moved up six places to 18th. They rose even higher later in the season (to 14th) and if only they had been able to string together a good run, they may well have finished in the top half of the table.

Owing to ground redevelopment, Albion had to play their first five League games away from home and during this period they also went out of the Coca-Cola Cup, beaten by Third Division Hereford United over two legs. In the F.A. Cup, Albion did well to draw at Premiership Coventry City, but after leading in the replay they eventually succumbed to their Midland rivals following the sending-off of Darren Bradley.

Injuries to, and suspensions of, key players certainly disrupted team selection, but defensively Albion had reasonable cover, likewise in attack. It was in midfield where they lacked impact and there's no doubt that it was in this department where a lot of games were lost.

Stuart Naylor, Paul Raven, Gary Strodder, 'Player of the Year', Paul Mardon, Kevin Donovan and Lee Ashcroft all had good campaigns. Ian Hamilton, Bob Taylor and Andy Hunt were not at their best, although the latter pair did suffer with injuries and illness, as did Daryl Burgess and Darren Bradley. The left-back position caused some concern throughout the season and this was finally solved when Buckley recruited Paul Agnew from his old club Grimsby, this after he had earlier signed striker Tony Rees as cover for Taylor and Hunt.

Albion, with their 25,000 all-seater stadium now complete, will certainly pull in the fans if they're doing well (their average in 1994-95 was over 15,200) and if manager Buckley can hold on to his key players, then there is no reason why the Baggies can't be a force to be reckoned with this coming season. Albion, with their 25,000 all-seater stadium now complete, will certainly pull in the fans if they're doing well (their average in 1994-95 was over 15,200) and if manager Buckley can hold on to his key players, then there is no reason why the Baggies can't be a force to be reckoned with this coming season.

TONY MATTHEWS.

WEST BROMWICH ALBION

Division One: 19th   **FA Cup:** 3rd Round   **Coca-Cola Cup:** 1st Round

M	DATE	COMP.	VEN	OPPONENTS	RESULT	H/T	LP	GOAL SCORERS/GOAL TIMES	ATT.
1	A 13	EL	A	Luton Town	D 1-1	1-0	12	Taylor 5	(8,640)
2	16	CC 1/1	A	**Hereford United**	D 0-0	0-0			**(5,425)**
3	28	EL	A	Wolverhampton Wand.	L 0-2	0-1	22		(27,764)
4	31	EL	A	Swindon Town	D 0-0	0-0	22		(11,188)
5	S 7	CC 1/2	H	**Hereford United**	L 0-1	0-0			**10,604**
6	10	EL	A	Millwall	D 2-2	1-1	24	Taylor 11, 54	(8,378)
7	14	EL	A	Middlesbrough	L 1-2	1-1	24	Ashcroft 34	14,878
8	17	EL	H	Grimsby Town	D 1-1	1-0	24	Ashcroft 26	(14,496)
9	24	EL	H	Burnley	W 1-0	0-0	23	Taylor 71	13,539
10	28	EL	H	Portsmouth	L 0-2	0-1	23		13,545
11	O 2	EL	A	Stoke City	L 1-4	1-2	23	Taylor 32	(14,203)
12	8	EL	H	Sunderland	L 1-3	0-2	23	Ashcroft 75	13,717
13	15	EL	A	Tranmere Rovers	L 1-3	1-2	24	Hunt 31	(7,397)
14	18	EL	H	Sheffield United	W 1-0	0-0	23	Mellon 64	12,713
15	22	EL	A	Barnsley	L 0-2	0-1	23		(5,082)
16	29	EL	H	Reading	W 2-0	0-0	23	Hunt 50, Ashcroft 76	14,312
17	N 2	EL	H	Port Vale	D 0-0	0-0	23		14,513
18	5	EL	A	Watford	L 0-1	0-0	23		(8,419)
19	13	EL	A	Charlton Athletic	D 1-1	0-1	23	Taylor 55	(10,878)
20	19	EL	H	Oldham Athletic	W 3-1	2-0	23	Donovan 18, Ashcroft 30, Taylor 85	14,616
21	26	EL	A	Notts County	L 0-2	0-1	23		(10,088)
22	D 3	EL	A	Barnsley	W 2-1	1-0	21	Heggs 13, Hamilton 81	13,921
23	10	EL	A	Sheffield United	L 0-2	0-1	21		(13,891)
24	18	EL	H	Luton Town	W 1-0	1-0	21	Donovan 35	14,392
25	26	EL	H	Bristol City	W 1-0	0-0	18	Munro 81 (og)	21,071
26	27	EL	A	Southend United	L 1-2	1-1	18	Ashcroft 4	(6,856)
27	31	EL	H	Bolton Wanderers	W 1-0	1-0	18	Hunt 41	18,134
28	J 2	EL	A	Derby County	D 1-1	1-1	17	Hamilton 9	(16,035)
29	7	FAC 3	A	**Coventry City**	D 1-1	0-1		**Ashcroft 85 (pen)**	**(16,555)**
30	14	EL	A	Reading	W 2-0	0-0	16	Hunt 51, Donovan 90	(9,390)
31	18	FAC 3R	H	**Coventry City**	L 1-2	0-0		**Raven 49**	**23,230**
32	F 1	EL	H	Watford	L 0-1	0-0	16		15,754
33	5	EL	H	Charlton Athletic	L 0-1	0-0	17		12,084
34	11	EL	A	Port Vale	L 0-1	0-0	18		(10,751)
35	18	EL	H	Notts County	W 3-2	1-0	15	Mardon 44, Hunt 47, 87	13,748
36	21	EL	A	Oldham Athletic	L 0-1	0-1	18		(7,690)
37	25	EL	A	Stoke City	L 1-3	1-1	18	Hamilton 24	16,591
38	M 4	EL	A	Burnley	D 1-1	0-0	19	Hunt 62	(11,885)
39	8	EL	A	Portsmouth	W 2-1	1-1	16	Taylor 43, 87	(7,160)
40	15	EL	H	Wolverhampton Wand.	W 2-0	0-0	15	Ashcroft 7, Taylor 48	20,661
41	19	EL	H	Swindon Town	L 2-5	0-0	16	Hunt 53, Rees 60	12,960
42	22	EL	H	Millwall	W 3-0	1-0	14	Hunt 16, 56, 80 (pen)	11,782
43	25	EL	A	Grimsby Town	W 2-0	1-0	14	Hunt 14, Donovan 76	(7,393)
44	A 1	EL	H	Middlesbrough	L 1-3	1-0	16	Rees 35	20,256
45	8	EL	A	Bolton Wanderers	L 0-1	0-0	16		(16,207)
46	15	EL	H	Southend United	W 2-0	1-0	15	Hamilton 16, Strodder 54	14,393
47	17	EL	A	Bristol City	L 0-1	0-0	17		(8,777)
48	22	EL	H	Derby County	D 0-0	0-0	19		15,255
49	30	EL	H	Tranmere Rovers	W 5-1	1-0	19	Donovan 41, Ashcroft 62, 68, 70 (pen), Taylor 84	17,486
50	M 7	EL	A	Sunderland	D 2-2	0-1	19	Hunt 47, Agnew 87	(18,232)
51									
52									
53									
54									
55									
56									
57									
58									
59									
60									

Best Home League Attendance: 21,071 v Bristol City   **Smallest:** 11,782 v Millwall   **Av Home Att:** 15,219

Goal Scorers:

League (51):   Hunt 13 (1 pen), Taylor 11, Ashcroft 10 (1 pen), Donovan 5, Hamilton 4, Rees 2, Agnew, Heggs, Mardon, Mellon, Strodder, Opponent   **Compared with 1993-94:** -1,621

C/Cola Cup (0):

FA Cup (2):   Ashcroft, Raven

362

Naylor S.	Parsley N.	Edwards P.	Phelan M.	Herbert C.	Burgess D.	Ashcroft L.	Hamilton I.	Taylor R.	Heggs C.	McNally B.	Donovan K.	Raven P.	Lange A.	Mellon M.	Darton S.	Strodder G.	Smith D.	Lilwall S.	Coldicott S.	Boere J.	Mardon P.	Hunt A.	O'Regan K.	Bradley D.	Rees A.	Referee
1	2	3	4	5	6	7*	8	9	10	11	12	S	S													G. Pooley 1
1	2	3	4	5			8	9	10	11*	7	6	S	12	S											J. Holbrook 2
1	2		4	5	6	14	8	9	10•	7*	11		S	12	3											P. Alcock 3
1	2		4	5	6		8	9	10	S	11		S	7	3	5										P. Harrison 4
1			4	6	2	8		9	S	10			S	7	3	5	11	S								E. Lomas 5
1			4	6	2	8•		9		14			S		3	5	11*	7	12	10						P. Foakes 6
1				6	2•	8		9		S			S		3	5	11	7	4	10	14					E. Parker 7
1	12			6		8*		9					S		3	5	11•	7	4	10	2	14				K. Lynch 8
1	2		4	6		8.		9		12	11		S		3	5		14		10	7*					T. West 9
1	2		4	6		8		9			14		S	11		5	10•	3			7*					J. Rushton 10
1	2		4			8		9	14				S	11		5	10•	3	14		7					J. Watson 11
1	2	6				8		9	14				S	11		5	10•	3	6		7	S				J. Kirkby 12
1	2	6				8		9	5				S	11			10	3	S		7				S	J. Lloyd 13
1	2	6	14			8.		9	12				S	10		5	11*	3	4		5•	7	14			E. Wolstenholme 14
1	2	3	4			8	11	9		7		6	S	S			S	4			7					W. Flood 15
1	2	3	4			8*	11	9		7		6	S	12			S				5	10				N. Barry 16
1	2	3	4			8	11	9	14	7*		6									5	10				S. Dunn 17
1	2	3	4•			8	11	9	12	7		6					S				5•	10	12			G. Pooley 18
1		3				8	11	9	10*	7		4	6	S			S				5	10*	14			I. Hemley 19
1	12	3				8	11	9	14	7*		4	6	S							5	12	2			C. Wilkes 20
1	12	3				8	11	9	14	7*		4	6	S							5	2	14			A. Dawson 21
1		3				8	11	9	10*	7•		4	6	S				3			5	12	2	14		K. Breen 22
1						8	11	9	10*	7•		4	6	S				3			5	12	2	14		K. Lynch 23
1	12					8	11	9*	14•			7	6					3			5	10	2	4		M. Brandwood 24
1	S	6				8	11	12	9*			7						3			5	10	2	4		T. West 25
1	12	6				8	11	9†				7					14	3			5	10	2•	4*		M. Pierce 26
1	2	3				8	11	9				7	6	S			S				5	10		4	S	A. Butler 27
1	2	3				8	11	9*				7	6	S			S				5	10	4	12	S	K. Poulain 28
1	2	3	S			8	11					7	6	S			12				5	10	4	9*		P. Durkin 29
1	2	3				8.	11					7	6•	S			14				5	10	2	4†		P. Foakes 30
1	2	3				8	11	12				7	6	S			14				5	10	2	4†		P. Durkin 31
1	2*	3	14				11•	9		12		7	6	GK			8				5	10	2	9*		D. Allison 32
1*	2					14	11	12				7	6				8•	3				10*	4	9		P. Wright 33
		3	11			2*	8	9				7	6	1							5	10	S	4	12	U. Rennie 34
		3	14			2	8	11	9			7•	6	1							5	10		4	12	J. Rushton 35
		3•	4			2	8*	11	9			14	6	1			7				5	10			12	J. Winter 36
	2*					5	8	11	9			7•	6	1								10	12	4	14	E. Wolstenholme 37
1				4		2	S	11	S				6	S		5	8					10	7		9	J. Kirkby 38
1				4		2	S	11	9		12	8*	6	S		5						10	7		9	G. Pooley 39
1				4•		2	8	11	9			7	6	S		5						10	14		S	W. Flood 40
1						2	8	11	9*		4	7	6	S		5.						10	14		12	W. Burns 41
1						2	8	11		S	4	7	6	S		5						10	S		9	T. Heilbron 42
1						2		11		S	8	7	6	S				4			5	10	12		9	J. Watson 43
1						2	8	11	12		4•	7	6	S		5						10	14		9*	A. D'Urso 44
1						2		11	12		4•	7	6	S		5	14	8				10			9*	A. Dawson 45
1						2	8	11	9			7	6	S		5	8					10		4	9	M. Bailey 46
1						2	8	11	9			7	6•	S		5	14*	8				10	4		12	D. Orr 47
1						2	8	11	9	S		7	6	S		5	10	4						S	9	R. Poulain 48
1						2	8	11	9			7•	6	S		5	10	4				12		14	S	K. Cooper 49
1						2	8	11	9			7	6	S		5	10*	4x				12		14		P. Wright 50
42	20	20	17	8	22	36	35	38	7	16	31	31	4	5	7	19	16	14	9	5	27	33	11	11	8	League Appearances
4		3			2			4	7	5	2			1	2			4	2	2		1	6	8	6	League Sub Appearances
2	1	1	2		2	1	1	1		1	2	1			1+1	1		1				2	2	1	2	C/Cola Cup Appearances
2	1	2				2	2	0+1			2	2					0+2				2	2	1	2	2	FA Cup Appearances

Also Played: Germaine S(24,25,26,34,35,36,37), Agnew 3(37,38,39,40,41,42,43,44,45,46,47,48,49,50)
Players on Loan: Boere (West Ham United)

† = Sent Off

WEST BROMWICH ALBION

CLUB RECORDS

BIGGEST VICTORIES
League: 12-0 v Darwen, Division 1, 4.4.1892 (League Record)
F.A. Cup: 10-1 v Chatham, Round 3, 2.3.1889.
League Cup: 6-1 v Coventry City, Round 4, 10.11.1965; v Aston Villa, Round 2,14.9.1966
Europe (UEFA): 4-0 v Dynamo Bucharest, Round 2, 27.11.1968

BIGGEST DEFEATS
League: 3-10 v Stoke City, Division 1, 4.2.1937.
F.A. Cup: 0-5 v Leeds United, Round 4, 18.2.1967
League Cup: 0-5 v Tottenham Hotspur, Round 4, 28.10.1970
1-6 v Nottingham Forest, Round 2, 6.10.1982
Europe: No more than 3 goals.

MOST POINTS
3 points a win: 85, Division 2, 1992-93
2 points a win: 60, Division 1, 1919-20

MOST GOALS
105, Division 2 1929-30
Cookson 33, Glidden 20, Carter 19, Wood 7, Cresswell 6, Evans 5, Shaw 4, Boston 3, Edwards 3, W.G. Richardson 2, Fitton 1, og 2.

MOST LEAGUE GOALS CONCEDED
98, Division 1, 1936-37

MOST FIRST CLASS MATCHES IN A SEASON
59 (42 League, 6 FA Cup, 3 League Cup, 8 UEFA Cup) 1978-79

MOST LEAGUE WINS: 28, Division 1, 1919-20

MOST LEAGUE DRAWS: 19, Division 1, 1979-80

MOST LEAGUE DEFEATS: 26, Division 1, 1985-86

INDIVIDUAL CLUB RECORDS

MOST GOALS IN A MATCH
6, Jimmy Cookson v Blackpool, Div 2, 17.9.1927

MOST GOALS IN A SEASON
'W.G.' Richardson 40 (League 39, FA Cup 1) 1935-36
4 goals twice=8, 3 goals twice=6, 2 goals 5 times=10, 1 goal 17 times=17

OLDEST PLAYER
Jesse Pennington, 38 years, 256 days v Liverpool, 6.5.1922

YOUNGEST PLAYER
Charlie Wilson, 16 years, 73 days v Oldham (Div 1), 1.10.1921
(Frank Hodgetts was 16 yrs 26 days when he played for Albion v Notts County in a wartime game on 26.10.1940)

BEST PERFORMANCES

League: 1919-20: Matches played 42, Won 28, Drawn 4, Lost 10, Goals for 104,Goals against 47, Points 60. (Champions)

F.A. Cup: 1887-88: 1st rnd. Wednesbury O.A. (a) 7-1; 2nd rnd. Mitchell St,George (a) 1-0; 3rd rnd. Wolves (h) 2-0; 4th rnd. bye; 5th rnd. Stoke City (h)4-1. 6th rnd. Old Carthusians (h) 4-2; Semi-Final, Derby Junction 3-0; Final Preston North End, 2-1
1891-92: 3rd rnd. Old Westminsters (a) 3-2; 4th rnd. Blackburn Rovers (h) 3-1;5th rnd. Sheffield Weds. (h) 2-1; Semi-Final Nottingham Forest 1-1, 1-1, 6-2;Final Aston Villa 3-0
1930-31: 3rd rnd. Charlton Athletic (h) 2-2, (a) 1-1, (n) 3-1; 4th rnd.Tottenham Hotspur (h) 1-0; 5th rnd. Portsmouth (a) 1-0; 6th rnd. Wolves (h) 1-1, (a) 2-1; Semi-Final Everton, 1-0; Final Birmingham 2-1
1953-54: 3rd rnd. Chelsea (h) 1-0; 4th rnd. Rotherham United (h) 4-0; 5th rnd.Newcastle United (h) 3-2; 6th rnd. Tottenham Hotspur (h) 3-0; Semi-Final Port Vale, 2-1; Final Preston North End, 3-2
1967-68: 3rd rnd. Colchester (a) 1-1, (h) 4-0; 4th rnd. Southampton (h) 1-1,(a) 3-2; 5th rnd. Portsmouth (a) 2-1; 6th rnd. Liverpool (h) 0-0, (a) 1-1, (n)2-1; Semi-Final Birmingham City, 2-0; Final Everton, 1-0

League Cup: 1965-66: 2nd rnd. Walsall (h) 3-1; 3rd rnd. Leeds United (a) 4-2;4th rnd. Coventry City (h) 1-1, (h) 6-1; 5th rnd. Aston Villa (h) 3-1; Semi-Final Peterborough United (h) 2-1, (a) 4-2; Final West Ham United (a) 1-2, (h)4-1

Europe (UEFA): 1978-79: 1st rnd. Galatasary, 3-1, 3-1; 2nd rnd. Sporting Braga,2-0, 1-0. 3rd rnd. Valencia, 1-1, 2-0; 4th rnd. Red Star, 0-1, 1-1.

ADDITIONAL INFORMATION
In 1956-57 Albion played 42 First Division games. They won 14, drew 14,and lost 14 for a total of 42 points and finished halfway in the table (11th)

Previous Name
West Bromwich Strollers 1878-80
Previous League:
None

Club colours: Navy blue/white striped shirts, white shorts, white socks.
Change colours: Yellow shirts light blue sleeves, blue shorts, yellow/blue socks.

Reserves League
Pontins Central League Division 1.

DIVISIONAL RECORD

	Played	Won	Drawn	Lost	For	Against	Points
Division 1	2,652	988	637	1,027	4,134	4,224	2,673
Division 2/1	1,074	462	261	351	1,746	1,373	1,279
Division 3/2	92	44	24	24	152	103	156
Total	3,818	1,494	922	1,402	6,033	5,700	4,108

RECORDS AND STATISTICS

COMPETITIONS

Div.1	Div.2/1	Div.3.2	ECWC	FMC	Texaco	A/Scot
1888-01	1901-02	1991-93	1968-69	1986	1970-71	1975-76
1902-04	1904-11			1987	1972-73	1976-77
1911-27	1927-31		EUFA	1988	1974-75	A/Ital.
1931-38	1938-49		1966-67	SC	Watney C	1969-70
1949-73	1973-76		1978-79	1988-89	1971-72	1970-71
1976-86	1986-91		1979-80	ZC		1994-95
	1993-		1981-82	1989-91	AGT	T/Cal
					1991-93	1977-78
						1978-79

HONOURS

Div.1	Div.2	FAC	Lge Cup	C/Shield
1919-20	1901-02	1887-88	1965-66	1920
	1910-11	1891-92		1954
		1930-31		
		1953-54		
		1967-68		

MOST GOALS IN A CAREER
Tony Brown - 261 (1963-80)

Year	League	FA Cup	Lge Cup	Europe
1963-64	5			
1964-65	9			
1965-66	17		10	
1966-67	14	1	1	3
1967-68	11	4		
1968-69	17	2	1	3
1969-70	10	1	2	
1970-71	28	2		
1971-72	17	1		
1972-73	12	1	1	
1973-74	19	4		
1974-75	12	1		
1975-76	8	4		
1976-77	8			
1977-78	19	3	1	
1978-79	10	2	1	2
1979-80	2	1	1	
Total	218	27	18	8

Current leading goalscorer: Bob Taylor - 67 (1992-95)

MOST APPEARANCES
Tony Brown 704+16 (1963-80)

Year	League	FA Cup	Lge Cup	Europe	Other
1963-64	13				
1964-65	17				
1965-66	35	1	9		
1966-67	31	2	4	3	
1967-68	35	10	1		
1968-69	42	4	2	6	1
1969-70	40	1	8+1		4
1970-71	42	4	2		6
1971-72	40	1	1		3
1972-73	38+1	5	3		4
1973-74	41	4	2		
1974-75	32+2	3	2		3
1975-76	37+3	4	1		1
1976-77	36+1	2	3		3
1977-78	41	6	2		1
1978-79	29+2	6	1	5+1	2
1979-80	12+4	0+1	5	2	
	561+13	53+1	46+1	16+1	28

RECORD TRANSFER FEE RECEIVED

Amount	Club	Player	Date
£1,500,000	Manchester Utd	Bryan Robson	10/81
£995,000	Real Madrid	Laurie Cunningham	6/79
£225,000	Manchester City	Asa Hartford	6/79
£75,000	Norwich City	Colin Suggett	2/73

RECORD TRANSFER FEE PAID

Amount	Club	Player	Date
£748,000	Manchester City	Peter Barnes	7/79
£516,000	Middlesbrough	David Mills	1/79
£138,000	Rangers	Willlie Johnson	12/72
£100,000	Sunderland	Colin Suggett	8/69

MANAGERS

Name	Seasons	Best	Worst
Thomas Foster	1885-87	5(1)	6(1)
Louis Ford	1887-90	5(1)	6(1)
W. Pierre Dix	1890-92	12(1)	12(1)
Henry Jackson	1892-94	8(1)	8(1)
E Stephenson	1894-95	13(1)	13(1)
Clement Keys	1895		
Frank Heaven	1896-02	7(1)	1(1)
Fred Everiss	1902-48	1(1)	11(2)
Jack Smith	1948-52	14(1)	3(2)
Jesse Carver	1952-53	4(1)	4(1)
Vic Buckingham	1953-59	2(1)	17(1)
Gordon Clark	1959-61	4(1)	10(1)
Archie Macauley	1961-63	9(1)	14(1)
Jimmy Hagan	1963-67	6(1)	14(1)
Alan Ashman	1967-71	8(1)	18(1)
Don Howe	1971-75	16(1)	16(2)
Johnny Giles	1975-77	7(1)	3(2)
Ronnie Allen	1977		
Ron Atkinson	1978-81	3(1)	10(1)
Ronnie Allen	1981-82	17(1)	17(1)
Ron Wylie	1982-84	11(1)	17(1)
Johnny Giles	1984-85	12(1)	12(1)
Nobby Stiles	1985		
Ron Saunders	1986-87	22(1)	22(1)
Ron Atkinson	1987-88	20(2)	20(2)
Brain Talbot	1988-91	9(2)	9(2)
Bobby Gould	1991-92	7(3)	7(3)
Ossie Ardiles	1992-93	4(3/2)	4(3/2)
Keith Burkinshaw	1993-94	21(1/2)	21(1/2)
Alan Buckley	1994-	19(1)	19(1)

LONGEST LEAGUE RUNS

of undefeated matches:	17 (23.11.1901 - 29.3.1902)	of league matches w/out a win:	12 (7.5.1985 - 19.10.1985)
of undefeated home matches:	19 (2.9.01-11.10.02, 7.9.08-6.9.09)	of undefeated away matches:	11 (23.4.57-14.12.57, 26.1.80-13.9.80)
without home win:	9 (2.5.21-26.11.21, 21.8.71-11.12.71)	without an away win:	27 (27.12.1969 - 12.4.1971)
of league wins:	11 (5.4.1930 - 8.9.1930)	of home wins:	11 (20.10.1906 - 1.4.1907)
of league defeats:	9 20.8.1985 - 28.9.1985)	of away wins:	7 (22.4.1953 - 31.10.1953)

WEST BROMWICH ALBION

PLAYERS NAME / Honours	Ht	Wt	Birthdate	Birthplace / Transfers	Contract Date	Clubs	APPEARANCES				GOALS			
							League	L/Cup	FA Cup	Other	Lge	L/C	FAC	Oth
G O A L K E E P E R S														
Neil Cutler			03.09.76	Birmingham	06.09.93	West Bromwich A.								
E: S.				Loan	09.12.94	Cheltenham Town								
				Loan	03.02.95	Cheltenham Town								
Stuart Naylor	6.4	11.3	06.12.62	Wetherby		Yorkshire Amateurs								
E: B.3, Y.1.				Free	19.06.80	Lincoln City	49	4	2	6				
				Loan	23.02.83	Peterborough Utd	8							
				£100,000	18.02.86	West Bromwich A.	327+1	18	12	15				
D E F E N D E R S														
Paul Agnew	5.9	10.7	15.08.65	Lisburn		Cliftonville								
NI: u23.1, Y.S.				£4,000	15.02.84	Grimsby Town	219+23	17+1	23+1	12+2	3			
				£65,000	23.02.95	West Bromwich A.	14				1			
Ian Brien	5.11	11.9	10.02.69	Dublin	13.02.87	Leicester City (A)	12+4	1	1	3	1			
				£90,000	16.12.88	Chesterfield	201+3	14	7	14	8			
					08.10.93	Rotherham United	41+2	2	4	6	4			
				Free	08.95	West Bromwich A.								
Daryl Burgess	5.11	12.3	24.01.71	Birmingham	01.07.89	West Bromwich A.(T)	173+5	8+2	6	8	5	1		
Paul Edwards	5.11	11.0	25.12.63	Birkenhead		Altrincham								
NPL LC'85.				Free	12.01.88	Crewe Alexandra	82+4	6	8	7+1	6			1
				£350,000	16.03.90	Coventry City	32+4	6	2	2				
				£100,000	13.08.92	Wolverhampton W.	43+3	2	2	1				
				£55,000	19.01.94	West Bromwich A.	35	1	2					
Craig Herbert			09.11.75	Coventry		Torquay United (T)								
				Free	18.03.94	West Bromwich A.	8	2						
Paul Mardon	6.0	12.0	14.09.69	Bristol	29.01.88	Bristol City (T)	29+13	3+3		1		1		
				Loan	13.09.90	Doncaster Rovers	3							
				£115,000	16.08.91	Birmingham City	54+10	11+1	1	3				
				£400,000	18.11.93	West Bromwich A.	49		2		2			
M I D F I E L D														
Stacy Coldicott	5.10	11.8	20.04.74	Redditch	04.03.92	West Bromwich A.(T)	23+7	3+1	1+1	4+1				
Shaun Cunnington	5.9	11.0	04.01.66	Bourne	11.01.84	Wrexham (J)	196+3	13	9	21	12		1	2
WFAC'86.				£55,000	19.02.88	Grimsby Town	182	11	11	9	13		3	
				£650,000	17.07.92	Sunderland	52+6	3	2	2	8		1	
				£200,000	08.95	West Bromwich A.								
Kevin Donovan	5.9	11.0	17.12.71	Halifax	11.10.89	Huddersfield T. (T)	11+9	1+1	1	4	1		2	
				Loan	13.02.92	Halifax Town	6							
				£25,000	01.10.92	West Bromwich A.	94+8	5	6+1	9+1	19	3	3	4
Dave Gilbert	5.4	10.4	22.06.63	Lincoln	29.06.81	Lincoln City (A)	15+15	5	3		1			
Div.4'87.				Free	18.08.82	Scunthorpe United	1	1						
via Boston Utd, 4 FAC App 2 gls.					30.06.86	Northampton Town	120	10	6	9	21	2	3	1
				£55,000	23.03.89	Grimsby Town	259	18	11	9	41	4	2	
					08.95	West Bromwich A.								
Ian Hamilton	5.9	11.3	14.12.67	Stevenage	24.12.85	Southampton (A)								
					29.03.88	Cambridge United	23+1	1	2	2	1			
					23.12.88	Scunthorpe United	139+6	6	6+1	14+1	18			3
				£170,000	19.06.92	West Bromwich A.	122+1	6	7	9+2	14		1	3
Mike Phelan	5.10	11.2	24.09.62	Nelson	29.07.80	Burnley (A)	166+2	16	16	8	9	2		2
E: 1, Y.5. Div.3'82. Div.2'86. FAC'90. CS'90.				£60,000	13.07.85	Norwich City	155+1	14	11	13	9		1	
ECEC'91. LC'92. Prem'93.				£750,000	01.07.89	Manchester United	88+14	14+2	10	15+3	2		1	
				Free	11.07.94	West Bromwich A.	17+3	2						
Paul Raven	6.0	12.3	28.07.70	Salisbury	06.06.88	Doncaster Rovers (J)	52	2	5	2	4			
ESFA u18.4.				£100,000	23.03.89	West Bromwich A.	135+4	7	6	9	9		2	
				Loan	27.11.91	Doncaster Rovers	7							
David Smith	5.8	10.2	29.03.68	Stonehouse	07.07.86	Coventry City (T)	144+10	17	6	4+1	19			
E: u21.10.				Loan	08.01.93	Bournemouth	1							
				P.E.	12.03.93	Birmingham City	35+3	4	0+1	1	3			
				£90,000	31.01.94	West Bromwich A.	34+6	1	0+2					
F O R W A R D S														
Lee Ashcroft	5.10	11.0	07.09.72	Preston	16.07.91	Preston N.E. (T)	78+13	3	5	6+2	13			1
E: u21.1				£225,000	01.08.93	West Bromwich A.	53+6	2+1	3	5+1	13		1	
Andrew Hunt	6.0	12.0	09.06.70	Grays		Kings Lynn								
				Free		Kettering Town								
				£150,000	29.01.91	Newcaslte United	34+9	3	2	3	11	1	2	
				£100,000	25.03.93	West Bromwich A.	77+7	3	3	3	34	1	1	2
James McCue			29.06.75	Glasgow	18.02.93	West Brom. A. (T)		0+1		0+1				

PLAYERS NAME / Honours	Ht	Wt	Birthdate	Birthplace / Transfers	Contract Date	Clubs	League	L/Cup	FA Cup	Other	Lge	L/C	FAC	Oth
Tony Rees	5.9	11.13	01.08.64	Merthyr Tydfil	01.08.82	Aston Villa (A)								
W: 1, u21.1, Y, S. FAYC'80.				Free	01.07.83	Birmingham City	75+20	7+1	5	1+2	12	2	2	
				Loan	01.10.85	Peterborough Utd	5				2			
				Loan	01.03.86	Shrewsbury Town	1+1							
					01.03.88	Barnsley	27+4	2	0+1	1	3			
					17.08.89	Grimsby Town	124+17	11+2	8+1	5	33	1		3
				£30,000	25.11.94	West Bromwich A.	8+6		2		2			
Bob Taylor	5.10	11.9	03.02.67	Horden		Horden CW								
				Free	27.03.88	Leeds United	33+9	5+1	1	4+1	9	3		1
				£175,000	23.03.89	Bristol City	96+10	6+1	9+1	3	50	2	5	1
				£300,000	31.01.92	West Bromwich A.	145+4	7	5+1	11+1	67	2	3	5
Gary Germaine			02.08.76	Birmingham	05.07.94	West Brom. A. (T)								

TOP GOALSCORER 1994/95
Andrew Hunt

Division One Goals (games) . . . . 13 (33+6)
Coca-Cola Cup Goals 0 (0)
F.A. Cup goals 0 (2)

Total . . . . **13 (35+6)**

Total goals for W.B.A. since 25.03.93 . . . . 38 (86+7)

Career total as at June 1st 1995 . . . . 52 (128+16)

THE MANAGER
ALAN BUCKLEY

Date of Birth . . . . 20th April 1951.
Place of Birth . . . . Eastwood.
Date of Appointment . . . . October 1995.

PREVIOUS CLUBS
As Manager . . . . Walsall, Kettering Town, Grimsby Town.
As Coach . . . .
As a Player . . . . Nottingham Forest, Walsall, Birmingham City, Walsall.

HONOURS
As a Manager
Guided Grimsby Town to promotion from Division 4 in 1990 and from Division 3 in 1991.

As a Player
None.

THE HAWTHORNS
West Bromwich B71 4LF
Tel: 0121 525 8888

Capacity ....25,117 (all seater)

First game...v Derby County, 1-1, 3.9.1900.
First floodlit game...v Chelsea, Div.1, 1-1, 18.9.1957)
Internationals ....England v N.Ireland 1922, v Belgium 1924, v Wales 1945.

ATTENDANCES
Highest...64,815 v Arsenal, FAC 6th Rnd, 6.3.1937.
Lowest ....405 v Derby County, Div 1, 29.11.1890.
OTHER GROUNDS ....Coopers Hill 1878. Dartmouth Park 1879-81.Bunns Field 1881-82.
.... Four Acres (Dartmouth CC) 1882-85.Stoney Lane 1885-1900. The Hawthorns 1900-

MATCHDAY TICKET PRICES

Halford Lane Centre	£15
Concessions	£10
Halford Lane Wings	£14
Concessions	£9
WBBS Centre	£14
Concessions	£9
WBBS Wings	£13
Concessions	£8
BRE/SME/Paddock	£10
Concessions	£7

Ticket Office Telephone no. ...... 0121 553 5472.

HOW TO GET TO THE GROUND
From all directions
Use motorway (M5) until junction 1.
Leave motorway and follow signs to Birmingham (A41) for West Bromwich Albion FC.

Car Parking
Car parks of Halfords Lane and Middlemore Road, street parking in some areas within 10 minutes walk of ground.

Nearest Railway Station
Rolfe St. Smethwick (One and a quarter miles).
Hawthorns Halt (400 yards).

CLUBCALL
0898 12 11 93
Calls cost 39p per minute cheap rate and 49p per minute at all other times.
Call costings correct at time of going to press.

MATCHDAY PROGRAMME

Programme Editor .... Tom Cardall.

Number of pages .... 40.

Price .... £1.50.

Subscriptions .... (Home only): UK £50, Eire & Europe £52.50.
... Outside Europe: Air £78.50. For home & away the cost is doubled.

Local Newspapers...................... Sandwell Evening Mail,
... Birmingham Post & Evening Mail, Express & Star Wolverhampton,
.... Sports Argus, Sporting Pink.l, Sunday Mercury.

Local Radio Stations....... BRMB Radio, Radio WM, Beacon Radio,
.... Mercia Sound, W.A.B. Radio.

WOLVERHAMPTON WANDERERS

(The Wolves)
ENDSLEIGH LEAGUE DIVISION 1
SPONSORED BY: GOODYEAR

Back Row (L-R): Jamie Smith, Gordon Cowans, Darren Ferguson, Geoff Thomas, Mike Stowell, Paul Jones, Neil Emblen, Neil Masters, Jermaine Wright, Robbie Dennison. **Middle Row:** Barry Holmes (Physio), Andy Thompson, Don Goodman, Brian Law, Dean Richards, Andy Debont, David Kelly, Jimmy Kelly, Mark Rankine, Paul Birch, Dave Hancock (Asst. Physio). **Front Row:** Chris Evans (Yth Dev. Officer), Ian Miller (Res. Coach), Steve Froggatt, Tony Daley, Peter Shirtliff (Capt), Graham Taylor (Manager), Bobby Downes (Asst. Manager), John De Wolf, Mark Venus, Steve Bull, Rob Kelly (Yth Manager), Steve Harrison (First team coach).

WOLVERHAMPTON WANDERERS
FORMED IN 1877
TURNED PROFESSIONAL IN 1888
LTD COMPANY IN 1892

PRESIDENT: Sir Jack Hayward
CHAIRMAN: Jonathan Hayward
DIRECTORS
Jack Harris, John Harris, John Richards,
Nic Stones, Keith Pearson, ACIS
SECRETARY
Keith Pearson ACIS (01902 712 181)
ASSISTANT SECRETARY: Dot Wooldridge
COMMERCIAL MANAGER
Gary Leaver

MANAGER: Graham Taylor
ASSISTANT MANAGER: Bobby Downes
COACH: Steve Harrison
RESERVE TEAM MANAGER
Ian Miller
YOUTH TEAM MANAGER
Chris Evans
PHYSIOTHERAPIST
Barry Holmes & Dave Hanock

STATISTICIAN FOR THE DIRECTORY
Les Smith

Manager Graham Taylor prepared for his first full season in charge at Molineux by adding three big signings, Tony Daley for a club record fee of £1,250,000, Steve Froggart for £1,000,000 and Neil Emblen for £600,000, to an already strong squad. Wolves were predictably and justifiably, on paper, made favourites for the one automatic promotion place. Unfortunately for Wolves, titles are not won on paper and things started to go wrong before the season started.

Daley was injured in training and when he finally made his debut in October he lasted eleven minutes before departing for the season. In the first match of the season Steve Bull was injured after ten minutes and so it went ton. All told, ten first team players required surgery during the worst season for injuries in the clubs history. To his credit Graham Taylor never complained about the injuries which decimated even his large squad, but got on with the job of going for promotion.

A good start was made with an opening win over fellow promotion favourites, Reading, with new boy Froggart scoring the only goal. The other new signing, Emblen, had a nightmare start at centre-half and was immediately dropped, but he soon came back in a midfield position and had a brilliant season in his new role. A win against local rivals, West Brom, and a run of five successive wins in September/October took Wolves to top spot where they started for two months.

At the end of November Wolves fell off the top and never regained those heights, although they never looked like missing out on the play-offs. A final position of fourth was just about right on the performances over the season. Wolves were playing well without being able to produce the results and so it proved against Bolton. In the first leg at Molineux Wolves won 2-1 but hit the bar twice, had two goals disallowed and won the corner count 19-1. In the return Bolton were the better side in a much closer match, but managed a 2-0 scoreline after extra-time to go through to the final.

The FA Cup provide the excitement for the fans last season. After coming back from 0-2 to beat Mansfield, Wolves met Sheffield Wednesday in the Fourth Round. After two draws the tie went to sudden death penalties. Again having to come from behind it was left to Don Goodman to see them through, he did and the home supporters went wild. Leicester City were put out in the next round, but the glory run came to a holt against, eventual Semi-finalists, Crystal Palace.

With mid-season signings of John De Wolf, who brought strength to a previously vulnerable defence, Don Goodman and Gordon Cowens being added to the squad and with the rest of the squad getting to full fitness, Wolves could once agin start the season as one of the teams to beat next year.

LES SMITH.

WOLVERHAMPTON WANDERERS

Division One: 4th   **FA Cup:** 6th Round   **Coca-Cola Cup:** 3rd Round   **Anglo Italian Cup:** Preliminary Round

M	DATE	COMP.	VEN	OPPONENTS	RESULT	H/T	LP	GOAL SCORERS/GOAL TIMES	ATT.
1	A 13	EL	H	Reading	W 1-0	1-0		Froggatt 11	27,012
2	21	EL	A	Notts County	D 1-1	0-1		Thompson 71 (pen)	(8,569)
3	24	AIC Pre	A	Lecce	W 1-0	0-0		Kelly 80	(1,795)
4	28	EL	H	West Bromwich A.	W 2-0	1-0	3	Thompson 22 (pen), Kelly 70	27,764
5	30	EL	A	Watford	L 1-2	0-1	6	Emblen 85	(10,108)
6	S 3	EL	A	Sunderland	D 1-1	1-1	5	Venus 43	(15,111)
7	6	AIC Pre	H	Ascoli	L 0-1	0-0			9,599
8	10	EL	H	Tranmere Rovers	W 2-0	1-0	3	Stewart 37, Emblen 52	27,030
9	13	EL	H	Southend United	W 5-0	3-0	2	Emblen 7, Kelly 10, Froggatt 38, Walters 63, Bull 67	23,608
10	17	EL	A	Burnley	W 1-0	0-0	1	Bull 59	(17,766)
11	20	CC 2/1	A	Chesterfield	W 3-1	0-1		Bull 63, 86, Kelly 77	(5,895)
12	24	EL	A	Portsmouth	W 2-1	1-1	1	Walters 35, Kelly 87	(13,466)
13	27	CC 2/2	H	Chesterfield	D 1-1	1-0		Froggatt 3	14,815
14	O 1	EL	A	Port Vale	W 2-1	0-0	1	Thompson 52, 79 (pens)	27,469
15	5	AIC Pre	A	Venezia	L 1-2	1-1		Venus 29	(750)
16	8	EL	A	Swindon Town	L 2-3	2-2	1	Kelly 13, 41	(14,036)
17	15	EL	H	Grimsby Town	W 2-1	1-1	1	Thompson 13 (pen), Venus 67	24,447
18	22	EL	H	Millwall	D 3-3	1-1	1	Bull 27, 53, Venus 79	25,059
19	26	CC 3	H	Nottingham Forest	L 2-3	1-2		Birch 41, Kelly 60	28,369
20	30	EL	A	Stoke City	D 1-1	1-1	1	Bull 40	(15,928)
21	N 1	EL	A	Bristol City	W 5-1	2-1	1	Walters 12, Thompson 36 (pen), Kelly 63, 65, 87	(10,400)
22	5	EL	H	Luton Town	L 2-3	0-1	1	Stewart 81, Johnson 85 (og)	26,749
23	15	AIC Pre	H	Atalanta	D 1-1	1-1		Mills 38	7,285
24	20	EL	A	Middlesbrough	L 0-1	0-0	2		(19,953)
25	23	EL	H	Bolton Wanderers	W 3-1	0-1	1	Thompson 53 (pen), Coleman 68 (og), Birch 75	25,903
26	27	EL	H	Derby County	L 0-2	0-1	2		22,768
27	D 4	EL	A	Millwall	L 0-1	0-0	3		(8,025)
28	10	EL	H	Notts County	W 1-0	0-0	2	Bull 46	25,786
29	18	EL	A	Reading	L 2-4	1-2	2	Bull 9, Quinn 58 (og)	(10,136)
30	26	EL	A	Oldham Athletic	L 1-4	1-0	4	Dennison 58	(11,962)
31	28	EL	H	Charlton Athletic	W 2-0	2-0	2	Bull 38, Chaple 42 (og)	27,500
32	31	EL	A	Barnsley	W 3-1	2-1	2	Dennison 1, Mills 4, Emblen 75	(9,207)
33	J 2	EL	H	Sheffield United	D 2-2	0-0	2	De Wolf 89 (pen), Emblen 90	27,809
34	7	FAC 3	A	Mansfield Town	W 3-2	0-2		Kelly 52, Dennison 59, Mills 71	(6,701)
35	14	EL	H	Stoke City	W 2-0	1-0	2	Kelly 17, Dennison 87	28,298
36	30	FAC 4	A	Sheffield Wednesday	D 0-0	0-0			(21,757)
37	F 4	EL	A	Bolton Wanderers	L 1-5	1-2	4	Goodman 26	(16,964)
38	8	FAC 4R	H	Sheffield Wednesday	D †1-1	1-0		Kelly 12 (Won 4-3 on penalties)	28,136
39	11	EL	A	Bristol City	W 2-0	1-0	2	Dennison 25, Kelly 61	25,451
40	18	FAC 5	H	Leicester City	W 1-0	1-0		Kelly 35	28,544
41	21	EL	A	Middlesbrough	L 0-2	0-0	6		27,611
42	25	EL	A	Port Vale	W 4-2	3-1	5	De Wolf 1, 43, 68 (pen), Bull 44	(13,676)
43	M 5	EL	H	Portsmouth	W 1-0	0-0	4	Bull 73	23,284
44	8	EL	H	Sunderland	W 1-0	0-0	3	Thompson 47 (pen)	25,926
45	11	FAC 6	H	Crystal Palace	D 1-1	0-0		Cowans 66	(14,604)
46	15	EL	A	West Bromwich A.	L 0-2	0-1	4		(20,661)
47	18	EL	H	Watford	D 1-1	1-0	5	Thomas 23	24,380
48	22	FAC 6R	H	Crystal Palace	L 1-4	1-3		Kelly 34	27,548
49	24	EL	H	Burnley	W 2-0	1-0	4	Bull 10, Emblen 58	25,703
50	A 1	EL	A	Southend United	W 1-0	0-0	3	Bull 83	(8,522)
51	4	EL	A	Luton Town	D 3-3	0-2	4	Kelly 48, 59, Emblen 90	(9,651)
52	8	EL	H	Barnsley	D 0-0	0-0	4		26,385
53	12	EL	A	Derby County	D 3-3	1-1	4	Goodman 11, Richards 75, 90	(16,040)
54	15	EL	A	Charlton Athletic	L 2-3	1-1	4	Bull, 66	(10,922)
55	17	EL	H	Oldham Athletic	W 2-1	1-1	4	Kelly 33, 82	25,840
56	22	EL	A	Sheffield United	D 3-3	0-1	4	Goodman 58, Bull 65, Kelly 83	(16,714)
57	29	EL	A	Grimsby Town	D 0-0	0-0	4		(10,112)
58	M 3	EL	A	Tranmere Rovers	D 1-1	0-1	4	Bull 73	(12,306)
59	7	EL	H	Swindon Town	D 1-1	1-0	4	Thompson 36 (pen)	26,245
60	14	PO SF/1	H	Bolton Wanderers	W 2-1	1-0		Bull 44, Venus 51	26,153
61	17	PO SF/2	A	Bolton Wanderers	L †0-2	0-1			(20,041)

Best Home League Attendance: 28,298 v Stoke City   **Smallest:** 22,768 v Derby County   **Av Home Att:** 26,001

Goal Scorers: **Compared with 1993-94:** +3,993

League (77): Bull 16, Kelly 15, Thompson 9, Emblen 7, Dennison 4, De Woolf 4, Goodman 3, Venus 3, Walters 3, Froggatt 2, Richards 2, Stewart 2, Birch, Mills, Thomas, Opponents

C/Cola Cup (6): Bull 2, Kelly 2, Birch, Froggat
FA Cup (7): Kelly 4, Cowans, Dennison, Mills
Anglo/Ital Cup (3): Kely Mills, Venus   **Play-Offs (2):** Bull, Venus

Stowell M.	Smith J.	Thompson A.	Ferguson D.	Emblen N.	Shirtliff P.	Keen K.	Thomas G.	Bull S.	Kelly D.	Froggatt S.	Mills L.	Jones P.	Blades P.	Rankine M.	Birch P.	Stewart P.	Dennison R.	Walters M.	Bennett T.	De Wolf J.	Goodman D.	Law B.	Cowans G.	Masters N.	Wright J.	Referee	
1	2	3	4	5	6	7	8	9*	10	11	S	14	G													E. Parker	1
1	2	3	4	5	6		8		10	11	7		6	5	9	S										I. Cruikshanks	2
G	2	3	4	12	6		8		10	11	7*		1	5	9•	14										J. Watson	3
1	2	3	4	7*	6		8		10	11	12		G	5	S	9										P. Alcock	4
1	2	3	4*	7	6		8		10•	11	12		G	5	14	9										J. Kirkby	5
1	2	3	8	4	6		S		10		11		G	5	14	7	9									D. Allison	6
G	2	3	8	4	6	10*					11		1	5	14	7*	9	12								M. Cardona	7
1	2	3	8	4	6		9	14	11	5		G			S	10•		7								I. Henley	8
1	2	3	8	4	6		9	10	11	5		G	S		S			7								R. Poulain	9
1	2	3	8	4	6		9	10	11	5		G	S		S			7								T. Heilbron	10
1	2	3	8	4	6	S		9	10	11	5		G	12		S		7								P. Danson	11
1	2	3	8		6	S		9	10	11	4		G	5		S		7								M. Bailey	12
1	2	3	8		6	14		9*	10•	11	4		G	5	12	7										K. Morton	13
1	2	3	8		6			9		11	4	S	G	5	10	S		7								E. Wolstenholme	14
G	S	3	8		S	11		9			4	10	1	5	2	7			6							A. Dawson	15
1	2	3	8*		6			9	10		4		G	S	S	7		11								P. Foakes	16
1	2	3	8		6			9	10	11	4		G	5	12			7								M. Pierce	17
1	2	3	8		6	S		9	10	11	4		G	5				7*								J. Kirkby	18
1	2	3	4*	12			8	9	10	11	6		G	5	S	7										P. Don	19
1	2•	3	12	4*			8	9	10	11	6		G	5				14		7						J. Holbrook	20
1	2	3	4				8	9•	10	11	6		G	5	S			14		7						C. Wilkes	21
1	2	3	4	12			8	9*	10	11	6		G	5				14		7•						E. Wolstenholme	22
1		3	4*	2			8			11	6	9	G	5	12	7	10	S								F. Treussi	23
1	S	3	11•	4			8		10	7	6		G	5	2	14	9									A. Flood	24
1	S	3	11	12			8		10	7	6		G	5*	2	4	9									K. Cooper	25
1	12	3*	4	14			8		10	11	6		G	5	2	7	9•									J. Lloyd	26
1	2		4	7			8	9	10	11	6	14	G	5	2			3								I. Hemley	27
1	2		4	6				9	14	11	3		G	12	7•			10*	5	8						E. Parker	28
1	2		10	4				9		11*	3	14	G	6	7	12•			5	8						P. Alcock	29
G	2		10*	4							3	9	1		7			11		S	5		6	8	12	J. Watson	30
G			4				9•				3	8	1	2				11		14	5	7*	6	10	12	P. Harrison	31
G			4					14			3	9•	1	2	S			11		8	5	7	6	10		S. Mathieson	32
G			4					8			3	9	1	2	S			11		S	5	7	6	10		P. Wright	33
G			4					8			3	9	1	2	14			11		S	5*	7	6	10		E. Wolstenholme	34
G			4					8			3	9	1	2	S	7*		11		S	5	7	6	10		J. Winter	35
G		3						8			12	9•	1	2		7*		11			5	14	6	10		A. Wilkie	36
		3	4*			14		8			9•	1	2					11		12	5	9	6	10		J. Kirkby	37
		3	4					8			14	1	2•	7*				11		12	5	9	6	10		A. Wilkie	38
G		3	4*					8			14	1	2	7•				11		12	5	9	6	10		M. Riley	39
G		2				S		8			3	S	1		7			11*		4	5	9	6	10		R. Hart	40
G		2		12		4		8			3•	14	1		7			11*			5	9	6	10		K. Breen	41
G	S	3			6		9*	8			12		1	2	4			11			5	14	6	10		J. Lloyd	42
1		3			6		9•	8				6G	2	4				11		S	5	7		10		G. Cain	43
1	2	3			6		9•	8					G		4			11		12	5*	7		10		P. Wright	44
1	2	3	12	6			9•	8					G		4			11*		S		7	5	10		G. Willard	45
1	2	3	12	6			9•	8					G		4			11			7	5	10*			M. Brandwood	46
1		3		6		8*		9			12		G	2	7•			11		4		10	5			R. Lupton	47
1		3	12	6				9	8				G	2				11	4*		7	5				G. Willard	48
1	S		10	6				9	8			3	G	2	4			11			7	5				P. Foakes	49
1			4					9	8		10		G	2		S		11			7	5			3	M. Pierce	50
1			4				14	9	8		11		G	2	7•			12			8	5	10		3*	G. Pooley	51
1		14	4*	12				9	8				G	2				11			7	5	10	3		P. Harrison	52
1	3			6				9	8		11		G	S	4						7	5	10•			J. Holbrook	53
1	3*			6•				9	8		11		G	12	4						7	5	10			A. D'Urso	54
1				6				9	8		3		G	S	4			11			7	5	10			C. Wilkes	55
1	12			6				9	8		3		G	2*	4			11			7	5	10			N. Barry	56
1	2			6				9	8		3		G	S	4			11			7	5	10			R. Poulain	57
1	2			6				9	8		3		G		4			11			7	5	10			J. Lloyd	58
1	2			6				9	8		3		G		4			11•			7	S	10			J. Watson	59
1	2			6				9	8		3		G		4			11			7	S	10			C. Wilkes	60
1	2			6				9	8		3		G		4			11•			7	S	10			S. Dunn	61
37	24	30	22	23	26	1	13	31	38	20	35	6	9	30	24	8	5	21	11	4	13	24	17	21	3	League Appearances	
	1	1	2	4	2		1		4		4	5			2	3	2	3	1			4			2	League Sub Appearances	
3	3	3	1+1	2	0+1		3	3	3		2+1	0+1	3													C/Cola Cup Appearances	
2	1	5	3+2	2			2	6		3+1	2+1	4	3	4+1	1		6			2+1	4	5+1	6	5		FA Cup Appearances	
1	2	4	4	2+1	2	2	1	1	2	4	2		3	4	2+2	3+1	2				2		2			Anglo/Ital Appearances	

Also Played: Richards 6(50,51,52),2(53,54),5(56,57,58,59,60,61), Daley 12(18), De Bont GK(37,38), Kelly S(50)

Players on Loan: Stewart (Liverpool), Walters (Liverpool), Richards (Bradford City)

WOLVERHAMPTON WANDERERS

CLUB RECORDS

BIGGEST VICTORIES
League: 10-1 v Leicester City, Division 1, 15.4.1938
9-0 v Fulham, Division 1, 16.9.1959
F.A. Cup: 14-0 v Crosswells Brewery, Rnd 2, 13.11.1886
League Cup: 6-1 v Shrewsbury, Rnd 2, 24.9.1991
Europe: 5-0 v F K Austria, 30.11.1960

BIGGEST DEFEATS
League: 1-10 v Newton Heath, Division 1, 15.10.1892
0-9 v Derby County, Division 1, 10.1.1891
F.A. Cup: 0-6 v Rotherham Utd, Rnd 1, 16.11.1985
League Cup: 0-5 v Fulham, Rnd 3, 5.10.1966
0-5 v Sunderland, Rnd 2 replay, 27.10.1982
Europe: 0-4 v Barcelona, European Cup Q-Final, 2.10.1960

MOST POINTS
3 points a win: 92, Division 3, 1988-89
2 points a win: 64, Division 1, 1957-58

MOST GOALS
115, Division 2, 1931-32.
Hartill 30, Bottrill 21, Phillips 18, Deacon 13, Lowton 9, Baraclough 7,Buttery 6, Hollingworth 4, Crook 2, Martin 1, Redfern 1, Richards 1, Smalley ,og 1.

MOST FIRST CLASS MATCHES IN A SEASON
61 (46 League, 3 FA Cup, 4 League Cup, 8 Sherpa Van Trophy) 1987-88

MOST LEAGUE GOALS CONCEDED
99, Division 1, 1905-06

MOST LEAGUE WINS
28, Division 1, 1957-58; Division 1, 1958-59

MOST LEAGUE DRAWS
19, Division 2, 1990-91

MOST LEAGUE DEFEATS
25, Division 1, 1964-65; Division 1, 1983-84; Division 2, 1984-85; Division3, 1985-86

INDIVIDUAL CLUB RECORDS

MOST GOALS IN A MATCH
5. J Brodie v Stoke, 8-0, FA Cup 3, 22.2.1890
5. J Butcher v Accrington, 5-3, Div 1, 19.11.1892
5. T Phillipson v Bradford City, 7-2, Div 2, 25.12.1926
5. W Hartill v Notts County, 5-1, Div 2, 12.10.1929
5. W Hartill v Aston Villa, 5-2, Div 1, 3.9.1934

MOST GOALS IN A SEASON
Steve Bull, 52, 1987-88.
League 34, FA Cup 3, League Cup 3, SVT 12.
League only: D Westcott 38, 1946-47

OLDEST PLAYER
Lawrie Madden 37 yrs 222 days v Derby County, 8.5.1993

YOUNGEST PLAYER
Jimmy Mullen, 16 years 43 days v Leeds United, 18.2.1939
Wartime: Cameron Buchanan, 14 yrs 57 days v W.B.A., 26.9.1942

MOST CAPPED PLAYER
Billy Wright, 105 for England

BEST PERFORMANCES

Wolverhampton are the only League Club to have been Champions of all Four Divisions: Div 1, 1954, 1958, 1959; Div 2, 1932, 1977; Div 3N 1924; Div 3,1989; Div 4, 1988

League: 1957-58: Played 42, Won 28, Drawn 8, Lost 6, Goals For 103, Goals Against 47, Points 64. First in Division One

Highest: Division One Champions 3 times

F.A. Cup: 1892-93: 1st rnd. Bolton Wanderers 1-1, 2-1; 2nd rnd. Middlesbrough 2-1; 3rd rnd. Darwen 5-0; Semi-Final Blackburn Rovers 2-1; Final Everton 1-0
1907-08: 1st rnd. Bradford City 1-1, 1-0; 2nd rnd. Bury 2-0; 3rd rnd. Swindon Town 2-0; 4th rnd. Stoke City 1-0; Semi-Final Southampton 2-0; Final Newcastle United 3-1
1948-49: 3rd rnd. Chesterfield 6-0, 4th rnd. Sheffield Utd 3-0; Liverpool 3-1;6th rnd. West Bromwich Albion 1-0; Semi-Final Manchester United 1-1, 1-0; Final Leicester City 3-1
1959-60: 3rd rnd. Newcastle United 2-2, 4-2; 4th rnd Charlton Athletic 2-1; 5th Luton Town 4-1; 6th rnd. Leicester City 2-1; Semi-Final Aston Villa 1-0; Final Blackburn Rovers 3-0

League Cup: 1973-74: 2nd rnd. Halifax Town 3-0; 3rd rnd. Tranmere Rovers 1-1,2-1; 4th rnd. Exeter City 5-1; 5th rnd. Liverpool 1-0; Semi-Final Norwich City 1-1, 1-0; Final Manchester City 2-1
1979-80: 2nd rnd. Burnley 1-1, 2-0; 3rd rnd. Crystal Palace 2-1; 4th rnd. Queens Park Rangers 1-1, 1-0; 5th rnd. Grimsby Town 0-0, 1-1, 2-0; Semi-Final Swindon Town 1-2, 3-1; Final Nottingham Forest 1-0

UEFA Cup: 1971-72: 1st rnd. Academica 3-0, 4-1; 2nd rnd. Den Haag 3-1, 4-0; 3rd rnd. Carl Zeiss 1-0, 3-0; Quarter-Final Juventus 1-1, 2-1; Semi-Final Ferencvaros 2-2, 2-1; Final Tottenham Hotspur 1-2, 1-1

ADDITIONAL INFORMATION
Previous Name: None.
Previous League: None.

Club colours: Gold shirts, black shorts, gold socks.

Change colours: All white.

Reserves League: Pontins Central League Division 1.

DIVISIONAL RECORD

	Played	Won	Drawn	Lost	For	Against	Points
Division 1	2,270	911	506	853	3,874	3,671	2,344
Division 2/1	1,332	535	306	491	2,105	1,895	1,507
Division 3	92	37	24	31	153	147	135
Division 3(N)	42	24	15	3	76	27	63
Division 4	92	51	16	25	151	93	169
Total	3,828	1,558	867	1,403	6,359	5,833	4,218

RECORDS AND STATISTICS

COMPETITIONS

Div.1	Div.2/1	Div.3N	Euro C	Texaco	Watney	C/Sld
1888-06	1906-23	1923-24	1958-59	1970-71	1972-73	1949-50
1932-65	1924-32		1959-60	1972-73		1954-55
1967-76	1965-67	Div.3	ECWC		F/SVT	1958-59
1977-82	1976-77	1985-86	1960-61		1985-86	1959-60
1983-84	1982-83	1988-89	UEFA	A/Ital	1986-87	1960-61
	1984-85		1971-72	1969-70	1987-88	
	1989-	Div.4	1973-74		1988-89	
		1986-88	1974-75			
			1980-81			

HONOURS

Div.1	Div.2	Div.3	Div.4	FAC	Lge C	C/S/Sld
1953-54	1931-32	1923-24	1987-88	1892-93	1973-74	1949-50*
1957-58	1976-77	1988-89		1907-08	1979-80	1954-55*
1958-59				1948-49		1959-60
				1959-60		1960-61*

*Shared

Also won the Texaco Cup - 1970-71 & SVT 1987-88

MOST APPEARANCES

Derek Parkin 607+2 (167-82)

Year	League	FA Cup	Lge Cup	Europe
1967-68	15			
1968-69	42	2	3	
1969-70	42	1	3	
1970-71	39	2	1	
1971-72	32	2	1	7
1972-73	18	3		
1973-74	39	3	6	4
1974-75	41	1	1	2
1975-76	30	6	3	
1976-77	42	5	1	
1977-78	38	3	1	
1978-79	42	7	1	
1979-80	40	3	11	
1980-81	19+1	6+1	1	2
1981-82	21	1	2	
	500+1	45+1	35	15

Includes 7 Texaco Cup 70-71, 4 Anglo-Itl 69-70, 1 Watney C. 72-73.

MOST GOALS IN A CAREER

Steve Bull - 251 (1986-94)

Year	League	FA Cup	Lge Cup	Others
1986-87	15			4
1987-88	34	3	3	12
1988-89	37		2	11
1989-90	24	1	2	
1990-91	26			1
1991-92	20		3	
1992-93	16	1	1	1
1993-94	14			1
1994-95	16		2	1
Total	202	5	13	31

MANAGERS

Name	Seasons	Best	Worst
Jack Addenbrooke	1885-1922	3(1)	19(2)
George Jobey	1922-24	22(2)	1(3)
Albert Hoskins	1924-26	4(2)	6(2)
Fred Scotchbrook	1926-27	15(2)	15(2)
Major Frank Buckley	1927-44	2(1)	17(2)
Ted Vizard	1944-48	3(1)	5(1)
Stan Cullis	1948-64	1(1)	18(1)
Andy Beattie	1964-65	21(1)	21(1)
Ronnie Allen	1965-68	17(1)	6(2)
Bill McGarry	1968-76	4(1)	20(1)
Sammy Chung	1976-78	15(1)	1(2)
John Barnwell	1978-81	6(1)	18(1)
Ian Greaves	1982		
Graham Hawkins	1982-84	22(1)	2(2)
Tommy Docherty	1984-85	22(2)	22(2)
Sammy Chapman	1985		
Bill McGarry	1985		
Sammy Chapman	1985-86	23(3)	23(3)
Brian Little	1986		
Graham Turner	1986-94	10(2)	4(4)
Graham Taylor	1994-	4(1)	4(1)

RECORD TRANSFER FEE RECEIVED

Amount	Club	Player	Date
£1,125,000	Manchester City	Steve Daley	9/79
£240,000	Arsenal	Alan Sunderland	11/77
£100,000	Liverpool	Alun Evans	6/68

RECORD TRANSFER FEE PAID

Amount	Club	Player	Date
£1,850,000	Bradford City	Dean Richards	5/95
£1,250,000	Aston Villa	Tony Daley	5/94
£1,150,000	Aston Villa	Andy Gray	9/80
£185,000	Hull City	Peter Daniel	3/78

LONGEST LEAGUE RUNS

of undefeated matches:	20 (24.11.1923 - 5.4.1924)	of league matches w/out a win:	19 (1.12.1984 - 6.4.1985)
of undefeated home matches:	27 (24.3.1923 - 6.9.1924)	of undefeated away matches:	11 (5.9.1953 - 2.1.1954)
without home win:	13 (17.11.1984 - 27.4.1985)	without an away win:	32 (4.3.1922 - 6.10.1923)
of league wins:	8 (13.3.1915-17.4.1915, 4.2.1967-28.3.1967)	of home wins:	14 (7.3.1953 - 28.11.1953)
	(14.3.1987 - 20.4.1987, 15.10.1988 - 26.11.1988)		
of league defeats:	8 (5.12.1981 - 13.2.1982)	of away wins:	5 (1.1.38-26.2.38, 20.8.62-22.9.62, 9.2.80-7.4.80)

WOLVERHAMPTON WANDERERS

PLAYERS NAME / Honours	Ht	Wt	Birthdate	Birthplace / Transfers	Contract Date	Clubs	League	L/Cup	FA Cup	Other	Lge	L/C	FAC	Oth
GOALKEEPERS														
Andrew De Bont	6.2	15.6	07.02.74	Wolverh'ton	07.07.92	Wolverh'ton W. (T)								
Paul S Jones	6.3	13.2	18.04.67	Chirk		Bridgnorth								
						Kidderminster H.			5					
				£40,000	23.07.91	Wolverhampton W.	25		5	4				
Michael Stowell	6.2	11.10	19.04.65	Preston		Leyland Motors								
				Free	14.02.85	Preston North End								
				Free	12.12.85	Everton				1				
				Loan	03.09.87	Chester City				2				
Loan York C., 24.12.87, 6 Lge App.				Loan	02.02.88	Manchester City	14	1						
				Loan	21.10.88	Port Vale	7			1				
Loan Wolves, 17.03.89, 7 Lge App.				Loan	08.02.90	Preston North End	2							
				£250,000	28.06.90	Wolverhampton W.	194	12	9	9				
DEFENDERS														
Johannes De Wolf	6.2	14.3	10.12.62	Schiedam		Feyenoord								
Dutch Int.				£600,000	06.12.94	Wolverhampton W.	13		4		4			
Neil Emblem			19.06.71	Bromley		Tonbridge								
						Sittingbourne								
				£175,000	08.11.93	Millwall	12			1				
				£600,000	14.07.94	Wolverhampton W.	23+4	1+1	3+2	2+1	7			
Neil Masters	6.1	13.3	25.05.72	Ballymena	31.08.90	Bournemouth (T)	37+1	4	5+2	2	2	1	1	
				£600,000	22.12.93	Wolverhampton W.	7+2							
Dean Richards	6.0	12.0	09.06.74	Bradford	10.07.92	Bradford City (T)	52+4	4	3	2+2	3			
				£1,850,000	08.95	Wolverhampton W.								
Peter Shirtliff	6.2	12.10	06.04.61	Hoyland	31.10.78	Sheffield Wed (A)	188	17+1	17+1		4		1	
LC'91.				£125,000	06.08.86	Charlton Athletic	102+1	10	5	7	7			2
				£500,000	26.07.89	Sheffield Wed.	104	18	9	4	4	1	2	
				£450,000	18.08.93	Wolverhampton W.	65+2	4	7	5				
Mark Venus	6.0	11.8	06.04.67	Hartlepool	22.03.91	Hartlepool Utd (J)	4			0+1				
Div.3'89.				Free	06.09.85	Leicester City	58+3	3	2	2+1	1			
				£40,000	23.03.88	Wolverhampton W.	216+9	12+1	12+1	17	7			2
MIDFIELD														
Paul Birch	5.6	10.9	20.11.62	Birmingham	15.07.80	Aston Villa (A)	153+20	21+4	9+5	5+2	16	5	3	1
ESC'82. FAYC'80.				£400,000	01.02.91	Wolverhampton W.	123+12	9	2+1	8+1	15	3		1
Gordon Cowans	5.7	10.6	27.10.58	Cornforth	01.09.76	Aston Villa (A)	276+10	23+4	19+1	23+1	42	5	3	2
E: 10, B.2, u21.5, Y. Div.1'81. EC'82. ESC'82.				£500,000	01.07.85	Bari								
CS'81. LC'77'94.				£250,000	13.07.88	Aston Villa	114+3	15	9	11+1	7			
				£200,000	28.11.91	Blackburn Rovers	49+1	4	5	3	2		1	
				Free	05.07.93	Aston Villa	9+2	2		4				
				£80,000	03.02.94	Derby County	19			3				1
				£25,000	19.12.94	Wolverhampton W.	21		5	2			1	
Darren Ferguson	5.10	10.9	09.02.72	Glasgow	11.07.90	Manchester Utd (T)	20+7	2+1						
S: u21.8, Y. Prem'93.				£250,000	13.01.94	Wolverhampton W.	34+4	3	4	4				
Stephen Froggatt	5.10	11.0	09.03.73	Lincoln	26.01.91	Aston Villa (T)	30+5	1+1	5+2		2		1	
E: u21.2.				£1,000,000	11.07.94	Wolverhampton W.	20	3			2	1		
Jim Kelly	5.10	11.10	14.02.73	Liverpool	05.07.91	Wrexham (T)	11+10		2	2+2				
					21.02.92	Wolverhampton W.	4+3	1						
				Loan	25.03.93	Walsall	7+3		2	2				
				Loan	05.03.94	Wrexham	9							
Geoff Thomas	6.1	12.0	05.08.64	Manchester	13.08.82	Rochdale	10+1			0+1	1			
E: 9, B.3. FMC'91.				Free	22.03.84	Crewe Alexandra	120+5	8	2	2+1	21			
				£50,000	08.06.87	Crystal Palace	192+3	24	13+1	15+1	26	3	2	4
				£800,000	18.06.93	Wolverhampton W.	21+1	1		4	5			
Andy Thompson	5.4	10.6	09.11.67	Cannock	16.11.85	West Bromwich A. (A)	18+6	0+1	2	1+1	1			
Div.4'88. Div.3'89. SVT'88.				£35,000	21.11.86	Wolverhampton W.	285+14	14	16	32	35		1	1
FORWARDS														
Jason Barnett			21.04.76	Shrewsbury	04.07.94	Wolverh'ton W. (T)								
Steve Bull	5.11	11.4	28.03.65	Tipton		Tipton Town								
E: 13, B.5, u21.5. Div.4'88. Div.3'89. SVT'88.				24.08.85	West Bromwich A.	2+2	2		1+2	2	1		
				£35,000	21.11.86	Wolverhampton W.	341	19	12	31+1	201	13	5	32
Tony Daley	5.8	10.8	18.10.67	Birmingham	31.05.85	Aston Villa (A)	189+44	22+2	15+1	15+2	31	4	2	1
E: 7, B.1, Y.8. LC'94.				£1,250,000	06.06.94	Wolverhampton W.	0+1							
Robert Dennison	5.7	11.0	30.04.83	Banbridge		Glenavon								
NI: 17, B.1. Div.4'88. Div.3'89. SVT'88.				£40,000	13.09.85	West Bromwich A.	9+7	1	2	1	1			
				£40,000	13.03.87	Wolverhampton W.	255+24	12+3	15+2	24+2	40	3	2	4
Don Goodman	5.10	11.7	09.05.66	Leeds		Collingham								
Div.3'85.				Free	10.07.84	Bradford City	65+5	5+1	2+3	4+1	14	2	4	2
				£50,000	27.03.87	West Bromwich A.	140+18	11	7	5	60	1	1	1
				£900,000	06.12.91	Sunderland	95+3	7	3	4	37	1	1	2
				£1,100,000	06.12.94	Wolverhampton W.	24		5+1	2	3			
David Kelly	5.11	11.3	25.11.65	Birmingham		Alvechurch								
Ei: 17, B.2, u23.1, u21.3. Div.1'93.				21.12.83	Walsall	115+32	11+1	12+2	14+3	63	4	3	10
				£600,000	01.08.88	West Ham United	29+12	11+3	6	2+1	7	5		2

PLAYERS NAME / Honours	Ht	Wt	Birthdate	Birthplace / Transfers	Contract Date	Clubs	APPEARANCES				GOALS			
							League	L/Cup	FA Cup	Other	Lge	L/C	FAC	Oth
David Kelly continued.				£300,000	22.03.90	Leicester City	83+3	6	1	2	22	2		1
				£250,000	04.12.91	Newcastle United	70	4	5	4	35	2	1	1
				£750,000	23.06.93	Wolverhampton W.	73+5	5	11	4	26	2	6	2
Dennis Pearce					07.06.93	Aston Villa								
				Free	08.95	Wolverhampton W.								
Stephen Piearce	5.11	10.10	27.09.74	Birmingham	06.07.93	Wolverh'ton W. (T)								
Mark Rankine	5.10	11.8	30.09.69	Doncaster	04.07.88	Doncaster Rov (T)	160+4	8+1	8	14	20	1	2	2
				£70,000	31.01.92	Wolverhampton W.	85+15	3+1	11+1	7+2	1			
James Smith	5.6	10.8	17.09.74	Birmingham	07.06.93	Wolverh'ton W. (T)	24+1	3	1	2				
Jermaine Wright	5.9	10.13	21.10.75	Greenwich	27.11.92	Millwall								
				£60,000	29.12.94	Wolverhampton W.	0+6			0+1				
Brian Law	6.2	11.12	01.01.70	Merthyr Tydfil	15.08.87	Q.P.R. (T)	19+1	2+1	3	1				
W: 1, u21.1, Y. S.				£134,000	23.12.94	Wolverhampton W.	17		6					
Mark Williams						RWD Molenbeek								
				£300,000	08.95	Wolverhampton W.								

TOP GOALSCORER 1994/95
Steve Bull

Division One Goals (games) 16 (31)
Coca-Cola Cup Goals 2 (3)
F.A. Cup goals 0 (2)
Anglo Italian 0 (1)
Play-offs 1 (2)
Total 19 (39)

Total goals for Wolves since 21.11.86 . . . . 251 (403+1)
Total for England (full caps only) 4 (13)

Career total as at June 1st 1995 . . . . 258 (421+5)

THE MANAGER
GRAHAM TAYLOR

Date of Birth . . . . 15th September 1944.
Place of Birth . . . . Worksop.
Date of Appointment . . . . March 1994.

PREVIOUS CLUBS
As Manager . . . . Lincoln City, Watford, Aston Villa, England.
As Coach . . . . None.
As a Player . . . . Grimsby Town, Lincoln City.

HONOURS
As a Manager
Lincoln City: Division 4 champions 1976.
Watford: Division 3 Runners-up 1979. Division 2 Runners-up 1982. Division 1 Runners-up 1983.
FA Cup finalists 1984.
Aston Villa: Division 1 Runners-up 1989-90.
As a Player
None.

MOLINEUX GROUND
Waterloo Road, Wolverhampton WV1 4QR
Tel: 01902 712 181

Capacity 28,500

First game ....v Aston Villa, 2.9.1889.
First floodlit game..v South Africa XI, 30.9.1953.

ATTENDANCES
Highest...61,315 v Liverpool, FA. Cup 5th Rnd, 11.2.1939.
Lowest ....900 v Notts County, Div.1, 17.10.1891.

OTHER GROUNDS ....None.

MATCHDAY TICKET PRICES

Jack Harris/Stand Cullis £10
Juv/OAP £7

John Ireland Stand. £12
Juv/OAP £8

Billy Wright Upper Wing £13
Juv/OAP £8.50
Billy Wright Upper Centre. £14
Juv/OAP £9

Young Wolves Family Enclosure £7.50

Ticket Office Telephone no. 01902 25899

CLUBCALL 0891 12 11 03
Calls cost 39p per minute cheap rate and 49p per
minute at all other times.
Call costings correct at time of going to press.

HOW TO GET TO THE GROUND

From the North
Use motorway M6 until junction 12, leave motorway and follow signs to
Wolverhampton (A5) then A449 and at roundabout take 2nd exit into Waterloo
Road, then turn left in Molineux Street for Wolverhampton Wanderers FC.
From the East
Use motorway M6 until junction 10, leave motorway and follow signs to
Wolverhampton 9A454). Then at crossroads turn right into Stafford Street. In 0.2
miles turn left into Ring Road. Then at next crossroads turn right into Waterloo
Road and shortly turn right into Molineux Street for Wolverhampton Wanderers FC.
From the South
Use motorway M5 until junction 12, leave motorway and follow signs to
Wolverhampton (A4123) turn right then shortly turn left into Ring Road. In 1 mile
turn left into Waterloo Road and shortly turn right into Molineux Street for
Wolverhampton Wanderers FC.
From the West
Use A454, sign posted Wolverhampton, and at roundabout turn left into Ring Road,
then left into Molineux Street for Wolverhampton FC.

Car Parking: Available around 'The West Park', in side streets and at the rear of
the North Bank.

Nearest Railway Station
Wolverhampton (01902 595 451)

MATCHDAY PROGRAMME

Programme Editor . . . . Paper Plane Publishing.

Number of pages . . . . 36.

Price . . . . £1.50.

Subscriptions . . . . Please contact club.

Local Newspapers . . . . . Express & Star, Sports Argus, The Chronicle.

Local Radio Stations. . . . . Beacon Radio, BRMB, Radio WM.

Division 2

FOOTBALL LEAGUE CHAMPIONSHIP

Endsleigh
League

Endsleigh
Insurance League

1995-96

ENDSLEIGH LEAGUE
DIVISION TWO

FINAL LEAGUE TABLE 1994-95

			HOME					AWAY				
		P	W	D	L	F	A	W	D	L	F	A	Pts
1	BIRMINGHAM CITY	46	15	6	2	53	18	10	8	5	31	19	89
PLAY-OFFS													
2	BRENTFORD	46	14	4	5	44	15	11	6	6	37	24	85
3	CREWE ALEXANDRA	46	14	3	6	46	33	11	5	7	34	35	83
4	BRISTOL ROVERS	46	15	7	1	48	20	7	9	7	22	20	82
5	HUDDERSFIELD TOWN	46	14	5	4	45	21	8	10	5	34	28	81
6	WYCOMBE WANDERERS	46	13	7	3	36	19	8	8	7	24	27	78
7	OXFORD UNITED	46	13	6	4	30	18	8	6	9	36	34	75
8	HULL CITY	46	13	6	4	40	18	8	5	10	30	39	74
9	YORK CITY	46	13	4	6	37	21	8	5	10	30	30	72
10	SWANSEA CITY	46	10	8	5	23	13	9	6	8	34	32	71
11	STOCKPORT COUNTY	46	12	3	8	40	29	7	5	11	23	31	65
12	BLACKPOOL	46	11	4	8	40	36	7	6	10	24	34	64
13	WREXHAM	46	10	7	6	38	27	6	8	9	27	37	63
14	BRADFORD CITY	46	8	6	9	29	32	8	6	9	28	32	60
15	PETERBOROUGH UNITED	46	7	11	5	26	29	7	7	9	28	40	60
16	BRIGHTON & H.A.	46	9	10	4	25	15	5	7	11	29	38	59
17	ROTHERHAM UNITED	46	12	6	5	36	26	2	8	13	21	35	56
18	SHREWSBURY TOWN	46	9	9	5	34	27	4	5	14	20	35	53
19	BOURNEMOUTH	46	9	4	10	30	34	4	7	12	19	35	50
RELEGATED													
20	CAMBRIDGE UNITED	46	8	9	6	33	28	3	6	14	19	41	48
21	PLYMOUTH ARGYLE	46	7	6	10	22	36	5	4	14	23	47	46
22	CARDIFF CITY	46	5	6	12	25	31	4	5	14	21	43	38
23	CHESTER CITY	46	5	6	12	23	42	1	5	17	14	42	29
24	LEYTON ORIENT	46	6	6	11	21	29	0	2	21	9	46	26

ENDSLEIGH LEAGUE DIVISION TWO 1995-96

BLACKPOOL
(The Seasiders)
ENDSLEIGH LEAGUE DIVISION 2
SPONSORED BY: REBECCA'S JEWELLERS

Back Row (L-R): Paul Symons, Darren Bradshaw, Jamie Murphy, Jason Lydiate, Craig Allardyce, Andy Preece, Phil Horner, Tony Ellis, Jon Sunderland, Scott Darton.

Middle Row: David Carroll, Stephen Torre, John Hooks, Graeme Craggs, Lee Martin, Tim Carter, Melvin Capleton, James Quinn, David Burke, Robert Ward, Jamie Sheppard.

Front Row: Stuart Parkinson, Micky Mellon, Chris Beech, Andy Morrison, Billy Bingham (Director of Football), Sam Allardyce (Manager), Phil Brown (Player Coach), Brian Croft, Andy Gouck, Mark Bonner, Andy Barlow.

BLACKPOOL
FORMED IN 1887
TURNED PROFESSIONAL IN 1887
LTD COMPANY IN 1896

PRESIDENT: C A Sagar B.E.M.
HON VICE PRESIDENTS: R P Gibrail,
J Armfield, K Chadwick,
Sir Stanley Matthews, W Beaumont
CHAIRMAN: O J Oyston
DIRECTORS:
Mrs V Oyston (Deputy Chairman)
W L Bingham MBE,
Mrs G Bridge (Managing)
G Warburton, J Wilde MBE
SECRETARY: Carol Banks
(01253 404 331)
COMMERCIAL MANAGER
Geoff Warburton (01253 752 222)

MANAGER: Sam Allardyce
PLAYER/COACH: Phil Brown

YOUTH TEAM MANAGER
Neil Bailey
PHYSIOTHERAPIST
Mark Taylor

CLUB STATISTICIAN FOR THE DIRECTORY
Roger Harrison

After the nail biting end to the previous season, with relegation avoided at the last hurdle, this season we finished in mid-table. At one stage a play-off place was a reality, but the season was one of ups and downs.

The season started badly, with new manager Sam Allardyce in charge, a 4-1 home defeat by Huddersfield Town and eliminated by Chesterfield from the Coca-Cola 1st Round. The campaign improved and by the end of November we were challenging for a play-off place, although we had lost in the FA Cup and Auto Windscreen 1st Round.

A bad Christmas period, losing at York (0-4) and at home to Stockport County (1-2) plus losing 1-7 at Birmingham City on New Years Eve, saw a slump into the bottom half of the table. The New Year brought better fortunes with a run of six wins and three draws from ten games putting the club back in the running for a play-off place, but a run of ten games without a win finally put paid to any promotion ambitions.

A crop of injuries meant experienced players Dave Bamber, Gary Briggs and Michael Davies hardly pictured while Kevin Sheedy did not manage a single outing. Signings were made during the season; Andy Morrison a record signing of £245,000 from Blackburn Rovers, Micky Mellon (West Brom), Darren Bradshaw (Peterborough), Jason Lydiate (Bolton W.) and Scott Darton (West Brom).

Tony Ellis finished up as top goalscorer with 18, closely followed by Andy Watson on 15. At the end of the season Bamber, Briggs, Sheedy, and Ian Gore were released, whilst Phil Brown and Michael Davies were offered coaching duties. New signings during the summer were Andy Preece (Crystal Palace), Brian Croft (QPR), Andy Barlow (Oldham Ath.), Tim Carter (Millwall) and John Hooks (Southampton) and hopefully the new stadium will be started within the next 12 months.

ROGER HARRISON.

BLACKPOOL

Division Two: 12th			**FA Cup:** 1st Round			**Coca-Cola Cup:** 1st Round		**Auto Windscreen Trophy:** 1st Round

M	DATE	COMP.	VEN	OPPONENTS	RESULT	H/T	LP	GOAL SCORERS/GOAL TIMES	ATT.
1	A 13	EL	H	Huddersfield Town	L 1-4	0-2		Gouck 58	8,343
2	16	CC 1/1	H	**Chesterfield**	**L 1-2**	**0-2**		**Quinn 70**	**2,570**
3	20	EL	A	Bournemouth	W 2-1	1-1	13	Ellis 8, 50	(3,098)
4	23	CC 1/2	A	**Chesterfield**	**L 2-4**	**2-3**		**Ellis 9, Brown 12**	**(2,516)**
5	27	EL	H	Shrewsbury Town	W 2-1	0-1	9	Horner 53, Ellis 56 (pen)	4,428
6	31	EL	A	Bristol Rovers	D 0-0	0-0	9		(3,762)
7	S 3	EL	A	Crewe A	L 3-4	2-2	12	Beech 32, Watson 36, Griffiths 64 (pen)	(4,915)
8	10	EL	H	Cardiff City	W 2-1	0-1	10	Brown 63, Ellis 74 (pen)	4,189
9	13	EL	H	Brighton	D 2-2	2-2	12	Brown 2, Beech 34	3,438
10	17	EL	A	Brentford	L 2-3	1-0	13	Horner 35, Quinn 61	(4,157)
11	24	EL	H	Wrexham	W 2-1	0-0	10	Brown 63, 80 (pen)	5,015
12	27	AWT	H	**Rochdale**	**L 1-2**	**1-0**		**Mitchell 19**	**1,817**
13	O 1	EL	A	Rotherham U	W 2-0	2-0	7	Quinn 24, Ellis 40	(3,517)
14	8	EL	A	Hull City	L 0-1	0-1	10		(3,829)
15	15	EL	H	Bradford City	W 2-0	0-0	8	Watson 65, Ellis 74	6,156
16	22	EL	H	Swansea City	W 2-1	2-0	8	Ellis 30 (pen), Watson 45	4,911
17	29	EL	A	Plymouth A	W 2-0	1-0	5	Watson 37, Ellis 63	(6,285)
18	N 1	EL	A	Oxford Utd	L 2-3	1-1	7	Watson 4, 63	(5,610)
19	5	EL	H	Leyton O	W 2-1	1-1	6	Ellis 35, Watson 64	4,653
20	8	AWT	A	**Wigan A**	**L 0-1**	**0-1**			**(1,161)**
21	14	FAC 1	A	**Preston NE**	**L 0-1**	**0-1**			**(14,036)**
22	19	EL	A	Chester City	L 0-2	0-1	6		(3,114)
23	26	EL	H	Wycombe W	L 0-1	0-0	8		4,846
24	D 10	EL	H	Bournemouth	W 3-1	2-1	6	Ellis 15, 90, Mitchell 25	3,847
25	17	EL	A	Huddersfield	D 1-1	0-0	8	Watson 72	(11,536)
26	26	EL	A	York City	L 0-4	0-2	11		(4,542)
27	27	EL	H	Stockport C	L 1-2	0-1	12	Mitchell 71	5,745
28	31	EL	A	Birmingham C	L 1-7	1-3	13	Bradshaw 8	(18,025)
29	J 2	EL	H	Peterborough U	W 4-0	1-0	10	Quinn 2, 69, Watson 67, Ellis 62	3,692
30	7	EL	A	Cardiff C	W 1-0	1-0	8	Watson 18	(3,467)
31	14	EL	H	Cambridge U	L 2-3	1-1	9	Mellon 40, Murphy 62	4,076
32	28	EL	H	Plymouth A	W 5-2	0-1	7	Watson 62,90, Ellis 65, Mellon 68,86	3,599
33	F 4	EL	A	Wycombe W	D 1-1	0-1	8	Quinn 47	(6,380)
34	7	EL	A	Leyton O	W 1-0	1-0	7	Watson 43	(3,301)
35	11	EL	H	Oxford U	W 2-1	0-0	6	Gouck 63, Quinn 79	5,206
36	18	EL	A	Cambridge U	D 0-0	0-0	6		(3,192)
37	21	EL	H	Chester C	W 3-1	2-1	5	Mitchell 37, Alsford 60 OG, Mellon 59 (pen)	4,649
38	25	EL	H	Rotherham U	D 2-2	1-1	5	Mitchell 21, Ellis 46	5,043
39	28	EL	A	Swansea C	L 0-1	0-0	6		(2,308)
40	M 4	EL	A	Wrexham	W 1-0	0-0	5	Watson 85	(4,261)
41	7	EL	H	Crewe A	D 0-0	0-0	6		5,859
42	11	EL	A	Shrewsbury Town	D 0-0	0-0	6		(4,261)
43	18	EL	H	Bristol Rovers	L 0-2	0-0	7		4,484
44	25	EL	H	Brentford	L 1-2	0-2	8	Brown 65	4,662
45	A 1	EL	A	Brighton	D 2-2	1-1	10	Ellis 19, Watson 87	(7,157)
46	4	EL	H	Birmingham C	D 1-1	1-1	9	Quinn 27	4,964
47	15	EL	A	Stockport C	L 2-3	0-2	11	Quinn 49, Ellis 60	(5,021)
48	18	EL	H	York C	L 0-5	0-3	11		3,517
49	22	EL	A	Peterborough U	L 0-1	0-0	13		(5,716)
50	29	EL	A	Peterborough U	L 0-1	0-0	13		(5,716)
51	M 6	EL	H	Hull	L 1-2	1-1	12	Ellis 44	4,251
52									
53									
54									
55									
56									
57									
58									
59									
60									

Best Home League Attendance: 8,343 v Huddersfield Town	**Smallest:** 3,438 v Brighton	**Av Home Att:** 4,763

Goal Scorers:

Compared with 1993-94: +7

League (64): Ellis 18 (3 pen), Watson 15, Quinn 8, Brown 5 (1 pen), Mellon 4, Beech 2, GoucK 2, Horner 2, Bradshaw, Griffiths (pen), Murphy, Opponent

Coca Cola Cup (3): Brown, Ellis, Quinn

FA Cup (0):

AW Trophy (3): Mitchell

1994-95

Sealy	Brown	Burke	Bonner	Horner	Gore	Rodwell	Gouck	Bamber	Ellis	Griffiths	Quinn	Martin	Beech	Stoneman	Cook	Watson	Thompson	Moore	Capleton	Mitchell	Murphy	Bradshaw	Mellow	Rowett	Referee	
1	2	3	4	5	6	7•	8*	9	10	11	14	S													P. Wright	1
1	2	3	4*		6	7•	12	9	10	11	14	S													S. Mathieson	2
1	2	3	4		6	12		S	10	11	9		5	7											G. Singh	3
1	2	3	4		6*	7	12	14	10	11•	9		5	5											J. Winter	4
1	2	3	4			7	11	9	10	S	8	S	6	5	S										I. Cruikshanks	5
1	2	3	9	4		7	11		10	12	8*	S	6	5											M. Pierce	6
1	2	3	12	4	6	7	11*			14	9	S	8	5											R. Poulain	7
1	2	5		4		7	11		10	S	9	S	8		3	5	6								W. Flood	8
1	2	5	12	4		7	11*		10		9		8		3	5	6	S							H. Lupton	9
	2	6*		4	12	7•	11		10		9	1	8		3	5	5								K. Leach	10
	2			4			S		10*	11*	9	1	8	7	3	5	6	S		12					U. Rennie	11
S	2	3		4		7			10	S	9	1	8		S	5*				11					J. Parker	12
S	2	3*		4		14	7		10		9	1	8	12		5	6			11•					P. Rejer	13
5	2	3		4		7*			10		9	1	8	12	14	5	6			11•					D. Allison	14
S	2	3	12	5		4			10	11	9*	1	8			7		6				S			E. Lomas	15
S	2	3		6		12			10	11	9*	1	8			7	5	S			4				T. Heildron	16
S	2	3		6					10	11	12	1	8			9*	5	S	7		4				R. Harris	17
	2	3		6					10	11	S	1	8			9	5	S							A. Durso	18
	2	3		6					10	11	S	1	8			9									J. Winter	19
	2	3	12	6		8*				11•	10	1				9	5	S	7		4				E. Wolstenholme	20
	2	3		6		S			10	11*	12	1	8			9	5	S	7		4				R. Dilkes	21
	2	3	8	6		14			10	11	12	1*				9*	5	15	7		4				R. Poulain	22
S		3	11	6					10	S	9					5		1	7	2	8*	4			P. Harrison	23
		3	7	6		14			10		9*	S				12	5	1		11	2	8	4•		N. Darry	24
		3	7	6		S			10		9*	S				12	5	1		11	2	8	4		G. Singh	25
	12	3	7•	6		14			10		S		4			9	5	1		11	2*	8			J. Lloyd	26
	2	3		6		7			10		S		4			9	5	1		11	S				K. Lynch	27
	2*	3		12		4			10		7					9		1		11	5				J. Rushton	28
	2	3		S		11			10		7	1	4			9	S	S	12			8	5		W. Burns	29
	2	3		6		11			10		7	1	4			9*	S	S	12			8	5		K. Cooper	30
				6		11			10		7	1	5			9	S	S	12	3*		8	5		M. Brandwood	31
	S			4		11			10		7	1				9		S	S	4		8	5	2	H. Lupton	32
	S			4		11			10		7	1				9		S	S	6		8	5	2	P. Alcock	33
	S			4		11			10		7*	1				9		S	12	6		8	5	2	A.N. Butler	34
	S			4		11			10		7	1				9		S	S	6		8	5*	2	R. Poulain	35
	12		14	4		11					7	1				9			10•	6		8		2	S. Dunn	36
	6		12	4		11					7*	1				9	5		10	S		8		2	R. Fernandez	37
	6*		12	4		11			10		7	1	S			9			5*			8		2	K. Drees	38
	S		12	4		11			10		7	1				9			6	8		2			C. Wilkes	39
			4	s		12			11		10	1				9			S	6	8		2		P. Rejer	40
			12			11			10		7•	1				9			14	6	8	4*	2		C. Cain	41
	S					11			10		7*	1	12			9			6	8†	4	2			S. Mathieson	42
	S					11			10		7	1	12			9•			6	8	4	2			M. Riley	43
	2		5			8			10		9	1	4*			14			11•	6	8†	4			I. Cruikshanks	44
	S					11			10		7	1	12			9•			6	8	4	2			G. Singh	45
	2		5			8			10		9	1	4*			14			11•	6			7		J. Lloyd	46
	2					8			10		9•	1	4*			12		S	11*	6			7		P. Harrison	47
	12					8			10		9•	1	4*			14		S	11	6		7	2		N. Barry	48
	2					7			10		9	1	S			12		S	11	6	8	4	2		J. Holbrook	49
	2	3				11*			10		12	1	7			9		S		6	8	4			A. Danson	50
	2	3				11			10		11†		4			9•			12	7*		6	8		K. Lynch	51

Sealy	Brown	Burke	Bonner	Horner	Gore	Rodwell	Gouck	Bamber	Ellis	Griffiths	Quinn	Martin	Beech	Stoneman	Cook	Watson	Thompson	Moore	Capleton	Mitchell	Murphy	Bradshaw	Mellow	Rowett		
7	28	23	9	33	3	7	35	2	40	12	37	31	25	4	4	24	17	7	6	25	6	26	26	18	League Appearances	
	3		8	1	1	2	4		2		4		3		2	9			1	5					League Sub Appearances	
2	2	2			2	2	2	0+2	1+1	2		1+1					1								C/Cola Appearances	
1	1		1				1		1	1	0+1	1	1		1	1		1		1		1			FA Cup Appearances	
1	1	0+1	2		1	1		1		1	2	2	1		2	1		2		1					AWS Appearances	

Also Played: Gibson 12(1) 8(2) 8(3) 8(4), Briggs 5+(2) 5*(3), Ward 5 (6)S/50), Thorpe 14(10), Sunderland 14 (20,51) 12/23), Allerdyce 3(27), Parkinson S(28,45),12(44), Davies 2(31), Miotto 5 (26), S(27,28,29,40,41,42,43), Cronsoalk S (44,48)   Players on Loan: Moore (Everton), Rowett (Everton)

CLUB RECORDS

BIGGEST VICTORIES
League: 8-4 v Charlton Athletic, Division 1, 27.9.1952.
7-0 v Reading, Division 2, 10.11.1928.
7-0 v Preston North End, Division 1, 1.5.1948.
7-0 v Sunderland, Division 1, 13.10.1957.
Most Goals Scored in a Cup Tie: 10-0 v Lanerossi, Anglo-Italian Cup, 10.6.1972.

BIGGEST DEFEATS
League: 1-10 v Small Heath, Division 2, 2.3.1901.
1-10 v Huddersfield Town, Division 1, 13.12.1930.
In a Cup Competition: 0-6 v Barnsley, FA Cup Round 1 Replay, 1909-10.

MOST POINTS
3 points a win: 86, Division 4, 1984-85.
2 points a win: 58, Division 2, 1929-30, 1967-68.

BEST PERFORMANCES
League: 2nd Division 1, 1955-56.
F.A. Cup: Winners in 1953.
League Cup: Semi-Final 1962.

HONOURS
Division 2 Champions 1929-30.
FA Cup Winners 1953.
Anglo-Italian Cup Winners 1971.

LEAGUE CAREER
Elected to Div 2 1896, Failed to gain re-election 1899, Re-elected to Div 2 1900, Promoted to Div 1 1929-30, Relegated to Div 2 1932-33, Promoted to Div 1 1936-37, Relegated to Div 2 1966-67, Promoted to Div 1 1969-70, Relegated to Div 2 1970-71, Relegated to Div 3 1977-78, Relegated to Div 4 1980-81, Promoted to Div 3 1984-85, Relegated to Div 4 1989-90, Promoted to Div 3 1991-92 (Now Div 2).

INDIVIDUAL CLUB RECORDS

MOST GOALS IN A SEASON
Jimmy Hampson - 46, Division 2,1929-30 (League 45, FA Cup 1).

MOST GOALS IN A MATCH
5, Jimmy Hampson v Reading, Division 2, 10.11.1928.
5, Jimmy McIntosh v Preston North End, Division 1, 01.05.1948.

OLDEST PLAYER
Sir Stanley Matthews, 46.

YOUNGEST PLAYER (In a League match)
Trevor Sinclair, 16 years 170 days v Wigan Athletic, 19.8.1989.

MOST CAPPED PLAYER

PREVIOUS MANAGERS

Jimmy Armfield (England) 43.
Since 1946: Joe Smith, Ron Stuart, Stan Mortensen, Les Shannon, Jimmy Meadows, Bob Stokoe, Harry Potts, Allan Brown, Jimmy Meadows, Bob Stokoe, Stan Ternent, Alan Ball (jnr), Allan Brown, Sam Ellis, Jimmy Mullen, Graham Carr, Billy Ayre.

ADDITIONAL INFORMATION
PREVIOUS NAME
In 1899 South Shore amalgamated with Blackpool who had been formed when Blackpool St John disbanded in 1887.

PREVIOUS LEAGUE
Lancashire League.

Club colours: Tangerine shirts with white collar, white shorts with tangerine trim, tangerine socks with navy trim.

Change colours: All white.

Reserves League: Pontins Central League Div 2.
Youth League: Lancashire League.

LONGEST LEAGUE RUNS

of undefeated matches:	17 (1968)	of league matches w/out a win:	19 (1970-71)
of undefeated home matches:	24 (1990-91)	of undefeated away matches:	10 (1973-74)
without home win:	16 (1966-67)	without an away win:	41 (1907-09)
of league wins:	9 (1936-37)	of home wins:	15 (1990-91)
of league defeats:	8 (1898-99)	of away wins:	6 (1936-37)

THE MANAGER

Sam Allardyce . . . . appointed in July 1994.

PREVIOUS CLUBS
As a Manager . . . . Limerick.
As an Assistant/Coach . . . . Preston North End (caretaker/Youth team coach).
As a Player . . . . Bolton Wanderers, Sunderland, Millwall, Tampa Bay, Coventry City, Huddersfield Town,
. . . . Bolton wanderers, Preston North End, West Bromwich Albion.

HONOURS
As a Manager . . . . None.
As a Player . . . . Division 2 Championship 1978, FLT 1983.

BLACKPOOL

PLAYERS NAME	Ht	Wt	Birthdate	Birthplace Transfers	Contract Date	Clubs	League	L/Cup	FA Cup	Other	Lge	L/C	FAC	Oth
G O A L K E E P E R S														
Melvin Capleton	5.11	12.0	24.10.73	London	01.07.92	Southend United (T)								
				Free	01.08.93	Blackpool	8+2							
Timothy Carter : Y.3.	6.2	13.8	05.10.67	Bristol	08.10.85	Bristol Rovers (A)	47	2	2	2				
				Loan	14.12.87	Newport County	1							
				£50,000	24.12.87	Sunderland	37	9		4				
oan 18.03.88 Carlisle Utd 4 Lge App. Loan					15.09.88	Bristol City	3							
oan 21.11.91 Birmingham C. 2 Lge 1 LC App.				Free	01.08.92	Hartlepool United	18	4	1	2				
				Free	06.01.94	Millwall	2							
oan 20.01.94 Blackpool				Free	08.95	Blackpool								
ell Hopper : S.	6.1	12.08	27.01.76	Southampton	01.07.94	Southampton (T)								
				Free	08.95	Blackpool								
ee B Martin	5.11	11.8	09.09.68	Huddersfield	01.07.87	Huddersfield T. (T)	54		4	5				
				Free	31.07.92	Blackpool	98	8	4	7				
D E F E N D E R S														
Craig Allardyce	6.3	13.07	09.06.75	Bolton		Preston North End	1							
					19.09.94	Blackpool								
hil Brown VT'89.	5.11	11.6	30.05.57	South Shields	07.07.78	Hartlepool United	210+7	12	11	3	8			1
				Free	30.07.85	Halifax Town	135	6	8	9	19	1	1	
				£17,000	23.06.88	Bolton Wanderers	254+2	25	23	28	14	1	1	1
				Free	25.07.94	Blackpool	28+3	2	1	2	5	1		
avid Burke : Y.2.	5.10	10.7	06.08.60	Liverpool	25.08.77	Bolton W. (A)	65+4	5	1+1		1			
				Free	16.06.81	Huddersfield Town	189	19	15		3			
				£78,000	09.10.87	Crystal Palace	80+1	4	3	9				
				£60,000	27.07.90	Bolton Wanderers	104+2	11+1	13	7			1	
				Free	27.07.94	Blackpool	23	2	1	2				
raham Craggs	6.1	13.06	05.06.76	Ashington	08.94	Blackpool (T)								
cott Darton oan 20.01.95 Blackpool	5.11	11.02	27.03.75	Ipswich	28.10.92	West Brom. A. (T)	15	1		5				1
					22.03.95	Blackpool	18							
hillip Horner oan 27.03.86 Rotherham Utd 3+1 Lge App.	6.1	12.1	10.11.68	Leeds	15.11.84	Leicester City (A)	7+3	1	0+1					
				Free	03.08.88	Halifax Town	70+2	6	6	8	4	2	1	
				£40,000	14.09.90	Blackpool	184+3	14	8	18+1	22			1
ason Lydiate	5.11	12.3	29.10.71	Manchester	01.07.90	Manchester Utd (T)								
				Free	19.03.92	Bolton Wanderers	29+1	4	2	1				
				£75,000	02.03.95	Blackpool	11							
ndy Morrison	5.11	12.0	30.07.70	Inverness	06.07.88	Plymouth A. (T)	105+8	10+1	6	2+1	6	1		
				£500,000	05.08.93	Blackburn Rovers	1+4		1					
					09.12.94	Blackpool	18							
ames Murphy	6.1	12.7	25.02.73	Manchester	23.08.90	Blackpool (J)	48+7	4	3	2+3	1	1		
M I D F I E L D														
ndrew Barlow iv.2'91. Loan 01.11.93 Bradford C. 2 Lge App.	5.9	11.1	24.11.65	Oldham	31.07.84	Oldham Ath. (J)	243+16	22	19	6	5			
				Free	08.95	Blackpool								
hris Beech : Y, S.	5.10	11.0	16.09.74	Blackpool		Blackpool (T)	25+3	1	1	1	2			
ark Bonner	5.10	10.10	07.06.74	Ormskirk	18.06.92	Blackpool (T)	58+17	6+2	4	3+3	7			
arren Bradshaw Y.2.	5.10	11.3	19.03.67	Sheffield		Sheffield Wed. (A)								
				via Matlock T. (F) to	12.08.87	Chesterfield	18	2						
				via Matlock T. (F) to	14.11.87	York City	58+1	2	2	3	3			
				£10,000	16.08.89	Newcastle United	32+6	3	2+1	3				
				Free	13.08.92	Peterborough U.	70+3	7	4	2	1	1		
					20.10.94	Blackpool	26		1	1	1			
ndrew Gouck	5.9	11.12	08.06.72	Blackpool	04.07.90	Blackpool (T)	113+19	7+3	3	7	11			3
ichael Mellon	5.8	11.3	18.03.72	Paisley	06.12.89	Bristol City (T)	26+9	3	1+1	5+3	1			
				£75,000	11.02.93	West Bromwich A.	38+7	3+2	0+1	6	6			1
				£50,000	23.11.94	Blackpool	26				4			
ell N Mitchell S.	5.6	10.0	07.11.74	Lytham	28.11.92	Blackpool (T)	39+28	0+3	2+1	5+1	8		1	1
uart Parkinson	5.8	10.0	18.02.76	Blackpool	18.07.94	Blackpool (T)	0+1							
ames Sheppard	5.8	10.10	18.09.75	Preston	18.09.75	Blackpool (T)								
				Loan	11.02.95	Horwich RMI								
ndrew Watson FAC'91.	5.9	11.2	01.04.67	Leeds		Harrogate Town								
				Free	23.08.88	Halifax Town	75+8	5+1	6	7	15	2	1	1
				£40,000	31.07.90	Swansea City	9+5	0+1		1+1	1			
				£30,000	19.09.91	Carlisle United	55+1	4	3	1	22	1	1	1
				£55,000	05.02.93	Blackpool	74+14	6	2	3	17	5		1
F O R W A R D S														
ony Ellis	5.11	11.0	20.10.64	Salford		Northwich Victoria								
				Free	22.08.86	Oldham Athletic	5+3	1		1				
				£23,000	06.10.87	Preston North End	80+6	3	5	11+1	26			5
				£250,000	20.12.89	Stoke City	66+11	5+1	1+4	3+2	19	1		
				£50,000+PE	14.08.92	Preston North End	70+2	4	6	6	48	2	3	3
				£165,000	25.07.94	Blackpool	40	2	1	1	18	1		
ndrew P Preece	6.1	12.0	27.03.67	Evesham		Evesham								
a Worcester City, Free				Free	31.08.88	Northampton Town	0+1	0+1		0+1				
				Free	22.03.90	Wrexham	44+7	5+1	1	5	7	1	2	1
				£10,000	18.12.91	Stockport County	89+8	2+1	7	12+1	42		3	9
				£350,000	23.06.94	Crystal Palace	17+3	4+2	2+3		4	1		
				£200,000	08.95	Blackpool								
mmy Quinn	6.2	11.11	15.12.74	Coventry		Birmingham City (T)	1+3							
				£25,000	05.07.93	Blackpool	75+21	3+5	0+3	4	18	3		
				Loan	04.03.94	Stockport County	0+1							
n Sunderland	5.11	11.9	02.11.75	Newcastle	18.07.94	Blackpool (T)	0+2			0+1				
aul Symons	5.11	12.0	20.04.76	North Shields		Blackpool (T)	0+1							
				Loan	12.09.94	Southport								
e Thorpe	6.0	11.06	14.12.75	W'hampton	18.07.94	Blackpool (T)	0+3							
				Loan	11.02.95	Horwich RMI								
A D D I T I O N A L C O N T R A C T P L A Y E R														
hn Hooks						Q.P.R.								
				Free	08.95	Blackpool								

Bloomfield Road

Blackpool, Lancashire FY1 6JJ
Tel: 01253 404 331   Fax: 01253 405 011

Capacity . . . . .9,654.
Covered Standing . . . . .2,800.
Seating . . . . .2,987.
First game . . . .(League) v Gainsborough Town, 1-1, 8.9.1900.
First floodlit game . . . . .v Hearts, 2-1, 13.10.1958.

ATTENDANCES
Highest . . . . .38,098 v Wolves, Division 1, 17.9.1955.
Lowest . . . . .1,228 v Rochdale, Sherpa Van Trophy, 6.12.1988.

MATCHDAY TICKET PRICES

Seats. £9
Concessions £5.50

Terraces £7.50
Concessions £4

Match and Ticket information
Bookable two weeks prior to match.

Ticket Office Telephone No. 01253 404 331

HOW TO GET TO THE GROUND

From the North, East and South
Leave M6 Motorway at junction 32 and follow signs to Blackpool M55. At end of motorway the ground is immediately on the right hand side of the Municipal Car Park.

Car Parking
Parking for 1,000 cars. Street Parking also available.

Nearest Railway Station
Blackpool North (01772 594 39).

TANGERINE CALL
0891 12 16 48

Calls cost 39p per minute cheap rate and 49p per minute at all other times.
Call costings correct at time of going to press.

MATCHDAY PROGRAMME

Programme Editor . . . . Geoff Warburton & Roger Harrison

Number of pages 40

Price £1.50

Subscriptions . . . . £55 for all home programmes.

Local Newspapers . . . . Blackpool Evening Gazette.

Local Radio Stations . . Red Rose Radio, Radio Lancashire, Radio Wave.

AFC BOURNEMOUTH
(The Cherries)
ENDSLEIGH LEAGUE DIVISION 2
SPONSORED BY: FRIZZELL

Back Row (L-R): Mike McElhatton, Matty Holland, Neil Young, Scott Mean, Rob Murray, Jason Brissett.
Middle Row: Larry Clay (Yth & Com. Dev. Officer), Sean O'Driscoll (Yth Dev. Manager), Steve Fletcher, Adrian Pennock, Alex Watson, Ian Andrews, Neil Moss, Steve Jones, Mark Morris, Jamie Victory, John Williams (Asst. Manager), Steve Hardwick (Physio).
Front Row: Russell Beardsmore, Mark Rawlinson, John Bailey, Mel Machin (Manager), Steve Robinson, Marcus Oldbury, David Town.

AFC BOURNEMOUTH
FORMED IN 1899
TURNED PROFESSIONAL IN 1912
LTD COMPANY IN 1914

PRESIDENT: P W Hayward
CHAIRMAN: K Gardiner
VICE-CHAIRMAN
B E Willis
DIRECTORS
E G Keep, G M C Hayward, G W Legg,
N Hayward
SECRETARY
Keith MacAlister
COMMERCIAL MANAGER
Terry Lovell

MANAGER: Mel Machin
ASSISTANT MANAGER: John Williams
RESERVE TEAM MANAGER
John Williams
YOUTH TEAM MANAGER
Sean O'Driscoll
PHYSIOTHERAPIST
Steve Hardwick

STATISTICIAN FOR THE DIRECTORY
Vacant

An end-of-season position of 19th - hardly a dream situation. But, until the penultimate game of an extremely worrying campaign, the Cherries had flirted with danger on a regular basis - in other words the prospect of finishing their campaign bottom of the pile and therefore automatic relegation.

Summer, in footballing terms, is the months of August and September and there is no Argument what is required is a good, solid start. In Endsleigh league terms, Bournemouth's beginning was of nightmare proportions - four games four defeats.

Certainly the portents were not there from the outset, with Manager John Pulis being shown the door in August plus all kinds of boardroom disruptions. Reserve team boss, the experienced and loyal John Williams, took temporary charge for four games before Mel Machin stepped into the hot seat.

By the first day of October, Bournemouth were already propping up the table, and this depressing situation continued until the New Year, when following six games unbeaten between 27th December and 21st January they managed to climb just two places.

Nine points from a possible fifteen, between 4th and 25th February was undoubtedly satisfactory, but the end result of this greater consistency was an upward move of just one place - to 21st! There is no doubt as to their most outstanding performance - a 2-1 home success over eventual champions, Birmingham City on 21st February.

Just one in March (v Stockport County) was compensated by a spate of useful draws, and as such April saw Machin's men still struggling in 20th spot. Survival was still very much the name of the game, but there was light at the end of a very dark tunnel in the shape of four April wins, followed by a more than convincing 3-2 home success over Shrewsbury Town. Five end-of-campaign wins out of seven and it was 19th place and not only survival, but also hope for the future.

In Cup football, the Cherries did not exactly set the world alight. Northampton Town were dispatched 3-0 on aggregate in the First Round of the Coca-Cola League, but 1-0 defeats in both legs of the tie with Chelsea put paid to any thoughts of giant-killing. Talking of giant-killing, Bournemouth were very nearly 2nd Round FA Cup Victims of Diadora outfit Worthing. Falling behind to the non-Leaguers they showed great spirit to eventually come out on top, 3-1. A Round Two exit at Plymouth, 2-1 to the Devon side, and all hopes of FA Cup glory had disappeared for another season at least. In the Auto Windscreens Shield two draws, 1-1 away to Bristol Rovers and 0-0 at home to Oxford United meant an early departure from this potentially lucrative tournament.

1995-96 should see an improvement, particularly if the spirit shown towards the latter stages of last season is repeated.   **GREG TESSER.**

AFC BOURNEMOUTH

M	DATE	COMP.	VEN	OPPONENTS	RESULT	H/T	LP	GOAL SCORERS/GOAL TIMES	ATT.
1	A 13	EL	A	Wrexham	L 0-2	0-2	21		(3,580)
2	16	CC 1/1	H	**Northampton Town**	W 2-0	2-0		**Russell 36, Cotterill 44**	**2,587**
3	20	EL	H	Blackpool	L 1-2	1-1	21	Cotterill 25	3,098
4	27	EL	A	Rotherham United	L 0-4	0-0	24		(2,306)
5	30	EL	H	Peterborough United	L 0-3	0-2			2,649
6	S 3	EL	H	York City	L 1-4	0-3	24	Aspinall 49 (pen)	3,181
7	6	CC 1/2	A	**Northampton Town**	W 1-0	1-0		**Cotterill 41**	**(3,249)**
8	10	EL	A	Stockport County	L 0-1	0-0	24		(4,054)
9	13	EL	A	Leyton Orient	L 2-3	1-1		Aspinall 34, Leadbitter 70	(2,536)
10	17	EL	H	Chester City	D 1-1	0-1		Leadbitter 70	3,025
11	21	CC 2/1	A	**Chelsea**	L 0-1	0-1			**(8,974)**
12	24	EL	H	Cardiff City	W 3-2	1-1	23	Beardsmore 3, 79, Aspinall 57 (pen)	3,177
13	O 1	EL	A	Hull City	L 1-3	1-2	24	Aspinall 10	(3,056)
14	4	CC 2/2	H	**Chelsea**	L 0-1	0-0			**9,784**
15	8	EL	A	Shrewsbury Town	L 0-3	0-1	24		(3,684)
16	15	EL	H	Brentford	L 0-1	0-1	24		4,411
17	19	AWT	A	**Bristol Rovers**	D 1-1	0-0		**Murray 66**	**(1,725)**
18	22	EL	H	Bradford City	L 2-3	1-2	24	Mean 35 (pen), Morris 48	3,037
19	29	EL	A	Huddersfield Town	L 1-3	0-2	24	Jones 77	(11,251)
20	N 2	EL	A	Brighton & H.A.	L 0-0	0-0			(5,631)
21	5	EL	H	Cambridge United	W 1-0	0-0	24	Robinson 60	3,272
22	N 8	AWT	H	**Oxford United**	D 0-0	0-0			**1,374**
23	12	FAC 1	H	**Worthing**	W 3-1	1-1		**Morris 41, Russell 65, McElhatton 88**	**3,922**
24	19	EL	A	Birmingham City	D 0-0	0-0			(15,477)
25	26	EL	H	Oxford United	L 0-2	0-1	24		4,277
26	D 3	FAC 2	A	**Plymouth Argyle**	L 1-2	0-2		**Jones 46**	**(6,960)**
27	10	EL	A	Blackpool	L 1-3	1-2	24	Jones 1	(3,847)
28	16	EL	H	Wrexham	L 1-3	1-1		Hughes 16	2,505
29	26	EL	A	Bristol Rovers	L 1-2	0-1		Pennock 78	(6,913)
30	27	EL	H	Crewe Alexandra	D 1-1	1-0		Beardsmore 8	3,325
31	31	EL	A	Wycombe Wanderers	D 1-1	1-0		Robinson 15	(5,990)
32	J 2	EL	H	Swansea City	W 3-2	2-1		Fletcher 29, 34, Pennock	3,816
33	7	EL	A	Bradford City	W 2-1	0-0	22	Robinson 56, Leadbitter 59	(5,426)
34	14	EL	H	Plymouth Argyle	D 0-0	0-0	22		4,913
35	21	EL	A	Cambridge United	D 2-2	0-1	22	Pennock 55, McElmatton 90	(2,834)
36	28	EL	H	Huddersfield Town	L 0-2	0-0	22		4,427
37	F 4	EL	A	Oxford United	W 3-0	2-0	21	Jones 22, 67, Fletcher 24	(5,473)
38	11	EL	H	Brighton & H.A.	L 0-3	0-2	21		5,247
39	18	EL	A	Plymouth Argyle	W 1-0	1-0	21	McElhatton 45	(5,435)
40	21	EL	H	Birmingham City	W 2-1	1-0		Jones 7, Mean 57	6,024
41	25	EL	H	Hull City	L 2-3	2-3	21	Jones 11, Pennock 27	4,345
42	M 4	EL	A	Cardiff City	D 1-1	1-1	20	Fletcher 37	(3,008)
43	7	EL	A	York City	L 0-1	0-0			(2,301)
44	11	EL	H	Rotherham United	D 1-1	0-0	20	Morris 89	5,666
45	16	EL	A	Peterborough United	D 0-0	0-0	21		(4,495)
46	21	EL	H	Stockport County	W 2-0	1-0		Fletcher 3, Jones 74	2,892
47	25	EL	A	Chester City	D 1-1	1-1		Fletcher 77	(1,618)
48	A 1	EL	H	Leyton Orient	W 2-0	1-0	20	Pennock 34, Holland 89	4,118
49	8	EL	H	Wycombe Wanderers	W 2-0	1-0	20	Mean 28 (pen), 54 (pen)	5,816
50	15	EL	A	Crewe Alexandra	L 0-2	0-1	20		(3,906)
51	18	EL	H	Bristol Rovers	W 2-0	1-0		Morris 43, Mean 62	7,020
52	22	EL	A	Swansea City	L 0-1	0-0	20		(2,664)
53	29	EL	A	Brentford	W 2-1	0-0	19	Mean 55, Jones 74	(10,079)
54	M 2	EL	H	Shrewsbury Town	W 3-0	3-0	19	Robinson 8, 20, Mean 13	10,737
55									
56									
57									
58									
59									
60									

Best Home League Attendance: 10,737 v Shrewsbury Town   **Smallest:** 2,649 v Peterborough United   **Av Home Att:** 4,390

Goal Scorers: Compared with 1993-94: -11

League (49):	Jones 8, Mean 7, Fletcher 6, Pennock 5, Robinson 5, Aspinall 4, Beardsmore 3, Leadbitter 3, Morris 3, McElmatton 2, Cotterill, Holland, Hughes
C/Cola Cup (3):	Cotterill 2, Russell
FA Cup (4):	Jones, McElmatton, Morris, Russell
AW Trophy (1):	Murray

Moss	O'Driscoll	O'Connor	Morris	Watson	Leadbitter	Beardsmore	Aspinall	Fletcher	Cotterill	Russell K.	Mean	McElmatton	Pennock	Reeves	Town	Murray	Andrews	Russell L.	Brissett	Barfoot	Jones	Holland	Robinson	Young	Chivers	Referee	
1	2	3	4	5	6	7	8	9*	10	11	12	S														Harrison P.	1
1	2	3	4	5	6	7	8*	9	10	11	12†		S													Alcock P.	2
1	2	3	4	5	6	7		9*	10	11	8	S		12												Singh G.	3
1	2	3	4	5†	6	7		9	10	11	8	S			S											Winter J.	4
1	2	3	4*	5•	6	7†	12	9	10	11		8				14										Wilkes C.	5
1	2	3			6	7	8	9	10	11•	4			12		5*										Pierce M.	6
S	2	3		5	6	7	8*	9	10•	11		4			14	12	1									Pooley G.	7
S	2*	3			6	7	8•	9	10	11	12	5		14			1	4								Wolstenholme E.	8
S	2	3		5	9		8•	6	10	11	14	7*		12			1	4								Dunn S.	9
S		3*	5	11	7		6	10•	9	8	2	14					1	4								Orr D.	10
S	2*	3		5	11	7	9•	6		10	8•	4	14				1				12					Vanes P.	11
S	2	3		5	11	7	9	6		10	8	4	S				1			S						D'Urso A.	12
S	2*	3		5	11	7	9	6		10	8	4•	12				1			14						Rushton J.	13
S	2*	3•		5	11	7	9	6			8	4		10		12	1									Durkin P.	14
S	2*			5	11	7	9	6			8	4		10			1			12						Rejer P.	15
S			4	5		7	9•	12			8	14	6†	10		1								2	3*	Harris R.	16
																											17
S			4			7		12			8	14	6			5•	1				9		10	2	3*	Cooper K.	18
S			4		6	7		5			8	S					1				10		12	2	3	Mathieson S.	19
S			4	5	6	7		11*			8	S					1				10		9	2	3	Pierce M.	20
S			4	5	6	7					8					12	1				10		9	2	3	Alcock P.	21
																											22
S			4	5	6	7*				11	8	12	3			14	1				10		9	2	3	Pooley G.	23
S			4	5	6	7					8	12	4				1				10		9	2		Furnandiz R.	24
S				5	6	7				8	S	3*				12	1				10		9	2		Barber G.	25
S			4	5	6	7•				11	8	12	11			14	1				10		9	2		Ashby G.	26
S		14	4	5	6•						8		6				1				10		9	2*		Barry N.	27
1†			4	5		7*				11	8		8			S			11		10		9•	9*	2	Pooley G.	28
S			4		6	7		14					6			5	1		11•		10		9*	2		Leach K.	29
S		14	4		8	7		10*					6		12	5	1		11•				9	2		D'Urso A.	30
			4		9	7		10			12	14	6			5	1		11				8*	2		Railey M.	31
			4		9•	7		10			12		6			5	1		11				8*	2		Singh G.	32
			4		9	7		10				S	6			5	1		11		12		8*	2		Heilbron T.	33
S		3*	4	14				10			9	7•	6			5	1		11		12		8	2		Alcock P.	34
S			4*	14			3	10			9	12	6			5	1		11•		7	14	8•	2		Lloyd J.	35
S			4		9*		3	10				12	6			5	1		11		7	11	8	2		Vanes P.	36
S			4	S	9	3		10				12	6			5	1		11		7	3	8	2		Mathieson S.	37
S			4*		11	7•		9			14		6			5	1		11*		10	7	8	2		Dunn S.	38
S			4				3	10			12	2			S	5	1		11		9	7	8			Cooper K.	39
1			4	12			3	10			6	2	8			5*	S		11		9	7	8	S		Pooley G.	40
1			4•	12			3	10			6	2	8		14	5	S		11•		9	7		3*		Holbrook J.	41
S			4	S			3	10			6*	14	8			5	1		11		9	7*	12	2		Brandwood J.	42
S			4	S			3	10			6	12	9			5	1		11		9	7		2		Burns B.	43
S			4	12	14		3	10			6		9			5*	1		11			7	8	2		Pierce M.	44
S			4	S	12		3	10			6*		8			5	1		11		S	8		2		Furnandiz R.	45
S			4				3	10			6	12	7*			5	1		11		9	12	7*	2		Orr D.	46
S			4				3	10			6		7		14	5	1		11*		9	14	8•	2		Lomas E.	47
S			4				3	10			6		7		S	5	1		11		9	12	8	2		Cooper K.	48
S			4				3	10			6		7*		S	5	1		11		9	14	8*	2		Rejer P.	49
S			4				3	10			6		7		12	5	1		11		9		8•	2		Lupton K.	50
S			4				3	10			6	12	7		S	5	1		11		9	12	8*	2		Barber G.	51
S			4•	14			3	10			6	2*	7			5	1		11		9	14	8			Leach K.	52
			4				3	10			6	12	7			5	1		11		9		8•	2*		Rutler A.	53
			4				3	10			6	12	7			5	1		11		9•		8	2*		Harris R.	54
8	10	11	38	16	25	43	8	37	8	13	32	13	31	2		28	38	3	25		27	8	30	32	5	League Appearances	
	2		6	2			1	3		7	13			5	5	3				2	2	8	2			League Sub Appearances	
1	4	4	1	4	4	4	4	4	2	3	2+1	3		1+1	0+1	0+2	3			0+1			2	2	1	C/Cola Cup Appearances	
			2	2	2	2					2	2	0+2	2		0+2	2				1		2	2	1	FA Cup Appearances	
					2	2					2	2	0+2	2		0+2	2				1		2	2	1	AW Trophy Appearances	

Also Played: Wells S(1,2,3,4,5,6,7,31,32,33) 14 (28), Williams 12(10), Brooks 3• (15), Adekola 12(14), Ferrett 14(15), Vincent S(23),3(24,26,27,28†,29,30,31,32), Strong 14(53),

AFC BOURNEMOUTH   RECORDS AND STATISTICS

CLUB RECORDS

BIGGEST VICTORIES
League: 7-0 v Swindon Town, Division 3(S), 22.9.1956.
Most Goals Scored in a Cup Tie: 11-0 v Margate, FA Cup, 20.11.1971.

BIGGEST DEFEATS
League: 0-9 v Lincoln City, Division 3, 1.12.1982.
Most Goals conceded in a Cup Tie: 0-7 v Burnley, FA Cup 3rd Round Replay, 1965-66.
0-7 v Sheffield Wednesday, FA Cup 4th Round, 1931-32.

MOST POINTS
3 points a win: 97, Division 3, 1986-87.
2 points a win: 62, Division 3, 1971-72.

RECORD TRANSFER FEE RECEIVED
£800,000 from Everton for Joe Parkinson, March 1994.

RECORD TRANSFER FEE PAID
£300,000 to Manchester City for Paul Moulden, July 1989.

BEST PERFORMANCES
League: 12th Division 2, 1988-89.
FA Cup: 6th Round, 1956-57.
League Cup: 4th Round, 1961-62, 1963-64.

HONOURS
Division 3 Champions 1986-87.
Associate Members Cup 1983-84.

LEAGUE CAREER
Elected to Div.3(S) 1923, Transferred to Div.3 1957-58, Relegated to Div.4 1969-70, Promoted to Div.3 1970-71, Relegated to Div.4 1974-75, Promoted to Div.3 1981-82, Promoted to Div.2 1986-87, Relegated to Div.3 (now Div.2) 1989-90.

INDIVIDUAL CLUB RECORDS

MOST GOALS IN A SEASON
Ted MacDougall - 49, 1970-71 (League 42, FA Cup 7).

MOST GOALS IN A MATCH
Ted MacDougall - 9 v Margate, FA Cup 1st Rnd. (11-0) 20.11.1971 (All time FA Cup record).

OLDEST PLAYER
Harry Kinghorn, 48 years v Brentford, 11.3.1929.

YOUNGEST PLAYER
Jimmy White, 15 years v Brentford, 30.4.1958.

MOST CAPPED PLAYER
Gerry Peyton (Eire) 7.

PREVIOUS MANAGERS

Harry Kinghorn 1920-25, Leslie Knighton 1925-28, Frank Richards 1928-30, Billy Birrell 1930-35, Bob Crompton 1935-36, Charles Bell 1936-39, Harry Kinghorn 1939-47, Harry Lowe 1947-50, Jack Bruton 1950-56, Freddie Cox 1956-58, Don Welsh 1958-61, Bill McGarry 1961-63, Reg Flewin 1963-65, Freddie Cox 1965-70, John Bond 1970-73, Trevor Hartley 1973-75, John Benson 1975-79, Alec Stock 1979-80, Dave Webb 1980-82, Don Megson 1982, Harry Redknapp 1983-92, Tony Pullis 1992-94.

ADDITIONAL INFORMATION
Previous League: Southern League.

Previous Names: Boscombe St Johns 1899.
Boscombe FC 1899-1923. Bournemouth & Boscombe AFC 1923-72.

Club colours: Black & red striped shirts, black shorts & black socks.

Change colours: Black & blue striped shirts blue shorts & socks.

Reserves League: Avon Insurance League Division 2.

LONGEST LEAGUE RUNS

of undefeated matches:	18 (1982)	of league matches w/out a win:	14 (1973-74)
of undefeated home matches:	33 (1962-63)	of undefeated away matches:	13 (1961)
without home win:	10 (1931-32)	without an away win:	26 (1976-77)
of league wins:	7 (1970)	of home wins:	12 (1968, 1971)
of league defeats:	7 (1955)	of away wins:	5 (1948)

THE MANAGER

MEL MACHIN. . . . . appointed September 1994.

PREVIOUS CLUBS
As Manager . . . . Manchester City, Barnsley.
As Asst.Man/Coach. . . . . Norwich City.
As a player. . . . . Port Vale, Gillingham, Bournemouth, Norwich City.

HONOURS
As a Manager . . . . None.
As a Player . . . . None.

BOURNEMOUTH

PLAYERS NAME / Honours	Ht	Wt	Birthdate	Birthplace / Transfers	Contract Date	Clubs	APPEARANCES League	L/Cup	FA Cup	Other	GOALS Lge	L/C	FAC	Oth
G O A L K E E P E R S														
Ian Andrews	6.2	12.2	01.12.64	Nottingham	06.12.82	Leicester City (A0	126	6	7					
E: u21.1, Y.10.				Loan	01.01.84	Swindon Town	1							
				£300,000	26.07.88	Celtic	5	2		1				
				Loan	15.12.88	Leeds United	1							
				£200,000	22.12.89	Southampton	10			1				
				£20,000	05.09.94	Bournemouth	38	3	2	2				
Neil Moss	6.1	12.11	10.05.75	New Milton	29.01.93	Bournemouth (T)	14+1	1	0+1					
D E F E N D E R S														
Mark Morris	6.1	13.8	26.09.62	Morden	26.09.80	Wimbledon (A)	167+1	11	11	1+1	9			
Div.4'83.				Loan	05.09.85	Aldershot	14		1					
				£35,000	21.07.87	Watford	41	5	7		1	1		
				£175,000	11.07.89	Sheffield United	53+3	5	5	2	3			
				£100,000	31.07.91	Bournemouth	162	11	14	7	7	1	1	
Adrian Pennock	5.11	12.1	27.03.71	Ipswich	04.07.89	Norwich City (T)	1							
				£30,000	14.08.92	Bournemouth	114	6	9	5	9		1	
Jamie Victory	5.10	12.0	14.11.75	Hackney	01.07.94	West Ham Utd (T)								
				Free	08.95	Bournemouth								
Alec Watson	6.0	11.9	05.04.68	Liverpool	18.05.85	Liverpool (A)	3+1	1+1	1+1	1				
E: Y.4. CS'88.				Loan	30.08.90	Derby County	5							
				£150,000	18.01.91	Bournemouth	145+6	14	12	5	5	1	1	
Neil Young	5.8	10.5	31.08.73	Harlow	17.08.91	Tottenham H. (T)								
				Free	11.10.94	Bournemouth	32		2	2				
M I D F I E L D														
Russell Beardsmore	5.6	9.0	28.09.68	Wigan	02.10.86	Manchester Utd (A)	30+26	3+1	4+4	2+5	4			
E: u21.5. ESC'91.				Loan	19.12.91	Blackburn Rovers	1+1							
				Free	29.06.93	Bournemouth	58+9	7	4	2	3	1		
Matthew Holland	5.9	11.4	11.04.74	Bury	03.07.92	West Ham Utd (T)								
				Loan	21.10.94	Bournemouth								
				£150,000	18.11.94	Bournemouth	9+7				1			
Scott Mean	5.11	11.11	13.12.73	Crawley	10.08.92	Bournemouth (T)	39+21	4+1	2	4	8			
Marcus Oldbury	5.7	10.02	29.03.76	Bournemouth	01.07.94	Norwich City (T)								
				Free	08.95	Bournemouth								
Mark Rawlinson	5.8	11.11	09.06.75	Bolton	05.07.93	Manchester Utd (T)								
				Free	08.95	Bournemouth								
F O R W A R D S														
John Bailey						Enfield								
				£10,000	08.95	Bournemouth								
Jason Brissett	5.11	11.10	07.09.74	Wanstead		Arsenal (T)								
				Free	14.06.93	Peterborough Utd	27+8	5+1	2+1	3+1		1	1	1
				Free	23.12.94	Bournemouth	24+1							
Stephen Cotterill	6.1	12.5	20.07.64	Cheltenham		Burton Albion								
				£30,000	27.02.89	Wimbledon	10+7	2	2+1	1+1	6	1		
				Loan	13.08.92	Brighton & H.A.	11				4			
				£80,000	14.08.93	Bournemouth	44+1	6	2+1	1	15	2	1	
Steven Fletcher	6.0	12.1	26.06.72	Hartlepool	23.08.90	Hartlepool Utd (T)	19+13	0+2	1+2	2+2	4	1		1
				£30,000	28.07.92	Bournemouth	97+10	10	2	2	16	1		
Stephen Jones	6.0	12.12	17.03.70	Cambridge		Billericay Town								
				£22,000	16.11.92	West Ham United	8+8		2+2	1+1	4		1	
				Loan	27.01.95	Bournemouth	27+3		1	1	8		1	
				Free	25.04.95	Bournemouth								
Michael McElhatton	6.1	12.8	16.04.75	Kerry (Eire)	05.07.93	Bournemouth (T)	19+19	3	0+2				1	
Robert Murray	5.11	11.7	21.10.74	Hammersmith	11.01.93	Bournemouth (T)	38+38	0+2	0+5	0+4	8			2
S: u21.1.														
Stephen Robinson	5.8	10.7	10.12.74	Lisburn	27.01.93	Tottenham H. (T)	1+1							
NI: B, u21.6, Y, S.				Free	20.10.94	Bournemouth	30+2		2	1	5			
David Town			09.12.76	Bournemouth	14.07.94	Bournemouth (T)	0+6	0+1						

DEAN COURT GROUND

Bournemouth, Dorset BH7 7AF
Tel: 01202 395 381

Capacity ....11,880.

First game ....In the League - 01.09.1923.
First floodlit game..v Northampton 27.09.1961.

ATTENDANCES
Highest ....28,799 v Manchester United, FA Cup 6th Round, 02.03.1957.
Lowest ....1,218 v Reading, Autoglass Trophy, 05.01.1993.

OTHER GROUNDS ....Castleman Road, Pokedown 1899-1910. Dean Court 1910-

MATCHDAY TICKET PRICES

South Stand (Terrace Standing). £7.50
Juv/OAP £4
New Stand (Enclosure Standing) £7.50
Juv/OAP £4
Centre Stand (Seating) £11.50
B Block (Seating) £10
E Block (Seating) £10
Juv/OAP £6.50
F Block (Family Stand - Seating) £8.50
Juv £4.50
(Adults must be accompanied by an u16-year-old)
A Block (Wing Stand - Seating) £8.50
Juv/OAP £4.50

Ticket Office Telephone no. 01202 395 381

CLUBCALL
0898 12 11 63
Calls cost 39p per minute cheap rate and 49p per
minute at all other times.
Call costings correct at time of going to press.

HOW TO GET TO THE GROUND

From the North and East
A338 to roundabout junction with A3060. Take second exit, then first
from next roundabout into Littledown Avenue. Turn right into
Thistlebarrow Road for Dean Court.

From the West
A3049 to Bournemouth. In 2 miles after, lights at Wallisdown, turn left
into Talbot Road. Take first exit from roundabout into Queens Park
South Drive, then second exit from next roundabout into Littledown
Avenue. Turn right into Thistle Road for Dean Court.

Car Parking
Parking for 1,500 cars.

Nearest Railway Station
Bournemouth. Tel: 01202 558 216.

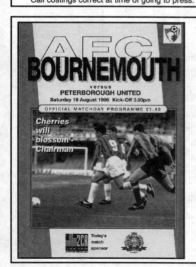

MATCHDAY PROGRAMME

Programme Editor . . . . John Hughes.

Number of pages . . . . 40.

Price . . . . £1.40.

Subscriptions. . . . . £37.50.

Local Newspapers . . . . Evening Echo.

Local Radio Stations . . . . Two Counties Radio, BBC Radio Solent.

BRADFORD CITY AFC
(The Bantams)
ENDSLEIGH LEAGUE DIVISION 2
SPONSORED BY: DIAMOND SEAL LTD

Back Row (L-R): Wayne Benn, Richard Liburd, Scott Jackson, Carl Shutt, Richard Huxford, Andy Kiwomya, Paul Showler, Chris Stabb, Neil Grayston.
Middle Row: Steve Redmond (Physio), Graham Mitchell, John Ford, Nicky Mohan, Gavin Ward, Ian Ormondroyd, Neil Tolson, Des Hamilton, Steve Smith (Yth Coach).
Front Row: Chris Dolby, Wayne Jacobs, Craig Midgley, Lennie Lawrence (Manager), Eddie Youds (Capt), Chris Kamara (Asst Manager), Gary Robson, Shaun Murray, Tommy Wright.

**BRADFORD CITY AFC
FORMED IN** 1903
TURNED PROFESSIONAL IN 1903
LTD COMPANY IN 1983

CHAIRMAN: G Richmond

DIRECTORS
T Goddard, FCCA, Miss E Richmond,
D Richmond
ASSOCIATE DIRECTORS
A Biggin, M Scott, M Smith, H Williams

SECRETARY
Shaun Harvey (01274 306 062)

COMMERCIAL MANAGER
Allan Gulliver

MANAGER: Lennie Lawrence
ASSISTANT MANAGER: Chris Kamara

RESERVE TEAM MANAGER
Steve Smith

YOUTH TEAM MANAGER
Steve Smith

PHYSIOTHERAPIST
Steve Redmond

STATISTICIAN FOR THE DIRECTORY
Terry Frost

Fifteen goals from their opening five League and Cup fixtures...........one unexpected point at Second Division champions-elect, Birmingham City, and no goals, in their closing five games of the 1994-95 Endsleigh League season!

Such a stark contrast in playing statistics epitomised the Bantams' vacillating fortunes during another highly-disappointing campaign, concluded with an ignominious run of eight matches without a victory that consigned them to 14th place in the table.

The inglorious ending to a season that began so promisingly - coming as it did during tenth anniversary commemorations of the tragic Valley Parade fire of May 11th 1985 - seemed an incongruous epitaph to the pioneering advances since that fateful day claimed 56 lives.

For all the suppositions of failure - an alarming catalogue of injuries at key moments, the introduction of relatively inexperienced youngsters etc. - City manager, Lennie Lawrence, never shirked the collective shortcomings.

He appeared to have bought wisely last summer, as witnessed by the early success of former Bristol Rovers sharpshooter John Taylor - at £300,000 the club's record purchase - Shaun Murray and Carl Shutt. Coupled with the free transfer acquisition of Wayne Jacobs from Rotherham United - recipient of five supporters' branch player of the year awards - the wholesale ineffectiveness of the squad became surprisingly enigmatic.

Solid backing from Chairman, Geoffrey Richmond, and his Board - both financially and morally - should have provided the springboard for a successful season, but a mini-slump around October and November saw the club plummet from third to tenth in the table.

Certainly all the unprecedented pre-season hype had whetted the appetites of City's long-suffering supporters but, over the rigorous ten months of competitive fixtures, that premature confidence proved too demanding.

It was all so different in the opening month of the season, when resounding away victories at Chester City on the opening day, and at Plymouth Argyle a fortnight later, established them as early divisional leaders. Such promotion form subsequently disposed of First Division Grimsby Town, in the Coca-Cola Cup first round, before succumbing to the Premiership skills of Sheffield Wednesday in the succeeding round.

Indifferent form led to spasmodic victories from thereon in - predominantly away from Valley Parade - and had their home form been as pleasing, their omission from the promotion play-offs may have been avoided.

Elimination from the FA Cup at the first hurdle was followed by an embarrassing walloping at Wrexham in the Auto Windscreens Shield and, but for a re-assuring revival, following the Christmas and New Year Holiday success of fixtures, the eventual outcome could have been disastrous.

The transfer deadline day departure of terrace favourites, Lee Duxbury and Lee Sinnott, to fierce rivals and neighbours, Huddersfield Town, and Endsleigh League XI representative, Dean Richards, to Wolves (on an initial loan period), did not endear supporters to the club management. Indeed, as some chose to vent their anger at Lennie Lawrence directly, others chose to vote with their feet as home attendances fell dramatically.

What the club needs is an injection of the spirit engendered by the VE Day veterans of fifty years ago. If that camaraderie, loyalty, and fierce determination could be transferred to the remaining personnel, and inevitable new recruits, maybe next season will have a more favourable conclusion.**TERRY FROST.**

BRADFORD CITY

Division Two: 14th   **FA Cup:** 1st Round   **Coca-Cola Cup:** 2nd Round   **Auto Windscreen Trophy:** 2nd Round

M	DATE	COMP.	VEN	OPPONENTS	RESULT	H/T	LP	GOAL SCORERS/GOAL TIMES	ATT.
1	A 13	EL	A	Chester City	W 4-1	1-0	4	Jewell 28,46,73,Taylor 62	(4,459)
2	16	CC I/I	H	Grimsby Town	W 2-1	0-0		Taylor 75, Duxbury 90	5,986
3	20	EL	H	Leyton Orient	W 2-0	1-0	3	Jewell 24, 87	(7,473)
4	23	CC 1/2	A	Grimsby Town	W 2-1	2-1		Murray 27, Richards 33	(3,498)
5	27	EL	A	Plymouth Argyle	W 5-1	4-0	1	Jewell 23,33,39 Shutt 41,48	(6,469)
6	30	EL	H	Oxford United	L 0-2	0-1	4		9,005
7	S 3	EL	H	Wycombe Wand.	W 2-1	1-0	3	Jewell 6, Shutt 59	8,010
8	10	EL	A	Swansea City	D 0-0	0-0	5		(3,445)
9	13	EL	A	Wrexham	W 1-0	1-0	2	Jewell 13	(4,179)
10	17	EL	H	York City	D 0-0	0-0	3		8,670
11	21	CC 2/1	A	Sheffield Wednesday	L 1-2	0-0		Shutt 69	(15,705)
12	24	EL	H	Huddersfield Town	L 3-4	0-1	3	Jewell 59, Kamara 78, Taylor 87	11,300
13	O 1	EL	A	Cambridge United	L 1-4	1-2	6	Liburd 1	(3,338)
14	4	CC 2/2	H	Sheffield Wednesday	D 1-1	0-1		Taylor 62	13,092
15	8	EL	H	Brighton & H.A.	W 2-1	1-0	6	Kamara 37, Taylor 78	6,970
16	11	AWT N1	H	Huddersfield Town	L 1-2	1-0		Kamara 43	3,772
17	15	EL	A	Blackpool	L 0-2	0-0	7		(6,156)
18	22	EL	A	AFC Bournemouth	W 3-2	2-1	7	Damara 10, Jewell 25, Huxford 50	(3,037)
19	30	EL	H	Cardiff City	L 2-3	1-3	10	Perry 9 (09), Murray 65	5,937
20	N 2	EL	H	Brentford	W 1-0	1-0	7	Jewell 10	4,105
21	5	EL	A	Bristol Rovers	L 0-4	0-2	9		(4,247)
22	8	AWT N1	A	York City	D 2-2	0-1		Murray 56, Tolson 90	(2,326)
23	12	FAC 1	H	Scunthorpe United	D 1-1	1-1		Tolson 1	5,478
24	19	EL	H	Crewe Alexandra	L 0-2	0-2	11		5,520
25	22	FAC1R	A	Scunthorpe United	L 2-3	0-0		Power 72, Richards 89	(4,514)
26	26	EL	A	Shrewsbury Town	W 2-1	1-0	9	Sinnett 11, Murray 76	(3,776)
27	29	AWT N2	A	Wrexham	L 1-6	0-4		Power 73	(1,407)
28	D 10	EL	A	Leyton Orient	D 0-0	0-0	10		(2,553)
29	17	EL	H	Chester City	D 1-1	1-0	12	Taylor 1	4,555
30	26	EL	A	Rotherham United	L 1-3	0-3	13	Taylor 89	(5,400)
31	28	EL	H	Hull City	W 1-0	0-0	12	Taylor 84	7,312
32	31	EL	A	Stockport County	W 2-1	1-0	9	Shutt 1, Taylor 46	(4,613)
33	J 2	EL	H	Birmingham City	D 1-1	1-0	9	Taylor 24	10,539
34	7	EL	A	AFC Bournemouth	L 1-2	0-0	10	Young 82 (og)	5,426
35	14	EL	A	Peterborough United	D 0-0	0-0	11		(4,400)
36	F 4	EL	H	Shrewsbury Town	D 1-1	1-0	12	Jacobs 12	4,817
37	7	EL	H	Bristol Rovers	W 2-1	1-0	11	Murray 37, Verveer 84	4,243
38	11	EL	A	Brentford	L 3-4	1-1	11	Robson 13, Murray 61, Power 73	(6,019)
39	18	EL	H	Peterborough United	W 4-2	2-0	10	Taylor 3, 73, Youds 39, 48	4,806
40	21	EL	A	Crewe Alexandra	W 1-0	0-0	8	Taylor 51,	(4,214)
41	25	EL	H	Cambridge United	D 1-1	0-0	8	Jewell 90	6,075
42	M 4	EL	A	Huddersfield Town	D 0-0	0-0	9		(17,404)
43	11	EL	H	Plymouth Argyle	W 2-0	0-0	10	Power 73, 87 (pen)	5,399
44	18	EL	A	Oxford United	L 0-1	0-0	12		(5,363)
45	21	EL	H	Swansea City	L 1-3	0-1	12	Richards 88	4,417
46	25	EL	A	York City	D 0-0	0-0	12		(5,431)
47	28	EL	A	Cardiff City	W 4.2	1-2	11	Tolson 38, 87, Murray 70, Showler 73	(2,560)
48	A 1	EL	H	Wrexham	D 1-1	1-1	11	Showler 45	4,461
49	4	EL	A	Wycombe Wanderers	L 1-3	0-3	12	Hamilton 78	(4,522)
50	8	EL	H	Stockport County	L 1-2	1-0	12	Youds 38	3,927
51	15	EL	A	Hull City	L 0-2	0-2	13		(4,368)
52	17	EL	H	Rotherham United	L 0-3	0-2	14		3,535
53	29	EL	H	Blackpool	L 0-1	0-1	14		5,036
54	M 2	EL	A	Birmingham City	D 0-0	0-0	14		(25,139)
55	6	EL	A	Brighton & H.A.	L 0-1	0-0	14		(7,701)
56									
57									
58									
59									
60									

Best Home League Attendance: 11,300 v Huddersfield Town   **Smallest:** 3,535 v Rotherham United   **Av Home Att:** 5,897

Goal Scorers: Compared with 1993-94:-498

League (57): Jewell 14, Taylor 11, Murray 5, Shutt 4, Kamara 3, Power 3 (1 pen), Youds 3, Opponents 2, Showler 2, Tolson 2, Hamilton, Huxford, Jacobs, Liburd, Richards, Robson, Sinnott, Verveer

C/Cola Cup (6): Taylor 2, Duxbury, Murray, Richards, Shutt

FA Cup (3): Power, Richards, Tolson

AW Trophy (4): Kamara, Murray, Power, Tolson

Tomlinson P.	Benn W.	Jacobs W.	Robson G.	Richards D.	Sinnott L.	Shutt C.	Kamara C.	Taylor J.	Jewell P.	Murray S.	Duxbury L.	Oliver G.	Bowling I.	Tolson N.	Liburd R.	Power L.	Hamilton D.	Sinclair R.	Huxford R.	Grayston N.	Midgley C.	McDonald C.	Stabb C.	Dow A.	Owen P.	Referee	
1	2	3	4*	5	6	7	8	9	10	11	12	S	S													D. Allison	1
1	2	3	4	5	6	7	8•	9	10	11*	14		S	12												P. Richards	2
1		3	8	6	5	7*	12	9	10	11	4		S	S	2											P. Harrison	3
1		3	8*	6	5	7		9	10	11	4		S	12	2	S										J. Parker	4
1		3		6	5	7	8	9	10	11	4				2	S	S	S								G. Singh	5
1		3		6	5•	7	8	9	10	11*	4				2	12	14	S								A. Dawson	6
1		3	S	6	5	7	8	9	10	11	4				2	S		S								I. Cruikshanks	7
1		3		6	5	7*	8	9	10	11	4				2	S	12	S								P. Vaner	8
1		3		6	5		8	9	10	11	4			12	2	7*	S	S								P. Wright	9
1		3		6	5*	7	8	9	10	11	4		S	S	2	12										T. Lunt	10
1	8	3		6		7	5	9	10*	11	4		S	S	2	12										T. Holbrook	11
1	5	3	6*		7•	8	9	10	11	4			S	14	2	12										R. Fernandez	12
1	12	3			7	8	9	10	11	4	5		S	14	2*	6•										J. Winter	13
1	2*	3	6•		7	8	9	10		4	5			12	11											R. Dilkes	14
1	12	3*	6		7	8	9	10		4	5			14	11•		2									S. Mathieson	15
1	6			7	8	9		4	5		10				2	3	11	S	S							J. Kirkby	16
	S		6		7*	8	9	10	11	4	5		1	12	2					3					S	E. Lomas	17
1			6	5	7	8	9	10*	11	4			S	S	12	2†				3						K. Cooper	18
1			6*	5	7•	8	9	10	11	4			S	12	14	2				3						A. Butler	19
1				5		8	9	10		4	6		S	12		S	7			2				3*		J. Lloyd	20
1				5		8	9	10•	12	4	6		S	14			7			2				3		R. Harris	21
1	S			5		8	9	10*	7	4	6		S	12			2			3						I. Cruikshanks	22
1			5	12	8	9•		7*	4	6		S	10	14	2					3						A. Wilkie	23
1		3	5	6	14	8	12		4		S	10	9*	7•		2										J. Watson	24
1†		3	6	5	7*	8	9	10•	11	4	12		14		2											A. Wilkie	25
1		3	6	5	7		9	10*	11	4	8				12	2									S	E. Wolstenholme	26
1		3	6*	5	7•		9	10	11	4	8	S			12	2									S	P. Richards	27
	8	3	6	5	7		9		11	4	S		10*		2										S	M. Pierce	28
	8*	3	6	5	7		9		11	4	S	14	10•	12	2										S	G. Cain	29
	8	3	4	6		7	9		11	S	S		10		2				S							J. Winter	30
1	S	3	4		7		9	10*	11	6	S				2											K. Lupton	31
1		3		6		7		9	10	11	4	S		S	8	2										D. Allison	32
1		3		6		7		9	10*	11	4	S		S	8	2										T. West	33
1		3	8	6		7•		9	10	11	4*	S		12		2†										T. Heilbron	34
1		3	8	6		7*		9	10	11	4	S		12		2	S									J. Parker	35
1		3	4	6		7*		9	10	11	S	S		8												J. Brandwood	36
1		3	8	6				9	14	11•	S		12	7	2											K. Breen	37
1		3	4•	6				9	12	11	S		14	7*	2											K. Cooper	38
1		3		6				9	S	11	S		S	7	2											N. Barry	39
1		3	4*	6				9	12	11	S		S		2											J. Holbrook	40
1		3	4	6				9•	14	11*	S		12		2											P. Harrison	41
1		3	4	6				9		S	S		S	11	2											K. Lupton	42
1		3	4	6		14		9		11*	S		12	10	2											E. Wolstenholme	43
1		3		6		14		9		12	S		10•	11	2											G. Barber	44
1		3	14	6				9		12	S		10	7	2											W. Burns	45
1		3	6			9			10	11	S	8	S	7	2											G. Cain	46
1		3	4			9			10•	11	S	8	14	7*	2											S. Dunn	47
1		3	4			9•	6*		14	11	S	8	10	12	2											J. Rushton	48
1		3	4			12	9		8	10	S		S	11	2				6*							C. Wilkes	49
1		3	4			9	8•		10*	14	S		12	11	2											D. Allison	50
S		3	4			9†	8		10•	7	1		14	11*	2											P. Vanes	51
S		3	4			S	8		10*	7	1		9		2		12									T. West	52
S	4						8		10	11	1		9*		2	3	12									A. Dawson	53
S	4					S			10	7	1		9	8	2	3	S									J. Parker	54
S	4					S			10	11*	1		9	8	2	3	12									S. Dunn	55
																											56
																											57
																											58
																											59
																											60
37	8	38	22	30	16	28	22	35	32	38	18	11	6	4	9	12	23		33	3	0		1		5	League Appearances	
	2		1			4	1	1	6	3	1			6		15	7				0					League Sub Appearances	
4	3	4	3	3	2	4	4	3	4	4	3+1	1		0+3	1	0+2	1									C/Cola Appearances	
2		1		1	2	1+1	2	2	1	2	2	1	0+1	1		0+2	1		2							FA Cup Appearances	
3	1	1		1	2	1+2	2	2	3	2	2	3	0+1	1+1			3	1	1							AWS Appearances	

Players on Loan: Dow (Chelsea), Owen (Stockport County), Petterson (Charlton Athletic), Sinclair (Stoke City), Verveer (Millwall) † = sent off

BRADFORD CITY

RECORDS AND STATISTICS

CLUB RECORDS

BIGGEST VICTORIES
League: 11-1 v Rotherham United, Division 3(N), 25.8.1928.
Most Goals Scored in a Cup Tie: 11-3 v Walker Celtic, FA Cup 1st Rnd. Replay, 1.12.1937.

BIGGEST DEFEATS
League: 0-8 v Manchester City, Division 2, 7.5..1927.
1-9 v Colchester United, Division 4, 30.12.1961.

MOST POINTS
3 points a win: 94, Division 3, 1984-85.
2 points a win: 63, Division 3(N), 1928-29.

Record Transfer Fee Received: £1.300,000 from Wolves for Dean Richards, May 1995.

Record Transfer Fee Paid: £300,000 to Bristol Rovers for John Taylor, June 1988.

BEST PERFORMANCES
League: 5th in Division 1, 1910-11.
F.A. Cup: Winners in 1911.
League Cup: 5th Round, 1964-65, 1987-88, 1988-89.

HONOURS
Division 2 Champions 1907-08.
Division 3(N) Champions 1928-29; Division 3(N) Cup 1939.
Division 3 Champions 1984-85.
FA Cup winners 1911.

LEAGUE CAREER
Elected to Div 2 1903, Div 1 1908, Div 2 1922, Div 3(N) 1927, Div 2 1929, Div 3(N) 1937, Transferred to Div 3 1958, Div 4 1961, Div 3 1969, Div 4 1972, Div 3 1977, Div 4 1978, Div 3 1982, Div 2 1985, Div 3 (now Div 2) 1990.

INDIVIDUAL CLUB RECORDS

MOST GOALS IN A SEASON
David Layne - 36 (League 34, FA Cup 2) Div 4, 1961-62.

MOST GOALS IN A MATCH
Albert Whitehurst - 7 v Tranmere Rovers, 8-0, Div 3(N), 6.3.1929.

MOST GOALS IN A CAREER
Robert Campbell - 143 (Lge 121, FAC 5, Lge Cup 11, Others 6).

MOST APPEARANCES
Cyril 'Cec' Podd 1970-84 (Lge 494+8, FAC 30, Lge C 33+1, Oth 8) Total: 574

OLDEST PLAYER
Tommy Cairns, 41 years 7 days v Bradford P.A., 7.11.1931.

YOUNGEST PLAYER
Robert Cullingford, 16 years 141 days v Mansfield Town, 22.4.1970.

MOST CAPPED PLAYER
Harry Hampton (Northern Ireland) 9.
Evelyn Lintott (England) 4.

PREVIOUS MANAGERS

R.Campbell 03-05, P.O'Rourke 05-21, D.Menzies 21-26, C.Veitch 26-28, P O'Rourke 28-30, J Peart 30-35, R.Ray 35-38, F.Westgarth 38-43, R.Sharp (Hon.) 43-46, J.Barker 46-47, J.Milburn 47-48, D.Steele 48-52, A.Harris (Hon.) 52, I.Powell 52-55, P.Jackson Snr. 55-61, R.Brocklebank 61-64, W.Harris 65-66, W.Watson 66-68, G.Hair 68, J.Wheeler 68-71, B.Edwards 71-75, R.Kennedy 75-78, J.Napier 1978, G.Mulhall 78-81, R.McFarland 81-82, T.Cherry 82-87, T.Dolan 87-89, T.Yorath 89-90, J.Docherty 90-91, F.Stapleton 91-94.

ADDITIONAL INFORMATION
Previous Names: None
Previous League: None (One of only two clubs to gain admission to Football League without playing a senior fixture - Chelsea being the other).
Club Colours: Amber/claret stripes, claret shorts, amber socks.
Change Colours: White shirts, white shorts, white socks.
Reserves League: Pontins Central League Division 2.

LONGEST LEAGUE RUNS

of undefeated matches:	21 (1968-69)	of league matches w/out a win:	16 (1948-49)
of undefeated home matches:	25 (1975-78)	of undefeated away matches:	10 (1968-69)
without home win:	10 (1962-64)	without an away win:	29 (1925-27)
of league wins:	10 (1983-84)	of home wins:	9 (1952-53, 1961-64)
of league defeats:	8 (1932-33)	of away wins:	5 (1928-29, 1981-82, 1984-85)

THE MANAGER

LENNIE LAWRENCE . . . . appointed May 1994.

PREVIOUS CLUBS
As Manager . . . . Plymouth Argyle (Caretaker), Charlton Athletic, Middlesbrough.
As Asst.Man/Coach . . . . Plymouth Argyle, Lincoln City.
As a player . . . . Croydon, Carshalton Athletic, Sutton United.

HONOURS
As a Manager . . . . Charlton Athletic: Division 2 runners-up 1985-86.
As Asst. Manager . . . . Promotion to Division 3 1980-81.

BRADFORD CITY

PLAYERS NAME / Honours	Ht	Wt	Birthdate	Birthplace / Transfers	Contract Date	Clubs	League	L/Cup	FA Cup	Other	Lge	L/C	FAC	Oth
G O A L K E E P E R S														
Paul Tomlinson	6.2	12.10	22.02.64	Brierley Hill	01.06.83	Sheffield United	37	1	5	3				
				Loan	20.03.87	Birmingham City	11							
				£47,500	23.06.87	Bradford City	293	28	15	14				
D E F E N D E R S														
Wayne Benn	5.10	11.0	07.08.76	Pontefract	01.06.94	Bradford City (T)	8+2	3		1				
Jonathan Ford	6.1	13.1	12.04.68	Birmingham		Cradley Town								
AGT'94.				£5,000	19.08.91	Swansea City	145+15	12+1	8+5	15+5	6		2	
				£210,000	08.95	Bradford City								
Neil Grayston	5.8	10.09	25.11.75	Keighley	27.05.94	Bradford City (T)	5		1					
Richard Huxford	5.10	11.6	25.07.69	Scunthorpe		Kettering Town								
					06.08.92	Barnet	33	2	2	2+1	1			
				Free	16.07.93	Millwall	25+7	1+1	1	3		1		
				Loan	21.02.94	Birmingham City	5							
Loan 11.08.94 Bradford City				£50,000	08.95	Bradford City	33		2	3	1			
Wayne Jacobs	5.9	10.2	03.02.69	Sheffield	03.01.87	Sheffield Wed. (A)	5+1	3		1				
				£27,000	25.03.88	Hull City	127+2	7	8	6	4			
				Free	05.08.93	Rotherham United	40+2	4	1	2	2			
				Free	.08.94	Bradford City	38	4	1	1	1			
Richard Liburd	5.9	11.1	26.09.73	Nottingham		Eastwood Town								
				£20,000	25.03.93	Middlesbrough	41	4	2	5	1			
				£200,000	21.07.94	Bradford City	9	2			1			
Graham Mitchell	6.1	11.4	16.02.68	Shipley	16.06.86	Huddersfield T. (T)	235+9	13+2	27	24	2	1	1	1
Loan 24.12.93 Bournemouth 4 Lge App.					23.12.94	Bradford City	26							
Nicholas Mohan	6.0	11.10	06.10.70	Middlesboro'	18.11.87	Middlesbrough (J)	93+6	11	9+1	11	4			
				Loan	26.09.92	Hull City	5				1			
				£330,000	07.07.94	Leicester City	23	2	1					
				£225,000	08.95	Bradford City								
Gavin J Ward	6.2	12.12	30.06.70	Sutton Coldfield		Aston Villa (T)								
WFAC'93; Div3'93				Free	26.09.88	Shrewsbury Town								
				Free	18.09.89	West Bromwich A.								
				Free	05.10.89	Cardiff City	58+1		1	7				
				£175,000	16.07.93	Leicester City	38	3	0+1	4				
				£175,000	08.95	Bradford City								
Edward Youds	6.0	10.10	03.05.70	Liverpool	10.06.88	Everton (T)	5+3	0+1		1				
Loan 29.12.89 Cardiff C. 0+1 Lge, 0+1 FAC App.				Loan	08.02.90	Wrexham	20				2			
				£250,000	15.11.91	Ipswich Town	38+12	1+2	5+1		1			
Loan 20.01.95 Bradford City				£150,000	17.03.95	Bradford City	17				3			
M I D F I E L D														
Derick Hamilton	5.11	11.10	15.08.76	Bradford	01.06.94	Bradford City (T)	25+7	1	1	1	2			
Gary Robson	5.7	10.12	06.07.65	Chester-Le-St.	05.05.83	West Brom. A. (A)	206+35	15+2	10+2	7+5	29		3	3
FLgXI.1.														
F O R W A R D S														
Chris Dolby	5.8	9.12	04.09.74	Dewsbury	05.08.93	Rotherham Utd (T)	0+1			1				
				Free	08.95	Bradford City								
Paul Jewell	5.8	10.8	28.09.64	Liverpool	30.09.82	Liverpool (A)								
FRT'85.				£15,000	20.12.84	Wigan Athletic	117+20	5+2	9	14+4	35		5	7
				£80,000	21.07.88	Bradford City	210+41	16+1	11+1	8+1	54	6	3	1
Andy Kiwomya	5.9	10.10	01.10.67	Huddersfield	16.07.85	Barnsley (A)	1							
				£5,000	07.10.86	Sheffield Wed.								
				Free	08.92	Dundee	11+10		0+1		1			
				Free	01.10.93	Rotherham United	4+3	0+1		0+2				
via Halifax Town (Free) to				Free	23.03.93	Scunthorpe United	9				3			
				Free	08.95	Bradford City								
Shaun Murray	5.7	10.5	07.12.70	Newcastle	10.12.87	Tottenham H. (T)								
E: Y.7.				£100,000	12.06.89	Portsmouth	21+13	2+1	1+3	2+2	1	1		
Loan 16.08.93 Millwall					01.11.93	Scarborough	29		2	2	5			
				£200,000	.08.94	Bradford City	38+3	3	2	2	5	1		1
Ian Ormondroyd	6.4	13.9	22.09.64	Bradford		Thackley								
					06.09.85	Bradford City	72+15	12+2	7	7+2	20	4	2	1
Loan 27.03.87 Oldham Ath. 8+2 Lge App. 1gl.				£600,000	02.02.89	Aston Villa	41+15	4+2	5	6+1	6	2	2	
				£350,000	19.09.91	Derby County	25	3	3		8		1	
					11.02.92	Leicester City	67+10	6	1+1	11	7	2		3
Loan 27.01.95 Hull City 10 Lge App. 6gls				£75,000	08.95	Bradford City								
Paul Showler	5.11	11.9	10.10.66	Doncaster		Sheffield Wed. (A)								
E: SP.2. NPL'90. NPLD1'89.				Free		Bentley Vics.								
via Goole Town (Free) & Colne Dynamoes (Free)						Altrincham			1					
				Free	15.08.91	Barnet	69+2	2	3+1	7	12		1	
				Free	04.08.93	Bradford City	43+12	3+1	3	2+1	7	1		
Carl Shutt	5.10	11.13	10.10.61	Sheffield		Spalding								
Div.1'92. Div'2'90.				Free	13.05.85	Sheffield Wed.	36+4	3	4+1		16	1	4	
				£55,000	30.10.87	Bristol City	39+7	5+2	7+1	10+1	10	4	4	4
				£50,000	23.03.89	Leeds United	46+33	6+2	10	4+5	17	2	1	4
				£50,000	23.08.93	Birmingham City	23+9	3			4			
Loan 11.08.94 Bradford City				£75,000	09.09.94	Bradford City	28+4	4	1+1	2	4	1		
Neil Tolson	6.2	12.4	25.10.73	Walsall	17.12.91	Walsall (T)	3+6		0+1	1+2	1	1		
				£150,000	24.03.92	Oldham Athletic	0+3							
				P.E.	02.12.93	Bradford City	20+12	0+3	1	1+1	4		1	2
				Loan	06.01.95	Chester City	3+1							
Tommy E Wright	5.7	9.9	10.01.66	Dunfermline	15.01.83	Leeds United (A)	73+8	3+2	4		24	1	3	
S: u21.1.				£80,000	24.10.86	Oldham Athletic	110+2	7+1	3	3	23	2	2	
				£350,000	14.08.89	Leicester City	122+7	7+1	4	10	22			7
				£650,000	01.07.92	Middlesbrough	44+9	3+1	3	5+1	5		1	
				Free	08.95	Bradford City								

THE PULSE STADIUM

Valley Parade, Bradford, West Yorkshire BD8 7DY
Tel: 01274 306 062

Capacity 14,359
Covered Standing 8,089
Seating 6,270

First game .... v Gainsborough Trin., Div 2 5.9.1903
First floodlit game .... v Hull City, 20.12.1954

ATTENDANCES
Highest .... 39,146 v Burnley, FAC 4th Rnd, 11.3.1911
Lowest .... 1,179 v Hartlepool United, AMC, 22.2.1984

MATCHDAY TICKET PRICES

M&P Stand £11
. . . . OAP £16, Juv £3
HSG Stand £10
. . . . OAP £5.50, Juv £2
Diamond Seal Kop £7
. . . . OAP £3.50, Juv £1

Match and Ticket Information
N&P Stand tickets available four weeks in
advance of matches.

Ticket Office Telephone No. . 01274 307 050

HOW TO GET TO THE GROUND

From the North
A650 to Bradford.
Join Ring Road, A6036.
Turn left into Valley Parade for ground.

From the South and West
M62 and A606 (M) to Bradford.
Fourth exit from roundabout to A6036 Ring Road.
Left at crossroads A650, left into Valley Parade.

From East
A647 to Bradford.
Right at crossroads, A6036.
Left at crossroads A650.
Left into Valley Parade.

MATCHDAY PROGRAMME

Programme Editor . . . . Kevin Mitchell.

Number of pages 16

Price £1.20

Subscriptions . . . . £25 per season

Local Newspapers . . . . Telegraph and Argus, Bradford Star

Local Radio Stations . . . . The Pulse 97.5 & 102.5 FM
. . . . BBC Radio Leeds (388 MW), Magic 828 (362 MW)

BRENTFORD
(The Bees)
ENDSLEIGH LEAGUE DIVISION 2
SPONSORED BY: ERICSSON MOBILE PHONES

Back Row (L-R): J Omigie, G Hurdle, J Bates, B Ashby, R Taylor, C Asaba, C Hutchings, C Campbell, K Burke.
Middle Row: B Booker, M Grainger, D McGhee, P Smith, T Fernandes, K Dearden, D Mundee, P Abraham, I Anderson, R Johnson.
Front Row: J Hooker, D Annon, L Harvey, D Webb, K Lock, N Forster, B Statham, C Ravenscroft.

BRENTFORD
FORMED IN 1889
TURNED PROFESSIONAL IN 1899
LTD COMPANY IN 1901

PRESIDENT: W Wheatley
CHAIRMAN: M M Lange
DIRECTORS
B R Evans, D Tana, J P Herting,
E J Radley-Smith, MS, FRCS, LRCR.

SECRETARY
Polly Kates
COMMERCIAL MANAGER
Peter Gilham

MANAGER: David Webb
ASSISTANT MANAGER: Kevin Lock

YOUTH TEAM MANAGER
Bob Booker
PHYSIOTHERAPIST
Roy Johnson

STATISTICIAN FOR THE DIRECTORY
Frank Coumbe

A highly entertaining season ended in despair for Brentford when they were eliminated from the Play-offs in a penalty shoot out by Huddersfield Town.

After a poor finish to the 1993/94 season hopes were raised by an opening day 5-1 victory at Plymouth, however, the first three months of the season saw good wins being balanced out by defeats and the Bees in a familiar mid-table position.

The turning point came on 26th November when Brentford beat Brighton 2-1. This started a run which saw just one defeat in 26 games and included memorable wins over Plymouth (7-0), Cambridge (6-0), Chester (4-1), Bradford City (4-3) and Leyton Orient (3-0) to name but a few.

The Bees hit the top of the table at the end of January and were only once outside the top two until the end of the season, but with only one club going up it was always going to be hard. Only one point was gained from the final three matches which included a defeat at Birmingham, which ultimately decided the destination of the championship. Two evenly contested matches with Huddersfield ended 2-2 on aggregate after 210 minutes of football, before the heartbreaking shoot-out saw Brentford remain in Division Two for 1995/96.

The Coca-Cola Cup saw Colchester beaten (4-0) before Brentford lost 1-0 to Tranmere, thanks to inspired goalkeeping by Tranmere's Eric Nixon. The FA Cup saw elimination in a First Round replay by Cambridge, while in the Auto Windscreens Shield Brighton and Gillingham were beaten before Oxford defeated the Bees.

In such a good season many players impressed, namely Kevin Dearden, Carl Hutchings, Brian Statham, Martin Grainger, Barry Ashby, captain and Player of the Year Jamie Bates, Paul Smith, Simon Ratcliffe, Lee Harvey, Denny Mundee and the 51 goal strike partnership of Robert Taylor and Nick Forster. With some promising players in reserve, Brentford must try to go one better in 1995/96 and lift the championship.

As long as the best players are retained there must be a good chance of this happening.

FRANK COUMBE.

BRENTFORD

Division Two: 2nd				**FA Cup:** 1st Round			**Coca-Cola Cup:** 2nd Round		**Auto Windscreen Trophy:** 2nd Round

M	DATE	COMP.	VEN	OPPONENTS	RESULT	H/T	LP	GOAL SCORERS/GOAL TIMES	ATT.
1	A 13	EL	A	Plymouth	W 5-1	3-1	1	Smith 25, Forster 37, 88 Stephenson 45, Taylor 71	(7,976)
2	16	CC 1/1	A	Colchester	W 2-0	1-0		**Stephenson 26, Taylor 56**	(2,521)
3	20	EL	H	Peterborough	L 0-1	0-1	11		5,561
4	24	CC 1/2	H	Colchester	W 2-0	1-0		**Parris 28, Smith 61**	2,315
5	27	EL	A	Stockport	W 1-0	1-0	7	Taylor 11	(4,399)
6	30	EL	H	Rotherham	W 2-0	1-0	5	Taylor 8, Forster 58	4,031
7	S 3	EL	H	Wrexham	L 0-2	0-2	7		5,820
8	10	EL	A	Wycombe	L 3-4	1-1	13	Taylor 16, Stephenson 81, Cousins 89 (og)	(6,847)
9	13	EL	A	York	L 1-2	1-1	15		(2,836)
10	17	EL	H	Blackpool	W 3-2	1-0	10	Forster 51, Smith 75, Grainger 79 (pen)	4,157
11	20	CC 2/1	A	Tranmere	L 0-1	0-1			(3,754)
12	24	EL	A	Crewe	W 2-0	1-0	8	Forster 41, Taylor 70	(3,839)
13	27	CC 2/2	H	Tranmere	D 0-0	0-0			4,076
14	O 1	EL	H	Shrewsbury	W 1-0	1-0	5	Taylor 44	4,556
15	8	EL	H	Bristol Rovers	W 3-0	2-0	5	Forster 3, 5, Taylor 79	5,330
16	15	EL	A	Bournemouth	W 1-0	1-0	4	Forster 31	(4,411)
17	19	AWT 1	A	Brighton	W 1-0	0-0		**Forster 77**	(1,104)
18	22	EL	H	Birmingham	L 1-2	0-1	5	Ward 83 (og)	7,779
19	29	EL	A	Cambridge	D 0-0	0-0	7		(3,102)
20	N 2	EL	A	Bradford City	L 0-1	0-1	9		(4,105)
21	5	EL	H	Hull	L 0-1	0-0	10		5,455
22	8	AWT	H	Gillingham	W 3-1	2-0		**Annen 14, Asaba 28, Ansah 74**	1,795
23	12	FAC 1	A	Cambridge	D 2-2	1-1		**Annen 5, Taylor 70**	(3,353)
24	19	EL	A	Huddersfield	L 0-1	0-0	13		(10,889)
25	22	FAC IR	H	Cambridge	L 1-2	1-2		**Grainger 25**	4,095
26	26	EL	H	Brighton	W 2-1	0-1	11	Ashby 48, Ansah 81	4,728
27	D 3	AWT	H	Oxford	L 1-2	0-0		**Grainger 49 (pen)**	2,410
28	10	EL	A	Peterborough	D 2-2	1-2	12	Taylor 11, Forster 68	(4,102)
29	17	EL	H	Plymouth	W 7-0	2-0	9	Annen 3, Smith 8, Taylor 48, 56 Forster 50, Mundee 74, Harvey 87	4,492
30	26	EL	H	Leyton Orient	W 3-0	3-0	8	Mundee 24, Ratcliffe 29, Forster 38	6,125
31	27	EL	A	Chester	W 4-1	3-1	6	Forster 8, 33, 69 Grainger 18	(2,261)
32	31	EL	H	Oxford	W 2-0	1-0	5	Forster 34, Taylor 80	7,125
33	J 2	EL	A	Cardiff	W 3-2	2-0	5	Harvey 7, Forster 33, Taylor 82	(5,235)
34	14	EL	H	Swansea	D 0-0	0-0	5		7,211
35	21	EL	A	Hull	W 2-1	0-0	2	Mundee 84, Grainger 86	(3,823)
36	28	EL	H	Cambridge	W 6-0	0-0	1	Forster 65, Taylor 68, 83 Grainger 80 (pen) Bailey 86, 90	6,390
37	F 4	EL	A	Brighton	D 1-1	1-0	2	Bailey 17	(9,499)
38	11	EL	H	Bradford City	W 4-3	1-1	1	Mundee 40, Taylor 64, Grainger 75 (pen), Forster 86	6,019
39	17	EL	A	Swansea	W 2-0	1-0	1	Forster 4, 74	(3,935)
40	21	EL	H	Huddersfield	D 0-0	0-0	1		9,562
41	25	EL	A	Shrewsbury	L 1-2	1-1	1	Forster 39	(4,570)
42	M 4	EL	H	Crewe	W 2-0	1-0	2	Mundee 9, Taylor 90	7,143
43	7	EL	A	Wrexham	D 0-0	0-0	1		(2,834)
44	11	EL	H	Stockport	W 1-0	1-0	1	Taylor 5	6,513
45	18	EL	A	Rotherham	W 2-0	2-0	1	Forster 26, Abrahams 39	(2,968)
46	21	EL	H	Wycombe	D 0-0	0-0	2		9,530
47	25	EL	A	Blackpool	W 2-1	2-0	2	Bates 3, Taylor 21	(4,663)
48	A 1	EL	H	York	W 3-0	1-0	1	Grainger 3, Forster 59, Taylor 60	6,474
49	8	EL	A	Oxford	D 1-1	1-1	2	Taylor 44	(7,800)
50	15	EL	H	Chester	D 1-1	0-1	3	Abrahams 88	8,020
51	17	EL	A	Leyton Orient	W 2-0	1-0	1	Bates (19) Forster (82)	(4,459)
52	22	EL	H	Cardiff	W 2-0	0-0	1	Grainger 54 (pen), Taylor 81	8,268
53	26	EL	A	Birmingham	L 0-2	0-0	2		(25,081)
54	29	EL	H	Bournemouth	L 1-2	0-0	2	Abrahams 67	10,079
55	M 6	EL	A	Bristol Rovers	D 2-2	0-1	2	McGhee 67, Taylor 71	(8,501)
56	14	P/O	A	Huddersfield	D 1-1	1-1		Forster 42	(14,160)
57	17	P/O	H	Huddersfield	D †1-1	1-1		Grainger 18 (pen) (lost 4-3 on pens)	11,161
58									
59									
60									

Best Home League Attendance: 10,079 v Bournemouth   **Smallest:** 4,031 v Rotherham United   **Av Home Att: 6,538**

Goal Scorers:

League (81): Forster 24, Taylor 23, Grainger 7 (4 pens), Mundee 5, Abrahams 3, Bailey 3, Smith 3, Bates 2, Stephenson 2, Annon, Ansah, Ashby, McGhee, Ratcliffe

C/Cola Cup (4): Parris, Smith, Stephenson, Taylor
FA Cup (3): Annon, Grainger, Taylor
AW Trophy (5): Annon, Asaba, Ansah, Forster, Grainger (pen)

Compared with 1993-94: +968

Play Offs (2): Forster, Grainger (pen)

1994-95

Squad numbers (across top, above selected players): 19 · 5 · 8 · 7 · 9 · 17 · 1 · 4 · 3 · 13 · 16 · 23 · 27 · 23 · 23

Fer	Hur	Bat	Wes	Hut	Smi	Par	Har	Tay	For	Ste	Rat	Ben	Dea	Ann	Ash	Mun	Gra	Sta	Rav	McG	Ans	Asa	Bai	Abr	#
X	X	X	X	X	X	X	X	X	X	X	X	S	S												1
S	X	X	X	X	X	X	X	X	X1	X	X	S1	X												2
S	X	X		X	X	X	X1	X	X	X	S		X	S1											3
S	X	X		X	X	X	X	X1	X2	X	S2		X		X	S1									4
S	X	X		X	X	X	X1	X	X	X			X		X	S1	S								5
S	X	X		X	X	X		X	X	X			X	S	X	X	S								6
S	X	X		X	X	X2	S1	X	X	X1			X		X	X	S2								7
S	X	X		X	X		X	X	X1	X	S		X		X	S1	X								8
S		X1		X	X		X	X	X	X	S1		X		X	S	X	X							9
S		X1	S1	X	X		X	X	X	X		X2	X		X	S2	X	X							10
S	S		X	X		X	X	X	X				X		X	S	X	X							11
S	S		X†	X		X	X1	X	X				X		X	S1	X	X							12
S	S		X	X		X	X	X	X				X		X	S1	X	X							13
S	S		X	X		X	X	X					X		X	S1	X	X						X1	14
S2	X2		X	X		X	X1	X	X				X		X	S1	X	X							15
S	S		X	X		X	X1	X2	X				X†		X	S2	X	X							16
S	S		X	X		X	X	X	X	X			X		X	X	X	X		S					17
S	S		X	X1		X	X	X					X		X	S1	X	X							18
X			X	S		X	X	X	X	X			X		X	S1	X	X							19
S			X	S	X	X	X	X1	X				X		X	S1	X	X							20
S			X	S	X	X	X	X1					X		X	S1	X	X			X				21
S1	X	X		X	X		X3	S2					X1	X	X		X		S3		X		X2		22
S	S1		X	X		X	X	X					X	X1	X		X	X			X	S			23
S1	S		X	X1	X	X	X						X		X		X	X			X			X	24
S			X	X	S1	X	X	X	X1				X		X	X	X†	X							25
S			X	X		X	X	X	X1				X	X2	X	S2	X	X				S1			26
S			X	X2	S1	X	X	X1					X	S2	X	X	X	X†		X					27
X	X		X		S	X	X	X	X				S	X1	X	X		X			X				28
S	S		X		X	X1	X	X	X				X	X	X	S1	X								29
S	S		X		X		X	X	X	X			X	X	X	X	X			S					30
S	S		X		X		X	X	X				X	X	X	X	X			S					31
S			X	X	X		X	X	X				X	X1		X	X	S1		S					32
S			X	X	X		X	X	X				X		X1	X	S1			S					33
S			X		X		X	X	X				X	X	X1	X	S1			S					34
S			X		X		X	X	X				X	X2	X	X	S1			S2					35
S			X		X			X	X1	X			X		X	X	S1			S		X			36
S			X		X			X	X1	X			X		X	X2	S1			S2		X			37
S			X		X			X	X	X	X1		X		X	X	S1			S		X			38
S			X		X			X	X	X			X		X	X	S1			S		X			39
S			X		X				X	X			X		X	X	S1	S	S	X1		X			40
S			X		X	X			X1	X2	X		X		X	X	X	S1		S2		X			41
S			X		X	X			X	X	X1		X		X	X	S1	S				X			42
S	S		X	X	X			X	X	X	X		X		X		X			S					43
S			X	X	X			X	X	X	X		X			X		X		S				S	44
S			X	X	X			X	X	X			X		S	X		X		X		X			45
S			X	X	S	X			X	X	X		X			X	X1	X		S1				X	46
S			X		X	X		X	X	X1			X			X	S1	X		S			X		47
S			X		X	X		X	X	X			X			X	S	X		S			X		48
S			X		X	X1		X	X	X			X			X	S1	X		X			X		49
S			X		X1	X		X	X	X2			X			X	S1	X†	X	S2			X		50
S			X		S	X		X	X	X	X		X			X	X	X		S			S		51
S			X		S1	X		X	X2	X1	X		X			X	X	X		S			S2		52
S			X		S	X		X	X	X1	X		X			X	X	X		S			S1		53
S			X		X	X		X	X2	X1	X		X			X	S1		X	S2			X		54
S			X		X	X		X	X2	X	X1		X			X	S1		X	S2			X		55
S			X		S1	X		X	X	X	X		X			X	X	X	X1	S					56
S			X		S	X		X	X	X	X		X			X	S1	X	X					X1	57

Fer	Hur	Bat	Wes	Hut	Smi	Par	Har	Tay	For	Ste	Rat	Ben	Dea	Ann	Ash	Mun	Gra	Sta	Rav	McG	Ans	Asa	Bai	Abr	
3	7	38	15	38	35	5	24	43	46	34	24	1	43	9	40	22	36	26	1	1	2		6	7	League Appearances
1	2		1	1			1				1			1		17	1	10		6	1			3	League Sub Appearances
2	2	2	4	4	2	4	4	4	4	0+1	0+1	4		3		0+1	2	2							C/Cola Appearances
0+1	1	2	1+1	2		2	2	2			2		1	2	1	2									FA Cup Appearances
0+1	1	2	2	2+1	1	2	2	2+1	1	1	3		1+1	3	2	3	2	0+1		2	1				AWT Appearances

Also Played: 25 Mason S. (1,19), 22 Hooker S.I. (28) Players on Loan: Parris (Birmingham City), Ansah (Southend United), Bailey (Queens Park Rangers) † = sent off

CLUB RECORDS

BIGGEST VICTORIES
League: 9-0 v Wrexham, Division 3, 15.10.1963.
F.A. Cup: 7-0 v Windsor & Eton (a), 1st Round, 20.11.1982.

BIGGEST DEFEATS
League: 0-7 v Swansea City, Division 3(S), 8.11.1924.
0-7 v Walsall, Division 3, 19.1.1957.
F.A. Cup: 1-7 v Manchester United, 3rd Round, 1927-28.

MOST POINTS
3 points a win: 85, Division 2, 1994-95.
2 points a win: 62, Division 3(S), 1932-33.
62, Division 4, 1962-63.

MOST GOALS SCORED
98, Division 4, 1962-63.

RECORD TRANSFER FEE RECEIVED
£720,000 from Wimbledon for Dean Holdsworth, July 1992.

RECORD TRANSFER FEE PAID
£275,000 to Chelsea for Joe Allon, November 1992.

BEST PERFORMANCES
League: 5th in Division 1, 1935-36.
F.A. Cup: 6th Round, 1938, 1946, 1949, 1989.
League Cup: 4th Round, 1982-83.

HONOURS
Champions Division 3(S), 1932-33.
Champions Division 2, 1934-35.
Champions Division 4, 1962-63.
Champions Division 3, 1991-92.

LEAGUE CAREER
Founder Members of Division 3, 1920.
Division 3(S) 1921-33, Div 2 1932-33, Div 1 1934-35, Div 2 1946-47, Div 3(S) 1953-54, Div 4 1961-62, Div 3 1962-63, Div 4 1965-66, Div 3 1971-72, Div 4 1972,73, Div 3 1977-78, Div 2 (now Div 1) 1991-92, Div 2 1992-93.

INDIVIDUAL CLUB RECORDS

MOST GOALS IN A SEASON
Jack Holliday: 39 goals in 1932-33. (League 38, FA Cup 1).

MOST GOALS IN A MATCH
5. Jack Holliday v Luton Town, Division 3 (S), (a) 28.1.1933 (5-5).
5. Billy Scott v Barnsley, Division 2, (h) 15.12.1934 (8-1).
5. Peter McKennan v Bury, Division 2, (h) 18.2.1949 (8-2).

OLDEST PLAYER
Dai Hopkins, 39 years 7 months 13 days, 26.5.1947.

YOUNGEST PLAYER
Danis Salman, 15 years 8 months 3days, 15.11.1975.

MOST CAPPED PLAYER
Dai Hopkins (Wales) 12.
Billy Scott & Leslie Smith (England) 1.

PREVIOUS MANAGERS

(Since 1945)
Harry Curtis (Sec./Manager) 1926-49; A.H.'Jackie'Gibbons (Sec./Man.) 1949-52; Jim Bain 1952-53; Tommy Lawton (players/manager) 1953; Bill Dodgin (Senior) 1953-57; Malcolm MacDonald 1957-65; Tommy Cavanagh 1965-66; Billy Gray 1966-67; Jimmy Sirrel 1967-69; Frank Blunstone 1969-73; Mike Everitt 1973-75; John Docherty 1975-76; Bill Dodgin (Junior) 1976-80; Fred Callaghan 1980-84; Frank McLintock 1984-87; Steve Perryman 1987-90; Phil Holder 1990-93;

ADDITIONAL INFORMATION
PREVIOUS NAMES
None.
PREVIOUS LEAGUES
Southern League.
Club colours: Red & white striped shirts, red shorts, red socks with white turnover.
Change colours: Blue & white striped shirts, navy shorts and sky socks with three stripes.
Reserves League: Wendy Fair Capital League.
Youth League: South East Counties.

LONGEST LEAGUE RUNS

of undefeated matches:	16 (1932, 1967)	of league matches w/out a win:	16 (1994)
of undefeated home matches:	24 (1934-35)	of undefeated away matches:	11 (1993)
without home win:	11 (1947)	without an away win:	21 (1965-66)
of league wins:	9 (1932)	of home wins:	21 (1929-30)
of league defeats:	9 (1925,1928)	of away wins:	5 (1956, 1981)

Brentford won all 21 home games in 1929-30, they also played 44 away League games without a draw between 1923-25.

THE MANAGER

DAVID WEBB . . . . appointed in May 1993.

PREVIOUS CLUBS
As Manager . . . . Torquay United, Bournemouth, Southend, Chelsea.
As a player . . . . Leyton Orient, Southampton, Chelsea, Q.P.R., Leicester City, Derby County, ... Bournemouth, Torquay.

HONOURS
As a Manager . . . . None.
As a Player . . . . Chelsea: FA Cup 1970. E.C.W.C. 1971.

BRENTFORD

PLAYERS NAME / Honours	Ht	Wt	Birthdate	Birthplace / Transfers	Contract Date	Clubs	League	L/Cup	FA Cup	Other	Lge	L/C	FAC	Oth
G O A L K E E P E R S														
Kevin Dearden	5.11	12.8	08.03.70	Luton	05.08.88	Tottenham H. (T)	0+1	1						
				Loan	09.03.89	Cambridge United	15							
				Loan	31.08.89	Hartlepool United	10							
Loan 23.03.90 Swindon T. 1 Lge App.				Loan	24.08.90	Peterborough Utd	7							
Loan 10.01.91 Hull C. 3 Lge App.				Loan	16.08.91	Rochdale	2							
Loan 19.03.92 Birmingham C. 12 Lge App.				Free	30.09.93	Brentford	78	4	4	9				
Tamer Fernandes	6.3	13.7	07.12.74	Paddington	12.07.93	Brentford	6+3			0+2				
E: Y.1.				Loan	12.10.93	Wealdstone								
D E F E N D E R S														
Ijah Anderson			30.12.75			Tottenham H. (T)								
						South End United								
				Free	08.95	Brentford								
Barry Ashby	6.2	13.2	21.11.70	Brent	01.12.88	Watford (T)	101+13	6	4	2+1	3			
FAYC'89.					22.03.94	Brentford	48	3	2	5	2			
Jamie Bates	6.1	13.0	24.02.68	Croydon	01.06.87	Brentford (T)	259+20	21+3	7+1	32	10	2	1	1
Div.3'92.														
Corey Campbell	5.11	11.06	06.03.76	Hammersmith	07.07.94	Brentford (T)								
Martin Grainger	5.10	11.7	23.08.72	Enfield	28.07.92	Colchester Utd (T)	37+9	3	3+2	3	7			1
GMVC'92.				£60,000	21.10.93	Brentford	67+1	2	4	5	9		1	2
Gus Hurdle	5.9	11.01	14.10.73	Kensington		Fulham (T)								
via Dorchester Town (Free)				Free	19.07.94	Brentford	7+2	2	0+1	1				
Denny Mundee	5.10	11.0	10.10.68	Swindon		Q.P.R. (A)								
				Free	21.08.86	Swindon Town								
via Salisbury to				Free	23.09.88	Bournemouth	76+24	3+2	9+2	5+1	6		4	2
Loan Yeovil T. 3 FAC App.				Loan	07.09.89	Torquay United	9							
				Free	12.08.93	Brentford	59+19	0+3	3	5+3	16			2
Brian Statham	5.8	11.6	21.05.69	Zimbabwe	03.08.87	Tottenham H. (T)	20+4	2	0+1					
E: u21.3, u19.2. Div.3'92.				Loan	28.03.91	Reading	8							
Loan 20.11.91 Bournemouth 2 Lge, 1 Oth.				£70,000	16.01.92	Brentford	120+10	6	6	10	6		1	
M I D F I E L D														
Carl Hutchings	5.11	11.0	24.09.74	Hammersmith	12.07.93	Brentford (T)	58+10	5+1	3+1	6+2				
Paul W Smith	5.11	13.7	18.09.71	Lenham	16.03.90	Southend Utd (T)	18+2			0+1	1			
SLP'93. (while on loan with Dover)				Free	06.08.93	Brentford	67	4	4	7	6	1		1
F O R W A R D S														
Paul Abrahams	5.8	10.6	31.10.73	Colchester	11.08.92	Colchester Utd (T)	30+25	2+3	4	3	8		2	2
				£30,000	09.03.94	Brentford	7+3			1	3			
Darren Annon	5.8	10.11	17.02.72	London		Carshalton Athletic								
				£20,000	08.03.94	Brentford	23+6		2	2+2	3		2	2
Carl Asaba	6.2	13.0	28.01.73	Dulwich Hamlet										
					09.08.94	Brentford				1				1
				Loan	16.02.95	Colchester United	9+3				2			
Nicholas Forster	5.9	11.5	08.09.73	Caterham		Shrewsbury T. (T)								
via Horley Town						Gillingham	54+13	3+2	6		24	2		
				£100,000	17.06.94	Brentford	46	4	2	4+1	24			2
Lee Harvey	5.11	11.7	21.12.66	Harlow	05.12.84	Leyton Orient (A)	135+49	13+3	10+4	19+4	23	3	2	3
E: Y.5.				Free	04.08.93	Nottingham Forest	0+2	0+1						
				Free	18.11.93	Brentford	47+4	5	4	6	2			
Jonathan Hooker	5.7	11.0	31.05.73	London		Hertford Town								
				Trial	07.11.94	Gillingham				1				
				£5,000	14.11.94	Brentford	0+1							
David McGhee	5.10	11.04	19.06.76	Sussex	15.07.94	Brentford (T)	26+8	4	2	1	4			
Joe Omigie	6.2	13.0	13.06.72	Hammersmith		Donna								
					26.08.94	Brentford								
Craig Ravenscroft	5.6	9.7	20.12.74	London	27.07.93	Brentford (T)	5+3			1+2	1			
				Loan	25.11.94	Woking								
Robert Taylor	6.0	11.6	30.04.71	Norwich	26.03.90	Northwich City (T)								
				Loan	28.03.91	Leyton Orient	0+3							
via Birmingham City 31.08.91				Free	21.10.91	Leyton Orient	54+19	1+1	2+1	2+1	20			
				£100,000	24.03.94	Brentford	48	4	2	4	25	1	1	

GRIFFIN PARK

Braemar Road, Brentford, Middx, TW8 0NT
Tel: 0181 847 2511

Capacity...13,800
Covered Standing..6,500
Seating..3,500

First game...v Plymouth Argyle, 1.9.1904.
First floodlit game...v Chelsea, 5.10.1954.

ATTENDANCES
Highest.......................................39,626 v Preston North End, FA Cup 6th Rnd, 5.3.1938.
Lowest..1,110 v Swindon Town, AMC, 6.1.1987.

OTHER GROUNDS..None.

MATCHDAY TICKET PRICES

A Block . . . . £9.80 (Juv/OAP £5)

E Block . . . . £13 (Juv/OAP £10.20)

B Block . . . . £11.50 (Juv/OAP £8.70)

D Block . . . . £14 (Juv/OAP £11.20)

Terraces (Home & away) . . . . £7.80 (Juv/OAP £5)

Away End Seats. . . . . £13 (Juv/OAP £10)

Ticket Office Telephone No. . . . . . . 0181 847 2511.

CLUBCALL
0891 12 11 08

Calls cost 39p per minute cheap rate and 49p per minute at all other times.
Call costings correct at time of going to press.

HOW TO GET TO THE GROUND

From the North:
Use M1 or A1 then A406 North Circular Road to Chiswick then follow signs for the South Circular Road. In 0.3 miles turn right A315 (S.P. Brentford). In 0.5 miles turn right into Ealing Road for Brentford FC.

From the East:
Use either A406 North Circular Road then as above or South Circular Road A205. Cross Kew Bridge and turn left A315 (S.P. Brentford). In 0.5 miles turn right into Ealing Road for Brentford FC.

From the South:
Use A240/A3/M3 or A316 to junction with South Circular Road. A205. Cross Kew Bridge and turn left A315 (S.P. Brentford). In 0.5 miles turn right into Ealing Road for Brentford FC.

From the West:
Use M4 until junction 1, leave Motorway and follow signs for South Circular Road. In 0.3 miles turn right A315 (S.P. Brentford). In 0.5 miles turn right into Ealing Road for Brentford FC. Alternative use M25/M4.

Car Parking: Street parking available.
Nearest Railway Station: Brentford or South Ealing (Tube), Piccadilly Line.

MATCHDAY PROGRAMME

Programme Editor . . . . Eric White.

Number of pages . . . . 40.

Price . . . . £1.50.

Subscriptions . . . . £55.

Local Newspapers. . . . . . Brentford & Chiswick Times, Ealing Gazette,
. . . . Middlesex Chronicle, Hounslow Informer, Weekend Recorder.

Local Radio Stations. . . . . Capital Gold, London Newstalk.

BRIGHTON & HOVE ALBION
(The Seagulls)
ENDSLEIGH LEAGUE DIVISION 2
SPONSORED BY: AKZO SANDTEX

Back Row (L-R): Peter Smith, Stuart Storer, Paul McCarthy, Mark Ormerod, Nicky Rust, Derek Coughlan, Steve Foster, Simon Fox.
Middle Row: George Petchey (Youth Dev. Officer), Gerry Ryan (Asst. Manager), Ross Johnson, John Byrne, Kevin McGarrigle, Mark Fox, John Ryan, Dean Wilkins, Jimmy Case (Coach), Malcolm Stuart (Physio). **Front Row:** Ian Chapman, Stuart Myall, Phillip Andrews, Jeff Minton, Liam Brady (Manager), Junior McDougald, James Virgo, Stuart Munday, Stuart Tuck.

**BRIGHTON & HOVE ALBION
FORMED IN** 1900
TURNED PROFESSIONAL IN 1901
LTD COMPANY IN 1904

PRESIDENT: G A Stanley
CHAIRMAN: W A Archer
DIRECTORS
R A Bloom, B E Clarke, P Kent, D Sizen, D Stanley, G A Stanley, D Sullivan
SECRETARY:
Derek Allan (01273 778 855)

COMMERCIAL MANAGER
D Bellotti (01273 778 855)

MANAGER: Liam Brady
ASSISTANT MANAGER: Gerry Ryan

RESERVE TEAM MANAGER
Jimmy Case
YOUTH TEAM MANAGER
George Petchey
PHYSIOTHERAPIST
Malcolm Stuart

STATISTICIAN FOR THE DIRECTORY
James Millen

By 10th September, Brighton were in a very promising 8th position, seemingly destined for a say in the promotion stakes. Come 1st October, Albion had suffered just two defeats in all competitions, but then things slowly, but surely began to go sour.

Autumn, in the shape of October, began with an away defeat at Huddersfield (3-0). Despite a brilliant performance against Premiership outfit Leicester City in the Coca-cola Cup, (a 3-0 aggregate scoreline certainly did not flatter the Division Two side), Liam Brady's men managed to go nine league games without a win, which pushed them down to a crisis-position of 18th.

The Leicester League Cup success was literally just one light in a very dark tunnel. In the FA Cup, the Seagulls went out sensationally at the first hurdle, away at Diadora League Premier Division Kingstonian, by the odd goal in three. In the Auto Windscreen Shield, Brighton could manage just a 1-1 draw at Gillingham - their 1-0 defeat by Brentford on 19th October meant curtains.

The Coca-Cola tournament began well with two excellent victories over much-fancied Wycombe Wanderers in Round One (2-1 & 3-1). Then came the much-talked -about two-legged success over Leicester at the second stage. In Round Three the Seagulls were paired with Swindon at the Goldstone Ground. Despite going 1-0 down, Brighton fought back well to equalise in the 66th minute, thanks to a Paul McCarthy strike. The replay at the County Ground proved to be a formality for the Wiltshire lads. 2-0 to the good at the interval, Swindon added two more in the second period, with just one reply from Brighton.

Christmas was a relatively fruitful time. Wins over Plymouth on 10th December (3-0), Shrewsbury on 27th (2-1) plus draws at Wycombe (0-0) and Hull (2-2) at least created a degree of optimism as the New Year dawned.

The second day of 1995 was celebrated with a home 2-0 victory over strong opposition, in the shape of Stockport County. However, just one haul of three points was all Albion could muster in the ensuing seven games, and this a 3-0 away drubbing of struggling Bournemouth, two goals here for Jeff Minton.

March, they say comes like a Lion. Three wins in succession with nine goals scored and none conceded, but still Brighton were amongst the also-rans in 15th spot.

Only one defeat between 1st April (at Stockport) and the final day of the season on 6th May was easily enough to prevent the Seagulls from dropping into the relegation area, but just 54 Endsleigh League goals, ten of these from David McDougald, was possibly the root-cause of their inability to challenge the division's leading lights.

GREG TESSER

BRIGHTON & HOVE ALBION

Division Two: 16th **FA Cup:** 1st Round **Coca-Cola Cup:** 3rd Round

M	DATE	COMP.	VEN	OPPONENTS	RESULT	H/T	LP	GOAL SCORERS/GOAL TIMES	ATT.
1	A 13	EL	A	Swansea City	D 1-1	0-1		Nogan 47 (pen)	(4,640)
2	17	CC 1/1	H	Wycombe Wanderers	W 2-1	1-0		McDougald 45, Nogan 90	6,884
3	20	EL	H	Plymouth Argyle	D 1-1	0-0	16	Chamberlain 54	8,309
4	23	CC 1/2	A	Wycombe Wanderers	W 3-1	3-0		Nogan 2, 44, McDougals 26	(5,281)
5	27	EL	A	Wrexham	L 1-2	0-1	17	McDougald 64	(3,339)
6	31	EL	H	York City	W 1-0	0-0	13	Nogan 67 (pen)	(6,996)
7	S 3	EL	H	Leyton Orient	W 1-0	0-0	10	Nogan 88	8,581
8	10	EL	A	Chester	W 2-1	1-0	8	Nogan 1, 59	(2,063)
9	13	EL	A	Blackpool	D 2-2	2-2	9	Bissett 24, Chamberlain 35	(3,438)
10	17	EL	H	Oxford United	D 1-1	1-0	9	Nogan 22	9,970
11	21	CC 2/1	H	Leicester City	W 1-0	0-0		Nogan 77	11,481
12	24	EL	H	Cambridge United	W 2-0	1-0	6	McDougald 38, Nogan 50	8,280
13	27	AWT	A	Gillingham	D 1-1	1-1		McDougald 43	(963)
14	O 1	EL	A	Huddersfield Town	L 0-3	0-1	11		(10,321)
15	5	CC 2/2	A	Leicester City	W 2-0	1-0		Munday 16, Nogan 84	(14,258)
16	8	EL	A	Bradford City	L 1-2	0-1	13	McDougald 65	(6,970)
17	15	EL	H	Birmingham City	L 0-1	0-0	14		11,004
18	19	AWT	H	Brentford	L 0-1	0-0			1,104
19	22	EL	A	Bristol Rovers	L 0-3	0-2	15		(4,107)
20	26	CC 3	H	Swindon Town	D 1-1	0-1		McCarthy 66	11,382
21	29	EL	H	Rotherham United	D 1-1	0-1		Smith 55	6,734
22	N 2	EL	H	AFC Bournemouth	D 0-0	0-0			5,631
23	5	EL	A	Cardiff City	L 0-3	0-0	17		(5,004)
24	9	CC 3R	A	Swindon Town	L 1-4	0-2		Chamberlain 67	(3,815)
25	12	FAC 1	A	Kingstonian	L 1-2	1-1		Codner 33	(3,815)
26	19	EL	H	Peterborough United	L 1-2	1-2	18	Codner 38	6,445
27	26	EL	A	Brentford	L 1-2	1-0	18	Chapman 40	(4,728)
28	D 10	EL	A	Plymouth Argyle	W 3-0	0-0	17	Codner 55, 68, Akinbiyi 70	(6,091)
29	17	EL	H	Swansea City	D 1-1	0-1	18	Codner 59	6,817
30	26	EL	A	Wycombe Wanderers	D 0-0	0-0	17		(7,085)
31	27	EL	H	Shrewsbury Town	W 2-1	0-1	16	McDougald 67, Akinbiyi 74	7,290
32	31	EL	A	Hull City	D 2-2	1-1	17	Minton 12, Akinbiyi 70	(5,099)
33	J 2	EL	H	Stockport County	W 2-0	0-0	16	Minton 58, Akinbiyi 60	8,842
34	14	EL	A	Crewe Alexandra	L 0-4	0-1	17		(4,286)
35	F 4	EL	H	Brentford	D 1-1	0-1		Bates 50 (og)	9,499
36	11	EL	A	AFC Bournemouth	W 3-0	2-0	16	Minton 22, 31, McDougald 49	(5,247)
37	14	EL	H	Bristol Rovers	L 1-2	1-0			5,232
38	18	EL	H	Crewe Alexandra	L 0-1	0-1	1		6,986
39	21	EL	A	Peterborough United	L 1-2	0-1	18	McDougald 74	(3,870)
40	25	EL	H	Huddersfield Town	D 0-0	0-0			7,751
41	M 4	EL	A	Cambridge United	W 2-0	1-0		Chapman 24, Myall 85	(3,856)
42	7	EL	A	Leyton Orient	W 3-0	1-0	16	Minton 18, McDougald 46, M. Fox 83	(2,983)
43	11	EL	H	Wrexham	W 4-0	0-0	15	J. Byrne 59, McCarthy 61, Parris 70, McDougald 76	7,514
44	15	EL	H	Cardiff City	D 0-0	0-0			6,956
45	18	EL	A	York City	L 0-1	0-1			(2,915)
46	22	EL	H	Chester	W 1-0	1-0		McDougald 3	5,979
47	25	EL	A	Oxford United	D 0-0	0-0			(6,725)
48	28	EL	A	Rotherham United	L 3-4	1-3		J. Byrne 18, P. Byrne 51, Myall 54	(2,316)
49	A 1	EL	H	Blackpool	D 1-1	2-2		McCarthy 26, J. Byrne 72	7,157
50	8	EL	H	Hull City	W 1-0	0-0		McDougald 87	6,083
51	15	EL	A	Shrewsbury Town	D 1-1	1-1	16	J. Byrne 32	(3,597)
52	19	EL	H	Wycombe Wanderers	D 1-1	1-0		Parris 34	8,094
53	22	EL	A	Stockport County	L 0-2	0-1			(3,789)
54	29	EL	A	Birmingham City	D 3-3	1-2		Munday 41, Storer 47, Chapman 67	(19,006)
55	M 6	EL	H	Bradford City	W 1-0	0-0		Munday 88	7,701
56									
57									
58									
59									
60									

Best Home League Attendance: 11,004 v Birmingham **Smallest:** 5,232 v Bristol Rovers **Av Home Att:** 7,560

Goal Scorers:

League (54): McDougald 10, Nogan 7 (2 pens), Minton 5, Akinbiyi 4, J. Byrne 4, Chapman 4, Codner 4, Chamberlain 2, McCarthy 2, Munday 2, Myall 2, Parris 2, Bissett, P. Byrne M. Fox, Smith

C/Cola Cup (10): Nogan 5, McDougald 2, Chamberlain, McCarthy, Munday

FA Cup (1): Codner

AW Trophy (1): McDougald

Compared with 1993-94: -168

Rust N.	Munday S	Pates C.	Chapman I.	Foster S.	McCarthy P.	Minton J.	McDougald J.	Nogan K.	Codner R.	Wilkins D.	Funnell S.	Smith P.	Omerod M.	Chamberlain M.	Bissett N.	Case J.	Simmonds D.	Tuck S.	Kerr S.	Andrews P.	Fox M.	Myall S.	Akinbiyi A.	McGarrigle K.	Parris G.	Referee	
1	2	3	4	5	6	7	8	9	10	11		S	S	S												C. Wilkes	1
1	2	3	4*	5	6	7	8	9	10	11		S		14	S											I. Hemley	2
1	2	3	4*	5	6	7	8	9	10	11		S		12	S											P. Foakes	3
1		3		5	6		8	9	10	11•	12	S				7*	2	4	14							P. Alcock	4
1		3		5	6	11	8	9	10			S				7	2	4*	12							A. Dawson	5
1		3		5	6	11*	8	9	10•	12		S				7	2	4	14							M. Bailey	6
1	6	14	5			10*	8	9	12				2	S		7		4	11•	3						D. Orr	7
1		3	11•	5			12	8*		9		10•	2				7	6	4		14					P. Harrison	8
1		3	11	5			8			9		10•	12	2			7	6	4*		14					K. Lupton	9
1	12	3	11	5			8*		9	10	4		2	S		7•	6									G. Pooley	10
1	12	3	11	5			7	8	9	10	4*		2	S			6									P. Durkin	11
1	7		11	5	10	8*	9	S				2	S				6		4	3						P. Vanes	12
1	4*		11	5	S	7	8	9	10			2	S				6			3	12					P. Foakes	13
1	4		11	5			7	8•	9	14		2	S				6	10		3						W. Flood	14
1		14	11	5		7	8	9	10•			2		6			4	3								J. Rushton	15
1	10	3	11•	5		7*	8	9				2	S	12	6	4		14	S							S. Mathieson	16
1	2	14		5			8	9	10	12		7*	6				4•	3								G. Barber	17
1	12	3	11•	5	6	10	8	9				7	2	4*			14			11						I. Hemley	18
1		3	11	5	6	10	8	9	14			4	7•	2			S		S							M. Brandwood	19
1	14	3	11•	5	6	7	8	9	10			4	12	2*			S		S							P. Alcock	20
	7	3	11	5	6		8	9	10			4	14	2•			S									A. D'Urso	21
S	4	5•	14		6	7	8*	9	10			2	12				3	1								M. Pierce	22
1	S	5	11		6	4	8*	9	10			2	7				3	1								J. Holbrook	23
1	14	5	11*		6	4	8	9	10			2	7•				3	S	12							R. Gifford	24
1	14	5	11		6	4	8*	9	10			2	S	7•			3	S	12							S. Dunn	25
1	S		3		6	4	S	9	10	11		2	S				5		12							G. Pooley	26
1	11•		3		6	4		9	10			2	S	S			5				7	8				G. Singh	27
1	S		3		6	4	12	9*	10	11		2	S				5				7	8	14			S. Dunn	28
1	14		3		6	4	S	9	10	11		2	S								7	8				K. Cooper	29
1		3		5	6			12	9	10*		2•	S	14		4					7	8•				G. Barber	30
1	4		3	5	6	10	12	9*		11•		2	S				14				7	8				P. Foakes	31
1		3		5	6	11	5	9	10	S		2	S				4				7	8				E. Wolstenholme	32
1	2		3	5	6	4	8	9	10	11		2	S				12		S		7	8				M. Bailey	33
1	12		11	5	6	10	8		S			2	S	4*			3				7*					R. Furnandiz	34
1		11		5	6	10	8	S				2	S	9*			3		S		7					C. Wilkes	35
1	14	11	5	6	10	8			12			2	S	9*			3		12					4		S. Dunn	36
1	12		3	5	6	10	8		14	11•		2	S	9*							7•			4		P. Foakes	37
1	11		3	5	6	10•	8					2	S								7			4		P. Vanes	38
1	14		3	5	6	10	9					2	S							14	9			4		P. Harrison	39
1		3	5	6	10	9						2	S	S					12		7•		11	4		R. Harris	40
1		3	5	6	10*		9					2	S				S			7		S	11	4		M. Riley	41
1		3	5	6		9						2*	S								12		11	4		A. D'Urso	42
1	2	3	5	6	12	9						14									7•		11	4		G. Pooley	43
1	2*	3	5	6		9						S	S								7•		11	4		M. Pierce	44
1	2	3	5	6		9						14	S								12	7	11	4		I. Cruikshanks	45
1	2	3	5	6		9						S	S								7•		11	4		J. Holbrook	46
1	2	3•	5	6		9						14	S								8	7*	11	4		J. Lloyd	47
1		5	6	10*	9							2	S				3				12	7*	11	4		K. Lynch	48
1		5	6	10	9							2	S	S			3				12	14	11	4		G. Singh	49
1	7•		5	6	10	9						2	S				3				S		11	4		D. Orr	50
1	14		5	6•	10	9						2	S				3		S	14	11	4				E. Parker	51
1	5	3			10	9						2	S				6			S	7		11	4		M. Pierce	52
1	4	3	5		10	9						2	S				6		12	4*	7		11			J. Kirkby	53
1	12	3•	5		10	9						2	S				6					12	11	S		U. Rennie	54
																					14		11	4		S. Dunn	55
44	18	15	38	38	37	37	37	26	21	11		35	12	12	9	2	18	2		4	23	7	16	18		League Appearances	
12	1	2			2	3		2	2	1		3	7			2	5			4	4	4			1	League Sub Appearances	
6	2+1	5	5	4	5	6	6	4+2	3			3	4	2		2				0+1						C/Cola Cup Appearances	
1	0+1	1	1		1	1	1	1				1				1				0+1						FA Cup Appearances	
2	2	0+1			2		1	2	2	1		1			1		2	2		2				0+1		AW Trophy Appearances	

Also Played: Byrne J. 8*(40,44),8(41,42,43,46,48,49,50,51,52,53,54,55), Byrne P. 10(43,44,45,46,47,48),7•(49),7(50), Meade 14(10),S(11),14(12),12(14), Coughlan S(20), Stapleton 12(22), 11(23), Hughes S(44), Fox (45),S(46),12(47), Virgo S(50), Johnson S(53), Storer 7(54), 7(55) Players on Loan: Akinbiyi (Norwich), Byrne P. (Celtic), Kerr (Celtic), Parris (Birmingham)   † = Sent Off

BRIGHTON & H.A.   RECORDS AND STATISTICS

CLUB RECORDS

BIGGEST VICTORIES
League: 9-1 v Newport, Division 3(S), 18.4.1951.
9-1 v Southend, Division 3, 27.11.1965.
F.A. Cup: 12-0 v Shoreham, 1.10.1932.
10-1 v Wisbech, FA Cup Round 1, 13.11.1965.

BIGGEST DEFEATS
League: 0-9 v Middlesbrough, Division 2, 23.8.1958.
League Cup: 0-8 v Northampton, 4th Round replay, 1.11.1966.

MOST POINTS
3 points a win: 84, Division 3, 1987-88.
2 points a win: 65, Division 3(S), 1955-56 & Division 3, 1971-72.

MOST GOALS SCORED
112, Division 3, 1955-56.

RECORD TRANSFER FEE RECEIVED
£900,000 from Liverpool for Mark Lawrenson, August 1981.

RECORD TRANSFER FEE PAID
£500,000 to Manchester United for Andy Ritchie, October 1980.

BEST PERFORMANCES
League: 13th Division 1, 1981-82.
F.A. Cup: Runners-up 1982-83. **League Cup:** 5th Round 1978-79.

HONOURS
Charity Shield Winners 1910. Champions Division 3(S) 1957-58.
Champions Division 4, 1964-65.

LEAGUE CAREER
Original members of Division 3 1920, Div 3(S) 1921, Div 2 1957-58, Div 3 1961-62, Div 4 1962-63, Div 3 1964-65, Div 2 1971-72, Div 3 1972-73, Div 2 1976-77, Div 1 1978-79, Div 2 1982-83, Div 3 1986-87, Div 2 1987-88, Div 3 (now Div 2) 1991-92.

INDIVIDUAL CLUB RECORDS

MOST GOALS IN A SEASON
Peter Ward: 36 goals in 1976-77 (League 32, FA Cup 1, League Cup 3)

MOST GOALS IN A MATCH
6. Arthur Attwood v Shoreham, 12-0, FA Cup, 1.10.1932.

OLDEST PLAYER
Jimmy Case, 40 years 228 days, 2.1.1995.

YOUNGEST PLAYER
Simon Fox, 16 years 238 days v Fulham, Div 2, 23.4.1994.

MOST CAPPED PLAYER
Steve Penney (Northern Ireland) 17.

PREVIOUS MANAGERS

(Since 1945) Charles Webb 1919-47; Tommy Cook 1947; Don Welsh 1947-51; Billy Lane 1951-61; George Curtis 1961-63; Archie Macauley 1963-68; Freddie Goodwin 1968-70; Pat Saward 1970-73; Brian Clough 1973-74; Peter Taylor 1974-76; Alan Mullery 1976-81; MIke Bailey 1981-82; Jimmy Melia 1982-83; Chris Cattlin 1983-86; Alan Mullery 1986-87; Barry Lloyd 1987-93.

ADDITIONAL INFORMATION
PREVIOUS NAMES
Brighton United 1898-1900.
Brighton & Hove Rangers 1900-1901.
PREVIOUS LEAGUES
Southern League.
Club colours: Blue & white striped shirts, blue shorts, white socks.
Change colours: Red shirts with red & white patterned sleaves, white shorts, red stockings with white trim.
Reserves League: Avon Insurance Football Combination Div.1.
Youth: South Eastern Counties League Division Two.

LONGEST LEAGUE RUNS

of undefeated matches:	16 (1930-31)	of league matches w/out a win:	15 (1947-48, 1972-73)
of undefeated home matches:	27 (1975-76)	of undefeated away matches:	9 (1938)
without home win:	10 (1972-73)	without an away win:	21 (1982-83)
of league wins:	9 (1926)	of home wins:	14 (1955-56. 1975-76)
of league defeats:	12 (1972-73)	of away wins:	4 (1926, 1936 twice)

THE MANAGER

LIAM BRADY . . . . appointed December 1993.

PREVIOUS CLUBS
As Manager . . . . Glasgow Celtic.
As Asst.Man/Coach . . . . None.
As a player . . . . Arsenal, Juventus, Sampdoria, Inter Milan, Ascoli, West Ham United.

HONOURS
As a Manager . . . . None.
As a Player . . . . None.

BRIGHTON & HOVE ALBION

PLAYERS NAME Honours	Ht	Wt	Birthdate	Birthplace Transfers	Contract Date	Clubs	League	L/Cup	FA Cup	Other	Lge	L/C	FAC	Oth
G O A L K E E P E R S														
Mark Ormerod	6.0	11.05	05.02.76	Bournemouth	21.07.94	Brighton & H. A. (T)								
Nicholas Rust	6.0	13.1	25.09.74	Cambridge		Arsenal (T)								
E: S.				Free	09.07.93	Brighton & H.A.	92	10	2	4				
D E F E N D E R S														
Ian Chapman	5.8	11.6	31.05.70	Brighton	05.06.87	Brighton & H.A. (T)	229+16	17+1	10+2	8+4	10		2	
E:S.														
Stephen Foster	6.0	14.0	24.09.57	Portsmouth	01.10.75	Portsmouth (A)	101+8	10	8		6		2	
E: 3, u21.1. LC'88.				£150,000	06.07.79	Brighton & H.A.	171+1	13	16		6	2		
				£200,000	03.03.84	Aston Villa	15	2			3			
				£150,000	29.11.84	Luton Town	163	20	27	2	11	1	2	
				£175,000	13.07.89	Oxford United	95	9	5	4	10	2		1
				Free	14.08.92	Brighton & H.A.	107	5	4	3	6			
Paul McCarthy	6.0	13.6	04.08.71	Cork	26.04.89	Brighton & H.A. (T)	147+1	9	9	10	5	1		
Ei: u21.10.														
Kevin McGarrigle	5.11	11.05	21.07.94	Newcastle	21.07.94	Brighton & H.A. (T)	17+1							
Stuart Munday	5.11	10.0	28.09.72	Newham	06.07.90	Brighton & H.A. (T)	72+14	6+1	2+1	6+1	4	1		
Stuart Myall	5.10	13.3	12.11.74	Eastbourne	09.07.93	Brighton & H.A. (T)	42+5	2		2	2			
Peter Smith	6.1	12.7	12.07.69	Stone		Alma Swanley								
				08.08.94	Free	Brighton & H.A.	35+3	4+1	1	1	1			
Stuart Tuck	5.9	10.8	22.07.93	Brighton	09.07.93	Brighton & H.A. (T)	23+11	3	1	3+1				
Ross Yorke-Johnson			01.02.78	Brighton	22.07.94	Brighton & H.A. (T)	1+1			1				
M I D F I E L D														
Mark Fox	5.11	10.11	05.07.57	Basingstoke	21.07.94	Brighton & H.A. (T)	8+13			1	1			
Dean Wilkins	5.8	11.8	12.07.62	Hillingdon	17.05.80	Q.P.R. (A)	1+5	1						
				Free	04.08.83	Brighton & H.A.	2		1					
				Loan	22.03.84	Leyton Orient	10							
						Zwolle								
				Free	28.07.87	Brighton & H.A.	264+11	20	15+1	18	22	3		3
F O R W A R D S														
John Byrne	6.0	12.4	01.02.61	Manchester	31.01.79	York City (A)	167+8	10+2	10+1	1	55	5	3	
Ei: 23. Div.4'84.				£115,000	30.10.84	Q.P.R.	108+18	12+1	7+2	1	30	4	2	
		via Le Havre (Fra) to		£120,000	01.09.90	Brighton & H.A.	47+4	2	2	2+1	14	2	2	
				£225,000	23.10.91	Sunderland	33	2	8		8			
				£250,000	28.10.92	Millwall	12+5				1			
				Loan	25.03.93	Brighton & H.A.	5+2				2			
				£50,000	01.11.93	Oxford United	52+3	4	5	2	17		2	
				Free	24.02.95	Brighton & H.A.	14				4			
David McDougald	5.11	10.12	12.01.75	Texas	12.07.93	Tottenham H. (T)								
E: S.					12.05.94	Brighton & H.A.	37+4	6	1	2	10	2		1
Stuart Storer	5.11	11.8	16.01.67	Rugby	23.08.83	Mansfield Town (T)	0+1							
SVT'89.		free via VS Rugby to		Free	10.01.85	Birmingham City	5+3	1						
P.E. 06.03.87 Everton.				Loan	23.07.87	Wigan Athletic	9+3	4						
				£25,000	24.12.87	Bolton Wanderers	95+28	9+2	7+3	16+5	12		2	1
				£25,000	25.03.93	Exeter City	54	4	3	2	6	1	1	
				£15,000	02.03.95	Brighton & H.A.	2				1			
John Ryan	5.8	11.06	07.12.75	Cork		Cork								
					18.03.94	Brighton & H.A.								
A D D I T I O N A L C O N T R A C T P L A Y E R														
J. Thompson-Minton						Brighton & H.A. (T)								

THE GOLDSTONE GROUND

Newtown Road, Hove, E.Sussex BN3 7DE.
Tel: 01273 739 535

Capacity 18,203
Covered Standing 4,500
Seating 5,110

First game ....v Southampton, 3.9.1898.
First floodlit game ....v Boldklubben Frem, Copenhagen 10.4.61.

ATTENDANCES
Highest ....36,747 v Fulham, Div 2, 27.12.1958.
Lowest ....1,150 v Norwich City, Div 3(S), 2.2.1929.

OTHER GROUNDS..None.

MATCHDAY TICKET PRICES

West Stand £12
Concessions £6

South Stand £9
Concessions. £4.50

Terraces £7
Concessions. £3.50

Ticket Office Telephone no. 01272 778 855

HOW TO GET TO THE GROUND

From the North
Use A23 with Pyecoumbe, then in 2 miles turn right (S.P. Hove). In 1.1 miles bear left into Nevill Road A2023. In 0.9 miles, at cross roads, turn left A27 into Old Shoreham Road for Brighton & Hove Albion.

From the East
From Lewes use A27 to Brighton then follow signs Worthing A27 along Old Shoreham Road for Brighton & Hove Albion.

From West
Use A27 (S.P. Brighton) along Old Shoreham Road for Brighton & Hove Albion.

Car Parking
Available at the Greyhound Stadium (Nevill Road). Limited parking adjacent to ground. Visitors beware - Police tow-away squad on duty on match days.

Nearest Railway Station
Hove (01273 206 755)

CLUBCALL
0898 80 06 09
Calls cost 39p per minute cheap rate and 49p per minute at all other times.
Call costings correct at time of going to press.

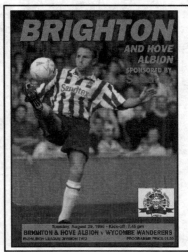

MATCHDAY PROGRAMME

Programme Editor . . . . Tony Millard Associates.

Number of pages . . . . 32.

Price . . . . £1.30.

Subscriptions . . . . . 23 home programmes £30 (saved) + £9 if posted.
. . . . 23 away programmes £28 (saved) + £9 if posted.

Local Newspapers . . . . Evening Argus.

Local Radio Stations . . . BBC Southern Counties Radio, Southern FM.

BRISTOL CITY
(The Robins)
ENDSLEIGH LEAGUE DIVISION 2
SPONSORED BY: AUTO WINDSCREENS

Back Row (L-R): Louis Carey, Rob Edwards, Matthew Hewlett, Vegard Hansen, Keith Welch, Mark Shail, Phil Klte, Jason Fowler, Scott Paterson, Matt Bryant, Alan McLeary. **Middle Row:** Dave Bell (Yth Coach), Tony Fawthrop (Chief Scout), Jim Brennan, Dominic Barclay, Paul Agostino, Mark Humphreys, Wayne Brown, Richard Dryden, Gary Owers, Brian Tinnion, Phil Barber, Mike Gibson (Coach), Buster Footman (Physio), Gerry Sweeney (Coach). **Front Row:** Stuart Munro, Dean Higgins, Junior Bent, Scott Partridge, Joe Jordan (Manager), John Gorman (Asst. Manager), David Seal, Martin Kuhl, Rodney McAree, Ian Baird.

BRISTOL CITY
FORMED IN 1894
TURNED PROFESSIONAL IN 1897
LTD COMPANY IN 1897

CHAIRMAN: David Russe
VICE-CHAIRMAN: Mike Fricker
DIRECTORS
John Clapp, Deryn Coller, Bob Neal,
Gary Williams
CHIEF EXECUTIVE
Michael Martin
SECRETARY
Miss Jean Harrison (01272 632 812)
COMMERCIAL MANAGER
John Cox

MANAGER: Joe Jordan
ASSISTANT MANAGER: John Gorman

PHYSIOTHERAPIST
Buster Footman

STATISTICIANS FOR THE DIRECTORY
David Woods & David Peacey

Last season I suggested that City needed a more reliable spread of goals amongst players and a good start to the campaign. I take no pleasure in being proved partly correct in that assessment and as yet another manager, (Joe Jordan being the club's sixth in seven years), plans for a new season, the side have it all to do again.

Nineteen league games out of forty six without scoring speaks volumes but, in fairness, fourteen league games were lost by the odd goal which offers either some hope or feelings of despair and frustration depending upon your outlook!

So, back to Division Two after five seasons at the higher level and a feeling that the make-up of the side will be much as before. The sale of Martin Scott to Sunderland helped finance the deals that brought the likes of Gary Owers, Martin Kuhl and Richard Dryden in but Joe Jordan's close-season announcement that "...until any sales are made, I am not in a position to sign anyone new" doesn't suggest an immediate impact will be made in Division Two this coming season.

With the City youngsters having a good season in the F.A. Youth Cup there is some light at the end of the tunnel and this may be the way ahead for a club that currently has 24 year old Bristolian Matt Bryant as a seasoned campaigner of some 150 plus league games and several other locally born players are "knocking on the door" of regular first team football. But this takes time and patience to achieve - the latter an attribute that is in short supply amongst some sections of the support at Ashton Gate.

It's a chicken-and-egg type situation, (some might say a vicious circle), - a splendid stadium that requires a successful team to complete the equation. Unfortunately, the one doesn't guarantee the other but every new season offers new hope. An increase in support on last season's average, (7,989 from an average of 11,500 three seasons ago), is vital to generate additional income if immediate transfer monies aren't available but I reckon that it's going to be another long hard season for the supporters, one of consolidation is likely rather than a challenge for the top end of the table.....

DAVE PEACEY.

BRISTOL CITY

Division One: 23rd **FA Cup:** 4th Round **Coca-Cola Cup:** 2nd Round

M	DATE	COMP.	VEN	OPPONENTS	RESULT	H/T	LP	GOAL SCORERS/GOAL TIMES	ATT.
1	A 13	EL	H	Sunderland	D 0-0	0-0			11,127
2	20	EL	A	Bolton Wanderers	W 2-0	1-0	4	Baird 25, Allison 68	(12,127)
3	27	EL	H	Port Vale	D 0-0	0-0	8		8,940
4	30	EL	A	Burnley	D 1-1	0-1	12	Allison 89	(11,067)
5	S 3	EL	A	Charlton Athletic	L 2-3	0-1	16	Allison 58, 70	(9,019)
6	10	EL	H	Notts County	W 2-1	1-1	10	Bent 16, Scott 54 (pen)	6,670
7	13	EL	H	Derby County	L 0-2	0-1	13		8,029
8	17	EL	A	Southend United	L 1-2	0-1	17	Baird 82	(3,663)
9	**20**	**CC 2/1**	**H**	**Notts County**	**L 0-1**	**0-0**			**2,546**
10	24	EL	H	Middlesbrough	L 0-1	0-0	20		8,642
11	**27**	**CC 2/2**	**A**	**Notts County**	**L 0-3**	**0-1**			**(2,721)**
12	O 1	EL	A	Luton Town	W 1-0	0-0	17	Baird 56	(6,633)
13	8	EL	H	Millwall	W 1-0	0-0	13	Baird 56	7,499
14	15	EL	A	Reading	L 0-1	0-0	15		(9,389)
15	22	EL	A	Grimsby Town	L 0-1	0-0	20		(4,025)
16	29	EL	H	Portsmouth	D 1-1	1-0	19	Scott 15 (pen)	7,238
17	N 1	EL	H	Wolverhampton Wand.	L 1-5	1-2	21	Baird 32	10,401
18	5	EL	A	Sheffield United	L 0-3	0-2	22		(11,568)
19	20	EL	H	Swindon Town	W 3-2	0-0	22	Bent 54, Allison 56, 63	9,086
20	26	EL	H	Oldham Athletic	L 0-2	0-0	22		(7,277)
21	D 3	EL	H	Grimsby Town	L 1-2	0-0	23	Partridge 60	6,030
22	7	EL	A	Barnsley	L 1-2	1-1	23	Bent 33	(4,305)
23	10	EL	H	Bolton Wanderers	L 0-1	0-1	23		6,144
24	17	EL	A	Sunderland	L 0-2	0-0	23		(11,661)
25	26	EL	A	West Bromwich A.	L 0-1	0-0	23		(21,071)
26	27	EL	H	Stoke City	W 3-1	0-0	23	Bryant 66, Allison 78,80	8,500
27	31	EL	A	Tranmere Rovers	L 0-2	0-2	23		(7,439)
28	J 2	EL	H	Watford	D 0-0	0-0	23		9,423
29	**7**	**FAC 3**	**H**	**Stoke City**	**D 0-0**	**0-0**			**9,683**
30	14	EL	A	Portsmouth	D 0-0	0-0	23		(8,803)
31	**18**	**FAC 3R**	**A**	**Stoke City**	**W 3-1**	**0-1**		**Bent 71, Baird 93, Tinnion 119**	**(11,579)**
32	21	EL	H	Sheffield United	W 2-1	0-0	23	Gayle 55 (og), Shail 75	10,211
33	**29**	**FAC 4**	**H**	**Everton**	**L 0-1**	**0-0**			**19,816**
34	F 4	EL	H	Barnsley	W 3-2	0-0	22	Dryden 53, Bryant 66, Allison 83	6,408
35	11	EL	A	Wolverhampton Wand.	L 0-2	0-1	22		(25,451)
36	15	EL	A	Swindon Town	W 3-0	1-0	20	Bent 7, Fleck 51, Bryant 57	(9,881)
37	18	EL	H	Oldham Athletic	D 2-2	2-1	20	Allison 8, 34	7,851
38	25	EL	H	Luton Town	D 2-2	0-1	21	Owers 65, Bent 85	7,939
39	M 4	EL	A	Middlesbrough	L 0-3	0-1	21		(17,371)
40	7	EL	H	Charlton Athletic	W 2-1	1-0	20	Kuhl 33, Tinnian 60	6,118
41	11	EL	H	Port Vale	L 1-2	1-1	21	Owers 10	(7,646)
42	18	EL	H	Burnley	D 1-1	1-0	21	Partridge 13	6,717
43	21	EL	A	Notts County	D 1-1	0-0	22	Baird 63	(5,692)
44	25	EL	H	Southend United	D 0-0	0-0	21		6,159
45	A 1	EL	A	Derby County	L 1-3	1-2	21	Allison 41	(14,555)
46	8	EL	H	Tranmere Rovers	L 0-1	0-1	23		6,723
47	15	EL	A	Stoke City	L 1-2	1-1	23	Shail 17	(10,172)
48	17	EL	H	West Bromwich A.	W 1-0	0-0	23	Bent 80	8,777
49	22	EL	A	Watford	L 0-1	0-0	23		(7,190)
50	29	EL	H	Reading	L 1-2	0-1	23	Tinnion 87	9,474
51	M 7	EL	A	Millwall	D 1-1	1-1	23	Allison	(8,805)
52									
53									
54									
55									
56									
57									
58									
59									
60									

Best Home League Attendance: 11,127 v Sunderland	**Smallest:** 6,030 v Grimsby Town	**Av Home Att:** 8,005

Goal Scorers:

League (42): Allison 13, Baird 6, Bent 6, Bryant 3, Owers 2, Partridge 2, Scott 2 (pens), Shail 2, Tinnion 2, Dryden, Fleck, Kuhl, Opponent

Compared with 1993-94: -851

C/Cola Cup (0):
FA Cup (3): Baird, Bent, Tinnion

410

Welch K.	Harriott M.	Scott M.	Shail M.	Bryant M.	Fowler J.	McAree R.	Bent J.	Baird I.	Allison W.	Edwards R.	Partridge S.	Munro S.	Kite P.	Loss C.	Owers	Kuhl	Tinnion B.	Simpson F.	Paterson S.	Jeal D.	Wyatt M.	Humphries M.	Hansen V.	Parris G.	Dryden R.	Referee	
1	2	3	4	5	6	7	8*	9	10	11	14	S	S													P. Alcock	1
1	2	3	4	5	6	7•	8*	9	10	11	14	12	S													Watson	2
1	2	3	4	5	6		8	9*	10•	11	14		S	7												G. Pooley	3
1	2	3	4	5	6		8	9	10	11	14	S	S	7*												D. Lupton	4
1	2	3	4	5	6		8	9	10	11	14	S	S	7*												T. West	5
1	2	3	4	5	6*		8	9*	10	11	7		S	14												J. Brandwood	6
1	2	3	4	5	6•		8	9	10	11	7		S	14												P. Vanes	7
1	2	3	4	5		S	8	9		11	7		S				6	10								M. Pierce	8
1	2	3	4	5		7	8			11	10	S	S	9*			6									P. Wright	9
1	2	3	4	5		7	8	9		11	14	S	S				6*	10								J. Lloyd	10
1		3	4	10	14	7*	8•			11		2					6		5							G. Cain	11
1	2	3	4	5		S	8*	9		11	14	6					10	7								P. Foakes	12
1	2	3	4		7*			9			14	6	8				11	10								J. Rushton	13
1	2		4	5		S		9	7	11	14	6•					10			8*		3				K. Leach	14
1	2		4	5			12	9	7	11	14	6•					10			8*		3				A. Dawson	15
1	2	3•	4	5			7*	9	10	11	8	12					6			14						A. Flood	16
1			4†	5	14		7*	9		11	S	2					6	10		8		3				C. Wilkes	17
1	2*		4	5	6			14	9	11	12			S					10	8•	7	3				B. Burns	18
	2	3		5	7	S	8	9	10	11			1				6						4			P. Wright	19
	2	3	4		7•	12	8	9	10	11			1	S			6						5			K. Breen	20
1		3	4	5	14		8	9	10	11				S			6						S	2		K. Cooper	21
1	2	3	4				8	9	10*	11	14			S			6						5	7		E. Wolstenholme	22
1	2	3	4				8	9	10•	11	14			S			6						5•	7		G. Singh	23
1		3	4				8	9	10•	11		6		S			12						5	7	S	D. Allison	24
1			4	5			8	9	10•			3		S	11		6						2	7	S	T. West	25
	2		4*	5			8	9•				3		S	11		6						2	7	14	P. Vanes	26
1			4	5			8	9	10•			3		S	11	7	6						2		S	P. Richards	27
1			4	5			8	9•	10			3		S	11	7	6			12			2		S	J. Kirby	28
1			4	5			8	9•	10			3		S	11	7	6						2		14	K. Cooper	29
1			4*	5			8	9	10•			3		S	11	7	6						2		14	M. Bailey	30
1			4	5			8	9	10•	14		3		S	11	7*	6						2		S	K. Cooper	31
1			4	5			8	9	10•	7		3		S	11	7	6						2		3	P. Alcock	32
1			4	5*			8	9•	10	7		3		S	11	7	6			12			2		14	T. Holbrook	33
1				5			8	12	10•			3		S	11	7	6						2		4	G. Singh	34
1			4	5			8*	12	10			3		S	11	7	6						2		S	M. Riley	35
1			4	5*			8	12	10			3		S	11	7	6						2		S	J. Lloyd	36
1				5			8	S	10			3		S	11•	7	6			12			2		14	G. Pooley	37
1			4	5*			8	12	10†			3		S	11	7	6						2		4	A. Flood	38
1			4	5*			8	12	10			3		S	11	7	6						2		14	J. Parker	39
1			S	5			8	12	10			3		S	11	7	6						2		4	J. Holbrook	40
1			14	5			8		10			3		S	11	7				12			2*		4	N. Barry	41
1			S	5			8	9				3		S	11	7					12		2		4	M. Pierce	42
1				5			8	9†		7	10	3		S	11		6		S				2		4	P. Harrison	43
1				5			8	9		7	10	3•		S	11		6						2		4	J. Brandwood	44
1			4				8		10			3•		S	11	7	6						2		5	J. Kirkby	45
1			4				8		12			3•		S	11	7	6						2		5	P. Vanes	46
1			4				8	12	10	14		3•		S	11	7	6						2		5	D. Allison	47
1			4				8		10	6•		3		S	11	7				12			2		5	D. Orr	48
1			4				8	9•	10			3		S	11	7						14	2		5	S. Mathieson	49
1			4	8	14			10	11	9•		3		S			6			12			2*		5	P. Wright	50
1			4•					9	10	11	6*	3		S		8							2		5	T. West	51
44	19	18	37	37	10	4	40	28	37	29	14	29	2	3	21	17	33	4	2	5	1	4	29	6	15	League Appearances	
					1			3			9			1	19	2		2		2		2	1	4	2	League Sub Appearances	
2	1	2	2	2	0+1	2	2	1		2	1	1			2		2			1						League Cup Appearances * Subs	
3		3	3			3	2	3	1+1	1+2	3				3	2	3			0+1			3		0+1	FA Cup Appearances * Subs	

Also Played: Brown 12 (3, 11), 14 (9), McKop 12 (6), S (7,8), Rosenior S(19), Brown S(20), Hewlett 14(51), Fleck 9(30*,32,34,35,36,37,38,39*,40*,41*) Martin S(34,43,44,45,46,47), 14(48),7(50),7(51), Flatts 12(44,45),9(46,47,48),6(49) Players on Loan: Simpson (Manchester C.), Parris (Birmingham C.), Watson (Tottenham), Fleck (Chelsea), Flatts (Arsenal)   † = Sent Off

BRISTOL CITY   RECORDS AND STATISTICS

CLUB RECORDS

BIGGEST VICTORIES
League: 9-0 v Aldershot, Division 3(S), 28.12.1946.
F.A. Cup: 11-0 v Chichester City, Round 1, 5.11.1960.
League Cup: 4-0 v Rotherham United, Round 2, 15.9.1970.
4-0 v Peterborough United, Round 3, 2.10.1979.
5-1 v Cardiff City, Round 1 2nd Leg, 25.8.92.
BIGGEST DEFEATS
League: 0-9 v Coventry City, Division 3(S), 28.4.1934.
F.A. Cup: 0-5 v Preston North End, Round 5 replay, 25.2.1935.
0-5 v Brentford, Round 4, 2nd leg, 31.1.1946.
1-6 v Sunderland, Round 4, 25.1.1964.
League Cup: 0-5 v Everton, Round 2, 13.9.1967.
1-6 v West Ham United, Round 2, 2nd leg, 9.10.1984.
1-6 v Sunderland, Round 2, 2nd leg, 8.10.1990.

MOST POINTS
3 points a win: 91, Division 3, 1989-90.
2 points a win: 70, Division 3(S), 1954-55.
MOST GOALS SCORED
104, Division 3(S), 1926-27.
MOST GOALS CONCEDED
97, Division 2, 1959-60.
MOST FIRST CLASS MATCHES IN A SEASON
64 (League 46, FA Cup 6, Lge Cup 9, AMC 3) 1988-89.
MOST LEAGUE WINS
30, Division 2, 1905-06; Division 3(S), 1954-55.
MOST LEAGUE DRAWS
17, Division 2, 1919-20, 1965-66; Division 4, 1982-83.
MOST LEAGUE DEFEATS
26, Division 2, 1959-60.
BEST PERFORMANCES
League: Champions of Division 2, 1905-06.
Highest Position: Runners-up in Division 1, 1906-07.
F.A. Cup: Runners-up in 1908-09.
League Cup: Semi-Finals in 1970-71, 1988-89.
HONOURS
Champions of Division 2, 1905-06.
Champions of Division 3(S), 1922-23, 1926-27, 1954-55.
Welsh Cup 1933-34. Anglo/Scottish Cup 1977-78.
Freight Rover Trophy 1985-86.

LEAGUE CAREER
Div 2 1901-06, Div 1 06-11, Div 2 11-22, Div 3(S) 22-23, Div 2 23-24, Div 3(S) 24-27, Div 2 27-32, Div 3(S) 32-55, Div 2 55-60, Div 3 60-65, Div 2 65-76, Div 1 76-80, Div 2 80-81, Div 3 81-82, Div 4 82-84, Div 3 84-90, Div 2 (now Div 1) 90-95, Div 2 95-

INDIVIDUAL CLUB RECORDS

MOST GOALS IN A SEASON
Don Clark: 41 goals in 1946-47 (League 36, FAC 5).

MOST GOALS IN A MATCH
6. 'Tot' Walsh v Gillingham, Division 3(S), 15.1.1927 (9-4).

OLDEST PLAYER
Terry Cooper, 40 years 86 days, 6.10.1984.

YOUNGEST PLAYER
Nyrere Kelly, 16 years 8 months, 16.10.1982.

MOST CAPPED PLAYER
Billy Wedlock (England) 26.

PREVIOUS MANAGERS
(Since 1945)
Bob Hewison 1945-49; Bob Wright 1949-50; Pat Beasley 1950-58; J Seed/L Bardsley (caretakers) 1958; Peter Doherty 1958-60; Les Bardsley (caretaker) 1960; Fred Ford 1960-67; Les Bardsley (caretaker) 1967; Alan Dicks 1967-80; T Collins/K Wimshurst (caretaker) 1980; Bob Houghton 1980-82; R Hodgson/G Sharpe (caretaker) 1982; Terry Cooper 1982-88; Joe Jordan 1988-90; Jimmy Lumsden 1990-92; Aizle'd/Osman/Shelton (caretakers) 1992; Denis Smith 1992-93; Russell Osman 1993-94.
ADDITIONAL INFORMATION
PREVIOUS NAMES
Bristol South End 1894-97.
PREVIOUS LEAGUES
Southern League 1897-1901.
Club colours: Red shirts, white shorts, red and white socks.
Change Colours:
Reserves League: The Avon Insurance Football Combination.
Youth League: South East Counties League.

LONGEST LEAGUE RUNS

of undefeated matches:	24 (9.9.1905 -10.2.1906)	of league matches w/out a win:	15 (29.4.1933 - 4.11.1933)
of undefeated home matches:	25 (24.10.1953 - 27.11.1954)	of undefeated away matches:	21 (16.9.1905 - 22.9.1906)
without home win:	10 (17.10.1931 - 5.3.1932)	without an away win:	23 (8.10.1932 - 28.10.1933)
of league wins:	14 (9.9.1905 - 2.12.1905)	of home wins:	12 (24.4.1926 - 29.1.1927)
of league defeats:	7 (5.9.1931- 3.10.1931 & 3.10.1970 - 7.11.71)	of away wins:	6 (16.9.1905 - 25.11.1905)

THE MANAGER

JOE JORDAN . . . . appointed November 1994.

PREVIOUS CLUBS
As Manager . . . . Bristol City, Hearts, Stoke City.
As Asst.Man/Coach . . . . Bristol City.
As a player . . . . Morton, Leeds United, Manchester United, AC Milan, Verona, Southampton, Bristol City.

HONOURS
As a Manager . . . . Division Three runners-up 1989-90.
As a Player . . . . Leeds United: Division 1 Champions 1974.
International Career . . . . 52 full caps and 1 U23 cap for Scotland.

BRISTOL CITY

PLAYERS NAME / Honours	Ht	Wt	Birthdate	Birthplace / Transfers	Contract Date	Clubs	League	L/Cup	FA Cup	Other	Lge	L/C	FAC	Oth
G O A L K E E P E R S														
Phillip Kite	6.1	14.7	26.10.62	Bristol	31.10.80	Bristol Rovers (A)	96	12	8	2				
E: Y.5, S.				£50,000	16.08.84	Southampton	4			1				
Loan 27.03.86 Middlesbrough 2 Lge App.				Free	07.02.87	Gillingham	70	5	4	10				
				£20,000	16.08.89	Bournemouth	7	1						
				£25,000	10.08.90	Sheffield United	11	5	1	1				
Loan 21.11.91 Mansfield 11 Lge, 1 Oth. App.				Loan	09.09.92	Plymouth Argyle	2							
Loan 24.10.92 Rotherham Utd 1 Lge App.				Loan	27.11.92	Crewe Alexandra	5		1	2				
Loan 25.03.93 Stockport C. 5 Lge App.				Free	01.07.93	Cardiff City	17+1	2	0+1	2				
				Free	11.08.94	Bristol City	2							
Keith Welch	6.2	12.5	03.10.68	Bolton		Bolton W. (T)								
				Free	03.03.87	Rochdale	205	12	10	12				
				£200,000	25.07.91	Bristol City	160	10	9	8				
D E F E N D E R S														
Matthew Bryant	6.1	12.4	21.09.70	Bristol	01.07.89	Bristol City (T)	170+1	7	10	6	7			
				Loan	24.08.90	Walsall	13	4						
Richard Dryden	6.0	12.0	14.06.69	Stroud	14.07.87	Bristol Rovers (T)	12+1	2+1	0+2	2				
Div.4'90.				Loan	22.09.88	Exeter City	6							
					08.03.89	Exeter City	86	7	2	4	13	2		
Loan 18.11.92 Plymouth Argyle 5 Lge, 1 Oth App.				£250,000	09.08.91	Notts County	30+1	1+1	2+1	2	1			
				£165,000	19.03.93	Birmingham City	45	4	1					
				£200,000	16.12.94	Bristol City	15+4		0+1	1				
Vergard Hansen	6.1	12.12	08.08.69	Dramen		Stromsgodset (Norway)								
					18.11.94	Bristol City	29		3					
Mark Humphries	5.11	12.0	23.12.71	Glasgow		Cove Rangers								
				Free		Aberdeen	2							
via Free 24.05.93 Leeds United					05.10.94	Bristol City	4							
Rodney McAree	5.7	10.9	19.08.74	Dungannon	21.08.91	Liverpool (T)								
NI: Y.				Free	26.07.94	Bristol City	4+2	2						
Henry McKop	5.11	12.0	08.07.67	Zimbabwe		Bonner SC								
Zimbabwe Int.					02.02.94	Bristol City	2+4							
Alan McLeary	5.10	10.9	06.10.64	Lambeth	12.10.81	Millwall (A)	289+18	16+1	24+1	22+1	5		2	2
E: B.2, u21.1, Y.6. FLT'83. Div.2'88.				Loan	23.07.92	Sheffield United	3							
Loan 16.10.92 Wimbledon 4 Lge, 2 LC App.				Free	27.05.93	Charlton Athletic	44	2	5	3	2			
				Free	08.95	Bristol City								
Stuart Munro	5.8	10.5	15.09.62	Falkirk		St. Mirren	1							
SPD'87'89'90'91. SLC'87'88'91.						Alloa	58+2	14	2		5	1	1	
						Glasgow Rangers	173+6	21+1	13+2	19+1	3			
				£350,000	12.08.91	Blackburn Rovers	1							
				Free	04.02.93	Bristol City	88+3	3	8	1				1
Mark Shail	6.1	13.03	15.10.66	Sweden		Worcester City			2					
ESP.1.				£5,000		Yeovil Town			8					
				£45,000	25.03.93	Bristol City	75+3	4	8	1	4		1	
Mark Tinnion	5.11	11.5	23.02.68	Stanley	26.02.86	Newcastle Utd (A)	30+2	5		1+1	2			
				£150,000	09.03.89	Bradford City	137+8	12	9	7+1	22	1	4	2
				£180,000	23.03.93	Bristol City	84+3	4	8		9		3	
M I D F I E L D														
Jim Brennan	5.9	11.06	08.05.77	Canada		Sora Lazio								
				Free	05.10.94	Bristol City								
Robert Edwards	6.0	11.10	01.07.73	Kendal	10.04.90	Carlisle United (T)	48	4	1	2+1	5			
W: B.2, u21.9, Y.				£135,000	27.03.91	Bristol City	86+20	6+1	8+1	5+1	3	1		1
Jason Fowler	6.0	11.12	20.08.74	Bristol	08.07.93	Bristol City (T)	10+5	0+1		1+1				
Matthew Hewlett	6.2	10.11	25.02.76	Bristol	12.08.93	Bristol City (T)	11+2	2						
E: Y.				Loan	30.12.94	Bath City								
Martin Kuhl	5.11	11.13	10.01.65	Frimley	13.01.83	Birmingham City (A)	103+8	13	8	1+1	5		1	1
					20.03.87	Sheffield United	38	2	1	1	4			
via 19.02.88 Watford 4 Lge App.				£125,000	30.09.88	Portsmouth	146+11	11	13	3	27	1		
				£650,000	26.09.92	Derby County	59	5	6	2	1			1
Loan 09.09.94 Notts County 2 Lge App.				£330,000	30.12.94	Bristol City	17		2		1			
Gary Owers	5.11	11.10	03.10.68	Newcastle	08.10.86	Sunderland (A)	241+8	25+1	10+2	11+1	24	1		1
Div.3'88. FLgXI.1.				£300,000	23.12.94	Bristol City	21		3		2			
Scott Patterson	5.11	11.9	13.05.72	Aberdeen		Cove Rangers			1+1					
				£15,000	19.03.92	Liverpool								
				Free	04.07.94	Bristol City	2+1	1						
F O R W A R D S														
Ian Baird	6.0	12.9	01.04.64	Rotherham	05.04.82	Southampton (A)	20+2	1+1			5			
E: S. Div.2'90.				Loan	01.11.80	Cardiff City	12				8			
Loan 01.12.86 Newcastle U. 4+1 Lge App. 1 gl.				£75,000	10.03.85	Leeds United	84+1	4	5	4	33		4	
				£285,000	12.08.87	Portsmouth	20	1	1		1			
				£120,000	04.03.88	Leeds United	76+1	5	3	6	17	1	2	
				£500,000	29.01.90	Middlesbrough	60+3	5+1	3	4	19		1	1
				£400,000	31.07.91	Hearts	64	5	7	3	15	2	1	1
				£295,000	06.07.93	Bristol City	44+12	3	2	1	11		1	
Phillip A Barber	5.11	12.6	10.06.65	Tring		Aylesbury								
				£7,500	14.02.84	Crystal Palace	207+27	13+6	14	19+2	35	3	1	2
				£100,000	25.07.91	Millwall	104+6	7	2	2+1	12			
				Loan	23.12.94	Plymouth Argyle	4		1					
				Free	08.95	Bristol City								
Junior Bent	5.5	10.6	01.03.70	Huddersfield	09.12.87	Huddersfield T. (T)	25+11	1	3+1	4	6		1	
				Loan	30.11.89	Burnley	2				3			
				£30,000	22.03.90	Bristol City	92+27	5+1	9+3	2+2	15		2	
				Loan	26.03.92	Stoke City	1							
Scott Partridge	5.9	10.09	13.10.74	Grimsby	10.07.92	Bradford City	0+5	1						
				Free	01.08.85	Bristol City	21+21	2+1	1+2		6			
David Seal	5.11	12.4	26.01.72	Sydney (Aust)		Eendracht Aalst (Belg)								
				£80,000	05.10.94	Bristol City	5+4		0+1					
A D D I T I O N A L C O N T R A C T P L A Y E R														
Paul Agostino						Young Boys of Berns								
				£50,000	08.95	Bristol City								

ASHTON GATE
Bristol BS3 2EJ
Tel: 01272 632 812

Capacity ....20,832.

First game ....v Bolton W. 3.9.1904.
First floodlit game...v Wolves 27.1.1953.

ATTENDANCES
Highest..43,335 v P.N.E. FA Cup 5th Rnd, 16.2.1935.
N.B. Over 50,000 were judged to be in the ground on 30.1.1935 for the FA Cup 4th Rnd replay v Portsmouth, when the gates were rushed and the crowd broke in. Official paid attendance was given as 42,885.
Lowest...1,515 v Oxford United, Anglo Italian Cup, 7.9.1993.

OTHER GROUNDS ....St John's Lane 1894-1904.

MATCHDAY TICKET PRICES

Atyeo Stand £8.50
Concessions £5

Dolman & Williams Stands £11
Concessions £7.50

Additional Information
Wheelchairs free, helper pays £8.50.

Ticket Office Telephone No. . . . . 01272 632 812.

CLUBCALL
0898 12 11 76

Calls cost 39p per minute cheap rate and 49p per minute at all other times.
Call costings correct at time of going to press.

HOW TO GET TO THE GROUND

From the North and West
Use motorway (M5) until junction 16. Leave motorway and follow signs to Bristol (A38). Follow signs to City Centre then follow signs to Taunton (A38). In 1.2 miles cross Cumberland Basin swing bridge, then branch left into Winterstoke Road for Bristol City FC.

From the East
Use motorway (M4), then M32 and follow signs to the City Centre, then follow signs to Taunton A38. In 1.2 miles cross Cumberland Basin swing bridge, then branch left into Winterstoke Road for Bristol City FC.

From the South
Use motorway (M5) until junction 18. Leave motorway and follow signs to Bristol (A4) along Portway then turn right and follow signs to Taunton over Cumberland Basin swing bridge, then branch left into Winterstoke Road for Bristol City FC. To use the Bristol City FC park and ride scheme follow AA signs to 'Bristol City car park', which is in Anchor Road.

Car Parking
Winterstoke Road car park £60. Wills £50. There is limited street parking around ground.
Nearest Railway Station
Temple Meads (01272 294 255).

MATCHDAY PROGRAMME

Programme Editor . . . . Paper Plane.

Number of pages . . . . 24.

Price . . . . £1.30.

Subscriptions . . . . £40 (home), £45 (away), £85 all programmes).

Local Newspapers . . . . Bristol Evening Post, Western Daily Press,
. . . . Sunday Independent.

Local Radio Stations. Radio Bristol, GWR/Brunel Radio, Galaxy Radio.

BRISTOL ROVERS
(The Pirates)
ENDSLEIGH LEAGUE DIVISION 2
SPONSORED BY: ELITE HAMPERS LTD

Back Row (L-R): Mike Wyatt, Billy Clark, Gareth Taylor, Shane Higgs, Brian Parkin, Andy Collett, Justin Skinner, Ian McLean, Ian Wright.
2nd Row: Lee Archer, Dave Pritchard, Marcus Stewart, Andy Tillson, Marcus Browning, Paul Miller, Worrell Sterling, Justin Channing.
3rd Row: Roy Dolling (Youth Dev. Manager), Ray Kendall (Kit Manager), Tony Gill (Youth Team Manager), John Ward (Manager), Steve Cross (Assistant Manager), Terry Connor (Reserve Team Manager), Keith James (Physio).
Front Row: Andy Gorney, John French, Matthew Hayfield, Mike Davis, Martin Paul, Paul Tovey, Tom White, Lee Maddison.

BRISTOL ROVERS
FORMED IN 1883
TURNED PROFESSIONAL IN 1897
LTD COMPANY IN 1896

PRESIDENT: Marquis of Worcester
CHAIRMAN: Denis M H Dunford
DIRECTORS
R Craig, G H M Dunford, V B Stokes,
R Andrews
SECRETARY
Ian Wilson
COMMERCIAL MANAGER
Graham Bolden (0117 986 9999)

MANAGER: John Ward
ASSISTANT MANAGER: Steve Cross
RESERVE TEAM MANAGER
Terry Connor
YOUTH TEAM MANAGER
Tony Gill
PHYSIOTHERAPIST
Keith James

STATISTICIAN FOR THE DIRECTORY
Mike Jay

The sale of last season's leading goalscorer John Taylor to second division rivals Bradford City, cast a shadow over the early part of the season. Taylor's replacement, Paul Miller, a £100,000 signing from Wimbledon, took a few matches to become accepted, but his striking partner, Marcus Stewart, finally proved what a valuable asset and consistent goalscorer he could be.

Stewart's absence due to injuries for two fairly lengthy spells ensured an opportunity for Gareth Taylor. The Welsh Under-21 player converted from a central defender to a targetman certainly improved Rovers attacking options. His power in the air and physical aggression was evident, while his goalscoring contribution was particularly useful.

Rovers had the previous season relied too much on his namesake, John Taylor. Rovers strong defence with goalkeeper Brian Parkin fully supported by David Pritchard, Billy Clark, Andy Tillson (player of the season) and Andy Gurney were assured. An impressive home record in the league (they were eliminated from both major Cups, FA and Coca-Cola by first division opponents) was unbeaten until 1st March, when Hull City went away from Twerton Park with maximum points. That was in fact the only home league defeat. Rovers put together an impressive 12 match unbeaten spell in the last quarter of the season to clinch a play-off place.

Good defending and a consistent spell of goalscoring ensured this. Only 40 goals were conceded and Stewart, Miller and Taylor contributed 42 goals of the 68 scored in the League. During the season the impressive Marcus Stewart managed to break a 39 year club goalscoring record of scoring in nine consecutive matches and then inexplicably went a further ten matches before scoring again, a vital winner at Cardiff City to secure a play-off place.

The final at Wembley, before a Division Two record crowd of over 59,000, resulted in a 2-1 defeat by Huddersfield, which on the balance of play was a major disappointment for over 33,000 Rovers fans. However, manager John Ward and his assistant, Dennis Booth, are to be congratulated on their achievements in organising and improving a squad of talented players on very limited resources.

With the relegation of Plymouth Argyle, Rovers can now claim a unique record of never having played in either the top or bottom divisions of the football league.

MIKE JAY.

BRISTOL ROVERS

Division Two: 4th **FA Cup:** 3rd Round **Coca-Cola Cup:** 1st Round

M	DATE	COMP.	VEN	OPPONENTS	RESULT	H/T	LP	GOAL SCORERS/GOAL TIMES	ATT.
1	A 13	EL	A	Peterborough United	D 0-0	0-0	13		(5,695)
2	17	CC 1/1	H	Port Vale	L 1-3	1-0		Tilson 39	3,307
3	20	EL	H	York City	W 3-1	1-1	8	Clark 30, Miller 48, Stewart 55	3,597
4	23	CC 1/2	A	Port Vale	D 1-1	0-1		Stewart 85,	(14,728)
5	27	EL	A	Wycombe Wanderers	D 0-0	0-0	11		(5,895)
6	31	EL	H	Blackpool	D 0-0	0-0			3,762
7	S 3	EL	H	Stockport County	D 2-2	2-1	13	Tilson 23, Archer 44	4,263
8	10	EL	A	Rotherham United	W 3-0	3-0	12	Miller 2, 34, Wilder 24 (og)	(2,596)
9	13	EL	A	Swansea City	D 0-0	0-0			(3,226)
10	17	EL	H	Wrexham	W 4-2	1-0	6	Clark 2, 87, Taylor 66, Miller 89	4,441
11	24	EL	A	Shrewsbury Town	L 0-1	0-1	11		(4,596)
12	S 27	AWT S1	A	Oxford United	D 2-2	0-1		Skinner 60 (pen), Clark 62	(1,518)
13	O 1	EL	H	Crewe Alexandra	D 2-2	0-2	12	Taylor 64, 85	4,862
14	8	EL	A	Brentford	L 0-3	0-2	15		(5,330)
15	15	EL	H	Cardiff City	D 2-2	0-1	13	Clark 67, Channing 79	3,936
16	O 19	AWT S1	H	Bournemouth	D 1-1	0-0		Steward 70 (pen)	1,728
17	22	EL	H	Brighton & H.A.	W 3-0	1-0	12	Stewart 7, Miller 25, 88	4,107
18	29	EL	A	Birmingham City	L 0-2	0-2	12		(15,886)
19	N 1	EL	A	Cambridge United	D 0-0	1-1	12	Tilson 67	(2,328)
20	5	EL	A	Bradford City	W 4-0	2-0	12	Stewart 20, 66, Oliver 21 (og), Browning 79	4,247
21	12	FAC 1	A	Bath City	W 5-0	1-0		Stewart 18, Miller 61,73,79,84	(6,751)
22	19	EL	A	Hull City	W 2-0	1-0	10	Stewart 37, 84	(4,450)
23	26	EL	H	Huddersfield Town	D 1-1	1-1	12	Miller 7	5,679
24	D 3	FAC 2	A	Leyton Orient	W 2-0	1-0		Stewart 20, 88	(5,071)
25	10	EL	A	York City	W 3-0	1-0	9	Skinner 6, Stewart 69, 86	(3,094)
26	17	EL	A	Peterborough United	W 3-1	0-1	7	Stewart 55 (pen), 72, Gurney 75	4,635
27	26	EL	H	Bournemouth AFC	W 2-1	1-0		Miller 37, Stewart 69	6,913
28	31	EL	H	Chester City	W 3-0	2-0		Archer 14, 70, Stewart 21	5,629
29	J 7	FAC 3	A	Luton Town	D 1-1	1-1	8	Stewart 20	(7,571)
30	14	EL	H	Oxford United	W 3-2	0-2	8	Taylor 73, Miller 78, Stewart 80	5,875
31	18	FAC 3R	H	Luton Town	L 0-1	0-0			8,218
32	F 4	EL	A	Huddersfield Town	D 1-1	1-1	9	Sterling 31	(10,389)
33	7	EL	A	Bradford City	L 1-2	0-1	9	Heggs 56	(4,243)
34	14	EL	A	Brighton & H.A.	W 2-1	0-1	9	Stewart 63, Archer 81	(5,316)
35	18	EL	A	Oxford United	D 0-0	0-0	8		(6,349)
36	25	EL	A	Crewe Alexandra	L 1-2	0-2	11	Miller 73	(4,222)
37	M 1	EL	H	Hull City	L 0-2	0-1			3,707
38	4	EL	H	Shrewsbury Town	W 4-0	1-0	10	Taylor 10, Archer 51, Browning 85, Miller 88	4,338
39	7	EL	A	Stock Port County	L 1-2	1-1	9	Miller 8	(3,580)
40	11	EL	H	Wycombe Wanderers	W 1-0	1-0	11	Taylor 2	5,118
41	15	EL	A	Cambridge United	W 2-1	2-1		Miller 16, Taylor 45	3,734
42	18	EL	A	Blackpool	W 2-0	0-0	6	Miller 57, Skinner 62	(4,484)
43	22	EL	H	Rotherham United	W 2-0	0-0		Taylor 77, Clark 86	4,420
44	25	EL	H	Wrexham	D 1-1	1-0	5	Archer 45	(3,170)
45	29	EL	H	Birmingham City	D 1-1	1-0		Whyte 44 (og)	8,010
46	A 1	EL	H	Swansea City	W 1-0	0-0	4	Taylor 64	7,062
47	4	EL	A	Plymouth Argyle	D 1-1	0-1		Miller 60	(6,743)
48	8	EL	A	Chester City	D 0-0	0-0	4		(2,241)
49	11	EL	A	Leyton Orient	W 2-1	0-0		Miller 44, Channing 65	(2,338)
50	15	EL	H	Plymouth Argyle	W 2-0	0-0	4	Taylor 51, Wright 65	7,068
51	18	EL	A	Bournemouth	L 0-2	0-1			(7,020)
52	22	EL	H	Leyton Orient	W 1-0	0-0	4	Clark 90	4,838
53	29	EL	A	Cardiff City	W 1-0	0-0	4	Stewart 87	(5,462)
54	M 6	EL	H	Brentford	D 2-2	1-0	4	Taylor 16, 86	8,501
55	14	PO	H	Crewe Alexandra	D 0-0	0-0			8,538
56	17	PO	A	Crewe Alexandra	D 1-1	0-0		Miller 106 (Bristol Rovers won away goals rule)	6,578
57	28	PO F	N	Huddersfield Town	L 1-2	1-1		Stewart 45	(59,175)
58									
59									
60									

Best Home League Attendance: 8,501 v Brentford **Smallest:** 3,597 v York City **Av Home Att:** 5,162

Goal Scorers:

League (70): Miller 16, Stewart 15, Taylor 12, Archer 6, Clark 5, Opponents 3, Browning 2, Channing 2, Skinner 2, Tilson 2, Guerney, Heggs, Skinner, Sterling, Wright **Compared with 1993-94:** -126

C/Cola Cup (2): Stewart, Tilson

FA Cup (8): Miller 4, Stewart 4

AW Trophy (3): Clark, Skinner, Stewart

Parkin	Pritchard	Maddison	Channing	Clark	Tillson	Sterling	Stewart	Paul	Skinner	Archer	Browning	Taylor	Law	Miller	Guerney	Wright	Towey	Davis	Higgs	McLean	Collett	Ward	Hardyman	Heggs	White	Referee	#
1	2	3	4	5	6	7	8*	9	10	11•	12	14	S													K. Breen	1
1	2	3	4	5	6	7	8		10	11	S	S	9													G. Singh	2
1	2		4	5	6	7	8		10	11*	12		S	9	3	S										G. Pooley	3
1	2		4*	5	6	7	8		10	11	12		S	9	3											T. Lunt	4
1	2		4	5	6	7	8*		10	11•	14	12	S	9	3											P. Foakes	5
1	2		4	5	6	7				11	S	10	S	9	3	S										M. Pierce	6
1	2		4	5	6	7		S	10*	11	12	9	S	8	3											P. Alcock	7
1	2		4	5	6	7		12	10	11		9*	S	8	3	S										J. Watson	8
1	2		4	5	6†	7	S		10	11	S	9	S	8	3	1	2									J. Holbrook	9
1	2		4	5	6	7		S	10	11	S	9	S	8	3											I. Hemley	10
1	2		4*	5	6	7			10	11	14	9•	S	8	3	12										S. Mathieson	11
1	2	14	4	5		7			10*	11	12	9	S	8•	3	6										M. Bailey	12
	2	12	4	5	6	7	8•		10	11	9		1	3*	6			14	S							M. Pierce	13
	2	3	4	5*	6	7			10•	11	8	9	1	14				S	12							E. Parker	14
	2		4	5	6	7	9		10		11	12	8*	3				S	1								M. Brandwood	15
			4	5	6	7	9*		10•	14	11	12	8	3				1	2								P. Harrison	16
	2		4	5	6	7	9*		10	S	11	S	8	3				1								T. Heilbron	17
S	2		4	5	6	7	9		10	12	11	14	8•	3				1								R. Harris	18
1	2		4*	5	6	7	9		10	12	11	S	8	3												M. Brandwood	19
1	2		4*	5	6	7	9	14	10•	12	11	9	S	3												K. Lynch	20
1	2			5	6	7	9	S	10	11	4	12	8*	3												J. Rushton	21
1	2			5	6	7	9		10	11*	4	S	8	3						12						G. Poll	22
1	2			5	6	7	9		10	11*	4	S	8	3						12						P. Wright	23
1			4	5		7	9		10	11*	6	S	8	3	2					12						C. Wilkes	24
1				5		7	9		10	11*	4	12	8	3	2*					12						K. Leach	25
1	2*			5	6	7	9		10	11	4	14	8•	3								12				G. Singh	26
1	S	4		5	6	7	9		10	11		12	8*	3								2				P. Rejer	27
1				5	6	7	9•	12		11	10	12	8	3								2*				G. Cain	28
1	2*			5	6	7				11	10	9	8	3		S	S					12				P. Rejer	29
1	2		4		6	7			10	S	11	12	8	3		S							9*			J. Watson	30
1	2		4		6	7			10	S	11	S	8	3		S						9	5		K. Breen	31
1	2		4		6	7	9*			11	10	14	8*	3		S						12	5		P. Foakes	32
1	2		4		6	7	9•			11	10	12	8*	3		S						14	5		D. Orr	33
1	2		4		6	7	9•			11	10*	8	14	3		S						12	5		J. Parker	34
1	2		4*	5	6	7	9		10	12	11		8	3		S									A. D'Urso	35
1	2		S	5	6	7			10	11	4	9	8	3		S						S			W. Flood	36
1	2		12	5	6	7			10	11	4	9*	8	3	S	S									J. Winter	37
1	2			5	6	7			10	11	4	9	8	3	S	S									R. Harris	38
1	2		12	5	6	7			10	11*	4	9	8	3	S	S									E. Wolstenholme	39
1	2	S	12	5	6	7			10	11*	4	9	8	3											M. Riley	40
1	2	3	12	5	6	7			10	11*	4	9	8		S	S									M. Bailey	41
1	2	3	12	5	6	7			10	11	4	9*	8	S						S					U. Rennie	42
1	2	3	4	5	6	7			10	11		12	8	S						S					D. Alcock	43
1	2	3	4	5	6	7	9•		10*	11	14	12	8						S						P. Vanes	44
1	2	3	4	5	6	7	9			11	10	S	8	S					S						P. Rejer	45
1	2	3	4	5	6	7	9			11•	10*	12	8	14					S						N. Barry	46
1	2	3	4	5	6*	7	9			12•	10	11	8	14					S						K. Cooper	47
1	2	3	4	5		7	9•		10*	12	14	11	8		6				S						J. Rushton	48
1	2	3*	4	5		7	9		10	12	11		8		6				S						G. Barber	49
1	2		4•	5	6	7	12		10	14	11*	9	8	3					S						P. Wright	50
1	2		4	5	6	7*	9		10	12	14	11•	8	3					S						K. Leach	51
1	2		4*	5	6	7	9•		10	14	12	11	8	3					S						J. Lloyd	52
1	2		12	5	6	7	9*		10	4	S	11	8	3					S						P. Alcock	53
1	2		4•	5	6	7	9		10*	14	12	11	8	3					S						J. Winter	54
40	42	12	35	42	40	46	26	2	38	32	31	23	2	41	35	6					4	1	1	2	4	League Appearances	
		2	5				1	3		10	10	14		1	3	1		1		1			4	3		League Sub Appearances	
2	2		2	2	2	2			2	2	0+1			2	1											C/Cola Cup Appearances + Subs	
4	3		3	4	4	4	3			3	3+1	3	1+1	4	4								0+1			FA Cup Appearances + Subs	

Also Played: Waddock 8(7)

† = sent off

CLUB RECORDS

BIGGEST VICTORIES
League: 7-0 v Swansea City, Division 2, 2.10.1954.
7-0 v Brighton & Hove Albion, Division 3(S), 29.11.1952.
7-0 v Shrewsbury Town, Division 3, 21.3.1964.
F.A. Cup: 6-0 v Merthyr Tydfil, Round 1, 14.11.1987.

BIGGEST DEFEATS
League: 0-12 v Luton Town, Division 3(S), 13.4.1936.
F.A. Cup: 1-8 v Queens Park Rangers, 27.11.1937.

MOST POINTS
3 points a win: 93, Division 3, 1989-90.
2 points a win: 64, Division 3(S), 1952-53.

MOST GOALS SCORED
92, Division 3(S), 1952-53.

RECORD TRANSFER FEE RECEIVED
£1,000,000 from Crystal Palace for Nigel Martyn, November 1989.

RECORD TRANSFER FEE PAID
£370,000 to Queens Park Rangers for Andy Tillson, November 1992.

BEST PERFORMANCES
League: 6th in Division 2, 1955-56, 1958-59.
Highest Position:
F.A. Cup: 6th Round 1950-51, 1957-58.
League Cup: 5th Round, 1970-71, 1971-72.

HONOURS
Division 3 South Cup 1934-35.
Champions of Division 3(S), 1952-53.
Champions of Division 3, 1989-90.

LEAGUE CAREER
Original members of Div 3 1920, Transferred to Div 3 South 1921, Div 2 1952-53, Div 3 1961-62, Div 2 1973-74, Div 3 1980-81, Div 2 (now Div 1) 1989-90, Div 2 1992-93.

INDIVIDUAL CLUB RECORDS

MOST GOALS IN A SEASON
Alfie Biggs: 37 goals in 1963-64 (League 30, FA Cup 1, League Cup 6).

MOST GOALS IN A MATCH
6. Jack Jones v Weymouth, FA Cup, 15-1, 17.11.1900.

OLDEST PLAYER
Jack Evans, 39 years, 9.4.1928.

YOUNGEST PLAYER
Ronnie Dix, 15 years 180 days v Norwich City, 3.3.1928.
(Youngest player to score in the Football League, in his second match).

MOST CAPPED PLAYER
Neil Slatter (Wales) 10, 1983-85.
Geoff Bradford (England) 1, 1955.

PREVIOUS MANAGERS

1899-1920 Alf Homer; 1920-21 Ben Hall; 1921-26 Andrew Wilson; 1926-29 Joe Palmer; 1929-30 David McLean; 1930-36 Albert Prince Cox; 1936-37 Percy Smith; 1938-49 Brough Fletcher; 1950-68 Bert Tann; 1968-69 Fred Ford; 1969-72 Bill Dodgin; 1972-77 Don Megson; 1977-79 Bobby Campbell; 1979-80 Harold Jarman; 1980-81 Terry Cooper; 1981-83 Bobby Gould; 1983-85 David Williams; 1985-87 Bobby Gould, 1987-91 Gerry Francis; 1991 Martin Dobson; 1991-92 Dennis Rofe; 1992-93 Malcolm Allison.

ADDITIONAL INFORMATION
Previous Names: Black Arabs, Eastville Rovers.
Previous Leagues: Southern League.

Club colours: Blue shirts with blue & white quarters & white trim, white shorts, blue socks.
Change colours: Green & white stripes, black shorts, black socks.

Reserves League: Avon Insurance Football Combination.
'A' Team: South East Counties League Div.2.

LONGEST LEAGUE RUNS

of undefeated matches:	32 (1973-74)	of league matches w/out a win:	20 (1980-81)
of undefeated home matches:	34 (1989-90)	of undefeated away matches:	17 (1973-74)
without home win:	10 (1980-81)	without an away win:	23 (1980-81)
of league wins:	12 (1952-53)	of home wins:	10 (1934-35)
of league defeats:	8 (1961-62)	of away wins:	5 (1952-53, 1964)

THE MANAGER

JOHN WARD . . . . appointed March 1993.

PREVIOUS CLUBS
As Manager . . . . York City.
As Asst.Man/Coach . . . . Watford, Aston Villa.
As a player . . . . Lincoln City, Watford, Grimsby Town, Lincoln City.

HONOURS
As a Manager . . . . None.
As a Player . . . . None.

BRISTOL ROVERS

PLAYERS NAME Honours	Ht	Wt	Birthdate	Birthplace Transfers	Contract Date	Clubs	League	L/Cup	FA Cup	Other	Lge	L/C	FAC	Oth
G O A L K E E P E R S														
Andrew A Collett	5.11	11.3	28.10.73	Stockton	06.03.92	Middlesbrough (T)	2			3				
Loan 18.10.94 Bristol Rovers				£10,000	23.03.95	Bristol Rovers	4			1				
Brian Parkin	6.1	12.0	12.10.65	Birkenhead	31.03.83	Oldham Athletic (J)	6	2						
Div3'90				Free	30.11.84	Crewe Alexandra	98	7	2	6				
				Free	01.07.88	Crystal Palace	20	3		2				
				Free	11.11.89	Bristol Rovers	221	11	12	21				
D E F E N D E R S														
Justin Channing	5.10	11.3	19.11.68	Reading	27.08.86	Q.P.R. (A)	42+13	4+1	2	5	5			
E: Y2				£250,000	24.10.92	Bristol Rovers	86+8	3	4	6+1	9			
William Clarke	6.0	12.3	19.05.67	Christchurch	25.09.84	Bournemouth (T)	4							
					16.10.87	Bristol Rovers	171+11	7+1	8+1	13+2	11		1	
Andrew Gurney	5.7	10.7	25.01.74	Bristol	10.07.92	Bristol Rovers (T)	37+4	1	4	7	1			
Matthew Hayfield			08.08.75	Bristol	13.07.94	Bristol Rovers (T)								
Lee Madison	5.11	11.0	05.10.72	Bristol	18.07.91	Bristol Rovers (T)	68+5	4	2	6+1				
				Loan	15.01.93	Bath City								
Ian McLean	6.2	13.2	18.08.66	Paisley	15.09.93	Bristol Rovers	17+11			2+2	2			1
				Loan	09.09.94	Cardiff City								
				Loan	21.12.94	Cardiff City								
David Pritchard	5.7	11.4	27.05.72	Wolverhampton		West Bromwich A.	1+4							
					.08.92	Telford			2					
				£15,000	25.02.94	Bristol Rovers	54	2	3	6				
Gareth Taylor	6.2	12.5	25.02.73	Weston-super-Mare		Southampton (T)								
				Free	29.07.91	Bristol Rovers	24+16	0+1	1+1	5	12			
Andrew Tillson	6.2	12.7	30.06.66	Huntingdon		Kettering Town								
				Free	14.07.88	Grimsby Town	104+1	8	10	5	6			
				£400,000	21.12.90	Q.P.R.	27+2	2		1	2			
				Loan	15.09.92	Grimsby Town	4			1				
				£370,000	07.11.92	Bristol Rovers	81+1	4	5	6	2	1		
Thomas White	5.11	12.02	26.01.76	Bristol	13.07.94	Bristol Rovers (T)	4							
Ian M Wright	6.1	12.4	10.03.72	Lichfield	11.07.90	Stoke City (T)	6	1+1		1				
					23.09.93	Bristol Rovers	35+1		1	4	1			
M I D F I E L D														
Lee Archer	5.6	9.6	06.11.72	Bristol	18.07.91	Bristol Rovers (T)	41+3	3	1	3	6		1	
Justin Skinner	6.0	11.6	30.01.69	Hounslow	17.11.86	Fulham (A)	11+24	10+1	5+1	10+1	23	4		1
				£130,000	27.08.91	Bristol Rovers	118+3	7	7	11+1	9			1
Paul Tovey	5.8	10.9	05.12.73	Wokingham	24.07.92	Bristol Rovers (T)	0+1							
F O R W A R D S														
Marcus Browning	6.1	13.0	22.04.71	Bristol	01.07.89	Bristol Rovers (T)	83+20	1+3	7	6+3	7		1	2
				Loan	18.09.92	Hereford United	7				5			
Michael Davis	6.0	12.0	19.10.74	Bristol		Yate Town								
				Free	26.04.93	Bristol Rovers	2+11			0+1	1			
				Loan	19.08.94	Hereford United								
Paul Miller	6.0	11.0	31.01.68	Woking		Wimbledon								
via Wealdstone and Yeovil Town				to	12.08.87	Wimbledon	65+15	3+3	3	1	11			
Loan Newport C., (20.10.87), 6 Lg Apps +2 Gls.				Loan	11.01.90	Bristol City	0+3			2				
				£100,000	16.08.94	Bristol Rovers	41+1	2	4	6	16		4	2
Martin Paul	5.8	10.8	02.02.75	Lancashire	19.07.93	Bristol Rovers (T)	2+7				2+1			
Worrell Sterling	5.7	10.11	08.06.65	Bethanal Green	10.06.83	Watford (A)		82+12	7+2	18	0+1	14	1	
2														
FAYC'82				£70,000	23.03.89	Peterborough United	190+3	15	14	14	28	3	5	2
				£140,000	29.07.93	Bristol Rovers	89	4	5	9	6	1		
Marcus Stewart	5.10	10.3	07.11.72	Bristol	18.07.91	Bristol Rovers (T)	93+34	7	6+1	9+1	36	1	3	9
E: S														
Michael Wyatt	5.10	11.3	12.09.74	Bristol	07.07.93	Bristol City (T)	11+2	2		1				
				Free	.08.95	Bristol Rovers								

TWERTON PARK

Bath BA2 1DB
Tel: 0117 986 9999

Capacity 8,730
Covered Standing 3,165
Seated...1,026 + 14 disabled

First game..v Reading, League Cup, 1986-87.
First floodlit game ....as above.

ATTENDANCES
Highest ....9,813 v Bristol City, Division 2, 2.5.1990.
Lowest ....1,490 v Ipswich Town, ZDS Cup, 2.10.1991.

OTHER GROUNDS ....Eastville.

MATCHDAY TICKET PRICES

Grandstand £13
Juv/OAP £8.50

Family Stand £10
Juv/OAP £7

Family Enclosure £7
Juv/OAP £4

Terraces. £8
Juv/OAP £4

Visitors Terracing £8
Juv £8

Ticket Office Telephone no. . . . . . . 01225 312 327.
(Matchdays only)

CLUBCALL 0891 66 44 22

Calls cost 39p per minute cheap rate and 49p per
minute at all other times.
Call costings correct at time of going to press.

HOW TO GET TO THE GROUND

From all directions
Use M4 and M5. Leave M5 at junction 18 via A46 to Bath, follow ring
road to Twerton for Bristol Rovers FC.

Car Parking
Restricted to permit holders only, at ground.
Very limited street parking.

Nearest Railway Station
Bath Spa (1mile from ground)

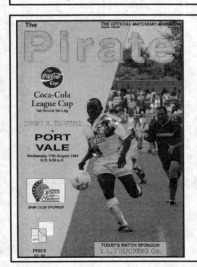

MATCHDAY PROGRAMME

Programme Editor . . . . Phil Tottle.

Number of pages . . . . 32.

Price . . . . £1.30.

Subscriptions . . . . £45.50 (inland), £56 (Europe), £90 (Overseas).

Local Newspapers . . . . Western Daily Press, Bristol Evening Post,
. . . . Bath Evening Chronicle, Sunday Independent,
. . . . Kingswood/North Avon Gazette.

Local Radio Stations . . . . Radio Bristol, GWR Radio.

BURNLEY
(The Clarets)
ENDSLEIGH LEAGUE DIVISION 2
SPONSORED BY: ENDSLEIGH INSURANCE

Back Row (L-R): Ted McMinn, Adrian Randall, Steve Thompson, Nathan Peel, Mark Winstanley, Tony Philliskirk, Peter Swan, John Pender, Glen Davies, Paul Smith. **Middle Row:** Terry Pashley (Yth Coach), Gary Parkinson, Warren Joyce, Alan Harper, Derek Adams, Wayne Dowell, Marlow Beresford, Wayne Russell, Andy Cooke, Kurt Nogan, Matthew Taylor, John Borland, Brian Miller (Chief Scout). **Front Row:** Harry Wilson (Res. Coach), Adrian Heath, Liam Robinson, Chris Brass, David Eyres, Jamie Hoyland, Jimmy Mullen (Manager), Clive Middlemass (Asst. Manager), Chris Vinnicombe, John Francis, Paul Weller, Gerry Harrison, Andy Jones (Physio).

BURNLEY
FORMED IN 1882
TURNED PROFESSIONAL IN 1883
LTD COMPANY IN 1897

CHAIRMAN: F J Teasdale
VICE-CHAIRMAN
Dr R D Iven MRCS(Eng), LRCOP (Lond), MRCGP
DIRECTORS
R B Blakeborough, B Dearing, C Holt
B M Rothwell, JP
SECRETARY
Mark Blackbourne (01282 427 777)
COMMERCIAL MANAGER
Tom Skelly

MANAGER: Jimmy Mullen
ASSISTANT MANAGER: Clive Middlemass
RESERVE TEAM MANAGER
Harry Wilson
YOUTH TEAM MANAGER
Terry Pashley
PHYSIOTHERAPIST
A Jones

STATISTICIAN FOR THE DIRECTORY
Wallace Chadwick

There was a feeling all along that hopes were unrealistically high. For all the euphoria of Wembley, many supporters knew that Burnley's promotion had been their benefit from an unfair system, and that serious team strengthening would be needed if consolidation in the First Division was to be a reality.

There was certainly no shortage of new arrivals...no less than 16 players made their Burnley debuts during the season, and the old incoming transfer record which had stood since 1978 was broken four times over. But there was an emphasis on proven experience which hindered the development of youth, and some of the newcomers' commitment to a club they arrived at relatively late in their careers was questionable to say the least.

The main problem was up front. Countless striking permutations failed to yield a successful blend, David Eyres' golden touch of the previous campaign seemed to have deserted him until too late, and only Paul Shaw, a loan signing from Arsenal who spearheaded the last-ditch escape attempt, really looked capable of finding the target regularly.

The Cup competitions brought some excitement, and in four matches against Liverpool, Burnley were only outplayed once (the Coca-Cola second leg), and then by a Reds team at the peak of their form. The home FA Cup match, a goalless draw, was the one bright spark of a dreadful start to 1995 which saw the club equal its record of eight consecutive League defeats.

Despite the problems, support stayed high. There were the predictable cries for Jimmy Mullen's head long before relegation was confirmed, and some of the criticisms levelled at his team selection, tactics and substitutions were certainly justified in 1994-95. He seems unlikely to go, though, and the real test now will be how he copes with the return to a lower level. The team's average age must be reduced, the striking positions must be resolved, and much may depend on how the likely influx of transfer cash for Steve Davis is spent.

Barring disasters, there is no indication that support for Burnley will diminish, and it is vital that the club realises its responsibility to that support.

WALLACE CHADWICK.

BURNLEY

Division One: 22nd   FA Cup: 4th Round   Coca-Cola Cup: 2nd Round

M	DATE	COMP.	VEN	OPPONENTS	RESULT	H/T	LP	GOAL SCORERS/GOAL TIMES	ATT.
1	A 13	EL	A	Middlesbrough	L 0-2	0-2			23,343
2	16	CC 1/1	H	York City	W 1-0	0-0		Joyce 73	6,390
3	20	EL	H	Stoke City	D 1-1	1-0	20	Davis 42	15,331
4	23	CC 1/2	A	York City	D 2-2	0-1		Robinson 64, Gayle 67	3,089
5	27	EL	A	Oldham Athletic	L 0-3	0-0	23		11,310
6	30	EL	H	Bristol City	D 1-1	1-0	21	Robinson 40	11,067
7	S 3	EL	H	Barnsley	L 0-1	0-0	2		11,968
8	10	EL	A	Luton Town	W 1-0	1-0	22	Robinson 44	6,911
9	14	EL	A	Millwall	W 3-2	0-0	20	Winstanley 52, 69, Robinson 79	7,375
10	17	EL	H	Wolverhampton Wand.	L 0-1	0-0	21		17,766
11	21	CC 2/1	A	Liverpool	L 0-2	0-1			23,359
12	24	EL	A	West Bromwich Albion	L 0-1	0-0	22		13,539
13	O 1	EL	H	Tranmere Rovers	D 1-1	0-1	22	Eyres 80 (pen)	12,427
14	5	CC 2/2	H	Liverpool	L 1-4	0-1		Robinson 84	19,032
15	8	EL	H	Bolton Wanderers	D 2-2	0-1	22	Davis 68, Deary 73	16,687
16	15	EL	A	Sunderland	D 0-0	0-0	22		17,700
17	22	EL	A	Charlton Athletic	W 2-1	0-1	21	Davis 52, Robinson 61	9,436
18	29	EL	H	Notts County	W 2-1	1-0	18	Eyres 7 (pen), Hoyland 52	12,876
19	N 1	EL	H	Watford	D 1-1	0-1	17	Eyres 74	11,739
20	5	EL	A	Reading	D 0-0	0-0	21		8,150
21	12	FAC 1	H	Shrewsbury Town	W 2-1	1-1		Heath 28, Deary 46	9,269
22	20	EL	H	Sheffield United	W 4-2	1-1	15	Robinson 24, Hoyland 54, Gayle 71, Davis 78	11,475
23	23	EL	A	Swindon Town	D 1-1	0-1	15	Gayle 68	7,654
24	26	EL	A	Grimsby Town	D 2-2	0-1	15	Davis 58, Parkinson 90	7,084
25	D 4	FAC 2	A	Chester City	W 2-1	0-0		Eyres 49 (pen), Heath 85	4,231
26	10	EL	A	Stoke City	L 0-2	0-0	18		13,040
27	18	EL	H	Middlesbrough	L 0-3	0-1	20		12,049
28	31	EL	H	Southend United	W 5-1	2-0	19	Saville 27, Gayle 34, Bressington (og), Davis 86, Robinson 90	10,561
29	J 2	EL	A	Portsmouth	L 0-2	0-1	20		9,097
30	7	FAC 3	A	Cambridge United	W 4-2	2-1		Eyres 24 (pen), Robinson 45, Randall 72, Gayle 76	6,275
31	14	EL	A	Notts County	L 0-3	0-0	22		8,702
32	21	EL	H	Reading	L 1-2	0-2	22	Parkinson 56	9,841
33	28	FAC	H	Liverpool	D 0-0	0-0			20,551
34	F 4	EL	H	Swindon Town	L 1-2	0-1	23	Harrison 85	10,960
35	7	FAC 4	A	Liverpool	L 0-1	0-1			32,109
36	11	EL	A	Watford	L 0-2	0-0	23		9,297
37	18	EL	A	Grimsby Town	L 0-2	0-1	23		10,511
38	21	EL	H	Sheffield United	L 0-2	0-1	23		13,349
39	25	EL	A	Tranmere Rovers	L 1-4	0-1	24	Garnett 89 (og)	9,909
40	M 4	EL	H	West Bromwich Albion	D 1-1	0-0	24	Robinson 89	11,885
41	7	EL	A	Barnsley	L 0-2	0-1	24		5,587
42	11	EL	H	Oldham Athletic	W 2-1	1-0	24	Nogan 7, Vinnicombe 75	11,620
43	15	EL	A	Derby County	L 0-4	0-1	24		13,922
44	18	EL	A	Bristol City	D 1-1	0-1	24	Eyres 65	6,717
45	21	EL	H	Luton Town	W 2-1	0-0	23	Mullin 73, Harrison 83	9,551
46	24	EL	A	Wolverhampton Wand.	L 0-2	0-1	23		25,703
47	28	EL	H	Port Vale	W 4-3	1-1	23	Nogan 45, Randall 60, Shaw 64, Sandeman (og) 66	10,058
48	A 1	EL	H	Millwall	L 1-2	0-1	23	Shaw 75	10,454
49	4	EL	H	Charlton Athletic	W 2-0	1-0	21	Eyres 24m Shaw 81	10,045
50	8	EL	A	Southend United	L 1-3	0-2	22	Nogan 82	5,037
51	15	EL	H	Derby County	W 3-1	2-0	22	Eyres 12, Shaw 19, Davis 70	11,534
52	17	EL	A	Port Vale	L 0-1	0-1	22		9,663
53	22	EL	H	Portsmouth	L 1-2	0-1	22	Eyres 81	10,666
54	29	EL	H	Sunderland	D 1-1	1-1	21	Eyres (pen) 36	15,121
55	M 7	EL	A	Bolton W.	D 1-1	0-0	22	Philliskirk 60	16,853
56									
57									
58									
59									
60									

Best Home League Attendance: 17,766 v Wolves   **Smallest:** 9,551 v Luton Town   **Av Home Att:** 12,008

Goal Scorers: Compared with 1993-94: +679

League (49): Eyres 8, Davis 7, Robinson 7, Shaw 4, Gayle 3, Nogan 3, Opponents 3, Harrison 2, Hoyland 2, Parkinson 2, Winstanley 2, Deary, Mullin, Philliskirk, Randall, Saville, Vinnicombe

C/Cola Cup (4): Robinson 2, Gayle, Joyce

FA Cup (8): Eyres 2, Heath 2, Deary, Gayle, Randall, Robinson

Beresford	Parkinson	Vinnicombe	Davis	Winstanley	Joyce	Harper	Deary	Heath	Robinson	McMinn	Lancashire	Dowell	Gayle	Harrison	Russell	Eyres	Randall	Phillskirk	Hoyland	Francis	Mullin	Armstrong	Saville	Brass	Peel	Referee	
1	2	3	4	5	6*	7	8	9	10	11	12															R. Poulain	1
1	2		4	5	6	7	8	9	10		11	3														T. Heilbron	2
1	2	3	4	5	6*	7	12	9	10	11*			8													W. Flood	3
1	2	3*	4	5	6*	7	12	9	10	11	14		8													M. Brandwood	4
1	3		4	5	6	7		9	10*	11			8	2	12											D. Allison	5
1	2	3	4	5	6	7		9	10*	11			8	12												K. Lupton	6
1	2	3	4	5	14	6*	8	12	10	7			9*			11										J. Watson	7
1	2	3	4	5		7		9	10	11				8	1		6									S. Dunn	8
1	2	3	4	5		7	6	9	10	11				8												M. Bailey	9
1	2	3	4	5		7	6	9	10*	11				8*		12		14								T. Heilbron	10
1	2	3	4	5		7	12	9	0*	11				8*		6		14								R. Dilkes	11
1	2	3	4	5		7	14	9	10	8*				6*		11		12								T. West	12
1	2	3	4	5		6		9	10	7				8*		11		12								K. Lynch	13
1	2	3	4	5		6*		9	10	7*		14	12			11	6	8								J. Worral	14
1	2*	3	4	5			9		10	7*		14	12			11	6	8								P. Harrison	15
1	2	3		5		7	9	12	10*				14			11	6	8*	4							K. Breen	16
1	2	3		5		7		9	10							11	6		8							M. Bailey	17
1	2	3	4	4		7	9	12	10							11	6*		8							J. Lloyd	18
1	2	3*	4	5		7*	9*	14	10							11	6	12	8							K. Breen	19
1	2	3*	4	5		7	9	8	10*				12			11	6				14					P. Foakes	20
1	2		4	5		7	8	9	10*			3				11	6				12					J. Worral	21
1	2		4	5		7		8	10			3	12			11	6		9							P. Vanes	22
1	2		4	5		7		8	10*			3*	12			11	6		9							P. Alcock	23
1	2		4	5		7		8	10*			3*	12			11	6		9		14					R. Poulain	24
1	2		4	5		7		8	10			3*	12			11	6		9							A. Wilkie	25
1	2		4	5*		7		8	10				9			11	6*	14	3		12					C. Wilkes	26
1	2		4	5		7*		8	10			3	12			11	6		9		14					P. Wright	27
1	2		4	5			11	8	10	12			9*	6									3	7		R. Furnandiz	28
1	2		4	5*			11	8	9				6*	12		10	15					3*	7	14		J. Holbrook	29
1	2			5		7	12	8	10	11*			9			3	6		4							N. Barry	30
1	2			5		7	14	8	10*	12			9			3	6*		11							G. Singh	31
1	2		4	5		7*			10	12			9		1	3	6		8			3*	14			G. Cain	32
1	2		4	5		7			10*	12					1	3	6		8	9	11					K. Morton	33
1	2		4	5		7			10	12			14			11	6		8	9		3*				N. Barry	34
1	2		4	5		7			10	12			11*			3	6		8	9					14	K. Morton	35
1	2			5		7		9	10	12			6*			3			8	11						A. D'Urso	36
1	3			5				12	14	7			2*			11	6		8	10						K. Leach	37
1	2		4	5		7*		9					6			3			8	11					12	M. Brandwood	38
1	2		4			7*		9	12				6			3			5							T. West	39
1	2		4			7*		12	14			3*				11	6		5							J. Kirkby	40
1	2	5	4	3												11	6		7						12	K. Lynch	41
1	2	5	4	3												11	6		7							A. Dawson	42
1	2	5	4	3												11	6		7				9*		12	G. Cain	43
1	14	5	4	3					12					2	1	11	6*		7							M. Pierce	44
		5	4	3					7					2	1	11	6		12							R. Poulain	45
		5	4	3					10*					2*	1	11	6		7							R. Foakes	46
		5	4	3										2*	1	11	6		10		14			12		W. Burns	47
1	2*		4	5					12							11	6		10		14	3				M. Riley	48
1	2	5	4	3					12	11*						9	6		10							K. Lupton	49
1	2	5	4	3					14	11						9*	6		10				8			G. Barker	50
1	2	5	4	3					12	7*						11	6	9	10							A. Butler	51
1	2	8	4	3*					12							11	6	9	10							R. Harris	52
1	2	5	4	3					14	7						11	6	9*	10							J. Winter	53
1	2	5	4	3						7*						11	6	9	10		12					W. Flood	54
1	2	5	4	3												11	6	9			7					W. Burns	55
																											56
																											57
																											58
																											59
																											60
40	42	29	43	44	4	27	12	21	29	17		5	7	16	6	38	32	7	30		6	4	3	2		League Appearances	
1					1	4	6	10		5	1						2		6		2	6	1	3	3	League Sub Appearances	
4	4	3	4	4	2	4	1+2	4	4	3	1+1	1	1+1	1+1		2		1+1								C/Cola Appearances	
4	5		4	5		5	1+1	3	5	1+2		2	1+1	1		1	5	5	4	0+1	2		1		0+1	FA Cup Appearances	

Also Played: Pender 4(36),4*(37),10(44),10*(45),S(52), Stewart 9(37,40,41,42),10(38,39), Thompson 8(39,40,41,42,43,44,45,46,47,48,49),10(55), Nogan 11(39),10(40,41*,42,43), 9(44*,45,46,47*),12(50,53), 14(52,54) 8(55), Shaw 12(46), 7(47,48,49,50*,52*),8(51,53*,54*)

CLUB RECORDS

BIGGEST VICTORIES
League: 9-0 v Darwen, Division 1, 9.1.1892.
F.A. Cup: 9-0 v Crystal Palace, 2nd Round, 10.2.1909.
9-0 v New Brighton, 4th Round, 26.1.1957.
9-0 v Penrith, 1st Round (a), 17.11.1984.
League Cup: 6-0 v Grimsby Town, 2nd Round, 10.9.1968.
BIGGEST DEFEATS
League: 0-10 v Aston Villa, Division 1, 29.8.1925.
0-10 v Sheffield United, Division 1, 19.1.1929.
F.A. Cup: 0-11 v Darwen Old Wanderers, 1st Round, 17.10.1885.
League Cup: 0-4 v Peterborough, 5th Round, 17.11.1965.
0-4 v Leeds United, 2nd Round, 6.9.1972.
0-4 v West Ham, 2nd Round, 2.9.1980.
0-4 v Manchester United, 2nd Round, 26.9.1984.
MOST POINTS
3 points a win: 83, Division 4, 1991-92.
2 points a win: 62, Division 2, 1972-73.
MOST GOALS SCORED: 102, Division 1, 1960-61.
MOST GOALS CONCEDED: 108, Division 1, 1925-26.
MOST FIRST CLASS MATCHES IN A SEASON
62 - 1960-61 (League 42, FA Cup 7, League Cup 8, European Cup 4, Charity Shield 1).
MOST LEAGUE WINS: 25, Division 4, 1991-92.
MOST LEAGUE DRAWS: 17, Division 3, 1981-82.
MOST LEAGUE DEFEATS: 23, Division 1, 1975-76.
BEST PERFORMANCES
League: 1972-73: Played 42, Won 24, Drawn 14, Lost 4, Goals for 72, Against 35, Points 62. Champions of Division 2.
Highest Position: Champions of Division 1 - 1920-21, 1959-60.
F.A. Cup: 1913-14: 1st Round South Shields 3-1; 2nd Round Derby County 3-2; 3rd Round Bolton Wanderers 3-0; 4th Round Sunderland 0-0,2-1; Semi-Final Sheffield United 0-0,1-0; Final Liverpool 1-0.
League Cup: Semi-Final in 1960-61, 1968-69.
1982-83: 1st Round Bury 5-3,3-1; 2nd Round Middlesbrough 3-2,1-1; 3rd Round Coventry 2-1; 4th Round Birmingham City 3-2; 5th Round Tottenham 4-1; Semi-Final Liverpool 0-3,1-0.
Europe: European Cup: 1960-61, 2nd Round Reims 2-0,2-3; 3rd Round Hamburg 3-1,1-4.
European Fairs Cup: 1966-67, 1st Round V.F.B.Stuttgart 1-1,2-0;

2nd Round Lausanne-Sports 3-1,5-0; 3rd Round Napoli 3-0,0-0; 4th Round Eintracht Frankfurt 1-1,1-2.
HONOURS: Champions of Division 1, 1920-21, 1959-60.
Champions of Division 2, 1897-98, 1972-73.
Champions of Division 3, 1982-83.Champions of Division 4, 91-92.
FA Cup winners in 1913-14.
Charity Shield winners in 1960-61, shared in 1973-74.
LEAGUE CAREER: Div 1 88-97, Div 2 97-98, Div 1 98-00, Div 2 00-13, Div 1 13-30, Div 2 30-47, Div 1 47-71, Div 2 71-73, Div 1 73-76, Div 2 76-80, Div 3 80-82, Div 2 82-83, Div 3 83-85, Div 4 85-92, Div 3/2 92-94, Div 2/1 94-95, Div.3/2 1995.

INDIVIDUAL CLUB RECORDS

MOST GOALS IN A SEASON
Jimmy Robson: 37 goals in 1960-61 (League 25, FA Cup 5, Lge Cup 4, EC 3).
Willie Irvine: 37 goals in 1965-66 (League 29, FAC 5, Lge Cup 3).
MOST GOALS IN A MATCH
6. Louis Page v Birmingham City (a), Division 1, 10.4.1926.
OLDEST PLAYER
Jerry Dawson, 40 years 282 days, (Christmas Day 1928).
YOUNGEST PLAYER
Tommy Lawton, 16 years 174 days, 28.3.1936.
MOST CAPPED PLAYER
Jimmy McIlroy (Northern Ireland) 51. Bob Kelly (England) 11.

PREVIOUS MANAGERS

Arthur Sutcliffe 1893-96; Harry Bradshaw 1896-99; Ernest Mangnall 1900-03; Spen Whittaker 1903-10; John Haworth 1910-24; Albert Pickles 1925-32; Tom Bromilow 1932-35; Alf Boland 1935-40; Cliff Britton 1945-48; Frank Hill 1948-54; Alan Brown 1954-57; Billy Dougall 1957-58; Harry Potts 1958-70; Jimmy Adamson 1970-76; Joe Brown 1976-77; Harry Potts 1977-79; Brian Miller 1979-83; Frank Casper 1983; John Bond 1983-84; John Benson 1984-85; Martin Buchan 1985; Tommy Cavanagh 1985-86; Brian Miller 1986-89; Frank Casper 1989-91.
ADDITIONAL INFORMATION
Previous Name: Burnley Rovers 1881-82.
Club colours: Claret shirts with light blue sleeves, white shorts & socks. **Change colours:** All yellow.
Reserves League: Pontins Central League Division 2.

LONGEST LEAGUE RUNS

of undefeated matches:	30 (1920-21)	of league matches w/out a win:	24 (1979)
of undefeated home matches:	34 (1911-13)	of undefeated away matches:	15 (1972-73)
without home win:	11 (1979)	without an away win:	31 (1901-03)
of league wins:	10 (1912-13)	of home wins:	17 (1920-21)
of league defeats:	8 (1889-90 & 1895)	of away wins:	7 (1991-92)

THE MANAGER

JIMMY MULLEN . . . . appointed October 1991.

PREVIOUS CLUBS
As Manager. . . . . Newport County, Cardiff City (joint manager), Blackpool.
As Asst.Man/Coach . . . . Aberdeen, Blackpool.
As a player . . . . Sheffield Wednesday, Rotherham, P.N.E. (Loan), Cardiff City.

HONOURS
As a Manager. . . . . 4th Division Championship, Promotion to Division 1 via the play-offs.
As a Player . . . . None.

BURNLEY

PLAYERS NAME / Honours	Ht	Wt	Birthdate	Birthplace / Transfers	Contract Date	Clubs	League	L/Cup	FA Cup	Other	Lge	L/C	FAC	Oth
G O A L K E E P E R S														
Marlon Beresford	6.1	12.6	02.09.69	Lincoln	23.09.87	Sheffield Wed. (T)								
Loan Bury, (25.08.89) 1 Lg				Loan	27.09.90	Northampton Town	13			2				
Loan Crewe Alexandra, (28.02.91) 3 Lg				Loan	15.08.91	Northampton Town	15							
				£95,000	28.08.92	Burnley	130	8	13	7				
Wayne L Russell	6.2	13.7	29.11.67	Cardiff		Ebbw Vale								
					28.10.93	Burnley	6+2		1					
D E F E N D E R S														
Christopher Brass	5.9	11.08	24.07.75			Burnley	2+3							
				Loan	14.10.94	Torquay	7		2	1				
Glen Davies	6.1	12.10	20.02.76	Brighton		Burnley (T)								
Wayne A Dowell	5.10	11.2	28.12.73	Durham	27.03.93	Burnley (T)	5	1	2					
Gary Parkinson	5.10	11.6	10.01.68	Thornaby		Everton (T)								
					17.01.86	Middlesbrough	194+8	20	17	19	5	1	1	
Loan 10.10.92 Southend United 6 Lge App.				Free	02.03.93	Bolton Wanderers				4				
				£80,000	27.01.94	Burnley	62+1	4	5	3	3			1
John Pender	6.0	12.3	19.11.63	Luton	08.11.81	Wolverhampton (A)	115+2	5	7		3			1
Ei: u21.1, Y; Div4'92				£35,000	23.07.85	Charlton Athletic	41	1	1	2				1
				£50,000	30.10.87	Bristol City	83	11	8	12	3			
				£70,000	18.10.90	Burnley	170	10	19	21	9	1	1	1
Matthew Taylor	5.7	11.12	06.03.76	Maidstone	1994-95	Burnley (T)								
Christopher Vinnicombe	5.9	10.4	20.10.70	Exeter		Exeter City (T)	35+4	5		2	1	1		
E: u21.12						Rangers	14+9	1	1+1		1			
				£200,000	30.06.94	Burnley	29	3			1			
M I D F I E L D														
Derek Adams	5.8	11.06	25.06.75	Aberdeen		Aberdeen								
					27.10.95	Burnley								
Alan Harper	5.8	9.7	01.11.60	Liverpool	22.04.78	Liverpool (A)								
E: Y1; Div1'85'87; CS'86'87				£100,000	01.06.83	Everton	103+24	17+2	10+8	13+1	4		1	
				£275,000	06.07.88	Sheffield Wednesday	32+3	1+1	1	1				
				£150,000	15.12.89	Manchester City	46+4	3	6	3	1	1		
				£200,000	12.09.91	Everton	45+6	5+1	2+1	2				
				Free	13.09.93	Luton Town	40+1		7		1			
				Free	11.08.94	Burnley	27	4	5					
Gerald R Harrison	5.10	12.12	15.04.72	Lambeth	18.12.89	Watford (T)	6+3							
				Free	23.07.91	Bristol City	24+13	2+2	1	4+1	1			
Loan 24.01.92 Cardiff City 10 Lge App. 1gl.				Loan	19.11.93	Hereford United	6	1		1				
				Free	24.03.94	Huddersfield Town								
				Free	05.08.94	Burnley	16+3	1+1	1		2			
Jamie Hoyland	6.0	12.8	23.01.66	Sheffield	12.11.83	Manchester City (A)	2	0+1						
E: Y3				Free	11.07.86	Bury	169+3	14+1	6	12	35	5		2
				£250,000	04.07.90	Sheffield United	72+15	3+3	8+2	2	6	1	1	1
Loan 04.03.94 Bristol City 6 Lge App.				Loan	14.10.94	Burnley								
				£130,000	08.11.94	Burnley	30		4		2			
Warren Joyce	5.9	11.11	20.01.65	Oldham	23.06.82	Bolton W. (J)	180+4	14+1	11	11	17	1	1	2
				£35,000	16.10.87	Preston North End	170+7	8	6	19	34	2	1	7
				£160,000	19.05.92	Plymouth Argyle	28+2	6	2	2	3	1	1	
				£140,000	07.07.93	Burnley	23+4	3	4	5	4	1	1	1
				Loan	20.01.95	Hull								
Kevin Ted C McMinn	6.0	12.11	28.09.62	Castle Douglas	01.01.82	Queen of the South	56+6	4+2	1		5			
SLC'87				£50,000	01.10.84	Glasgow Rangers	37+26	4+2		2+3	4	2		
via Seville, Spain, (05.02.88), £225,000 to				£225,000	05.02.88	Sevill (Spa)								
				£300,000	05.02.88	Derby County	108+15	11	6+1	12	9	3	1 1	
				£115,000	28.07.93	Birmingham City	19+3	1+1	1	1				
					05.04.94	Burnley	31+5	3	1+2	3	3			
Adrian J Randall	5.11	11.0	10.11.68	Amesbury	02.09.86	Bournemouth (A)				1+2				
E: Y; Div4'92					15.09.88	Aldershot	102+5	3	11	10	12		3	2
				£40,000	12.12.91	Burnley	125+17	4	12+3	2	9		1	
Stephen J Thompson	5.9	11.0	02.11.64	Oldham	04.11.82	Bolton W. (A)	329+6	27	21	39	49	2	4	2
SVT'89				£180,000	13.08.91	Luton Town	5	2						
					22.10.91	Leicester City	105+3	6	5	11+3	18	2	1	4
				£200,000	24.02.95	Burnley	12							
F O R W A R D S														
Andrew Cooke	6.0	12.0	02.01.74	Shrewsbury		Newtown								
					01.05.95	Burnley								
David Eyres	5.10	11.0	26.02.64	Liverpool		Rhyl								
				£10,000	15.08.89	Blackpool	147+11	11+1	11	13+2	38	1	2 4	
				£90,000	29.07.93	Burnley	83+1	6	9	5	27	3	6	2
John Francis	5.8	11.2	21.11.63	Dewsbury		Emley								
Div4'92					08.02.85	Halifax Town	1+3			2				1
via Emley				£10,000	15.09.88	Sheffield United	14+28	0+2	0+1	0+1	6			1
				£90,000	24.01.90	Burnley	99+2	6	8	11+1	27			4
				£95,000	13.08.92	Cambridge United	2+2	0+1	0+1	3	1			
				£70,000	25.03.93	Burnley	40+14	3+1	4+1	4+1	8	1		2
Adrian Heath	5.6	10.1	11.01.61	Stoke	12.01.79	Stoke City (A)	94+1	9	4		16		1	
E: u21.8' UEFA u21'82; Div1'85'87;				£700,000	07.01.82	Everton	206+20	33+4	24+5	14+3	71	11	6 5	
FAC'84; CS'84'85'86'87				£800,000	15.11.88	Espanol								
				£360,000	14.08.89	Aston Villa	8+1	1+1	0+1					
				£300,000	23.02.90	Manchester City	58+1	7+1	2+1	1+1	4	1		
				£50,000	27.03.92	Stoke City	5+1			3+1				
				Free	21.08.92	Burnley	105+6	7+1	12	6	29		6	
Kurt Nogan	5.10	11.1	09.09.70	Cardiff	11.07.89	Luton Town(T)	17+16	1+3		1+1	3	1		
W: u21.2				Free	30.09.92	Peterborough United				0+1				
				Free	17.10.92	Brighton & H.A.	71	4	4+1	5	42	2	4	
				£300,000	24.02.95	Burnley	11+4							
Nathan Peel	6.1	12.7	17.05.72	Blackburn	09.07.90	Preston North End	1+9	1		1+1	1			
				£50,000	01.08.91	Sheffield United	0+1							
Loan 03.02.93 Halifax Town 3 Lge App.				£60,000	24.09.93	Burnley	4+12	1	0+3	1+2	2			
Anthony Philliskirk	6.1	11.2	10.02.65	Sunderland	16.08.83	Sheffield United (J)	62+18	4+1	5	3+2	20	1	1	
E: S Loan 16.10.86 Rotherham U. 6 Lge Ap.1gl. £25,000					13.07.88	Oldham Athletic	3+7	0+2		1	1		1	
					10.02.89	Preston North End	13+1				6			
				£50,000	22.06.89	Bolton Wanderers	139+2	18	10	13	52	12	7	5
				£85,000	17.10.92	Peterborough United	37+6	2	4	2	15	1	1	1
				£80,000	21.01.94	Burnley	33+12	2+2			8			
Spencer L Robinson	5.7	11.5	29.12.65			Nottingham Forest (J)								
				Free	05.01.84	Huddersfield Town	17+4				2			
Loan 18.12.85 Tranmere Rovers 4 Lge App. 3gls.				£60,000	08.07.86	Bury	248+14	17+3	9	24	89	6	1	4
				£130,000	14.07.93	Bristol City	31+10	1	5	1	4	1		
				£250,000	26.07.94	Burnley	29+10	4	5		7	2	1	
Paul Weller	5.8	10.13	06.03.75	Brighton	1993-94	Burnley (T)								

TURF MOOR

Brunshaw Road, Burnley, Lancs BB10 4BX
Tel: 01282 427 777

Capacity 20,912
Seating: 7,437

First game ....v Rawtemstall, 17.02.1883.
First floodlit game ....v Blackburn (friendly), .12.1957.

ATTENDANCES
Highest ....54,775 v Huddersfield Town, FA Cup Round 3, 23.2.1924.
Lowest ....1,138 v Darlington, AMC, 13.3.1986.

OTHER GROUNDS..None.

MATCHDAY TICKET PRICES

Endsleigh Stand. . . . . £9.50.
Concessions . . . . £4.50.

Bob Lord . . . . £11.50.
Concessions. . . . . £6.

Terraces . . . . £7.50 (covered).
. . . . £7 (uncovered).
Concessions . . . . £4 (covered).
. . . . £3.50 (uncovered).

Ticket Office Telephone No. . . . . . . 01282 427 777.

CLUBCALL
0898 12 11 53

Calls cost 39p per minute cheap rate and 49p per minute at all other times.
Call costings correct at time of going to press.

HOW TO GET TO THE GROUND

From the North
Follow signs to Burnley (A56) into Town Centre, at roundabout take first exit into Yorkshire Street, shortly over crossroads into Brunshaw Road for Burnley FC.

From the East:
Follow signs Burnley (A646) then join A671 enter town centre by Todmorden Road and at the end turn right at crossroads into Brunshaw Road for Burnley FC.

From the South:
(or use route from west). Use M62, M66 and A56 signposted Burnley into town centre, then at roundabout take 3rd exit in Yorkshire Street, shortly at crossroads forward into Brunshaw Road for Burnley FC.

From the West and South:
Use M6 to junction 31, then Blackburn bypass and A679 into Burnley town centre and at roundabout take third exit into Yorkshire Street, shortly over crossroads into Brunshaw Road for Burnley FC.

Car Parking
Parks in Church Street and Fulledge Recreation Ground for approx 500 vehicles each (chargeable). Both are five minutes walk from ground.

Nearest Railway Station: Burnley Central.

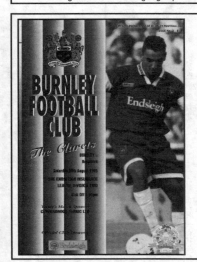

MATCHDAY PROGRAMME

Programme Editor . . . . John Stringer.

Number of pages . . . . 48.

Price . . . . £1.50.

Subscriptions . . . . Apply to club.

Local Newspapers . . Lancashire Evening Telegraph, Burnley Express.

Local Radio Stations . . . . Radio Lancashire, Red Rose Radio.

CARLISLE UNITED
(The Cumbrians)
ENDSLEIGH LEAGUE DIVISION 2
SPONSORED BY: CONWAY VAUXHALL

Back Row (L-R): Marc Clelland, Jeff Thorpe, Lee Peacock, Rory Delap, Paul Conway, David Currie, Tony Gallimore, Will Varty, Gareth McAlindon, Nathan Murray. **Middle Row:** David Wilkes (Yth Coach), Peter Hampton (Physio), Tony Hopper, Richard Prokas, Darren Edmondson, Tony Caig, Tony Elliott, Jamie Robinson, Glynn Snodin, Rod Thomas, Joe Joyce (Coach), Neil Dalton (Asst. Physio). **Front Row:** Warren Aspinall, Steve Hayward, David Reeves (Capt), Mick Wadsworth (Director of Coaching), Michael Knighton (Chairman & Chief Executive), Mervyn Day (Coach), Dean Walling, Derek Mountfield, Paul Murray.

CARLISLE UNITED
FORMED IN 1904
TURNED PROFESSIONAL IN
LTD COMPANY IN 1921
PRESIDENT: J C Monkhouse JP
VICE-PRESIDENTS
J A Doweck, J B Lloyd,
Dr T Gardner, MB ChB MBE, H A Jenkins,
J R Sheffield, R S Liddell FCA, T A Bingley
CHAIRMAN & CHIEF EXECUTIVE
Michael Knighton
DIRECTORS
B Chaytow (Vice-Chairman), A Dowbeck,
R McKnight
SECRETARY
Philip Vine (01228 26237)
COMMERCIAL MANAGER
Donna Wenn (01228 24014)
DIRECTOR OF COACHING: Mick Wadsworth
COACHES: Joe Joyce & Mervyn Day
RESERVE TEAM MANAGER

YOUTH TEAM MANAGER
David Wilkes
PHYSIOTHERAPIST
Peter Hampton
STATISTICIAN FOR THE DIRECTORY
Bill Rodger

When the 1993-94 season ended on a note of great hope fed by a late-season surge which led to an ultimately unsuccessful play-off place, not even the most optimistic of the club's followers could have anticipated the delights which were to unfold during the 1994-95 season.

The first sign that this was to be no ordinary campaign came in the first round of the Coca-Cola Cup against second division Rotherham United. Languishing two goals in arrears at half-time in the second leg, a magnificent second-half performance brought the goals necessary for the aggregate victory. This was to set the scene for a run of six successive league victories until Queen's Park Rangers from the Premiership proved too strong in the next round of the League Cup. Apart from a narrow defeat at Northampton on the rebound from the home Q.P.R. fixture, it was to be February and the 42nd match of the season before the side were to be beaten again by Third Division opposition.

By then not only had the club established themselves as strong favourites for promotion but they had also enjoyed great success in the other cup competitions. The early rounds of the FA Cup brought convincing wins over Guiseley and Darlington before running up against the same third round opposition as the previous year in the shape of first division Sunderland. The pattern was familiar, a praiseworthy draw at Roker Park being followed by the inability to finish the job in the replay. However any fears that this reverse might disrupt the season were soon dispelled as the leadership of the division was extended and further progress was made in the early rounds of the Auto-Windscreen Shield. After victories over Darlington and Hartlepool in the local preliminaries Chesterfield, Wrexham, Crewe Alexandra and finally Rochdale were disposed off to set up the Wembley appearance which had been so tantalisingly missed the previous year. Appropriately this final turned out to be between the champions elect of the second and third divisions with Birmingham gaining the verdict in overtime on a magnificent family occasion before a crowd which exceeded that of the Coca-Cola final between Liverpool and Bolton Wanderers.

Almost predictably league form had slipped around this time from the previous majestic standard with successive defeats against Bury and Hartlepool (this the first home reverse of the season) when no doubt a subconscious eye was being turned in the direction of the forthcoming Wembley appearance, but the league championship was clinched with praiseworthy victories at Colchester and Chesterfield which led to a rapturous series of events in the final weekend of the season with the presentation of the League trophy and a civic reception to reflect the successes of the season.

With average gates now treble the level of three seasons ago, when Michael Knighton took over the club, great credit must go to him and the coaching staff of Mick Wadsworth, Mervyn Day, Joe Joyce, David Wilkes and Peter Hampton who have fostered a great level of team spirit among the senior players while also developing a youth structure which grows ever stronger by the year.

W. RODGER.

CARLISLE UNITED

Division Three: 1st   **FA Cup:** 3rd Round   **Coca-Cola Cup:** 2nd Round   **Auto Windscreen Trophy:** Runners-up

M	DATE	COMP.	VEN	OPPONENTS	RESULT	H/T	LP	GOAL SCORERS/GOAL TIMES	ATT.
1	A 13	EL	H	Wigan Athletic	W 2-1	1-0	3	Reeves 45, Walling 56	6,231
2	16	CC 1/1	A	**Rotherham United**	**L 0-1**	**0-0**			**(2,055)**
3	20	EL	A	Torquay United	D 1-1	0-0	5	Reeves 76	(3,506)
4	23	CC 1/2	H	**Rotherham United**	**W 3-1**	**0-1**		**Reeves 50, 67, Walling 65**	**5,004**
5	27	EL	H	Scarborough	W 2-0	2-0	4	Mountfield 14, Reeves 25	5,720
6	30	EL	A	Walsall	W 2-1	1-1	3	Reeves 26,71	(3,610)
7	S 3	EL	A	Scunthorpe United	W 3-2	0-2	1	Gallimore 80, Thorpe 89, 90	(3,217)
8	10	EL	H	Exeter City	W 1-0	1-0	1	Thomas 38	6,213
9	13	EL	H	Mansfield Town	W 2-1	0-0	1	Thomas 58, Currie 77	6,136
10	17	EL	A	Wigan Athletic	W 2-0	0-0	1	Edmondson 63, Reeves 78	(3,003)
11	20	CC 2/1	H	**Queens Park Rangers**	**L 0-1**	**0-1**			**9,570**
12	24	EL	A	Northampton Town	L 1-2	0-1	2	Reeves 68	(3,508)
13	27	AWT	A	**Darlington**	**W 3-2**	**2-2**		**Currie 17, 53 Gallimore 20 (pen)**	**(1,583)**
14	O 1	EL	H	Darlington	W 2-1	0-1	1	Gallimore 55 (pen), Walling 78	6,100
15	5	CC 2/2	A	**Queens Park Rangers**	**L 0-2**	**0-2**			**(6,500)**
16	8	EL	A	Lincoln City	D 1-1	0-0	1	Reeves 47	(3,097)
17	15	EL	H	Colchester United	D 0-0	0-0	2		5,817
18	18	AWT (NP)	H	**Hartlepool United**	**W 2-0**	**0-0**		**Thomas 51, Arnold 75**	**2,536**
19	22	EL	H	Barnet	W 4-0	1-0	2	Reeves 32, Conway 73, Davey 81, Thomas 82	6,155
20	29	EL	A	Fulham	W 3-1	2-0	2	Reeves 7, Mountfield 37, Conway 62	(5,563)
21	N 5	EL	H	Rochdale	W 4-1	1-0	2	Davey 45, 61 Reeves 58, Edmondson 88	5,984
22	13	FAC 1	A	**Guiseley**	**W 4-1**	**2-0**		**Reeves 19, 81, Conway 30, Mountfield 65**	**(6,548)**
23	19	EL	A	Hereford United	W 1-0	1-0	1	Conway 41	(2,531)
24	26	EL	A	Doncaster Rovers	D 1-1	0-0	1	Walling 83	7,781
25	29	AWT N(1)	H	**Chesterfield**	**W 1-0**	**0-0**		**Currie 88**	**3,591**
26	D 3	FAC 2	H	**Darlington**	**W 2-0**	**0-0**		**Conway 73, Currie 81**	**8,365**
27	10	EL	H	Torquay United	W 1-0	1-0	1	Thomas 12,	5,141
28	17	EL	A	Scarborough	W 2-1	1-1	1	Gallimore 28 (pen), Currie 49	(1,910)
29	26	EL	A	Hartlepool United	W 5-1	1-0	1	Mountfield 6, Conway 58, Reeves 65, 72, Gallimore 79 (pen)	(3,854)
30	27	EL	H	Bury	W 3-0	1-0	1	Currie 19, Conway 50, Reeves 76	12,242
31	31	EL	A	Gillingham	W 1-0	0-0	1	Walling 71	(3,682)
32	J 7	FAC 3	A	**Sunderland**	**D 1-1**	**0-0**		**Davey 78,**	**(15,523)**
33	10	AWS N(2)	H	**Wrexham**	**W 2-1**	**1-0**		**Thomas 27, (og) 77**	**8,771**
34	14	EL	H	Preston North End	D 0-0	0-0	1		10,684
35	17	FAC 3R	H	**Sunderland**	**L 1-3**	**0-2**		**Walling 61,**	**12,201**
36	21	EL	A	Rochdale	D 1-1	0-0	1	Walling 68	(3,289)
37	24	EL	A	Barnet	W 2-0	0-0	1	Currie 75, Davey 85	(2,413)
38	28	EL	H	Fulham	D 1-1	1-1	1	Thomas 11	6,891
39	F 4	EL	A	Doncaster Rovers	D 0-0	0-0	1		(3,587)
40	11	EL	H	Hereford United	W 1-0	1-0	1	Gallimore 6 (pen)	5,676
41	14	AWS NSF	A	**Crewe Alexandra**	**W 1-0**	**1-0**		**Thomas 40**	**(4,046)**
42	18	EL	A	Preston North End	L 0-1	0-1	1		(11,867)
43	25	EL	A	Darlington	W 2-0	1-0	1	Thomas 7, Reeves 87	(3,992)
44	28	AWS NFl	H	**Rochdale**	**W 4-1**	**3-0**		**Currie 14, Thomas 26, 44, Conway 80**	**8,647**
45	M 4	EL	H	Northampton Town	W 2-1	2-0	1	Walling 32, 45	6,755
46	11	EL	A	Exeter City	D 1-1	1-1	1	Reeves 10	(2,673)
47	14	AWS NF2	A	**Rochdale**	**L 1-2**	**1-2**		**Mountfield 39**	**(4,082)**
48	18	EL	H	Walsall	W 2-1	0-1	1	Reeves 75, 87	7,769
49	25	EL	H	Scunthorpe United	W 2-1	0-0	1	Aspinall 63, Hayward 80	6,704
50	A 1	EL	A	Mansfield Town	W 2-1	1-1	1	Prokas 39, Thorpe 87	(5,197)
51	4	EL	H	Chesterfield	D 1-1	0-0	1	Robinson 66	8,478
52	8	EL	H	Gillingham	W 2-0	2-0	1	Thorpe 14, Hayward 34	6,786
53	15	EL	A	Bury	L 0-2	0-0	1		(5,507)
54	17	EL	H	Hartlepool United	L 0-1	0-1	1		10,242
55	23	AW SF	A	**Birmingham City**	**L 0-1**	**0-0**			**(16,663)**
56	29	EL40	A	Colchester United	W 1-0	0-0	1	Reeves 58	(3,333)
57	M 2	EL41	A	Chesterfield	W 2-1	1-1	1	Reeves 10, 58	(7,290)
58	6	EL42	H	Lincoln City	L 1-3	0-1	1	Conway 90	12,412
59									
60									

Best Home League Attendance: 12,412 v Lincoln City   **Smallest:** 5,141 v Torquay United   **Av Home Att:** 7,425

Goal Scorers:

League (67): Reeves 29, Walling 7, Thomas 6, Conway 6, Gallimore 5, Davey 4, Thorpe 4, Currie 4, Mountfield 3, Hayward 2, Edmondson 2, Aspinall, Robinson, Prokas   Compared with 1993-94: +1,901

C/Cola Cup (3): Reeves 2, Walling

FA Cup (8): Reeves 2, Conway 2, Walling, Mountfield, Currie, Davey

AW Trophy (14): Thomas 5, Currie 4, Mountfield, Gallimore, Conway, Arnold, Opponent

Caig A.	Joyce J.	Gallimore T.	Walling D.	Mountfield D.	Edmondson D.	Thomas R.	Currie D.	Reeves D.	Davey S.	Reddish S.	Thorpe G.	Elliott T.	Pearson J.	Valentine P.	Prokas R.	Peacock L.	Robinson J.	Arnold I.	Conway P.	Murray P.	Peters R.	Delap R.	Aspinall W.	Hayward S.	Hopper T.	Referee	
1	2	3	4	5	6*	7	8•	9	10	11	12	13	14													S. Mathieson	1
1	2	3	4	5†	6	7	8*	9	10	11	12															N. Barry	2
1	2	3	4	5	6	7	8	9		10*	12				11											C. Wilkes	3
1	2	3	4	5*	6	7	8	9	10		12				11											K. A. Lupton	4
1	2	3	4	5	6•	7*	8	9	10		14				11	12										P. Richards	5
1	2	3	4		6*		8•	9	10		14			5	11*	12										D. Orr	6
1	2	3	4		6*		8*	9	10		14			5	11	12										E. Wolstenholme	7
1	2	3	4		12	7	8*	9	10		6*			5	11			14								U. Rennie	8
1	2	3	4		6	7	8*	9	10		12			5	11			S								D. Allison	9
1	2	3	4		6	7	8*	9	10	S	8			5	11											R. Furnandez	10
1	2	3	4		6	7	8*	9	10		14			5	11*											J. Winter	11
1	2	3	4	6	12	7	8	9	10					5•	14											J. Kirby	12
1	2	3	4		6	7	8	9*	10		12			5	11											K. Lynch	13
1	2	3	4		6*	7•	8†	9	10		12			5	11			14								E. Lomas	14
1	2*	3	4	8	6	7•	12	9	10					5	11			14								B. Hill	15
1	2	3	4	12	6	7*	8•	9	10		14			5	11											A. D'Urso	16
1	2	3	4		6*	7		9	10					5	11	14		8•								G. Cain	17
S		3	4	5	2*	7•		9	10		14		1		11			8	6	12						P. Wright	18
1			4	5	2	7	8	9	10		12				11				6	3						R. Poulain	19
1		3	4	5	2	7	8	9	10						11				6							T. West	20
1		3	4	5	2	7	8	9*	10						11		12	6	14							I. Cruikshank	21
1	12	3	4	5	2	7	8*	9	10		14				11				6							P. Richards	22
1	12	3	4	5	2	7	8*	9	10						11				6							E. Wolstenholme	23
1		3	4	5	2	7	8	9	10						11				6							E Parker	24
1		3	4	5	2	7	8	9	10						11				6							G. Cain	25
1		3	4	5	2	7*	8*	9	10		12				11			14	6							J. Worrall	26
1		3	4	5	2	7	8	9			12	13			11				6		10					S. Mathieson	27
1†		3	4	5	2	7•	8•	9			12	13			11				6		10					W. Flood	28
1	14	3	4	5	2		8•	9			*7				11				6		10	12				R. Fernandez	29
1		3	4	5	2	7*	8	9	10		12				11				6							D. Allison	30
1		3	4	5	2		8	9	10		7	1			11				6		12					P. Alcock	31
1		3	4	5	2	7	8	9	10						11				6							P. Don	32
1		3	4	5	2	7*	8	9	10		12				11		5		6		14					J. Winter	33
1		3	4	5	2	7*	8	9	10		12				11				6		S					W. Burns	34
1		3	4	5	2	7		9	10		8*				11				6		12					J. Worrall	35
1		3	4	5	2	7*	8	9	10		12				11				6							M. Reilly	36
1	2*	3	4	5		7	8	9	10						11	12			6							G. Pooley	37
1		3	4	5	2	7	8	9	10		12				11*				6							E. Wolstenholme	38
1		3	4	5*	2	7	8	9	10						11	12			6							K. Leach	39
1		3	4	5	2	7*	8	9	10						11				6		12					A. Dawson	40
1		3	4	5	2	7	8•	9	10							14			6	11•	12					J. Kirkby	41
1		3	4	5	2	7	8	9	10						12				6	11*	14					T. West	42
1		3	4	5	2	7	8	9							11		12		6		10					N. Barry	43
1		3	4	5	2	7	8•	9			14				11		12		6		10		6*			W. Flood	44
1		3	4	5	2*	7	8	9			14				11		12		6		10		6•			K. Breen	45
1		3	4	5	2	7*	8	9			12				11				6		10		6			C. Wilkes	46
1		3	4	5	2		8	9			7*				11				6		10		6			G. Singh	47
1		3	4	5	2		8	9			7*				11				6		10		6	7*		J. Rushton	48
1		3		5	2		8*	9			12				11	14	4		10				6	7		P. Richards	49
1	2	3	4	5		7	8*	9			12				11	14			10				6•	10		C. Wilkes	50
1	11•	3	4		2	7		9			8*					6	5			12				10	14	J. Watson	51
1	14		4	5	2	7*		9			8•				11									10	12	K. Lupran	52
1	2	3	4	5			8	9			7				11		S				10				6	W. Burns	53
1	2	3	4	5		7	8	9							11•		14						6*	10	12	P. Harrison	54
1		3	4	5*	2	7	8	9			12				11*	14		6						10		P. Foakes	55
1	14	3	4		2	7*	8	9			12				11		5	6						10		S. Dunn	56
S		3	4		2			9			11•	1				12	5		14		7	6*	10	8		G. Heilbron	57
1		3	4		2	7	8	9							11*		5	6			12	10				G. Cain	58
40	**17**	**40**	**41**	**30**	**36**	**36**	**38**	**42**	**25**	**2**	**7**	**2**	**0**	**9**	**37**	**2**	**6**	**1**	**24**	**2**	**5**	**2**	**6**	**9**	**2**	League Appearances	
	4			1	2						21	1	1		2	5	8	3		3	3	1	1		3	League Sub Appearances	
4	0+1	4	4	4	4	3	4	4			1+2				3		1	0+1	4				0+1			FA Cup Appearances	
4	4	4	4	3+1	4	4	3+1	4	4		1			2	3			0+1	4							C/Cola Appearances	
7	1	8	8	6	8	7	7	8	5		1+5	1		1	7		1+3	1	7		1+1	1+2		2		AW Trophy Appearances	

Also Played: Lowe *11(12)12(17), Smith (31) Loan Players: Lowe K, Smith S, Aspinall W

CARLISLE UNITED   RECORDS AND STATISTICS

CLUB RECORDS

BIGGEST VICTORIES
League: 8-0 v Hartlepool United, Division 3(N), 1.9.1928.
8-0 v Scunthorpe United, Division 3(N), 25.12.1952.
F.A. Cup: 6-1 v Billingham Synthonia, Round 1, 1.17.1956.

BIGGEST DEFEATS
League: 1-11 v Hull City, Division 3(N), 14.1.1939.
F.A. Cup: 0-5 v West Ham United, lst Round replay, 1909-10.
1-6 v Wigan Athletic, 1st Round, 1934-35.
1-6 v Bradford City, 1st Round, 1951-52.
0-5 v Bristol City, 4th Round replay, 28.1.1981.

MOST POINTS
3 points a win: 80, Division 3, 1981-82.
2 points a win: 62, Division 3(N), 1950-51.

RECORD TRANSFER FEE RECEIVED
£275,000 from Vancouver Whitecaps for Peter Beardsley, April 1981.

RECORD TRANSFER FEE PAID
£121,000 to notts County for David Reeves, October 1993.

BEST PERFORMANCES
League: 22nd in Division 1, 1974-75.
F.A. Cup: 6th Round, 1974-75.
League Cup: Semi-Finals in 1969-70.

HONOURS
Champions of Division 3, 1964-65, 1994-95.

LEAGUE CAREER
Elected to Div 3N 1928, Transferred to Div 4 1958, Div 3 1961-62, Div 4 1962-63, Div 3 1963-64, Div 2 1964-65, Div 1 1973-74, Div 2 1974-75, Div 3 1976-77, Div 2 1981-82, Div 3 1985-86, Div 4 (now Div 3) 1986-87, Div 2 1994-95.

INDIVIDUAL CLUB RECORDS

MOST GOALS IN A SEASON
Hugh McIlmoyle: 44 goals in 1963-64 (League 39, League Cup 5).

MOST GOALS IN A MATCH
5. H.Mills v Halifax Town, Division 3(N), 11.9.1937.
5. Jim Whitehouse v Scunthorpe United, 8-0, Division 3(N), 25.12.1952.

OLDEST PLAYER
Bryan 'Pop' Robson, 39 years 321 days v Shrewsbury Town, 28.9.1985.

YOUNGEST PLAYER
Rory Delap, 16 years 306 days v Scarborough, 8.5.1993.

MOST CAPPED PLAYER
Eric Welsh (Northern Ireland) 4.

PREVIOUS MANAGERS

W.Clark; Ivor Broadis; Bill Shankly; Fred Emery; Andy Beattie; Ivor Powell; Alan Ashman; Tim Ward; Bob Stokoe; Ian MacFarlane; Alan Ashman; Dick Young; Bobby Moncur; Martin Harvey; B.S.Robson; Bob Stokoe; Harry Gregg; Aidan McCaffery.

ADDITIONAL INFORMATION
PREVIOUS NAMES
None.

PREVIOUS LEAGUES
North Eastern League.

Club colours: Blue shirts with white pinstripe, white collar with red and blue trim, white shorts and blue stockings.
Change colours: Green, red and white stripes.

Reserves League: Midland Senior League.

'A' Team: Lancashire League Division 2.

LONGEST LEAGUE RUNS

of undefeated matches:	15 (1950-51, 1983-84)	of league matches w/out a win:	14 (1935)
of undefeated home matches:	22 (1950-51)	of undefeated away matches:	12 (1950-51)
without home win:	8 (1954, 1991-92)	without an away win:	20 (1970-71)
of league wins:	6 (1937, 1981-82)	of home wins:	7 (1930-35)
of league defeats:	8 (1935)	of away wins:	4 (1964-65)

THE MANAGER

MICK WADSWORTH . . . . appointed June 1993.

PREVIOUS CLUBS
As Manager . . . . None.
As Asst.Man/Coach . . . . Carlisle United.
As a player . . . . Scunthorpe United.

HONOURS
As a Manager . . . . None.
As a Player . . . . None.

CARLISLE UNITED — APPEARANCES — GOALS

PLAYERS NAME / Honours	Ht	Wt	Birthdate	Birthplace / Transfers	Contract Date	Clubs	League	L/Cup	FA Cup	Other	Lge	L/C	FAC	Oth
G O A L K E E P E R S														
Anthony Caig	6.1	12.0	11.04.74	Whitehaven	10.07.92	Carlisle United (T)	61	4	6	13				
Mervyn Day	6.2	15.1	26.06.55	Chelmsford	01.03.73	West Ham Utd (A)	194	14	14	10				
E: u23.5, Y; FAC'75; Div2'90				£100,000	01.07.79	Leyton Orient	170	8	10					
				£15,000	12.08.83	Aston Villa	30	3						
Loan Luton Town 05.03.92 4 Lg Apps.				£30,000	01.02.85	Leeds United	227	14	11	16				
Loan Sheffield United (01.05.92) 1 Lg App.				Free	14.07.93	Carlisle United	16	2	1	2				
Anthony Elliott	6.0	12.12	30.11.69	Nuneaton	03.12.86	Birmingham City (A)	1							
E: Y.2, S; WFAC'90				Free	22.12.88	Hereford United	75	5	6	9				
				Free	29.07.92	Huddersfield Town	15	2	3	3				
				Free	28.06.93	Carlisle United	8+1		1	2				
D E F E N D E R S														
Darren Edmondson	6.0	12.2	04.11.71	Coniston	17.07.90	Carlisle United (T)	146+6	11	12	17	7	1	2	1
Joseph Joyce	5.9	10.5	18.03.61	Consett		Barnsley	332+2	26+1	24	3	4	1	1	
				Free	20.02.91	Scunthorpe United	91	5		11	2			
				Free	05.08.93	Carlisle United	45+5	4+1	4+1	9				1
				Loan	23.09.93	Darlington	4							
Derek Mountfield	6.0	13.6	02.11.62	Liverpool	04.11.80	Tranmere R. (A)	26	2	1		1			
E: B1, u21.1; Div1'85'87; UEFAu21'84;				£30,000	02.06.82	Everton	100+6	16	17	14+1	19	3	2	1
FAC'84; CS'84'85; ECWC'85				£450,000	06.06.88	Aston Villa	88+2	13	6	11	9	2	1	5
				£150,000	07.11.91	Wolverhampton W.	79+4	4	2	2	4	1		
				Free	03.08.94	Carlisle United	30+1	3+1	4	6	3	1	1	1
Nathan Murray	6.1	12.7	10.09.75	South Shields	23.04.93	Newcastle United (T)								
E: S, Y				Free	.08.95	Carlisle United								
Glynn Snodin	5.6	10.5	14.02.60	Rotherham		Doncaster Rov. (A)	288+21	12+2	15	5	61	1	1	1
				£115,000	19.06.85	Sheffield Wed.	51+8	3+1	9	1	1			
				£135,000	31.07.87	Leeds United	83+1	9+1	5+2	4	10	3		
				Loan	15.08.91	Oldham Athletic	8	1			1			
Loan 28.02.92 Rotherham Utd 3 Lge App.				Free	31.03.92	Hearts	20+14	0+2	2+1	2+1			1	1
				Free	23.07.93	Barnsley	18+7	3						
				Free	08.95	Carlisle United								
M I D F I E L D														
Rory Delap	6.0	11.11	06.07.76	Coldfield	18.07.94	Carlisle United (T)	4+4			0+1				
Anthony Gallimore	5.11	11.3	21.02.72	Crewe	11.07.90	Stoke City (T)	6+5							
Loan Carlisle United, (03.10.91) 8 Lg Apps.				Loan	26.02.92	Carlisle United	8							
Loan Carlisle United, (25.03.93) 8 Lg +1 Gl.				£15,000	13.07.93	Carlisle United	80	6	7	17	6		1	1
Steve Hayward	5.10	11.7	08.09.71	Pelsall	17.09.88	Derby County (J)	12+11	0+2	1	2+4	1			
E: Y13; Flg u18.1				£100,000	13.03.95	Carlisle United	9		2	2	2			
Tony Hopper	5.11	11.07	31.05.76	Carlisle	18.07.94	Carlisle United	5+6							
Paul Murray	5.8	10.5	31.08.76	Carlisle	14.06.94	Carlisle United	12+6			3+2				
Richard Prokas	5.8	11.4	22.01.76	Penrith	18.07.94	Carlisle United (T)	37+2	3	3	7	1			
Jamie Robinson	6.1	12.3	26.02.72	Liverpool	04.06.90	Liverpool (T)								
				Free	17.07.92	Barnsley	8+1		3					
				Free	28.01.94	Carlisle United	16		4	1				1
Jeffery Thorpe	5.10	12.8	17.11.72	Cockermouth	02.07.91	Carlisle United (T)	70+41	6+3	3+2	6+10	6			1
F O R W A R D S														
Warren Aspinall	5.9	11.12	13.09.67	Wigan	31.08.85	Wigan Athletic (A)	39+12	1	2+3	3+5	22		2	4
E: u19.1, Y2; FRT'85				£150,000	05.05.86	Everton	0+7	0+1		0+2				
				£300,000	19.02.87	Aston Villa	40+4	4	1+1		14	2		
				£315,000	26.08.88	Portsmouth	97+35	8+3	4+5	6+1	21	3	2	2
				Loan	27.08.93	Bournemouth	4+2				1			
				Loan	14.10.93	Swansea City	5		1					
				£20,000	31.12.93	Bournemouth	18		1		5			
Loan 09.03.95 Carlisle United				Free	.08.95	Carlisle United								
Paul Conway	6.1	12.6	17.04.70	London	29.10.93	Carlisle United	64+2		8	16	16		4	2
David Currie	6.0	11.3	27.11.62	Stockton	05.02.82	Middlesbrough	94+19	6	5+1	2	31	1		
FlgXI.1; Div2'91				Free	17.06.86	Darlington	76	6	3	5	33			3
				£150,000	26.02.88	Barnsley	80	3	5	1	30	1	4	
				£750,000	19.01.90	Nottingham Forest	4+4				1			
				£460,000	23.08.90	Oldham Athletic	17+14	2+1	1	0+1	3	2		
				£250,000	05.09.91	Barnsley	53+22	2+1	4+1	1+1	12			1
				Loan	15.10.92	Rotheram united	5				2			
				Loan	10.01.94	Huddersfield TOwn	7			1	1			
				Free	18.07.94	Carlisle United	38	3+1	3	7	4		1	4
Lee Peacock	6.0	12.8	09.10.76	Paisley	10.03.95	Carlisle United (T)	2+6							
S: Y.														
David Reeves	6.0	11.7	19.11.67	Birkenhead		Heswall								
Loan Scunthorpe Utd, (17.12.86), 3+1 App. 2 Gls				Free	06.08.86	Sheffield Wed.	8+9	1+1	1+1	0+1	2	1		
Loan Scunthorpe Utd, (01.10.87), 6 Lg App. 4 Gls				Loan	20.11.87	Burnley	16		2		8			1
				£80,000	17.08.89	Bolton Wanderers	111+23	14+1	8+5	9+2	30	1	5 7	
				£80,000	25.03.93	Notts County	9+4	1+1			2			
					01.10.93	Carlisle United	76	4	8	16	33	2	3	3
Roderick Thomas	5.6	10.6	10.10.70	Brent	03.05.88	Watford (T)	63+21	3+2	0+1	3+1	9			
E: u21.1, Y8, S; FAYC'89				Loan	27.03.92	Gillingham	8		1		1			
				Free	12.07.93	Carlisle United	73+1	6	8	16	15	1		7
Dean Walling	6.0	10.8	17.04.69	Leeds		Leeds United (A)								
FAV'91				Free	30.07.87	Rochdale	43+22	3	0+1	1+1	8			
via Guiseley (Free) to				Free	01.07.91	Carlisle United	135+6	11	9+1	21	17	1	1	3
A D D I T I O N A L C O N T R A C T P L A Y E R														
Gareth McLindon						Newcastle								
				Free	.08.95	Carlisle United								

BRUNTON PARK
Warwick Road, Carlisle, Cumbria CA1 1LL
Tel: 01228 26237

Capacity...10,925 at present.
By Christmas the capacity will rise to 17,300, and eventually the stadium will accomadate for 28,000 all seated spectators.

First game...Not known.
First floodlit game ....Not known.

ATTENDANCES
Highest ....27,500 v Birmingham City, FA Cup 3rd Round, 5.1.1957
.... & Middlesbrough, FA Cup 5th Round, 7.2.1970.
Lowest...859 v Hartlepool, AMC 1st Round, 15.12.1992.

OTHER GROUNDS: .... None.

MATCHDAY TICKET PRICES

A, B & D	£9.50
Juv/OAP	£5.50
C Stand	£10
Platinum Stand	£10
Terraces	£7.50
Juv/OAP	£4.50

Foxy's Restaurant

Eat & View (Viewing Gallery)	£28
Eat & View (Platinum Stand)	£23

Ticket Office Telephone no. 01228 26237

CLUBCALL
0891 12 16 32

Calls cost 39p per minute cheap rate and 49p per minute at all other times.
Call costings correct at time of going to press.

HOW TO GET TO THE GROUND

From the North, East, South
Use Motorway M6 until junction 43. Leave motorway and follow signs to Carlisle (A69) into Warwick Road for Carlisle United FC.

From the West
Follow signs into Carlisle then forward (A69) along Warwick Road for Carlisle United FC.

Car Parking
Car park for 1,500 vehicles next to ground. Entrance in St Aidan's Road. 50p cars, 32.00 coaches. Limited street parking permitted.

Nearest Railway Station
Carlisle Citadel (01228 4471)

MATCHDAY PROGRAMME

Programme Editor. . . . . Jim Thoburn.

Number of pages . . . . 32.

Price . . . . £1.20.

Subscriptions . . . . £28 per season (home), £56 (home & away).

Local Newspapers. . . . . Cumbrian Newspapers.

Local Radio Stations . . . . BBC Radio Cumbria, CFM Radio.

CHESTERFIELD
(The Spireites)
ENDSLEIGH LEAGUE DIVISION 2
SPONSORED BY: N.DERBYS HEATH AUTH. & G K GROUP

Back Row (L-R): Mark Williams, Kevin Davies, Andy Beasley, Chris Marples, Darren Roberts, Tony Lormor.
Middle Row: Mark Stuart, Jon Howard, Darren Carr, David Moss, Andy Morris, Nicky Laws, Shaun Dyche, Des Hazel, Phil Robinson, Lee Rogers.
Front Row: Mark Jules, Tom Curtis, Chris Perkins, Dave Rushbury (Physio), John Duncan (Manager), Kevin Randall (Assistant Manager), Jon Narbett, Wayne Fairclough, Jamie Hewitt.

CHESTERFIELD
FORMED IN 1866
TURNED PROFESSIONAL IN 1891
LTD COMPANY IN 1871

PRESIDENT
His Grace The Duke of Devonshire MC,DL,JP

CHAIRMAN: J Norton-Lea
VICE-CHAIRMAN: B W Hubbard
DIRECTOR: R F Pepper, Mike Warner
SECRETARY
Nicola Bellamy (01246 209 765)
COMMERCIAL MANAGER
Jim Brown

MANAGER: John Duncan
ASSISTANT MANAGER: Kevin Randall

PHYSIOTHERAPIST
Dave Rushbury

STATISTICIAN FOR THE DIRECTORY
Richard West

Manager John Duncan worked the miracle at Saltergate for a second time as he led the Spireites to promotion via the play-offs exactly ten years after winning the Division Four Championship with Chesterfield during his previous spell in charge.

Despite hovering around the play-off zone for the first half of the season, there was little talk about promotion before Christmas. Then came the inspirational signing of midfielder Phil Robinson and striker Tony Lormor to add and extra dimension to the team. Starting with the Boxing Day victory over Doncaster Rovers, the Blues embarked on a club record run of 21 league games without defeat.

It looked as though the superb unbeaten sequence would be enough to pip Walsall for second place, but a heartbreaking defeat at home to champions Carlisle United in the penultimate game scuppered hopes of automatic promotion. Duncan's gutsy squad was not about to surrender after coming so close, however, and a mouth-watering pairing with local rivals Mansfield Town in the play-off semi-finals produced one of the all time classic games at Saltergate as Chesterfield twice came from behind to thrash the Stags 5-2 in extra time.

And so to Wembley. The Derbyshire club's only previous visit to the Twin Towers in 1990 led to a narrow defeat by John Beck's Cambridge United in the first ever play-off Final to be held at Wembley. This time around, first-half strikes form Lormor and Robinson put Chesterfield firmly in control and the Spireites held their nerve to defeat Bury 2-0 and step up to Division Two.

GREG TESSER.

CHESTERFIELD

Division Three: 3rd   **FA Cup:** 1st Round   **Coca-Cola Cup:** 2nd Round

M	DATE	COMP.	VEN	OPPONENTS	RESULT	H/T	LP	GOAL SCORERS/GOAL TIMES	ATT.
1	A 13	EL	H	Scarborough	L 0-1	0-1			3,099
2	16	CC 1/1	A	Blackpool	W 2-1			Perkins, Cheetham	(2,570)
3	20	EL	A	Rochdale	L 1-4	0-1	17	Norris	(2,122)
4	23	CC 1/2	H	Blackpool	W 4-2			Norris (Pen), Davies, Morris, Curtis	2,516
5	27	EL	H	Mansfield Town	L 0-1		19		4,210
6	30	EL	A	Wigan Athletic	W 3-2	2-1		Robertson (og), Morris, Moss	(1,231)
7	S 3	EL	A	Hartlepool United	W 2-0	0-0	11	Morris, Moss	(2,173)
8	10	EL	H	Walsall	D 0-0	0-0	12		3,027
9	13	EL	H	Exeter City	W 2-0	1-0		Davies, Norris	2,136
10	17	EL	A	Scarborough	W 1-0	1-0	10	Curtis	(1,475)
11	20	CC 2/1	H	Wolverhampton W.	L 1-3			Moss	5,895
12	24	EL	A	Bury	L 1-2	1-1	12	Davies	(3,031)
13	27	CC 2/2	A	Wolverhampton W.	D 1-1			Jules	(14,815)
14	O 1	EL	H	Torquay United	W 1-0	0-0	9	Burton (og)	2,465
15	8	EL	A	Colchester United	W 3-0	1-0	8	Davies, Moss, Morris	(3,476)
16	15	EL	H	Darlington	D 0-0	0-0	6		2,836
17	18	AWS 1	A	Rotherham United	D 1-1			Roberts	(1,585)
18	22	EL	H	Fulham	D 1-1	1-0	7	Roberts	2,860
19	29	EL	A	Barnet	L 1-4	1-2	9	Hewitt	(2,130)
20	N 5	EL	H	Hereford United	W 1-0	1-0	7	Norris	2,448
21	8	AWS 1	H	Scunthorpe United	D 1-1			Davies	1,424
22	12	FAC 1	H	Scarborough	D 0-0	0-0			2,902
23	19	EL	A	Gillingham	D 1-1	1-0	7	Davies	(2,722)
24	22	FAC 1R	A	Scarborough	L 0-2				(1,564)
25	26	EL	H	Preston North End	W 1-0	0-0	7	McAuley	3,191
26	29	AWS 2	A	Carlisle United	L 0-1				(3,531)
27	D 10	EL	H	Rochdale	D 2-2	2-1	7	Hewitt (2)	2,457
28	18	EL	A	Mansfield Town	L 2-4	0-2	7	Davies, Robinson	(3,519)
29	26	EL	H	Doncaster Rovers	W 2-0	1-0	7	Robinson (2)	4,226
30	27	EL	A	Northampton Town	W 3-2	2-1	7	Moss (2), Madden	(6,329)
31	31	EL	H	Lincoln City	W 1-0	0-0	5	Robinson	8,325
32	J 8	EL	A	Fulham	D 1-1	1-0	4	Moss	(3,927)
33	14	EL	H	Scunthorpe United	W 3-1	3-0	3	Lormor, Moss (2)	3,245
34	24	EL	A	Hereford United	W 2-0	1-0		Lormor, Davies	(1,673)
35	F 4	EL	A	Preston North End	D 0-0	0-0	3		(8,544)
36	11	EL	H	Gillingham	W 2-0	2-0	2	Lormor, Law	3,070
37	14	EL	H	Barnet	W 2-0	0-0		Moss, Davies	2,978
38	18	EL	A	Scunthorpe United	W 1-0	0-0	2	Robinson	(3,566)
39	25	EL	A	Torquay United	D 3-3	1-1	2	Lormor, Davies (2)	(3,236)
40	M 4	EL	H	Bury	D 0-0	0-0	2		4,429
41	11	EL	A	Walsall	W 3-1	1-0	2	Carr, Lormor, Howard	(6,219)
42	18	EL	H	Wigan Athletic	D 0-0	0-0			8,808
43	25	EL	H	Hartlepool United	W 2-0	1-0	2	Lormor (2)	4,125
44	A 1	EL	A	Exeter City	W 2-1	0-0	2	Davies, Morris	(2,144)
45	4	EL	A	Carlisle United	D 1-1	0-0		Moss	(8,478)
46	8	EL	A	Lincoln City	W 1-0	1-0	2	Robinson	(5,141)
47	15	EL	H	Northampton	W 3-0	1-0	2	Morris (2), Robinson	4,884
48	17	EL	A	Doncaster Rovers	W 3-1	1-1	2	Robinson, Carr, Curtis	(4,796)
49	29	EL	A	Darlington	W 1-0	1-0	2	Lormor	(3,387)
50	M 2	EL	H	Carlisle United	L 1-2	1-1		Davies	7,283
51	6	EL	H	Colchester United	D 2-2	1-1	3	Lormor (2)	4,133
52	14	PO 1	A	Mansfield Town	D 1-1			Robinson	(6,582)
53	17	PO 2	H	Mansfield Town	W 5-2	1-2		Lormor, Howard (2), Law (2)	8,165
54	27	PO F	N	Bury	W 2-0	2-0		Lormor, Robinson	(22,814)
55									
56									
57									
58									
59									
60									

Best Home League Attendance: 8,808 v Wigan Athletic   **Smallest:** 2,136 v Exeter City   **Av Home Att:** 3,773

Goal Scorers:

League (62): Davies 11, Lormor 10 (2 pens), Moss 10, Robinson 8, Morris 6, Hewitt 3, Norris 3, Carr 2, Curtis 2, Howard 1, Law 1, McAuley 1, Madden 1, Roberts 1, Opponents 2.

C/Cola Cup (8): Cheetham 1, Curtis 1, Davies 1, Jules 1, Morris 1, Moss 1, Norris 1, Perkins 1.

AWS (2): Roberts, Davies.

FA Cup (0)

Play-offs (8): Howard 2, Law 2, Lormor 2, Robinson 2.

Compared with 1993-94: +632

434

1994-95

Marples	Hewitt	Rogers	Fairclough	Carr	Law	Curtis	Norris	Davies	Moss	Cheetham	Perkins	Roberts	Beesley	Marshall	Spooner	Morris	Jules	Hill	Madden	Reddish	Dyche	McAuley	Robinson	Lormor	Narbett	Referee
1	2	3•	4	5	6	7	8*	9	10	11	14	12	S													1
1	2	3	4	5		7	8	9	10	11	6		S	S												2
1	2	3	4	5		7	8	9		11	6*		S	12	10	S										3
1	2	3	4	5		7	8	9		6	S		S		10	11*	12									4
1	2	3	4	5	6	7	8	9	10				S			11	S	S								5
1	2	3	S	5	6	7		9	10				S			8	11	4								6
1	2	3		5	6	7		9	10			S	S			8	11	4								7
1	2	3		5	6	7		9	10		14		S		12	8	11*	4								8
1	2	3		5	6	7	12	9	S		10*		S		11	8			4							9
1	2	3		5	6	7		9	10		12		S		11	8			4							10
1	2	3		5	6	7	12	9*	10		8•		S		11		14		4							11
1	2	3	12	5	6	7		9	10•		14		S		4	8	11*									12
	2	3	10	5	6	7	S		S	8	1			4	9	11										13
1	2			5	6	7		10	S		8*		S	4*	9	11		3	12							14
	3	2		6•	7		8	10			14	S			9	12	5	11								15
	2	3	6			7		8•	10*		14	S			9	12	5	4	11							16
	2	3	6			7		8	10	12	4	14	1		9•		5*	11								17
1	2	3	6	5		7*		8	12	10*	4	9	S						11							18
1	2	3	6	5		7		8	10		4*	S	S		9				12							19
1	2	3	6	5		7	8	S			4	11	S		9				10							20
	2		6	5		S	8	12	10		4	9•	1			11					7					21
1	2	3	6	5		7•		8	14		4*	S			9	12			11		10					22
	3	6	5			7		8	9		4	S	S		11		2	S								23
1	3	6	5			7•		8	9		10	4	S		12	11*			2	14						24
	11	3	7	5	6		S	8	S		4	1			9				2	10						25
	7	3	4	5	6		S	8	S			1			9	11			2							26
	2	3			6		14	8	10		4	1				12			5		11*		7			27
	2	3			6	12		9	10		4*	1							5		11		7			28
1	2	3		5	6	4		9	10			S				14					11	S	7	8		29
1	2		5•		6	4		8	10			S				14			3		11	S	7	9		30
1	2	5		6		4		8	10	3		S				12					11	S	7	9*		31
1	2		5	6		4		8	10			S				12					11	S	7	9*		32
1*	2	3		5	6	4		8•	10			S*			S	14					11		7	9		33
	2	3	5	6	4		8•					1			10	14					11		7	9	12	34
	2	3	S	5	6	4		8	10			1			12						11		7	9*		35
	2	3	S	5	6	4		8	10*			1			12						11		7	9		36
	2	3		5	6	4		8	10*			1			12	S					11		7	9		37
	2	3	S	5	6	4		8	10	11		1											7	9	S	38
	2	3	S	5	6	4		8	10			1				11							7	9*		39
	2	3		5	6	4		8	10•	S		1*			14						11		7	9	S	40
	2	3		5	6	4		8*	10			1				7					11		7	9	S	41
	2	3		5	6	4		8*	10			1				14					11			9	7•	42
	3			6•		4		8			2	1				14	5		11					9	7	43
	3			6	4		8	S				1			10		5		11*				7	9		44
	2	3		5	6	4		8	12			1			10*	11•							7	9		45
	2	3		5	6	4		8*	10	11		1					S				11		7	9		46
	2	3		5	6	4		8*	10	11		1									11		7	9•		47
	2	3		5	6	4		8		11		1			10								7	9		48
	2	3		5	6	4		8•		11		1			10*								7	9		49
	2	3		5	6	4		8	10	11*		1			12								7	9•		50
	2	3		5		4		8*	14	11		1			10•								7	9		51
	2	3	S	5	6	4		8*	10	11		1											7	9		52
	2	3	S	5	6	4				14		1*			10								7	9		53
																										54

21	38	39	12	35	35	39	5	41	28	5	17	4	20		6	21	10	3	10	2	22	1	22	23	2	League Appearances
		1				1	2		4	1	7	1	1	1	5	13			1						1	League Sub Appearances
3	4	4	3	4	2	4	2+1	3	2	2	1	2	1		3	2	1+2	1								C/Cola Cup Appearances
2	1	2	2	2		2	2	1+1	1		2					1+1	1+1				2		1+1			FA Cup Appearances
3	2	3	2	1	1	1	2+1	2	0+1	2	1+1	2				2	1		1		1		3	1		A.W.S Appearances

Also Played: Lewis S (2), Brown S (34,35,50), Bibbo S(36-39, 41,42) 12 (40), Stewart 1 (42), S (43-49, 51,52) 12 (53),
Howard 12 (39, 41-44, 46,47,51,52), 14 (45,49,50), S (48), 8 (53), Hazell 11 (53*).

CHESTERFIELD RECORDS AND STATISTICS

CLUB RECORDS

BIGGEST VICTORIES
League: 10-0 v Glossop, Division 2, 17.1.1903.
F.A. Cup: 5-0 v Wath Athletic (a), 1st Round, 1925-26.
League Cup: 5-0 v Mansfield (a), 1st Round, 1971-72.
5-0 v Scunthorpe United, 1st Round replay, 1972-73.

BIGGEST DEFEATS
League: 0-10 v Gillingham (a), Division 3, 5.9.1987.
F.A. Cup: 1-8 v West Ham United, 1st Round, 1913-14.
0-7 v Burnley, 3rd Round, 1956-57.

MOST POINTS
3 points a win: 91, Division 4, 1984-85.
2 points a win: 64, Division 4, 1969-70.

MOST GOALS SCORED
102, Division 3(N), 1930-31.

RECORD TRANSFER FEE RECEIVED
£200,000 from Wolves for Alan Birch, August 1981.

RECORD TRANSFER FEE PAID
£150,000 to Carlisle United for Phil Bonnyman, March 1980.

BEST PERFORMANCES
League: 4th Division 2, 1946-47.
F.A. Cup: 5th Round 1932-33, 1937-38, 1949-50.
League Cup: 4th Round 1964-65.

HONOURS
Champions Division 3(N) 1930-31, 1935-36.
Champions Division 4, 1969-70, 1984-85.
Anglo-Scottish Cup winners 1980-81.

LEAGUE CAREER
Elected to Div 2 1899, Failed re-election 1908-09, Re-elected to Div 3(N) 1921-22, Div 2 1930-31, Div 3(N) 1932-33, Div 2 1935-36, Div £(N) 1950-51, Transferred to Div 3 1958, Div 4 1960-61, Div 3 1969-70, Div 4 1982-83, Div 3 1984-85, Div 4 (now Div 3) 1988-89, Div 2 1994-95.

INDIVIDUAL CLUB RECORDS

MOST GOALS IN A SEASON
Jimmy Cookson: 46 goals in 1925-26 (League 44, FA Cup 2).

MOST GOALS IN A MATCH
No player has ever scored more than 4 goals in a match, but this feat has been achieved on 19 occasions.

OLDEST PLAYER
Billy Kidd, 40 years 232 days v Southampton, Division 2, 20.9.1947.

YOUNGEST PLAYER
Dennis Thompson, 16 years 160 days v Notts County, Division 2, 26.12.1950.

MOST CAPPED PLAYER
Walter McMillan (Northern Ireland) 4.

PREVIOUS MANAGERS

1945-49 Bob Brocklebank; 1949-52 Bob Marshall; 1952-58 Ted Davison; 1958-62 Dugald Livingstone; 1962-67 Tony McShane; 1967-73 Jimmy McGuigan; 1973-76 Joe Shaw; 1976-80 Arthur Cox; 1980-83 Frank Barlow; 1983-87 John Duncan; 1987-88 Kevin Randall; 1988-91 Paul Hart; 1991-93 Chris McMenemy.

ADDITIONAL INFORMATION
PREVIOUS NAMES
Chesterfield Municipal until 1915, Chesterfield Town 1919-22.

PREVIOUS LEAGUES
Midland League.

Club colours: Blue shirts, white shorts, blue socks.
Change colours: Green & white striped shirts, navy shorts, navy socks.

Reserves League: Pontins League.

LONGEST LEAGUE RUNS

of undefeated matches:	21 (1994-95)	of league matches w/out a win:	16 (1960-61, 1983)
of undefeated home matches:	27 (1925-26)	of undefeated away matches:	12 (1994-95)
without home win:	9 (1963)	without an away win:	26 (1907-08)
of league wins:	10 (1933)	of home wins:	17 (1929-30)
of league defeats:	9 (1960)	of away wins:	6 (1933)

THE MANAGER

JOHN DUNCAN . . . . appointed February 1993.

PREVIOUS CLUBS
As Manager . . . . Hartlepool United, Chesterfield, Ipswich Town.
As Player Manager . . . . Scunthorpe United.
As a player . . . . Dundee, Tottenham Hotspur, Derby County, Scunthorpe United.

HONOURS
As a Manager . . . . Chesterfield: Division 4 Champions 1985. Promotion to Division 2 via the play-offs 1995.
As a Player . . . . Scottish Football League.

CHESTERFIELD

PLAYERS NAME Honours	Ht	Wt	Birthdate	Birthplace Transfers	Contract Date	Clubs	League	L/Cup	FA Cup	Other	Lge	L/C	FAC	Oth
G O A L K E E P E R S														
Andy Beasley	6.2	12.2	05.02.64	Sedgley	23.02.82	Luton Town (A)								
				Free	06.07.84	Mansfield Town	94	5	3	7				
				Loan	28.07.86	Peterborough Utd	7	3						
				Loan	01.03.88	Scarborough	4							
Loan 11.92 Kettering 1 FAC App.				Loan	25.03.93	Bristol Rovers	1							
				Free	30.07.93	Doncaster Rovers	37	2	1	2				
				Free	12.08.94	Chesterfield	20+1	1		5				
D E F E N D E R S														
Darren Carr	6.2	13.0	04.09.68	Bristol	20.08.86	Bristol Rovers (T)	26+4	2+2	3	2				
via Newport Co, 30.10.87, £3,000, 9 Lge App.				£8,000	10.03.88	Sheffield United	12+1	1	3+1	1	1			
				£35,000	18.09.90	Crewe Alexandra	96+8	8	12	10	5		2	
				£30,000	21.07.93	Chesterfield	63	7	3	7	3			
Sean Dyche	6.0	11.7	28.06.71	Kettering	20.05.89	Nottingham F. (T)								
				Free	01.02.90	Chesterfield	144+10	5	5	13	8			
Wayne Fairclough	5.10	9.12	27.04.68	Nottingham	28.04.86	Notts County (A)	39+32	1+2	3	10+3				
				£80,000	05.03.90	Mansfield Town	131+10	5	4+1	10	12		1	
				Free	23.06.94	Chesterfield	12+1	3	2	3				
Jamie Hewitt	5.10	10.8	17.05.68	Chesterfield	22.04.86	Chesterfield (T)	240+9	10	8+1	11+2	14	1		
				Free	01.08.92	Doncaster Rovers	32+1	3+1	1	3		1		
					08.10.93	Chesterfield	66+1	4	2	8	5			
Nicholas Law	6.0	13.5	08.09.61	Greenwich	17.07.79	Arsenal (A)								
E: S.				Free	04.08.81	Barnsley	113+1	5	6		1			
				Free	28.08.85	Blackpool	64+2	2	2	3	1			
				£40,000	12.03.87	Plymouth Argyle	37+1	2	2	0+1	5			
				£70,000	17.06.88	Notts County	44+3	4	1	4	4			
Loan 10.11.89 Scarborough 12 Lge, 1 FAC App.				£35,000	01.08.90	Rotherham United	126+2	12	12	7	3	1		
					08.10.93	Chesterfield	66	2	1	6	3			2
Lawrence Madden	5.11	13.1	28.09.55	London		Arsenal (T)								
				Free	01.03.75	Mansfield Town	9+1	2	2					
via Manchester University				Free	04.03.78	Charlton Athletic	109+4	4+2	8		7			
				£10,000	25.03.82	Millwall	44+3	2	1		2			
				Free	24.08.83	Sheffield Wed.	200+12	26+2	20+1	5	2	3		
				Loan	17.01.91	Leicester City	3							
				Free	15.08.91	Wolverhampton W.	62+5	4	3	2	1			
				Free	03.09.93	Darlington	5			1				
				Free	04.10.93	Chesterfield	46	3	1	2	2			
Chris Perkins	5.11	10.9	09.01.74	Nottingham	19.11.92	Mansfield Town (T)	3+5			0+1				
				Free	15.07.94	Chesterfield	17+1	1	2	3+2		1		
Lee Rogers	5.11	12.1	28.10.66	Doncaster	27.07.84	Doncaster Rov. (T)				1				
				Free	29.08.86	Chesterfield	274+19	15+1	10+1	25+1	1			
Mark S Williams	6.0	13.0	28.09.70	Hyde		Newtown								
Div.3'94.				Free	27.03.92	Shrewsbury Town	98+6	7+1	6	6	3			1
				£20,000	08.95	Chesterfield								
M I D F I E L D														
Tommy Curtis	5.8	11.4	01.03.73	Exeter	01.07.91	Derby County (J)								
				Free	12.08.93	Chesterfield	74+2	8	3	5	5	1		
David Moss	6.2	13.7	15.11.68	Doncaster		Boston United								
					10.03.93	Doncaster Rovers	18	2		0+1	5			
				Free	08.10.93	Chesterfield	53+5	2	2+1	3	16	1		
Jonathan Narbett	5.11	12.3	21.05.68	Birmingham	19.09.86	Shrewsbury T. (A)	20+6	4	1		3			
				£30,000	06.10.88	Hereford United	148+1	8	10	14	31	1	2	3
				£65,000	07.07.92	Oxford United	13+2	1	2	2+1				
Free to Kalmar FF 30.03.94						Merthyr Tydfil								
					23.12.94	Chesterfield	2+1							
Philip Robinson	5.9	10.10	06.01.67	Stafford	08.01.85	Aston Villa (A)	2+1				1			
Div.4'88. Div.3'89. AMC'88'91.				£5,000	03.07.87	Wolverhampton W.	63+8	6	3	8+2	8	1		
				£67,500	18.08.89	Notts County	65+1	6	1+1	9+1	5	1		
Loan 18.03.91 Birmingham C. 9 Lge, 2+1 Oth. Ap.					01.09.92	Huddersfield Town	74+1	4	8	8	4		1	
					09.12.94	Chesterfield	22		3	8	8			2
				Loan	30.12.94	Telford United								
F O R W A R D S														
Kevin Davies	6.0	12.12	26.03.77	Sheffield	18.04.94	Chesterfield (T)	57+8	4+1	1	5+2	15	1		1
Desmond Hazel	5.10	10.4	15.07.67	Bradford	29.07.85	Sheffield Wed (A)	5+1	1		0+1				
Div.4'89.				Loan	23.10.86	Grimsby Town	9				2			
				£45,000	13.07.88	Rotherham United	204+34	17+1	17	18	28	3	1	6
					23.03.95	Chesterfield				2				
Jonathan Howard	5.10	11.7	07.10.71	Sheffield	10.07.90	Rotherham Utd (T)	25+11	0+1	4	3+1	5		2	
					09.12.94	Chesterfield	1+11			2+1	1			2
Mark Jules	5.10	11.1	05.09.71	Bradford	03.07.90	Bradford City (T)		0+1						
				Free	14.08.91	Scarborough	57+20	6+4	1+1	6	16	2		4
				£40,000	21.05.93	Chesterfield	38+18	5+7	1+2	4	1	2		
Anthony Lormor	6.0	11.5	29.10.70	Ashington	25.02.88	Newcastle Utd (T)	6+2				3			
				£25,000	29.01.90	Lincoln City	90+10	1+2	4	6	30	2	2	
Loan 03.03.94 Halifax Town				Free	04.07.94	Peterborough Utd	2+3		1	1+1				
				Free	23.12.94	Chesterfield	23			3	10			2
Andrew Morris	6.4	15.7	17.11.67	Sheffield	29.07.85	Rotherham Utd (J)	0+7	0+1						
					12.01.88	Chesterfield	183+29	15	9+1	14+4	46	8	3	3
				Loan	04.03.92	Exeter City	4+3				2			
Darren Roberts	6.0	12.4	12.10.69	Birmingham		Burton Albion								
				£20,000	23.04.92	Wolverhampton W.	12+9	0+1		1+1	5			
				Loan	18.03.94	Hereford United	5+1				5			
				Free	18.07.94	Chesterfield	4+7	2		1+1	1			1
				Loan	30.12.94	Telford United								

RECREATION GROUND
Chesterfield S40 4SX
Tel: 01246 209 765

Capacity 11,308
Seating..2,608

First game ....v Lincoln City, 9.9.1899.
First floodlit game..v Lincoln City, 23.10.1967.

Attendances
Highest...30,968 v Newcastle United, Division 2, 7.4.1939.
Lowest ....1,053 v Burnley, AMC, 21.1.1986.

Other Grounds..None.

MATCHDAY TICKET PRICES

Centre Stand £9
Juv/OAP £4.50

Wing Stand £8
Juv/OAP £4

Family Stand (1 Adult + 2 children). £8

Terraces. £7
Juv/OAP £3.50

Ticket Office Telephone no. . . . . . . 01246 209 765.

HOW TO GET TO THE GROUND

From the North
Use motorway (M1) until junction 30, then follow signs to Chesterfield (A619). In town centre follow signs to Old Brampton into Saltergate for Chesterfield FC.

From East and South
Follow signs to Chesterfield (A617) into town centre then follow signs to Old Brampton into Saltergate for Chesterfield FC.

From the West
Follow signs to Chesterfield (A619) then at roundabout take first exit into Foljambe Road at the end turn right into Saltergate for Chesterfield FC.

Car Parking
Street parking near ground allowed. Car parks 0.5 miles from ground in Saltergate.

Nearest Railway Station
Chesterfield (01246 74371)

SPIREITES HOTLINE
0891 55 58 18
Calls cost 39p per minute cheap rate and 49p per minute at all other times.
Call costings correct at time of going to press.

MATCHDAY PROGRAMME

Programme Editor . . . . K Barson.

Number of pages . . . . 36.

Price . . . . £1.30.

Subscriptions . . . . £30 + £5 P&P.

Local Newspapers . . . . Derbyshire Times, Sheffield Star,
. . . . Chesterfield Star.

Local Radio Stations . . . . Radio Hallam, Radio BBC Sheffield.

CREWE ALEXANDRA
(The Railwaymen)
ENDSLEIGH LEAGUE DIVISION 2
SPONSORED BY: BOLDON JAMES

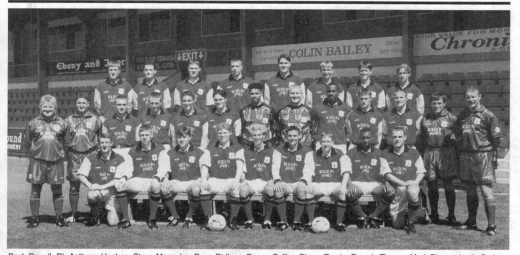

Back Row (L-R): Anthony Hughes, Steve Macauley, Dave Ridings, Danny Collier, Simon Turpin, Francis Tierney, Mark Rivers, Justin Parker.
Middle Row: John Fleet (Kit Manager), Steve Holland (Yth Coach), Rob Edwards, Billy Barr, Lee Unsworth, Steven Pope, Mark Gayle, Mark Smith, Dele Adebola, Ashley Westwood, Shaun Smith, Dario Gradi (Manager), Neil Baker (Asst. Manager).
Front Row: Phil Clarkson, Dale Hawtin, Martyn Booty, Neil Lennon, Robbie Savage, Gareth Whalley, Steve Garvey, Wayne Collins, Danny Murphy. **Photo:** Steve Finch LRPS.

CREWE ALEXANDRA
FORMED IN 1877
TURNED PROFESSIONAL IN 1893
LTD COMPANY IN 1892

PRESIDENT: N Rowlinson
CHAIRMAN: J Bowler MPS
VICE-CHAIRMAN
N Hassall FCCA
DIRECTORS
K Potts, J McMillan, D Rowlinson, R Clayton,
D Gradi, E Weetman, R G Holmes.
SECRETARY
Mrs Gill Palin (01270) 213 014)
COMMERCIAL MANAGER
Gill Palin

MANAGER: Dario Gradi
ASSISTANT MANAGER: Neil Baker
RESERVE TEAM MANAGER
Neil Baker
YOUTH TEAM MANAGER
Steve Holland
PHYSIOTHERAPIST
Bernadette Oakes
STATISTICIAN FOR THE DIRECTORY
Harold Finch

Following their promotion to Division Two on the final day of the previous season, there were many who wondered just how would this young Crewe team fare in a higher Division. They did not have long to wait and they won their first five league games to go to the top of the table.

That run of success did not last and after a spell of six matches without a win, they bounced back again once more. A n early dismissal from the Coca-Cola Cup was to some extent a disappointment but they did not let it effect their game. Two results really set them back on their heels, a 7-1 reverse at Hull followed by a 5-0 defeat at the hands of Birmingham City.

The F.A. Cup brought them into contact with non-League side Gresley Rovers and they recorded their highest win to date in the competition proper with centre forward Ashley Ward getting a hat-trick. In a spell of just six games, Ashley scored ten goals including that F.A. Cup hat-trick and another in the A.W.S. competition and Norwich City were alerted and signed him for a fee of £500,000.

The loss of the leading striker could have been a problem but goals started coming from all quarters to keep the fans happy. A late winner by Bury ended their run in the F.A. Cup but it may have been a blessing in disguise, the team were able to concentrate on their league games, with the A.W.S. as a secondary string to their bow.

Carlisle United managed to hold out in the A.W.S. Semi-Final at Gresty Road and so in the end a Wembley dream came to nought. It was now that the attention turned to the league position and with a fairly settled side, apart from a hiccup during the month of March the club managed to always keep in touch with the leading group.

April arrived and a run of eight games brought 22 out of 24 points, the Manager, his second Manager of the Month award and above all into the play-off positions. A draw in the final game against Cardiff City ensured them of third place in the table, and so, for the third time in a period of four years, a place in the play-offs. It had been a great season for everyone, we did far better than expected, this young side have gained valuable experience and could go on to even greater things.

The play-off semi-finals against Bristol Rovers were both close affairs. A goalless draw at Twerton Park set up an exciting finale. After 90 minutes the sides were still level and although Crewe went ahead in extra time Bristol gained a fortuitous equaliser. The away goal ruling applied and there was to be no play-off appearance at Wembley.

HAROLD FINCH.

CREWE ALEXANDRA

Division Two: 3rd   FA Cup: 2nd Round   Coca-Cola Cup: 1st Round   Auto Windscreen Trophy:

M	DATE	COMP.	VEN	OPPONENTS	RESULT	H/T	LP	GOAL SCORERS/GOAL TIMES	ATT.
1	A 13	EL	A	York City	W 2-1	0-0		Macauley 61,87	(4,420)
2	16	CC	H	**Wigan Athletic**	W 2-1	1-0		**Garvey 35, Ward 70**	**3,054**
3	20	EL	H	Rotherham United	W 3-1	2-0	4	Rowbotham 8, Tierney 41, Ward 58	3,505
4	23	CC	A	**Wigan Athletic**	L 0-3	0-0			**(1,421)**
5	27	EL	A	Peterborough	W 5-1	3-0	2	Rowbotham 6, 7, Collins 44, Smith (pen) 52, Ward 64	(4,579)
6	30	EL	H	Stockport City	W 2-1	0-0	1	Booty 56, collins 57	5,050
7	S 9	EL	H	Blackpool	W 4-3	2-2	1	Garvey 44, Smith (pen) 23, Barr 74, Booty 89	4,915
8	10	EL	A	Wrexham	L 0-1	0-0	1		(6,399)
9	13	EL	A	Oxford United	L 1-2	0-2	2	Savage 51	(6,499)
10	17	EL	H	Wycombe Wanderers	L 1-2	0-2	5	Walters 86	4,466
11	24	EL	H	Brentford	L 0-2	0-1	7		3,839
12	27	AWT	H	Wrexham	D 0-0	0-0			1,573
13	O 1	EL	A	Bristol Rovers	D 2-2	2-0	8	Ward 30, Garvey 44	(4,862)
14	8	EL	A	Cardiff City	W 2-1	0-1	7	Ward 89, Edwards 90	(4,126)
15	15	EL	H	Shrewsbury	L 1-0	1-0	6	Ward 11	4,296
16	22	EL	H	Huddersfield	D 3-3	3-2	6	Garvey 26, Macauley 35, Edwards 42	5,352
17	29	EL	A	Hull City	L 1-7	0-2	9	Ward 55	(4,694)
18	N 1	EL	A	Birmingham City	L 0-5	0-3	10		(14,212)
19	5	EL	H	Swansea City	L 1-2	0-1	11	Smith (pen) 66	3,242
20	8	AWT	A	Mansfield	D 2-2	1-1		Collins 17, Ward 65	(1,250)
21	12	FAC 1	H	**Gresley Rovers**	W 7-1	1-0		Rowbotham 30,78, Ward 72,79,86, Elliott 60 (0g), Garvey 82	4,539
22	19	EL	A	Bradford City	W 2-0	2-0	8	Ward 2 , Adebola 27	(5,520)
23	26	EL	H	Cambridge United	W 4-2	1-0	6	Smith (pen) 11, Collins 48, 72, Ward 55	3,656
24	29	AWT	A	**Chester**	W 6-0	3-0		Ward 13, 31(pen) 80	**(1,890)**
25	D 3	FAC 2	H	**Bury**	L 1-2	1-0	8	**Ward 26**	**4,875**
26	10	EL	A	Rotherham United	D 2-2	2-0	8	Collins 45, Lennon 45	(3,907)
27	16	EL	H	York City	W 2-1	2-0	6	Adebola 13, Lennon 20	3,432
28	26	EL	H	Chester	W 2-1	0-1	6	Adebola 55, Lennon 82	5,428
29	27	EL	A	Bournemouth	D 1-1	0-1	7	Collins 75,	(3,325)
30	31	EL	H	Leyton Orient	W 3-0	0-0	6	Clarkson 59, Murphy, Bellamy (og)	3,792
31	J 2	EL	A	Plymouth	L 2-3	2-1	7	Murphy 13, Clarkson 40	(6,802)
32	7	EL	A	Huddersfield	W 2-1	1-0	6	Smith 15, Collins 55	(11,466)
33	14	EL	H	Brighton	W 4-0	1-0	3	Adebola 24, Collins 54, Smith 59, Clarkson 83	4,286
34	F 4	EL	A	Cambridge	W 2-1	0-0	4	Murphy 46, Collins 54	(3,339)
35	7	AWT	A	**Wigan Athletic**	W 3-1	2-0		**Whalley 4, Macauley 19, Adebola 75**	**(2,063)**
36	11	EL	H	Birmingham	W 2-1	1-0	4	Clarkson 31, Murphy 64	6,359
37	14	AWT	H	**Carlisle United**	L 0-1	0-1			**4,046**
38	18	EL	A	Brighton	W 1-0	1-0	4	Savage 5	(6,986)
39	21	EL	H	Bradford City	L 0-1	0-0	4		4,214
40	26	EL	H	Bristol Rovers	W 2-1	2-0	4	Adebola 31, Murphy 45	4,222
41	M 4	EL	A	Brentford	L 0-2	0-1	4		(7,143)
42	7	EL	A	Blackpool	D 0-0	0-0	4		(5,859)
43	11	EL	H	Peterborough	L 1-3	0-2	5	Rowbotham 47	3,983
44	18	EL	A	Stockport City	L 0-1	0-1		Lennon 86	(4,974)
45	21	EL	H	Wrexham	L 1-3	0-3	6	Smith (pen)	3,632
46	25	EL	A	Wycombe Wanderers	D 0-0	0-0	7		(6,288)
47	A 1	EL	H	Oxford United	W 3-2	1-2	6	Rowbotham, Smith, Adebola	3,928
48	8	EL	A	Leyton Orient	W 4-1	2-1	6	Whalley, Rowbotham, Tierney, Lennon	(2,797)
49	15	EL	H	AFC Bournemouth	W 2-0	1-0	6	Collins 23, Tierney 83	3,906
50	17	EL	A	Chester	W 1-0	0-0	6	Tierney 55	(3,054)
51	22	EL	H	Plymouth	D 2-2	2-1	7	Lennon 7, Adebola 27	3,786
52	25	EL	A	Swansea	W 1-0	1-0	5	Clarkson 3	(2,600)
53	29	EL	A	Shrewsbury	W 2-1	2-1	5	Collins 18, Barr 32	4,381
54	M 2	EL	H	Hull City	W 3-2	2-2	3	Macauley 26, Clarkson 42, Adebola 56	3,870
55	6	EL	H	Cardiff City	D 0-0	0-0	3		4,382
56	14	POSF	A	Bristol Rovers	D 0-0	0-0			(8,538)
57	17	POSF	H	Bristol Rovers	D 1-1	0-0		Rowbotham 97 (Bristol won on away goals rule)	6,578
58									
59									
60									

Best Home League Attendance: 6,359 v Birmingham City   Smallest: 3,242 v Swansea City   Av Home Att: 3,974

Goal Scorers: Compared with 1993-94: +141

League (80):   Collins 11, Ward 8 (1 pen), Adebola 8, Smith 8 (5 pens), Rowbotham 6, Lennon 6, Clarkson 6, Murphy 5, Macauley 4,
               Tierney 4, Garvey 3, Booty 2, Edwards 2, Savage 2, Barr 2, Whalley, Walters, Opponent
C/Cola Cup (2):   Ward, Garvey
FA Cup (8):   Ward 4, Rowbotham 2, Garvey, Opponent
AW Trophy (11):   Ward 4, Collins 2, Adebola 2, Whalley 2, Macauley   PLAY-OFFS (1): Rowbotham

1994-95

Smith M.	Booty M.	Gardiner M.	Wilson G.	Macauley S.	Barr B.	Tierney F.	Walters S.	Ward A.	Whalley G.	Rowbotham D.	Adebola D.	Collier D.	Gayle M.	Annan R.	Garvey S.	Smith S.	Collins W.	Murphy D.	Savage R.	Edwards R.	Lennon N.	Clarkson P.	McCarthy S.	Woodward A.	Wilkinson I.	Referee	
1	2	3*	4	5	6	7	8	9	10	11	12	S	S													E. Wolstenholme	1
1	2		4•	5	6	7	8	9	10		12	14	S	3	11*											U. Rennie	2
1	2	3		5	6	7	8	9	10	11*		S	S		12	4										D. Allison	3
1	2			5	6	7		9	10	11		S	S		S	3	4	8								J. Kirkby	4
S	2			5	6	7		9•	10	11		14	3	1		4*	8	12								T. West	5
S	2			5	6			9	10	11		S	3	1		4	8	12								K. Breen	6
S	2			5	6		12	9	3	11		S	1		7	4	8	10*								R. Poulain	7
S	2			5	6		4	9	10•	11		14	1		7	3	8		9*	12						K. Lynch	8
S	2*			5	6		4	9	10				1		7	3	8	12	11	S						P. Alcock	9
S	2			5	6•		4	9	10			14	1		7	3		8		11*	12					J. Parker	10
S	2	10			6		4•	9			12	5*	1		7	3	8	14		11						A. Butler	11
	2	10			6			9	5	11		S	1		7	3	8	4		S						T. Lunt	12
S	2	10	5*	S	6			9	4	11	S		1		7	3	8	12								M. Bailey	13
S	2		4	5	14		14	9*		11			1		7•	3	8	10*		12						K. Cooper	14
S	2		4	5	14		14	9*		11			1		7•	3	8	10		6						M. Riley	15
S	2		4	5				6*	11	9	S		1		7	3	8	12		10						P. Vanes	16
S	2		4	5			14	9	6•	11	12		1		7*	3	8	10								T. Heilbron	17
S	2		4	5		12	8	9*	6	11			1			3	14	10		7•						G. Cain	18
S	2		4	5			8	6•	11				1		12	3	14	10*		7						K. Lynch	19
S	2		4		5			9	6	11	S	14	1		7•	3	8			10						C. Wilkes	20
1	2	S	4	5				9	6	11	S		S		7	3	8			10						T. Holbrook	21
1	2	S	4	5				9	6		11		S		7	3	8			10	S					J. Watson	22
1	2	S	4	5				9	6		11		S		7	3	8			10	S					E. Lomas	23
1	2	14	4	5				9	6•		11		S		7*	3	8			10	12					U. Rennie	24
1	2	S	4	5				9	6		11		S		7	3	8			10	S					T. West	25
1	2		4	5					6		11		S		7	3	8	S		10	9	S				B. Burns	26
1	2	14	4	5					6		11		S		7•	3	8			10	9	S				P. Harrison	27
1	2	6	4						6		11*		S		7	3	8	12		10*	10	9	5	14		R. Harris	28
1	2	6	4						6		11*		S		7	3	8•	12	14	10	10	9	5			A. Durso	29
1	2	6	4	5	14	12							7*	3	8	11•			10	9			S		T. Lunt	30
1	2	6•	4	5	14	7								3	8	7		12	10	9*			S		M. Pierce	31
1	2		4	5	14			6		9			S		3	8	7		11*	10	14			S		K. Lupton	32
1	2		4	5	14			6		11			S		3	8	7		10*	9			S			R. Furnandiz	33
1	2		4	5	14	12		6		9•			S		3	8	7*			10	11					P. Rejer	34
1	2			5	4	12		6		9*	14		S		3	8•	7			10	11					M. Brandwood	35
1	2			5	4	8		6		9*	S	S	S		12	3		7		10	11					I. Winter	36
1	2			5	4	8*		6	12		S	S	S		9	3		7		10	11					J. Kirby	37
1	2			5	4	12		6					S		8*	3		7	9•	10	11		S			P. Vanes	38
1	2			5	4	12		6					S		14	3		7	9•	10	11		14			J. Holbrook	39
1	2			5	4			6		9*			S		14	3		7•		12	10	11				J. Parker	40
1		2•		5	4	14			6		9			S		3	8	7		12	10	11*				M. Bailey	41
1	2		S	5	4				6		9*			S		3	8	7		11	10	12				G. Cain	42
1	2•		14	5	4				6	12				S		3	8	7*		11	10	9				P. Richards	43
1			4•	5	2				6	9	12			S	14	3	8			7	10	11*				E. Lomas	44
1	2			5	4	S			6	11•	9			S	12	3	8		7*	10						D. Allison	45
	2			5	4	S			6	11•	9		1		7	3	8	14			10				S	G. Pooley	46
	2			5	4	12			6	11•	9		1		7*	3	8			12	14				S	K. Lynch	47
	2	S		5	4	7			6	11	9		1			3	8	12		10*					S	A. Butler	48
	2	14		5	4	7•			6	11*	9		1			3	8	12		10					S	K. Lupton	49
	2	S		5	4	7			6	11*	9		1			3	8	12		10					S	E. Wolstenholme	50
	2	6*		5	4	7			6		9		1			3	8	12		14	10	11*			S	K. Breen	51
	2	10		5	4	7			6		9*	S	1			3	8			14		11			S	G. Barber	52
	2			5	4	7			6		9	S	1			3	8	12			10	11			S	R. Furnandiz	53
	2			5	4	7			6		9	S	1			3	8	12			10	11*			S	R. Poulain	54
	2			5	4	7			6		9*		1			3	8	11		12	10	14*			S	N. Barry	55
S	2	12		5	4	7			6		9•		1		3*	8		11			10	14				P. Alcock	56
S	2	3		5	4	7			6	14	9•		1			8*		11		12	10					J. Winter	57
22	44	9	20	43	29	13	8	16	40	20	25	3	24		22	45	38	20	5	8	31	19	2			League Appearances	
2		1	1		5	7	3					1	5	2	1		6		2	15	1	9	4		2	League Sub Appearances	
2	2		1	2	2			2	1	2	1		1	1+1	2	2				2	2					C/Cola Cup Appearances	
2	2		2	2				2	2	1	1				2	2	2			4	2+1					FA Cup Appearances	
3	5	1+1	1+1	3	4			3	5	2+1	2	+2		2	4	5	4	3								AW Trophy Appearances	
	2		1+1	2	2	2				2	0+1	2		2			1	2	2	0+1	2	0+1				Play-Off Appearances	

Loan Players: McCarthy (ex. Millwall)

CREWE ALEXANDRA — RECORDS AND STATISTICS

CLUB RECORDS

BIGGEST VICTORIES
League: 8-0 v Rotherham United, Division 3(N), 1.10.1932.
F.A. Cup: 7-1 v Gresley Rovers, 1st Round, 12.11.1994.
5-0 v Druids, 1st Round, 1887-88.
5-0 v Billingham Synthonia 1st Round, 1948-49.
6-1 v Wrexham, 1st Round, 14.11.1992.
6-1 v Accrington Stanley, 2nd Round, 5.12.1992.
AMC: 6-0 v Chester City (a), 2nd Round, 29.11.1994.
BIGGEST DEFEATS
League: 1-11 v Lincoln City, Division 3(N), 29.9.1951.
F.A. Cup: 2-13 v Tottenham Hotspur, 4th Round replay, 3.2.1960.

MOST POINTS
3 points a win: 83, Division 2, 1994-95
2 points a win: 59, Division 4, 1962-63.

MOST GOALS SCORED: 95, Division 3(N), 1931-32.

RECORD TRANSFER FEE RECEIVED
£600,000 from Liverpool for Rob Jones, October 1991. (A further instalment will be due if Rob plays a given number of Full Internationals).

RECORD TRANSFER FEE PAID
£80,000 to Barnsley for Darren Foreman, March 1990.
£80,000 to Leicester City for Ashley Ward, December 1992.

BEST PERFORMANCES
League: 10th Division 2, 1892-93.
F.A. Cup: Semi-Final 1888.
League Cup: 3rd Round 1960-61, 1974-75, 1975-76, 1978-79, 1992-93.   Welsh Cup: Winners (2).
HONOURS
Welsh Cup Winners 1936, 1937.

LEAGUE CAREER
Original members of Div 2 1892, Failed to gain re-election 1896, re-joined Div 3(N) 1921, Transferred to Div 4 1958, Div 3 1962-63, Div 4 1963-64, Div 3 1967-68, Div 4 1968-69, Div 3 1988-89, Div 4 (now Div 3) 1990-91, Div 2 1993-94.

INDIVIDUAL CLUB RECORDS

MOST GOALS IN A SEASON
Terry Harkin: 35 goals in 1964-65, Division 4.

MOST GOALS IN A MATCH
5. Tony Naylor v Colchester United, 7-1, Division 3, 24.4.1993.

OLDEST PLAYER
Kenny Swain, 39 years 281 days v Maidstone, 5.11.1991.

YOUNGEST PLAYER
Steve Walters, 16 years 119 days v Peterborough United, 6.5.1988.

MOST CAPPED PLAYER
Bill Lewis (Wales) 12.
J.H.Pearson (England) 1.

PREVIOUS MANAGERS

(Since 1946)
George Lillycrop, Frank Hill, Arthur Turner, Harry Catterick, Ralph Ward, Maurice Lindley, Harry Ware, Jimmy McGuigan, Ernie Tagg, Dennis Violete, Jimmy Melia, Ernie Tagg, Harry Gregg, Warwick Rimmer, Tony Waddington, Arfon Griffths, Peter Morris.

ADDITIONAL INFORMATION
PREVIOUS NAMES
None.

PREVIOUS LEAGUES
Central League.

Club colours: Red shirts, white shorts, red socks.
Change colours: White shirts, white or red shorts.

Reserves & 'A' Team League: Lancashire League.

LONGEST LEAGUE RUNS

of undefeated matches:	14 (1990)	of league matches w/out a win:	30 (1956-57)
of undefeated home matches:	28 (1967-68)	of undefeated away matches:	7 (1966-67, 1990, 1993)
without home win:	15 (1979)	without an away win:	56 (1955-57)
of league wins:	7 (1928-29, 1986)	of home wins:	16 (1938)
of league defeats:	10 (1923, 1957-58, 1979)	of away wins:	5 (1986)

THE MANAGER

Dario Gradi . . . . appointed May 1983.

PREVIOUS CLUBS
As Manager . . . . Wimbledon, Crystal Palace.
As Asst.Man/Coach. . . . . Chelsea, Derby County, Wimbledon, Orient (Youth Team).
As a player . . . . Sutton United.

HONOURS
As a Manager. . . . . Wimbledon: Promotion to Division 3, 1978-79.
. . . . Crewe: Promotion to Division 3, 1989-90. Promotion to Division 2 (what was Div 3) 1993-94.
As a Player. . . . . England Semi-Professional.

CREWE ALEXANDRA

PLAYERS NAME / Honours	Ht	Wt	Birthdate	Birthplace Transfers	Contract Date	Clubs	League	L/Cup	FA Cup	Other	Lge	L/C	FAC	Oth
G O A L K E E P E R S														
Mark S R Gayle	6.2	12.3	21.10.69	Bromsgrove	01.07.88	Leicester City (T)								
				Free	15.08.89	Blackpool		1						
				Free		Worcester City								
				£15,000	08.05.91	Walsall	74+1	8	1	8				
				£35,000	21.12.93	Crewe Alexandra	32+1			4				
Mark A Smith	6.1	13.9	02.0.73	Birmingham	07.02.91	Nottingham F. (T)								
				Free	24.02.93	Crewe Alexandra	61+2	4	5	10				
Ian M Wilkinson	5.11	13.4	02.07.73	Warrington	05.06.91	Manchester United		1						
				Free	20.07.93	Stockport County								
				Free	29.10.93	Crewe Alexandra	2+1							
				Loan	02.09.94	Doncaster Rovers								
				Loan	10.03.95	Congleton Town								
D E F E N D E R S														
Martyn J Booty	5.8	11.2	30.05.71	Kirby Muxloe	30.05.89	Coventry City (T)	4+1	2	2					
				Free	07.10.93	Crewe Alexandra	74+1	2	5	11	3			
Anthony B Hughes E: Y.4.	6.0	12.0	03.10.73	Liverpool	31.05.94	Crew Alexandra (T)	18+5	2+1	3	2+1	1			
				Loan	28.02.92	Witton Albion								
Neil F Lennon NI: 1, B1, u23.1, u21.2	5.9	12.4	25.06.71	Lurgan, N. I.	26.08.89	Manchester City (T)	1							
				Free	09.08.90	Crewe Alexandra	117+5	4+1	11	12+1	13		1	
Steven R Macauley FAVC'86	6.1	12.0	04.03.69	Lytham	05.11.87	Manchester City (T)								
						Fleetwood Town			1					
				£25,000	24.03.92	Crewe Alexandra	94	6	5	10	12			2
Gareth Shaun Smith	5.10	11.0	09.04.71	Leeds	01.07.89	Halifax Town (T)	6+1			1				
				Free		Emley			1					
				Free	31.12.91	Crewe Alexandra	118+10	3+1	5	14+1	19		2	1
Ashley Westwood	6.0	11.3	31.08.76		01.07.94	Manchester Utd (T)								
				£40,000	08.95	Crewe Alexandra								
M I D F I E L D														
William J Barr	5.11	10.8	21.01.69	Halifax	06.07.88	Halifax Town (T)	178+18	8+1	11+1	14+3	13	2	2	
				Free	17.06.94	Crewe Alexandra	29+5	2		6	2			
Philip I Clarkson	5.10	10.8	13.11.68	Garstang		Fleetwood Town		1						
				£22,500	15.10.91	Crewe Alexandra	75+18	6+1	3+1	6+5	27	1	2	1
Wayne A Collins	6.0	12.0	04.03.69	Manchester		Winsford United								
				£10,000	29.07.93	Crewe Alexandra	65+10	2	4+1	10	13			1
Daniel B Murphy	5.9	10.8	18.03.77	Chester	21.03.94	Crewe Alex. (T)	25+22	1		6+1	7			1
Francis Tierney E: S	5.10	11.0	10.09.75	Liverpool	22.03.93	Crewe Alex. (T)	17+12	2	0+2	4+1	5			2
Gareth Whalley	5.10	11.6	19.12.73	Manchester	29.07.92	Crewe Alex. (T)	74+6	5+1	7+1	14	3		3	2
F O R W A R D S														
Bamberdele Adebola	6.3	12.6	23.06.75	Liverpool	21.06.93	Crewe Alex. (T)	25+12	0+1	1	4	7			2
				Loan	02.02.94	Northwich Victoria								
Robert Edwards	5.8	11.7	23.02.70	Manchester	11.07.88	Crewe Alex. (T)	81+42	5	8+5	7+8	29	1	3	5
Stephen H Garvey	5.9	10.9	22.11.73	Stalybridge	25.10.91	Crewe Alex. (T)	33+17	4+4	2+1	5	4	2	1	
Daniel J Collier	6.1	10.5	15.01.74	Eccles	07.07.92	Wolves (T)								
				Free	15.06.94	Crewe Alexandra	3+2	1		0+2				
Robert Savage W: S, Y. FAYC'92.	6.0	10.1	18.10.74	Wrexham	05.07.93	Manchester Utd (T)								
				Free	22.07.94	Crewe Alexandra	5+1				2			
A D D I T I O N A L C O N T R A C T P L A Y E R S														
(D) Justin N Parker			11.11.76	Stoke	23.09.94	Crewe Alex. (T)								
Dave Ridings				Ashton										
					08.95	Crewe Alexandra								
(D) Mark A Rivers			26.11.75	Crewe	06.05.74	Crewe Alex. (T)								
(D) Simon A Turpin			11.08.75	Blackburn	20.08.94	Crewe Alex. (T)								
				Loan	30.12.94	Chorley								
				Loan	10.03.94	Northwich Victoria								
(D) Lee P Unsworth			25.02.73	Eccles		Ashton								
					17.02.94	Crewe Alexandra								

GRESTY ROAD

Crewe, Cheshire CW2 6EB
Tel: 01270 213 014

Capacity 6,000

First game ....v Basford, 1877.
First floodlit game..v All Stars XI, 29.10.1958.

ATTENDANCES
Highest ....20,000 v Tottenham, FA Cup 4th Round, 30.1.1960.
Lowest ....994 v Stockport, AMC, 14.1.1986.

OTHER GROUNDS..Earle Street, Edleston Road, Nantwich Road.

MATCHDAY TICKET PRICES

Ringwings Stand...................... £9.50
Juv/OAP £7

Family Stand......................... £9.50
Juv/OAP £7

South Stand £9.50
Juv/OAP £7

Paddock £8
Juv/OAP £6

Gresty Road Visitors Stand £9.50
Juv/OAP £7

ALEX HOTLINE
0891 66 45 64

Calls cost 39p per minute cheap rate and 49p per minute at all other times.
Call costings correct at time of going to press.

HOW TO GET TO THE GROUND

From the North
Use motorway (M6) until junction 17 and follow signs to Crewe (A534). At Crewe roundabout follow signs to Chester into Nantwich Road. Then take next turning on left into Gresty Road for Crewe Alexandra FC.

From the East and South
Use A52 then A5020 (sign posted Crewe), then at Crewe roundabout follow signs to Chester into Nantwich Road. Then take next turning on left into Gresty Road for Crewe Alexandra FC.

From the West
Use A534 (sign posted Crewe) and immediately before Crewe Railway Station turn right into Gresty Road for Crewe Alexandra FC.

Car Parking
Barker Street

Nearest Railway Station
Crewe (5mins) 01270 255 245)

MATCHDAY PROGRAMME

Programme Editor .... Harold Finch.

Number of pages .... 32.

Price .... £1.30.

Subscriptions ..... Subscription rates on request from the club editor.

Local Newspapers............. Crewe Chronicle, Crewe Guardian,
.... Evening Sentinel, Hanley.

Local Radio Stations .... Radio Stoke (200 MW),
.... Signal Radio 102.6 & 96.9 FM.

HULL CITY
(The Tigers)
ENDSLEIGH LEAGUE DIVISION 2
SPONSORED BY: PEPIS

Back Row (L-R): Andy Williams, Neil Allison, Rob Dewhurst, Alan Fettis, Steve Wilson, Gary Hobson, Andrew Mason, Paul Fewings.
Middle Row: Billy Legg (u16 Manager), Bernard Ellison (Yth Coach), Chris Lee, Linton Brown, Neil Mann, Richard Peacock, Simon Dakin, Gavin Haigh, Craig Lawford, Adam Lowthorpe, Rod Arnold (Goalkeeping Coach), Jeff Radcliffe (Physio). **Front Row:** Ian Plant, Michael Quigley, Dean Windass, Terry Dolan (Manager), Martin Fish (Chairman), Jeff Lee (Asst. Manager), Greg Abbott, Jimmy Graham, David Chambers.
Photo: Innes Photograhpers.

HULL CITY
FORMED IN 1904
TURNED PROFESSIONAL IN 1904
LTD COMPANY IN 1904

PRESIDENT: T C Waite, FIMI, MIRTE
CHAIRMAN: M W Fish
VICE-CHAIRMAN
R M Chetham
DIRECTORS
G H C Needler BA, FCA,
M St. Quinton BA (Hon.)
SECRETARY
Tom Wilson
COMMERCIAL MANAGER
Simon Cawkill

MANAGER: Terry Dolan
ASSISTANT MANAGER: Jeff Lee
RESERVE TEAM MANAGER

YOUTH TEAM MANAGER
Bernard Ellison
PHYSIOTHERAPIST
Jeff Ratcliffe MCSP, SRP

STATISTICIAN FOR THE DIRECTORY
Vacant

Who would have thought on 20th August, when after just two games the Tigers were already propping up the Division Two table, that come Guy Fawkes Day they would be up there in 4th spot challenging the leaders.

Day one of the season and it was definitely nightmare time. Only 45 minutes gone at Oxford and City were four goals to the bad. Thankfully, further embarrassment was avoided, thanks to a goalless second period. In the second game of the campaign Hull again failed to score and were, on this occasion, on the wrong end of a 2-0 scoreline (home v Swansea).

24th at the end of August; 17th on the final day of September; November dawned and City found themselves in the top six following a 7-1 home crushing of Crewe (a hat-trick here for Linton Brown), and a fine 3-0 home success over York City on the first day of the month.

Top scorer Dean Windass certainly had a fruitful festive season, with five strikes between 10th December and 7th January. Unfortunately, a basic lack of consistency was the real reason why the Tigers never managed to make the big breakthrough into the division's top three.

During February and March they hovered between 7th and 9th, and following a 1-0 defeat at Brighton on 8th April, City had dropped to 11th. Their end of season run-in - only one defeat in six - resulted in a final position of 8th, which was not quite enough to put them in a play-off place. Their wins tally was only one less than play-off finalists Bristol Rovers but not enough draws were obtained to really threaten the top five.

There was no glory to speak of in cup competitions. Scarborough put paid to any Hull Coca-Cola aspirations in Round One, going through to the next stage 3-2 on aggregate. In the FA Cup they went down by the only goal at home to Lincoln City. In the Auto Windscreen Shield they also fell at the first stage, again to Lincoln, again by the same score but not this occasion on their opponents' patch.

Their fortunes for 1995-96 are not easy to predict, but there is no reason why they should not be amongst the front runners come next May.

GREG TESSER.

HULL CITY

Division Two: 8th   **FA Cup:** 1st Round   **Coca-Cola Cup:** 1st Round

M	DATE	COMP.	VEN	OPPONENTS	RESULT	H/T	LP	GOAL SCORERS/GOAL TIMES	ATT.
1	A 13	EL	A	Oxford United	L 0-4	0-4	23		(5,485)
2	16	CC 1/1	H	Scarborough	W 2-1	1-0		Peacock 21, Lee 65	2,546
3	20	EL	H	Swansea City	L 0-2	0-0	24		3,799
4	23	CC 1/2	A	Scarborough	L 0-2	0-0			(2,287)
5	27	EL	A	Leyton Orient	D 1-1	0-0	2	Brown 84	(3,243)
6	30	EL	H	Plymouth Argyle	W 2-0	0-0		Mann 52, Lee 62	3,384
7	S 3	EL	H	Chester City	W 2-0	1-0	14	Brown 43, Windass 82	3,615
8	10	EL	A	Peterborough United	L 1-2	1-1	17	Peacock 25	(5,044)
9	13	EL	A	Wycombe Wanderers	W 2-1	1-0		Dakin 4, Abbott 55	(4,626)
10	17	EL	H	Rotherham United	L 0-2	0-2	16		4,431
11	24	EL	A	Birmingham	D 2-2	1-1	17	Windass 41 (pen), Peacock 54	(12,192)
12	O 1	EL	H	Bournemouth	W 3-1	2-1	14	Brown 15, Dewhurst 32, Atkinson 53	3,056
13	8	EL	H	Blackpool	W 1-0	1-0	12	Gouck 11 (og)	3,829
14	15	EL	A	Wrexham	D 2-2	1-0	11	Lanford 44, Windass 87 (pen)	(3,418)
15	22	EL	A	Shrewsbury Town	W 3-2	2-0	11	Peacock 33, Dewhurst 45, Lawford 81	(3,685)
16	29	EL	H	Crewe Alexandra	W 7-1	2-0	8	Windass 8, 58, Peacock 45, Brown 63, 67, 70, Dewhurst 80	4,694
17	N 1	EL	H	York City	W 3-0	3-0	6	Brown 11, Windass 29, Lawford 36	6,551
18	5	EL	A	Brentford	W 1-0	0-0	4	Dewhurst 74	(5,455)
19	8	AWT	A	Lincoln City	L 0-1	0-0			(1,626)
20	12	FAC 1	H	Lincoln city	L 0-1	0-0			5,758
21	19	EL	H	Bristol Rovers	L 0-2	0-1	5		4,450
22	25	EL	A	Cardiff City	W 2-0	2-0	5	Brown 15, Windass 29 (pen)	(4,226)
23	D 10	EL	A	Swansea City	L 0-2	0-1	5		(4,903)
24	17	EL	H	Oxford United	W 3-1	2-1	5	Windass 17, 28, Ferris 88	4,884
25	26	EL	H	Huddersfield Town	W 1-0	0-0		Peacock 82	10,220
26	28	EL	A	Bradford City	L 0-1	0-0			(7,312)
27	31	EL	H	Brighton & H.A.	D 2-2	1-1		Brown 33, Windass 74	5,099
28	J 2	EL	A	Cambridge United	D 2-2	2-0		Brown 8, Windass 9	(3,569)
29	7	EL	H	Shrewsbury Town	D 2-2	0-2	6	Windass 47 (pen), Cox 73	4,369
30	14	EL	A	Stockport County	L 0-4	0-1	7		(4,516)
31	21	EL	H	Brentford	L 1-2	0-0	7	Joyce 68	3,82
32	F 4	EL	H	Cardiff City	W 4-0	2-0	7	Ormondroyd 28, 44, Brown 49, Joyce 88	3,903
33	18	EL	H	Stockport County	D 0-0	0-0	9		4,576
34	25	EL	A	Bournemouth	W 3-2	3-2	9	Ormondroyd 8, 20, Mann 38	(4,345)
35	M 1	EL	A	Bristol Rovers	W 2-0	1-0	9	Brown 20, Ormondroyd 50	(3,707)
36	4	EL	H	Brimingham City	D 0-0	0-0	8		9,854
37	11	EL	H	Leyton Orient	W 2-0	1-0	7	Dewhurst 13, Joyce 60	4,519
38	16	EL	A	Plymouth Argyle	L 1-2	1-2	9	Ormondroyd 14	(4,839)
39	21	EL	H	Peterborough United	D 1-1	1-1		Breen 17 (og)	4,609
40	25	EL	A	Rotherham United	L 0-2	0-1			(3,692)
41	28	EL	A	Chester City	W 2-1	0-0		Abbott 80, Lund 82	(1,191)
42	A 1	EL	H	Wycombe Wanderers	D 0-0	0-0	9		5,054
43	4	EL	A	York City	L 1-3	0-1		Windass 47	(4,612)
44	8	EL	A	Brighton & H.A.	L 0-1	0-1	11		(6,083)
45	15	EL	H	Bradford City	W 2-0	2-0	10	Windass 26, 28 (pen)	4,368
46	17	EL	A	Huddersfield Town	D 1-1	0-0		Dewhurst 46	(12,402)
47	22	EL	H	Cambridge United	W 1-0	0-0	9	Dewhurst 80	3, 483
48	29	EL	H	Wrexham	W 3-2	2-1	9	Dewhurst 4, Lund 20, Windass 54,	3,683
49	M 2	EL	A	Crewe Alexandra	L 2-3	2-2		Abbott 32, Lund 37	(3,870)
50	6	EL	A	Blackpool	W 2-1	1-1	8	Windass 19, Ferris 90	(4,251)
51									
52									
53									
54									
55									
56									
57									
58									
59									
60									

Best Home League Attendance: 10,220 v Huddersfield Town   **Smallest:** 3,056 v Bournemouth   **Av Home Att:** 4,793

Goal Scorers: **Compared with 1993-94:** -1,163

League (68):   Windass 17, Brown 12, Dewhurst 8, Ormondroyd 6, Peacock 5, Abbott 3, Joyce 3, Lawford 3, Lund 3, Fettis 2, Mann 2, Opponents 2, Atkinson, Cox, Dakin, Lee

C/Cola Cup (2):   Lee, Peacock

Fettis	Dakin	Graham	Allison	Dewhurst	Abbott	Peacock	Lee	Hargreaves	Windass	Lawford	Hobson	Brown	Wilson	Mann	Atkinson	Lowthorpe	Mail	Garside	Edeson	Carroll	Wallace	Cox	Joyce	Ormondroys	Lund	Referee	
1	2	3	4*	5	6	7	8•	9†	10	11	12	14	S													K. Cooper	1
1	2	3		5	6*	7	8		10	11•	4	9	S	12	14											I. Cruikshanks	2
1	S	3		5		7	8	6	10	11*	4	9	S		12	2										K. Lupton	3
1	12	3		5		7		8*	10	11•	4	9	S	6	14	2										P. Harrison	4
1		3	S	5		7*	8		10	12	4	9	S	6	11	2										M. Bailey	5
1		3		5	S	S	8		10	11	4	9	S	6	7	2										K. Lynch	6
1		3		5	12	14	8		10	11	4	9	S	6*	7•	2										J. Kirkby	7
1	S	3		5	6	S	8	S	10			9	S	11	2	4										E. Parker	8
1	7*	3		5	6	12	8	14	10			9•	S	11	2	4										G. Singh	9
1		3	S	5	6†	7	8	9	10	S		9•	S	11	2	4										W. Burns	10
	2	3		5	6	7	8		10		4	9	1	S		11										P. Richards	11
S	2	3		5		7		8	10	11	4	9	1	6			S									J. Rushton	12
S	2	3		5		7*	8		10	12	4	9	1	6			S									D. Allison	13
S	S	3		5		7	8	12	10	11	4	9	9*	6												E. Wolstenholme	14
S		3		5	12	7	8		10	11	4	9	9•	6		2										P. Wright	15
S		3		5	12	7•	8	14	10	11	4	9	1	6		2*										T. Heilbron	16
S	2	3		5	S	7	8	12	10	11	4	9	9*	6												A. Dawson	17
A	U	T	O	W	I	N	D	S	C	R	E	E	N													S. Dunn	18
S	2	3		5		7	8		10		4	9	1	6*													19
S	2*	3		5	14		8	7•	10		4	9	1	6			12									E. Lomas	20
	2	3		5		7	8		10		4	9	1	S			12									K. Lynch	21
S	2	3	12	5*	6	7•		8	10		4	9	1	14												G. Pooley	22
12		3	5		6	7			10		4	9	1	8			S									J. Rushton	23
S		3		5	6	7*	12	8	10		4	9	1	8							2	5				A. Butler	24
S		3	5*		6	7•	8	14	10		4	9	1				12				2					U. Rennie	25
S		3			6*	7	12	8	10		4	9	1	8							2	5				K. Lupton	26
S		3				7	6	12	10		4	9	1	8*			S				2	5				E. Wolstenholme	27
S		3				7•	6	14	10		4	9	1	8			12				2	5				G. Barber	28
S	S	3		7		12	6		10			9*	1	8			4				2	5				D. Allison	29
1	S	3	S	5		6	9		10	11	4			8			4				2	5				I. Cruikshanks	30
1		3	6	5		12	14		10		4	9	S	8•	2								7			J. Winter	31
1		3	6	5	S	S	2		10		4	9	S	8	2*								7	11		G. Cain	32
1		3	6	5	S	S	2		10		4	9	S	8									7	11		A. Dawson	33
1		3	6	5	S	S	2		10		4	9	S	8									7	11		J. Holbrook	34
1		3	6	5	S	12	2		10		4†	9	S	8*									7	11		A. D'Urso	35
1		3	6	5	S	12	2		10		4	9	S	8*									7	11		R. Furnandiz	36
1	4	3*	6	5			2		10	12		9	S	8•									7	11		E. Parker	37
1		3	6*	5		8	2	S	10	12	4	9	S										7	11		P. Rejer	38
12		3	6*	5	8•	7	2		10	14	4		1										7	11		E. Lomas	39
4		3•		5		8	2*		10	14	4		1					S		S				11	9	A. Flood	40
1	5	3				8	12	2*		10	14		1	7			11•	6		S				11	9	P. Richards	41
1	5	3•		6		8			10	11	4		S	12		2*	14								9	T. Heilbron	42
1				5		8	12	7		10	3	4	S	11		2*	6		S						9	M. Bailey	43
1	12			5	6	7	8		10	3*	4		S	11•		2			S						9	D. Orr	44
1	4		S	5	6	7	8	11	10				S			2	3		S						9	P. Vanes	45
1	4		S	5	6	7*	8	11	10				S			2	3		12						9	I. Cruikshanks	46
1	4		12	5	6	7	8	11	10				S			2	3*								9	K. Lupton	47
1	4		3*	5	6	7	8	11	10				S			2									9	S. Mathieson	48
8	4			5	6*	7•	2	11	10				1			3			14	S					9	A. Poulain	49
																										K. Lynch	50
27	19	39	11	41	22	28	42	13	43	25	35	32	20	29	7	21	10				7	5	9	10	11	League Appearances	
1	2		2		4	9	3	8	1	6	1	1		2	2	1	4		3							League Sub Appearances	
2	1+1			2	1	2	1	1	2	2	2			1+1	0+2	1										C/Cola Cup Appearances	
	1	1		1	1	1	1	1	0+1	1	1	1	1	1												FA Cup Appearances	

Also Played: Fewings S(48),12(49,50), Plant S(49)   Players on Loan: Ormondroyd (Leicester), Lund

† = Sent Off

CLUB RECORDS

BIGGEST VICTORIES
League: 10-0 v Halifax Town, Division 3(N), 26.12.1930.
11-1 v Carlisle United, Division 3(N), 14.1.1939.
F.A. Cup: 8-2 v Stalybridge Celtic, 1st Round, 26.11.1932.

BIGGEST DEFEATS
League: 0-8 v Wolverhampton Wndrs, Division 2, 4.11.1911.
F.A. Cup: 0-5 v Fulham, 3rd Round, 9.1.1960.
League Cup: 0-5 v Lincoln City, 1st round, 9.8.1980.
0-5 v Manchester United, 2nd Round 1st leg, 23.9.1987.

MOST POINTS
3 points a win: 90, Division 4, 1982-83.
2 points a win: 69, Division 3, 1965-66.

RECORD TRANSFER FEE RECEIVED
£750,000 from Middlesbrough for Andy Payton, November 1991.
(Installments could take fee to £1,000,000)

RECORD TRANSFER FEE PAID
£200,000 to Leeds United for Peter Swan, March 1989.

BEST PERFORMANCES
League: 3rd Division 2, 1909-10.
F.A. Cup: Semi-Finalists 1929-30.
League Cup: 4th Round 1973-74, 1975-76, 1977-78.

HONOURS
Champions of Division 3(N) 1932-33, 1948-49.
Champions of Division 3 1965-66.

LEAGUE CAREER
Elected to Div 2 1905, Div 3(N) 1930-31, Div 2 1933-34, Div 3(N) 1936-37, Div 2 1948-49, Div 3(N) 1956-57, Transferred to Div 3 1958-59, Div 2 1959-60, Div 3 1960-61, Div 2 1966-67, Div 3 1978-79, Div 4 1981-82, Div 3 1983-84, Div 2 1985-86, Div 3 (now Div 2) 1990-91.

INDIVIDUAL CLUB RECORDS

MOST GOALS IN A SEASON
Bill McNaughton: 42 goals in 1932-33 (League 39, FA Cup 3).

MOST GOALS IN A MATCH
5. Ken McDonald v Bristol City, 5-1, Division 2, 17.11.1928.
5. Slim Raleigh v Halifax Town, 10-0, Division 3(N), 26.12.1930.

OLDEST PLAYER
Eddie Burbanks, 40 years 15 days, 16.4.1953.

YOUNGEST PLAYER
Matthew Edeson, 16 years 63 days v Fulham, 10.10.1992.

MOST CAPPED PLAYER
Terry Neill (Northern Ireland) 15.

PREVIOUS MANAGERS

1905-13 Ambrose Langley, 1913-14 Harry Chapman, 1914-16 Fred G Stringer, 1916-21 David M Menzies, 1921-23 P Lewis, 1923-31 Bill McCracken, 1931-34 Hayden Green, 1934-36 Jack Hill, 1936 David Menzies, 1936-46 Ernie Blackburn, 1946-48 Major Buckley, 1948-51 Raich Carter, 1952-55 Bob Jackson, 1955-61 Bob Brocklebank, 1961-70 Cliff Britton, 1970-74 Terry Neill, 1974-77 John Kaye, 1977-78 Bobby Collins, 1978-79 Ken Houghton, 1980-82 Mike Smith, 1982-84 Colin Appleton, 1984-88 Brian Horton, 1988-90 Eddie Gray, 1990 Colin Appleton, 1990-91 Stan Ternant.

ADDITIONAL INFORMATION
PREVIOUS NAMES
None.

PREVIOUS LEAGUES
None.

Club colours: Amber and black striped shirts, black shorts, black and amber socks.
Change colours: Green shirts, white shorts, white socks.

Reserves League: Pontins Central League Division 2.

LONGEST LEAGUE RUNS

of undefeated matches:	15 (1964-65, 1983)	of league matches w/out a win:	27 (1990)
of undefeated home matches:	25 (1932-33, 1965-66)	of undefeated away matches:	13 (1948-49)
without home win:	15 (1990)	without an away win:	35 (1979-81)
of league wins:	10 (1948, 1966)	of home wins:	19 (1965-66)
of league defeats:	8 (1934)	of away wins:	5 (Several occasions)

THE MANAGER

TERRY DOLAN . . . . appointed April 1991.

PREVIOUS CLUBS
As Manager . . . . Bradford City, Rochdale.
As Asst.Man/Coach . . . . Bradford City.
As a player . . . . Bradford P.A., Huddersfield Town, Bradford City, Rochdale.

HONOURS
As a Manager . . . . Bradford City: Promotion to Division 2, 1988.
As a Player . . . . None.

HULL CITY

PLAYERS NAME Honours	Ht	Wt	Birthdate	Birthplace Transfers	Contract Date	Clubs	League	L/Cup	FA Cup	Other	Lge	L/C	FAC	Oth
G O A L K E E P E R S														
Alan Fettis NI: 3, B1	6.1	11.4	01.07.72	Belfast £50,000	14.08.91	Ards Hull City	127+1	7	5	6				
Stephen L Wilson	5.10	10.7	24.04.74	Hull	13.07.92	Hull City (T)	60	3	3	5				
D E F E N D E R S														
Neil J Allison	6.2	11.10	20.10.73	Hull	13.07.92	Hull City (T)	51+9	6	2	3+1	1			
Simon M Dakin	5.11	11.7	30.11.74	Nottingham Free	24.03.94	Derby County(T) Hull City	27+3	1+1	1	1	1			
Robert M Dewhurst	6.3	12.0	10.09.71	Keighley Loan Loan Free	15.10.90 20.12.91 02.10.92 05.11.93	Blackburn Rovers (T) Darlington Huddersfield Town Hull City	13 11 7 68	2 2	1 3	1 1 3	1 10			
Craig B Lawford	5.10	11.0	25.11.72	Dewsbury Free	02.07.91 05.08.94	Bradford City (T) Hull City	13+7 25+6	3 2	2+1 1	1+1 2	1 3			
James Graham	6.0	11.8	05.11.69	Glasgow Loan £15,000 Free	12.09.88 03.11.89 09.07.90 05.08.94	Bradford City (T) Rochdale Rochdale Hull City	6+1 11 120+6 39	13+1 2	4 8 1	3 6 2	1			1
Gary Hobson	6.1	12.10	12.11.71	Hull	17.07.91	Hull City (T)	107+6	10	1+1	4				
M I D F I E L D														
Gregory S Abbott Div3'85 via Guisley to	5.9	10.7	14.12.63	Coventry free £25,000 Free	05.01.82 10.09.82 22.07.91 14.12.92	Coventry City (A) Bradford City Halifax Town Hull City	256+25 24+4 89+4	22+3 2 3	15+1 2 0+3	19+2 2 4+2	38 1 9	6 1	3 5	2
Christopher Lee	5.10	11.10	18.06.71	Batley Free Free Free	01.07.89 14.06.90 14.03.91 30.07.93	Bradford City (T) Rochdale Scarborough Hull City	24+2 75+3 42+3	4 11 1	2 2 1	3 4+2 2	2 3 1	1 2 1		
Neil Mann	5.10	12.0	19.11.72	Nottingham Free Free	06.09.90 30.07.93	Notts County (T) Grimsby Town Spalding United Grantham United Hull City	31+5	1+2	1	2+1	2			
Richard J Peacock	5.11	11.0	29.10.72	Sheffield	14.10.93	Hull City	32+16	2	1	2	6	1		
Michael Quigley	5.7	9.13	02.10.70	Manchester Free	01.07.89 08.95	Manchester City (T) Hull City	3+9			1				
Andy Williams Div.2'90.	6.0	11.10	29.07.62	Birmingham £20,000 £175,000 Loan £115,000 Loan Free	24.07.85 16.10.86 11.11.88 11.12.91 04.02.93 13.09.93 21.10.93 08.95	Solihull Borough Coventry City Rotherham United Leeds United Port Vale Notts County Huddersfield Town Rotherham United Hull City	3+6 87 25+21 5 32+7 4+2 51	8 3+3 3 2	6 2 1 3	0+1 5 5+2 4	13 3 2 2			2 2
Dean Windass	5.9	12.3	01.04.69	Hull £2,000	24.10.91	North Ferriby Utd Hull City	157+3	7	6	9	53	1		2
F O R W A R D S														
Linton J Brown	5.9	11.0	12.04.68	Driffield Loan Free	18.12.92 008.01.93	Guisley Halifax Town Hull City	3 90+8	4	3	2	10		1	
Adam Lowthorpe	5.7	10.06	07.08.75	Hull	02.07.93	Hull City	21+1	1						
Andrew Mason	5.11	11.11	22.11.74	Bolton Free	21.05.93 08.95	Bolton W. (T) Hull City								

BOOTHFERRY PARK

Boothferry Road, Hull, North Humberside HU4 6EU
Tel: 01482 51119

Capacity...15,828
Covered Standing...9,203
Seating..5,515

First game...31st August 1946.
First floodlit game ....19th January 1953.

ATTENDANCES
Highest ....55,019 v Manchester United, FA Cup 6th Round, 26.2.1949.
Lowest..890 v Doncaster Rovers. AMC, 27.9.1994.

OTHER GROUNDS..None.

MATCHDAY TICKET PRICES

Best Stand............................ £10
Juv/OAP £5

Family Stand £8
Juv/OAP £4

South Stand.......................... £8
Juv/OAP £4

Ground £7
Juv/OAP £3

Ticket office Telephone no......... 01482 51119

CLUBCALL
0898 88 86 88

Calls cost 39p per minute cheap rate and 49p per
minute at all other times.
Call costings correct at time of going to press.

HOW TO GET TO THE GROUND

From the North
Use A1 or A19 then A1079, sign posted Hull, into town centre. Then follow signs
to Leeds (A63) into Anlaby Road. At roundabout take first exit into Boothferry
Road for Hull City FC.

From the West
Use motorway (M62) then A63, sign posted Hull, into Boothferry Road for Hull
City FC.

From the South
Use motorway (M1), M18 then M62 and A63, sign posted Hull, into Boothferry
Road for Hull City FC.

Car Parking
Limited parking in front of ground.

Nearest Railway Station
Hull Paragon (01482 260 33) or Boothferry Halt by the ground.

MATCHDAY PROGRAMME

Programme Editor .... Robert Smith.

Number of pages .... 36.

Price .... £1.50.

Subscriptions...................................... £37.50.

Local Newspapers .... Hull Daily Mail.

Local Radio Stations . BBC Radio Humberside (95.5FM, MW1485KHZ)
.... Viking Radio (96.6 FM)

NOTTS COUNTY
(The Magpies)
ENDSLEIGH LEAGUE DIVISION 2
SPONSORED BY: BANK'S BITTER

Unfortunately the 1995-96 team photo had not been taken before going to press,so the 1993-94 photo has been used.
Back row L-R: Richard Walker, Tony Agana, Steve Slawson, Shaun Murphy, Steve Cherry, Dean Yates, Michael Emenalo, Gary Lund, Colin Hoyle. **Middle:** Dean Thomas, Paul Sherlock, Ron Matthews, Paul Cox, Paul Reece, Gavin Worboys,Michael Johnson, chris Short, Gary McSwegan. **Front:** Russell Slade (Asst.manager), Tommy Gallagher, Paul Devlin, Derek Pavis (Chairman), Phil Turner,Mick Walker (Manager), Andy Legg, Michael Simpson, Dennis Pettitt (Physio).

NOTTS COUNTY
FORMED IN 1862 (Oldest League Club)
TURNED PROFESSIONAL IN 1885
LTD COMPANY IN 1890

PRESIDENT: F Sherwood
CHAIRMAN: D C Pavis
VICE-CHAIRMAN
J Mounteney
DIRECTORS
W Barrowcliffe, W Hopcroft, Mrs V Pavis,
D Ward, M Youdell MBE
SECRETARY
Ian Moat
SALES & MARKETING MANAGER
Neal Hook, M Inst M

GENERAL MANAGER: Colin Murphy
TEAM MANAGER: Steve Thompson

YOUTH TEAM MANAGER
John Gant
PHYSIOTHERAPIST
Dennis Pettitt

STATISTICIAN FOR THE DIRECTORY
Ian Moat

When reviewing a club's season, all kinds of league problems can often be discounted if the club concerned has not only reached a Wembley cup final, but has come away with the trophy to boot.

Unfortunately, in the case of Notts County this situation does not apply as the cup in question, the Anglo-Italian Variety, was hardly a success of which dreams are made. However, win it they did at the famous old stadium in March, the winning goal coming from Tony Agana in front of less than 12,000 fans. The opposition, in the shape of Ascoli, was certainly strong, but no one could say that this well-earned Wembley success made up for all the many traumas of life in Division One.

Just two league successes were gained between 13th August and Guy Fawkes Day, hardly a record to inspire confidence.

The one beacon in this gloom was a truly sensational 3-0 Coca-cola defeat of Spurs at Meadow Lane. Just under 17,000 supporters were there on that late October evening, many I am sure rubbing their eyes in disbelief.

1994 ended with a defeat by the only goal at home to Luton. County were now well-established in 24th spot, and apart from one short period in February when they managed to climb one rung, position twenty-four was where they were to remain.

After their tremendous victory over Tottenham, confidence was obviously quite high when they were drawn out of the hat, away to Norwich City. County played well enough, but one Norwich goal was enough to put to an end any hopes of further progress in this competition.

In the FA Cup, another top-drawer display in Round Three against Premiership opposition, this time Manchester City, brought them a fully-merited 2-2 draw. Unfortunately, the replay at Maine Road brought the Endsleigh outfit back to earth with a bump, going down 5-2.

In the league, just 45 goals were scored, nine coming from Paul Delvin. Just one win from their final eleven games probably just about sums up their Division One season!

GREG TESSER.

NOTTS COUNTY

Division One: 24th   **FA Cup:** 3rd Round   **Coca-Cola Cup:** 4th Round   **Anglo Italian Cup:** Winners

M	DATE	COMP.	VEN	OPPONENTS	RESULT	H/T	LP	GOAL SCORERS/GOAL TIMES	ATT.
1	A 13	EL	A	Portsmouth	L 1-2			Sherlock	(10,487)
2	21	EL	H	Wolverhampton	D 1-1			Simpson	8,569
3	24	AIC	A	Ascoli	D 1-1			Devlin	(1,300)
4	27	EL	A	Sheffield United	W 3-1			McSwegan (2), Lund	(15,301)
5	30	EL	H	Oldham Athletic	L 1-3			McSwegan	6,603
6	S 3	EL	H	Swindon Town	L 0-1		19		6,537
7	6	AIC	H	Lecce	W 1-0			Turner	2,495
8	10	EL	A	Bristol City	L 1-2		22	Jemson	(6,670)
9	13	EL	A	Barnsley	D 1-1		22	Lund	(3,928)
10	17	EL	H	Stoke City	L 0-2				8,281
11	20	C/C 2/1	A	Bristol City	W 1-0			Devlin	(2,546)
12	24	EL	H	Charlton Athletic	D 3-3		24	Lund, Agana, (og)	5,726
13	27	C/C 2/2	H	Bristol City	W 3-0			Lund (2), Jemson	(2,721)
14	O 1	EL	A	Reading	L 0-2				7,465
15	5	AIC	A	Atalanta	D 1-1			Agana	(2,300)
16	8	EL	H	Port Vale	D 2-2		23	Williams, Agana	6,903
17	15	EL	A	Watford	L 1-3		23	Williams	(7,008)
18	23	EL	H	Derby County	D 0-0		24		6,389
19	26	C/C 3	H	Tottenham Hotspur	W 3-0			McSwegan (2), Agana	16,952
20	29	EL	A	Burnley	L 1-2		24	(og)	(12,876)
21	N 1	EL	A	Southend United	L 0-1		24		(4,302)
22	5	EL	H	Sunderland	W 3-2		24	Devlin (2), Legg	8,890
23	15	AIC	H	Venezia	D 3-3			Devlin, Marsden, Murphy	2,861
24	19	EL	A	Bolton Wanderers	L 0-2		24		(11,698)
25	26	EL	H	West Bromwich	W 2-0		24	Turner, Lund	10,088
26	30	C/C 4	A	Norwich City	L 0-1				(14,030)
27	D 3	EL	A	Derby County	D 0-0		24		(14,078)
28	6	EL	H	Tranmere Rovers	W 1-0		24	Devlin	4,703
29	10	EL	A	Wolverhampton	L 0-1		24		(25,786)
30	17	EL	H	Portsmouth	L 0-1		24		6,382
31	26	EL	H	Millwall	L 0-1		24		6,758
32	28	EL	A	Middlesbrough	L 1-2		24	McSwegan	(21,558)
33	31	EL	H	Luton Town	L 0-1		24		6,249
34	J 8	FAC 3	H	Manchester City	D 2-2			White, Matthews	12,376
35	14	EL	A	Burnley	W 3-0		24	Devlin, White, McSwegan	8,702
36	18	FAC 3R	A	Manchester City	L 2-5			McSwegan, Matthews	(14,261)
37	21	EL	A	Sunderland	W 2-1		24	Lund, Matthews	(14,334)
38	24	AIC	H	Stoke City	D 0-0				5,135
39	28	EL	A	Grimsby Town	L 1-2		24	White	(5,161)
40	31	AIC S/F	A	Stoke City	W †3-2			Mills, Legg, Nicol (won on pens)	(10,741)
41	F 4	EL	A	Tranmere Rovers	L 2-3		24	Legg, Devlin	(6,105)
42	7	EL	H	Bolton Wanderers	D 1-1		24	Matthews	7,553
43	11	EL	H	Southend United	D 2-2		24	Legg, Matthews	6,768
44	18	EL	A	West Bromwich	L 2-3		24	Devlin (2)	(13,748)
45	25	EL	H	Reading	W 1-0		23	Agana	7,183
46	M 3	EL	A	Charlton Athletic	L 0-1		23		(13,638)
47	11	EL	H	Sheffield United	W 2-1		23	Simpson, White	11,102
48	14	EL	A	Oldham Athletic	D 1-1		23	Devlin	(5,469)
49	19	AIC F	A	Ascoli	W 2-1			White, Agana	(11,704)
50	21	EL	H	Bristol City	D 1-1		24	White	5,692
51	25	EL	A	Stoke City	L 1-2		24	White	(10,204)
52	A 1	EL	H	Barnsley	L 1-3		24	Devlin	6,834
53	8	EL	A	Luton Town	L 0-2		24		(6,482)
54	15	EL	H	Middlesbrough	D 1-1		24	White	9,377
55	19	EL	A	Millwall	D 0-0		24		(5,471)
56	22	EL	H	Grimsby Town	L 0-2		24		5,286
57	29	EL	H	Watford	W 1-0		24		5,083
58	M 3	EL	A	Swindon Town	L 0-3		24		
59	7	EL	A	Port Vale	D 1-1		24	McSwegan	
60									

Best Home League Attendance: 11,102 v Sheffield United   **Smallest:** 4,703 v Tranmere Rovers   **Av Home Att:** 7,195

Goal Scorers:

Compared with 1993-94: -1462

League (45): Devlin 9, White 7, McSwegan 6, Lund 5, Agana 3, Legg 3, Matthews 3, Simpson 2, Williams 2, Jemson, Sherlock, Turner

C/Cola Cup (7): Lund 2, McSwegan 2, Agana, Devlin, Jemson

FA Cup (4): Matthews 2, McSwegan, White

Anglo-Ital Cup (11): Agana 2, Devlin 2, Marsden, Murphy, Turner, White, Legg (pen), Mills (pen), Nicol (pen)

Player appearance grid (shirt numbers by match). Columns left-to-right: Cherry S., Hoyle C., Johnson M., Turner P., Yates D., Murphy S., Agana T., Legg A., Lund G., McSwegan G., Simpson M., Cox P., Sherlock P., Reece P., Emenalo M., Matthews R., Devlin P., Gallagher T., Jemson N., Kuhl M., Walker R., Mills G., Williams J., Butler P., Daniel R., Kelly D.

Ch	Ho	Jo	Tu	Ya	Mu	Ag	Le	Lu	McS	Si	Cx	Sh	Re	Em	Ma	De	Ga	Je	Ku	Wa	Mi	Wi	Bu	Da	Ke	Referee	No
1	2	3*	4	6	5	7	8	9	10	11	12	14	S												13	P. Foakes	1
1	2		4	6	5	7	8	9	10	11	12			15	3	14			11							I. Cruikshanks	2
1	2		4	5	6	10		9		11	12	8		15	3	14	7		11	3						I. Hemley	3
1			4	6	5	7	8	9	10	12				15	3	14	11			14						K. Lupton	4
1			4	5		7	8	9	10	14	6	2		15	3	12	11									G. Singh	5
1		14	6	5	12	8	9	10			2			15	3	11	7									K. Lynch	6
	5	4	6	15	9	8	14	10	12	16			1		3	11	7	2		14	2					P. Rodomonti	7
	5	4	6	12		8	14	10					15	3	9		2	7		14	2					M. Brandwood	8
	5	4	6			8	12	10		14			15			9	2	7		8	2					J. Rushton	9
	5	4	6			8	12	10	11				15	3		9	2	7		8	2	10				E. Wolstenholme	10
	5	4	6	3	12	8	9	10	11		2		15			7		14	14	2	10	8				P. Wright	11
	5	4	6	3	11	8	9	12			2		15		14	7			10	3	2	10	8			N. Barry	12
	3	4	5	6	11	8	9						15		12	7			10	3	2		8			G. Cain	13
	3	4	5	6	11	8	9						15		12	7			10	3	14	8	6			J. Kirkby	14
	15	4	5	6	11	12	9					14	13	3	7				10	6	14	8	3	13		A. Flood	15
	3	4	5	6	11		9						15		14	7			12		12	8	3			R. Poulain	16
	3		5	6	11		9			4			15			7			12			8	3			A. Flood	17
15		6	4	5	12	11		9					1			7			14	2		8	3			D. Allison	18
15		6	4	5	12	11	9						1		14	7				2		8	3			K. Burge	19
15			4	5	12	11	9						1			7	2			2		8				J. Lloyd	20
		4	5		11							10				7	2			2		8				P. Foakes	21
15		6	4	5		11	10				12	1		9		7	2			2		8				M. Bailey	22
13		6	4	5	12	11	16			14		1		9		7	2	15		2		8				D. Tombolini	23
13		6	4		5	11		12			14	1		9		7				2		8				K. Lupton	24
1		6	4	5		11		9	14			13			7	10				2		8				A. Dawson	25
1		6	4	5		14	11	3	9	10		13			7				2		8				K. Morton	26
1		6	4	5		14	11	3	9	10		13			7				2		8				J. Watson	27
1		6		5		14	11	3	9	10		13			7	12				2		8				J. Winter	28
1		6	4	5		14	11	3	9			13			7	12				2		8				E. Parker	29
1		6	4	5		14	11	3	9			13			7	12				2		8				T. West	30
1	6	4	5			11	3		10			13				7	12			2		8				K. Breen	31
1	6	4		5	11	3			10			13		14		7			12	2		8				J. Kirkby	32
1	6	4		5		3		11				13		14	7				12	2		8				R. Harris	33
1	6	4		5		10				14	13			11	7				12	2		8				M. Reed	34
1	6	4		5	12	3		10			14	13		11	7					2						G. Singh	35
1	6	4		5		3	14	10			12	13		11	7					2						M. Reed	36
	6	4	5			3	9			14	13		11	7						2						W. Burns	37
13	6	4		5		3	9			15			14	12	7					2						P. Vanes	38
13	6	4		5		3	9			14				11	7					2						M. Brandwood	39
	16	4		5	9	3	15			7		13		12	14					2						E. Parker	40
	11	4		5	9	3			14			13			7					2						K. Lynch	41
	11	4		5	9	3		8				13		12	7					2						P. Alcock	42
	11	4		5	9	3	12			14		13		8	7					3						S. Mathieson	43
	3	4		5		8	12	9	14			13		11	7					2						J. Rushton	44
13	14		5	12	11			10				8	7							14						A. Dawson	45
13	14		5	11								7								3						C. Wilkes	46
			5	14	11			4				13			7					3						S. Dunn	47
			5	14	11			4				13			7					3						I. Cruikshanks	48
1		6		5	9	11			10			13	14		7	12				3						C. Agius	49
1		12	14		9	11						13			7					3		4				P. Harrison	50
1		4		5		11						13	9		7					3		4				N. Barry	51
1		12	4			11		9				13			7					3		4				P. Richards	52
1	6	11	4		5					7		13			12				4	3						M. Pierce	53
13		4		5	14	12				7		1														J. Holbrook	54
13		4		5		14				7		1			12											P. Rejer	55
13				5		14				7		1			12											G. Singh	56
13				5				14	7			1			9											E. Wolstenholme	57
13			5			12	7				1			9												D. Orr	58
13			5			9	7				1															R. Poulain	59

Ch	Ho	Jo	Tu	Ya	Mu	Ag	Le	Lu	McS	Si	Cx	Sh	Re	Em	Ma	De	Ga	Je	Ku	Wa	Mi	Wi	Bu	Da	Ke	
46	33	35	37	20	25	31	37	31	25	31	37	20	24	8	18		19	3		3	18		6			League Appearances
1	1	2	6	13	2	4	5	1	3		7	2		4	1	8	2	1	2							League Sub Appearances
4	3	4	2	4	3	1+2	4	4	4	2	3+1	2+2		0+1			0+1									C/Cola Cup Appearances
1	1	1		1	1	1	1	1	1	0+1	1	0+1	1													FA Cup Appearances
3	3		3	3		3	3	0+2	3	3	3	0+2				3					3					Play-Off Appearances

Players on Loan: Barnard (Chelsea), Viveash (Swindon Town)

CLUB RECORDS

BIGGEST VICTORIES
League: 10-0 v Port Vale, Division 2, 26.2.1895.
11-1 v Newport County, 15.1.1949.
F.A. Cup: 15-0 v Thornhill (no Rotherham), 1st Round, 24.10.1885.
League Cup: 5-0 v Mansfield, 30.8.1988.
5-0 v Swindon Town, 17.10.1962.
BIGGEST DEFEATS
League: 1-9 v Blackburn Rovers, Division 1, 16.11.1889.
1-9 v Aston Villa, Division 3(S), 29.9.1930.
1-9 v portsmouth, Division 2, 9.4.1927.
0-8 v West Bromwich Albion, Division 1, 25.10.1919.
0-8 v Newcastle United, Division 1, 26.10.1901.
F.A. Cup: 1-8 v Newcastle united, 3rd Round, 8.1.1927.
League Cup: 1-7 v Newcastle United (h), 2nd Round, 5.10.1993.
MOST POINTS: 3 points a win: 87, Division 3, 1989-90.
2 points a win: 69, Division 4, 1970-71.
MOST GOALS SCORED: 107, Division 4, 1959-60.
Newsham 24, Forrest 19, Bircumshaw 17, Roby 11, Joyce 10,
Withers 8, Hateley 8, Horobin 7, Carver 2, Opponents 1.
MOST GOALS CONCEDED: 97, Division 2, 1934-35.
MOST FIRST CLASS MATCHES IN A SEASON
62 - 1993-94 (League 46, FA Cup 3, League Cup 4, Anglo/Italian 9).
MOST LEAGUE WINS: 30, Division 4, 1970-71.
MOST LEAGUE DRAWS: 18, Division 4, 1968-69.
MOST LEAGUE DEFEATS: 28, Division 3, 1963-64.

BEST PERFORMANCES
League: 1970-71: Matches played 46, Won 30, Drawn 9, Lost 7,
Goals for 89, Goals against 36, Points 69. First in Division 4.
Highest Position: 3rd in Division 1, 1890-91, 1900-01.
F.A. Cup: 1893-94: 1st Round Burnley (h) 1-0; 2nd Round Burton
(a) 2-1; 3rd round Nottingham Forest (a) 1-1 (h) 4-1; Semi-final
Blackburn Rovers 1-0; Final Bolton Wanderers 4-1.
League Cup: 5th Round in 1963-64, 1972-73.
Most recent success: 1975-76: 2nd Round Sunderland (h) 2-1;
3rd Round Leeds United (a) 1-0; 4th Round Everton (a) 2-2, (h) 2-0;
5th Round Newcastle United (a) 0-1.
HONOURS: Division 2 Champions 1896-97, 1913-14, 1922-23.
Division 3(S) Champions 1930-31, 1949-50.
Division 4 Champions 1970-71. FA Cup 1893-94.
Anglo-Italian Cup winners in 1994-95. Runners-up 1993-94.
LEAGUE CAREER: Founder member of Football League 1988, Div
2 1892-93, Div 1 1896-97, Div 2 1912-13, Div 1 1913-14, Div 2
1919-20, Div 1 1922-23, Div 2 1925-26, Div 3(S) 1929-30, Div 2
1930-31, Div 3(S) 1934-35, Div 2 1949-50, Div 3 1957-58, Div 4
1958-59, Div 3 1959-60, Div 4 1963-64, Div 3 1970-71, Div 2 1972-
73, Div 1 1980-81, Div 2 1983-84, Div 3 1984-85, Div 2 (now Div 1)
1989-90, Div 2 1994-95.

INDIVIDUAL CLUB RECORDS

MOST GOALS IN A SEASON
Tom Keetley: 41 goals in 1930-31 (League 39, FA Cup 2).

MOST GOALS IN A MATCH
9. Harry Curshaw v Wednesbury Strollers, FA Cup 2nd Round
replay, 10.12.1881.

OLDEST PLAYER: Albert Iremonger, 41 years 320 days.

YOUNGEST PLAYER: Tony Bircumshaw, 16 years 54 days.

MOST CAPPED PLAYER
Kevin Wilson (Northern Ireland) 13.
Harry Curshaw (England) 8.

RECORD TRANSFER FEE RECEIVED
£2,500,000 from Derby County for Craig Short, 9/92.

RECORD TRANSFER FEE PAID
£750,000 for Tony Agana from Sheffield United, 11/91.

PREVIOUS MANAGERS

Albert Fisher 1913-27, Horace Henshall 1927-34, Charles Jones
1934, David Platt 1934, Percy Smith 1935-36, Jim McMullen 1936-
37, Harry Parkes 1938-39, Tony Towe 1939-42, Frank Womack
1942-43, Frank Buckley 1944-46, Arthur Strolley 1946-49, Eric
Houghton 1949-53, George Dryser 1953-57, Tommy Lawton 1957-
58, Frank Hill 1958-61, Tim Coleman 1961-63, Eddie Lowe 1963-
65, Tim Coleman 1965-66, Jack Burkitt 1966-67, Andy Beattie 1967,
Bill Gray 1967-68, Jack Wheeler 1968-69, Jimmy Sirrell 1969-75,
Ronnie Fenton 1975-77, Jimmy Sirrell 1977-82, Howard Wilkinson
1982-83, Larry Lloyd 1983-84, Ritchie Barker 1984-85, Jimmy Sirrell
1985-87, John Barnwell 1987-88, Neil Warnock 1988-92, Mick
Walker 1992-94, Howard Kendal 1995.

ADDITIONAL INFORMATION
PREVIOUS NAMES: None.
PREVIOUS LEAGUES: None.

Club colours: Black and white striped shirts, black shorts, white
socks.

Change colours: Tartan shirts, black shorts & black socks.

Reserves League: Pontins Central League Division 1.
Youth League: Melville Youth League.

LONGEST LEAGUE RUNS

of undefeated matches:	19 (26.4.1930 - 6.12.1930)	of league matches w/out a win:	18 (26.11.1904 - 8.4.1905)
of undefeated home matches:	25 (17.8.1970 - 14.8.1971)	of undefeated away matches:	10 (24.7.1971 - 30.10.1971)
without home win:	13 (3.12.1904 - 23.9.1905, 24.11.79 - 26.4.80)	without an away win:	24 (23.12.1933 - 30.1.1935)
of league wins:	8 (17.1.1914 - 14.3.1914)	of home wins:	14 (17.9.1959 - 13.2.1960)
of league defeats:	7 (1888-89, 1912, 1933, 1983)	of away wins:	5 (15.9.1896 - 31.10.1896)

GENERAL MANAGER

COLIN MURPHY . . . . appointed July 1995.

PREVIOUS CLUBS
As Manager . . . . . Derby, Lincoln (11 years), Stockport,
. . . . Southend.
As Asst.Man/Coach . . . . Derby, Leicester, Luton.
As a player . . . Crystal Palace, Cork Hibs, Wimbledon.

HONOURS
As a Manager . . Promotion gained on three occasions.
As a Player . . . . None.

TEAM MANAGER

Steve Thompson . . . . .appointed July 1995.

. . . . .Lincoln, Southend.

. . . . .Doncaster Rovers.
. . . . .Lincoln, Charlton Athletic, Sheffield United.

. . . . .Promotion gained on two occasions.
. . . . .None.

NOTTS COUNTY

PLAYERS NAME / Honours	Ht	Wt	Birthdate	Birthplace / Transfers	Contract Date	Clubs	League	L/Cup	FA Cup	Other	Lge	L/C	FAC	Oth
G O A L K E E P E R S														
Paul J Reece	5.10	12.7	16.07.68	Nottingham	18.07.86	Stoke City(A)	2							
				via Kettering Town £10,000	18.07.88	Grimsby Town	54	3	5	4				
				via Kettering Town Free	25.09.92	Doncaster Rovers	1							
				Free	02.10.92	Oxford United	39	3	2	1				
				Free	02.08.94	Notts County	11	1		2+1				
Darren Ward	5.11	12.9	11.05.74	Nottingham	27.07.92	Mansfield Town (T)	81	5	5	6				
				£150,000	08.95	Mansfield Town								
D E F E N D E R S														
Michael Emenalo	5.11	11.4	14.07.65	Nigeria	Nigeria	Molenbeek								
Nigerian Int.				Free	12.08.94	Notts County	7			3+1				
Michael E Forsyth	5.11	12.2	20.03.66	Liverpool	16.11.83	West Brom. A. (A)	28+1	1	2	1				
E: B.1, u21.1, Y.8. Div.2'87.				£25,000	28.03.86	Derby County	323+1	36	15+1	29	8	1		
				£200,000	23.02.95	Notts County	7							
Thomas D Gallacher	5.10	11.0	25.08.74	Nottingham	01.06.92	Notts County (T)	20			5+2				
Michael O Johnson	5.11	11.6	04.07.73	Nottingham	09.07.91	Notts County	102+5	9	4	15+1				
Shaun P Murphy	6.0	12.0	05.11.70	Sydney, Aus		Perth Italia (Aus)								
					04.09.92	Notts County	45+9	2+2	3	6+1	2			1
Stephen Nicol	5.10	11.2	11.12.61	Irvine		Aye United	68+2	16	3		7	1		
S: 27, u21.14. Div.1'84'86'88'90. FAC'86'89'92.				£300,000	26.10.81	Liverpool	328+15	42	50	32+2	36	4	3	3
EC'84. CS'89. SC'86. FLg.XI.1.				Free	20.01.95	Notts County	19			2				1
Christian M Short	5.10	12.2	09.05.70	Munster		Pickering Town								
				Free	11.07.88	Scarborough	42+1	5	1	3+1	1			
				£100,000	05.09.90	Sheffield United	77+15	5	4+1	7	2		1	
				Loan	23.12.94	Huddersfield Town	6			1				
						Notts County								
Gary Strodder	6.1	11.4	01.04.65	Cleckheaton	08.04.83	Lincoln City (A)	122+10	7+1	2+1	5+1	6			
				20.03.87	West Ham United	59+6	8	4+2	2	2			
				£190,000	22.08.90	West Bromwich A.	123+17	8+1	7	10	8	1		
				£145,000	08.95	Notts County								
Richard N Walker	5.11	10.12	09.11.71	Derby	03.07.90	Notts County (T)	39+1	6		5+1	4			
				Loan	23.03.95	Mansfield Town	4							
M I D F I E L D														
Peter J Butler	5.9	11.1	27.08.66	Halifax	21.08.84	Huddersfield T. (A)	0+5							
				Loan	24.01.86	Cambridge United	14			1	1			
Free 08.07.86 Bury 9+2/2/-/1/-/1/-/-				Free	10.12.86	Cambridge United	55	4	2	2	9			
				£75,000	12.02.88	Southend United	135+7	12	2	11	9	1		2
Loan 24.03.92 Huddersfield Town 7 Lge App.				£125,000	12.08.92	West Ham United	70	4	3	1	3			
				£350,000	04.10.94	Notts County	20	2	2	3				
Michael A Galloway	5.11	11.5	13.10.74	Nottingham	15.06.93	Notts County	6+1							
Andrew Legg	5.8	10.7	28.07.66	Neath		Britton Ferry								
WFAC'89'91				12.08.88	Swansea City	155+8	9+1	16	15+3	29		4	5
				£275,000	23.07.93	Notts County	61+3	7	4+1	10	5			4
Christopher Marsden	5.11	10.12	03.01.69	Sheffield	06.01.87	Sheffield Utd (A)	13+3	1		1	1			
				15.07.88	Huddersfield Town	113+8	15+1	6+2	10	9			
Loan 02.11.93 Coventry City 5+2 Lge App.				£150,000	11.01.94	Wolverhampton W.	8		3					
				£250,000	15.11.94	Notts County	7			1				1
Philip Turner	5.8	10.7	12.02.62	Sheffield	05.02.80	Lincoln City (A)	239+2	19	12	5	19			
				22.08.86	Grimsby Town	62	6	6	3	9			1
				£42,000	19.02.88	Leicester City	18+6	1+1	1		2			
				03.03.89	Notts County	211+14	14+3	13	33+1	15	3	3	
Michael Simpson	5.9	10.6	28.02.74	Nottingham	01.07.92	Notts County (T)	20+5	2+1		4+3	3			
F O R W A R D S														
Patrick A O Agana	5.11	12.0	02.10.63	Bromley		Weymouth				2				
ESP.1				£35,000	13.08.87	Watford	12+3	1+1	2	1	1	2		
				£45,000	19.02.88	Sheffield United	105+13	12	14	4+1	42	3	5	1
Loan Leeds United, 27.2.92, 1+1 Lg Apps.				£750,000	12.11.91	Notts County	77+16	5+1	5	11+1	10	2	1	3
Paul J Devlin	5.8	10.10	14.04.72	Birmingham	01.11.90	Stafford Rangers	0+1							
				£40,000	22.02.92	Notts County	106+9	9+1	5	14+1	19	1	1	4
Nigel B Jemson	5.10	11.10	10.08.69	Hutton	06.07.87	Preston N.E. (T)	28+4		2	5+1	8			1
E: u21.1. LC'90.				£150,000	24.03.88	Nottingham Forest	45+2	9	3+1	1	13	4	3	
Loan 03.12.88 Bolton Wanderers 4+1 Lg App.				Loan	15.03.89	Preston North End	6+3							
				£800,000	17.09.91	Sheffield Wed.	26+25	3+4	3+3	2+2	9	1		1
Loan 10.09.93 Grimsby Town 6 Lg 1gl, 1 Oth. App.				£300,000	08.09.94	Notts County	5+6	1+1		1	1	1		
Loan 13.01.95 Watford 3+1 Lg App.				Loan	25.04.95	Coventry City								
Gary J Lund	5.11	11.0	13.09.64	Grimsby	27.07.93	Grimsby Town (J)	47+13	6+2	4	2	24	1		5
E: u21.1				Free	22.08.86	Lincoln City	41+3	4	1	3	13	1	1	1
Loan Hull City, 14.8.92, 11Lg Apps +3 Gl				£40,000	17.06.87	Notts County	223+25	15+3	13+3	28+6	63	5	4	8
				Loan	23.03.95	Hull City	11				3			
Gary J McSwegan	5.8	10.9	24.09.70	Glasgow		Glasgow Rangers	9+9	1	0+2	0+3	4			
SFAC'93				£400,000	13.07.93	Notts County	47+12	6	4+1	6	21	3	1	1
Gary R Mills	5.8	11.1	11.11.61	Northampton	13.11.78	Nottingham F. (A)	50+8	7+3	3	4+2	8	2		
E: u21.2, Y2, S. EC'80.				13.10.82	Derby County	18	2	3		2			
via Seattle Sounders to				02.12.83	Nottingham Forest	63+15	9+2	2	3+1	4	1		
via Seattle Sounders to				14.08.87	Notts County	75	6	5	10	8	1		
				02.03.89	Leicester City	194+5	9+1	7	15	15	1		
				£50,000	26.09.94	Notts County	33+1	3	2	4				1
Graeme J Hogg	6.1	12.4	17.06.64	Aberdeen	01.06.82	Manchester Utd (A)	82+1	7+1	8	12	1			
AIC'95.				Loan	03.11.87	West Bromwich A.	7			1				
				£150,000	25.08.88	Portsmouth	97+3	2	6	2	2			
				£200,000	23.08.91	Hearts	49+8	5	1	4	3		1	
Loan 03.10.94 Notts County				£75,000	27.01.95	Notts County	17			1				
Colin R Hoyle	5.11	12.3	15.01.72	Wirksworth	29.01.90	Arsenal								
Loan 08.02.90 Chesterfield 3 Lge App.				Free	01.07.90	Barnsley								
				£25,000	28.08.92	Bradford City	55+7	1	3+1	4	1			
				Free	06.08.94	Notts County	3			1				
				Loan	03.10.94	Mansfield Town	4+1	2		1				
Devon W White	6.3	13.8	02.03.64	Nottingham		Arnold Kingswell								
				Free	14.12.84	Lincoln City	21+8			2+1	4			2
£2,000 via Boston United to				Free	21.08.87	Bristol Rovers	190+12	9	10	19	54	2	3	2
				£100,000+P.E	28.03.92	Cambridge United	157	4	1	1	4	1		1
				£100,000	26.01.93	Q.P.R.	15+10	1+1			9			
				£100,000	23.12.94	Notts County	16+4		2	3	7		1	
Ian D Ridgeway	5.8	10.6	28.12.75	Reading	15.07.94	Notts County (T)	0+1							

ADDITIONAL CONTRACT PLAYERS: James M Hunt 15.07.94 Notts County (T). **Christopher D Pearson** 15.07.94 Notts County (T)

MEADOW LANE

Nottingham NG2 3HJ
Tel: 0115 952 9000

Capacity ....20,300.

First game ....v Nottingham Forest, September 1910.
First floodlit game...v Derby County, 23.3.1953, 1-1, Att: 20,193.

ATTENDANCES
Highest...47,310 v York City, FACup 6th Round, 10.3.1955.
Lowest ....1,616 v Peterborough United, FMC, 12.12.1989.

OTHER GROUNDS...None.

MATCHDAY TICKET PRICES

New Stand Centre £14

Wings £12

Jimmy Sirrel Stand. £10

Family Stand £10
Juv/OAP £5

Additional Information
Under 10s pay £20 per season for membership and are then admitted free of charge.

Ticket Office Telephone no. 01159 557 210

CLUBCALL
0898 88 86 84

Calls cost 39p per minute cheap rate and 49p per minute at all other times.
Call costings correct at time of going to press.

HOW TO GET TO THE GROUND

From the North
Use motorway (M1) until junction 26, leave motorway and follow signs into Nottingham A610. Follow signs to Melton Mowbray, Trent Bridge A606. On near-side of River Trent turn left into Meadow Lane for Notts County FC.

From the East
Use A52 sign posted Nottingham to Trent Bridge, cross River and then turn right into Meadow Lane for Notts County FC.

From the South
Use motorway (M1) until junction 24, leave motorway and follow signs to NOttingham (South) to Trent Bridge, cross river and then right into Meadow Lane for Notts County FC.

From the West
Use A52 into Nottingham, then follow signs to Melton Mowbray, Trent Bridge A606 on nearside of River Trent turn left into Meadow Lane for Notts County FC.

Car Parking: Limited street parking near ground but ample space in the City of Nottingham Corporation car park only 20 minutes walk.

Nearest Railway Station: Nottingham Midland (all enquiries to Derby Station 01332 32051)

MATCHDAY PROGRAMME

Programme Editor . . . . Terry Bowles.

Number of pages . . . . 40.

Price . . . . £1.30.

Subscriptions . . . . Apply to club.

Local Newspapers. . . . . Nottingham Evening Post.

Local Radio Stations. . . . . Radio Nottingham, Radio Trent.

OXFORD UNITED
(The U's)
ENDSLEIGH LEAGUE DIVISION 2
SPONSORED BY: UNIPART

Back Row (L-R): Mickey Lewis, Matt Murphy, Paul Milsom, Elliot Jackson, Phil Whitehead, Danny Cullip, Mark Druce, Chris Allen.
Middle Row: John Clinkard (Physio), Maurice Evans (General Manager), Simon Marsh, Alex Dyer (departed), Steve Wood, Paul Moody, Matt Elliott, Phil Gilchrist, Malcolm Elias (Youth Dev.), Mark Harrison (Res/Youth Coach).
Front Row: Bobby Ford, Stuart Massey, Wayne Biggins, Les Robinson, Denis Smith (Director of COaching), Malcolm Crosby (1st Team Coach), Mike Ford, David Smith, David Rush.

OXFORD UNITED
FORMED IN 1893
TURNED PROFESSIONAL IN 1949
LTD COMPANY IN 1949

PRESIDENT: The Duke of Marlborough
CHAIRMAN: R Herd CBE
DIRECTORS
K Cox, G Coppock, N Hams, D Smith
SECRETARY
Mick Brown (01865 61503)
MARKETING
Tony Watson

MANAGER: Denis Smith
ASSISTANT MANAGER: Malcolm Crosby
RESERVE/YOUTH TEAM MANAGER
Mark Harrison
PHYSIOTHERAPIST
John Clinkard

STATISTICIAN FOR THE DIRECTORY
Roy Grant

If season 1993/94 was frustrating for Oxford supporters then 1994/95 must have been even worse. The old football adage of a game of two halves was much in evidence to describe United's season, with the first half seeing the side as one of the best in the division, but the second half being mediocre in comparison.

Following their win at Peterborough on Boxing Day the side was four points clear at the top of the table, and looked to end the year on a high (despite one of the surprises of the season - losing at Marlow in Round One of the FA Cup), but a run of four defeats (and 7 in 9) soon saw them drop to 7th - their lowest placing of the season - and the position in which they were to ultimately end. The team did enjoy a good February/March which saw them rise again to third but another disappointing run of results cost them dear with no time left to recover.

Of course, there were highs - Paul Moody's 24 often spectacular goals was the best total by an Oxford player for ten years. The emergence of Bobby Ford and Simon Marsh, the shrewd signing of Phil Gilchrist, the goals from midfield from Matt Murphy and the consistent displays of Les Robinson all helped on the playing front. However, the lows were frustrating results - Marlow has already been mentioned but defeats at Chester (ending a 13 game unbeaten run), Bristol Rovers and Crewe (where Oxford led both by 2-0 only to lose 3-2) cost them dearly, especially as the latter two just pipped us for a play-off spot. Injuries also played a big part, Steve Wood, Mike Ford, Phil Whitehead, Anton Rogan and speedy winger Chris Allen all had long spells out injured, and youngster Mark Druce joined them later on just when he had started to establish himself as Moody's partner following the surprise mid-season move of experienced striker, John Byrne.

On their day, there is no doubt that this United side is good enough to regain their Division One status and, Manager, Denis Smith, will look for a good start to next season to be a platform for the hoped promotion. Good news off the field in the quest for a new stadium has seen Oxford aiming to play at the new Minchery Farm site early in 1997 - that news is probably the best United fans have had during the frustrations of 1994/95 after an end of term report that reads ëcould do betterí.

The return of derby matches with Swindon will also add spice to the season, and the Oxford fans would dearly love to finish above their arch rivals after the disappointments of finishing one place below (and conceding both league games to) temporary local rivals Wycombe.

Come on you yellows.

OXFORD UNITED

	Division Two: 7th		FA Cup: 1st Round		Coca-Cola Cup: 2nd Round		Auto Windscreen Trophy: 3rd Round		

M	DATE	COMP.	VEN	OPPONENTS	RESULT	H/T	LP	GOAL SCORERS/GOAL TIMES	ATT.
1	A 13	EL	H	Hull City	W 4-0	4-0		Byrne 19, 30, 45, Moody 33	5,691
2	16	CC 1/1	H	**Peterborough United**	**W 3-1**	**1-1**		**Moody 1 (pen), Massey 73, Robinson 81**	**4,183**
3	20	EL	A	Cardiff City	W 3-1	2-1	2	Moody 29, 35, 57	(7,281)
4	23	CC 1/2	A	**Peterborough United**	**W 1-0**	**1-0**		**Dyer 34**	**(3,351)**
5	27	EL	H	Cambridge United	W 1-0	1-0	3	Moody 29 (pen)	5,525
6	30	EL	A	Bradford City	W 2-0	1-0	2	Moody 22, Jacobs 89 (og)	(9,005)
7	S 3	EL	A	Huddersfield Town	D 3-3	2-1	2	Moody 28 (pen), Druce 34, Rogan 67	(10,122)
8	10	EL	H	Birmingham City	D 1-1	0-0	2	Moody 47 (pen)	8,072
9	13	EL	H	Crewe Alexandra	W 2-1	2-0	1	Byrne 41, 45	6,499
10	17	EL	A	Brighton & H.A.	D 1-1	0-1	1	Moody 64	(9,970)
11	20	CC 2/1	H	**Olham Athletic**	**D 1-1**	**1-1**		**Ford M. 35**	**5,070**
12	24	EL	H	Leyton Orient	W 3-2	0-0	1	Moody 65, Elliott 79, Rush 89	5,824
13	27	AWT 1	H	**Bristol Rovers**	**D 2-2**	**1-0**		**Moody 20, 86**	**1,518**
14	O 1	EL	A	Chester City	L 0-2	0-1	2		(2,324)
15	4	CC 2/2	A	**Oldham Athletic**	**L 0-1**	**0-0**			**(4,525)**
16	8	EL	H	Plymouth Argyle	W 1-0	1-0	2	Byrne 18	6,551
17	15	EL	A	Swansea City	W 3-1	3-1	2	Elliott 10, Moody 26, Byrne 43	(3,724)
18	22	EL	A	Wrexham	L 2-3	2-2	2	Moody 17, Hunter 41 (og)	(3,925)
19	29	EL	H	Shrewsbury Town	D 0-0	0-0	3		6,091
20	N 1	EL	H	Blackpool	W 3-2	1-1	2	Elliott 36, Byrne 57, Rush 90	5,610
21	5	EL	A	Stockport County	W 2-0	1-0	2	Moody 9 (pen), 64	(5,132)
22	8	AWT 1	A	**Bournemouth**	**D 0-0**	**0-0**			**(1,374)**
23	13	FAC1	A	**Marlow**	**L 0-2**	**0-0**			**(3,050)**
24	19	EL	H	Rotherham United	W 2-1	2-1	2	Moody 28, 38	5,802
25	26	EL	A	Bournemouth	W 2-0	1-0	1	Byrne 34, Butters 65	(4,277)
26	D 3	AWT 2	A	**Brentford**	**W 2-1**	**0-0**		**Murphy 47, Ashby 52 (og)**	**(2,410)**
27	10	EL	H	Cardiff City	W 1-0	1-0	1	Murphy 37	6,181
28	17	EL	A	Hull City	L 1-3	1-2	1	Elliott 45	(4,884)
29	26	EL	A	Peterborough United	W 4-1	2-1	1	Ford R 14, Rush 40, 84, Murphy 90	(5,803)
30	27	EL	H	Wycombe Wanderers	L 0-2	0-1	1		9,540
31	31	EL	A	Brentford	L 0-2	0-1	2		(7,125)
32	J 2	EL	A	York City	L 0-2	0-1	3		6,384
33	10	AWT 3	H	**Swansea City**	**L 1-2**	**0-1**		**Ford R 46**	**2,309**
34	14	EL	A	Bristol Rovers	L 2-3	2-0	4	Druce 12, 15	(5,875)
35	28	EL	A	Shrewsbury Town	D 1-1	1-1	4	Byrne 13	(3,768)
36	F 4	EL	H	Bournemouth	L 0-3	0-2	6		5,473
37	11	EL	A	Blackpool	L 1-2	0-0	7	Rush 87	(5,206)
38	18	EL	H	Bristol Rovers	D 0-0	0-0	7		6,349
39	21	EL	A	Rotherham United	D 1-1	1-0	7	Murphy 2	(2,833)
40	25	EL	H	Chester City	W 1-0	0-0	7	Gilchnot 52	4,930
41	28	EL	H	Stockport County	W 4-0	1-0	5	Murphy 12, Lewis 64, Rush 73 (pen), Allen 85	4,594
42	M 4	EL	A	Leyton Orient	D 1-1	0-1	6	Moody 63	(4,052)
43	7	EL	H	Huddersfield Town	W 3-1	0-0	5	Elliott 51, Murphy 68, Moody 74	7,161
44	11	EL	A	Cambridge United	W 2-1	1-0	3	Rush 45, 90	(3,558)
45	18	EL	H	Bradford City	W 1-0	0-0	3	Moody 72	5,427
46	21	EL	A	Birmingham City	L 0-3	0-1	4		(19,781)
47	25	EL	H	Brighton & H.A.	D 0-0	0-0	4		6,724
48	A 1	EL	A	Crewe Alexandra	L 2-3	2-0	5	Moody 8, Allen 16	(3,928)
49	4	EL	H	Wrexham	D 0-0	0-0	5		4,729
50	8	EL	H	Brentford	D 1-1	1-1	5	Dyer 25	7,845
51	15	EL	A	Wycombe Wanderers	L 0-1	0-1	7		(7,683)
52	17	EL	H	Peterborough United	W 1-0	1-0	6	Moody 33	5,163
53	22	EL	A	York City	W 2-0	1-0	6	Murphy 15, 83	(3,732)
54	30	EL	H	Swansea City	L 1-2	1-1	7	Rush 23	5,219
55	M 6	EL	A	Plymouth Argyle	D 1-1	0-1	7	Ford R 51	(4,953)
56									
57									
58									
59									
60									

Best Home League Attendance: 9,540 v Wycombe Wanderers   **Smallest:** 4,594 v Stockport County   **Av Home Att:** 6,148

Goal Scorers:

Compared with 1993-94: -729

League (66): Moody 21 (4 pens), Byrne 10, Rush 9 (1 pen), Murphy 7, Elliott 5, Druce 3, Allen 2, Ford R 2, Opponents 2 Butters, Dyer, Gilchrist, Lewis
C/Cola Cup (5): Dyer Ford M, Massey, Moody, Robinson
FA Cup (0):
AW Trophy (5): Moody 2, Ford R, Murphy, Opponent

Whitehead P.	Robinson L.	Ford M.	Dyer A.	Elliott M.	Rogan A.	Massey S.	Smith D.	Moody P.	Byrne J.	Allen C.	Lewis M.	Cusack N.	Deegan M.	Druce M.	Wood S.	Murphy M.	Ford R.	Marsh S.	Collins D.	Rush D.	Butters G.	Wanless P.	Cullip D.	Dobson T.	Carter J.	Referee	
1	2	3	4	5	6*	7	8	9	10•	11	12	14		S												Cooper K.	1
1	2	3	4*	5	6	7	8	9	10†	11			S	12	S											Wright P.	2
1	2	3	4	5	6•	7	8	9	10	11	14		S	S												Pierce M.	3
1	2	3	4	5	6	7	8	9	10	11•	14		S	S												Lynch K.	4
1	2	3	4	5	6	7	8	9	10•	11	S		S	12												Flood A.	5
1	2	3	4	5	6	7	8			11	S		S	10	S											Dawson A.	6
1	2	3	4	5	6	7	8	9		11	S		S	10•		12										Burns W.	7
1	2	3	4	5	6	7	8	9		11	S		S	10•	12											Lloyd J.	8
S	2	3	4	5	6*	7	8	9*	10	11	14		S	12												Alcock P.	9
S	2	3		5		7	8	9	10	11	4		1					S	6	S						Pooley G.	10
1	2	3		5		7	8	9*	10	11	4		S	12				6	S							Morton K.	11
1	2	3		5		7	8	9*	10	11	4		S					6	S	12						Hemley I.	12
S	2	3	6	5		7	8	9	10*	11	4		1				S			12						Wilkes C.	13
1	2	3	6*	5		7	8	9	10	11	4		S						S	12						Richards P.	14
1	2	3	4	5		7	8	9	10	11	S		S					6*		12						Kirkby J.	15
1	2	3	4	5	6	7	8	9*	10	11•	14		S							12						Wright P.	16
1	2	3	4	5	6	7	8	9•	10	11*	14		S							12						Lunt T.	17
1	2	3	4	5	6	7	8	9	10*		14	12	S			11•										Cain G.	18
1	2	3	4	5	6•	7	8*		10		14		S			11				12						Rushton J.	19
1	2		4	5		7*	8	9	10		S					11	6	3		12						D'urso A.	20
1	2		4	5		7	8	9	10*		14		S			11•	6			12	3					Rennie U.	21
S	2						8			4		1	7*		12	11	6	5	10	3	9	S				Dunn S.	22
1	2		4	5		7	8	9	10		S					11	6*	3		12						Bailey C.	23
1	2		4	5			8	9•	10		6		S			11	S			12	3					Singh G.	24
1	2		4	5			8	9•	10		6		S	14		11				12	3	7*				Barber G.	25
1	2		4	5			8		10	3	S	S	6•	7		11				9		14				Leach K.	26
1	2		4	5			8	9†	10•	3	S	14		7*		11				12	6					Foakes P.	27
1	2		4	5			8	9	10	3	S	14		7•		11*				12			6			Butler A.	28
1	2		4	5	12		8		10*	3	S			14		11				9			6	7•		Riley M.	29
1	2		4	5	12		8	14	10	3	S			11•		9							6	7*		Cooper K.	30
1	2		4	5			8	9	10•	3*	S			14	11		10					12	6	7		Holbrook J.	31
1	2		4	5			8	9		14	3*		S			7•		11		10			6	12		Vanes P.	32
	2		4*	5	6		8			11			1	9		12	7	3		10			S			Wilkes C.	33
	2		4*	5	6		8			11•			1	9		12	7	3		10	14					Cain G.	34
	2		4	5	6		8	9•	10	11	12		S	14		7*		3								Orr D.	35
	2		4	5	6		8	9	10•	11			S	14	3*	7				12						Mathieson S.	36
	2		12	5	6		8	14	10•	11*	4		S	3		7				9						Poulain R.	37
	2		11	5			8		10•	12	4		S	14		7		3		9*						Orr D.	38
	2		11	5			8	14	10•	12	4		S			7		3*		9						Wolstenholme E.	39
S	2		3	5		S	8	9		11	4		S			7				10						Vanes P.	40
1	2*		3	5•		12	8			11	4		S	9		7				10	14					Brandwood J.	41
1	2	3		5	S		8	12		11	4		S	9		7				10*						Foakes P.	42
1	2		5	3	S	S	8	12		11	4		S	9		7				10						Pierce M.	43
1	2		14	5	3		8	9*		11•	4		S	12		7				10						Winter J.	44
1	2		14	5	3		8•	12		11	4		S	9*		7				10						Barber G.	45
1	2		14	5	3		8•	12		11	4		S	9*		7				10						Barry N.	46
1	2		11•	5	3		8	9		14	4		S	12		7*				10						Lloyd J.	47
1	2		14	5	3	7	8*	9		11	4		S			12				10•						Lynch K.	48
1	2		14	5	3•	7	8*	9		11	4		S					12		10						Flood A.	49
1	2		10	5	3	7*	8•	9		11	4		S					12				14†				D'Urso A.	50
1	2	12	10*	5+				9		11	4•		S			7			8		14					Cooper K.	51
1	2	12		5	12			9		11	4		S			8	7			10•		14				Rejer P.	52
1	2	S		5	3			9		11	4		S			8	7		S	10•						Parker J.	53
1	2	12			3*	14		9		11	4		S			8•	7		3	10	5					Singh G.	54
1	2			5		9*	12			11	4		S			8	7			10	14					Wilkes C.	55
38	46	15	32	45	27	20	41	34	25	32	30		2	9	2	17	20	8	3	22	3	3		5	3	League Appearances	
	3	6		2	2	1	7			4	9	2		10		5	3			12		7			1	League Sub Appearances	
4	4	4	3	4	2	4	4	4	4	4	1+1			+2						+1						C/Cola Cup Appearances	
1	1		1	1			1	1	1	1							1	1	1		+1					FA Cup Appearances	
1	4	1	3	3	1		4	1		2	2	3		3		3	1+2	3	2	1	3+1	1		1+1		AW Trophy Appearances	

Also Played: Key (1(35,36,37,38,39,40), Gilchrist 6(38,39,40,41,42,43,44,45,46,47,48,49,50,51,52,53,54,55•), Jackson S(33,34)
Players on Loan: Butters, Dobson (Portsmouth), Carter (Arsenal), Key (Sheffield Wednesday)

† = Sent Off

CLUB RECORDS

BIGGEST VICTORIES

7-0 v Barrow,Division 4, 19.12.1964.
6-0 v Gillingham, League Cup, Rnd 2, 24.9.86.

BIGGEST DEFEAT

0-6 v Liverpool, Div. 1, 22.3.1986

MOST LEAGUE POINTS

(3pts for win) 95, Div 3, 1983-84
(2pts for win) 61, Div 4,1964-65

RECORD TRANSFER FEE RECEIVED

£1,100,000 from Derby County for Dean Saunders, October 1988.

RECORD TRANSFER FEE PAID

£285,000 to Gillingham for Colin Greenall, February 1988.

BEST PERFORMANCES

League: 18th Div 1 1983-84,1986-87 FA Cup: 6th Rnd. 1963-64
League Cup: Winners (1) 1985-86

HONOURS

League Division 2, 1984-85; Division 3, 1967-68, 1983-84; League
Cup1985-86.

LEAGUE CAREER

Elected to Div 4 1962
Promoted to Div 3 1965
Promoted to Div 2 1968
Relegated to Div 3 1976
Promoted to Div 2 1984
Promoted to Div 1 1985
Relegated to Div 2 1988
Relegated to Div 2 1994.

INDIVIDUAL CLUB RECORDS

MOST APPEARANCES

John Shuker: League 473+5 + FA Cup 29 + League Cup 24 + Anglo
Italian 3. Total 529+5 (1962-77)

MOST CAPPED PLAYER

Jim Magilton (N. Ireland) 18

RECORD LEAGUE GOALSCORER IN A SEASON

John Aldridge 34 (League 30, FAC 1,League Cup 3) 1984-85.
3 goals twice = 6; 2 goals 8 times = 16; 1 goal 12 times = 12.

RECORD LEAGUE GOALSCORER IN A CAREER

John Aldridge 90 (League 72; FAC 2;League Cup 14; FMC 2) 1983-87.

OLDEST PLAYER IN A LEAGUE MATCH

Colin Todd, 35 years 4 months.

YOUNGEST PLAYER IN A LEAGUE MATCH

Jason Seacole, 16 years 5 months.

PREVIOUS MANAGERS

(Since 1959) 1959-69 A Turner, 1969 R Saunders, 1969-75 G
Summers, 1975-79 M Brown, 1979-80 W Asprey, 1980 R Barry,
1980-82 I Greaves,1982-85 J Smith, 1985-88 M Evans, 1988 M
Lawrenson, 1988-93 B Horton.

ADDITIONAL INFORMATION

Previous League: Southern League
Previous Names: Headington United (until 1960)

Club colours: Yellow shirts blue sleeves, blue shorts, yellow socks.

Change colours: Red & black striped shirts, black shorts, red/black
shorts or Grey shirts & shorts and blue socks.

Reserves League: Avon Insurance Football Combination.

LONGEST LEAGUE RUNS

of undefeated matches:	20 (17.3.1984 - 29.9.1984)	of league matches w/out a win:	27 (14.11.1987 - 27.8.1988)
of undefeated home matches:	20 (3.10.1964 - 25.8.1965)	of undefeated away matches:	12 (28.2.1984 - 22.9.1984)
without home win:	13 (21.11.1987 - 2.5.1988)	without an away win:	24 (14.9.1974 - 27.9.1975)
of league wins:	6 (14.1.67-26.2.67, 16.3.68-6.4.68, 4.12.82-3.1.83)	of home wins:	10 (15.9.1984 - 29.12.1984)
of league defeats:	7 (4.5.1991 - 7.9.1991)	of away wins:	4 (4.12.1982 - 3.1.1983, 7.5.1984 - 22.9.1984)

THE MANAGER

DENNIS SMITH . . . . appointed September 1993

PREVIOUS CLUBS

As Manager . . . . York City, Sunderland, Bristol City.
As Asst.Man/Coach . . . . None.
As a player . . . . Stoke City, York City.

HONOURS

As a Manager . . . . York: Division 4 champions 1984. Sunderland: Promotion to Division 1, 1990.
As a Player . . . . Stoke: League Cup 1972.

OXFORD UNITED

PLAYERS NAME / Honours	Ht	Wt	Birthdate	Birthplace / Transfers	Contract Date	Clubs	League	L/Cup	FA Cup	Other	Lge	L/C	FAC	Oth
G O A L K E E P E R S														
Philip M Whitehead	6.3	13.7	17.12.69	Halifax	01.07.88	Halifax Town (T)	42	2	4	4				
				£60,000	09.03.90	Barnsley	16							
Loan Halifax T., 7.3.91, 9 Lg App.				Loan	29.11.91	Scunthorpe Utd	8			2				
Loan Scunthorpe U., 4.9.92, 8 Lg + 2 LC App.				Loan	19.11.92	Bradford City	6			4				
				£75,000	01.11.93	Oxford United	77	4	5	1				
D E F E N D E R S														
Matthew S Elliot	6.3	13.6	01.11.68	Wandsworth		Epsom & Ewell								
				£5,000	09.09.88	Charlton Athletic		1						
				£10,000	23.03.89	Torquay United	123+1	9	9	16	15	2	2	1
				£50,000	26.03.92	Scunthorpe United	61	6	2	8	8			
				£150,000	05.11.93	Oxford United	77	4	5	3	10	2		
Michael P Ford	6.0	11.6	09.02.66	Bristol	11.02.84	Leicester City (A)								
				Free	01.08.84	Devizes Town								
				Free	19.09.84	Cardiff City	144+1	6	9	7	13			
				£150,000	10.06.88	Oxford United	166+15	13+1	5+1	5	10	1	1	
Philip A Gilchrist	6.0	11.12	25.08.73	Stockton-on-T	05.12.90	Nottingham F. (T)								
				Free	10.01.92	Middlesbrough								
				Free	27.11.92	Hartlepool United	77+5	4+1	4	5				
				£100,000	17.02.95	Oxford United	18				1			
Leslie Robinson	5.8	11.1	01.03.67	Shirebrook		Chesterfield (J)								
				Free	06.10.84	Mansfield Town	11+4		1					
					27.11.86	Stockport County	67	2	4	4	3			
				£10,000	24.03.88	Doncaster Rovers	82	4	5	5	12		1	1
				£150,000	19.03.90	Oxford United	167+2	14	8+1	9	2	1		
Stephen A Wood	6.1	12.7	02.02.63	Bracknell	19.02.81	Reading (A)	216+3	10	15	4	9			
Div3'86, Div2'88				£80,000	17.06.87	Millwall	108+2	10	10	3+1				
				£400,000	09.10.91	Southampton	46	2+1	2	4			7	
				Free	20.07.94	Oxford United	2			1				
M I D F I E L D														
Robert J Ford	5.8	11.0	22.09.74	Bristol	06.10.92	Oxford United (T)	32+5	0+1	3	4	2			1
Michael Lewis	5.6	10.6	15.02.65	Birmingham	18.02.82	West Brom. A. (A)	22+2	4+1	4					
E:Y7				£25,000	16.11.84	Derby County	37+6	2	0+1	4	1			
					25.08.88	Oxford United	271+10	15+2	12+1	11+1	7			
Stuart A Massey	5.11	11.8	17.11.64	Crawley		Sutton United				4				
				£20,000	17.07.92	Crystal Palace	1+1			1				
				Free	05.07.94	Oxford United	20+2	4	1	1		1		
Matthew S Murphy	5.10	11.5	20.08.71	Northampton		Corby Town								
				£20,000	12.02.93	Oxford United	19+5			1+2	7			1
				Loan	28.01.94	Kettering Town								
David C Smith	5.8	11.2	26.12.70	Liverpool	04.07.89	Norwich City (T)	13+5		2+1	1+1				
				£100,000	05.07.94	Oxford United	41+1	4	1	4				
F O R W A R D S														
Chris A Allen	5.11	12.2	18.11.72	Oxford	14.05.91	Oxford United (T)	97+29	7+2	4+3	4+3	9	2	1	
Mark Angell			23.08.75	Newcastle	31.12.93	Sunderland								
				Free	08.95	Oxford United								
Wayne Biggins	5.11	11.0	20.11.61	Sheffield	22.11.79	Lincoln City (A)	8				1			
Div.2'88. AGT'92. via Kings Lynn & Matlock				£7,500	04.02.84	Burnley	78	6	3	7	29	1	1	5
				£40,000	17.10.85	Norwich City	66+13	6	4	6+2	16	2		3
				£150,000	15.07.88	Manchester City	29+3	4	2		9	1		
				£250,000	10.08.89	Stoke City	120+2	10	6	10	46	2		5
				£200,000	02.10.92	Barnsley	44+3		3+1		16			
					25.11.93	Celtic	4+5		0+1					
				£125,000	24.03.94	Stoke City	18+9	1+1		3+1	6			2
				Free	08.95	Oxford United								
Mark A Druce	5.11	11.11	03.03.74	Oxford	03.12.91	Oxford United (T)	17+27	1+3		2+1	4			
Alex C Dyer	5.10	12.0	14.11.65	Forest Gate		Watford (A)								
				Free	20.10.83	Blackpool	101+7	8+1	4+1	7	19		1	1
				£37,000	13.02.87	Hull City	59+1	2	4		14		1	
				£250,000	11.11.88	Crystal Palace	16+1	3+1	1+1	3+1	2			3
				£100,000	30.11.90	Charlton Athletic	60+18	2+1	1	3+1	13		1	
				Free	26.07.93	Oxford	62+14	4	5	5	6	1	1	
Paul Moody	6.3	12.6	13.06.67	Portsmouth		Fareham				1				
				£4,000		Waterlooville				1				
				£50,000	15.07.91	Southampton	7+5	1	0+1					
				Loan	09.12.92	Reading	5		1	1	1			
				£60,000	19.02.94	Oxford United	49+7	4	1	1	29	1		2
Simon T Marsh	5.11	11.2	29.01.77	Ealing	22.11.94	Oxford United (T)	8	2	1	2				
David Rush	5.11	10.3	15.05.71	Sunderland		Notts County (T)								
					21.07.89	Sunderland	40+19	1+1	9	1+1	12		1	
Loan 15.08.91 Hartlepool 8 Lge App. 2gls.				Loan	27.10.93	Peterborough Utd	2+2	1			1	1		
				Loan	12.09.94	Cambridge United	2							
				£100,000	23.09.94	Oxford United	22+12	0+1	0+1	3+1	9			

MANOR GROUND

London Road, Headington, Oxford OX3 7RS
Tel: 01865 61503

Capacity 9,572
Standing 6,769
Seating 2,803

First game 1.10.1898
First floodlit game......................................v Banbury, 18.12.1950(first club to stage a floodlit game)
ATTENDANCES
Highest ....22,750 v Preston North End, FA Cup 6th Round, 29.2.1964.
Lowest ....1,055 v Portsmouth, ZDS Cup, 12.12.1990.

OTHER GROUNDS...None.

MATCHDAY TICKET PRICES

Seats . . . . £8 - £11
Juv/OAP . . . . £4 - £7.50

Terraces . . . . £7 - £8
Juv/OAP . . . . £5 - £5.50
(all prices dependant on category of match)

Ticket Office Telephone no. 01865 61503

CLUBLINE
0891 44 00 55
Calls cost 39p per minute cheap rate and 49p per
minute at all other times.
Call costings correct at time of going to press.

HOW TO GET TO THE GROUND

From the North: From North (M40) leave at junction 9. Follow signs for A34 to Oxford. Take slip road A44 marked Witney, Woodstock. At roundabout take first exit (Pear Tree). Follow to next roundabout A44 junction with A40 Woodstock Road, take second exit marked A40 London. Down to next roundabout (Banbury Road), take second exit on to Northern by-pass. Cars should take next left turn at slip road marked New Marston half-a-mile and JR Hospital 1 mile. (Coaches should follow diversions to avoid week bridge, next roundabout A40, Green Road, take fifth exit, follow signs for A40 junction with (B4105) Marston). Down to mini-roundabout turn left. Straight up Headley Way, coaches should take second junction right marked Franklin Road which leads into coach park.

From South: A34 by-pass to junction A44 Pear Tree. Follow directions as North.

From the East: Cars and coaches should follow coach diversion directions as from Green Road roundabout.

From the West: Take A34 following signs to M40. Take exit A44 marked Woodstock, take third exit Pear Tree, follow as North.

Car Parking: Street parking near ground. Take care for matchday parking restrictions.

Nearest Railway Station: Oxford (01865 722 333)

MATCHDAY PROGRAMME

Programme Editor . . . . Roy Grant.

Number of pages . . . . 32 (sometimes 36).

Price . . . . £1.30.

Subscriptions . . . . £40 per season.

Local Newspapers . . . . Oxford Mail, Oxford Times.

Local Radio Stations . . . . Radio Oxford, Fox FM.

PETERBOROUGH UNITED
(The Posh)
ENDSLEIGH LEAGUE DIVISION 2
SPONSORED BY: THOMAS COOK

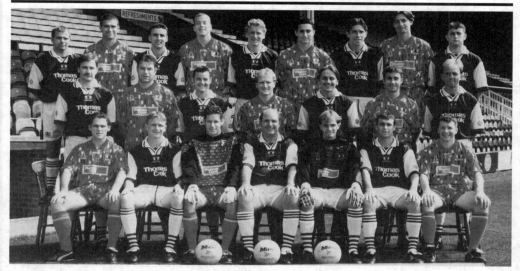

Back Row (L-R): Kevin Ashley, Simon Clark, Danny Carter, Greg Heald, Lee Power, David Morrison, Neil Le Bihan, Gary Breen, Ryan Semple. **Middle Row:** Keith Oakes (Physio), Sean Farrell, David Gregory, Marcus Ebdon, Billy Manuel, Andy Furnell, Michael Halsall (Asst. Manager). **Front Row:** Lee Williams, Gary Martindale, Mark Tyler, John Still (Manager), Jon Sheffield, Scott McGleish, Tony Spearing.

PETERBOROUGH UNITED
FORMED IN 1934
TURNED PROFESSIONAL IN 1934
LTD COMPANY IN 1934

CHEIF EXECUTIVE: Chris Turner
CHAIRMAN: Alf Hand
DIRECTORS
P Sagar, N Hands, R Terrell
ASSOCIATE DIRECTORS
M Judson, T Judson, T Elisgood
SECRETARY
Mis Caroline Hand
COMMERCIAL MANAGER
Mick Vincent

MANAGER: John Still
ASSISTANT MANAGER: Mick Halsall

YOUTH TEAM MANAGER
Bob Higgins
PHYSIOTHERAPIST
Keith Oakes

STATISTICIAN FOR THE DIRECTORY
Mick Robinson

1994/94 was to some extent going to be a trip into the unknown. John Still had been appointed as Manager the day after the last game of the 1993/94 season. The name did not mean alot to the majority of supporters as John had not managed a league team before and it was going to be down to him to attract the right players to steady the ship and prevent a second successive relegation. John said that he would not be looking for players just to see the club through but would be looking to buy youth and to build for the future. Gary Breen aged 20, Greg Heald aged 22, Neil Le Bihan aged 18, David Morrison aged 19, were among the players signed to further this hope.

The 14 players to figure in the opening league game saw six making their Posh debuts and a further four who had only started nine games for the club between them. As it turned out the club finished in mid-table but the season seemed to have more lows than highs with relegation a distinct possibility until the last third of the season. The team just could not seem to get any consistency into their game. A run of 12 league games without a victory followed by eight games undefeated. Fine victories at Crewe 3-1, Huddersfield 2-1 and Brighton 2-1, where a large part of the second half was played with only nine men after Morrison and Charlery had been dismissed, were offset by poor results at Leyton Orient 1-4, at Blackpool 0-4 and, a candidate for the worst ever Posh performance, a 1-5 defeat at home to Crewe.

The cups did not really add any light to the gloomy season, first round elimination by Oxford in the Coca-Cola Cup, a first round dismissal in the Autoglass Windscreen Shield by Hereford and a second round defeat by county rivals, Cambridge in the FA Cup.

What went wrong? I do not really know. Certainly the number of young players John Still brought in possibly added to the lack of consistency but by the end of the season, David Morrison and Greg Heald, who both started off slowly showed that they are capable of becoming more than useful players and Gary Breen had a fine season, which saw him play regularly for the Eire U21 Team. The one position that did cause the club a great deal of concern was the goalkeeper. By the end of the season seven players had been named as the No.1. Scott Cooksey looked to lack confidence from the start, Mark Tyler, a youth international, looks a fine 'keeper but was not given an extended run, which was a surprise given John Still's views on youth, Mark Prudhoe was taken on loan from Stoke and proved a very useful 'keeper and popular with the fans but Stoke's demands rising from £50,000, at the start of the loan to a reported £200,000 by the end, killed any hopes of a permanent move. Ex-Posh player Fred Barber was the next to arrive but a broken collar bone in his fifth game brought a premature end to his season. In stepped No.5, John Keeley an experienced goalkeeper but after three poor displays he walked out on the club saying, he could not stand the barracking from the fans!! This led to Ian Feuer arriving from West Ham United, Ian's arrival saw the start of Posh's best run of the season and he seemed to inspire a great deal of confidence in the players around him. The last player to wear a goalkeepers shirt for Posh was Glyn Knight but he only managed to sit on the subs bench.

So what for next season? Well assuming that John Still will not give Mark Tyler an extended run in the team a goalkeeper has got to be high on the list of needs. Someone to share the burden of finding the net along with Ken Charlery, and a midfielder who will score double figures. This along with the years experience that the younger players have gained could see a play-off place in the offering. M.ROBINSON.

PETERBOROUGH UNITED

Division Two: 15th   FA Cup: 2nd Round   Coca-Cola Cup: 1st Round   Auto Windscreen Trophy: 1st Round

M	DATE	COMP.	VEN	OPPONENTS	RESULT	H/T	LP	GOAL SCORERS/GOAL TIMES	ATT.
1	A 13	EL	H	Bristol Rovers	D 0-0	0-0	13		5,695
2	16	CC 1/1	A	Oxford United	L 1-3	1-1		Morrison 22	(4,185)
3	20	EL	A	Brentford	W 1-0	1-0	10	Charlery 14	(5,516)
4	23	CC 1/2	H	Oxford United	L 0-1	0-1			3,3351
5	27	EL	H	Crewe Alexandra	L 1-5	0-3	15	Morrison 78	4,579
6	30	EL	A	Bournemouth	W 3-0	2-0	8	Farrell 16, Morrison 38,. Charlery 74	(2,644)
7	S 3	EL	A	Shrewsbury Town	D 2-2	2-0	9	Henry 2,41	(3,879)
8	10	EL	H	Hull City	W 2-1	1-1	7	Morrison 36, Charlery 64	5,044
9	13	EL	H	Huddersfield Town	D 2-2	2-1	8	Farrell 14, Charlery 43	5,316
10	18	EL	A	Birmingham City	L 0-4	0-3	12		(10,600)
11	24	EL	H	Rotherham United	D 2-2	1-2	13	Henry 2, 78	4,894
12	27	AWT	H	Birmingham City	L 3-5	2-3		Henry 1, Brissett 30, Charlery 70	2,044
13	O 1	EL	A	Cardiff City	W 2-1	1-1	10	McGorry 24, Charlery 54	(4,225)
14	8	EL	A	York City	D 1-1	0-0	11	Williams 88	(3,601)
15	15	EL	H	Stockport County	L 0-1	0-0	12		5,369
16	22	EL	H	Wycombe Wanderers	L 1-3	1-1	13	Henry 4	5,924
17	29	EL	A	Swansea	L 0-2	0-1	14		(2,733)
18	N 1	EL	A	Plymouth Argyle	W 1-0	1-0	13	Henry 5	(4,145)
19	5	EL	H	Chester City	W 2-0	1-0	13	Charlery 32, Farrell 89	4,610
10	8	AWT	A	Walsall	W 3-2	0-1		Heald 52, Breen 55, Henry 68	(2,104)
21	12	FAC 1	H	Northampton Town	W 4-0	0-0		Charlery 70, 85, (pen.), Williams 74, Henry 87	8,739
22	19	EL	A	Brighton	W 2-1	2-1	12	Charlery 20, Ebdon 33	(6,445)
23	26	EL	H	Leyton Orient	D 0-0	0-0	13		5,114
24	29	AWT	A	Hereford United	L 0-2	0-1			(1,301)
25	D 3	FAC 2	H	Cambridge United	L 0-2	0-2			9,576
26	10	EL	H	Brentford	D 2-2	2-1	14	Henry 4, Kelly 12	4,102
27	17	EL	A	Bristol Rovers	L 1-3	1-0	1	Farrell 37	(4,635)
28	26	EL	H	Oxford United	L 1-4	1-2	14	Charlery 15	5,803
29	27	EL	A	Wrexham	D 3-3	2-0	14	Morrison 14, 54 Ebdon 44	(4,689)
30	31	EL	H	Cambridge United	D 2-2	1-1	14	Charlery 16,84	7,412
31	J 2	EL	A	Blackpool	L 0-4	0-1	15		(3,692)
32	14	EL	H	Bradford City	D 0-0	0-0	16		4,400
33	28	EL	A	Chester City	D 1-1	0-1	16	Morrison 76	(1,501)
34	F 4	EL	A	Leyton Orient	L 1-4	0-2	16	Ebdon 68	(3,447)
35	11	EL	H	Plymouth Argyle	L 1-2	0-1	16	Farrell 54	4,318
36	18	EL	A	Bradford City	L 2-4	0-2	18	Farrell 46, Ebdon 60	(4,806)
37	21	EL	H	Brighton	W 2-1	1-0	17	Charlery 25, Farrell 84	3,870
38	25	EL	H	Cardiff City	W 2-1	1-1	16		4,226
39	M 4	EL	A	Rotherham United	D 0-0	0-0	16		(3,123)
40	7	EL	H	Shrewsbury Town	D 1-1	0-0	18	Charlery 85	3,554
41	11	EL	A	Crewe Alexandra	W 3-1	2-0	16	Ebdon 18, Morrison 30, Breen 52	(3,983)
42	18	EL	H	Bournemouth	D 0-0	0-0	16		4,495
43	21	EL	A	Hull City	D 1-1	1-1	16	McGorry 22	(4,601)
44	25	EL	H	Birmingham City	D 1-1	0-0	16	Charlery 70	8,796
45	28	EL	A	Wycombe Wanderers	L 1-3	0-1	17	Gordon 50	(4,590)
46	A 1	EL	A	Huddersfield	W 2-1	1-0	16	Ebdon 43, McGorry 62	(11,324)
47	4	EL	H	Swansea City	W 1-0	1-0	15	Kelly 43 (pen.)	3,764
48	8	EL	A	Cambridge United	L 0-2	0-1	16		(5,828)
49	15	EL	H	Wrexham	W 1-0	1-0	15	Manual 39	4,309
50	17	EL	A	Oxford Utd	L 0-1	0-1	15		(5,163)
51	22	EL	H	Blackpool	W 1-0	0-0	15	Farrell 76	5,716
52	29	EL	A	Stockport	D 1-1	0-1	15	Morrison 86	(4,387)
53	M 6	EL	H	York City	D 1-1	0-0	15	Charlery 74 (pen.)	4,963
54									
55									
56									
57									
58									
59									
60									

Best Home League Attendance: 8,756 v Birmingham City   Smallest: 3,554 v Shrewsbury Town   Av Home Att: 5,055

Goal Scorers: Compared with 1993-94: -2,377

League (54):   Charlery 16 (1 pen), Farrell 8, Morrison 8, Henry 7, Ebdon 6, McGorry 3, Kelly 2,(1 pen.), Breen, Gordon, Manual, Williams
Coca Cola Cup (1): Morrison
FA Cup (4):   Charlery 2 (1 pen), Henry, Williams
AW Trophy (6):   Henry 2, Breen, Brissett, Charlery, Heald

Cooksey	Ashley	Clarke	Ebdon	Heald	Walsh	Morrison	Breen	Farrell	Charlery	Moran	Williams	Funnell	Tyler	McGorry	Heney	Brissett	Dunphy	Spearing	Lormor	Webster	Prudhoe	Thomas	Kelly	Barber	Lebihan	Referee	
1	2	3	4	5	6	7	8*	9	10	11	12*	S	S													K. Breen	1
1	2	3	4	5	6	7*	8	9*	10	11	12*			14*												P. Wright	2
1	2	3	4		6	7*	5		9	10	11	8		S	S	12*										J. Rushton	3
1	2	3	4		6		5		9	10	11*	8		14*	12*	7*										K. Lynch	4
1	2	3	4		6	7	5	9*	10			8*		S	12*	11		14*								T. West	5
1	2	3*		5	6	7			9	10			14*	S	4	11*		12*	8							C. Wilkes	6
1	2	3		5	6	7	12*	9	10		4*	S	S		S	11		8								P. Harrison	7
1	2	3		5	6	7	8	9*	10		4			S	12*	11			S							J. Parker	8
1	2*	3		5	6	7	8	9	10					S	4	11	S	12*								K. A. Cooper	9
S	2	3		5	6	7	8	9*	10		12*		1	4	11	14*										R. Poulain	10
S	2*	3	4		5	6	7	8	14*	10	9*		1	12*	11											G. Barber	11
S		S	4	5			7*	8		10			1	8	11	9		3	12*		2					I. Hemley	12
S	2	3	4		6	7	5		10			S		8	11	9			S			1				G. Singh	13
S	2	3	4		6	7*	5		10	14*			8	11*	9			12*	12*			1				J. Watson	14
	2*	3	4		6	7*	5	12*	10		14*		S	8	11	9*						1				S. Dunn	15
	2	3	4	S	6	7*	5	9	10		12*	S	8	11								1				U. Rennie	16
	2	3	4*		6	7*	5	12*	10		9		S	8	11			14*				1				G. Cain	17
	2	6	4		S	S	5	7	10		9		S	8	11			3				1				J. Holbrook	18
1	2	6	4				12*	5	7	10*	9		S	8	11			3				S				T. Heilbron	19
1			4	2		10	5	7		9			S	8	11	S	3	S				6				P. Harrison	20
1	2	6	4			12*	5	7*	10		9		S	8	11		3	S				S				K. Morton	21
1	2	6	4			7	5		10		9		S	8	11		3	S				S				G. Pooley	22
1	2	6	4			12*	5		10		9		S	8*		7*	3	11	8*			6				K. Lynch	23
S	12*	4*	2			5			10	7	9		1			14*	3	11	8*			6				S. Dunn	24
1	2	6*	4			5		7*	9		S	8	10	12*	3	11			14*							P. Alcock	25
1	2*	6	4			7	12*		9			S	10		3	11*		14*	8							A. Flood	26
1	2	6	4		S	7	5	11*	9			S	10		3	12*			8							C. Wilkes	27
	2		4	12*		7	5		10	9*	14*	S	11*		3			6	8	1						M. Riley	28
	2		4	7		9	5		10		11*	S	12*		3			6	8	1			S			R. Poulain	29
	2	6	4	S		5	12*	10		9		S	7	11*		3			8	1						J. Kirby	30
	2	6		4		7*		12*	10		9		S	11	S		3		5	8	1					W. C. Burns	31
		6		2		7	5	9*	10		11	12*	15*	4				3				1*	S			E. J. Parker	32
S		6		2		7	5	9*	10	12*	11		1	4				3					S			J. Watson	33
S	2	6	4		S	11		5		10	12*	7						3				6	4			T. West	34
S	2	6	4	S		12*	5	9	10	11*	7							3								P. Folkes	35
	6	4	2			12*	5	9	10	11*	7		S	8				3				S				N. Barry	36
	6	4	2			12*	5	9	10	7			S	8	11*			3				S				P. Harrison	37
	6	4	2			12*	5	9	10	7*			S	8	11*			3				14*				K. Lupton	38
2*	6	4	12*			S	5	9	10	7			S	8				3								D. Allison	39
	6	4	S			7	5	9	10	11*	7		S	12*				3								G. Barber	40
		4	6			7*	5	9*	10	2		14*	S	11	12*			3								P. Richards	41
		4	6			7	5	9	10	2			S	11*	12*			3				S				R.D. Furnandiz	42
		4	6			7	5	9*	10	2			S	11	12*			3				S				E. Lomas	43
		4	6			7	5		10	2			S	11	S			3				S				P. Folkes	44
		4	6			7	5		10	2				11*	12*			3				S				M. Pierce	45
	S	4	6				5		10	2			S	11	S			3				7				K. Wolstenholme	46
	S	4	6			5			10	2			S	11	S			3				7				K. Breen	47
		4	6			12*	5		10	2			S	11*	14*			3				7				K. Leach	48
		4	6			11	5	12*	10	2			S		9*			3				7				M.A. Riley	49
	S		6			11	5	9*	10	2			S		12*			3				7		4		P. Rejer	50
	7*		6			11	5	12*	10	2			1	8				3						4		J. Holbrook	51
		8	6			14*	5	9	10	2			S	7*	12*			3						4*		W. Burns	52
	3		6			11	5	9*	10	2			S	4*	14*			3						12*		A. Butler	53
12	27	32	35	27	14	33	43	26	44	5	35	3	4	31	22	4		31	2		6	6	12	5	3	League Appearances	
			2			8	1	8		2	5	4	1	4	10	1	2	2	2			2	1		1	League Sub Appearances	
2	2	2	2	1	2	1	2	2	2	2	1+1			0+2	0+1	1										C/Cola Cup Appearances	
2	2	2	2			0+1	2	1	1	1	2			2	2	0+1		2	1			0+1				FA Cup Appearances	
	0+1	3	3			2	3	1	2	1	2			2	2	2		1+1	2			2				AW Trophy Appearances	

Also Played: Soloman 8(32,33,34,35), Keeley (134,35,36), Feuer 1(37,38,39,40,41,42,43,44,45,46,47,48,49,50,51,52,53), Manual 11(39)8(40,41,42,43,44,45,46,47,48,49,50,53),11(52), Gordon 9(44,45,46,47,48*51*), Knight *(45,51), Semple 14"(51) Players on Loan: Prudoe (Stoke City), Barber (Luton Town), Soloman (Watford), Feuer (W.H.U.), Gordon (W.H.U)   † = Sent Off

PETERBOROUGH UNITED RECORDS AND STATISTICS

CLUB RECORDS

BIGGEST VICTORIES
League: 8-1 v Oldham Athletic, Div 4, 26.11.1969; 7-0 v Barrow, Div 4, 9.10.1971.

MOST GOALS SCORED IN A CUP TIE
9-1 v Rushden, 6.10.45.

BIGGEST DEFEAT
League: 0-7 v Tranmere Rovers, Div 4, 29.10.1985

MOST LEAGUE POINTS
(3pts for win) 82, Div 4, 1981-82
(2pts for win) 66, Div 4,1960-61

MOST LEAGUE GOALS
134, Division 4, 1960-61
Bly 52, Hails 21, Smith 17, Emery 15, McNamee 16, Ripley 5, Dunne 1, Raymor 1,og 6.

RECORD TRANSFER FEE RECEIVED
£350,000 from Watford for Ken Charlery, October 1992.
£350,000 from Birmingham for Ken Charlery, July 1995.

RECORD TRANSFER FEE PAID
£170,000 to Watford for Ken Charlery, December 1993

BEST PERFORMANCES
League: 10th Div 1, 1992/93, FA Cup: 6th rnd. 1964-65
League Cup: Semi Final 1965-66

HONOURS
League Division 4 Champions, 1960-61, 1973-74.

LEAGUE CAREER
Elected to Div 4 1960
Promoted to Div 3 1961
Demoted to Div 4 1968
Promoted to Div 3 1974
Relegated to Div 4 1979
Promoted to Div 3 1990
Promoted to Div 1 1992
Relegated to Div 2 1994

INDIVIDUAL CLUB RECORDS

MOST APPEARANCES
Tommy Robson: League 440+42 + FA Cup 43+2 + League Cup 31+1 +Texaco 3 Total 517+45 (1968-81)

MOST CAPPED PLAYER
A Millington (Wales) 8

RECORD LEAGUE GOALSCORER IN A SEASON
Terry Bly 54 (League 52, FAC 2) 1960-61
4 goals 2 times = 8; 3 goals 5 times = 15; 2 goals 6 times = 12; 1 goal 17times = 17.

RECORD LEAGUE GOALSCORER IN A CAREER
Jim Hall 122 0In All Competitions: JimHall 137 (League 122, FAC 11, Lge Cup 4) 1967-75

OLDEST PLAYER IN A LEAGUE MATCH
Norman Rigby, 38 years 333 days, 21.4.1962.

YOUNGEST PLAYER IN A LEAGUE MATCH
Mark Heeley, 16 years 229 days, 24.4.1976.

PREVIOUS MANAGERS

1934-36 Jock Porter, 1936-37 Fred Taylor, 1937-38 VicPoulter, 1938-48 Sam Haden, 1948-50 Jack Blood, 1950-52 Bob Gurney, 1952-54Jack Fairbrother, 1954-58 George Swindin, 1958-62 Jimmy Hagan, 1962-64 JackFairbrother, 1964-67 Gordon Clark, 1967-69 Norman Rigby, 1969-72 Jim Iley,1972-77 Noel Cantwell, 1977-78 John Barnwell, 1978-79 Billy Hails, 1979-82Peter Morris, 1982-83 Martin Wilkinson, 1983-86 John Wile, 1986-88 NoelCantwell, 1988-89 Mick Jones, 1989-90 Mark Lawrenson, 1990-91 Dave Booth, 1991-93 Chris Turner, 1993-94 Lil Fuccillo, 1994 Chris Turner, 1994 John Still.

ADDITIONAL INFORMATION
Previous League: Midland League.
Previous Names: None
Club colours: Blue shirt white sleeve, white shorts, blue & white socks.
Change colours: Red with yellow and green flecks shirt and shorts, red socks.
Reserves League: Capital League.
Youth League: Midland Intermediate.

LONGEST LEAGUE RUNS

of undefeated matches:	17 (17.12.1960 - 15.4.1961)	of league matches w/out a win:	17 (28.9.1978 - 30.12.1978)
of undefeated home matches:	32 (21.4.1973 - 9.11.1974)	of undefeated away matches:	8 (28.1.69-19.4.69, 19.3.88-10.9.88)
without home win:	9 (1.2.1992 - 14.3.1992)	without an away win:	26 (7.1.1976 - 22.3.1977)
of league wins:	9 (1.2.1992 - 14.3.1992)	of home wins:	15 (3.12.1960 - 28.8.1961)
of league defeats:	5 (26.12.1988 - 21.1.1989)	of away wins:	5 (22.3.1988 - 7.5.1988)

THE MANAGER

JOHN STILL. . . . . appointed May 1994.

PREVIOUS CLUBS
As Manager. . . . . Leyton Stone (x3), Dartford, Maidstone, Dagenham.
As Asst.Man/Coach . . . . None.
As a player . . . . Leyton Orient.

HONOURS
As a Manager. . . . . Maidstone: GM Vauxhall Conference plus other non-League championships.
As a Player . . . . None.

PETERBOROUGH UNITED

PLAYERS NAME / Honours	Ht	Wt	Birthdate	Birthplace / Transfers	Contract Date	Clubs	APPEARANCES				GOALS			
							League	L/Cup	FA Cup	Other	Lge	L/C	FAC	Oth
G O A L K E E P E R S														
Scott Cooksey	6.3	13.10	24.06.72	Birmingham	25.07.90	Derby County (T)								
SLP'92.				Free	07.02.91	Shrewsbury Town								
				Free		Bromsgrove Rovers			3					
				£25,000	30.12.93	Peterborough Utd	15	2	2	1				
Joathan Sheffield	6.0	12.0	01.02.69	Bedworth	16.02.87	Norwich City (A)	1							
				Loan	22.09.89	Aldershot	11		1					
Loan 21.08.90 Aldershot 15 Lge, 1 Oth App.				Loan	28.01.94	Cambridge United	28	3	5					
Loan 23.12.93 Colchester United 6 Lge App.				Loan	28.01.94	Swindon Town	2							
Loan 15.11.94 Hereford United 8 Lge, 2 Oth.				Free	08.95	Peterborough Utd								
Mark Tyler	6.0	12.9	02.04.77	Norwich	07.12.94	Peterborough Utd	4+1			2				
D E F E N D E R S														
Kevin Ashley	5.7	10.4	31.12.68	Birmingham	07.01.87	Birmingham City (A)	56+1	5	3	1+1	1			
				£500,000	13.09.90	Wolverhampton W.	87+1	5	1+1	4	1			
				Free	10.08.94	Peterborough Utd	27	2	2					
Gary Breen	6.1	12.7	12.12.73	Hendon		Charlton Athletic (T)								
Ei: u21.1.				Free	06.03.91	Maidstone United	19							
				Free	02.07.92	Gillingham	45+6	4	5	1				
				£70,000	05.08.94	Peterborough Utd	43+1	2	2	3	1			1
Simon Clark	6.1	12.06	12.03.67			Stevenage Borough								
				Free	25.05.94	Peterborough Utd	32	2	2	0+1				
Nick Dunphy	6.0	12.0	03.08.74			Hednesford Town								
				Free	26.08.94	Peterborough Utd	0+2							
Loan 17.11.94 Dagenham & Red.				Loan	11.02.95	Hednesford Town								
David Gregory	5.11	11.6	23.01.70	Sudbury	31.03.87	Ipswich Town (T)	16+16	3+2	1	3+2	2			4
Loan 09.01.95 Hereford Utd 2 Lge, 1 Oth App.				Free	08.95	Peterborough Utd								
Greg Heald	6.1	12.08	26.09.71	London		Enfield								
				£20,000	08.07.94	Peterborough Utd	27+2	1		3				1
Greg Rioch	5.11	10.09	24.06.75	Sutton C'field		Luton Town								
				Loan		Barnet	3							
				Free	08.95	Peterborough Utd								
Tony Spearing	5.9	10.12	07.10.64	Romford	11.10.82	Norwich City (A)	67+2	5	4	4				
FAYC'83.				Loan	01.11.84	Stoke City	9							
Loan Oxford United, 01.02.85, 5 Lge App.				£100,000	12.07.88	Leicester City	71+2	2+1	1	2	1			
				Free	01.07.91	Plymouth Argyle	35	6	1	2+1				
				Free	21.01.93	Peterborough Utd	85+4	4	2+1	5	1			
M I D F I E L D														
Marcus Ebdon	5.9	11.0	17.10.70	Pontypool	16.08.89	Everton (T)								
W: u21.2, Y.				Free	15.07.91	Peterborough Utd	85+3	9+1	6+1	9+1	12			
Neil Le Bihan	5.11	11.1	14.03.76			Tottenham H. (T)								
				Free	13.07.94	Peterborough Utd								
				Loan	23.09.94	Bishop Stortford								
				Loan	10.03.95	Yeovil Town								
Brian McGorry	5.10	11.0	16.04.70	Liverpool		Weymouth								
				£30,000	13.08.91	Bournemouth	56+5	7	7+3	5	11		2	1
				£60,000	10.02.94	Peterborough Utd	44+8	0+2	2	2	6			
Lee Williams	5.7	11.13	03.02.73	Birmingham	26.01.91	Aston Villa (T)								
E: Y.1, S.				Loan	08.11.92	Shrewsbury Town	2+1		1+1	2			1	
					23.03.94	Peterborough Utd	51+7	1+1	2	2	1		1	
F O R W A R D S														
Tony Adcock	5.11	11.9	27.02.63	Bethnal Green	31.03.81	Colchester Utd (A)	192+18	16+1	12+2	9	98	5	3	6
				£75,000	01.06.87	Manchester City	12+3	2+1	2	2	5	1		3
				£85,000	25.01.88	Northampton Town	72	6	1	4	30	3		1
				£190,000	06.10.89	Bradford City	33+5	1	0+1	2	6			
				£75,000	11.01.91	Northampton Town	34+1	1	1	2	10		1	1
				£35,000	30.12.91	Peterborough Utd	107+4	8+1	5	3+2	35	3	1	
				£20,000	04.08.94	Luton Town	0+2		0+1					
				Free	08.95	Peterborough Utd								
Darren S Carter	5.11	11.12	29.06.69	Hackney		Billericay Town								
					04.07.88	Leyton Orient	168+20	13+3	10	17+2	22	2	3	1
				£25,000	08.95	Peterborough Utd								
Sean Farrell	6.1	12.8	28.02.69	Watford	05.03.87	Luton Town (A)	14+11		2+1	1+2	1		1	2
Loan Northampton T., 13.09.91, 4 Lge App, 1 gl.				Loan	01.03.88	Colchester United	4+5				1			
				£100,000	19.12.91	Fulham	93+1	5+1	2	8	31	3	1	3
				£120,000	05.08.94	Peterborough Utd	25+8	2	1	1	8			
Andy Furnell			13.02.77	Peterborough		Peterborough U. (T)	5+5	1	0+1		1			
Gary Martindale	5.11	11.9	24.06.71	Liverpool		Burscough								
					24.03.94	Bolton Wanderers								
				Free	08.95	Peterborough Utd								
Scott McGleish	5.9	10.08	10.02.74	St Pancras		Edgware Town								
				Free	24.05.94	Charlton Athletic								
				Free	08.95	Peterborough Utd								
Paul Moran	5.10	11.0	22.05.68	Enfield	15.07.85	Tottenham H. (T)	14+22	1+6	3+1	0+1	2			
Loan Leicester City, 2.11.89, 10 Lge App, 2 gls.				Loan	11.01.89	Portsmouth	3							
Loan Southend Utd., 21.03.91, 1 Lge App.				Loan	14.02.91	Newcastle United	1							
				Free	08.07.94	Peterborough Utd	5+2	2	1	1				
David Morrison						Chelmsford City								
				£30,000	12.05.94	Peterborough Utd	34+8	1	0+1	2	8	1		
Lee Power	5.10	10.10	30.06.72	Lewisham	06.07.90	Norwich City (T)	28+16	1	0+1	0+2	10			
Ei: B.1, u21.12, Y.				Loan	04.12.92	Charlton Athletic	5							
				Loan	13.08.93	Sunderland								
				Loan	15.10.93	Portsmouth	1+1		1					
				£200,000	08.03.94	Bradford City	14+16	0+2	0+2	1+1	3		1	1
				£80,000	08.95	Peterborough Utd								
				Loan	09.01.95	Millwall								

LONDON ROAD GROUND
Peterborough PE2 8AL
Tel: 01733 53947

Capacity 10,675
Covered Standing 6,000
Seating 4,675
New stand seating 5,000 to be completed 01.01.1996.

First game ....v Gainsborough, 01.09.34.
First floodlit game ....v Arsenal, 08.02.60.

ATTENDANCES
Highest ....30,096 v Swansea City, FA Cup 5th Round, 20.2.1965.
Lowest...279 v Aldershot, AMC, 17.4.1986.

OTHER GROUNDS: .... None.

MATCHDAY TICKET PRICES

Main Stand £11
Juv/OAP £5.50

Wing Stand/Enclosure £9
Juv/OAP £4.50

Terraces £7
Juv/OAP £3.50

Match & Ticket Inforamtion
Tickets bookable 14 days in advance.

Ticket Office Telephone no 01733 63947

CLUBCALL
0898 12 16 54
Calls cost 39p per minute cheap rate and 49p per
minute at all other times.
Call costings correct at time of going to press.

HOW TO GET TO THE GROUND

From the North and West
Use A1 then A47 sign posted Peterborough into town centre. Follow signs to Whittlesey and cross river bridge into London Road for Peterborough United FC.

From East
Use A47 into Peterborough town centre and follow signs to Whittlesey and cross river bridge into London Road for Peterborough United FC.

From the South
Use A1 then A15 sign posted Peterborough into London Road for Peterborough United FC.

Car Parking
Ample parking available at ground.

Nearest Railway Station
Peterborough (01733 68181)

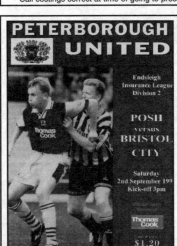

MATCHDAY PROGRAMME

Programme Editor . . . . Russell Plummer.

Number of pages . . . . 32.

Price . . . . £1.20.

Subscriptions . . . . Please apply to club.

Local Newspapers . . . . Herald & Post, Evening Telegraph.

Local Radio Stations . . . . Radio Cambridgeshire, Hereward Radio.

ROTHERHAM UNITED
(The Merry Millers)
ENDSLEIGH LEAGUE DIVISION 2
SPONSORED BY: PARKGATE RETAIL WORLD (Stadium Development)

ROTHERHAM UNITED
1995-96

ROTHERHAM UNITED
FORMED IN 1884
TURNED PROFESSIONAL IN 1905
LTD COMPANY IN 1920

PRESIDENT: Sir J Layden
CHAIRMAN: K F Booth
VICE-CHAIRMAN
R Hull
DIRECTORS
C Luckock, J A Webb
SECRETARY
N Darnill (01709 562 434)
COMMERCIAL MANAGER
D Nicholls (01709 562 760)

MANAGERS
Archie Gemmill & John McGovern

YOUTH TEAM MANAGER
Bill Russell
PHYSIOTHERAPIST
Ian Bailey

STATISTICIAN FOR THE DIRECTORY
Mike Smith

Though we started the season with a few new faces, there was no great improvement in standard of play or results. A swift exit from the Coca-Cola Cup followed by three successive defeats saw the elevation of Phil Henson to General Manager and the appointment of our new dual management team. Initially a greater sense of urgency and working for the team was noted and this resulted in improved results, though from January onwards old failings seemed to re-emerge and standards dip.

Throughout the season we suffered from injuries to key players and rarely had a settled side or a full squad to call on. The use of loan players was a frequent stop-gap measure, as was the elevation from the reserves of a number of youngsters. Again, lack of cash for the purchase of proven replacements meant that far too often we were 'making do' rather than putting out a really competitive team.

Eventually, we survived - but at a cost in terms of attendances, which were at their lowest for a long time.There is no doubt that investing in quality players would ultimately see rewards, not only in results and pride, but in increasing attendances and revenue.

With our new management team ready for their first full season and some reasonable moves in the transfer market underway, there is reason for optimism, but wouldn't it be nice for a change to have confidence.

MIKE SMITH.

ROTHERHAM UNITED

Division Two: 17th   **FA Cup:** 2nd Round   **Coca-Cola Cup:** 1st Round   **Auto Windscreen Trophy:** 3rd Round

M	DATE	COMP.	VEN	OPPONENTS	RESULT	H/T	LP	GOAL SCORERS/GOAL TIMES	ATT.
1	A 13	EL	H	Shrewsbury Town	L 0-4	0-3			3,762
2	16	CC 1/1	H	**Carlisle United**	W 1-0	0-0		**Varadi 59**	**2,055**
3	20	EL	A	Crewe Alexandra	L 1-3	0-2	20	Varadi 68	(3,505)
4	23	CC 1/2	A	**Carlisle United**	L 1-3	1-0		**Hayward 45**	**(5,004)**
5	27	EL	H	Bournemouth	W 4-0	0-0	16	Goater 47, 76, Hayward 49 (og), 69	2,306
6	30	EL	A	Brentford	L 0-2	0-1	18		(4,031)
7	S 3	EL	A	Cambridge United	L 1-2	0-1	20	Goater 88	(2,885)
8	10	EL	H	Bristol City	L 0-3	0-3	20		2,596
9	13	EL	H	Birmingham City	D 1-1	1-0	22	Hazel 37	3,799
10	17	EL	A	Hull City	W 2-0	2-0	20	Goodwin 7, Goater 40	(4,431)
11	24	EL	A	Peterborough United	D 2-2	2-1	18	Goodwin 13, Goater 20	(4,894)
12	27	AWT	A	**Scunthorpe United**	W 3-1	3-1		**Helliwell 11, Goater 14, Todd 26**	**(1,404)**
13	O 1	EL	H	Blackpool	L 0-2	0-2	20		3,517
14	8	EL	A	Stockport County	L 0-1	0-0	21		(4,991)
15	15	EL	H	York City	W 2-1	2-0	21	Goater 42, Goodwin 44	3,380
16	18	AWT	H	**Chesterfield**	D 1-1	0-0		**Goater 59**	**1,585**
17	22	EL	H	Leyton Orient	W 2-0	1-0	18	Marginson 37, Goater	2,700
18	29	EL	A	Brighton & H.A.	D 1-1	1-0	18	Davison 28	(6,734)
19	N 1	EL	A	Swansea City	L 0-1	0-0	18		2,511
20	5	EL	H	Plymouth Argyle	W 3-1	1-0	16	Goater 15, 80, Varadi	2,848
21	12	FAC 1	A	**York City**	D 3-3	1-1		**Goater 14, 83, Helliwell 77**	**(4,020)**
22	19	EL	A	Oxford United	L 1-2	1-2	16	Helliwell 3	(5,801)
23	22	FAC 1	H	**York City**	W 3-0	3-0		**Davison 1, 40, Goater 28**	**4,391**
24	26	EL	A	Chester	W 2-0	0-0	16	Goater 62, 76	2,947
25	29	AWT	H	**Wigan Athletic**	L 1-3	0-2		**Goater 77**	**1,587**
26	D 3	FAC 2	A	**Wrexham**	L 2-5	1-1		**Davison 11, Hurst 60**	**(4,521)**
27	10	EL	A	Crewe Alexandra	D 2-2	0-2	16	McGlashan 61, Hayward 77	2,907
28	16	EL	A	Shrewsbury Town	L 0-1	0-1	17		(3,243)
29	26	EL	H	Bradford City	W 3-1	3-0	15	Roscoe 2, Goater 7, Davison 22	5,400
30	27	EL	A	Huddersfield Town	L 0-1	0-1	17		(15,557)
31	31	EL	H	Cardiff City	W 2-0	1-0	16	Monnington 42, Breckin 67	3,064
32	J 7	EL	A	Leyton Orient	D 0-0	0-0	17		(2,796)
33	14	EL	H	Wycombe Wanderers	W 2-0	1-0	15	Hayward 8 (og), 82	3,437
34	21	EL	A	Plymouth Argyle	D 0-0	0-0	15		(5,484)
35	F 4	EL	A	Chester	D 4-4	2-3	15	Monnington 22, McGlashan 29, 64, Wilder 83	(1,794)
36	11	EL	H	Swansea City	D 3-3	3-1	15	Roscoe 17, Hayward 20, Davison 28	2,858
37	18	EL	A	Wycombe Wanderers	L 0-2	0-1	16		(5,153)
38	22	EL	H	Oxford United	D 1-1	0-1	16	Goater 56	2,833
39	26	EL	A	Blackpool	D 2-2	1-1	16	Davison 44, Goater 54	(5,043)
40	M 4	EL	H	Peterborough United	D 0-0	0-0	17		3,123
41	7	EL	H	Cambridge United	W 1-0	1-0	15	Goater 36	2,208
42	11	EL	A	AFC Bournemouth	D 1-1	0-0	17	Goater 75	(5,666)
43	14	EL	A	Wrexham	L 1-3	1-1	18	Goater 45	(1,823)
44	18	EL	H	Brentford	L 0-2	0-2	18		2,968
45	22	EL	A	Bristol Rovers	L 0-2	0-0	18		(4,420)
46	25	EL	H	Hull City	W 2-0	1-0	18	Peel 8, Roscoe 60	3,692
47	28	EL	H	Brighton & H.A.	W 4-3	3-1	16	Breckin 25, (og) 37, Roscoe 44, Goater 70	2,316
48	A 1	EL	A	Birmingham City	L 1-2	1-0	17	Goater 17	(16,077)
49	8	EL	A	Cardiff City	D 1-1	0-1	17	Peel 86,	(6,412)
50	15	EL	H	Huddersfield Town	D 1-1	0-0	17	Hayward 56	6,687
51	17	EL	A	Bradford City	W 3-0	2-0	17	Farelly 8, Hayward 10, Peel 72	(3,535)
52	22	EL	A	Wrexham	L 0-1	0-0	17		2,628
53	29	EL	A	York City	L 0-2	0-0	17		(3,138)
54	M 6	EL	H	Stockport County	W 1-0	0-0	17	Farelly 80	3,469
55									
56									
57									
58									
59									
60									

Best Home League Attendance: 6,687 v Huddersfield   **Smallest:** 2,208 v Cambridge   **Av Home Att:** 3,280

Goal Scorers:

League (57): Goater 19, Hayward 6, Davison 4, Roscoe 4, Goodwin 3, McGlashan 3, Peel 3, Opponents 3, Breckin 2, Farelly 2, Monnington 2, Varadi 2, Hazel, Helliwell, Marginson Wilder

C/Cola Cup (2): Hayward, Varadi

FA Cup (8): Davison 3, Goater 3, Helliwell, Hurst

AW Trophy: (5) Goater 3, Helliwell, Todd

Compared with 1993-94: -443

Clarke	Smith	Hurst	Wilder	Breckin	Richardson	Hazel	Goodwin	Goater	Varadi	James	Helliwell	Brien	Mercer	Williams A.	Hayward	Williams C.	Todd	Pike	Foran	Dolby	McGlashan	Marginson	Davison	Pierce	Roscoe	Referee	
1	2	3	4	5	6	7	8	9	10	11	S	12	S													Lunt T.	1
S			2		6	7	9	11•	10	3	9	5*	1	4	12	14										Barry N.	2
S			2		6	7	9	11•	10	3	9*	5	1	4	12	14										Allison D.	3
S		S	2	6		7	8		10•		3		5	1	4	9	12	11								Lupton K.	4
1			2			7•	8			11	10		S	4	9	S	6	3	5	12						Winter J.	5
1			2			7	8			11•	10		S	4	9		6	3	5	12						Vanes P.	6
1			2			7	8	12		11*	10		S	4	9•		6	3	5							Howes T.	7
1			2			7	8			11	10		S	4	9	S	6	3		S						Watson J.	8
1			2	5		7•	8	10			9	6	S	4			11	3								Helbron T.	9
1			2	5	S	7	8	10		3	9	6	S	4			11			S						Burns B.	10
1			2	5	S	7	8	10	S	3	9	6	S	4			11									Barber G.	11
1			2	5	S	7	8	10•	12	3	9	6	S	4			11									Cruikshanks I.	12
1			2	5		7	8	10	12	3	9•	6	S	4			11									Rejer P.	13
1			2	5	S		8	10		7		6	S	4		12	11•	3			9					West T.	14
1			2	5		7•	8	10		11		6		4	12			3			S	9	S			Furnandiz R.	15
1			2	5				10		3		6		4	7				11		8	9	S			Parker J.	16
1			2	5			8	10	12	3		6		4	7			S			11	9•	S			Lomas E.	17
1			2	5			8•	10	14	3		6		4	7						12	9*	S		11	D'Urso A.	18
1			2	5				10	9	3		6		4	7						8		S		11	Vanes P.	19
1		12	2	5	S			10	9	3		6		4	7						8•		S		11	Richards P.	20
1	8		2	5	S			10	9	3•	12	6		4				7			11		S			Mathieson S.	21
1	7		2	5	12			10	9•	3	8*	6		4	14								S		11	Singh G.	22
1		11	2	5	8			10	12	3	S	6		4	7							9•	S			Mathieson S.	23
1		14	2	5	8			10•	12	3		6		4*	7							9	S		11	Holbrook J.	24
1		11•	2	5	8			10	12	3		6			7							9	S			Heilbron T.	25
1	4	11	2	5	8			10	S	3	12	6			7•							9	S			Flood A.	26
1	S	11	2		4			10		3	S	6			7						8	9	S			Burns W.	27
1	S	11	2	6	4			10		3	S				7						8	9	S			Vanes P.	28
1		14	2	6	4			10		3	12				7*						8	9•	S			Leach K.	29
1	S		2	6	4	12		10		3					7						8	9	S		11•	Cruikshanks I.	30
1		14	2	6	4	12		10		3					7						8	9•	S		11*	Watson J.	31
1			2	6	4•	10				3	12				7						8	14	9•	S	11	Dunn S.	32
1	S		2	6	4	12		10•		3					7						8		9	S	11	Lupton K.	33
1			2	6	4	S		10	12	3					7						8	9•	S		11	Wilkes C.	34
1			2	6	4	12		10	S	3					7•						8	9	S		11	Butler A.	35
1			2	6	4•	12		10	S	3					7						8	9	S		11	Lomas E.	36
1			2	6	4			10	14	3					7						8	12	9•	S	11	Foakes P.	37
1			2	6	4	7		10	S	3											8	S	9	S	11	Wolstenholme E.	38
1			2	6	4	7		10	S	3											8	S	9	S	11	Breen K.	39
1	12		2	6	4	7		10*	15	3•											8		9	S	11	Allison D.	40
1		3	2	6	4			10	12						7						8	9•	S		11	Singh G.	41
1		3	2	6	4			10	S			S			7		9				8		S		11	Pierce M.	42
1		3	2	6	4			10	12						7•		9			8			S		11	Barry N.	43
1	2	3		6	4•			10	9*						12		14			8			S		11	Cain G.	44
1		3	2	6	4•			10	14						7*		9			8			S		11	Bailey M.	45
1			2	6				10		3					7		S			8	S		S		11	Flood A.	46
1			2	6				10	S	3		5			7		S			8			S		11	Lynch K.	47
1			2	6	S			10		3					7		12			8			S		11	Lupton K.	48
1			2	6	S			10	S	3					7		S			8			S		11	Wright P.	49
1			2	6	S			10		3					7					8		S	S		11	Furnandiz R.	50
1			2	6*	14			10•		3					7					8		12	S		11	West T.	51
1			2	6	S			10		3					7					8		12	S		11	Watson J.	52
1	12		2	6	5			10		3					7•					8			S		11	Heilbron T.	53
1			2	6	5			10		3					7					8			S		11	Rushton J.	54
45	3	8	45	41	23	16	10	45	6	40	10	16	1	17	33		12	7	3		27	5	19		31	League Appearances	
	1	5		2	5			11		2	1			4	2	2				2		3	2			League Sub Appearances	
		2	1	1	2	2		1	2	2	1	2	2	2	1+1	0+2	1									League Cup Appearances	
3	2	3	3	3	1	1	1	3	1+1	3	1	3		2	2					1			1	2		FA Cup Appearances	
3	0+1	1	3	3	1	1	1	3	0+2	3	1	3		2	2		1					1	2			AW Trophy Appearances	

Also Played: Peel 9(46,47,48•,49,50,51•,52,53,54) Monnington 5(27,28,29,30,31,32,33,34,35,36,37,38,39,40,41,42,43,44,45,46,48,50,51,52,54), Farrelly 12(45),4(46,47,48,49,50,51,52,53,54) Boucken S(53,54), Ayrton 4•(25), Roberts S (6), 14 (7), 9 (12)

CLUB RECORDS

RECORD LEAGUE VICTORY
8-0 v Oldham Athletic, Div 3N, 26.5.1947
Record Cup Victory and Most Goals Scored in a Cup Tie
6-0 v Spennymoor United,FA Cup Round 2, 1977-78   6-0 v
Wolverhampton Wanderers, FA Cup Round 1,16.11.1985

RECORD LEAGUE DEFEAT
1-11 v Bradford City, Div 3N, 25.8.1928*
* First match of the season. Rotherham United won their second
match at home!
Record Cup Defeat
0-15 v Notts County, FA Cup Round 1, 24.10.1885

MOST LEAGUE POINTS
(2pts for win) 71, Div 3N, 1950-51
(3pts a win) 82, Div4, 1988-89

MOST LEAGUE GOALS
14, Div 3N, 1946-47

RECORD TRANSFER FEE RECEIVED
£180,000 from Everton for Bobby Mimms, May 1985
RECORD TRANSFER FEE PAID
£100,000 to Cardiff City for Ronnie Moore, August 1980

BEST PERFORMANCES
League: 3rd Div 2, 1954-55
FA Cup: 5th Round 1952-53,1967-68
League Cup: Finalists 1960-61

HONOURS
Division 3N Champions 1950-51
Division 3 Champions 1980-81
Division 4 Champions1988-89

LEAGUE CAREER
Rotherham Town: Elected to Div 2 1893   Not re-elected to Div 2
1896
Rotherham County: Elected to Div 2 1919   Relegated to Div 3N
1923   Promoted to Div 2 1951   Relegated to Div 3 1968
Relegated to Div 4 1973   Promoted to Div 3 1975   Promoted to
Div 2 1981   Relegated to Div 3 1983
Relegated to Div 4 1988   Promoted to Div 3 1989   Relegated to
Div 4 1991   Promoted to Div 3 (now Div 2) 1992

INDIVIDUAL CLUB RECORDS

MOST APPEARANCES FOR CLUB
Danny Williams (1946-60): 459

MOST CAPPED PLAYER
Shaun Goater, Bermuda (6+), Harold Millership, 6 Wales

RECORD GOALSCORER IN A MATCH
No player has scored more than four goals

RECORD LEAGUE GOALSCORER IN A SEASON
Wally Ardron, 38, Div 3N, 1946-47

RECORD LEAGUE GOALSCORER IN A CAREER
Gladstone Guest, 130, 1946-56

OLDEST PLAYER IN A LEAGUE MATCH
Chris Hutchings, 36 years 175 days v Bradford City, Div.2
27.12.1993

YOUNGEST PLAYER IN A LEAGUE MATCH
Kevin Eley, 16 years 72 days v Scunthorpe (h), 3-0, 15.5.1984

PREVIOUS MANAGERS

(Since 1946): Reg Freeman   Andy Smailes   Tom Johnston   Danny
Williams   Jack Mansell   Tommy Docherty   Jimmy McAnearney
Jimmy McGuigan   Ian Porterfield   Emlyn Hughes   George Kerr
Norman Hunter   Dave Cusack   Billy McEwan   Phil Henson

ADDITIONAL INFORMATION
Previous League: Midland League

Previous Names: Thornhill United (1884), Rotherham County
(1905), amalgamated in 1925 with Rotherham Town as Rotherham
United

Club colours: Red and white.

Change colours: White with black & red.

Reserves League: Pontins Central League Division 1.

Youth League: Northern Intermediate.

LONGEST LEAGUE RUNS

of undefeated matches:	18 (1950-51)	of league matches w/out a win:	14 (1934, 1977-78)
of undefeated home matches:	27 (1939-46-47, 1980-81)	of undefeated away matches:	16 (1950-51)
without home win:	9 (1983)	without an away win:	33 (1894-96-1919 - non-League club)
of league wins:	9 (1982)	of home wins:	22 (1939-46-47)
of league defeats:	8 (1956)	of away wins:	8 (1948)

THE MANAGERS

ARCHIE GEMMILL & JOHN McGOVERN . . . . appointed September 1994.

PREVIOUS CLUBS
As Manager . . . . None for both.
As Asst.Man/Coach . . . . JM - Plymouth.
As a player. . . . . AG - Derby, Nottingham Forest. JM - Nottingham Forest.

HONOURS
As a Manager . . . . None.
As a Player . . . . Division 1 championship and European Cup for both, while at Nottingham Forest.
International: AG- Full caps for Scotland.

ROTHERHAM UNITED

PLAYERS NAME Honours	Ht	Wt	Birthdate	Birthplace Transfers	Contract Date	Clubs	APPEARANCES League	L/Cup	FA Cup	Other	GOALS Lge	L/C	FAC	Oth
G O A L K E E P E R S														
Matthew Clarke	6.3	11.7	03.11.73	Sheffield	28.07.92	Rotherham Utd (T)	83+1		3	3				
Steve Farrelly				Manchester		Chester City								
via Knowsley United & Maccles field Town to				£20,000	08.95	Rotherham United								
D E F E N D E R S														
Paul Blades	6.0	11.0	05.01.65	Peterborough	29.12.82	Derby County (A)	157+9	9+3	12	8+2	1			
E: Y.3. Div.2'87.				£700,000	18.07.90	Norwich City	47	8	2	5				
				£325,000	14.08.92	Wolverhampton W.	103+4	4+1	9	6	2		1	
				£110,000	08.95	Rotherham United								
Ian Breckin	6.1	12.9	24.02.75	Rotherham	01.11.93	Rotherham Utd (T)	51	1	3	3	1			
Shaun Goodwin	5.7	8.10	14.06.69	Rotherham	01.07.87	Rotherham Utd (T)	218+15	13+7	16+1	15+2	30	1	3	1
Div.4'89														
Paul Hurst	5.7	10.4	25.09.74	Sheffield	12.08.93	Rotherham Utd (T)	11+6		2	3			1	
Mark Monington	6.1	13.0	21.10.70	Bilsthorpe	23.03.89	Burnley (J)	65+19	5	4+1	4+2	5		1	
Div.4'92.					28.11.94	Rotherham United	25			2				
Martin Pike	5.10	11.7	21.10.64	South Shields	26.10.82	West Brom. A. (A)								
				Free	18.08.83	Peterborough Utd	119+7	8	10	5	8			1
Loans from Sheffield United				£20,000	22.08.86	Sheffield United	127+2	10	12	5+1	5			
Loan Tranmere R., 10.11.89, 2 Lge, 1 LC, 1 FAC App.				£65,000	08.02.90	Fulham	187+3	10	5	12	14		1	2
Loan Bolton W., 14.12.89, 5 Lge 1gl, 1 Oth App.				Free	.08.94	Rotherham United	7							
Neil Richardson	5.10	13.5	03.03.68	Sunderland		Brandon United								
					18.08.89	Rotherham United	94+8	8+1	4+1	4+1	4			
Scott Smith	5.8	11.6	06.03.75	Christchurch, NZ	01.10.93	Rotherham Utd (T)	10+1		2	0+1				
Chris Wilder	5.11	10.10	23.09.67	Stockbridge	26.09.85	Southampton (A)								
				Free	20.08.86	Sheffield United	89+4	8+1	7	3	1			
Loan Walsall, 2.11.89, 4 Lge, 1 FAC, 2 Oth App.				Loan	12.10.90	Charlton Athletic	1							
Loan Chalton Athletic, 28.11.91, 2 Lge App.				Loan	27.02.92	Leyton Orient	16		1		1			
				£50,000	30.07.92	Rotherham United	111+4	7	15+2	5+1	10		1	
M I D F I E L D														
Gary Bowyer	6.0	12.13	22.06.71	Manchester	01.08.85	Westfields								
WFAC'90.				Free	02.12.89	Hereford United	12+2				2			
				Free	15.09.90	Nottingham Forest								
				Free	08.95	Rotherham United								
Martin James	5.10	11.7	18.05.71	Crosby	19.07.89	Preston N.E. (T)	92+6	6	4	8+1	11			
				£50,000	16.03.93	Stockport County	13+19	2	0+1	0+2				
				£50,000	.08.94	Rotherham	40	2	3	3				
John McGlashan	6.1	13.3	03.06.67	Dundee		Montrose	67+1	2	4		11			
				£50,000	22.08.90	Millwall	9+7		0+1	1				
				Loan	11.12.92	Fulham	5			1	1			
				Loan	15.01.93	Cambridge United	0+1							
				£75,000	27.01.93	Peterborough Utd	44+2	4+1	1	2	3	1		1
				Free	04.11.94	Rotherham United	27				3			
Glyn Roberts	5.11	12.2	19.10.74	Ipswich		Norwich City (T)								
				Free	05.08.93	Rotherham United	11+5				1			
Andrew Roscoe	5.11	12.0	04.06.73	Liverpool		Liverpool (T)								
				Free	17.07.91	Bolton Wanderers	2+1			1+1				
Loan 27.10.94 & 22.12.94 Rotherham Utd					02.02.95	Rotherham United	31				4			
Mark Todd	5.7	10.2	04.12.67	Belfast	07.08.85	Manchester Utd (T)								
NI: u23.1				Free	01.07.87	Sheffield United	62+8	5+1	10+1	5+1	5		1	
				Loan	14.03.91	Wolverhampton W.	6+1							
				£35,000	11.09.91	Rotherham United	60+4	5	3	2	7	2		1
F O R W A R D S														
Leonardo Goater	5.11	11.4	25.02.70	Bermunda		Manchester Utd (J)								
Bermunda				Free	25.10.89	Rotherham United	125+40	9+4	11+3	7+5	52	1	5	4
				Loan	12.11.93	Notts County	1							
Andy Hayward						Frickley Athletic								
				Free	.08.94	Rotherham United	33+4	1+1	2	2	6	1		
Bobby Davison	5.10	11.5	17.07.59	South Shields		Seaham CW								
Div.2'87'90.				£1,000	02.07.80	Huddersfield Town	1+1							
				£20,000	28.08.81	Halifax Town	63	4	2		29	4		
				£90,000	02.12.82	Derby County	203+3	18	11	4	83	6	7	2
				£350,000	27.11.87	Leeds United	79+12	4	2+4	7+2	31	1	1	3
Loan 19.09.91 Derby Co. 10 Lge App. 8 gls				£50,000	12.08.92	Leicester City	21+4	3		2+1	6	1		2
Loan 06.03.92 Sheffield Utd 6+5 Lge App. 4 gls				Free	04.11.93	Sheffield United	9+3	2		2	1	1		
				Free	14.10.94	Rotherham United	19+2		2	2	4		3	
Michael R Jeffrey	5.9	10.6	11.08.71	Liverpool	09.02.89	Bolton W. (T)	9+6	1+2	1	2+1				
				£20,000	05.03.92	Doncaster Rovers	48+1	4		2	19		1	
				£60,000 + PE	04.10.93	Newcastle United	2	1		0+2			1	
				£100,000	08.95	Rotherham United								
ADDITIONAL CONTRACT PLAYER														
Darren Garner						Dorchester Town								
				£30,000	08.95	Rotherham United								

MILLMOOR GROUND
Rotherham, South Yorkshire YO12 4HF
Tel: 01709 562 434

Capacity 11,533
Covered Standing 6,951
Seating 4,582

First game ....v Tranmere, 31.8.1925.
First floodlit game ....v Bristol Rovers, Lge Cup 2nd Rnd, 23.11.1960.

ATTENDANCES
Highest ....25,000 v Sheffield Utd, Div.2, 13.12.1952.
Lowest ....1,182 v Scarborough, AMC, 27.11.1990.

OTHER GROUNDS ....None.

MATCHDAY TICKET PRICES

Main Stand £9.50
Juv/OAP £6
Millmoor Lane Stand £7.50
Juv/OAP £5
Enclosure Stand £8
Juv/OAP £5
Tivoli Terrace £7
Juv/OAP £4.50
Visiting Seats £9.50
Juv/OAP £6

Ticket Office Telephone no........ 01709 562 434

CLUBCALL
0891 12 16 37
Calls cost 39p per minute cheap rate and 49p per minute at all other times.
Call costings correct at time of going to press.

HOW TO GET TO THE GROUND

From the North
Use motorway M1 until junction 34, leave motorway and follow signs to Rotherham (A6109). Cross railway bridge and then turn right into Millmoor Lane for Rotherham United FC.

From the East
Use A630 into Rotherham and then follow signs to Sheffield into Masborough Street, then turn left into Millmoor Lane for Rotherham United FC.

From the South and West
Use motorway M1 until junction 34, leave motorway and follow signs to Rotherham (A6178). At roundabout take 1st exit into Ring Road and at next roundabout 1st exit in Masborough Street (A6109). Take 1st turning left into Millmoor for Rotherham United FC.

Car Parking
There are parks within easy distance of the ground in Kimberworth Road and Main Street.

Nearest Railway Station
Rotherham Central (Town Centre)

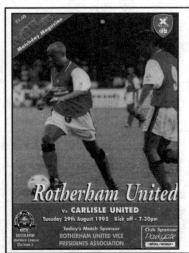

MATCHDAY PROGRAMME

Programme Editor............................. Dave Nicholls.

Number of pages .... 32.

Price .... £1.40.

Subscriptions .... £35 for full season (includes postage).

Local Newspapers................. Sheffield Morning Telegraph,
.... Sheffield Star (including Saturday special).

Local Radio Stations .... Radio Hallam (194 MWs),
.... Radio Sheffield (290 MW).

SHREWSBURY TOWN

(The Town or Blues)
ENDSLEIGH LEAGUE DIVISION 2
SPONSORED BY: GREENHOUS LEYLAND DAF & VAUXHALL

Back Row (L-R): Darren Rowbotham, Ian Stevens, Darren Simkin, Martin Jefferies, Ray Woods, Austin Berkley, Nathan King.
Middle Row: Malcolm Musgrove, Dean Spink, Shaun Wray, Mark Hughes, Tony Grenham, Tim Clarke, Paul Edwards, Tommy Lynch, Dave Walton, Steve Anthrobus, Kevin Summerfield. **Front Row:** Chris Withe, Ian Reed, Paul Evans, Mark Taylor, Fred Davies, Kevin Seabury, Richard Scott, Lee Martin, Mark Dempsey.

SHREWSBURY TOWN
FORMED IN 1886
TURNED PROFESSIONAL IN 1905
LTD COMPANY IN 1936

PRESIDENT: F C G Fry
VICE-PRESIDENT: Dr J Millard Bryson
CHAIRMAN: R Bailey
VICE-CHAIRMAN
R Wycherley
DIRECTORS
K R Woodhouse, M J Starkey, G W Nelson, W H Richards
SECRETARY
M J Starkey (01743 360 111)
COMMERCIAL MANAGER
M Thomas (01743 356 316)

MANAGER: Fred Davies

PHYSIOTHERAPIST & COACH
M Musgrove
STATISTICIAN FOR THE DIRECTORY
Richard & Nicola Stocken

After last season's Division 3 Championship the season of 'consolidation' was a little disappointing. After an opening day 4-0 victory at Rotherham, biggest win of the season, Town spent the remainder of the season flirting with relegation, securing Division 2 status with a hard fought 2-1 home win over Huddersfield with just two games to go, both subsequently lost.

Despite the lowly position though, only Birmingham and Crewe of the top teams completed doubles over the team, whilst wins were recorded over Bristol Rovers and Brentford in addition to Huddersfield at Gay Meadow. There weren't enough of them to make an impact, only 13, of which four were away at Rotherham, Wrexham, Chester and Cardiff. The mediocrity of the season produced no more than two successive victories in the league and four successive league defeats. There was never really a significant run good or bad.

An important factor for a club like Shrewsbury is to avoid injuries, but the club were savaged by them to a number of key players, making stability in the side impossible. Dave Hockaday, Tommy Lynch, Wayne Clarke, who still managed 11 league goals in 26 games, Ray Woods, Mark Hughes and new signing Darren Simkin on his debut all suffered lay offs. Add to that the mid-season departure of fans favourite Michael Brown to Preston and Gary Patterson to Wycombe the ranks were often severely depleted. Brown's departure was especially damaging, as he took advantage of freedom of contract, which has often robbed Shrewsbury of their better players. A positive result though was the emergence of two home grown players, Paul Evans who acquired the knack of scoring vital goals and Kevin Seabury.

Equal leading scorer Dean Spink worked tirelessly, supported by either Wayne Clarke or Ian Stevens with eight goals. Mark Taylor had another excellent season in midfield and the central defence was in the care again of Dave Walton and Mark Williams, with no small contribution from Mark Hughes. Dave Hockaday, Chris Withe, Tommy Lynch and Kevin Seabury shared the full-back roles whilst two goalkeepers were used, Paul Edwards and Tim Clarke.

Progress in the Coca-Cola Cup and FA Cup ended in round one courtesy of Birmingham and Burnley respectively, but the twin towers beckoned in the Auto Windscreen Shield. After defeating Wycombe and Exeter at Gay Meadow interest in the Regional Semi-Final ended at Leyton Orient.

The retained list saw Smith, Hockaday and Clarke released and manager Davies's season long search to replace some width into the side should guarantee new faces by August. On limited resources Davies will always need to utilise his choices to the limit. It remains to be seen if the consolidation of 1994/95 pays dividends in 1995/96 season. **RICHARD STOCKEN.**

SHREWSBURY TOWN

Division Two: 18th   **FA Cup:** 1st Round   **Coca-Cola Cup:** 1st Round   **Auto Windscreen Trophy:** R. Semi-Final

M	DATE	COMP.	VEN	OPPONENTS	RESULT	H/T	LP	GOAL SCORERS/GOAL TIMES	ATT.
1	A 13	EL	A	Rotherham United	W 4-0	3-0		Taylor 15, Spink 32, 68, Clarke 39	(3,762)
2	16	CC 1/1	H	**Birmingham City**	**W 2-1**	**1-0**		**Clarke 16, Spink 79**	**5,049**
3	20	EL	H	Wrexham	D 2-2	1-2	6	Clarke 13, Brown 66	5,748
4	23	CC 1/2	A	**Birmingham City**	**L 0-2**	**0-2**			**(9,847)**
5	27	EL	A	Blackpool	L 1-2	1-0	12	Clarke 17 (pen)	(4,428)
6	S 3	EL	H	Peterborough United	D 2-2	0-2	16	Spink 47, Clarke 89	3,879
7	6	EL	H	Swansea City	D 3-3	1-0	15	Clarke 37, Currie 52, Stevens 80	3,534
8	10	EL	A	York City	L 0-3	0-1	18		(3,196)
9	13	EL	A	Stockport County	L 1-2	0-0	19	Patterson 85	(3,473)
10	17	EL	H	Leyton Orient	W 3-0	3-0	17	Brown 30, Clarke 31, Currie 33	3,560
11	24	EL	H	Bristol Rovers	W 1-0	1-0	14	Stevens 42	4,596
12	O 1	EL	A	Brentford	L 0-1	0-1	15		(4,556)
13	8	EL	H	AFC Bournemouth	W 3-0	1-0	14	Brown 16, Clarke 49, 68	3,684
14	15	EL	A	Crewe Alexandra	L 0-1	0-1	15		(4,296)
15	22	EL	H	Hull City	L 2-3	0-2	16	Clarke 74, Stevens 80	3,685
16	29	EL	A	Oxford United	D 0-0	0-0	16		(6,094)
17	N 1	EL	A	Wycombe Wanderers	L 0-1	0-1	17		(4,620)
18	5	EL	H	Birmingham City	L 0-2	0-1	18		5,942
19	12	FAC 1	A	**Burnley**	**L 1-2**	**1-1**		**Spink 36**	**(9,269)**
20	19	EL	A	Cambridge United	L 1-3	1-1	19	Stevens 38	(2,748)
21	26	EL	H	Bradford City	L 1-2	0-1	19	Stevens 63	3,776
22	29	AWT 2	H	**Wycombe Wanderers**	**W 2-0**	**1-0**		**Williams 7, Stevens 89**	**1,785**
23	D 10	EL	A	Wrexham	W 1-0	0-0	18	Evans 84	(5,859)
24	16	EL	A	Rotherham United	W 1-0	1-0	16	Walton 22	3,243
25	26	EL	H	Cardiff City	L 0-1	0-0	18		4,933
26	27	EL	A	Brighton & H.A.	L 1-2	1-0	18	Clarke 2	(7,290)
27	J 2	EL	A	Huddersfield Town	L 1-2	1-1	19	Withe 45	(12,748)
28	7	EL	A	Hull City	D 2-2	2-0	19	Clarke 20, Jeffers 29	(4,369)
29	10	AWT QF	H	**Exeter City**	**W 3-1**	**1-0**		**Spink 4, Stevens 72, 86**	**1,960**
30	14	EL	H	Chester City	W 1-0	0-0	19	Evans 70	3,879
31	28	EL	H	Oxford United	D 1-1	1-1	19	Stevens 3	3,768
32	31	AWT SF	A	**Leyton Orient**	**L 1-2**	**0-1**		**Stevens 57**	**(2,913)**
33	F 4	EL	A	Bradford City	D 1-1	0-1	19	Spink 78	(4,817)
34	7	EL	H	Plymouth Argyle	W 3-2	0-1	17	Spink 49, 81, Withe 59	3,029
35	11	EL	H	Wycombe Wand.	D 2-2	1-0	17	Spink 20, Taylor 58	3,945
36	18	EL	H	Chester City	W 3-1	1-0	15	Evans 45 (pen), Spink 64, Walton 66	(2,720)
37	21	EL	H	Cambridge United	D 1-1	0-1	15	Evans 63	3,200
38	25	EL	H	Brentford	W 2-1	1-1	15	Spink 34, Lynch 50	4,570
39	M 4	EL	A	Bristol Rovers	L 0-4	0-1	15		(4,338)
40	7	EL	A	Peterborough United	D 1-1	0-0	17	Spink 53	(3,554)
41	11	EL	H	Blackpool	D 0-0	0-0	18		4,261
42	17	EL	A	Swansea City	D 0-0	0-0	17		(4,130)
43	21	EL	H	York City	W 1-0	1-0	15	Evans 31	2,849
44	25	EL	A	Leyton Orient	L 1-2	1-1	17	Williams 2	(2,724)
45	A 1	EL	H	Stockport City	D 1-1	0-1	18	Stevens 75	3,655
46	8	EL	A	Plymouth Argyle	L 0-1	0-1	18		(5,089)
47	11	EL	A	Birmingham City	L 0-2	0-1	18		(18,366)
48	15	EL	H	Brighton & H.A.	D 1-1	1-1	18	Scott 13	3,597
49	17	EL	A	Cardiff City	W 2-1	1-0	18	Smith 44, Spink 64	(4,677)
50	22	EL	H	Huddersfield Town	W 2-1	1-0	18	Walton 9, Stevens 16	4,758
51	29	EL	H	Crewe Alexandra	L 1-2	1-2	18	Smith 3	4,381
52	M 2	EL	A	AFC Bournemouth	L 0-3	0-3	18		(10,747)
53									
54									
55									
56									
57									
58									
59									
60									

Best Home League Attendance: 5,942 v Birmingham City   **Smallest:** 2,849 v York City   **Av Home Att:** 4,021

Goal Scorers: **Compared with 1993-94:** -362

League (54): Spink 11, Clarke 11 (1 pen), Stevens 8, Evans 5 (1 pen), Brown 3, Walton 3, Taylor 2, Currie 2, Smith 2, Withe 2, Patterson, Jeffers, Lynch, Williams, Scott
C/Cola Cup (2): Clarke, Spink
FA Cup (1): Spink
AW Trophy (6): Stevens 4, Williams, Spink

Edwards P.	Hockaday D.	Lynch T.	Taylor M.	Williams M.	Patterson G.	Brown M.	Clarke W.	Spink D.	Walton D.	Woods R.	Summerfield K.	Hughes M.	Clarke T.	Wthe C.	Stevens I.	Currie D.	Seabury K.	Evans P.	Smith M.	Slawson S.	Harford P.	Simkin D.	Jeffers J.	Scott R.	Reed I.	Referee	
1	2	3	4	5	6	7*	8	9	10	11	12		S	S												T. Lunt	1
1	2	3	4	5	6	7•	8	9	10	11*			S		12	14										A. Butler	2
1	2	3	4	5	6	7	8	9	10			S	S	11	S											T. West	3
1	2	3	4	5	6	7	8*	9	10		12	S	S	11												A. Flood	4
1	2	3	4	5	6	7*	8	9	10		12	14	S	11•												I. Cruikshanks	5
1	2	3	4	S	6		8	9	10	11	7*	5	S			12										P. Harrison	6
1	2*	3	4	12	6		8	9	10	11		5	S		14	7•										E. Wolstenholme	7
S		3	4	5	6		8*	9		11•		10	1	12		7	2	14								D. Allison	8
S		3	4	5	8	7•		9	10		6*	1			12	11	2	14								G. Cain	9
1		3	4•		6	7	8	9*	10			S	2	12	11		14									J. Lloyd	10
1	2	3	4	5	6	7*	8		10			S	S	9		11		12								S. Mathieson	11
1	2*	3	4	5	6	7	8		10			S	12	9	11•			14								G. Barber	12
1	2	3	4	5	6	7*	8		10			S		9	11		S	12								P. Rejer	13
1		3	4	5	6		8		10			S		9	11	2	7*	12								M. Riley	14
1		3	4	5	6		8	12	10	7	S		S	9	11•	2										P. Wright	15
1			4	5	6		8*		10	7	11	S	S	3	9	12•	2									J. Rushton	16
1		9	4	5	6				10	7	8	S	S	3		12	2			11*						A. Butler	17
1		3*	4	5	6	7		12		14	10	8	S		11•	2		9								E. Lomas	18
1	2		4	5	6		9			7	10	8	S	3	11		S	S								J. Worrall	19
1	2	3	4	5	12		9			7	8	6*		S	10		S			11						A. D' Urso	20
1		3	4	5	8		9			7*		6	S		10		2	S	12	11						E. Wolstenholme	21
1	S	3	4	5	8		9*			6	S				10		2	11	7	12						R. Poulain	22
1	2	3*	4	5			14	9•	10		6	S			7		12	8		11						R. Furnandiz	23
1.	2		4				12	9	10		6	13.	3	7*		5	8		11t	14						P. Vanes	24
1	2		4				8	9		7*		6	S	3	12	5	11		S	10						P. Richards	25
1		6	4*	5			8	9		14	10		S	3	7		11		12	2•						P. Foakes	26
1	2*	S	4	5			8	9	10		6		S	3	7		11		12							T. Heilbron	27
1	2	3*	4	5			8	9*	10	7	6		S	3	12							11				D. Allison	28
1	2	14	4•	5			8	9*	10	7	6		S	3	12							11				R. Furnandiz	29
1	2		4	5			8	9*	10	7	6•		S	3	12							11				K. Leach	30
1	2	6		5			8*	12		7			S	3	9		S	4			10	11				D. Orr	31
1	2	6	4	5			9			7*			S	3	10		12	8		S		11				G. Pooley	32
1		6	4	S			9	10					S	3	7	11	12	8	S*			2				M Brandwood	33
1		6	4	S			9	10					S	3	7	11	12	8				2				R. Poulain	34
1		6	4	S			S	9	10				S	3	7	11	5	8				2				K. Lynch	35
1		6	4				14	9	10			12	S	S	3	7•	11	5	8			2*				M. Riley	36
1		6	4				S	9	10			S	S	3	7	11	5	8				2				U. Rennie	37
1		6	4				S	9	10			11	S	3	7	S	5	8				2				J. Kirkby	38
1		6*	4	5			9	10		14	11•	S	3	7			5	8				2				A. Flood	39
S		6	4	5	12		8	9		11	S	1	3	12		2	10	7*								G. Barber	40
S		6	4	5			8*	9		11	7	1	3	12		2	10	S								S. Mathieson	41
S		6	4*	5			8	9	3	11	7	1	S			2	10	12								A. Butler	42
S		3	4	5			8	10		S	7	1	9			2*	6	11				12				K. Breen	43
S		3	4	5			8	9	10		7	1	14				6	11•				2*		12		M. Pierce	44
S		3*	4	5			8	9	10			1	12	14		2	6	11•					7			G. Cain	45
S		3*	4	5			8•	9	10			1	12	14		2	6	11					7			S. Dunn	46
S			4	5				9	10	7•	14	6*	1	3	11		2	8	12							P. Harrison	47
S			4	5*				9	10	7		1	3	8•		2	6	12					11	14		E. Parker	48
S			4*					9	10		5	1	3	8•		2	6	11				14	7	12		K. Cooper	49
S			4	5				9	10	12		1	3	7*		2	6	11				S	8			D. Allison	50
S			4•	5			12	9	10			1	3	8*		2	6	7				11	14			R. Furnandiz	51
S			14	9			12		10•	5	1	3			2	4	7*			6			8	11		B. Harris	52
31	16	34	44	33	17	9	26	36	36	15	14	18	15	27	26	15	27	27	10	6	3	10	3	7	1	League Appearances	
				1			5	3		4	4	2	1	4	12	2	3	5	7		3	2		1	3	League Sub Appearances	
2	2	2	2	2	2	2	2	2	2	1	0+1		1	1+1	0+1		1	1								C/ColaCup Appearances	
1	1	1	1	1	1			1				1	1	1	1											FA Cup Appearances	
3	2	2+1	3	3	1		1	3	1	2	1	1		2	2+1		1+1	2	1		0+1		2			AW Trophy Appearances	

Players on Loan: Jeffers (Port Vale), Harford (Blackburn Rovers), Currie (W.H.U.), Slawson (Notts County)

† = Sent Off

SHREWSBURY TOWN   RECORDS AND STATISTICS

CLUB RECORDS

RECORD LEAGUE VICTORY
7-0 v Swindon Town, Div 3S, 6.5.1955
Most Goals Scored in a League Match
7-2 v Luton Town (a), Div 3, 10.3.1965 7-1 v Blackburn Rovers (h),
Div 3, 2.10.1971 7-4 v Doncaster Rovers, Div 4,1.2.1975
Most Goals Scored in a Cup Tie
7-1 v Banbury Spencer (h), FA Cup 1st Round,4.11.1961
RECORD LEAGUE DEFEAT
1-8 v Norwich City (h), Div 3S, 13.9.1952 1-8 v Coventry City (a),
Div 3, 22.10.1963 0-7 v Bristol Rovers (a), Div 3, 21.3.1964

MOST LEAGUE GOALS
101, Division 4, 1958-59

MOST LEAGUE POINTS
(3pts for win) 79, Div 3, 1993-94
(2pts for win) 62,Division 4, 1974-75

RECORD TRANSFER FEE RECEIVED
£450,000 from Manchester City for Carl Griffiths,29.10.93
RECORD TRANSFER FEE PAID
£100,000 to Aldershot for John Dungworth in November1979.
£100,000 to Southampton for Mark Blake, August 1990

BEST PERFORMANCES
League: 8th Division 2, 1983-84, 1984-85
FA Cup: 6th Round1978-79, 1981-82
League Cup: Semi-Final 1960-61
Welsh Cup: Winners 1891,1938, 1977, 1979, 1984, 1985
HONOURS
Champions Div 3 1978-79, 1993-94
Welsh Cup Winners (6 times)

LEAGUE CAREER
Elected to Div 3N 1950 Reverted to Div 3S 1951 Joined Div4
1958
Promoted to Div 3 1958-59 Relegated to Div 4 1973-74
Promoted to Div 31974-75 Promoted to Div 2 1978-79
Relegated to Div 3 1988-89 Relegated to Div 4 (now Div 3) 1991-
92 Promoted to Div 2 1993-94

INDIVIDUAL CLUB RECORDS

MOST APPEARANCES FOR CLUB
Colin Griffin 1975-89: League 402+4 + FA Cup 30 +League Cup 25
+ Others 9 Total 466+4 subs

MOST CAPPED PLAYER
Jimmy McLoughlin 5, Northern Ireland & Bernard McNally
5,Northern Ireland For England: None

RECORD GOALSCORER IN A MATCH
Alf Wood 5 v Blackburn Rovers (h), 7-1, Div 3,2.10.1971

RECORD LEAGUE GOALSCORER IN A SEASON
Arthur Rowley 38, Div 3, 1958-59 In All Competitions: Alf Wood
40 (League 35, FA Cup 2, League Cup 3) 1971-72

RECORD LEAGUE GOALSCORER IN A CAREER
Arthur Rowley 152, 1958-65 In All Competitions: Arthur Rowley
167 (League 152, FA Cup 11, League Cup 4) 1958-65

OLDEST PLAYER IN A LEAGUE MATCH
Asa Hartford, 40 years 69 days v Brentford1.1.1991

YOUNGEST PLAYER IN A LEAGUE MATCH
Gerry Nardiello, 17 years 9 days, 14.5.1983

PREVIOUS MANAGERS

(Since 1950): 1950-52 Sammy Crooks 1952-54 Walter Rowley
1954-56 Harry Potts 1956-57 John Spuhler 1957-68 Arthur
Rowley 1968-72Harry Gregg 1972-74 Maurice Evans 1974-78
Alan Durban 1978 Ritchie Barker 1978-84 Graham Turner 1984-
87 Chic Bates 1987 Ken Brown 1987-90 Ian McNeil 1990-91
Asa Hartford 1991-93 John Bond Fred Davies 1993-

ADDITIONAL INFORMATION
Previous League: Birmingham League Midland League
Club colours: Blue shirts, blue shorts, blue socks.
Change colours: All red with white side stripes and white trim, red
socks with white trim.
Reserves League: Pontins League.
'A' Team: Midland Intermediate.

LONGEST LEAGUE RUNS

of undefeated matches:	16 (30.10.1993 - 26.2.1994)	of league matches w/out a win:	17 (1992)
of undefeated home matches:	31 (1978-79)	of undefeated away matches:	14 (30.10.1993 - 30.4.1994)
without home win:	9 (1992)	without an away win:	20 (1981-82)
of league wins:	7 (1955)	of home wins:	8 (1955, 1975)
of league defeats:	7 (1951-52, 1987)	of away wins:	5 (6.11.1993 - 1.1.1994)

THE MANAGER

FRED DAVIES . . . . appointed May 1993.

PREVIOUS CLUBS
As Manager. . . . . Merthyr Tydfil.
As Asst.Man/Coach . . . . Norwich City, Bournemouth, Blackpool, Swansea, Birmingham, Shrewsbury.
As a player . . . . Wolverhampton, Cardiff, Bournemouth.

HONOURS
As a Manager. . . . . Division 3 Championship 1993-94.
As a Player . . . . None.

SHREWSBURY TOWN

PLAYERS NAME / Honours	Ht	Wt	Birthdate	Birthplace / Transfers	Contract Date	Clubs	League	L/Cup	FA Cup	Other	Lge	L/C	FAC	Oth
G O A L K E E P E R S														
Tim Clarke	6.3	13.7	19.09.68	Stourbridge		Halesowen Town			1					
				£25,000	22.10.90	Coventry City								
				£15,000	22.07.91	Huddersfield Town	70	7	6	8				
Loan Rochdale, 12.02.93, 2 Lge App.					21.10.93	Shrewsbury Town	15+1							
Paul Edwards	5.11	11.5	22.02.65	Liverpool		Leek Town								
Div.3'94.				Free	24.08.88	Crewe Alexandra	29	4	3	4				
				Free	06.08.92	Shrewsbury Town	115	10	7	7				
D E F E N D E R S														
Mark Hughes	6.0	12.8	05.02.62	Port Talbot	05.02.80	Bristol Rovers (A)	73+1	1	9+1	3	3			1
W: Y. LCD'90.				Loan	24.12.82	Torquay United	9		3		1		1	
Free via Swansea, 30.07.84, 12 Lge App.					07.02.85	Bristol City	21+1	1		3				
				£3,000	19.09.85	Tranmere Rovers	258+8	27	11+3	36+1	9	2		1
				Free	04.07.94	Shrewsbury Town	18+2		1	1				
Tom Lynch	6.0	12.6	10.10.64	Limerick		Limerick								
Div.3'94.				£20,000	11.08..88	Sunderland	4		1					
				£20,000	16.01.90	Shrewsbury Town	198+11	14	12	14+1	11			1
Richard Scott	5.9	10.10	29.09.74	Dudley	17.05.93	Birmingham City (T)	11+1	3+1		3				
				22.03.95	Shrewsbury Town	7+1				1			
Kevin Seabury	5.9	11.06	24.11.73	Shrewsbury	06.07.92	Shrewsbury Town	27+4			1+1				
Darren Simkin	6.0	12.0	24.03.70	Walsall		Blakenhall								
				£10,000	03.12.91	Wolverhampton W.	14+1	1						
				£36,000	20.12.94	Shrewsbury Town	10+2							
Dean Spink	6.1	13.6	22.01.67	Birmingham		Halesowen Town			1					
Div.3'94.				£30,000	01.07.89	Aston Villa								
				Loan	20.11.89	Scarborough	3			1	2			
Loan Bury, 01.02.90, 6 Lge, 1 gl.				£75,000	15.03.90	Shrewsbury Town	173+25	16+2	13+1	10+1	43	1	3	3
David Walton	6.2	13.4	10.04.73	Bedlington		Ashington								
Div.3'94.				Free	15.05.91	Sheffield United								
					05.11.93	Shrewsbury Town	63	2	3	1	8		1	
Christopher Withe	5.10	11.3	25.09.62	Liverpool	10.10.80	Newcaslte Utd (A)	2							
Div.3'85'94.				Free	01.06.83	Bradford City	141+2	14	7	6	2			
				£50,000	02.10.87	Notts County	80	4	5	12	3			1
				£40,000	31.07.89	Bury	22+9	2+2		0+3	1			
Loan Chester City, 18.10.90, 2 Lge App.					24.01.91	Mansfield Town	75+1	4	2	2	5			
				Free	15.05.93	Shrewsbury Town	50+7	5+2	2	2+1	2			
M I D F I E L D														
Mark A Dempsey	5.7	10.9	0.12.72	Dublin	09.08.90	Gillingham (T)	27+21	0+1	5	6	2			
Ei: u21.6				Free	04.07.94	Leyton Orient	43	2	1+1	5	1			1
				Free	08.95	Shrewsbury T. (T)								
Paul S Evans	5.6	10.8	01.09.74	Oswestry	02.07.93	Shrewsbury T. (T)	42+9	5+1	1+1	2	5	1		
Div.3'94.														
Nathan King	6.0	12.06	01.08.75	West Brom	08.94	Shrewsbury T. (T)								
Ian Reed	5.8	10.09	04.09.75	Lichfield	04.07.94	Shrewsbury Town	1+3							
Kevin Summerfield	6.0	10.7	07.01.59	Walsall	01.01.77	West Brom A. (A)	5+4	2			4			
FAYC'76. EY'77. Div.3'94.				Free	31.05.82	Birmingham City	2+3	1	1+1		1		1	
				Free	14.12.82	Walsall	42+12	5+2			17	2		
Free via Cardiff C., 06.07.84, 10 Lge 1 gl, LC 2 App. Free					21.12.84	Plymouth Argyle	118+21	6+1	13	4	26	3	4 1	
Loan Exeter City, 22.03.90, 4 Lge App.				Free	10.10.90	Shrewsbury Town	140+22	13+1	11+1	8	21	7	1	
Raymond Woods	5.11	11.6	07.06.65	Birkenhead	08.06.83	Tranmere Rovers (A	9+5	1		0+1	2			
via Bangor City & Northwich Victoria to				Free		Runcorn								
via Caernarfon (5 FAC) & Colne Dynamoes to				Free	01.03.89	Wigan Athletic	25+3	2	4	2	3		1	
				£200,000	30.01.91	Coventry City	21	1	0+1		1			
				Loan	08.01.93	Wigan Athletic	12+1			4				3
				Free	23.03.94	Shrewsbury Town	22+6	1	1	2	1			
F O R W A R D S														
Steve Anthrobus	6.2	12.13	10.11.68	Lewisham	04.08.86	Millwall (J)	19+2	3		1	4			
Loan Southend Utd, 9.2.90, 0 App.				£150,000	16.02.90	Wimbledon	27+1	1	2					
				Loan	21.01.94	Peterborough Utd								
				Loan	26.08.94	Chester City	7							
				£25,000	08.95	Shrewsbury Town								
Darren Rowbotham	5.10	11.5	22.10.66	Cardiff	07.11.84	Plymouth A. (J)	22+24	1	0+3	1+1	2		1	
W: Y. Div.4'90.					31.10.87	Exeter City	110+8	11	8	5	46	6	5	1
				£25,000	13.09.91	Torquay United	14		3	2	3		1	
				£20,000	02.01.92	Birmingham City	31+5	0+1		3+1	6			
Loan 18.12.92 Mansfield Town 4 Lge App.				Loan	25.03.93	Hereford United	8				2			
				Free	06.07.93	Crewe Alexandra	59+2	3	4	6+2	21	1	3	1
				Free	08.95	Shrewsbury Town								
Ian Stevens	5.9	12.0	21.10.66	Malta	22.11.84	Preston N.E. (T)	9+2		1		2			
SVT'89				Free	27.10.86	Stockport County	1+1		0+1	0+1				
via Lancaster City				Free	25.03.87	Bolton Wanderers	26+21	1+2	4	3+1	7		2	
				Free	03.07.91	Bury	100+10	3+1	2+2	7+1	38			3
				£20,000	.08.94	Shrewsbury Town	26+12	0+1	1	2+1	8			4
R Mark Taylor	5.8	11.8	22.02.66	Birmingham	24.07.84	Walsall (T)	100+13	7+1	3+4	10	4			
Div.3'94.				£50,000	22.06.89	Sheffield Wed.	8+1	2						
				£70,000	13.09.91	Shrewsbury Town	175	11	9	9	13			1

GAY MEADOW
Shrewsbury SY2 6AB
Tel: 01743 360 111

Capacity...8,000
Covered Standing...2,000
Seating...3,500

First game...v Wolves Res. (Birmingham Lge), 10.9.1910.
First floodlit game ....v Q.P.R., Div.3, 21.11.1959.

ATTENDANCES
Highest ....18,917 v Walsall, Div.3, 26.4.1961.
Lowest ....520 v Torquay Utd, 16.1.1991.

OTHER GROUNDS ....Old Racecourse. Copthorne.

MATCHDAY TICKET PRICES

Wakeman Stand . . . . (members only) £9
Juv/OAP £5

Centre Stand £10
Juv/OAP £10

Station Stand (away) £10
Family Stand (1+1) £8
Extra child £2, extra adult £10
Terraces. £7
Juv/OAP (members). £4

Ticket Office Telephone no. 01743 360 111

TOWN TALK
0891 888 611
Calls cost 39p per minute cheap rate and 49p per
minute at all other times.
Call costings correct at time of going to press.

HOW TO GET TO THE GROUND

From the North
Use A49 or A53 and at roundabout take 2nd exit (A5112) into Telford Way. In 0.8 miles at roundabout take 2nd exit. Then at 'T' junction turn right into Abbey Foregate (A458) for Shrewsbury Town FC.

From the East
Use A5 then A458 into Shrewsbury and into Abbey Foregate for Shrewsbury Town FC.

From the South
Use A49 and follow signs Shrewsbury Town centre then at end of Coleham Head turn right in to Abbey Foregate for Shrewsbury Town FC.

From the West
Use A458 then A5 around Shrewsbury Ring Road, Roman Road, then turn left A49 into Hereford Road, and at end of Coleman Head turn right into Abbey Foregate for Shrewsbury Town.

Car Parking
Park adjacent to ground and a public car park five minutes away.

Nearest Railway Station
Shrewsbury (01743 64041)

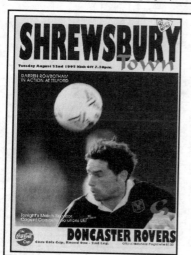

MATCHDAY PROGRAMME

Programme Editor . . . . Pemandos A & M.

Number of pages . . . . 32.

Price . . . . £1.20.

Subscriptions . . . . Aply to club for details.

Local Newspapers . . . . Shropshire Star, Shrewsbury Chronicle.

Local Radio Stations . . . . Radio Shropshire, Beacon Radio.

STOCKPORT COUNTY
(The Hatters)
ENDSLEIGH LEAGUE DIVISION 2
SPONSORED BY: FREDERIC ROBINSON LIMITED

Back Row (L-R): Alun Armstrong, Tony Dinning, Richard Landon, Ian Helliwell, Jim Gannon, Matthew Bound, Jeff Eckhardt. **Middle Row:** Rodger Wylde (Physio), Tom Bennett, Michael Oliver, Neil Edwards, John Sainty (Asst. Manager), Matt Dickins, Chris Beaumont, Paul Ware, Dave Philpotts (Yth Manager). **Front Row:** Sean Connelly, Phil Johnson, Gavin Allen, Martyn Chalk, Dave Jones (Manager), Michael Flynn (Capt), Lee Marshall, Lee Todd, Marc Lloyd Williams.

This was without doubt the most disrupted season of Danny Bergara's managerial reign, and it finally resulted in his departure, although this was not caused by the results.

Most of the new players settled in well, and with the players in dispute all re-signing, County looked like they were going to carry on where they left off in previous seasons. An early boost was the fact that despite much speculation Kevin Francis started the season with the club. By the end of OCtober the club were in second place, having scored four goals in four of their matches. One of these saw County go through to the second round of the League Cup, where they lost to Sheffield United 1-6 on aggregate.

Unfortunately, the start of November began the worst spell for Stockport County since 1988. The first match saw County lose 0-1 at Chester with Kevin Francis suffering an injury. At this stage Francis had scored 11 goals. He was to play only three more games spread over the next two months before leaving the club in a record move to Birmingham City.

From Francis' injury at Chester, County failed to score a League goal in November, and continued patchy form over the next three months saw the club drop into the bottom half of the table for the first time since they were promoted. This period also saw County lose in the FA Cup and Auto Windscreen Shield in the early rounds.

Once Ian Helliwell had been signed as the new centre-forward, the promising Alun Armstrong began to score regularly for the first time in three months. He eventually became the top scorer for the season.

The results improved a little but County still hovered either side of half way, mainly due to poor away form. On 28 March at Plymouth they finally won an away game. The 100 or so County fans who made that trip for a Tuesday night match did not realise that Bergara would have left by the following match. A much publicised incident at a club function caused the board to terminate the manager's contract.

Promoting internally Dave Jones was appointed to his first managerial role. As often occurs the results improved immediately, with only two defeats in the remaining seven matches.

With the young players signed last summer having experienced a years football the fans and officials are hoping for a more enjoyable season. Especially if the manager pursues the tactics that he has described in his various meetings with the public. Perhaps they will even be challenging for promotion again after their year off.

IAN WATTS.

481

STOCKPORT COUNTY

Division Two: 11th   **FA Cup:** 1st Round   **Coca-Cola Cup:** 2nd Round

M	DATE	COMP.	VEN	OPPONENTS	RESULT	H/T	LP	GOAL SCORERS/GOAL TIMES	ATT.
1	A 13	EL	H	Cardiff City	W 4-1	1-1	3	Ward 14, Francis 47, 51, Armstrong 57	5,139
2	17	CC 1/1	A	**Preston North End**	D 1-1	1-0		Chalk 4	**(2,385)**
3	20	EL	A	Cambridge United	W 4-3	2-1		Eckhardt 21, Armstrong 43, Gannon 49, Francis 73	(3,163)
4	24	CC 1/2	H	**Preston North End**	**W 4-1**	0-0		**Emerson 48, Armstrong 53, Ward 69, Beaumont 70**	4,547
5	27	EL	H	Brentford	L 0-1	0-1	6		4,399
6	30	EL	A	Crewe Alexandra	L 1-2	0-0	10	Armstrong 79	(5,050)
7	S 3	EL	A	Bristol Rovers	D 2-2	1-2	11	Sterling 42 (og), Eckhardt 88	(4,263)
8	10	EL	H	AFC Bournemouth	W 1-0	0-0	9	Francis 85	4,054
9	13	EL	H	Shrewsbury Town	W 2-1	0-0	6	Flynn 60, Armstrong 82	3,473
10	17	EL	A	Huddersfield Town	L 1-2	1-1	9	Chalk 23	(9,526)
11	20	CC 2/1	H	**Sheffield United**	**L 1-5**	0-1		**Francis 58**	**5,109**
12	24	EL	H	Wycombe Wanderers	W 4-1	3-0	4	Francis 9, 82, Armstrong 16, Chalk 45	4,607
13	27	CC 2/2	A	**Sheffield United**	**L 0-1**	0-1			**(5,065)**
14	O 1	EL	A	York City	W 4-2	2-2	3	Tutill 2 (og), Slinn 45, Francis 70, Ward 79	(3,790)
15	8	EL	H	Rotherham United	W 1-0	0-0	3	Francis 79	4,991
16	15	EL	A	Peterborough United	W 1-0	0-0	3	Armstrong 60	(5,369)
17	22	EL	H	Plymouth Argyle	L 2-4	1-2	4	Chalk 1, Francis 68	5,652
18	29	EL	A	Leyton Orient	W 1-0	0-0	2	Francis 57	(3,267)
19	N 2	EL	A	Chester City	L 0-1	0-0	5		(2,400)
20	5	EL	H	Oxford United	L 0-2	0-1	7		5,132
21	12	FAC 1	A	**Wrexham**	**L 0-1**	0-0			**4,740**
22	19	EL	A	Swansea City	L 0-2	0-0	7		(3,019)
23	26	EL	H	Birmingham City	L 0-1	0-0	10		5,577
24	29	AWT 1	H	**Scarborough**	**W 3-1**	0-0		**Dinning 54, Bound 60, Ward 83**	**2,310**
25	D 10	EL	H	Cambridge United	W 2-1	0-0	7	Gannon 53, 90	3,903
26	17	EL	A	Cardiff City	D 1-1	0-0	11	Gannon 82	(3,448)
27	26	EL	H	Wrexham	D 1-1	1-0	10	Todd 37	5,636
28	27	EL	A	Blackpool	W 2-1	1-0	9	Wallace 39, Gannon 89	(5,745)
29	31	EL	A	Bradford City	L 1-2	0-1	10	Francis 88	4,613
30	J 2	EL	A	Brighton & H.A.	L 0-2	0-0	11		(8,842)
31	10	AWT 2	A	**Rochdale**	**L 1-2**	1-1		**Wallace 43**	**(2,154)**
32	14	EL	H	Hull City	W 4-0	1-0	10	Beaumont 12, Helliwell 48, 80, Armstrong 90	4,516
33	28	EL	H	Leyton Orient	W 2-1	1-0	10	Ware 44, Armstrong 68	4,250
34	F 4	EL	A	Birmingham City	L 0-1	0-0	10		(17,160)
35	11	EL	H	Chester City	D 2-2	0-2	10	Wallace 47, Beaumont 86	4,405
36	18	EL	A	Hull City	D 0-0	0-0	11		(4,576)
37	21	EL	H	Swansea City	L 0-1	0-1	13		3,088
38	25	EL	H	York City	L 2-3	1-2	13	Armstrong 5, Gannon 87	3,570
39	28	EL	A	Oxford United	L 0-4	0-1	14		(4,594)
40	M 4	EL	A	Wycombe Wanderers	D 1-1	1-0	14	Gannon 9	(5,275)
41	7	EL	H	Bristol Rovers	W 2-1	1-1	13	Flynn 12, Armstrong 47	3,580
42	11	EL	A	Brentford	L 0-1	0-1	13		(6,513)
43	18	EL	H	Crewe Alexandra	W 3-1	1-0	13	Chalk 10, 55, Armstrong 73	4,946
44	21	EL	A	AFC Bournemouth	L 0-2	0-1	14		(2,892)
45	25	EL	H	Huddersfield Town	L 1-2	0-1	14	Armstrong 56	5,383
46	28	EL	A	Plymouth Argyle	W 2-0	1-0	14	Graham 2, Dinning 57	(4,618)
47	A 1	EL	A	Shrewsbury Town	D 1-1	1-0	14	Graham 1	(3,655)
48	8	EL	A	Bradford City	W 2-1	0-1	13	Armstrong 69, Ward 87	(3,927)
49	15	EL	H	Blackpool	W 3-2	2-0	12	Helliwell 6, 51, Todd 29	5,021
50	17	EL	A	Wrexham	L 0-1	0-0	12		(3,041)
51	22	EL	H	Brighton & H.A.	W 2-0	1-0	11	Chalk 26, Davenport 88	3,789
52	29	EL	H	Peterborough United	D 1-1	1-0	11	Armstrong 28	4,387
53	M 6	EL	A	Rotherham United	L 0-1	0-0	11		(3,469)
54									
55									
56									
57									
58									
59									
60									

Best Home League Attendance: 5,652 v Plymouth Argyle   **Smallest:** 3,088 v Swansea City   **Av Home Att:** 4,526

Goal Scorers:

Compared with 1993-94: -568

League (63): Armstrong 14, Francis 11, Gannon 7, Chalk 6, Helliwell 4, Ward 3, Beaumont 2, Eckhardt 2, Flynn 2, Graham 2, Todd 2, Wallace 2, Opponents 2, Davenport, Dinning, Slinn, Ware

C/Cola Cup (6): Armstrong, Beaumont, Chalk, Emerson, Francis, Ward

FA Cup (0):

AW Trophy (4): Bound, Dinning, Wallace, Ward

482

Keeley J.	Connelly S.	Todd L.	Eckhardt J.	Flynn M.	Gannon J.	Emerson D.	Ward P.	Francis K.	Armstrong A.	Chalk M.	Miller D.	Graham D.	Ironside I.	Frain D.	Slinn K.	Wallace M.	Beaumont C.	Dinning A.	Ware P.	Brock K.	Edwards N.	Bound M.	Oliver M.	Young R.	Helliwell I.	Referee	
1	2	3	4	5+	6	7*	8	9	10•	11	12	14	S													K. Lynch	1
1	4	3	7	5	6		8	9	10	11	2		S	S	S											P. Rejer	2
1†	2	3	4	5	6		8	9	10•	11	12		13	7*	14											R. Poulain	3
1	2*	3•	4	5	6	7	8	9	10	11			S			12	14									I. Cruikshanks	4
1	5		4*		6		8	9	10	11			14	S	7•		3	2	12							T. Heilbron	5
1	2		4		6		8	9	10	11	S	7	S				3	S	5							K. Breen	6
1	2		4		6	14	8	9	10	11•	12	7*	S				3		5							P. Alcock	7
1	2	3	4	5	7	S	8	9	10	11			S				S		6							E. Wolstenholme	8
1	2	3	4	5	7		8	9	10	11			S				S		6		S					G. Cain	9
1	2	3	4	5	7	14	8	9	10•	11†			S						6		S					K. Lupton	10
1	2	3	4	5	7	10	8	9		11•		S	S						6		14					T. Lunt	11
1	2	3	4•	5	7		8	9	10	11			S			S			6		14					M. Riley	12
1	2	3*	4	5	7			9	10•				S		14	12		6	8	11						G. Singh	13
1	2	3	4	5	7		8	9*					S		11•		14	6	12							W. Burns	14
	2	3	4	5	7		8	9	10	11•			1			14	6	S			S					T. West	15
		3	4	5	7		8	9	10	S			1		S	11	6	2			S					S. Dunn	16
	2	3*	4	5	7•		8	9	10	11			1/			14	6	12	13							N. Barry	17
	2		4	5	7		8	9	10	S			1			3	11	S			S	6				G. Pooley	18
	2		4	5	7		8*	9•	10	14			1			3	11	12			S	6				J. Kirkby	19
	2		4	5	7		8•		9	11			1			3	10	S	8		S	6	S			U. Rennie	20
	2		9	5	7		8•		14	11			1			3	10	12	4*		S	6				M. Reed	21
	2		9	5	7			9		11			1		S	3	10	8			S	6				P. Rejer	22
S	2	3	4	5	7•			9	10				S		14	S	11	8			1	6				K. Lupton	23
S		3	4	5	7		8*		9	14					11•	12	10	2			1	6				K. Lynch	24
S	2	3	9•	5	7				14	11		S				8	10	4			1	6				A. Butler	25
S	2	3	9	5	7		S		14	11•						8	10	4			1	6				K. Leach	26
	2	3	8	5	7		12		9•	14				S		11*	10	4			1	6				E. Wolstenholme	27
	2	3	9	5	7		8*		S	11						12	10	4			1	6				K. Lynch	28
	2•	3	9*	5	7			12	14	11						S	10	4			1	6				D. Allison	29
	2*			5	7			9	11					S		3	10	4	8		1	6				M. Bailey	30
	2*	3		5	12			9	11					S		3	10	4•	7		1	6		14		N. Barry	31
	2	3	S	5	7				10	S						8	11	6	4		1				9	I. Cruikshanks	32
	2	3	S	5	7				10	S						8	11	6	4		1				9	T. Heilbron	33
	2	3	12	5	7*				10•	14						8	11	6	4		1				9	E. Parker	34
	2	3	7	5	12				10•	14						8	11	6	4*		1				9	P. Wright	35
	2	3	9	5	7				12	S					10*	8	11	6	4		1					A. Dawson	36
	2	3	9•	5	7				14	11						8	10	6	4		1				9	P. Richards	37
	2•	3		5	7				10	14						8	11	6	4		11†				9	J. Watson	38
			5	7•					10	8*		12				3	11	2	4			8	6	14	9/	J. Brandwood	39
			5	7					10	14						3	11	6	4		S	S	8		9	A. D'Urso	40
		2	5	7					10	12						3	11*	6	4		1		8		9	J. Winter	41
S	2		5	7		8			10•							3	9	6	4•		S		14		9	G. Singh	42
	2	S	5	7		8			10•	11		14				3	9	6	4		S				9	E. Lomas	43
	6	2		5	7		8•		10	11						3	9	6	4•		S	S	14		9	D. Orr	44
	2	3		5	7				10			14				S	9	6			S	4	8		9	T. West	45
	2	3		5	7		8		10•			11				S	14	6			S	4			9	C. Wilkes	46
	2	3		5	7		8	10		11•							14	6			S	4			9	G. Cain	47
	2	3		5			8		10			12				S	7	6			S	4			9	D. Allison	48
	2	3		5	12		8		10			S				7		6			S	4			9	P. Harrison	49
	2	3		5	7		8		10	12						11*	6•				S	4			9	E. Parker	50
14	3		5	7		8		10	11							2		6			1		4		9	J. Kirkby	51
14	3		5	7		8		10	11*							2•		6			1		4		9	W. Burns	52
S	3		5	7		8		10	11							2		6			1	6*			9	J. Rushton	53
10	37	37	26	43	43	1	27	16	40	24		5	7	2	2	24	33	38	16		18	14	10		17	League Appearances	
	2		1		2	2	1	1	5	9	3	6	1		2	1	5	2	3		1		3			League Sub Appearances	
4		4	4	4	4		2	3	4	3	3		1		0+1	0+2	0+1	2	1+1	1						C/Cola Cup Appearances	
1		1	1	1	1		1		1			1				1	0+1	1								FA Cup Appearances	
1	2	1	2	1+1	1		2	1+1				1	1+1	2	2	1		2	2		0+1				9	AW Trophy Appearances	

Also Played: Dickens 13(38),1(39,40,42,43,44,45,46,47,48,49,50),S(41,51,52,53), Gray S(39), Brown 2•(40),S(41), Davenport 11•(45)11*(48,49),S(47), 14(50),12(51,52), Marshall 4(53), Lloyd-Williams 14(53)

† = Sent Off

CLUB RECORDS

RECORD VICTORY
13-0 v Halifax Town, Div 3N, 6.1.1934 (Joint League record victory)
Record First Class Cup Victory: 6-2 v West Auckland (a), FA Cup
Round 1, 14.11.1959

RECORD LEAGUE DEFEAT
1-8 v Chesterfield, Div 2, 19.4.1902   0-7 v Burton Utd, Div 2,
10.10.1903   0-7 v Bristol City, Div 2, 20.1.1906   0-7 v Fulham, Div
2,8.3.1913   0-7 v Port Vale, Div 3N, 10.4.1954   0-7 v Aldershot,
Div 4, 22.2.1964   0-7 v Hull City, Div 4, 29.1.1983
Record Cup Defeat: 0-7 v Portsmouth, FA Cup Round 3, 8.1.1949
0-7 v Crystal Palace, League Cup Round 2 2nd leg, 4.9.1979   0-7
v Sheffield Wednesday, League Cup Round 2 2nd leg, 6.10.1986

MOST LEAGUE POINTS
(2pts a win) 64, Div 4, 1966-67
(3pts a win) 85, Div 2, 1993-94

MOST LEAGUE GOALS
115, Div 3N, 1933-34

RECORD TRANSFER FEE RECEIVED
£800,000 from Birmingham City for Kevin Francis, January 1995.

RECORD TRANSFER FEE PAID
£150,000   to Preston North End for Mike Flynn, March 1993.

BEST PERFORMANCES
League: 10th Div 2 1905-06
FA Cup: 5th Round 1935, 1950
League Cup: 4th Round 1972-73
HONOURS: Champions Div 3N 1921-22, 1936-37   Champions Div
4 1966-67   Lancashire League 1899-00   Lancashire Combination
1904-05   Division 3N Cup Winners 1934-35   Autoglass Trophy
Finalists 1992, 1993

LEAGUE CAREER: Elected to Div 2 1900   Failed Re-election
1904   Elected to Div 2 1905 Relegated to Div 3N 1920-21
Promoted to Div 2 1921-22   Relegated to Div 3N 1925-26
Promoted to Div 2 1936-37   Relegated to Div 3N 1937-38
Transferred to Div 3 1958   Relegated to Div 4 1958-59
Promoted to Div 3 1966-67   Relegated to Div 4 1969-70
Promoted to Div 3 (now Div 2) 1990-91

INDIVIDUAL CLUB RECORDS

MOST APPEARANCES FOR CLUB
Andy Thorpe 1978-86 & 1987-92: Lge 484+5 + FAC 14 + Lge Cup
32+1 + Others 18+1. 0Total 548+7

MOST CAPPED PLAYER
Harry Hardy 1, England

RECORD GOALSCORER IN A MATCH
Joe Smith 5 v Southport (h), 6-3, Div 3N,7.1.1928   Joe Smith 5 v
Lincoln City (h), 7-3, Div 3N, 15.9.1928   F Newton 5 v Nelson, 6-1,
Div 3N, 21.9.1929   Alf Lythgoe 5 v Southport, 6-1, Div 3N,
25.8.1934   W McNaughton 5 v Mansfield Town, 6-1, Div 3N,
14.12.1935   Jack Connor 5 v Workington (h), 6-0, Div 3N,
8.11.1952   Jack Connor 5 v Carlisle United (h), 8-1, Div 3N, 7.4.1956

RECORD LEAGUE GOALSCORER IN A SEASON
Alf Lythgoe 46 In All Competitions: Alf Lythgoe 47 (League 46 + FA
Cup 1) 1933-34

RECORD LEAGUE GOALSCORER IN A CAREER
Jack Connor 132 In All Competitions Jack Connor 140 (League
132 + FAC 8) 1951-56

OLDEST PLAYER IN A LEAGUE MATCH
Alec Hard 40 years 47 days, 25.12.1951, Crewe Alexandra (H).

YOUNGEST PLAYER IN A LEAGUE MATCH
Steve Massey 16 years 337 days, 28.02.1975, Darlington (H) (sub).

PREVIOUS MANAGERS

-1895 George Ellis, 1895-1903 Fred Stewart, 1903-04 Sam Ormerod
1904-11 Fred Stewart   1911-14 Harry P Lewis   1914-19 David
Ashworth   1919-24 Albert Williams   1924-26 Fred Scotchbrook
1926-31 Lincoln Hyde   1931-32 No Manager   1932-33 Andrew
Wilson   1933-36 Fred Westgarth   1936-38 Bob Kelly   1938-39 No
Manager   1939-49 Bob Marshall   1949-52 Andy Beattie   1952-56
Dick Duckworth   1956-60 Willie Moir   1960-63 Reg Flewin 1963-65
Trevor Porteous   1965 Bert Trautmann   1965-66 Eddie Quigley
1966-69 Jimmy Meadows   1969-70 Walter Galbraith   1970-71 Matt
Woods   1971-72 Steve Fleet (acting)   1972-74 Brian Doyle   1974-75
Jimmy Meadows 1975-76 Roy Chapman   1976-77 Eddie Quigley
1977-78 Alan Thompson   1978-79 Mike Summerbee   1979-82
Jimmy McGuigan   1982-85 Eric Webster   1985 Colin Murphy
1985-86 Les Chapman   1986 Jimmy Melia   1986-87 Colin Murphy
1987-89 Asa Hartford   1989-95 Danny Bergara

ADDITIONAL INFORMATION

Previous Name: Heaton Norris Rovers 1883-88   Heaton Norris
1988-90

Previous League: The Combination 1891-94; Lancashire League
1894-1900; Lancashire Combination 1904-05

Club colours: White shirts and shorts with blue pinstripe & trim,
white socks with blue trim.

Change colours: Red and black striped shirts with black trim, black
shorts, and white socks.

Reserves League: Pontins League Division Three.

 'A' Team: Lancashire League Division 2.

LONGEST LEAGUE RUNS

of undefeated matches:	18 (1933)	of league matches w/out a win:	15 (1989)
of undefeated home matches:	48 (1927-29)	of undefeated away matches:	8 (1921-22, 1929, 1929-30)
without home win:	12 (1986)	without an away win:	37 (1901-03)
of league wins:	8 (1927-28)	of home wins:	13 (1928-29, 1930)
of league defeats:	9 (1908-09)	of away wins:	7 (1951)

THE MANAGER

DAVID JONES . . . . appointed March 1995

PREVIOUS CLUBS
As Manager. . . . . None.
As Asst.Man/Coach . . . . Morecambe, Stockport County.
As a player . . . . Everton, Coventry City, Seiko FC (Hong Kong), Preston North End, Morecambe.

HONOURS
As a Manager . . . . None.
As a Player . . . . England Under-21. 1 caps, England Youth.

STOCKPORT COUNTY

PLAYERS NAME / Honours	Ht	Wt	Birthdate	Birthplace / Transfers	Contract Date	Clubs	APPEARANCES				GOALS			
							League	L/Cup	FA Cup	Other	Lge	L/C	FAC	Oth
G O A L K E E P E R S														
Matthew Dickins	6.4	14.0	03.09.70	Sheffield	01.07.89	Sheffield Utd (T)								
				Free	27.02.91	Lincoln City	27	1	1	2				
				£250,000	27.03.92	Blackburn Rovers	1							
Loan 19.11.93 Lincoln City 1 Oth. App.				Loan	22.01.93	Blackpool	19							
Loan 09.09.94 Grimsby Town				Loan	14.10.94	Rochdale	4			1				
Loan 12.01.95 Stockport County					17.03.95	Stockport County	11+1							
Neil Edwards	5.10	11.10	05.12.70	Aberdare	10.03.89	Leeds United (T)				1				
W: u21.1, Y.				£5,000	03.09.91	Stockport County	118+1	6	7	27				
D E F E N D E R S														
Thomas Bennett	5.11	11.8	12.12.69	Falkirk	16.12.87	Aston Villa (A)								
				Free	05.07.88	Wolverhampton W	103+12	73+1	4+2	3				
				£75,000	08.95									
Matthew Bound	6.2	12.0	09.11.72	Melksham	03.05.91	Southampton (T)	2+3							
				Loan	27.08.93	Hull City	7			1				
				£125,000	26.10.95	Stockport County	14		1	2				1
Sean Connelly	5.10	11.10	26.06.70	Sheffield Hallam										
				Free	12.08.92	Stockport County	74+4	4	2+1	8				
Tony Dinning	6.2	12.11	12.04.75	Wallsend	01.10.93	Newcastle Utd (T)								
				Free	23.06.94	Stockport County	38+2	2	0+1	2	1			1
Jeff Eckhardt	6.0	11.7	07.10.65	Sheffield	23.08.84	Sheffield United (J)	73+1	7	2	5	2			
				£50,000	20.11.87	Fulham	245+4	13	5+1	15	25			3
				£50,000	21.07.94	Stockport County	26+1	4	1	1	1			
James Gannon	6.2	12.6	07.09.68	Southwark Dundalk										
To Sheffield United, 27.04.89				Loan	22.02.90	Halifax Town	2							
				£40,000	07.03.90	Stockport County	211+6	13	9	31+2	46	1	1	8
				Loan	14.01.94	Notts County	2							
Phil Johnson	5.8	10.06	07.04.75	Liverpool	09.07.93	Tranmere Rov. (T)								
				Free	08.95	Stockport County								
Lee Todd	5.5	10.3	07.03.72	Hartlepool		Hartlepool United (T)								
				Free	23.07.90	Stockport County	133+11	10+1	9	24+1	2			2
M I D F I E L D														
Michael Flynn	6.0	11.0	23.02.69	Oldham	07.02.87	Oldham Ath. (A)	37+3	1+1	1	2	1			
E: u19.2.				£100,000	22.12.88	Norwich City								
				£125,000	04.12.89	Preston North End	134+2	6	6+1	13	7		1	
				£125,000	25.03.93	Stockport County	98+1	6	5	12	3			
Lee Marshall	5.9	9.12	01.08.75	Nottingham	03.08.92	Nottingham F. (T)								
				Free	20.03.95	Stockport County	1							
Michael Oliver	5.10	12.4	02.08.75	Cleveland	19.08.92	Middlesbrough	0+1							
				£15,000	07.07.94	Stockport County	10+3							
Paul Ware	5.8	11.2	07.11.70	Congelton	15.11.88	Stoke City (T)	92+23	7+1	4+1	12+2	10			4
Div.2'93.					08.09.94	Stockport County	16+3	1+1	1	1	1			
F O R W A R D S														
Gavin Allen	5.8	10.05	17.06.76	Bangor	12.07.94	Tranmere Rov. (T)								
E: u21.2.				Free	08.95	Stockport County								
Alun Armstrong	6.1	11.13	22.02.75	Gateshead	01.10.93	Newcastle United								
				£50,000	23.06.94	Stockport County	40+5	3	0+1	2	14	1		
Chris Beaumont	5.11	11.7	05.12.65	Sheffield Denaby United										
				Free	21.07.88	Rochdale	31+3	0+1	2	2	7	1	1	
				£8,000	21.07.89	Stockport County	200+15	9+3	11	32+2	39	3	1	6
Martyn Chalk	5.6	10.0	30.08.69	Louth Louth United										
				£10,000	23.01.90	Derby County	4+3		3	0+1	1		1	
				£40,000	30.06.94	Stockport County	24+9	3	1	1+1	6	1		
Ian Helliwell	6.3	13.12	07.11.62	Rotherham Matlock Town										
				£10,000	23.10.87	York City	158+2	8	5	9+1	40	1		7
				£80,000	16.08.91	Scunthorpe United	78+2	8	4	9	22	5	2	2
				£50,000	01.08.93	Rotherham United	37+3	3+1	1	1+1	3			
Loan 12.01.95 Stockport County					10.02.95	Stockprot County	17			4				
Richard Landon	6.3	13.05	22.03.70	Worthing Bedworth										
				£30,000	26.01.94	Plymouth Argyle	21+9	0+1	0+1	2	12			
				£30,000	08.95	Stockport County								
Marc L Williams	5.10	10.12	08.02.73	Bangor Bangor City										
				£10,000	23.03.95	Stockport County	0+1							

EDGELEY PARK
Hardcastle Road, Edgeley, Stockport, Cheshire SK3 9DD
Tel: 0161 480 8888

Capacity ....

First game .... v Gainsborough Trinity 1-1, Div.2, 13.09.02.
First floodlit game .... v Fortuna '54 Geleen (Neth) 0-3, 16.10.56

ATTENDANCES
Highest .... 27,833 v Liverpool, FAC 5th Rnd, 11.2.1950.
Lowest .... 1,000 v Carlisle Utd, AMC, 8.12.1986.

OTHER GROUNDS .... Heaton Norris Rec. Ground 1883-84,
Heaton Norris W'derers Cricket Ground 1884-85, Chorlton's Farm 1885-87, Wilkes' Field 1887-89,
.... Green Lane 1899-1902.

MATCHDAY TICKET PRICES

Main Stand £9
Juv/OAP £3

Barlow Stand £8
Juv/OAP £3

Cheadle Stand £7
Juv/OAP £3

Railway End (Visitors) £7

Ticket Office Telephone no. 0161480 8888

HOW TO GET TO THE GROUND

From the North, South and West
Use motorway (M63) until junction 11, sign posted Cheadle (A560). At round-about follow A560 to Stockport and in 0.3 miles turn right at lights, sign posted Stockport County FC). In 1 mile turn right into Caroline Street for Stockport County FC.

From the East
Use A6 into Stockport Town centre and turn left into Greek Street, opposite the Town Hall. At roundabout go straight over and into Mercian Way and in 0.2 miles left into Caroline Street for Stockport County FC.

Car Parking
Ample street parking around the ground.

Nearest Railway Station
Edgeley (short walk to the ground).

CLUBCALL
0891 12 16 38

Calls cost 39p per minute cheap rate and 49p per minute at all other times.
Call costings correct at time of going to press.

MATCHDAY PROGRAMME

Programme Editor . . . . Steve Bellis.

Number of pages . . . . 56.

Price . . . . £1.50.

Subscriptions . . . . £40 inc. postage.

Local Newspapers . . . . Stockport Express Advertiser,
. . . . Stockport Messenger, Edgeley Park Echo.

Local Radio Stations . . . . Radio Piccadilly, G.M.R., Signal Radio.

SWANSEA CITY
(The Swans)
ENDSLEIGH LEAGUE DIVISION 2
SPONSORED BY: GULF OIL

Back Row (L-R): Denis Spiteri, Darren Perrett, Lee Jones, Roger Freestone, Ben Miles, David Barnhouse, Jamie Rickard.
Middle Row: Mark Clode, David Thomas, Michael Basham, Christian Edwards, Stephen Torpey, Carl Heggs, Keith Walker, Jason Price, Shaun Chapple.
Front Row: David Beresford, Jonathan Coates, John Hodge, Colin Pascoe, John Cornforth, David Penney, Andy Cook, Kwame Ampadu, Stephen Jenkins

SWANSEA CITY
FORMED IN 1900
TURNED PROFESSIONAL IN 1912
LTD COMPANY IN 1912

PRESIDENT: Ivor Pursey MBE
CHAIRMAN: D J Sharpe
VICE-CHAIRMAN
D G Hammond FCA MBIM
DIRECTORS
M Griffiths
SECRETARY
G M Taylor (01792 474 114)
COMMERCIAL MANAGER
Karen Finney

MANAGER: Frank Burrows
ASSISTANT MANAGER: Bobby Smith

YOUTH TEAM MANAGER
Jimmy Rimmer
PHYSIOTHERAPIST
Mike Davenport

STATISTICIAN FOR THE DIRECTORY
Prof. David Farmer

Whilst, at the end of the campaign, the Swans proved to have been what one paper called a 'nearly side', there were times during the season when success appeared to have been within the grasp of the team. For example, in a remarkable run from late October to the end of 1994, the team surged up the table moving from 19th to 10th. In the process, seven league matches were played and only one lost.

A similar spell during March saw the Swans win six matches out of seven, whilst the other was drawn, to take the side to sixth in the table and to result in Frank Burrows getting a 'Manager of the Month' award. In addition, there were fine performances against Norwich City in the Coca-Cola Cup, and against Middlesbrough, and Newcastle in the FA Cup. The victory over the 'Boro on their own pitch was particularly impressive. Brian Robson said, on that occasion, as did Kevin Keegan after the next round match, that the Swans were a credit to their division.

Furthermore, many informed people in the game thought that Swansea were the best passing side in the lower divisions. However, as Frank Burrows was obliged to point out time and again, passes don't win matches, it's goals that count. Even when the side dominated poorer sides, on occasions they failed to finish.

In an effort to overcome this goal-shyness, manager Frank Burrows permutated his small squad, but with little success. In due course, unable to buy, he ventured into the loan market, bringing John Hendry to the Vetch from Spurs for a two month loan spell. Had that move been made permanent, the general consensus of opinion was that the Swans would, at least, have made the play-offs. Sadly though, with an average 'gate' throughout the season of only 3,500, the money was not available for the hard-working Scot to strengthen his side.

To finish tenth in the table at the end of a season would have satisfied many sets of supporters, but at the Vetch, it is clear that the fans are demanding the excitement of goals being scored. And, as Frank Burrows put it, "We need to capture the imagination of the supporters, again!" With no Jack Walker in sight, it is clear that much of the growth to enable that to happen must come from within, and there was encouragement in that regard, as a result of the success of the reserve side. Among other things, they were champions of the Avon Combination Division Two league, beating big-spending Birmingham into second place, and, in addition, they won the Division Two cup to do 'the double'.

All in all, the season illustrated, yet again, how narrow the margin is between success and 'almost getting there'. Clearly, whatever Frank Burrows does during the close season , as he 'wheels and deals' will have a big impact on the outcome of the season ahead. Every Swans fan will wish him well in his search for that key striker and tough mid-field man. The right fresh faces could turn Swansea dreams into reality yet again. It's been done before, so why not during the 1995-96 campaign?

Up the Swans!

PROF. DAVID FARMER.

SWANSEA CITY

Division Two: 10th   **FA Cup:** 5th Round   **Coca-Cola Cup:** 2nd Round   **Auto Windscreen Trophy:** 5th Round

M	DATE	COMP.	VEN	OPPONENTS	RESULT	H/T	LP	GOAL SCORERS/GOAL TIMES	ATT.
1	A 8	EL	H	Brighton	D 1-1			Penney (pen) 30	4,638
2	17	CC 1/1	A	**Exeter City**	D 2-2			**Harris 54, Hodge 81**	**(2,850)**
3	20	EL	A	Hull City	W 2-0		8	Cornforth 79, Ampadu 89	(3,797)
4	23	CC 1/2	H	**Exeter City**	W 2-0			**Penney 68 (pen), 72**	**(2,523)**
5	27	EL	H	Birmingham City	L 0-2		13		5,797
6	S 3	EL	A	Cardiff City	D 1-1		17	Hayes 44	(5,523)
7	6	EL	A	Shrewsbury Town	D 3-3		16	Hodge 53, Pascoe 58, Ford 60	(3,534)
8	10	EL	H	Bradford City	D 0-0		16		3,448
9	13	EL	H	Bristol Rovers	D 0-0		16		3,326
10	17	EL	A	Cambridge United	W 3-1		15	Penney 3, 44, Torpey 73	(2,795)
11	21	CC 2/1	A	**Norwich City**	L 0-3				**(8,053)**
12	24	EL	H	York City	D 0-0		16		2,875
13	O 1	EL	A	Wycombe Wanderers	L 0-1		17		(4,151)
14	5	CC 2/2	H	**Norwich City**	W 1-0			**Pascoe 55**	**3,568**
15	8	EL	A	Chester City	D 2-2		17	Ampadu 12, Ford 84	(2,186)
16	15	EL	H	Oxford United	L 1-3		17	Hendry 16	3,724
17	18	AWT	A	**Torquay United**	W 3-1			**Hendry 32, 42, Bowen 90**	**(885)**
18	22	EL	A	Blackpool	L 1-2		19	Ampadu 79	(4,911)
19	29	EL	H	Peterborough	W 2-0		17	Hendry 37, Bowen 90	2,733
20	N 1	EL	H	Rotherham United	W 1-0		14	Pascoe 82	2,511
21	5	EL	A	Crewe Alexandra	W 2-1		14	Bowen 47, 89	(3,242)
22	8	AWT	H	**Hereford United**	D 1-1			**Torpey 75**	**1,215**
23	19	EL	H	Stockport County	W 2-0		14	Ampadu 70, Cornforth 89	3,019
24	21	FAC	A	**Walton & Horsham**	W 2-0			**Ford 22, Ampadu 89**	**(2,230)**
25	26	EL	A	Wrexham	L 1-4		15	Ford 68	(3,598)
26	29	AWT	A	**Northampton Town**	W 1-0			**Hendry 18**	**(2,706)**
27	D 4	FAC	A	**Bashley**	W 1-0			**Torpey 61**	**(2,047)**
28	10	EL	H	Hull City	W 2-0		13	Torpey 40, 68	2,903
29	17	EL	A	Brighton	D 1-1		13	Torpey 3	(6,817)
30	26	EL	H	Plymouth	W 3-0		12	Hodge 4, Hayes 28, 43	3,816
31	27	EL	A	Leyton Orient	W 1-0		10	Hayes 4	(3,259)
32	31	EL	H	Huddersfield Town	D 1-1		11	Torpey 87	5,438
33	J 2	EL	A	Bournemouth	L 2-3		12	Hodge 4, Penney 83	(3,816)
34	7	FAC	H	**Middlesbrough**	D 1-1			**Ford 35**	**8,407**
35	10	AWT	A	**Oxford United**	W 2-1			**Torpey 25, Hayes 49**	**(2,321)**
36	14	EL	A	Brentford	D 0-0		14		(7,211)
37	17	FAC	A	**Middlesbrough**	W 2-1			**Torpey 21, Penney 56**	**(13,940)**
38	28	FAC	A	**Newcastle United**	L 0-3				**(34,372)**
39	31	AWT	A	**Birmingham**	L †2-3			**Pascoe 3 (og), 42**	**(20,326)**
40	F 4	EL	H	Wrexham	D 0-0		14		4,563
41	11	EL	A	Rotherham United	D 3-3		14	Williams 25, Pascoe 45, Hodge 82	(3,816)
42	17	EL	H	Brentford	L 0-2		14		3,935
43	22	EL	A	Stockport	W 1-0		14	Torpey 14	(3,088)
44	25	EL	H	Wycombe Wanderers	D 1-1		14	Torpey 90	3,699
45	28	EL	H	Blackpool	W 1-0		13	Torpey 63	2,308
46	M 4	EL	A	York City	W 4-2		11	Bowen 41, 55, Torpey 79, Hodge 80	(2,920)
47	8	EL	H	Cardiff City	W 4-1		9	Williams 10, Penney 16, Pascoe 18, Chapple 85	3,942
48	11	EL	A	Birmingham	W 1-0		8	Hodge 38 (pen)	(16,191)
49	17	EL	H	Shrewesbury	D 0-0		10		4,130
50	21	EL	A	Bradford City	W 3-1		7	Cornforth 33, Ampadu 54, 61	(4,417)
51	25	EL	H	Cambridge United	W 1-0		6	Torpey 5	4,007
52	A 1	EL	A	Bristol Rovers	L 0-1		7		(7,062)
53	4	EL	A	Peterborough United	L 0-1		8		(3,764)
54	8	EL	A	Huddersfield	L 0-2		9		(10,105)
55	15	EL	H	Leyton Orient	W 2-0		9	Torpey 9, Pascoe 28	3,277
56	17	EL	A	Plymouth Athletic	L 1-2		10	Hodge 40	(5,890)
57	22	EL	H	Bournemouth	W 1-0		10	Clode 46	2,684
58	26	EL	H	Crewe Alexandra	L 0-1		10		2,600
59	30	EL	A	Oxford United	W 2-1		9	Chapple 56, Freestone 33 (pen)	(5,244)
60	M 6	EL	H	Chester City	L 0-1		10		2,065

Best Home League Attendance: 5,797 v Birmingham City   **Smallest:** 2,065 v Chester City   **Av Home Att:** 3,541

Goal Scorers: Compared with 1993-94: -5,148

League (57): Torpey 11, Hodge 8, Ampadu 5, Pascoe 5, Penney 5, Bowen 5, Hayes 4, Cornforth 3, Ford 3, Hendry 2, Williams 2, Chapple 2, Freestone, Clode

C/Cola Cup (5): Penney 2, Harris, Hayes, Pascoe

FA Cup (6): Torpoy 2, Ford 2, Hayes, Harris

AW Trophy (9): Hendry 3, Torpey 2, Bowen, Hayot, Pascoe, Opponent

Welsh Cup (20): Bowen 3, Perrett 3, Hayes 3, Hendry 2, McFarlane 2, Ampadu, Hayes, Thomas, Torpoy, Cornforth, Bowen, Opponent

1994-95

	Freestone	Jenkins	Clode	Ford	Harris	Ampadu	Gowen	Penney	Hayes	Comforth	Hodge	Pascoe	Torpey	Perrott	Hendry	Jones	Basham	Chapple	Barnhouse	Walker	Burns	Macfarlane	Williams	Edwards	Coates	Cook	Referee	
	1	2	3	4	5	6	7	8	9	10	11*	12															Wilkes C.	1
1		2	3	4	5	6	7	8	9	10	11	12															Pierce M.	2
1		2	3	4	5	6	7	8	9*	10	11		12														Lupton K.	3
1		2	3	4	5	6	7	1	14	10	11	8	9														Singh G.	4
1		2	3	4	5	6*		8	7†	10	11	12*	9	14													Dunn S.	5
1		2	3	4	5	6		8	7	10	11*	12	9	14													Hamley I.	6
1		2	3	4	5			8	7	10	11*	6	9	12													Wolstenholme C.	7
1		2	3	4	5	12	14	8	7	10	11	6*	9														Vanes P.	8
1		2	3	4	5	12	14	8		10	11	6	9	7													Holbrook J.	9
1		2	3	4	5	14	7	8		10	12	6	9	11													Brandwood M.	10
1		2	3	4	5		7	8		10		6	9	11													West T.	11
1		2	3	4	5	14	7	8		10	11	6	9	12													Harris R.	12
1		2	3	4	5	14	7	8		10	11	6	9	12													Pooley A.	13
1		2	3	4	5	7	12	8		10	14	6	9	11													West T.	14
1		2	3	4	5	7	12	8		10	14	6	9		11												Rennie W.	15
1		2	3	4	5	7	12	8	14		11	6	9		10												Lunt T.	16
		2		3	5		7	8	12		11	6		9	1		4	10									Down S.	17
S		2		3	5	10	7	8			11	6		9	1		4	12									Heilbron T.	18
1		2	3		5	12	7	8	14	10	11	6		9			4										Cain G.	19
1		2	3		5	12	7	8	14	10	11	6		9			4										Vanes P.	20
1		2	3		5	6	7	8	14	10	11			9			4	12									Lynch K.	21
1		2	3		5		7	8	12	10	11	6		9			4										Singh G.	22
1		2	3		5	6	7	8		10	11	14	12	9			4										Rujer P.	23
1		2	3		5	6	7	8		10	11			9			4										Holbrook J.	24
1		2	3		5	6	7	8		10	11	14		9			4										Rushton J.	25
1		2			5		7	8	12	10	11			9			4	6	3								Butler A.	26
1		2			5	10	7	8			11			9			4	6	3	12							Rushton J.	27
1		2	3				7	8	10	11	9						5	6	4	12							Harris R.	28
1		2				10	7	8		11	9	14					5	6	4	3	12						Cooper K.	29
1					5	10		14	7	11	9	12					4	6	2	3	8						Vanes P.	30
1					5	10		8	7	6	11	9	12				4		2	3							Bailey M.	31
1					5	8		14	7	6	11	9	12				4		2	3	10						Brandwood M.	32
1					5	8		14	7	10	11	9	12				4		2	3	6						Singh G.	33
1			3			6		8	7	10	11	9					5		2	4		12					Morton K.	34
1		2			5	6		8	7	10	11	9					4	12		3		12					Wilkes C.	35
1		2			5	6		8	7	10	11	9					4			3							West T.	36
1		2			5	6		8	7	10	11	9					4	12		3		12					Morton K.	37
1		2			5			8	7	10	11	9					4			3		12					Hill B.	38
1		2			5		12	8	7	10	11	6	9				4			3		14					Flood W.	39
1		2			5			8	7	10		6	9					4				11					Pierce M.	40
1		2			5		3	8	7	10	12	6	9					4		14	11						Lloyd J.	41
1		2	3		5			8	7	10	12	6	14					4		9	11						Mathieson J.	42
1		2	3		5	10	7			12	6	9				14		4			11	8					Richards P.	43
1		2	3		5	10	7			12	6	9				14		4			11	8					Dunn S.	44
1		2	3		5	10	7	8			11	6	9					4				8					Wilkes C.	45
1		2	3		5	10	7				11	6	9					4			8						Harrison P.	46
1		2	3		5	10		8			11	6	9				12	4			7						Lloyd J.	47
1		2	3		5	10	7	12			11	6	9					4				8	14				Cruikshank I.	48
1		2	3		5	10	7	8		14	11	6	9					4				12					Butler A.	49
1		2	3		5	7		12		10	11	6	9					4			8						Burns W.	50
1		2	3		5	7		8		10	11	6	9					4				12					Wright P.	51
1		2			5	7				10	11	6	9	8				4			3						Vanes P.	52
1		2	3		5	7				10	11	6	9	12				4			8						Breen K.	53
1		2	3		5	7	14		12	10	11	6	9					4			8		3				Lynch K.	54
1		2	3		5	8	7		12	10	11	6	9					4									Rejer P.	55
1		2	3		5	8	7		12	10	11	6	9					4									Holbrook J.	56
1		2	3		5	8	7		12		11	6	9					4			8						Leach K.	57
1		2	3		5	10	7		12		11	6	9		1			4									Barber G.	58
1		2	3		5	11	7			10		6	9				8	4									Singh G.	59
1		2	3		5	12	7			10	11	6	9					4									D'Urso A.	60
44	**42**	**33**	**46**	**14**	**36**	**25**	**29**	**14**	**32**	**37**	**32**	**37**	**3**	**8**	**2**	**13**	**4**	**4**	**28**	**3**	**1**	**6**	**9**		**1**	**League Appearances**	
1						8	5	5	10	1	6	3	4	12			5			2	2			3		**League Sub Appearances**	
4	4	4	4	4	3+1	3+1	3+1	1+1	4	2+1	3+1	3	2													**C/Cola Cup Appearances**	
5	4	1	5		3	2	5	3+1	5	5	5	0+1	5	2+1	1	4		0+1	0+2							**FA Cup Appearances**	
4	5	1	5	1	1	3+1	5	2+3	4	5	2	2+1		3	1	5	2+1	1	2			0+1				**AW Trophy Appearances**	

Also Played: Thomas 14(56,58),10(57)8(60) Loan Players: Hendry (Tottenham Hotspur), Williams J (Coventry), Burns (Porstmouth) † = Sent Off

CLUB RECORDS

RECORD LEAGUE VICTORY
8-0 v Hartlepool United, Div 4, 1.4.1978
Most Goals Scored in a Cup Tie: 12-0 v Sliema Wanderers (Malta), 1st rnd 1st leg, European Cup Winners Cup, 15.9.1982

RECORD LEAGUE DEFEAT
1-8 v Fulham, Div 2, 22.1.1938 1-8 v Newcastle United,Div 2, 2.9.1939 0-7 v Tottenham Hotspur, Div 2, 3.12.1932 0-7 v Bristol Rovers, Div 2, 2.10.1954 0-7 v Workington, Div 3, 4.10.1960
Record Cup Defeat
0-8 v Liverpool, FA Cup Round 3 replay, 9.1.1990 0-8 v Monaco, ECWC 1st rnd 2nd leg, 1.10.1991
European Competitions entered: European Cup Winners Cup 1961-62, 1966-67, 1981-82, 1982-83, 1983-84, 1989-90, 1991-92

MOST LEAGUE POINTS
(3pts a win) 73, Division 2 1992-93
(2pts a win) 62, Div3S, 1948-49

MOST LEAGUE GOALS
92, Div 4, 1976-77

RECORD TRANSFER FEE RECEIVED
£375,000 from Crystal Palace for Chris Coleman, June 1991 (Fee paid in installments. Final payment made when Coleman played his 50th game for Palace). £375,000 from Nott'm Forest for Des Lyttle, July 1993

RECORD TRANSFER FEE PAID
£340,000 to Liverpool for Colin Irwin, Aug 1981

BEST PERFORMANCES
League: 6th Div 1 1981-82
FA Cup: Semi-finals 1926, 1964
League Cup: 4th Round 1964-65, 1976-77
European Cup Winners Cup: 2nd round
Welsh Cup Winners (10)

HONOURS
Champions Div 3S 1924-25, 1948-49 Welsh Cup Winners (10 times) Autoglass Trophy 1993-94

LEAGUE CAREER
Original Members of Div 3 1920 Promoted to Div 2 1924-25
Relegated to Div 3S 1946-47 Promoted to Div 2 1948-49
Relegated to Div 31964-65 Relegated to Div 4 1966-67
Promoted to Div 3 1969-70 Relegated to Div 4 1972-73
Promoted to Div 31977-78 Promoted to Div 2 1978-79
Promoted to Div 1 1980-81 Relegated to Div 2 1982-83
Relegated to Div 31983-84 Relegated to Div 4 1985-86
Promoted to Div 3 (now Div 2) 1987-88

INDIVIDUAL CLUB RECORDS

MOST APPEARANCES FOR CLUB
`Wilfy' Milne (1920-37): League 585 + FA Cup 44 +Welsh Cup 28
Total 657

MOST CAPPED PLAYER
Ivor Allchurch, 42 Wales For England: None

RECORD GOALSCORER IN A MATCH
Jack Fowler 5 v Charlton Athletic, 6-1 Div 3S,27.9.1924
RECORD LEAGUE GOALSCORER IN A SEASON
Cyril Pearce 35, 1931-32 In All Competitions: Cyril Pearce 39 (Lge 35 + Welsh Cup 4)
RECORD LEAGUE GOALSCORER IN A CAREER
Ivor Allchurch 166 (1949-58 & 1965-68) In All Competitions: Ivor Allchurch, 189 (League 166 + FA Cup 9 + League Cup 4+ Welsh Cup 10)

OLDEST PLAYER IN A LEAGUE MATCH
Tommy Hutchison 43 years 171 days v Southend,12.3.91
YOUNGEST PLAYER IN A LEAGUE MATCH
Nigel Dalling, 15 years 10 months

PREVIOUS MANAGERS

1912-14 Walter Whittaker 1914-15 William Bartlett 1919-26 Joe Bradshaw 1927-31 James Thompson 1934-39 Neil Harris 1939-47 Haydn Green 1947-55 Billy McCandless 1955-58 Ron Burgess 1958-65 Trevor Morris 1965-66 Glyn Davies 1967-69 Billy Lucas 1969-72 Roy Bentley 1972-75 Harry Gregg 1975-78 Harry Griffiths 1978-84 John Toshack 1984 Colin Appleton 1985-86 John Bond 1986-89 Terry Yorath 1989-90 Ian Evans 1990-91 Terry Yorath 1991- Frank Burrows
In addition B Watts-Jones, Joe Sykes, Walter Robins, Doug Livermore, Wyndham Evans, Les Chappel, and Tommy Hutchison all acted in a `caretaker' capacity for short periods.

ADDITIONAL INFORMATION
Previous Name: Swansea Town (until Feb 1970)
Previous League: Southern League.

Club Colours: All white.
Change Colours: Orange & white shirts, blue shorts.
Reserves League: Neville Ovenden Football Combination.

LONGEST LEAGUE RUNS

of undefeated matches:	19 (1970-71)	of league matches w/out a win:	15 (1989)
of undefeated home matches:	28 (1925-27)	of undefeated away matches:	12 (1970-71)
without home win:	9 (1938)	without an away win:	46 (1982-84)
of league wins:	8 (1961)	of home wins:	17 (1948-49)
of league defeats:	9 (1990-91)	of away wins:	4 (1955-56, 1987-88, 1993)

THE MANAGER

FRANK BURROWS . . . . appointed March 1991.

PREVIOUS CLUBS
As Manager . . . . Portsmouth, Cardiff City.
As Asst.Man/Coach . . . . Portsmouth, Swindon, Sunderland.
As a player . . . . Raith Rovers, Scunthorpe, Swindon, Mansfield.

HONOURS
As a Manager . . . . None.
As a Player . . . . Swindon: League Cup Winners 1969.

SWANSEA CITY

PLAYERS NAME / Honours	Ht	Wt	Birthdate	Birthplace / Transfers	Contract Date	Clubs	League	L/Cup	FA Cup	Other	Lge	L/C	FAC	Oth
G O A L K E E P E R S														
Roger Freestone	6.2	14.6	19.08.68	Newport	02.04.86	Newport Co. (T)	13			1				
W: u21.1. Div.2'89. AGT'94.				£95,000	10.03.87	Chelsea	42	2	3	6				
				Loan	29.09.89	Swansea City	14			1				
				Loan	09.03.90	Hereford United	8							
				£50,000	05.09.91	Swansea City	178+1	12	15	24	1			
Lee Jones	6.3	14.4	09.08.70	Pontypridd		AFC Porth								
				£7,500	24.03.94	Swansea City	2			1				
Ben Miles	6.1	11.07	13.04.74	Southall	04.07.94	Swansea City (T)								
				Loan	03.03.95	Trowbridge Town								
D E F E N D E R S														
Michael Basham	5.10	11.0	27.09.73	Barking	03.07.92	West Ham U. (T)								
E: Y.2, S. AGT'94.				Loan	18.11.93	Colchester United	1							
				Free	24.03.94	Swansea City	18		5	8				
Andy Cook	5.9	10.12	10.08.69	Romsey	06.07.87	Southampton (A)	11+5	4	1	1	1			
				£50,000	13.09.91	Exeter City	70	2	7	6	1		1	1
				£125,000	23.07.93	Swansea City	24+5	2	2	7+1				2
Christian Edwards	6.3	11.7	23.11.75	Caerphilly	20.07.94	Swansea City (T)	9			1+1				
Mark Harris	6.1	13.0	15.07.63	Reading		Wokingham Town								
AGT'94.				£25,000	29.02.88	Crystal Palace	0+2							
				Loan	07.08.89	Burnley	4	2						
				£22,500	22.09.89	Swansea City	228	16	18	26	14	1	1	2
Stephens Jenkins	5.10	10.9	16.07.72	Merthyr Tydfil	01.07.90	Swansea City (T)	140+10	10+1	10+1	25	1			
W: u21.2, Y. AGT'94.														
M I D F I E L D														
David Barnhouse	5.9	10.9	19.03.75	Swansea	08.07.93	Swansea City (T)	6+2		1	2				
Shaun Chappell	5.10	12.3	14.02.73	Swansea	15.07.91	Swansea City (T)	44+19	2+1	7+2	8+2	7	1		1
W; u21.6.														
Mark Clode	5.7	10.6	24.02.73	Plymouth	30.03.91	Plymouth A. (T)								
AGT'94.				Free	23.07.93	Swansea City	59+2	6	3	7	2			
John Cornforth	6.1	12.8	07.10.67	Whitley Bay	11.10.85	Sunderland (A)	21+11	0+1		1+3	2			
Div.3'88. AGT'94.				Loan	06.11.86	Doncaster Rovers	6+1			2	3			
				Loan	23.11.89	Shrewsbury Town	3			2				
				Loan	11.01.90	Lincoln City	9			1				
				£50,000	02.08.91	Swansea City	130+2	12	14	19	14		1	1
David Penney	5.8	10.7	17.08.64	Wakefield		Pontefract								
WFAC'91.				£1,500	26.09.85	Derby County	6+13	2+3	1	1+3		1	1	
				£175,000	23.06.89	Oxford United	76+34	10+1	2+2	3+1	15	1		
				Loan	28.03.91	Swansea City	12			3				
				£20,000	24.03.94	Swansea City	40+6	3+1	5	8	7	2	1	
Keith Walker	6.0	11.9	17.04.66	Edinburgh		Stirling Albion	82+9	5	5		16	3	2	
						St Mirren	41+2	3	1	3	6			
				£80,000	23.11.89	Swansea City	159+7	6	20	18	5		1	
F O R W A R D S														
Kwame Ampadu	5.10	10.10	20.12.70	Bradford	19.11.88	Arsenal (T)	0+2							
Ei: u21.4, u17.2, Y.1. AGT'94.				Loan	31.10.90	Plymouth Argyle	6		1		1			
				£50,000	24.06.91	West Bromwich A.	27+22	6+1	1	5	4			1
				£15,000	16.02.94	Swansea City	47+10	3+1	3	9	6		1	
Jonathan Coates	5.8	10.4	27.06.75	Swansea	08.07.93	Swansea City (T)	0+9			1				
Carl Heggs	6.0	11.10	11.10.70	Leicester		Leicester United								
					22.08.91	West Bromwich A.	13+27	2	0+1	6+3	3			1
				Loan	27.01.95	Bristol Rovers	2+3			1				
				£60,000	08.95	Swansea City								
John Hodge	5.6	10.0	01.04.69	Skelmersdale		Falmouth Town								
AGT'94.				Free	12.09.91	Exeter City	57+8	3	2	8+2	10	1		1
				£20,000+P.E.	14.07.93	Swansea City	53+18	4+2	5	11+3	9	1		
Colin Pascoe	5.10	10.0	09.04.65	Port Talbot	12.04.83	Swansea City (T)	167+7	11	9	7	39	3	2	1
W: 10, u21.4, Y. WFAC'83. AGT'94.				£70,000	25.03.88	Sunderland	116+10	12	4+2	5	22	3		
				Loan	24.07.92	Swansea City	15	2			4			
				£70,000	01.08.93	Swansea City	63+5	7+1	2	12	10	2	2	1
Darren Perrett	5.9	11.6	29.12.69	Cardiff		Cheltenham Town								
				Free	09.07.93	Swansea City	11+15	1	1+1	3+1	1		1	3
Stephen Torpey	6.3	13.3	08.12.70	Islington	14.02.89	Millwall (T)	3+4	0+1						
AGT'94.				£70,000	21.11.90	Bradford City	86+10	6	2+1	8	22	6		
				£80,000	03.08.93	Swansea City	73+8	6+1	7	10+2	20	1	4	4
ADDITIONAL CONTRACT PLAYER														
Jason Price				Aberavon										
				Free	08.95	Swansea City								

VETCH FIELD

Swansea SA1 3SU
Tel: 01792 474 114

Capacity 16,550
Covered Standing 13,003
Seating 3,547

ATTENDANCES
Highest ....32,796 v Arsenal, FA Cup 4th Round, 17.2.1968.
Lowest ....1,311 v Brentford, Division 4, 26.4.1976.

OTHER GROUNDS ....None.

MATCHDAY TICKET PRICES

Centre Stand £11

East Stand . . . . Adult £10
. . . . 1+1 - £14, 1+2 - £16

Jewson Stand . . . . Adult £10
. . . . 1+1 £14, 1+2 - £16

Wing Stand £9
OAP £6.50

Terraces £7.50
Juv/OAP £4

Ticket Office Telephone no. 01792 462 584

CLUBCALL
0891 12 16 39

Calls cost 39p per minute cheap rate and 49p per
minute at all other times.
Call costings correct at time of going to press.

HOW TO GET TO THE GROUND

Five minutes walk from city bus station or take South Wales
Transport Co Ltd from High Street General Station to Lowere Oxford
Street.
Car parking near ground at Quadrant.

Car Parking
Car park 200 yards from ground in the Kingsway. Covered super-
vised parking within 75 yards.
There is also ample street parking.

Nearest Railway Station
Swansea High Street (01792 467 777)

MATCHDAY PROGRAMME

Programme Editor . . . . Major Reg Pike, I.S.M, T.D.

Number of pages . . . . 32.

Price . . . . £1.30.

Subscriptions . . . . Please contact club (01792 463 584)

Local Newspapers . . . . Evening Post, Western Mail.

Local Radio Stations . . . . Swansea Sound, BBC Radio Wales.

SWINDON TOWN
(The Robins)
ENDSLEIGH LEAGUE DIVISION 2
SPONSORED BY: CASTROL (UK LTD)

Back Row (L-R): Wayne Allison, Paul Bodin, Shaun Taylor, Fraser Digby, Mark Seagreaves, Andy Thomson, Peter Thorne.
Middle Row: Ian Culverhouse, Kevin Horlock, Jason Drysdale, Stephen Finney, Dean Hooper, Mark Robinson, Luc Nijholt, Ty Gooden, Edwin Murray.
Front Row: Martin Ling, Wayne O'Sullivan, Andy Rowland (1st Team Coach), Steve McMahon (Player/Manager), Ross MacLaren (Reserves Manager), Jonathan Trigg (Physio), Jamie Pitman, Ben Worrall.

SWINDON TOWN
FORMED IN 1879
TURNED PROFESSIONAL IN 1894
LTD COMPANY IN 1894

PRESIDENT: C Green
CHAIRMAN: J M Spearman
VICE-CHAIRMAN
P T Archer
DIRECTORS
P R Godwin CBE, Sir D Seton Wills, Bt,
C J Puffett, J R Hunt (Associate Director)
SECRETARY
Jon Pollard (01793 430 430)
MARKETING CONTROLLER
Phil Alexander

MANAGER: Steve McMahon
FIRST TEAM COACH: Andy Rowland
RESERVE TEAM MANAGER
Rolff MacLaren
YOUTH TEAM MANAGER
John Trollope MBE
PHYSIOTHERAPIST
Jonathan Trigg

STATISTICIAN FOR THE DIRECTORY
Vacant

Swindon Town are not the first club to discover that promotion to the top flight of English football can have serious drawbacks if that success cannot be consolidated. Premier Division fare lasted only one season and this was sadly followed by a further immediate drop from Division One to Division Two, where the club will operate this coming campaign with hopes that nothing worse will follow.

The club will also hope that , after a disastrous initial spell as Manager, Steve McMahon can not only enjoy some success but also set a good personal example and not literally ësee redí again. Is it too much to ask from the former Liverpool star, who took over from the amiable but unlucky John Gorman before Christmas.

In playing terms Swindon had a reasonable start to the competition and by the end of October they appeared to have a chance of challenging for one of the play-off positions, but then league form nosedived and McMahon arrived to face the prospect of trying to save the side from relegation, which became virtually impossible when a goal famine - relieved only by a surprise 5-2 win at West Bromwich - descended on the team. A final position of 21st was the ultimate humiliation.

It was almost incomprehensible that such poor league form was accompanied by a Coca-Cola Cup run that took Swindon past Charlton Athletic (a 3-1 home defeat was followed by a shock 4-1 victory at the Valley), Brighton & Hove Albion (1-1 away and 4-1 in the home reply), Derby County (2-1 at home) and Millwall (3-1 also at the County Ground) with the home leg of the semi-final against Bolton also being won (2-1), before the Lancashire side in an inspired spell turned a 3-1 aggregate deficit into a 4-3 triumph at Burnden Park. The FA Cup saw a 2-0 home win against Marlow followed by a single goal exit at Watford, while the Anglo Italian Cup saw only one win from four outings (3-1 at home to Lecce) with Atlanta winning at Swindon and away losses at Venezia and Ascoli.

In the new season the eccentric Norwegian striker Fjortoft will no longer be with the club, so goals may still be a problem. Consistent performers last campaign were in short supply - not helped by injury problems - but keeper Fraser Digby was still reliable even though he did have to make way for Hammond for a spell. Defenders Robinson, Nijholt and Taylor were also consistent in trying conditions as was Beauchamp in a midfield role, but loss of form and confidence was all too evident elsewhere.

Swindon will need a good start and subsequent consistency to avoid further catastrophes over the next few months.

SWINDON TOWN

Division One: 21st   FA Cup: 4th Round   Coca-Cola Cup: Semi-Finalists

M	DATE	COMP.	VEN	OPPONENTS	RESULT	H/T	LP	GOAL SCORERS/GOAL TIMES	ATT.
1	A 14	EL	H	Port Vale	W 2-0	1-0		Fjortoft 22, Scott 80	10,431
2	20	EL	A	Tranmere Rovers	L 2-3	2-1	8	Fjortoft 9, 43	(8,482)
3	24	AIC	H	Atalanta	L 0-2	0-0			5,167
4	27	EL	H	Watford	W 1-0	1-0	4	Ling 8	9,781
5	31	EL	H	West Bromwich Albion	D 0-0	0-0			11,188
6	S 3	EL	A	Notts County	W 1-0	1-0	2	Fjortoft 40	(6,537)
7	6	AIC	A	Venezia	L 0-1	0-0			(7,000)
8	11	EL	H	Derby County	D 1-1	1-1		Fjortoft 16	9,054
9	14	EL	H	Reading	W 1-0	1-0		Scott 81	11,551
10	17	EL	A	Charlton Athletic	L 0-1	0-1	4		(9,794)
11	21	CC 2/1	H	Charlton Athletic	L 1-2	0-0		Scott 67	4,932
12	24	EL	H	Grimsby Town	W 3-1	1-1	3	Bodin 18, 89 (pen), Scott 90	8,219
13	26	CC 2/2	A	Charlton Athletic	W 4-1	3-0		Fjortoft 2, 27, 42, Petterson 105 (og)	(4,932)
14	O 1	EL	A	Barnsley	L 1-2	0-1	4	Taylor 67	(3,911)
15	5	AIC	H	Lecce	W 3-1	2-0		Mutch 32, 88, Scott 44	2,375
16	8	EL	A	Wolverhampton Wand.	W 3-2	2-2		Bodin 15, Scott 28, Beauchamp 60	14,036
17	15	EL	A	Portsmouth	L 3-4	1-2	5	Bodin 32 (pen), Fjortoft 84, 86	(10,610)
18	22	EL	H	Southend United	D 2-2	1-2	5	Fjortoft 15, 90	9,909
19	26	CC 3	A	Brighton & H.A.	D 1-1	1-0		Thomson 25	(11,382)
20	29	EL	A	Middlesbrough	L 1-3	0-1	5	Fjortoft 56	17,328
21	N 1	EL	A	Bolton Wanderers	L 0-3	0-1	9		(10,046)
22	5	EL	H	Millwall	L 1-2	0-0		Bodin 76 (pen)	9,311
23	9	CC 3R	H	Brighton & H.A.	W 4-1	2-0		Scott 7, 63, Fjortoft 8, 76	6,482
24	15	AIC	A	Ascoli	L 1-3	0-0		Hamon	(750)
25	20	EL	A	Bristol City	L 2-3	0-0		Scott 58, 89	(9,086)
26	23	EL	H	Burnley	D 1-1	1-0		Scott 17	7,654
27	26	EL	H	Luton Town	L 1-2	1-1	19	Scott 11	9,455
28	30	CC 4	H	Derby County	W 2-1	1-1		Fjortoft 8, 84	8,920
29	D 3	EL	A	Southend United	L 0-2	0-1	19		(5,803)
30	10	EL	H	Tranmere Rovers	D 2-2	2-1	20	Rodin 14, Fjortoft 41	8,608
31	17	EL	A	Port Vale	D 2-2	1-1	19	Taylor 25, Fjortoft 50	(7,747)
32	26	EL	A	Stoke City	D 0-0	0-0			(17,662)
33	27	EL	H	Sheffield United	L 1-3	0-	1	Fjortoft 54	11,007
34	31	EL	A	Oldham Athletic	D 1-1	1-1		Ling 24	(8,917)
35	J 7	FAC 3	H	Marlow	W 2-0	0-0		Fjortoft 46, Nijholt 58	7,007
36	11	CC 5	H	Millwall	W 3-1	2-0		Mutch 26, 61, Fjortoft 36	11,772
37	15	EL	H	Middlesbrough	W 2-1	1-1	20	Fjortoft 23, Horlock 57	8,888
38	28	FAC 4	A	Watford	L 0-1	0-1			(11,202)
39	F 4	EL	A	Burnley	W 2-1	1-0	19	Thorne 43, 72	(10,960)
40	12	CC S/F 1	H	Bolton Wanderers	W 2-1	1-1		Thorne 38, 76	15,341
41	15	EL	H	Bristol City	L 0-3	0-1			9,881
42	18	EL	A	Luton Town	L 0-3	0-1	22		(6,595)
43	25	EL	A	Barnsley	D 0-0	0-0	22		8,158
44	M 1	EL	A	Millwall	L 1-3	0-0		Beauchamp 68	(5,950)
45	4	EL	A	Grimsby	D 1-1	0-1	22	Taylor 90	(4,934)
46	8	CC S/F2	A	Bolton Wanderers	L 1-3	0-0		Fjortoft 57	(19,851)
47	11	EL	A	Watford	L 0-2	0-0	22		(7,123)
48	15	EL	H	Sunderland	W 1-0	1-0		Thorne 20	8,233
49	19	EL	A	West Bromwich Albion	W 5-2	0-0	21	Thorne 57, 85, 89, Fjortoft 73, Gooden 81	(12,960)
50	22	EL	A	Derby County	L 1-3	0-2		Viveash 19	(16,839)
51	25	EL	H	Charlton Athletic	L 0-1	0-0	21		9,106
52	A 1	EL	A	Reading	L 0-3	0-2	22		(12,565)
53	5	EL	H	Bolton Wanderers	L 0-1	0-0			8,110
54	8	EL	H	Oldham Athletic	W 3-1	2-1	21	Viveash 24, Beauchamp 27, Taylor 56	7,488
55	15	EL	A	Sheffield United	D 2-2	1-0	21	Gooden 27, Ling 53	(12,217)
56	17	EL	H	Stoke City	L 0-1	0-1			10,549
57	22	EL	A	Sunderland	L 0-1	0-1	21		(16,794)
58	29	EL	H	Portsmouth	L 0-2	0-1	22		9,220
59	M 3	EL	H	Notts County	W 3-0	1-0	21	Hamon 8, Thorne 58, 65	6,553
60	7	EL	A	Wolverhampton Wand.	D 1-1	1-1	21	Thorne 38	(26,254)

Best Home League Attendance: 14,036 v Wolverhampton Wand.   **Smallest:** 6,553 v Notts County   **Av Home Att:** 9,408

Goal Scorers:

Compared with 1993-94: -5,148

League (53):   Fjortoft 16, Thorne 9, Scott 8, Bodin 6, Taylor 4, Beauchamp 3, Gooden 2, Ling 2, Viveash 2, Hamon, Horlock
C/Cola Cup (18):   Fjortoft 9, Scott 3, Mutch 2, Thorne 2, Thomson, Opponent
FA Cup (2):   Fjortoft, Nijholt
Anglo-Ital Cup (4):   Mutch 2, Hamon, Scott

Digby	Robinson	Odin	Whitebread	Nijholt	Taylor	Ling	Fenwick	Fjortoft	Mutch	Horlock	O'Sullivan	Scott	Hammond	Kilkline	Beauchamp	Thomson	Berkley	Murray	Webb	Tiler	Maclaren	Hamon	McMahon	Culver House	Thorne	Referee	
1	2	3	4	5	6	7*	8	9	10•	11	12	14	S													M. Pierce	1
1	2	3		5	6	7	8	9	10•	11		12	S	4*	14											A. Dawson	2
																											3
1	2	3		5	6	7		9	S	11		10	S		8	4										P. Vanes	4
1	2	3		5	6	7		9	S	S	11	10	S		8	4										P. Harrison	5
1	2			5	6	7		9*	12	14	11•	10	S		8	4										K. Lynch	6
S*	2			5		7		9	3	11			1*	4	8	6	10	14			12						7
1	2	3		5	6	7		9	12	11•	14	10*			8	4										G. Singh	8
1	2	3		5	6	7				11*	10	12	S	S	8	4										M. Brandwood	9
1	2	3		5	6*	7		9	14	11	10•				8	S	12									S. Dunn	10
1	2	3		5*		7		9	10	11			S	6	8	4		12	S							D. Gallagher	11
1	2	3		5	6	10		9	14	7*	12	11	S		8•	4										T. Lunt	12
1	2	3		5	6	10		9	12	S	7	11*	S		8	4										G. Pooley	13
1	2	3		5	6			12	9	7	11	S		4	8	S	10									K. Lupton	14
1	2	3		5	6	10		9	S	7	11		S		8	4	S										15
1	2	3		5	6	10•		9	12	S	11*		S		8	4										P. Foakes	16
1	2	3		5	6	10•		9	14	12	11		S	4	8			7*								P. Vanes	17
1	2	3		5	6	10		9	12	14	11		S		8•	4*		7								A. Flood	18
1	2	3		5	6	10		9	S	7	11		S	S	8	4										P. Alcock	19
1	2	3		5	6*	10		9	14	7*	11		S		8	4		12								E. Lomas	20
1	2	3		5*		12		9	14	7	11		S	6	8•	4		10								W. Burns	21
1	2	3		5		14		9	12	7*	11		S	6		4†		10•								E. Parker	22
1	2	3		5		7		9	10	S	11		S	6	8	4	S									R. Gifford	23
12	2					10		9	3	7	11		1*	6	8	5	S	S			4	12					24
1	2	3						9	10	7	14	11	S	5*	8			12	4	6•						P. Wright	25
1	2	3						9	10	8	7•	11	S		12	5		6		4*	S					P. Alcock	26
1	2	3						9	19•	8	7•	11	S	6	12	5				4*	14					C. Wilkes	27
1	2	3		5				9	8	7		11	S	6*	14	4					6†					J. Kirkby	28
1	2	3		5				9	12	S	7	S	11	S	8	4					6†					S. Dunn	29
1	2	3		5	6	10		9	12	7	S				8	4						10	6			P. Harrison	30
		3		5	6	10		9	S	7	S	11	S		8	5							2			E. Wolstenholme	31
1	2	3		5	6	10		9	S	7	12	11	S		8	5							4			D. Allison	32
1	2	3*		5•	6	10		9	12	7	14	11	S		8								4			A. Flood	33
S	2	3		5	6	11		9	8	7			1		12		S						10*		4	M. Riley	34
S	2	3		5	6	11		9	10	7			S		8•							14			4*	P. Vanes	35
S	2	3		5	6	11		9	10	7			S		8			S							4	P. Foakes	36
S	2	3		5	6	11		9	10	7			S		8			S							4	G. Pooley	37
S	2	3		5*	6	11		9	10•	7					8			3						12	4	P. Danson	38
S	2	3		5	6	11		9	S	7					8			3					4*		10	N. Barry	39
S	2+	3		5		11		9	S	7		4	1		8		S	3							10	P. Alcock	40
S	2			5		11		9	S	7		4	1		8	6*		3					12		10	J. Lloyd	41
S	2					11		9	12	5		4	1		8			3				6			10	J. Kirkby	42
S	2			5	6			9	3	7			1		8			3				11	4		10	M. Pierce	43
S					6	12		9	3	7			1		8	5•						11	2*		10	P. Foakes	44
1					6			9	7		2		S		8		S					11			10	T. Heilbron	45
1				5	6	S		9	7		2		S		8							11			10	I. Cruickshanks	46
1				5	6			9	8	2*			S		12							11			10	P. Harrison	47
1				5	6	S		9	5	2			S		8							11			10	K. Breen	48
1	5					S		9	7	2*			S		8							11			10	W. Burns	49
1	11			5*	6	12		9		2			S		8	S						11			10	J. Winter	50
1	5				6	9*				12			S		8							11			10	K. Leach	51
1	5*			S	6	7			3				S		8						12	11			10	S. Dunn	52
1	5			S	6	S			3	7			S		8							11†			10	G. Barber	53
1	2			5	6*	3				6					8							11			10	J. Holbrook	54
1	2			5	6	7				S		S			8	S						11			10	E. Lomas	55
1	2*			5	6	7•				14					8	12						11			10	G. Singh	56
1	2			5	6	11				7		S			8								12		10	T. West	57
1				5	6	11				7		S			8	3									10	J. Brandwood	58
1	2			5	6	11			3	14		S			8•				9						10	D. Orr	59
1	2			5	6	12			3+	4		S			8			14	9						10	J. Watson	60

Digby	Robinson	Odin	Whitebread	Nijholt	Taylor	Ling	Fenwick	Fjortoft	Mutch	Horlock	O'Sullivan	Scott	Hammond	Kilkline	Beauchamp	Thomson	Berkley	Murray	Webb	Tiler	Maclaren	Hamon	McMahon	Culver House	Thorne		
39	40	25	1	35	37	31	2	36	7	32	21	21	7	6	39	20	4	5	2	3	2	16	9		20	League Appearances	
					5				14	4	8			1	4	1						1	1	3	1	League Sub Appearances	
6	7	6		8	5	6+1		8	3+1	5	5	5	2		1	4	1					1		3	1	C/Cola Cup Appearances	
2	1		2	2	2		2	2	0+2	2	2	2		1								0+1	2	0+1	2	FA Cup Appearances	

Also Played: Gooden S(38),12(39,49),7*(42,45),14(44),11(46),7,(47),7(48,50,51),9(52,53,54,55,56,57)9.(58), Drysdale 3(51), Hamblin S(52,53,54) Todd 4(44,45) ,3(47,48,49,50,55,56) ,3*(57),2*(58) Viveash 5(45),4(46,47,48,49,50,51,52,53,54,55,56,57,58,59), Worrall 12(58,59),11(60) Hooper 12(45,47,54),S(46),14(57), Pitman 14(58),7(59*60*) Loan Players: Webb (Notts Forest)

SWINDON TOWN

RECORDS AND STATISTICS

CLUB RECORDS

BIGGEST VICTORIES
League: 9-1 v Luton Town, Division 3S, 28.4.1921
8-0 v Newport County, Div 3S, 26.12.1938
8-0 v Bury, Division 3, 8.12.1979
F.A. Cup: 10-1 v Farnham United Breweries FC (a), Round 1, 28.11.1925
League Cup: 6-0 v Torquay United (a), Rnd 2 1st leg 23.9.1992
BIGGEST DEFEATS
League: 0-9 v Torquay United, Division 3S, 8.3.1952
F.A. Cup: 1-10 v Manchester City, Round 2, 29.1.1930
League Cup: 0-5 v Notts County, Round 3, 1962-63
0-5 v Liverpool, Round 3, 1980-81
MOST POINTS
3 points a win: 102, Division 4, 1985-86 (League record)
2 points a win: 64, Division 3, 1968-69
MOST GOALS
100, 1926-27, Division 3S.
Morris 47, Eddelston 11, Thom 8, Wall 7, Petrie 6, Denyer 5, Dickinson 3, Flood 3, Jeffries 3, Archer 1, Weston 1, Brown 1, Bailey 1, Johnson 1, Daniel 1, og1.
MOST LEAGUE GOALS CONCEDED
105, Division 3S, 1932-33
MOST FIRST CLASS MATCHES IN A SEASON
64 (46 League, 4 FA Cup, 4 League Cup, 5 Freight Rover Trophy, 5 Play-offs)1986-87
MOST LEAGUE WINS: 32, Division 4, 1985-86
MOST LEAGUE DRAWS: 17, Division 3, 1967-68
MOST LEAGUE DEFEATS: 25, Division 3S, 1956-57

BEST PERFORMANCES
League: 1985-86: Matches played 46, Won 32, Drawn 6, Lost 8, Goals for 82,Goals against 43, Points 102. First in Division 4.
Highest: 1989-90: 4th Division 2.
F.A. Cup: 1910: 1st rnd. Crystal Palace 3-1; 2nd rnd. Burnley 2-0; 3rd rnd.Tottenham Hotspur 3-2; 4th rnd. Manchester City 2-0; Semi-Final Newcastle Utd. 0-2.
1912: 1st rnd. Division 3S, Notts County 2-0; 3rd rnd. West Ham United1-1, 4-0; 4th rnd. Everton 2-1; Semi-Final Barnsley 0-0, 0-1.
League Cup: 1968-69: 1st rnd. Torquay 2-1; 2nd rnd. Bradford City 1-1;4-3; 3rd rnd. Coventry City 2-2, 3-0; 4th rnd. Derby County 0-0, 1-0; Semi-Final Burnley 2-1; Final Arsenal 3-1.
HONOURS: Division 4 champions 1985-86. League Cup winners 1968-69. Anglo Italian Cup winners 1970.
LEAGUE CAREER
Division 1/P: 1993-94.
Division 2/1: 1963-65, 1969-74, 1987-93, 1994-95
Division 3: 1920-21, 1958-63, 1965-69, 1974-82, 1986-87, **1995-**
Division 3(S): 1921-58.
Division 4: 1982-86.

INDIVIDUAL CLUB RECORDS

MOST GOALS IN A MATCH
5. Harry Morris v Queens Park Rangers, 18.12.1927, Div 3S (6-2).
5. v Norwich City, 26.4.1930, Div 3S (5-1).
5. Keith East v Mansfield, 20.11.1965, Div 3. (6-2).

MOST GOALS IN A SEASON
Harry Morris 48, (47 League, 1 FA Cup) 1926-27.
5 goals once=5; 4 goals once=4; 3 goals 3 times=9; 2 goals 5 times=10; 1 goal 20 times=20.

OLDEST PLAYER
Alex Ferguson 43 years 103 days, v Bristol City (Div. 3S), 15.11.1947.

YOUNGEST PLAYER
Paul Rideout, 16 years 107 days v Hull (Div 3), 29.11.1980).

MOST CAPPED PLAYER
Rod Thomas (Wales) 30

PREVIOUS MANAGERS

Ted Vizard 1933-39, Neil Harris 1939, Louis Page 1945-53, Maurice Lindley 1953-58, Bert Head 1958-65, Danny Williams 1965-69, Fred Ford 1969-71, Dave Mackay 1971-72, Les Allen 1977-74, Danny Williams 1974-78, Bob Smith 1978-80, John Trollope 1980-83, Ken Beamish 1983-84, Lou Macari 1984-89, Osvaldo Ardiles 1989-91, Glenn Hoddle 1991-93, John Gorman 1993-94.

ADDITIONAL INFORMATION
Previous Name: None.

Previous League: Southern League.

Club colours: Red shirts, shorts & socks with white & green trim.

Change colours: Blue & black shirts, blue shorts, blue socks.

Reserves League: Avon Insurance Combination Division 1.

LONGEST LEAGUE RUNS

of undefeated matches:	22 (12.1.1986 - 23.8.1986)	of league matches w/out a win:	9 (17.4.1993 - 20.11.1993)
of undefeated home matches:	26 (24.2.1968 - 29.3.1969)	of undefeated away matches:	13 (18.1.1986 - 6.9.1986)
without home win:	10 (28.2.56-15.9.56, 17.4.93-20.11.93)	without an away win:	30 (25.11.1972 - 15.4.1974)
of league wins:	8 (2.1.26-27.3.26, 12.1.86-15.3.86)	of home wins:	14 (26.8.1985 - 15.3.1986)
of league defeats:	6 (1967, 3.5.8.1980 - 6.9.1980)	of away wins:	6 (18.1.1986 - 8.3.1986).

THE MANAGER

STEVE McMAHON . . . . appointed November 1994.

PREVIOUS CLUBS
As Manager. . . . . None.
As Asst.Man/Coach . . . . None.
As a player. . . . . Everton, Aston Villa, Liverpool, Manchester City, Swindon.

HONOURS
As a Manager . . . . None.
As a Player . . . . Liverpool: Division 1 championship 1986, 1988, 1990. FA Cup 1986, 1989.
. . . . Charity Shield 1986,1988,1989. Super Cup 1986.

SWINDON TOWN

PLAYERS NAME / Honours	Ht	Wt	Birthdate	Birthplace / Transfers	Contract Date	Clubs	APPEARANCES League	L/Cup	FA Cup	Other	GOALS Lge	L/C	FAC	Oth
G O A L K E E P E R S														
Fraser Digby	6.1	12.12	23.04.67	Sheffield	25.04.85	Manchester Utd (A)								
E: S, u21.5, u19.1, Y.7.				£32,000	25.09.86	Swindon Town	323	30	13	30+1				
D E F E N D E R S														
Ian Culverhouse	5.10	11.2	22.09.64	Bishop's Stort	24.09.82	Tottenham H. (A)	1+1							
E: Y.6. Div.2'86.				£50,000	08.10.85	Norwich City	295+1	23	28	22	1			
				£250,000	30.12.94	Swindon Town	9	1	2					
Jason Drysdale	5.10	12.0	17.11.70	Bristol	08.09.88	Watford (T)	135+10	8+1	2	4	11	2		
E: Y.5. FAYC'89.				£425,000	02.08.94	Newcaslte United								
				£340,000	23.03.95	Swindon Town	1							
Kevin Horlock	6.0	12.0	01.11.72	Bexley	01.07.91	West Ham U. (T)								
NI: B.1.				Free	27.08.92	Swindon Town	79+11	7+1	5	4	2			
Brian Kilcline	6.2	12.0	07.05.62	Nottingham	01.04.80	Notts County (A)	156+2	16	10		9	1	2	
E: u21.2. FAC'87. Div.1'93.				£60,000	11.06.84	Coventry City	173	16+1	15	8	28	4	3	
				£400,000	01.08.91	Oldham Athletic	8	2						
				£250,000	19.02.92	Newcaslte United	20+12	3+2	1+2	5				
				£90,000	20.01.94	Swindon Town	16+1	3		4				
Ross MacLaren	5.10	12.12	14.04.62	Edinburgh		Glasgow Rangers (J)								
Div.2'87. WFAC'85.				Free	15.08.80	Shrewsbury Town	158+3	11	7+1		18	3	1	
				£67,000	11.07.85	Derby County	113+9	13	9	5	4	1		
				£165,000	04.08.88	Swindon Town	195+2	21	11	16	9	2		1
Lee Middleton	5.11	10.12	10.09.70	Nuneaton	30.05.89	Coventry City (T)	0+2							
				Free	20.07.92	Swindon Town								
Edwin Murray	5.11	12.0	31.08.73	Ilford	09.07.91	Swindon Town (T)	4+3	2	1+1					
Mark Seagraves	6.0	12.10	22.10.66	Bootle	04.11.83	Liverpool (A)		1	1					
E: Y.4, S.				Loan	21.11.86	Norwich City	3							
				£100,000	25.09.87	Manchester City	36+6	3	3	2				
				£100,000	24.09.90	Bolton Wanderers	152+5	8	17	13	8		1	1
				Free	08.95	Swindon Town								
Shaun Taylor	6.1	12.8	26.02.63	Plymouth		Bideford								
Div.4'90.				Free	10.12.86	Exeter City	200	12	9	12	17			
				£200,000	26.07.91	Swindon Town	167	17	8	7	23	2		1
Andrew Thomson	6.3	12.0	28.03.74	Swindon	01.05.93	Swindon Town (T)	21+1	5		3	1			
Adrian Viveash	6.1	11.9	30.09.69	Swindon	14.07.88	Swindon Town (T)	51+3	6+1	0+1	2	3			
Loan 04.01.93 Reading 5 Lge. 1 Oth. App. 1 Oth. gl.				Loan	20.01.95	Reading	6							
M I D F I E L D														
Austin Berkley	5.9	10.10	28.01.73	Dartford	13.05.91	Gillingham (T)	0+3			0+3				
				Free	16.05.92	Swindon Town	0+1	0+1		3+1				1
Paul Bodin	5.10	10.11	13.09.64	Cardiff		Chelsea (J)								
W: 22, u21.1, Y.				Free	28.01.82	Newport County								
				Free	01.08.82	Cardiff City	68+7	11	4		4			
				Free		Bath City			8				3	
				£15,000	27.01.88	Newport County	6			1				
				£30,000	07.03.88	Swindon Town	87+6	12	6	8	9			1
				£550,000	20.03.91	Crystal Palace	8+1	1						
				Loan	05.12.91	Newcaslte United	6							
				£225,000	10.01.92	Swindon Town	103+5	10	6	7	26			1
Ty Gooden	5.8	12.06	23.10.72	Canvey Island		Arsenal (T)								
via Wycombe Wands. (Free) to				Free	31.01.94	Swindon Town	15+5	1		0+1	2			
Dean Hooper	5.10	11.06	13.04.71	Harefield		Hayes								
					03.03.95	Swindon Town	0+4	0+1						
Paul Hughes	6.1	11.5	19.04.76	Hammersmith	11.07.94	Chelsea (J)								
				Free	08.95	Swindon Town								
Steve McMahon	5.9	12.1	20.08.61	Liverpool	29.08.79	Everton (A)	99+1	11	9		11	3		
E: 17, u21.6, B.2. Div.1'86'88'90. FAC'86'89.				£175,000	20.05.83	Aston Villa	74+1	9	3	4	7			
CS'86'88'89. SC'86. FLgXI.1.				£375,000	12.09.85	Liverpool	202+2	27	30	16	29	13	7	1
				£900,000	24.12.91	Manchester City	77+3	7	3		1			
					01.12.94	Swindon Town	16+1							
Luc Nijholt	5.11	11.8	29.07.61	Amsterdam		Basle O.B.								
SFAC'91.				£125,000	01.08.90	Motherwell	91+5	6	9	2	5		1	
				£175,000	20.07.93	Swindon Town	66+1	11	3+1	3	1		1	
Wayne O'Sullivan	5.11	11.2	25.02.74	Cyprus	01.05.93	Swindon Town (T)	22+8	5	0+2	2			1	
Jamie Pitman	5.9	10.09	06.01.76	Trowbridge	08.07.94	Swindon Town (T)	2+1							
Mark Robinson	5.9	10.6	21.11.68	Rochdale	10.01.87	West Brom. A. (A)	2	0+1						
				Free	23.06.87	Barnsley	117+20	7+2	7+1	3+2	6			1
				£450,000	09.03.93	Newcaslte United	14+11		1					
				£600,000	22.07.94	Swindon Town	40	7	2	4				
Ben Worrall	5.8	10.06	07.12.75	Swindon	08.07.94	Swindon Town (T)	1+2							
E: Y.1.														
F O R W A R D S														
Wayne Allison	6.1	13.5	16.10.68	Huddersfield	06.07.87	Halifax Town (T)	74+10	3	4+1	8+1	21	2		3
				£250,000	26.07.89	Watford	6+1							
				£300,000	09.08.90	Bristol City	112+46	4+5	9+1	6+2	35	2	5	3
				£475,000	08.95	Swindon Town								
Joseph Beauchamp	5.10	11.10	13.03.71	Oxford	16.05.89	Oxford United (T)	117+7	6+1	8	5+1	20	2	3	
FLg.u18.1.				Loan	30.10.91	Swansea City	5		1		2			
				£1,000,000	22.06.94	West Ham United								
				£850,000	22.06.94	Swindon Town	38+4	7+1	2	4	3			
Stephen K Finney	5.10	12.0	31.01.73	Hexham	02.05.92	Preston N.E. (T)	1+5		0+1	1+1	1			
				Free	12.02.93	Manchester City	1		1					
Chris Hamon	6.2	12.6	27.04.70	Jersey		St. Peters								
				Free	08.07.92	Swindon Town	3+5		0+1	0+2	1			1
Martin Ling	5.8	10.2	15.07.66	West Ham	13.01.84	Exeter City (A)	109+8	8	4	5	14			
				£25,000	14.07.86	Swindon Town	2	1+1						
				£15,000	16.10.86	Southend United	126+12	8	7	11+1	31	2	1	3
Loan 24.01.91 Mansfield Town 3 Lge App.				£15,000	28.03.91	Swindon Town	120+13	11+1	8	9+1	10	1		
Andy Mutch	5.10	11.3	28.12.63	Liverpool		Southport								
E: B.3, u21.1, Div.4'88. Div.3'89. SVT'88.					25.02.86	Wolverhampton W.	277+12	14	11+1	23	99	4	1	4
				£250,000	16.08.93	Swindon Town	34+16	6+1	4	3	6	3	1	2
Peter Thorne	6.0	12.3	21.06.73	Manchester	20.06.91	Blackburn Rovers								
Loan 11.03.94 Wigan Ath. 10+1 Lge App.				£200,000	18.01.95	Swindon Town	20+1	2	0+1		9	2		

COUNTY GROUND
Swindon SN1 2ED
Tel: 01793 430 430

Capacity 15,341

First game ....v Old St Stephens, 13.5.1893.
First floodlit game ....v Bristol City, 02.04.1951.

ATTENDANCES
Highest ....32,000 v Arsenal, FA Cup, 15.1.1972. 29,106 v Watford, Division 3, 29.3.1969.
Lowest ....1,681 v Darlington, Division 4, 17.4.1984.

OTHER GROUNDS..Bradford's Field, Globe Field, The Croft (1884-1895)

MATCHDAY TICKET PRICES

Seats . . . . £9 - £12.50

Juv/OAP . . . . £4.50 - £7

Ticket Office Telephone no. 01793 529 000

HOW TO GET TO THE GROUND

From all directions
Two miles towards Town Centre from M4, junction 15.

Car Parking
Town centre car parks. No off street parking.

Nearest Railway Station
Swindon (01793 536 804) 10-15 minutes walk.

CLUBCALL
0891 12 16 40
Calls cost 39p per minute cheap rate and 49p per minute at all other times.
Call costings correct at time of going to press.

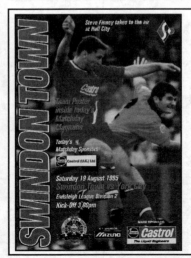

MATCHDAY PROGRAMME

Programme Editor. . . . . Jon Pollard.

Number of pages . . . . 40.

Price . . . . £1.50.

Subscriptions . . . . £50.

Local Newspapers . . . . . . Wiltshire Newspapers (Evening Advertiser),
. . . . Western Daily Press.

Local Radio Stations . . . . GWR, BBC Wiltshire Sound.

WALSALL
(The Saddlers)
ENDSLEIGH LEAGUE DIVISION 2
SPONSORED BY: CHOICE PERSONNEL

Back Row (L-R): Charlie Ntamark, Wayne Evans, Chris Marsh, James Walker, Adrian Thompson, Trevor Wood, Ian Roper, Stuart Ryder, Darren Bradley.
Middle Row: Eric McManus (Youth Team Coach), Stuart Watkiss, Charlie Palmer, Kyle Lightbourne, David Richards, Darren Rogers, Martin Butler, James Rollo, Ray Daniels, Tom Bradley (Physio).
Front Row: Colin Gibson, Scott Houghton, Kevin Wilson, Chris Nicholl (Manager), Martin O'Connor, John Keister, Chris Smith.

WALSALL
FORMED IN 1888
TURNED PROFESSIONAL IN 1888
LTD COMPANY IN 1921

CHAIRMAN: J W Bonser
DIRECTORS
K R Whalley, M N Lloyd, C Welch,
R Tisdale
SECRETARY
Roy Whalley (01922 22791)
COMMERCIAL MANAGER
Roy Whalley

MANAGER: Chris Nicholl
PLAYER/COACH: Kevin Welson

YOUTH TEAM COACH
Eric McManus
PHYSIOTHERAPIST
Tom Bradley

STATISTICIAN FOR THE DIRECTORY
Mervyn Sargeant

Few Saddler's fans can have expected the excitement and success of 1994/95. Two key signings arrived during the summer - Trevor Wood, who fully deserved his international call-up to the Northern Ireland squad, and Kevin Wilson who easily won the player of the season award. His experience and skill helped to turn Kyle Lightbourne into the clubs 27 goal top scorer, and Wilson chipped in with 22 goals himself. Between them they scored over half of Walsall's goals, and many were of the highest quality.

Yet the season started badly with only one of the first four league games being won. Even so, many were surprised with the timing of Kenny Hibbitt's dismissal. Paul Taylor took over on a Caretaker basis before, out of the blue, experienced Chris Nicholl became manager.

Nicholl's only transfer activity was to sell McDonald to Partick, but the transformation in skill, commitment, passion and play was at times breathtaking. Experienced players were given a new lease of life, and promising players began to realise their potential with Stuart Ryder earning a call up for the England Under 21 squad.

In the cup competitions West Ham were beaten 2-1 at Bescot in the first leg of the Coca-Cola cup, and Leeds were 4 minutes away from defeat before securing a replay in the FA Cup. Both needed extra-time to eventually gain victory. The only disappointment was failure to progress in the Auto Windscreen Shield.

Comfortably placed with games in hand throughout most of the second half of the season, defeat by Chesterfield in March, then one point from matches against Wigan and Rochdale in April, meant that their mathematical advantage had gone. The final three games, against play-off hopefuls Scunthorpe, form team Scarborough, and promotion rivals Bury were all to be played inside six days.

Walsall travelled to Scarborough on the same night that Chesterfield played 'champions-elect' Carlisle. A nerve-racking 90 minutes followed with Walsall securing victory, whilst fans were listening to radios for the Chesterfield score. Carlisle's victory meant that one point from the final game at Bury would give Walsall promotion.

The Bury match was even more stressful as the Saddler's dug in to earn the draw that secured promotion and signalled celebrations for over 3,000 travelling fans. If Walsall can retain Chris Nicholl as manager, supporters can look forward to 1995-96 with renewed optimism.

MERVYN SARGEANT.

WALSALL

Division Two: 2nd **FA Cup:** 3rd Round **Coca-Cola Cup:** 2nd Round

M	DATE	COMP.	VEN	OPPONENTS	RESULT	H/T	LP	GOAL SCORERS/GOAL TIMES	ATT.
1	A 13	EL	A	Fulham	D 1-1	1-0	8	Lightbourne 8	(5,308)
2	16	CC 1/1	H	**Plymouth Argyle**	W 4-0	0-0		**Wilson 53, 72, Lightbourne 74, O'Connor 83**	2,810
3	20	EL	H	Lincoln City	W 2-1	1-0	5	O'Connor 39 (pen), Marsh 57	3,813
4	23	CC 1/2	A	**Plymouth Argyle**	L 1-2	0-1		**Wilson 75**	(2,801)
5	27	EL	A	Hereford United	D 0-0	0-0	10		(3,004)
6	30	EL	H	Carlisle United	L 1-2	1-1	12	Marsh 12	3,610
7	S 3	EL	H	Northampton Town	D 1-1	1-1	12	Lightbourne 10	4,249
8	10	EL	A	Chesterfield	D 0-0	0-0	13		(3,027)
9	13	EL	A	Colchester United	L 2-3	1-0	16	Lightbourne 23, Houghton 89	(2,239)
10	17	EL	H	Fulham	W 5-1	3-0	11	Marsh 3, 42, Lightbourne 24, 49, 52	3,378
11	20	CC 2/1	H	**West Ham United**	W 2-1	1-1		**Watkiss 25, Potts 74 (og)**	5,994
12	24	EL	H	Gillingham	W 2-1	1-0	10	Wilson 45, Ryder 61	3,654
13	O 1	EL	A	Preston North End	W 2-1	0-1	7	O'Connor 55, Marsh 64	(7,852)
14	5	CC 2/2	A	**West Ham United**	L 0-2	0-0			(13,553)
15	8	EL	H	Scarborough	W 4-1	1-1	5	O'Connor 6 (pen), Ryder 52, Houghton 77	3,601
16	15	EL	A	Scunthorpe United	W 1-0	1-0	3	Wilson 3	(3,609)
17	18	AWS P	A	**Birmingham City**	L 0-3	0-1			(10,089)
18	22	EL	A	Hartlepool United	D 1-1	1-1	4	Lightbourne 24	(1,704)
19	29	EL	H	Bury	L 0-1	0-0	5		5,255
20	N 5	EL	A	Darlington	D 2-2	0-1	5	Gregan 52 (og), Marsh 84	(2,186)
21	8	AWS P	H	**Peterborough United**	L 2-3	1-0		Gibson 18, Marsh 78	2,104
22	12	FAC 1	H	**Rochdale**	W 3-0	2-0		**Lightbourne 34, Butler 42, 78**	3,619
23	19	EL	H	Exeter City	W 1-0	1-0	5	O'Connor 45	3,629
24	26	EL	A	Mansfield Town	W 3-1	2-0	5	Wilson 34, O'Connor 42, Ntamark 74	(2,733)
25	D 3	FAC 2	A	**Preston North End**	D 1-1	1-1		**Wilson 33**	(9,767)
26	10	EL	A	Lincoln City	D 1-1	1-1	5	Wilson 12	(2,717)
27	13	FAC 2R	H	**Preston North End**	W 4-0	2-0		**Houghton 33, Wilson 42, Lightbourne 64, 77**	6,468
28	17	EL	A	Hereford United	W 4-3	1-2	5	Houghton 27, Lightbourne 47, 55, Ryder 58	3,652
29	26	EL	H	Barnet	W 4-0	2-0	3	Palmer 14, Wilson 30, Lightbourne 48, 64	5,392
30	27	EL	A	Rochdale	W 2-0	1-0	3	Wilson 38 (pen), Lightbourne 74	(2,438)
31	31	EL	A	Doncaster Rovers	W 1-0	0-0	2	Marsh 77	4,561
32	J 7	FAC 3	H	**Leeds United**	D 1-1	1-0		**Marsh 29**	8,619
33	14	EL	A	Torquay United	L 2-3	1-0	2	Houghton 45, Marsh 62	(2,976)
34	17	FAC 3R	A	**Leeds United**	L 2-5	1-2		**O'Connor 29 (pen), Wilson 69**	(17,881)
35	F 4	EL	H	Mansfield Town	W 1-0	0-0	2	Wilson 78	4,369
36	18	EL	H	Torquay United	W 1-0	0-0	3	Ryder 64	3,708
37	28	EL	H	Preston North End	D 2-2	1-1	3	Marsh 14, Wilson 48	4,429
38	M 4	EL	A	Gillingham	W 3-1	0-0	3	Lightbourne 53, 56, Houghton 80	(3,669)
39	7	EL	H	Hartlepool United	W 4-1	1-1	3	O'Connor 4, Houghton 55, 90, Wilson 83	3,314
40	11	EL	H	Chesterfield	L 1-3	0-1	4	Lightbourne 81	6,219
41	14	EL	H	Darlington	W 2-0	1-0	3	Lightbourne 19, Wilson 60	3,154
42	18	EL	A	Carlisle United	L 1-2	1-0	3	Wilson 13	(7,769)
43	25	EL	A	Northampton Town	D 2-2	1-1	3	Lightbourne 35, Wilson 82	(6,282)
44	A 1	EL	H	Colchester United	W 2-0	0-0	3	Lightbourne 71, O'Connor 83 (pen)	3,622
45	4	EL	A	Exeter City	W 3-1	1-0	3	O'Connor 41, Lightbourne 68, 89	(1,551)
46	8	EL	A	Doncaster Rovers	W 2-0	1-0	3	Wilson 6, 56	(2,368)
47	11	EL	A	Wigan Athletic	L 0-1	0-1	3		(2,176)
48	15	EL	H	Rochdale	D 0-0	0-0	3		3,766
49	17	EL	A	Barnet	W 3-1	2-1	3	Ryder 24, Wilson 37, Lightbourne 58	(2,078)
50	22	EL	H	Wigan Athletic	W 2-0	0-0	3	O'Connor 49, Lightbourne 72	3,508
51	29	EL	H	Scunthorpe United	W 2-1	0-0	3	Palmer 69, Lightbourne 78	4,539
52	M 2	EL	A	Scarborough	W 2-1	0-0	2	Houghton 48, Wilson 59	(2,841)
53	4	EL	A	Bury	D 0-0	0-0	2		(6,790)
54									
55									
56									
57									
58									
59									
60									

Best Home League Attendance: 6,219 v Chesterfield **Smallest:** 3,154 v Darlington **Av Home Att:** 4,068

Goal Scorers: **Compared with 1993-94:** -165

League (75): Lightbourne 23, Wilson 16 (1 pen), O'Connor 10 (4 pens), Marsh 9, Houghton 8, Ryder 5, Palmer 2, Ntamark, Gregan
Opponent
C/Cola Cup (7): Wilson 3, Lightbourne, O'Connor, Watkiss, Opponent
FA Cup (11): Lightbourne 3, Wilson 3, Butler 2, Houghton, Marsh, O'Connor (pen)
AW Trophy (2): Gibson, Marsh

1994-95

Wood	Evans	Rogers	Watkiss	Marsh	Palmer	O'Conner	N/Amark	Lightbourne	Wilson	Mehew	Keester	Ullis	Butler	Rider	Embleton	Peer	Houghton	Gibson	Wacker	Thompson	Referee	
1	2	3	4†	5	6	7	8	9	10	11*	12	S									A. D'Urso	1
1	2*	3	4	5	6	7	8	9	10	11	S	12									G. Pooley	2
1	2	3	4	5	6	7*	8	9	10	11•	12	14									E. Lomas	3
1	2	3	4	5	6	7	8	9*	10	11			12	8	S						C. Wilkes	4
1	2	3		5	6	7	8	9	10	11*			4•	S	12	14					S. Mathieson	5
1†	2	3	4	5	6	7	8	9	10	11*			12	S	S						D. Orr	6
1	2	3	4	5	6	7	8	9	10					S	S	11	S				G. Lane	7
	2*	3		5	6	7	8	9	10				12	S	S	11	4	1			A. Butler	8
S		3		5	6		8	9	10	S	S		2		7	11	4	1			R. Harris	9
1	2	3	S	5	6	7	12	9	10*					8	11	4	S				M. Riley	10
1	2	3	4	5	6*	7	11•	9	10	14			12		8		S				P. Harrison	11
1	2	3	4*	S		7		9	10	S			12		8	11	6	S			P. Wright	12
1		3	4	S			7	S	9	10	S		2		8	11	6	S			R. Furnandiz	13
1	14	3	4	5*	6	7•	12	9	10	11			2		8		S				J. Holbrook	14
1	5•	12	4*		6	7		9	10	8			14	2		11	3	S			E. Wolstenholme	15
1	S	4			6	7*	S	9	10	8			2		12	11	3	S			K. Lupton	16
1	S	4			6		S	9	10	8*	12		2		7	11	3	S			G. Singh	17
1		4		5	6	7	8	9*	10			S	12	2		11	3	S			J. Watson	18
1		4		5	6	7	8	9	10	12			2		S	11*	3	S			G. Barber	19
1		4		5	6	7	8	9	10	S			2		S	11	3	S			T. West	20
1	2	4		5	6	7	8	S	10		S		9			11	3	S			P. Harrison	21
1	2	4		5	6	7	8	10*		12			9•		14	11	3	S	S		G. Ashby	22
1	2			5	6	7	8	9	10				12	4	S	S	11*	3			K. Breen	23
1	2			5	6	7*	8	9	10	14				4	S	12	11•	3			I. Hemley	24
1	2	S		5	6	7	8	9	10				12	4	S		11*	3			R. Hart	25
1	2	S		5	6	7	8*	9	10				12	4	S		11	3			P. Richards	26
1	2			5	6	7*	8	9	10•				14	4	S	12	11	3			R. Hart	27
1	2			5	6	7	8	9	10*		S		12	4	S		11	3			N. Barry	28
1	2	12		5	6	7*	8	9	10•	14				4			11	3	S		E. Parker	29
1	2	12		5	6		8	9	10		7			4		14	11•	3*	S		J. Winter	30
1	2	S		5	6	7	8	9	10	8				4			11	3	S		M. Pierce	31
1	2	S		5	6	7	8	9	10	12				4			11	3*	S		J. Winter	32
1	2	S		5	6	7	8	9	10	S				4			11	3	S		K. Cooper	33
1		14	2	5	6	7•	8	9	10*	12				4			11	3	S		J. Winter	34
1	2	3		5	6	7	8	9	10	S	S			4			11		S		I Crukshanks	35
1	2	3		5	6	7	8	9	10	S	S			4			11		S		T. Heilbron	36
1	2	S		5	6	7	8	9	10	S				4			11	3	S		S. Mathieson	37
1	2	12		5	6		8	9	10•	14				4			11	3*	S		S. Dunn	38
1	2	S		5	6	7	8	9*	10	12				4			11	3	S		U. Riennie	39
1	2	S		5	6	7	8	9	10	S				4			11	3	S		E. Lomas	40
1	2	12		5	6		8	9	10•	14	7			4			11	3*	S		K. Lynch	41
1	2	3		5	6	7		9	10	S	8			4		S	11		S		J. Rushton	42
1	2	S	6	5	6	7		9*	10	12	8			4			11	3	S		M. Riley	43
1	2			5*	6	7	12	9	10		8	8		4			11	3	S		P. Harrison	44
1	2			5	6	7	8	9	10*	12	8			4			11	3	S		M. Pierce	45
1	2	12		5	6	7	8	9	10		8			4			11	3*	S		T. West	46
1	2	S		S*	6	7	12	9	10		8			4			11	3	S		O. Alleson	47
1	2	S		5	6	7	12	9	10		8*			4			11	3	S		U. Rennie	48
1	2	12			6	7	8	9	10•				14	4		5	11*	3	S		P. Foulkes	49
1	2	12		5	6	7	8	9	10					4		5	11	3*	S		A. Dawson	50
1	2	3		12	6	7*	8	9	10			S		4		S	11		S		G. Barber	51
1•	2	3		12	6	7	8	9	10					4		S*	11•	14	15•		J. Winter	52
	2	3	S	5	6	7*	8	9	10					4	8		11	12	1		G. Cain	53
39	36	20	8	36	39	39	31	42	42	6	9		1	34	8	38	31	3			League Appearances	
	7		2			4			7	2	1	7	2	1	4		2	1			League Sub Appearances	
4	3+1	4	4	4	4	4	3+1	4	4	3+1		0+1	0+1	1+1	2						C/Cola Cup Appearances	
5	1+1	1+1	1	5	5	5	5	5	4	0+3			1+2	4		0+2	5	5			FA Cup Appearances	
2	1	2		1	2	1	2	1	2	1	0+1		1	1		1	2	2			AW Trophy Appearances	

CLUB RECORDS

RECORD LEAGUE VICTORY
10-0 v Darwen,Div 2, 4.3.1899
Most Goals Scored in a First Class Cup Tie: 6-1 v Leytonstone (a),
Round 1,30.11.1946   6-1 v Margate, Round 1, 24.11.1955

RECORD LEAGUE DEFEAT
0-12 v Small Heath, Div 2, 17.12.1892   0-12 v Darwen,Div 2,
26.12.1896
Record Cup Defeat: 0-6 v Wednesday Town, FA Cup Round 2,
1883-84   0-6 v West Bromwich Albion, FA Cup Rnd 1 replay, 1899-
1900   0-6 v Aston Villa, FA Cup Round 1, 1911-12

MOST LEAGUE POINTS
(3pts for win) 82, Div 3, 1987-88
(2pts for win) 65, Div4, 1959-60

MOST LEAGUE GOALS
102, Division 4, 1959-60

RECORD TRANSFER FEE RECEIVED
£600,000 from West Ham United for David Kelly, August 1988

RECORD TRANSFER FEE PAID
£175,000 to Birmingham City for Alan Buckley, June1979

BEST PERFORMANCES
League: 6th Div 2 1898-99
FA Cup: 5th Round 1939, 1975,1978 and last sixteen 1889
League Cup: Semi-Final 1983-84

HONOURS
Champions Div 4 1959-60

LEAGUE CAREER
Elected to Div 2 1892   Failed to gain re-election 1895
Rejoined Div 2 1896   Failed re-election 1901   Elected as original
members of Div 3N 1921   Transferred to Div 3S 1927
Transferred to Div 3N 1931   Transferred to Div 3S 1936
Joined Div 4 1958   Promoted to Div 3 1959-60
Promoted to Div 2 1960-61   Relegated to Div 3 1962-63
Relegated to Div 41978-79   Promoted to Div 3 1979-80
Promoted to Div 2 1987-88   Relegated to Div 3 1988-89
Relegated to Div 4(now Div 3) 1989-90 Promoted to Div 2 1994-95

INDIVIDUAL CLUB RECORDS

MOST APPEARANCES FOR CLUB
Colin Harrison (1964-82): League 452+15 + FA Cup 36+ League
Cup 19 Total 507+15 subs
Most Capped Player: Mick Kearns 15, Eire   For England: None
RECORD GOALSCORER IN A MATCH
Johnny Devlin 5 v Torquay United (h), 7-1, Div3S, 1.9.1949   Gilbert
Alsop 5 v Carlisle Utd (a), 6-1, Div 3N, 2.2.1935   W.Evans 5 v
Mansfield Town, 7-0, Div 3N, 5.10.1935
RECORD LEAGUE GOALSCORER IN A SEASON
Gilbert Alsop 40, Div 3N, 1933-34, 1934-35 In All Competitions:
Gilbert Alsop 44 (League 40 + FA Cup 4) 1934-35
RECORD LEAGUE GOALSCORER IN A CAREER
Tony Richards 184, 1954-63   In All Competitions: Alan Buckley 204
(League 174 + Cups 30) 1973-84
OLDEST PLAYER IN A LEAGUE MATCH
Des Bremner 37 years 240 days v Bristol City, 5.5.1990
YOUNGEST PLAYER IN A LEAGUE MATCH
Geoff Morriss 16 years 218 days v Scunthorpe, 14.9.1965

PREVIOUS MANAGERS

1921-26 J Burchell   1926-27 D Ashworth   1927-28 J Torrance   1928-
29 J Kerr   1929-30 S Scholey   1930-32 P O'Rourke   1932-34 W
Slade   1934-37 Andy Wilson   T Lowes 1937-44   1944-51 Harry
Hibbs   1951-52 G McPhee   1952-53 Brough Fletcher   1953-56
Frank Buckley   1956-57 John Love   1957-64 Bill Moore   1964 Alf
Wood   1964-68 Ray Shaw   1968 Dick Graham   1968-69 Ron Lewin
1969-72 Bob Moore   1972-73 John Smith   1973 Jim McEwan   1973
Ronnie Allen   1973-77 Doug Fraser   1977-78 Dave Mackay   1978
Alan Buckley   1978Alan Ashman   1978 Frank Sibley   1978-81 Alan
Buckley   1981-82 Neil Martin   1982-86 Alan Buckley   1986-88
Tommy Coackley   1988-89 Ray Train   1989-90 John Barnwell
1990 Paul Taylor   1990-94 Kenny Hibbitt   1994- Chris Nichol

ADDITIONAL INFORMATION
Previous Name: Walsall Swifts (1877) and Walsall Town (1879)
amalgamated and played as Walsall Town Swifts until 1895

Club Colours: Red/black and white trim, black shorts with red and
white trim, red socks with black & white trim.
Change Colours: Claret & royal blue stripes, royal blue shorts with
claret and white trim, royal blue socks with claret hoops.

Reserves League: Midland Senior League **Youth Team:** Purity Lge

LONGEST LEAGUE RUNS

of undefeated matches:	21 (1979-80)	of league matches w/out a win:	18 (1988-89)
of undefeated home matches:	26 (1960-61)	of undefeated away matches:	13 (1979-80)
without home win:	10 (1988-89, 1989-90)	without an away win:	29 (1953-54)
of league wins:	7 (1933-34)	of home wins:	9 (1973)
of league defeats:	15 (1988-89)	of away wins:	6 (24.4.1993 - 18.9.1993)

THE MANAGER

Chris Nicholl . . . . appointed September 1994.

PREVIOUS CLUBS
As Manager . . . . Southampton.
As Asst.Man/Coach . . . . Grimsby Town.
As a player . . . . Burnley, Witton Albion, Halifax Town, Luton Town, Aston Villa, Southampton, Grimsby Town.

HONOURS
As a Manager . . . . Division 3 championship 1972. League Cup 1975.
As a Player . . . . None.

WALSALL

PLAYERS NAME Honours	Ht	Wt	Birthdate	Birthplace Transfers	Contract Date	Clubs	League	L/Cup	FA Cup	Other	Lge	L/C	FAC	Oth
							APPEARANCES				**GOALS**			
G O A L K E E P E R S														
Adrian Thompson			13.03.77	Sydney	24.04.95	Walsall (T)								
James Walker	5.11	11.8	09.07.73	Nottingham	09.07.91	Notts County (T)								
				Free	04.08.93	Walsall	34+1		4	1				
Trevor Wood	6.0	12.6	03.11.68	Jersey	07.11.86	Brighton & H.A. (A)								
				Free	08.07.88	Port Vale	42	4	2	2				
				Free	18.07.94	Walsall	39	4	5	2				
D E F E N D E R S														
Ray Daniel	5.10	11.0	10.12.64	Luton	07.09.82	Luton Town (A)	14+8	2	5+1		4			
				Loan	01.09.83	Gillingham	5							
				Free	30.06.86	Hull City	55+3	1	1+1	0+1	3			
				£40,000	22.08.89	Cardiff City	56	5	5	1	1			
				£80,000	09.11.90	Portsmouth	91+9	7+2	6	6+1	4			1
				Free	03.08.95	Walsall								
Wayne D Evans	5.10	12.0	25.08.71	Welshpool		Welshpool								
				Free		Walsall	77	5+1	8	3				
Colin Gibson	5.08	10.10	06.04.60	Bridport	13.04.78	Aston Villa (A)	181+4	26	12	14+1	10	4	1	2
E: B.1, u21.1, Y. ESC'82. Div.1'81.				£275,000	29.11.85	Manchester United	74+5	7	8+1	2	9			1
				Loan	27.09.90	Port Vale	5+1				2			
				£100,000	21.12.90	Leicester City	50+9	4	1+1	7+1	4			
				Free	12.08.94	Blackpool	1+1	2						
				Free	02.09.94	Walsall	31+2		5	2				1
Charles Palmer	5.11	12.05	10.07.63	Aylesbury	13.07.81	Watford (A)	10	2		4	1			
				Free	12.07.84	Derby County	51	7	1	2	2			
				£32,000	13.02.87	Hull City	69+1	3	3	2	1			
				£25,000	15.02.89	Notts County	178+4	9	10	19	7			2
				Free	22.07.94	Walsall	39	4	5	2	2			
Darren Rogers	5.9	11.2	09.04.70	Birmingham	05.07.88	West Brom A. (T)	7+7		0+1	1	1			1
				Free	01.07.92	Birmingham City	15+3	2	0+1	5				
				Loan	05.11.93	Wycombe W.	0+1			1				
				Free	19.07.94	Walsall	20+7	4	1+2	2				
Ian Roper	6.4	14.0	20.06.77	Nuneaton	15.05.95	Walsall (T)								
Stuart Ryder	6.0	12.1	06.11.73	Sutton C'field	16.07.92	Walsall (T)	74+10	3+1	8	4+1				
Stuart Watkiss	6.2	13.7	08.05.66	Wolverhampton	13.07.84	Wolverhampton (T)	2							
				Free	28.02.86	Crewe Alexandra	3							
				Free		Rushall Olympic								
				Free	05.08.93	Walsall	46+1	6	4	2	3			
M I D F I E L D														
Darren Bardley	5.7	11.10	24.11.65	Birmingham	19.12.83	Aston Villa (A)	16+4	3						
E: u19.3, Y.3.					14.04.86	West Bromwich A.	236+18	13	10	11	9	1	2	1
				Free	01.08.95	Walsall								
Scott Houghton	5.05	11.06	22.10.71	Hitchin	24.08.90	Tottenham H. (T)	0+10	0+2		0+2	2			
E: Y.7, S.. FAYC'90.				Loan	26.03.91	Ipswich Town	7+1				1			
				Loan	17.12.92	Gillingham	3							
				Loan	26.02.93	Charlton Athletic	6							
				Free	10.08.93	Luton Town	7+9	2+1	0+1	2	1			
				£15,000	07.09.94	Walsall	38		5	2	8		1	
John Kiester	5.8	11.0	11.11.70	Manchester	18.09.93	Walsall	26+7		4	0+1	1			
Sierra Leonne Int.														
Charles Ntamark	5.8	11.12	22.07.64	Paddington		Boreham Wood								
Cameroon Int.				Free	22.08.90	Walsall	186+10	13+1	14	15	11	1		1
Martin O'Connor	5.8	10.8	10.12.67	Walsall		Bromsgrove Rovers			1					
SLP'92.				£25,000	26.06.92	Crystal Palace	2		1+1					
				Loan	24.03.93	Walsall	10		2	1				1
				Loan	14.02.94	Walsall	14				2			
				£40,000	.08.94	Walsall	39	4	5	1	10	1	1	
Chris Smith			03.01.77	Birmingham	15.05.95	Walsall (T)								
F O R W A R D S														
Martin Butler	5.10	11.3	15.09.74	Wordsley	24.05.93	Walsall (T)	10+13	0+1	1+2	1	3		2	
Kyle Lightbourne	6.2	11.0	29.09.68	Bermuda	11.12.92	Scarborough	11+8	1		0+1	3			
Bermuda Int.				Free	17.09.93	Walsall	76+1	4	9	3	30	1	5	
Chris Marsh	6.0	12.10	14.01.70	Sedgley	11.07.88	Walsall (T)	129+28	7+2	11+1	11+1	9		2	
David Richards			31.12.76	Birmingham	24.04.95	Walsall (T)								
Kevin Wilson	5.7	10.7	18.04.61	Banbury		Banbury United								
NI: 40. Div.2'89. FMC'90.				£20,000	21.12.79	Derby County	106+16	8+3	8		30	8	3	
				£100,000	05.01.85	Ipswich Town	94+4	8	10	7	34	8	3	4
				£335,000	25.06.87	Chelsea	124+28	10+2	7+1	14+5	42	4	1 8	
				£225,000	27.03.92	Notts County	58+11	3+1	2	5+1	3			
				Loan	13.01.94	Bradford City	5							
				Free	02.08.94	Walsall	42	4	4	2	16	2	3	

BESCOT STADIUM

Bescot Crescent, Walsall WS1 4SA
Tel: 01922 22791

Capacity 10,400
Seating 4,500

First game ....v Aston Villa, Friendly, 18.8.1991.
First floodlit game ....v Cambridge Utd, Lge Cup, 28.8.1991.

ATTENDANCES
Highest ....10,628, England 'B' v Switzerland, 20.5.1991.
Lowest ....1,837 v Mansfield Town, AMC Rnd 1, 8.12.1992.

OTHER GROUNDS ....Fellows Park.

MATCHDAY TICKET PRICES

Gilbert Alsop Terrace Advanced £7.50/Matchday £8
Juv/OAP . . . . £5/£6
H.L.Fellows Stand Centre . . . . £11/£12
Juv/OAP Block J,K,Q,R, only. . . . . £7/£8
Highgate Stand Non-Members. . . . . £11/£12
Family Area (2 adults per Juv.). . . . . £10/£11
Adults. . . . . £8/£9
Juv . . . . £2/£2
Non-Members . . . . £13/£14
Adults . . . . £11/£12
Juv . . . . £2/£2
William Sharp Stand. £10
Juv £6
Swifts Club. £20
Reserve Games. £3

HOW TO GET TO THE GROUND

From the North
Use A461, sign posted Walsall, then join A4148 Broadway North around Ring Road. Turn left at traffic lights into Bescot Crescent, ground on left.

From the East, South and West
Use motorway M6 until junction 9, leave motorway and follow signs Walsall A461, then turn right A4148 into Broadway West. Turn right at first set of traffic lights into Bescot Crescent Stadium on left.

Car Parking
Car park for 1,200 vehicles at ground.

Nearest Railway Station
Bescot Stadium Station 5 yards from Ground.

OFFICIAL CLUBCALL
0898 55 58 00
Calls cost 39p per minute cheap rate and 49p per minute at all other times.
Call costings correct at time of going to press.

MATCHDAY PROGRAMME

Programme Editor. . . . . Don Stanton.

Number of pages . . . . 32.

Price . . . . £1.50.

Subscriptions. . . . . Apply to club shop.

Local Newspapers . . . . Wolverhampton Express & Star,
. . . . Birmingham Evening Mail, Birmingham Post & Mail,
. . . . Walsall Observer.

Local Radio Stations . . . . . . BBC Radio West Midlands, BRMB Radio,
. . . . Beacon Radio.

WREXHAM
(The Robins)
ENDSLEIGH LEAGUE DIVISION 2
SPONSORED BY: WREXHAM LAGER

Back Row (L-R): Lewis Coady, Karl Connolly, Scott Williams, Barry Jones, Mark Cartwright, Barry Hunter, Andy Marriott, Mark McGregor, Ken Dixon, Paul Jones, Jonathan Cross, Stephen Futcher, Gareth Owen. **Middle Row:** Mel Pejic (Player/Physio), Joey Jones (Coach), Steve Morris, Kieron Durkan, Peter Ward, Wayne Phillips, Mike Cody, Steve Watkin, David Ridler, Craig Skinner, Richard Barnes, Kevin Russell, Mike Buxton (Schoolboy Dev. Officer), Cliff Sear (Yth Dev. Officer). **Front Row:** Steve Weaver (Community Officer), Bryan Hughes, David Brammer, Tony Humes, Kevin Reeves (Asst. Manager), Brian Flynn (Manager), Phil Hardy, Deryn Brace, Richard Rawlins, Dudley Hall (Res. Team Physio).

WREXHAM
FORMED IN 1872
TURNED PROFESSIONAL IN 1912
LTD COMPANY IN 1912

PRESIDENT: G Mytton
CHAIRMAN: W P Griffiths
VICE-CHAIRMAN
B Williams
DIRECTORS
C Griffiths, S F Mackreth, D Rhodes, C G Paletta
SECRETARY
D Rhodes (01978 262 129)
COMMERCIAL MANAGER
P Stokes (01978 352 536)

MANAGER: Brain Flynn
ASSISTANT MANAGER: Kevin Reeves
COACHES: Brian Prandle & Dudley Hall
SCHOOLBOY, YOUTH & RESERVE TEAM MANAGEMENT
Cliff Sear, Mike Buxton, Joey Jones
PHYSIOTHERAPIST
Mel Pejic

STATISTICIAN FOR THE DIRECTORY
Gareth Davies

Same again with a bonus could well be a summing up of Wrexham's season, while 'hot and cold', 'hit and miss' could also be apt descriptions of the club's second campaign in the Second Division after ten season's in the basement.

To finish one place below the previous season's 12th position perhaps shows no improvement, but there 'are' signs of further progress in the Racecourse club's bid to emulate past glories in the late seventies.

On their day the present Wrexham side are a match for any team in the Second Division 'and' further up the scale, illustrated in the FA Cup win over Premier League club Ipswich Town and the trip to Old Trafford, when the Robin's took the game to Manchester United. Performing far better than the scoreline suggests and making the FA Cup holders sweat more than a little.

Inconsistency however, plagued many of the league performances, but with so many youngsters now establishing themselves and learning their trade, the Division's more physical sides are coming out on top with the junior members of the Wrexham team unable to match them in this aspect of the game, prompting a call for Brian Flynn to persuade an experienced midfield general to join the ranks at the Racecourse, to supplement the obvious skills present.

The fact that eight own goals were conceded during the season also points fingers at lack of understanding in the back four but now that full-back Barry Jones has joined new international Barry Hunter in the heart of the defence, there is a more solid look about the rearguard, with young Deryn Brace at right-back progressing apace with his committed displays (ala Joey Jones!).

Perhaps another two quality players are required to provide a 'serious' challenge for promotion to augment the talent already at the club, for example, 'a goalscorer' to hopefully replace Gary Bennett who has now sadly departed, 'Benno' had scored his 100th goal in two and half seasons by the end of February, a phenomenal record for a player who, prior to his move to Wrexham, had played wide right for most of his career; Karl Connolly with his dazzling wing play, Barry Jones, Gareth Owen, who must begin to produce the goods more consistently soon, Phil Hardy and the afore mentioned Barry Hunter joining his father Victor, plus Uncle's Alan Hunter and Willie McFaul as a full Northern Ireland international.

Of the players, the final mention must go to Bryan Hughes, who is the real find of the season among the current staff at the Racecourse, and seems destined to reach the very top level if he continues his present rate of progress. Awareness, movement, first touch and a penchant for scoring quality goals are just some of the attributes of this latest product from the Wrexham F.C. youth factory.

The club is now running on the right lines on the field but the Racecourse is fast becoming 'off track'. In the ground development stakes, something needs to be done now if they are to keep up with other ambitious clubs in the league - the three sided ground can't help the players' moral and does not show the club in good light when trying to attract new talent.

Wrexham's 66th! match of the season, against Cardiff City in the Welsh Cup final, brings us to the 'bonus'.....a Cup final victory that will bring further chances of European glory next season.

GARETH M DAVIES.

WREXHAM

Division Two: 13th   **FA Cup:** 4th Round   **Coca-Cola Cup:** 2nd Round   **Auto Windscreen Trophy:** 2nd Round

M	DATE	COMP.	VEN	OPPONENTS	RESULT	H/T	LP	GOAL SCORERS/GOAL TIMES	ATT.
1	A 13	EL	H	Bournemouth	W 2-0	2-0	7	Pejic 37, Bennett 42 (pen)	3,580
2	15	CC 1/1	A	Doncaster Rovers	W 4-2	0-1		Bennett 46, Connolly 64, Watkin 86, 90	(1,925)
3	20	EL	A	Shrewsbury Town	D 2-2	2-1	7	Bennett 6, 12	(5,748)
4	23	CC 1/2	H	Doncaster Rovers	D 1-1	1-0		Watkin 12	2,215
5	27	EL	H	Brighton & H.A.	W 2-1	1-0	4	Bennett 34, 88 (pen)	3,339
6	30	EL	A	Cardiff City	D 0-0	0-0	7		(4,903)
7	S 3	EL	A	Brentford	W 2-0	2-0	4	Watkin 12, Phillips 22	(5,820)
8	10	EL	H	Crewe Alexandra	W 1-0	1-0	3	Owen 58	6,399
9	13	EL	H	Bradford City	L 0-1	0-1	5		4,179
10	17	EL	A	Bristol Rovers	L 2-4	0-1	7	Brammer 49, Connolly 85	(4,441)
11	20	CC 2/1	H	Coventry City	L 1-2	1-1		Jones 43	5,286
12	24	EL	A	Blackpool	L 1-2	0-0	12	Cross 74	(5,015)
13	27	AWS PR	A	Crewe Alexandra	D 0-0	0-0			(1,573)
14	O 1	EL	H	Birmingham City	D 1-1	1-0	13	Connolly 39	6,002
15	5	CC 2/2	A	Coventry City	L 2-3	1-1		Cross 42, Bennett 71 (pen)	(8,561)
16	8	EL	A	Cambridge United	W 2-1	0-0	8	Bennett 48, 74 (pen)	(3,221)
17	15	EL	H	Hull City	D 2-2	0-1	10	Hughes 66, Bennett 77 (pen)	3,418
18	18	AWS PR	H	Mansfield Town	W 2-0	1-0		Bennett 40, 89	1,002
19	22	EL	H	Oxford United	W 3-2	2-2	10	Richardson 19, 60, Connolly 26	3,925
20	30	EL	A	Chester	D 1-1	0-1	11	Owen 56	(4,974)
21	N 1	EL	A	Huddersfield Town	L 1-2	0-1	11	Connolly 86	(9,639)
22	5	EL	H	Wycombe Wanderers	W 4-1	2-0	8	Bennett 15, 57, 65, Connolly 30	3,747
23	12	FAC 1	H	Stockport County	W 1-0	0-0		Watkin 80	4,748
24	19	EL	A	Plymouth Argyle	L 1-4	0-3		Durkan 21	(6,936)
25	26	EL	H	Swansea City	W 4-1	2-0	7	Hughes 24, Watkin 35, 66, Owen 71	3,598
26	29	AWS 1	H	Bradford City	W 6-1	4-0		Bennett 2, 14, 55, Watkin 17, 42, Owen 52	1,407
27	D 3	FAC 2	H	Rotherham United	W 5-2	1-1		Connolly 35, 90, Bennett 58, Hughes 61, Watkin 81	4,521
28	10	EL	H	Shrewsbury Town	L 0-1	0-0	11		5,859
29	16	EL	A	Bournemouth	W 3-1	1-1	6	Hughes 34, Watkin 75, Bennett 85	(2,505)
30	26	EL	A	Stockport County	D 1-1	0-1	9	Bennett 67	(5,636)
31	27	EL	H	Peterborough United	D 3-3	0-2	11	Bennett 46 (pen), 82, Morris 67	4,689
32	J 7	FAC 3	H	Ipswich Town	W 2-1	0-0		Durkan 59, Bennett 86 (pen)	8,324
33	10	AWS 2	H	Carlisle United	L 1-2	0-1		Bennett 61	(8,773)
34	14	EL	H	Leyton Orient	W 4-1	1-0	13	Bennett 6, 48, 64, Connolly 58	6,616
35	28	FAC 4	A	Manchester United	L 2-5	1-2		Durkan 9, Cross 89	(43,222)
36	F 4	EL	H	Swansea City	D 0-0	0-0	13		(4,563)
37	7	EL	A	York City	W 1-0	1-0	12	Bennett 33	(3,140)
38	11	EL	H	Huddersfield Town	L 1-2	1-0	12	Bennett 9	5,894
39	14	EL	H	Chester	D 2-2	2-1	12	Connolly 15, Bennett 18	5,698
40	18	EL	A	Leyton Orient	D 1-1	0-1	12	Hughes 83	(3,135)
41	21	EL	H	Plymouth Argyle	W 3-1	0-1	10	Bennett 61, 90, Hughes 68	3,030
42	25	EL	A	Birmingham City	L 2-5	2-1	12	Bennett 12, 27	(18,884)
43	M 4	EL	H	Blackpool	L 0-1	0-0	13		4,251
44	7	EL	H	Brentford	D 0-0	0-0	14		2,834
45	11	EL	A	Brighton & H.A.	L 0-4	0-0	14		(7,514)
46	14	EL	H	Rotherham United	W 3-1	1-1	13	Hughes 35, Durkan 72, Bennett 89	1,823
47	18	EL	H	Cardiff City	L 0-3	0-1	14		3,023
48	21	EL	A	Crewe Alexandra	W 3-1	0-0	13	Morris 55, Connolly 67, Bennett 82	(3,632)
49	25	EL	H	Bristol Rovers	D 1-1	0-1	13	Hughes 72	3,170
50	A 1	EL	A	Bradford City	D 1-1	1-1	13	Bennett 11	(4,461)
51	4	EL	A	Oxford United	D 0-0	0-0	13		(4,729)
52	8	EL	H	York City	D 1-1	0-0	14	Connolly 88	2,558
53	11	EL	A	Wycombe Wanderers	L 0-3	0-3	14		(5,115)
54	15	EL	A	Peterborough United	L 0-1	0-1	14		(4,309)
55	17	EL	H	Stockport County	W 1-0	0-0	14	Hughes 66	3,049
56	22	EL	A	Rotherham United	W 1-0	0-0	12	Bennett 59	(2,628)
57	29	EL	A	Hull City	L 2-3	1-2	13	Connolly 31, Hughes 72	(3,683)
58	M 6	EL	H	Cambridge United	L 0-1	0-1	13		3,172
59									
60									

Best Home League Attendance: 6,616 v Leyton Orient   **Smallest:** 1,823 v Rotherham United   **Av Home Att:** 4,080

Goal Scorers:

Compared with 1993-94: + 147

League (65): Bennett 29, Connolly 10, Hughes 9, Watkin 4, Owen 3, Richardson 2, Durkan 2, Morris 2, Brammer, Cross, Pejic, Phillips
C/Cola Cup (8): Watkin 3, Bennett 2, Connolly, Cross, Jones
FA Cup (10): Connolly 2, Bennett 2, Watkin 2, Durkan 2, Hughes, Cross
AW Trophy (9): Bennett 6, Watkin 2, Owen

Marriott	Jones B	Hardy	Hughes	Humes	Hunter	Pejic	Brace	Phillips	Williams	Brammer	Durran	Lake	Owen	Taylor	Connolly	Cross	Watkin	Bennett	Morris	Pugh	Richardson	Quigley	Coady	Barnes	McGregor	Referee	
1	2	3		5	S	6		12			4		8*		9	11	10	7								P. Harrison	1
1	2	3		5	S	6		11*			8		4	12	9		10	7								J. Watson	2
1	2	3		5	14	6·		12			8		4·	11	9		10	7								T. West	3
1	2	3		5	6		S	4			8		11		9		10	7								M. Riley	4
1	2	3	S	5	6		S	4			8		11		9		10	7								A Dawson	5
1	2	3	14	5	6			12			4		8	11·	9		10	7*								K. Leach	6
1	2	3	S	5*	5	6		12			4		8	11	9		7	10·								P. Foakes	7
1	2	3	S	5	6			12	4*		11		8		9	14	10·	7								K. Lynch	8
1	2	3	S	5	6			S	4		11		8		9		10	7								P. Wright	9
1	2	3		5	6			S	4		11		8		9	12	10	7*								J. Hemsley	10
1	2	3		5	6			S	4		11		8		9		S	7								E. Lomas	11
1	2·	3		5	6	14			4		11		8*		9	12	10	7								U. Rennie	12
1	2	3	4·	5	6					14	11		8		9	10*	S	7								J. Brandwood	13
1	2	3	4	5	6				S		11		8		9	10·	S	7								K. Breen	14
1	2	3	4*	S	5	6					11		8		9	10	S	7								K. Burge	15
1	2		4	6	5			S			11		8		9	10	S	7								N. Barry	16
1	2	3	4	3	5	6		12			11*		8		9	10	S	7								E. Wolstenholme	17
1	2	3	11	6	5				4				8		9	10	S	7								A. Flood	18
1	2	3	11	6	5								8		9	10	S	7			4					G. Cain	19
1	2	3	11	6	5			S					8		9	10	S	7			4					J. Cruikshanks	20
1	2	3	11*	6	5			S					8		9	10	12	7			4					J. Watson	21
1	2	3	11*	6	5			12					8		9	10	S	7			4					S. Mathieson	22
1	2	3	11	6	5			4·			14		8		9	10	12	7								M. Reed	23
1	2	3	4	6*	5			12					8		9	10*	10	7·								K. Cooper	24
1	5	3	4			6	2						8		9	14	10	7	S							J. Kirkby	25
1	6*	3	4		5		2	12			11·		8		9	S	14	10	7							P. Richards	26
1	5	3	4			6	2	12					8		9	14	10	7	S							A. Flood	27
1	5	3	4			6	2	S		11*			8		9		10	7								R. Furnandiz	28
1	2	3	4	5		6			S				11		8	9*	10	7								G. Pooley	29
1	2	3	4	5	S	6					11		8		9	10	7		10	S						E. Wolstenholme	30
1	2	3	4	5	14	6·					11*		8		9	10*	7		10	12						R. Poulain	31
1	2	3	4	6	5	S					11		8		9	10*	7	S								J. Rushton	32
1	2	3	4	5	14						11		8		9	12	7	12								J. Winter	33
1	2	3	4	6	5·						11		8		9	11	7	12								P. Richards	34
1	2	3	4·	6	5			14			11		8		9*	S	10	7								M. Bodenham	35
1	2	3	4	6	5			8	S						9	S	10	7	S							M. Pierce	36
1	2	3	4	6*	5	12					8		11		9	12	10	7								T. West	37
1	2	3	4	5	6			8*			11				9	11	10	7								J. Parker	38
1	2	3	4	5	6			S			11*		8		9	11	10	7								A. Dawson	39
1	2	3	4	5	6			S							9	11*	10	7	S			8				C. Wilkes	40
1	2	3	4	5	6			S			12				9		10	7	S			8				K. Lynch	41
1	2	3	4	5	6			S			11*		12		9		10	7				8				A. Butler	42
1	2	3	4	6	5										9	9·	10	7				8				P. Rejer	43
1	2	3	4	5		6		11	S				8*		9		10	7	S							R. Poulain	44
1	2	3	4	5		6		11	12	14	11		8		9·		10	7								G. Pooley	45
1	6	3	10	5			2	4	S				8		9		S	7								N. Barry	46
1	2	3	11	6	5			4	S		11				9	10*	10*	7	12							P. Harrison	47
1	6	3	4		5		2	S	8		11				9		S	7	10							D. Allison	48
1	6	3	4		5		2	S	8		11				9		12	7								U. Rennie	49
1	6	3	4		5		2	S	8		11				9		S	7	10*							J. Rushton	50
1	6	3	4		5		2	S	8		11				9		12	7	10*							A. Flood	51
1	6	3	4	S	5			2	8		11				9		12	7	10*							G. Singh	52
1	6	3	4		5		2	12	8*		11				9		14	7	10·							J. Holbrook	53
1	6	3	4		5			2			8	11*	12		9		10·	7	S							M. Riley	54
1	6	3	14	5			2		8·		12				9		10*	7						11		J. Parker	55
1		3	4	6	5		2	S	8		S				9			7	10					11		J. Watson	56
1			4*	3	5	6		2			8	11			9		S	7	10						12	S. Mathieson	57
1	6	3	4					2			8·	11	14		9		12	7*	10						5	P. Richards	58
46	44	44	37	28	35	18	10	13	8	13	28	2	24	3	45	18	24	45	10		4	4	2		1	League Appearances	
	1		1		2	2	4	5	2	1	2					6	7		2	1					1	League Sub Appearances	
4	4	4	1	3	2			2			3	2	1		2	1+1	4	1+1	3+1	4						C/Cola Cup Appearances	
4	4	4	4	2	4	1	1	0+1	0+1	1	3		4		4	2+2	2	4	0+1							FA Cup Appearances	

Players on Loan: Richardson (Cardiff City) Quigley (Manchester City)

† = Sent Off

WREXHAM   RECORDS AND STATISTICS

CLUB RECORDS

RECORD LEAGUE VICTORY
10-1 v Hartlepool, Div 4, 3.3.1962
Most Goals Scored in a Cup Tie: 11-1 v New Brighton (h), Div 3N
Cup, 1933-34
RECORD LEAGUE DEFEAT
0-9 v Brentford, Div 3, 15.10.1963
Record Cup Defeat: 1-9 v Wolverhampton Wanderers, FA Cup Rnd
3, 1930-31
MOST LEAGUE POINTS
(2pts for win) 61, Div 4, 1969-70, Div 3, 1977-78
(3pts for win) 80 Div 3, 1992-93
MOST LEAGUE GOALS
106, Div 3N, 1932-33

RECORD TRANSFER FEE PAID
£210,000 to Liverpool for Joey Jones, Oct 1978
RECORD TRANSFER FEE RECEIVED
£300,000 from Manchester United for Mickey Thomas, Nov 1978
£300,000 from Manchester City for Bobby Shinton, July 1979
£300,000 + further £300,000 on completion of set amount of first
team appearances from Liverpool for Lee Jones, March 1992
£300,000 from Tranmere Rovers for Gary Bennett, June 1995.

BEST PERFORMANCES
League: 15th Div 2, 1978-79
FA Cup: 6th Round 1973-74,1977-78
League Cup: 5th Round 1961, 1978   Welsh Cup: Winners (23),
Runners-up (22). This is a record number of victories and appear-
ances in the Final
European Cup Winners Cup: Quarter-Final 1975-76
European Competitions entered
European Cup Winners Cup: 1972-73, 1975-76,1978-79, 1979-80,
1984-85, 1986-87, 1990-91
HONOURS
Div 3 Champions 1977-78   Welsh Cup Winners (23)
Welsh Cup Runners-Up (22)

LEAGUE CAREER
Original members of Div 3N 1921   Transferred to Div 3 1958
Relegated to Div 4 1959-60 Promoted to Div 3 1961-62
Relegated to Div 4 1963-64 Promoted to Div 31969-70
Promoted to Div 2 1977-78   Relegated to Div 3 1981-82
Relegated to Div 4 1982-83 (now Div 3) Promoted to Div 2 1992-93

INDIVIDUAL CLUB RECORDS

MOST APPEARANCES FOR CLUB
Arfon Griffiths (1959-61 & 1962-79) Total 586+6 subs (not including
Cup ties)
MOST CAPPED PLAYER
Joey Jones (Wales) 29   0For England: None
RECORD GOALSCORER IN A MATCH
A Livingstone 7 v Tranmere Rovers, Wartime Football League
North, 25.10.1943   T Bamford 6 v New Brighton (h), 11-1, Div3N
Cup, 1933-34   T H Lewis 5 v Crewe Alexandra (h) 7-0, Div 3N,
20.9.1930   T Bamford 5 v Carlisle United (h) 8-1, Div 3N, 17.3.1934
RECORD LEAGUE GOALSCORER IN A SEASON
Tommy Bamford, 44, Div 3N, 1933-34
RECORD LEAGUE GOALSCORER IN A CAREER
Tommy Bamford, 175, 1929-35
OLDEST PLAYER IN A LEAGUE MATCH
W. Lot Jones 46 years, 1921-22
YOUNGEST PLAYER IN A LEAGUE MATCH
Ken Roberts 15 years 158 days v Bradford Park Avenue, 1.9.1951
Ken shares this record with Albert Geldard (Bradford P.A.) as the
two youngest players to play in the Football League.

PREVIOUS MANAGERS

1924-26 Charles Hewitt   1929-31 Jack Baynes   R Burkinshaw Dec
1931-Jan 1932   1932-36 Ernest Blackburn   Captain Logan 1937-
38   1939-42Tommy Morgan   1942-49 Tom W Williams   C Lloyd
March-May 1949   1949-50 Leslie J McDowall   1951-54 Peter
Jackson   1954-57 Clifford Lloyd   1957-59 John Love   1960-61 Billy
Morris   1961-65 Ken Barnes   1965-66 Billy Morris   1966-67Jack
Rowley   1967 Cliff Lloyd   1967-8 Alvan Williams   1968-77 John
Neal   1977-81 Arfon Griffiths   1981-82 Mel Sutton   1982-85 Bobby
Roberts   Dixie McNeil 1985-89   Brian Flynn 1989-

ADDITIONAL INFORMATION
Previous Names: Wrexham Athletic 1881-82.
Wrexham Olympic 1884-88.

Previous Leagues: The Combination, Birmingham League

Club colours: Red shirts, white socks with red trim, red socks.
Change colours: Old gold shirts, black shorts with gold trim, black
socks.
Reserves League: Pontins Central League Division 3.

LONGEST LEAGUE RUNS

of undefeated matches:	16 (1966)	of league matches w/out a win:	14 (1923-24, 1950)
of undefeated home matches:	38 (1969-70)	of undefeated away matches:	9 (1992-93)
without home win:	10 (1980-81)	without an away win:	31 (1982-83)
of league wins:	7 (1961, 1978)	of home wins:	13 (19832-33)
of league defeats:	9 (1963)	of away wins:	7 (1961)

THE MANAGER

BRIAN FLYNN . . . . appointed November 1989.

PREVIOUS CLUBS
As Manager . . . . None.
As Asst.Man/Coach . . . . None.
As a player . . . . Burnley, Leeds Utd, Cardiff City, Doncaster Rovers, Bury, Limerick, Doncaster Rovers.

HONOURS
As a Manager . . . . Promotion to Division 2, 1992-93.
As a Player . . . . 66 full caps, 2 U23 and Schools honours for Wales.

WREXHAM

PLAYERS NAME / Honours	Ht	Wt	Birthdate	Birthplace / Transfers	Contract Date	Clubs	League	L/Cup	FA Cup	Other	Lge	L/C	FAC	Oth
G O A L K E E P E R S														
Mark Cartwright		13.01.73		Chester		York City (T)								
				Free	17.08.91	Stockport County								
					05.03.94	Wrexham								
Kenneth Dixon	5.11	11.0	24.02.76	Knowsley	07.07.94	Wrexham (T)								
Andrew Marriott	6.1	13.3	11.10.70	Sutton-in-Ashfield	22.10.88	Arsenal (T)								
E: u21.1, Y..2, S. FLg u18.1. Duv.4'92. FMC'92.				£50,000	20.06.89	Nottm. Forest	11	1		1				
				Loan	06.09.89	West Bromwich A.	3							
				Loan	29.12.89	Blackburn Rovers	2							
				Loan	21.03.90	Colchester United	10							
				Loan	29.08.91	Burnley	15			2				
				£200,000	08.10.93	Wrexham	82	4	6	14				
D E F E N D E R S														
Deryn Brace	5.9	10.8	15.03.75	Haverfordwest	06.07.93	Norwich City (T)								
W: Y.				Free		Wrexham	11+4		1	4				
Phil Hardy	5.10	10.2	09.04.73	Ellesmere Port	24.11.90	Wrexham (T)	176	13	13	26				
E: u21.3.														
Tony Humes	5.11	11.0	19.03.66	Blyth	26.05.83	Ipswich Town (A)	107+13	6	4	10	10		1	1
				£40,000	27.03.92	Wrexham	99+3	7	6	10	1			
Barry Hunter	6.4	12.0	18.11.68	Coleraine		Crusaders								
NI: B.1				£50,000	20.08.93	Wrexham	58+2	4	5	13	1			1
Barry Jones	6.0	12.10	30.06.70	Liverpool		Prescot Town								
					19.01.89	Liverpool				0+1				
				Free	10.07.92	Wrexham	119	10	5	16	4	1		
Melvin Pejic	5.7	10.6	27.04.59	Newcastle -U-Lyme	22.07.77	Stoke City (J)	1							
WFAC'90				Free	13.06.80	Hereford United	404+8	23+2	20+1	26+1	14	3	3	
				£7,000	09.01.92	Wrexham	103+3	7	3	8	4	2		
Scott Williams	6.0	11.0	07.08.74	Bangor	02.07.93	Wrexham (T)	20+5	1		2+2				
M I D F I E L D														
Richard Barnes	5.8	10.0	06.09.75	Wrexham	31.05.94	Wrexham (T)	0+1							
David Brammer	5.9	11.0	28.02.75	Bromborough	02.07.93	Wrexham (T)	30+8	3	1	3+2	3			
Jonathan Cross	5.10	11.4	02.03.75	Wallasey	15.11.92	Wrexham (T0	75+17	4+2	4+1	7+4	10	1	1	1
Michael Lake	6.1	13.7	16.11.66	Manchester		Cuzon Ashton								
E:S-P.2. NPL'87.						Macclesfield			3					
				£60,000	11.10.89	Sheffield United	19+16	3+2	5	0+1	4		1	
				£60,000	26.11.92	Wrexham	56+3	2	1	6	6			
Gareth Owen	5.10	11.4	21.10.71	Chester	06.07.90	Wrexham (T)	151+21	5+1	12+2	26	18			
W: u21.8.														
Wayne Phillips	5.10	11.0	15.12.70	Bangor	23.08.89	Wrexham (T)	101+16	12	6+2	13+5	5		1	1
W: B.														
Peter Ward	5.10	11.7	15.10.64	Durham		Chester-Le-Street								
					07.01.87	Huddersfield Town	24+13	1+1	2	1	2			
				Free	20.07.89	Rochdale	83+1	5	7	5	10		1	
					06.06.91	Stockport County	140+2	8	7	26	10	1		6
				Free	08.95	Wrexham								
F O R W A R D S														
Karl Connolly	6.1	12.6	09.02.70	Prescot	08.05.91	Wrexham	156+6	12	12	19+1	29	2	3	3
Kieron Durkan	5.10	10.8	01.12.73	Chester	16.07.92	Wrexham (T)	37+5	2	3+1	14	3		2	1
Bryan Hughes	5.9	10.0	19.06.76	Liverpool		Wrexham (T)	40+9	1	4	12	9		1	2
Steve Morris	5.10	11.01	13.05.76	Liverpool		Liverpool (T)								
				Free	.08.94	Wrexham	10+2			3+1	2			
Kevin J Russell	5.8	10.10	06.12.66	Brighton		Brighton & H.A. (A)								
E: Y.6. Div.2'93.				Free	09.10.84	Portsmouth	3+1	0+1	0+1	1+1	1			
				£10,000	17.07.87	Wrexham	84	4	4	8	43	1		3
				£175,000	20.06.89	Leicester City	24+19	0+1	1	5	10			2
				Loan	06.09.90	Peterborough	7				3			
				Loan	17.01.91	Cardiff City	3							
				Loan	07.11.91	Hereford United	3		1		2			
				Loan	02.01.92	Stoke City	5		1					
				£95,000	16.07.92	Stoke City	30+10	3	2	4+1	5			1
				£150,000	28.06.93	Burnley	26+2	4	4	1	6	1		1
				£125,000	03.03.94	Bournemouth	17				1			
				£60,000	24.02.95	Notts County	9+2							
				£60,000	08.95	Wrexham								
Craig Skinner	5.10	11.0	21.10.70	Heywood	13.06.89	Blackburn Rov (T)	11+5	0+1	1	3				1
					21.08.92	Plymouth Argyle	42+11	4	5+2	3+1	3		1	
				£50,000	08.95	Wrexham								
Stephen Watkin	5.10	11.0	16.06.71	Wrexham	24.07.89	Wrexham (J)	127+14	8+1	9+2	14+5	40	3	8	4
W: B.2.														

RACECOURSE GROUND
Mold Road, Wrexham
Tel: 01978 262 129

Capacity 11,500
Covered Standing 6,500
Seating..5,026

First game...v Past & Present Grove Park School, 19.10.1872.
First floodlit game...v Swindon Town (h), Div.3, 30.09.1959.

ATTENDANCES
Highest ....34,445 v Manchester United, FA Cup 4th Round, 26.1.1991.
Lowest................................627 v Mansfield Town, AMC Preliminary Round, 15.10.1991.
OTHER GROUNDS .... Rhosddu Recreation Ground 1880-83. Grosvenor Road 1884.

MATCHDAY TICKET PRICES

Yall Stand (Centre)...................... £10
Yall Stand (Wings) £9
Juv/OAP £7

Terraces.. £7
Juv/OAP £5

Away Supporters
Marston's Stand .... £10/£7(Juv/OAP)
Marston's Paddock........... £7/£5 (Juv/OAP)

Ticket office Telephone no. 01978 262 129

CLUBCALL
0898 12 16 42
Calls cost 39p per minute cheap rate and 49p per minute at all other times.
Call costings correct at time of going to press.

HOW TO GET TO THE GROUND
From the North and West
Use A483 and Wrexham bypass until junction with A541, then branch left and at roundabout follow signs to Wrexham into Mold Road for Wrexham FC.

From the East and South
Follow signs into Wrexham on A543 or A525 then follow signs A541 into Mold Road for Wrexham FC.

Car Parking
Parking at St Marks, Bodhyfryd Square, Eagles Meadow, Old Guild Hall, Hill Street, Holt Street and Town Hall (Hill Street.

Nearest Railway Station
Wrexham General.

MATCHDAY PROGRAMME

Programme Editor .... D Roberts, G Parry, and P Jones.

Number of pages .... 32.

Price .... £1.40.

Subscriptions.......... £49.50 for all 1st team home programmes.
.... £100 for home and away.

Local Newspapers .... Wrexham Evening Leader, Daily Post,
.... Wrexham Weekly Leader, Shropshire Star.

Local Radio Stations ...... Radio City, Marcher Sound, Radio Clwyd,
.... BBC Radio Wales, B.B.C. Radio Cymru.

WYCOMBE WANDERERS
(The Chairboys)
ENDSLEIGH LEAGUE DIVISION 2
SPONSORED BY: VERCO OFFICE FURNITURE LTD

Back row (L-R): Jason Soloman, Sean Stevens, Terry Howard, Paul Hyde, Terry Evans, Chuck Moussadik, Matt Crossley, Simon Stapleton, Gary Patterson. **Middle Row:** Dave Jones (Physio), Jim Melvin (Youth Dev. Officer), Miquel Desouza, Tony Hemmings, Keith Ryan, Jason Cousins, Dave Carroll, Steve Thompson, David Kemp (Assistant Manager), Neil Smillie (Youth Team Manager). **Front Row:** Steve Brown, Mickey Bell, Paul Hardyman, Alan Smith (Manager), Anthony Clark, Simon Garner, Steve McGavin.

**WYCOMBE WANDERERS
FORMED IN** 1884
TURNED PROFESSIONAL IN 1974
LTD COMPANY IN 1980

PATRON: J Adams
PRESIDENT: M E Seymour
CHAIRMAN: I L Beeks
DIRECTORS
G Cox, B R Lee, A Parry, G Peart,
G Richards, A Thibault
SECRETARY
John Reardon
COMMERCIAL MANAGER
Mark Austin, BA

MANAGER: Alan Smith
ASSISTANT MANAGER: David Kemp

YOUTH TEAM MANAGER
Neil Smillie
PHYSIOTHERAPIST
Dave Jones

STATISTICIAN FOR THE DIRECTORY
Dave Finch

Yet another excellent season, with the Blues going so close to promotion for the third successive time. As in previous seasons, Martin O'Neill kept faith with the squad that had gained promotion. The only new addition being Cyrille Regis, a free transfer from Wolverhampton. He formed possible the oldest strikeforce in the league with Simon Garner.

Their experience told in the first half of the season as the team comfortable held a play-off place. Several superb wins were recorded over the main promotion rivals. However, Cyrille sustained an injury in November that kept him out for a month, and when he returned he was not the same player. Since the departure of Keith Scott in November 1993 the club have struggled to find a regular goalscorer, but this problem seemed to have been solved with the signing of Miquel Desouza from Birmingham in January. He scored twice on his debut at Chester and had netted six goals in as many games when he picked up an injury whilst on a training trip to Spain.

This all coincided with a long-term injury to buy midfielder Keith Ryan. Consequently, the Blues struggled and during February and March played eight games without a win. A record fee of £140,000 was then paid out to Birmingham for Steve McGavin, while Jason Soloman from Watford and Peter Garland (on loan) from Charlton were also acquired. Despite losing only twice in the last twelve games, the damage had been done and the Blues had to settle for sixth place, one off the play-offs.

Defeats against Brighton and Shrewsbury saw early exits from the Coca-Cola Cup and the Auto Windscreens Shield, but the Third Round of the FA Cup was reached for the second successive season. Chelmsford and Hitchin were beaten quite comprehensively before West Ham were drawn at home. A record crowd of 9,007 packed Adams Park but the Hammers were not seriously threatened.

Steve Brown, silencing his critics, had an outstanding season and easily won the player of the year award. Paul Hyde, as good as any keeper at his level, Matt Crossley and Keith Ryan until his unfortunate injury, also had fine seasons.

During the summer, Martin O'Neill left to take on the challenge as manager at Norwich. There can be no praise high enough to describe his achievements in his time at the club - the finest period in it's history. The club has risen fifty places in that time with average attendances rising by almost 4,000, plus three wins at Wembley. In Alan Smith, though, a worthy successor has been appointed and the new season is eagerly anticipated.

DAVE FINCH.

WYCOMBE WANDERERS

Division Two: 6th   **FA Cup:** 3rd Round   **Coca-Cola Cup:** 1st Round   **Auto Windscreen Trophy:** 1st Round

M	DATE	COMP.	VEN	OPPONENTS	RESULT	H/T	LP	GOAL SCORERS/GOAL TIMES	ATT.
1	A 13	EL	H	Cambridge United	W 3-0	1-0	7	Garner 3, Hemmings 78, Cousins 81 (pen)	5,782
2	17	CC 1/1	A	**Brighton & H.A.**	L 1-2	0-1		**Regis 53**	(6,884)
3	20	EL	A	Huddersfield Town	W 1-0	1-0	5	Garner 41	(13,334)
4	23	CC 1/2	H	**Brighton & H.A.**	L 1-3	0-3		**Turnbull 86**	5,281
5	27	EL	H	Bristol Rovers	D 0-0	0-0	5		5,895
6	30	EL	A	Birmingham City	W 1-0	0-0	4	Regis 67	(14,305)
7	S 3	EL	A	Bradford City	L 1-2	0-1	6	Cousins 90 (pen)	(8,010)
8	10	EL	H	Brentford	W 4-3	1-1	6	Evans 8, Garner 65, 69, Regis 83	6,847
9	13	EL	H	Hull City	L 1-2	0-1	7	Evans 76	4,676
10	17	EL	A	Crewe Alexandra	W 2-1	2-0	4	Regis 13, Carroll 45	(4,466)
11	24	EL	A	Stockport County	L 1-4	0-3	5	Turnbull 74	(4,607)
12	O 1	EL	H	Swansea City	W 1-0	1-0	4	Carroll 21	4,388
13	8	EL	H	Leyton Orient	W 2-1	1-0	4	Regis 35, Thompson 74	5,668
14	15	EL	A	Plymouth Argyle	D 2-2	1-2	5	Regis 28, 84	(6,864)
15	22	EL	A	Peterborough United	W 3-1	1-1	3	Regis 43, Garner 54, Thompson 61	(5,924)
16	29	EL	H	York City	D 0-0	0-0	4		7,140
17	N 1	EL	H	Shrewsbury Town	W 1-0	1-0	4	Regis 18	4,626
18	5	EL	A	Wrexham	L 1-4	0-2	5	Ryan 70	(3,747)
19	12	FAC 1	H	**Chelmsford City**	**W 4-0**	**1-0**		**Stapleton 27, 61, Bell 58, Ryan 87**	**5,654**
20	19	EL	H	Cardiff City	W 3-1	1-0	4	Ryan 25, 76, Hemmings 75	5,391
21	26	EL	A	Blackpool	W 1-0	0-0	4	Kerr 80	(4,846)
22	29	AWT 2	A	**Shrewsbury Town**	**L 0-2**	**0-1**			(1,785)
23	D 3	FAC 2	A	**Hitchin Town**	**W 5-0**	**2-0**		**Garner 7, 47, 62, Ryan 37, Bell 57**	(2,765)
24	10	EL	H	Huddersfield Town	W 2-1	0-1	3	Evans 69, Garner 83	6,790
25	16	EL	A	Cambridge United	D 2-2	1-1	2	Patterson 37, Evans 60	(3,713)
26	26	EL	H	Brighton & H.A.	D 0-0	0-0	3		7,085
27	27	EL	A	Oxford United	W 2-0	1-0	2	Ryan 31, Garner 57	(9,540)
28	31	EL	H	AFC Bournemouth	D 1-1	0-1	3	Carroll 89	5,990
29	J 7	FAC 3	H	**West Ham United**	**L 0-2**	**0-0**			9,007
30	14	EL	A	Rotherham United	L 0-2	0-1	6		(3,537)
31	31	EL	A	Chester City	W 2-0	2-0	4	Desouza 26, 43	(1,524)
32	F 4	EL	H	Blackpool	D 1-1	1-0	5	Desouza 7	6,380
33	11	EL	A	Shrewsbury Town	D 2-2	0-1	5	Stapleton 56, Desouza 75 (pen)	(3,945)
34	18	EL	H	Rotherham United	W 2-0	0-0	5	Desouza 50, Stapleton 89	5,153
35	21	EL	A	Cardiff City	L 0-2	0-0	6		(3,024)
36	25	EL	A	Swansea City	D 1-1	0-0	6	Desouza 68	(3,699)
37	M 4	EL	H	Stockport County	D 1-1	0-1	7	Evans 66	5,265
38	11	EL	A	Bristol Rovers	L 0-1	0-1	9		(5,118)
39	14	EL	A	York City	D 0-0	0-0	8		(2,800)
40	18	EL	H	Birmingham City	L 0-3	0-2	11		7,289
41	21	EL	A	Brentford	D 0-0	0-0	11		(9,530)
42	25	EL	H	Crewe Alexandra	D 0-0	0-0	10		6,288
43	28	EL	H	Peterborough United	W 3-1	1-0	7	Garner 11, 59, Brown 70	4,590
44	A 1	EL	A	Hull City	D 0-0	0-0	8		(5,054)
45	4	EL	H	Bradford City	W 3-1	3-0	6	Soloman 2, Hemmings 30, Carroll 38	4,522
46	8	EL	A	AFC Bournemouth	L 0-2	0-1	7		(5,815)
47	11	EL	H	Wrexham	W 3-0	3-0	6	McGavin 21, Bell 28, 37	5,115
48	15	EL	H	Oxford United	W 1-0	1-0	5	Carroll 41	7,683
49	19	EL	A	Brighton & H.A.	D 1-1	0-1	6	Carroll 65	(8,094)
50	22	EL	H	Chester City	W 3-1	2-1	5	Hemmings 8, 28, McGavin 64	5,284
51	29	EL	H	Plymouth Argyle	L 1-2	0-1	6	Bell 48	6,850
52	M 6	EL	A	Leyton Orient	W 1-0	0-0	6	Regis 46	(4,698)
53									
54									
55									
56									
57									
58									
59									
60									

Best Home League Attendance: 7,683 v Oxford United   **Smallest:** 4,388 v Swansea City   **Av Home Att:** 5,856

Goal Scorers: Compared with 1993-94: +386

League (60): Garner 9, Regis 9, Carroll 6, Desouza 6, Evans 5, Hemmings 5, Ryan 4, Bell 3, Cousins 2, McGavin 2, Stapleton 2, Thompson 2, Brown, Kerr, Patterson, Solomon, Turnbull

C/Cola Cup (2): Regis, Turnbull

FA Cup (9): Garner 3, Bell 2, Ryan 2, Stapleton 2

Hyde P.	Cousins J.	Titterton D.	Crossley M.	Evans T.	Ryan K.	Carol D.	Thompson S.	Regis C.	Garner S.	Stapleton S.	Creaser G.	Hemmings A.	Moussaddik C.	Brown S.	Turnbull L.	Hutchinson S.	Langford T.	Bell M.	Reid N.	Patterson G.	Desouza M.	Howard T.	Skiverton T.	Garland P.	Soloman J.	Referee	
1	2	3	4	5	6	7	8	9	10•	11*	12	14		S												J. Holbrook	1
1	2	3*		5	6	7	8	9	10•	11	4	14		S	12											I. Hemley	2
1	2			5	6	7	8	9*	10	11	4•	14		S	3	12										T. Lunt	3
1	2			5	6	7	8	9*	10	11	4•	14		S	3	12										P. Alcock	4
1	2			5	6	7	8	9	10*	11		14		S	3											P. Fookes	5
1	2			5	6	7	8	9	10	11				S	3		14									D. Allison	6
1	2	12		5	6	7	8	9	10	11*				S	4•		14									I. Cruickshanks	7
1	2	4		5	6	7	8	9	10	11				S			S									M. Bailey	8
1	2	4		5	6*	7	8	9	10	S				S			12									G. Singh	9
1	2	4		5	6	7	8	9	10	S				S			S									E. Parker	10
1	2	4		5	6	7		9*	10	11	S			S	3	12	8									M. Riley	11
1	2	4		5	6	7	8	9	10	12		14		S	3	11*										G. Pooley	12
1	2	4		5	6	7	8	9		10		14		S	3	11•	S									R. Harris	13
1	2	4		5	6	7	8•	9		10*	11			S	3		14	12								C. Wilkes	14
1	2			5	6	7	11	9	10	4	S	3			S	8										U. Rennie	15
1	2			5	6	7	11*	9	10	4	S				S	12	8									K. Leach	16
1	2	4		5	6	7	12•	9	10*	11				S	3	14	8									A. Butler	17
1	2*	4		5	6	7	12	9	10	11				S	3		8	S								S. Mathieson	18
1	2	4		5	6	7	12		10•	11				S	3	9*	8	14								P. Durkin	19
1	2	4		5	6	7	9		10*	11		12		S	3		8	S								M. Brandwood	20
1	2	4		5	6	7	9			10*	11			S	3		8+	S								P. Harrison	21
1	2	4		6				11	5	12			S	3	9*	14	8	10								R. Poulain	22
1	2	4		5	6	7	9		10•	11*		14		S	3	12	8									C. Wilkes	23
1	2	4		5	6	7	9		10		11•			S	3	14	S		8†							I. Hemley (P. Taylor)	24
1	2	4		5	6	7	9		10		11*			S	3	12	8									J. Rushton	25
1	2	4		5	6	7	8	9	10	11•				S	3	S										G. Barber	26
1	2	4		5	6	7	12	9*	10*	11				S	3	14	8									K. Cooper	27
1	2	4		5	6•	7	14	9	10*	11				S	3	12	8									M. Bailey	28
1	2	4		5	6	7	11*	9•	10	12				S	3		8									G. Willard	29
1	2	4		5	6	7	11*	9•	10	12		14		S	3		8									K. Lupton	30
1	2	4		5		7	12	9*	10•	11				S	3	14	8			6						J. Winter	31
1	2	4		5		7	12	9*	10	11				S	3	S	8			6						P. Alcock	32
1	2	4		5				9	10	11	12	S		S			8	7*	6	3						K. Lynch	33
1		4		5				12	9	10	11			S		S	8	7*	6	3	2					P. Fookes	34
1		4		5				12	9•	10	11*		14	S		7	8		6	3	2					G. Singh	35
1				5				7	9	10		S	S	S	3	11	8		6	4	2					S. Dunn	36
1	2			5				12				S		S	8	11*		4	6							A. D'Urso	37
1	2	S		5				7	4					S	6		8	S	14	3						R. Harris (D. Spicer)	38
1	2	S		5				7	12	9*				S	4		8	6	11	3						M. Lomas	39
1	2			5				7	9	10				S	4*	14	8			3		12	6•	11		T. West	40
1	2	3		5				7		12	10			S	14		8			4			6•	11*		K. Leach	41
1	2	3		5				7		12	10			S	8		11*			4			6•			G. Pooley	42
1	2•	3		5				7			10*		12	S	6		8		11	4		14				M. Pierce	43
1		3		5				7	S		10*		12	S	6		8		11	4	2					T. Heilbron	44
1		3		5				7	14		12		10*	S	6		8		4•				11			C. Wilkes	45
1	2*	3		5				7		12	14		10	S	6		8		4				11•			P. Rejer	46
1	2	4		5				7		S			10	S	6		8		3			11		S		J. Holbrook	47
1	2	4		5				7		14			10*	S	6		8		3			11		S		K. Cooper	48
1	2			4				7		12	14		10*	S	6		8		3	5		11				M. Pierce	49
1	2	4		5				7	11	14	5*		10•	S	6		8		3	2		12				M. Riley	50
1	2	4		5				7	11*		12		10	S	6		8		3	S						J. Lloyd	51
1	2	3		5				7		14				S	6		8		11	12	4					M. Bailey (R. Saunders)	52

Hyde P.	Cousins J.	Titterton D.	Crossley M.	Evans T.	Ryan K.	Carol D.	Thompson S.	Regis C.	Garner S.	Stapleton S.	Creaser G.	Hemmings A.	Moussaddik C.	Brown S.	Turnbull L.	Hutchinson S.	Langford T.	Bell M.	Reid N.	Patterson G.	Desouza M.	Howard T.	Skiverton T.	Garland P.	Soloman J.		
46	41	1	35	44	24	41	25	30	35	24	2	10		38	2	1	31	3	9	6	20	8	5	5	5	League Appearances	
		1						10	5	6	2	2	10	2	3	4	5		4	1		2			1	League Sub Appearances	
2	2	1		2	2	2	2	2	2	2	0+2	1+1	0+1													C/Cola Cup Appearances	
3	3		3	3	3	3	2+1	1	3	2+1		0+2		3	1		0+1	3	0+1							FA Cup Appearances	
1	1		1	1	1	1		1	1	1		1	1	0+1	1		0+1	1	1							AW Trophy Appearances	

Also Played: McGavin 9(41,42,43,44,45,46,47,48,50,51),9•(49,52), Clark 10(52*) Turner 4•(5,6),14(8),11(9),S(10), Skinner 12(5),S(6),3(7,8,9,10), Kerr 12(21),7•(22), Wallace 14(42)
Players on Loan: Turner (Tottenham), Skinner (Wimbledon), Skiverton (Chelsea), Garland (Charlton)
† = Sent Off

WYCOMBE WANDERERS RECORDS AND STATISTICS

CLUB RECORDS

RECORD LEAGUE VICTORY
4-0 v Scarborough (h), Division 3, 2.11.1993
Most Goals Scored in a Cup Tie: 15-1 v Witney Town (h), FA Cup
Prelim Rnd replay,14.9.1955
(First Class) 5-0 v Hitchin Town (a), Second Round, 3.12.1994.

RECORD LEAGUE DEFEAT
2-5 v Colchester United (h) Division 3, 18.9.1993; 0-3 v Mansfield
Town, Division 3, 12.2.1994. 1-4 v Stockport (a) Div.2 24.9.94. 1-4 v
Wrexham (a) Div.2, 1.11.94. 0-3 v Mansfield (a) Div.3, 12.2.94.
0-3 v Birmingham (h) Div.2, 18.3.95.
Record Cup Defeat: 0-8 v Reading (h), FA Cup 1st Qualifying Rnd,
28.10.1899 (First Class) 1-5 v Watford (a), FA Cup 2nd Rnd,
5.12.1959

MOST LEAGUE POINTS
(3pts for win) 78, Division 2 1994-95

MOST LEAGUE GOALS
67, Division 3 1993-94

RECORD TRANSFER FEE RECEIVED
£375,000 from Swindon for Keith Scott, November 1993
RECORD TRANSFER FEE PAID
£140,000 to Birmingham City for Steve McGavin, March 1995.

BEST PERFORMANCES
League: 6th Division 2 1994-95
FA Cup: 3rd Round 1974-75,1985-86, 1993-94
League Cup: 2nd Round 1993-94

HONOURS: Third Division Play-off Winners 1993-94; GM Vauxhall
Conference Champions 1992-93; F.A. Amateur Cup Winners
1930-31; F.A. Trophy Winners1990-91, 1992-93; Isthmian
League Champions 1955-56, 1956-57, 1970-71, 1971-72, 1973-74,
1974-75, 1982-83, 1986-87; Spartan League Champions 1919-
20,1920-21;   Bob Lord Trophy Winners 1991-92;   Anglo-Italian
Trophy Winners1975-76;   Conference Shield Winners 1991-92,
1992-93, 1993-94; Hitachi(League) Cup Winners 1984-85;   Berks
& Bucks Senior Cup Winners 24 times

LEAGUE CAREER
Promoted to Division 3 1992-93   Promoted to Division 2 1993-94

INDIVIDUAL CLUB RECORDS

MOST APPEARANCES FOR CLUB
Paul Hyde 59 (1993-94)

MOST CAPPED PLAYER
(England Semi-Pro.) Larry Pritchard 26 (1970-74)
RECORD LEAGUE GOALSCORER IN A SEASON
Keith Scott 14 Division 3, (10 League, 2 Lge Cup, 2 Others) 1993-94

RECORD LEAGUE GOALSCORER IN A CAREER
20 - Somon Garner (13 League, 3 FAC, 4 Others) 1993-95.
MOST GOALS IN A MATCH
3 - Simon Garner v Hitchin Town (a), FAC 2nd Rnd, 3.12.1994.

OLDEST PLAYER IN A LEAGUE MATCH
Cyrille Regis, 37 years 86 days v Leyton Orient (a) Div.2, 6.5.1995.
YOUNGEST PLAYER IN A LEAGUE MATCH
Anthony Clark, 18 years 29 days v Leyton Orient (a) Div.2, 6.5.1995.

PREVIOUS MANAGERS

First coach appointed 1951: (Coaches) 1951-52 James McCormack
1952-61 Sid Cann   1961-62 Graham Adams   1962-64 Don Welsh
1964-68 Barry Darvill   (Managers): 1969-76 Brian Lee   1976-77
Ted Powell   1977-78 John Reardon   1978-80 Andy Williams
1980-84 Mike Keen   1984-86 Paul Bence   1986-87 Alan Gane
1987-88 Peter Suddaby   1988-90 Jim Kelman   1990-95 Martin
O'Neill

ADDITIONAL INFORMATION
Previous League: 1896-1908 Southern Div 2; 1898-99 Bucks &
Contiguous Counties;1901-03 Berks & Bucks Senior; 1908-14 Great
Western Suburban; 1919-21 Spartan;1921-85 Isthmian; 1985-86
Gola; 1986-87 Vauxhall-Opel; 1987-93 GM Vauxhall Conference

Club Colours: Light & dark blue quartered shirts, dark blue shorts,
light blue socks with light blue turnovers.
Change Colours: Yellow shirts with blue flashes, yellow shorts &
socks or Black & red striped shirts, black shorts & red socks with
black tops.

Reserves League: Springheath Print Capital League

LONGEST LEAGUE RUNS

of undefeated matches:	7 (19.11.1994 - 31.12.1994)	of league matches w/out a win:	8 (21.2.1995 - 25.3.1995)
of undefeated home matches:	11 (1.10.1994 - 4.3.1995)	of undefeated away matches:	9 (14.8.1993 - 27.11.1993)
without home win: 3 (19.4.94-7.5.94, 26.12.95-4.2.95,4.3.95-25.3.95)		without an away win:	9 (11.2.1995 - 19.4.1995)
of league wins: 4 (3.1.1994-25-1.1994, 26.2.1994-19.3.1994)		of home wins:	6 (2.11.1993 - 25.1.1994)
of league defeats:	3 (29.1.1994 - 19.2.1994)	of away wins: 3 (31.8.1993 - 2.10.1993, 26.2.1994 - 19.3.1994)	

THE MANAGER

ALAN SMITH. . . . . appointed June 1995.

PREVIOUS CLUBS
As Manager . . . . Dulwich Hamlet, Crystal Palace.
As Asst.Man/Coach . . . . Wimbledon (twice), Crystal Palace.
As a player . . . . Brentford.

HONOURS
As a Manager . . . . Crystal Palace: Division 1 Champions 1993-94.
As a Player . . . . None.

WYCOMBE WANDERERS

PLAYERS NAME Honours	Ht	Wt	Birthdate	Birthplace Transfers	Contract Date	Clubs	League	L/Cup	FA Cup	Other	Lge	L/C	FAC	Oth
G O A L K E E P E R S														
Paul Hyde GMVC'93. FAT'93	6.1	15.8	07.04.63	Hayes		Hillingdon Borough								
						Hayes			7					
				£15,000	06.07.93	Wycombe Wands	88	6	11	11				
Chuck Moussaddik Morocco: u21.	5.11	12.3	23.02.70	Morocco		Wimbledon								
						Tottenham Hotspur								
						Wycombe Wands								
D E F E N D E R S														
Jason Cousins GMVC'93. FAT'93	6.0	11.8	04.10.70	Hayes	13.07.89	Brentford (T)	20+1	3		2+2				
				Free	01.07.91	Wycombe Wands	78	6	11	10	3	1		
Glyn Creaser GMVC'93. FAT'91.	6.4	14.7	01.09.59	London		Wolverton								
						Barnet			1					
				£15,000		Wycombe Wands	17+2	2	10+1	7+1	2		2	2
				Loan	02.02.94	Yeovil Town								
Matt Crossley GMVC'93. FAT'91'93.	6.2	12.9	18.03.68	Basingstoke		Aldershot (T)								
						Newbury Town								
						Overton Ut.								
						Basingstoke Town								
						Wycombe Wands	74+1	4	14	9	2			
Terry Evans Div.3'92.	6.4	12.0	12.04.65	Hammersmith		Hillingdon Borough								
				£5,000	22.07.85	Brentford	228+1	15+1	17	23	23	4	2	1
				£40,000	26.08.93	Wycombe Wands	64+2	4	6	4	11	1		1
Paul Hardyman E: u21.2.	5.8	11.4	15.09.65	Manchester		Fareham								
						Waterford								
				Free	08.07.83	Portsmouth	113+4	5	6	8	3			
				£130,000	25.07.89	Sunderland	101+5	11	8+1	3	9	2	1	
				£160,000	03.08.92	Bristol Rovers	54+13	3	3+1	3	5			1
				Free	08.95	Wycombe Wands								
Terry Howard E: u19.3. Loan 23.01.87 Chester C. 2 Lge, + 2 FAC App.	6.1	11.7	26.02.66	Stepney	01.03.84	Chelsea (A)	6							
				Loan	09.01.86	Crystal Palace	4							
				£10,000	19.03.87	Leyton Orient	323+5	26	23+1	29	31	1	3	1
					10.02.95	Wycombe Wands	20							
Jason Soloman E: Y.6. FAYC'89.	6.0	12.2	06.10.70	Welwyn G. C.	09.12.88	Watford (T)	79+21	9	1	5+1	5	1		
				Free	06.03.95	Wycombe Wands	5+1							
Shuan Stevens	5.10	11.05	08.03.76	Chertsey	21.07.94	Wycombe Wands								
M I D F I E L D														
Stephen Brown	5.10	10.12	06.07.66	Northampton	11.08.83	Northampton T. (J)	14+1				3			
				Free		Irthlingborough D.								
				Free	21.07.89	Northampton Town	145+13	10	12	10+1	19	1	2	1
				£40,000	09.02.94	Wycombe Wands	87+3	3+1	6	1+1	8			
Dave Carroll E: S. GMVC'93. FAT'91'93.	6.0	12.0	20.09.66	Paisley		Ruislip Manor								
				£6,000		Wycombe Wands	41	4	12	8	6		3	3
Gary Patterson Div 3'94.	6.1	12.5	27.10.72	Newcastle	17.07.91	Notts County (T)								
				Free	02.07.93	Shrewsbury Town	52+5	5	4	3	2			
				£75,000	09.12.94	Wycombe Wands	9+4				1			
Keith Ryan GMVC'93. FAT'91'93.	6.0	11.7	25.06.70	Northampton		Berkhamsted								
						Wycombe Wands	66	6	6+3	10+1	5	1	3	
Simon Stapleton E: S-P.1. GMVC'93. FAT'91.	5.8	11.4	10.12.68	Oxford	16.12.86	Portsmouth (A)								
				Free	19.07.88	Bristol Rovers	4+1	1	1	1				
				Free	01.08.89	Wycombe Wands	45+3	3	12+1	4	3		3	
Steve Thompson E: S-P.1. GMVC'93. FAT'93. Isth Prem'90	5.8	11.4	12.01.63	Plymouth	31.07.81	Bristol City (J)	10+2	3	0+1		1			
				Free	01.02.83	Torquay United	0+1							
						Saltash								
						Slough Town			3					
				£15,000		Wycombe Wands	41+21	5	5+2	7+1	3	1	1	2
F O R W A R D S														
Michael Bell	5.8	10.4	15.11.71	Newcastle	01.07.90	Northampton T. (T)	133+20	7+1	5	9+2	10		1	1
					21.10.94	Wycombe Wands	31		3	1	3		2	
Juan Desouza via Yeovil, Dorchester, Bashley, Dag & Red	5.10	11.0	11.02.70	Newham		Clapton								
					04.07.89	Charlton Athletic								
				Free	01.08.90	Bristol City								
				£25,000	01.02.94	Birmingham City	5+10	2		1				
				Loan	25.11.94	Bury	2+1							
				Loan	27.01.95	Wycombe Wands	1				2			
				£100,000	03.02.95	Wycombe Wands	5+1				4			
Tony Hemmings	5.10	12.10	21.09.67	Burton		Northwich Victoria								
				£25,000	08.09.93	Wycombe Wands	28+18	1+3	2+2	3+3	12		1	1
Steve McGavin GMVC'92. FAT'92.	5.10	10.10	24.01.69	North Walsham		Ipswich Town (T)								
				Free		Sudbury								
				£10,000	28.07.92	Colchester United	55+3	2	6	4	17	2		
				£150,000	07.01.94	Birmingham City	6+2				1			
				£175,000	20.03.95	Wycombe Wands	12				2			
David Sargent				Free	20.02.95	Watford								
						Wycombe Wands								

ADAMS PARK

Hillbottom Road, High Wycombe, Buckinghamshire HP12 4HJ
Tel: 01494 472 100

Capacity 9,649
Covered Standing 8,382
Seating 1,267

First game .... 9.8.1990 v Nottingham Forest, friendly.
First floodlit game .... As above.

ATTENDANCES
Highest .... 7,802 v Norwich City, FAC 3rd Rnd, 8.1.1994.
Lowest .... 2,323 v Barnet, AMC 1st Rnd, 28.9.1993.

OTHER GROUNDS .... Loakes Park, Daws Hill Park, Spring Gardens, The Rye.

MATCHDAY TICKET PRICES

Stand .... £12 (no conc.)

Family Stand ...... £10 (max 3 juniors per adult)
Juniors................................ £5

Terraces .... £7 (conc. £4.50)

Adult terrace tickets available on the day only, all others available up to 2 weeks in advance by personal or postal application (with SAE), on credit card hotline (£10 and over only) or on match day.

Ticket Office Telephone no 01494 472 100
Credit Card Only no............. 01494 441 118

'RINGING THE BLUES'
0891 446 855

Calls cost 39p per minute cheap rate and 49p per minute at all other times.
Call costings correct at time of going to press.

HOW TO GET TO THE GROUND

From all Directions
Exit M40 at junction 4 and take A4010 John Hall Way, sign posted Aylesbury. Cross over three mini roundabouts into New Road, continue down hill to two mini roundabouts at bottom. Turn sharp left at first into Lane End Road and turn right at next mini roundabout into Hillbottom Road. Continue through industrial Estate to Adams Park at end.

From Town Centre
Take A40 west, sign posted Aylesbury, after 1.5 miles turn left after second set of traffic lights into Chapel Lane. Turn right and right again at mini roundabouts into Lane End Road (then as above).

Car Parking
Club car park (340 spaces) or on adjacent Industrial Estate (some charging).

Nearest Railway Station
High Wycombe (01494 441 561)
London Marylebone to Birmingham Snow Hill Line - 2.9 miles from ground. Special buses depart station at 1.55pm and 2.25pm Saturdays, 6.35pm and 7.05pm midweek, returning 10 minutes after the match.

MATCHDAY PROGRAMME

Programme Editor .... Adrian Wood (01865 63007)

Number of pages .... 44.

Price .... £1.30.

Subscriptions .... Apply to club.

Local Newspapers ... Bucks Free Press, Wycombe/South Bucks Star.

Local Radio Stations. Chiltern Radio (Dunstable), Radio 210 (Reading) .... Radio Berkshire (Reading), Eleven Seventy Am (High Wycombe).

YORK CITY
(The Minster Men)
ENDSLEIGH LEAGUE DIVISION 2
SPONSORED BY: PORTAKABIN LTD

Back Row (L-R): Scott Oxley, Neil Campbell, Paul Baker (Player coach), Nick Scaife, Dean Kiely, Andy Warrington, Tony Barras, Steve Tutill, Wayne Osborne, Paul Atkin.
Middle Row: Paul Stancliffe (Assistant Manager), Paul Wilson, Paul Barnes, Jon McCarthy, Nigel Pepper, Graeme Murty, Andy McMillan, Glenn Naylor, Nick Peverell, Jeff Mille (Physio).
Front Row: Darren Williams, Wayne Hall, Scott Jordan, Alan Little (Manager), Steve Bushell, Jason Cutler, Andy Curtis.

YORK CITY
FORMED IN 1922
TURNED PROFESSIONAL IN 1922
LTD COMPANY IN 1922

CHAIRMAN: D M Craig OBE, JP, BSc, FICE
DIRECTORS
B A Houghton, C Webb, E B Swallow,
J E H Quickfall, F.C.A.
SECRETARY
Keith Usher (01904 624 447)
COMMERCIAL MANAGER
Mrs Maureen Leslie (01904 645 941)

MANAGER: Alan Little
ASSISTANT MANAGER: Paul Stancliffe
COACH: Paul Baker
YOUTH TEAM MANAGER
Derek Bell
PHYSIOTHERAPIST
Jeff Miller

STATISTICIAN FOR THE DIRECTORY
David Batters

Although failing in their bid to make a third successive promotion play-off appearance, 1994-95 was another good season for York City. A final position of 9th with 72 points was a respectable achievement considering injuries to key players, notably Paul Barnes, Steve Bushell and Nigel Pepper. Owing to both injuries and loss of form, several changes also had to be made in the defence in direct contrast to the previous campaign.

A poor start was made with just one point from the opening four games, but results improved and a run of four successive wins early in the New Year raised hopes of another promotion charge. They were to remain, however, on the fringe of the leading pack and although keeping in touch until the closing weeks, never really mounted a serious challenge. On their day City were a match for anyone in the Division and outstanding performances were recorded at home to Huddersfield Town (3-0), Birmingham City (2-0), Hull City (3-1) and Brentford (2-1), whilst on their travels notable successes were at Oxford United (2-0) and Blackpool where remarkably for the 2nd successive season they triumphed 5-0.

Paul Barnes, who was the subject of much transfer speculation, again was the leading marksman and included in his 17 goals were a couple of hat-tricks. Paul Baker, who was signed from Gillingham following the departure of Steve Cooper to Airdrie, did well and was second top scorer with 14 goals, whilst Jon McCarthy, who won all the club's Player of the Year awards had another fine season. The only ever present was 'keeper Dean Kiely who last missed a senior game back in December 1992. Young players Graeme Murty and Scott Jordan continued to show fine progress. At the end of the season Tony Canham was released after eleven years splendid service. Only four players in City's history have exceeded his total number of 413 senior appearances.

Average League attendances fell from 4,633 in 1993-94 to 3,685 and again the performances in the various cup competitions were very disappointing. Not since 1985-86 have City progressed beyond the 2nd Round of any of the cups and for the third successive season they fell at the first hurdle in the FA Cup.

On a brighter note the intermediates had a fine season and were only pipped on goal difference by Newcastle United for the Northern Intermediate League title. During the campaign Youth Team Manager Ricky Sbragia left to take up a similar appointment at Sunderland and his replacement was Derek Bell.

The structure of the club remains very sound and manager Alan Little, at the end of the term, stated that he was just two or three players short of a perfect promotion pursuing squad.

DAVID BATTERS.

YORK CITY

| Division Two: 9th | | FA Cup: 1st Round | | Coca-Cola Cup: 1st Round | | Auto Windscreen Trophy: 1st Round | |

M	DATE	COMP.	VEN	OPPONENTS	RESULT	H/T	LP	GOAL SCORERS/GOAL TIMES	ATT.
1	A 13	EL	H	Crewe Alexandra	L 1-2	0-0	16	Cooper 64	4,420
2	16	CC 1/1	A	**Burnley**	**L 0-1**	**0-0**			**(6,390)**
3	20	EL	A	Bristol Rovers	L 1-3	1-1	19	McCarthy 35	(3,957)
4	23	CC 1/2	H	**Burnley**	**D 2-2**	**1-0**		**Pepper 17, Cooper 71**	**3,089**
5	27	EL	H	Cardiff City	D 1-1	0-0	18	Barnes 71	2,861
6	31	EL	A	Brighton & H.A.	L 0-1	0-0	21		(6,996)
7	S 3	EL	A	AFC Bournemouth	W 4-1	3-0	18	Barnes 11, 35, 59, McCarthy 44	(3,181)
8	10	EL	H	Shrewsbury Town	W 3-0	1-0	14	Barnes 15, Pepper 49, Naylor 85	3,196
9	13	EL	H	Brentford	W 2-1	1-1	13	Pepper 33, Jordan 56	2,836
10	17	EL	A	Bradford City	D 0-0	0-0	14		(8,670)
11	24	EL	A	Swansea City	D 0-0	0-0	15		(2,875)
12	O 1	EL	H	Stockport County	L 2-4	2-2	16	Barnes 18 (pen), Naylor 44	3,790
13	8	EL	H	Peterborough United	D 1-1	0-0	16	McCarthy 52	3,601
14	15	EL	A	Rotherham United	L 1-2	0-2	16	Pepper	(3,380)
15	18	AWT 1	A	**Huddersfield Town**	**L 0-3**	**0-1**			**(4,183)**
16	22	EL	H	Chester City	W 2-0	1-0	14	McCarthy 19, Barnes 55	2,820
17	29	EL	A	Wycombe Wanderers	D 0-0	0-0	13		(7,140)
18	N 1	EL	A	Hull City	L 0-3	0-3	15		(6,551)
19	5	EL	H	Huddersfield Town	W 3-0	2-0	15	Baker 7, Naylor 41, Barnes 83	6,345
20	8	AWT 1	H	**Bradford City**	**D 2-2**	**1-0**		**Barnes 37, Baker 68**	**2,326**
21	12	FAC 1	H	**Rotherham United**	**D 3-3**	**1-1**		**Naylor 5, 61, McCarthy 72**	**4,020**
22	19	EL	A	Leyton Orient	W 1-0	0-0	15	Barnes 68	(3,532)
23	22	FAC 1R	A	**Rotherham United**	**L 0-3**	**0-3**			**(4,391)**
24	26	EL	H	Plymouth Argyle	W 1-0	0-0	14	McCarthy 78	3,185
25	D 10	EL	H	Bristol Rovers	L 0-3	0-1	15		3,094
26	16	EL	A	Crewe Alexandra	L 1-2	0-2	15	Barnes 76 (pen)	(3,432)
27	26	EL	H	Blackpool	W 4-0	2-0	14	Barnes 27, 38, 74, Naylor 48	4,542
28	28	EL	A	Cambridge United	L 0-1	0-0	15		(3,285)
29	J 2	EL	A	Oxford United	W 2-0	1-0	14	Naylor 6, Marsh (og) 58	6,386
30	7	EL	A	Chester City	W 4-0	0-0	13	Barnes 56, Jordan 63, McCarthy 77, Alsford (og) 90	(1,844)
31	14	EL	H	Birmingham City	W 2-0	1-0	12	McCarthy 33, Canham 72	(6,828)
32	F 4	EL	A	Plymouth Argyle	W 2-1	0-1	11	Baker 70, Naylor 82	(5,572)
33	7	EL	H	Wrexham	L 0-1	0-1	13		3,140
34	18	EL	A	Birmingham City	L 2-4	0-2	13	Baker 58, McCarthy 70	(14,846)
35	21	EL	H	Leyton Orient	W 4-1	2-1	12	Bellamy (og) 4, Baker 31, 69, Naylor 83	2,926
36	25	EL	A	Stockport County	W 3-2	2-1	10	Baker 38, Pepper 48, Dinning (og) 88	(3,570)
37	28	EL	A	Huddersfield Town	L 0-3	0-1	10		(10,468)
38	M 4	EL	H	Swansea City	L 2-4	1-1	12	Canham 21, Barnes 51	2,920
39	7	EL	H	AFC Bournemouth	W 1-0	0-0	12	Jordan 55	2,301
40	11	EL	A	Cardiff City	W 2-1	2-1	12	Naylor 8, 11	(2,689)
41	14	EL	H	Wycombe Wanderers	D 0-0	0-0	10		2,800
42	18	EL	H	Brighton & H.A.	W 1-0	1-0	8	Barnes 12	2,915
43	21	EL	A	Shrewsbury Town	L 0-1	0-1	10		(2,849)
44	25	EL	H	Bradford City	D 0-0	0-0	8		5,431
45	A 1	EL	A	Brentford	L 0-3	0-1	12		(6,474)
46	4	EL	H	Hull City	W 3-1	1-0	11	Baker 30, 52, Murty 74	4,612
47	8	EL	A	Wrexham	D 1-1	0-0	8	Peverell 71	(2,558)
48	15	EL	H	Cambridge United	W 2-0	1-0	8	Barras 23, McMillan 88	3,278
49	18	EL	A	Blackpool	W 5-0	3-0	8	Baker 12, 66 (pen), Bushell 31, McCarthy 40, Murty 69	(3,517)
50	22	EL	H	Oxford United	L 0-2	0-1	8		3,732
51	29	EL	H	Rotherham United	W 2-0	0-0	8	Baker 69, 80 (pen)	3,183
52	M 6	EL	A	Peterborough United	D 1-1	0-0	9	Baker 64	(4,983)
53									
54									
55									
56									
57									
58									
59									
60									

| Best Home League Attendance: 6,828 v Birmingham City | Smallest: 2,301 v Bournemouth | Av Home Att: 3,685 |

Goal Scorers:

Compared with 1993-94: -948

League (67):	Barnes 16, Baker 13, Naylor 9, McCarthy 9, Pepper 4, Jordan 3, Canham 2, Murty 2, Barras, Couper, Bushell, McMillan, Peverell, Opponents
C/Cola Cup (2):	Couper, Pepper
FA Cup (3):	Naylor 2, McCarthy
AW Trophy (2):	Barnes, Baker

518

Reily D.	McMillan A.	Hall W.	Pepper N.	Tutill S.	Stancliffe P.	McCarthy J.	Cooper S.	Barnes P.	Bushell S.	Canham T.	Naylor G.	Barras T.	Warrington A.	Atkin P.	Jordan S.	Simpson E.	Wilson P.	Baker P.	Mocker P.	Murty G.	Williams D.	Barratt T.	Peverell N.	Cresswell R.	Scaife N.	Referee	
1	2	3	4	5	6	7	8	9*	10	11	12	S	S													E. Wolstenholme	1
1	2	3	4	5		7	8	9	10	11	S	6	S	S												T. Heilbron	2
1	2	3	4	5		7	8	9	10	11	S	6*	S		12											S. Pouley	3
1	2	3	4	5		7	8	9	10	11	S	6	S	S												J. Brandwood	4
1	2	3	4	5		7	8	9	10	11		6	S	S	S											K. Breen	5
1	2	3	4	5		7	8	9	10*	11	S	6	S	12												M. Bailey	6
1	2	12	4	5		7	8	9		11	S	6	S	3	10*											M. Pierce	7
1	2	12	4	5		7	8•	9		11	14	6*	S	3	10											D. Allison	8
1	2		4	5		7	8	9		11*	S	12	S	6	10	3										N. Barry	9
1	2	3	4	5		7	8*	9	S		12	6	S	11	10											T. Lunt	10
1	2	3	4	5		7	8	9		S	S	6	S	11	10											R. Harris	11
1	2	3	4	5	S	7		9		12	8	6	S	11*	10											W. Burns	12
1	2		4	5		7		9		11	8	6	S	S	10*		3	S								J. Watson	13
1	2		4	5		7		9		11	8•	6	S	12	10*		3†	12								R. Furnandiz	14
1	2		4	5		7		9		11	8	6	S	12	10*		3†	14								T. West	15
1	2		4	5		7		9		11	8	6	S	S	10		3	S								K. Lupton	16
1	2	12	4	5*		7		9		11	8	6	S		10		3	S								K. Leach	17
1	2	3	4		5	7		9		11	8	6	S		10*			12	S							A. Dawson	18
1	2	3	4		5	7		9		11*	8	6	S	S	12			10								M. Riley	19
1	2	3	4			7		9		11	8	6	S	S	S		S	10								I. Cruikshanks	20
1	2	S		5		7		9		11	8	6	S	4	S		3	10								S. Mathieson	21
1	2	S		5		7		9		11	8*	6	S	4	12		3	10								J. Holbrook	22
1	2	S		5		7		9		11	8	6	S	4	S		3	10								S. Mathieson	23
1	2	3	4			7		9		11*	8*	6	S	5	12		3	10								G. Cain	24
1	2•	3	4	14		7		9		11	12	6	S	5	5	8*		10								P. Wright	25
1	2	3	4	12		7		9		11		6*	S	6*	8			10		14						P. Harrison	26
1	2	3	4	5		7		9		11*	8		S	6	10•			12	14							J. Lloyd	27
1	2	3	4	5		7		9		11	8		S	6	10		S			S						P. Alcock	28
1	2	11	4	5		7		9			8		S	6	10		3	S		S						P. Vanes	29
1	2	11	4	5		7		9•			8*		S	6	10		3	12		14						S. Mathieson	30
1	2	11	4	5		7				12			S	6	10		3	9		8*	S					U. Rennie	31
1	2	11	4	5•		7				12	14		S	6	10		3	9		8*						J. Holbrook	32
1	2	11•	4	5		7		12		14	8		S	6	10		3	9*								T. West	33
1	2	14	4	5		7		9*		11	8		S	6	10•		3	12								E. Wolstenholme	34
1	2		4	5		7				11	8	S	S	6			3	9		10		S				A. Dawson	35
1	2	10	4	5						11			S	6	8*		3	9		12		7		S		J. Watson	36
1	2	10	4	5		7†		8•		11	12		S	6*			3	9					14			P. Richards	37
1	2		4*	5		7		8		11†	S		S	6	10		3	9				12				P. Harrison	38
1		3		5		7•		8†		11	12	14	S	6	10			9		4	2					W. Burns	39
1	S	3		5		7		8			11	12	S	6	10*			9		4	2					J. Rushton	40
1	12	11		5				8			10*		S	6	7		3	9		4	2	S				E. Lomas	41
1	12	11		5		7†		9			14		S	6	4		3	10•		8	2					I. Cruikshanks	42
1	12	11		5		7		9			S		S	6	4		3*	10		8	2					K. Breen	43
1	12	11†	4	5		7		9			10•		S	6			3	14		8	2					G. Cain	44
1	2		4†	5		7		9	8•			6	S	14			3	10		11	12					P. Foakes	45
1	2	3		5		7			8		9†	6	S	S	4			10		11		12				M. Bailey	46
1	2	3				7		4*		12	10•	6	S	5	8			9		11		14				G. Singh	47
1	2	3		5		7		4*		11		6	S		8•			9		10		12		14		J. Kirkby	48
1	2	3		5		7		4*		11		6	S	5	8			9		10		12				N. Barry	49
1		3		5*		7				11	14	6	S	12	4			9		10	2		8•			J. Parker	50
1	2	3	4			7		8*		11•		6	S	5	14			9		10		12				T. Heilbron	51
1	2	3†	4			7		8*		11		6	S	5			12	9•		10		14				A. Butler	52

46	39	33	35	37	4	44	9	35	10	30	21	27		30	33	1	21	25		17		7	2			League Appearances	
	4		4			2			1		5	8	1	46	4	4		1	5		3	1	3	7		1	League Sub Appearances	
2	2	2	2	2		2	2	2	2		2	2		0+2	2		1	5		3	1	3	7		1	C/Cola Cup Appearances	
2	2	1	2	1		2		2		2	2	2		0+2	1+1	1	1	1								FA Cup Appearances	

† = Sent off

CLUB RECORDS

RECORD LEAGUE VICTORY
9-1 v Southport,Div 3N, 2.2.1957
Most Goals Scored in a Cup Tie: 7-1 v Horsforth (h), Prelim. Round FA Cup,1924-25 7-1 v Stockton Malleable (h), FA Cup 3rd Qualifying Round, 1927-28 7-1 v Stockton (h), FA Cup 1st Qualifying Round, 1928-29 6-0 v South Shields(a), FA Cup 1st Round, 1968-69
7-1 v Hartlepool Utd (h), Leyland Daf Cup,1989-90.

RECORD LEAGUE DEFEAT
0-12 v Chester, Div 3N, 1.2.1936
Record Cup Defeat: 0-7 v Liverpool, FA Cup Round 5 replay, 20.2.1985

MOST LEAGUE POINTS
(3pts a win) 101, Div 4, 1983-84
(2pts a win) 62, Div 4,1964-65

MOST LEAGUE GOALS
96, Div 4, 1983-84

RECORD TRANSFER FEE RECEIVED
£350,000 from Port Vale for Jon McCarthy, August 1995.

RECORD TRANSFER FEE PAID
£50,000 to Aldershot for Dale Banton, Nov 1984 £50,000 to Stoke City for Paul Barnes, July 1992

BEST PERFORMANCES
League: 15th Div 2, 1974-75
FA Cup: Semi-final Replay,1954-55 (as a Third Division club)
League Cup: 5th Round, 1961-2

HONOURS
Champions Div 4, 1983-84

LEAGUE CAREER
Elected to Div 3N 1929 Transferred to Div 4 1958 Promoted to Div 3 1958-59
Relegated to Div 4 1959-60   Promoted to Div 3 1964-65
Relegated to Div 41965-66   Promoted to Div 3 1970-71
Promoted to Div 2 1973-74   Relegated to Div 3 1975-76
Relegated to Div 41976-77   Promoted to Div 3 1983-84
Relegated to Div 4 (now Div 3) 1987-88   Promoted to Div 2 1992-93

INDIVIDUAL CLUB RECORDS

MOST APPEARANCES FOR CLUB
Barry Jackson (1958-70): League 481 + FA Cup 35 +League Cup 22 Total 538

MOST CAPPED PLAYER
Peter Scott, 7 Northern Ireland For England: None

RECORD GOALSCORER IN A MATCH
Alf Patrick 5 v Rotherham United, 6-1, Div 3,20.11.1948
RECORD LEAGUE GOALSCORER IN A SEASON
Bill Fenton, 31, Div 3N, 1951-52 Arthur Bottom 1954-55 and 1955-56, Div 3N In All Competitions: Arthur Bottom, 39(League 31, FA Cup 8) 1954-55
RECORD LEAGUE GOALSCORER IN A CAREER
Norman Wilkinson, 127, 1954-66 In All Competitions: Norman Wilkinson, 143, (League 127, FA Cup 16) 1954-66

OLDEST PLAYER IN A LEAGUE MATCH
Matt Middleton, 42 years 6 months, May 1950
YOUNGEST PLAYER IN A LEAGUE MATCH
Reg Stockill, 15 years 6 months, Aug 1929

PREVIOUS MANAGERS

1929-30 John Collier 1930-33 G W Sherrington 1933-37John Collier 1937-50 Tom Mitchell 1950-52 Dick Duckworth 1952-53 Charlie Spencer 1953-54 Jim McCormick 1956-60 Sam Bartram 1960-67 Tom Lockie 1967-68 Joe Shaw 1968-75 Tom Johnston 1975-77 Wilf McGuinness 1977-80Charlie Wright 1980-81 Barry Lyons 1982-87 Denis Smith 1987-88 Bobby Saxton 1988-91 John Bird 1991-93 John Ward

ADDITIONAL INFORMATION
Previous League: Midland League

Club Colours: Red shirts, navy blue shorts, red stockings
Change Colours: Blue shirts, navy blue shorts, navy blue stockings

Reserves League: Pontins Central League Div 2
`A' Team: Northern Intermediate League

LONGEST LEAGUE RUNS

of undefeated matches:	21(1973-74)	of league matches w/out a win:	17 (May-Oct 1987)
of undefeated home matches:	32 (1970-71)	of undefeated away matches:	10 (1973-74)
without home win:	12 (1981-82)	without an away win:	38 (Sept 1986 - Mar 1988)
of league wins:	7 (1964)	of home wins:	14 (1964-65)
of league defeats:	8 (1966)	of away wins:	5 (1983, 1984)

THE MANAGER

ALAN LITTLE . . . . appointed March 1993.

PREVIOUS CLUBS
As Manager. . . . . York City (Caretaker).
As Asst.Man/Coach . . . . Hartlepool United (C), York City (A.M.).
As a player. . . . . Aston Villa, Southend United, Barnsley, Doncaster Rovers, Torquay United,
. . . . Halifax Town, Hartlepool United.

HONOURS
As a Manager. . . . . Promotion to Division 2, 1992-93 (via the play-offs).
As a Player . . . . None.

YORK CITY

PLAYERS NAME Honours	Ht	Wt	Birthdate	Birthplace Transfers	Contract Date	Clubs	League	L/Cup	FA Cup	Other	Lge	L/C	FAC	Oth
G O A L K E E P E R S														
Dean Kiely	6.1	11.8	10.10.70	Salford	30.10.87	Coventry City (T)								
E: Y.4.					09.03.90	York City	170	6	4	13				
Andrew Warrington	6.3	12.13	10.06.76	Sheffield	11.06.94	York City (T)								
D E F E N D E R S														
Paul Atkin	6.0	12.4	03.09.69	Nottingham	06.07.87	Notts County (T)								
E: Y.1,S.					22.03.89	Bury	14+7			2+1	1			
				Free	01.07.91	York City	100+12	3+1	6	8+1	3			
Tony Barras	6.0	12.3	29.03.71	Billingham	06.07.89	Hartlepool Utd (T)	9+3	2	1	1				
				Free	23.07.90	Stockport County	94+5	2	7	19+1	5			
				Loan	25.02.94	Rotherham United	5				1			
					18.07.94	York City	27+4	2	2	2	1			
Wayne Hall	5.8	10.2	25.10.68	Rotherham	19.12.88	Darlington (T)								
				Free		Hatfield Main								
				Free	15.03.89	York City	224+12	10+1	9+1	17	8		1	1
Andy McMillan	5.10	10.13	22.06.68	South Africa	17.10.87	York City	254+12	11	12	18	3			
John Scaife	6.2	11.0	14.07.75	Middlesbrough		Whitby Town								
					04.03.95	York City	0+1							
Steve Tutill	5.11	11.0	01.10.69	York	27.01.88	York City (T)	253+6	14	14	16+3	6			1
Michael Wallace	5.8	11.10	05.10.70	Farnworth	01.07.89	Manchester City (T)								
E: Y.				Free	30.09.92	Stockport County	65+5	2+2	4+1	10+3	5		1	1
				Free	08.95	York City								
Paul Wilson	5.10	10.6	02.08.68	Bradford	12.06.86	Huddersfield T (T)	15	1						
				£30,000	23.07.87	Norwich City								
				£30,000	12.02.88	Northampton Town	132+9	10	7	6+3	6	1		
				£30,000	19.12.91	Halifax Town	45	2	1	2	7			
					01.02.93	Burnley	31		0+1					
				Loan	06.10.94	York City	5							
					09.10.94	York City	16+1		2	1				
M I D F I E L D														
Paul Baker	6.1	12.10	05.01.63	Newcastle		Bishop Auckland								
				£4,000	01.07.94	Southampton								
				Free	02.07.85	Carlisle United	66+5	4	3	2+1	11	1		
				Free	31.07.87	Hartlepool United	192+5	12	16	16	65	4	6	5
				£77,500	01.08.92	Motherwell	5+4	1			1			
				£40,000	07.01.93	Gillingham	58+5	2	3	2	16		1	
					03.10.94	York City	25+5		2	1+1	13			1
Stephen Bushall	5.7	10.5	28.12.72	Manchester	25.02.91	York City (T)	73+7	2	2	6	5			1
Scott Jordan	5.10	11.2	19.07.75	Newcastle	21.10.92	York City (T)	33+5		1	1+1	3			
Graeme Murty	5.10	11.2	13.11.74	Middlesbro'	23.03.93	York City (T)	18+3			1	2			
Nigel Pepper	5.10	10.3	25.04.68	Rotherham	26.04.86	Rotherham Utd (A)	35+10	1	1+1	3+3	1	1		
				Free	18.07.90	York City	158+8	8+1	8	11+1	19	1	1	
F O R W A R D S														
Paul Barnes	5.10	10.6	16.11.67	Leicester	16.11.85	Notts County (A)	36+17		0+1	4+6	14			5
				£30,000	23.03.90	Stoke City	10+14	0+2		3+1	3			2
				Loan	08.11.90	Chesterfield	1		1				1	
				£50,000	15.07.92	York City	117+1	5	4	11	61			2
Andrew Curtis	5.8	12.0	02.12.72	Doncaster	01.07.91	York City (T)	6+6	0+1						
						Peterborugh Utd	7							
				Free	08.95	York City								
Glenn Naylor	5.10	11.10	11.08.72	Howden	05.03.90	York City (T)	58+27	2+2	4+1	3+4	23		2	
Nicky Peverall	5.11	11.10	28.04.73	Middlesbrough	03.07.91	Middlesbrough								
				Free	27.11.92	Hartlepool United	14+21		1+2	1+2	3		1	
				Free	1994	Hong Kong								
				Free	16.12.94	Hartlepool United	0+1							
				Free	03.02.95	York City	2+7				1			
Paul Stephenson	5.10	10.0	02.01.68	Wallsend	02.01.86	Newcastle Utd (A)	58+3	3+1	2	2	1			
E: Y.2.				£300,000	10.11.88	Millwall	81+17	3	9	8	6	1	2	1
				Loan	21.11.92	Gillingham	12			2	2			
				£30,000	04.03.93	Brentford	70	6	1+1	5	2	1		
					08.95	York City								

521

BOOTHAM CRESCENT
York YO3 7AQ
Tel: 01904 62447

Capacity...9,534
Covered Standing...5,865
Seating...3,669

First game ....v Stockport County, 1932.
First floodlit game ....v Q.P.R., September 1959.

ATTENDANCES
Highest...28,123 v Huddersfield, FAC 6th Rnd, 5.3.1938.
Lowest.................................957 v Carlisle Utd, AMC Prelim Rnd, 22.10.1991.

OTHER GROUNDS...Fulfordgate 1922-23.

MATCHDAY TICKET PRICES

Main Stand £10
Juv/OAP £6

Popular Stand £8
Juv/OAP £5

Ground £7
Juv/OAP £4
Popular Stand transfer £1

Enclosure. £10
Juv/OAP £6
(Only obtainable from Ticket Office)

Family Stand (max. 3 children) £7.50
Child £4

Ticket Office Telephone no. 01904 624 447

CLUBCALL 0891 66 45 45
Calls cost 39p per minute cheap rate and 49p per minute at all other times.
Call costings correct at time of going to press.

HOW TO GET TO THE GROUND

From the North
Use A1 then A59, sign posted York. Cross railway bridge and in 1.9 miles turn left into Water End. At end turn right A19, sign posted City Centre. In 0.4 miles turn left into Bootham Crescent for York City FC.

From the East
Use A1079 into York City centre and follow signs for Thirsk (A19) into Bootham. Cross railway bridge and then take 2nd turning on right into Bootham Crescent for York City FC.

From the South
Use A64. Turn left onto by-pass and follow signs for Thirsk (A19). Then turn left sign posted York and then take left into Bootham Crescent for York City FC.

From the West
Use B1224, sign posted York into city centre and follow signs to Thirsk (A19) into Bootham. Cross railway bridge and then take 2nd turning on right into Bootham Crescent for York City FC.

Car Parking
Ample parking in side streets.

Nearest Railway Station: York (01904 642 155)

MATCHDAY PROGRAMME

Programme Editor . . . . Maureen Leslie.

Number of pages . . . . 32.

Price . . . . £1.30.

Subscriptions . . . . Apply to club.

Local Newspapers . . . . Yorkshire Evening Press.

Local Radio Stations . . . . BBC Radio York & Minster FM.

Division 3

FOOTBALL LEAGUE CHAMPIONSHIP

Endsleigh League

Endsleigh
Insurance League

1995-96

FINAL LEAGUE TABLE

		P	W	D	L	F	A	W	D	L	F	A	Pts
			HOME						**AWAY**				
1	CARLISLE UNITED	42	14	5	2	34	14	13	5	3	33	17	91
2	WALSALL	42	15	3	3	42	18	9	8	4	33	22	83
PLAY-OFFS													
3	**CHESTERFIELD**	42	11	7	3	26	10	12	5	4	36	27	81
4	BURY	42	13	7	1	39	13	10	4	7	34	23	80
5	PRESTON NORTH END	42	13	3	5	37	17	6	7	8	21	24	67
6	MANSFIELD TOWN	42	10	5	6	45	27	8	6	7	39	32	65
7	SCUNTHORPE UNITED	42	12	2	7	40	30	6	6	9	28	33	62
8	FULHAM	42	11	5	5	39	22	5	9	7	21	32	62
9	DONCASTER ROVERS	42	9	5	7	28	20	8	5	8	30	23	61
10	COLCHESTER UNITED	42	8	5	8	29	30	8	5	8	27	34	58
11	BARNET	42	8	7	6	37	27	7	4	10	19	36	56
12	LINCOLN CITY	42	10	7	4	34	22	5	4	12	20	33	56
13	TORQUAY UNITED	42	10	8	3	35	25	4	5	12	19	32	55
14	WIGAN ATHLETIC	42	7	6	8	28	30	7	4	10	25	30	52
15	ROCHDALE	42	8	6	7	25	23	4	8	9	19	44	50
16	HEREFORD UNITED	42	9	6	6	22	19	3	7	11	23	43	49
17	NORTHAMPTON TOWN	42	8	5	8	25	29	2	9	10	20	38	44
18	HARTLEPOOL UNITED	42	9	5	7	33	32	2	5	14	10	37	43
19	GILLINGHAM	42	8	7	6	31	25	2	4	15	15	39	41
20	DARLINGTON	42	7	5	9	25	24	4	3	14	18	33	41
21	SCARBOROUGH	42	4	7	10	26	31	4	3	14	23	39	34
22	EXETER CITY	42	5	5	11	25	36	3	5	13	11	34	34

ENDSLEIGH LEAGUE DIVISION THREE 1995-96

BARNET
(The Bees)
ENDSLEIGH LEAGUE DIVISION 3
SPONSORED BY: THE PRINTING COMPANY LTD

Back Row (L-R): Alan Hamlet, Linvoy Primus, Shaun Gale, Mark Cooper, Lee Pearce, Lee Hodges, Alan Pardew, Paul Smith, Kieran Adams. **Middle Row:** Terry Bullivant (First Team Coach), Laird Budge (Kit Manager), Kieran Gallagher, Jamie Campbell, Paul Newell, Glen Thomas, Maik Taylor, Graeme Hall, Terry Harvey (Yth Coach), David Mott (Physio), Terry Gibson (Yth Manager). **Front Row:** Mickey Tomlinson, Terry Robbins, Peter Scott, Ray Clemence (Manager), Paul Wilson, David McDonald, Dougie Freedman (Now Crystal Palace).

BARNET
FORMED IN 1888
TURNED PROFESSIONAL IN 1965

CHAIRMAN: A A Kleanthous

DIRECTORS:
D J Buchler FCA, D B Edwards OBE,
F W Higgins FCA, S Glynne

SECRETARY: A Ashworth

COMMERCIAL MANAGER
Brian Wheeler

MANAGER: Ray Clemence

YOUTH TEAM MANAGER
Terry Gibson

PHYSIOTHERAPIST
David Mott

The goalscoring exploits of Dougie Freedman (29 goals in total) undoubtedly made sure the Hertfordshire side were never ignored by the media.

The league season began with a defeat at home to Scunthorpe, but several good wins soon lifted them to the lofty heights of number two spot and despite a less than convincing 2-2 home draw with Hereford on 8th October, the Bees were still up there in the top three.

Christmas was very much an in-an-out period, with just two wins and three defeats between 10th December and New Year's Eve. A 1-1 away draw at Colchester on 14th January and Barnet were down to sixth, and then, if the truth be told, the rot set in.

February, March and April were dismal months indeed. Thankfully, Freedman was still finding the net on a regular basis, but by the second week in March an away draw with Doncaster (1-1) and a 3-0 reverse at Bury had thrown all hopes of a play-off place out of the proverbial window.

Down to twelfth, a Freedman hat-trick against Hartlepool at Underhill moved back into the top ten, and even though a 2-1 home success over Lincoln City on 4th April lifted them one more place, just to be satisfied with a respectable mid-table slot.

In cup football the Bees put on a display at home to Manchester City in Round Two of the Coca-cola. A Freedman effort after just one minute put the frighteners into the Premiership outfit, but in the second leg City ran out easy 4-1 victors. A scintillating 4-4 draw in Round One of the FA Cup with those doughty Conference Cup fighters Woking was all the more remarkable when you consider that at the interval Woking led 3-0!

Just two appearances in the Auto Windscreen Shield, both defeats, hardly kept any continuity going. On the attendance front, a paltry 995 watched their 2-0 shield defeat at the hands of Cambridge at Underhill, and low gates were much in evidence throughout the campaign.

GREG TESSER.

BARNET

Division Three: 11th   **FA Cup:** 1st Round   **Coca-Cola Cup:** 2nd Round   **Auto Windscreen Trophy:** 1st Round

M	DATE	COMP.	VEN	OPPONENTS	RESULT	H/T	LP	GOAL SCORERS/GOAL TIMES	ATT.
1	A 13	EL	H	Scunthorpe United	L 1-2	0-1	16	Cooper 65	2,208
2	16	CC 1/1	H	**Leyton Orient**	W 4-0	0-0		**Freedman 46, 75, Cooper 55, 84**	**2,187**
3	20	EL	A	Scarborough	W 1-0	0-0	14	Cooper 84	(1,471)
4	23	CC 1/2	A	**Leyton Orient**	D 1-1	1-0		**Freedman 43**	**(2,464)**
5	27	EL	H	Preston North End	W 2-1	0-0	7	Freedman 58, Hodges 73	2,441
6	30	EL	A	Hartlepool	W 1-0	1-0	3	Freedman 22	2,019
7	S 3	EL	A	Wigan Athletic	W 2-1	1-1	3	Cooper 22, Wilson 64	(1,438)
8	10	EL	H	Doncaster	D 0-0	0-0	5		2,625
9	13	EL	H	Rochdale	W 6-2	4-1	2	Gale 89, Freedman 12, 16, 39,56,Cooper 33	1,688
10	17	EL	A	Scunthorpe	L 0-1	0-0	3		(2,481)
11	20	CC 2/1	H	**Manchester City**	W 1-0	1-0		**Freedman 1**	**3,120**
12	24	EL	A	Torquay United	W 2-1	2-0	3	Newson 12, Hodges 21	(3,280)
13	27	AWT 1	H	**Cambridge**	L 0-2	0-2			**995**
14	O 1	EL	H	Fulham	D 0-0	0-0	3		3,579
15	5	CC 2/2	A	**Manchester City**	L 1-4	0-0		**Freedman 57**	**(11,545)**
16	8	EL	H	Hereford	D 2-2	1-1	3	Newson 3, Hodges 49	2,116
17	15	EL	A	Northampton	D 1-1	0-0	4	Freedman 68	(7,461)
18	22	EL	A	Carlisle United	L 0-4	0-1	5		(6,155)
19	29	EL	H	Chesterfield	W 4-1	2-1	4	McMahon 7, Freedman 1,55, (og)	2,130
20	N 1	AWT 1	A	**Northampton**	L 1-3			**Cooper**	**(2,168)**
21	5	EL	A	Lincoln City	W 2-1	1-1	4	Freedman 67, Cooper 15	2,741
22	12	FAC 1	H	**Woking**	D 4-4	0-3		**McMahon 56, Hodges 75, Cooper 61,79**	**3,114**
23	19	EL	H	Bury	D 1-1	1-0	4	McMahon 10	3,006
24	22	FAC 1	A	**Woking**	L 0-1	0-1			**(3,748)**
25	26	EL	A	Darlington	W 1-0	0-0	4	(og)	(2,157)
26	D 10	EL	H	Scarborough	W 3-1	0-0	4	Freedman 78, Wilson 56, Cooper 70	1,988
27	17	EL	A	Preston North End	L 0-1	0-0	4		(6,429)
28	26	EL	A	Walsall	L 0-4	0-2	5		(5,392)
29	27	EL	H	Gillingham	W 1-0	0-0	4	Freedman 59	3,074
30	31	EL	A	Mansfield Town	L 0-3	0-1	4		(2891)
31	J 14	EL	A	Colchester	D 1-1	1-0	6	Hodges 44	(3,706)
32	24	EL	H	Carlisle United	L 0-2	0-0	7		2,413
33	F 4	EL	H	Darlington	L 2-3	0-2	10	Walker 51, Cooper 61	2,034
34	14	EL	A	Chesterfield	L 0-2	0-0	11		(2,978)
35	18	EL	H	Colchester United	L 0-1	0-1	11		2,242
36	25	EL	A	Fulham	L 0-4	0-3	12		(6,195)
37	28	EL	H	Exeter City	D 1-1	1-0	11	Gibson38	1,325
38	M 4	EL	H	Torquay United	W 2-0	1-0	11	Gale 68, Freedman 30	1,816
39	11	EL	A	Doncaster	D 1-1	0-0	12	Freedman 53	(1,979)
40	14	EL	A	Bury	L 0-3	0-3	12		(2,380)
41	18	EL	H	Hartlepool	W 4-0	1-0	10	Freedman 39, 56, 67, Tomlinson 63	1,557
42	25	EL	H	Wigan Athletic	D 1-1	1-1	10	Freedman 20	2,362
43	A 1	EL	A	Rochdale	D 2-2	1-1	11	Freedman 44, 52	(1,834)
44	4	EL	H	Lincoln City	W 2-1	1-1	9	Freedman 3, Wilson 71	1,616
45	8	EL	H	Mansfield Town	D 2-2	1-1	9	Cooper 14, 47	2,115
46	15	EL	A	Gillingham	L 1-2	1-2	10	Freedman 23	(3,448)
47	17	EL	A	Walsall	L 1-3	1-2	11	Inglethorpe 15	2,078
48	22	EL	A	Exeter City	W 2-1	1-0	10	Inglethorpe 41, Cooper 60	(1,903)
49	29	EL	H	Northampton	L 2-3	1-2	11	Freedman 31, Inglethorpe 67	2,796
50	M 6	EL	A	Hereford	L 2-3	1-3	11	Cooper 18, Freedman 61	
51									
52									
53									
54									
55									
56									
57									
58									
59									
60									

Best Home League Attendance: 3,579 v Fulham   **Smallest:** 1,325 v Exeter   **Av Home Att:** 2,248

Goal Scorers:

League (54): Freedman 24, M. Cooper 11, Hodges 4, Wilson 3, Gale 2, Inglethorpe 3, McMahon 2, Newson 2, Gibson, Tomlinson, Walker

C/Cola Cup (7): Freedman 5, Cooper 2

FA Cup (4): Cooper 2, McMahon 1, Hodges 1

Compared with 1993-94: - 175

Phillips G.	McDonald D.	Gale S.	Hoddle C.	Walker A.	Newson M.	Tomlinson M.	Freedman D.	Hodges L.	Cooper M.	Wilson	Scott P.	Primus L.	Newell P.	Alexander T.	Haynes J.	Mitchell R.	Gibson T.	Smith G.	Inglethorpe A.	Adams K.	Hamlet A.	Thomas G.	Cooper G.	Carmichael M.	Watson K.	Referee	
1	2	3	4	5	6	7*		9	10	11	12	14	S													P. Rejer	1
1	2	3	4	5	6•	7*	8	9	10	11	12	14	S													G. Barber	2
1	2	3	4	5		7	8	9*	10	11	12	6	S	14												M. Riley	3
1	*2	3	4	5		7	*8	9	10	11	12	6	S	14												G. Pooley	4
1	2	3	4	5		7	8	9	10	11	12	6	S	14												R. Harris	5
1	2	3	4	5		7*	8	9	10	11	12	6*	S	14												S. Mathieson	6
1	2	3	4	5•		7	8*	9	10	11	12	6	S													N. Barry	7
1	2	3	4			7	8	9	10	11	12	6	S	14												A. D'Urso	8
1	2	3	4			7	8	9	10*	11	12	6	S	5	14											C. Wilkes	9
1	2	3	4	5*	14		8	9		11	10	6	S													P. Richards	10
1	2	3	4	5			8	9		11	10	6	S	12	7	14										S. Dunn	11
1	2	3	4	5			8	9		11	7	6	S	12	14									10*		K. Leach	12
1	2	3	4	5			8	9		11	10	6*	S	12•	7											D. Orr	13
1	2	3	4	5	14		8	9		11	10	6	S	12										7*		P. Vanes	14
1	2	3•	4	5		7*	8	9	12	11	10	6	S		14											S. Lodge	15
1	2		4	5		7	8	9	12	11	10*	6	S			3								14		M. Bailey	16
1	2	3	4*	5		7•	8	9	10	11		6	S		14									12		P. Harrison	17
1	2	3*	4	5		12	8	9	10	11		6	S											14		R. Poulain	18
1	2		4	3	5	14	8	9	10	12	11	6	S													C. Wilkes	19
S	2•		4	3	5	14	8	9*	10	12	11	6	1													D. Orr	20
1			4	2	5	14	8	9	10	12	11	6	S													R. Furnandiz	21
1	2		4	3	5*	14	8	9•	10	12	11	6	S													P. Don	22
1	2		4	3	S	14	8		10*	9	11	6	S			12										A. Butler	23
1	2		4	3	S*	14	8		10•	9	11	6	S			12										P. Don	24
S	2		4	5		10*	8	9		11		6	1	14	3								12			W. Flood	25
S	2		4	3	5	14	8	9	10	11		6	1			12										J. Holbrook	26
S	2		4	3	5	14	8	9	10	11		6	1			12										U. Rennie	27
S	2	4*	3•	5		12	8	9	10	14	11	6	1													E. Parker	28
S	2			5		14	8	4	10	9	11	6	1			3			12							K. Leach	29
S						12	8	4		9		6	1	11*	3•				14	2				S		E. Lomas	30
S		4		5		7	8	9		11			1	3	14		10		12	2						J. Rushton	31
S	2		4	5		7	8	9*	10	11		6	1	3	12		14									G. Pooley	32
S	2		4	5		7	8	9	10	3		6*	1			12	14									P. Foakes	33
S	2		4*	5		7	8	9	10	3	11	6	1			12	14									P. Richards	34
1	2	14		5	3	7•	8	9	10	11*		6	S			12									4	R. Harris	35
1	2	7	11	5	3	14	8	9	10			6	S			12									4	P. Alcock	36
1	2	3	12	5		14	8	9	10	11		6	S			7									4	M. Bailey	37
1	2	3	12	5			8*	9	14	11	10	6	S			7									4•	G. Barber	38
1		3	2	5	12		8	9*		11	10	6	S			7	14								4	T. Lunt	39
1		3	2	5	9		8			11	10	6	S			7*	12		14						4	J. Kirby	40
1	2	3	12	5	9		8•		10	11		6	S			7*			14						4	J. Lloyd	41
1	2	3	7	5	9		8		10	11		6	S						12	14					4*	J. Holbrook	42
1	2	3		S	9	8*			10	11	7	6	S				12					14			4	M. Brandwood	43
1	2	3••		5	7	8			10	11		6	S				12					14		4*		S. Dunn	44
1	2•	3		5	7*	8	14		10	11		6	S				12					4		9		G. Pooley	45
S		2	12	5		8	9	10	11		6*	1					7	14	3					4		M. Pearce	46
S	2	3*		5		8	9	10	11			1					12	7	14	6				4		P. Foakes	47
S	2	3	12	5		8	9	10	11			1					7	4*	14	6						C. Wilkes	48
S	2*	12		5		8	9	10	3	11	4	1		14			7					6				P. Rejer	49
S				5		8	9	10	11			6	1				7	4	2	3						E. Lomas	50
28	35	25	26	21	29	21	42	32	33	37	23	39	15	2	2	6	4	3	5	2	3	6	1	2	13	League Appearances	
15		2	5		1	13		2	2	3	7	1	27	6	6	3	10	4	1	8	2	2	1	3		League Sub Appearances	
4	4	4	4	2	3	3	4	4	3	4	4	4	4	3	2	1										C/Cola Cup Appearances	
2	2	2	2	2	2	1	2	2	2	2	2	2	2											1		FA Cup Appearances	

Also Played: McMahon 7(18-28,29*,30), Gallagher 14(50), Brady 12(50) Players on Loan: Inglethorpe, Carmichael, Watson, McMahon   † = Sent Off

CLUB RECORDS

SINCE JOINING THE FOOTBALL LEAGUE
RECORD LEAGUE VICTORY
6-0 v Lincoln City (away), Division 4.9.1992.
Most Goals scored in a Cup tie: 9-0 v Wealdstone, FAC, 1961-62
First Class Cup tie: 6-3 v Brentford, AMC, 17.12.1991.
5-0 v Tiverton Town, FA Cup 1st Round, 16.11.1992.

RECORD LEAGUE DEFEAT
1-5 v York City (h), Division 3, 13.3.1993.

RECORD TRANSFER FEE RECEIVED
£350,000 from Wimbledon for Andy Clarke, 1991.

RECORD TRANSFER FEE PAID
£40,000 to Barrow for Kenny Lowe, 1991. £40,000 to Runcorn for Mark Carter, 1991.

BEST PERFORMANCES
League: 3rd in Division 4/3, 1992-93.
FA Cup: 3rd Round in 1964-65, 1970-71, 1972-73, 1981-82, 1990-91(As a non-League club) 1991-92, 1993-94 (As a League club).
League Cup: 2nd Round in 1993-94, 1994-95.

HONOURS SINCE JOINING THE FOOTBALL LEAGUE
None.

LEAGUE CAREER
Promoted to Division 4/3 1990-91, Promoted to Division 2 1992-93.

INDIVIDUAL CLUB RECORDS

MOST APPEARANCES
Gary Bull - 106 (1989-93): League 83, FA Cup 11, League Cup 4, AMC 6, Play-offs 2.

MOST CAPPED PLAYER
No Barnet player has won a full cap.

RECORD GOALSCORER IN A MATCH
4 - Douglas Freedman v Rochdale, 6-2, 13.9.95.

RECORD LEAGUE GOALSCORER IN A SEASON
Gary Bull 20, 1991-92.
In All Competitions: Mark Carter - 32 (1991-92): League 19, FA Cup 5, League Cup 2, AMC 5, Play-offs 1.

RECORD LEAGUE GOALSCORER IN A CAREER
Gary Bull - 37 (1991-93).
In All Competitions: Mark Carter - 47 (1991-93): League 31, FA Cup 6, League Cup 2, Others 8.

PREVIOUS MANAGERS

(Since 1946): Lester Finch, George Wheeler, Dexter Adams, Tommy Coleman, Gerry Ward, Gordon Ferry, Brian Kelly, Bill Meadows, Barry Fry, Roger Thompson, Don McAllister, Barry Fry, Gary Phillips.

ADDITIONAL INFORMATION
Previous Leagues: Olympian, London Athenian, Southern, Alliance, Gola, GM Vauxhall Conference.
Previous Name: Barnet Alston F.C.

Club colours: Amber shirts, black shorts, black socks.
Change colours: Green & white stripe, green shorts, green socks.

Reserves League: Springheath Print Capital League.

LONGEST LEAGUE RUNS

of undefeated matches:	12 (1992-93)	of league matches w/out a win:	6 (1993)
of undefeated home matches:	16 (1992-93)	of undefeated away matches:	5 (1992-93)
without home win:	2 (1993)	without an away win:	9 (1991-92)
of league wins:	5 (1993)	of home wins:	8 (1991)
of league defeats:	3 (1992, 1993)	of away wins:	2 (1991, 3 TIMES 1993)

THE MANAGER

Ray Clemence . . . . appointed in January 1994.

PREVIOUS CLUBS
As a Manager . . . . None.
As an Asst.Man/Coach . . . . Tottenham Hotspur, Barnet.
As a player . . . . Scunthorpe United, Liverpool, Tottenham Hotspur.

HONOURS
As a Manager . . . . None.
As a Player . . . . Div.1 championship (x5), FAC (x2), Lge Cup, EC (x3), UEFA (x2), ESC. E: 61, U23-4.

BARNET

PLAYERS NAME / Honours	Ht	Wt	Birthdate	Birthplace / Transfers	Contract Date	Clubs	League	L/Cup	FA Cup	Other	Lge	L/C	FAC	Oth
G O A L K E E P E R S														
Paul Newell	6.1	12.8	23.02.69	Woolwich	17.06.87	Southend Utd (T)	15		2	1				
				£5,000	06.08.90	Leyton Orient	61	3	3	4				
				Loan	12.08.92	Colchester United	14	2						
				Free	26.07.94	Barnet	15			1				
Gary Phillips	5.11	14.5	20.09.61	St. Albans		Brighton & H.A. (A)								
E: SP.1. GMVC'91.				Free	27.06.79	West Bromwich A.								
				Free		Barnet			9					
				£5,000	07.12.84	Brentford	143	8	5	15				
					25.08.88	Reading	24		7	3				
				Loan	01.09.89	Hereford United	6							
				£12,500	01.12.89	Barnet	117	10	14	7				
Maik Taylor			08.11.63			Basingstoke Town								
Army Rep. BHLP.						Farnborough								
				Free	08.95	Barnet								
D E F E N D E R S														
Shaun Gale	6.0	11.6	08.10.69	Reading	12.07.88	Portsmouth	2+1			0+1				
				Free	13.07.94	Barnet	25+2	4		1	2			
David McDonald	5.10	11.0	02.01.71	Dublin	05.08.88	Tottenham H. (T)	2							
Ei: B, u21.2, Y.				Loan	27.09.90	Gillingham	10			2				
				Loan	28.08.92	Bradford City	7							
				Loan	06.03.93	Reading	11							
				Free	13.08.93	Peterborough Utd	28+1	4	2	1				
				Free	24.03.94	Barnet	45	4	2	2				
Linvoy Primus	6.0	14.0	14.09.73	Forest Gate	14.08.92	Charlton Ath. (T)	4	0+1		0+1				
				Free	18.07.94	Barnet	39	3+1	2	2				
Glen Thomas	61.	11.0	06.10.67	Hackney	09.10.85	Fulham (A)	246+5	21	8	14+1	6			
				Free	04.11.94	Peterborough Utd	6+2	0+1		2				
				Free	23.03.95	Barnet	6+1							
Paul Wilson	5.9	10.11	26.09.64	Forest Gate		Billericay Town								
GMVC'91.						Barking								
					01.03.88	Barnet	101+3	6	14+1	6+2	7			
M I D F I E L D														
Jamie Campbell	6.1	11.3	21.10.72	Birmingham	01.07.91	Luton Town (T)	10+26	1	1+3	1+2	1			
				Loan	25.11.94	Mansfield Town	3		2		1			
				Loan	10.03.95	Cambridge United	12							
				Free	08.95	Barnet								
Alan Pardew	5.11	11.0	18.07.61	Wimbledon		Yeovil Town								
				£7,000	17.03.87	Crystal Palace	111+17	9+3	8	20	8	1	1	2
				Free	21.11.91	Charlton Athletic	98+6	3+1	9+1	6	24		1	1
				Free	08.95	Barnet								
Paul Smith			02.11.71	Lewisham	1994-95	Barnet (T)								
F O R W A R D S														
Mark D Cooper	6.1	13.0	05.04.67	Watford	16.10.84	Cambridge Utd (A)	61+10	7	4	2	17	3		
					02.04.87	Tottenham Hotspur								
				Loan	10.09.87	Shrewsbury Town	6				2			
				£105,000	09.10.87	Gillingham	38+11	2+1	3+1	4	11			
					02.02.89	Leyton Orient	117+33	6	8+2	10+2	45	2	5	4
				Free	13.07.94	Barnet	32+2	2+1	2	1	11	2	2	1
Douglas Freedman	5.9	11.2	21.01.74	Glasgow	15.05.92	Q.P.R. (T)								
				Free	26.07.94	Barnet	42	4	2	2	24	5		
Lee L Hodges	5.9	10.9	04.09.73	Epping	29.02.92	Tottenham H. (T)	0+4							
E: Y.4.				Loan	26.02.93	Plymouth Argyle	6+1				2			
				Loan	31.12.93	Wycombe W.	2+2		1	1				
				Free	31.05.94	Barnet	32+2	4	1	2	4		1	
Terry Robbins	5.5	10.0	14.01.65	Southwark		Tottenham Hotspur								
E: SP. LSC. Middx Wand.						Gillingham								
						Maidstone United								
						Crawley Town								
						Welling United								
				Free	08.95	Barnet								
Peter Scott	5.8	11.0	01.10.63	Notting Hill	02.10.81	Fulham (A)	268+9	18+2	9	15	27	6	1	
				Free	14.08.92	Bournemouth	9+1	2	1	0+1				
				Free	04.11.93	Barnet	53	2+2	6	2	2			
Michael Tomlinson	5.9	10.7	15.09.72	Lambeth	05.07.91	Leyton Orient (T)	7+7	4	1	0+1	1	1		
				Loan	28.01.94	St Albans City								
				Free	21.03.94	Barnet	37+7	3	0+2	0+2	1			

Underhill Stadium

Barnet Lane, Herts EN5 2BE
Tel: 0181 441 6932

Capacity. 3,887

First game . . . . v Crystal Palace, 7.9.1907 (London Lge).

ATTENDANCES
Highest . . . . 11,026 v Wycombe W., FA Amateur Cup
. . . . 4th Round, 1951-52.
Lowest . . . . 248 v Milton Keynes City,Southern League
. . . . First Division North, 1975-76.

MATCHDAY TICKET PRICES

Main Stand. . . . . £12 (Concessions £6)

Family Stand. £10 (£5)
Restricted £10 (£6)
East Terrace. £7 (£3.50)
North & West Terrace £6 (£2)
South Stand £10 (£7)

Ticket Office Telephone No. 0181 364 9601

HOW TO GET TO THE GROUND

From North, South, East and West
Use M1 then M25, turn off at junction 23. Follow signs for Barnet (A100). Ground is located at the foot of Barnet Hill, behind the Old Red Lion Public House.

Car Parking
Surrounding roads under police control or HIgh Barnet underground station car park.

Nearest Railway Station
High Barnet (LT Northern Line) New Barnet (British Rail).

CLUBCALL
0891 12 15 44
Calls cost 39p per minute cheap rate and 49p per minute at all other times.
Call costings correct at time of going to press.

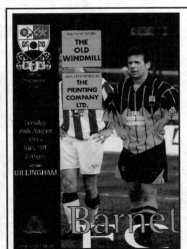

MATCHDAY PROGRAMME

Programme Editor . . . . D Bracegirdle.

Number of pages 32

Price £1.50

Subscriptions . . . . Apply to club

Local Newspapers . . . . . . Barnet & Finchley Press, Barnet Advertiser, Barnet Independent, Barnet Borough Times, Hendon & Finchley Times.

Local Radio Stations . . . . LBC, Capital, Chiltern, Three Counties.

BURY
(The Shakers)
ENDSLEIGH LEAGUE DIVISION 3
SPONSORED BY: BIRTHDAYS (RON WOOD GREETING CARDS LTD)

Back Row (L-R): Ian Hughes, Mark Sertori, Trevor Matthewson, John Paskin, Ryan Cross, Nick Daws, Chris Lucketti.
Middle Row: Alan Raw (Physio), Stan Ternent (Asst. Manager), Andy Woodward, Dave Lancaster, Gary Kelly, Michael Jackson, Lee Bracey, Tony Rigby, Dave Johnson, Cliff Roberts (First Team Coach). **Front Row:** Phil Stant, Kevin Hulme, Lenny Johnrose, David Pugh, Mike Walsh (Manager), Jimmy Mulligan, Stuart Bimson, Shaun Reid, Mark Carter.

BURY
FORMED IN 1885
TURNED PROFESSIONAL IN 1885
LTD COMPANY IN 1897

CHAIRMAN: T Robinson
VICE-CHAIRMAN
Canon J R Smith, MA
DIRECTORS
J Smith, C H Eaves FCA, F Mason
SECRETARY
Mr J Heap
COMMERCIAL MANAGER
N Neville (0161 705 2144)

MANAGER: Mike Walsh
ASSISTANT MANAGER: Stan Ternant

PHYSIOTHERAPIST
Alan Raw

STATISTICIAN FOR THE DIRECTORY
Paul Greenlees

A bridesmaid, but not quite the bride. Season 1994-95 is best summed-up with these words. At the end of September, the Shakers headed the division, following a 2-1 win over Chesterfield. A surprising defeat at Colchester by the only goal on the first day October was the only early season hiccup, as following the Layer Road disappointment, just one league game was lost from eight starters.

At the turn of the year, they were still very much involved in the promotion stakes, but four games without one haul of three points early in 1995 and they found themselves in the comparatively lowly position of ninth. Ironically, a 4-1 home demolition of Colchester on 25th February moved them down one more place to tenth!

In the next game, Torquay were brushed aside 3-1 and it was play-off place time again (fifth).

Throughout April, they remained in fourth spot, and a final 2-1 victory over Darlington at Gig Lane, with goals from the evergreen Mark Carter (penalty) and Phil Stant confirmed their place in the end-of-season play-offs. A 2-0 win over Lancashire rivals Preston North End in the semi-finals and it was off to the Twin Towers and Wembley Stadium. Their opponents in the Third Division Play-Off Final were Chesterfield and even though Bury had taken four points off the Derbyshire outfit in their league encounters (a win and a draw), this counted for nothing in what is always a dramatic one-off situation.

So, promotion at one stage looked an odds-on certainty, was lost in the tension-filled cauldron that is Wembley on a play-off final day. And other dramas were to be acted out in cup competitions.

Despite a relatively comfortable First Round first leg success over Hartlepool in the Coca-cola League Cup, the Shakers were blasted out of the competition in the second leg 5-1! In the FA Cup, they came up against one of the great names of the old FA Amateur Cup in the shape of Bishop Auckland, at the first hurdle. A dour 0-0 draw on 12th November was followed ten days later by a much more exciting affair at Gigg Lane in the replay. 1-1 after extra-time, the tie was decided by penalty-kicks - Bury winning this competition 4-2. In Round Two, they gained a memorable away win at in-force Crewe (2-1).

Crowd support was certainly extremely variable. Over 9000 watched them in the play-off semi-final, but surprisingly only 2612 turned up for their vital final home league fixture. In an area awash with some of the country's most successful clubs, it would undoubtedly need something special from the Shakers to bring out the towns people in force. **GREG TESSER.**

BURY

Division Three: 4th   FA Cup: 3rd Round   Coca-Cola Cup: 1st Round   Auto Windscreen Trophy: 3rd Round

M	DATE	COMP.	VEN	OPPONENTS	RESULT	H/T	LP	GOAL SCORERS/GOAL TIMES	ATT.
1	A 13	EL	H	Rochdale	L 0-1	0-0	19		3,230
2	16	CC 1/1	H	Hartlepool United	W 2-0	1-0		Carter 22 (pen), Lynch 74 (og)	1,515
3	20	EL	A	Exeter City	W 4-0	3-0	10	Carter 10, 16, 89, Jackson 37	(2,164)
4	22	CC 1/2	A	Hartlepool United	L 1-5	1-1		Rigby 31	(1,505)
5	27	EL	H	Hartlepool United	W 2-0	1-0	6	Carter 40 (pen), 89	2,145
6	30	EL	H	Preston North End	D 0-0	0-0			3,623
7	S 3	EL	A	Mansfield Town	W 2-0	1-0	5	Carter 29, Paskin 90	(2,576)
8	10	EL	H	Scunthorpe United	W 2-0	1-0	3	Johnrose 44, Carter 58	2,540
9	13	EL	H	Doncaster Rovers	W 2-0	1-0		Pugh 40, Paskin 69	2,395
10	17	EL	A	Rochdale	W 3-0	0-0	2	Carter 69, Paskin 75, 87	(3,748)
11	24	EL	H	Chesterfield	W 2-1	1-1	1	Pugh 45, Carter 56	3,031
12	O 1	EL	A	Colchester United	L 0-1	0-0	2		(3,288)
13	8	EL	A	Darlington	W 2-0	0-0	2	Carter 74, Pugh 84	(2,352)
14	15	EL	H	Lincoln City	W 2-0	2-0	1	Johnrose 24, Pugh 38	3,139
15	18	AWT 1	A	Chester City	L 1-3	0-2		Rigby 85	(841)
16	22	EL	H	Gillingham	W 3-2	2-0	1	Carter 4 (pen), Paskin 11, 64	2,976
17	29	EL	A	Walsall	W 1-0	1-0	1	Pugh 78 (pen)	(5,255)
18	N 5	EL	H	Scarborough	W 1-0	0-0	1	Johnrose 52	3,016
19	8	AWT 1	H	Preston North End	W 1-0	0-0		Sertori 53	1,756
20	12	FAC 1	A	Bishop Auckland	D 0-0	2-0			(3,135)
21	19	EL	A	Barnes	D 1-1	0-1	2	Mulligan 83	(3,006)
22	22	FAC 1R	H	Bishop Auckland	D 1-1	1-1		Paskin 42 (Bury won 4-2 on pens.)	3,517
23	26	EL	A	Fulham	D 0-0	0-0	2		3,323
24	D 3	FAC 2	A	Crewe Alexandra	W 2-1	0-1		Johnrose 64, Rigby 89	(4,875)
25	10	EL	H	Exeter City	D 0-0	0-0	2		2,876
26	17	EL	A	Hartlepool United	L 1-3	0-2	2	Daws 49	(1,746)
27	26	EL	H	Wigan Athletic	D 3-3	2-2		Lucketti 9, Carter 45, Matthews 52	3,616
28	27	EL	A	Carlisle United	L 0-3	0-1	3		(12,242)
29	J 2	FAC 3	H	Tranmere Rovers	D 2-2	2-0		Lucketti 3, Stanislaus 24	5,755
30	14	EL	H	Hereford United	D 1-1	1-0	4	Carter 39	2,708
31	24	AWT 1/4	H	Huddersfield Town	W 2-1	1-0		Kelly 37, 67	3,311
32	F 4	EL	A	Fulham	L 0-1	0-0	5		(3,941)
33	18	EL	A	Hereford United	L 0-1	0-1	9		(1,827)
34	25	EL	H	Colchester Utd	W 4-1	1-0	10	Stant 32, Hughes 47, Betts 57 (og), Lucketti 68	2,484
35	28	EL	H	Torquay United	W 3-1	1-0		Kelly T 8, Lucketti 48, Stant 76	2,241
36	M 4	EL	A	Chesterfield	D 0-0	0-0	5		(4,429)
37	7	EL	A	Northampton Town	W 5-0	1-0		Pugh 39, 47, 87 (pen), Kelly 50, Stant 64	(4,211)
38	11	EL	A	Scunthorpe United	L 2-3	1-1	5	Pugh 42, Mulligan 67	(2,767)
39	14	EL	H	Barnet	W 3-0	3-0		Rigby 11, Stant 45, Johnrose 45	2,380
40	18	EL	A	Preston North End	L 0-5	0-2	5		(9,626)
41	21	EL	A	Scarborough	W 2-1	1-0		Pugh 35, 89	(1,744)
42	25	EL	H	Mansfield Town	D 2-2	1-0		Kelly 12, Pugh 55 (pen)	4,188
43	A 1	EL	A	Doncaster Rovers	W 2-1	1-1	4	Stant 54, 83	(2,485)
44	4	EL	A	Gillingham	D 1-1	1-1		Lancaster 32	(2,945)
45	8	EL	A	Torquay United	D 2-2	1-1	4	Stant 19, 64	(1,969)
46	15	EL	H	Carlisle United	W 2-0	0-0	4	Stant 51, Jackson 58	5,507
47	22	EL	H	Northampton Town	W 5-0	1-0		Daws 37, Stant 60, Pugh 68 (pen), Rigby 84, Paskin 87	2,921
48	29	EL	A	Lincoln City	W 3-0	2-0	4	Pugh 24, 45, Stant 88	(3,928)
49	M 4	EL	H	Walsall	D 0-0	0-0			6,790
50	6	EL	H	Darlington	W 2-1	1-1	4	Carter 45 (pen), Stant 83	2,612
51	14	PO SF 1	A	Preston North End	W 1-0	1-0		Pugh 40	(13,297)
52	17	PO SF 2	H	Preston North End	W 1-0	0-0		Rigby 88	9,094
53		PO F	N	Chesterfield	L 0-2	0-2			(28,814)
54									
55									
56									
57									
58									
59									
60									

Best Home League Attendance: 6,790 v Walsall	Smallest: 1,515 v Bury	Av Home Att: 3,433

Goal Scorers:

League (71): Pugh 16, Carter 14, Stant 12, Paskin 7, Johnrose 4, Lucketti 3, Kelly 3, Rigby 3, Jackson 2, Mulligan 2, Daws 2, Matthews 1, Hughes 1, Lancaster 1

C/Cola Cup (2): Carter, Rigby

FA Cup (5): Paskin, Johnrose, Rigby, Lucketti, Stanislaus

Kelly	Cross	Jackson	Lucketti	Stanislaus	Mulligan	Mauge	Reid	Daws	Pugh	Hulme	Carter	Paskin	Bracey	Hughes	Johnrose	Kelly T.	Rigby	Matthewson	Sertori	Mulloy	Embleton	De Sousa	Banks	Matthews	Stant	Referee	
1	2	3	4	5	6	7	8*	12.	9	10	11	12	S													P. Richards	1
1	2	5	6	3	7	4			11	9	8	S	S	10*	12											K. Breen	2
1	2	6	5	3	7	4			11	9*	8	12	S		10•	S										J. Holbrook	3
1	2	6	5	3	7	4	S			8	9	S		10	S	11										R. Poulain	4
1	2	3	4	5	6*	7			9	10•	11	14	S		12		8									U. Rennie	5
1	2	3	4	5	6*	7			9	10	11	12	S		14		8*									G. Cain	6
1	2		5	3	7*	4			11	9•	8	14	S		10		12	6								J. Lloyd	7
		2	3	5	6	8*			9	11•	10	14	1		7			4	12	S						R. Furnandiz	8
		2	3	5	6*				7	9	10	11	12	1		8			4	S		S				I. Cruikshanks	9
1		2	3	5		4*			12	11	9•	8	7	S		10		14	6							J. Winter	10
1		2	3	5					8	9	6	11	10*	S		7		12	4	S						W. Flood	11
1		2	5	3					4	11	9	8	7	S		10		12	6*	S						P. Alcock	12
1		2*	5	3					4	11	9	8	7	S		10	12	S	6							A. Dawson	13
1		2*	3	5					8	9		11	10	S		7	S	6	4	12						T. West	14
AUTO WINDSCREEN SHIELD																										J. Rushton	15
1	2			5	3		S		8	9	12	10	11*	S		7		6	4							P. Rejer	16
1	2			5	3	12.			4	11	9	8*			S	14	10	7	6							G. Barber	17
		2	3	5		11			7	9*	10			S	S	8	12	6	4							N. Barry	18
AUTO WINDSCREEN SHIELD																										D. Allison	19
1	2			5	3	12	10		4	11				S	S	8*		7	6	9						R. Furnandiz	20
1	2*			5	3	12	10		4	11			9	14	S	8		7•	6							A. Butler	21
1	2			5	3	14	10		4*	11			9	S	12	8		7•	6							R. Furnandiz	22
1	2			3	5		7		9	10		11*	S	S	8	6		4				12				W. Burns	23
		2	5	3			S	4	11			1	8	10	7	12	6	9*		S						T. West	24
1	2*	3	5						8	9		14	S	7	10	11•	12	4				10				L. Riley	25
1	2	5	3				S		4	11		8		S	7	10		12	6*			9				K. lynch	26
1	2*	3	5			7			14	9		10		S	12	8		6•	4					9		P. Harrison	27
1	12	2	5	3					4	6*	11		8	S	7	10		S						9		D. Allison	28
1	2		3	5					7			9	6*	11	10.	S	12	8		14	4					A. Wilkie	29
1	2			5	12				S	9	6*	11	10	S	3	8			4							R. Poulain	30
AUTO WINDSCREEN SHIELD																											31
1		2*	5	3				4		12†	11		8	9.	5	6	10	7							14	D. Orr	32
1	2*		5							11	12		8	S	6	10	7	4	S						9	M. Pierce	33
1			3	2					8	9	12		11	S	4	S	6*	7							10	J. Winter	34
1			3	2			S		8	9	S		11	S	4		6	7							10	J. Watson	35
1			3	2				12	10	11	14	8.		S	6		7*	4							9	T. West	36
1			5	2		14	12		10.	11	8*			S	6		7	4							9	S. Dunn	37
1			5	2		12			10	11	8			S	6	S	7*	4							9	P. Wright	38
1			3	2		6*			8	9		14		S	4	12	7								9	J. Kirkby	39
1		7		2*					10	11	8			S	6	S	4	5							9	A. Dawson	40
1			5	2					10	11	8	S		14	6		12	4							9.	R. Furnandiz	41
1			3	2					8	9	10	12		S	4*		6	7•								R. Poulain	42
1			5	2					4	11		S		S	6	10	7								9	N. Barry	43
			5				12		4	11		14		1	6	10	7*							S	9	G. Singh	44
			5				12†		4	11		8*		1	6		7	10					S		9	C. Wilkes	45
1		4	3						8	9	11*		12	S			6	7							10	W. Burns	46
1		4	3						7	9	11*		12	S	S		6	8							10	K. Lynch	47
1		6	5						4	11	8*		14	S	12		7	10							9	A. D'Urso	48
1		4	3*						8	9			11	S	S		6	7							10	G. Cain	49
1		4					14	12	7*	9		11•		S	3		6	8							9.	T. Holbrook	50
1		6	5						4	11	8•		14	S	12		7	10							9	J. Winter	51
1		4	3	5					7	9		11*	12	S	S		6	8							10	J. Kirkby	52
39	12	25	40	34	16	21	1	35	44	27	27	26	7	23	25	23	32	18	2	0	0	3	0	2	21	League Appearances	
0	0	0	0	0	1	3	0	1	0	1	2	0	36	6	3	2	1	2	3	1	1	0	2	0	0	League Sub Appearances	
2	2	2	2	2	2	0	0	1	1	2	0	0	1	1+1	0	1	0	0	0	0	0	0	0	0	0	C/Cola Cup Appearances	
3	3	1	4	4	2	3	0+1	3	4	1	1	2	1+3	3+1	4	1	4	4	2	0	0	0	0+1	0	0	FA Cup Appearances	
																										AW Trophy Appearances	

Also Played: Bimson 3(33,37,38,41,43,44,45,48,51*),5(34,35,3639,42,46,47,49,50), Simpson 3(40), Rowe 7*(41),14(42),S(43),7(44), Woodward 2(44,45*),46,47,48*,49,50,51,52), Cartwright 14(49)

† = Sent Off

BURY

BURY — RECORDS AND STATISTICS

CLUB RECORDS

BIGGEST VICTORIES
League: 8-0 v Tranmere Rovers, Division 3, 10.1.1970 (Bury have scored eight goals four times in the League).
F.A. Cup: 12-1 v Stockton, 1st Round, 2.2.1897.

BIGGEST DEFEATS
League: 0-8 v Sheffield United, Division 1, 6.4.1896.
0-8 v Swindon Town, Division 3, 8.12.1979.
League Cup: 0-10 v West Ham United, Round 2, 25.10.1983.

MOST POINTS
3 points a win: 84, Division 4, 1984-85.
2 points a win: 68, Division 3, 1960-61.

MOST GOALS SCORED
108, Division 3, 1960-61.

BEST PERFORMANCES
League: 4th in Division 1, 1925-26.
F.A. Cup: Winners in 1900, 1903.
League Cup: Semi-Final 1963.

HONOURS
Champions of Division 2, 1894-95.
Champions of Division 3, 1960-61.
FA Cup winners 1900, 1903.

LEAGUE CAREER
Elected to Div 2 1894, Div 1 1894-95, Div 2 1911-12, Div 1 1923-24, Div 2 1928-29, Div 3 1956-57, Div 2 1960-61, Div 3 1966-67, Div 2 1967-68, Div 3 1968-69, Div 4 1970-71, Div 3 1973-74, Div 4 1979-80, Div 3 1984-85, Div 4/3 1991-92.

INDIVIDUAL CLUB RECORDS

MOST GOALS IN A SEASON
Craig Madden: 43 goals in 1981-82 (League 35, FA Cup 4, League Cup 3, Group Cup 1)

MOST GOALS IN A MATCH
5. Ray Pointer v Rotherham United, 6-1, Division 2, 2.10.1965.
5. Eddie Quigley v Millwall (h), 5-2, Division 2, 15.2.1947.

OLDEST PLAYER
Derek Fazackerley, 37 years 182 days, 6.5.1989.

YOUNGEST PLAYER
Brian Williams, 16 years 133 days, 18.3.1972.

MOST CAPPED PLAYER
Bill Gorman (Eire) 11.

PREVIOUS MANAGERS

(Since 1946)
Norman Bullock, John McNeil, Dave Russell, Bob Stokoe, Bert Head, Les Shannon, Jack Marshall, Les Hart, Colin McDonald, Tommy McAnearney, Allan Brown, Bobby Smith, Bob Stokoe, Dave Hatton, Dave Connor, Jim Iley, Martin Dobson, Sam Ellis.

ADDITIONAL INFORMATION
PREVIOUS NAMES
None.

PREVIOUS LEAGUE
Lancashire League.

Club Colours: White shirts, royal blue shorts, royal blue socks.
Change colours: Green & purple striped shirts, purple shorts, purple socks.

Reserves League: Midland Senior League.

LONGEST LEAGUE RUNS

of undefeated matches:	18 (1961)	of league matches w/out a win:	19 (1911)
of undefeated home matches:	25 (1967-68)	of undefeated away matches:	8 (1961)
without home win:	13 (1937, 1978)	without an away win:	42 (1910-1912)
of league wins:	9 (1960)	of home wins:	15 (1894-95)
of league defeats:	6 (1953, 1967)	of away wins:	6 (1960)

THE MANAGER

MIKE WALSH . . . . appointed November 1990.

PREVIOUS CLUBS
As Manager . . . . None.
As Player/Coach . . . . Blackpool, Bury.
As a player . . . . Bolton W., Everton, Norwich (loan), Burnley (loan), Fort Lauderdale,
. . . . Manchester City, Blackpool, Bury.

HONOURS
As a Manager . . . . 3rd Division play-offs 1990-91.
As a Player . . . . Bolton: Division 2 Championship 1979-80. Blackpool: Promotion to Division 3, 1984-85.
International . . . . 4 full caps for Eire.

BURY

PLAYERS NAME / Honours	Ht	Wt	Birthdate	Birthplace / Transfers	Contract Date	Clubs	League	L/Cup	FA Cup	Other	Lge	L/C	FAC	Oth
G O A L K E E P E R S														
Lee Bracey	6.1	12.8	11.09.68	Barking	06.07.87	West Ham U. (T)								
WFAC'91.				Free	27.08.88	Swansea City	99	8	11	10				
				£47,500	17.10.91	Halifax Town	73	2	1	2				
				£20,000	23.08.93	Bury	44+2	1	2	3				
Gary Kelly	5.11	12.3	03.08.66	Preston	20.06.84	Newcastle Utd (A)	53	4	3	2				
Ei: B.1, u21.7. FAYC'85.				Loan	07.10.88	Blackpool	5							
				£60,000	05.10.89	Bury	173	10	8	19				
D E F E N D E R S														
Stuart Bimson	5.11	11.8	29.09.69	Liverpool		Macclesfield Town								
				£12,500	06.02.95	Bury	19			2				
Ryan Cross	6.0	11.8	11.10.72	Plymouth	30.03.91	Plymouth Argyle (T)	18+1	2		1				
				£75,000	11.06.92	Hartlepool United	49+1	8	5	5	2			
					07.12.93	Bury	27+2	2	4	1				
Michael Jackson	5.11	11.9	04.12.73	Chester	29.07.92	Crewe Alexandra (T)	5	1	1	2				
E: Y.2, S.				£13,000	13.08.93	Bury	61+2	4	2	9	2			
Chris Lucketti	6.0	12.1	28.09.71	Littleborough		Rochdale (T)	1							
via Free 23.08.90 Stockport County				Free		Halifax Town	73+5	2	2	4	2	1		
				£50,000	01.10.93	Bury	66+1	2	6	10	4		1	
Trevor Matthewson	6.1	12.5	12.02.63	Sheffield	12.02.81	Sheffield Wed. (A)	3		2					
GMVC'88. ANMC'91.				Free	15.10.83	Newport County	73+2	2	7	6				
				Free	27.09.85	Stockport County	79+1	3	2	3				
				£13,000	01.08.87	Lincoln City	43	3	3	2	2			
				£45,000	03.08.89	Birmingham City	167+1	11	8	16	12			1
					20.08.93	Preston North End	12	1		1	1			
				£10,000	02.09.95	Bury	18		4	4				
Nicholas Richardson	6.1	12.6	11.04.67	Halifax		Emley								
WFAC'93. Div.3'93.				Free	15.11.88	Halifax Town	89+12	6+4	2+1	6	17	2	1	1
				£35,000	13.08.92	Cardiff City	106+5	7	6	12+2	13			2
Loan 21.10.94 Wrexham 4 Lge App. 2 gls.				Loan	16.12.94	Chester City	6				1			
					08.95	Bury								
Mark Setori	6.3	13.4	01.09.67	Manchester	07.02.87	Stockport County	3+1	1						
GMVC'88.				Free	01.07.88	Lincoln City	43+7	6	4	5	9		1	2
				£30,000	09.02.90	Wrexham	106+4	8+1	6	9+1	3			
					22.07.94	Bury	0+2		2	1+1				1
Andrew Woodward	5.10	10.12	23.09.73	Stockport	29.07.92	Crewe Alex. (T)	9+11	2		0+3				
					13.03.95	Bury	8			3				
M I D F I E L D														
Nicholas Daws	5.11	13.2	15.03.70	Manchester		Altrincham				2+1				
				£10,000	13.08.92	Bury	98+9	6+1	9	10+2	4			
Ian Hughes	5.10	10.9	02.08.64	Bangor	19.11.91	Bury (T)	81+12	5	5+2	12+3	1			
W: u21.6.														
Lennie Johnrose	5.10	11.5	29.11.69	Preston	16.06.88	Blackburn Rov (T)	20+22	2+1	0+3	2	11	1		
Loan 21.01.92 Preston NorthEnd 1+2 Lge App. 1 gl				£50,000	28.02.92	Hartlepool United	59+7	5+1	5	5	11	4	1	
					07.12.93	Bury	34+6	1+1	5	5	4		1	
David Pugh	5.10	11.0	19.09.64	Liverpool		Runcorn				2+2				
				£35,000	21.07.89	Chester City	168+11	13	11+1	9	23		1	
				£22,500	05.07.95	Bury	42	1	4	7	16			
Shaun Reid	5.8	11.10	13.10.65	Huyton	20.09.83	Rochdale (A)	126+7	10	5	12	4	2	1	2
Loan 12.12.85 Preston North End 3 Lge App.				£32,500	23.12.88	York City	104+2	7	4	5	7			1
				Free	16.08.92	Rochdale	106	6	7	8+1	10		1	2
				£15,000	08.95	Bury	1			1				
Tony Rigby	5.7	10.8	10.08.72	Ormskirk	16.05.90	Crewe Alexandra (T)								
via Lancaster C. & Burscough				Free	06.01.93	Bury	54	1	1	6	8			
F O R W A R D S														
Mark Carter	5.9	11.6	17.12.60	Liverpool		South Liverpool								
E: S.P.11.			via Bangor C., 4 FAC App.			Runcorn			12					
				£40,000	20.02.91	Barnet	62+20	5	4+1	7+2	31	2	6	8
				£6,000	10.09.93	Bury	57+5	2	3	8+1	34	1		
Kevin Hulme	5.10	11.9	02.12.67	Farnworth		Radcliffe Borough								
				£5,000	16.03.89	Bury	82+28	4+3	4+1	4+8	21	2	1	2
Loan 26.10.89 Chester C. 4 Lge App.				£42,500	14.07.93	Doncaster Rovers	33+1	2	1	2	8	1		
				£42,500	11.08.94	Bury	24+4	1	2	2				
David Johnson	5.6	12.03	15.08.76	Kingston		Manchester Utd (T)								
				Free	08.95	Bury								
David Lancaster	6.3	14.0	08.09.61	Preston		Colne Dynamoes								
				Free	15.09.90	Blackpool	7+1	2		0+1	1			
Loan 26.02.91 Chesterfield 12 Lge App. 4 gls.				£70,000	27.08.91	Chesterfield	66+3	5	2	6	16	3		3
				Free	05.07.93	Rochdale	37+3	4	2	1	14	1		
via Free 20.07.94 Halifax Town				Free	13.05.95	Bury	3+2				1			
James Mulligan	5.5	10.0	22.04.74	Dublin	07.07.92	Stoke City (T)								
Loan 19.02.93 Malmo				Loan	19.03.93	Telford United								
Loan 28.08.93 Northwich Victoria				Loan	05.11.93	Bury	2+1			0+1				
				£15,000	05.07.94	Bury	9+6	2	0+2	1+1	2	1		
William J Paskin	5.11	12.2	01.02.62	Capetown		K. V. Kortrikj (Bel)								
				Free	27.08.88	West Bromwich A.	14+11	1	0+2					
				£75,000	26.06.89	Wolverhampton W.	21+13	2+1	2	0+1	2			
Loan 11.09.91 Stockport C. 3+2 Lge App. 1 gl.				Loan	21.11.91	Birmingham City	8+2	0+1			3			
Loan 13.02.92 Shrewsbury T. 1 Lge App.					21.02.92	Wrexham	28+3	1+3		3+2	11	3		2
				Free	22.07.94	Bury	15+11	1	3	3+3	8		1	1
Phil Stant	6.1	12.7	13.10.62	Bolton	19.08.82	Reading	3+1		1					
WFAC'93. Div.3'93.			via Army to	Free	25.11.86	Hereford United	83+6	3	3	11	38	2	2	7
				£175,000	18.07.89	Notts County	14+8	2	0+1	3+2	6	1		
Loan 05.09.90 Blackpool 12 Lge App. 5 gls.				Loan	05.10.90	Huddersfield Town	5				1			
Loan 22.11.90 Lincoln C. 4 Lge App.				£60,000	08.02.91	Fulham	19			1	5			
				£50,000	01.08.91	Mansfield Town	56+1	4	2	2	32	1		
				£100,000	04.12.92	Cardiff City	77+2	2	6+1	10	35	2	4	3
Loan 12.06.93 Mansfield Town 4 Lge 1gl, 1 LC 1gl.					26.01.95	Bury	19+1		3		13			
A D D I T I O N A L C O N T R A C T P L A Y E R														
Andrew Oakes						Burnley								
				Free	08.95	Bury								

GIGG LANE

Bury, Lancashire, BL9 9HR
Tel: 0161 764 4881

Capacity ....11,614.
Covered Standing ....4,825.
Seating..6,787.

First game ....Accrington v Church, 18.6.1885.
First floodlit game...v Wolverhampton Wanderers, 3-1, 6.10.1953.

ATTENDANCES
Highest ....35,000 v Bolton Wanderers FA Cup 3rd Round, 9.1.1960.
Lowest...416 v Tranmere Rovers, AMC, 26.2.1986.

OTHER GROUNDS ....None.

MATCHDAY TICKET PRICES

Main Stand £10
Juv/OAP £5

Family & Cemetery Enclosure £8
Juv/OAP £4
Family Ticket (1+1) £11

South Stand. £9
Juv/OAP £4

Ticket Office telephone no. . . . . 0161 764 4881.

HOW TO GET TO THE GROUND

From the North
Use motorway (M66) until junction 2, then leave motorway and follow signs to Bury A58. In half a mile turn left into Heywood Street and at end forward into Parkhills Road. At end turn left (A56) into Manchester Road, then shortly turn left into Gigg Lane for Bury FC.

From the East, South and West
Use motorway (M62) until junction 17. Leave motorway and follow signs to Bury (A56). In 3.1 miles turn right into Gigg Lane for Bury FC.

Car Parking
Ample side-street parking is available.

Nearest Railway Station
Bury Metro Interchange.

CLUBCALL
0898 12 11 97

Calls cost 39p per minute cheap rate and 49p per minute at all other times.
Call costings correct at time of going to press.

MATCHDAY PROGRAMME

Programme Editor . . . . N Neville.

Number of pages . . . . 32.

Price . . . . £1.20.

Subscriptions . . . . £1.20 per match +50p P&P or SAE.

Local Newspapers . . . . Bury Times, Bolton Evening News,
. . . . Manchester Evening News.

Local Radio Stations . . . . Piccadilly Radio, G.M.R.

CAMBRIDGE UNITED
(The U's)
ENDSLEIGH LEAGUE DIVISION 3
SPONSORED BY: PREMIER HOLIDAYS AND TRAVEL

Back Row (L-R): Jody Craddick, Ollie Morah, Steve Butler, David Thompson, Shane Westley, Russell Stock, David Adekola, Danny Granville.
Middle Row: Tony Richards, Leon Gutzmore, Martin Davies, Colin Vowden, Marc Joseph, Lee Palmer.
Front Row: Soner Zumrutel, Matt Joseph, John Fowler, Craig Middleton, Andy Jeffrey, Lenny Pack, Carlo Corazzin, Michael Kyd.
Photo: David Smith - Photo Finish.

After the exciting end to the 1993-94 season Cambridge United fans were hopeful of another high finish in the table but sadly the last week of the season bought relegation to division 3 - manager Gary Johnson had paid the price for the team's failure with dismissal at the start of April and the manager for the new season will be Tommy Taylor, the former West Ham United defender.

The squad that completed the 1994 season remained largely intact for 1994/1995. Departures were Michael Cheetham and Richard Wilkins with only two additions - Ollie Morah at a cost of £50,000 from Sutton and Efon Elad from neighbours Northampton Town who left after only a few games.

The season started disastrously - five defeats before a won against bottom club Chester at the end of August. Thereafter the club's poor league performance saw them in the bottom seven of the table for the remainder of the season.

There were some notable highlights to the season - a 4-1 demolition of Bradford in the league, FA Cup victories at Brentford and Peterborough and end of season league victories against Peterborough and Birmingham City at the Abbey. On the downside a 6-0 defeat at Brentford and the loss of vital points with opposition goals in the last minutes of games.

The squad has many younger players - the season saw Michael Kyd, Lenny Pack and Jon Rattle progress via the youth team whilst other former youth players Jody Craddock and Danny Granville caught the scouts eye. Goalkeeper John Filan moved to Coventry City after Jon Sheffield reclaimed the keeper's position whilst Darren Hay moved to Woking. The strike force of Carlo Corazin and Steve Butler was very effective with 40 goals between them.

And so to 1995-96 - the nucleus of the squad is young and promising and with experience from older players they should do well and hopefully see United challenging for promotion at the end of the season.

CCF.

CAMBRIDGE UNITED

Division Two: 20th   **FA Cup:** 3rd Round   **Coca-Cola Cup:** 1st Round

M	DATE	COMP.	VEN	OPPONENTS	RESULT	H/T	LP	GOAL SCORERS/GOAL TIMES	ATT.
1	A 13	EL	A	Wycombe Wanderers	L 0-3	0-1			(5,782)
2	17	CC 1/1	A	Portsmouth	L 0-2	0-2			(3,854)
3	20	EL	H	Stockport	L 3-4	1-2	18	Joseph 17, Morah 85, Corazzin 89	3,163
4	23	CC 1/2	H	Portsmouth	L 2-3	1-1		Craddock 3, Barrick 72	2,571
5	27	EL	A	Oxford United	L 0-1	0-1	22		(5,513)
6	30	EL	H	Chester City	W 2-1	0-0	17	Barrick 60, Corazzin 72	2,520
7	S 3	EL	H	Rotherham United	W 2-1	1-0	15	Corazzin 24, 76	2,885
8	10	EL	A	Leyton Orient	D 1-1	0-0	15	Morah 47	(3,699)
9	13	EL	A	Plymouth	D 0-0	0-0	17		(3,824)
10	17	EL	H	Swansea City	L 1-3	1-2	18	Granville 40	2,795
11	27	EL	A	Brighton	L 0-2	0-1	20		(8,280)
12	27	AWT	A	Barnet	W 2-0			Lillis, Corazzin	(995)
13	O 1	EL	H	Bradford City	W 4-1	2-1	18	Corazzin 19, Lillis 35, Butler 69, 88	3,338
14	18	EL	H	Wrexham	L 1-2	0-0	18	Corazzin 85	3,221
15	15	EL	A	Huddersfield	L 1-3	1-0	19	Butler 42	(10,742)
16	18	AWT	H	Northampton	L 1-3	1-0		Lillis 29	1,497
17	22	EL	A	Cardiff City	L 1-3	1-1	20	Jeffrey 38	(3,580)
18	29	EL	H	Brentford	D 0-0	0-0	21		3,102
19	N 1	EL	H	Bristol Rovers	D 1-1	0-0	22	Corazzin 54	2,328
20	5	EL	A	AFC Bournemouth	L 0-1	0-0	22		(3,272)
21	12	FAC 1	H	Brentford	D 2-2	1-1		Lillis 13, Butler 47	3,353
22	19	EL	H	Shrewsbury	W 3-1	1-1	21	Butler 10, 90, Lillis 15	2,748
23	22	FAC 1R	A	Brentford	W 2-1	2-1		Lillis 6, Butler 45	(4,096)
24	26	EL	A	Crewe	L 2-4		21	Corazzin	(3,636)
25	29	AWT	A	Bristol Rovers	L 2-4			Corrazin, Hay	(2,373)
26	D 3	FAC 2	A	Peterborough	W 2-0			Barrick, Hay	(9,576)
27	10	EL	A	Stockport County	L 1-2		21	Butler	(3,903)
28	16	EL	H	Wycombe Wanderers	D 2-2	1-1	20	Butler 7, Corazzin 63	3,713
29	26	EL	A	Birmingham City	D 1-1	0-1	20	Otto 82 (og)	(20,090)
30	28	EL	H	York City	W 1-0	0-0	19	Corazzin 63	3,285
31	31	EL	A	Peterborough	D 2-2	1-1	18	Lillis 20, 82	(7,412)
32	J 2	EL	H	Hull City	D 2-2	0-2	18	Hay 61, 82	3,569
33	7	FAC 3	H	Burnley	L 2-4	1-2		Butler 17 (pen), 85	6,275
34	14	EL	A	Blackpool	W 3-2	1-1	18	Butler 14, Corazzin 66,73	(4,076)
35	17	EL	H	Cardiff	W 2-0	1-0	18	Corazzin 18, Butler 65 (pen)	2,460
36	21	EL	H	Bournemouth	D 2-2	1-0	17	Butler 4, 77	2,834
37	28	EL	A	Brentford	L 0-6	0-0	17		(6,390)
38	F 4	EL	H	Crewe	L 1-2	0-0	18	Corazzin 78	3,339
39	18	EL	H	Blackpool	D 0-0	0-0	19		3,192
40	21	EL	A	Shrewsbury	D 1-1	1-0	19	Hay 26	(3,200)
41	15	EL	A	Bradford City	D 1-1	1-0	19	Jeffrey 90	(6,075)
42	M 4	EL	H	Brighton	L 0-2	0-1	19		3,856
43	7	EL	A	Rotherham	L 0-1	0-1	19		(2,208)
44	11	EL	H	Oxford	L 1-2	0-1	19	Corazzin 90	3,558
45	15	EL	A	Bristol Rovers	L 1-2	1-2	19	Kyd 34	(3,734)
46	18	EL	A	Chester City	W 3-1	3-0	19	Corazzin 12, 40, Butler 32	(1,720)
47	21	EL	H	Leyton Orient	D 0-0	0-0	19		3,048
48	24	EL	A	Swansea City	L 0-1	0-1	19		(4,007)
49	A 1	EL	H	Plymouth Argyle	D 1-1	0-0	19	Butler (pen)	3,913
50	8	EL	H	Peterborough United	W 2-0	1-0	19	Joseph 17, Butler 62	5,828
51	15	EL	A	York City	L 0-2	0-1	19		(3,278)
52	17	EL	H	Birmingham City	W 1-0	0-0	19	Heathcote 62	5,317
53	22	EL	A	Hull City	L 0-1	0-0	19		(3,483)
54	29	EL	H	Huddersfield	D 1-1	1-1	20	Granville 27	5,188
55	M 6	EL	A	Wrexham	W 1-0	1-0	20	Corazzin 29	(3,172)
56									
57									
58									
59									
60									

Best Home League Attendance: 5,828 v Peterborough   **Smallest:** 2,328 v Bristol Rovers   **Av Home Att:** 3,443

Goal Scorers:

Compared with 1993-94: -243

League (52):	Corazzin 15, Butler 14, Lillis 4, Hay 3, Granville 2, Jeffrey 2, Joseph 2, Morah 2, Barrick 1, Heathcote, Kyd, Opponent
C/Cola Cup (2):	Barrick 2, Craddock
FA Cup (8):	Butler 4, Lillis 2, Hay, Barrick
AW Trophy (5):	Corazzin 2, Lillis 2, Hay

Filan	Hunter	Barrick	Craddock	Heathcote	O'Shea	Hyde	Elad	Butler	Corrazin	Nyamah	Fowler	Murah	Rattie	Joseph	Granville	Danzey	Kyd	Lillis	Hayrettin	Walker	Manuel	Jeffrey	Sheffield	Hay	Pack	Referee	
1	2	3	4	5	6	7	8	9	10	11	12															T. Holbrook	1
1	2	3	4	5	6	7		12	10			9	8	11												D. Orr	2
1	2	3	4	5	6	7	14	9	10			12	8	11												R. Poulain	3
1	2	3	4	5	6	7	14	9	10			12		11	8											K. Cooper	4
1	2	3	4	5	12	7	8	14	10	11	6	9														A. Flood	5
1	2	3	4	5				9	10			7		11			8	12								P. Alcock	6
1	2	3	4	5		14		9	10			7		11			8	12									
1	2	3	4	5		14		9	10			7		11	6			12	8							K. Leach	8
1	2	3	4	5		14		9	10			7		12	6				8							E. Pearce	9
1	2	3	4	5		14		9	10			7		12	6				8							D. Bryan	10
1	2	3	4	5		14		9	10			7		12					6	8						P. Vanes	11
1	2	3	4	5				9	10	14				12				7	6	8						D. Orr	12
1	2	3	4	5	12			9	10	14				11				7	6	8						J. Winter	13
1	2	3	4	5				9	10	14				11		12		7	6	8						N. Barry	14
1		3	4	5				9	10	2				11	14	6		7		8				12		P. Richards	15
1		3	4	5				9	10	2				11	14	6		7		8				12		G. Pooley	16
1	4	3		5				9	10					11	14	6		7		8		2		12		S. Dunn	17
1	6	3	4	5				9	10		12			11	7						8	2				R. Furnandiz	18
1	2	3	4	5		14		9	10		6			11	7						8	2				T. Heilbron	19
1	2	3	4	5	6			9	10		14			11	7						8			12		P. Alcock	20
	12	3	4	5	6			9	10					2				8			7		1	11		P. Foakes	21
		3	4	5	6			9	10				14	2				8			7		1	11		A. D'Urso	22
		3	4	5	6			9	10	12		7		2				8					1	11		P. Foakes	23
		3	4	5	6			9	10	12		7		2				8				14	1	11		E. Lomas	24
	14	3	4		6			9	10			7		2	8			12				5	1	11		G. Barber	25
	2	3	4		6			9	10				14	8				12			7	5	1	11		P. Alcock	26
	2	3	4		6			9	10					8				12			7	5	1	11		A. Butler	27
	2	3	4		6			9	10					8				12			7	5	1	11		J. Rushton	28
	2	3	4		6	8			10					11	14			12			7	5	1			S. Mathieson	29
	2	3	4		6	9			10					11	14			8			7	5	1	12		P. Alcock	30
	2	3	4		6	9			10			7		11				8				5	1	12		J. Kirkby	31
	2	3	4		6	9			10	14				11				8				5	1	12		G. Barber	32
	12	3			6	7		9	10					2				8				5	1	12		N. Brady	33
		3	4	5	6	7		9	10					11				8				3	1	12		J. Brandwood	34
	14	3	4	5	6	7		9	10					11				8				3	1	12		T. West	35
		3	4	5	6			9	10			7		11					14		8	3	1	12		J. Lloyd	36
		3	4	5	6			9	10			7		11							8	12	1	14		G. Pooley	37
		3	4		6			9	10					2	7	5		8				11	1			P. Rejer	38
		3	4	5		7		9	10					2	8							11	1			S. Dunn	39
	7	3	4	5				9						2			14	12	6			11	1	8		U. Rennie	40
	7	3	4	5				9	10		12			2			14	6				11	1	8		P. Harrison	41
		3	4	4				9	10			7		2	1		8	6				11	2	12		M. Riley	42
		3	4	5	6	14		9	10					2			8		7			11	1	12		G. Singh	43
			4	5	6	14		9	14					2			8	10				11	1	7		J. Winter	44
		3		5	6			9	10					2	7		8					11	1	12		E. Wolstenholme	45
		3	4	5	6			9	10					2	11		8		14				1	12		T. Heilbron	46
		3		5	6			9	10					2			8		7			14	1	12	11	R. Harris	47
		3		5		4		9	10					2			8		7				1	12	11	P. Wright	48
	12			5		7		9	10	14				2			8		6				1		11	D. Orr/ R. Saunders	49
		3	4	5				9	10	8				2		6	12					11	1			K. Leach	50
		3	4	5				9	10	8				2		14	12					11	1			J. Kirby	51
	12	3	4	5					10					2		14	9	8				11	1			R. Poulain	52
		3		5				9	10					2	6	14	12	8				11	1			K. Lupton	53
		3		5				9	10					2	6	14	12	8				11	1			P. Foakes	54
		3	8	5				9	10					2	6	S		S				11	1			P. Richards	55
16	23	44	38	24	30	18	2	35	45	5	12	8	6	39	11	7	10	14	15	5	10	25	28	7	3	League Appearances	
	3				1	9	1	2	1	4	4	6					5	4	9	5	2			3		League Sub Appearances	19
2		2	2	2	2	2	2	0+1	1+1	2				1+1	1	2	1									C/Cola Appearances	
	1+2	4	3	1	3	4		4	4	0+1	1+1			4	0+1			3+1			2	2	4	4		FA Cup Appearances	
2	1+1	3	3		2	1		3	3	1	1+1	0+1		3	1+1	1		2+1	1	2		1	1	1+1		AW Trophy Appearances	

Also Played: Livett 6(6,7), Lomas S(43),1(46), Rush 9(9,10), Campbell S(2)   Loan Players: Campbell J (Luton), Rush (Sunderland), Walker (Port Vale)

CAMBRIDGE UNITED   RECORDS AND STATISTICS

CLUB RECORDS

BIGGEST VICTORIES
League: 6-0 v Darlington, Division 4, 18.9.1971.
6-0 v Hartlepool United, Division 4, 11.2.1989.
7-2 v Cardiff City (a) Division 2, 30.4.1994.
F.A. Cup: 5-1 v Bristol City, 5th Round 2nd replay, 27.2.1990.

BIGGEST DEFEATS
League: 0-6 v Aldershot (a) Division 3, 13.4.1974.
0-6 v Darlington (a), Division 4, 28.9.1974.
0-6 v Chelsea (a), Division 2, 15.1.1983.
League Cup: 0-5 v Colchester United, 1st Round, 1970-71.
0-5 v Derby County, Round 2, 4.10.1989.

MOST POINTS
3 points a win: 86, Division 3, 1990-91.
2 points a win: 65, Division 4, 1976-77.

MOST GOALS SCORED
87, Division 4, 1976-77.

RECORD TRANSFER FEE RECEIVED
£1,000,000 from Manchester United for Dion Dublin, August 1992.

RECORD TRANSFER FEE PAID
£195,000 to Luton Town for Steve Claridge, November 1992.

BEST PERFORMANCES
League: 5th in Division 2, 1991-92.
F.A. Cup: 6th Round 1989-90, 1990-91.
League Cup: 5th Round, 1992-93.

HONOURS
Champions of Division 4, 1976-77.
Champions of Division 3, 1990-91.

LEAGUE CAREER
Elected to Div 4 1970, P. Div 3 1972-73, R. Div 4 1973-74, P. Div 3 1976-77, P. Div 2 1977-78, R. Div 3 1983-84, R. Div 4 1984-85, P. Div 3 1989-90, P. Div 2 (now Div 1) 1990-91, R. Div 2 1992-93, R. Div 3 1994-95.

INDIVIDUAL CLUB RECORDS

MOST GOALS IN A SEASON
David Crown: 27 goals in 1985-86 (League 24, FA Cup 1, Freight Rover Trophy 2).

MOST GOALS IN A MATCH
5. Steve Butler v Exeter City, Division 2, 4.4.1994.

OLDEST PLAYER
John Ryan, 37 years 134 days v Derby County, 1.12.1984.

YOUNGEST PLAYER
Andy Sinton, 16 years 228 days v Wolverhampton W., 2.11.1982.

MOST CAPPED PLAYER
Tom Finney (Northern Ireland) 7.

PREVIOUS MANAGERS

(Since 1951)
Bill Whittaker 1951-55; Gerald Williams 1955; Bert Johnson 1955-59; Bill Craig 1959; Alan Moore (was player coach from 1959-60) 1960-63; Roy Kirk (caretaker) 1963-64; Roy Kirk 1964-66; Matt Wynn (caretaker) 1966-67; Bill Leivers 1967-74; Ray Freeman (caretaker) 1974; Ron Atkinson 1974-78; John Docherty 1978-83; John Ryan 1984-85; John Cozens (caretaker) 1984-85; Ken Shellito 1985-86; Chris Turner 1986-90; John Beck 1990-92; Gary Johnson (caretaker) 1992; Ian Atkins 1992-93; Gary Johnson 1993-95.

ADDITIONAL INFORMATION
PREVIOUS NAMES
Abbey United until 1951.
PREVIOUS LEAGUES
Southern League.

Club Colours: Amber shirts with black sleeves, black shorts amber flash, black socks with amber trim.
Change colours: All white.
Reserves League: Springheath Print Capital League.
Youth League: South East Counties.

LONGEST LEAGUE RUNS

of undefeated matches:	14 (1972)	of league matches w/out a win:	31 (1983-84. A League Record)	
of undefeated home matches:	22 (1977-78)	of undefeated away matches:	12 (1990)	
without home win:	16 (1983-84. A League Record)	without an away win:	32 (1981-83)	
of league wins:	7 (1977)	of home wins:	10 (1977-78)	
of league defeats:	7 (1983, 1984, 1984-85, 1985)	of away wins:	4 (20.3.1994 - 30.4.1994)	

Cambridge United played 12 successive home league games without conceding a goal in 1982-83.

THE MANAGER

TOMMY TAYLOR . . . . appointed April 1995.

PREVIOUS CLUBS
As Manager . . . . None.
As Asst.Man/Coach . . . . Maidstone.
As a player . . . . West Ham United, Orient.

HONOURS
As a Manager . . . . None.
As a Player . . . . FA Cup 1975.

CAMBRIDGE UNITED

PLAYERS NAME Honours	Ht	Wt	Birthdate	Birthplace Transfers	Contract Date	Clubs	League	L/Cup	FA Cup	Other	Lge	L/C	FAC	Oth
							APPEARANCES				**GOALS**			
G O A L K E E P E R S														
Scott Barrett	6.0	12.11	02.04.63	Ilkeston		Ilkeston Town								
GMVC'92, FAT'92					27.09.84	Wolverhampton W.	30	1	1	3				
				£10,000	24.07.87	Stoke City	51	2	3	4				
				Loan	10.01.90	Colchester United	13							
				Loan	22.03.90	Stockport County	10			2				
						Colchester United				5				
				Free	14.08.92	Gillingham	47	5	4	2				
				Free	.08.95	Cambridge United								
Martin Davies	6.1	12.4	28.06.74	Swansea	02.07.92	Coventry City (T)								
				Loan	23.11.93	Stafford Rangers								
				Free	.08.95	Cambridge United								
D E F E N D E R S														
Jody Craddock	6.0	11.10	25.07.75	Bromsgrove		Christchurch								
				Free	13.08.93	Cambridge United	57+1	2	3	3		1		
				Loan	04.10.93	Woking								
Micah A Hyde	5.9	10.5	10.11.74	Newham	19.05.93	Cambridge Utd (T)	31+14	2	4+2	2+1	2			
Andrew Jeffrey	5.10	11.0	15.01.72	Bellshill	13.02.90	Leicester City (T)								
via Cambridge City, (23.7.91) to				£8,500	09.07.93	Cambridge United	62+6	4	5	4	2			
Matthew N A Joseph	5.7	10.2	30.09.72	Bethnal Green	17.11.90	Arsenal (T)								
				Free	07.12.92	Gillingham								
					19.11.93	Cambridge United	105	4	8	6	6			
Lee Palmer	6.0	12.4	19.09.70	Croydon	28.07.89	Gillingham (T)	99+11	5+1		7+1	6	4		
				Free	.08.95	Cambridge United								
David Thompson	6.3	12.7	20.11.68	Ashington	26.11.86	Millwall (A)	88+9	4	4	6	6		1	
					18.06.92	Bristol City	17	4		5+1				
				Free	01.02.94	Brentford	9+1				1			
				Loan	09.09.94	Blackpool								
					07.11.94	Blackpool								
				Free	23.03.95	Cambridge United	7							
Colin Vowden	6.0	13.0	13.09.71	Newmarket		Cambridge City								
				£15,000	19.05.95	Cambridge United								
Shane Westley	6.2	12.10	16.06.65	Canterbury	08.06.83	Charlton Athletic (A)	8		1					
				£15,000	01.03.85	Southend United	142+2	10+1	5	7	10	1		1
				£150,000	19.06.89	Wolverhampton W.	48+2	5		2	1	1		
				£100,000	31.10.92	Brentford	46+2	2	3	4	1	2		
				Free	.08.95	Cambridge United								
M I D F I E L D														
Dean Barrick	5.9	11.4	30.09.69	Hemsworth	07.05.88	Sheffield Wed. (T)	11				2			
				£50,000	14.02.91	Rotherham United	96+3	6	8	5	7			1
				£50,000	11.08.93	Cambridge United	88	6	7	6	2	1	1	
John A Fowler	5.9	10.7	27.10.74	Preston	18.04.92	Cambridge Utd (T)	30+9	2+4	4+1	3+1	1			
				Loan	19.02.93	Preston North End	5+1							
Daniel Granville	5.11	12.5	19.01.75	Islington	19.05.93	Cambridge Utd (T)	21+6	1	0+1	1+2	7			
				Loan	12.01.94	Saffron Walden								
Michael Kyd	5.8	12.10	21.05.77	Hackney		Cambridge Utd (T)	10+9				1			
F O R W A R D S														
Stephen Butler	6.2	13.0	27.01.82	Birmingham		Wokingham Town								
E: S-P3; GMVC'89						Windsor		1						
				Free	19.12.84	Brentford	18+3			2	3			
				Free	01.08.86	Maidstone United	76	4	18	10	41	3	7	4
				£150,000	13.03.91	Watford	40+22	4+3	1	2+1	9			
Loan Bournemouth, (18.12.92), 1Lg App.				£75,000	23.12.92	Cambridge United	91+2	4+1	5	3	41		4	
Giancarlo Corazzin	5.9	12.5	25.12.71	Canada		Vancouver								
Canada				£20,000	10.12.93	Cambridge United	73+1	2	4	3	29			2
Craig Middleton	5.11	10.13	10.09.70	Nuneaton	30.05.89	Coventry City (T)	2+1	1						
				Free	20.07.93	Cambridge United	17+2	1			2			
Olisa Morah	5.11	13.2	03.09.72	Islington	17.08.91	Tottenham H. (T)								
E: S, Y1; FAYC'90				Loan	20.11.91	Hereford United	0+2							
				Free	13.11.92	Swindon Town								
via Sutton United, 3 Apps. + 1Gl FAC, (Free), to				£50,000	08.06.94	Cambridge United	8+6	1+1		0+1	2			
				Loan	23.03.95	Torquay United	2							

ABBEY STADIUM

Newmarket Road, Cambridge CB5 8LN
Tel: 01223 566 500

Capacity 9,667
Covered Standing 6,425
Seating 3,242

First game ....v University Press, Friendly, 31.8.1932.
First floodlit game ....v Great Yarmouth, East Anglian Cup, 21.10.57.

ATTENDANCES
Highest...14,000 v Chelsea (friendly), 1.5.1970.
Lowest ....857 v Colchester United, AMC 24.11.1987.

OTHER GROUNDS...None.

MATCHDAY TICKET PRICES

Blocks A & G £10
Juv/OAP/Students £5

Family B Block. £7
Juv/OAP/Students £4

Blocks C,D,E £12
Juv/OAP/Student £6

Terraces. £7
Juv/OAP/Students £4

Match and Ticket Information
Postal application with payment & SAE one week in advance. (Access & Visa accepted)
Ticket Office Telephone no. 01223 566 500

CLUBCALL
0891 55 58 85

Calls cost 39p per minute cheap rate and 49p per minute at all other times.
Call costings correct at time of going to press.

HOW TO GET TO THE GROUND

From the North
Use A1 and A14 signposted to Cambridge, then follow signs for Newmarket. Leave A14 to join B1047 to Cambridge. Turn right into Newmarket Road for Cambridge United FC.

From the East
Follow signs A14 to Cambridge, use A1303 to Cambridge, then follow signs for Newmarket Road for Cambridge United FC.

From the South
Use A10 or M11, follow signs for A14 to Newmarket. Leave A14 to join B1047 to Cambridge, turn right into Newmarket Road for Cambridge United FC.

From the West
Follow signs A428 to Cambridge, then A14 to Newmarket and as for North.

Car Parking
Limited parking at main entrance. Off-street parking permitted. Also at Coldhams Common for visitors.

Nearest Railway Station
Cambridge (01233 311 999)

MATCHDAY PROGRAMME

Programme Editor. . . . . B Pope.

Number of pages . . . . 32.

Price . . . . £1.30.

Subscriptions. . . . . £50.00.

Local Newspapers . . . . Cambridge Evening News.

Local Radio Stations . . . . BBC Radio Cambridgeshire, Q103,
. . . . Chiltern Radio.

CARDIFF CITY
(The Bluebirds)
ENDSLEIGH LEAGUE DIVISION 3
SPONSORED BY: THE SOUTH WALES ECHO

Back Row (L-R): Chris Davies, Andy Scott, Simon Haworth, Scott Young, Paul Shaw, Derek Brazil. **Middle Row:** Harry Parsons (Kit Manager), Keith Downing, Lee Baddeley, Patrick Mountain, Nathan Wigg, David Williams, Anthony Bird, Steve Williams, Chris Ingram, Bill Coldwell (director of football), Ian Jones, Jimmy Goodfellow (physio). **Front Row:** Ian Rodgerson, Damon Searle, Jason Perry (club captain), Kenny Hibbitt (coach), Paul Harding (captain), Carl Dale, Darren Adams.

CARDIFF CITY
FORMED IN 1899
TURNED PROFESSIONAL IN 1910
LTD COMPANY IN 1910

CHAIRMAN: Samesh Kumar
DIRECTORS
Will Dixon, David Henderson
SECRETARY
Jim Finney
COMMERCIAL MANAGER
Howard King

DIRECTOR OF FOOTBALL: Bill Caldwell
COACH: Terry Hibbitt

YOUTH TEAM MANAGER
Gavin Tait

STATISTICIAN FOR THE DIRECTORY
Alan Jenkins

Speculation throughout the close season on who would become the new owners led to an unsettled period at Ninian Park. No new players coming in meant that the team were going to struggle. Only one league win in the first twelve outings, knocked out in the first round of the Coca-Cola Cup and the FA Cup; and beyond that the club were unable to string more than two victories together throughout the season.

The consortium that Rick Wright chose to become the new owners of the club didn't have the money that they said would be available. In the end they had to leave the club. Not before Eddie May had been removed and replaced by a reluctant Terry Yorath, who had been part of the consortium take-over. When the consortium failed, Yorath had to go, and in typical Wright fashion the press conference convened to announce his replacement, and the Chairman introduced Eddie May! A run of just one defeat in seven league and cup games brought what turned out to be false hope.

At the beginning of the season Wright said the club would be aiming for a play-off place. The supporters knew that that would be unlikely and even Wright would have realised that if he'd attended more than just a couple of games throughout the whole of the season. He then stated that the club wouldn't be relegated. In the end the fans would probably have been happy with Second Division survival. But even that was too much to ask for.

So it's Division Three for the new season and we don't even have the added incentive of European football at Ninian Park.

At the moment there's talk over another consortium taking over. Two deadlines have passed already. The rumour is that former Maidstone United and Gillingham chairman is involved. He failed to do anything with either of these clubs (one is now defunct and according to press reports Gillingham's future doesn't look too rosy). If he does take over from Wright, will Cardiff City go the same way as Maidstone and Gillingham?

ALAN JENKINS.

543

CARDIFF CITY

Division One: 22nd   **FA Cup:** 4th Round   **Coca-Cola Cup:** 2nd Round   **Auto WindScreen Trophy:** 2nd Round   **Welsh Cup:** Finalists

M	DATE	COMP.	VEN	OPPONENTS	RESULT	H/T	LP	GOAL SCORERS/GOAL TIMES	ATT.
1	A 13	EL	A	Stockport County	L 1-4	1-1		Stant 30	(5,139)
2	16	CC 1/1	H	**Torquay United**	W 1-0	0-0		**Oatway 58**	**2,690**
3	20	EL	H	Oxford United	L 1-3	1-2	20	Stant 7	7,281
4	23	CC 1/2	A	**Torquay United**	L 2-4	2-2		**Stant 40, 43**	**(2,719)**
5	27	EL	A	York City	D 1-1	0-0	19	Millar 79	(2,861)
6	30	EL	H	Wrexham	D 0-0	0-0	20		4,903
7	S 3	EL	H	Swansea City	D 1-1	0-1	22	Richardson 53	5,523
8	10	EL	A	Blackpool	L 1-2	1-0	21	Richardson 4	(4,189)
9	13	EL	A	Chester City	W 2-0	0-0	20	Stant 51, Aizlewood 67	(2,671)
10	17	EL	H	Plymouth Argyle	L 0-1	0-0	21		5,674
11	24	EL	A	AFC Bournemouth	L 2-3	1-1	22	Scott 27, Aizlewood 80	(3,177)
12	27	AWT 1	H	**Plymouth Argyle**	W 2-0	0-0		**Griffith 56, Dale 75**	**1,299**
13	O 1	EL	A	Peterborough United	L 1-2	1-1	22	Fereday 41	4,225
14	8	EL	H	Crewe Alexandra	L 1-2	1-0	22	Stant 24	4,126
15	15	EL	A	Bristol Rovers	D 2-2	1-0	22	Richardson 14, Millar 53	(3,936)
16	22	EL	H	Cambridge United	W 3-0	1-0	22	Stant 14, 55, 85	3,580
17	30	EL	A	Bradford City	W 3-2	3-1	20	Millar 4 (pen), 44 Stant 26	(5,937)
18	N 1	EL	A	Leyton Orient	L 0-2	0-0	21		(2,558)
19	5	EL	H	Brighton & H.A.	W 3-0	0-0	19	Baddeley 49, Stant 71, 78	5,004
20	7	WC 3	A	**Ebbw Vale**	D 1-1	0-0		**Millar 58**	**1,316**
21	12	FAC 1	A	**Enfield**	L 0-1	0-0			**(2,345)**
22	15	AWT 1	A	**Exeter City**	D 1-1	0-0		**Young 66**	**(1,203)**
23	19	EL	A	Wycombe Wanderers	L 1-3	1-0	20	Stant 82	(5,391)
24	22	WC3 R	H	**Ebbw Vale**	W 2-0	0-0		**Richardson 54, Thompson 90**	**1,343**
25	25	EL	A	Hull City	L 0-2	0-2	20		4,226
24	29	AWT 2	A	**Exeter City**	L 0-1	0-0			**(1,452)**
25	D 10	EL	A	Oxford United	L 0-1	0-1	20		(6,181)
26	17	EL	H	Stockport County	D 1-1	0-0	21	Dale 89	3,448
27	26	EL	A	Shrewsbury Town	W 1-0	0-0	19	Stant 79	(4,933)
28	28	EL	H	Birmingham City	L 0-1	0-0	20		7,420
29	31	EL	A	Rotherham United	L 0-2	0-1	20		(3,064)
30	J 2	EL	H	Brentford	L 2-3	0-2	21	Stant 58, Bird 84	5,235
31	7	EL	H	Blackpool	L 0-1	0-1	21		3,467
32	14	EL	H	Huddersfield Town	D 0-0	0-0	21		3,808
33	17	EL	A	Cambridge United	L 0-2	0-1	21		(2,460)
34	F 4	EL	A	Hull City	L 0-4	0-2	22		(3,903)
35	8	WC 3R	H	**Ebbw Vale**	W 7-0	3-0		**Bird 20, Thompson 21, Aizelwood 34, Ware 48, (og) Dale**	**1,292**
36	15	WC 4	H	**Risca United**	W 4-0	0-0		**Dale 57, 73, 84, Brazil 64**	**1,294**
37	18	EL	H	Huddersfield Town	L 1-5	0-4	22	Brazil 73	(10,035)
38	21	EL	H	Wycombe Wanderers	W 2-0	0-0	22	Dale 48, Richardson 65	3,024
39	25	EL	A	Peterborough United	L 1-2	1-1	22	Dale 2	(4,226)
40	28	WC 5	A	**Llandudno**	W 1-0	0-0		**Dale 89**	**(800)**
41	M 4	EL	H	AFC Bournemouth	D 1-1	1-1	22	Dale 13	3,008
42	7	EL	A	Swansea City	L 1-4	0-3	22	Wigg 86	(3,943)
43	11	EL	A	York City	L 1-2	1-2	22	Griffith 32	2,689
44	15	EL	A	Brighton & H.A.	D 0-0	0-0	22		(6,956)
45	18	EL	A	Wrexham	W 3-0	1-0	22	Nicholls 24, Griffith 56, Humes 89 (og)	(3,023)
46	25	EL	H	Plymouth Argyle	D 0-0	0-0	22		(5,611)
47	28	EL	H	Bradford City	L 2-4	2-1	22	Perry 36, Millar 40	2,560
48	A 1	EL	H	Chester	W 2-1	1-0	22	Dale 44, Millar 87	4,405
49	4	EL	H	Leyton Orient	W 2-1	0-0	22	Bird 87, Nicholls 90	4,324
50	8	EL	A	Rotherham United	D 1-1	1-0	22	Griffith 33	6,412
51	11	WC S/F1	A	**Swansea City**	W 1-0	0-0		**Millar 88**	**(2,654)**
52	15	EL	A	Birmingham City	L 1-2	1-1	22	Millar 14	(17,455)
53	17	EL	H	Shrewsbury Town	L 1-2	0-1	22	Bird 60	4,677
54	22	EL	A	Brentford	L 0-2	0-0	22		(8,268)
55	29	EL	H	Bristol Rovers	L 0-1	0-0	22		5,462
56	M 2	WC S/F2	H	**Swansea City**	D 0-0	0-0			**4,227**
57	6	EL	A	Crewe Alexandra	D 0-0	0-0	22		(4,382)
58	21	WC F	N	**Wrexham**	L 1-2	0-2		**Dale 78**	**12,810**
59									
60									

Best Home League Attendance: 7,420 v Birmingham City **Smallest:** 2,560 v Bradford City   **Av Home Att:** 5,519

Goal Scorers:
League (46): Stant 13, Millar 7, Dale 5, Richardson 4, Griffith 3, Bird 3, Aizlewood 2, Nicholls 2, Baddeley, Brazil, Fereday, Perry Scott, Wigg, Opponent   **Compared with 1993-94:** -1,069
C/Cola Cup (3): Stant 2, Oatway
FA Cup (0):
AW Trophy (3): Dale, Griffith, Young
Welsh Cup (17): Dale 8, Millar 2, Thompson 2, Aizelwood, Bird, Brazil, Richardson, Opponent

Williams	Evans T.	Scott	Aizlewood	Perry	Oatway	Griffith	Richardson	Stant	Bird	Fereday	Dale	Brazil	Williams D.	Millar	Adams	Street	Young	Wigg	Thompson	Searle	Baddeley	McLean	Evans A.	Ramsey	Fleming	Referee	
1	2•	3	4	5	6	7	8	9	10*	11	12	14	S													K. Lynch	1
S	2		4	5	6	7	8	9	10*	11•	12	3	1	14												R. Harris	2
S	2		4•	5	6		8	9	10	11*	S	3	1	7	S											M. Pearce	3
S	2																									P. Vanes	4
S	2			6		8	9	7		10	5	1	11	S	3•	4	S									K. Breen	5
S	2	3		6	7	8		9*	11	10	5	1	12			4	S									K. Leach	6
S	2	3		6	7	8		12	11*	10	5	1	9			4	S	9	11*	14						I. Hemley	7
S	2•	3	4		6	7	8				10	5	1	12			14				5					A. Flood	8
S	2	3	*4		7	11•	8	9•			10	6	1	12							5					E. Lomas	9
S		3	4	6	7	11	8	9•	14		10	2	1	S			9			14	5•					J. Rushton	10
S		3	4	6	*7	11	8		12		10	2	1				9				5					A. D'Urso	11
S	2•	3	4	6	7	11	8				10		1	12			14			3	5					P. Vanes	12
S		4	2	6	8	12		9			10	7	1	11*				S	3	5						G. Singh	13
S		4	2	6	8	14	9	12	11	10*		1	7•					3	S			14				K. A. Cooper	14
S		4	5	6	7	8	9	11•		2	1	10					3	5			14					J. Parker	15
S			6	4	7	8	9	11•		2	1	12	*10					5								S. Dunn	16
S		3		6	4	7		9	11	10	2	1	8	S			S		5							A. Butler	17
S		3		6	4	7		9	11	10	2	1	8			S	S		5							G. Barber	18
S		3		6	4	7		9	11	10	2	1	8			S	S		5			7				J. Holbrook	19
S		3		6	4•	8		9	12	11*		2	1	10			14	12		5			7			R. Gifford	20
S	3		4	6	8*		9	11		2•	1	10			14	7	12		5			7				P. Vanes	21
S	2	3	14	6	4	8*		11		1	10•					10	3	5			7	S				M. Pearce	22
S		4		8	9			1	6	11*	2	12	10	3	5			7								J. Brandwood	23
S		4	6	8	12		S		1	11	2	10	3	5			7									R. Gifford	24
S		4	6	8		12	9	S		1	11	2*	10	3			7									G . Polley	25
S		4*		6	12	8	9	14		5	1	11•	2	10	3	5			7							J. Holbrook	26
1	2*			4	14	8	9		11*	12	6	S	10	3	5											P. Floakes	27
S			4	12	8	9		14	7	6	1	11•	2*	10	3	5			7							K. Leach	28
S		6*		4	S		9	11	8		1	12	2	3	5	2*	10	7								P. Richards	29
S			6	4	12		9	11	8		1	S	3	5	10	7										C. Wilkes	30
S			6	4•	11*		9	2	8	1	12	14	3	5	10											J. Watson	31
S	*		6	4•	14		9	12	2	8	1	11	7	10	3	5			7							P. Rejer	32
S		*11	6	4		9	12	2•	8		1	14	10	3	5			12	7							K.A. Cooper	33
S			6	8	11*		2•	9		1	14	10	3	5			7									P. Wright	34
S			6	8•		12	2	11		1	14	9•	10	3	5			7								T. West	35
S			6	4	14		12	8		1	11	9•	2	12	3	5			6							G. Cain	36
			4			8			11	7		1				14	9	3	5			14				R. Gifford	37
			4		11•		7	2*	8	12	1		6	10	3	5			14							V. Reed	38
			4	11		9•	2	8	12	1	10*		6	7	3	5										W. Burns	39
			4	14	10	2	8	6	1	12		11	3	5			12									G. Singh	40
			4•	6	14	10	11	8		1		7	3	5			9									K. Lupton	41
			6	14	10	11	8	4		1		12	7	3	5			9								B. Lawtor	42
			4	6	14	10	11•	8	2	1		12	7	3*	5			14								J. Brandwood	43
			4	6	10	11	8•	12	1		7	3	5													J. Lloyd	44
			4*	6	8	10	11	12	1	14		7	3	5												J. Rushton	45
S			6	4	10*	3	12	1	11		7	5*														M. Pierce	46
S			6	4	10	3	1	11	12	7	3	S	S													P. Harrison	47
S			6	4	10	1	11	5	7	3	12															P. Vanes	48
S			6	4	10	2*	1	11	5	7•	3	5														S. Dunn	49
S			6	4	10	S	1	11	5	7•	3	5														J. Holbrook	50
S			6	11	8	12	10	2	1	7	4•	3	5													P. Alcock	51
S			6•	11	8	12	10	2	1	7	4	3	5			12										P.Wright	52
S			6	11	8	9	10	2	1	*7	4•	3	5													A. Howells	53
S			6	11	8	9	10	2	1	7	S	4	3	5												K. Lynch	54
1			6*	11	8	9	10	2	7	12	4	3	5			12										K. Cooper	55
1			11	8	9	10	2	7	6•	4	3	5														M. Pierce	56
1			12	11	8	9*	10	2	7	14	6•	4	3	5			12									K. Leach	57
1			14	11	10	8	2•	7	6	4	3	5														R. Gifford	58
1			6	S	11	10	8	2	7	14	4	3	5			12										N. Barry	59
1			6	14	11	8	10	2	9•	7*	14	4														V. Reed	60

Williams	Evans T.	Scott	Aizlewood	Perry	Oatway	Griffith	Richardson	Stant	Bird	Fereday	Dale	Brazil	Williams D.	Millar	Adams	Street	Young	Wigg	Thompson	Searle	Baddeley	McLean	Evans A.	Ramsey	Fleming	
6	7	13	17	34	27	31	32	19	7	26	33	26	40	25	4	9	15	18	11	32	33	4	4	11		League Appearances
			3	9	1		1	12	1	1	4			10	1		8	1	2		3		9			League Sub Appearances
2		1	1	2	2	2	2	2	1	1	2			2		1	1	0								C/Cola Cup Appearances
1		1	0+1	1	1	1		1			1		1	1		1								1		FA Cup Appearances
1	1		2	1	2	2+1	1+1	2	1	5		1+1	2	2	2		1	0+1	2	3	3		2			AW Trophy Appearances
2+1		1	5	6	1+1	6+1	4+1	2	5	3	6	5+2	6	6		3+4	7	2+1	7	8		1+2	1			Welsh Cup

Also Played: Nicholls 4(31,32)10(34)14(43,44,48,49,50,53)8(45,46,47)S(51,52) , Honor 2(34,38,39,41,42,43,44,45,47)7(37), Pearson 9(34,37,38,41,42,43,44,45,46,47,48,49), Mountain S(34,35,36,56,58), Morris S(37,38,39,40,41,42,52,53,54,55,57), Vick 8(43,44), Milsom 14(46,47)9(55,56)

545

CARDIFF CITY   RECORDS AND STATISTICS

CLUB RECORDS

BIGGEST VICTORIES
League: 7-0 v Burnley, Division 1, 1.9.1928.
9-2 v Thames, Division 3(S), 6.2.1932.
7-0 v Barnsley, Division 2, 7.12.1957.
F.A. Cup: 8-0 v Enfield 1st Round, 1931-32.
(Scored 16 in a Welsh Cup tie, 20.1.1961)
Europe: 8-0 v P.O.Larnaca (Cyprus), ECWC 1st Round, 1970-71.
BIGGEST DEFEATS
League: 2-11 v Sheffield United, Division 1, 1.1.1926.
0-9 v Preston North End, Division 2, 7.5.1932.
F.A. Cup: 1-6 v Aston Villa, 3rd Round, 1928-29.
0-5 v Charlton Athletic, 3rd Round, 1937-38.
MOST POINTS
3 points a win: 86, Division 3, 1982-83.
2 points a win: 66, Division 3(S), 1946-47.
MOST GOALS SCORED: 93, Division 3(S), 1946-47.
RECORD TRANSFER FEE RECEIVED
£215,000 from Portsmouth for Jimmy Gilligan, September 1989.
RECORD TRANSFER FEE PAID
£200,000 to San Jose Earthquakes for Godfrey Ingram, Sept 1982.
BEST PERFORMANCES
League: Runners-up Division 1, 1923-24.
Highest Position: 2nd Division 1, 1923-24.
F.A. Cup: Winners in 1926-27.
League Cup: Semi-Finals in 1965-66.
Welsh Cup: Winners 22 times.
Europe: (ECWC) Semi-Finals in 1967-68
HONOURS
Champions of Division 3(S), 1946-47.
Champions of Division 3, 1992-93.
FA Cup winners in 1926-27.
Charity Shield winners in 1927.
Welsh Cup winners 22 times.
LEAGUE CAREER
Elected to Div 2 1920, Div 1 1920-21, Div 2 1928-29, Div 3(S) 1930-31, Div 2 1946-47, Div 1 1951-52, Div 2 1956-57, Div 1 1959-60, Div 2 1961-62, Div 3 1974-75, Div 2 1975-76, Div 3 1981-82, Div 2 1982-83, Div 3 1984-85, Div 4 1985-86, Div 3 1987-88, Div 4 (now Div 3) 1989-90, Div 2 1992-93, Div 3 1994-95

INDIVIDUAL CLUB RECORDS

MOST GOALS IN A SEASON
John Toshack: 31 goals in 1968-69 (League 22, Cup ties 9).

MOST GOALS IN A MATCH
6. Derek Tapscott v Knighton Town (Welsh FA Cup) 20.01.61.

OLDEST PLAYER
George Latham, 42 v Blackburn Rovers, Division 1, 2.1.1922.

YOUNGEST PLAYER
John Toshack, 16 v Leyton Orient, Division 2, 13.11.1965.

MOST CAPPED PLAYER
Alf Sherwood (Wales) 39.

PREVIOUS MANAGERS

Davy McDougall 1910-11; Fred Stewart 1911-33; Bartley Wilson 1933-34, B Watts Jones 1934-37; Bill Jennings 1937-39; Cyril Spiers 1939-46; Billy McCandless 1946-48; Cyril Spiers 1948-54; Trevor Morris 1954-58; Bill Jones 1958-62; George Swindin 1962-64; Jimmy Schoular 1964-73; Frank O'Farrell 1973-74; Jimmy Andrews 1974-78; Richie Morgan 1978-81; Graham Williams 1981-82; Len Ashurst 1982-84; Jimmy Goodfellow & Jimmy Mullen (caretakers) 1984; Alan Durban 1984-86; Frank Burrows 1986-89; Len Ashurst 1989-91; Eddie May 1991-94; Terry Yorath 1994-95; Eddie May 1995.

ADDITIONAL INFORMATION
PREVIOUS NAMES
Riverside FC (1899-1908) amalgamated with Riverside Albion (1902). Cardiff City from 1908.

PREVIOUS LEAGUES
Southern League. Cardiff & District F.L. South Wales League.

Club colours: Royal blue shirts with white collar, white shorts, blue stockings.
Change colours: All yellow.
Reserves League: Neville Ovenden Football Combination.

LONGEST LEAGUE RUNS

of undefeated matches:	21 (1946-47)	of league matches w/out a win:	15 (1936-37)
of undefeated home matches:	27 (1939/46/47)	of undefeated away matches:	10 (1946-47)
without home win:	10 (1986-87)	without an away win:	44 (1971-73)
of league wins:	9 (1946)	of home wins:	9 (1922-23, 1951-52)
of league defeats:	7 (1933)	of away wins:	7 (1993)

THE MANAGER

KENNY HIBBITT . . . . appointed July 1995.

PREVIOUS CLUBS
As Manager . . . . Walsall.
As Asst.Man/Coach . . . . Bristol Rovers.
As a player . . . . Chelsea, Aston Villa, Nottingham Forest, Portsmouth, Crewe Alexandra.

HONOURS
As a Manager . . . . None.
As a Player . . . . Wolves: League Cup 1974, 1980. Division 2 Championship 1977. UEFA Cup runners-up.
International . . . . 1 u23 cap for England.

CARDIFF CITY

PLAYERS NAME / Honours	Ht	Wt	Birthdate	Birthplace / Transfers	Contract Date	Clubs	League	L/Cup	FA Cup	Other	Lge	L/C	FAC	Oth
G O A L K E E P E R S														
David P Williams	6.0	12.0	18.09.68	Liverpool	15.08.87	Oldham Athletic (T)								
					23.03.88	Burnley	24	2		2				
Loan Rochdale, (02.09.91) 6 Lge, 1LC.					12.08.94	Cardiff City	40	2	1	8				
Stephen Williams	6.3	12.12	16.10.74	Cardigan		Coventry City (T)								
				Free	13.08.93	Cardiff City	24		1	5+1				
D E F E N D E R S														
Lee Baddeley	6.1	12.10	12.07.74	Cardiff	13.08.91	Cardiff City (T)	81+13	0+2	7	20	1			
Derek Brazil	6.0	12.1	14.12.68	Dublin	12.03.86	Manchester United	0+2							
Ei: B1, u23.1, u21.7; WFAC'93; Div3'93				Loan	20.11.90	Oldham Athletic	1			1				
				Loan	12.09.91	Swansea City	12	2		2	1			
				£85,000	26.08.92	Cardiff City	30+5	6	8	12+3	1			1
Terry Evans	5.8	10.7	08.01.76	Pontypridd	08.07.94	Cardiff City (T)	11+1	2	1	2+1				
Jason Perry	5.11	10.4	02.04.70	Newport	21.08.87	Cardiff City (T)	230+2	16	13+1	20+1	5			
W: 1, B2, u21.3, Y; WFAC'92'93; Div'93														
Andrew M Scott	6.0	12.0	27.06.75	Manchester	04.01.93	Blackburn Rov (T)								
				Free	09.08.94	Cardiff City	13		1	1	1			
Damon Searle	5.11	10.5	26.10.71	Cardiff	20.08.90	Cardiff City (T)	191+2	5	11	26	2	1		
W: B1, Y, u21.7; WFAC'93; Div3'93														
M I D F I E L D														
Paul Harding	5.10	12.5	06.03.64	Mitcham		Enfield				2				
FAT'88		via Barnet to		£60,000	28.09.90	Notts County	45+9	1	6	7+1	1			2
				Loan	26.08.93	Southend United	2+3			2				
				Loan	02.11.93	Watford	1+1							
				£50,000	03.12.93	Birmingham City	14+2		1				1	
				Free	.08.95	Cardiff City								
Anthony C. Oatway	5.7	10.10	28.11.73	Hammersmith		Yeading				2				
				Free	04.08.94	Cardiff City	27+3	2	1	3+1		1		
Ian Rodgerson	5.8	10.7	09.04.66	Hereford	03.07.85	Hereford United (J)	95+5	7	4	7+1	6			
				£35,000	03.08.88	Cardiff City	98+1	8	10	6+1	4			
				£50,000	04.12.90	Birmingham City	87+8	7+1	2	11	13	2		1
				£140,000	23.07.93	Sunderland	2+2							
				Free	.08.95	Cardiff City								
Nathan Wigg	5.9	10.5	27.09.74	Pontypool	04.08.93	Cardiff City (T)	26+12		0+1	7+3	1			
F O R W A R D S														
Darren Adams	5.7	10.7	12.01.74	Bromley		Bashley								
				Free	21.01.94	Cardiff City	13+7			2+1	1			
Anthony Bird	5.10	11.9	01.09.74	Cardiff	04.08.93	Cardiff City (T)	35+28	5	4+1	11+3	9	1	1	3
W: u21.2														
Carl Dale	6.0	12.0	24.04.66	Colwyn Bay		Bangor City								
WFAC'92'93; Div3'93				£12,000	19.05.88	Chester City	106+10	7+1	9	6	41		5	2
				£100,000	19.08.91	Cardiff City	100+11	5+1	4	14+1	38	2		13
David Andrew Evans	6.1	12.1	25.11.75	Aberystwyth		Cardiff City (T)	4+9			1+2				
Paul William Millar	6.2	12.7	16.11.66	Belfast		Portadown								
NI: B1, YPoY(NI)'86; IFAC'86; WFAC'92'93; Div3'93			£35,000	29.12.88	Port Vale	44+31	1+1	1+2	9+1	12			2
				Loan	11.10.90	Hereford United	5				2			
				£20,000	21.08.91	Cardiff City	66+19	6	7+1	5+2	10	1	1	1
Scott Young	6.1	12.0	14.01.76	Pontypridd	04.07.90	Cardiff City (T)	18+10	1		4+3				1

NINIAN PARK
Sloper Road, Cardiff CF1 8SX
Tel: 01222 398 636

Capacity ....21,000.
Seating..14,000.

First game ....v Ton Pentre, Southern Lge Div 2, 24.9.1910.
First floodlit game...v Grasshoppers Zurich
....(Friendly) 5.10.1960.

ATTENDANCES
Highest ....61,566 Wales v England, 14.10.1961. 57,893 v Arsenal, Division 1, 22.4.1953.
Lowest ....1,006 v Swansea City, AMC, 28.1.1986. 581 v Taffs Well, Welsh Cup, 25.11.1986.

OTHER GROUNDS: .... None.

MATCHDAY TICKET PRICES

Grandstand C&D £9
Juv/OAP £6

Grandstand elsewhere................... £8
Juv/OAP £5

Family Enclosure...................... £6
Juv/OAP £3

Additional Information
There are sometimes surcharges for important games of £1 or more per ticket.

Ticket Office Telephone no....... 01222 398 636

BLUEBIRDS CALL
0898 88 86 03

Calls cost 39p per minute cheap rate and 49p per minute at all other times.
Call costings correct at time of going to press.

HOW TO GET TO THE GROUND

From the North
Follow signs to Cardiff (A470) until junction with Cardiff bypass. At roundabout take 3rd exit A48 (sign posted Port Talbot). In 2 miles at roundabout take 1st exit (A4161) into Cowbridge Road . In half a mile turn right along Lansdowne Road. At end at crossroads turn right (A4055) into Leckwith Road. In 0.2 miles turn left into Sloper Road to Cardiff City FC.

From the East
Use motorway (M4), then A48 into Cardiff bypass. Follow Port Talbot then in 2 miles at roundabout take first exit A4161 into Cowbridge Road. In half a mile turn right along Lansdowne Road. At end at crossroads turn right (A4055) into Leckwith Road. In 0.2 miles turn left into Sloper Road for Cardiff City FC.

From the West
Use the M4 and leave at junction 33, taking the A4232 (traffic from the A48 can also join the A4232 at the Culverhouse Cross junction). Leave the A4232 at the exit the City Centre, B4267 for Cardiff City FC.

Car Parking
(Shared with the Leckwith athletic stadium) across the road from Ninian Park.

Nearest Railway Station
Cardiff Central (0122 228 000)

MATCHDAY PROGRAMME

Programme Editor . . . . Steve Groves & David Chapman.

Number of pages . . . . 32.

Price . . . . £1.

Subscriptions . . . . Apply to the club.

Local Newspapers . . . . South Wales Echo, Western Mail.

Local Radio Stations . . . . . BBC Radio Wales, Red Rose Radios (ILR),
. . . . BBC Radio Cymru.

CHESTER CITY
(The Blues)
ENDSLEIGH LEAGUE DIVISION 3
SPONSORED BY: CORBETTS

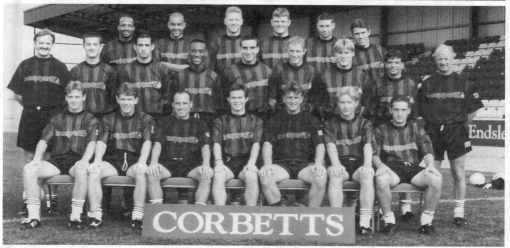

Back Row (L-R): Cyrille Regis, Spencer Whelan, Billy Stewart, Ray Newland, John Murphy, Eddie Bishop.
Middle Row: Stuart Walker (Physio), David Rogers, Scott Blenchley, Leroy Chambers, Julian Alsford, Andy Milner, David Flitcroft, Stuart Rimmer, Derek Mann (Yth Coach/Physio).
Front Row: Chris Priest, Iain Jenkins, Gary Shelton (Player/Coach), Roger Preece, Kevin Ratcliffe (Manager), Jason Burnham, Neil Fisher.

Photo: Dale Miles.

CHESTER CITY
FORMED IN 1884
TURNED PROFESSIONAL IN 1902
LTD COMPANY IN 1909

PATRON: Duke of Westminster

CHAIRMAN: M.S Guterman
VICE-CHAIRMAN: I G Morris

SECRETARY
D E Barber J.P. Amitd

GENERAL MANAGER: W Wingrove
MANAGER: Kevin Ratcliffe
PLAYER COACH: Gary Shelton

YOUTH TEAM MANAGER
and PHYSIOTHERAPIST
D Mann

STATISTICIAN FOR THE DIRECTORY
John Martin

After the celebrations of promotion at the end of 1993/94 season, no-one could have predicted what was to follow during the summer of last year.

Manager Graham Barrow left the club in June, and with most of the players out of contract, the club had only three players signed on when Mike Pejic was appointed as manager. Pejic was appointed in July along with ex-Everton and Wales captain Kevin Ratcliffe, who joined the club as player-coach.

After a great deal of activity in the transfer market a squad was assembled just before the start of the season of free transfer players and many fans thought that the team would struggle in a higher division. Their fears came true as the team failed to pick a point in the first seven league games, winning in the league at the ninth attempt when Oxford United were beaten at the Deva.

This form was to set the pattern for the season, with only three league wins registered before the turn of the year. After a disastrous Christmas period in which the team conceded thirteen goals, Mike Pejic was relieved of his duties as manager, to be replaced by Derek Mann on a caretaker basis. Although performances improved the team could not produce the results to get them away from the bottom of the table and the formality of relegation to Division Three. Kevin Ratcliffe was appointed caretaker manager for the last three games of the season, the team drew one and won two of these games, recording their only away win of the season at Swansea in the final game, leaving the club in 23rd position.

On the cups front City fared little better, Lincoln won a two-legged Coca-Cola 1st Round tie 5-2 on aggregate, whereas a 6-0 thrashing by Cheshire neighbours Crewe ended any hopes of success in the Auto Windscreen Shield. After beating Witton Albion 1-0 in the First round of the FA Cup Burnley visited the Deva Stadium in round two along with the Sky TV cameras. Despite giving a good account of themselves, City fell to a late goal from Aidrian Heath, losing the game 2-1.

During the summer Ratcliffe was appointed as manager on a permanent basis, with midfielder Gary Shelton becoming player/coach. New players brought in include goalkeeper Billy Stewart who returns to the club after a season at Northampton, ex-Bolton midfielder Neil Fisher and ex-England International Cyrille Regis from Wycombe Wanderers.

It is not only on the pitch that changes have taken place however. With new owners now in control a complete new management structure is in place with the emphasis firmly on youth development. Ex-City manager Ken Roberts has returned to the club as Chief Scout and is working closely with Derek Mann to establish a successful youth policy which the club sees as vitally important to its future. As well as the Lancashire League, City will be competing in the Pontins League Division 3 this season and have increased the number of YTS recruits by nine during the summer.

With the new owners in control and a stable squad in place, the club are looking to the future with renewed optimism and will be hopeful of a quick return to Division Two.

JOHN MARTIN.

CHESTER CITY

DivisionTwo: 23rd   FA Cup: 2nd Round   Coca-Cola Cup: 1st Round   Auto Windscreen Trophy: 3rd Round

M	DATE	COMP.	VEN	OPPONENTS	RESULT	H/T	LP	GOAL SCORERS/GOAL TIMES	ATT.
1	A 13	EL	H	Bradford City	L 1-4	0-1		Milner 88	4,459
2	17	CC 1/1	A	Lincoln City	L 0-2	0-1			(2,531)
3	20	EL	A	Birmingham City	L 0-1	0-1			(12,188)
4	23	CC 1/2	H	Lincoln City	L 2-3	0-3		Whelan 55, Chambers 71	(1,568)
5	27	EL	H	Huddersfield	L 1-2	0-1	23	Bishop 71	2,895
6	30	EL	A	Cambridge United	L 1-2	0-0	23	Page 58	(2,520)
7	S 3	EL	A	Hull City	L 0-2	0-1	23		(3,615)
8	10	EL	H	Brighton & H.A.	L 1-2	0-1	23	Page 60	2,063
9	13	EL	H	Cardiff City	L 0-2	0-0	23		1,671
10	17	EL	A	AFC Bournemouth	D 1-1	1-0	23	Lightfoot 43	(3,025)
11	24	EL	A	Plymouth Argyle	L 0-1	0-1	23		(5,329)
12	27	AWT	A	Preston North End	D 1-1	1-1	24	Page 28	(3,242)
13	O 1	EL	A	Oxford United	W 2-0	1-0	24	Hackett 8, Priest 70	2,324
14	8	EL	H	Swansea City	D 2-2	1-1	24	Page 16 (pen), Shelton 83	2,186
15	15	EL	A	Leyton Orient	L 0-2	0-1	23		(3,309)
16	18	AWT	H	Bury	W 3-1	2-0	23	Shelton 16, 27, Page 89	841
17	22	EL	A	York City	L 0-2	0-1	23		(2,820)
18	30	EL	H	Wrexham	D 1-1	1-0	23	Hackett 29	4,974
19	N 2	EL	H	Stockport County	W 1-0	0-0	23	Shelton 65	2,400
20	5	EL	A	Peterborough	L 0-2	0-1	23		(4,610)
21	19	EL	H	Blackpool	W 2-0	1-0	23	Milner 3, Page 89	3,114
22	26	EL	A	Rotherham United	L 0-2	0-0	23		(2,949)
24	29	AWT	H	Crewe Alexandra	L 0-6	0-3	23		1,890
25	D 4	FAC 2	H	Burnley	L 1-2	0-0	23	Milner 76	4,231
26	10	EL	H	Birmingham City	L 0-4	0-2	23		3,946
27	17	EL	A	Bradford City	D 1-1	0-1	23	Milner 71	(4,555)
28	26	EL	A	Crewe Alexandra	L 1-2	1-0	24	Page 33 (pen)	(5,428)
29	27	EL	H	Brentford	L 1-4	1-3	24	Richardson 4	2,266
30	31	EL	A	Bristol Rovers	L 0-3	0-2	24		(5,629)
31	J 7	EL	H	York City	L 0-4	0-0	24		1,844
32	14	EL	A	Shrewsbury Town	L 0-1	0-0	24		(3,879)
33	28	EL	H	Peterborough United	D 1-1	0-0	24	Hackett 57	1,501
34	31	EL	H	Wycombe Wanderers	L 0-2	0-2	24		1,524
35	F 4	EL	H	Rotherham United	D 4-4	3-2	24	Hackett 13, Milner 32, Rimmer 24, Preece 57	1,794
36	11	EL	A	Stockport City	D 2-2	2-0	24	Preece 22, Dinning (og) 24	(4,405)
37	14	EL	A	Wrexham	D 2-2	1-2	24	Bishop 14 (pen), Milner 85	(5,698)
38	18	EL	H	Shrewsbury Town	L 1-3	0-1	24	Bishop 82 (pen)	2,720
39	21	EL	A	Blackpool	L 1-3	1-2	24	Milner 38	(4,649)
40	25	EL	A	Oxford United	L 0-1	0-0	24		(4,930)
41	M 4	EL	H	Plymouth Argyle	W 1-0	1-0	24	Rimmer 3	1,823
42	11	EL	A	Huddersfield Town	L 1-5	1-3	24	Booth (og) 16	(9,606)
43	18	EL	A	Cambridge United	L 1-3	0-3	24	Milner 69	1,720
44	22	EL	A	Brighton & H.A.	L 0-1	0-1	24		(5,679)
45	25	EL	H	AFC Bournemouth	D 1-1	0-0	24	Jackson 50	1,618
46	28	EL	H	Hull City	L 1-2	0-0	24	Lightfoot 67	1,191
47	A 1	EL	A	Cardiff City	L 1-2	0-1	24	Hackett 88	(4,405)
48	8	EL	H	Bristol Rovers	D 0-0	0-0	24		2,241
49	15	EL	A	Brentford	D 1-1	1-0	24	Lightfoot 4	(8020)
50	17	EL	H	Crewe Alexandra	L 0-1	0-0	24		3,054
51	22	EL	A	Wycombe Wanderers	L 1-3	1-2	24	Whelan 42	(5,284)
52	29	EL	H	Leyton Orient	W 1-0	0-0	23	Bishop 59	(1,596)
53	M 6	EL	A	Swansea City	W 1-0	1-0	23	Milner 41	(2,065)
54									
55									
56									
57									
58									
59									
60									

Best Home League Attendance: 4,974 v Wrexham   **Smallest:** 1191 v Hull City   **Av Home Att:** 2,388

Goal Scorers:

Compared with 1993-94: - 802

League (37): Milner 8, Page 5, Hackett 5, Bishop 4, Lightfoot 3, Shelton 2, Preece 2, Rimmer 2, Richardson 2, Whelan, Priest, Jackson, Chambers, Alsford

C/Cola Cup (2): Whelan, Chambers

FA Cup (3): Alsford, Page, Hackett

AW Trophy (4): Page 2, Shelton 2

550

Felgate	Jenkins	Burnham	Ratcliffe	Alsford	Whelan	Flitcroft	Rimmer	Preece	Milner	Chambers	Page	Lightfoot	Newland	Bishop	Priest	Jackson	Shelton	Hackett	Richardson	Anthrobus	Gardiner	Aunger	Toson	Murphy	Bagnall	Referee	
1	2	3	4	5*	6	7	8•	9	10	11	12	14		S												D. Allison	1
1	2	3	4	S	5	7	10	6	9	S	11			S	8†											J. Rushton	2
1	2	3	4	9	5	14	10*	6	7•	12	11			S	8											M. Bailey	3
1	2	3	4	9	5	S	10*	6†	12	7	11			S	8											T. West	4
S	2	3	4	5*	11	7		6	9	12	8•		1	14				10								E. Parker	5
S	2	3	4•	8	5	7		6	9*	12	11	14	1					10								P. Alcock	6
1	2	3	4	5	S	6			12	11	9*	SG	8					7		10						J. Kirkby	7
	2	3	4	5	S				S	11	9		1	8	6			7†		10					S	P. Harrison	8
	2	3	4*	5	8				12	11	9		1		6			7•		10					S	E. Lomas	9
	2	3	4	5	S				14	11	9		1	8	6	7				10.					S	D. Orr	10
	2	3	4	5•	12				14	10	7	9	1	8*	6			11							S	P. Rejer	11
	2	3•	14	4	11				5	10*	7	9	1	8	6			11					12		S	A. Dawson	12
	1	S	3	4					12	7				10	9	1	8	5	6*	11					S	P. Richards	13
1	2		3	4					12	7	14		10	9•			8*	5	6*	11						U. Rennie	14
S	2	S	3						9			7	14	10	4†	1	8•	5	6	11						A. D'Urso	15
1	2		3	4					S	9	S	7	10	5			8	5	6	11						J. Rushton	16
1	2		3						12	9	14	7•	10	4	S		8*	5	6	11						K. Lupton	17
1	2		3	4					12	9*		7•	10		S		8	5*	6	11				14		I. Cruikshank	18
1	2		3	4					12	9		7•	10		S		8	5	6	11				14		J. Kirkby	19
1	2		3	4					12	9		7•	10*		S		8	5	6	11				14		T. Heilbron	20
1	2	3	5	4					8	14	9	7*	10		S			6•		11				12		P. Danson	21
1	2		3	4					8	14	9	7•	10		S		5	6		11				S		R. Poulain	22
1	2		3	4					8	12	9	7	10•		S		5	6*		11				14		J. Holbrook	23
1	2		3	4					8	12	6	7	10		S	14	5			11*				9•		U. Rennie	24
1	2	S		4					7		9	14•	10	3	S	8•	5	6		11						A. Wilkie	25
1		3		4					8	9			14	10*	8		5	6		11•				12		M. Brandwood	26
1			3	4				S		2	7	10•	9		S		5	6	11	8		14				G. Cain	27
1			3	4				S		2	7	10•	9		S		5	6	11	8		14				R. Harris	28
1	S		3	4						2	7	12	9		S	11	5	6*	12	8		10				E. Parker	29
1			3	4						2	7	10•	9		S	11	5	6*		8		12	10			G. Singh	30
1	2		3•	4						7	11		9		S	14	5	6*		8	12	10				S. Mathieson	31
1	3			2					7		4	9		14	6	S	12	11*	8			10*				K. Leach	32
1	3			2					7	14	4	9		S	5	5	8	11•				10				A. Butler	33
1	3*			2					7	10	4	9•			6	8	5	12	11			14				J. Winter	34
1	3			2					10•	4	9		14	6	S	8	S	5	7	11						A. Butler	35
1	2		3	5					10	4	9*		12	6	S	8	14		7	11•						P. Wright	36
1	3	14		5				7•	10*	2	9		12	6†	S	11†	8		4							A. Dawson	37
1	3	S		2					7	10	4	9		S	6†	S	11	8	5							M. Riely	38
1	2†	3	5*					14	10	7	9		S	4	S	8	11	6†								R. Furnandez	39
1	2	14	3					6	7	10•	4	9			S	8*	5	12	11							P. Vanes	40
1	2		3					5	14	10	4			9	S	7*	6	8	11•		12					U. Rennie	41
1		3	6	2					5	10	4	9			S	7*	8	14	11•		11•					P. Rejer	42
SG		3		2	66			14	S	10	4	9			1	12	5	7	11•		8*					T. Heilbron	43
1	2	3		14	6		S	10	4	9				S	7	5	8	11•								J. Holbrook	44
1	2	3		6	S			10	4	9				S	7	5	8	11								E. Lomas	45
1	2	3*		6	12			10	4	9				S	8	S	7	5	11							P. Richards	46
1	2	3•		S	6			8	10	4	9			S	14	5	7	11								P. Alcock	47
1	2	3		S	6			S	10	4	9			S	7†	5	8	11								N. Bailey	48
1	2	3	12	6	7			10	4	9				S*	S		8	S								D. Orr	49
1	2	3	S	6	7			10	4	9				S	11		8	5	8*	14						E. Wolstenholme	50
1	2*	3	12	6	7			10	4	9•				S	11		5	8	14							M. Riely	51
1	2	3	S	6	7			10	4	9				S	11		5	8	S							K. Lynch	52
1	2	3	S	6	7•			10	4	9				S	11		5	8	14							A. D'Urso	53

Felgate	Jenkins	Burnham	Ratcliffe	Alsford	Whelan	Flitcroft	Rimmer	Preece	Milner	Chambers	Page	Lightfoot	Newland	Bishop	Priest	Jackson	Shelton	Hackett	Richardson	Anthrobus	Gardiner	Aunger	Toson	Murphy	Bagnall		
37	40	22	21	32	22	19	20	41	32	6	22	26	9	14	22	32	31	30	6	7	2	1	3	1		League Appearances	
1		2		3		11	3	1	4	6	8	2	1	3	2		2	5			1	4	1		5	League Sub Appearances	
2	2		2	2		1	2	2	1+1	1	2				2											League Cup Appearances	
2	2	1	1	2	0	2	0+1	2	1+1	0	2	1	0	1	0	1	2	2						0+1		FA Cup Appearances	
2	3	2	2+1	2	0	2	0+1	3	1	2	3	2	1	0+1	2	1	2	2						1+1		AW Trophy Appearances	

Loan Players: Richardson, Antribus, Tolson, Gardiner

† = sent off

CHESTER CITY — RECORDS AND STATISTICS

CLUB RECORDS

BIGGEST VICTORIES
League: 12-0 v York City, Division 3(N), 1.2.1936.
F.A. Cup: 6-1 v Darlington, 1st Round, 25.11.1933.
5-0 v Crewe Alexandra, 1st Round, 1964-65.
5-0 v Runcorn (a), 1st Round replay, 28.11.1978.

BIGGEST DEFEATS
League: 0-9 v Barrow, Division 3(N), 10.2.1934.
2-11 v Oldham Athletic, Division 3(N), 19.1.1952.
F.A. Cup: 0-7 v Blackburn Rovers, 2nd Round, 1890-91.
League Cup: 2-9 v Leyton Orient, 3rd Round, 1962-63.

MOST POINTS
3 points a win: 84, Division 4, 1985-86.
2 points a win: 57, Division 4, 1974-75.

MOST GOALS SCORED
119, Division 4, 1964-65.
(in this season 4 players scored 20 goals or more, the only occasion this has ever happened in the Football League. The 119 goals were shared between just 8 players).

RECORD TRANSFER FEE RECEIVED
£300,000 from Liverpool for Ian Rush, May 1980.

RECORD TRANSFER FEE PAID
£120,000 to Barnsley for Stuart Rimmer, August 1991.

BEST PERFORMANCES
League: 5th Division 3, 1977-78.
F.A. Cup: 5th Round replay, 1976-77, 1979-80.
League Cup: Semi-Final 1974-75. Welsh Cup: Winners (3).

HONOURS
Division 3(N) Cup winners 1935-36, 1936-37.
Debenhams Cup winners 1977. Welsh Cup winners (3).

LEAGUE CAREER
Elected to Div 3(N) 1931, Div 4 1957-58, Div 3 1974-75, Div 4 1981-82, Div 3 (now Div 2) 1985-86, Div 3 1992-93.

INDIVIDUAL CLUB RECORDS

MOST GOALS IN A SEASON
Dick Yates: 44 goals in 1946-47 (League 36, Others 8).

MOST GOALS IN A MATCH
5. T.Jennings v Walsall, 5-1, Division 3(N), 30.1.1932.
5. Barry Jepson, York City, 9-2, Division 4, 8.2.1958.

OLDEST PLAYER
Graham Barrow, 39 years 234 days v P.N.E., Division 3, 2.4.1994.

YOUNGEST PLAYER
Aidan Newhouse, 15 years 350 days v Bury, 7.5.1988.

MOST CAPPED PLAYER
Bill Lewis (Wales) 7.

PREVIOUS MANAGERS

1930-36 Charles Hewitt; 1936-38 Alex Raisbeck, 1938-53 Frank Brown; 1953-56 Louis Page; 1956-59 John Harris; 1959-61 Stan Pearson; 1961-63 Bill Lambton; 1963-68 Peter Hauser; 1968-76 Ken Roberts; 1976-82 Alan Oakes; 1982 Cliff Sear*; 1982-83 John Sainty*; 1983-85 John McGrath; 1985-92 Harry McNally; Graham Barrow* 1992-94; Mike Pejic 1994-95; Derek Mann* 1995.
*Includes period as caretaker manager.

ADDITIONAL INFORMATION
PREVIOUS NAMES
Chester until 1983.

PREVIOUS LEAGUES
Cheshire League.

Club colours: Blue & white striped shirts, blue shorts, white socks with blue tops.
Change colours: Jade/black striped shirts, black shorts, black socks with jade tops.

Reserves League: Lancashire League, Pontins League.

LONGEST LEAGUE RUNS

of undefeated matches:	18 (1934-35)	of league matches w/out a win:	26 (1961-62)
of undefeated home matches:	27 (1973-75)	of undefeated away matches:	12 (1939-46)
without home win:	13 (1961-62)	without an away win:	29 (1971-72, 1977-78)
of league wins:	8 (1934, 1936, 1978)	of home wins:	10 (1932, 1963-64)
of league defeats:	9 (7.4.1993 - 21.8.1993)	of away wins:	4 (1934, 1936)

THE MANAGER

KEVIN RATCLIFFE . . . . appointed April 1995

PREVIOUS CLUBS
As Manager . . . . None.
As Asst.Man/Coach . . . . None.
As a player. . . . . Everton, Dundee, Cardiff City, Derby County, Chester City.

HONOURS
As a Manager . . . . None.
As a Player . . . . Division 1 championship 1985, 1987. FA Cup 1984. ECWC 1985.
. . . . Charity Shield 1984, 1985, 1986,1987. Division 3 championship 1993.
International . . . . 56 full caps, 2 U21, Youth and Schoolboy level for Wales.

CHESTER CITY

PLAYERS NAME Honours	Ht	Wt	Birthdate	Birthplace Transfers	Contract Date	Clubs	League	L/Cup	FA Cup	Other	Lge	L/C	FAC	Oth
G O A L K E E P E R S														
Ray Newland	6.2	12.4	19.07.71	Liverpool	12.09.91	St Helens								
				Free	03.07.92	Plymouth Argyle	25+1	1	2					
				Free	18.07.94	Chester City	9+1			1				
Billy Stewart	5.11	11.7	01.01.65	Liverpool	05.01.83	Liverpool (A)								
				Free	02.07.84	Wigan Athletic	14			1				
				Free	11.08.86	Chester City	272	21	19	20				
				Free	04.07.94	Northampton Town	26+1	2	1	1				
				Free	08.95	Chester City								
D E F E N D E R S														
Julian Alsford	6.2	12.11	24.12.72	Poole	30.04.91	Watford (T)	9+4	1		2	1			
				Loan	28.03.94	Slough Town								
				Free	11.08.94	Chester City	32+3	1	2	2	1			
Jason Burnham	5.10	10.10	08.05.73	Mansfield	23.07.73	Northampton T. (T)	79+9	4+2	6	8	2			
				Free	29.07.94	Chester City	22+2	2	1	2				
Peter Jackson	6.1	12.6	06.04.61	Bradford	07.04.79	Bradford City (A)	267+11	27	10+1	4	24	1		
Div.3'85.				£250,000	23.10.86	Newcastle United	60	3	6	3	3			
				£290,000	15.09.88	Bradford City	55+3	7	4	2	5			
				Free	06.09.90	Huddersfield Town	152+3	11	13	18	3		1	1
				Loan	29.09.94	Chester City								
				Free	23.11.94	Chester City	32		1	1	1			
Iain Jenkins	5.10	11.6	24.11.72	Prescot	04.06.91	Everton (T)	3+2	0+1						
				Loan	31.12.92	Bradford City	6			1				
				Free	13.08.93	Chester City	70+4	2+2	6	7				
Kevin Ratcliffe	5.11	10.2	04.12.62	Mancot	18.11.78	Everton (A)	356+3	46	57	29+1	2			
W: 59, u21.2, Y, S. CS'84'85'86'87. FAC'84.				Loan	01.08.92	Dundee	4	1						
Div.1'85'87. ECWC'85. Div.3'93.				Free	12.08.93	Cardiff City	25	1		3	1			
				Free	20.01.94	Derby County	6							
				Free	19.07.94	Chester City	23	2	1	2+1				
Spencer Whelan	6.1	11.13	17.09.71	Liverpool		Liverpool (T)								
				Free	03.04.90	Chester City	108+8	6+1	5+1	2+1	1	1		
M I D F I E L D														
Neil Fisher	5.10	11.0	07.11.70	St Helens	12.07.89	Bolton W. (T)	7+6	2	1		1			
				Free	08.95	Chester City								
David Flitcroft	5.11	12.0	14.01.74	Bolton	02.05.92	Preston N.E. (T)	4+4	0+1		0+1	2			
				Loan	17.09.93	Lincoln City	2	0+1						
				Free	09.12.93	Chester City	24+16	1	2	2	1			
Roger Preece	5.9	10.4	09.06.69	Much Wenlock		Coventry City (T)								
				Free	15.08.86	Wrexham	89+21	2+1	5	8+1	12			1
				Free	14.08.90	Chester City	164+5	10	8	11	4		1	
Chris Priest	5.10	10.10	18.10.73	Leigh	01.06.92	Everton (T)								
				Loan	09.09.94	Chester City								
				Free	11.01.95	Chester City	22+2			2	1			
Dave Rogers	6.0	11.01	25.08.75	Liverpool		Tranmere Rov. (T)								
				Free	08.95	Chester City								
Gary Shelton	5.7	10.12	21.03.58	Nottingham	01.03.76	Walsall (A)	12+12	0+1	2+2				1	
E: u21.1.				£80,000	18.01.78	Aston Villa	24	2+1			7	1		
Loan 13.03.80 Notts County 8 Lge App.				£50,000	25.03.82	Sheffield Wed.	195+3	19	23+1	1	18	3	3	
				£150,000	24.07.87	Oxford United	60+5	7+1	5	1	1	2		
					24.08.89	Bristol City	149+1	12	9	9	24			3
				Loan	11.02.94	Rochdale	3							
				Free	22.07.94	Chester City	31+2		2	2	2			2
F O R W A R D S														
Leroy Chambers	5.10	11.7	25.10.72	Sheffield	13.06.91	Sheffield Wed. (T)								
				Free	12.08.94	Chester City	6+7	1		2	1	1		
Andrew Milner	6.0	11.12	10.02.67	Kendal		Netherfield								
via Manchester City, No Apps.,				£20,000	18.01.90	Rochdale	103+24	9+4	6+2	4	25	5	1	2
				Free	12.08.94	Chester City	32+4	1+1	1+1	1	8		1	
Cyrille Regis	6.0	13.4	09.02.58	French Guyanna		Molesey								
E: 5, B.3, u21.6. FAC'87.		via Hayes to	£5,000	01.05.77	West Bromwich A.	233+4	27+1	25	10	82	16	10	4
				£250,000	11.10.84	Coventry City	231+7	24	15+1	4	47	12	3	
				Free	02.07.91	Aston Villa	46+6	3+1	5+2		12			
				Free	03.08.93	Wolverhampton W.	8+11		1+2	1	2			
				Free	08.94	Wycombe W.	30+5	2	1		9	1		
				Free	08.95	Chester City								
Stuart Rimmer	5.8	11.0	12.10.64	Southport	15.10.82	Everton (A)	3							
E: Y.3.				£10,000	17.01.85	Chester City	110+4	6	4+3	11+1	68	6		3
				£205,000	18.03.88	Watford	10	0+1			1	1		
				£200,000	10.11.88	Notts County	3+1		2	3	2			
				£150,000	02.02.89	Walsall	85+3	6	5	7	31	4	2	7
				£150,000	05.03.91	Barnsley	10+5			1	1			
				£150,000	15.08.91	Chester City	135+12	9	6+2	6+2	43	3		1
				Loan	02.09.94	Rochdale	3							
				Loan	05.12.94	Preston North End	0+2							

DEVA STADIUM
Bumpers Lane, Chester, Cheshire
Tel: 01244 371 376

Capacity 6,000
Covered Standing 2,640
Seating 3,094

First game .... v Stockport Co., Lge Cup, 25.8.1992.
First floodlit game .... As above.

ATTENDANCES
Highest .... 5,638 v P.N.E., Div 3, 2.4.1994.
Lowest .... 841 v Bury, AMC, 18.10.1994.

OTHER GROUNDS .... Sealand Road

MATCHDAY TICKET PRICES

Seats £9
Juv/OAP £6

Terraces. £7
Juv/OAP £4.50

Additional Information
£20 membership charge for Supporters Club Lounge.

Ticket Office Telephone no. . . . . . . 01244 371 376.

SPORTSLINES
0891 66 45 54
Calls cost 39p per minute cheap rate and 49p per minute at all other times.
Call costings correct at time of going to press.

HOW TO GET TO THE GROUND

From the North
Use motorway (M56), A41 or A56 sign posted to Chester, into Town Centre, then follow signs to Queensferry (A548) onto Sealand Road, turn into Bumpers Lane for Chester City FC.

From the East
Use A54 or A51 sign posted Chester, into Town Centre, then follow signs to Queensferry (A548) into Sealand Road as above.

From the South
Use A41 or A483 sign posted Chester Town Centre, then follow signs to Queensferry (A548) into Sealand Road as above.

From the West
Use A55, A494 or A548 sign posted Chester, then follow signs to Queensferry. Follow signs to Birkenhead (A494), then in 1.2 miles branch left to join the A548 Chester into Sealand Road as above.

Car Parking
Parking at the ground.

Nearest Railway Station
British Rail, Chester (01244 340 170)

MATCHDAY PROGRAMME

Programme Editor . . . . J Stanley.

Number of pages . . . . 32.

Price . . . . £1.30.

Subscriptions . . . . Available on request (-1244 371 376).

Local Newspapers . . . . Chester Chronicle, Evening Leader.

Local Radio Stations . . . . . . Radio Merseyside, Marcher Sound Radio.

COLCHESTER UNITED
(The U's)
ENDSLEIGH LEAGUE DIVISION 3
SPONSORED BY: SGR FM

Back Row (L-R): Adam Locke, Steve Ball, Tony McCarthy, Carl Emberson, Peter Cawley, Mark Kinsella, Simon Betts.
Middle Row: Steve Foley (Yth Manager), Tony English (Capt), Tony Adcock, Michael Cheetham, Chris Fry, Robbie Reinelt, Nicky Haydon, Paul Gibbs, Brian Owen (Physio).
Front Row: Kelvin Wagner (Kit Manager), Gus Ceaser, Tony Dennis, Steve Mardenborough, Steve Wignall (Manager), Steve Whitton (Asst. Manager), James Siddons, Tony Lock, Jean Dalli, Paul Dyer (Chief Scout).

COLCHESTER UNITED
FORMED IN 1937
TURNED PROFESSIONAL IN 1937
LTD COMPANY IN 1937

CHAIRMAN: Gordon Parker
VICE-CHAIRMAN
Peter Heard
DIRECTORS
Peter Powell, John Worsp
SECRETARY
Sue Smith
COMMERCIAL MANAGER
Marie Partner

MANAGER: Steve Wignall
ASSISTANT MANAGER: Steve Whitton
RESERVE TEAM MANAGER
Paul Dyer
YOUTH TEAM MANAGER
Steve Foley
PHYSIOTHERAPIST
Brian Owen

STATISTICIAN FOR THE DIRECTORY
Vacant

Only one goal and six consecutive defeats at the start of the season saw `The U's' at the foot of the table and out of the Coca-Cola Cup. The only way was up!

For George Burley to turn `his club's' form upside down and achieve six victories and a draw with the same squad of players was nothing short of miraculous and no doubt this fact was noted by neighbouring Ipswich who were later to appoint their ex-player as manager.

Twelve goals were scored in the second half dozen games and the form of Steve Whitton, who scored in four consecutive games, certainly lifted morale. He finished as leading scorer with thirteen by the end of the season but more all round fire power will be needed if a promotion challenge is to be mounted.

Last season the more optimistic supporters may have started to think of play-offs during a good mid season run of results but the required consistency could never be found.

The FA Cup didn't inspire any heroics either, although seven goals in a replay against Yeading was enjoyed and an away win after coming from behind at Exeter did give Colchester a trip to Wimbledon. Sadly the attendance was only 6,903 and the result equally disappointing.

The only ever present during the season was Mark Kinsella but experienced defender Gus Caesar and Simon Betts also had successful campaigns.

In goal Carl Emberson forced his way in as first choice in place of John Cheesewright but while the defence was solid, Steve Wigley (a popular `old boy' at Layer Road) will need to strengthen the attack.

On a cheerful note the youth team often impressed and a good youth policy will obviously be the best way for the club to prepare for a successful future.

COLCHESTER UNITED

Division Three: 10th   FA Cup: 3rd Round   Coca-Cola Cup: 1st Round   Auto Windscreen Trophy:

M	DATE	COMP.	VEN	OPPONENTS	RESULT	H/T	LP	GOAL SCORERS/GOAL TIMES	ATT.
1	A 13	EL	H	Torquay United	L 1-3	1-2	14	Kinsella 11	3,175
2	16	CC 1/1	H	**Brentford**	**L 0-2**	**0-1**			**2,521**
3	20	EL	A	Mansfield Town	L 0-2	0-0	18		(2,247)
4	22	CC 1/2	A	**Brentford**	**L 0-2**	**0-1**			**(2,315)**
5	27	EL	H	Doncaster Rovers	L 0-3	0-2	21		2,320
6	30	EL	A	Exeter City	L 0-1	0-1			(1,804)
7	S 3	EL	A	Scarborough	W 1-0	0-0	20	Dennis 70	(1,494)
8	10	EL	H	Hartlepool United	W 1-0	0-0	18	Whitton 53	2,428
9	13	EL	H	Walsall	W 3-2	0-1		Kinsella 86, 90, Whitton 88	2,239
10	17	EL	A	Torquay United	D 3-3	0-1	12	Whitton 63, Brown 72, Dennis 89	(3,390)
11	24	EL	A	Darlington	W 3-2	2-1	11	Whitton 27, 77, Brown 36	(2,260)
12	27	AWT	H	**Leyton Orient**	**W 1-0**	**0-0**		**Abrahams 63**	**1,486**
13	O 1	EL	H	Bury	W 1-0	0-0	8	Cawley 78	3,288
14	8	EL	H	Chesterfield	L 0-3	0-1	9		3,476
15	15	EL	A	Carlisle United	D 0-0	0-0	11		(5,817)
16	22	EL	H	Preston North End	W 3-1	1-0	9	Brown 11, 77, Whitton 48	3,015
17	29	EL	A	Wigan Athletic	W 2-1	2-0	6	Kinsella 31, Fry 39	(1,621)
18	N 5	EL	H	Gillingham	D 2-2	1-2	6	Fry 29, Brown 53	3,817
19	8	AWT	A	Fulham	**L 2-3**	**0-1**		**Abrahams 63, Kinsella 66**	**(1,451)**
20	12	FAC 1	A	Yeading	**D 2-2**	**1-1**		**Kinsella 9, Abrahams 55**	**(1,780)**
21	19	EL	A	Rochdale	D 0-0	0-0	6		(1,903)
22	22	FAC 1R	H	**Yeading**	**W 7-1**	**3-1**		**Abrahams 2, Whitton 28, 52, Brown 33, 54, Kinsella 77**	**4,016**
23	26	EL	H	Scunthorpe United	W 4-2	2-0	6	Brown 25, Abrahams 45, 86, Whitton 78	2,904
24	D 3	FAC 2	A	**Exeter City**	**W 2-1**	**0-1**		**Whitton 47, English 85**	**(3,528)**
25	10	EL	H	Mansfield Town	D 1-1	1-0	6	Fry 8	3,016
26	16	EL	A	Doncaster Rovers	W 2-1	0-0	6	Cawley 61, Brown 84	(2,460)
27	26	EL	H	Northampton Town	L 0-1	0-1			5,064
28	27	EL	A	Fulham	W 2-1	1-1		Kinsella 32, 89 (og)	(4,243)
29	31	EL	H	Hereford United	D 2-2	0-2	7	Stoneman 76, Whitton 89	3,322
30	J 7	FAC 3	A	**Wimbledon**	**L 0-1**	**0-1**			**(6,903)**
31	10	EL	A	Preston North End	L 1-2	0-1		Fry 83	6,377
32	14	EL	H	Barnet	D 1-1	0-1	8	Putney 49	3,706
33	28	EL	H	Wigan Athletic	L 0-1	0-0	11		3,067
34	F 4	EL	A	Scunthorpe United	W 4-3	2-3	9	Locke 25, English 28, Thompson 80, 84	(2,748)
35	11	EL	H	Rochdale	D 0-0	0-0	7		3,080
36	18	EL	A	Barnet	W 1-0	1-0	5	Asaba 18	(2,242)
37	21	EL	A	Lincoln City	L 0-2	0-0			(1,969)
38	25	EL	A	Bury	L 1-4	0-1	6	Fry 77	(2,484)
39	M 4	EL	H	Darlington	W 1-0	1-0	7	Asara 4	6,055
40	11	EL	A	Hartlepool	L 1-3	1-2	9	Fry 17	(1,371)
41	18	EL	H	Exeter City	W 3-1	1-0	9	Thompson 4, Betts 77 (pen), Lock 87	2,375
42	25	EL	H	Scarborough	L 0-2	0-0	8		3,025
43	A 1	EL	A	Walsall	L 0-2	0-0	9		(3,622)
44	8	EL	A	Hereford United	L 0-3	0-2	11		(1,669)
45	11	EL	A	Gillingham	W 3-1	0-1		Betts 58 (pen), Thompson 87, 88	(3,328)
46	15	EL	H	Fulham	W 5-2	4-1	8	Cheetham 6, English 10, Caesar 18, Fry 36, 55	3,448
47	17	EL	A	Northampton Town	D 1-1	0-1		Whitton 67	(5,011)
48	22	EL	H	Lincoln City	L 1-2	1-1	9	McCarthy 38	2,654
49	29	EL	H	Carlisle United	L 0-1	0-0	10		3,333
50	M 6	EL	A	Chesterfield	D 2-2	1-1	10	Whitton 38, Putney 65 (pen)	(4,133)
51									
52									
53									
54									
55									
56									
57									
58									
59									
60									

Best Home League Attendance: 6,055 v Darlington   **Smallest:** 2,239 v Walsall   **Av Home Att:** 3,201

Goal Scorers: Compared with 1993-94: +342

League (56): Whitton 10, Fry 8, Brown 7, Kinsella 5, Thompson 5, Abrahams 2, Ashba 2, Betts 2, Cawley 2, Dennis 2, English 2, Locke 2, Putney 2, Cheetham, McCarthy, Stoneman, Opponent

C/Cola Cup (0):

FA Cup (10): Whitton 3, Abrahams 2, Brown 2, Kinsella 2, English

AW Trophy (3): Abrahams 2, Kinsella 1

556

Cheesewright	Culling	Dali	English	Caesar	Dennis	Fry	Brown	Whitton	Kinsella	Abrahams	Allpress	Roberts	Emberson	Partner	Davis	Burley	Scott	Putney	Cawley	Allen	Betts	Locke	Thompson	Stoneman	Lock	Referee	
1	2	3*	4	5	6	7	8	9	10	11	12	S	S													G. Barber	1
1	2		4	5	6	7*	8	9	10	11	3	12	S	S												A. D'Urso	2
1	2		7	5	6	12	8	9	10*	11	4		S	S	3											N. Barry	3
S			2*	5	6		8	9	10	11	4	7	1		3	12	S									D. Orr	4
1				5	6	S	8	9	10	11	4		S	S	3	2		7								I. Hemley	5
1				5*	6*	14	8	9	10	11	4		S	12	3	2		7								S. Dunn	6
1			2	5	6	12	8*	9	10	11		S		3			S	7	4							E. Lomas	7
1			3	5	6		8	9	10	11*		S		2				7	4	12						G. Pooley	8
1			3	5	6		8	9	10	11		S		2				7	4	S	12					R. Harris	9
1			3	5	6		8	9	10	11*		S		12				7	4	S	2					J. Holbrook	10
1			3	5	6	11•	8*	9	10			S						7	4	12	2	14				W. Burns	11
1			3	5	6	S	8	9	10	11		S		S					4		2	7				P. Alcock	12
1			3	5	6	12	8	9	10	11*		S		14					4		2	7				S. Dunn	13
1			3	5	6*	11•	8	9	10	14		S						7	4		2	12				G. Cain	14
1			3	5		11*	8	9	10	12	S	S						7	4		2	6				K. Leach	15
1			3	5	12	11•	8	9	10	14		S						7	4		2	6*				K. Lynch	16
1			3	5	S	11*	8	9	10	12		S						7	4		2	6				M. Pierce	17
S			3	5	7	S	8	9	10	11	S		1						4		2	6				G. Barker	18
1			3	5	6*	12	8	9	10	11	S		S						4		2	7				U. Rennie	19
1			3	5	12	7	8	9*	10	11		S							4		2	6*	14			G. Barber	20
1			3	5	S	S	8	9	10	11		S						7	4		2	6				K. Cooper	21
1			3	5	12	14	8•	9	10	11		S						7*	4		2	6				P. Durkin	22
1			5	3	7		8	9	10	11	S		S						4		2	6	S			G. Barker	23
1			S*	11	4	12	8*	9	10•	14	12		S		2				4	3		6				I. Cruikshanks	24
1			3	5	4	11	8•	9	10	14	12		S					7			2	6				P. Alcock	25
1			3		4	11•	8	9	10	14	12		S					7*	4		2	6	5			S. Dunn	26
1			3	5		11•	8	9	10	14	12		S					7*	4		2	6	5			S. Pooley	27
1			3	5	12	S	8	9	10	11*		S						7	4		2	6				P. Danson	28
1*			3†	5	6	14	8	9	10	11•		12						7	4		2		S			N. Barry	29
S			3	5	8	12		10	11		1						7	4		2	6	9*				J. Rushton	30
S			5	8		12		10	11		1						7*	4		2	6	9*	3	14		A. D'Urso	31
S			3	5	8	7		11	9	10		1						4		2	6*	12	S			R. Furnandiz	32
S			3	5	6*	7	8	9•	10	14	12		1					4		2	4	11				M. Pierce	33
S			3	5	6	7		9*	10	11•	12		1						2	4	14					R. Harris	34
S			3	5	6	7			10	11	S		1						2	4	9*	S		12	M. Bailey	35
S			3	5	6	9			10	11*	12		1					7†		2	4	S				J. Winter	36
S				5	6	7	12	9*	10		S		1			8	4		2	3						A. Butler	37
S				5	6	7	8•		10		12		1						4*		2	14				J. Kirkby	38
S			4	6				9	10		S		1			7*				2	8	12				J. Holbrook	39
S			4	6		S		9	10				1			7*				2	7					D. Orr	40
S			3	5	6	S		9	10				1			8				2	14					P. Harrison	41
S			3	5	6*	12	11		10				1			8				2	12					S. Mathieson	42
S			3	5		7*		9	10				1			6				2	12					P. Rejer	43
S			3	5		7		9•	10				1			6				2	14					K. Leach	44
S			3	5*		7		9	10				1			6				2	14					U. Rennie	45
S			3	5		7•		9	10				1			6		2*								M. Bailey	46
S				5	6	7•		9	10				1			8				2						S. Dunn	47
S				5	6	7*		9	10				1			8	S			2						A. Dawson	48
																											49
																											50
23	2	1	33	40	32	24	26	36	42	20	3		19	4	5			28	23		34	20	5	3		League Appearances	
	1				9	2				8	8		1	1		2				2	1	2	8		3	League Sub Appearances	
1	1		2	2	2	1	2	2	2	2	2	1+1	1		1		0+1									C/Cola Cup Appearances	
3			4	4	1+3	4	4	4	4		1				2			4	4		4	4	0+1			FA Cup Appearances	
2			2	2	0+1	2	2	2	2		2								2		4	2	2	2		AW Trophy Appearances	

Also Played: Asaba 8 (36,37,38,42,43), 11 (39), 9 (40,41,44), 12 (47), 14 (48), Gibbs 3 (40,41,42,49), 11 (45,46,47,48), 12 (50), Williams 11 (40,41*,42), McCarthy 5 (41,42) 4 (43,44,45,46,47, 48, 49, 50), Cheetham S (42), 11 (43), 7 (44), 8(45, 46*, 47, 48), 11 (49, 50) Reinett S (43), 14 (45, 46), 12 (48), 2 (49), 3 (50)

† = sent off

COLCHESTER UNITED   RECORDS AND STATISTICS

CLUB RECORDS

BIGGEST VICTORIES
League: 9-1 v Bradford City, Division 4, 30.12.1961.
F.A. Cup: 7-0 v Yeovil Town, 2nd Round, 1958.

BIGGEST DEFEATS
League: 0-8 v Leyton Orient, 15.10.1988.

MOST POINTS
3 points a win:
2 points a win:

RECORD TRANSFER FEE RECEIVED
£120,000 from Wimbledon for P McGee, February 1989.

RECORD TRANSFER FEE PAID
£45,000 to Sporting Lochern for D Tempest, August 1987.

BEST PERFORMANCES
League: 3rd Division 3(S), 1956-57.
Highest Position:
F.A. Cup: 6th Round (shared record for Division 4) 1970-71.
League Cup: 5th Round 1974-75.

HONOURS
GMVC winners 1991-92.
FA Trophy winners 1991-92.

LEAGUE CAREER
Elected to Div.3(S) 1950, Transferred to Div.3 1958, Relegated to Div.4 1960-61, Promoted to Div.3 1961-62, Relegated to Div.4 1964-65, Promoted to Div.3 1965-66, relegated to Div.4 1967-68, Promoted to Div.3 1973-74, Relegated to Div.4 1975-76, Promoted to Div.3 1976-77, relegated to Div.4 1980-81, Relegated to GM Vauxhall Conference 1989-90, Promoted to Div 3 (Old 4) 1991-92.

INDIVIDUAL CLUB RECORDS

MOST GOALS IN A SEASON
Bobby Hunt: 38 goals in 1961-62 (League 37, FA Cup 1).

MOST GOALS IN A MATCH
No one has scored more than four.

OLDEST PLAYER
Benny Fenton, 39 years 6 months.

YOUNGEST PLAYER
Lindsay Smith, 16 years 218 days v Grimsby Town, 24.4.1971.

MOST CAPPED PLAYER
None.

PREVIOUS MANAGERS

(Since joining the Football League)
Ted Fenton; Jimmy Allen, Jack Butler, Benny Fenton, Neil Franklin, Dick Graham, Jim Smith, Bobby Roberts, Allan Hunter, Cyril Lea, Jock Wallace, Mick Mills, Ian Atkins, Roy McDonough, George Burley.

ADDITIONAL INFORMATION
PREVIOUS NAMES
None.

PREVIOUS LEAGUES
Southern League; Alliance Premier (Vauxhall Conference).

Club Colours: Royal blue & white striped shirts, royal blue shorts, white socks.
Change colours: Red & black quarters, black shorts, red socks.

Reserves League: Springheath Print Capital League.

LONGEST LEAGUE RUNS

of undefeated matches:	20 (1956-57)	of league matches w/out a win:	20 (1968)
of undefeated home matches:	27 (1956-57)	of undefeated away matches:	9 (1956-57)
without home win:	11 (1958)	without an away win:	19 (1950-51, 1959-60)
of league wins:	7 (1968-69)	of home wins:	13 (1976-77)
of league defeats:	8 (1954)	of away wins:	5 (1981, 1987)

THE MANAGER

STEVE WIGNALL . . . . appointed January 1995.

PREVIOUS CLUBS
As Manager. . . . . Aldershot.
As Asst.Man/Coach. . . . .
As a player . . . . Doncaster Rovers, Colchester United, Brentford, Aldershot.

HONOURS
As a Manager . . . . None.
As a Player . . . . None.

COLCHESTER UNITED

PLAYERS NAME / Honours	Ht	Wt	Birthdate	Birthplace / Transfers	Contract Date	Clubs	League	L/Cup	FA Cup	Other	Lge	L/C	FAC	Oth
G O A L K E E P E R S														
Carl W Emberson	6.1	12.5	13.07.93	Epsom	04.05.91	Millwall (T)				1				
				Loan	17.12.92	Colchester United	13							
				Free	06.07.94	Colchester United	19+1	1	1					
D E F E N D E R S														
Steven J Ball	6.0	12.1	02.09.69	Colchester	20.09.87	Arsenal (T)								
				Free	29.12.89	Colchester United	3+1			1				1
				Free	18.09.90	Norwich City	0+2	0+2						
via Cambridge United, Free (07.08.92)				Free	14.09.92	Colchester United	46+10	2	2	14+1	6		3	1
Simon R Betts	5.9	11.4	03.03.73	Middlesbrough	02.07.91	Ipswich Town (T)								
				Free	13.08.92	Wrexham								
				Free	03.11.92	Scarborough								
				Free	11.12.92	Colchester United	88+3	1	5+1	6	3			
Gus C Caeser	6.0	12.0	05.03.66	Tottenham	10.02.84	Arsenal	27+17	3+2	0+1	1				
E: u21.3				Loan	28.11.90	Q.P.R.	5							
				Free	31.07.91	Cambridge United								
				Free	06.09.91	Bristol City	9+1	1	1	1				
				Free	.01.92	Airdrie	57	4	7+1	1	1			
				Free	11.08.94	Colchester United	39	2	4	2	1			
Peter Cawley	6.4	14.8	15.09.65	Walton-on-Thames		Chertsey Town								
					26.01.87	Wimbledon	1		1					
				Loan	26.02.87	Bristol Rovers	9+1							
				Loan	14.12.88	Fulham	3+2							
				Free	17.07.89	Bristol Rovers	1+2							
				Free	06.07.90	Southend United	6+1	1	1	1	1			
					22.11.90	Exeter City	7							
				Free	08.11.91	Barnet	3		1					
				Free	09.10.92	Colchester United	81+2		7	6	6			
Anthony P McCarthy	6.0	12.0	09.11.69	Dublin		Shelbourne								
Ei: u21.5.				£100,000	25.06.92	Millwall	20+4	3			1			
				Loan	09.12.94	Crewe Alexandra	2							
				Free	17.03.95	Colchester United	10				1			
Andrew N Partner	6.4	13.6	21.10.74	Colchester	24.06.93	Colchester Utd (T)	1+2		1					
M I D F I E L D														
Michael M Cheetham	5.11	11.5	30.06.67	Amsterdam		Basingstoke Town								
Div.3'91.				Loan	10.10.88	Ipswich Town	1+3			0+1				
				£50,000	11.10.89	Cambridge United	123+9	8+1	17	12+1	22	1	1	3
				Free	15.07.94	Chesterfield	5	2		0+1		1		
				Free	23.05.95	Colchester United	8+1				1			
John A Dennis	5,7	10.11	01.12.63	Maidenhead	03.12.81	Plymouth Argyle (A)	7+2	1	0+1			1		
Div3'91				Free	15.08.83	Exeter City	3+1	1						
				Free		Slough Town								
				£15,000	22.02.89	Cambridge United	89+22	6+2	2+4	7+2	10			1
				£20,000	15.06.93	Chesterfield	4+6	2		2				
				Free	10.08.94	Colchester United	32+1	2	1+3	2	2			
Anthony K English	5.11	11.2	19.10.66	Luton		Coventry City (A)								
E: Y9, GMVC'92, FAT'92				Free	24.12.84	Colchester United	325+15	14	28	21+1	42	1	2	
Christopher D Fry	5.9	9.6	23.10.69	Cardiff	03.08.88	Cardiff City (T)	22+33	1+2	0+2	0+2	1			
W: S				Free	02.08.91	Hereford United	76+14	6+2	8+2	6	6		1	
					24.10.93	Colchester United	36+14	1	1+1	0+1	8			
Mark A Kinsella	5.9	11.2	12.08.72	Dublin		Home Farm								
Ei: u21.8, GMVC'92, FAT'92				Free	18.08.89	Colchester United	122+6	6+1	10	6+2	20	1	1	2
Anthony C Lock	5.11	11.0	03.09.76	Harlow	18.04.95	Colchester Utd (T)	0+3				1			
Adam S Locke	5.10	12.7	20.08.70	Croydon	21.06.88	Crystal Palace (T)								
				Free	06.08.90	Southend United	56+17	5	2+1	6+1	3			
				Loan	08.10.93	Colchester United	4			1				
						Colchester United	20+2		4	2	1			
Robert S Reinholt	5.10	11.13	11.03.74	Loughton		Aldershot (T)	3+2							
				Free		Wivenhoe Town								
				Free	19.03.93	Gillingham	16+9	1	2+1	2	1	1		
				Swap	22.02.95	Colchester United	2+3							
F O R W A R D S														
Tony Adcock	5.11	11.9	27.02.63	Bethnal Green	31.03.81	Colchester Utd (A)	192+18	16+1	12+2	9	98	5	3	6
				£75,000	01.06.87	Manchester City	12+3	2+1	2	2	5	1		3
				£85,000	25.01.88	Northampton Town	72	6	1	4	30	3		1
				£190,000	06.10.89	Bradford City	33+5	1	0+1	2	6			
				£75,000	11.01.91	Northampton Town	34+1	1	1	2	10		1	1
				£35,000	30.12.91	Peterborough Utd	107+4	8+1	5	3+2	35	3	1	
				£20,000	04.08.94	Luton Town	0+2		0+1					
Paul Gibbs	5.10	11.3	26.10.72	Gorleston		Diss Town								
					06.03.95	Colchester United	8+1							
Stephen P Whitton	6.0	12.7	04.02.60	East Ham	15.09.78	Coventry City (A)	64+10	3+2	2		21		2	
Div2'92				£175,000	11.07.83	West Ham United	35+4	6	1		6	2		
				Loan	31.01.86	Birmingham City	8				2			
				£60,000	28.08.86	Birmingham City	94+1	7+1	5	3	28	4		1
				£275,000	03.03.89	Sheffield Wed	22+10	3	0+1	0+1	4	4		
				£150,000	11.01.91	Ipswich Town	80+8	7+1	8+1	4	15	2	2	
				£10,000	24.03.94	Colchester United	44	2	4	2	12		2	

LAYER ROAD GROUND
Colchester, Essex CO2 7JJ
Tel: 01206 574 042

Capacity..7,944
Covered Standing..4,591
Seating..1,150

First game...Not known.
First floodlit game ....Not known.

ATTENDANCES
Highest..19,073 v Reading, FA Cup Round 1, 27.11.1948.
Lowest ....Not known.

OTHER GROUNDS...None.

MATCHDAY TICKET PRICES

Terraces.................................. £6
Juniors.................................... £4

Family Enclosure £5
Juniors..................................... £2

Seats.................... £6.50, £7.50 or £8
Juniors .... £4.50, £5 or £5.50

Ticket Office Telephone no........ 01206 574 042

CLUBCALL
0898 66 46 46

Calls cost 39p per minute cheap rate and 49p per
minute at all other times.
Call costings correct at time of going to press.

HOW TO GET TO THE GROUND

From the North
Follow signs in Colchester on A133/B1508 or A12, then follow signs to Layer B1026 into Layer Road for Colchester United FC.

From the East
Follow signs into Colchester on A604 or A133 then follow signs to Layer B1026 into Layer Road for Colchester United FC.

From the South and West
Follow signs into Colchester on A604 or A12 then follow signs to Layer B1026 into Layer Road for Colchester United FC.

Car Parking
Street parking only.

Nearest Railway Station
Colchester North (01206 564 777)

MATCHDAY PROGRAMME

Programme Editor .... Jim French & Rob Hadcroft.

Number of pages .... 32.

Price .... £1.30.

Subscriptions .... £63 per season (home & away).

Local Newspapers .... Evening Gazette (Mon-Fri evenings),
.... East Anglian Daily Times (Mon-Fri mornings),
.... Essex County Standard (weekly-Fridays).

Local Radio Stations..................... SGR FM (Colchester),
.... Essex Radio (Southend & Chelmsford) 257 MW.

DARLINGTON
(The Quakers)
ENDSLEIGH LEAGUE DIVISION 3
SPONSORED BY: HUTCHINSON TELECOM

Back Row (L-R): Rui Neves, Andy Crosby, Sean Gregan, Mike Pollitt, Steve Gaughan, Gary Himsworth, Pedro Paulo.
Middle Row: Steohen Morgon (Director), Peter Ellis (Asst. Director), Paul Mattison, Michael Pugh, Robert Blake, Anthony Carrs, Robbie Painter, Simon Shaw, Gavin Worboys, Nigel Carnell (Physio), Gordon Hodgson (Director), Ian Parker (Asst. Director). **Front Row:** Paul Olsson, Mattie Appleby, Jim PLatt (Director of Coaching), Bernard Lowery (Chairman), Stephen Weeks (Vice Chairman), David Hodgson (Director of Coaching), Gary Bannister, Phil Brumwell.

DARLINGTON
FORMED IN 1883
TURNED PROFESSIONAL IN 1908
LTD COMPANY IN 1891

PRESIDENT: Alan Noble
CHAIRMAN: B Lowery
VICE-CHAIRMAN
Gordon Hodgson
DIRECTORS
Steve Morgan, Stephen Weeks
COMMERCIAL MANAGER
K Agar
GENERAL MANAGER
S Morgan

DIRECTOR OF COACHING: David Hodgson
ASSISTANT MANAGER: Jim Platt
FIRST TEAM COACH
Gary Bannister

YOUTH TEAM MANAGER
Tony Kenworthy
PHYSIOTHERAPIST
Nigel Carnell
STATISTICIAN FOR THE DIRECTORY
Frank Tweddle

Yet again Darlington flattered to deceive after one of the club's better starts to a season, with only two defeats in the first ten games. After occupying a mid-table position until the turn of the year the side slumped to finish third from bottom, with only thirteen points from a possible sixty gained during 1995. Three managers were tried during the season with Alan Murray being replaced by Paul Futcher in early March. After ten games without a win (and seven without a goal) Futcher also left and assistant manager, Eddie Kyle, took charge for the remaining three games. Now David Hodgson has been appointed as director of coaching, assisted by former Northern Ireland goalkeeper, Jim Platt, so hopefully a more stable period is in prospect.

The side had been strengthened by the arrival of the experienced Ian Banks from Rotherham, the promising Matty Appleby from Newcastle (who had previously been on loan) and giant goalkeeper Mike Pollitt from Lincoln City. A s mentioned earlier, the season started well for the Quakers and after four wins and two draws in the first eight league games they lay in seventh place in the division by mid-September. However they could not maintain this form and despite playing some attractive football were unable to win games. Gavin Worboys was signed from Notts County in November to boost the attack and did end up as leading scorer, but only with eleven goals. Murray's departure coincided with the start of a dreadful run of seven games without a goal (a club record) under his replacement Paul Futcher and by the time he resigned, with just three games to go, the club did well to avoid bottom spot for the second year in succession.

At least there was a little success in the cups, for after fifteen cup ties without a win, stretching back to November 1991, Darlington won two cup ties in five days! The jinx was broken at Hartlepool in the Auto Windscreens Shield and then the Quakers survived a difficult trip to Hyde United in the First Round of the FA Cup. However, the second rounds proved more awkward with a defeat on penalties at Rochdale in the Shield and an exit at Carlisle in the FA Cup. The highlight of an otherwise dismal season was undoubtedly the two draws played with First Division Barnsley in the Coca-Cola Cup. After a 2-2 draw at Feethams, the Quakers were unlucky to lose on the away goals rule after a 0-0 draw after extra-time at Oakwell.

So again Darlington look forward to better things under the new management team with a return to the traditional strip of black and white hoops (not used since the fifties) and talks underway with the council about the siting of a new stadium at Maidendale on the South Eastern edge of the town.

FRANK TWEDDLE.

DARLINGTON

Division Three: 20th   **FA Cup:** 2nd Round   **Coca-Cola Cup:** 1st Round   **Auto Windscreen Trophy:** 2nd Round

M	DATE	COMP.	VEN	OPPONENTS	RESULT	H/T	LP	GOAL SCORERS/GOAL TIMES	ATT.
1	A 13	EL	H	Preston North End	D 0-0	0-0	10		3,800
2	16	CCC 1/1	H	Barnsley	D 2-2	0-2		Cross 65, Slaven 80	2,207
3	20	EL	A	Hartlepool United	L 0-1	0-0	16		(3,035)
4	23	CCC 1/2	A	Barnsley	D 0-0	0-0			(3,263)
5	27	EL	H	Exeter City	W 2-0	0-0	13	Gaughan 63, Painter 83	1,861
6	30	EL	A	Mansfield Town	W 1-0	0-0		Gaughan 77	(2,427)
7	S 3	EL	A	Doncaster Rovers	D 0-0	0-0	9		(2,967)
8	10	EL	H	Torquay United	W 2-1	1-1	8	Painter 9, Gaughan 89	2,161
9	13	EL	H	Scunthorpe United	L 1-3	1-2	8	Painter 25	2,181
10	17	EL	A	Preston North End	W 3-1	1-0	7	Appleby 43, Olsson 59. Chapman 77	(8,884)
11	24	EL	H	Colchester United	L 2-3	1-2	9	Chapman 45, Himsworth 46	2,260
12	27	AWT PR	H	Carlisle United	L 2-3	2-2		Himsworth 16, Olsson 44	1,583
13	O 1	EL	A	Carlisle United	L 1-2	1-0	12	Painter 36	(6,100)
14	8	EL	H	Bury	L 0-2	0-0	14		2,352
15	15	EL	A	Chesterfield	D 0-0	0-0	13		(2,836)
16	22	EL	H	Hereford united	W 3-1	0-0	11	Gregan 71, Olsson 77, Painter 90	1,996
17	29	EL	A	Gillingham	L 1-2	1-1	13	Painter 38	(2,785)
18	N 5	EL	H	Walsall	D 2-2	1-0	13	Painter 7, Gregan 64	2,163
19	8	AWT PR	A	Hartlepool United	W 2-0	0-0		Worboys 58, 88	(1,211)
20	12	FAC 1	H	Hyde United	W 3-1	1-1		Slaven 37, Worboys 52, 53	(2,315)
21	19	EL	A	Wigan Athletic	L 1-4	1-2	15	Worboys 39	(1,785)
22	26	EL	H	Barnet	L 0-1	0-0	16		2,157
23	29	AWT 2	A	Rochdale	L 2-2	2-1		Worboys 13, Appleby 22 (pen)	(1,069)
24	D 4	FAC 2	A	Carlisle United	L 0-2	0-0			(8,365)
25	10	EL	H	Hartlepool United	L 1-2	1-1	16	Burgess 31 (og)	3,193
26	17	EL	A	Exeter City	W 2-0	1-0	15	Gaughan 7, Worboys 52	(2,336)
27	26	EL	H	Scarborough	W 1-0	1-0	14	Slaven 43	2,958
28	27	EL	A	Lincoln City	L 1-3	1-1	15	Slaven 11	(2,964)
29	31	EL	H	Northampton Town	W 4-1	1-0	13	Slaven 2, Banks 48, Gaughan 51, Shaw 68	2,250
30	J 7	EL	A	Hereford United	D 0-0	0-0	13		(2,237)
31	14	EL	H	Fulham	D 0-0	0-0	13		2,113
32	F 4	EL	A	Barnet	W 3-2	2-0	14	Worboys 17,49 Gaughan 35	(2,034)
33	11	EL	H	Wigan Athletic	L 1-3	0-1	15	Worboys 67	1,780
34	18	EL	A	Fulham	L 1-3	0-1	15	Slaven 86	(3,864)
35	21	EL	H	Gillingham	W 2-0	0-0	14	Slaven 76, Painter 85	1,548
36	25	EL	H	Carlisle United	L 0-2	0-1	16		3,992
37	M 4	EL	A	Colchester United	L 0-1	0-1	16		(6,055)
38	11	EL	A	Torquay United	L 0-1	0-0	16		(2,332)
39	14	EL	A	Walsall	L 0-2	0-1	16		(3,144)
40	18	EL	H	Mansfield Town	D 0-0	0-0	16		1,613
41	21	EL	A	Rochdale	L 0-2	0-0	16		(1,471)
42	25	EL	H	Doncaster Rovers	L 0-2	0-0	16		2,017
43	A 1	EL	a	Scunthorpe United	L 1-2	1-1	17	Olsson 6	(2,449)
44	8	EL	A	Northampton Town	L 1-2	0-1	18	Painter 54	(4,496)
45	15	EL	H	Lincoln City	D 0-0	0-0	18		1,664
46	18	EL	A	Scarborough	L 1-3	0-1	18	Olsson 83	(2,182)
47	22	EL	H	Rochdale	W 4-0	2-0	17	Worboys 20 (pen), Gaughan 32,48, Himsworth 73	1,886
48	29	EL	H	Chesterfield	L 0-1	0-1	19		3,387
49	M 6	EL	A	Bury	L 1-2	1-1	20	Reed 18	(6,790)
50									
51									
52									
53									
54									
55									
56									
57									
58									
59									
60									

Best Home League Attendance: 3,992 v Carlisle United	**Smallest:** 1,548 v Gillingham	**Av Home Att:** 2,349

Goal Scorers:

Compared with 1993-94: +216

League (43): Painter 9, Gaughan 8, Worboys 6(1 pen), Slaven 5, Olsson 4, Chapman 2, Gregan 2, Himsworth 2, Appleby, Banks, Shaw, Reed, Opponent
Coca Cola Cup (2): Cross, Slaven
FA Cup (3): Worboys 2, Slaven
AW Trophy (6): Worboys 3, Himsworth, Olsson, Appleby (1 pen)

Politt	Appleby	Cross	Banks	Crosby	Gregan	Slaven	Painter	Gaughan	Olsson	Mattison	Himsworth	Chapman	Collier	Reed	Shaw	Scott	Taylor	Worboys	Kirkham	Blake	Bolton	Referee	
1	2	3	4†	5	6	7	8	9	10	11*	12	S	S									U.D. Rennie	1
1	2	3	4	5	6	7	8	9	10	S	11*	12	S									D.B. Allison	2
1	2	3*	4	5	6•	7	8	9	10		12	11	S	14								J. Parker	3
1	2	3	4			7	8	9	10	11*	12		S	6	S							E. Wolstenholme	4
1	2	3		5		7	8	9	10	S	11	4	S	6	S							R. Furnandiz	5
1	2	3	4	5		7	8	9	10		S	11	S	6	S							P. D'Urso	6
1	2	3	4	5		7	8*	9	10		12	11	S	6	S							J. Holbrook	7
1	2	3	4	5		7	8	9	10	14	12*	11*	S	6								P. Richards	8
1	2	3	4	5		7	8	9	10	S	12	11*	S	6								P. Harrison	9
1	2	3	4	5			8	9	10	S	7	11	S	6	S							A. Butler	10
1	2	3	4	5		12	8*	9	10	S	7	11	S	6								W. Burns	11
1	2	3	4	5	14	12	8	9	10		7*	11	S	6•								K.M. Lynch	12
1	2	3	4	5	6	7	8*	9	10	S	11	12	S	S								E. Lomas	13
1	2	3	4	5	6	7		9	10	14	11•	8	S	12								A. Dawson	14
1	2	3	4	5•	6			9	10	7	S	11	S	14								R. Poulain	15
		3•	4	5	6	12	8	0	14	7	11*	1	2			S						M. Riley	16
S	2		4	5	6	7*	8	9	10		11	12	1	S			3					K. Cooper	17
1	2*		4	5	6	S	8	9	10		11			S	12		3	7				T.E. West	18
1	2		4	5	6	S	8	9	10		11			S	S		3	7				J. Winter	19
1	2		4	5	6	7	8	9	10		3	S	S	S				11				A.N. Butler	20
1	2†		4			6†	S	8	9	10		7	S	S	5		3	11				N. Barry	21
1	2		4			6	7	8	12	10		11*	S	S	5		3	9				W. Flood	22
1	2		4			6		7	10		11*	8	S	S	5	S	3	9	12			M. Riley	23
1			4	5		7	8*	2	10		3	11	S	6				9	12			J. Worrall	24
1	2		4	5		7	8	12	10		11*	14	S	6			3	9•				K. Breen	25
1	2*		4	5		7•	8	11	10		12	14	S	6			3	9				G. Barber	26
1			4	5		7	8*	11•	10	12	2	14		6		S	3	9				K.A. Lupton	27
1			4	5		7	8*	11•	10	12	2	14		6		S	3	9				E. Wolstenholme	28
1	2		4*	5		7		8	10		3	14	S	6	12			9	11•			G. Cain	29
1	2		4	6	12	7*		8	11	10•	3	14	S	6				9				J. Brandwood	30
1	2		4	5		S		8	11	10	3		S	6				9	7			S. Mathieson	31
1	2*		4	5		12	7•	8	11	10	3	14	S	6				9				P. Foakes	32
1	2		4	5		S	7	8*	11	10	3	14	S	6		S		9				J. Watson	33
1	2		4•			5	3	7	8	11	10	14	S	6		S		9	S			A. D'Urso	34
1						5	3	7	8	11	10	4	2	S	6	S	9					J. Lloyd	35
1	12					5	3	7	8	11	10	4	2	S	6	S	9					N. Barry	36
1	2		4			5		7	8	11	10	3		6*	S		9		12		S	A. Butler	37
1	2		4				8	11	10	3	12		S	5	6		9*	7•	14			K. Leach	38
1	2		4	5			8	11	10	3	12		S	6*	7		9•		14			K. Lynch	39
1			4	5	2		8•	11	10	7*	3		S	6			14	9				U. Rennie	40
1			4	5	2	7	12		10	8*	3		S	6	14		11	9*				J. Rushton	41
1	7		4	5†	2		8	11	10*	3		S	6	14			9*		12			A. Dawson	42
1	7*		4	5	2		8	11	10	3		S	6	S			9	12				M. Bailey	43
1	7		4		5		8*	11	10	14	3		S	6	2•		9	S	12			E. Lomas	44
1	7		4		5			11	10	3	9	S	6	2			12	14	8*			W. Flood	45
1	7		4		5			11	10	3	9	S	6	2•			12		8*			T. West	46
1	7		4•	5			12	11	10	3*	8	S	6	2			9	14				W.C. Burns	47
1	7		4	5	14		12	11	10	3*	8	S	6	2			9					G. Cain	48
1	7		4	5	3		12	11	10	S	8*	S	6	2			9					J. Holbrook	49

Politt	Appleby	Cross	Banks	Crosby	Gregan	Slaven	Painter	Gaughan	Olsson	Mattison	Himsworth	Chapman	Collier	Reed	Shaw	Scott	Taylor	Worboys	Kirkham	Blake	Bolton		
40	35	13	39	35	22	24	34	39	42	4	32	19	2	34	9	8	24	3	3	1		League Appearances	
	1			3	2	4	2			6	6	14		4	3		3	1	6	1		League Sub Appearances	
2	2	2	2	1	2	2	2	2	1	1+1	0+1	1										C/Cola Cup Appearances	
2	1		2	2	1	2	2	2	2	1		1		2				0+1				FA Cup Appearances	
3	3	1	3	2	2+1	0+1	2	3	3		3	2		2				2	0+1			AW Trophy Appearances	

Players on Loan: Appleby (Newcastle United), Taylor (Middlesbrough), Worboys (Notts County)

† = Sent Off

CLUB RECORDS

BIGGEST VICTORIES
League: 9-2 v Lincoln City, Division 3(N) 7.1.1928.
F.A. Cup: 7-2 v Evenwood, 1st Round, 17.11.1958.
Freight Rover Trophy: 7-0 v Halifax Town, 3.3.1985.

BIGGEST DEFEATS
League: 0-10 v Doncaster Rovers, Division 4, 25.1.1964.

MOST POINTS
3 points a win: 85, Division 4, 1984-85 (87, GMVC, 1989-90).
2 points a win:

RECORD TRANSFER FEE RECEIVED
£200,000 from Leicester City for Jimmy Willis, December 1991.

RECORD TRANSFER FEE PAID
£95,000 to Motherwell for Nick Cusack, January 1992.

BEST PERFORMANCES
League: 15th Division 2, 1925-26.
F.A. Cup: 3rd Round 1910-11, 5th Round 1957-58 (both last 16).
League Cup: 5th Round 1967-68.

HONOURS
Division 3(N) Champions 1924-25.
Division 3(N) Cup 1933-34.
G.M.V.C. Champions 1989-90.
Division 4 Champions 1991.

LEAGUE CAREER
Original member of Div 3(N) 1921, Div 2 1924-25, Div 3(N) 1926-27, Transferred to Div 4 1958, Div 3 1965-66, Div 4 1966-67, Div 3 1984-85, Div 4 1986-87, G.M.V.C. 1988-89, Div 4 1989-90, Div 3 1990-91, Div 4 (now Div 3) 1991-

INDIVIDUAL CLUB RECORDS

MOST GOALS IN A SEASON
David Brown: 39, Division 3(N), 1924-25.

MOST GOALS IN A MATCH
5. Tom Ruddy v South Shields, Division 2, 23.4.1927.
5. Maurice Wellock, Division 3(N), 15.2.1930.

OLDEST PLAYER
Jimmy Case, 39 years 128 days v Wycombe W., Division 3, 23.10.1993.

YOUNGEST PLAYER
Dale Anderson, 16 years 254 days, 4.5.1987.

MOST CAPPED PLAYER
None.

PREVIOUS MANAGERS

(Since 1946)
Bill Forrest, George Irwin, Bob Gurney, Dick Duckworth, Eddie Carr, Lol Morgan, Jimmy Greenhalgh, Ray Yeoman, Len Richley, Frank Brennan, Allan Jones, Ralph Brand, Dick Connor, Bill Horner, Peter Madden, Len Walker, Billy Elliott, Cyril Knowles, Paul Ward (Player/manager), David Booth, Brian Little, Frank Gray, Ray Hankin, Alan Murray, Paul Futcher, Eddie Kyle (Caretaker)

ADDITIONAL INFORMATION
PREVIOUS NAMES
None.

PREVIOUS LEAGUES
Northern League, North Eastern League, G.M.Vauxhall League.

Club colours: Black white hooped shirts,
Change colours: Yellow, blue sleeves.

Reserves League: Pontins League.

LONGEST LEAGUE RUNS

of undefeated matches:	17 (1968)	of league matches w/out a win:	19 (1988-89)
of undefeated home matches:	36 (1923-25)	of undefeated away matches:	14 (1968-69)
without home win:	18 (1988-89)	without an away win:	36 (1952-54)
of league wins:	5 (1922, 1924, 1975, 1985, 1989 (GMVC)	of home wins:	8 (1923-24, 1924, 1935-36)
of league defeats:	8 1985)	of away wins:	4 (1948) 5 (1989 GMVC)

THE MANAGER (DIRECTOR OF COACHING)

DAVID HODGSON . . . . appointed June 1995.

PREVIOUS CLUBS
As Manager . . . . None.
As Asst.Man/Coach . . . . None.
As a player . . . . Middlesbrough, Liverpool, Sunderland.

HONOURS
As a Manager . . . . None.
As a Player . . . . Division 1 championship 1983.
International . . . . 6 u21 caps for England.

DARLINGTON

PLAYERS NAME / Honours	Ht	Wt	Birthdate	Birthplace / Transfers	Contract Date	Clubs	League	L/Cup	FA Cup	Other	Lge	L/C	FAC	Oth
G O A L K E E P E R S														
Michael F Pollitt	6.3	14.1	24.0972	Farnworth	01.07.90	Manchester Utd (T)								
				Free	10.07.91	Bury								
				Free	01.12.92	Lincoln City	57	5	2	4				
				Free	11.08.94	Darlington	40	2	2	3				
D E F E N D E R S														
Matthew W Appleby	5.10	11.0	16.04.72	Middlesbrough	04.05.90	Newcastle Utd (T)	18+2	2+1	2	2+2				
				Loan	25.11.93	Darlington	10		1		1			
				Free	15.06.94	Darlington	35+1	2	1	3	1			1
Andrew K Crosby	6.2	13.0	03.03.73	Rotherham		Leeds United (T)								
				Free	04.07.91	Doncaster Rovers	41+10	1+1	2	4+1				1
Loan Halifax Town, (12.10.93), 0 Apps.				Free	10.12.93	Darlington	60	2	2	2				
Sean M Gregan	6.2	12.5	29.03.74	Guisborough	20.12.91	Darlington (T)	75+7	3	4	5+1	4			
M I D F I E L D														
Steven E Gaughen	5.11	11.2	14.04.70	Doncaster		Hatfield Main								
				Free	21.01.88	Doncaster Rovers	42+25	2+2	4+1	5+1	3			
				Free	01.07.90	Sunderland								
				£10,000	21.01.92	Darlington	125+5	6	4	5+1	12			
Peter J Kirkham	6.0	11.4	28.10.74	Newcastle		Newcastle Utd (J)								
				Free	03.09.93	Darlington	5+8		0+2	0+1				
Paul Olsson	5.8	10.11	24.12.65	Hull	07.01.84	Hull City (A)				1				1
				Free	13.03.87	Exeter City	38+5	2	0+1		2			
				Free	17.08.88	Scarborough	34+14	5+1	2	8	5			
				£5,000	26.12.89	Hartlepool United	162+19	11+2	10	11+1	13			2
				Free	01.07.90	Darlington	42	2	2	3	4			1
Paul A Mattison	5.8	11.04	24.04.73	Wakefield		North Ferriby								
					12.08.94	Darlington	4+6	1						
Simon R Shaw	6.0	12.0	21.09.73	Middlesbrough	14.08.92	Darlington (T)	46+20	2+1	1	2+1	6			
F O R W A R D S														
Gary Bannister	5.8	11.3	22.07.60	Warrington	10.05.78	Coventry City (A)	17+5	2	2		3			
E: u21.1.				£100,000	03.08.81	Sheffield Wed.	117+1	13	12		55	6	4	
				£200,000	13.08.84	Q.P.R	136	23	9	4	56	9	1	6
				£300,000	10.03.88	Coventry City	39+4	5			11	2		
				£250,000	09.03.90	West Bromwich A.	62+10	3+1	1+1	2+1	18	1		1
				Loan	19.03.92	Oxford United	7+3				2			
				Free	01.08.92	Nottingham Forest	27+4	2+1	3		8	1	1	
				Free	21.05.93	Stoke City	10+5		2	0+1	2			
			via Hong Kong	Free	14.09.94	Lincoln City	25+4	2	1+1	1	7		1	
				Free	08.95	Darlington								
Robert J Blake	5.11	12.0	04.03.76	Middlesbrough	01.07.94	Darlington (T)	3+6							
Gary P Himsworth	5.8	10.6	19.12.69	Pickering	27.01.88	York City (T)	74+14	5		5+2	8			
				Free	05.12.90	Scarborough	83+9	7+2	1+1	6+1	6	1		
				Free	16.07.93	Darlington	60+6	3+1	3	6	5			4
Peter Robert Painter	5.10	11.0	26.01.71	Wigan	01.07.88	Chester City (T)	58+26	2+2	7+1	3+4	8		3	
				£30,000	16.08.91	Maidstone United	27+3	2	1+1	0+2	5			
				£25,000	27.03.92	Burnley	16+10	2	1		2			
					16.09.93	Darlington	69+5	2	3	5	20		1	2
Gavin A Worboys	6.2	12.0	14.07.74	Doncaster	01.04.92	Doncaster Rov. (T)	6+1				2			
				£100,000	01.05.92	Notts County								
				Free	18.11.94	Darlington	24+3		2	2	6		2	3

FEETHAMS
Darlington, Co.Durham DL1 5JB
Tel: 01325 465 097

Capacity...9,984
Covered Standing...2,822
Seating...973

First game...1883.
First floodlit game...v Millwall, 19.9.1960.

ATTENDANCES
Highest...21,023 v Bolton, Lge Cup 3rd Rnd, 14.11.1960.
Lowest...657 v Halifax, AMC, 3.3.1985.

OTHER GROUNDS...None.

MATCHDAY TICKET PRICES

Seats. £6
Juv/OAP £3

Terraces. £6
Juv/OAP £3

Transfer to seat £2
Juv/OAP £2

Transfer to paddock. £1
Juv/OAP £1

Transfer to West £1
Juv/OAP £1
Ticket Office Telephone no. 01325 465 097

HOW TO GET TO THE GROUND

From the North
Use motorway (A1M) then A167 sign posted Darlington into town centre, then follow signs to Northallerton into Victoria Road for Darlington FC.

From the East
Use A67 sign posted Darlington into town centre, then follow signs to Northallerton into Victoria Road for Darlington FC.

From the South
Use motorway (A1M) and A66M then A66 sign posted Darlington and at round-about take the fourth exit into Victoria Road for Darlington FC.

From the West
Use A67 sign posted Darlington into town centre and at roundabout take 3rd exit into Victoria Road for Darlington FC.

Car Parking
Adequate space in adjacent side streets.

Nearest railway Station
Darlington (01325 55111)

CLUBCALL
0898 10 15 55
Calls cost 39p per minute cheap rate and 49p per minute at all other times.
Call costings correct at time of going to press.

MATCHDAY PROGRAMME

Programme Editor. . . . . Ken Lavery.

Number of pages . . . . 28.

Price £1

Subscriptions . . . . £34 (all home games).

Local Newspapers . . . . Northern Echo, Evening Gazette.

Local Radio Stations . . . . BBC Radio Cleveland, T.F.M. Radio.

DONCASTER ROVERS
(The Rovers)
ENDSLEIGH LEAGUE DIVISION 3
SPONSORED BY: DONCASTER FREE PRESS

Back Row (R-L): Jason Knight, Kevin Noteman, Mark Proctor, Paul Marquis, Mickey Norbury, Perry Suckling, Graeme Jones, Lee Warren, Darren Moore, Hakan Hayrettin. **Middle Row:** Phil McLoughlin (Physio), Jim Golze (Yth Coach), Ian Clarke, John Schofield, Ian Measham, Mark McCluskie, Warren Hackett, Lee Saunders, Paul Haywood, Duane Darby, Ryan Kirby, Peter Schofield (Chief Scout), George Foster (Coach). **Front Row:** Scott Maxfield, James Meara, Steve Gallen, Ken Richardson, Russ Wilcox, Steve Beaglehole (Asst. Manager), Scott Colcombe, Sean Parrish, Steve Harper, Gary Brabin.

DONCASTER FREE PRESS
FORMED IN 1879
TURNED PROFESSIONAL IN 1885
LTD COMPANY IN 1905 & 1920

CHAIRMAN: R Kennan
VICE-CHAIRMAN
K Chappell
DIRECTORS
J J Burke, K Haran, J Ryan,
V T Nuttall, T Sedgewick
SECRETARY
Mrs K J Oldale (01302 539 441)

MANAGER: Sammy Chung
ASSISTANT MANAGER: Steve Beaglehole
FIRST TEAM COACH
George Foster

RESERVES & YOUTH TEAM MANAGER
Steve Beaglehole

PHYSIOTHERAPIST
Phil McCloughlin

STATISTICIAN FOR THE DIRECTORY
Ernest Wiles

A final league placing of 9th was satisfactory enough, but when you consider that in December Rovers occupied a top three position, the words anti-climax certainly come into mind. But there again 9th was a great improvement on the previous term's disappointing 16th.

By the end of August they had occupied top spot - riches indeed! An obvious lack of punch up front was, however, a major problem. Ex-non-Leaguer Graeme Jones, signed from Bridlington Town in August 1993 for £10,000, was initially regular on the scoresheet, but even his final tally of twelve was probably less than expected.

The Christmas/New Year period was far from rewarding. Seven league games took place between 10th December and 14th January and not once did Rovers pick up three points. However, two 1-0 victories in January over west-country opposition, Torquay and Exeter, plus an impressive 0-0 draw with high-flying Carlisle and they were once more in the top four.

Unfortunately, just four wins from their final fifteen games was a lack-lustre end to the season and certainly not promotion form.

Gary Barbin, a semi-pro international signed from Conference club Runcorn for £40,000 in July 1994, was a great success. Eight goals from mid-field was an excellent strike record from someone new to the League scene.

Round One exits in both major cup competitions (Coca-cola and FA) were bitter blows, but there is no doubt that in the long term, Rovers can look forward to an extremely positive period.

In the Auto Windscreen Shield, Bury put paid to their hopes in Round Two.

GREG TESSER.

DONCASTER ROVERS

Division Three: 9th **FA Cup:** 1st Round **Coca-Cola Cup:** 1st Round **Auto Windscreens Trophy:** 2nd Round

M	DATE	COMP.	VEN	OPPONENTS	RESULT	H/T	LP	GOAL SCORERS/GOAL TIMES	ATT.
1	A 13	EL	A	Hereford United	W 1-0	0-0	5	Jones 41	(3,076)
2	15	CC 1/1	H	Wrexham	L 2-4	1-0		Jones 21, Torfason 85	1,925
3	20	EL	H	Northampton Town	W 1-0	1-0	4	Jones 35	2,194
4	22	CC 1/2	A	Wrexham	D 1-1	0-1		Swailes 48	(2,215)
5	27	EL	A	Colchester United	W 3-0	2-0	1	Jones 12, Donaldson 33, 74	(2,320)
6	30	EL	H	Fulham	D 0-0	0-0			3,003
7	S 3	EL	H	Darlington	D 0-0	0-0	4		2,967
8	10	EL	A	Barnet	D 0-0	0-0	6		(2,625)
9	13	EL	A	Bury	L 0-2	0-1			(2,395)
10	16	EL	H	Hereford	W 3-0	2-0	5	Brabin 4, Thew 22, Harper 71	1,938
11	24	EL	H	Preston NE	W 2-1	1-0	4	Harper 63, Brabin 69	3,321
12	27	AWT I	A	Hull City	W 2-0	1-0		Thew 44, Jones 64	(890)
13	O 1	EL	A	Rochdale	L -02	0-0	5		(2,445)
14	8	EL	H	Wigan	W 5-3	3-1		Roche 35 (pen), Brabin 40, 52, Harper 45,63	2,060
15	5	EL	A	Scarborough	D 2-2	0-2	5	Roche 87 (pen) 90 (pen)	(1,641)
16	17	AWT	A	Lincoln City	W 1-0	1-0		Turner 37	1,480
17	22	EL	A	Mansfield Town	W 1-0	0-0	3	Jones 76 (pen)	(2,988)
18	29	EL	H	Torquay United	W 3-0	0-0	3	Hackett 50, Jones 86, Lawrence 89	2,697
19	N 5	EL	A	Exeter City	W 5-1	4-0	3	Parrish 5, 38, Turner 36, Harper 42, Jones 83	(2,813)
20	12	FAC 1	H	Huddersfield Town	L 1-4	0-2		Jones 86	6,626
21	19	EL	H	Hartlepool United	W 3-0	1-0	3	Brabin 45, Harper 49, Meara 77	2,509
22	26	EL	A	Carlisle United	D 1-1	0-0	3	Lawrence 60	7,781
23	28	AWT 2	H	Bury	L 0-1	0-1			2,859
24	D 10	EL	A	Northampton Town	D 0-0	0-0	3		(4,538)
25	16	EL	H	Colchester	L 1-2	0-0		Brabin 80	2,460
26	26	EL	A	Chesterfield	L 0-2	0-1			(4,226)
27	27	EL	H	Scunthorpe United	D 1-1	1-0		Bryan 23	3,852
28	31	EL	A	Walsall	L 0-1	0-0			(4,561)
29	J 10	EL	H	Mansfield Town	L 0-2	0-0	9		2,577
30	14	EL	A	Lincoln C	L 0-1	0-0	9		(2,771)
31	28	EL	A	Torquay United	W 1-0	0-0	8	Hackett 71	(2,852)
32	30	EL	H	Exeter City	W 1-0	0-0	6	Brabin 75	1,611
33	F 2	EL	H	Carlisle United	D 0-0	0-0	4		3,587
34	7	EL	H	Gillingham	L 1-2	1-1	4	Schofield 37	1,740
35	18	EL	A	Lincoln City	W 3-0	1-0	4	Wilcox 15, Finlay 73, Harder 75	2,291
36	25	EI	H	Rochdale	L 0-1	0-1	3		2,246
37	M 4	EL	A	Preston NE	D 2-2	1-0	6	Jones 36, Wilcox 76	(9,624)
38	11	EL	H	Barnet	D 1-1	0-1	7	Harper 67	1,979
39	18	EL	A	Fulham	W 2-0	1-0	7	Jones 34, Parrish 61	(403)
40	21	EL	A	Hartlepool	L 1-2	0-2	7	Jones 67	(1,354)
41	25	EL	A	Darlington	W 2-0	0-0	7	Wilcox (pen)48, Brabin 81	(2,017)
42	A 1	EL	H	Bury	L 1-2	1-1		Wilcox 34 (pen)	2,485
43	8	EL	H	Walsall	L 0-2	0-1	7	Norbury 13,51,61 Warren 43, Harper 45	(2,368)
44	15	EL	A	Scunthorpe United	W 5-0	3-0	7	Norbury 13,51,61 Warren 43, Harper 45	(4,366)
45	17	EL	H	Chesterfield	L 1-3	1-1		Jones 41	4,796
46	22	EL	A	Gillingham	L 2-4	2-3	8	Norbury 7, Warren 36	(2,826)
47	29	EL	H	Scarborough	W 1-0	0-0	7	Jones 59	1,710
48	M 8	EL	A	Wigan	L 2-3	0-0	9	Jones 61, Norbury 70	(1,576)
49									
50									
51									
52									
53									
54									
55									
56									
57									
58									
59									
60									

Best Home League Attendance: 4,796 v Chesterfield **Smallest:** 1,710 v Scarborough **Av Home Att:** 59,804

Goal Scorers:

Compared with 1993-94: +315

League (58): Jones 12, Harper 9, Brabin 8, Norbury 5, Wilcox 4, Parrish 3, Roche 3, Donaldson 2, Hackett 2, Lawrence 2, Warren 2, Bryan 1, Finlay, Schofield, Thew, Turner, Meara

C/Cola Cup (3): Jones, Torfason, Swailes

FA Cup (1): Jones

AW Trophy (3): Thew, Jones, Turner

Suckling	Kitchen	Hackett	Brabin	Wilcox	Swailes	Lawrence	Thew	Jones	Findlay	Parrish	Kirby	Donaldson	Williams D.	Harper	Meara	Warren	Roche	Schofield	Norbury	Bryan	Maxfield	Turner	Limber	Torfason	Marquis	Referee	
1	2	3*	4	5	6	7	8	9	10	11	12	14	S													R. Harris	1
1	2	5	4		6	7	8	9	12	11		10	S										3	14		J. Watson	2
1		3	4	5	6	7	8	9		S	2	12	S	11										10		S. Mathieson	3
S		3	4	5	6	7			11	14	12	10	1		8							2	9			M. Riley	4
1*		3		5	6	7	8	9		11	2	10	12	S	4									14		I. Hemley	5
		3		5	6	7		9		11	2	10	1		4	8								14		N. Barry	6
		3	12	5	6			9		11	2	10	1		4	8								14		J. Holbrook	7
		3	4	5	6	7	12	9		11	2	10	1				5	8								A. P. D'Urso	8
		5	8	4		3	6	10		9	2	11	1	12		14	7									I. Cruikshanks	9
		3	4	5	6		7		S		11	2	10	1	9		S	8								G. Cain	10
		3	4	5	6	7		12		11	2		1	9		8									S	J. Brandwood	11
		3		5	6	7	4	9		11	2		1	10		8									S		12
		3	4		6		7	9	S	11	2		1	10	S		8							5		J, Lloyd	13
S		3	4	5	6	7		9		11		2		1	10	S	8							12*		A. Flood	14
		3	4	5	6	7		12		11		2		1	10		8		9						S	T. Heilbron	15
		3	4	5	6	7			12	11		2		1	10		8		9						S	J. Watson	16
		3	4	5	6	7		12		11		2		1	10	S	8		9							J. Winter	17
S		3	4	5	6	7		12		11		2		1	10	S	8		9							K. Breen	18
S		3	4	5	6	7	S	12		11		2		1	10	9	8		9							J, Lloyd	19
S		3	4	5	6	7		14	12	11		2		1	10	9	8									E.J. Parker	20
S		3	4	5	6	7		S	12	1	2	1	10	9		8										D. Allison	21
S		3	4	5	6	7		12		11	2	10	1			8	14	9								J. Parker	22
S	6	3	4	5		7	11	9			2	12	1		8	14		10								S. Mathieson	23
S	S	3		5	6	7		9		11	2		1		8		12	10	4							A.P. D'Urso	24
S		3	4	5	6		12			2		1	9	11	S		8	10	7							I. Cruikshanks	25
S		3	4	5	6	12	14			2		1	10	11		8	9	7								E. Lomas	26
S	6		4	5			7	11		10		2		1			12	8	S	9	3					A. Butler	27
S	6	4	3	5			7	10		12		2		1			11	8	9	S						M. Pierce	28
	5	3	4		6		7			11	2		1	9	14		10	8	12							K. Lynch	29
S		3			6		7	12	4	11	2		1	9	5	14	10	8								J. Kirkby	30
S		3	4	5	6		9				2		1	7	S		10	8	12		11					R. Harris	31
S		3	4	5	6		9				2		1	7	S		10	8	12		11					T. Hielbron	32
S		3		5	6		S	9		11	2		1	7	4		10	8	12							K. Leach	33
S		3		5	6		11				2		1	7	4	12	10	8	9							G. Cain	34
1				5	6		S		11		2		S	7	4	S		8	9	3						P. Rejer	35
1				5	6		12		11		2		S	7	4	S		8	9	3						U. Rennie	36
1		3	4	5	6		S	9		11	2		S	7	S		8	10								J.L. Watson	37
1*		3	4	5	6		S	9		11	2*		12*	7		14	8	10								T. Lunt	38
	S	3	4		6		12*	9		11*	2		1	7		5	8	10								C. Wilkes	39
	S	3	4		6			9		11	2		1	7		S	5	8	10							A. Flood	40
S	6	3	4	5			S	9		11*	2		1	7		10		8	S							A. Dawson	41
S	6	3		5			12*	9		11	2		1	7	S	4		8	10							N. Barry	42
S	6	3		5			11*	9			2		1	7		4		8	12	S						T. West	43
S		3		5				9*			2		1	7	S	4		8	10	6						G. Singh	44
S		3		5				9			2		1	7	S	4		8	10	6						K. Lynch	45
S		3		5				9	12*		2		1	7	S	4		8	10	6						G. Pooley	46
1	S	3	4		5			9			2		1	7	S	4		8	10	6						P. Harrison	47
1	12	3		5			S	9			2					11	4	8	10	6						I. Cruikshank	48
																											49
																											50
																											51
																											52
																											53
																											54
																											55
																											56
																											57
																											58
																											59
																											60
10	8	39	27	37	32	14	15	25	6	25	40	7	32	31	14	10	19	25	18	5	10	4		1	1	League Appearances	
	1		1				2	5	6	1		1					2	1	4	1	2	4		3	1	League Sub Appearances	
1	1	2	2	1	2	2	1	1	1+1	1+1	0+1	2	1	1							2	1+1				C/Cola Appearances	
	1	1	1	1	1	0+1	0+1		1	1		1	1	1		1					1					FA Cup Appearances	
	1	3	2	3	2	3	2+1	2		0+1	2	3	0+1	3	2	1	0+1	2		1	1					AWT Appearances	

Also Played: Williams P. 10(35,36*,43),11(44,45,46*) 12(47),S(48), Williams D.A. 10(11), Hoy 12(44)S(34,45), Buxton S(6,29,39,40), Gallen S(12), Measham 7(48), Hilton S(17)

CLUB RECORDS

BIGGEST VICTORIES
League: 10-0 v Darlington, Division 4, 25.1.1964.
F.A. Cup: 7-0 v Blyth Spartans, 1st Round, 1937-38.

BIGGEST DEFEATS
League: 0-12 v Small Heath, Division 2, 11.4.1903.
F.A. Cup: 0-8 v Everton, 4th Round, 1938-39.

MOST POINTS
3 points a win: 85, Division 4, 1983-84.
2 points a win: 72, Division 3(N), 1946-47.

MOST GOALS SCORED
123, Division 3(N), 1946-47.

RECORD TRANSFER FEE RECEIVED
£250,000 from Q.P.R. for Rufus Brevett, February 1991.
£175,000 from Leicester for Jamie Lawrence - Further installments could take the fee to £300,000.

RECORD TRANSFER FEE PAID
£60,000 to Stirling Albion for John Philliben, March 1984.
£60,000 to Hull City for Russ Wilcox, July 1993.

BEST PERFORMANCES
League: 7th in Division 2, 1901-02.
F.A. Cup: 5th Round 1951-52, 1953-54, 1954-55, 1955-56.
League Cup: 5th Round 1975-76.

HONOURS
Division 3(N) champions 1934-35, 1946-47, 1949-50.
Division 4 champions 1965-66, 1968-69.

LEAGUE CAREER
Elected to Div 2 1901, Failed to gain re-election 1903, Re-elected to Div 2 1904, Failed to gain re-election 1905, Re-elected to Div 3(N) 1923, Div 2 1934-35, Div 3(N) 1936-37, Div 2 1946-47, Div 3(N) 1947-48, Div 2 1949-50, Div 3 1957-58, Div 4 1958-59, Div 3 1965-66, Div 4 1966-67, Div 3 1968-69, Div 4 1970-71, Div 3 1980-81, Div 4 1982-83, Div 3 1983-84, Div 4 (now Div 3) 1987-88.

INDIVIDUAL CLUB RECORDS

MOST GOALS IN A SEASON
Clarrie Jodan: 44 goals in 1946-47 (League 42, FA Cup 2).

MOST GOALS IN A MATCH
6. Tom Keetley v Ashington (a), 7-4, Division 3(N), 16.2.1929.

OLDEST PLAYER
Mitchell Downie, 40 years 252 days.

YOUNGEST PLAYER
Alick Jeffrey, 15 years 229 days.

MOST CAPPED PLAYER
Len Graham (Northern Ireland) 14.
Ian Snodin (England U21) 4.

PREVIOUS MANAGERS

(Since 1946)
Bill Marsden, Jackie Bestall, Peter Doherty, Jack Hodgson, Syd Bycroft, Jack Crayston, Jack Bestall, Norman Curtis, Danny Malloy, Oscar Hold, Bill Leivers, Keith Kettleborough, George Raynor, Lawrie McMenemy, Maurice Setters, Stan Anderson, Billy Bremner, Dave Cusack, Dave Mackay, Billy Bremner, Steve Beaglehole.

ADDITIONAL INFORMATION
PREVIOUS NAMES
None.

PREVIOUS LEAGUES
Midland League.

Club colours: Red shirts with white sleeves & red/green trim, white shorts, red socks with white/green tops.
Change colours: Dark blue shirts, with white sleeves/red trim, white shorts with red trim, red socks with blue/white tops.

Reserves League: Central League Division 3.

LONGEST LEAGUE RUNS

of undefeated matches:	21 (1968-69)	of league matches w/out a win:	16 (1991-92)
of undefeated home matches:	33 (1931-33)	of undefeated away matches:	17 (1939, 1946)
without home win:	13 (1989)	without an away win:	44 (1902-03, 1904-05, 1923-24)
of league wins:	10 (1947)	of home wins:	11 (1934-35)
of league defeats:	9 (1905)	of away wins:	9 (1939, 1946)

THE MANAGER

SAMMY CHUNG . . . . appointed July 1994.

PREVIOUS CLUBS
As Manager . . . . Wolves, IFK Vastern, Tamworth.
As Asst.Man/Coach . . . . Watford, Ipswich, Wolves, United Arb Em., Stoke, Colchester.
As a player . . . . Reading, Norwich, Watford.

HONOURS
As a Manager . . . . Wolves: Division 2 Champions 1977.
As a Player . . . . None.

DONCASTER ROVERS

PLAYERS NAME Honours	Ht	Wt	Birthdate	Birthplace Transfers	Contract Date	Clubs	APPEARANCES League	L/Cup	FA Cup	Other	GOALS Lge	L/C	FAC	Oth
G O A L K E E P E R S														
Perry J Suckling	6.1	11.2	12.10.65	Leyton	19.10.83	Coventry City (A)	27	2						
E: u21.10, Y14					05.06.86	Manchester City	39	3	1	3				
				£100,000	14.01.88	Crystal Palace	59	4	1	7				
				Loan	15.12.89	West Ham United	6							
				Loan	11.10.91	Brentford	8			1				
				Free	13.07.92	Watford	39	4	1	2				
				Free	08.07.94	Doncaster Rovers	9	1						
Dean P Williams	6.0	12.8	05.01.72	Lichfield	11.07.90	Birmingham City (T)	4		1					
				Free	01.03.92	Tamworth								
				£2,000	08.08.93	Brentford	6+1							
				Free	12.08.94	Doncaster Rovers	33+2	1	1	3				
D E F E N D E R S														
Stephen J Gallen	6.0	12.0	21.11.73	London	08.05.92	Q.P.R. (T)								
Ei: u21.4, Y					15.07.94	Doncaster Rovers								
Warren J Hackett	5.9	10.7	16.12.71	Plaistow		Tottenham H. (T)								
FAYC'90					Free	03.07.90	Leyton Orient	74+2	4	8	7	3		1	
				Free	26.07.94	Doncaster Rovers	39	2	1	3	2			
Paul Haywood	5.11	10.02	04.10.75	Barnsley	08.92	Nottingham F. (T)								
				Free	08.95	Doncaster Rovers								
Ryan M Kirby	5.11	12.0	06.09.74	Redbridge	06.07.93	Arsenal (T)								
				Free	06.07.94	Doncaster Rovers	41+1	0+1	1	3				
Paul R Marquis	6.1	11.12	29.08.72	Enfield	01.07.91	West Ham Utd (T)	0+1							
				Free	10.03.94	Doncaster Rovers	11+2							
Scott Maxfield	5.8	10.7	13.07.76	Doncaster	08.07.94	Doncaster R. (T)	20		0+1					
Ian Meaham	5.11	11.1	14.12.64	Barnsley	16.12.82	Huddersfield T. (A)								
Div4'92					Loan	18.10.85	Lincoln City	6							
				Loan	21.03.86	Rochdale	12							
				Free	08.08.86	Cambridge United	46	6	3	2				
				Free	10.11.86	Burnley	181+1	8	19	19	2			
					16.09.93	Doncaster Rovers	22		2	2				
Darren Moore	6.2	12.0	22.04.74	Birmingham	18.11.92	Torquay United (T)	102+1	6	7	8	7		1	2
				£62,500	08.95	Doncaster Rovers								
Lee J Saunders			23.03.77	Nuneaton	08.94	Doncaster Rov. (T)								
Russell Wilcox	6.0	11.0	25.03.64	Hemsworth	28.05.80	Doncaster R. (A)	1							
E: S-P3; Div4'87					Free		Frickley athletic		7					1	
				£15,000	30.06.86	Northampton Town	137+1	6	10	8	9			1
				£120,000	06.08.90	Hull City	92+8	5	5	5+1	7		1	
				£60,000	30.07.93	Doncaster Rovers	77	3	3	3	6	1		
Paul L Williams	6.0	11.0	25.09.70	Liverpool	21.07.89	Sunderland (T)	6+4	1		2				
WFAC'91					Loan	28.03.91	Swansea City	12							
				Free	14.07.93	Doncaster Rovers	6+2							
M I D F I E L D														
Gary Brabin	5.11	14.8	09.12.70	Liverpool		Stockport Co. (T)	1+1							
						Gateshead								
						Runcorn			1					
				£45,000	26.07.94	Doncaster Rovers	27+1	2	1	2	8			
James S Meara	5.7	10.6	07.10.72	Hammersmith	30.04.91	Watford (T)	1+1							
FAYC'89					Free	15.07.94	Doncaster Rovers	39+1	2+1	2	3	4			
Sean Parrish	5.9	10.0	14.03.72	Wrexham	12.07.90	Shrewsbury T. (T)	1+2	1		3				1
				Free		Telford United			4					
				£20,000	28.05.94	Doncaster Rovers								
John D Schofield	5.11	11.3	16.05.65	Barnsley		Gainsborough T.								
				Free	10.11.88	Lincoln City	209+10	11	5+2	12+1	10	2		
				Free	18.11.94	Doncaster Rovers	25+2			1				
F O R W A R D S														
Scott Colcombe	5.5	10.6	15.12.71	West Bromwich	05.07.90	West Brom. A. (T)								
				Free	14.08.91	Torquay United	68+11	8+1	4+1	5	1		1	
				Free	08.95	Doncaster Rovers								
Duane Darby	5.11	11.2	17.10.73	Birmingham	03.07.92	Torquay United (T)	60+48	4+3	1+4	5+3	25	1		2
				£35,000	08.95	Doncaster Rovers								
Steven J Harper	5.10	11.5	03.02.69	N'castle-u-Lyme	29.06.87	Port Vale(T)	16+12	1+2		1+1	2			
Div4'92					23.03.89	Preston North End	57+20	1+1	1+2	6+1	10			1
				Free	23.07.91	Burnley	64+5	1+2	10	8	8		3	
				Free	07.08.93	Doncaster Rovers	56+8	2	3	4	11	1		
Graeme A Jones	6.0	12.12	13.03.70	Gateshead		Bridlington								
NPL Div1'93; FA Vase'93					£10,000	02.08.93	Doncaster Rovers	49+11	2+1	1+1	3	16	1	1	1
Michael S Norbury	6.0	12.0	22.01.69	Hemsworth		Ossett Town								
				30.12.89	Scarborough								
via Ossett Town & Bridlington Town to					13.02.92	Cambridge United	11+15			1+2	3			
				£32,500	23.12.92	Preston North End	32+10	1+1	0+3	3+1	13			1
				£10,000	28.11.94	Doncaster Rovers	17+5			1	5			
Lee A Warren	6.0	11.10	28.02.69	Manchester	27.07.87	Leeds United (T)								
				Free	28.10.87	Rochdale	31		1	2	1			
				£100,000	25.08.88	Hull City	141+12	8	5+1	4+1	1		1	
				Loan	20.09.90	Lincoln City	2+1				1			
				Free	21.07.94	Doncaster Rovers	10+4			0+1	2			

571

BELLE VUE GROUND
Doncaster, South Yorkshire DN4 5HT
Tel: 01302 539 441

Capacity 7,794
Covered Standing 2,125
Seating 1,259

First game ....v Gainsborough Trinity, 08/1922.
First floodlit game ....v Hiberbian, 4.3.1952.

ATTENDANCES
Highest ....37,149 v Hull City, Div 3(N), 2.10.1948.
Lowest ....613 v Blackpool, AMC, 17.12.1991.

OTHER GROUNDS ....None.

HOW TO GET TO THE GROUND

From the North
Use motorway (A1(N)) then A638 sign posted Doncaster into Town Centre. Then follow signs to Bawtry (A368) and in 1.2 miles at roundabout take 3rd exit into Bawtry Road for Doncaster FC.

From the East
Use motorway (M18) then A630 sign posted Doncaster. In 2.7 miles at roundabout take first exit (A18). In 2.5 miles at roundabout take first exit into Bawtry Road (A638) for Doncaster FC.

From the South
Use motorway (M1) then M18, take junction 3, sign posted to Doncaster (A6182) in 2 miles at roundabout take 3rd exit, sign posted Racecourse and Scunthorpe (A18). In 1.25 miles at roundabout take 3rd exit (A638) into Bawtry Road for Doncaster FC.

From the West
Use (A635) in Doncaster Town Centre then follow signs to Bawtry (A638) and in 1.2 miles at roundabout take 3rd exit into Bawtry Road for Doncaster FC.

Car Parking: Very large car and coach park adjacent to ground. Entrance direct from Great North Road.
Nearest Railway Station: Doncaster (01302 340 222)

MATCHDAY TICKET PRICES

Seats £9
Juv/OAP/Unemployed £5

Terraces £7
Juv/OAP/Unemployed £3.50

Ticket Office Telephone no. 01302 539 441

MATCHDAY PROGRAMME

Programme Editor .... K Avis.

Number of pages .... 32.

Price £1.20

Subscriptions .... £30.

Local Newspapers .... Doncaster Star, Yorkshire Post.

Local Radio Stations .... Radio Hallam, Radio Sheffield.

EXETER CITY
(The Grecians)
ENDSLEIGH LEAGUE DIVISION 3
SPONSORED BY: ALC WINDOWS

Unfortunately the 1995-96 team photo had not been taken before going to press,so the 1993-94 photo has been used.
Back row L-R: Wayne Edwards, Nicky Medlin, Matthew Hare, Barry McConnell, PhilJoon, Peter Fox, Andy Woodman, Ross Bellotti, Andy Rollason, Marc Baines, RogerDerham, Jamie Littley. **3rd Row:** Mark Gavin, Mark Cooper, Dave Cooper, AnthonyThirlby, Gary Rice, Martin Phillips, Danny Bailey, Mickey Ross, Jason Minett,Russell Coughlin. **2nd Row:** Matthew Moxey, Ronnie Robinson, Mike Cecere, PeterWhiston, Mark Came, Robbie Turner, Stuart Storer, Scott Daniels, JonRichardson, Richard Pears, Colin Anderson, Jon Brown, Chris Grant. **Front:** R.Anderson (Club Doctor), Mike Chapman (Physio), Trevor Morgan (Asst. Manager),Mr Murry Couch (Financial Director), Mr Gerald Vallance (Director), TerryCooper (Manager), Mr Ivor Doble (Chairman), Mr Stuart Dawe (Director), AlecLynn (ALC), Les Phillips (ALC), George Kent (Kit Manager), Mike Radford (YthDev. Officer).

EXETER CITY
FORMED IN 1904
TURNED PROFESSIONAL IN 1908
LTD COMPANY IN 1908

CHAIRMAN:
DIRECTORS
M Couch, S Dawe, G Vallance
SECRETARY
Margaret Bond (01392 54073)
COMMERCIAL MANAGER
Steve Birley

MANAGER: Peter Fox
ASSISTANT MANAGER: Noel Blake

RESERVE TEAM MANAGER
Mike Radford
YOUTH TEAM MANAGER
Mike Radford (01395 232 784)

STATISTICIAN FOR THE DIRECTORY
Graham Lucas

On the final day of August, City managed to scrape a 1-0 home win over Colchester United Four days later, Gillingham were dismissed 3-0, thanks to a brace from Mark Cooper. Fourteenth in their division at the time, the Grecians looked on paper to be more than capable of finishing in a respectable mid-table position, but a lack of any real punch up front plus an obvious naivety at the back always meant trouble was never far away!

In terms of league respectability, 22nd position at the end of August and 22nd come May probably summed it all up.

Striker Michele Cecere was, without question, a success. More goalscorers in his mold and the Grecians would have found the task of trying to win three points not such a complicated business.

In the FA Cup, an unconvincing 1-0 home win over the non-Leaguers from Sussex, Crawley, in the First Round did not exactly set the world alight. In Round Two, a Morgan goal after 23 minutes at home to Colchester proved to be the club's final positive act in the season's competition. Two second-half strikes from the Essex outfit and Exeter were out!

There was no real joy in the Coca-cola Cup. Drawn against Swansea City, they deservedly led 2-0 at half-time in the first leg, thanks to goals from Turner and Cecere, but another poor performance in the second 45 minutes enabled the Swans to claw their way back and go into the second leg on equal terms, 2-2. At the Vetch Field, two goals in the second half put paid to Exeter's Coca-cola aspirations.

In Endsleigh League terms, it was all very depressing. However, in the Auto Windscreen Shield, wins over Plymouth Argyle (3-1), Cardiff City(1-0) led to a quarter-final pairing with Shrewsbury Town. Despite a goal from Richardson after 50 minutes, the Grecians were easily pushed aside 3-1 in front of just 1960 fans at Gay Meadow.

Despite a regular supply of goals from the talented Cecere, their end-of-season run-in was disappointing to say the least - sixteen games without a win!!

GREG TESSER.

EXETER CITY

Division Three: 22nd   **FA Cup:** 2nd Round   **Coca-Cola Cup:** 1st Round   **Auto Windscreen Trophy:** 1/4 Finals

M	DATE	COMP.	VEN	OPPONENTS	RESULT	H/T	LP	GOAL SCORERS/GOAL TIMES	ATT.
1	A 13	EL	A	Lincoln City	L 0-2	0-2	22		(3,439)
2	17	CC 1/1	H	**Swansea City**	D 2-2	2-0		**Turner 18, Cecere 32**	**2,050**
3	20	EL	H	Bury	L 0-4	0-3	22		2,164
4	22	CC 1/2	A	**Swansea City**	L 0-2	0-0			**(2,423)**
5	27	EL	A	Darlington	L 0-2	0-0	22		(1,861)
6	30	EL	H	Colchester United	W 1-0	1-0		Bailey 19	1,804
7	S 3	EL	H	Gillingham	W 3-0	2-0	14	Cooper 22, 58, Dunne 27	2,241
8	10	EL	A	Carlisle United	L 0-1	0-1	17		(6,213)
9	13	EL	A	Chesterfield	L 0-2	0-1			(2,136)
10	17	EL	H	Lincoln City	W 1-0	0-0	15	Thirley 84	2,180
11	24	EL	A	Mansfield Town	D 1-1	0-0	14	Morgan 80	(2,486)
12	O 1	EL	A	Hartlepool United	W 2-1	1-1	14	Gavin 21, Cooper 84	2,390
13	8	EL	H	Northampton Town	D 0-0	0-0	15		3,015
14	15	EL	A	Fulham	L 0-4	0-2	16		(4,314)
15	18	AWT 1	A	**Plymouth Argyle**	W 3-1	1-0		**Cecere 5, 75, Cooper 47**	**(1,847)**
16	22	EL	H	Scunthorpe United	D 2-2	1-1	15	Game 23, Cecere 74	2,511
17	29	EL	A	Preston North End	W 1-0	1-0	14	Cecere 44	(6,808)
18	N 5	EL	A	Doncaster Rovers	L 1-5	0-4	15	Turner 66	2,813
19	12	FAC 1	H	**Crawley**	W 1-0	1-0		**Cecere 7**	**3,214**
20	19	EL	A	Walsall	L 0-1	0-1	16		(3,629)
21	26	EL	H	Scarborough	W 5-2	2-1	14	Cecere 27, 52, Gavin 36, Phillips 65, Storer 77	2,179
22	29	AWT 2	H	**Cardiff City**	W 1-0	0-0		**Brown 87**	**1,452**
23	D 3	FAC2	H	**Colchester United**	L 1-2	1-0		**Morgan 23**	**3,528**
24	10	EL	A	Bury	D 0-0	0-0	15		(2,876)
25	17	EL	H	Darlington	L 0-2	0-1			2,336
26	26	EL	H	Torquay United	L 1-2	1-0		Storer 33	5,538
27	27	EL	A	Hereford United	L 0-3	0-2			(2,567)
28	J 7	EL	A	Scunthorpe United	L 0-2	0-2	18		(2,463)
29	10	AWT 1/4	A	**Shrewsbury Town**	L 1-3	0-1		**Richardson 50**	**(1,960)**
30	14	EL	H	Rochdale	D 0-0	0-0	17		2,316
31	31	EL	A	Doncaster Rovers	L 0-1	0-0			(1,611)
32	F 4	EL	A	Scarborough	W 2-0	1-0	17	Anderson 15, Pears 74	(1,512)
33	18	EL	A	Rochdale	W 1-0	1-0	17	Cooper 26	(1,945)
34	21	EL	H	Wigan Athletic	L 2-4	1-2		Richardson 13, Cecere 83	2,370
35	25	EL	A	Hartlepool United	D 2-2	1-1	18	Cecere 11, Thirley 79	(1,440)
36	28	EL	A	Barnet	D 1-1	0-1		Cooper M. 59	(1,325)
37	M 4	EL	H	Mansfield Town	L 2-3	1-1	18	Phillips 21, Minett 68 (pen)	2,458
38	11	EL	M	Carlisle United	D 1-1	1-1	18	Brown 25	2,673
39	18	EL	A	Colchester United	L 1-3	0-1	18	Cecere 82	(2,375)
40	21	EL	H	Preston North End	L 0-1	0-0			2,057
41	25	EL	H	Gillingham	L 0-3	0-2			(3,332)
42	A 1	EL	H	Chesterfield	L 1-2	0-0		Brown 74	2,144
43	4	EL	H	Walsall	L 1-3	0-1	21	Cecere 51	1,551
44	8	EL	A	Wigan Athletic	L 1-3	0-2	21	Cecere 59	(1,417)
45	15	EL	H	Hereford United	D 1-1	0-1	21	Cecere 61	2,083
46	18	EL	A	Torquay United	D 0-0	0-0			(4,155)
47	22	EL	H	Barnet	L 1-2	0-1	21	Cooper M. 88	1,903
48	29	EL	H	Fulham	L 0-1	0-0	22		3,388
49	M 6	EL	A	Northampton	L 1-2	0-1		Minett 83	(6,734)
50									
51									
52									
53									
54									
55									
56									
57									
58									
59									
60									

Best Home League Attendance: 5,538 v Torquay United   **Smallest:** 1,551 v Walsall   **Av Home Att:** 2,489

Goal Scorers:

League (36): Cecere 10, Cooper 6, Thirley 2, Gavin 2, Phillips 2, Storer 2, Brown 2, Minett 2, Pears, Anderson, Richardson, Game, Morgan, Dunne, Bailey, Turner

C/Cola Cup (2): Turner, Cecere

FA Cup (2): Cecere, Morgan

AW Trophy (5): Cecere 2, Cooper, Brown, Richardson

Compared with 1993-94: -860

Woodman	Daniels	Anderson	Cooper M	Game	Richardson	Storer	Coughlin	Turner	Ross	Gavin	Thirley	Brown	Fox	Bailey	Phillips	Cecere	Pears	Rice	Minett	Noon	Robinson	Morgan	Bellotti	Barrett	Cooper D.	Referee	
1	2	3	4*	5	6	7	8	9•	10	11	12	14	S													A. Butler	1
1	2	3*		5	6			9		11	8	12	S	4	7	10*	14									M. Pierce	2
1	2		12	5				9		11	8*	6	S	4	7	10•	14	3								J. Holbrook	3
			7	5			S			11	8	6	1	4	S	9	10	3	2	S						G. Singh	4
			7	5	6	12				11	8	14	1	4		9*	10	3	2	S						R. Furnandiz	5
		3	9	5	6	7	10*			11	8	12	1	4	S				2	S						S. Dunn S	6
			9	5	6	7	10*			11	8	S	1	4	12				2	S	3					J. Brandwood	7
			9	5	6	7	10				8	11	1	4*	S		12		2	S	3					U. Rennie	8
			9*	5	6	7	10•			11	8	4	1		14		12		2	S	3					E. Wolstenholme	9
				5	6	7	10			11	8	4	1			12	S		2	S	3	9*				P. Vanes	10
		10				6†	7*	5	9		8	4	1			S	11		2	S	3	12				J. Rushton	11
S	10•	4		5	6			9		11	8*	14	1						2		3	12				C. Wilkes	12
S		4		5		7	10	9*		11	8	S	1		S				2		3	12				K. Leach	13
S		4		5	6	7	10	9		11	8	S	1						2		3	S				J. Holbrook	14
																											15
1		4		5		7	10	9		11	8	3	S		S	6	S		2							G. Singh	16
1		4		5	6	7	10	9		11	S	S	S		8				2		3					J. Kirkby	17
1		4		5	6	7*	10	12		11		3	S		8•		14		2							J. Lloyd	18
S		4		5	6	12	8	9*		11	7*	3	1			10•			2		3	14				M. Pierce M	19
S		14		5	6		8	9		11	7*	3	1	4	12	10•			2							K. Breen	20
1		12			6*	7	10	9•		11		3		4	5	8	14		2				S			P. Rejer	21
																											22
1	5	9•			6	7	8*			11	14	3		4					2		12	10	S			P. Durkin	23
	3	8	4		7	10	6*			11	5	9							2		12	S	1			L. Riley	24
		8	12	5	6					11	10	4				S			2		3	9*	S	1		S. Dunn	26
	5	8	10		6	7				11		4		4	12	9*	S		2		3	S	S	1		J. Lloyd	27
	5	3	8		6	7				11	S	4		4		10	S		2		9	S	S	1		D. Adcock	28
																											29
S	5	10	8		6	7*		9			12	1	4		11•	14			2		3					R. Harris	30
S	3	8	5	6	7	4				11	9	1			10*	12			2		S					T. Heilbron	31
S	4	8	5	6	7	12				11	S	3	1		10	9*			2		3					P. Richards	32
S	4	8	5	6						11	7	3	1		12	10	9*		2				S			A. Butler	33
	4*	8	5	6	12					11	7	3	1		14	10	9•		2				S			K. Cooper	34
S		8		6		4				11	14	2	1	4	7	10	9*		2		5	12			3*	G. Cain	35
S		8		6		4				11	12	5	1		7	10	9*		2		5				3	M. Bailey	36
S		8*		6		4				11	12	9	1		7	10	S		2		5				3	P. Vanes	37
			12	5*	6					11	8	4	1		7	10	9		2			S	S		3	C. Wilkes	38
		4	12	5						11	10	6	1	S	7	8	9*		2				S		3*	J. Holbrook	39
		4	12	5	6					11	10•	9	1		7	8	14		2				S		3	G. Singh	40
		4	12	5	6					11	S	3	1		7	10			2		9*		S		3	P. Rejer	41
		4	8	5	6		14				11•	10	1		7	12			2		9*		S		3	K. Leach	42
		4	8	5	6					11	S	9	1		7	10	S		2			S	S		3	M. Pierce.	43
		4	8	5	6					11		10	1		7	9*	12		2			S	S		3	W. Flood	44
		4	8		6		11				12	2	1	9	7	10	S	3*	2			S	S		5	G. Barber	45
		4*		5	6		8			11	S	9	1		7	10	12		2			S	S		3	S. Dunn	46
S			12	5*	6		4			11	S	8	1		7	10	9		2			S	S		3	C. Wilkes	47
		3	8	5	6		12			11	14	4*	1		7	10	9•		2			S	S			M. Pierce	48
			10*	9	6					11	S	4	1		7	8	12	3	2			S			5	E. Wolstenholme	49
6	6	21	39	31	37	22	25	11	1	36	25	36	31	13	24	28	19	10	37	0	16	8	1	3	14	League Appearances	
11	0	0	0	0	0	0	0	0	0	6	4	5	1	5	1	5	3	0	7	0	5	9	8	1		League Sub Appearances	
1	1	1	1	2	1	0	0+1	1	0	2	2	1	1+1	2	1+1	2	2	1	1	0+1	0	0	0	0	0	C/Cola Cup Appearances	
1+1	1	0	2	1	2	2	2	1	0	2	1	2	1	1	0	1	0	0	2	0	2	2	0+1	0	0	FA Cup Appearances	

† = sent off

CLUB RECORDS

BIGGEST VICTORIES
League: 8-1 v Coventry, Division 3(S) 4.12.1926.
8-1 v Aldershot, Division 3(S) 4.5.1935.
7-0 v Crystal Palace, Division 3(S) 9.1.1954.
F.A. Cup: 9-1 v Aberdare, 1st Round, 26.11.1927.
Other: 11-6 v Crystal Palace, Division 3(S) Cup, 24.1.1934.

BIGGEST DEFEATS
League: 0-9 v Notts County, Division 3(S), 16.10.1948.
0-9 v Northampton Town, Division 3(S), 12.4.1958.
League Cup: 1-8 v Aston Villa, 2nd Round 7.10.1985.

MOST POINTS
3 points a win: 89, Division 4, 1989-90.
2 points a win: 62, Division 4, 1976-77.

MOST GOALS SCORED: 88, Division 3(S), 1932-33.

RECORD TRANSFER FEE RECEIVED
£300,000 from Glasgow Rangers for Chris Vinicombe, November 1989. (Initial £200,000 + £100,000 for completion of 20 first team appearances paid Oct'91)

RECORD TRANSFER FEE PAID
£10,000 + £5,000 + £125,000 to Bristol Rovers for Richard Dryden, March 1989, May 1989, July 1991.

BEST PERFORMANCES
League: 2nd Division 3(S) 1932-33.
F.A. Cup: 6th Round replay 1930-31.
League Cup: 4th Round.

HONOURS
Champions of Division 4, 1989-90.
Division 3(S) Cup winners 1933-34.

LEAGUE CAREER
Elected to Div 3 1920, Transferred to Div 3(S) 1921, Div 4 1957-58, Div 3 1963-64, Div 4 1965-66, Div 3 1976-77, Div 4 1983-84, Div 3(now Div 2) 1989-90, Div 3 1993-94

INDIVIDUAL CLUB RECORDS

MOST GOALS IN A SEASON
Rod Williams: 37 goals in 1936-37 (League 29, FA Cup 7, Division 3(S) Cup 1).

MOST GOALS IN A MATCH
6. James Bell v Weymouth, 1st Preliminary Rnd., 3.10.1908.
6. Fred Whitlow v Crystal Palace, Division 3(S) Cup, 24.1.1934 (11-6).

YOUNGEST PLAYER
Cliff Bastin, 16 years 31 days v Coventry City, 14.4.1928.

MOST CAPPED PLAYER
Dermot Curtis (Eire) 1.

PREVIOUS MANAGERS

1908-22 Arthur Chadwick, 1923-27 Fred Mavin, 1928-29 David Wilson, 1929-35 Billy McDevitt, 1935-40 Jack English, 1945-52 George Roughton, 1952-53 Norman Kirkman, 1953-57 Norman Dodgin, 1957-58 Bill Thompson, 1958-60 Frank Broome, 1960-62 Glen Wilson, 1962-63 Cyril Spiers, 1963-65 Jack edwards, 1965-66 Ellis Stuttard, 1966-67 Jock Basford, 1967-69 Frank Broome, 1969-76 John Newman, 1977-79 Bobby Saxton, 1979-83 Brian Godfrey, 1983-84 Gerry Francis, 1984-85 Jim iley, 1985-87 Colin Appleton, 1988 John Delve (caretaker), 1988-91 Terry Cooper, 1991-94 Alan Ball.

ADDITIONAL INFORMATION
PREVIOUS NAMES
None.
PREVIOUS LEAGUES
None.

Club colours: Red & white striped shirts, black shorts, red socks.
Change colours: All white.
Reserves League: Avon Combination Division 2.
'A' Team: Devon & Exeter Premier.

LONGEST LEAGUE RUNS

of undefeated matches:	13 (1986)	of league matches w/out a win:	18 (1984)
of undefeated home matches:	23 (1989-90)	of undefeated away matches:	8 (1964)
without home win:	9 (1984)	without an away win:	27 (1986-87)
of league wins:	7 (1977)	of home wins:	13 (1932-33)
of league defeats:	7 (1921, 1923, 1925, 1936, 1984)	of away wins:	6 (1977)

THE MANAGER

PETER FOX . . . . appointed June 1995.

PREVIOUS CLUBS
As Manager . . . . None.
As Asst.Man/Coach . . . . None.
As a player . . . . Sheffield Wednesday, Barnsley, Stoke City.

HONOURS
As a Manager . . . . None.
As a Player . . . . None.

EXETER CITY

PLAYERS NAME Honours	Ht	Wt	Birthdate	Birthplace Transfers	Contract Date	Clubs	League	L/Cup	FA Cup	Other	Lge	L/C	FAC	Oth
G O A L K E E P E R S														
Peter Fox	5.10	12.4	05.07.57	Scunthorpe	01.06.75	Sheffield Wed. (A)	49		3					
AGT'92, Div.2'93.				Loan	22.12.77	Barnsley	1	1						
				£15,000	04.03.78	Stoke City	409	32	22	14				
				Free	15.07.93	Exeter City	56+1	5	5	2				
D E F E N D E R S														
Noel Blake	6.0	13.11	12.01.62	Kingston (Jam)		Sutton Coldfield T.								
					01.08.79	Aston Villa	4							
				Loan	01.03.82	Shrewsbury Town	6							
				£55,000	15.09.82	Birmingham City	76	12	8		5			
				£150,000	24.08.84	Portsmouth	144	14	10	5	10	1	2	1
				Free	04.07.88	Leeds United	51	4+1	2	4	4			
				£175,000	09.02.90	Stoke City	74+1	6	3+1	4+1	3			
				Loan	27.02.92	Bradford City	6							
				Free	20.07.92	Bradford City	31+1	2	3	3	3		1	
					12.93	Dundee United								
				Free	08.95	Exeter City								
Mark R Came	6.1	13.0	14.09.61	Exeter		Winsford United								
					28.04.84	Bolton Wanderers	188+7	15+4	16+2	27	7	2		2
					04.12.92	Chester City	47	2	3	6	1			1
				Free	14.07.94	Exeter City	32	2	1	1	1			
Neil Parsley	5.9	10.12	25.04.66	Liverpool		Witton Albion								
				£20,000	08.11.88	Leeds United								
				Loan	13.12.89	Chester City	6			1				
				Free	25.07.90	Huddersfield Town	55+2	6	6	6		1		
				Loan	20.02.91	Doncaster Rovers	2+1							
				£25,000	09.09.93	West Bromwich A.	38+5	3	1	1				
				Free	08.95	Exeter City								
M I D F I E L D														
Colin R Anderson	5.8	10.6	26.04.62	Newcastle	29.04.80	Burnley (A)	3+3							
				Free	18.09.82	Torquay United	107+2	5	7	3	11		1	
				£20,000	27.03.85	West Bromwich A.	131+9	5+2	2	2+1	10		2	
				Free	22.08.91	Walsall	25+1		2	4	2			
				Free	13.08.92	Hereford United	67+3	4+1	2+2	5	1			
				Free	14.07.94	Exeter City	21	1		1	1			
Mark N Cooper	5.8	10.10	18.12.68	Wakefield	10.09.87	Bristol City (T)								
				Free	03.10.89	Exeter City	46+4	4+1	3+1	5	12		1	
				Loan	22.03.90	Southern United	4+1							
					05.09.91	Birmingham City	30+9		2	3	4			1
				£40,000	21.11.92	Fulham	10+4	2		3				
				Loan	25.03.93	Huddersfield Town	10				4			
				Free	10.01.94	Wycombe W.	0+2				1			
				Free	11.02.94	Exeter City	52+9	1	2	4	14			
F O R W A R D S														
Michael J Cecere	6.0	11.4	04.01.68	Chester	17.01.86	Oldham Athletic (A)	35+17	4+1	1+2	2+1	8		1	1
				£100,000	11.11.88	Huddersfield Town	50+4	4	7+1	5	8	1	3	1
				Loan	22.03.90	Stockport County	0+1							
				£25,000	23.08.90	Walsall	92+20	10+1	4+2	12	32			2
					13.01.94	Exeter City	29+1	2	1	3	11	1	1	2
Mark W Gavin	5.8	10.7	10.12.63	Bailleston	24.12.81	Leeds United (A)	20+10	4+1	0+1		3	1		
				Loan	29.03.85	Hartlepool United	7							
				Free	04.07.85	Carlisle United	12+1	2		1	1	1		
				Free	27.03.86	Bolton Wanderers	48+1	1	5	10	3		1	1
					14.08.87	Rochdale	23	3	1	2	6			
via Hearts, (£30,000), 5+4 S.Lg Apps.				£30,000	04.10.88	Bristol City	62+7	8	13	6	6		1	1
				£100,000 + P.E	09.08.90	Watford	8+5							
				£60,000	06.12.91	Bristol City	34+7	0+1	4	4	2			
					11.02.94	Exeter City	49	2	2	3	2			
Richard J Pears	6.0	12.6	16.07.76	Exeter	07.07.94	Exeter City (T)	18+12	1+1		0+1	2			
Martin J Phillips	5.11	12.08	13.03.76	Exeter	04.07.94	Exeter City (T)	25+14	1+1	1+2	0+5	2			
Jonathan Richardson	6.0	12.0	29.08.75	Nottingham	07.07.94	Exeter City (T)	42+3	1	2	3	1			
Anthony D Thirlby NI: S	5.10	11.5	04.03.76	Berlin	04.07.94	Exeter City (T)	27+10	2+1		1				
Robert P Turner	6.3	14.1	18.09.66	Ripon	19.09.84	Huddersfield T. (A)	0+1	1						
				Free	19.07.85	Cardiff City	34+5	3	1	1	8	1		
Loan Hartlepool United, (02.10.86), 7 Lg Apps. +1Gl				Free	31.12.86	Bristol Rovers	19+7	2		0+1	2			
				£15,000	17.12.87	Wimbledon	2+8	1+1	0+1	3+1			1	1
				£45,000	27.01.89	Bristol City	45+7		7	2	12		3	
				£150,000	23.07.90	Plymouth Argyle	66	5	3	3	17	1		1
Loan Shrewsbury Town, (25.03.93), 9Lg Apps.				£90,000	21.11.92	Notts County	7+1		1		1			
				Free	04.02.94	Exeter City	32+1	1	1	2	4	1		1

ST. JAMES PARK
Well Street, Exeter, Devon EX4 6PX
Tel: 01392 54073

Capacity 8,960
Covered Standing 3,200
Seating..1,664

First game ....Not Known.
First floodlit game...Not Known.

ATTENDANCES
Highest...20,984 v Sunderland, FA Cup 6th Round replay, 4.3.1931.
Lowest ....1,515 v Darlington, Division 4, 30.4.1988.

OTHER GROUNDS...None.

MATCHDAY TICKET PRICES

Seat. £8
Juv/OAP £5

Terraces. £5
Juv/OAP £3

Covered standing. £6
Juv/OAP £3

HOW TO GET TO THE GROUND

From the North
Use motorway (M5) until junction 30. Leave motorway and follow signs to City Centre along Sidmouth Road for Heavitree Road, then at roundabout take 4th exit into Western Way and at roundabout take 2nd exit into Old Tiverton Road, then take next turning left into St. James Road for Exeter FC.

From the East
Use A30 sign posted Exeter, into Heavitree Road, then at roundabout take 4th exit into Western Way and at roundabout take 2nd exit into Old Tiverton Road, then take next turning left into St James Road for Exeter FC.

From the South and West
Use A38 and follow signs to the City Centre into Western Way and at round-about take 3rd exit passing Coach Station, then at next roundabout take 2nd into Old Tiverton Road, and turn left into St James Road for Exeter City FC.

Car Parking
Use City Centre car parks and local street parking.

Nearest Railway Station
Exeter St Davids (01392 33551)

CLUBCALL
0891 44 68 68
Calls cost 39p per minute cheap rate and 49p per minute at all other times.
Call costings correct at time of going to press.

MATCHDAY PROGRAMME

Programme Editor . . . . Mike Blackstone (01395 274 564).

Number of pages . . . . 48.

Price . . . . £1.

Subscriptions. . . . . £30 for all home, £35 for all away games.

Local Newspapers . . . . Express & Echo, Western Morning News, ... Sunday Independent.

Local Radio Stations . . . . BBC Radio Devon, The New Devonair.

FULHAM
(The Cottagers)
ENDSLEIGH LEAGUE DIVISION 3
SPONSORED BY: G.M.B.

Back Row (L-R): Tony Lange, Lee Harrison. **3rd Row:** Chris Smith (Physio), Lea Barkus, Carl Williams, Danny Bolt, Tony Finnigan, Danny Bower, Rory Hamill, Paul Brooker. **Middle Row:** Len Walker (Asst. Manager), Martin Thomas, Nicky Andrews, Carl Bartley, Michael Mison, Mike Conroy, Terry Angus, Duncan Jupp, David Smith, Alan Cork (Yth Manager), Micky Adams (First Team Coach). **Front Row:** Gary Brazil, Nick Cusack, Kevin Moore, Ian Branfoot (Manager), Simon Morgan, Mark Blake, Robbie Herrera.

FULHAM
FORMED IN 1879
TURNED PROFESSIONAL IN 1898
LTD COMPANY IN 1903

CHAIRMAN: Jimmy Hill
DIRECTORS
W F Muddyman (Vice-Chairman),
D E Shrimpton, C A Swain,
A M Muddyman, T Wilson
SECRETARY
Mrs Janice O'Doherty (0171 736 6561)
COMMERCIAL MANAGER
Ken Myers

MANAGER: Ian Branfoot
ASSISTANT MANAGER: Len Walker
COACH: Micky Adams

YOUTH MANAGER
Alan Cork
PHYSIOTHERAPIST
Chris Smith
STATISTICIAN FOR THE DIRECTORY
Dennis Turner

This was Fulham's first-ever season at this level after dropping down in May 1994 with 52 points, one of the highest tallies for a relegated club. The 1994 close season saw the appointment of Ian Branfoot as manager in succession to the sacked Don Mackay. Coach Ray Lewington, who was in temporary charge on Mackay's departure, was another to leave, for Crystal Palace. Relegation also spelt the end of the Fulham road for regulars Jeff Eckhardt (to Stockport), Sean Farrell (to Peterborough), Martin Pike (to Rotherham) and Udo Onwere (to Lincoln). Early in the season, two more were on their way on free transfers, and both ended in higher divisions, Glen Thomas at Peterborough and Julian Hails at Southend.

Several new faces arrived at the Cottage, usually with a Southampton connection, reflecting manager Branfoot's previous job. Another common denominator was the age of the new recruits, for virtually all were longer on experience than potential. Mickey Adams and Kevin Moore were at the Dell in 1993-94, whilst Terry Hurlock came via Millwall. Alan Cork, never a Saint, was also signed, on a free transfer rom Sheffield United. These four had almost 2,000 League appearances between them with 17 clubs, and their combined ages was 139, hardly long-term prospects. There were some recruits under 30. Branfoot signed Martin Thomas from Orient (ex-Southampton), Mark Blake from Shrewsbury (ex-Southampton) and Nick Cusack from Oxford. In the second half of the season, a promising striker emerged, Rory Hamill was still in his teens and new to League football, but had once been a junior.........at Southampton!

The supporters' worst fears about football in the League basement were confirmed. The quality of the football was poor and Fulham's inconsistency meant they never imposed themselves on the division. The Cottagers were never really in the promotion race, although they harboured play-off ambitions until the final month of the season. Goalscoring was an obvious problem. Adams topped the list in all competitions, but every one of his 12 goals came from either a free-kick or penalty. The only other player to reach double figures was skipper Simon Morgan, who played in midfield or defence. It was also curious that on at least half a dozen occasions, Fulham's opponents played half the game with ten men, yet the Cottagers failed to win.

Whether there was a more physical approach in the Third Division, or a new attitude amongst the players, or a tougher line from referees is not clear, but Fulham received an unprecedented (for them) seven red cards during the season. Hurlock, moreover, became the first player in English football to accumulate 61 disciplinary points, for which he received a total suspension of 15 games. Too often, the Cottagers tried to compete on the basis of aggression and directness, and whilst their commitment could not be faulted, skill seemed to take a back seat. Since they finished in mid-table, moreover, it cannot be claimed the policy was a success.

As ever, the football was played out against a backdrop of uncertainty about the future of Craven Cottage and a parlous financial situation. Although the ground issue is nearing a resolution, there are few bright spots on the financial horizon. Manager Branfoot must build from the bottom, since he has little scope for buying on the transfer market. Although there seems to be a lot of promise amongst the juniors, the lack of a reserve side in the Football Combination makes it more difficult to develop this talent. There is potential at the younger end of the age range at the club, in the likes of Ducan Jupp (who won Scottish Under 21 honours during the season), Martin Thomas, Rory Hamill, Michael Mison and Danny Bolt, who did well alongside the more experienced and reliable players, such as Stannard, Morgan, Herrera and Brazil. If they are retained and then encouraged and allowed to use their skills, these players might help Fulham make a more sustained promotion challenge in 1995-96.

DENNIS TURNER.

FULHAM

Division Three: 8th **FA Cup:** 2nd Round **Coca-Cola Cup:** 2nd Round **AutoWindscreens Trophy:**

M	DATE	COMP.	VEN	OPPONENTS	RESULT	H/T	LP	GOAL SCORERS/GOAL TIMES	ATT.
1	A 13	EL	H	Walsall	D 1-1	0-1	8	Moore 82	5,300
2	18	CC 1/1	A	Luton Town	D 1-1	0-0		Moore 82	(3,287)
3	20	EL	A	Scunthorpe	W 2-1	1-1	6	Cork (2) 13, 90	(3,167)
4	23	CC 1/1	H	Luton Town	D 1-1	1-0		Haworth 10	5,134
5	27	EL	H	Wigan	W 2-0	1-0	5	Morgan 10, Cork 76	4247
6	30	EL	A	Doncaster Rovers	D 0-0	0-0			(3,003)
7	S 3	EL	A	Torquay United	L 1-2	1-2	8	Moore 26	(4,739)
8	10	EL	H	Preston NE	L 0-1	0-0	10		5,001
9	13	EL	H	Scarborough	L 1-2	1-2		Hails 16	2,729
10	17	EL	A	Walsall	L 1-5	0-3	17	Brazil 84	(3,378)
11	20	CC 2/1	H	Stoke City	W 3-2	0-0		Moore 55, Haworth 74, Blake 85	3,721
12	24	EL	H	Hereford United	D 1-1	0-1	15	Brazil 78	3,740
13	28	CC 2/2	A	Stoke City	L 0-1	0-1			(7,440)
14	O 1	EL	A	Barnet	D 0-0	0-0	17		(3,579)
15	8	EL	A	Rochdale	W 2-1	0-1	16	Brazil 65, Haworth 79	(2,573)
16	15	EL	H	Exeter City	W 4-0	2-0	12	Stallard 1,9,53, Morgan 76	4,134
17	18	AWT	A	Leyton Orient	L 2-5	1-4		Mison, Haworth	(1,282)
18	22	EL	A	Chesterfield	D 1-1	1-1	15	Moore 90	(1,860)
19	29	EL	H	Carlisle United	L 1-3	0-2	15	Morgan 82	5,563
20	N 5	EL	A	Northampton Town	W 1-0	1-0	12	Adams 43	(7,366)
21	8	AWT	H	Colchester United	W 3-2	1-0		Haworth 3, Adams 71, Cusack 88	1,457
22	12	FAC 1	A	Ashford Town	D 2-2	0-1		Adams 81, 83, (2pens)	(3,363)
23	19	EL	H	Lincoln City	D 1-1	1-0	13	Adams 10	3,955
24	22	FAC 1R	H	Ashford Town	W 5-3	2-1		Morgan 8, Adams 19, 89 Blake, Cork	6,539
25	26	EL	A	Bury	D 0-0	0-0	11		(3,323)
26	29	AWT 2	A	Leyton Orient	L 0-1	0-1			(1,757)
27	D 3	FAC 2R	A	Gillingham	D 1-1	0-1		Hamill 74	(6,253)
28	10	EL	H	Scunthorpe United	W 1-0	1-0	8	Morgan 33	3,358
29	13	FAC 2	H	Gillingham	L 1-2	0-1		Hamill	6,531
30	17	EL	A	Wigan Athletic	D 1-1	0-1	10	Marshall 81	(1,791)
31	26	EL	A	Gillingham	L 1-4	0-1	12	Morgan 80	(4,677)
32	27	EL	H	Colchester	L 1-2	1-1	13	Hamill 6	4,243
33	31	EL	A	Hartlepool United	W 2-1	1-1	12	Cusack 42, Brazil 64	(1,698)
34	J 2	EL	H	Mansfield T	W 4-2	1-0	12	Hamill 1, Cusack 46, Blake 81, Thomas 89	4,091
35	8	EL	A	Chesterfield	D 1-1	0-1	11	Brazil 68,	3,927
36	14	EL	A	Darlington	D 0-0	0-0	12		(2,113)
37	28	EL	A	Carlisle United	D 1-1	1-1	12	Walling 44 (og)	(6,891)
38	F 4	EL	H	Bury	W 1-0	0-0	12	Thomas 52	3,941
39	14	EL	H	Northampton	D 4-4	2-1		Morgan 35, Marshall 44, Adams 86, Hamill 89	3,423
40	18	EL	H	Darlington	W 3-1	0-0	8	Adams 11, 62, Hamill 72	3,864
41	25	EL	H	Barnet	W 4-0	3-0	6	Cusack 7, Marshall 14, Morgan 44, Hamill 79	6,195
42	M 4	EL	A	Hereford United	D 1-1	0-0	8	Jupp 44	(2,895)
43	11	EL	A	Preston North End	L 2-3	1-1	10	Jupp 45, Blake 81 (pen)	(8,601)
44	18	EL	A	Doncaster Rovers	L 0-2	0-1	11		4,021
45	25	EL	H	Torquay United	W 2-1	0-1	9	Adams 73, Cusack 78	4,941
46	A 1	EL	A	Scarborough	L 1-2	0-1	11	Adams 61	(2,050)
47	8	EL	H	Hartlepool United	W 1-0	0-0	11	Blake	3,465
48	11	EL	A	Lincoln City	L 0-2	0-1	11		(2,932)
49	15	EL	A	Colchester United	L 2-5	1-4	11	Morgan 4, Mison 80	(3,448)
50	17	EL	H	Gillingham	W 1-0	0-0	10	Morgan 83	3,612
51	22	EL	A	Mansfield Town	D 1-1	0-1	10	Morgan 64	(2,861)
52	29	EL	A	Exeter City	W 1-0	0-0	9	Brazil 68	(3,388)
53	M 6	EL	H	Rochdale	W 3-0	5-0	8	Cusack 6, 11, 73, Thomas 16, Brazil 59	4,342
54									
55									
56									
57									
58									
59									
60									

Best Home League Attendance: 6,195 v Barnet **Smallest:** 2,729 v Scarborough **Av Home Att:** 4,204

Goal Scorers: **Compared with 1993-94:** -450

League (60): Morgan 10, Brazil 7, Adams 7, Cusack 7, Hamill 5, Morre 3, Blake 3, Stallard 3, Marshall 3, Thomas 3, Cork 3, Jupp 2, Hails, Hurlock, Mison, Opponent
C/Cola Cup (5): Moore 2, Haworth 2, Blake
FA Cup (9): Adams 4, Hamill 2, Cork, Morgan, Blake
AWS (5): Haworth 2, Mison, Adams, Cusack

580

Stannard	Morgan	Marshall	Wilson	Moore	Thomas G.	Thomas M.	Bedrossian	Cork	Brazil	Herrera	Jupp	Harrison	Haworth	Ferney	Hurlock	Hails	Angus	Adams	Blake	Stallard	Bartley	Finnigan	Cusack	Gregory	Hamill	Referee	
1	2.	3	4	5	6		7*	8	9	10	11	12	S	14												A.P. D'Urso	1
1	2	7	4	5	6		S	9	10	3	8	S	11	S													2
1	2	7	4.	5	6		S	9	10	3	8	S	11	14												T.E. Heilbron	3
1	2	7.	4	5	6			9	10	3	8	S	11*		12	14										M.E. Pierce	4
1	2	7	11	5	6			9.	10	3	8	S		S	4	14										G.P. Barber	5
1	2	7	11	5	6		S		10		8	S		S	4	9	3									N. Barry	6
1	2	7*	11	5	6.			9	10		8	S	14		4	12		3								S. Dunn	7
1	2	7	S	5	6			9	10		8	S	12		4	11*		3								C.R. Wilkes	8
1	2	12	7	5	6	14		9	10		8*	S			4	11		3.								I. Hemley	9
1	2	7			6*			9	10	3	8	S	14		4	11.										M. Riley	10
1	2	7	S	5				9	10	3	8	S	11		4	S										M.C. Bailey	11
1	2	7	4	5			S	9	12	3*	8	S					10	6	11							P.L. Foakes	12
1	2	7	4	5.	11	14		10		8	S	12					S			9*						J. Watson	13
1	6	3.	4		11	7*		10			S	12		8		14	5	9		2						P. Vanes	14
1	6	8			11	7*		10		2	S	12		4		3	5	9		S						J. Brandwood	15
1	8	7	5		11			10		2	S	S		4	S	3	6	9								J.H. Holbrook	16
1	8	7	5		11			10		2	S	12		4	9*	3		6								M. Pierce	17
1	8	7	5					10		2	S	9*		4	11.	3	12	6									18
1	8	4	7			S		12	10*	3	S						5	11	6			14				T. E. West	19
	8	4	7						3	12	1	10					5	11	6	2		9				W.A. Flood	20
1	8	4	7	5				9	3	12	S	10					S	11	6	2*		9.	S			G. A. Pooley	21
1	8	10	7.					9	3	2	13				4		S	11	6	2*						A.P. D'Urso	22
1	8	10	7.					9	3	2	S	14			4		S	11	6				9			R.J. Harris	23
1	8	7		5				10	S	3	2	S			4		S	11	6							A.P. D'Urso	24
1	8	7.		5				10		3	2	S			4		S	11	6				9			W.C. Burns	25
1	8	7		5				11	10	3	2	1			4		S		6				9		14	P. Rejer	26
1	8	7		5				11.	10	3	2	S			4		S		6				9	S	14	M. Pierce	27
1	8	7	4	5				11.	10	3	2	S					S		6				9		14	M.C. Bailey	28
1	8	7	4.	5					10	3	2	S		14			S		6				9		14	M.E. Pierce	29
1	8	14		5					10	3	2	S	7*		4	12			6				9		11	K.A. Lupton	30
1	8	S		5					10	3	2	S			4	3			6				9.		11	A. D'Urso	31
1	8		5	7					10	S	2	S			4	3			6			7	9		11	S.W. Dunn	32
1	8	S	5	7					10	12	2	S			4	3*			6		S		9		11	N. Barry	33
1	8		5	7					10	3	2.	S		14	4		S		6				9		11	P.L. Foakes	34
1	8	S	5	7					10	3		S			4		S		6				9		11	G.P. Barber	35
1	8	S	5	7					10		S	S			4	3			6	2			9		11	S. Mathieson	36
1	8	4	5	7					10	2	S					3			6	2			9		11	E. Wolstenholme	37
1	8	4	5.	7					10	2	S					3	14		6	S			9		11	D. Orr	38
1	8	4		7				S		3	2	S				5	10*		6	S			9		11	P.W. Vanes	39
1	8	4	14	7						3	2	S				5	10*		6			12	9		11	A.P. D'Urso	40
1	8	7	14						12	3	2	S		4.		5	10*		6			12	9		11	P.E. Alcock	41
1	8	7	10*						12	3	2	S		S	4	5			6				9		11		42
1	8	7.	5	14						3	2	S			4		S	10	6				9		11	K. Lynch	43
1	8	S	5	7						3	2	S			4		S	10	6				9		11	C.A. Wilkes	44
1	8	11	5	7						S	2	S			4	3		10	6				9		11	A.N. Butler	45
	8	7*	S	5				12		3	2	1			4			10	6				9		14	J. Watson	46
	8	14	5	7.				9		3	2	1			4			10	6			9.		13	11	P.L. Foakes	47
	8	7	14	5				12		3	2	1		4.				S	6			12	S		11*	K. Breen	48
	8	7.	14		4					11*	3	2	1					S	6				9	S		Leach	49
1	8	4		7						11*	3	2		S		5		10	6				9	S	12	P.E. Alcock	50
	8	14		7						11	3	1		4.			S	S	6				9	S	12	P. Harrison	51
	8	14		7						11	3	1		4.			S	S	6	2		9	S	S		M. Pierce	52
	8	14		7						11	3	1		4				S	6	2		9	S		12	P. Rejer	53
																											54
																											55
																											56
																											57
																											58
																											59
																											60
36	42	25	17	31	7	21	3	11	30	26	35	6	3	5	27	6	21	18	34	4	1	7	26		18	League Appearances	
		2		7		2		4	2	1	1	7	2		2		2	3	1			4	1	1	5	League Sub Appearances	
4	4	4	3	4	2	1	0+1	3	4	3	4			3+1	1+1	0+1		1				2	1			C/Cola Appearances	
3	4	4	3	4				4	2	4	3+1	1		1+1	2			2	4			1	2			FA Cup Appearances	
2	3	2	2	2				2	2	2+1	1			1+1	2	1	2	2	3			1	2	0+1		AWT Appearances	

Also Played: Williams 14(21), Bolt 10(52,53*)

FULHAM
RECORDS AND STATISTICS

CLUB RECORDS

BIGGEST VICTORIES
League: 10-1 v Ipswich Town, Division 1, 26.9.1963.
10-2 v Torquay United, Division 3, 10.9.1931.
F.A. Cup: 6-0 v Wimbledon, 1st Round replay, 1930-31.
6-0 v Bury, 3rd Round, 7.1.1939.
8-3 v Luton Town (a), 1st Round, 1907-08.

BIGGEST DEFEATS
League: 0-9 v Wolverhampton Wanderers, Division 1, 16.9.1959.
League Cup: 0-10 v Liverpool, 2nd Round, 23.9.1986.

MOST POINTS
3 points a win: 78, Division 3, 1981-82.
2 points a win: 60, Division 2, 1958-59. Division 3, 1970-71.

MOST GOALS SCORED
111, Division 3(S), 1931-32.

RECORD TRANSFER FEE RECEIVED
£333,333 from Liverpool for Money, May 1980.

RECORD TRANSFER FEE PAID
£150,000 to Orient for Peter Kitchen, February 1979.
£150,000 to Brighton for Teddy Maybank, December 1979.

BEST PERFORMANCES
League: 10th Division 1, 1959-60.
F.A. Cup: Runners-up 1974-75.
League Cup: 5th Round 1967-68, 1970-71.

HONOURS
Champions of Division 3(S) 1931-32.
Champions Division 2, 1948-49.

LEAGUE CAREER
Elected to Div 2 1907, Div 3(S) 1927-28, Div 2 1931-32, Div 1 1948-49, Div 2 1951-52, Div 1 1958-59, Div 2 1967-68, Div 3 1968-69, Div 2 1970-71, Div 3 1979-80, Div 2 1981-82, Div 3 (now Div 2) 1985-86, Div 3 1993-94.

INDIVIDUAL CLUB RECORDS

MOST GOALS IN A SEASON
Frank Newton: 43, Division 3(S), 1931-32.

MOST GOALS IN A MATCH
6. Ronnie Rooke v Bury, 6-0, FA Cup 3rd Round, 7.1.1939.

OLDEST PLAYER
Jimmy Sharpe, 40 years, April 1920 (Played in an emergency and scored his only goal for the club many years after officially retiring!)

YOUNGEST PLAYER
Tony Mahoney, 16 years, 1976.

MOST CAPPED PLAYER
Johnny Haynes (England) 56.

PREVIOUS MANAGERS

1904-09 Harry Bradshaw, 1909-24 Phil Kelso, 1924-26 Andy Ducat, 1926-29 Joe Bradshaw, 1929-31 Ned Liddell, 1931-34 James McIntyre, 1934-35 Jimmy Hogan, 1935 Joe Edelston (acting), 1935-48 Jack Peart, 1948-49 Frank Osborne, 1949-53 Bill Dodgin, 1956-58 Dug Livingstone, 1958-64 Bedford Jezzard, 1964-65 Arthur Stevens (acting), 1965-68 Vic Buckingham, 1968 Bobby Robson, 1968 Johnny Haynes (acting), 1968-72 Bill Dodgin (jnr), 1972-76 Alec Stock, 1976-80 Bobby Campbell, 1980-84 Malcolm MacDonald, 1984-86 Ray Harford, 1986-90 Ray Lewington, 1990-91 Alan Dicks, 1991 Ray Lewington (caretaker), 1991-94 Don Mackay.

ADDITIONAL INFORMATION
PREVIOUS NAMES
Fulham St Andrews 1879-98.
PREVIOUS LEAGUES
Southern League.

Club colours: White shirts with black trim, white shorts and white socks with black trim.
Change colours: All red.
Youth League: South East Counties.

LONGEST LEAGUE RUNS

of undefeated matches:	15 (1957, 1970)	of league matches w/out a win:	15 (1950)
of undefeated home matches:	28 (1921-22)	of undefeated away matches:	9 (1958, 1970)
without home win:	9 (8.5.1993 - 6.11.1993)	without an away win:	31 (1964-66)
of league wins:	8 (1963)	of home wins:	12 (1959)
of league defeats:	11 (1961-62)	of away wins:	5 (1966, 1981)

THE MANAGER

IAN BRANFOOT . . . . appointed June 1994.

PREVIOUS CLUBS
As Manager . . . . Reading, Southampton.
As Asst.Man/Coach . . . . Crystal Palace.
As a player . . . . Sheffield Wednesday, Lincoln City, Doncaster Rovers.

HONOURS
As a Manager . . . . Reading: Promotion to Division 3, Division 3 Champions, Simod Cup winners.
As a Player . . . . None.

FULHAM							APPEARANCES				GOALS			
PLAYERS NAME Honours	Ht	Wt	Birthdate	Birthplace Transfers	Contract Date	Clubs	League	L/Cup	FA Cup	Other	Lge	L/C	FAC	Oth
G O A L K E E P E R S														
Lee D Harrison	6.2	11.0	12.09.71	Billericay	03.07.90	Charlton Athletic (T)								
				Loan	18.11.91	Fulham				1				
				Loan	24.03.92	Gillingham	2							
				Loan	18.12.92	Fulham				1				
				Free	15.07.93	Fulham	6+1		1	1		2		
Tony Lange	6.0	12.9	10.12.64	West Ham	15.12.82	Charlton Ath. (A)	12			1				
Loan 22.08.85 Aldershot 7 Lge App.				Free	07.07.88	Aldershot	125	5	10	16				
				£150,000	13.07.89	Wolverhampton W.	8	2						
				Loan	23.11.90	Aldershot	2			1				
Loan 12.09.91 Torqauay U. 1 Lge App.				Free	12.08.92	West Bromwich A.	45+3	3	1	7				
				Free	08.95	Fulham								
D E F E N D E R S														
Terence N Angus	6.0	13.9	14.01.66	Coventry		V S Rugby								
				£15,000	22.08.90	Northampton Town	115+1	7	5+1	9	6			
				Free	12.07.93	Fulham	49+10	1+1	1	7	2			1
Roberto Herrera	5.7	10.6	12.06.70	Torquay	01.03.88	Q.P.R. (A)	4+2	1+2		1+1				
Loan 17.03.92 Torquay Utd 11 Lge App.				Loan	24.10.92	Torquay United	5							
					29.10.93	Fulham	49+1	3	4	4	1			
Duncan A Jupp	6.0	13.4	25.01.75	Haslemere	12.07.93	Fulham (T)	66+3	7+1	4+1	7+1	2			
Kevin T Moore	5.11	12.2	29.04.58	Grimsby	01.07.76	Grimsby Town (J)	397+3	41	25	2	28	3	3	
E: S; Div3'80; FLGC'82				£100,000	20.02.87	Oldham Athletic	13			2	1			
				£125,000	03.08.87	Southampton	144+4	18+1	13	5	10	2		1
Loan Bristol Rovers, (09.09.92), 7Lg Apps.				Loan	17.10.92	Bristol Rovers	4				1			
				Free	27.07.94	Fulham	31	4	4	2	3	2		
Simon C Morgan	5.10	11.7	05.09.68	Birmingham	15.11.84	Leicester City (T)	147+13	14	4+1	3	3	1		
E: u21.2				£100,000	12.10.90	Fulham	182+4	12	9	10	27		1	2
Martin R Thomas	5.8	10.8	12.09.73	Lymington	19.06.92	Southampton (T)								
				Free	24.03.94	Leyton Orient	5				2			
				Free	21.07.94	Fulham	21+2	1		1	3			
M I D F I E L D														
Michael R Adams	5.6	10.4	08.11.61	Sheffield	01.11.79	Gillingham (A)	85+7	5	6		5			
E: Y4				£75,000	19.07.83	Coventry City	85+5	9	7	2	9	1		
				£110,000	23.01.87	Leeds United	72+1	4	6	6	2		1	
				£250,000	14.03.89	Southampton	141+3	16	8	6	7			
				Free	24.03.94	Stoke City	10				3			
				Free	14.07.94	Fulham	18+3	1	2	2	7		4	1
Daniel A Bolt	6.0	12.5	05.02.76	Wandsworth	15.07.94	Fulham (T)	2							
Terence A Hurlock	5.9	13.2	22.09.58	Hackney		Leytonestone Ilford								
E: B3; ILP'80; Div3'86; Div2'88; SPD'91; SLC'91				£6,000	28.08.80	Brentford	220	17	17	9	18	2	4	
				£82,000	20.02.86	Reading	29	3	1	2				
				£95,000	12.02.87	Millwall	103+1	9	5	5	8	2		
				£325,000	01.09.90	Glasgow Rangers	29	3+1	2		2			
				£400,000	09.09.91	Southampton	59+2	7	5	6				1
				Free	01.03.94	Millwall	13			2				
				Free	21.07.94	Fulham	27	1+1	2	2	1			
John P Marshall	5.9	11.4	18.08.64	Balham	20.08.82	Fulham (A)	379+16	33	17+1	20	29	2	3	2
Michael Mison	6.3	13.2	08.11.75	London	15.07.94	Fulham (T)	18+10	3	3	2+1	1			1
F O R W A R D														
Lea Barkus	5.6	9.13	07.12.74	Reading	13.08.92	Reading (T)	8+7		0+1	1	1			
				£20,000	08.95	Fulham								
Gary Brazil	5.11	9.13	19.09.62	Tunbridge Wells		Crystal Palace (A)								
				Free	11.08.80	Sheffield United	39+23	4+1	4+5	1+1	9	1		
				Loan	24.08.84	Port Vale	6				3			
				£12,500	15.02.85	Preston North End	163+3	13	10	13	50	6	3	5
				£50,000 + P.E.	09.02.89	Newcastle United	7+16	1+1	0+1	2	1			
				£110,000	06.09.90	Fulham	190+6	10	7	14	46	3	1	7
Mark C Blake	6.1	12.8	19.12.67	Portsmouth	23.12.85	Southampton	18	2	3	1+2	2			
E: Yth				Loan	05.09.89	Colchester United	4				1			
				£100,000	22.03.90	Shrewsbury Town	142	12	9	12	3			
				Free	16.09.94	Fulham	34+1	2	4	3	3	1	1	
Michael Conroy	6.0	11.0	31.12.65	Glasgow		Coventry City (A)								
Div.4'92.						Clydebank	92+22	4+1	5+2		38			
						St Mirren	9+1		0+1		1			
				£50,000	28.09.88	Reading	65+12	3+2	8+2	2+2	7		1	
				£35,000	16.07.91	Burnley	76+1	4	9+1	7+1	30	1	4	4
				£85,000	20.08.93	Preston North End	50+7	2+1	7	2+3	22		2	
Nicholas J Cusack	6.0	11.13	24.12.65	Maltby		Alvechurch								
					18.06.87	Leicester City	5+11		0+1	1+1	1			
				£40,000	29.07.88	Peterborough Utd	44	4	4	2	10	1	1	
				£100,000	02.08.89	Motherwell	68+9	5	3+1	1+1	17	4	2	1
				£95,000	24.01.92	Darlington	21				6			
				£95,000	16.07.92	Oxford United	48+11	3	4+2	2+1	10	2	1	
				Loan	24.03.94	Wycombe W.	2+2				1			
Loan 04.11.94 Fulham				Free	06.01.95	Fulham	26+1		2	2	7			1
Rory Hamill	5.8	12.3	04.05.76	Coleraine		Port Stewart								
				Free	18.11.94	Fulham	18+5		0+2	0+1	5		2	

CRAVEN COTTAGE

Stevenage Road, Fulham, London SW6 6HH
Tel: 0171 736 6561

Capacity 11,600

First game...v Minerva, 5-0, Middx Snr Cup, 10.10.1896.
First floodlit game ....v Sheffield Wednesday, 4-1,
....League, September 1962.

ATTENDANCES
Highest..49,335 v Millwall, Div 2, 8.10.1938.
Lowest ....1,108 v Gillingham, Autoglass Trophy, 28.11.1991.

OTHER GROUNDS ....None as a professional club.

MATCHDAY TICKET PRICES

Seats £10.50
Juv/OAP £5

Terraces £7
Juv/OAP £3.50

CLUBCALL
0891 44 00 44

Calls cost 39p per minute cheap rate and 49p per minute at all other times.
Call costings correct at time of going to press.

HOW TO GET TO THE GROUND

From the North
Use motorway (M1) sign posted London then take North Circular Road (A406), sign posted West to Neasden, follow signs to Harlesden (A404), then Hammersmith (A219) and at Broadway follow sign to Fulham and in 1 mile turn right into Harbord Street and at end turn left for Fulham FC.

From the East & South
Use South Circular Road (A205) and take sign to Putney Bridge (A219). Cross bridge and follow sign to Hammersmith and in 0.5 miles turn left into Bishops Park Road and at end turn right for Fulham FC.

From the West
Use motorway (M4) then A4 and in 2 miles branch left, sign posted, other routes into Hammersmith Broadway, follow sign Fulham (A219) and in 1 mile turn right into Harbord Street and at end turn left for Fulham FC.

Car parking
Ample in adjacent streets.

Nearest Railway Station
Putney
Nearest Tube Stations
Putney Bridge or Hammersmith.

MATCHDAY PROGRAMME

Programme Editor . . . . Ken Myers.

Number of pages . . . . 32.

Price . . . . £1.30.

Subscriptions . . . . All League & Cup matches £40.

Local Newspapers. . . . . Fulham Chronicle,
. . . . Hammersmith & Fulham Gazette.

Local Radio Stations . . . . London News, Capital Radio.

GILLINGHAM
(The Gills)
ENDSLEIGH LEAGUE DIVISION 3
SPONSORED BY: INVICTA RADIO FM 103.1 + 102.8

Back Row (L-R): Dominic Naylor, Joe Dunne, Neil Smith, Richard Carpenter, John Byrne, Jim Stannard, Rusell Eggleton, Steve Brown, Scott Linsey, Gary Micklewhite, Mark O'Connor. **3rd Row:** Malcolm Machin (Yth De. Officer), Wayne Jones (Physio), Andy Arnott, Darren Freeman, Dave Martin,Lindsay Parsons (Asst. Manager), Tony Butler, Mark Harris, Richard Green, Simon Ratcliffe, Tony Pullis (Manager), Kevin Bremner. **2nd Row:** Lee Quigley, Sam Tydeman, Paul Watson, Leo Fortune-West, Paul Wilson, Paul Scally (Chairman/Chief Executive), Dennis Bailey, Adrian Foster, Kevin Rattray, Steve Norman, Chris Hall, Craig Roser. **Front Row:** Kevin Clifford, Adam Flanagan, Lee Spiller, Jay Saunders, Darren Smith, Lee Bacon, Tommy Butler, Mark Barnes, Andrew Sambrooke, Roland Edge.

GILLINGHAM
FORMED IN 1893
TURNED PROFESSIONAL IN 1894
LTD COMPANY IN 1893

PRESIDENT: J W Leech
CHAIRMAN/CHIEF EXECUTIVE
Paul Scally

DIRECTORS
A Smith FRICS, P Spokes FCCA
SECRETARY
Gwen Poynter
COMMERCIAL MANAGER
Mike Ling

MANAGER: Tony Pulis
ASSISTANT MANAGER: Lindsay Parsons
YOUTH TEAM MANAGER
Kevin Bremner

PHYSIOTHERAPIST
Javed Mughal

STATISTICIAN FOR THE DIRECTORY
Roger Triggs

Season 1994-95 was indeed a traumatic year for Gillingham Football Club. Optimism was high back in August, but the club soon found themselves at the wrong end of the table and the financial burden was beginning to take its toll.

It reached a crisis point, when just one hour after their FA Cup third round tie against Sheffield Wednesday, director Tony Smith placed the hands of the receivers. Supporters rallied around the club, with attendances far better than clubs in the top half of the table. But would anybody come in to save Kent's only Football League side?

That anybody took the shape of Sevenoaks businessman Paul Scally, who having looked at the club, he decided it was worth purchasing. Weeks of protracted discussions went on and although the Football League kept asking for different assurances nearly every day of the week, he saved the club just hours before the League's deadline.

He quickly appointed Tony Pulis as manager, and he has completely changed the playing side with quality players. Season ticket sales are up and everybody is pulling to make this club one of the leading figures in Division Three this season.

The only bright notes from last season was that FA Cup run, which produced a full house against Wednesday and record receipts. The emergence of full-back/midfielder Paul Watson and Chris Pike who after his signing from Hereford United for just £15,000, scored 20 goals in just 35 appearances.

ROGER TRIGGS.

GILLINGHAM

Division Three: 19th   **FA Cup:** 3rd Round   **Coca-Cola Cup:** 1st Round   **Auto Windscreens Trophy:** 1st Round

M	DATE	COMP.	VEN	OPPONENTS	RESULT	H/T	LP	GOAL SCORERS/GOAL TIMES	ATT.
1	A 13	EL	H	Hartlepool United	D 0-0	0-0	11		2,956
2	16	CC 1/1	H	**Reading**	L 0-1	0-0			2,556
3	20	EL	A	Wigan Athletic	W 3-0	1-0	4	Foster 36, Reinelt 53, Watson 83	(1,514)
4	23	CC 1/2	A	**Reading**	L 0-3	0-0			3,015
5	27	EL	H	Rochdale	D 1-1	0-1	9	Butler 83	3,015
6	30	EL	A	Scunthorpe United	L 0-3	0-0	12		(2,098)
7	S 3	EL	A	Exeter City	L 0-3	0-2	16		(2,241)
8	10	EL	H	Scarborough	W 3-1	1-0	9	Palmer 43, Ritchie 66, Baker 88	2,414
9	13	EL	H	Preston North End	L 2-3	2-2	14	Smith 23, Baker 38	2,555
10	17	EL	A	Hartlepool United	L 0-2	0-1	16		(1,756)
11	24	EL	A	Walsall	L 1-2	0-1	17	Micklewhite 81	(3,654)
12	27	AWS SP	H	**Brighton & H.A.**	D 1-1	1-1		**Carpenter 13**	963
13	O 1	EL	H	Mansfield Town	L 0-2	0-1	20		2,555
14	8	EL	H	Torquay United	W 1-0	1-0	17	Pike 24	2,439
15	15	EL	A	Hereford United	L 1-2	-01	19	Arnott 90	(2,472)
16	22	EL	A	Bury	L 2-3	0-2	20	Pike 87, 89 (pen)	(2,976)
17	29	EL	H	Darlington	W 2-1	1-1	17	Pike 18, Smillie 51	2,785
18	N 5	EL	A	Colchester United	D 2-2	2-1	17	Reinelt 8, Pike 27	(3,817)
19	8	AWS SP	A	**Brentford**	L 1-3	0-2		**Pike 61**	(1,795)
20	11	FAC 1	A	**Heybridge Swifts**	W 2-0	0-0		**Reinelt 52, Pike 86**	(4,614)
21	19	EL	H	Chesterfield	D 1-1	0-1	17	Reinelt 85	2,722
22	26	EL	A	Lincoln City	D 1-1	0-0	17	Arnott 87	(2,919)
23	29	AWS 1	A	**Birmingham City**	L 0-3	0-2			(17,028)
24	D 3	FAC 2	H	**Fulham**	D 1-1	1-0		**Pike 26**	6,253
25	10	EL	H	Wigan Athletic	L 0-1	0-0	19		2,257
26	13	FAC 2R	A	**Fulham**	W 2-1	1-0		**Pike 26, Reinelt 112**	(6,536)
27	17	EL	A	Rochdale	L 1-0	0-2	19	Foster 64	(1,665)
28	26	EL	H	Fulham	W 4-1	1-0	18	Reinelt 44, Micklewhite 63, Foster 78,82	4,677
29	27	EL	A	Barnet	L 0-1	0-0	18		(3,074)
30	31	EL	H	Carlisle United	L 0-1	0-0	19		3,682
31	J 7	FAC 3	H	**Sheffield Wednesday**	L 1-2	1-2		**Pike 43 (pen)**	10,425
32	14	EL	A	Northampton Town	L 0-2	0-0	21		(5,529)
33	F 4	EL	H	Lincoln city	D 0-0	0-0	20		4,196
34	7	EL	A	Doncaster Rovers	W 2-1	1-1	19	Pike 14, 81	(1,740)
35	11	EL	A	Chesterfield	L 0-2	0-2	19		(3,070)
36	18	EL	H	Northampton Town	W 3-1	1-0	19	Ramage 24, Green 67, Foster 70	4,075
37	21	EL	A	Darlington	L 0-2	0-0	19		(1,548)
38	25	EL	A	Mansfield Town	L 0-4	0-1	20		(3,182)
39	M 4	EL	H	Walsall	L 1-3	0-0	20	Foster 70	3,669
40	11	EL	A	Scarborough	D 0-0	0-0	21		(1,949)
41	18	EL	H	Scunthorpe United	D 2-2	0-1	20	Foster 60, Pike 66	2,459
42	25	EL	H	Exeter City	W 3-0	2-0	19	Foster 1, Pike 42 (pen), Butler 61	3,332
43	A 1	EL	A	Preston North End	D 1-1	0-1	19	Dunne 49	(9,100)
44	4	EL	H	Bury	D 1-1	1-1	18	Brown 3	2,945
45	8	EL	A	Carlisle United	L 0-2	0-2	19		(6,786)
46	11	EL	H	Cochester United	L 1-3	1-0	19	Watson 15	3,328
47	15	EL	H	Barnet	W 2-1	2-1	18	Thomas 2 (og), Pike 39	3,448
48	17	EL	A	Fulham	L 0-1	0-0	19		(3,612)
49	22	EL	H	Doncaster Rovers	W 4-2	3-2	18	Kirby 2 (og), Pike 26, 38, 50	2,826
50	29	EL	H	Hereford United	D 0-0	0-0	17		4,208
51	M 6	EL	A	Torquay United	L 1-3	0-1	19	Stamps (og) 76	(2,638)
52									
53									
54									
55									
56									
57									
58									
59									
60									

Best Home League Attendance: 4,677 v Fulham   **Smallest:** 2,257 v Wigan Athletic   **Av Home Att:** 3,169

Goal Scorers:

Compared with 1993-94: +30

League (46): Pike 13 (2 pens), Foster 8, Reinelt 4, Opponents 3, Arnott 2, Baker 2, Butler 2, Micklewhite 2, Watson 2, Brown, Dunne, Green, Palmer, Ramage, Ritchie, Smillie, Smith

C/Cola Cup (0):

FA Cup (6): Pike 4 (1 pen), Reinelt 2

AWS (2): Carpenter, Pike

Barrett S.	Dunne J.	Palmer L.	Micklewhite G.	Green R.	Butler T.	Smillie N.	Smith N.	Foster A.	Arnott A.	Watson P.	Baker P.	Ramage A.	Banks S.	Reinelt R.	Trott R.	Carpenter R.	Watts G.	ritchie P.	Pike C.	Hutchinson I.	Bodley M.	Lindsey S.	Freeman D.	Knott G.	Martin E.	Referee	
1	2	3	4	5	6	7.		8	9	10*	11	12	14	S												D. Orr	1
1	2	3	4	5	6		8	9	12	11	10*			S	7	S										M. Bailey	2
1	2	3	4	5	6		8	9	S	11	10			S	7											J. Winter	3
1	2	3	4	5	6		8	9	12	11	10*			S	7											J. Lloyd	4
1	2	3	4	5	6		8	9.	12	11	10*			S	7		14									A. D'Urso	5
1	2	3.	4	5	6		8		9	11	10*			S	7		14									E. Lomas	6
S	2.		4	5	6		11	8		9	3		1	7		14	10*									J. Brandwood	7
S	2	3	S	5	6		8			11	9		1	7		4			10							G. Barber	8
S	2	3.	14*	5	6		8			11	9		1	7		4			10							P. Foakes	9
S	2		S	5	6		8			11	9		1	7	3	4			10*							T. West	10
S	2		7	5	6	11	8			3	9*		1	12	S	4		10								P. Wright	11
S	2		7	5	6	11	8			3			1	9*	S	4	12	10								P. Foakes	12
S	2	3	7	5	6		8			11			1	12	S	4		10*	9							M. Pierce	13
S	2	3	7	5	6		8		14	11			1	10.		4	12	9*								G. Pooley	14
S	2	3	7	5	6		8		14	11			1	10		4*	9.		12							A. Butler	15
S	2	3	7	5	6		8.			12	11	14	1	10*		4		9								P. Rejer	16
S	2		7	5	6	11	8			S	3		1	10		4		9	S							S. Dunne	17
S	2*		7	5	6	11			8	3			1	10		4		9	12							M. Pierce	18
1		3	12		6				2			14	S	10	5	4		9*	7							P. Alcock	19
S	2		7	5	6	11			8	3		S	1	10		4		9	S							P. Alcock	20
S	2.		7		6	11	12	8*	5	3			1	10	14	4		9								M. Bailey	21
S			7			11	2*	8	5	3			1	10	S	4		9	12	6						T. Heilbron	22
1		3						8*	5	11	12		S	10	S	4		9	7	6	2					A. D'Urso	23
S			7	6		11	4	9	5	3			1	8	S	2		10				S				M. Pierce	24
S			14		5	11	7	9	2	3+			1	8.	S	2		10		6						R. Harris	25
S			7	6	8	11	4	9.	5	3			1	14	S	2		10								M. Pierce	26
S			8	6	5*	11	7.	9	2	3			1	14		4		10		12						J. Kirby	27
S			7	6	5		8	9	2			S	1	11		4		10	3	S						A. D'Urso	28
S			8	6	5		7	9	2			S	1	11		4		10	12	3.	S	14				K. Leach	29
S			7	6	5		8	9	2*				1	11		4		10	12	3.						P. Alcock	30
S		S	7	6	5		8	9	2	3			1	11		4		10								M. Bodeham	31
S	S		7	6	5		8	9	2	11*			1	12		4		10		3						J. Holbrook	32
	2	S	7	5				10		3		4	1	12	6			9*			8	S				G. Barber	33
S	2	S	8	5		11		9		3		4	1	S	6			10		7						G. Cain	34
S	2		7	5	S	11*		10		3		4	1	12	6			9		8						P. Harrison	35
S	2		8	5	11		S	10		3		4	1	S	6			9					7			M. Bailey	36
S	2		7	5	8			10	S	3		4	1	12	6			9					11*			J. Lloyd	37
S	2		7	5	6			9	8	11		4	1	14	3.			10					S			W. Burns	38
S	7		8	5	6*		4	10	2	3			14					9				12	11.			S. Dunn	39
S	7		8	5	6		4	10	2	3		12	1					9				S	11*			R. Poulain	40
S	2.		8	5	6		4	10		3			1		S	7		9				14	11			A. D'Urso	41
S	2		8	5	6		4	10		11			1		S	7		9				S		3		P.Rejer	42
S	4			5				10	6	11		8	1		S	7		9				2	S	3		J. Winter	43
S	7		8	5				10	6	11			1			4		S				2	S	3		G. Singh	44
S	7			5	14			10*	6	11			1			8		12				2*		3		K. Lupton	45
S	2		8	5				10	6	11			1		S	7		9				S		3		P. Rejer	46
S	7			5		11	4	10	6	3		14	1		12	8*		10				2				M. Pierce	47
S	7			5		11	4	10	6	3		14	1	12	8*							2*				P. Alcock	48
S	7		8	5.	14		4	12	6*	11			1									2		3		G. Pooley	49
S	7		8	5			4	10	6	11		S	1		S							2		3		D. Orr	50
S	7			5	11		4	12	6	11		3	8	1		S						2*				J. Brandwood	51
																											52
																											53
																											54
																											55
																											56
																											57
																											58
																											59
																											60
4	35	10	33	37	31	15	32	27	24	39	7	8	38	18	7	26	2	5	26	1	6	11		5	7	League Appearances	
	2		2				1	2	4		1	5		9	2	3	1		1	4	1	1	2			League Sub Appearances	
2	2	2	2	2	2		2	0+2	2	2			2	2												C/Cola Appearances	
	1		4	4	3	3	3	4	4				4	3+1		4			4							FA Cup Appearances	
2	2	1	2	1+1	2	1	1	2	2			0+2	1	3	1	3	0+1	1	2	2	1	1				AWT Appearances	

Also Played: S. Brown, P. Hague S(3,4). P. Wilson 12 (6) 12 (7), A. Kennedy S (8), 12(9) 12(10), A. Kamara 8 (19), J. Hokker 11 (19)

Loan Palyers: Ritchie (Dundee), Bodley (Southend United), Knott (Tottenham Hotspur)

CLUB RECORDS

BIGGEST VICTORIES
League: 10-0 v Chesterfield, Division 3, 5.9.1987 (Div. 3 record).
F.A. Cup: 10-1 v Gorleston (h), 1st Round, 16.11.1957.

BIGGEST DEFEATS
League: 0-8 v Luton Town, Division 3(S), 14.4.1929.
League Cup: 0-6 v Oxford United, 2nd Round, 24.9.1986.

MOST POINTS
3 points a win: 83, Division 3, 1984-85.
2 points a win: 62, Division 4, 1973-74.

RECORD TRANSFER FEE RECEIVED
£300,000 from Tottenham Hotspur for Peter Beadle, June 1992.

RECORD TRANSFER FEE PAID
£102,500 to Tottenham Hotspur for Mark Cooper, October 1987.

MOST GOALS IN A SEASON
Ernie Morgan: 33 goals in 1954-55 (League 31, FA Cup 2).

BEST PERFORMANCES
League: 4th Division 3, 1978-79, 1984-85.
F.A. Cup: 5th Round 1969-70.
League Cup: 4th Round 1963-64.

HONOURS
Champions of Division 4, 1963-64.

LEAGUE CAREER
Original members of Div 3 1920, Transferred to Div 3(S) 1921, Failed to gain re-election 1938, Southern League 1938-44, Kent League 1944-46, Southern League 1946-50, Re-elected to Div 3(S) 1949, Transferred to Div 4 1958, Div 3 1963-64, Div 4 1970-71, Div 3 1973-74, Div 4 (now Div 3) 1988-89.

INDIVIDUAL CLUB RECORDS

MOST GOALS IN A MATCH
6. Fred Cheesmur v Merthyr Town (h), 6-0, Division 3(S), 26.4.1930.

OLDEST PLAYER
John Simpson, 39 years 137 days.

YOUNGEST PLAYER
Billy Hughes, 15 years 275 days v Southend, 13.4.1976.

MOST CAPPED PLAYER
Tony Cascarino (Eire) 3.

PREVIOUS MANAGERS

(Since 1920)
1920-23 John McMillian, 1923-26 Harry Curtis, 1926-30 Albert Hoskins, 1930-32 Dick Hendrie, 1932-37 Fred Mavern, 1937-38 Alan Ure, 1938-39 Bill Harvey, 1939-58 Archie Clark, 1958-62 Harry Barratt, 1962-66 Freddie Cox, 1966-71 Basil Hayward, 1971-74 Andy Nelson, 1974-75 Len Ashurst, 1975-81 Gerry Summers, 1981-87 Keith Peacock, Paul Taylor 1987-88, 1988-89 Keith Burkinshaw, 1989-92 Damien Richardson, 1992-93 Glenn Roeder, 1993-95 Mike Flanagan, Neil Smillie 1995.

ADDITIONAL INFORMATION
PREVIOUS NAMES
New Brompton 1893-1913.

PREVIOUS LEAGUES
Southern League, Kent League.

Club colours: Blue shirts, white shorts, white socks.
Change colours: Red shirts, red shorts, red socks.

Reserves League: Capital League.
Youth League: South East Counties.

LONGEST LEAGUE RUNS

of undefeated matches:	20 (1973-74)	of league matches w/out a win:	15 (1972)
of undefeated home matches:	48 (1963-65)	of undefeated away matches:	10 (1973-74)
without home win:	9 (1961)	without an away win:	28 (21.3.1992 - 18.9.1993)
of league wins:	7 (1954-55)	of home wins:	10 (1963)
of league defeats:	10 (1988-89)	of away wins:	4 (1953-1981)

Missing seasons in 'away without a win' , between 1938-50, was when they were a non-League club.

THE MANAGER

TONY PULIS . . . . appointed July 1995.

PREVIOUS CLUBS
As Manager. . . . . Bournemouth.
As Asst.Man/Coach . . . . Bournemouth.
As a player . . . . Bristol Rovers, Hong Kong, Bristol Rovers, Newport County, Bournemouth,
. . . . Gillingham, Bournemouth.

HONOURS
As a Manager . . . . None.
As a Player . . . . Newport County: Division 3 Championship 1987.

GILLINGHAM

PLAYERS NAME Honours	Ht	Wt	Birthdate	Birthplace Transfers	Contract Date	Clubs	League	L/Cup	FA Cup	Other	Lge	L/C	FAC	Oth
G O A L K E E P E R S														
Steven Banks	5.11	12.4	09.02.72	Hillingdon	24.03.90	West Ham Utd (T)				1				
				Loan	25.03.93	Gillingham								
				Free	24.06.93	Gillingham	67		7	2				
James Stannard	6.0	13.6	06.10.62	Harold Hill		Ford United								
					05.08.80	Fulham	41	3	1					
				Loan	17.09.84	Southend United	6							
				Loan	01.02.85	Charlton Athletic	1							
				£12,000	28.0.85	Southend United	103	6	4	5				
				£50,000	14.08.87	Fulham	348	22	13	18	1			
				Free	08.95	Gillingham								
D E F E N D E R S														
Phillip A Butler	6.2	10.10	28.09.72	Stockport	13.05.91	Gillingham (T)	108+4	10	11	3+1	3			
Richard E Green	6.0	12.8	22.11.67	Wolverhampton	19.07.86	Shrewsbury T. (T)	120+5	11	5	5	5	1		1
				Free	25.10.90	Swindon Town								
				Free	06.03.92	Gillingham	126+1	7	9+1	4	12		1	
Scott Lindsey	5.9	11.10	04.05.72	Walsall		Bridlington								
				Free	28.07.94	Gillingham	11+1			1				
David Martin	6.1	12.2	25.04.63	East Ham	10.05.80	Millwall (A)	131+9	10+2	7	4	6	3	1	1
E: Y.4. FAYC'79. FLT'83. FAT'92.				£35,000	14.09.84	Wimbledon	30+5	2	2+1	3	3			
				Free	23.08.86	Southend United	212+9	25	9+1	10+1	19	4		3
				Free	19.07.93	Bristol City	36+2		5	2	1			
				Loan	13.02.95	Northampton Town	7				1			
				Free	08.95	Gillingham								
Elliot J Martin	5.8	10.6	27.09.72	Plumstead	13.05.91	Gillingham (T)	59+1	2	4	4	1			
Simon Ratcliffe	5.11	11.9	08.02.67	Urmston	13.02.85	Manchester Utd (A)								
E: u19.3, Y.1, S. Div.3'92.				£40,000	16.06.87	Norwich City	6+3	2						
				£100,000	13.01.89	Brentford	197+17	13+3	9+1	23+2	16			2
				Free	08.95	Gillingham								
Neil J Smith	5.7	11.10	30.09.71	Lambeth	24.07.90	Tottenham H. (T)								
FAYC'90				£40,000	17.10.91	Gillingham	126+8	7	12	7	8		2	2
Paul D Watson	5.8	10.10	04.01.75	Hastings	08.12.92	Gillingham (T)	54	4	4	3+3	2			
M I D F I E L D														
Richard Carpenter	6.0	12.0	30.09.72	Sheerness	13.05.91	Gillingham (T)	99+10	2+1	9	5	4			1
Kevin Hunt	5.10	11.0	04.07.75	Chatman	23.03.95	Gillingham (T)								
Gary Micklewhite	5.7	10.4	21.03.61	Southwark	23.03.78	Manchester Utd (A)								
Div2'83'87				Free	04.07.79	Q.P.R.	97+9	12+1	4+2	1+1	11	5	1	
				£90,000	26.02.85	Derby County	223+17	23+3	8+3	8+3	31	2	4	6
				Free	22.07.93	Gillingham	61+3	4	6	1+1	3			
Kevin Rattray				London		Woking (Y)								
FAT'94				£5,000	08.95	Gillingham								
F O R W A R D S														
Andrew J Arnot	6.1	12.5	18.10.73	Chatham	13.05.91	Gillingham (T)	40+22	2+3	10+2	3+1	12		1	
Stephen R Brown	6.0	11.6	06.12.73	Southend	10.07.92	Southend Utd (T)	10		0+1	1	2			
				Free	05.07.93	Scunthorpe United								
				Free	27.08.93	Colchester United	56+6	2	5	5	17		1	1
				Swap	22.03.95	Gillingham	8				1			
Joseph J Dunne	5.9	11.0	25.05.73	Dublin	09.08.90	Gillingham (T)	107+6	6	5	3+1	1			
Ei: u21.1, Y														
Leo Fortune-West						Stevenage Boro'								
				Free	08.95	Gillingham								
Adrian M Foster	5.9	11.0	19.03.91	Kidderminster	20.07.89	West Brom. A. (T)	13+14	1+3	0+2		2			
				Free	03.07.92	Torquay United	55+20	5+1	3	4+3	24	3	1	
				£60,000	11.12.94	Gillingham	27+2	2	3	1	8			
Darren B A Freeman	5.11	13.0	22.08.73	Brighton		Horsham Town								
				Free	31.01.95	Gillingham	0+2							
Mark O'Connor	5.7	10.2	10.03.63	Southend	01.06.80	Q.P.R. (A)	2+1							
Div.3'87				Loan	07.10.83	Exeter City	38		2	3	1		1	1
				£20,000	13.08.84	Bristol Rovers	79+1	8	7	4	10	1	1	1
				£25,000	27.03.86	Bournemouth	115+13	5+3	7	4+1	12			
				£70,000	15.12.89	Gillingham	107+9	8	7+1	6+2	8			1
				Free	05.07.93	Bournemouth	56+2	7+1	4	1	3			
				Free	08.95	Gillingham								
Neil Smillie	5.6	10.7	19.07.58	Barnsley	01.10.75	Crystal Palace (A)	71+12	7	7		7			
SC'88; Div3'92				Loan	01.01.77	Brentford	3							
					09.08.82	Brighton & H.A.	62+13	2	8+1		2		1	
				£100,000	24.06.85	Watford	10+6	1	2		3		1	
				Free	04.12.86	Reading	38+1	3		5+1				2
				Free	15.08.88	Brentford	163+9	21	12	18+1	18		1	3
				Free	26.07.93	Gillingham	53	2	4	1	3			
Christopher Pike	6.2	12.7	19.10.61	Cardiff		Barry Town								
WFAC'92'93. Div.3'93.				Free	14.03.85	Fulham	32+10	3+1		3	4	1		1
				Loan	12.12.86	Cardiff City	6				2			
				Free	01.08.89	Cardiff City	134+14	6+2	5+2	9	65	2	2	2
				Free	09.07.93	Hereford United	36+2	4+1	2	2+1	18			
				£15,000	30.09.95	Gillingham	26+1		4	2	13		4	1
Paul A F Wilson	5.8	11.0	22.02.77	Maidstone	25.04.95	Gillingham	0+2							

589

PRIESTFIELD STADIUM
Redfern Avenue, Gillingham, Kent ME7 4DD
Tel: 01634 851 854/576 828

Capacity 10,422
Covered Standing 4,823
Seating...1,225

First game...v Woolwich Arsenal, Friendly, 2.9.1893.
First floodlit game ....v Bury, Lge Cup, 25.9.1963.

ATTENDANCES
Highest ....23,002 v Q.P.R., FA Cup 3rd Rnd, 10.1.1948.
Lowest...963 v Colchester, AMC, 23.1.1985.

OTHER GROUNDS..None.

MATCHDAY TICKET PRICES

Enclosure	£9
OAP.	£7
Juv	£5
Main Stand	£11.50
no concessions	
Terraces	£7
OAP.	£5
Juv	£3

Ticket Office Telephone no. . . . 01634 851 854/576 828.

HOW TO GET TO THE GROUND
Use motorway (M2) until junction 4.
Leave motorway and follow signs to Gillingham.
Straight over two roundabouts, at 3rd roundabout turn left (A2).
In 500 yards straight over roundabout.
Traffic lights in 200 yards Woodlands Road.
Go straight over until next traffic lights.
Stadium on left.
One block street parking.

Nearest Railway Station
Gillingham (10 minutes walk from ground).

CLUBCALL
0891 800 676
Calls cost 39p per minute cheap rate and 49p per minute at all other times.
Call costings correct at time of going to press.

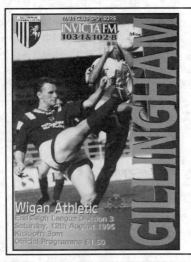

MATCHDAY PROGRAMME

Programme Editor . . . . Roger Evans.

Number of pages . . . . 32.

Price . . . . £1.20.

Subscriptions . . . . £30 including postage.

Local Newspapers. . . . . Kent Today, Medway News and Standard.

Local Radio Stations . . . . BBC Radio Kent, Invicta Radio.

HARTLEPOOL UNITED
(The Pool)
ENDSLEIGH LEAGUE DIVISION 3
SPONSORED BY: CAMERONS BREWERY COMPANY

Back Row (L-R): Sean McAuley, Chris Homer, Neil Maughan, Ian McGuckin, Damian Henderson, Denny Ingram.
Middle Row: Shane Reddish, Chris Lynch, Brian Horne, Gary Henderson (Physio), Steve Jones, Scott Sloan, Tony Canham.
Front Row: Billy Horner (Youth Team Coach), Keith Oliver, Mick Tait (Player Coach), Keith Houchen (Player Manager), Stephen Halliday, Brian Honour (Assistant Youth Team Coach).

HARTLEPOOL UNITED
FORMED IN 1908
TURNED PROFESSIONAL IN 1908
LTD COMPANY IN 1908

PRESIDENT: E Leadbitter
VICE-PRESIDENT: R Boyes, MP
CHAIRMAN: Harold Hornsey
DIRECTORS
A Bamford, D Jukes
CHIEF EXECUTIVE
Stuart Bagnall
COMMERCIAL EXECUTIVE
Frankie Baggs

MANAGER: Keith Houchen
COACH: Mick Tait

YOUTH TEAM MANAGER
Billy Horner
Brian Honour (Assistant Youth Team Coach)

STATISTICIAN FOR THE DIRECTORY
Gordon Small

After two disappointing years and with the club's on-going financial problems, 1994-95 was always going to be a difficult season. In practice this did prove to be the case, but with considerable changes made in the past year there is a real optimism that the worst is now over.

Hartlepool made an average start to the 1994-95 season, then things began to go wrong as problems off the field returned to unsettle the players. The result was a gradual decline with Pool eventually going bottom of the table in November. Three consecutive wins saw a temporary reprieve, but as the season progressed Pool were never too far from the dreaded bottom place. In the last quarter of the season they were again struggling, and a return to the bottom looked highly likely. However an inspired 1-0 win at Carlisle made all the difference, and under new manager Keith Houchen the last two home games were won to take Hartlepool up to the heady heights of 18th position.

In the Coca-Cola Cup Hartlepool did well to come back from a 2-0 defeat at Bury to win the tie 5-3 on aggregate after extra time in the second leg. They were rewarded with two games against the mighty Arsenal, but there was never any likelihood of a surprise - although one or two players did get a chance to impress. With three defeats and no goals scored, Hartlepool's performances in the other two cup competitions are perhaps best forgotten.

It was certainly a year of managerial changes. John MacPhail began the season in charge, but early on he fell out with Chairman Harold Hornsey when it was revealed he had been in contact with the previous Chairman. 'Mr Hartlepool' Billy Horner took over as caretaker for a month, before David McCreery was appointed on a one year contract. He was in charge for most of the season, but struggled to get the desired results. He resigned shortly after it was announced his contract would not be renewed, and for the last three games Keith Houchen filled the hot seat.

Despite the lack of success there were some bright points. Keith Houchen had a remarkable season - he re-discovered his goalscoring boots as Pool's top scorer, he realised his ambition to become Player-Manager, then finally was voted Player of the Year by the supporters. Ian McGuckin developed into a more mature player at the heart of the defence, and Hartlepool will expect a large fee when he is inevitably transferred. Nicky Southall was another to attract the interest of bigger clubs, while goalkeeper Brian Horne also place himself back in the shop-window as a player with a future. Much was expected of teenager Stephen Halliday - he gained valuable first team experience then finished off the season with a fine hat-trick. Hartlepool's other young players had mixed fortunes. Denny Ingram and Keith Oliver quietly established themselves as regular first teamers, but Chris Lynch, Antony Skedd, and Paul Thompson, will all be disappointed with their progress. Scott Sloan struggled as a goalscorer, but new signings Damian Henderson and Shane Reddish both showed promise, and hopefully all three will do even better next season. In 1994-95 Hartlepool utilised a number of players at the veteran stage of their careers - in this category must come Mick Tait who continues to play every game with total commitment.

During the close season there has been a transformation of the Victoria Ground - or Victoria Park as it is now known. For years the ground resembled a building site, but now the 1,640 seater Cyril Knowles Stand is in place, while improvements at the Town-End mean that there is now cover all round the ground. Chairman Harold Hornsey has worked wonders to improve the facilities in such a short time, and now has ambitions that Hartlepool make comparable advancements on the playing side.
GORDON SMALL.

HARTLEPOOL UNITED

Division Three: 18th   **FA Cup:** 1st Round   **Coca-Cola Cup:** 2nd Round

M	DATE	COMP.	VEN	OPPONENTS	RESULT	H/T	LP	GOAL SCORERS/GOAL TIMES	ATT.
1	A 13	EL	A	Gillingham	D 0-0	0-0	11		(2,956)
2	16	CC 1/1	A	Bury	L 0-2	0-1			(1,515)
3	20	EL	H	Darlington	W 1-0	0-0	9	Lynch 64	3,035
4	22	CC 1/2	H	Bury	W 5-1	1-1		Houchen 8, Southall 73, 78, Jackson 107 (og), Thompson 116	1,505
5	27	EL	A	Bury	L 0-2	0-1	14		(2,145)
6	30	EL	H	Barnet	L 0-1	0-1			2,095
7	S 3	EL	H	Chesterfield	L 0-2	0-0	18		2,173
8	10	EL	A	Colchester United	L 0-1	0-0	20		(2,428)
9	13	EL	A	Northampton Town	D 1-1	0-0		Halliday 71	(2,466)
10	17	EL	H	Gillingham	W 2-0	1-0	18	Houchen 39, Walsh 69(pen)	1,756
11	21	CC 2/1	H	Arsenal	L 0-5	0-2			4,421
12	24	EL	H	Lincoln City	L 0-3	0-3	19		1,419
13	O 1	EL	A	Exeter City	L 1-2	1-1	21	Halliday 38	(2,390)
14	5	CC 2/2	A	Arsenal	L 0-2	0-0			(20,520)
15	8	EL	A	Mansfield Town	L 0-2	0-1	21		(2,545)
16	15	EL	H	Preston North End	W 3-1	2-1	20	Houchen 6, Ainsley 39, Foster 58	2,002
17	18	AWT	A	Carlisle United	D 0-2	0-0			(2,563)
18	22	EL	H	Walsall	D 1-1	1-1	19	Houchen 36	1,704
19	29	EL	A	Scunthorpe United	D 0-0	0-0	20		(2,624)
20	N 5	EL	H	Wigan Athletic	L 0-1	0-1			1,683
21	8	AWT	H	Darlington	L 0-2	0-0			1,211
22	12	FAC 1	A	Port Vale	L 0-6	0-3			(6,199)
23	19	EL	A	Doncaster Rovers	L 0-3	0-1	22		(2,507)
24	26	EL	H	Rochdale	W 1-0	1-0	19	Sloan 22	1,387
25	D 10	EL	A	Darlington	W 2-1	1-1	17	Southall 13, Houchen 63	(3,193)
26	17	EL	H	Bury	W 3-1	2-0		Houchen 27, 45, 70	1,746
27	26	EL	H	Carlisle United	L 1-5	0-1		Caig 73 (og)	3,854
28	27	EL	A	Torquay United	D 2-2	1-1		Southall 35, Thompson 82	(3,172)
29	31	EL	H	Fulham	L 1-2	1-1	16	Southall 19 (pen)	1,698
30	J 14	EL	H	Scarborough	D 3-3	0-1	16	Thompson 67, 77, Sloan 75	1,784
31	28	EL	H	Scunthorpe United	L 1-4	0-1	17	Thompson 49	1,660
32	F 4	EL	A	Rochdale	L 0-1	0-1	19		(1,848)
33	18	EL	A	Scarborough	D 2-2	1-1	21	McGuckin 18, Houchen 48	(1,517)
34	21	EL	A	Hereford United	L 0-1	0-0			(1,685)
35	25	EL	H	Exeter City	D 2-2	1-1	19	Houchen 2, McGuckin 62	1,440
36	28	EL	A	Wigan Athletic	L 0-2	0-1			(1,452)
37	M 4	EL	A	Lincoln City	L 0-3	0-0	21		(6,477)
38	7	EL	A	Walsall	L 1-4	1-1		McGuckin 25	(3,314)
39	11	EL	H	Colchester United	W 3-1	2-1	20	Southall 12 (pen), 35,85 (pen)	1,371
40	16	EL	A	Barnes	L 0-4	0-1	20		(1,557)
41	21	EL	H	Doncaster Rovers	W 2-1	1-0		Houchen 13, 38	1,354
42	25	EL	A	Chesterfield	L 0-2	0-1			(4,125)
43	A 1	EL	H	Northampton Town	D 1-1	1-0	20	Houchen 11	2,113
44	8	EL	A	Fulham	L 0-1	0-0	20		(3,465)
45	15	EL	H	Torquay United	D 1-1	0-0	20	Henderson 90	1,770
46	17	EL	A	Carlisle United	W 1-0	1-0		Houchen 30	(10,243)
47	22	EL	H	Hereford United	W 4-0	0-0	19	Holmes 51, 72, Henderson 64, 89	1,596
48	29	EL	A	Preston North End	L 0-3	0-2	20		(9,129)
49	M 6	EL	H	Mansfield Town	W 3-2	1-0	18	Halliday 45, 48, 90	3,049
50									
51									
52									
53									
54									
55									
56									
57									
58									
59									
60									

Best Home League Attendance: 3,854 v Carlisle United   **Smallest:** 1,354 v Doncaster Rovers   **Av Home Att:** 1,938

Goal Scorers: **Compared with 1993-94:** -159

League (43): Houchen 13, Southall 6, Halliday 5, Thompson 4, Henderson 3, McGuckin 3, Holmes 2, Sloan 2, Ainsley, Foster, Lynch, Walsh, Opponent

C/Cola Cup (5): Southall 2, Houchen, Thompson, Opponent

FA Cup (0):

AW Trophy (0):

Horne	Ingram	Sweeney	Gilchrist	McGuckin	Oliver	Ainsley	Sloan	Houchen	Honour	Southall	Thompson	Lynch	Jones	Cook	Lynyard	Skedd	Halliday	Garrett	Hyson	Tait	Reddish	Burgess	Walsh	McCreery	Foster	Referee	
1	2	3	4	5	6†	7	8	9	10	11	S	S	S													D. Orr	1
	2	3*	4	5	6	7	8		10	11	14	12	1	S												K. Breen	2
1	2		4	5	6		8	9		11	7*	10	S			3	12	S								J. Parker	3
1	2		4	5	6		8*	9		11	7	10	S			3	12									R. Poulain	4
1	2		4	5		8*		9		11	7	10	S			3	6	S	12							U. Rennie	5
1	2		4	5	6	S		9		11	7	10	S			3	8*		12							S. Mathieson	6
1	2		4	5*	6		8	9		11•	7	10	S			3	14		12							T. Lunt	7
1	2		4		6	8	11	9•			7		S			3+		14	12	5						G. Pooley	8
1	2		4		6	8*	11	9			7	10	S			3		S		5						G. Barber	9
1	S		4	5	6*			9		11	7	12					10			8		2	3			T. West	10
1	10		4	5	6*			9•		11	7						10	14		8		2	3			D. Allison	11
1			4	5	6*			9			7	12				14	10	11•		8		2	3			E. Wolstenholme	12
1	8		4	5	6	11	12	9			7*					S	10					2	3			C. Wilkes	13
1	8		4	5	6•	11	12	9			7	14				S	10					2	3*			P. Richards	14
1	3		4	5	6	7	11	9					S			S	S				2			8	10	W. Burns	15
A		U		T		O		W		I		N		D		S		C		R		E		E	N		16
1	3		4	5		6	7	9*		11	12					S					2			8	10	J. Watson	17
1	3		4	5		6	7	9		11	S	S	S								2			8	10	J. Brandwood	18
1	3		4	5		6	7*	9		11	14					12					2			8	10•	A. Butler	19
A		U		T		O		W		I		N		D		S		C		R		E		E	N		20
1	2		4	5		6*	14	9		11	7					12	10					3		8•		S. Lodge	21
1	10		4	5		6*	9•			11	7				3		14			8	2			12		D. Allison	22
1			4					10		11	9	S	S		3	6	12			8	2					T. West	23
1	S		4	5				10		11	9	S	S		3	6					8	2				K. Breen	24
1	2		4	5				10	9†	11		S	S	S	3	6					8	S				K. Lynch	25
1	2		4					10*		11	S	S	S		3	6	12			5	8					R. Furnandiz	26
1	2		4				8	10		11	9	S	S		3	S				6	S					C. Wilkes	27
1	2		4	5			8	10		11	9*	S	S		3					6	S					N. Barry	28
1†	2			5			S	10•		11	9	14	3				12			6	8					E. Wolstenholme	29
1	2			5			S	10		11	9	1	3	S			12			6	8					M. Riley	30
1	2		4				14	10		11	9	S	3			12				6	8•					R. Poulain	31
1	2			5†			S	10	9•	11	4	S	3			S				6	8			14		K. Breen	32
1	2			5	S			10	9	11	4	S	3			S				6	8					P. Rejer	33
1	2			5				10	9	11	4*	S	3			12	14			6	8					G. Cain	34
1	2*			5				10	9	11		S	3			14	7			6	8•					J. Lloyd	35
1				5	5			10	9	11		S	3				7		6†		8			S		T. Lunt	36
1			5	4				10		11		S	3			12	7			6	2			8*		U. Rennie	37
1	S		5	8				S	9	11		S	3			12	7			6	2					J. Kirkby	38
1	2		5					9		11		S	S	3		S	7				2					J. Lloyd	39
1	2		5				12	9		11		S			3	7		6•		8						A. Flood	40
1	2		5					9		11	4	S	S	S	3	7				6						S. Mathieson	41
1	2		5					9		11	4	S	S	12	3	7				6			8*		D. Allison	42
1	9									11	4	12	S	3	5	7				2			8*		P. Foakes	43
1	6				4		10*	9		11	8	S	S		3	7				2					K. Breen	44
1	2		5	4				9		11		S	S	7	3	5				8					P. Harrison	45
1	2		5	4				9		11	3	S	7		3					8					E. Wolstenholme	46
1	2		5	4				9		11	3			7	S	6				8					A. Riley	47
1	2		5	4				9		11	S	3				8				6					R. Furnandiz	48
41	35	1	23	34	18	14	25	32	1	37	24	8	2	21		16	20		1	20	23	11	4	7	4	League Appearances	
												3	3	1	1							4			2	League Sub Appearances	
3	3+1	1	4	4	4	3	2+1	3		1	2	3	2+1			1+1	2+1	1					2	2		C/Cola Cup Appearances	
1	1		1	1		1	0+1	1		1	1					0+1	1			1			2	2		FA Cup Appearances	

Also Played: Hichen 9(2), Gourlay 12(9), McPhail 5(23,26),4(29,30,35,36),   Peverell 12(27),Daughtry 7*(23,24,25,26,27,28,29*,30*,31*,32*,33,34*) ,S(36),8(39), 14(40),8(41), Sunley 12(35),2(36),S(37), Henderson 9(37), 10(38,39,40,41,42,43),5(44),10(45,46,47,48), Holmes 4(38,39,40*),6(45,46), Homer 6(43), S(48), Maugham S(43)

† = Sent Off

CLUB RECORDS

BIGGEST VICTORIES
League: 10-1 v Barrow, Division 4, 4.4.1959.
F.A. Cup: 6-0 v North Shields, 1st Round, 30.11.1946.
6-1 v Scarborough, 1st Round, 20.11.1971.
6-3 v Marine, 2nd Round replay, 15.12.1975.

BIGGEST DEFEATS
League: 1-10 v Wrexham, Division 4, 3.3.1962.
F.A. Cup: 0-6 v Manchester City, 3rd Round, 3.1.1976.
Other: 1-7 v York City, Leyland Daf Cup 7.11.1989.

MOST POINTS
3 points a win: 82, Division 4, 1990-91.
2 points a win: 60, Division 4, 1967-68.

MOST GOALS SCORED
90, Division 3(N) 1956-57.

RECORD TRANSFER FEE RECEIVED
£250,000 from Plymouth Argyle for Paul Dalton, May 1992.

RECORD TRANSFER FEE PAID
£60,000 to Barnsley for Andy Saville, March 1992.

BEST PERFORMANCES
League: 2nd Division 3(N) 1956-57.
F.A. Cup: 4th Round 1954-55, 1977-78, 1988-89, 1992-93.
League Cup: 4th Round 1974-75.

HONOURS
None.

LEAGUE CAREER
Original members of Div 3(N) 1921, Transferred to Div 4 1958, P. Div 3 1967-68, R. Div 4 1968-69, P. Div 3 (now Div 2) 1990-91.

MOST GOALS IN A SEASON
Joe Allon: 35 goals in 1990-91. (League 28, FA Cup 3, League Cup 2, Leyland Daf 2).

INDIVIDUAL CLUB RECORDS

MOST GOALS IN A MATCH
7. Billy Smith v St Peters Albion (10-1), FA Cup, 17.11.1923.
5. Harry Simmons v Wigan Borough (6-1), Division 3(N), 1.1.1931.
5. Bobby Folland v Oldham Athletic (5-1, Division 3(N), 15.4.1961.

OLDEST PLAYER
Jackie Carr, 39 years 360 days, 21.11.1931.

YOUNGEST PLAYER
John McGovern, 16 years 205 days, 21.5.1966.

MOST CAPPED PLAYER
Amby Fogarty (Eire) 1.

PREVIOUS MANAGERS

1908-12 Fred Priest, 1912-13 Percy Humphreys, 1913-20 Jack Manners, 1920-22 Cecil Potter, 1922-24 David Gordon, 1924-27 Jack Manners, 1927-31 Bill Norman, 1931-35 Jackie Carr, 1935-39 Jimmy Hamilton, 1943-57 Fred Westgarth, 1957-59 Ray Middleton, 1959-62 Bill Robinson, 1962-63 Allenby Chilton, 1963-64 Bob Gurney, 1964-65 Alvan Williams, 1965 Geoff Twentyman, 1965-67 Brian Clough, 1967-70 Angus McLean, 1970-71 John Simpson, 1971-74 Len Ashurst, 1974-76 Ken Hale, 1976-83 Billy Horner, 1983 John Duncan, 1983 Mick Docherty, 1983-86 Billy Horner, 1986-88 John Bird, 1988-89 Bobby Moncur, 1989-91 Cyril Knowles, 1991-93 Alan Murray; 1993 Viv Busby, 1993-94 John MacPhail, 1994-95 David McCreery.

ADDITIONAL INFORMATION
PREVIOUS NAMES
Until 1968 Hartlepool United: 1968-77 Hartlepool.
PREVIOUS LEAGUES
North Eastern League.

Club colours: Light blue & white striped shirts, light blue shorts with dark blue trimmings.
Change colours: Green shirts, dark blue shorts.

Youth League: Northern Intermediate

LONGEST LEAGUE RUNS

of undefeated matches:	17 (1968)	of league matches w/out a win:	18 (1962-63, 1993)
of undefeated home matches:	27 (1967-68)	of undefeated away matches:	8 (1992)
without home win:	8 (1977, 1984, 1986, 1993)	without an away win:	31 (1937-38)
of league wins:	7 (1956, 1968)	of home wins:	12 (1933, 1951)
of league defeats:	8 (1950, 1993)	of away wins:	4 (1921-22, 1979, 1991)

THE MANAGER

KEITH HOUCHEN . . . . appointed April 1995.

PREVIOUS CLUBS
As Manager . . . . None.
As Asst.Man/Coach . . . . None.
As a player . . . . Chesterfield, Hartlepool, Leyton Orient, York City, Scunthorpe Utd, Coventry City, Hibernian, ... Port Vale, Hartlepool United.

HONOURS
As a Manager . . . . None.
As a Player . . . . FA Cup 1987.

HARTLEPOOL UNITED

<table>
<tr><th rowspan="2">PLAYERS NAME
Honours</th><th rowspan="2">Ht</th><th rowspan="2">Wt</th><th rowspan="2">Birthdate</th><th rowspan="2">Birthplace
Transfers</th><th rowspan="2">Contract
Date</th><th rowspan="2">Clubs</th><th colspan="4">APPEARANCES</th><th colspan="4">GOALS</th></tr>
<tr><th>League</th><th>L/Cup</th><th>FA Cup</th><th>Other</th><th>Lge</th><th>L/C</th><th>FAC</th><th>Oth</th></tr>

<tr><td colspan="15">G O A L K E E P E R S</td></tr>
<tr><td>Brian S Horne</td><td>5.11</td><td>12.4</td><td>05.10.67</td><td>Billericay</td><td>10.10.85</td><td>Millwall (A)</td><td>163</td><td>14</td><td>9</td><td>10</td><td></td><td></td><td></td><td></td></tr>
<tr><td>E: u21.5, u19.2, Y8; Div2'88</td><td></td><td></td><td></td><td>Loan</td><td>28.08.92</td><td>Middlesbrough</td><td>3+1</td><td></td><td></td><td></td><td></td><td></td><td></td><td></td></tr>
<tr><td></td><td></td><td></td><td></td><td>Loan</td><td>02.10.92</td><td>Stoke City</td><td>1</td><td>1</td><td></td><td></td><td></td><td></td><td></td><td></td></tr>
<tr><td></td><td></td><td></td><td></td><td>Free</td><td>24.12.92</td><td>Portsmouth</td><td>3</td><td></td><td></td><td>2</td><td></td><td></td><td></td><td></td></tr>
<tr><td></td><td></td><td></td><td></td><td>Free</td><td>02.08.94</td><td>Hartlepool United</td><td>41</td><td>3</td><td>1</td><td>2</td><td></td><td></td><td></td><td></td></tr>
<tr><td>Steven Jones</td><td>5.11</td><td>12.2</td><td>31.01.74</td><td>Stockton</td><td>07.05.92</td><td>Hartlepool Utd (T)</td><td>38+1</td><td>1</td><td>2</td><td></td><td></td><td></td><td></td><td></td></tr>

<tr><td colspan="15">D E F E N D E R S</td></tr>
<tr><td>Stuart Denevan Ingram</td><td>5.10</td><td>11.8</td><td>27.06.76</td><td>Sunderland</td><td>05.07.94</td><td>Hartlepool Utd (T)</td><td>48</td><td>3+1</td><td>1</td><td>2</td><td></td><td></td><td></td><td></td></tr>
<tr><td>Sean McAuley</td><td>6.0</td><td>11.9</td><td>23.06.72</td><td>Sheffield</td><td>1991</td><td>Manchester Utd (T)</td><td></td><td></td><td></td><td></td><td></td><td></td><td></td><td></td></tr>
<tr><td>S: u21.</td><td></td><td></td><td></td><td></td><td>1992-95</td><td>St Johnstone</td><td>62</td><td></td><td></td><td></td><td></td><td></td><td></td><td></td></tr>
<tr><td></td><td></td><td></td><td></td><td>Loan</td><td>1994-95</td><td>Chesterfield</td><td>1</td><td></td><td></td><td></td><td></td><td></td><td>1</td><td></td></tr>
<tr><td></td><td></td><td></td><td></td><td>Free</td><td>08.95</td><td>Hartlepool United</td><td></td><td></td><td></td><td></td><td></td><td></td><td></td><td></td></tr>
<tr><td>Thomas Ian McGuckin</td><td>6.2</td><td>12.2</td><td>24.04.73</td><td>Middlesbrough</td><td>20.06.91</td><td>Hartlepool Utd (T)</td><td>86+4</td><td>8</td><td>3</td><td>5</td><td>6</td><td></td><td></td><td></td></tr>
<tr><td>Shane Reddish</td><td>5.10</td><td>11.10</td><td>05.05.71</td><td>Bolsover</td><td>25.07.89</td><td>Mansfield Town (T)</td><td></td><td></td><td></td><td></td><td></td><td></td><td></td><td></td></tr>
<tr><td></td><td></td><td></td><td></td><td>Free</td><td>07.02.90</td><td>Doncaster Rovers</td><td>51+9</td><td>1</td><td>2</td><td>2</td><td>3</td><td></td><td></td><td></td></tr>
<tr><td></td><td></td><td></td><td></td><td>Free</td><td>07.07.93</td><td>Carlisle United</td><td>35+2</td><td>3</td><td>3+1</td><td>7+2</td><td>1</td><td></td><td></td><td></td></tr>
<tr><td></td><td></td><td></td><td></td><td>Free</td><td>18.11.94</td><td>Hartlepool United</td><td>23</td><td></td><td></td><td></td><td></td><td></td><td></td><td></td></tr>

<tr><td colspan="15">M I D F I E L D</td></tr>
<tr><td>Tony Canham</td><td>5.9</td><td>11.8</td><td>08.06.60</td><td>Leeds</td><td></td><td>Harrogate R.I.</td><td></td><td></td><td></td><td></td><td></td><td></td><td></td><td></td></tr>
<tr><td></td><td></td><td></td><td></td><td>Free</td><td>16.01.85</td><td>York City</td><td>309+38</td><td>18</td><td>20</td><td>24+4</td><td>56</td><td>2</td><td>6</td><td>4</td></tr>
<tr><td></td><td></td><td></td><td></td><td>Free</td><td>08.95</td><td>Hartlepool United</td><td></td><td></td><td></td><td></td><td></td><td></td><td></td><td></td></tr>
<tr><td>Keith Oliver</td><td>5.8</td><td>10.3</td><td>15.01.76</td><td>South Shields</td><td>05.07.94</td><td>Hartlepool Utd (T)</td><td>18+1</td><td>4</td><td></td><td>2</td><td></td><td></td><td></td><td></td></tr>

<tr><td colspan="15">F O R W A R D S</td></tr>
<tr><td>Stephen W Halliday</td><td>5.10</td><td>11.2</td><td>03.05.76</td><td>Sunderland</td><td>05.07.94</td><td>Hartlepool Utd (T)</td><td>26+13</td><td>2+1</td><td>1</td><td>1+1</td><td>5</td><td></td><td></td><td></td></tr>
<tr><td>Damian Henderson</td><td>6.2</td><td>13.8</td><td>12.05.73</td><td>Leeds</td><td>05.07.91</td><td>Leeds United (T)</td><td></td><td></td><td></td><td></td><td></td><td></td><td></td><td></td></tr>
<tr><td></td><td></td><td></td><td></td><td>Loan</td><td>01.11.91</td><td>Yeovil Town</td><td></td><td></td><td>0+1</td><td></td><td></td><td></td><td></td><td></td></tr>
<tr><td></td><td></td><td></td><td></td><td>Free</td><td>01.08.93</td><td>Scarborough</td><td>17</td><td>2</td><td>2</td><td>3</td><td>5</td><td></td><td></td><td></td></tr>
<tr><td></td><td></td><td></td><td></td><td>Free</td><td>10.12.93</td><td>Scunthorpe United</td><td>31+6</td><td>2</td><td>1</td><td>1</td><td>4</td><td>1</td><td></td><td></td></tr>
<tr><td></td><td></td><td></td><td></td><td>Free</td><td>08.95</td><td>Hartlepool United</td><td></td><td></td><td></td><td></td><td></td><td></td><td></td><td></td></tr>
<tr><td>Keith M Houchen</td><td>6.2</td><td>11.4</td><td>25.07.60</td><td>Middlesbrough</td><td></td><td>Chesterfield (J)</td><td></td><td></td><td></td><td></td><td></td><td></td><td></td><td></td></tr>
<tr><td>FAC'87</td><td></td><td></td><td></td><td>Free</td><td>09.02.78</td><td>Hartlepool United</td><td>160+10</td><td>8</td><td>4+1</td><td></td><td>65</td><td>1</td><td></td><td></td></tr>
<tr><td></td><td></td><td></td><td></td><td>£25,000</td><td>26.03.82</td><td>Leyton Orient</td><td>74+2</td><td>3</td><td>3</td><td>0+1</td><td>20</td><td>1</td><td></td><td></td></tr>
<tr><td></td><td></td><td></td><td></td><td>£151,000</td><td>22.03.84</td><td>York City</td><td>56+11</td><td>6</td><td>9+2</td><td>4</td><td>19</td><td>3</td><td>3</td><td>2</td></tr>
<tr><td></td><td></td><td></td><td></td><td>£40,000</td><td>28.03.86</td><td>Scunthorpe United</td><td>9</td><td></td><td></td><td></td><td>2</td><td></td><td></td><td></td></tr>
<tr><td></td><td></td><td></td><td></td><td>£60,000</td><td>03.07.86</td><td>Coventry City</td><td>43+11</td><td>2+1</td><td>5+1</td><td>2+1</td><td>7</td><td></td><td>5</td><td></td></tr>
<tr><td></td><td></td><td></td><td></td><td>£100,000</td><td></td><td>Hibernian</td><td>51+6</td><td>5</td><td>6</td><td>4</td><td>11</td><td>1</td><td>4</td><td>1</td></tr>
<tr><td></td><td></td><td></td><td></td><td>£100,000</td><td>09.08.91</td><td>Port Vale</td><td>44+5</td><td>2+1</td><td>2</td><td>1+1</td><td>10</td><td>1</td><td></td><td></td></tr>
<tr><td></td><td></td><td></td><td></td><td>Free</td><td>01.08.93</td><td>Hartlepool United</td><td>66</td><td>5</td><td>2</td><td>3</td><td>21</td><td>1</td><td></td><td></td></tr>
<tr><td>Christopher J Lynch</td><td>6.0</td><td>11.0</td><td>18.11.74</td><td>Middlesbrough</td><td>02.08.93</td><td>Hartlepool Utd (T)</td><td>25+6</td><td>2+1</td><td></td><td></td><td>1</td><td></td><td></td><td></td></tr>
<tr><td>Scott M Sloan</td><td>5.10</td><td>11.6</td><td>14.12.67</td><td>Wallsend</td><td></td><td>Berwick Rangers</td><td>58+5</td><td>2</td><td>4</td><td></td><td>20</td><td>2</td><td>1</td><td></td></tr>
<tr><td></td><td></td><td></td><td></td><td>£75,000</td><td>31.07.90</td><td>Newcastle United</td><td>11+5</td><td></td><td>1</td><td>1</td><td>1</td><td></td><td></td><td></td></tr>
<tr><td></td><td></td><td></td><td></td><td></td><td></td><td>Falkirk</td><td>49+15</td><td>2</td><td>7+1</td><td>3+1</td><td>11</td><td></td><td>4</td><td>2</td></tr>
<tr><td></td><td></td><td></td><td></td><td>Loan</td><td>25.02.94</td><td>Cambridge United</td><td>4</td><td></td><td></td><td></td><td></td><td></td><td></td><td></td></tr>
<tr><td></td><td></td><td></td><td></td><td>Free</td><td>12.08.94</td><td>Hartlepool United</td><td>26+3</td><td>2+1</td><td>0+1</td><td>1</td><td>2</td><td></td><td></td><td></td></tr>
<tr><td>Michael P Tait</td><td>5.11</td><td>12.5</td><td>30.09.56</td><td>Wallsend</td><td>08.10.74</td><td>Oxford United (A)</td><td>61+3</td><td>2+1</td><td>2</td><td></td><td>23</td><td>1</td><td></td><td></td></tr>
<tr><td>Div.3'83. SC'88. Div.4'91.</td><td></td><td></td><td></td><td>£65,000</td><td>03.02.77</td><td>Carlisle United</td><td>101+5</td><td>7</td><td>7</td><td></td><td>20</td><td></td><td>2</td><td></td></tr>
<tr><td></td><td></td><td></td><td></td><td>£150,000</td><td>06.09.79</td><td>Hull City</td><td>29+4</td><td></td><td>1</td><td></td><td>3</td><td></td><td>1</td><td></td></tr>
<tr><td></td><td></td><td></td><td></td><td>£100,000</td><td>11.06.80</td><td>Portsmouth</td><td>227+12</td><td>33+1</td><td>13</td><td>2+1</td><td>31</td><td>1</td><td>1</td><td></td></tr>
<tr><td></td><td></td><td></td><td></td><td>£50,000</td><td>01.09.87</td><td>Reading</td><td>98+1</td><td>9</td><td>16</td><td>9</td><td>10</td><td>2</td><td></td><td>3</td></tr>
<tr><td></td><td></td><td></td><td></td><td>Free</td><td>03.08.90</td><td>Darlington</td><td>79</td><td>5</td><td>4</td><td>3</td><td>2</td><td></td><td></td><td></td></tr>
<tr><td></td><td></td><td></td><td></td><td>Free</td><td>31.07.92</td><td>Hartlepool United</td><td>35</td><td>4</td><td>2</td><td></td><td>1</td><td></td><td></td><td></td></tr>
<tr><td></td><td></td><td></td><td></td><td>Free</td><td>08.94</td><td>Gretna</td><td></td><td></td><td></td><td></td><td></td><td></td><td></td><td></td></tr>
<tr><td></td><td></td><td></td><td></td><td>Free</td><td>09.09.94</td><td>Hartlepool United</td><td>20</td><td>1</td><td></td><td></td><td></td><td></td><td></td><td></td></tr>

<tr><td colspan="15">ADDITIONAL CONTRACT PLAYER</td></tr>
<tr><td>Steve Howard</td><td></td><td></td><td></td><td></td><td></td><td>Tow Law Town</td><td></td><td></td><td></td><td></td><td></td><td></td><td></td><td></td></tr>
<tr><td></td><td></td><td></td><td></td><td>Free</td><td>08.95</td><td>Hartlepool United</td><td></td><td></td><td></td><td></td><td></td><td></td><td></td><td></td></tr>
</table>

THE VICTORIA PARK
Hartlepool, Cleveland TS24 8BZ
Tel: 01429 272 584

Capacity 7,229
Seating 1,650
Town End Terrace 1,775

First game .... v Newcastle Utd Res. (F) 6-0, 2.9.1908.
First floodlit game .... v Southend Utd, Div 4, 1-2, 6.1.1967.

ATTENDANCES
Highest .... 17,426 v Manchester Utd, FA Cup 3rd round, 18.1.1957.
Lowest .... 655 v Bradford City, Football League Trophy, 18.8.1982.
.... 790 v Stockport County, Division 4, 5.5.1984.

OTHER GROUNDS .... None.

MATCHDAY TICKET PRICES

Seats £9
Juv/OAP £6

Terraces £7
Juv/OAP £5

Ticket Office Telephone no 01429 222 077

HOW TO GET TO THE GROUND

From the North
Use A1, A19 then A179, sign posted Hartlepool to Hart. In 2.5 miles at traffic signals forward, then at crossroads turn right into Clarence Road for Hartlepool United FC.

From the South and West
Use A1, A19 and A689 into Hartlepool town centre, then bear right into Clarence Road for Hartlepool United FC.

Car Parking
Side street parking is ample.

Nearest Railway Station
Hartlepool Church Street (01429 274 039).

CLUBCALL
0891 12 11 47

Calls cost 39p per minute cheap rate and 49p per minute at all other times.
Call costings correct at time of going to press.

MATCHDAY PROGRAMME

Programme Editor .... Lisa Charlton & Mike Challards.

Number of pages .... 32.

Price £1.20

Subscriptions .... Please apply to club.

Local Newspapers .... Hartlepool Mail, Northern Echo.

Local Radio Stations .... T.F.M, Radio Cleveland.

HEREFORD UNITED
(United)
ENDSLEIGH LEAGUE DIVISION 3
SPONSORED BY: SUN VALLEY

Back Row (L-R): Dean Clarke, Steve White, John Brough, Tony James, Chris McKenzie, Neil Lyne, Kevin Lloyd, Rob Warner.
Front Row: Phil Preedy, Murray Fishlock, Andy Preece, Gary Pick, Graham Turner, Dean Smith, Richard Wilkins, Nicky Cross, Tim Steele.

HEREFORD UNITED
FORMED IN 1924
TURNED PROFESSIONAL IN 1924
LTD COMPANY IN 1939

LIFE-VICE-PRESIDENT: A Bush
CHAIRMAN: P S Hill, FRICS
DIRECTORS
M B Roberts (Vice-Chairman),
D H Vaughan, D Jones, J Duggan,
R Fry (Managing)
SECRETARY
D H Vaughan (01432 276 666)
COMMERCIAL MANAGER
(01432 273 155)

MANAGER
Graham Turner

STATISTICIAN FOR THE DIRECTORY
Lawrence Appleby

Hereford United reached the dizzy heights of 16th position last season, the highest for some time. To some this may not seem much, but to the long suffering fans, especially in the second half of the season, the change in form was a welcome sight.

Greg Downs left early in the season and within a short period John Layton was appointed as manager, followed closely by Dick Bate as coach. The difference was certainly clear, three wins in the first 16 games followed by three defeats in the last 16.

The biggest problem all season was a lack of goals. Leading scorer was Steve White with 14 League goals, no one else could manage more than six. A goalscorer is certainly needed this coming season.

The FA Cup came and went within a couple of weeks, while the League Cup provided the first interest of the season. After a draw at home to West Bromwich Albion, a difficult tie looked certain at the Hawthorns. But a great Steve White goal was enough to book a place in the second round against Nottingham Forest. A close 1-2 defeat at the City Ground set up a great second leg match which, alas, resulted in a goalless draw, a result to be proud of but a result that saw Forest go through.

In the Auto Windscreen Trophy the quarter-final stage was reached once again. Birmingham City were the opponents and proved to strong, despite a sterling performance by Hereford, infront of Birmingham home support.

Apart from the good run at the end of the season, it was some fine individual performances that had the interest of the fans. Chris McKenzie was outstanding in goal, Dean Smith skippered the team with superb leadership and other excellent performances were shown by Richard Wilkins, Kevin Lloyd, Gareth Davies and Neil Lyne and with the emergence of Robert Warner and Murray Fishlock (Andy Browngg was sold after only eight League appearances, to Norwich).

I am sure a great season is ahead for everyone at the club.

LAWRENCE APPLEBY.

HEREFORD UNITED

Division Three: 16th **FA Cup:** 1st Round **Coca-Cola Cup:** 2nd Round **Auto Windscreen Trophy:** Qtr-Finalists

M	DATE	COMP.	VEN	OPPONENTS	RESULT	H/T	LP	GOAL SCORERS/GOAL TIMES	ATT.
1	A 13	EL	H	Doncaster	L 0-1	0-0			(3,076)
2	16	CC 1/1	H	West Brom A	D 0-0	0-0			5,425
3	20	EL	H	Preston NE	L 0-2	0-0	21		3,039
4	27	EL	H	Walsall	D 0-0	0-0	18		3,004
5	30	EL	A	Scarborough	L 1-3	0-1		Reece (75)	(1,490)
6	S 3	EL	A	Rochdale	W 3-1	1-0	17	Preedy (26), James (46), White (89)	(2,258)
7	7	CC 1/2	A	West Brom A	W 1-0	0-0	-	White (52)	(10,604)
8	10	EL	H	Wigan Ath	L 1-2	1-0	19	White (27)	2,771
9	13	EL	H	Torquay	D 1-1	1-0	-	White (33)	2,153
10	16	EL	A	Doncaster	L 0-3	0-2	20		(1,938)
11	21	CC 2/1	A	Nottingham F	L 1-2	1-0	-	White (6)	(10,076)
12	24	EL	A	Fulham	D 1-1	1-0	21	White (30)	(3,740)
13	27	AWT SP	H	Torquay	W 4-2	2-0	-	Smith (23), Preed (39), White (30), Cross (59)	1,046
14	O 1	EL	H	Scunthorpe	W 2-1	1-0	18	Cross (2), White (61)	2,267
15	3	CC 2/2	H	Nottingham F	D 0-0	0-0	-		9,865
16	8	EL	A	Barnet	D 2-2	1-1	18	White (21), Reece (55)	(2,116)
17	15	EL	H	Gillingham	W 2-1	1-0	17	Cross (1), Davies (88)	2,472
18	22	EL	A	Darlington	L 1-3	0-0	19	Cross (62)	(1,996)
19	29	EL	H	Lincoln	L 0-3	0-1	19		2,485
20	N 5	EL	A	Chesterfield	L 0-1	0-1	19		(2,448)
21	8	AWT SP	A	Swansea	W 1-0	1-0	-	Reece (25)	(1,215)
22	12	FAC 1	H	Hitchin	D 2-2	0-2	-	Lynne (49,55)	(3,078)
23	19	EL	H	Carlisle	L 0-1	0-1	21		2,531
24	22	FAC 1R	A	Hitchin	L 2-4	2-1	-	White (7), Pick (44)	(3,078)
25	26	EL	A	Northampton	W 3-1	0-0	18	Pick (52), Reece (79), White (84)	(5,148)
26	29	AWT S1	H	Peterborough	W 2-0	1-0	-	James (30), Reece (82)	1,301
27	D 10	EL	A	Preston NE	L 2-4	0-3	20	Reece (85), Cross (90)	(6,581)
28	17	EL	A	Walsall	L 3-4	2-1	20	Cross (36), James (43), White (89)	(3,652)
29	26	EL	A	Mansfield	L 1-7	0-1	-	Wilkins (60)	(2,887)
30	27	EL	H	Exeter C	W 3-0	2-0	-	Lyne (36), Cross (39), Wilkins (55)	2,567
31	31	EL	H	Colchester U	D 2-2	2-0	20	Brough (11), Whitton OG (37)	3,322
32	J 7	EL	H	Darlington	D 0-0	0-0	19		2,237
33	10	AWT Q/F	A	Birmingham	L 1-3	1-1	-	Lyne (45)	(24,000)
34	14	EL	A	Bury	D 1-1	0-1	19	Reece (85 P)	(2,708)
35	28	EL	A	Lincoln C	L 0-2	0-0	19		(2,545)
36	F 4	EL	H	Northampton	W 2-1	1-1	18	Lloyd (25), White (63)	2,365
37	11	EL	A	Carlisle	L 0-1	0-1	18		(5,676)
38	18	EL	H	Bury	W 1-0	1-0	18	Lloyd (19)	1,827
39	21	EL	H	Hartlepool	W 1-0	0-0	-	White (87)	1,685
40	25	EL	A	Scunthorpe	L 0-1	0-1	17		(2,193)
41	M 4	EL	A	Fulham	D 1-1	0-1	17	Pick (86)	2,895
42	18	EL	H	Scarborough	W 2-1	0-0	17	Smith (64, 89)	1,497
43	25	EL	H	Rochdale	D 0-0	0-0	17		1,954
44	29	EL	A	Wigan A	D 1-1	0-0	-	Pounder (57)	(1,492)
45	A 1	EL	A	Torquay	W 1-0	1-0	16	White (6)	(2,410)
46	8	EL	H	Colchester	W 3-0	2-0	16	White (4,35), Smith (57)	1,669
47	15	EL	A	Exeter	D 1-1	1-0	16	White (25)	(2,083)
48	17	EL	H	Mansfield T	D 0-0	0-0	-		2,743
49	22	EL	A	Hartlepool	L 0-4	0-0	16		(1,596)
50	29	EL	A	Gillingham	D 0-0	0-0	16		(24)
51	M 6	EL	H	Barnet	W 3-2	3-1	16	White (8), Pounder (13), Lloyd (36)	2,069
52									
53									
54									
55									
56									
57									
58									
59									
60									

Best Home League Attendance: 3, 076 v Doncaster Rovers **Smallest:** 1,497 v Scarborough **Av Home Att:** 2,252

Goal Scorers: **Compared with 1993-94:** -21

League (45): White 15, Cross 6, Reece 5 (1 pen), Smith 3, Lloyd 3, James 2, Pick 2, Wilkins 2, Pounder 2 (1 og), Brough, Preedy,, Davies, Lynne
C/Cola Cup (2): White 2
FA Cup (4): Lyne 2, White, Pick
AW Trophy: (3): Reece 2, White, Cross, James, Lyne, Preedy, Smith

Pennock T.	Reece A.	Preedy P.	Davies G.	Smith D.	James T.	Wilkins R.	Pick G.	Cross N.	Clark H.	Steele T.	Downs G.	Clarke D.	Williams C.	Pike C.	Gonzague M.	Eversham P.	McLenzie C.	Lyne N.	Fishlock M.	Llewelyn A.	Farringdon M.	Brough J.	Lloyd K.	Warner R.	Browning A.	Referee
1	2	3	4	5	6	7	8	9	10+	11	12															1
1	2	3	4	5	6	7	12	9		11	8			10+												2
1	2	3	4*	5	6	7	12	9		11	8	14	10-													3
1	4	11		5	6	7		9	2	8	3				10											4
1	4-	11	3	5	6	7	12	9	2				8+		10											5
1	12	3		5	6	7	4+	9	2						10	11-	14									6
1		3		5	6	7	4	9	2						10	11										7
1	4		3	5	6	7		9	2						10	11+		12								8
	4		3	5	6	7+		9	2						10	11		1		12						9
	4	3		5	6		12	9	2	7					10		8+			11						10
	4	3		5	6	7	8	9	2	11					10											11
	4	3	11	5	6	7	8	9	2						10											12
1	4	3		5	6		8	9	2						10	12	7+			11						13
	4	11		5	6		8	9	2						10		7				3					14
	4	11		5	6	7	8	9	2						10						3					15
	4	11+	12	5	6	7	8	9	2						10						3		14			16
	4	11	14	5-	6	7-	8	9	2						10						3		12			17
	4	11	5		6		8+	9							10	2	12				3					18
	4	11	5		6	8		9							10	2					3					19
	4	11	5		6	8		9							10+					12	3	2-		14		20
1	4		5-	14	6	8		9		7					12					10	11+	2			3	21
1	5	3		4	6	8		9		7-					10+					11	2					22
1	6		5	4		8	11	9												10	3		2			23
1	2	3	5	4		8	6	9							10					11						24
1	2		5-	4		8	11	12							9+					10	6		14		3	25
1	2			4	6	8	11	12							9+					10	5		14		3	26
1	2+		11	4	6	8									9					10	5	12			3	27
1	4	11		5	6	7	8								9					10		2			3	28
1	4	11		5	6+	7	8								9					10		2			3	29
	4			5		7+	11	8										1		10				9	3	30
	4	7+		5			11	8							9			1		10				9	3	31
	4	2		5			11		7						8			1		10				9	3	32
	4			5			11		7						9			1		10					3	33
	4			5		7	11	12							10+			1		9				8	3	34
1	4	2	5			6		12							14			1		9				10	3	35
	4	8	5			7									10			1		11					3	36
	4	8		7		14									10			1		11			5		3+	37
	4	8		7											12			1		9+			5		3	38
	4	8		7											12			1		10			5		3	39
	4		5	7		9												1		10			6		3	40
	4*	8	5	7		14	12	3+							9			1		10			6			41
13		8	5	7		14	9	12										1		10	3		6	2		42
		8	5	7	4	9									10			1		12			6		3	43
1			5	7	4										9+					10	3		6	8		44
		8	5	7	4										9			1		10	14		6	3+		45
																										46
																										47
																										48
																										49
																										50
																										51
																										52
																										53
																										54
																										55
																										56
																										57
																										58
																										59
																										60
13	30	15	23	29	18	30	17	22	13	4	2	1	1		26	2	2	2	14	20	11	3		15	18	League Appearances
1	1		2				4	4	1			1	1		3		1	2		2	2	1		2	2	League Sub Appearances
2	3	4	1	4	4	4	3+1	4	3	2	1			1	3	1				1						C/Cola Appearances
2	2	2	1	2	1	2	1+1	2	1				1		2				1		2					FA Cup Appearances
3	4	1	2	1+1	3	2	3	2+1	3	1					3+1	0+1	1		1	3	2	1		0+1	3	AWT Appearances

Also Played: D, Gregory 8(33,35), D. Henderson 11(35),9(36,37,39*) 10(38), G. Stockoe 4(42*),2(43*,44,45), J. Reeve 14(43),12(44,46), T Pounder 8(6,7,8,9), 7(18,19,20,23,24,25,26,27) 14(22), 12(28,29,3,37), 11(38,39,40,41,42,43,44,45), Sheffield 1(10,11,12,14,15,16,17,18,19,20)

CLUB RECORDS

BIGGEST VICTORIES
League: 6-0 v Burnley (a), Division 4, 24.1.1987.
F.A. Cup: 6-1 v Queens Park Rangers, 2nd Round, 7.12.1957.

BIGGEST DEFEATS
League: 0-6 v Rotherham United (a), Division 4, 29.4.1989.
F.A. Cup: 2-7 v Arsenal, 3rd Round replay, 21.1.1985.
League Cup: 0-5 v Newport County 1st round, 11.8.1981.
0-5 v Nottingham Forest 2nd Round, 7.10.1987.
0-5 v Torquay United, 1st round 2nd leg, 25.8.1992.

MOST POINTS
3 points a win: 77, Division 1, 1984-85.
2 points a win: 63, Division 3, 1974-75.

MOST GOALS SCORED
86, Division 3, 1975-76.

RECORD TRANSFER FEE RECEIVED
£250,000 from Q.P.R. for Darren Peacock, March 1991, plus another £240,000 after moving to Newcastle United from QPR, March 1994.

RECORD TRANSFER FEE PAID
£75,000 to Walsall for Dean Smith, July 1994.

BEST PERFORMANCES
League: 22nd Division 2, 1976-77.
F.A. Cup: 4th Round 1971-72, 1976-77, 1981-82, 1989-90, 1991-92.
League Cup: 3rd Round, 1974-75.
Welsh Cup: Finalists (4 times), Winners 1989-90.

HONOURS
Division 3, 1975-76.
Welsh FA Cup 1989-90.

LEAGUE CAREER
Elected to Div 4 1972, Div 3 1972-73, Div 2 1975-76, Div 3 1976-77, Div (now Div 3) 1977-78.

INDIVIDUAL CLUB RECORDS

MOST GOALS IN A SEASON
'Dixie' McNeil: 37 goals in 1975-76 (League 35, FA Cup 2).

MOST GOALS IN A MATCH
4.'Dixie' McNeil v Chester, Division 3, 10.3.1976.

OLDEST PLAYER
John Jackson, 40 years 6 days.

YOUNGEST PLAYER
Stuart Phillips, 16 years 112 days.

MOST CAPPED PLAYER
Brian Evans (Wales) 1.

PREVIOUS MANAGERS

(Since joining the Football League)
1971-74 Colin Addison, 1974-78 John Sillett, 1978 Tony Ford, 1978-79 Mike Bailey, 1979-82 Frank Lord, 1982-83 Tommy Hughes, 1983-87 John Newman, 1987-90 Ian Bowyer, 1990-91 Colin Addison, 1991-92 John Sillett, 1992-94 Greg Downs, John Layton 1994-95.

ADDITIONAL INFORMATION
PREVIOUS NAMES
None.

PREVIOUS LEAGUES
Southern League, Birmingham Lge, Birmingham Combination.

Club colours: White shirts with black trim, black shorts with white trim, black socks with white hooped tops.
Change colours: red/white/black/diamond pattern, white shorts, white socks.

Reserves League
Avon Insurance Football Combination. (Youth Team)

LONGEST LEAGUE RUNS

of undefeated matches:	14 (1972-73, 1984)	of league matches w/out a win:	13 (1977-78, 1978)
of undefeated home matches:	21 (1972-73)	of undefeated away matches:	6 (1972-73, 1984)
without home win:	11 (1981-82)	without an away win:	28 (1977-78)
of league wins:	5 (twice 1984)	of home wins:	12 (1973)
of league defeats:	8 (1986-87)	of away wins:	3 (1975-76, 1976-77, 1984-85, 1987-88)

THE MANAGER

GRAHAM TURNER . . . . appointed Summer 1995.

PREVIOUS CLUBS
As Manager. . . . . Shrewsbury Town, Aston Villa, Wolverhampton Wanderers.
As Asst.Man/Coach . . . . None.
As a player . . . . Wrexham, Chester City, Shrewsbury Town.

HONOURS
As a Manager. . . . . Shrewsbury Town: Division 3 Championship 1979.
. . . . Wolves: Division 4 Championship 1987-88. Sherpa Van Trophy 1987-88. Division 3 Champions 1988-89.
As a Player . . . . None.

HEREFORD UNITED

PLAYERS NAME Honours	Ht	Wt	Birthdate	Birthplace Transfers	Contract Date	Clubs	League	L/Cup	FA Cup	Other	Lge	L/C	FAC	Oth
G O A L K E E P E R S														
Christopher Mackenzie	6.0	12.6	14.05.72	Northampton		Corby								
				Free	20.07.94	Hereford United	21+1			1				
				Loan	07.10.94	Rushden & Dia.								
D E F E N D E R S														
Murray Fishlock	5.7	11.0	23.09.73	Marlborough		Trowbridge								
				Free	30.09.94	Hereford United	12+2	1		2				
Anthony C James	6.3	13.8	27.06.67	Sheffield		Gainsborough Town								
				£20,000	22.08.88	Lincoln City	24+5	2		0+1				
				£150,000	23.08.89	Leicester City	79+28	6	2	3+1	11		1	
				Free	25.07.94	Hereford United	18	4	1	3	2			1
Kevin G Lloyd	6.0	12.1	26.09.70	Llanidloes		Caersws								
				Free	07.11.94	Hereford United	24			3	3			
Phillip Preedy	5.10	10.8	20.11.75	Hereford	13.07.94	Hereford United (T)	24+5	4	2	1	1			1
Dean Smith	6.1	12.0	19.03.71	West Brom	01.07.89	Walsall (T)	137+5	10	4	10	2			
				£75,000	17.06.94	Hereford United	35	4	2	3+1	3			1
Robert M Warner	5.9	11.07	20.04.77	Stratford	18.01.95	Hereford United (T)	15+1							
M I D F I E L D														
John Brough	6.0	12.6	08.01.73	Ilkeston	09.07.91	Notts County								
				Free	06.07.92	Shrewsbury Town	7+9	1+1	1	1	1			
						Telford United								
				Free	04.11.94	Hereford United	16+2			0+2	1			
Gary M Pick	5.8	11.8	09.07.71	Leicester		Leicester United								
					19.08.92	Stoke City								
				Free	16.01.92	Hereford United	23+6	3+1	1+1	3	2		1	
Andrew J Reece Div3'90	5.11	12.0	05.09.62	Shrewsbury Free		Walsall (A) Worcester City								
via Willenhall & Dudley Town to					11.08.87	Bristol Rovers	230+9	11+1	10+2	21	17		3	3
				Loan	20.11.92	Walsall	9			3	1			
				Loan	12.08.93	Walsall	6	2						
					05.11.93	Hereford United	63+2	3	4	5	5			2
Timothy W Steele	5.9	11.0	01.12.67	Coventry	07.12.85	Shrewsbury T (A)	41+20	3+1		1+1	5	1		
				£80,000	22.02.89	Wolverhampton W.	53+22	5	1	4	6	3		
				Loan	20.02.92	Stoke City	7			1				
				Free	16.07.93	Bradford City	2+3	2+1			1	1		
				Free	14.01.94	Hereford United	24+1	2	1	1				2
Gareth Stoker	5.9	10.10	22.02.73	Bishop Auckland		Leeds United (J)								
				Free	13.09.91	Hull City	24+6	3	2+1	0+2	2			
					16.03.95	Hereford United	10							
Richard J Wilkins Div3'91	6.0	11.6	28.05.65	Lambeth		Haverhill Rovers								
				Free	20.11.86	Colchester United	150+2	6	7+2	9+3	24		4	3
				£65,000	25.07.90	Cambridge United	79+2	6	8+1	9	7			
				Free	20.07.94	Hereford United	34+1	4	2	2	2			
F O R W A R D S														
Nicholas J R Cross AGT'93	5.9	11.2	07.02.61	Birmingham	12.02.79	West Brom.A. (A)	68+37	6+2	5	0+!	15	2	1	
				£48,000	15.08.85	Walsall	107+2	10	12+1	6+1	45	2	3	1
				£65,000	22.01.88	Leicester City	54+4	3+2	1	1	15	1		
				£125,000	28.06.89	Port Vale	120+24	2+4	12	12+1	40		1	2
				Free	13.07.94	Hereford United	24+4	4	2	2+1	6			1
Neil G F Lyne	6.1	12.2	04.04.70	Leicester		Leicester United								
					16.08.89	Nottingham Forest		0+1						
				Loan	22.03.90	Walsall	6+1							
				Loan	14.03.91	Shrewsbury Town	16				6			
					11.07.91	Shrewsbury Town	61+3	6	3	3	11	2	2	
				£75,000	15.01.93	Cambridge United	5+12							
Loan Chesterfield, (24.04.93) 3Lg + 1Gl				Loan	24.03.94	Chesterfield	2+1							
				Free	27.07.94	Hereford United	27+4		2	4	1			1
Stephen J White Div.2'82.	5.10	11.4	02.01.59	Chipping Sodbury		Mangotsfield								
				Free	11.07.77	Bristol Rovers	46+4	2	3		20	1	3	
				£200,000	24.12.79	Luton Town	63+9	3+1	2+1		25	1		
				£150,000	30.07.82	Charlton Athletic	29	2			12			
				Loan	28.01.83	Lincoln City	2+1							
				Loan	24.02.83	Luton Town	4							
				£45,000	26.08.83	Bristol Rovers	89+12	8	7+1	5+2	24	2	2	1
				Free	08.07.86	Swindon Town	200+44	21+8	9+2	22+6	83	11	2	15
				Free	26.08.94	Hereford United	31+5	3	2	3+1	14	2	1	1

EDGAR STREET

Hereford HR4 9JU
Tel: 01432 276 666

Capacity..13,752
Covered Standing..10,855
Seating..2,897

First game..v Atherstone (2-3), 30.8.24.
First floodlit game ....v Merthyr (3-1), 14.3.53

ATTENDANCES
Highest ....18,114 v Sheffield Wednesday, FA Cup 3rd Round, 4.1.1958.
Lowest ....662 v Shrewsbury, AMC 1st Round, 22.12.1992.

OTHER GROUNDS..None.

MATCHDAY TICKET PRICES

Merton Stand (A/B) . . . . £8/£9
*Juv/OAP . . . . £5/£6

Len Weston Stand. . . . . £8/£9
*Juv/OAP . . . . £5/£6

Ground . . . . £6/£7
*Juv/OAP . . . . £3/£4

*Concessionary prices are only available to holders
of 'Bulls Membership' otherwise full prices apply.

Ticket Office Telephone no. . . . . . . 01432 276 666.

CLUBCALL
0898 55 58 08
Calls cost 39p per minute cheap rate and 49p per
minute at all other times.
Call costings correct at time of going to press.

HOW TO GET TO THE GROUND

From the North
Use A49 (sign posted Hereford) into Edgar Street for Hereford United FC.

From the East
Use A465 or A438 (sign posted Hereford) into town centre, then follow signs
Leominster A49 into Edgar Street for Hereford United FC.

From the South
Use A49 or A465 (sign posted Hereford) into town centre, then follow signs
Leominster A49 into Edgar Street for Hereford United FC.

From the West
Use A438 (sign posted Hereford) into town centre, then follow signs Leominster
A49 into Edgar Street for Hereford United FC.

Car Parking
Available near ground for 1,000 cars (approx)

Nearest Railway Station
Hereford (01432 266 534)

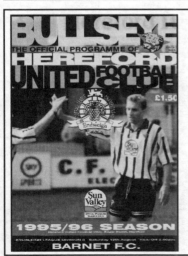

MATCHDAY PROGRAMME

Programme Editor . . . . Dave Bradley.

Number of pages . . . . 28.

Price . . . . £1.

Subscriptions . . . . £28 (All home programmes)

Local Newspapers. . . . . Herefordshire Times, Evening News.

Local Radio Stations. . . . . Radio Wyvern.

LEYTON ORIENT
(The O's)
ENDSLEIGH LEAGUE DIVISION 3
SPONSORED BY: H.E.A.T.

Back Row (L-R): Danny Chapman, Ian Hendon, Lee Shearer, Peter Caldwell, Colin West, Mark Warren, Kevin Austin.
Middle Row: Tommy Cunningham (Director of Coaching), Roger Stanislaus, Barry Lakin, Glen Wilkie, Darren Purse, Paul Hayne, Alex Inglethorpe, Voe Baker, Andy Taylor (Physio).
Front Row: Tony Flynn (Kit Manager/Asst. Physio), Lee Williams, Tony Kelly, Glenn Cockerill, Pat Holland (Manager), Barry Hearn (Chairman), Gary Bellamy, Shaun Brooks, Andy Gray, Steve Shorey (Youth Dev. Officer).

LEYTON ORIENT
FORMED IN 1881
TURNED PROFESSIONAL IN 1903
LTD COMPANY IN 1906

CHAIRMAN: Barry Hearn
VICE-CHAIRMAN
D L Weinrabe

DIRECTORS
A Pincus, H Linney, M Pears

SECRETARY
David Burton (0181 539 2223)
COMMERCIAL MANAGER
F Woolf

MANAGER: Pat Holland

DIRECTOR OF COACHING
Tommy Cunningham

PHYSIOTHERAPIST
Andy Taylor

STATISTICIAN FOR THE DIRECTORY
Don Hales

Orient's season started promisingly with a 2-1 home win over promotion favourites Birmingham City before what was to be their biggest home crowd of the season, 7,578. From then on however it was downhill all the way. The writing was on the wall when a few days later they lost 0-4 to a Third Division Barnet side whose squad included several players signed on free transfers from the Orient.

Only five more home League wins were recorded, whilst the run of away League games without a win - which began in October 1993 - continued unbroken throughout the season to reach a total of 39 matches.

Lack of goals was the team's main problem with only 30 being scored throughout the League campaign. The club gradually dropped down the table reaching 23rd position at the turn of the year and hitting the bottom spot in the penultimate game, when they lost to Chester City, the previous occupants of the position. As the season progressed the results got worse and worse with only one win in the last 19 League games and finishing with nine straight defeats without scoring in the last five.

Severe economic problems also dogged the club all season with chairman Tony Wood's coffee business being lost in the Rwanda civil war. For most of the season the club were barred from buying or loaning players due to the financial difficulties and at one stage Wood offered to sell the club - apparently losing £10,000 a week- to anyone for a fiver. The management team of John Sitton and Chris Turner, appointed in April 1994, were inexperienced and appeared to have difficulty in gaining the respect of the players. Public denouncements of players efforts, refusing them a half-time drink and suspending overweight players all told the same story and matters reached a head in February when long serving Terry Howard was apparently sacked at half-time against Blackpool for lack of effort, although he subsequently proved good enough for promotion contenders Wycombe Wanderers.

Barry Hearn took over control of the club from Wood in March and the following month he dismissed Sitton and Turner, putting Cockerill in charge as acting player-manager for one match before appointing Pat Holland as manager with two matches to go. Hearn had already decreed that he would not be a Blackburn style Jack Walker chairman and that the club would concentrate on developing local talent. To prove the point Darren Purse at 18-years-old was appointed team captain - the youngest in the Premier and Endsleigh Leagues - and fellow teenagers Wilkie, Perifimou, Rufus and Shearer were all given first team places at the end of the season.

Early exits from both the Coca-Cola and F.A.Cups did not help Orient's finances but the one highlight of the campaign occurred in the Autoglass Windscreen Cup where the O's reached the Southern Final. A narrow 1-0 away defeat to Birmingham City before 24,000 in the first leg gave hope that Wembley could be reached. However a 3-2 home defeat before 10,830 put an end to the dreams for another year. Soon after this disappointment Hendon and Bogie - two of the better performers - were sold for somewhat less than their real value to relieve the pressure on finances.

Now the club must pull themselves together as they face the future in the Third Division. At least they now have a chairman with a clear vision of the future and a definite strategy. The commitment to build by developing local talent is the stuff of dreams and could lead to exciting times ahead.

DON HALES.

LEYTON ORIENT

Division Two: 24th   **FA Cup:** 2nd Round   **Coca-Cola Cup:** 2nd Round   **Auto Windscreen Trophy:** Southern Final

M	DATE	COMP.	VEN	OPPONENTS	RESULT		H/T	LP	GOAL SCORERS/GOAL TIMES	ATT.
1	A 13	EL	H	Birmingham City	W	2-1	1-1		Purse 6, Bogie 66	7,578
2	16	CC 1/1	A	Barnet	L	0-4	0-0			(2,158)
3	20	EL	A	Bradford City	L	0-2	0-1	15		(7,473)
4	23	CC 1/2	H	Barnet	D	1-1	0-1		Cockerill 70	2,464
5	27	EL	H	Hull City	D	1-1	0-0	14	Gray 49	3,243
6	30	EL	A	Huddersfield Town	L	1-2	1-0	18	Purse 23	(8,552)
7	S 3	EL	A	Brighton & H.A.	L	0-1	0-0	19		(8,581)
8	10	EL	H	Cambridge United	D	1-1	0-0	19	West 66	3,699
9	13	EL	H	AFC Bournemouth	W	3-2	1-1	19	West 66 (pen), 86 (pen), Cockerill 44	2,536
10	17	EL	A	Shrewsbury Town	L	0-3	0-3	19		(3,560)
11	29	EL	A	Oxford United	L	2-3	0-0	19	Hague 81, Howard 85	(5,814)
12	27	AWT 1	A	Colchester United	L	0-1	0-0			(1,486)
13	O 1	EL	H	Plymouth Argyle	L	0-1	0-2	21		4,740
14	8	EL	A	Wycombe Wanderers	L	1-2	0-1	20	Gray 77,	(5,668)
15	15	EL	H	Chester City	W	2-0	1-0	20	Cockerill 13, West 86	3,309
16	18	AWT 1	H	Fulham	W	5-2	4-1		Purse 10, Dempsey 16, West 29 (pen), 33, 66	1,282
17	22	EL	A	Rotherham United	L	0-2	0-1	21		(2,700)
18	29	EL	H	Stockport County	L	0-1	0-0	21		3,267
19	N 1	EL	A	Cardiff City	W	2-0	0-0	20	Purse 51, West 89	2,558
20	5	EL	A	Blackpool	L	1-2	1-1	21	West 45	(4,653)
21	12	FAC 1	A	Tiverton Town	W	3-1	3-1		Gray 33, Carter 39, West 48	(3,000)
22	19	EL	A	York City	L	0-1	0-0	22		3,532
23	26	EL	A	Peterborough United	D	0-0	0-0	22		(5,114)
24	29	AWT 2	H	Fulham	W	1-0	1-0		West 12	1,757
25	D 3	FAC 2	H	Bristol Rovers	L	0-2	0-1			5,071
26	10	EL	H	Bradford City	D	0-0	0-0	22		2,553
27	17	EL	A	Birmingham City	L	0-2	0-1	22		20,022
28	26	EL	H	Brentford	L	0-3	0-3	22		(6,125)
29	27	EL	H	Swansea City	L	0-1	0-1	22		3,259
30	31	EL	A	Crewe Alexandra	L	0-3	0-0	22		(3,792)
31	J 7	EL	A	Rotherham Utd	D	0-0	0-0	23		2,797
32	10	AWT 3	H	Bristol Rovers	W	†0-0	0-0		(Won on penalties)	1,381
33	14	EL	A	Wrexham	L	1-4	0-1	23	Bogie 69 (pen)	(6,616)
34	28	EL	A	Stockport County	L	1-2	1-0	23	West 77	(4,250)
35	31	AWT S/F	H	Shrewsbury Town	W	2-1	1-0		Warren 18, Brooks 85	2,913
36	F 4	EL	H	Peterborough United	W	4-1	2-0	23	Warren 17, 36, 68, West 80	3,458
37	7	EL	A	Blackpool	L	0-1	0-1	23		3,301
38	18	EL	H	Wrexham	D	1-1	1-0	23	Cockerill 43	3,135
39	21	EL	A	York City	L	1-4	1-2	23	Cockerill 28	(2,926)
40	25	EL	A	Plymouth Argyle	L	0-1	0-0	23		(5,173)
41	28	AWT Fin	A	Birmingham City	L	0-1	0-1			(24,002)
42	M 4	EL	H	Oxford Utd	D	1-1	1-0	23	West 5	4,052
43	7	EL	A	Brighton & H. A.	L	0-3	0-1	23		2,983
44	11	EL	A	Hull City	L	0-2	1-0	23		(4,519)
45	14	AWT Fin	H	Birmingham City	L	2-3	0-1		Purse 60, McGleish 84	10,830
46	18	EL	H	Huddersfield Town	L	0-2	0-0	23		3,177
47	21	EL	A	Cambridge United	D	0-0	0-0	23		(3,048)
48	25	EL	H	Shrewsbury Town	W	2-1	1-1	23	Austin 20, Gray 76	2,724
49	A 1	EI	A	AFC Bournemouth	L	0-2	0-1	23		(4,118)
50	4	EL	A	Cardiff City	L	1-2	0-0	23	McGleish 65	(4,324)
51	8	EL	H	Crewe Alexandra	L	1-4	1-2	23	Austin 25	2,797
52	11	EL	H	Bristol Rovers	L	1-2	0-1	23	Dempsey 71	2,338
53	15	EL	A	Swansea City	L	0-2	0-2	23		(3,277)
54	17	EL	H	Brentford	L	0-2	0-1	23		4,459
55	22	EL	A	Bristol Rovers	L	0-1	0-0	23		(4,838)
56	29	EL	A	Chester City	L	0-1	0-0	24		(1,596)
57	M 6	EL	H	Wycombe Wanderers	L	0-1	0-0	24		4,698
58										
59										
60										

Best Home League Attendance: 7,578 v Birmingham City   **Smallest:** 2,338 v Bristol Rovers   **Av Home Att:** 3,487

Goal Scorers: **Compared with 1993-94:** -752

League (30): West 9, Cockerill 4, Gray 3, Purse 3, Warren 3, Austin 2, Bogie 2, Dempsey, Hague, Howard, McGleish
C/Cola Cup (1): Cockerill
FA Cup (3): Carter, Gray, West
AWS (10): West 4, Purse 2, Brooks, Dempsey, McGleish, Warren

1994-95

Heald	Warren	Austin	Purse	Hendon	Lakin	Barnett	Ryan	Bogie	West	Dempsey	Cockerill	Turner	Gray	Howard	Carter	Martin	Hague	Putney	Bellamy	Brooks	Wilkie	McGleish	Read	Barry	Perfirmou	Referee	
1	2	3	4	5	6	7•	8*	9	10	11	12	S	14													West T.	1
1	2	3	4	5	6	7•	S	9	10	11	8	S	14													Barber G.	2
1		3	4	5	12	7*	6	14	10	11	8	S		2	9•											Harrison P.	3
1		3	4	5	6•	7*		9	10	11	8	S	14	2	12											Pooley G.	4
1		3	4	5	12	S		6	10	11	8	S	9	2	7*											Bailey M.	5
1	14	3	4	2	12		6*	7•	10	11	8	S	9	5												Watson J.	6
1	2	3	4		6	14	7•		10	11	8	S	9*	5	12											Orr D.	7
1		3	4	2	6		7•		10	11	8	S	9*	5	14	12										Leech K.	8
1		3	4	2		14	7•		10	11	8	S	9*	5	6	12										Dunn S.	9
1		3	4*	2	7		14		10	11	8	S		5	6		9•	12								Lloyd J.	10
1		3	4	2	7•				10	11*	8	S	12	6	9		14	5								Hemley I.	11
1	2•	3	4		14				10		8	S	5	9	11*		6	7								Bailey M.	12
1		3	4		7	14		12	10	11•	8	S	9	2	6*		5									Butler A.	13
1	14	3	12		7			6	10	11	8	S	9•	2	5*				4							Harris R.	14
1	S	3	9*	5	7			6	10	11	8	S		2	12				4							D'Urso A.	15
1	14	3	9*	5	7			6	10	11	8			2•	12				4							Pierce M.	16
1	12	3	9	5	7			6	10	11		S		2	8*		S		4							Lomas E.	17
1		3	9*	5	7	12		6	10	11			S	2	8		S		4							Pooley G.	18
1		3	9	5	7	12		6	10	11		S		2	8*		S		4							Barber G.	19
1	2*	3	9•		7	12		6	10	11	8	S	14	5					4							Winter J.	20
1		3		2	14	7•		6	10	12	8	S	9*	5	11				4							Wilkes C.	21
1		3		2	14	7•		6	10	11	8	S	9	5					4	S						Holbrook J.	22
1		3		2	14	7*		6	10	11	8	S	9•	5					4	12						Lynch K.	23
1	14	3	9*	2				7	12	10•	8	S		5	11				4	6						Rejer P.	24
1		3	5		14	7*		6	10	11	8	S		2	9				4•	12						Poll G.	25
1		3	5		7*	12		6		11	8	S	14	2	9				4	10•						Pierce M.	26
1	14	5	2		8•	7*		11			12	S	3	9			4			10						Breen A.	27
	14		2		S			6		11	8	S	7	3	9•		5			4	10					Foakes P.	28
1	10		2		12			6		11	8	S	7*	3	9		5		4		S					Bailey M.	29
1	10	3	5		12			6		11	8	S	7*	2•	9				4		14					Lunt T.	30
1	9•	3	4		7*			6		11	8	S	14	2	12		5			10						Dunn S.	31
1	9*	3	4	8	12			6		11		S		2	7		5			10	S					Pierce M.	32
1	9*	3	4	8				6	12	11		S		2	7		5			10	S					Richards P.	33
1	S	5	2					12	10	11	8	S	9	3	7				4	6						Heilbron T.	34
1	10	5	2	S				9*		11	8	S	12	3	7				4	6						Pooley G.	35
1	10	5	2	6*				9	12	11	8	S	S	3	7				4							West T.	36
1	10	5	2	6				9	12	11	8	S		3*	7				4	S						Butler A.	37
1	9•	3	5	2		14		6		11	8	S			7				4	S						Wilkes C.	38
1	9	3	5	2	S			6	10	11	8	S			7	S			4							Dawson A.	39
1	9	3	5	2	S			6	10	11	8	S			7	S			4							Singh G.	40
1	12	3	5	2	9*			6	10	11	8	S			7	S			4							Kirkby	41
1	S	3	5	2				6	10•	11	8	S	14		7				4			9				Foakes P.	42
1	10	3	5	2	7•			6	S	11	8	S							4		14	9				D'Urso A.	43
S	12	3	5	2				6	10	11	8	1					S		4		7*	9				Parker E.	44
1	12	3	5	2				6	10*	11	8	S					14		4		7	9•				Wilkes C.	45
1	9	3		2	7			6	10	11	8	S			5		S		4	S						Alcock P.	46
1	9•		2		12			6	10	11	8	S	14		5				4		7*			3		Rejer P.	47
1	9*	3	4		14				10•	11	8	S	12		5					6	7		2	3		Pierce M.	48
1	9	3	4	8						11*	S	S			5					7	6	12	10	2		Cooper K.	49
1	9	3	4	8						14	S	S			5					7	6	10*	9	2	11•	Holbrook J.	50
1	10*	3	4	S						11	8	S	12		5					7	6		9	2		Butler A.	51
1	10	3	4	8*						11		S	14		5		2				9•	12	7			Cooper K.	52
1	11	3		8						11	S	S			5				4		2	9	7			Rejer P.	53
1	10	3		7						11	S	S	8						4		2	9			S	Vanes R.	54
1	S	S	11		7					8		S			10	3			4	2		7				Wright P.	55
1	2	3	9		7										11*	5		6	4	8		10				Lynch K.	56
1	2	3	9		7										5			6	4	8*					12	Bailey M.	57
45	24	39	37	29	16	16	6	28	27	43	32	1	13	27	25	1	7	1	32	9	10	4	11	5	3	League Appearances	
	3	1	1		5	12	1	3	3		1		12	4		1		1		1	2		1	1	1	League Sub Appearances	
2	1	2	2	2		2		2	2	2	2		0+2	1	0+1											C/Cola Cup Appearances	
2		2	1	1	0+2	2		2	2	1+1	2		1	2	2				2	0+1						FA Cup Appearances	
7	3+4	6	7	6	1+1	2+2		5+1	5	5	6		0+1	5	5+1		2+1		5	3		1	1			AW Trophy Appearances	

Also Played: Rufus 12(50,56),6(52,53,54,55)11(57), Shearer S(53,56),5(54),10(57), Sopp - Non-playing GK (55,56,57), Bird - Non-playing Sub (57)   † = Sent Off
Players on Loan: Martin (Southend) McGleish (Charlton Athletic), Read (Arsenal)

CLUB RECORDS

BIGGEST VICTORIES
League: 9-2 v Aldershot, Division 3(S), 10.2.1934.
8-0 v Crystal Palace, Division 3, 12.11.1955.
8-0 v Rochdale, Division 4, 20.10.1987.
8-0 v Colchester United, Division 4, 15.10.1988.
League Cup: 9-2 v Chester, 3rd Round, 15.10.1962.

BIGGEST DEFEATS
League: 1-7 v Torquay United (A) Division 3(S), 16.4.1949.
1-7 v Stoke City (a), Division 2, 7.9.1956, also 0-6 on seven occasions.
F.A. Cup: 0-8 v Aston Villa, 4th Round, 30.1.1929.

MOST POINTS
3 points a win: 75, Division 4, 1988-89.
2 points a win: 66, Division 3, 1955-56.

MOST GOALS SCORED
106, Division 3(S), 1955-56.

RECORD TRANSFER FEE RECEIVED
£600,000 from Notts County for John Chiedozie, August 1981.

RECORD TRANSFER FEE PAID
£175,000 to Wigan Athletic for Paul Beesley, October 1989.

BEST PERFORMANCES
League: 22nd Division 1, 1962-63.
F.A. Cup: Semi-final 1977-78.
League Cup: 5th Round 1963.

HONOURS
Champions of Division 3(S), 1955-56.
Champions of Division 3, 1969-70.

LEAGUE CAREER
Elected to Div 2 1905, Div 3(S) 1928-29, Div 2 1955-56, Div 1961-62, Div 2 1962-63, Div 3 1965-66, Div 2 1969-70, Div 3 1981-82, Div 4 1984-85, Div 3 (now Div 2) 1988-89.

INDIVIDUAL CLUB RECORDS

MOST GOALS IN A SEASON
Tom Johnston: 36 goals in 1957-58 (League 35, FA Cup 1).

MOST GOALS IN A MATCH
5. R Heckman v Lovells Athletic (h), 7-1, 1st Round, 19.8.1955.

OLDEST PLAYER
John Rutherford, 42 years v Portsmouth (h) Division 2, 2.4.1927.

YOUNGEST PLAYER
Chris Bart-Williams, 16 years 232 days v Tranmere Rovers (h), Division 3, 2.2.1991.

MOST CAPPED PLAYER
John Chiedozie (Nigeria) 8.
J Townrow & O Williams (England) 2.

PREVIOUS MANAGERS

S Ormerod 1905-07; W Holmes 1907-22; P Proudfoot 1923-28; A Grimsdell 1929-30; P Proudfoot 1930-31; J Seed 1931-33; D Pratt 1933-35; P Proudfoot 1935-39; W Wright 1939-40; W Hall 1945; W Wright 1945-46; C Hewitt 1946-48; N McBain 1948-49; A Stock 1949-56; L Gore (caretaker) 1956; A Stock 1956-57; L Gore (caretaker) 1957-58; A Stock 1958-59; J Carey 1961-63; L Gore (caretaker) 1963; B Fenton 1963-64; L Gore (caretaker) 1964-65; D Sexton 1965; L Gore (caretaker) 1965-66; R Graham 1966-68; J Bloomfield 1968-71; G Petchey 1971; J Bloomfield 1971-81; P Went 1981; K Knighton 1981-83; Frank Clark 1983-91; Peter Eustace 1991-94; John Sitton & Chris Turner 1994

ADDITIONAL INFORMATION
Previous Names: 1881-86 Glyn Cricket & Football Club, 1886-88 Eagle FC, 1888-98 Orient FC, 1898-1946 Clapton Orient, 1946-67 Leyton Orient, 1967-87 Orient, 1987 Leyton Orient.
Previous Leagues: None.

Club colours: Red with white shirts, white shorts, red socks.
Change colours: Yellow with blue shirts, blue shorts, yellow socks.
Reserves League: Capital League. **Youth League:** S.E. Counties.

LONGEST LEAGUE RUNS

of undefeated matches:	14 (1954-55)	of league matches w/out a win:	23 (1962-63)
of undefeated home matches:	25 (1913-14)	of undefeated away matches:	9 (1954-55)
without home win:	14 (1962-63)	without an away win:	34 (1938-47)
of league wins:	10 (1956)	of home wins:	12 (1954)
of league defeats:	8 (1927-28)	of away wins:	6 (1956)

THE MANAGER

PAT HOLLAND . . . . appointed April 1995.

PREVIOUS CLUBS
As Manager . . . . None.
As Asst.Man/Coach . . . . Leyton Orient.
As a player . . . . West Ham, Bournemouth (Loan).

HONOURS
As a Manager . . . . None.
As a Player . . . . FA Cup winner 1975. ECEC runners-up 1976.

LEYTON ORIENT

PLAYERS NAME / Honours	Ht	Wt	Birthdate	Birthplace / Transfers	Contract Date	Clubs	League	L/Cup	FA Cup	Other	Lge	L/C	FAC	Oth
G O A L K E E P E R S														
Peter Caldwell	6.1	12.3	05.06.72	Dorchester	09.03.90	Q.P.R. (T)								
				Free	08.95	Leyton Orient								
D E F E N D E R S														
Kevin Austin	5.9	10.12	12.02.73	London		Saffron Walden								
				£1,000	19.08.93	Leyton Orient	69	2	5	6	2			
Gary Bellamy	6.2	11.5	04.07.62	Worksop	25.06.80	Chesterfield (A)	181+3	12	7	4	7		1	1
Div4'85'88; Div3'89; SVT'88; WFAC'92 Honours				£17,000	21.07.87	Wolverhampton W.	133+3	9	3	16	9			
Loan Cardiff City (18.03.92), 9 Lg Apps.				£30,000	10.09.92	Leyton Orient	97+3	1	6	12	5			
Andrew Gray	5.6	10.10	25.10.73	Southampton	03.07.92	Reading(T)	8+9	0+1		1+1	3	1		
				Loan	08.10.93	Woking		1						
				Free	20.07.94	Leyton Orient	13+12	0+2	1	0+1	3		1	
Paul Hague	6.2	13.3	16.09.72	Shortley Bridge	13.05.91	Gillingham (T)	8+1			4				
				Loan	13.01.94	Sittingbourne								
					09.09.94	Leyton Orient	17+1			2+1	1			
Ian M Hendon	6.0	12.0	05.12.71	Ilford	20.12.89	Tottenham H. (T)	0+4	1		0+2				
E: Y19, u21.7; FAYC'90; CS'91				Loan	16.01.92	Portsmouth	1+3							
				Loan	26.03.92	Leyton Orient	5+1							
Loan Barnsley (17.3.93), 6Lg Apps.				£50,000	09.08.93	Leyton Orient	64+1	4	4	9	2			
				Loan	23.03.95	Birmingham City	4							
Darren J Purse	6.0	12.4	14.02.77	London	22.02.94	Leyton Orient (T)	76+5	4	2	14	6			4
Roger Stanislaus	5.9	12.6	02.11.68	Hammersmith	31.07.86	Arsenal (A)								
				Free	18.09.87	Brentford	109+2	8	7	9	4	1		
				£90,000	30.07.90	Bury	167+9	9	10	21	5	1	1	
				Free	08.95	Leyton Orient								
Glen Wilkie	5.10	12.4	22.01.77	Stepney	17.03.95	Leyton Orient (T)	10+1							
M I D F I E L D														
Joseph P J Baker			19.04.77	London		Charlton Athletic								
				Free	08.95	Leyton Orient								
Shaun Brooks	5.7	11.0	09.10.62	London	16.10.79	Crystal Palace (A)	47+7	5+1	5		4	1		
				Free	17.10.83	Leyton Orient	140+8	10	12	7+3	26	1	4	1
				£20,000	22.06.87	Bournemouth	114+14	12	4+1	3	13		1	
						Dorchester Town								
				Free	06.10.94	Leyton Orient	1							
				Free	18.11.94	Leyton Orient	8+1		0+1	3				1
Danny Chapman	5.11	13.6	21.11.74	Deptford	18.03.93	Millwall	4+8	0+1						
				Free	08.95	Leyton Orient								
Glen Cockerill	6.0	12.4	25.08.55	Grimsby		Louth United								
				Free	01.11.76	Lincoln City	65+6	2	2		10			
				£11,000	06.12.79	Swindon Town	23+3	3			1			
				£40,000	12.08.81	Lincoln City	114+1	167	1	25	1			
				£125,000	23.03.84	Sheffield United	62	6	1		10	1		
				£225,000	17.10.85	Southampton	272+15	35+2	20+2	12	32	5	2	
				Free	10.12.93	Leyton Orient	51+1	2	2	9	6	1		
F O R W A R D S														
Alex M Inglethorpe	5.11	11.0	14.11.71	Epsom	01.07.90	Watford (J)	2+10	1+2		1+1	2			1
					18.05.95	Leyton Orient								
Tony Kelly	5.9	10.12	14.02.66	Meridan		Bristol City (A)	2+4				1			
via Dulwich H., Cheshunt, Enfield & St.Albans				£20,000	29.01.90	Stoke City	33+25	5+4		3+3	5	3		
				Loan	30.01.92	Hull City	6				1			
				Loan	30.10.92	Cardiff City	5				1			
				£10,000	17.09.93	Bury	53+4	0+1	1+1	8	10			3
				£30,000	08.95	Leyton Orient								
Barry Lakin	5.9	12.6	19.09.73	Dartford	06.07.92	Leyton Orient (T)	36+10	4	2+2	1+1	2		1	
				Loan	04.02.94	Woking								
Mark W Warren	5.9	10.5	12.11.74	Clapton	06.07.92	LeytonOrient(T)	43+9	1	1	6+4	3			1
E: Y2														
Colin West	6.1	13.2	13.11.62	Wallsend	09.07.80	Sunderland (A)	88+14	13+4	3+1		21	5	2	
				£115,000	28.03.85	Watford	45	2+1	8		20	3		
				£180,000	23.05.86	Glasgow Rangers	4+6	2	0+1	0+2	2	1		
				£150,000	07.09.87	Sheffield Wed.	40+5	6	6	3	8	3	1	1
				P.E.	24.02.89	West Bromwich A.	64+9	2	4	2	22		1	1
				Loan	01.11.91	Port Vale	5				1			
				Free	05.08.92	Swansea City	29+4	0+1	5	3+2	12		2	1
				Free	26.07.93	Leyton Orient	69+4	2	4	5	23		1	4

BRISBANE ROAD

Leyton, London E10 5NE
Tel: 0181 539 2223

Capacity..18,869
Seating..7,171

First game ....v Cardiff City, 28.8.1937.
First floodlit game ....v Brighton & Hove Albion, 10.9.1959.

ATTENDANCES
Highest ....34,345 v West Ham United, FA Cup 4th Round, 25.1.1964.
Lowest...749 v Brentford, AMC, 15.12.1986.

OTHER GROUNDS..None.

MATCHDAY TICKET PRICES

Main Centre £11
Juv/OAP £6

Main North (members) £9
Juv/OAP £4.50

Main South £9
Juv/OAP £4.50

Terraces. £7
Juv/OAP £3.50

Ticket Office Telephone no. 0181 539 2223

CLUBCALL
0891 12 11 50

Calls cost 39p per minute cheap rate and 49p per
minute at all other times.
Call costings correct at time of going to press.

HOW TO GET TO THE GROUND

From the North and West
Use A406 North Circular Road (sign posted Chelmsford) to Edmonton, then in
2.6 miles at roundabout take 3rd exit A112 (sign posted Leyton). Pass Leyton
Midland Road Station and in half-a-mile turn right into Windsor Road, then turn
left into Brisbane Road for Leyton Stadium.

From the East
Use A12 (sign posted London then City) to Leytonstone and follow signs
Hackney into Grove Road. At Leyton cross main road and forward into Ruckholt
Road, then turn right then left into Leyton High Road and in 0.2 miles turn left
into Buckingham Road then right into Brisbane Road for Leyton Orient FC.

Car Parking
Street parking around the ground.

Nearest Railway Station
Leyton Central.

Nearest Tube Station
Leyton (Central Line).

MATCHDAY PROGRAMME

Programme Editor . . . . Tim Reder.

Number of pages . . . . 42.

Price . . . . £1.50.

Subscriptions. . . . . Rates obtainable from the shop manager.

Local Newspapers . . . . Waltham Forest Guardian, Ilford Recorder,
. . . . Hackney Gazette, East London Advertiser, Stratford Express.

Local Radio Stations . . . . Radio Goodmayes,
. . . . Whipps Cross Hospital Radio.

LINCOLN CITY
(The Red Imps)
ENDSLEIGH LEAGUE DIVISION 3
SPONSORED BY: LINCOLNSHIRE ECHO

Back Row (L-R): Sam Ellis (Manager), Neil Davis, Phil Daley, Ben Dixon, Matt Carbon, Andy Leaning, David Johnson, Grant Brown, Alan Johnson, Paul Wanless, Frank LOrd (Asst. Manager).
Front Row: Joe Allon, Tony Daws, Udo Onwere, Steve Williams, Jason Minett, Colin Greenall, Dean West, David Puttman, Paul Mudd, Darren Huckerby.

LINCOLN CITY
FORMED IN 1884
TURNED PROFESSIONAL IN 1885
LTD COMPANY IN 1895

PRESIDENT: H Dove
CHAIRMAN: K J Reames
VICE-CHAIRMAN
G R Davey
DIRECTORS
H C Sills, J Hicks
SECRETARY
Phil Hough
COMMERCIAL MANAGER
David Teague

MANAGER: Sam Ellis

YOUTH TEAM MANAGER
Mark Smith

STATISTICIAN FOR THE DIRECTORY
Ian Nannestad

The return of former Lincoln hero Sam Ellis as Manager promised great things, but although there were many clear improvements in the teamís performances they failed to achieve a top ten position at any point in the campaign. The final position of 12th was a vast improvement on the 18th place gained in 1993/94, but the Imps were well adrift of a play-off spot.

Ellisís main achievement was to produce a team which was very difficult to beat. Visitors to Sincil Bank had to really graft to come away with even one point - something which has not been the case for many seasons. Away from home the side did not fare as well as they have in recent campaigns and often seemed to be short of fire power up front. There were, however, signs that this had been corrected towards the end of the season with three victories coming from the final five away trips. Overall, the team generally kept its shape even when under pressure and showed grit and determination throughout, even if the tactics employed may not always have been adventurous. The development of the clubís promising youngsters continued and positional changes for both Matt Carbon (to striker) and Ben Dixon (to full back) proved inspirational moves.

Notable League performances included both home and away encounters with champions Carlisle United, but the seasonís high points came in the cup competitions. Premiership Crystal Palace were defeated 1-0 in the first leg of the Coca-cola Cup tie and the team performed heroics in the second leg at Selhurst Park only to concede a controversial equalizer well into injury time and eventually go out to two extra time goals. Fine displays in the FA Cup saw the Imps eliminate Second Division Hull City and Huddersfield Town to reach the third round for the first time since 1976/77. Drawn at Crystal Palace again the team were well beaten in the Sunday lunchtime encounter.

Off the field the ten year re-development of Sincil Bank was completed with the opening of the Linpave Stand. raising the ground capacity back up to around 11,000 with over 9,000 seats. The ënewí stadium is certainly impressive and it is to be hoped that the playing performances will soon begin to match the surroundings.

IAN NANNESTAD.

LINCOLN CITY

Division Three: 12th   **FA Cup:** 3rd Round   **Coca-Cola Cup:** 2nd Round   **Auto Windscreen Trophy:** Group Rounds

M	DATE	COMP.	VEN	OPPONENTS	RESULT	H/T	LP	GOAL SCORERS/GOAL TIMES	ATT.
1	A 13	EL	H	Exeter City	W 2-0	2-0	2	Daws 31, Johnson 40 (pen)	3,439
2	16	CC 1/1	H	Chester City	W 2-0	1-0		Carbon 26, Schofield 64	2,531
3	20	EL	A	Walsall	L 1-2	0-1	11	60	(3,813)
4	22	CC 1/2	A	Chester City	W 3-2	3-0		Schofield 1, West 17, Johnson 34 (pen)	(1,568)
5	27	EL	H	Torquay United	L 1-2	1-1	15		3,154
6	30	EL	A	Rochdale	L 0-1	0-0			(1,974)
7	S 3	EL	A	Preston North End	L 0-4	0-0	19		(8,837)
8	10	EL	H	Mansfield Town	W 3-2	1-1	14	Daley 39, West 66, Puttman 87	2,575
9	13	EL	H	Wigan Athletic	W 1-0	0-0		Schofield 68	2,030
10	17	EL	A	Exeter City	L 0-1	0-1	13		(2,180)
11	20	CC 2/1	H	Crystal Palace	W 1-0	0-0		Johnson 61	4,310
12	24	EL	A	Hartlepool United	W 3-0	3-0	13	West 4, Greenall 26, Puttman 45	(1,419)
13	O 1	EL	H	Northampton Town	D 2-2	1-2	13	Brown 12, Puttman 66	3,248
14	4	CC 2/3	A	Crystal Palace	L 0-3	0-3			(6,870)
15	8	EL	H	Carlisle United	D 1-1	0-0	12	Bannister 74	3,097
16	15	EL	A	Bury	L 0-2	0-2	15		(3,139)
17	17	AWT 1	A	Doncaster Rovers	L 0-1	0-1			(1,480)
18	22	EL	H	Scarborough	W 2-0	1-0	13	Bannister 45 (pen), Daley 83	2,396
19	29	EL	A	Hereford United	W 3-0	1-0	11	Matthews 9, Daley 48, Puttman 57	(2,485)
20	N 5	EL	A	Barnet	L 1-2	1-1	11	Matthews 22	2,741
21	8	AWT 1	H	Hull City	W 1-0	0-0		West 73	1,626
22	12	FAC1	A	Hull City	W 1-0	0-0		Bannister 53	(5,758)
23	19	EL	A	Fulham	D 1-1	0-1	12	Bannister 59 (pen)	(3,955)
24	26	EL	H	Gillingham	D 1-1	0-0	10	West 82	2,919
25	D 3	FAC 2	H	Huddersfield Town	W 1-0	0-0		Johnson 57	4,143
26	10	EL	H	Walsall	D 1-1	1-1	11	Brown 41	2,717
27	17	EL	A	Torquay United	L 1-2	0-1	13	Daws 59	(2,004)
28	26	EL	A	Scunthorpe United	L 0-2	0-0			(4,785)
29	27	EL	H	Darlington	W 3-1	1-1		Johnson 33, Carbon 62, 84	2,964
30	31	EL	A	Chesterfield	L 0-1	0-0			(3,325)
31	J 8	FAC 3	A	Crystal Palace	L 1-5	0-3		Greenall 66	(6,541)
32	14	EL	H	Doncaster Rovers	W 1-0	0-0	15	Daws 52 (pen)	2,771
33	28	EL	H	Hereford United	W 2-0	0-0	13	Hill 50, Carbon 53	2,545
34	F 4	EL	A	Gillingham	D 0-0	0-0	15		(4,196)
35	7	EL	A	Scarborough	D 1-1	1-0	14	Daws 40	(1,217)
36	18	EL	A	Doncaster Rovers	L 0-3	0-1	14		(2,291)
37	21	EL	H	Colchester United	W 2-0	0-0		Bannister 79, Johnson 88	1,969
38	25	EL	A	Northampton Town	L 1-3	0-1	12	Greenall 82	(4,821)
39	M 4	EL	H	Hartlepool United	W 3-0	0-0	12	Bannister 68, Carbon 70, Daws 80 (pen)	6,477
40	11	EL	A	Mansfield Town	L 2-6	0-1	13	Daws 64, Brown 90	(3,396)
41	18	EL	H	Rochdale	D 2-2	2-0	13	West 10, Johnson 44	2,939
42	25	EL	H	Preston North End	D 1-1	1-0		West 24	5,487
43	A 1	EL	A	Wigan Athletic	W 1-0	1-0	13	Hill 12	(1,696)
44	4	EL	A	Barnet	L 1-2	1-1		Carbon 2	(1,616)
45	8	EL	H	Chesterfield	L 0-1	0-1	14		5,141
46	11	EL	H	Fulham	W 2-0	1-0		Carbon 41, Hill 51	2,932
47	15	EL	A	Darlington	D 0-0	0-0	13		(1,644)
48	17	EL	H	Scunthorpe United	D 3-3	2-2		Carbon 19, Greenall 22, Williams 66	3,330
49	22	EL	A	Colchester United	W 2-1	1-1	12	Bannister 22, Huckerry 72	(2,654)
50	29	EL	H	Bury	L 0-3	0-2	12		3,928
51	M 6	EL	A	Carlisle United	W 3-1	1-0	12	Bannister 35, Huckerry 84, Daws 89	(12,412)
52									
53									
54									
55									
56									
57									
58									
59									
60									

Best Home League Attendance: 6,477 v Hartlepool United   **Smallest:** 1,969 v Colchester United   **Av Home Att:** 3,276

Goal Scorers: **Compared with 1993-94:** + 98

League (54): Daws 7, Carbon 7, Bannister 7, West 5, Puttman 4, Daley 3, Greenall 3, Brown 3, Hill 3, Matthews 2, Huckerry 2, Schofield 1, Williams 1

C/Cola Cup (6): Schofield 2, Johnson 2, Carbon 1, West 1

FA Cup (2): Johnson, Greenall

Auto Windscreen (1): Bannister

Hoult	Schofield	Platnauer	Hebberd	Greenall	Brown	West	Onwere	Daley	Daws	Johnson D.	Johnson A.	Matthews	Leaning	Carbon	Parkinson	Putman	Book	Smith	Foley	Bannister	Lucas	Hill	Dixon	De Garis	Dixon	Referee	
1	2	3*	4	5	6	7	8†	9	10•	11	12	14	S													A. Butler	1
	2	3	4	5	6	7	8	9		11	S	S	1	10												J. Rushton	2
1	2	3	6	4	5	7		10		9	11	12	S	8*	S											E. Lomas	3
	2	3	4	5	6	7		9		11	8		1	10*	S	12	S									T. West	4
1	2	3	4	5	6	7		9		11	8		S	10	S			S								P. Rejer	5
1	2	3	14	5	6	7	4	9	12•	11	8		S	10*												J. Holbrook	6
1	2	3	12	5	6	7	4*	9		11	8		S	10•		14										G. Singh	7
1	2	3	S	5	6	7	S	9		11	8		S	10					4							J. Kirkby	8
1	2	3	12	5	6	7	S	9		11*	8		S	10					4							M. Riley	9
1	2	3	S	5	6	7		9*		11	8		S	10					4	12						P. Vanes	10
	2	3	S	5	6	7	8			11	S		1	10	S				4	9						W. Burns	11
1	2	3	S	5	6	7	8				S	S		11		10			4	9						E. Wolstenholme	12
1	2	3	12	5	6	7	8	14					S	11•		10			4*	9						U. Rennie	13
	2	3	4*	5	6	7	8	14		11			1	10•	S	12				9						G. Willard	14
1	2	3*	4	5	6	7	8	9		11			S	12				S		10						A. D'Urso	15
1	2		14	4	3	6	7	11•					S	9		12			8*	10	5					T. West	16
																											17
1	S		7	5	6		2	9				3	S	11*		12			4	10	8					S. Mathieson	18
1	S		4	5	6		2	9				3	8	S		11*				10	7	12				K. Cooper	19
1	S		4	5	6		2	9				3	8	S		12			10*	7		11				R. Furnandiz	20
																											21
			8	5	6		2	S		S	3	7	1	11				S	4	9		10				E. Lomas	22
			8	5	6		2	9*		S	3	7	1	12					4	10	11		S			R. Harris	23
			8*	5	6		2	9		14	12	3	7	1					4	10•	11		S			T. Heilbron	24
			8	5	6		2	9		12	10•	3	7	1		4†			S	14	11		S			J. Rushton	25
			8*	5	6		2	9		12	10•	3	7	1		4			14	11•			S		3	P. Richards	26
			4	5†	6		2	9	8	10		7*	1	12		14				11•			S		3	J. Holbrook	27
			8	5	6		2	9	10		3*	1	4	12				S	7	11			S			R. Poulain	28
			7	5	6		2	9	14	11	3	1	4	10•		12			8*				S			E. Wolstenholme	29
			8		6		2	12	14	10	3	1	4*	11		7			9•				S		5	W. Burns	30
			4	5	6		2	10	11	3	1	9	8*	S		7			S				S		12	P. Wright	31
			4		2		10	11	3	1	9	6	8	S		7			S				S		5	J. Kirkby	32
			4		6		2	10*	7	3	1	9	12	8		S			11				S		5	J. Winter	33
			4*	5	6		2	10	7	3	9	1	12	8					11				S		S	G. Barber	34
			S	5	6		2	10	7	3	9	1	4	8					11				S		S	A. Dawson	35
				5	6		2	10	7	3*	9•	1	8			4				11		S			12	P. Rejer	36
			10	5	6		2	7	3		1	8	4			12				11		S			S	M. Bailey	37
			8	5	6		2	7	3		1	9	4	10						11		S			S	K. Leach	38
			8*	5	6		2	12	7	S	1	9	4	10						11		S			3	T. Lunt	39
			S	5	6		2*	8	7	12	1	9	4	10						11		S			3	T. Heilbron	40
			S	5	6		2	8	7	12	1	9*	4	10						11		S			3	P. Foakes	41
				5	6		2	10	7*	12	1	9	S	4					8	11					3	R. Furnandiz	42
				5	6		2	10	7*	1*	9	12	4	8						11					3	T. West	43
				5	6		2	10•	7	1	14	4	8*	11								S			3	S. Dunn	44
				5	6		2	10	7	9	12	4*	8	11								S			3	E. Parker	45
				5	6		2	8	7	9	S	4	10	11								S			3	K. Breen	46
				5	6		2	8•	7*	9	4	10	11									S			3	W. Flood	47
				5	6•		2	8	12	9	4*	10	11									S			3	D. Allison	48
			4	S	5			8	7	9	S	10	11						S				S		3	M. Railey	49
			S	5	6		2	8	7	1	9	12	11												3	A. D'Urso	50
			4	5			2	8	7	1	9	6	11												3	G. Cain	51

15	12	13	25	39	39	36	13	20	26	25	24	23	21	32	0	17	0	17	16	29	4	26	0	0	17	League Appearances	
0	3	0	7	0	0	0	2	0	0	0	0	0	15	0	2	3	0	2	0	2	0	0	14	9	4	League Sub Appearances	
0	4	4	3+1	4	4	4	3	3	0	4	1+2	0+1	4	2	0+1	3	0+3	1	1	2	0	0	0	0	0	C/Cola Cup Appearances	
0	0	0	3	3	3	1	2	1+1	2	3	2	3	2	3	0	0	0+1	0	2	1+2	0	3	0+1	0+1	1	FA Cup Appearances	

Also Played: Williams 14(36,47,48),9*(37),4*(50), Sherwood S(42,50),12(43),1(44,45,46,47,48,49), Craven 9(44) Huckerry S(32,38,43,45,46),12(44,47),7(48),2(49)10(50,51)

611

CLUB RECORDS

BIGGEST VICTORIES
League: 11-1 v Crewe Alexandra, Division 3(N), 29.9.1951.
F.A. Cup: 13-0 v Peterborough (a), 1st Qualifying Round, 12.10.1895.
8-1 v Bromley, 2nd Round, 10.12.1938.
BIGGEST DEFEATS
League: 3-11 v Manchester City, Division 2, 23.3.1895.
0-8 v Notts County, Division 2, 23.1.1897.
0-8 v Preston North End, Division 2, 28.12.1901.
1-9 v Wigan Borough, Division 3(N), 3.3.1923.
0-8 v Stoke City, Division 2, 23.2.1957.
F.A. Cup: 0-5 v Grimsby Town, 4th Qualifying Round, 10.12.1892.
0-5 v Stoke City, 1st Round, 11.01.1907.
League Cup: 0-5 v Leicester City, 3rd Round, 05.10.1966.
Others: 2-7 v Doncaster Rovers, Division 3(N) Cup Round 1, 28.10.1937.

MOST POINTS: 3 points a win: 77, Division 3, 1981-82.
2 points a win: 74, Division 4, 1975-76.
MOST GOALS SCORED: 121, Division 3(N), 1951-52.
RECORD TRANSFER FEE RECEIVED
£250,000 from Blackburn Rovers for Matt Dickins, March 1992.
(+£150,000 installment)
RECORD TRANSFER FEE PAID
£60,000 to Southampton for Gordon Hobson, September 1988.
£60,000 to Sheffield United for Alan Roberts, October 1989.
£60,000 to Leicester City for Grant Brown, January 1990.
BEST PERFORMANCES
League: 5th Division 2, 1901-02.
F.A. Cup: Equivalent 5th Round 1886-87, 18889-90, 1901-02.
League Cup: 4th Round 1967-68.
HONOURS
Champions of Division 3(N), 1931-32, 1947-48, 1951-52.
Champions of Division 4, 1975-76. Champions of GMVC 1987-88.
LEAGUE CAREER: Original members of Div 2 1892, Not re-elected to Div 2 1908, re-elected Div 2 1909, Not re-elected 1911, Re-elected Div 2 1912, Not re-elected 1920, Re-elected Div 3(N) 1921, Div 2 1931-32, Div 3(N) 1933-34, Div 2 1947-48, Div 3(N) 1948-49, Div 2 1951-52, Div 3 1960-61, Div 4 1961-62, Div 3 1975-76, Div 4 1978-79, Div 3 1980-81, Div 4 1985-86, GMVC 1986-87, Div (now Div 3) 1987-88.

INDIVIDUAL CLUB RECORDS

MOST GOALS IN A SEASON
Allan Hall: 42 goals in 1931-32, Division 3(N).

MOST GOALS IN A MATCH
6. Andy Graver v Crewe Alexandra (h) 11-1, Division 3(N), 29.9.1951.
6. Frank Keetley v Halifax Town (h) 9-1, Division 3(N), 16.1.1932.

OLDEST PLAYER
John Burridge, 42 years 57 days v Rochdale, Division 3, 29.1.1994.

YOUNGEST PLAYER
Shane Nicholson, 16 years 112 days, League Cup v Charlton, 23.9.1986.

MOST CAPPED PLAYER
David Pugh (Wales) 3.
George Moulson (Eire) 3.

PREVIOUS MANAGERS

(since 1947)
Bill Anderson 1947-64; Con Moulson (coach) 1965; Roy Chapman (player/coach) 1965-66; Ron Gray 1966-70; Bert Loxley 1970-71; David Herd 1971-72; Graham Taylor 1972-77; George Kerr 1977; Willie Bell 1977-78; Colin Murphy 1978-85; John Pickering 1985; George Kerr 1985-87; Peter Daniel (caretaker) 1987; Colin Murphy 1987-90; Alan Clarke 1990; Steve Thompson 1990-93; Keith Alexander 1993-94.

ADDITIONAL INFORMATION
PREVIOUS NAMES
None.
PREVIOUS LEAGUES
None.
Club colours: red shirts, with two white stripes, black sleeves, black shorts with red trim, red socks with black & white trim.
Change colours: Green shirt with two purple stripes, black sleeves, black shorts with red trim, red socks with black & white trim.
Reserves League: Midland Senior League.
Youth League: (Juniors) Midland Purity Youth League.

LONGEST LEAGUE RUNS

of undefeated matches:	18 (1980)	of league matches w/out a win:	19 (1978)
of undefeated home matches:	35 (1975-76)	of undefeated away matches:	12 (1980)
without home win:	11 (1978-79)	without an away win:	35 (1896-98)
of league wins:	10 (1930)	of home wins:	14 (1982)
of league defeats:	12 (1896-97)	of away wins:	5 (1968, 1975, 1989, 1992)

THE MANAGER

SAM ELLIS . . . . appointed June 1994.

PREVIOUS CLUBS
As Manager . . . . Blackpool, Bury.
As Asst.Man/Coach . . . . Manchester City.
As a player . . . . Sheffield Wednesday, Mansfield, Lincoln City, Watford (coach).

HONOURS
As a Manager . . . . None.
As a Player . . . . Blackpool: Division 4 runners-up 1985.
International . . . . 3 U23 caps for England.

LINCOLN CITY

PLAYERS NAME Honours	Ht	Wt	Birthdate	Birthplace Transfers	Contract Date	Clubs	APPEARANCES League	L/Cup	FA Cup	Other	GOALS Lge	L/C	FAC	Oth
G O A L K E E P E R S														
Andrew J Leaning	6.0	13.0	18.05.63	Howden		Rowntree Mack.								
				Free	01.07.85	York City	69	4	8	5				
				Free	28.05.87	Sheffield United	21	2	2					
				£12,000	27.09.88	Bristol City	75	5	7	2				
				Free	24.03.94	Lincoln City	29	4	3	2				
D E F E N D E R S														
Grant A Brown	6.0	11.12	19.11.69	Sunderland	01.07.88	Leicester City (T)	14	2						
				£60,000	20.08.89	Lincoln City	220	13	9	13	11	1		1
Matthew P Carbon	6.2	12.4	08.06.75	Nottingham	13.04.93	Lincoln City (T)	40+3	3	3	2+2	7	1		
Colin A Greenall	5.11	11.10	30.12.63	Billinge	17.01.81	Blackpool (A)	179+4	12	9	2	9	2		
E: Y5				£40,000	10.09.88	Gillingham	62	3	6	9	5	1	1	2
				£285,000	15.02.88	Oxford United	67	4	1	2	2			
Loan Bury, 4.1.90, 3Lg + 1 Other App.				£125,000	16.07.90	Bury	66+2	3	2	8	5			1
				£50,000	27.03.92	Preston North End	29				1			
				Free	13.08.93	Chester City	42	2	4	4	1			1
				Free	27.07.94	Lincoln City	39	4	3	2	3		1	
Alan K Johnson	6.0	12.0	19.02.71	Wigan	01.04.89	Wigan Athletic (T)	163+17	7+2	14+2	14+3	13	1	1	3
					15.02.94	Lincoln City	40+1	2	3	2+1				1
M I D F I E L D														
Ben Dixon	6.1	11.0	16.09.74	Lincoln	04.11.92	Lincoln City (T)	23+8		0+1	1+2				
				Loan	28.10.93	Witton Albion								
Darren C Huckerby	5.11	10.8	23.04.76	Nottingham	14.07.94	Lincoln City (T)	4+8				3			
Jason Minett	5.9	10.4	12.08.71	Peterborough	04.07.89	Norwich City (T)	0+3							
				Loan	19.03.93	Exeter City	11+1			1				1
				Free	21.07.93	Exeter City	42+4	4	6	6	3			1
				Free	08.95	Lincoln City								
Paul Mudd	5.9	11.4	13.11.70	Hull	01.07.89	Hull City (T)	1							
E: SFA 19.2				£5,000	25.07.90	Scarborough	95+3	10	3	6	2			
				Free	26.07.93	Scunthorpe United	66+2	4	8	5	4			
				Free	08.95	Lincoln City								
Udo A Onwere	6.0	11.3	09.11.71	Hammersmith	11.07.90	Fulham (T)	66+19	4+2	1+1	9	7			
				Free	12.08.94	Lincoln City	7+1	3		1				
Paul Wanless	6.1	13.4	14.12.73	Banbury	03.12.91	Oxford United (T)	9+13	0+3		1+1		1		
				Free	08.95	Lincoln City								
Dean West	5.10	11.7	05.12.72	Morley	17.08.91	Lincoln City (T)	86+25	9	6	5+2	19	1	1	1
				Loan	27.08.93	Boston United								
F O R W A R D S														
Joe Allon	5.11	12.2	12.11.66	Gateshead	16.11.84	Newcastle Utd (T)	9	1			2			
E: Y.1. FAYC'85.				Free	06.08.87	Swansea City	27+7	2	2	2	12			1
				Free	29.11.88	Hartlepool United	112	5	6+1	7	51	2	5	2
				£250,000	14.08.91	Chelsea	3+11	0+2		1+1	2			1
				Loan	27.07.92	Port Vale	2+4							
				£275,000	19.11.92	Brentford	38+7	2	2	7	19		2	7
				Loan	16.09.93	Southend United	2+1							
					24.03.94	Port Vale	13+10	0+1	2		9		1	
				£42,500	08.95	Lincoln City								
Phillip Daley	6.2	12.9	12.04.67	Liverpool		Newtown								
					12.10.89	Wigan Athletic	152+9	9	11+1	16	39	1		6
				£40,000	01.08.94	Lincoln City	19+1	2+1	1	2+1	4			1
Anthony Daws	5.8	11.10	10.09.66	Sheffield	18.09.84	Notts County (A)	6+2				1			
E:Y1				Free	21.08.86	Sheffield United	7+4		1	0+1	3			
				Free	02.07.87	Scunthorpe United	166+17	15+1	9	23+1	63	4	2	3
				£50,000	25.03.93	Grimsby Town	14+2	2		1+1	1			1
				£50,000	15.02.94	Lincoln City	34+6		1	1	10			
David A Johnson	6.2	13.8	29.10.70	Dinnington	01.07.89	Sheffield Wed. (T)	5+1							
				Loan	31.10.91	Hartlepool United	7		2		2		1	
				Loan	20.11.92	Hartlepool Uinted	3			2				1
					20.08.93	Lincoln City	59+4	5+1	4	7	12	4	2	2
David P Puttnam	5.10	11.9	03.02.67	Leicester		Leicester United								
				£8,000	09.02.89	Leicester City	4+3	0+1						
				35,000	21.01.90	Lincoln City	156+16	12+1	4	8+1	20	1		
Steven R Williams	6.1	11.7	03.11.75	Sheffield	11.06.94	Lincoln City (T)	10+10		0+1	0+2	3			
ADDITIONAL CONTRACT PLAYER														
Neil Davis						Fleetwood								
				Free	08.95	Lincoln City								

SINCIL BANK

Lincoln LN5 8LD
Tel: 01522 522 224

Capacity 10,898

ATTENDANCES
Highest ....23,196 v Derby County, League Cup 4th Round, 15.11.1967.
Lowest ....1,003 v Scunthorpe, AMC, 25.11.1986.

OTHER GROUNDS...None.

MATCHDAY TICKET PRICES

St Andrews Stand Ticket Sales Tel: 01522 522224
Adult £8
Juv/OAP £6
Family 1+1..£10
1+2 - £13 ....1+3 - £16
Stacey West Stand (Covered seating or standing)
Adult £6
Juv/OAP £4.50
Family 1+1...£8
1+2 - £11.50 ....1+3 - £15
Linpave Stand £8
Juv/OAP £6
South Park Stand (Away - covered seating)
Adult £8
E.G.T. Family Stand
Family 1+1...£8
1+2 - £11.50 ....1+3 - £15

CLUBCALL 0891 66 46 66
Calls cost 39p per minute cheap rate and 49p per
minute at all other times.
Call costings correct at time of going to press.

HOW TO GET TO THE GROUND

From the North, East and West
Use A15, A57, A46 or A158 into Lincoln City centre then follow Newark (A46) in
High Street, left into Scorer Street and right into Cross Street for Lincoln City FC.

From South
Use A1 then A46 (sign posted Lincoln) then following signs city centre into High
Street and turn right into Scorer Street and right again into Cross Street for
Lincoln City FC.

Car Parking
Club Car Park 32, plus street parking available.

Nearest Railway Station
Lincoln Central (01522 39502).

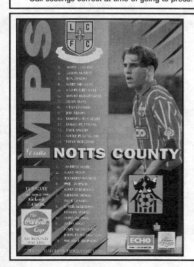

MATCHDAY PROGRAMME

Programme Editor .... David Teague.

Number of pages .... 32.

Price .... £1.30.

Subscriptions .... £36.

Local Newspapers .... Lincolnshire Echo, Adscene, Lincoln Standard.

Local Radio Stations .... BBC Radio Lincolnshire, Lincs FM.

MANSFIELD TOWN
(The Stags)
ENDSLEIGH LEAGUE DIVISION 3
SPONSORED BY: ABACUS - LIGHTING FOR SPORT

Back Row (L-R): Iffy Onoura, Matt Carmichael, Jason Trinder, Lee Howarth, Ian Bowling, Mark Gale, Mark Peters.
Middle Row: Paul Handford, John Dodlan, Chris Timmons, Scott Eustace, Ian Baraclough, Steve Slawson, Stewart Hadley, Kevin Lampkin.
Front Row: Keith Alexander (Asst. Manager), Bob Shaw (Chief Scout), Aidy Boothroyd, Steve Parkin, Andy King (Manager), Paul Sherlock, Simon Ireland, Barry Statham (Physio).

MANSFIELD TOWN
FORMED IN 1910
TURNED PROFESSIONAL IN 1910
LTD COMPANY IN 1921

CHAIRMAN: Keith Haslam
DIRECTORS
M Haslam, K Walker
SECRETARY
Michael Horton (01623 23567)
COMMERCIAL MANAGER
Lou Smith

MANAGER: Andy King
RESERVE/YOUTH TEAM MANAGER
Keith Alexander

PHYSIOTHERAPIST
Barry Statham

STATISTICIAN FOR THE DIRECTORY
Pete Stevenson

Although defeated by local neighbours Chesterfield in the play-offs, the club enjoyed a wonderful season. One hundred goals were scored in all competitions, Premier League Leeds United were beaten in the Second Round of the Coca-Cola Cup, the Third Round of the FA Cup was reached before being eliminated by Wolverhampton Wanderers and sixth position in Division Three was achieved.

The defeat of Leeds United was undoubtedly the high point of the first-half of the season because, although the first four games of the season were won, the next four were all lost and indeed the 'Stags' were lying in fourteenth position in early December. However, a remarkable spell of results either side of Christmas moved the club to within striking distance of the play-off qualification positions. During this period twenty-one goals were scored in just five matches. By mid March the club were safely ensconced in the top five and although only one league victory was obtained during the last nine matches the 'Stags' reached the play-offs.

The enthusiasm of manager Andy King certainly succeeded in bringing out the best of his players with Paul Holland (P.F.A. Division 3 team) and Steve Wilkinson (club Player of the Year) enjoying fine seasons.

Providing the club are able to resist transfer offers for their players a successful promotion attempt will be accomplished during season 1995-96.

PETE STEVENSON.

MANSFIELD TOWN

Division Three: 6th   **FA Cup:** 3rd Round   **Coca-Cola Cup:** 3rd Round   **Auto Windscreen Trophy:** 1st Round

M	DATE	COMP.	VEN	OPPONENTS	RESULT	H/T	LP	GOAL SCORERS/GOAL TIMES	ATT.
1	A 16	CC 1/1	A	Rochdale	W 2-1	0-1		Wilkinson 56, 87	(1,746)
2	20	EL	H	Colchester United	W 2-0	0-0	13	Holland 80, Hadley 90	2,247
3	23	CC 1/2	H	Rochdale	W 1-0	1-0		Wilkinson 32	2,234
4	27	EL	A	Chesterfield	W 1-0	0-0	8	Hadley 85	(4,210)
5	30	EL	H	Darlington	L 0-1	0-0			2,427
6	S 3	EL	H	Bury	L 0-2	0-1	15		2,576
7	10	EL	A	Lincoln City	L 2-3	1-1	15	Wilkinson 19, Noteman 72	(2,575)
8	13	EL	A	Carlisle United	L 1-2	0-1	15	Hadley 76	(6,245)
9	17	EL	H	Northampton Town	D 1-1	0-1	19	Holland 63	2,557
10	21	CC 2/1	A	Leeds United	W 1-0	1-0		Ireland 17	(7,884)
11	24	EL	H	Exeter City	D 1-1	0-0	18	Howarth 67	2,486
12	O 1	EL	A	Gillingham	W 2-0	1-0	15	Holland 19, Wilkinson 86	(2,555)
13	4	CC 2/2	H	Leeds United	D 0-0	0-0			7,227
14	8	EL	H	Hartlepool United	W 2-0	1-0	13	Holland 24, Wilkinson 60	2,545
15	11	EL	A	Northampton Town	W 1-0	1-0		Wilkinson 18	(4,993)
16	15	EL	A	Torquay United	L 1-2	1-1	10	Peters 36	(2,900)
17	18	AWT	A	Wrexham	L 0-2	0-1			(1,002)
18	22	EL	H	Doncaster Rovers	L 0-1	0-0	14		2,988
19	25	CC 3	H	Millwall	L 0-2	0-1			5,359
20	29	EL	A	Rochdale	D 3-3	2-1	12	Hadley 31, Noteman 44 (pen), Wilkinson 51	(1,968)
21	N 5	EL	H	Preston North End	L 1-2	1-2	14	Hadley 39	2,602
22	8	AWT	H	Crewe Alexandra	D 2-2	0-1		Alexander 66, 78	1,250
23	19	EL	A	Scunthorpe United	W 4-3	0-1	11	Holland 63, Hadley 66, Noteman 74, Peters 77	(2,975)
24	22	FAC 1	H	Northwich Victoria	W 3-1	1-1		Hadley 16, Holland 69, 83	2,999
25	26	EL	H	Walsall	L 1-3	0-1	13	Wilkinson 51	2,733
26	D 3	FAC 2	A	Halifax Town	D 0-0	0-0			(2,396)
27	10	EL	A	Colchester United	D 1-1	0-1	14	Wilkinson 48	(3,016)
28	13	FAC 2R	H	Halifax Town	W 2-1	0-1		Aspinall 71, Holland 89	2,648
29	18	EL	H	Chesterfield	W 4-2	2-0		Campell 2, Wilkinson 25, 79, 82	3,519
30	26	EL	H	Hereford United	W 7-1	1-0		Donaldson 23, 51, Baraclough 47, Hadley 48, Howarth 53, Ireland 66, Wilkinson 89	2,887
31	27	EL	A	Scarborough	W 5-2	2-1		Donaldson 1, 76, Baraclough 6, Wilkinson 48, Noteman 87	(1,926)
32	31	EL	H	Barnet	W 3-0	1-0		Donaldson 31, 77, Ireland 47	2,891
33	J 2	EL	A	Fulham	L 2-4	1-1		Baraclough 3, Hadley 53	(4,006)
34	7	FAC 3	H	Wolverhampton Wand.	L 2-3	2-0		Donaldson 7, Ireland 10	6,701
35	10	EL	A	Doncaster Rovers	W 2-0	0-0		Hadley 73,80	(2,577)
36	14	EL	H	Wigan Athletic	W 4-3	1-0	5	Holland 8, Peters 60, Wilkinson 72, Doolan 90	2,618
37	21	EL	A	Preston North End	L 1-2	1-1	5	Lampkin 5	(8,448)
38	F 4	EL	A	Walsall	L 0-1	0-0	8		(4,369)
39	18	EL	A	Wigan Athletic	W 4-0	2-0	7	Holland 17, 52, Hadley 27, 74	(1,884)
40	21	EL	H	Scunthorpe United	W 1-0	0-0		Wilkinson 48	3,079
41	25	EL	H	Gillingham	W 4-0	1-0	3	Holland 12, Ireland 58, Parkin 77, Wilkinson 89	3,182
42	M 4	EL	A	Exeter City	W 3-2	1-1	4	Wilkinson 3, 49, Onoura 89	(2,458)
43	7	EL	H	Rochdale	D 1-1	0-1		Wilkinson 80	2,931
44	11	EL	H	Lincoln City	W 6-2	1-0	3	Noteman 6, 89 (pen), Hadley 75, Onoura 78, 83, 85	3,396
45	18	EL	A	Darlington	D 0-0	0-0	4		(1,613)
46	25	EL	A	Bury	D 2-2	0-1	5	Onoura 68, Wilkinson 77	(4,188)
47	A 1	EL	H	Carlisle United	L 1-2	1-1	5	Lampkin 33	5,197
48	8	EL	H	Barnet	D 2-2	1-1	5	Wilkinson 44, Phillips 73 (og)	(2,115)
49	15	EL	H	Scarborough	W 3-2	2-2	5	Ireland 19, Wilkinson 42, Hadley 81	2,931
50	17	EL	A	Hereford United	D 0-0	0-0			(2,743)
51	22	EL	H	Fulham	D 1-1	1-0	5	Peters 23	2,861
52	29	EL	H	Torquay United	D 2-2	1-1	6	Onoura 34, Wilkinson 48	3,216
53	M 6	EL	A	Hartlepool United	L 2-3	0-1	6	Ireland 60, Onoura 71	(3,049)
54	14	PO S/F1	H	Chesterfield	D 1-1	0-0		Hadley 72	6,582
55	17	PO S/F2	A	Chesterfield	L 2-5	2-1		Holland 3, Wilkinson 32	(8,165)
56									
57									
58									
59									
60									

Best Home League Attendance: 5,197 v Carlisle United   **Smallest:** 2,247 v Colchester United   **Av Home Att:** 2,946

Goal Scorers:

Compared with 1993-94: +228

League (84): Wilkinson 22, Hadley 14, Holland 9, Onoura 7, Donaldson 6, Noteman 6 (2 pens), Ireland 5, Peters 4, Baraclough 3, Howarth 2, Lampkin 2, Campbell, Doolan, Parkin, Opponent

C/Cola Cup (4): Wilkinson 3, Ireland

FA Cup (7): Holland 3, Aspinall, Donaldson, Hadley, Ireland

AW Trophy (2): Alexander 2

Play-Offs (3): Hadley, Holland, Wilkinson

616

Ward	Boothroyd	Baraclough	Holland	Howarth	Aspinall	Ireland	Parkin	Wilkinson	Hadley	Noteman	Castledine	Timons	Pearcey	Alexander	Doolan	Frain	Peters	Hoyle	Williams	Trinder	Pearson	Campbell	Lampkin	Donaldson	Onoura	Referee	#
1	2	3	4	5	6	7	8	9	11*	12	S	S														Fernandiz R.	1
1	2	3	4	5	6	7	8	9	10	11	S		S													Barry N.	2
1	2	3*	4	5	6	7	8	9	10	11			S													Heilbron T.	3
1	2		4	5	6	7	8	9	10	11	12	S	S													Riley M.	4
1	2		4	5	6	7*	8	9	10	11	14	S	12•													D'Urso A.	5
1	2		4	5	6•	7	8	9	10	11*	14		S		3	12										Lloyd J.	6
1	2		4	5	6	7	8*	9	10	12	S	S	S		3	11										Kirkby J.	7
1	2	3	4	5	6	7		9	12	11•	14	S	S		8	10*										Allison D.	8
1	2	3	4	5	6	7		9	10	11	S	S			8*	12										Lomas E.	9
1	2	3	4	5	6	7		9	10	11*	S	12	S		8											Worrall J.	10
1	2	3	4	5	6	7*		9	10	11	12	S	S		8											Rushton J.	11
1	2	3	4	5	S	7		9	10	11	S		S		8		6									Pierce M.	12
1	2	3	4	5		7*		9	10	11	S		S		10		6	8								Danson P.	13
1	2	3	4	5		7		9	S	11	S		S		10		6	8								Richards P.	14
S	2	3	4*	5		7•		9	12	11	14		1		10		6	8								Foakes P.	15
S	2	3		5	12	7		9	8	11	4*	S	1		10		6									Singh G.	16
S	2			5	3*	7	S	9	11	8	4		1		10		6									Flood A.	17
S	2	3	4	5		7*		9	12	11	8•		1		10		6	14								Winter J.	18
1	2†	3	4	5		7*		9	12	11	8		S		10		6	8								Dawson A.	19
1	2	3	4*	5		7*		9	10	11	12	S	S		8		6									Allison D.	20
1	2	3	4	5		S		9	10	11	7	S	S		6		8									Breen K.	21
1		3	4*	5		7		9		11		2	S	12	6		8				8					Wilkes C.	22
1*		3	4	5	14	7•	8	9	10	11					6		2		S	12						Mathieson S.	23
1	2	3	4	5	12	7	8	9	10	11*			S		6			S								Barry N.	24
1	2	3	4	5	12			9	10	11•	6				8*				S		14	7				Hemley I.	25
1	2	3	4	5	6	7		9	10	S					8				S		S	11				Harrison P.	26
1*		3	4		6	7		9		11•	15	5			8						12	14	10			Barber G.	27
1	2	3	4	5		7		9		11		S	S				6				10	8				Harrison P.	28
1	2	3	4*	5		7		9		11				12	10		6		S		8					Parker J.	29
1*	2	3		5	14	7			10•	11	S						6		12		4		8			Kirkby J.	30
	2	3		5	6	7		9	10	11									S	1	4		8			West T.	31
S	2	3	4	5	12	7		9	10*	11	14									1	6•		8			Lomas E.	32
S	2	3	4	5	14	7		9	10	11*							12			1	6		8•			Foakes P.	33
1	2	3	4	5		7*	12	9•	10								6		S		14	11	8			Wolstenholme E.	34
1	2		4	5		7	8*	9	10	S	12						6		S				11			Lynch P.	35
1	2		4	5	12	7*		9	10	11	S				3		6		S				8			Refer P.	36
1	2	3	4	14		7		9	10•	12	11*						6		S				8			Flood A.	37
1	2†	3	4	5	S	7	8	9	10*								6		S				11			Cruickshanks I.	38
1		3	4*	5	2	7	8	9•	10								6		S				11		14	Winter J.	39
1		3	4	5	S	7	8	9	10						2		6		S				11		S	Rushton J.	40
1		3	4	5		7*	8	9	10•	12					2		6		S				11		14	Burns W.	41
1		3	4	5		7	8	9	10•	12					2		6*		S				11		14	Vanes P.	42
1	14	3	4	5		7	8	9	10*						2•		6		S				11		12	Parker J.	43
1	2	3		5		7*	8•	9	12	11					14		6		S				4		10	Holbron T.	44
1	2	3		5		S	8	9		11	S				7		6		S				4		10	Rennie V.	45
1	2	3		5		7*	8	9	12	11					S		6		S				4		10	Poulain R.	46
1	2	3		5		14	8	9	12	11•					7*		6		S				4		10	Wilkes C.	47
1	2	3	4*	5		7•	8	9	14						12		6		S				11		10	Pooley G.	48
1	2	11	4	5		7•	8	9	14								6		S				12		10	Dunn S.	49
1	2	3	S	5		7	8	9	12	11*							6		S				4		10	Wright P.	50
1	2	3	4	5		7	8	9	12	S							6		S				11*		10*		51
1	2	3	4	5		7	8	9	14		S						6		S				11*		10•	Lomas E.	52
S			12		6	7*		9		11		5			3				14	1			4		10	Furnandiz R.	53
1	2	3	4	5		7	8	9		11	S						6		S				12		10	Foakes P.	54
1	2*	3	4	5		7	8	9	10•						12		6†		S				11†			Wilkes C.	55
35	35	36	33	39	13	38	22	41	28	27	3	4	3		21	4	25	4	4		3		22	4	10	League Appearances	
	1			1	7	2							2	3		2	1	1	1		3	2	1		4	League Sub Appearances	
5	5	5	5	5	3	5	2	5	3+2	5		0+1	0+1		2	1	2	2								C/Cola Cup Appearances	
4	4	4	4	3	2+1	4	1+1	4	3	2					2		2				1+1	2	1	1		FA Cup Appearances	
1	1	1	1	2	2	1	1	2	1	2	1	2	1	0+1	1		2	1								AW Trophy Appearances	
2	2	2	2	2		2	2	2	2							0+1	2						1+1			Play-Off Appearances	

Also Played: Walker 6(46,47,48)3*(49), Sherlock S(46),12(52),8(53),14(55), Fleming 11*(2),12(3),3*(4), Marrows 12(17), Stark 10(22), Elad 12(38,39), Clifford 2•(53)

Players on Loan: Frain (Stockport County), Hoyle (Notts County), Campbell (Luton Town), Donaldson (Doncaster Rovers), Walker (Notts County)

† = Sent Off

CLUB RECORDS

BIGGEST VICTORIES
League: 9-2 v Rotherham United, Division 3(N), 27.12.1932.
8-1 v Q.P.R., Division 3, 15.3.1965.
7-0 v Scunthorpe United, Division 4, 21.4.1975.
F.A. Cup: 8-0 v Scarborough (a), 1st Round, 22.11.1952.
9-2 v Hounslow, 1st Round replay, 5.11.62.

BIGGEST DEFEATS
League: 1-8 v Walsall, Division 3(N), 19.1.1933.
F.A. Cup: 0-5 v Sheffield Wednesday (a), 3rd Round 10.1.1946.
0-5 v Bristol Rovers (a), 3rd Round, 4.1.1958.
League Cup: 0-5 v Chesterfield (h), 1st Round replay 23.8.1971.
0-5 v Notts County (a) 1st Round, 30.8.1988.
2-7 v Luton Town (a), 2nd Round, 3.10.1989.

MOST POINTS
3 points a win: 81, Division 4, 1985-86.
2 points a win: 68, Division 4, 1974-75.

MOST GOALS SCORED
108, Division 4, 1962-63.

RECORD TRANSFERS FEE RECEIVED
£638,500 from Swindon Town for Colin Calderwood (£27,000 7/85 + £611,500 8/93 when Calderwood moved on to Tottenham).

RECORD TRANSFER FEE PAID
£80,000 to Leicester City for Steve Wilkinson, Oct 1989 & to Notts County for Wayne Fairclough, March 1990.

BEST PERFORMANCES
League: 21st Division 2, 1977-78.
F.A. Cup: 6th Round, 1968-69.
League Cup: 5th round 1975-76.

HONOURS
Division 4 champions 1974-75.
Division 3 champions 1976-77.
Freight Rover Trophy winners 1986-87.

LEAGUE CAREER: Elected to Div 3(S) 1931, Transferred to Div 3(N) 1932, Transferred to Div 3(S) 1937, Transferred to Div 3(N) 1947, Transferred to Div 3 1958, Div 4 1959-60, Div 3 1962-63, Div 4 1971-72, Div 3 1974-75, Div 2 1976-77, Div 3 1977-78, Div 4 1979-80, Div 3 1985-86, Div 4 1990-91, Div 3 (now Div 2) 1991-92, Div 3 1992-93.

INDIVIDUAL CLUB RECORDS

MOST GOALS IN A SEASON
Ted Harston: 58 goals in 1936-37 (League 55, FA Cup 3).

MOST GOALS IN A MATCH
7. Ted Harston v Hartlepool United, Division 3(N), 8-2, 23.1.1937.

OLDEST PLAYER
David Owen 'Dai' Jones, 38 years 207 days v Wrexham (a), Division 3(N), 4.5.1949.

YOUNGEST PLAYER
Cyril Poole, 15 years 351 days v New Brighton (h), Division 3(N), 27.2.1937.

MOST CAPPED PLAYER
John McClelland (Northern Ireland) 6.

PREVIOUS MANAGERS

J Baynes 1922-25; E Davison (player/manager) 1926-27; J Hickling 1928-33; H Martin 1933-35; C Bell 1935; H Wightman 1936; H Parkes 1936-38; J Poole 1938-44; C Barke 1944-45; R Goodall 1945-49; F Steele 1949-51; G Jobey 1952-53; S Mercer 1953-56; C Mitten 1956-58; S Weaver 1958-60; R Carter 1960-63; T Cummings 1963-67; T Eggleston 1967-70; J Basford 1970-71; D Williams 1971-74; D Smith 1974-76; P Morris 1976-78; B Bingham 1978-79; M Jones 1979-81; S Boam 1981-83; I Greaves 1983-89; George Foster 1989-93.

ADDITIONAL INFORMATION
PREVIOUS NAMES
None.
PREVIOUS LEAGUES
Midland League.
Club colours: Amber & blue striped shirts, blue shorts with yellow trim.
Change colours: White shirts with green trim, green shorts with white trim, black with green socks with white trim.
Reserves League: Pontins League Division 2.
'A' Team: Midland Purity Youth League.

LONGEST LEAGUE RUNS

of undefeated matches:	20 (1976)	of league matches w/out a win:	12 (1959, 1974, 1979-80)
of undefeated home matches:	38 (1976-77)	of undefeated away matches:	8 (1976, 1991)
without home win:	11 (1959)	without an away win:	37 (1931-33)
of league wins:	7 (1962, 1991)	of home wins:	10 (1949)
of league defeats:	7 (1947)	of away wins:	7 (1976, 1991)

THE MANAGER

ANDY KING . . . . appointed November 1993.

PREVIOUS CLUBS
As Manager . . . . None.
As Asst.Man/Coach . . . . Luton Town.
As a player . . . . Luton, Everton, QPR, WBA, Everton, Wolves, Cambuut (Netherlands), Luton, Aldershot.

HONOURS
As a Manager . . . . None.
As a Player . . . . 2 caps for England U21.

MANSFIELD TOWN

PLAYERS NAME / Honours	Ht	Wt	Birthdate	Birthplace / Transfers	Contract Date	Clubs	League	L/Cup	FA Cup	Other	Lge	L/C	FAC	Oth
G O A L K E E P E R S														
Jason Trinder	5.11	14.2	03.03.70	Leicester	23.12.92	Grimsby Town								
						Oadby Town								
				Free	18.11.94	Mansfield Town	4+3							
D E F E N D E R S														
Adrian N Boothroyd	5.7	11.0	08.02.71	Bradford	01.07.89	Huddersfield T. (T)	9+1							
				£30,000	20.06.90	Bristol Rovers	10+6	1	0+1					
				Free	19.11.92	Hearts	0+4		0+2				2	
				Free	01.08.94	Mansfield Town	57+2	5	4	3+1	1			
Lee Howarth	6.1	12.6	03.01.68	Bolton		Chorley								
				Free	16.08.91	Peterborough Utd	56+6	8	3	3+2				1
				£15,000	05.08.94	Mansfield Town	39+3	5	3	4	2			
Stephen J Parkin	5.6	10.7	07.11.65	Mansfield	12.11.83	Stoke City (A)	104+9	9	9	6	5			
E: u21.5, Y6, S				£190,000	16.06.89	West Bromwich A.	44+4	3		2+1	2			
				Free	16.07.92	Mansfield Town	59+2	4	3+1	5+1	2			
Mark Peters	6.0	11.3	06.07.72	St Asaph	05.07.90	Manchester City (T)								
W: B.1, u21.3.				Free	02.09.92	Norwich City								
				Free	10.08.93	Peterborough Utd	17+2	2		2				
				Free	30.09.94	Mansfield Town	25+1	2	2	4	4			
Christopher B Timons	6.1	12.6	08.12.74	Nottingham	01.02.94	Mansfield Town (T)	17+3	0+1		2+1	1			
				Loan	22.03.95	Stafford Rangers								
M I D F I E L D														
Simon P Ireland	5.10	10.7	23.11.71	Barnstaple	01.07.90	Huddersfield T. (J)	10+9	1	0+1	1+1		1		
ESFAu18.4				Loan	11.03.92	Wrexham	2+3							
				£200,000	03.11.92	Blackburn Rovers	0+1							
				Loan	18.03.94	Mansfield Town	8+1				1			
				£60,000	12.08.94	Mansfield Town	38+2	5	4	3	5	1	1	
Kevin Lampkin	5.10	11.8	20.12.72	Liverpool (T)	17.05.91	Liverpool								
				Free	01.07.92	Huddersfield Town	13	1						
				Free	18.02.94	Mansfield Town	33+3		1	1+1	3			
Ifem Onuora	6.0	11.10	28.07.67	Glasgow	28.07.89	Huddersfield Town	115+50	10+6	12+3	13+3	30	4	3 3	
				Free	20.07.94	Mansfield Town	10+4			1	7			
Paul Sherlock	5.11	11.9	17.11.73	Wigan	01.07.92	Notts County (T)	8+4	1	2	2+1	1			
				£15,000	22.03.95	Mansfield Town	1+1			0+1				
F O R W A R D S														
Ian R Baraclough	6.1	11.10	04.12.70	Leicester	15.12.88	Leicester City (T)			1	0+1				
E: FLg, u18.1				Loan	22.03.90	Wigan Athletic	8+1				2			
				Loan	21.12.90	Grimsby Town	1+3							
				Free	13.08.91	Grimsby Town	1							
				Free	21.08.92	Lincoln City	68+5	7	4	7	10	1		
				Free	06.06.94	Mansfield Town	36	5	4	3	3			
Scott Eustace	6.0	13.6	13.06.75	Leicester	09.07.93	Leicester City (T)	0+1							
				Free	08.95	Mansfield Town								
Stewart Hadley	6.0	11.7	30.12.72	Dudley		Halesowen Town								
				Free	06.07.92	Derby County								
					09.02.94	Mansfield Town	42+11	3+2	3	3	19		1	1
Mark Sale	6.5	13.8	27.02.72	Burton-on-Trent	10.07.90	Stoke City (T)	0+2							
				Free	31.07.91	Cambridge United								
via Rocester					26.03.92	Birmingham City	11+10	2		3+1		1		2
				£10,000	05.03.93	Torquay United	30+14	1	2	3+1	8		1	
				£20,000	26.07.94	Preston North End	10+3	1+1	0+1	4	6			
				Free	08.95	Mansfield Town								
Stephen Slawson	6.1	12.2	13.11.72	Nottingham	09.07.91	Notts County (T)	16+21	1+1	0+3	3+3	4			1
				Loan	12.02.93	Burnley	5				2			
				Free	08.95	Mansfield Town								

FIELD MILL GROUND

Quarry Lane, Mansfield, Nottingham NG18 5DA
Tel: 01623 23567

Capacity 10,315
Covered Standing 1,638
Seating..3,329

First game..v Swindon Town, August 1931.
First floodlit game...v Cardiff City, (friendly), 5.10.1961.
An experimental match under artificial lights took place at Field Mill on 22.2.1930.
ATTENDANCES
Highest ....24,467 v Nott'm Forest, FAC Rnd 3, 10.1.1963.
Lowest ....1,086 v Darlington, AMC, 22.2.1984.

OTHER GROUNDS: ....None.

MATCHDAY TICKET PRICES

Seats. £10
Juv/OAP £5

Family Stand £8
Juv £4
1+1 . . . . £9
1+2 . . . . £12

Terraces. £8
Juv/OAP £3

Ticket Office Telephone no. . . . . 01623 23567.

CLUBCALL
0898 88 86 56

Calls cost 39p per minute cheap rate and 49p per
minute at all other times.
Call costings correct at time of going to press.

HOW TO GET TO THE GROUND

From the North
Use motorway M1 until junction 29. Leave motorway and follow signs to
Mansfield A617. In 6.3 miles turn right into Rosemary Street B6030. In 1 mile
turn right into Quarry Lane for Mansfield Town FC.

From the East
Use A617 to Rainworth. In 3 miles, at crossroads, turn left (B6030) into Windsor
Road. At end turn right into Nottingham Road. Shortly turn left into Portland
Street, then turn left into Quarry Lane for Mansfield Town FC.

From the South and West
Use motorway M1 until junction 28 then follow signs to Mansfield (A38). In 6.4
miles at crossroads turn right into Belvedere Street (B6030). In 0.4 miles turn
right into Quarry Lane for Mansfield Town FC.

Car Parking
Space for 500 cars at the ground.

Nearest Railway Station
Mansfield Alfreton Parkway.

MATCHDAY PROGRAMME

Programme Editor . . . . Lou Smith.

Number of pages . . . . 32.

Price . . . . £1.20.

Subscriptions . . . . £32 per person.

Local Newspapers . . . Chronicle Advertiser, Nottingham Evening Post.

Local Radio Stations. . . . . Radio Trent, Radio Nottingham.

NORTHAMPTON TOWN
(The Cobblers)
ENDSLEIGH LEAGUE DIVISION 3
SPONSORED BY: CHRONICLE & ECHO

Back Row (L-R): Michael Warner, Martin Aldridge, Ollie Cahill, Jason White, Darren Hughes, Christian Lee.
Middle Row: Dennis Casey (Physio), Jason Beckford, Dean Peer, Andy Woodman, Chris Burns, Billy Turley, Ian Sampson, Gary Thompson, Paul Curtis (Youth Team Coach).
Front Row: Gareth Williams, Neil Grayson, Ray Warburton, Ian Atkins (Manager), Danny O'Shea, Lee Colkin, David Norton. **Photo:** Pete Norton.

NORTHAMPTON TOWN
FORMED IN 1897
TURNED PROFESSIONAL IN 1897
LTD COMPANY IN 1922

CHAIRMAN: B J Ward
DIRECTORS
B Hancock, B Stonhill, D Kerr, B Collins,
B Lomax, M Church, R Church
SECRETARY
Rebecca Kerr
COMMERCIAL MANAGER
Bob Gorrill

MANAGER: Ian Atkins
PLAYER COACH: Danny O'Shea

YOUTH TEAM MANAGER
Paul Curtis
PHYSIOTHERAPIST
Dennis Casey

STATISTICIAN FOR THE DIRECTORY
Frank Grande

There were great expectations for the start of the season, Manager John Barnwell had cleared out many of the previous season's players to bring in his own men. He paid out £65,000 for a centre-back pairing of Ray Warburton from York, and Ian Sampson from Sunderland, and then brought in a host of players from non-League football as well as Peter Morris, as his number two. Unfortunately the results were the same, it was the eighth league game that the club registered its first win, ironically v. Carlisle, the runaway leaders, and their next was to be on the 22nd of October v. Wigan, their second game at the brand new Sixfields stadium, their first being against Barnet on the 15th October in front of a new record crowd of 7,461.

Just one win in the next ten games saw the club hit the bottom of the League again. A board meeting was held just after Christmas, where it was decided that John Barnwell's services at the club were no longer needed, Peter Morris was to follow a few weeks later.

Ian Atkins, a man who at one stage last season was going to join the Cobbler's as a player, joined as manager, and in no time he brought in experienced men in an attempt to pull away from the bottom, most experienced was Garry Thompson, the ex-Villa, Coventry and Cardiff forward, who found a new lease of life at Sixfields.Atkins started with a bang, beating Gillingham 2-0, but he did not have all his own way, not only did Bury do the double over Northampton, but won both games 5-0, and there was also a home defeat by struggling Scarborough, but on the plus side, there was a league victory at Barnet for the first time, a thrilling 4-4 draw at Fulham, and home wins over Torquay, Lincoln and Darlington, finishing the season with a 2-1 victory over Exeter, one of the clubs oldest opponents, in what could be their last league game. This lifted the club to 17th position.

Sixfields, not only gave the club a brand new stadium, it also brought back the crowds, an average of 5,362 for league games, over 1,500 up on last season, and the best since 1987-88, when the club were attracting 5,500, while pushing for a play-off place in the then Division Two.

Once again the cup competitions were disappointing for the club, Bournemouth ended the clubs interest in the Coca-Cola cup, and Peterborough won at London Road in the F.A.Cup, as in most seasons, Northampton won through the early stage of the Auto Windscreen Trophy, only to fail at the first hurdle in the knock out stages.

Now, with a new ground, and a new manager, supporters of the club look forward to 95/96, and hope that for the first time in three seasons, Northampton Town F.C. will not be fighting for its League life. **FRANK GRANDE.**

NORTHAMPTON TOWN

Division Three: 17th   **FA Cup:** 1st Round   **Coca-Cola Cup:** 1st Round   **Auto WindScreen Trophy:** 2nd Round

M	DATE	COMP.	VEN	OPPONENTS	RESULT	H/T	LP	GOAL SCORERS/GOAL TIMES	ATT.
1	A 16	CC 1/1	A	Bournemouth	L 0-2	0-2			(2,587)
2	20	EL	A	Doncaster Rovers	L 0-1	0-1			(2,195)
3	27	EL	A	Scunthorpe United	D 1-1	1-1	17	Trott 38	(2,409)
4	30	EL	A	Torquay United	L 1-2	0-2	21	Sampson 50	(3,619)
5	S 3	EL	A	Walsall	D 1-1	1-1	21	Trott 27	(4,249)
6	6	CC 1/2	H	Bournemouth	L 0-1	0-1			3,249
7	10	EL	H	Rochdale	L 1-2	1-0	22	Trott 38	2,887
8	13	EL	H	Hartlepool United	D 1-1	0-0		Aldridge 85	2,466
9	17	EL	A	Mansfield Town	D 1-1	0-0	21	Aldridge 48	(2,557)
10	24	EL	H	Carlisle United	W 2-1	1-0	20	Aldridge 34, Bell 69	3,508
11	10	EL	A	Lincoln City	D 2-2	2-1	19	Harmon 23, Warburton 32	(3,248)
12	8	EL	A	Exeter City	D 0-0	0-0	20		(3,015)
13	11	EL	H	Mansfield Town	L 0-1	0-1			4,993
14	15	EL	W	Barnet	D 1-1	0-0	21	Aldridge 61	7,461
15	18	AWT 1	A	Cambridge United	W 3-1	0-1		Warburton 50, Grayson 80, Aldridge 88	(1,497)
16	22	EL	H	Wigan Athletic	W 1-0	1-0	18	Grayson 35	6,379
17	29	EL	A	Scarborough	D 0-0	0-0	18		(1,468)
18	N 1	AWT 2	H	Barnet	W 3-1	1-0		Aldridge 11, Harmon 67, Grayson 82	2,618
19	5	EL	H	Fulham	L 0-1	0-1	18		7,366
20	12	FAC1	A	Peterborough United	L 0-4	0-0			(8,739)
21	19	EL	A	Preston North End	L 0-2	0-1	18		(7,927)
22	26	EL	H	Hereford United	L 1-3	0-0	21	Cahill 72	5,148
23	29	AWT 3	H	Swansea	L 0-1	0-1			2,706
24	D 10	EL	H	Doncaster Rovers	D 0-0	0-0	21		4,463
25	16	EL	H	Scunthorpe United	L 0-1	0-1	21		8,845
26	26	EL	A	Colchester United	W 1-0	1-0	20	Harmon 20 (pen)	(5,064)
27	27	EL	H	Chesterfield	L 2-3	1-2		Brown 39, Harmon 85 (pen)	6,329
28	31	EL	A	Darlington	L 1-4	0-1		Grayson 72	(2,250)
29	J 7	EL	A	Wigan	L 1-2	0-1	21	Colkin 75	(1,911)
30	14	EL	H	Gillingham	W 2-0	0-0	20	Harmon 79 (pen), Trott 83	5,529
31	28	EL	H	Scarborough	L 0-3	0-0	20		5,737
32	F 4	EL	A	Hereford	L 1-2	1-1	21	Grayson 2	(2,365)
33	11	EL	H	Preston North End	W 2-1	0-0	20	Burns 57, Smith 62	5,195
34	14	EL	A	Fulham	D 4-4	2-1		Aldridge 30, 84, Grayson 57, Brown 56	(3,423)
35	18	EL	A	Gillingham	L 1-3	0-1	20	Thompson 52	(4,075)
36	25	EL	H	Lincoln City	W 3-1	1-0	21	G. Brown 33 (og), Grayson 55, Aldridge 67	4,821
37	M 4	EL	A	Carlisle United	L 1-2	0-1	21	Martin 90	(6,755)
38	7	EL	H	Bury	L 0-5	0-1			4,208
39	11	EL	A	Rochdale	D 0-0	0-0	19		(1,894)
40	18	EL	H	Torquay United	W 2-0	0-0	19	Grayson 65, Brown 90	3,832
41	25	EL	H	Walsall	D 2-2	1-1	21	Grayson 9, Warburton 87	6,282
42	A 1	EL	A	Hartlepool	D 1-1	0-1	18	Thompson 12	(2,113)
43	8	EL	H	Darlington	W 2-1	1-0	17	Thompson 30, Grayson 59	4,496
44	15	EL	A	Chesterfield	L 0-3	0-1	17		(4,884)
45	17	EL	H	Colchester	D 1-1	1-0		Brown 8	5,011
46	22	EL	A	Bury	L 0-5	0-1	20		(2,921)
47	29	EL	A	Barnet	W 3-2	2-1	18	Burns 24, Thompson 37, Warburton 60	(2,796)
48	M 6	EL	H	Exeter City	W 2-1	1-0	17	O'Shea 36, Sampson 62	6,734
49									
50									
51									
52									
53									
54									
55									
56									
57									
58									
59									
60									

Best Home League Attendance: 7,461 v Barnet   **Smallest:** 2,466 v Hartlepool   **Av Home Att:** 5,086

Goal Scorers: Compared with 1993-94: +1,643

League (45): Grayson 8, Aldridge 7, Brown 4, Harman 4 (3 pens), Thompson 4, Trott 4, Warburton 3, Burns 2, Sampson 2, Bell, Cahill, Colkin, O'Shea, Smith, Thompson, Opponent

C/Cola Cup (0):
FA Cup (0):
AW Trophy (6): Aldridge 2, Grayson 2, Harmon, Warburton

Stewart	Pascoe	Curts	Norton	Warburton	Sampson	Harmon	Trott	Grayson	Bell	Wilkin	Colkin	Ovendale	Aldridge	Robinson (L)	Williams	Brown	Hughes	Burns	Smith (L)	Daniels	Thompson	Martin (L)	Turner	Woodman	O'Shea	Referee	
1	2*	3	4	5	6	7	9	10	11	12	S	S														Alcock P.	1
1	2	3*	4	5	6	7	9	10	11	14	12	S														Mathiewson S.	2
1	2		4	5	6	7	9	12	11	10*	3	S	S													Butler A.	3
1	2	6*	8	5	4	7	9	10	11		3	S	12													Brandwood M.	4
1	S	6	2	5	4	7	9	10	11*		3	S	12	8												Cain G.	5
1	S	6*	2	5	4	7	9	10	12		3	S	11	8												Pooley G.	6
1	S		2	5	4	7	9	10	11*	8	3	S		6												Harris R.	7
1	6		2	5	4	7	9	10*	11		3	S	12	8												Barber G.	8
1	S	6	2	5	4	7	9	S	11		3	S	10	8	S											Lomas E.	9
1	S	6	2	5	4	7	9	S	11		3	S	10	8												Kirkby J.	10
1	S	6	2	5	4	7	9		11		3	S	10	8	S											Rennie U.	11
1	S	6	2	5	4	7	9	S	11		3	S		8	10											Leach K.	12
1		6*	2	5	4	7	9	12	11		3	S	14	8	10*											Foakes P.	13
1	2	S		5	4	7	9	12	11		3*	S	10	6	8											Harrison P.	14
S	2•	6		5	4	7		11		12		1	10		8											Pooley G.	15
1	2	6*		5	4	7		9			3	S	10	11	8								S			Rushton J.	16
1	2			5	4	7	9	8		11*		S	12	10	6								S			Parker J.	17
S	2			5	4	7		8				3	1	9	10	6							11*			Bailey M.	18
1	2*		12	5	4	7		8				3	S	9	10	6							S			Flood A.	19
1	2		11	5	4	7	9	8*				3	S	12	10	6							S			Morton K.	20
S	14		2	5	4	7*	9	11			3		S	8	10	6•										Riley M.	21
1		S	2	5	4	7	9	12					S	8*	10	6										Richards P.	22
1		12	2	5*	4	7	9•	8					S	10	6											Butler A.	23
1	3*		2	5	4	7	9	8					S	12	6								S			D'Urso A.	24
1	14		2	5	4	7	9*	3		12			S	8		6										Burns W.	25
1	12	5	2		4	7		9			3		S		11	8										Alcock P.	26
1	2	5	6		4	7		9			3		S		11*	8										Furnandiz R.	27
1	S	6	2	5	4			10			3		S		12	11	7									Cain G.	28
1	12	6	2	5	4			11			10	S	9			8										Cruikshanks I.	29
1		2	5	4	7	12	11				6	S	9*			8	3	10								Holbrook J.	30
1		2	5	4	7	9	11					S				8	3	10	6*							Mathiewson S.	31
S		2	5	6	14	7	10					1				8	12	7†	4	3*						Rushton J.	32
S	S	2	5	4	6		11					1	7			8	3	10			9					Kirkby J.	33
S		2	5	4		12	11					1	7			8	3	10		6*	9		S			Vanes P.	34
		2	5	4		12	11					1	7			8	3	10		6*	9					Bailey M.	35
		2	5	4		10	11				7	1	7		S	8*				6	9	12				Leach K.	36
12		2	5	4		12	11				3		7*		14	8*				6	9					Breen K.	37
1		2	5	4		12	11				3		7•			8		10*		6	9		14			Dunn S.	38
		2	5	4			11				14	S	12			8*	3	10		6	9	7*		1		Watson J.	39
		2	5	4			11				12	S	7*			8	3	10		6	9			1		Lynch K.	40
		2	5	4		12	11				6	S			14	8*	3	10	7*		9			1		Riley M.	41
		2*	5	4			11				12	S				8	3	10	7		9			1	6	Allison D.	42
		2	5	4			11				7*	S			S	8	3	10	12		9			1	6	Lomas E.	43
	5	2•		4		14	12	11			7					8	3*	10			9			1	6	Winter J.	44
	12		5	4			11				7	S			S	8	3	10	2*		9			1	6	Rennie U.	45
	S		5	4		10	9	11			7					8	3	12	2*		9			1	6	Lynch K.	46
		2	5	4			11•				12					8*	3	10	12		9			1	6	Rejer P.	47
		2	5	4			11•				12					8	3	10	14		9			1	6	Wolstenholme E.	48
30	11	13	36	39	42	26	20	34	12	2	28	6	18	14	13	23	12	16	6	5	15	7	2	10	7	League Appearances	
1	4	2				7	2	4			2		5		9	2			1	1	3		2		3	League Sub Appearances	
2	1	2	2	2	2	2	2	2	1+1	+1	1		1		1											VC/Cola Cup Appearances	
1	1	1	1	1	1	1	1			+1	1		1		1	1	1			3						FA Cup Appearances	
1	2	1+1	3	3	3	1	3			+1	1		2	2	3										1	AW Trophy Appearances	

Also Played: Patmore 14(26),12(27,31),9(28*),S(29), Flounders 10(26•,27•) Byrne 8(1,2,3),S(4,8), McNamara 12(7),9(15*), Kelly 3(15,17),S(18),3(22)
Cahill 14(15,27),12(16,18,21),11(19,22,23,24,25•),7(48*), Harrison 14(23),10(24,25),7(28,29),S(30,31,40),11(32•), Sedgemore 6(26*)

Players on Loan: Robinson (Huddersfield Town), Sedgemore (Birmingham City), Smith (Sudbury), Martin (Bristol City)

† = Sent Off

CLUB RECORDS

BIGGEST VICTORIES
League: 10-0 v Walsall, Division 3(S), 5.11.1927.
F.A. Cup: 10-0 v Sutton, 7.12.1907.
League Cup: 8-0 v Brighton, 1.11.1966.

BIGGEST DEFEATS
League: 0-10 v Bournemouth, Division 3(S), 2.9.1939.
F.A. Cup: 2-8 v Manchester United (h), 5th Round, 7.2.1970.
League Cup: 0-5 v Fulham, 13.10.1965.
0-5 v Ipswich, 30.8.1977.

MOST POINTS
3 points a win: 99, Division 4, 1986-87.
2 points a win: 68, Division 4, 1975-76.

MOST GOALS SCORED
109, Division 3(S), 1952-53, Division 3, 1962-63.

RECORD TRANSFER FEE RECEIVED
£265,000 from Watford for Richard Hill, March 1987.

RECORD TRANSFER FEE PAID
£85,000 to Manchester City for Tony Adcock, January 1988.

BEST PERFORMANCES
League: 21st Division 1, 1965-66.
F.A. Cup: 5th Round 1911-12, 1933-34, 1949-50, 1969-70.
League Cup: 5th Round 1964-65, 1966-67.

HONOURS
Champions Division 3, 1962-63.
Champions Division 4, 1986-87.

LEAGUE CAREER
Original members of Division 3 1920, Transferred to Div 3(S) 1921, Div 4 1957-58, Div 3 1960-61, Div 2 1962-63, Div 1 1964-65, Div 2 1965-66, Div 3 1966-67, Div 4 1968-69, Div 3 1975-76, Div 4 1976-77, Div 3 1986-87, Div 4 (now Div 3) 1989-90.

INDIVIDUAL CLUB RECORDS

MOST GOALS IN A SEASON
Cliff Holton: 39 goals in 1961-62 (League 36, FA Cup 3).

MOST GOALS IN A MATCH
5. R Hoten v Crystal Palace (h) 8-1, Division 3(S), 27.10.1928.
5. A Dawes v Lloyds Bank (h) 8-1, FA Cup 1st Round, 26.11.1932.

OLDEST PLAYER
Steve Sherwood, 40 years 24 days v Crewe Alexandra, Division 3, 3.1.1994.

YOUNGEST PLAYER
Adrian Mann, 16 years 297 days v Bury, 5.5.1984.

MOST CAPPED PLAYER
E Lloyd-Davies (Wales) 12.

PREVIOUS MANAGERS

1903-12 Herbert Chapman, 1912-13 Walter Bull, 1913-19 Fred Lessons, 1920-25 Bob Hewison, 1925-31 Jack Tresadern, 1931-36 Jack English Snr., 1936-37 Sid Puddlefoot, 1937-War Warney Cresswell, War-1949 Tom Smith, 1949-55 Bob Dennison, 1955-59 Dave Smith, 1959-63 Dave Bowen, 1963 Jack Jennings (caretaker), 1963-67 Dave Bowen, 1967-68 Tony Marchi, 1968-69 Ron Flowers, 1969-72 Dave Bowen, 1972-73 Bill Baxter, 1973-76 Bill Dodgin, 1976-77 Pat Crerand, 1977 Committee*, 1977-78 John Petts, 1978-79 Mike Keen, 1979-80 Clive Walker, 1980-81 Bill Dodgin, 1981-84 Clive Walker, 1984-85 Tony Barton, 1985-90 Graham Carr, 1990-92 Theo Foley, 1992-93 Phil Chard, 1993- 95 John Barnwell.
*Committee: 1 director, 1 coach, 2 senior players.

ADDITIONAL INFORMATION
PREVIOUS NAMES
None.
PREVIOUS LEAGUES
Northants League and Midland League.
Club colours: Claret shirts, with white shoulders, white shorts, claret socks.
Change colours: White shirts with claret shoulders, claret shorts, white socks
Youth Team League: South East Counties League.

LONGEST LEAGUE RUNS

of undefeated matches:	21 (1986-87)	of league matches w/out a win:	18 (1969)
of undefeated home matches:	29 (1932-33, 1975-76)	of undefeated away matches:	12 (1986-87)
without home win:	11 (1989-90)	without an away win:	33 (1921-23)
of league wins:	8 (1960)	of home wins:	12 (1927)
of league defeats:	8 (1935)	of away wins:	5 (1978)

THE MANAGER

IAN ATKINS . . . . appointed January 1995.

PREVIOUS CLUBS
As Manager . . . . . . Colchester United (player-manager), Cambridge United (player-manager), Doncaster Rovers.
As Asst.Man/Coach . . . . Birmingham City.
As a player . . . . Shrewsbury Town, Sunderland, Everton, Ipswich Town, Birmingham.

HONOURS
As a Manager . . . . None.
As a Player . . . . None.

NORTHAMPTON TOWN

PLAYERS NAME / Honours	Ht	Wt	Birthdate	Birthplace / Transfers	Contract Date	Clubs	League	L/Cup	FA Cup	Other	Lge	L/C	FAC	Oth
GOALKEEPERS														
Andrew Woodman	6.1	12.4	11.08.71	Camberwell	01.07.89	Crystal Palace (T)								
				Free	04.07.94	Exeter City	6	1	1	2				
				Free	10.03.95	Northampton Town	10							
DEFENDERS														
Lee Colkin	5.11	11.1	15.07.74	Nuneaton	31.08.92	Northampton T. (T)	59+10	3	1	1	2			
Martin Matthews	5.10	11.03	22.12.75	Peterborough	08.94	Derby County (T)								
					08.95	Northampton Town								
David Norton	5.7	11.3	03.03.65	Cannock	23.03.83	Aston Villa (A)	42+2	8	2+1	2	2			
E: Y.7.				£30,000	24.08.88	Notts County	22+5	3+1		4+1	1			
				Loan	18.10.90	Rochdale	9			2				
Loan 10.01.91 Hull City 15 Lge App.				£80,000	16.08.91	Hull City	134	7	7	9	5		1	1
Loan 15.08.94 Northampton Town					03.11.94	Northampton Town	36+2	2	1	1				
Daniel E O'Shea	6.0	12.8	26.03.63	Kennington	23.12.80	Arsenal (A)	6	3						
Div.3'91.				Loan	23.02.84	Charlton Athletic	9							
				Free	24.08.84	Exeter City	45	2	2	2	2			
				£5,000	09.08.85	Southend United	116+2	8	5+1	6	12			
				Free	18.08.89	Cambridge United	186+17	18+1	15+3	12+2	1			
				Free	23.03.95	Northampton Town	7				1			
Ian Sampson	6.2	12.8	14.11.68	Wakefield		GooleTown								
					13.11.90	Sunderland	13+4	1	0+2	0+1	1			
				Loan	08.12.93	Northampton Town	8							
				Free	05.08.94	Northampton Town	42	2	1	3	2			
Richard B Skelly	5.11	11.7	24.03.72	Norwich		Newmarket Town								
				Free	14.01.94	Cambridge United	2							
				Free	19.06.94	Northampton Town	3			2				
				Loan	03.02.95	Sudbury								
Raymond Warburton	6.0	11.5	07.10.67	Rotherham	05.10.85	Rotherham Utd (A)	3+1		2	2				
				Free	08.08.89	York City	86+4	8	6	7	9	1	1	
				£35,000	04.02.94	Northampton Town	56	2	1	3	4			1
MIDFIELD														
Christopher Burns	6.0	12.0	09.11.67	Manchester		Cheltenham Town								
				£25,000	15.03.91	Portsmouth	78+12	7+2	7	9+1	9	2		
Loan 17.12.93 Swansea City 4 Lge App. 1gl				Loan	11.03.94	Bournemouth	13+1				1			
				Free	25.11.94	Swansea City	3+2		0+1					
				Free	13.01.95	Northampton Town	16+1				2			
Neil Grayson	5.10	12.4	01.01.64	York		Rowntree Mac.								
				Free	22.03.90	Doncaster Rovers	21+8		1+1	2+1	6			1
				Free	26.04.91	York City	0+1							
				Free	16.08.91	Chesterfield	9+6	2	1	1				
Free Gateshead, via Boston United to					19.06.94	Northampton Town	34+4	2	1	3	8			2
Darren J Harmon	5.5	9.12	0.01.73	Northampton	17.07.91	Notts County (T)								
				Free	21.02.92	Shrewsbury Town	1+5				2			
					24.10.92	Northampton Town	76+13	2+1	5	9	12			1
Roy Hunter	5.9	10.12	29.10.73	Middlesbrough	04.03.92	West Brom. A. (T)	3+6			4+1	1			
					08.95	Northampton Town								
Dean Peer	6.2	11.5	08.08.69	Stourbridge	09.07.87	Birmingham City (T)	106+14	14+1	2+1	11+1	8	3		1
AMC'91.				Loan	18.12.92	Mansfield Town	10			1				
				Free	16.11.93	Walsall	41+4	2	4+2	3	8			
				Free	08.95	Northampton Town								
Graham Mark Turner	6.0	11.1	04.02.72	Bebbington		Paget Rangers								
					02.07.91	Wolverhampton W.	1							
				Free	01.07.94	Northampton Town	2+2			1				
FORWARDS														
Martin J Aldridge	5.11	11.4	06.12.74	Northampton	27.08.93	Northampton T. (T)	50+20	1+2	1+1	5	17		1	4
Jason N Beckford	5.9	12.4	14.02.70	Manchester	18.08.87	Manchester C. (T)	8+12	1+4			1	1		
Loan 14.03.91 Blackburn Rovers 3+1 Lge App.				Loan	26.09.91	Port Vale	4+1				1			
				£50,000	02.01.92	Birmingham City	5+2			1	2			
Loan 24.04.94 Bury 3 Lge App.				Free	10.08.94	Stoke City	2+2			1				
				Free	15.12.94	Millwall	6+3							
				Free	15.05.95	Northampton Town								
Oliver F Cahill	5.10	11.02	29.09.75	Clonmel		Clonmel								
					02.09.94	Northampton Town	5+3			1+2	1			
Garry L Thompson	6.1	13.13	07.10.59	Birmingham	29.06.77	Coventry City (A)	127+7	12+1	11		38	7	4	
E: u21.6. FMC'91.				£225,000	17.02.83	West Bromwich A.	91	9	5		39	5	1	
				£450,000	12.08.85	Sheffield Wed.	35+1	2+1	5		7	1	1	
				£450,000	05.06.86	Aston Villa	56+4	6	4	3	17	2		
				£325,000	24.12.88	Watford	24+10	0+1	7+1		8			
				£200,000	24.03.90	Crystal Palace	17+3			0+1	3	1		
				£125,000	19.08.91	Q.P.R.	10+9	3+2	1		1	3		
				Free	15.07.93	Cardiff City	39+4	2	5+2	6+3	5		1	3
				Free	10.02.95	Northampton Town	15				4			
Jason White	6.2	12.0	19.10.71	Meriden	04.07.90	Derby County (T)								
				Free	06.09.91	Scunthorpe United	44+24	1+1	3+3	4+4	16		1	1
Loan Darlington, 20.08.93, 4 Lge App, 1gl.				Free	10.12.93	Scarborough	60+3	2+1	5	1	20	1		
				£35,000	08.95	Northampton Town								
Gareth J Williams	5.10	11.8	12.03.67	Isle of Wight		Gosport Borough								
				£30,000	09.01.88	Aston Villa	6+6	0+1	2	0+1				
				£200,000	06.08.91	Barnsley	23+11	1	1+1	1+1	6			
Loan 17.09.92 Hull City 4 Lge App.				Loan	06.01.94	Hull City	16				2			
Free 23.08.94 Wolverhampton Wanderers				Free	16.09.94	Bournemouth	0+1							
				Free	27.09.94	Northampton Town	13+2		1	3				

A D D I T I O N A L   C O N T R A C T   P L A Y E R S

Christian Lee - Free from Doncaster Rovers 08.95.
Billy Turley - Free from Evesham 08.95.
Michael Warner - Free from Tamworth 08.95.

SIXFIELDS

Upton Way, Northampton NN5 4EG
Tel: 01604 75 77 73

Capacity..7,673.

First game ....v Barnet, Division 3, 15.10.1994.
First floodlit game..v Barnet, AMC, 1.11.1994.

ATTENDANCES
Highest..7,461 v Barnet, Division 3, 15.10.1994.
Lowest...2,618 v Barnet, AMC, 1.11.1994.

OTHER GROUNDS ....County Ground 1897-94.

MATCHDAY TICKET PRICES

West Stand Upper Centre £10
Upper Wing. £9.50
Concessions £7
Family Enclosure . . . . £7.50.
Family Tandem. £10
Family Tricycle. £12
Concessions £4
Lower Centre. £9
Lower Wing £8
Concessions £6
East Stand Centre £8.50
Family Enclosure. £7.50
Family Tandem. £10
Family Tricycle. £12
Concessions £4
Away Section £8.50
North Stand £7.50
Concessions £5

Ticket Office Telephone no. 01604 75 77 73

CLUBCALL 0839 66 44 77

Calls cost 39p per minute cheap rate and 49p per
minute at all other times.
Call costings correct at time of going to press.

HOW TO GET TO THE GROUND

From the North and West
M1 to junction 16. Take A45 (signposted Northampton/Duston). After approx.
3.25 miles there is a roundabout; take the fourth exit onto Upton Way for the
ground.

From the South
M1 to junction 15a, then A43 (signposted Northampton) to A45 Northampton
Ring Road. Bear left (signposted Daventry) at second roundabout, then take first
exit into Upton Way and the ground is immediately on the left.

From the East
Either A43 or A428 to A45. Once on the A45, follow signs for Daventry until you
pass the Rugby Ground (Franklin Gardens). At the second roundabout after this,
take the first exit into Upton Way for the ground.

Car Parking
There is on-site parking at Six Fields with six overflow car parks to take the
strain on busy days.

Nearest Railway Station
Castle Station (01908 370 883 - Milton Keynes Enqs.)

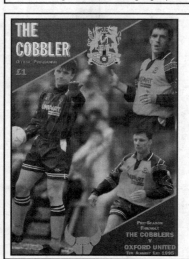

MATCHDAY PROGRAMME

Programme Editor . . . . Brian Barrow.

Number of pages . . . . 32.

Price . . . . £1.40.

Subscriptions . . . . Apply to club.

Local Newspapers . . . . Chronicle and Echo, Evening Telegraph,
. . . . Northants Post.

Local Radio Stations . . . . Northants Radio, Radio Northampton.

PLYMOUTH ARGYLE
(The Pilgrims)
ENDSLEIGH LEAGUE DIVISION 3
SPONSORED BY: ROTOLOK

Back Row (L-R): Andy Comyn, Keith Hill, Mick Heathcoat, Kevin Blackwell, Nicky Hammond, Kevin Nugent, Adrian Viveash, Michael Evans.
Middle Row: Mick JOnes (Asst. Manager), Wayne Burnett, Steve McCall, Chris Twiddy, James Dungey, Ronnie Mauge, Mark Patterson, Chris Leadbitter, Norman Meadhurst.
Front Row: Mark Saunders, Paul Williams, Micky Ross, Neil Warnock, Dan McCauley (Chairman), Martin Barlow, Adrian Littlejohn, Sam Shilton.

PLYMOUTH ARGYLE
FORMED IN 1886
TURNED PROFESSIONAL IN 1903
LTD COMPANY IN 1903

PRESIDENT: S Rendell
CHAIRMAN: D McCauley
DIRECTORS
P Bloom, G Jasper, D Angilley, I Jones
SECRETARY
M Holladay (01752 562 561/2/3)
COMMERCIAL MANAGER
Steve Birley

MANAGER: Neil Warnock
ASSISTANT MANAGER: Mick Jones
YOUTH TEAM MANAGER
Kevin Blackwell
PHYSIOTHERAPIST
Norman Medhurst

STATISTICIAN FOR THE DIRECTORY
Jonathan Brewer

As most people expected Plymouth Argyle changed divisions at the end of the 1994-95 season. The fact that they ended up in Division 3, and not Division 1 owed a lot to off the field wrangling. The much publicised dismissal of Peter Shilton dominated a season which promised so much and produced nothing.

Having finished third the previous season much was expected of the team, which was by and large the same. the team, however, never reproduced any of the form that made them top goalscorers in all four divisions the previous year. They lacked direction and this was indicative of the problems behind the scenes at Home Park. Long term injury problems to key players such as Steve Castle, Steve McCall and Paul Dalton made Shilton's job even more demanding. The team's ailing fortunes, along with his own personal problems, saw Shilton depart halfway through the season.

McCall took over the role of player-manager on Shilton's departure. At the time this was a very popular decision with fans and players alike. However, with hindsight, his appointment was a bad decision. McCall failed to halt the slide towards Division 3 and his stay in charge lasted only 16 games. Next in line, (albeit with a different title), was Russell Osman. The team managed to show some improvement under his guidance but it was all a little too late. Plymouth were relegated to the lowest division for the first time in their history.

During the close season Argyle acquired the services of the much respected Neil Warnock as their next manager. After his arrival he quickly stamped his own ideas at Home Park bringing in a number of new faces to the squad.

As for last season Argyle will start the campaign as favourites to gain promotion. With Neil Warnock in charge the future again looks bright. Hopefully, this time the team will deliver what they are capable of and regain their Second Division status at the first time of asking.

JONATHAN BREWER.

PLYMOUTH ARGYLE

Division Two: 21st   **FA Cup:** 3rd Round   **Coca-Cola Cup:** 3rd Round   **Auto Windscreen Trophy:** 2nd Round

M	DATE	COMP.	VEN	OPPONENTS	RESULT	H/T	LP	GOAL SCORERS/GOAL TIMES	ATT.
1	A 13	EL	H	Brentford	L 1-5	1-3		Swan 18	7,976
2	16	CC 1/1	A	**Walsall**	**L 0-4**	**0-0**			**(2,810)**
3	20	EL	A	Brighton & H.A.	D 1-1	0-0		Bradshaw 69	(8,309)
4	23	CC 1/2	H	**Walsall**	**W 2-1**	**1-0**		**Swan 33, Castle 55**	**2,801**
5	27	EL	H	Bradford City	L 1-5	0-4	20	Dalton 83	6,469
6	30	EL	A	Hull City	L 0-2	0-0	22		(3,384)
7	S 3	EL	A	Birmingham City	L 2-4	0-2	22	Castle 59, Daish 80 (og)	(13,202)
8	10	EL	H	Huddersfield Town	L 0-3	0-2	22		5,464
9	13	EL	H	Cambridge United	D 0-0	0-0	22		3,824
10	17	EL	A	Cardiff City	L 0-2	0-0			(1,299)
11	24	EL	H	Chester City	W 1-0	1-0	21	Twiddy 4	5,329
12	27	AWT S1	A	**Cardiff City**	**L 0-2**	**0-0**			**(1,299)**
13	O 1	EL	A	Leyton Orient	W 2-0	2-0	19	Landon 14,38	(4,140)
14	8	EL	A	Oxford United	L 0-1	0-1	19		(6,550)
15	15	EL	H	Wycombe Wanderers	D 2-2	2-1	18	Skinner 25 (pen), Barlow 29	6,864
16	18	AWT S1	H	**Exeter City**	**L 1-3**	**0-1**		**Naylor 58**	**1,847**
17	22	EL	A	Stockport County	W 4-2	2-1	17	Edworthy 24, O' Hagan 30, Landon 55,87	(5,652)
18	29	EL	H	Blackpool	L 0-2	0-1	19		6,285
19	N 1	EL	H	Peterborough United	L 0-1	0-1	19		4,145
20	5	EL	A	Rotherham United	L 1-3	0-1	20	Skinner 75	(2,848)
21	13	FAC 1	A	**Kettering Town**	**W 1-0**	**0-0**		**Skinner 46**	**(4,602)**
22	19	EL	H	Wrexham	W 4-1	2-1	17	Hughes 6 (og), Burnett 39, Phillips 75 (og), Barlow 89	6,936
23	26	EL	A	York City	L 0-1	0-0	17		(3,185)
24	D 3	FAC 2	H	**A.F.C. Bournemouth**	**W 2-1**	**2-0**		**Ross 4, 30**	**6,960**
25	10	EL	H	Brighton & H.A.	L 0-3	0-0	19		6,091
26	17	EL	A	Brentford	L 0-7	0-2	19		(4,492)
27	26	EL	A	Swansea City	L 0-3	0-3	21		(4,859)
28	J 2	EL	H	Crewe Alexandra	W 3-2	1-2	20	Patterson 30, Evans 83, 90	6,802
29	7	FAC 3	A	**Nottingham Forest**	**L 0-2**	**0-2**			**(19,821)**
30	14	EL	A	A.F.C. Bourrnemouth	D 0-0	0-0	20		(4,931)
31	21	EL	A	Rotherham United	D 0-0	0-0	20		5,484
32	28	EL	A	Blackpool	L 2-5	1-0	20	Patterson 30, Dalton 60	(3,599)
33	F 4	EL	H	York City	L 1-2	1-0	20	Hall 45 (og)	5,572
34	8	EL	A	Shrewsbury Town	L 2-3	1-0	20	Nugent 21, Evans 86	(3,029)
35	11	EL	A	Peterborough United	W 2-1	1-0	20	McCall 3, Nugent 85	(4,318)
36	18	EL	H	A.F.C. Bournemouth	L 0-1	0-1	20		5,435
37	21	EL	A	Wrexham	L 1-3	1-0	21	Castle 32	(3,030)
38	25	EL	H	Leyton Orient	W 1-0	0-0	20	Landon72	5,173
39	M 4	EL	A	Chester City	L 0-1	0-1	21		(1,820)
40	11	EL	A	Bradford City	L 0-2	0-0	21		(5,399)
41	18	EL	H	Hull City	W 2-1	2-1	20	Nugent 11, Evans 19	4,839
42	21	EL	A	Huddersfield Town	L 0-2	0-1	21		(12,099)
43	25	EL	H	Cardiff City	D 0-0	0-0	21		5,611
44	28	EL	H	Stockport County	L 0-2	0-1	21		4,618
45	A 1	EL	A	Cambridge Utd	D 1-1	0-0	21	Landon 62	(3,913)
46	4	EL	H	Bristol Rovers	D 1-1	1-0	21	Nugent 6	6,743
47	8	EL	H	Shrewsbury Town	W 1-0	1-0	21	Patterson 25	5,089
48	15	EL	A	Bristol Rovers	L 0-2	0-0	21		(7,068)
49	17	EL	H	Swansea City	W 2-1	1-1	21	Swan 43, Nugent 61	5,890
50	19	EL	H	Birmingham City	L 1-3	0-0	21	Dalton 90	8,550
51	22	EL	A	Crewe Alexandra	D 2-2	1-2	21	Gardiner 45 (og), Dalton 81 (pen.)	(3,786)
52	29	EL	A	Wycombe Wanderers	W 2-1	1-0	21	Hills 5, Landon 65	(6,850)
53	M 6	EL	H	Oxford United	D 1-1	1-0	21	Nugent 12	4,953
54									
55									
56									
57									
58									
59									
60									

Best Home League Attendance: 8,550 v Birmingham City   **Smallest:** 3,824 v Cambridge United   **Av Home Att:** 5,832

Goal Scorers:

Compared with 1993-94: -3171

League (45):	Landon 7, Nugent 6, Opponents 5, Evans 4, Dalton 4, (1 pen), Castle 3, Patterson 3, Swan 2, Barlow 2, Skinner 2, (1 pen), Bradshaw, Burnett, Edworthy, Hill, McCall, O'Hagan, Twiddy
Coca Cola Cup (2):	Swan, Castle
FA Cup (3):	Ross 2, Skinner
AW Trophy (1):	Naylor

Hodge M.	Patterson M.	Hill K.	Comyn A.	Swan P.	Barlow M.	Burnett W.	Nugent K.	Evans M.	Skinner C.	Landon R.	Dungey J.	Edworthy M.	Twiddy C.	Naylor D.	Castle S.	Nicholls A.	Morgan J.	Ross M.	Dalton P.	Crocker M.	Dawe S.	McCall S.	Wotton P.	Payne I.	O'Hagan D.	Referee	
1	2•	3	4	5	7	8	9	10	11	12		S	14										6*			S. Dunn	1
1	6	4†	5	7†	8	9	10	11•	S	3		S					14							2		G. Pooley	2
1	6	4	5*	7	12	9	10				S	2	S	3					11							P. Foakes	3
1	6	4	5	7		9	10*		12			2•	14	3					11							C. Wilkes	4
1	S	4	5	7		9						2•	14	3	8	S			11							G. Singh	5
1	2	4	5		7	9						S	14	3	8	S			11•							K. Lynch	6
1	2*	6	4	5	7	9		S					11	3	8	S										J. Parker	7
1•		12	4*	5	7	6	9					11	3	8	13†					S						J. Holbrook	8
		4	5		7	6	9					S	11	3	8	1				S						M. Pierce	9
S		4	5	12	7	6	9*			14			11	3	8	1										J. Rushton	10
1	2	4•	5	14	7	6	9	12		10*			11	3				8								P. Rejer	11
S	2	4	5		7	6*		9•	14	10		12	11	3		1	8									P. Vanes	12
	2	4	5		7•	6	S		9	10		14	11	3		1	8									A. Butler	13
	2•	4	5		7	6*	12		9	10	S	14	11	3		1	8									P. Wright	14
	2	5	4	7	6			9	10	S	11	3		1	8•									14		C. Wilkes	15
	4	5		7	6		14	8	10	S	2	11	3		1							S		9		K. Cooper	16
	2	4*	5		7	6	S		9	10	13	8	11•	3		1†								12		N. Barry	17
	2		5		7	6			8	10	S	4	11	3		1	S		12					9*		R. Harris	18
	2		5		7	6	14			10*	S	4	11	3		1	8		9					S		J. Holbrook	19
1	2		5		7	6•	9	12	11	14	S	4		3			8		10*							P. Richards	20
1	2		5		7	6	10	8	S	S	4	11	3											S		G. Singh	21
S	2		5	S	7	6	9	11*		8		4		3		1	12									K.A. Cooper	22
S	2		5	S	14	7	6	9•		8		4†	11*	3		1										G. Cain	23
S	8		5	4	7	6	9•	11*		14		2		3		1		10								G. Ashby	24
S	2		5	4	7	6		12		S				3		1		10		8*						S. Dunn	25
1	2		5	4	7	6	8	9			S			3		1		10	11	3				S		B. Harris	26
S	2	3	5	4	7	6*	12	9•							1		10	14	8							P. Vanes	27
S	2	5			4	7	10	9	14	8		6		3		1		10•								M. Pierce	28
S	2	5			4	7	10	9	12	8		6		3		1						S				D. Ellery	29
S	2*	4	5		7	6	9•	10	8	14				3		1					12					P. Alcock	30
S		4	5		8	6		10	7	9		2		3		1			12				S			C. Wilkes	31
S	2	4	5		8	14		7	10*			6		3		1			12		11•					K. Lupton	32
S	2	4	5		8	11	10	14	7•					3		1			12		6*					J. Holbrook	33
S	2	4	5		7		10†							3	12	1			11		6*	8				R. Poulain	34
S	2	4		5	7		10	12						3	12	1			11		6•	8				P. Foakes	35
1	2†	4		5	7			14	9	S				3	8	1			11		6•	14		S		K. Cooper	36
1	2	4	5		7		14		12	9	S			3	8•	1			11			6*				K. Lynch	37
1	2	4	5		7			9*	12	10	S	6•		3	8	1			11			14				G. Singh	38
1		5	4		6	9	10•		7		S	2		3	8	1		10	11			7*				U. Rennie	39
1		5	4		6	9	7				S	2		3	8	1		10	11		S			S		E. Wolstenholme	40
1	14		4	12	6	9	7					2		3	8	1		10	11				7*			P. Rejer	41
1	2•	14		4	6	5	9					5		3	8	S		10	11					6		G. Cain	42
1	2			4	7*		9	12				5		3	8	S		10	11		S					P. Vanes	43
	2	6		4	7	14	9			10*		5		3	8	1		12	11.							C. Wilkes	44
	2	6		4	7•	14	9			10*	S	5		3	8	1		12	11							D. Orr (R. Saunders L/E)	45
	2	6		8	S	9		7	10•			5		3	12	1		14	11		4*					P. Rejer	46
	2	6		8	4•	9		7	10	5	S		3	1		14	11									S. Dunn	47
	2	6		4	14		7•	S	S	5			3	8	1		10	11								J. Rushton	48
	2	6		4	S	9		7*	12	S	5		3	8	1		10	11								J. Holbrook	49
	2	6	4		S	9		7	12	1		5		3	8		10*	11								R. Harris	50
	2	6		4•	5	14	9		7	12	1			3	8		10*	11							S	K. Breen	51
	2	4			6	S	14	9	7•	10•	1	5		3	8			11							S	J. Lloyd	52
	2	6			4	12	9	14	7*	10•	1	5		3	8			11							S	C. Wilkes	53
17	37	32	30	24	40	25	34	12	21	18	3	24	13	42	23	26	6	11	23	3	3	7	5	1	1	League Appearances	
	1		2	3	2	7	3	11	3	6	1	3	2		3	1	2	6	3	2	1		2		2	League Sub Appearances	
2		2	2	2	2	1	2	2	1		0+1		2	0+1		1		0+1	1					1		C/Cola Cup Appearances	
1		3	1	2	2	3	3	2+1	2		3	1	3		2	1									1	FA Cup Appearances	
	1	2	2		2	2	0+1	1	1+1	2		1+1	2	2	2	1									1	AW Trophy Appearances	

Also Played: Bradshaw 8(3),2(4),6(5),6(6),12(7),2(8),2(9), Gee 9(32,33),9.(34),9*(36),10(37,38), Shaw 10(5,6,7,8,9,10), Shilton P S(9,11,13), Quinn 10(22,23), Barber 11(27,28,29*30,31*), Shilton S 12(24),14(25), Osman S(51,52,53).

Players on Loan: Bradshaw (Peterborough), Shaw (Stoke City), Quinn (Coventry City), Barber (Millwall), Gee (Leicester City)

† = Sent Off

CLUB RECORDS

BIGGEST VICTORIES
8-1 v Millwall,Division 2, 16.1.1932   8-1 v Hartlepool U. (a),
Division 2, 7.5.1994   7-0 v Doncaster Rovers, Division 2, 5.9.1936
6-0 v Corby, FA Cup Round 3,22.1.1966

BIGGEST DEFEATS
0-9 v Stoke City, Division 2, 17.12.1960
Record Cup Defeat
1-7 v Tottenham Hotspur, FA Cup Rnd 4, 1966-67   0-6 v West Ham
United, League Cup Rnd 2, 26.9.1962

MOST LEAGUE POINTS
(3pts for win) 87, Division 3, 1986-87
(2pts for win)68, Division 3S, 1929-30

MOST LEAGUE GOALS
107, Division 3S, 1925-26 (42 games)   107, Division 3S,1951-52
(46 games)

RECORD TRANSFER FEE RECEIVED
£350,000 from Southend for Gary Poole, July 1993
£350,000 from Crystal Palace for Marc Edworthy, May 1995

RECORD TRANSFER FEE PAID
£300,000 to Port Vale for Peter Swan, July 1994

BEST PERFORMANCES
League: Third in Div 2 1931-32, 1952-53   FA Cup: Semi-Finalists
1983-84
League Cup: Semi-Finalists 1964-65, 1973-74

HONOURS
Champions Division 3S 1929-30, 1951-52   Champions Division 3
1958-59

LEAGUE CAREER
Founder Members of Division 3 1920   Transferred to Division 3S
1921-22
Promoted to Div 2 1929-30   Relegated to Div 3S 1949-50
Promoted to Div 21951-52   Relegated to Div 3S 1955-56
Transferred to Div 3 1958-59   Promoted to Div 2 1958-59
Relegated to Div 31967-68   Promoted to Div 2 1974-75
Relegated to Div 3 1976-77   Promoted to Div 2 1985-86
Relegated to Div 3/21991-92 Relegated to Div 3 1994/95

INDIVIDUAL CLUB RECORDS

MOST APPEARANCES FOR CLUB
Kevin Hodges (1978-93): League 502+28, FA Cup 39,League Cup
32+3, Other 9+2 Total 582+33

MOST CAPPED PLAYER
Moses Russell (Wales) 20, 1920-28

RECORD GOALSCORER IN A MATCH
Wilf Carter, 5 v Charlton Athletic, 6-4, Div 2,27.12.1960

RECORD LEAGUE GOALSCORER IN A SEASON
Jack Cock, 32, 1926-27 In All Competitions: Jack Cock, 32 (all
league) 1926-27   W Carter 32 (League 26, FA Cup 6) 1957-58
Tommy Tynan, 32 (League 31, FA Cup 1) 1984-85

RECORD LEAGUE GOALSCORER IN A CAREER
Sam Black, 176, 1924-37 In All Competitions: Sam Black, 185
(League 176, FA Cup 9) 1924-37

OLDEST PLAYER IN A LEAGUE MATCH
Peter Shilton, 44 years 21 days v Burnley Div 2, 9.10.1993.

YOUNGEST PLAYER IN A LEAGUE MATCH
Sam Shilton, 16 years 4 months 19 days v Brighton, 10.12.94.

PREVIOUS MANAGERS

1903-05 Frank Brettall   1905-06 Bob Jack   1906-07 Will Fullerton
1910-38 Bob Jack   1938-48 Jack Tresadern   1948-55 Jim Rae
1955-60 Jack Rowley   1960-61 George Taylor/ Neil Dougall
1961-63 Ellis Stuttard   1963 Vic Buckingham   1963-64 Andy
Beattie   1964-65 Malcolm Allison   1965-68 Derek Ufton   1968-
70 Billy Bingham   1970-72 Ellis Stuttard   1972-77 Tony Waiters
1977-78 Mike Kelly   1978 Lennie Lawrence   1978-79 Malcolm
Allison   1979-81 Bobby Saxton   1981-83 Bobby Moncur   1983-
84 John Hore   1984-88 Dave Smith   1988-90 Ken Brown   1990-
92 David Kemp 1992-95 Peter Shilton, 1995 Steve McCall.

ADDITIONAL INFORMATION
Previous Name: Argyle Athletic Club 1886-1903
Club colours: Green & white diagonals with black flashes, black
shorts with green and white trim, green & white hooped socks with
black trim. **Change colours:** Yellow shirts with green & black
flashes, green shorts, yellow socks.
Reserves League: Avon Combination

LONGEST LEAGUE RUNS

of undefeated matches:	22 (1929)	of league matches w/out a win:	13 (1962-63)
of undefeated home matches:	47 (1921-23)	of undefeated away matches:	9 (1929)
without home win:	8 (1989-90)	without an away win:	27 (1975-76)
of league wins:	9 (1930,1986)	of home wins:	17 (1922)
of league defeats:	9 (1947)	of away wins:	6 (1929)

THE MANAGER

NEIL WARNOCK . . . . appointed 22nd June 1995.

PREVIOUS CLUBS
As Manager . . . . Gainsborough Trinity, Burton Albion, Scarborough, Notts County, Huddersfield Town.
As Asst.Man/Coach . . . . None.
As a player . . . . Chesterfield, Rotherham United, Hartlepool United, Scunthorpe United, Aldershot, Barnsley,
. . . . York City, Crewe Alexandra.

HONOURS
As a Manager . . . . Notts County: Div.2 promotion 1991, Div.3 promotion 1990.
. . . . Huddersfield: Promotion to Div.1, 1995. Scarborough: Conference League Champions 1987.
As a Player . . . . None.

PLYMOUTH ARGYLE

PLAYERS NAME / Honours	Ht	Wt	Birthdate	Birthplace / Transfers	Contract Date	Clubs	League	L/Cup	FA Cup	Other	Lge	L/C	FAC	Oth
GOALKEEPERS														
Nicky Hammond	6.0	11.13	07.09.67	Hornchurch	12.07.85	Arsenal (A)								
				Loan	23.08.86	Bristol Rovers	3							
				Free	01.07.87	Swindon Town	65+2	11	10	6				
				£40,000	08.95	Plymouth Argyle								
Martin Hodge	6.2	14.2	04.02.59	Southport	01.02.77	Plymouth A. (A)	43	1	1					
Loans from Everton:				£135,000	01.07.79	Everton	25		6					
Preston N.E., 13.12.81, 28 Lge App.				£50,000	01.08.83	Sheffield Wednesday	197	24	25	3				
Oldham Ath., 22.07.82, 4 Lge App.				£250,000	31.08.88	Leicester City	75	4	1	1				
Gillingham, 13.01.83, 4 Lge App.				Free	07.08.91	Hartlepool United	69	8	6	6				
Preston N.E., 27.02.83, 16 Lge App.				Free	12.07.93	Rochdale	42	4	2	1				
				£10,000	.08.94	Plymouth Argyle	17	2	1					
Alan Nicholls	5.11	12.0	28.08.73	Birmingham		Wolverhampton (T)								
E: u21.1.				Free		Cheltenham Town								
				£5,000	01.08.93	Plymouth Argyle	64+1	1	7	6				
D E F E N D E R S														
Andrew Comyn	6.1	11.12	02.08.68	Wakefield	05.08.86	Manchester Utd (J)								
				Free		Alvechurch								
				£34,000	22.08.89	Aston Villa	12+3	2+1	2	1				
				£200,000	08.08.91	Derby County	59+4	7	3+1	9	1		1	2
				£200,000	01.08.93	Plymouth Argyle	76	4	7	6	5			
Micky Heathcote	6.1	12.7	10.09.65	Kelloe		Spennymoor								
				£15,000	19.08.87	Sunderland	6+3			0+1				
				Loan	17.12.87	Halifax Town	7		1		1			
				Loan	04.01.90	York City	3			1				
				£55,000	12.07.90	Shrewsbury Town	43+1	6	5	4	6			
				£150,000	12.09.91	Cambridge United	123+5	7	5+2	7	13	1	2	2
				£70,000	08.95	Plymouth Argyle								
Keith Hill	6.0	11.3	17.05.69	Bolton	09.05.87	Blackburn Rov. (J)	89+7	6	5+1	3+2	4	1		
					23.09.92	Plymouth Argyle	96+3	7	7	7	2			
Steve McCall	5.11	11.3	15.10.60	Carlisle	05.10.78	Ipswich Town (A)	249+1	29	23+1	18+1	7		1	3
E: B.1, u21.6, Y.6. UEFAC'81. UEFA u21'82.				£300,000	03.06.87	Sheffield Wednesday	21+8	2+3	1	0+1	2			
				Loan	08.02.90	Carlisle United	6							
				£25,000	26.03.92	Plymouth Argyle	88+1	5	6	6	4			
Dominic Naylor	5.10	11.7	12.08.70	Watford	20.09.88	Watford (T)								
FAYC'89.				Loan	06.12.89	Halifax Town	5+1			1+1	1			
via Hong Kong (Free)				Free	12.08.91	Barnet	50+1	2	5	4			1	
				Free	16.07.93	Plymouth Argyle	84+1	2	8	4+1	1			
Mark Patterson	5.10	11.5	13.09.68	Leeds	30.06.86	Carlisle United (T)	19+3	4						
				£60,000	10.11.87	Derby County	41+10	5+2	4	5+1	3			2
				£85,000	23.07.93	Plymouth Argyle	78+1	2	6	5	3			
Peter Swan	6.2	12.0	28.09.66	Leeds	06.08.84	Leeds United (T)	43+6	3	3	1+2	11	2		
AGT'93.				£200,000	23.03.89	Hull City	76+4	2+3	2	1	24	1		
				£300,000	16.08.91	Port Vale	105+6	6	9	12	6		1	1
				£300,000	22.07.94	Plymouth Argyle	24+3	2		2	2	1		
Paul R C Williams	5.6	10.7	11.09.69	Leicester	01.07.88	Leicester City (T)								
					05.07.89	Stockport County	61+9	3	4	7+5	4			1
				£150,000	12.08.93	Coventry City	8+6	3+1	1					
				Loan	19.11.93	West Bromwich A.	5							
				Loan	17.03.95	Huddersfield Town	9			1				
				£50,000	08.95	Plymouth Argyle								
M I D F I E L D														
Martin Barlow	5.7	10.3	26.06.71	Plymouth	01.07.89	Plymouth A. (T)	127+25	6+1	7	8+1	9	2		
Wayne Burnett	6.0	12.6	04.09.71	Lambeth	13.11.89	Leyton Orient (T)	34+6	3+1	3+1	4	1	1		
E: Y.1.				£90,000	19.08.92	Blackburn Rovers								
					09.08.93	Plymouth Argyle	55+9	1	8	3+1	3			
Gary Clayton	5.10	11.7	02.02.63	Sheffield		Rotheram Utd (A)								
ESP1			via Burton Albion to		23.08.86	Doncaster Rovers	34+1	2	3	2	5			
				£10,000	02.07.87	Cambridge United	166+13	17+1	9	7	14	3		2
Loan Peterborough Utd, (25.01.91), 4 Lg Apps.				£20,000	18.02.94	Huddersfield Town	15+4		0+1	4	1			2
				P.E.	08.95	Plymouth Argyle								
Chris Leadbitter	5.9	10.6	17.10.67	Middlesbrough	04.09.85	Grimsby Town (A)								
Div.3'91.				Free	21.08.86	Hereford United	32+4	2	2	3	1			
				Free	02.08.88	Cambridge United	144+32	14	16+2	11+2	18	3	3	1
				£25,000	16.08.93	Bournemouth	20+7	2+1	3	1				
				Free	08.95	Plymouth Argyle								
Adrian Littlejohn	5.9	10.5	26.09.70	Wolverhampton		West Brom A. (T)								
E: S.				Free	24.05.89	Walsall	26+18	2+1	1+1	4+1	1			
				Free	06.08.91	Sheffield United	44+25	5+1	3+2	1	12		1	1
				£100,000	08.95	Plymouth Argyle								
Ron Mauge	5.10	10.6	10.03.69	Islington	22.07.87	Charlton Athletic (T)								
				Free	21.09.88	Fulham	47+3	4	1	2	2			
				£40,000	30.07.90	Bury	92+15	8+2	8	10+2	10	2	2	
				Loan	26.09.91	Manchester City				0+1				
				£40,000	08.95	Plymouth Argyle								
Mark Saunders				Tiverton										
				Free		Plymouth Argyle								
F O R W A R D S														
Chris Billy	6.0	10.9	02.01.73	Huddersfield	01.07.91	Huddersfield T (T)	46+11	5+1	3	9+1	2			
				P.E.	08.95	Plymouth Argyle								
Michael Evans	6.0	11.5	11.01.73	Plymouth	30.03.91	Plymouth A. (T)	56+29	6	4+2	2	14		1	
Kevin Nugent	6.1	12.4	10.04.69	Edmonton	08.07.87	Leyton Orient (T)	86+8	9+3	9	9+1	19	6	3	1
Ei: Y.				£200,000	23.03.92	Plymouth A. (T)	120+5	9	10	4+3	31	2	3	
Daniel O'Hagan	6.1	13.08	24.04.76	Truro	29.06.94	Plymouth A. (T)	1+2			1	1			
Michael Ross	5.7	9.13	02.09.71	Southampton	30.12.88	Portsmouth (T)	0+4		0+1	2+3				
				£35,000	01.08.93	Exeter City	27+1	4	3	2+1	9		1	
					22.11.94	Plymouth Argyle	11+6		1				1	
Chris Twiddy	5.11	11.06	19.01.76	Pontypridd	29.06.94	Plymouth Argyle (T)	13+2	0+1	1	2	1			
W: Y.1.														

HOME PARK

Plymouth, Devon PL2 3DQ
Tel: 01752 562 561

Capacity 19,700
Covered Standing 7,000
Seating 6,400

First game .... v Northampton T, Sth Lge, 2-0, 5.9.1903.
First floodlit game .... v Exeter, 26.10.1953.

ATTENDANCES
Highest .... 43,596 v Aston Villa, Division 2, 10.10.1936.
Lowest .... 1,875 v Hull, 11.5.1979.

OTHER GROUNDS .... None.

MATCHDAY TICKET PRICES

Grandstand Centre £10
OAP £8
Grandstand Wing £9
Juv/OAP £7
Mayflower £9
OAP £7
Lynhurst £8
Juv/OAP £6
Standing
Lynhurst/Devonport £6
Juv/OAP £4.50
Mayflower £6
Juv/OAP £4.50
Barn Park (Visitors) £5.50
Ticket Office Telephone no. 01752 562 561

HOW TO GET TO THE GROUND

From all directions
Use A38 Plymouth bypass as far as the Tavastock Road (A386).
Then branch left and follow signs to Plymouth (A386).
In 0.7 miles turn right then left (A3041) into Outland Road for Plymouth Argyle FC.

Car Parking
Free car park adjoining ground, space for 1,000 cars.

Nearest Railway Station
Plymouth (01752 21300)

CLUBCALL
0898 12 16 88

Calls cost 39p per minute cheap rate and 49p per
minute at all other times.
Call costings correct at time of going to press.

MATCHDAY PROGRAMME

Programme Editor .... Gordon Sparks.

Number of pages .... 48.

Price .... £1.30.

Subscriptions .... £46 per year for all home programmes.

Local Newspapers .... Evening Herald.

Local Radio Stations .... Plymouth Sound AM (11.52 Kz).

PRESTON NORTH END
(The Lillywhites)
ENDSLEIGH LEAGUE DIVISION 3
SPONSORED BY:BAXI PARTNERSHIP

Back Row (L-R): Gareth Ainsworth, Lee Cartwright, Simon Davey, Allan Smart, Barry Richardson, David Lucas, John Vaughan, Steve Wilkinson, Kevin Magee, Graeme Atkinson. **Middle Row:** Geoff McDougle (Chief Scout), Brian Hickson (Kit Manager), Paul Raynor, Ryan Kidd, Andy Saville, Jamie Squires, John Calligan, Steve Holmes, Kevin Kilbane, Mick Rathbone (Physio), Jim Parker (Yth Physio). **Front Row:** Joe Jakub (Yth Dev. Officer), Chris Borwick, Terry Fleming, Andy Fensome, David Moyes (Player Coach), Gary Peters (Manager), Ian Bryson Capt), Graham Lancashire, Mickey Brown, Raymond Sharp, Chris Sulley (Yth Manager).

PRESTON NORTH END
FORMED IN 1881
TURNED PROFESSIONAL IN 1885
LTD COMPANY IN 1893

PRESIDENT: Tom Finney, OBE,CBE,JP
VICE-PRESIDENT: T C Nicholson, JP,FCIOB
CHAIRMAN: Bryan Gary
VICE-CHAIRMAN
M J Woodhouse
DIRECTORS
J E Starkie LL.B (Lond), D Shaw (MD),
M J Woodhouse (jnr)
SECRETARY
Mrs Audrey Shaw (01772 795 919)
GENERAL MANAGER
Phil Critchley
MANAGER: Gary Peters

YOUTH TEAM MANAGER
Chris Sulley
PHYSIOTHERAPIST
Mick Rathbone

STATISTICIAN FOR THE DIRECTORY
Lawrence Bland

An interesting season, finished disappointingly when we lost both the play-off games with Bury. It was a season of many changes, which mostly should be beneficial in the long term. The pre-season transfer of Tony Ellis to Blackpool, left the side short of a regular goalscorer, and he was never satisfactorily replaced. Seven league defeats during September and October found the side in 16th place and ruined any chances of automatic promotion, and ultimately led to the resignation of manager John Beck on December 2nd. His assistant, Gary Peters, became the new manager, and he did well to lift the North End to 5th place and the play-offs. We shall have to leave promotion until next season. There was little cup success, although the FA Cup win over Blackpool brought much local satisfaction, in a game televised live by Sky.

September saw the take-over of the club by Baxi Partnership Limited, with Bryan Gray becoming the new Chairman. Money being provided for new signings, with the ground being bought back from the local council. The rebuilding of the ground will being during the summer with the demolition of the old 1906 West Stand, to be replaced by an all-seater stand, which will incorporate a National Football Museum. At long last grass returned to Deepdale (first used on September 3rd), with the pitch being widened in January by four yards to encourage more attacking play. The club were the best supported in Division 3, with Gary Peters being manager of the month for March. Andy Fensome was the player of the season.

There were again many signings and transfers. John Beck signed Terry Fleming and Barry Richardson (Northampton), Mark Sale (Torquay), Neil Trebble (Scunthorpe), John Vaughan (Charlton), Graham Atkinson (Hull), Richard Sharp (Dunfermline), Dean Emerson (Stockport), Allan Smart (Caledonian) and Micky Brown (Shrewsbury), Gary Peters added Graham Lancashire (Burnley), Simon Davey (Carlisle United) and Matt Carmichael (Scunthorpe). Transfers were Tony Ellis (Blackpool), Liam Watson (Marine), Steve Woods (Motherwell), Trevor Matthewson (Bury), Kelham O'Hanlon (Dundee United), Mike Norbury (Doncaster), Greg Challender (Southport), Stuart Hicks and Neil Trebble (Scarborough), Dean Emerson (Chorley) and Neil Whalley (Altrincham). Gavin Nebbeling retired. David Beckham (Manchester United), Stuart Rimmer (Chester) and Steve Welsh (Peterborough) came on loan.

Junior players signed on professional terms were Chris Borwick, John Calligan, Kevin Kilbane, David Lucas and Jamie Squires. Chris Sulley became the club's youth development officer, being assisted by Gavin Nebbeling and latterly by David Hamilton. At the end of the season, Michael Carmichael and Richard Lucas were released. David Moyes becoming player-coach with ex-player Mick Rathbone returning as physio. **LAWRENCE BLAND.**

PRESTON NORTH END

Division Three: 5th | **FA Cup:** 2nd Round | **Coca-Cola Cup:** 1st Round

M	DATE	COMP.	VEN	OPPONENTS	RESULT	H/T	LP	GOAL SCORERS/GOAL TIMES	ATT.
1	A 13	EL	A	Darlington	D 0-0	0-0			(3,315)
2	16	CC 1/1	H	**Stockport County**	D 1-1	0-1		Fensome 90 (pen)	2,385
3	20	EL	A	Hereford United	W 2-0	0-0	8	Conroy 82, Sale 86	(3,039)
4	23	CC 1/2	A	**Stockport County**	L 1-4	0-0		Moves 86	(4,547)
5	27	EL	A	Barnet	L 1-2	0-0	10	Sale 49	(2,441)
6	30	EL	A	Bury	D 0-0	0-0	14		(3,623)
7	S 3	EL	A	Lincoln City	W 4-0	0-0	7	Moves 48, Sale 50, Ainsworth 53, Greenall 85 (og)	(8,837)
8	10	EL	A	Fulham	W 1-0	0-0	7	Trebble 88	(5,001)
9	13	EL	A	Gillingham	W 3-2	2-2	5	Sale 22, 26, Fleming 78	(2,555)
10	17	EL	H	Darlington	L 1-3	0-1	6	Trebble 76	8,484
11	24	EL	A	Doncaster Rovers	L 1-2	0-0	8	Fleming 89	(3,321)
12	27	AWT 1	H	**Chester City**	D 1-1	1-1		Trebble 29	3,242
13	O 1	EL	H	Walsall	L 1-2	1-0	11	Whalley 41	7,852
14	8	EL	H	Scunthorpe United	L 0-1	0-0	11		6,895
15	15	EL	A	Hartlepool United	L 1-3	1-2	14	Atkinson 27	(2,002)
16	22	EL	A	Colchester United	L 1-3	0-1	16	Trebble 46	(3,015)
17	29	EL	H	Exeter City	L 0-1	0-1	16		6,808
18	N 5	EL	A	Mansfield Town	W 2-1	2-1	16	Conroy 28, 41	(3,602)
19	8	AWT 1	A	**Bury**	L 0-1	0-0			(1,756)
20	14	FAC 1	H	**Blackpool**	W 1-0	1-0		Conroy 14	14,036
21	19	EL	H	Northampton Town	W 2-0	1-0	14	Moves 36, Raynor 72	7,297
22	26	EL	A	Chesterfield	L 0-1	0-0	15		(3,191)
23	D 3	FAC 2	H	**Walsall**	D 1-1	1-1		Smart 5	9,767
24	10	EL	H	Hereford United	W 4-2	3-0	10	Bryson 31, (pen), 58 (pen), Magee 13, Conroy 21	6,581
25	13	FAC 2R	A	**Walsall**	L 0-4	0-2			(6,468)
26	17	EL	H	Barnet	W 1-0	0-0	9	Kidd 88	6,429
27	26	EL	H	Rochdale	W 3-0	3-0	9	Smart 10, Kidd 28, Conroy 41	10,491
28	31	EL	H	Scarborough	W 1-0	0-0	10	Smart 79	8,407
29	J 2	EL	A	Torquay United	L 0-1	0-1	11		(3,770)
30	10	EL	H	Colchester United	W 2-1	1-0	10	Smart 44, Trebble 85	6,377
31	14	EL	A	Carlisle United	D 0-0	0-0	10		(10,684)
32	21	EL	H	Mansfield Town	W 2-1	1-1	6	Bryson 23, Smart 62	8,448
33	24	EL	A	Wigan Athletic	D 1-1	0-1	6	Cartwright 81	(3,618)
34	F 4	EL	H	Chesterfield	D 0-0	0-0	7		8,544
35	11	EL	A	Northampton Town	L 1-2	0-0	8	Smart 64	(5,195)
36	18	EL	H	Carlisle United	W 1-0	1-0	6	Conroy 38	11,867
37	28	EL	A	Walsall	D 2-2	1-1	6	Conroy 6, Raynor 87	(4,492)
38	M 4	EL	H	Doncaster Rovers	D 2-2	0-1	9	Davey 47, Beckham 56	9,624
39	11	EL	H	Fulham	W 3-2	1-1	6	Conroy 23, Raynor 48, Beckham 50	8,601
40	18	EL	H	Bury	W 5-0	2-0	6	Carmichael 41, 89, Conroy 45, 77, Moyes 52	9,626
41	21	EL	A	Exeter City	W 1-0	0-0	6	Bryson 55	(2,057)
42	25	EL	A	Lincoln City	D 1-1	0-1	6	Kidd 78	(5,487)
43	A 1	EL	H	Gillingham	D 1-1	1-0	6	Carmichael 38	9,100
44	8	EL	A	Scarborough	D 1-1	1-1	6	Bryson 32	(4,266)
45	15	EL	H	Wigan Athletic	W 1-0	1-0	6	Smart 23	10,238
46	17	EL	A	Rochdale	W 1-0	1-0	5	Davey 39	(4,012)
47	22	EL	H	Torquay United	L 0-1	0-0	6		9,173
48	29	EL	H	Hartlepool United	W 3-0	2-0	5	Moyes 11, Holmes 16, Davey 51	9,129
49	M 6	EL	A	Scunthorpe United	L 1-2	1-2	5	Sale 10,	(3,691)
50	14	PO	H	Bury	L 0-1	0-1			13,297
51	17	PO	A	Bury	L 0-1	0-0			(9,094)
52									
53									
54									
55									
56									
57									
58									
59									
60									

Best Home League Attendance: 11,867 v Carlisle United | **Smallest:** 6,377 v Colchester | **Av Home Att:** 8,514

Goal Scorers:

League (58): Conroy 10, Sale 6, Smart 6, Bryson 5 (2 pens), Moyes 4, Trebble 4, Carmichael 3, Davey 3, Kidd 3, Raynor 3, Beckham 2, Fleming 2, Ainsworth, Atkinson, Cartwright, Holmes, Magee, Whalley, Opponent

C/Cola Cup (2): Fensome (pen), Moyes

FA Cup (2): Conroy, Smart

AW Trophy (1): Trebble

Compared with 1993-94: +1,137

Richardson B	Fensome A	Fleming T	Whalley D	Hicks S	Moyes D	Ainsworth G	Cartwright L	Raynor P	Treble N	Bryson J	O'Hanlon K	Squires J	Sale M	Kidd R	Conroy M	Vaughan J	Lucas D	Atkinson G	Sharp R	Holmes S	Emerson D	Smart A	Magee K	Rimmer S	Lancashire G	Referee	
1	2	3	4	5	6	7	8	9	10	11	S	S	S													Rennie U.	1
1	2	3	4	5	6		7	9	10•	11*	S		14	8	12											Rejer P.	2
1	2	11	4	5	6	7	8	9*			S	S	10	3	12											Orr D.	3
1	2	11	4	5	6	7*	8	14		12			9•	3	10	S										Cruikshanks I.	4
1	2	3	4	5		7	8	14	9*	11			12	6	10•	S										Harris R.	5
1	2	S	4		6	7	S	9		8		5		10	3	11	S									Cain G.	6
1	2	12	4		6	7	14	9		8•		5		10	3	11*	S									Singh G.	7
1	2	11•	4	5	6	7*	14	9	12	8				10+	3		S									Wilkes C.	8
1	2	11	4•	5	6	7	14	9*	12	8				10	3		S									Foakes P.	9
1	2	11	4		6	7	14	9	12	8		5	10*	3•			S									Butler A.	10
1	2	9	4		S	6	7	S	11	10	8			5	3		S									Brandwood J.	11
1	2	12	4•		6	7	14	11†	10*	8		5	9	3		S										Dawson A.	12
1	2	12	4		6	7	14	11*	10	8*		5	9	3			S									Furnandiz P.	13
1	2	10	4	5	6	7		11	12	8			9*	3		S		S								Vanes P.	14
S	2	14	4*	5+		7	12	10	8			9•	6+		1		11	3	3							Burns W.	15
S	2	12	4	5		6	7*		9	8			14		10•	1		11	3								Leach K.	16
S	2	7	4*		6		14	9		8			12		10•	1		11	3	5							Kirkby J.	17
S	2	7	12		6		4	9		8	5*	S		10	1		11	3									Breen K.	18
S	2	11*	12		6		4	9	7	8			10		1			3	5							Allison D.	19
1	2		12		6	7*	4	9	11	8			14		10•		S		3	5						Dilkes R.	20
1	2	14		6	7	4	9	11•	8*				10		S		3	5	12							Riley M.	21
1	2			6		4	12	7*	8				11		S		3	5	S	9						Wright P.	22
1	2	12			6		4	11•	7*	8				10		S		3	5	14	9					Hart R.	23
1	2	14			6		4	11	8				10		S		3	5	9•	7•	12					Heilbron T.	24
1	2*	4		6		7	11•	14	8				10		S		3	5	12	9	12					Hart R.	25
1	2	S		6		7	11		8			5	10		S		3	4	9*	12						Rennie U.	26
1	2		6		4	11		8			5	10	S		12	3		9•	7•		14				Cain G.	27
1**	2		6		4	11		8			5	10•	12**		14	3*		9	7	15						Cruikshanks I.	28
2	3		6	7*		12	8			5	14	1		S	11		9•			10						Brandwood J.	29
2	3		6		4	11	14	8			5		1	S	12		9•	7•	10							Barry N.	30
S	2	3		6		4	11	12	8			5		1	14		9*	7•	10							Burns W.	31
S	3	3		6		4	11	14	8			5		1	12		9•	7*	10							Flood A.	32
S	2	14		6	7	4	11	12	8			5		1	3*		9•		10							Lomas E.	33
S	2		6		4	11	14	8			5		1	12	3		9•	7*	10							Lupton K.	34
S	2		6	7*	4	11	12	8			5		1	10	3		9	S								Kirkby J.	35
S	2		6		4	11		8			5	10	1		12	3		9•	7*		14					West T.	36
S	2		6		4	11		8			5	10	1		5	3		9•		12						Mathieson S.	37
S	2		6		4	11*	8			5	10	1			3		14			9.						Watson J.	38
S	2		6		12	9		8*			5	10	1		3		S	11								Lynch K.	39
S	2		6		S		12	8			5	10	1		3		S	11								Dawson A.	40
S	2		6		14	12	8			5	10	1			3		S	11*								Singh G.	41
S	2		6		12	4	8		5		5	10	1			3		11•								Furnandiz R.	42
S	2		6		11	4	8		5			10	1		10	3		14	11*							Winter J.	43
S	2	3		6		11	4	8		5			10	1	S					12						Rushton J.	44
S	2	3		6*	4	11	8			5	10	1				9•			14							Watson J.	45
S	2	3		4	11	8		6		5	14	1			9*			12								Cain G.	46
S	2	3		4	11	8		6		5*	10•	1		10	3		9		14	11*						Flood A.	47
S	2	3		6		4	8			1		S	5		S	11		9								Riley M.	48
S	2*	3		6		12	4	8		10•	5	1		11			9									Heilbron T.	49
S	2	3		6		14	4•	8		10•	5	12	1						11			9				Winter J.	50
S	2•	3		6	14	11	4		8		10*	5						9			1	1			1	Kirby J.	51
17	42	20	14	8	38	16	25	34	8	41		11	10	32	22	25		8	21	5	1	17	14		9	League Appearances	
	7	1			11	4	11					3			3	1	7			1		2		2	8	League Sub Appearances	
2	2	2		2	2	1	2	1+1	1	1+1			1+1	2	1+1											C/Cola Cup Appearances	
3	3	0+1	1+1		3	1	3	2+1	3		0+1								3	3	0+2	2				FA Cup Appearances	
1	1+1	1+1		2	1	1+1	2	2	2		1	2	1		1	1										AW Trophy Appearances	
2	2		2	0+1	1+1	2		2			2	2	0+2	2							1	1		1		Play-Offs Appearances	

Also Played: Davey 7(37,38,39,40,41,42,43,44,45,46,47,48,49,50,51), 9(40,41)9*(42,44),9.(43),12(45,47),10.(46),10(48),14(49) Welsh S(19), Beckham 12(38),4(39,40,41,42)

Players on Loan: Beckham D. (Manchester United), Rimmer S. (Chester City), Welsh S (Peterborough United)

† = Sent Off

PRESTON NORTH END   RECORDS AND STATISTICS

CLUB RECORDS

RECORD LEAGUE VICTORY
10-0 v Stoke City (h), Div 1, 14.9.1889
Most Goals Scored in a Cup Tie
26-0 v Hyde, FA Cup 1st Round, 15.10.1887

RECORD LEAGUE DEFEAT
0-7 v Blackpool (h), Div 1, 1.5.1948   0-7 v Nottingham Forest (a),
Div 2, 9.4.1927
Record Cup Defeat
0-6 v Charlton Athletic, FA Cup Round 5, 1945-46

MOST LEAGUE POINTS
(2pts for win) 61, Div 1, 1970-71
(3pts for win) 90 1986-87

MOST LEAGUE GOALS
100 Div 2, 1927-28   100 Div 1, 1957-58

RECORD TRANSFER FEE RECEIVED
£765,000 Manchester City for Michael Robinson, June 1979

RECORD TRANSFER FEE PAID
£125,000 to Norwich City for Mike Flynn, 4.12.89

BEST PERFORMANCES
League: Champions Div 1 (2) FA Cup: Winners (2)
League Cup: 4th Round 1963, 1966, 1972, 1981

HONOURS
Champions Div 1 *1888-89 (first winners), 1889-90   Champions
Div 2,1903-04, 1912-13, 1950-51   Champions Div 3 1970-71   FA
Cup Winners *1889,1938
*League and FA Cup Double

LEAGUE CAREER
Original Members of Football League 1888   Relegated to Div
21900-01   Promoted to Div 1 1903-04
Relegated to Div 2 1911-12   Promoted to Div 1 1912-13
Relegated to Div 21913-14   Promoted to Div 1 1914-15
Relegated to Div 2 1924-25   Promoted to Div 1 1933-34
Relegated to Div 21948-49   Promoted to Div 1 1950-51
Relegated to Div 2 1960-61   Relegated to Div 3 1969-70
Promoted to Div 21970-71   Relegated to Div 3 1973-74
Promoted to Div 2 1977-78   Relegated to Div 3 1980-81
Relegated to Div 41984-85   Promoted to Div 3 (now Div 2) 1986-
87   Relegated to Div 4/3 1992-93

INDIVIDUAL CLUB RECORDS

MOST APPEARANCES FOR CLUB
Alan Kelly (1961-75): League 447+Cup games 65 Total512

MOST CAPPED PLAYER: TOM FINNEY, 76 ENGLAND
Record Goalscorer in a Match: Jimmy Ross, 8 v Hyde (h), 26-0, 1st
Round FA Cup,15.10.1887

RECORD LEAGUE GOALSCORER IN A SEASON
Ted Harper 37, Div 2, 1932-33 In All Competitions: Ted Harper 37
(League 37) 1932-33

RECORD LEAGUE GOALSCORER IN A CAREER
Tom Finney 187 In All Competitions: Tom Finney 210 (League 187
+ FA Cup 23) 1946-60

OLDEST PLAYER IN A LEAGUE MATCH
Bob Kelly 40 years 50 days, 5.1.1935 v Everton(h)

YOUNGEST PLAYER IN A LEAGUE MATCH
Steve Doyle, 16 years 166 days, 15.11.1974 v Tranmere Rovers (a)

PREVIOUS MANAGERS

1919 V Hayes   1924 T Lawrence   1925 F Richards   1927 A
Gibson   1931-32 L Hyde   1932-36 No Manager   1936-37 T
Muirhead   1937-49 No Manager   1949-53 W Scott   1953-54 Scot
Symon   1954-56 F Hill   1956-61 C Britton   1961-68 J Milne
1968-70 R Seith   1970-73 A Ball (Snr)   1973 F Lord (Caretaker)
1973-75 R Charlton   1975-77 H Catterick   1977-81 N Stiles   1981
T Docherty   1981-83 G Lee   1983-85 A Kelly   1985 T Booth
1986 B Kidd   1986 J Clark (Caretaker)   J McGrath 1986-90   L
Chapman 1990-92   S Allardyce (Caretaker) 1992   John Beck 1992-
94 Gary Peters 1994-
ADDITIONAL INFORMATION
Club colours: White & green shirt, green shorts, white socks with
green hoops.
Change colours: Red shirts green sleeves, red shorts, red socks
with green hoops or as red shirts but in yellow.
Reserves League: Pontins League Div 2. **Youth:** Lancs Lge 1 & 2.

LONGEST LEAGUE RUNS

of undefeated matches:	23 (1888-89)	of league matches w/out a win:	15 (1923)
of undefeated home matches:	31 (1903-04)	of undefeated away matches:	11 (1888-89)
without home win:	9 (1965-66)	without an away win:	33 (1897-99)
of league wins:	14 (1950-51 - joint League record)	of home wins:	20 (1891-92)
of league defeats:	8 (1983, 1984)	of away wins:	8 (1950-51)

THE MANAGER

GARY PETERS . . . . appointed December 1994.

PREVIOUS CLUBS
As Manager . . . . None.
As Asst.Man/Coach . . . . Cambridge United, Preston North End.
As a player. . . . . Reading, Fulham, Wimbledon, Aldershot, Reading, Fulham.

HONOURS
As a Manager . . . . None.
As a Player . . . . Reading: Division 4 championship 1978-79. Division 3 Championship 1985-86.
. . . . Wimbledon: Division 4 championship 1982-83.

PRESTON NORTH END

PLAYERS NAME Honours	Ht	Wt	Birthdate	Birthplace Transfers	Contract Date	Clubs	League	L/Cup	FA Cup	Other	Lge	L/C	FAC	Oth
G O A L K E E P E R S														
Barry Richardson	6.1	12.1	05.08.69	Wallsend	20.05.88	Sunderland (T)								
					21.03.89	Scunthorpe United								
via Seaham Red Star, Free				Free	03.08.89	Scarborough	30	1		1				
				Free	16.06.91	Stockport County								
				Free	10.09.91	Northampton Town	96	4	5	8				
				£20,000	25.07.94	Preston North End	17	2	3	1				
John Vaughan	5.10	13.1	26.06.82	Isleworth	30.06.82	West Ham U. (A)								
Div.3'91.				Loan	11.03.85	Charlton Athletic	6							
Loan 05.09.85 Bristol Rovers 6 Lge App.				Loan	23.10.85	Wrexham	4							
Loan 04.03.86 Bristol City 2 Lge App.				£12,500	21.08.86	Fulham	44	4	4	3				
Loan 21.01.88 Bristol City 3 Lge App.				Free	06.06.88	Cambridge United	178	13	24	16				
				Free	05.08.93	Charlton Athletic	5+1		2	1+1				
				Free	26.07.94	Preston North End	25+1			3				
D E F E N D E R S														
Steven Holmes	6.2	13.0	13.01.71	Middlesbrough	17.07.89	Lincoln City (T)								
Free Gainsborough T. via Guisborough T.				£10,000	14.03.94	Preston North End	5		3	3	1			
				Loan	31.03.94	Bromsgrove Rovers								
				Loan	10.03.95	Hartlepool United	5				2			
Ryan Kidd	5.11	10.0	06.10.71	Radcliffe	12.07.90	Port Vale (T)	1	0+2		0+1				
				Free	15.07.92	Preston North End	80+3	3	4	5	4			
David Moyes	6.1	11.5	25.04.63	Blythswood			19+5	8+1		2+1				
SPD'92.				Free	28.10.83	Cambridge United	79	3	1	3	1			
				£10,000	10.10.85	Bristol City	83	6	5	15	6			
				£30,000	30.10.87	Shrewsbury Town	91+5	4	3	5	11		1	
					01.08.90	Dunfermline	105	7	5		13	1		
via Hamilton Acc. 5 Lge App.					01.08.95	Preston North End	67	2		10	7	1	1	1
Raymond Sharp	5.11	12.06	16.11.69	Stirling			151				1			
Loan Stenhousemuir 5 Lge App.					04.10.94	Preston North End	21		3	1				
James Squires	6.1	12.0	15.11.75	Preston	26.04.94	Preston N.E. (T)	15			2				
				Loan	08.95	Stafford Rangers								
M I D F I E L D														
Graeme Atkinson	5.8	10.5	11.11.71	Hull	06.05.90	Hull City (T)	129+20	6+3	4+1	7	23	2	1	
					07.10.94	Preston North End	8+7				1			
James Ian Bryson	5.11	11.11	26.11.62	Kilmarnock			194+21	12+7	14+2		40	1	3	
				£40,000	24.08.88	Sheffield United	138+17	11+2	18+4	7	36	1	4	3
				£20,000	12.08.93	Barnsley	16	2		2	3	1		
				£42,500	29.11.93	Preston N.E. (T)	65+1	1+1	4+1	7	2			1
Lee Cartwright	5.8	10.6	19.09.72	Rossendale	30.07.91	Preston N.E. (T)	138+18	6	11	9+2	10	1		
Andrew Fensome	5.7	10.10	18.02.69	Northampton	16.02.87	Norwich City (A)								
Div.3'91.				Free		Bury Town								
				Free	21.11.89	Cambridge United	122+4	11	17+2	9+1	1			
					08.10.93	Preston North End	73	2	7	9	1	1		
David A Lucas	5.10	11.4	22.09.70	Chapletown	01.07.89	Sheffield United (T)	8+2		1	0+1				
				£40,000	24.12.92	Preston North End	47+3		4	4+1				
				Loan	14.10.94	Lincoln City	4			2				
F O R W A R D S														
Gareth Ainsworth	5.9	11.9	10.05.73	Blackburn			Blackburn Rov (T)								
				Free	31.10.91	Northwich Victoria								
					21.01.92	Preston North End	2+3			1		1		
				Free	17.08.92	Cambridge United	1+3	0+1		1				
				Free	23.12.92	Preston North End	76+4	3	3+1	8+1	12		1	
Michael Brown	5.9	10.12	08.02.68	Birmingham	11.02.86	Shrewsbury T. (A)	174+16	17	10	11	9	2	1	
Div.3'94				£100,000	15.08.91	Bolton Wanderers	27+6	0+1	3	2	3			
				£25,000	23.12.92	Shrewsbury Town	66+1	8	3	2	11	1		
				£75,000	02.12.94	Preston North End								
Simon Davey	5.10	11.2	01.10.70	Swansea	03.07.89	Swansea City (T)	37+12	1	1+2	2+3	4		1	
WFAC'91.				Free	05.08.92	Carlisle United	105	10	7	15	18	1	2	2
				£75,000	23.02.94	Preston North End	13			2	3			
Terry Fleming	5.9	10.9	05.01.73	Marston Green	02.07.91	Coventry City (T)	8+5	0+1						
				Free	03.08.93	Northampton Town	26+5	2	0+1	0+1	1			
				Free	18.07.94	Preston North End	20+7	2	0+1	3+1	2			
Graham Lancashire	5.10	11.12	19.10.72	Blackpool	01.07.91	Burnley (T)	11+19		2+2	2+4	8		1	
Div.4'92.				Loan	20.11.92	Halifax Town	2			1+1				
				Loan	21.01.94	Chester City	10+1				7			
				£55,000	23.12.94	Preston North End	9+8			1				
Paul Raynor	5.8	11.12	29.04.66	Nottingham	02.04.84	Nottm. Forest (A)	3	1						
WFAC'89/'91.				Loan	28.03.85	Bristol Rovers	7+1							
				Free	15.08.85	Huddersfield Town	38+12	3	2+1	1	9			
				Free	27.03.87	Swansea City	170+21	11+1	8+1	15+1	27	3	1	3
Loan 17.10.88 Wrexham 6 Lge App.				Free	10.03.92	Cambridge United	46+3	5	1	2+1	2		1	
				£36,000	23.07.93	Preston North End	70+7	3+1	7	10	9		1	2
Andy Saville	6.0	12.0	12.12.64	Hull	23.09.83	Hull City	74+27	6	3+2	4+2	18	1	1	
				£100,000	23.03.89	Walsall	28+10	2		1+1	5			
				£80,000	09.03.90	Barnsley	71+11	5+1	2+1	4	20			1
				£60,000	13.03.92	Hartlepool United	37	4	4	3	13	1	5	1
				£155,000	22.03.93	Birmingham City	51+8	4	1	1	17	1		
Loan 30.12.94 Burnley 3+1 Lge, 1 FAC, 1 Lge gl				£100,000	08.95	Preston North End								
Allan Smart	6.2	12.07	08.07.74	Perth			Caledonian	4							
				£15,000	22.11.94	Preston North End	17+2		2	1	6		1	
Stephen J Wilkinson	5.10	10.9	01.09.68	Lincoln	06.09.86	Leicester City (A)	5+4		1		1			
				Loan	08.09.88	Crewe Alexandra	3+2				2			
				£80,000	02.10.89	Mansfield Town	214+18	13+1	10+1	17	83	4	2	1
				£90,000	08.95	Preston North End								

DEEPDALE

Preston PR1 6RU
Tel: 01772 795 919

Capacity...10,173
Seating 2,000
(New West Stand should be opened early 1996- approximate capacity of stand 8,000)
First game...v Eagley (F) 0-1, 5.10.1878.
First floodlit game ....v Bolton W., Lancs Senior Cup 1st Rnd, 3-0, Att: 12,000, 21.10.53.

ATTENDANCES
Highest ....42,684 v Arsenal, Div 1, 23.4.1938.
Lowest ....751 v Bury, AMC, 29.1.1986.

OTHER GROUNDS ....None.

MATCHDAY TICKET PRICES

Pavillion Stand........................ £10
Juv/OAP £6

West Stand . . . . *Under construction.*

Paddocks £7.50
Juv/OAP............................ £4.50

Kop & Town End £7
Juv/OAP .... Juv/OAP £4

Ticket Office Telephone no....... 01772 709 170

P.N.E. CLUBCALL
0891 66 02 20

Calls cost 39p per minute cheap rate and 49p per
minute at all other times.
Call costings correct at time of going to press.

HOW TO GET TO THE GROUND

From the North
Use motorway (M6) then M55 until junction 1, leave motorway and follow signs
to Preston A6. In 1.9 miles at crossroads turn left A5085 into Blackpool Road. In
0.8 miles turn right A6063 into Deepdale for Preston North End FC.

From the East and South
Use motorway (M6) until junction 31, leave motorway and follow signs Preston
A59. In 1 mile at roundabout take 2nd exit into Blackpool Road. In 1.3 miles turn
left A6063 into Deepdale for Preston North End FC.

From the West
Use motorway (M55) until junction 1, leave motorway and follow signs Preston
A6. In 1.9 miles at crossroads turn left A5085 into Blackpool Road. In 0.8 miles
turn right (A6063) into Deepdale for Preston North End FC.

Car Parking
Club park on Deepdale Road (West Stand) side of ground for 500 vehicles.
Limited off-street parking Cost (match-days): £1.00.

Nearest Railway Station
Preston (01772 59439)

MATCHDAY PROGRAMME

Programme Editor . . . . George Hodkinson.

Number of pages . . . . 32.

Price . . . . £1.30.

Subscriptions . . . . Home £31. Away £31. Home & Away £62.

Local Newspapers . . . . Lancashire Evening Post.

Local Radio Stations . . . . Red Rose Radio, Radio Lancashire.

ROCHDALE
(The Dale)
ENDSLEIGH LEAGUE DIVISION 3
SPONSORED BY: CARCRAFT

Back Row (L-R): Steve Whitehall, Mark Stewart, Paul Butler, Paul Williams, Ian Thompstone, Peter Valentine, David Bayliss.
Middle Row: Jimmy Robson, Graham Shaw, Darren Ryan, Ian Gray, Chris Clarke, Dean Martin, John Deary, Mick Docherty.
Front Row: Derek Hall, Jason Peeke, Dave Thompson, Kevin Formby, Alex Russell, Jamie Taylor, Andy Thackery.

ROCHDALE
FORMED IN 1907
TURNED PROFESSIONAL IN 1907
LTD COMPANY IN 1910

PRESIDENT: Mrs L Stoney
CHAIRMAN: D F Kilpatrick
DIRECTORS
J Marsh, G Morris, C Dunphy,
M Mace, G R Brierley
SECRETARY
Keith Clegg (01706 44648)
COMMERCIAL MANAGER
Stephen Walmsley (01706 47521)

MANAGER: Mick Docherty
RESERVE TEAM MANAGER
Jimmy Robson
YOUTH TEAM MANAGER
Keith Hicks
PHYSIOTHERAPIST
John Dawson

STATISTICIAN FOR THE DIRECTORY
Stephen Birch

A season promising so much ended with Rochdale facing a somewhat uncertain future. The team set off with the now familiar bang, winning four of the first six league games and holding top spot during August. As with similar promising starts in each of the past three seasons, form began to tail off, only this time the decline was sooner, sharper and more prolonged.

The tailspin coincided with the sale of central defender Alan Reeves to Premiership contenders Wimbledon. Over the next 12 games 32 goals were conceded. Just three league wins during the next four months saw the Dale in the bottom half of the table by the turn of the year. At this stage manager, Dave Sutton, who had achieved so much with so little but had also promised so much more, decided enough was enough and resigned.

An embarrassing month ensued during which a replacement was promised weekly but never emerged. Following a pointless Christmas, in all senses of the word, the board were left with little choice but to appoint Sutton's assistant Mick Docherty. Although Docherty's baptism coincided with a run of just one loss in 13 league games to open the New Year, Rochdale slipped further in the standings as draw piled upon draw. With just one win and five goals in the final nine games attendances dropped below the 2000 mark for the first time since the 1980s and the penultimate game against Scarborough 'attracted' just 1,170 fans, a seasonal low for the Football League.

Both major cup competitions brought first round dismissals, but the form book was turned upside down in the Autoglass trophy with five straight victories, two over second division opposition. Just one step away from the twin towers Rochdale lost badly in the first leg of the Northern Final at Carlisle and left themselves just too much to do in the return.

Rochdale's quartet of away wins again came in the most unlikely of places with full points being brought home from Bury, Northampton, Doncaster and Scarborough (first ever win in eight trips to the seaside). Victories had been achieved just eight times in 76 previous trips to these venues. The opening day victory at Bury was the home team's only league home loss all season but Rochdale emphasised their liking for Gigg Lane by repeating the trick in the Autoglass Trophy.

Steve Whitehall once again topped the scoring charts with just ten strikes, two of which were from penalties and was alone in playing in all 42 league games (one being started on the subs bench). Only six times in 66 previous league seasons, have fewer goals been scored than the 44 in 1994-95. With the Chairman assuming responsibility for the failure to escape division three and promising resignation over the summer prospects for a reversal in fortunes, as opposed to a return to the dark days of the less recent pass, appear slim. STEPHEN BIRCH.

ROCHDALE

Division Three: 15th   **FA Cup:** 1st Round   **Coca-Cola Cup:** 1st Round   **Auto Windscreen Trophy:** Winners

M	DATE	COMP.	VEN	OPPONENTS	RESULT	H/T	LP	GOAL SCORERS/GOAL TIMES	ATT.
1	A 13	EL	A	Bury	W 1-0	0-0		Thompson 52	(3,230)
2	16	CC1	H	**Mansfield Town**	L 1-2	1-0		**Whitehall 14**	1,746
3	20	EL	H	Chesterfield	W 4-1	1-0	1	Reid 16, Thompson 50, Thackeray 55, Whitehall 69	2,122
4	23	CC1	A	**Mansfield Town**	L 0-1	0-1			(2,234)
5	27	EL	A	Gillingham	D 1-1	1-0	2	Hall 32	(3,015)
6	30	EL	H	Lincoln City	W 1-0	1-0		Whitehall 45	1,974
7	S 3	EL	H	Hereford United	L 1-3	0-1	6	Williams 83	2,258
8	10	EL	A	Northampton Town	W 2-1	0-1	4	Reid 62, Thompson 66	(3,052)
9	13	EL	A	Barnet	L 2-6	1-4		Reid 36 (pen), Williams 55	(1,688)
10	17	EL	H	Bury	L 0-3	0-0	9		3,748
11	24	EL	A	Scarborough	W 4-2	1-1	6	Williams 12, 61, Whitehall 55, Butler 65	(1,200)
12	27	AWT	A	**Blackpool**	W 2-1	0-1		**Stuart 63, Burke (og) 66**	(1,817)
13	O 1	EL	H	Doncaster Rovers	W 2-0	0-0	4	Williams 74, Peake 81	2,445
14	8	EL	H	Fulham	L 1-2	1-0	6	Whitehall 21	2,573
15	15	EL	A	Wigan Athletic	L 0-4				(2,118)
16	17	AWT	H	**Wigan Athletic**	W 1-0	0-0		**Taylor 89**	1,004
17	22	EL	A	Torquay United	L 1-4	0-1	10	Thackeray 58	(2,547)
18	29	EL	H	Mansfield Town	D 3-3	1-2	10	Butler 8, Whitehall 53, 76	1,968
19	N 5	EL	A	Carlisle United	L 1-4	0-1	10	Gallimore 89 (og)	(5,984)
20	12	FAC 1	A	**Walsall**	L 0-3				(3,619)
21	19	EL	A	Colchester United	D 0-0	0-0	10		1,903
22	26	EL	A	Hartlepool	L 0-1	0-1	12		(1,387)
23	29	AWT 1	H	**Darlington**	D 2-2	1-2		**Whitehall 10, 58**	1,069
24	D 10	EL	A	Chesterfield	D †2-2	1-2	13	Russell 15, Whitehall (pen) 84 (Won on penalties)	(2,457)
25	17	EL	H	Gillingham	W 2-1	2-0	12	Stuart 25, Valentine 31	1,665
26	26	EL	A	Preston North End	L 0-3	0-3	14		(10,491)
27	27	EL	H	Walsall	L 0-2	0-1			2,438
28	31	EL	A	Scunthorpe United	L 1-4	0-2	14	Butler 87	(2,653)
29	J 7	EL	H	Torquay United	W 2-0	0-0	14	Sharpe 46, Thompson 49	1,636
30	11	AWT QF	H	**Stockport County**	W 2-1	1-1		**Whitehall 13, 64**	2,154
31	14	EL	A	Exeter City	D 0-0	0-0	14		(2,316)
32	21	EL	A	Carlisle United	D 1-1	0-0			3,289
33	F 4	EL	H	Hartlepool	W 1-0	1-0	13	Deary 44	1,848
34	7	AWC SF	A	**Bury**	W 2-1	2-1		**Sharpe 13, Reid 40**	(3,341)
35	11	EL	A	Colchester United	D 0-0	0-0	13		(3,080)
36	18	EL	H	Exeter City	L 0-1	0-1	13		1,945
37	25	EL	A	Doncaster Rovers	W 1-0	1-0	14	Sharpe 41	(2,246)
38	28	AWC F	A	**Carlisle United**	L 1-4	0-3		**Whitehall (pen) 46**	(8,647)
39	M 7	EL	A	Mansfield Town	D 1-1	1-0		Whitehall 34	(2,931)
40	11	EL	H	Northampton Town	D 0-0	0-0	15		1,894
41	14	AWC F	H	**Carlisle United**	W 2-1	0-0	15	**Whitehall 13, Reid 22**	4,082
42	18	EL	H	Lincoln City	D 2-2	0-2	15	Thompson 52, Valentine 56	(2,939)
43	21	EL	H	Darlington	W 2-0	0-0	13	Thompson 64, Whitehall 89	1,471
44	25	EL	A	Hereford United	D 0-0	0-0	13		(1,954)
45	A 1	EL	H	Barnet	D 2-2	1-1	14	McDonald (og) 26, Thackeray 88	1,834
46	8	EL	H	Scunthorpe United	L 1-2	1-0	15	Ryan 13	1,720
47	15	EL	A	Walsall	D 0-0	0-0	15		(3,766)
48	17	EL	H	Preston North End	L 0-1	0-1			4,012
49	22	EL	A	Darlington	L 0-4	0-2	15		(1,886)
50	25	EL	H	Scarborough	D 1-1	0-0		Ryan 82	1,170
51	29	EL	H	Wigan Athletic	W 1-0	1-0	15	Whitehall (pen) 28	1,949
52	M 6	EL	A	Fulham	L 0-5	0-3	15		(4,342)
53									
54									
55									
56									
57									
58									
59									
60									

Best Home League Attendance: 4,012 v Preston North End   **Smallest:** 1,170 v Scarborough   **Av Home Att:** 2,184

Goal Scorers:
League (44): White Hall 10 (2 pens), Thompson 6, Williams 5, Butler 3, Reid 3 (1 pen), Thackeray, Peake 2, Ryan 2, Sharpe 2, Valentine 2, Opponents 2, Dreary, Hall, Russell, Stuart
C/Cola Cup (1): Whitehall
FA Cup (0):
AW Trophy (12): Whitehall 6 (1 pen), Reid 2, Sharpe, Stuart, Taylor, Opponent

Compared with 1993-94: -472

1994-95

Clarke	Thackery	Formby	Reid	Reeves	Matthews	Thompson	Peake	Bowden	Whitehall	Stuart	Ryan	Hall	Dunford	Williams	Doyle	Butler	Rimmer	Russell	Oliver	Creighton	Dickens	Sharpe	Taylor	Bayliss	Shore	Referee	No.
1	2	3	4	5	6	7	8	9	10	11*	12*	S	G													Richards P.	1
1	2	3	4	5	6	7•	8*	9	10	11	14•	12*														Furnandiz R.	2
1	2	3	4	5	6	7•	8*		10	11	14•		G	9	12*											Cain G.	3
1	2	3	4	5	6	7			10	12*	11*	8	G	9	S	6										Heilbron T.	4
1	2	3	4	5	S	7	12*		10*	11		8		9		6										D'Urso A.	5
1	2	3	4	5		7	14•		10	11•		8*		9	12*	6										Holbrook J.	6
1	2	3	4	5		7	8		10	14•				9	12*#	6*	11•									Lypton K.	7
1	2	3	4		5	7	8		12*	S				9*	10	6	11									Harris R.	8
1	2	3	4		5	7	8*		10			12*		14•	11	6	9•									Wilkes C.	9
1	2	3	4		5	7	S		10	11	S	8		9		6										Winter J.	10
1	2	3	4•		5	7	14•		10	11		8*		9		6		12*	S							Dawson A.	11
1*	2	3			5	7	8		10	11	12*			9		6		4								Parker J.	12
	2	3	14•			7*	8		10	11	12*		1	9	5	6		4•		G						Lloyd J.	13
	2	3	4				12*	8	10	11•	7*		1	9	5	6		14•		G						Brandwood J.	14
	2	3	4			7•	8		10	*	12*		G	9	5	6					1					Wright P.	15
	2	3	4			7•			10		14•	8	G	9	5	6					1	11*	12*			Burns W.	16
	2	3	4			7			10	11•		8		9	5*	6					1	12*	14•			Pierce M.	17
	2		4		5	7	8		10	11			G			6			3		1	9*	12*	S		Allison D.	18
	2	3*	4		5	12*	8		10	9	11		G			6			7•		1	14•				Cruikshanks I.	19
	2	3*	4		5		8•		10	11	14•		1	9	7	6						12*			G	Ashby G.	20
	2	3	4		5				10	11	S		G	9*	7	6							12*			Rennie U.	21
	2		4		5		7*		10	11•					12*	6			3			14•#				West T.	22
	2	3	4		5	7•			10	12*	11				8*	6						9	14•			Riley M.	23
	2					7	8•	9	10	11	14•		12*			6		4*	3							Rejer P.	24
	2					7	8	9*	10	4•	11	12*				6			3				14•		G	Kirkby J.	25
G	2	3•				7	8	9	10	4	11*					6		12*	14•							Cain G.	26
G	2		4			7	8	9•	10*	11						6		14•	3#			12*				Winter J.	27
	2		4			7	8	12*	10•	11	14•					6			3			9*				Heilbron T.	28
G	2		4			7	8	9	10	S						6		S	3			11				Furnandiz R.	29
	2	3	4*		5	7	8		10	11		12*				6		14•				9•				Barry N.	30
G	2	3	4*		14•	7	8		10	12*						6						11•				Harris R.	31
G	2	3	4		S	7	8		10	11						6						S				Riley M.	32
G	2	3	4			7	8•		10	11*						6						12*				Poulain R.	33
G	2*	3	4		5	7	8		10	14•						6		12*				9•				Lloyd J.	34
G	2	3•	4			7	8		10	12*						6						11*				Pierce M.	35
1	2	3	4*		14•	7•	8		10	11						6							12*		G	Butler A.	36
1	2*	3	4		12*	7	8•		10							6						11			G	Rennie U.	37
1	2	3	4		5	7	8		10		14•	12*				6						11•			G	Flood A.	38
1	2	3	4			7	8		10	14•	12*					6						11			G	Parker J.	39
1	2	3•	4			7	8		10	12*	14•					6						11*			G	Watson J.	40
1	2	3•	4*		5	7	8		10	14•	12*					6						9			G	Singh G.	41
1	2	3*				7	8		10	14•	12*					6						9•			G	Foakes P.	42
1	2					7	3	S	10	9*	8					6						12*			G	Rushton J.	43
1	2					7	3	S	10	11						6						12*			G	Dunn S.	44
1	2	S				7	3	12*	10	11*														6	G	Brandwood J.	45
1	2					7	3•	12*	10*	11						6							14•		G	Cruikshanks I.	46
1	2	s				7	3	12*		11	G					6									G	Rennie U.	47
1	2	12*				7	3	s		9	11					6									G	Cain G.	48
1	2#	3*				7	4	14•	10	9	11					6									G	Burns B.	49
1	2					7	3	s	10*	9	11					6							12*		G	Barry N.	50
1	2					7•	3	s	10	9	11					6							12*		G	Richards P.	51
1		2*				7	3		10	9	12*					6							11	S	G	Rejer P.	52
24	41	27	27	5	10	38	36	6	41	26	15	5	2	12	7	39	3	2	8		4	9	1	1		League Appearances	
	1	1		3	2	3	5	1	5	10	4	2		4				5	1			7	8			League Sub Appearances	
2	2	2	2	2	1	2	1	1	2	1+1	1+1	1+1	1	1		1										C/Cola Cup Appearances	
	1	1	1			1			1				1	1		1						0+1				FA Cup Appearances	
3	7	7	6		6	7	5		7	2+3	1+4	1+2		2	2	7		1+2			1	6	0+2			AW Trophy Appearances	

Also Played: Gray 1(21-35), Valentine 8(21,22), 5(24-29, 31-33,35-37,39-40,42-52), Whitington 9(22), Martin 9(31,32),14(33,35) 4(42-48*,50-52),12(49),
Shaw 9(44*-47*), Deary 9(33,35,36,37,38*,39*40), 11(34,41,42,43), 8(44-51#,52)

Players on Loan: Dickens (Blackburn Rovers), Martin (Scunthorpe United), Whitington (Huddersfield Town), Gray (Oldham Athletic), Rimmer (Chester)

CLUB RECORDS

RECORD LEAGUE VICTORY
8-1 v Chesterfield, Div 3N, 18.12.1926   7-0 v Walsall,Div 3N, 24.12.1921   7-0 v York City (a), Div 3N, 14.1.1939   7-0 v Hartlepool,Div 3N, 2.11.1957

RECORD LEAGUE DEFEAT
1-9 v Tranmere Rovers, Div 3N, 25.12.1931   0-8 v Wrexham(a), Div 3, 28.9.1929   0-8 v Leyton Orient (a), Div 4, 20.10.1987
Record Cup Defeat
0-6 v Wigan Athletic, Freight Rover Trophy, 28.1.1986

MOST LEAGUE POINTS
(2pts a win) 62 Div 3N, 1923-24
(3pts a win) 67 Div 4,1991-92

MOST LEAGUE GOALS
105, Div 3N, 1926-27

RECORD TRANSFER FEE RECEIVED
£200,000 plus 25% of any future fee from Bristol City for Keith Welch, July 1991

RECORD TRANSFER FEE PAID
£80,000 to Scunthorpe Utd for Andy Flounders, July 1991

BEST PERFORMANCES
League: 9th Div 3, 1969-70   FA Cup: 5th Round, 1989-90
League Cup: Runners-Up 1962 (4th Div Record)

HONOURS
None

LEAGUE CAREER
Elected to Div 3N 1921   Transferred to Div 3 1958   Relegated to Div 4 1958-59
Promoted to Div 3 1968-69   Relegated to Div 4 (now Div 3) 1973-74

INDIVIDUAL CLUB RECORDS

MOST APPEARANCES FOR CLUB
Graham Smith (1966-74): League 316+1, FA Cup 15,League Cup 13 Total 344+1 sub

MOST CAPPED PLAYER
No Rochdale player has won an international cap

RECORD GOALSCORER IN A MATCH
Tommy Tippett 6 v Hartlepool (a), 8-2, Div 3N,21.4.1930

RECORD LEAGUE GOALSCORER IN A SEASON
Albert Whitehurst 44 (1926-27)   In All Competitions: Albert Whitehurst, 46 (League 44 + FA Cup 2)

RECORD LEAGUE GOALSCORER IN A CAREER
Reg Jenkins 119   In All Competitions: Reg Jenkins 130 (League 119 + FA Cup 5 + League Cup 6) 1964-73

MOST GOALS SCORED IN A FIRST CLASS MATCH
Record League Victory (above)   8-2 v Crook Town (h), 1st Round FA Cup, 26.11.1927   8-2 v Hartlepool United (a), Div3N, 22.4.1930

OLDEST PLAYER IN A LEAGUE MATCH
Jack Warner (player/manager) 41 years 195 days v Chesterfield, Div 3N, 4.4.1953

YOUNGEST PLAYER IN A LEAGUE MATCH
Zac Hughes, 16 years 105 days v Exeter City, Div 4, 19.9.1987

PREVIOUS MANAGERS

1920-21 William Bradshaw   1921-22 No appointment made   1922-23 Thomas C Wilson   1923-30 Jack Peart   1930 Harry Martin (caretaker)   1930-31 William Smith Cameron   1931-32 Vacant   1932-34 Herbert Hopkinson   1934-35 William H Smith   1935-37 Ernest Nixon (caretaker)   1937-38 Sam Jennings   1938-52 Ted Goodier   1952 Jack Warner   1953-58 Harry Catterick   1958-60 Jack Marshall   1960-67 Tony Collins   1967-68 Bob Stokoe   1968-70 Len Richley   1970-73 Dick Connor   1973-76 Walter Joyce   1976-77 Brian Green   1977-78 Mike Ferguson   1978-79 Peter Madden (caretaker)   1979 Doug Collins   1979-83 Peter Madden   1983-84 Jimmy Greenhoff   1984-86 Vic Halom   1986-88Eddie Gray   1988-89 Danny Bergara   1989-91 Terry Dolan   1991-94 Dave Sutton 1994- Mick Docherty (caretaker).

ADDITIONAL INFORMATION
Club colours: Blue shirts blue shorts.

Change colours: White shirts blue shorts.

Reserves League: Midland Senior League.

LONGEST LEAGUE RUNS

of undefeated matches:	20 (1923-24)	of league matches w/out a win:		28 (1931-32)
of undefeated home matches:	34 (1923-25)	of undefeated away matches:		9 (1923-24)
without home win:	16 (1931-32)	without an away win:		37 (1977-78)
of league wins:	8 (1969)	of home wins:		16 (1926-27)
of league defeats:	17 (1931-32)	of away wins:	4 (1923-24, 1926, 1946, 1947, 1969)	

THE MANAGER

MICK DOCHERTY. . . . . appointed January 1995

PREVIOUS CLUBS
As Manager . . . . Hartlepool.
As Asst.Man/Coach . . . . Sunderland, Blackpool, Burnley, Wolverhampton Wanderers, Rochdale.
As a player . . . . Burnley, Manchester City, Sunderland.

HONOURS
As a Manager . . . . None.
As a Player . . . . England Youth.

ROCHDALE

PLAYERS NAME Honours	Ht	Wt	Birthdate	Birthplace Transfers	Contract Date	Clubs	League	L/Cup	FA Cup	Other	Lge	L/C	FAC	Oth
G O A L K E E P E R S														
Chris Clarke	6.1	12.10	01.05.74	Barnsley		Bolton W. (T)								
				Free	04.07.94	Rochdale	24	2		3				
Ian J Gray	6.2	12.0	25.02.75	Manchester	16.07.93	Oldham Athletic(T)								
Loan 18.11.94 Rochdale 12 Lge, 3 Oth. App.				£20,000	08.95	Rochdale								
D E F E N D E R S														
Paul Butler	6.3	13.0	02.11.72	Manchester	05.07.91	Rochdale (T)	113+7	6+1	3+2	9+1	7			
Peter Valentine	5.10	12.0	16.04.63	Huddersfield	16.04.81	Huddersfield T. (A)	19	2	1		1			
				Free	18.07.83	Bolton Wanderers	66+2	4	4	5	1			
				Free	23.07.85	Bury	314+5	28	17	23+1	16	3	1	
				£10,000	18.08.93	Carlisle United	27+2	3		4	2			1
				£15,000	18.11.94	Rochdale	27				2			
M I D F I E L D														
John Deary	5.10	11.11	18.10.62	Ormskirk	13.03.80	Blackpool (A)	285+18	20	16+2	14	43	5	4	1
Div.4'92.				£30,000	18.07.89	Burnley	209+6	13+3	20+1	21	23	1	2	1
					30.01.95	Rochdale	17			3	1			
Kevin Formby	5.11	12.0	22.07.71	Ormskirk		Burscough								
RN rep.				Free	24.03.94	Rochdale	29+4	2	1	7				
Derek Hall	5.8	11.2	05.01.65	Ashton-U-Lyme	08.10.82	Coventry City (A)	1							
				Free	23.03.84	Torquay United	55	2	2	3	6			1
				Free	29.07.85	Swindon Town	9+1		2	1+1				
				Free	21.08.86	Southend United	120+3	13	6	8	15	1	2	1
				Free	25.07.89	Halifax Town	48+1	5	2	5	4	1		1
				Free	18.07.91	Hereford United	98+5	8	11	9	18	2	1	1
				£10,000	.08.94	Rochdale	5+4	1+1		1+2	1			
Dean Martin	5.10	10.2	09.09.67	Halifax	10.09.85	Halifax Town (A)	149+4	7	10	12	7			3
				Free	08.07.91	Scunthorpe United	100+6	8	7	13+1	7	1		1
Loan 13.01.95 Rochdale						Rochdale	12+3							
Jason Peake	5.10	11.5	29.09.71	Leicester	09.01.90	Leicester City (T)	4+4			1+1	1			
E: Y.1.				Loan	13.02.92	Hartlepool United	5+1				1			
				Free	26.08.92	Halifax Town	32+1		3	1	1		1	
					23.03.94	Rochdale	46+3	1	1	5	2			
Alex Russell			17.03.73	Crosby		Liverpool (T)								
				Free	01.03.93	Stockport County								
via Morecambe & Burscough				Free	11.07.94	Rochdale	2+5			1+2	1			
Darren Ryan	5.9	11.0	03.07.72	Oswestry	23.10.90	Shrewsbury T. (T)	3+1			0+1				
				Loan	15.10.91	Telford United								
				Free	14.08.92	Chester City	5+12	2	1+1	1+1	2		1	
				P.E.	25.01.93	Stockport County	29+7	2	1+1	5+1	6	1		
				Free	21.07.94	Rochdale	15+10	1+1	0+1	1+4	2			
Andy Thackeray	5.9	11.0	13.02.68	Huddersfield	15.02.86	Manchester City (J)								
FAYC.				Free	01.08.86	Huddersfield Town	2			0+1				
				£5,000	27.03.87	Newport County	53+1	3+1	1	2+1	4			1
				£5,000	20.07.88	Wrexham	139+13	10	6	13+2	14	1		
				£15,000	15.07.92	Rochdale	117+2	8	5	8+2	13			2
Ian Thompstone	6.0	11.3	17.01.71	Bury	01.09.89	Manchester City (T)	0+1							
				Free	25.05.90	Oldham Athletic								
				Free	23.01.92	Exeter City	15				3			
				Free	14.07.92	Halifax Town	31	1+1	1	2	9			
				£15,000	25.03.93	Scunthorpe United	48+13	2	4+2	2	8		1	
				Free	08.95	Rochdale								
F O R W A R D S														
Graham Shaw	5.8	10.1	07.06.67	Stoke	10.06.85	Stoke City (A)	83+16	7	2+4	3+2	18	2	1	2
Div.2'93.				£70,000	24.07.89	Preston North End	113+8	5	5	13	29	6	1	6
					12.08.92	Stoke City	23+13	2+1	2+1	2+4	5	1		
				Free	22.03.95	Rochdale	4							
Mark R Stuart	5.10	10.11	15.12.66	Chiswick	03.07.84	Charlton Athletic (J)	89+18	7+3	1	9+1	28	2	1	1
				£150,000	04.11.88	Plymouth Argyle	55+2	4	3	2	11			1
				Loan	22.03.90	Ipswich Town	5				2			
				£80,000	03.08.90	Bradford City	22+7	6	0+1	1+1	5	1		
				Free	30.10.92	Huddersfield Town	9+6		2	4	3			1
				Free	05.07.93	Rochdale	67+6	5+1	3	3+3	15	1	1	1
Jamie Taylor	5.6	9.12	11.01.77	Bury	12.01.94	Rochdale (T)	2+17	0+1		0+2	1			1
Dave S Thompson	5.9	11.6	27.05.62	Manchester	26.09.81	Rochdale	147+8	7	7+1	6	13			
					22.08.86	Notts County	52+3	3+1	3	2	8			
				£35,000	20.10.87	Wigan Athletic	107+1	5	3+1	6	16	2		1
				£77,500	01.08.90	Preston North End	39+7	1+1		3+1	4			
				Free	14.08.92	Chester City	70+10	4	4	4	9			
				£6,000	.08.94	Rochdale	38+2	2		7	6			
Steve Whitehall	5.10	11.0	08.12.68	Bromborough		Southport								
					23.07.91	Rochdale	139+18	7+3	7+2	11	45	3	2	7
Paul A Williams	6.4	14.0	08.09.63	Sheffield		Nuneaton Borough								
NI: 1, Y.				Free	18.12.86	Preston North End	1		1					
				Free	17.07.87	Carlisle United								
				Free	12.08.87	Newport County	26	2		2	3			
				£17,000	07.03.88	Sheffield United	6+2			2+1				
				Free	10.10.89	Hartlepool United	7+1		1	1				
				Free	23.08.90	Stockport County	24	2		3	14	1		1
				£250,000	28.03.91	West Bromwich A.	26+18	1+1	1+2	1+2	5		1	1
Loan 23.19.92 Coventry City 1+1 Lge App.				£25,000	12.01.93	Stockport County	6+10	1		5	3			1
				Free	05.11.93	Rochdale	21+4	1	1	2	7			

SPOTLAND
Willbutts Lane, Rochdale OL11 5DS
Tel: 01706 44648

Capacity 5,800
Covered Standing 3,076
Seating 1,852

First game ....v Oldham Ath., Friendly, 3.9.1907.
First floodlit game ....v St. Mirren, 16.2.1954.

ATTENDANCES
Highest ....24,231 v Notts County, FAC 2nd Rnd, 10.12.1949
Lowest..588 v Cambridge Utd, Div 3, 5.2.1974
(played on a Tuesday afternoon during power cuts)

OTHER GROUNDS..None.

MATCHDAY TICKET PRICES

Seats. £8
Juv/OAP £4.50

Family £8
Juv/OAP £1

Terraces. £6
Juv/OAP £3

Away Stand . . . . £6-£8
Juv/OAP £4.50

Executive Club per match £20

Ticket Office Telephone no. 01706 44648

CLUBCALL
0891 55 58 58
Calls cost 39p per minute cheap rate and 49p per
minute at all other times.
Call costings correct at time of going to press.

HOW TO GET TO THE GROUND

From all directions
Use motorway M62 until junction 20 then follow signs to Rochdale.
On to A627 (M), at first roundabout keep left and at second go straight ahead
signed Blackburn.
At traffic lights after 1 mile go straight ahead into Sandy Lane.
Ground on right after half-a-mile.

Car Parking
At the ground (£1) and in adjacent streets.

Nearest Railway Station
Rochdale.

MATCHDAY PROGRAMME

Programme Editor . . . . Stephen Walmsley.

Number of pages . . . . 32.

Price . . . . £1.20.

Subscriptions. . . . . £31 for home matches.

Local Newspapers . . . Rochdale Observer, Manchester Evening News.

Local Radio Stations . . . . Radio Manchester, Radio Piccadilly.

SCARBOROUGH
(The Boro)
ENDSLEIGH LEAGUE DIVISION 3
SPONSORED BY: YORKSHIRE COAST RADIO

Back Row (L-R): Don Page, Lee Thew, Craig Boardman, Kevin Martin, Gavin Kelly, Stuart Hicks, Ian Ironside, Jason Rockett, Lee Harper, Neil Trebble. **Front Row:** Oliver Heald, Steve Charles, David D'Auria, Andy Ritchie, Ian Kerr, Phil Chambers, Ray McHale, John Murray, Darren Knowles, Mark Wells, Richard Lucas, Alex Willgrass.

SCARBOROUGH
FORMED IN 1879
TURNED PROFESSIONAL IN 1926
LTD COMPANY IN 1933

PRESIDENT & CHIEF EXECUTIVE
J R Birley
CHAIRMAN: J Russell
DIRECTORS
Mrs C Russell
SECRETARY
Eric V Hall

MANAGER: Ray McHale
ASSISTANT MANAGER: Phil Chaberd
RESERVE TEAM MANAGER
&
YOUTH TEAM MANAGER
Phil Chaberd

PHYSIOTHERAPIST
J Murray

STATISTICIAN FOR THE DIRECTORY
Vacant

Since Scarborough joined The Football League in 1987 they have kept a very low profile. A few exiting Cup victories have given brief respite from dour battles for survival season after season in the lowest senior division.

There is always a threat of financial problems and managers have lived by their wits. Better players have had to be sold while every signing has to be carefully planned within the budget just to keep the club afloat. The 1994-95 season was again a desperate affair.

The new that Macclesfield Town's ground would not meet the required criteria for promotion gave great relief to the clubs at the foot of Division Three and in the end 'Borough' did avoid bottom place but finished in 21st position.

The seasons traumas would have seemed a long way away when a victory was recorded at much fancied Chesterfield on the first day of the season. But a slump took the club into the danger zone and they were never out of the bottom two places in 1995.

Luckily the consistency of Jason White, who only missed five games in the season and scored twelve goals, with six in a vital period near the end of the season, always gave Scarborough a chance. Good support also came from Alan D'Aurea with seven goals from 34 games. But only two other players; Knowles (38) and Charles (39) managed over thirty League appearances.

The cups didn't bring much cheer either, although a Coca-Cola Cup visit to high flying Middlesbrough gave the supporters a lift and the FA Cup gave Scarborough another victory over Chesterfield which produced a tie with Watford, which was lost in a replay at Vicarage Road.

The return of the popular Steve Norris (on loan from Carlisle United) created some excitement and he did manage four goals in eight games including a vital victory over Northampton.

The end of season battle was fought out with spirit and hopefully the club will have strengthened in the close season and will be able to avoid another desperate struggle for survival.

SCARBOROUGH

Division Three: 21st   **FA Cup:** 3rd Round   **Coca-Cola Cup:** 2nd Round

M	DATE	COMP.	VEN	OPPONENTS	RESULT	H/T	LP	GOAL SCORERS/GOAL TIMES	ATT.
1	A 13	EL	A	Chesterfield	W 1-0	1-0	7	Charles 39, (pen)	(3,099)
2	16	CC1/1	A	Hull City	L 1-2	0-1		Young 67	(2,546)
3	20	EL	H	Barnet	L 0-1	0-0	15		1,471
4	22	CC1/2	H	Hull City	W 2-0	0-0		Blackstone 2, 67	2,287
5	27	EL	A	Carlisle United	L 0-2	0-2	16		(5,720)
6	30	EL	H	Hereford United	W 3-1	1-0		Foreman 34, Rowe 85, White 90	1,490
7	S 3	EL	H	Colchester United	L 0-1	0-0	13		1,494
8	10	EL	A	Gillingham	L 1-3	0-1	16	Calvert 49	(2,414)
9	13	EL	A	Fulham	W 2-1	2-1		Swann 15, D'Auria 43	(2,729)
10	17	EL	H	Chesterfield	L 0-1	0-0	14		1,475
11	20	CC 2/1	H	Middlesbrough	L 1-4	1-4		Rowe 18	4,751
12	24	EL	H	Rochdale	L 2-4	1-1	16	Charles 22 (pen), White 52	1,200
14	27	CC 2/2	A	Middlesbrough	L 1-4	1-4		Rowe 18	4,751
13	O 1	EL	A	Wigan Athletic	D 1-1	1-1	16	Charles 26 (pen)	(1,403)
15	8	EL	A	Walsall	L 1-4	1-1	19	White 21	(3,601)
16	15	EL	H	Doncaster Rovers	D 2-2	2-0	18	Rutherford 33, Swann 44	1,641
17	22	EL	A	Lincoln City	L 0-2	0-1	21		(2,396)
18	29	EL	H	Northampton Town	D 0-0	0-0	21		1,468
19	N 5	EL	A	Bury	L 0-1	0-0			(3,016)
20	12	FAC 1	A	Chesterfield	D 0-0	0-0			(2,902)
21	19	EL	H	Torquay United	D 1-1	1-0	20	White 43	1,241
22	22	FAC 1R	H	Chesterfield	W 2-0	1-0		Toman 2, White 62	1,564
23	26	EL	A	Exeter City	L 2-5	1-2	22	Young 26, D'Auria 90	(2,179)
24	D 3	FAC 2	H	Port Vale	W 1-0	0-0		Swann 68	2,382
25	10	EL	A	Barnet	L 1-3	0-0	22	White 89	(1,988)
26	17	EL	H	Carlisle United	L 1-2	1-1	19	Rodwell 24	1,910
27	26	EL	A	Darlington	L 0-1	0-1			(2,958)
28	27	EL	H	Mansfield Town	L 2-5	1-2		Griffiths 36, Thompson 82	1,926
29	31	EL	A	Preston North End	L 0-1	0-0	22		(8,407)
30	J 7	FAC 3	H	Watford	D 0-0	0-0			3,544
31	14	EL	A	Hartlepool United	D 3-3	1-0	22	Norris 13, 72 (pen), D'Auria 87	(1,784)
32	17	FAC 3R	A	Watford	L 0-2	0-0			(7,047)
33	28	EL	A	Northampton Town	W 3-0	0-0	22	Swann 56, Norris 68, D'auria 81	(5,737)
34	F 4	EL	H	Exeter City	L 0-2	0-1	22		1,512
35	7	EL	H	Lincoln City	D 1-1	0-0	22	D'Auria 64	1,217
36	18	EL	H	Hartlepool United	D 2-2	1-1	22	Norris 10, Wells 84	1,517
37	25	EL	H	Wigan Athletic	L 0-1	0-1	22		1,416
38	28	EL	H	Scunthorpe United	W 3-0	0-0	22	Trebble 57, Swailes 61, D'Auria 69	1,179
39	M 7	EL	A	Torquay United	L 1-2	1-1	22	White 25	(1,492)
40	11	EL	H	Gillingham	D 0-0	0-0	22		1,949
41	18	EL	A	Hereford	L 1-2	0-0	22	White 70	(1,497)
42	21	EL	H	Bury	L 1-2	1-1	22	White 16	1,744
43	25	EL	A	Colchester United	W 2-0	0-0	22	Charles 46, Trebble 56	(3,025)
44	A 1	EL	H	Fulham	W 3-1	0-0	22	White 53, D'Auria 64, Scott 69	2,050
45	8	EL	H	Preston North End	D 1-1	1-1	22	Charles 7	4,266
46	15	EL	A	Mansfield Town	L 2-3	2-2	22	White 29, 42	(2,931)
47	18	EL	H	Darlington	W 3-1	1-0	22	Davis 43, Scott 58, 76	2,182
48	22	EL	A	Scunthorpe United	L 1-3	0-1	22	Trebble 66	(2,079)
49	25	EL	A	Rochdale	D 1-1	0-1		Davis 10	(1,170)
50	29	EL	A	Doncaster Rovers	L 0-1	0-0	21		(1,710)
51	M 2	EL	H	Walsall	L 1-2	0-0	21	Calvert 81	2,841
52									
53									
54									
55									
56									
57									
58									
59									
60									

Best Home League Attendance: 4,266 v Preston North End   **Smallest:** 1,179 v Scunthorpe United   **Av Home Att:** 1,771

Goal Scorers: Compared with 1993-94: +92

League (49):   White 11, D' Auria 7, Charles 5, Norris 4, Scott 3, Swann 3, Trebble 3, Calvert 2, Davis 2, Foreman, Griffiths, Rodwell, Rowe, Rutherford, Swailes, Thompson, Wells, Young

C/Cola Cup (4):   Blackstone 2, Young, Rowe

FA Cup (3):   Swann, Toman, White

Kelly	Knowles	Charles	Meyer	Calvert	Rockett	Rowe	Swann	Young	White	Blackstone	Thompson	Toman	Martin	Wells	Foreman	D'Auria	Talbot	Dunelly	Rutherford	Davis	Ford	Swayles	Rodwell	Griffiths	Norris	Referee
1	2	3	4	5	6	7	8	9	10	11	S	S	S													R. Furnandiz 1
1	2	3	5	4	6	7	8	9		11	10	S	S	S												I. Cruikshanks 2
1	2	3	5	4	6	7	8	9*		11	10	S	S		12											M. Riley 3
1	2	3	5	4	6		8	12	10.				S			9*	14									P. Harrison 4
1	2	3			6	7*	8	14	10	11			S			9•		12	4	5						P. Richards 5
1	2	3	4		6	12	8	14	10	11			S			9•		7*		5						U. Rennie 6
1	2	3	14		6	7	8	12	10•	11			S			9*		4		5						E. Lomas 7
1		3	7		6	12	8		10	11†	2		S			4*				5	9	S				G. Barber 8
1		3	7		6	9	8	S	10	11	2	12				4*				5						I. Hemley 9
1		3	7		6*	9	8•	14	10	11	2	12	S			4				5						T. Kirkby 10
1	2	3†	6		7			12	14	11	10	8			4*				5			S				S. Lodge 11
1	2	3	6	4		7			11	10		8	S		9	S			5			S				A. Dawson 12
																										S. Lodge 14
1	2	3	4			7*	12			11•	8			9	10		5	14	6	S						D. Allison 13
1	2*		4		14	8	7	10		3	12				11	9•			6	S	5					E. Wolstenholme 15
	2	4		S	12	8	7	10*	3					11	9				6	S	5					T. Heilbron 16
	2	4	14			8	7	10	12	3		S	9		11•				6	1	5*					S. Mathieson 17
	2	4		7*		8	12	11			S	9			S	10	6	1	3							J. Parker 18
S	2	4	3	7	8	12	14			1	9†		5*	10	6			11•								N. Barry 19
S	2	4	6	7	12	9		8	1	11	S		10*	5	3											M. Riley 20
S	2	8	11•	6	7	12	9		4	1	14		10*	5	3											J. Rushton 21
S	2	8		6	7	10*	9		4	1	11•		14	12	5	3										M. Riley 22
S	2	8		6	7	10	9		4.	1	11	12	14		3*											P. Rejer 23
1	2	8	5		6	7		9	14	12	4*	5	3	11	10•											D. Allison 24
S	2	8	5		7	9	12	S	3	11*		6	1	4	10											J. Holbrook 25
S	2	8	5		7*	9	12	S	3†	11		1	4	10•												W. Flood 26
S	2	3	5	4*	6	10	9	14	12	11		1	7•	11	8											K. Lupton 27
S	2	3	5	S	6†	10	9	7	4	S		1	11	8												T. West 28
1	2	3	5	6*		10	9	7	4			12	S	S	11	8										I. Cruikshanks 29
1	2	3	5	S		10	9	7	4			4	6	S	S	11	8									G. Singh 30
1	2	3	5	S		10	9	7	11	S	4	6	S	8												E. Wolstenholme 31
1	2	5	14			10•	9	12	7*	11	4	6	8													G. Singh 32
1	2	3	5	14		10	9	7*	12	11	14	7*	4	6	S	8•										S. Mathieson 33
1	2	3	5	14		10•	9	12	11	7*	4	6	S	8												P. Richards 34
1	2	3	5	4		9*	S	7	S	11	10	6	8													A. Dawson 35
1	2	3	4		6	12	12	14	9•	10	11	7	5*	8												K. Breen 36
1	2	3	4*	6	12	9	7•	11	14	8																T. Heilbron 37
1	2		5	6	4	9	11	7	8					S	3	S										K. Lynch 38
1	2	4	S	6	9	11	7	8						S	3	S										P. Vanes 39
1	2	4	14	6	9	11•	7*	8					S	3	12											R. Poulain 40
1	2	4	11	6	9	S	S	8					3	7												E. Parker 41
1	2		11	6	9	12	14	8					3	7•												R. Furnandiz 42
S	4	5*	11	6	9	12	5	8					3		8											D. Orr 43
	2	4	11	6	9	S	S	S	8				5	3												J. Watson 44
	2	4	11	6	9	S	S	S	8				5	3												J. Rushton 45
S	2	4	11		9	6	S	S	S	8				5	3											S. Dunn 46
S	2	4	11		9†	6	S	S	S	8				5	3											T. West 47
S	2	4	11		9	6	S	S	S	8				5	3											E. Lomas 48
S	2	4	11	6	9	S	S	8					5	3												N. Barry 49
S	2	4	11	6	9		8						5	3	12											P. Harrison 50
S	2	4	11		9	S	6	9	8				5	3	7											J. Winter 51
24	38	39	13	25	27	10	24	7	36	11	14	9	3	15	10	31	1	10	6	22	6	21	6	5	8	League Appearances
			4				4	3		6	3	2	2		7			2		1		2				League Sub Appearances
3	3	4	3	0+1	3		5	1+1	4	0+2	2+1	3		2	4			3+1		2+1	4		3	2		FA Cup Appearances

Also Played: Hicks 5(36,37,38,39,40) 5*(41), McHugh S(29,S1), Hoard S(31), Chilos 3(31), Mardenborough 12(34), Ironside 1(42,43,44,45,46,47,48,49,50), Love 2(42), Scott 7(42,43,44,45,46,47,48,49*), McKew S(48), Harper S(51)

CLUB RECORDS

RECORD LEAGUE VICTORY & MOST GOALS SCORED
4-0 v BoltonWanderers, Division 4, 29.8.1987 4-0 v Newport
County (a), Division 4,12.4.19880 4-0 v Doncaster R., Division 3,
23.4.94 5-2 v Torquay Utd,Division 4, 29.9.1988
Most Goals Scored in a First Class Cup Tie
6-0 v Rhyl Athletic, FA Cup Round1, 29.11.1930

RECORD LEAGUE DEFEAT
1-5 v Barnet, Division 4, 8.2.1992
Record Cup Defeat
 0-8 v Mansfield Town (h), FA Cup Rnd 1, 22.11.1952

MOST LEAGUE GOALS
67, Division 4, 1988-89

MOST LEAGUE POINTS
(3pts for win) 77, Division 4, 1988-89

RECORD TRANSFER FEE RECEIVED
£350,000 (´100,000 7/89 + ´250,000 9/92) from Notts County for
Craig Short

RECORD TRANSFER FEE PAID
£100,000 to Leicester City for Martin Russell,February 1989

BEST PERFORMANCES
League: 5th Division 4, 1988-89 FA Cup: Third Round
(1931,1938, 1976, 1978) League Cup: Fourth Round, 1992-93

HONOURS
FA Trophy Winners 1973, 1976, 1977 (Record) GM Vauxhall
ConfereneceChampions 1987 Midland League Champions 1930
Scarborough & District LeagueChampions 1946 North Easter
League Champions 1963 Vauxhall Floodlit League Winners 1973,
1975 Northern Premier League Cup Winners 1977 Bob Lord
TrophyWinners 1984 North Eastern Counties League Cup
Winners 1963 East Riding CupWinners (8 times) 1888, 1889,
1891, 1892, 1893, 1897, 1901, 1902 North RidingSenior Cup
Winners 1909, 1929, 1939, 1948, 1956, 1959, 1961, 1962, 1969,
1973,1974, 1977, 1978, 1981, 1982, 1985, 1988 Festival of
Football Winners 1990

INDIVIDUAL CLUB RECORDS

MOST APPEARANCES FOR CLUB
Steve Richards (1987-91): (League 164 + FA Cup 5 +League Cup
15 + Others 12) 0Total 196

MOST CAPPED PLAYER
Kyle Lightbourne, Bermuda

RECORD GOALSCORER IN A MATCH
Darren Foreman 3 v Northampton, Div 3, 10.10.1992(4-2) & Darren
Foreman 3 v York City, Div 3, 19.12.1992 (4-2)

RECORD LEAGUE GOALSCORER IN A SEASON
(Football League only) Darren Foreman 27,Div 4/3, 1992-93
In All Competitions: Darren Foreman, 31 (League 27, Lge Cup 2,
Autoglass 2)1992-93

RECORD LEAGUE GOALSCORER IN A CAREER
(Football League only) Darren Foreman,34, 1991-93
In All Competitions: Darren Foreman 40 (League 34, League Cup
4, Others 2)1991-93

OLDEST PLAYER TO PLAY IN A LEAGUE MATCH
John Burridge, 41 years 338 days v Doncaster Rovers, Division 3,
6.11.1993

YOUNGEST PLAYER IN A LEAGUE MATCH
Lee Harper, v Scunthorpe Utd, Division 3,2.10.1993

PREVIOUS MANAGERS

(Since the war): G Hall H Taylor F Taylor A Bell RHalton C
Robson G Higgins A Smailes E Brown A Frank S Myers
GShaw C Appleton K Houghton C Appleton J McAnearney J
Cottam H Dunn N Warnock R McHale P Chambers B Ayre

ADDITIONAL INFORMATION
Previous Leagues: Northern (1898-1910) Yorkshire Combination
(1910-14) Northern (1914-26) Yorkshire (1926-27) Midland
(1927-40) Scarborough &District (1945-46) Midland (1946-60)
Northern Counties (1960-62) NorthEastern (1962-63) Midland
(1963-68) Northern Premier (1968-79) Alliance Premier (1979-87)
Football League (1987-)
Club colours: Red & black stripes, black shorts, black socks.
Change colours: Yellow & black stripes, black shorts, black socks.

Reserves League: Midland Intermediate.

LONGEST LEAGUE RUNS

of undefeated matches:	9 (1988, 1990, 1990-91)	of league matches w/out a win:	6 (1989)
of undefeated home matches:	13 (1992)	of undefeated away matches:	6 (1.5.1993 - 2.10.1993)
without home win:	13 (23.3.1993 - 16.10.1993)	without an away win:	11 (1990,1992)
of league wins:	3 (x2 1987-88, 1988-89, x2 1989-90, x2 1992-93,94)	of home wins:	6 (1987)
of league defeats:	6 (1989)	of away wins:	3 (1992)

THE MANAGER

RAY MCHALE . . . . appointed December 1994

PREVIOUS CLUBS
As Manager . . . . Scarborough.
As Asst.Man/Coach . . . . None.
As a player . . . . Chesterfield, Halifax, Swindon, Brighton, Barnsley, Sheffield Utd, Swansea,
 . . . . Rochdale, Scarborough.

HONOURS
As a Manager . . . . None.
As a Player . . . . Promotion with three clubs.

SCARBOROUGH

PLAYERS NAME Honours	Ht	Wt	Birthdate	Birthplace Transfers	Contract Date	Clubs	League	L/Cup	FA Cup	Other	Lge	L/C	FAC	Oth
GOALKEEPERS														
Ian Ironside	6.1	11.9	08.03.64	Sheffield	17.09.82	Barnsley (J)								
				Free		North Ferriby United								
				Free	08.03.88	Scarborough	88	2	2	10				
				£80,000	15.08.91	Middlesbrough	12+1	2						
					23.09.93	Stockport County	17+2		1	1				
Loan 05.03.92 Scarborough 7 Lge				Free	23.03.95	Scarborough	9							
Gavin Kelly	6.1	13.0	29.09.68	Beverley	09.05.87	Hull City (T)	11	1		1				
				Free	01.07.90	Bristol Rovers	30		2					
				Free	04.07.94	Scarborough	24	4	3					
D E F E N D E R S														
Craig Boardman			30.11.70	Barnsley		Nottingham Forest								
						Peterborough Utd								
						Halifax Town								
				Free	08.95	Scarborough								
Lee Harper	5.11	12.5	24.03.75	Bridlington	08.04.94	Scarborough (T)	0+2							
				Loan	06.03.95	Goole Town								
Stuart Hicks	6.1	12.6	30.05.67	Peterborough	10.08.84	Peterborough U (T)								
				Free		Wisbech								
				Free	24.03.88	Colchester United	57+7	2	5	5			1	
				Free	19.08.90	Scunthorpe United	67	4	4	8	1		1	
				Free	10.08.92	Doncaster Rovers	36	2	1	2				
					27.08.93	Huddersfield Town	20+2	3	3	1	1			
					24.03.94	Preston North End	3+1			1				1
					22.02.95	Scarborough	6							
Adrian Meyer	5.11	11.4	22.09.70	Yate	10.06.89	Scarborough (T)	114	12	4+1	4+1	9			1
Ronald Robinson	5.9	11.0	22.10.66	Sunderland		SC Vaux								
				Free	06.11.84	Ipswich Town								
				Free	22.11.85	Leeds United	27							
				£5,000	25.02.87	Doncaster Rovers	76+2	6	5	3	5			
				£80,000	22.03.89	West Bromwich A.	1							
				£40,000	18.08.89	Rotherham United	86	9	6	7	2	1		1
				Free	10.12.91	Peterborough Utd	44+3	3	3	10				
				£25,000	24.07.93	Exeter City	37+2	4	2+1	3+1	1			
Loan 13.01.94 Huddersfield Town 2 Lge App.				Free	08.95	Scarborough								
Carl Stead			03.09.71	Hull		Doncaster Rovers								
				Free	24.11.94	Scarborough								
M I D F I E L D														
David D'Auria	5.8	11.0	26.03.70	Swansea	02.08.88	Swansea City (T)	27+18	2+2	1	4	6			
Free Merthyr Tydfil, via Barry Town					22.08.94	Scarborough	31+3	1+2	3+1	1	7			
Darren Knowles	5.6	10.1	08.10.70	Sheffield	01.07.89	Sheffield Utd (T)								
				£3,000	14.09.89	Stockport County	51+12	2+4		14+1				
				Free	04.08.93	Scarborough	81	6	7	4	1			
Richard Lucas	5.10	11.4	22.09.70	Chapeltown	01.07.89	Sheffield United (T)	8+2		1	0+1				
				£40,000	24.12.92	Preston North End	47+3		4	4+1				
				Free	08.95	Scarborough								
Jason Rockett	5.11	11.5	26.09.69	London	25.03.92	Rotherham United								
				Free	04.08.93	Scarborough	60+1	4	5	3				
Lee Thew	5.10	11.05	23.10.74	Sunderland	03.08.93	Doncaster Rov. (T)	21+11	1	0+2	2	2			1
				Free	08.95	Scarborough								
Andy Toman	5.10	11.7	07.03.62	Northallerton		Bishop Auckland								
GMVC'90. Div.4'91.				£10,000	16.08.85	Lincoln City	21+3	2		0+1	4			
						Bishop Auckland								
				£6,000	23.01.87	Hartlepool United	112	4	9	7	28	4		
				£40,000	01.08.89	Darlington	108+7	8	8	6	10	2	3	
				Free	20.08.93	Scunthorpe United	15	1	2	1	4	1		
Loan Scarborough, 25.2.93, 6 Lge App.				Free	10.12.93	Scarborough	21+8	1	3	1	1	1		
Mark Wells	5.9	10.1	15.10.71	Leicester	03.07.90	Notts County (T)	0+2			0+1				
				Free	09.08.93	Huddersfield Town	21+1	4	3	2+1	4			
				Free	21.07.94	Scarborough	16+2		4	1	1			
Alex Willgrass			08.04.76		14.07.94	Scarborough (T)								
F O R W A R D S														
Ian Blackstone	6.0	13.2	07.08.64	Harrogate		Harrogate R.I.								
					09.09.90	York City	107+22	3+1	3+1	11	37	1	2	2
					.08.94	Scarborough	11+2	4	0+2		2			
Mark Calvert	5.9	11.8	11.09.70	Consett	01.07.89	Hull City (T)	24+6	1+1		2+1	1			
				Free	04.08.93	Scarborough	68+4	6	2+1	3+1	5			1
Oliver Heald	6.0	12.0	13.03.75	Vancouver	06.10.93	Port Vale								
				Free	08.95	Scarborough								
Don Page	5.11	11.0	18.01.64	Manchester		Altrincham			1					
						Runcorn			7			1		
					23.03.89	Wigan Athletic	62+12	5	5	4+2	15	2	2	3
					16.08.91	Rotherham United	40+15	2+2	3	1+2	13		2	1
Loan 17.02.93 Rochdale 3+1 Lge App.					17.11.93	Doncaster Rovers	18+4				4			
				Free	29.07.94	Chester City	22+8	2	2	3	5	1	1	2
				Free	08.95	Scarborough								
Andy Ritchie	5.10	11.10	28.11.60	Manchester	05.12.77	Manchester Utd (A)	26+7	3+2	3+1		13			
E: u21.1, Y.4, S. Div.2'91.				£500,000	17.10.80	Brighton & H.A.	82+7	3+1	9		23	1	2	
				£150,000	25.03.83	Leeds United	127+9	11	9	2+1	40	3	1	
				£50,000	14.08.87	Oldham Athletic	187+30	18+2	8+2	3	83	18	4	
				Free	08.95	Scarborough								
Neil Trebble	6.3	13.10	16.02.69	Hitchin		Stevenage Boro'								
				Free	08.07.93	Scunthorpe United	8+6	0+1	1	1+1	2			
				Free	18.07.94	Preston North End	8+11	1	2+1	2	4			1
Loan 20.02.95 Scarborough					16.03.95	Scarborough	15				3			

THE MCCAIN STADIUM

Seamer Road, Scarborough TO12 4HF
Tel: 01723 375 094

Capacity 6,899
Covered Standing 1,000
Seating...2,150 + 1,350 under construction.
Terracing ....600, 2,150 by November 1995.

First game...Not known.
First floodlit game ....Not known.

ATTENDANCES
Highest ....11,162 v Luton Town, FAC 3rd Rnd, 1938.
Lowest ....412 v Scunthorpe Utd, AMC, 27.9.1993.

OTHER GROUNDS...None.

HOW TO GET TO THE GROUND

The ground is situated on the main Scarborough-York Road (A64). Half-a-mile on left past Plaxton's Coach Works coming from Town.

Car Parking
In streets around the ground.

Nearest Railway Station
Scarborough Central (2 miles)

MATCHDAY TICKET PRICES

Main Stand Transfer £2.50

Terraces. £7
Juv/OAP £3.50

Ticket Office Telephone no. . . . . . . 01723 375 094.

MATCHDAY PROGRAMME

Programme Editor. . . . . Eric Pickup.

Number of pages . . . . 36.

Price . . . . £1.20.

Subscriptions . . . . £30.

Local Newspapers . . . . Scarborough Evening News, The Mercury.

Local Radio Stations. . . . . Radio York, TFM Radio.

SCUNTHORPE UNITED
(The Iron)
ENDSLEIGH LEAGUE DIVISION 3
SPONSORED BY: BRIKENDEN

Back Row (L-R): R Wake, C Hope, M Ziccardi, A Knill, M Samways, R Bradley, A Murfin.
Middle Row: I White (Youth Development Officer), L Field, C Sansam, M Walsh, S Housham, L Turnbull, W Bullimore, S Thornber, J Exley.
Front Row: R Vickers, S Heath, P Wilson, P Spark.

SCUNTHORPE UNITED
FORMED IN 1904
TURNED PROFESSIONAL IN 1912
LTD COMPANY IN 1912

CHAIRMAN: K Wagstaff
VICE-CHAIRMAN
R Garton
DIRECTORS
B Borrill, C Plumtree, B Collen, S Wharton,
J Godfrey
SECRETARY
A D Rowing (01724 848 077)
COMMERCIAL MANAGER
A Chapman

MANAGER: David Moore
YOUTH TEAM MANAGER
Ian White

STATISTICIAN FOR THE DIRECTORY
Michael Norton

Right from the start United could never consider themselves serious challengers for an automatic promotion place and despite being in contention for a play-off spot for much of the season they were always a few points short of achieving that hangers-on position.

Four home defeats before the end of November did not help the cause. There was a serious problem in attack with no-one able to score consistently and deficiences were exposed in midfield and defence. Whilst Steve Thornber was always full of running and Wayne Bullimore's ball skills earned him a place in the division's representative Team of the Year, the midfield was somewhat lightweight and lacked height. This was all too evident against the more physical sides and when the midfield were brushed aside the defence too often wilted under pressure.

Home games against Carlisle, Mansfield and Colchester were prime examples where defeat was snatched from the jaws of victory. Because of the lack of fire-power most supporters could not understand why previous season's leading scorer Matt Carmichael was left out of the side. Manager Dave Moore considered Carmichael's best asset to be as a defender and preferred to combine experience with youth, pairing the rapidly-slowing Ian Juryeff with the willing-but-not-able Damian Henderson. Two goals from each of this duo in the opening three games flattered to deceive.

Having made early exits from the League Cup and Auto Windscreen Shield, it was left to the FA Cup in which to gain some glory. A solid display at Bradford City followed by another terrific performance in the replay took them into round two for lucrative games against Birmingham City, both matches being shown live on Sky TV. In all these games United showed they could match the standard of football played by higher level teams but they all too often failed to do it against teams at their own level. During the FA Cup run they lost all three league games thus extending the run without a victory to seven games.

With the onset of Christmas and the team down in mid-table Moore introduced a new attacking partnership with John Eyre on loan from Oldham paired with Stuart Young from Scarborough. The effect was almost immediate and the ball began to hit the back of the net regularly. In an eight-match spell United took 19 points and moved up to fifth place with Moore getting the Manger of the Month award for January. Sadly, Eyre was then recalled by Oldham and with Young affected by injury the attack lost it's bite. A bad spell was once again brought to an end with good signings by the manager. Neil Gregory on loan from Ipswich got the goals, Wycombe loanee Lee Turnbull strengthened the midfield whilst new signing Andy Kiwomya from Halifax was an instant hit with the fans.

The team finished just three points short of a play-off place but had surrendered a staggering 27 points to five of the top six teams, four of them doing the 'double'! As only three victories were recorded against teams finishing in the top ten places it is not difficult to see what points were lost.

MICHAEL NORTON.

SCUNTHORPE UNITED

Division Three: 7th   **FA Cup:** 2nd Round   **Coca-Cola Cup:** 1st Round   **Auto Windscreen Trophy:** 2nd Round

M	DATE	COMP.	VEN	OPPONENTS	RESULT	H/T	LP	GOAL SCORERS/GOAL TIMES	ATT.
1	A 13	EL	A	Barnet	W 2-1	2-0		Hendersun 27, Juryeff 45	(2,208)
2	16	CC 1/1	H	**Huddersfield Town**	**W 2-1**	**1-0**		**Hendersun 17, Bullimore 82**	**2,841**
3	20	EL	H	Fulham	L 1-2	1-1	12	Juryeff 8	3,165
4	23	CC 1/2	A	**Huddersfield Town**	**L 0-3**	**0-3**			**(6,455)**
5	27	EL	H	Northampton Town	D 1-1	1-1	11	Bradley 10	2,499
6	30	EL	H	Gillingham	W 3-0	0-0		Thornber 69, Henderson 78, Smith 90	2,098
7	S 3	EL	H	Carlisle United	L 2-3	2-0	10	Juryeff 24, Thornber 34	3,217
8	10	EL	A	Bury	L 0-2	0-1			(2,540)
9	13	EL	A	Darlington	W 3-1	2-1		Bullimore 42, Ford 45, Alexander 47	(2,181)
10	17	EL	H	Barnet	W 1-0	0-0	8	Juryeff 47	2,481
11	24	EL	H	Wigan Athletic	W 3-1	1-0	8	Thornber 44, Alexander 49, Bullimore 80 (pen)	2,602
12	27	AWT	H	**Rotherham United**	**L 1-3**	**0-3**		**Alexander 56**	**1,404**
13	O 1	EL	A	Hereford United	L 1-2	1-1	6	Bradley 23	(2,267)
14	8	EL	A	Preston North End	W 1-0	0-0	7	Alexander 79	(6,895)
15	15	EL	A	Walsall	L 0-1	0-1	8		3,609
16	22	EL	A	Exeter City	D 2-2	1-1	8	Hendersun 4, Juryeff 89	(2,511)
17	29	EL	H	Hartlepool United	D 0-0	0-0	8		2,624
18	N 5	EL	A	Torquay United	D 1-1	0-0	9	Juryeff 47	(3,036)
19	8	AW T	A	**Chesterfield**	**D 1-1**	**0-0**		**Bullimore 73 (pen)**	**(1,424)**
20	12	FAC 1	A	**Bradford City**	**D 1-1**	**1-1**		**Hope 3**	**(5,468)**
21	19	EL	H	Mansfield Town	L 3-4	1-0	9	Bullimore 38, Nicholson 78, Juryeff 90	2,975
22	22	FAC 1R	H	**Bradford City**	**W 3-2†**	**0-0**		**Carmichael 49, Alexander 64, Thompstone 96**	**4,514**
23	26	EL	A	Colchester United	L 2-4	0-2	9	Thornber 54, Knill 85	(2,904)
24	D 2	FAC 2	A	**Birmingham City**	**D 0-0**	**0-0**			**(13,832)**
25	10	EL	A	Fulham	L 0-1	0-1	12		(3,358)
26	14	FAC 2R	H	**Birmingham City**	**L 1-2**	**0-0**		**Bullimore 80**	**6,280**
27	16	EL	A	Northampton Town	W 1-0	1-0		Knill 9	(3,845)
28	26	EL	H	Lincoln City	W 2-0	0-0	11	Juryeff 59, Eyre 88	4,785
29	27	EL	A	Doncaster Rovers	D 1-1	0-1	10	Carmichael 85	(3,852)
30	31	EL	H	Rochdale	W 4-1	2-0	9	Mudd 11, Bullimore 45 (pen), Eyre 57, Thompstone 90	2,653
31	J 7	EL	H	Exeter City	W 3-0	2-0	8	Eyre 25, Alexander 34, Eyre 90	2,463
32	14	EL	A	Chesterfield	L 1-3	0-0	8	Bullimore 80 (pen)	(3,245)
33	21	EL	H	Torquay United	W 3-2	2-2	8	Smith 19, Eyre 23, Carmichael 47	2,229
34	28	EL	A	Hartlepool United	W 4-1	1-0	5	Knill 2, Young 78, Thornber 87, Eyre 90	(1,660)
35	F 4	EL	H	Colchester United	L 3-4	3-2	6	Eyre 4, Bullimore 16, Eyre 18	2,748
36	18	EL	A	Chesterfield	L 0-1	0-0	10		3,566
37	21	EL	A	Mansfield Town	L 0-1	0-0			(3,079)
38	25	EL	H	Hereford United	W 1-0	1-0	8	Nicholson 22	2,193
39	28	EL	A	Scarborough	L 0-3	0-0			(1,179)
40	M 11	EL	H	Bury	W 3-2	1-1	8	Gregory 45, 62 (og), Hughes 86	2,767
41	18	EL	A	Gillingham	D 2-2	1-0	9	Young 35, Turnbull 85	(2,459)
42	25	EL	A	Carlisle United	L 1-2	0-0	10	Kiwomya 81	(6,704)
43	A 1	EL	H	Darlington	W 2-1	1-1	8	Gregory 15, 65	2,449
44	4	EL	A	Wigan Athletic	D 0-0	0-0	8		(1,307)
45	8	EL	A	Rochdale	W 2-1	0-1	7	Turnbull 60, Kiwomya 72	(1,720)
46	15	EL	H	Doncaster Rovers	L 0-5	0-3	9		4,366
47	17	EL	A	Lincoln City	D 3-3	2-2	9	Turnbull 6, Gregory 40, Nicholson 54	(3,330)
48	22	EL	H	Scarborough	W 3-1	1-0	7	Gregory 37, Nicholson 59, Kiwomya 89	2,079
49	29	EL	A	Walsall	L 1-2	0-0	8	Gregory 60	(4,539)
50	M 6	EL	H	Preston North End	W 2-1	2-1	7	Ford 14, Knill 43	3,691
51									
52									
53									
54									
55									
56									
57									
58									
59									
60									

Best Home League Attendance: 4,785 v Lincoln City   **Smallest:** 2,079 v Scarborough   **Av Home Att:** 2,917

Goal Scorers:

Compared with 1993-94: -264

League (68): Eyre 8, Juryeff 8, Gregory 7, Bullimore 6 (3 pens), Thornber 5, Alexander 4, Nicholson 4, Knill 4, Henderson 3, Turnbull 3, Kiwomya 3, Bradley 2, Smith 2, Ford 2, Carmichael 2, Young 2, Mudd, Thompstone, Opponent

C/Cola Cup (2): Henderson, Bullimore

FA Cup (5): Hope, Carmichael, Alexander, Thompstone, Bullimore

AW Trophy : (2): Alexander, Bullimore (pen)

652

Samways M.	Ford A.	Mudd P.	Thomber S.	Knill A.	Bradley R.	Alexander G.	Bullimore W.	Juryeff I.	Henderson D.	Smith M.	Carmichael M.	Goodacre S.	Martin D.	Hope C.	Sansam C.	Thompstone I.	Nicholson M.	Eyre J.	Young S.	Eli R.	Turnbull L.	Gregory N.	Kwomya A.	Housham S.	Walsh M.	Referee	
1	2	3	4	5	6	7	8	9	10	11	S	S														Rejer P.	1
1	2	3	4	5	6	7	8	9+	10	11	S	S														Cain G.	2
1	2	3	4*	5	6	7	8	9	10•	11	12	14														Heilbron T.	3
1	2	3		5*	6	7	8	9	10	11•	12	14	4													Dawson A.	4
1	2	3	4		6	7	8•	9*	10	11	12		14	5												Butler A.	5
1	2	3	4	5	6	7*	8		10	11	S	9	12													Lomas E.	6
1	2	3	4	5	6	7	8	9*	10	11	12	14														Wolstenholme E.	7
1	4	3		5	6	7	8	9	10	11	2	S	S													Furnandiz R.	8
1	4*	3		5	6	7	8	9	10	11	2	5	12													Harrison P.	9
1	2	3	4	5	6	7	8	9	10	11	S	S														Richards P.	10
1	2	3	4	5	6	7	8	9	10	11		S	S													Poulain R.	11
1	2	3	4	5	6	7	8*	9•	10	11	12	14														Cruikshanks I.	12
1	2	3	4*	5	6	7	8	9	10	11•	12	14														Dunn S.	13
1	2	3	4	5	6	7	8	9	10			S	11		S											Vanes P.	14
1	2	3	4	5	6	7	8*	9	10•	12			1		14											Lupton K.	15
1	2	3	4	5•	6	7		9	10•	11	12				8	14										Singh G.	16
1	2	3	4	5	6	7		9*	10•	11	12				14	8										Brandwood J.	17
1	2	3	4	5	6	7		9	10•	11	12				S	8										Rejer P.	18
1		6•	5	3	7	8				11	9	10•	2	12	4									14		Lupton K.	19
1	8	3		5	6	7	4	9		11	S		2	10	S											Wilkie A.	20
1	4	3		5	6	7	8	9			2	10	S	11												Mathieson S.	21
1	4	3	11	5	6*	7	8	9		12		2	10•	14												Wilkie P.	22
1	2	3	4			7	8	9		6		12	10•	14	11*											Cooper K.	23
1	2	3	4	5	6	7	8	9*	10•	11	12						14									Dilkes R.	24
1	2	3	4	5	6	7	8	9*	10•	11	12						14									Bailey M.	25
1	2	3•	4	5	6	7	8	9		11	12						14	10*								Dilkes R.	26
1	2	3	4		6	7	8	9•		11	12						14	10*								Burns W.	27
1	2	3	4	5	6	7*	8	9•		11	12						14	10								Poulain R.	28
1	2	3	4	5	6	7	8	9•		11	12						14	10*								Butler A.	29
1	2	3	4		6	7	8			11	5						12	10	9*							Heilbron T.	30
1	2	3	4		6	7	8			11	5				S		S	10	9							Lomas E.	31
1	2	3	4		6	7	8			11*	12						14	9	10•							Allison D.	32
1	2*	3	4		6	7	8			11	12						S	10	9							Rennie U.	33
1	2	3	4			7	8*			11•	6				12		14	10	9							Riley M.	34
1	2	3	4			7	8			14	6				12		11•	10*	9							Furnandiz R.	35
1	2		4	5		7				s	6			3	8		11				9	12				Flood A.	36
1	2		4	5		7•				12	6				10*		8	11			9	14				Rushton J.	37
1	2	3	4	5		7	8			s	12			6			10	11	9*							Allison D.	38
1	2	3	4	5		7	11			12				6			9	10•	8*							Lynch K.	39
1	2	3	4	5			s			12				6			7	11	9*		8	10				Wright P.	40
1	2	3	4	5		7	14			12				6				11•	9*		8	10				D'Urso A.	41
1	2	3	4	5		s				s				6							8	10	11			Richards P.	42
1	2*	3	4	5		7	9			s				6		12					8	10	11			Bailey M.	43
1		3	4	5	s	7	9			s				6		2					8	10	11			Mathieson S.	44
1		3*	4	5		7				12				6	2			9•	14		8	10	11			Cruikshanks I.	45
1			4•	5	12	7	9			3				6	2*			9	14		8	10	11			Singh G.	46
1				5		7	4			3				6	9		S				8	10	11	2	S	Allison D.	47
1	7		4*			8				12				6	s				9			10	11	2	3	Lomas E.	48
1	7			5		12	8							6	14				9*		4	10	11	2•	3	Barber G.	49
1	7		12	5		14	8							6	10•				9*		4		11	2†	3	Heilbron T.	50
42	38	35	36	39	24	38	34	21	16	24	9	1		22	4	8	14	9	12		10	10	9	4	3	League Appearances	
		1			1	2	1		1		8	11	4	5	2	2	11	1			2	2				League Sub Appearances	
2	2	2	1	2	2	2	2	2		1	0+1	0+1		2	2	2	1									C/Cola Cup Appearances	
4	4	4	3	4	4	4	4	4	1	3	0+3			2	2+1		1+2									FA Cup Appearances	
2	1	1	2	2	2	2	2		1	2	1			2	0+1	1					0+2	1				AW Trophy Appearances	

Also Played: Heath SubGK(1-40,46,47), Ziccardi Sub GK (41-45,48-50). Players on Loan: Eyre (Oldham), Gregory (Ipswich), Turnbull (Wycombe)

† = Sent Off

SCUNTHORPE UNITED   RECORDS AND STATISTICS

CLUB RECORDS

RECORD LEAGUE VICTORY
8-1 v LutonTown, Div 3, 24.4.1965
Most Goals Scored in a Cup Tie
9-0 v Boston United, FA Cup 1st Round,21.11.1953

RECORD LEAGUE DEFEAT
0-8 v Carlisle United, Div 3N, 25.12.1952
Record Cup Defeat
0-7 v Coventry City, FA Cup Round 1, 29.11.1934

MOST LEAGUE POINTS
(3pts a win) 83, Div 4, 1982-83
(2pts a win) 66, Div 3N,1957-58

MOST LEAGUE GOALS
88, Div 3N, 1957-58

RECORD TRANSFER FEE RECEIVED
£400,000 from Aston Villa for Neil Cox, February1991

RECORD TRANSFER FEE PAID
£80,000 to York City for Ian Helliwell, August 1991

BEST PERFORMANCES
League: 4th Div 2, 1961-62 FA Cup: 5th Round 1957-58,1969-70
League Cup: Never beyond 3rd Round

HONOURS
Div 3N Champions 1957-58

LEAGUE CAREER
Elected to Div 3N 1950   Promoted to Div 2 1957-58
Relegated to Div 3 1963-64
Relegated to Div 4 1967-68   Promoted to Div 3 1971-72
Relegated to Div 41972-73   Promoted to Div 3 1982-83
Relegated to Div 4 (now Div 3) 1983-84

INDIVIDUAL CLUB RECORDS

MOST APPEARANCES FOR CLUB
Jack Brownsword (1950-65): League 597 + Cup 54 Total 651

MOST CAPPED PLAYER
No Scunthorpe player has won an international cap

RECORD GOALSCORER IN A MATCH:
Barrie Thomas 5 v Luton Town (h), 8-1, Div 3,24.4.1965

RECORD LEAGUE GOALSCORER IN A SEASON
Barrie Thomas 31, Div 2, 1961-62 In AllCompetitions: Barrie
Thomas, 31 (all league)

RECORD LEAGUE GOALSCORER IN A CAREER
Steve Cammack 110 In All Competitions: Steve Cammack 120
(League 110, FA Cup 6, League Cup 2, AMC 2) 1979-81 & 1981-86

OLDEST PLAYER IN A LEAGUE MATCH
Jack Brownsword, 41 years, 1965

YOUNGEST PLAYER IN A LEAGUE MATCH
Mike Farrell, 16 years 240 days, 8.11.1975

PREVIOUS MANAGERS

Leslie Jones 1950-51   Bill Corkhill 1951-56   Ron Stuart1956-58
Tony Macshane 1958-59   Bill Lambton (3 days) 1959   Frank Soo
1959-60   Dick Duckworth 1960-64   Freddie Goodwin 1964-67
Ron Ashman 1967-73   Ron Bradley 1973-74   Dickie Rooks 1974-
76   Ron Ashman 1976-81   John Duncan1981-83   Allan Clarke
1983-84   Frank Barlow 1984-87   Mick Buxton 1987-91 Bill Green
1991-93   Richard Money 1993-95   Dave Moore 1994-

ADDITIONAL INFORMATION
Previous League: Midland League
Previous Name: Merged with Lindsey United in 1910 to become
Scunthorpe and Lindsey United. Dropped the name Lindsey in 1958
Club colours: White shirts with claret and blue trim, sky blue
shorts, sky blue socks.
Change colours: Red shirts & shorts with claret, blue & yellow
'splashes', red socks.
Reserves League: Pontins Central League Div 3.

LONGEST LEAGUE RUNS

of undefeated matches:	15 (1957-58, 1971-72)	of league matches w/out a win:	14 (1973-74-1974-75)
of undefeated home matches:	21 (1950-51)	of undefeated away matches:	9 (1981-82-1982-83)
without home win:	7 (1963-64, 1972-73, 1989)	without an away win:	30 (1977-78)
of league wins:	6 (1954, 1965)	of home wins:	7 (1984-85, 1987)
of league defeats:	7 (1972-73)	of away wins:	5 (1965-66)

THE MANAGER

David Moore . . . . appointed March 1994.

Previous Clubs
As Manager. . . . . None.
As Asst.Man/Coach . . . . None.
As a player. . . . . Grimsby, Carlisle United, Blackpool, Grimsby, Darlington.

Honours
As a Manager . . . . None.
As a Player . . . . None.

SCUNTHORPE UNITED

PLAYERS NAME / Honours	Ht	Wt	Birthdate	Birthplace / Transfers	Contract Date	Clubs	League	L/Cup	FA Cup	Other	Lge	L/C	FAC	Oth
GOALKEEPERS														
Mark Samways	6.0	11.12	11.11.68	Doncaster	20.08.87	Doncaster Rov (A)	121	3	4	10				
					26.03.92	Scunthorpe United	122	6	10	13				
DEFENDERS														
Russell Bradley WFAC'90	6.2	12.5	28.03.66	Birmingham		Dudley Town								
				Nottingham Forest	20.05.88								
				Loan	13.11.88	Hereford United	12		1	3	1			
				£15,000	26.07.89	Hereford United	75+2	7		5+1	3			
				£45,000	06.09.91	Halifax Town	54+2	2	3	4	3			
				Free	30.06.93	Scunthorpe United	58+1	2	7	6	3			
Christopher Hope	6.1	12.2	14.11.72	Sheffield		Darlington (T)								
				Free	23.08.90	Nottingham Forest								
				£50,000	05.07.93	Scunthorpe United	59+6	2	6	5			1	
Alan Knill W: 1, Y. WC'89	6.2	11.7	08.10.64	Slough	14.10.82	Southampton (A)								
				Free	13.07.84	Halifax Town	118	6	6	6	6			
				£15,000	14.08.87	Swansea City	89	4	5	7	3			
				£95,000	18.08.89	Bury	141+3	7	8	14+1	9	1	1	1
				Loan	24.09.93	Cardiff City	4							
					05.11.93	Scunthorpe United	64	2	8	4	5			
MIDFIELD														
Wayne Bullimore E: S.	5.9	10.6	12.09.70	Sutton-in-Ash.	16.09.88	Manchester Utd (T)								
				Free	09.03.91	Barnsley	27+8	2+1	1+1		1			
				Free	11.10.93	Stockport County								
				Free	19.11.93	Scunthorpe United	51+2	2	5	3	9	1	1	1
John R Eyre	6.1	11.3	09.10.74	Hull	16.07.93	Oldham Athletic (T)	4+6	0+2			1			
				Loan	15.12.94	Scunthorpe United	9				8			
				£40,000	08.95	Scunthorpe United								
Tony Ford E: B.2. Div.3'80. FLGC'82.	5.9	12.2	14.05.59	Grimsby	01.05.77	Grimsby Town (A)	321+33	31+3	14+4	2	55	4	2	
				Loan	27.03.88	Sunderland	8+1				1			
				£35,000	08.07.86	Stoke City	112	8	9	6	13			1
				£145,000	24.03.89	West Bromwich A.	114	7	4	2+1	14		1	
				£50,000	21.11.91	Grimsby Town	59+9	1	3		3			
				Loan	16.09.93	Bradford City	5	2						
				Free	.08.94	Scunthorpe United	38	2	4	1	2			
Steve Housham	5.10	11.07	24.02.76	Gainsborough	23.12.93	Scunthorpe Utd (T)	4			0+1				
Andy McFarlane AGT'94.	6.3	12.6	30.11.68	Wolverhampton		Cradley Heath								
				£20,000	20.11.90	Portsmouth	0+2							
				£20,000	06.08.92	Swansea City	33+22	3	0+6	7+5	8	1	3	2
				£15,000	08.95	Scunthorpe United								
Christian Sansom	6.0	11.07	26.12.75	Hull	23.12.93	Scunthorpe Utd (T)	8+8		2+1	0+3				
Steve Thornber WFAC'89	5.10	11.2	11.10.65	Dewsbury	24.01.83	Halifax Town (J)	94+10	3+1	9	11	4	1	1	
				£10,000	23.08.88	Swansea City	98+19	7	9+2	8+3	5	3	1	
				Free	13.08.92	Blackpool	21+3	3		1				
				Free	12.07.93	Scunthorpe United	57+4	2	3+1	3	7			
Lee Turnbull	6.0	11.9	27.09.67	Stockton	07.09.85	Middlesbrough (T)	8+8	0+1		1+1	4			1
					24.08.87	Aston Villa								
				£17,500	03.11.87	Doncaster Rovers	108+15	3+1	5+1	9+1	21	2		2
				£35,000	14.02.91	Chesterfield	80+7	2+3	3	5	26	1	1	
					08.10.93	Doncaster Rovers	10+1		2	1	1			
				£20,000	21.01.94	Wycombe Wands	8+3	0+1	1	1	1	1		
				Loan	06.03.95	Scunthorpe United	10				3			
				£12,000	08.95	Scunthorpe United								

GLANFORD PARK

Doncaster Road, Scunthorpe DN15 8TD
Tel: 01724 848 077

Capacity 9,200
Covered Standing 2,773
Seating 6,427

First game ....v Hereford Utd, League, 27.8.1988.
First floodlit game ....Huddersfield, Lge Cup, 30.8.1988.

ATTENDANCES
Highest ....8,775 v Rotherham, Div 4, 1.5.1989.
Lowest ....859 v Chesterfield, AMC, 18.12.1990.

OTHER GROUNDS ....Old Show Ground.

MATCHDAY TICKET PRICES

British Steel Stand (home terrace) £6
Juv/OAP £3
Clugston Stand (all seated) £7.50
Juv/OAP £3.75
Evening Telegraph Stand (all seated) £8.50
Juv/OAP £5.50
South Stand (Away supporters) £8
Juv/OAP £4
Executive
Members £10.95
OAP £7.50
Non-Members £13
OAP £8.50
Family tickets (1+1) available if reserved in advance.

Ticket Office Telephone no. . . . . . . 01724 848 077.

HOW TO GET TO THE GROUND

From all Directions
Use motorway (M18) to junction 5, exit on to M180, at junction 3 exit on to M181, at roundabout take third exit.
The ground can clearly be seen on the right as you approach the roundabout.

Car Parking
Club park adjacent to ground for 800 vehicles.
£1 per car.

Nearest Railway Station
Scunthorpe.

CLUBCALL 0898 12 16 52

Calls cost 39p per minute cheap rate and 49p per
minute at all other times.
Call costings correct at time of going to press.

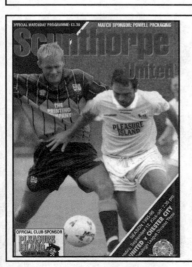

MATCHDAY PROGRAMME

Programme Editor . . . . John Curtis & Andy Skeels.

Number of pages . . . . 28.

Price . . . . £1.30.

Subscriptions . . . . Home & away combined £60.

Local Newspapers . . . . Scunthorpe Evening Telegraph.

Local Radio Stations . . . . Radio Humberside, Viking Radio.

TORQUAY UNITED
(The Gulls)
ENDSLEIGH LEAGUE DIVISION 3
SPONSORED BY: MOD DEC WINDOWS

Back Row (L-R): Michael Preston, Simon Travis, Neil Aggett, Scot Kaasikmae, Lee Barrow, Ellis Laight, Richard Hancox, Scott Stamps, Michael Shannon, Damien Davey (Physio), Lee Setter. **Middle Row:** Paul Compton (Yth Dev. Officer), Neil Povey, Matthew Wright, Neil Male, Matthew Gregg, Ashley Bayes, Paul Beswick, David Byng, Darren Horn, Robert King, John James (Scout). **Front Row:** Paul Buckle, Mark Hall, Chris Curran, Don O'Riordan (Manager), Mike Bateson (Chairman), Kevin Hodges (Caoch), Gregory Goodridge, Tom Kelly, Ian Hathaway

TORQUAY UNITED
FORMED IN 1898
TURNED PROFESSIONAL IN 1921
LTD COMPANY IN 1921

PRESIDENT: A J Boyce
CHAIRMAN: M Bateson
DIRECTORS
Mrs S Bateson, D Turner, M Beer, M Benney,
I Hayman, H Kinoelet, T Lilley, B Palk,
W Rogers
SECRETARY
David Turner (01803 328 666)
COMMERCIAL MANAGER
Cedric Munslow

MANAGER: Don O'Riordan

RESERVE TEAM MANAGER
Kevin Hodges
YOUTH TEAM MANAGER
Paul Compton
PHYSIOTHERAPIST
Damien Davey

STATISTICIAN FOR THE DIRECTORY
John Lovis

This proved to be a very disappointing season when one considers that the squad was virtually the same as that which came so close to promotion during the previous campaign. Very few players enhanced their reputations and there was a worrying tendency to give away soft goals, coupled with a lack of graft in the vital midfield and attacking areas.

Manager Don O'Riordan tried many permutations in an effort to pep up the attack but there were only occasional glimpses of what he was looking for. There was a good start and finish to the season but little else to cheer for the loyal Gulls fans. The Cup competitions brought little cheer and the defeat by Enfield in the F.A.Cup meant that for the fourth season running the club had been eliminated by non-League opposition.

Bright spots were the form of defender Lee Barrow who was far and away the most consistent performer and deservedly won the Player of the Year award and young midfielder Neil Povey, who earned a full contract after getting his first team chance at the latter end of the season. Off the pitch the club's financial position again improved, and the future of the club is in good hands.

Don O'Riordan faces a dilemma for the new campaign ahead. Does he make major changes to the personnel or attempt to fine tune the undoubted talent already within the club by adding a couple of experienced players to the squad?

JOHN LOVIS.

TORQUAY UNITED

Division Three: 13th   **FA Cup:** 2nd Round   **Coca-Cola Cup:** 2nd Round   **Auto Windscreen Trophy:**

M	DATE	COMP.	VEN	OPPONENTS	RESULT	H/T	LP	GOAL SCORERS/GOAL TIMES	ATT.
1	A 13	EL	A	Colchester United	W 3-1	2-1		Okorie 13, Buckle 41, Trollope 51	(3,175)
2	16	CC 1/1	A	**Cardiff City**	L 0-1	0-0			**(2,690)**
3	20	EL	H	Carlisle United	D 1-1	0-0	3	Hancox 62	3,506
4	23	CC 1/2	H	**Cardiff City**	W 4-2	2-2		**Goodridge 23, Hancox 40, 53, 74**	**2,719**
5	27	EL	A	Lincoln City	W 2-1	1-1	3	Hancox 3, 56	(3,154)
6	30	EL	H	Northampton Town	W 2-1	2-0	1	Okorie 19, 41	3,619
7	S 3	EL	H	Fulham	W 2-1	2-1	1	Stamps 31, Okorie 34	4,739
8	10	EL	A	Darlington	L 1-2	1-1	2	Trollope 14	(2,161)
9	13	EL	A	Hereford United	D 1-1	0-1	4	Goodridge 88	(2,153)
10	17	EL	H	Colchester United	D 3-3	1-0	4	Trollope 3, Hancox 67, Darby 88	3,390
11	20	CC 2/1	A	**Wimbledon**	L 0-2	0-2			**(2,451)**
12	24	EL	H	Barnet	L 1-2	0-2	7	Newson 69 (og)	3,280
13	27	AWS PR	A	**Hereford United**	L 2-4	0-2		**Laight 76, Darby 88**	**(1,046)**
14	O 1	EL	A	Chesterfield	L 0-1	0-0	10		(2,465)
15	5	CC 2/2	H	**Wimbledon**	L 0-1	0-1			**4,244**
16	8	EL	A	Gillingham	L 0-1	0-1	10		(2,439)
17	15	EL	H	Mansfield Town	W 2-1	1-1	9	Trollope 21, Pearcey 82 (og)	2,800
18	18	AWS PR	H	**Swansea City**	L 1-3	1-2		**Moore 22**	**885**
19	22	EL	H	Rochdale	W 4-1	1-0	6	Goodridge 38, 86, Hodges 64, Hathaway 77	2,547
20	29	EL	A	Doncaster Rovers	L 0-3	0-0	7		(2,697)
21	N 5	EL	H	Scunthorpe United	D 1-1	1-0	8	Barrow 15	3,036
22	12	FAC 1	A	**Kidderminster Harriers**	D 1-1	0-1		**Hathaway 73**	**(4,144)**
23	19	EL	A	Scarborough	L 1-1	0-1	8	Buckle 60	1,241
24	23	FAC 1R	H	**Kidderminster Harriers**	W 1-0	0-0		**Hancox 90**	**3,809**
25	26	EL	H	Wigan Athletic	D 0-0	0-0	8		2,509
26	D 3	FAC 2	A	**Enfield**	D 1-1	1-1		**Okorie 1**	**(2,326)**
27	10	EL	A	Carlisle United	L 0-1	0-1	9		(5,141)
28	13	FAC 2R	H	**Enfield**	L 0-1	0-0			**3,174**
29	17	EL	H	Lincoln City	W 2-1	1-0	8	Hancox 42, Sturridge 88	2,004
30	26	EL	A	Exeter City	W 2-1	0-1	8	Moore 63, O'Riordan 87	(5,538)
31	27	EL	H	Hartlepool United	D 2-2	1-1	9	Sturridge 23, Kelly 88	3,172
32	J 2	EL	H	Preston North End	W 1-0	1-0	9	Sturridge 44	3,770
33	7	EL	A	Rochdale	L 0-2	0-0	10		(1,636)
34	14	EL	H	Walsall	W 3-2	0-1	7	Okorie 60, Hathaway 63, Sturridge 69	2,976
35	21	EL	A	Scunthorpe United	L 2-3	2-2	9	Curran 38, Hancox 40	(2,229)
36	28	EL	H	Doncaster Rovers	L 0-1	0-0	10		2,852
37	F 4	EL	A	Wigan Athletic	D 1-1	1-0	11	Sturridge 35	(1,609)
38	18	EL	A	Walsall	L 0-1	0-0	12		(3,708)
39	25	EL	H	Chesterfield	D 3-3	1-1	13	Hathaway 5, 55, Darby 85	3,236
40	28	EL	A	Bury	L 1-3	0-1		Darby 89	(2,241)
41	M 4	EL	A	Barnet	L 0-2	0-1	14		(1,816)
42	7	EL	H	Scarborough	W 2-1	1-1	12	Barrow 35, Byng 59	1,492
43	11	EL	H	Darlington	W 1-0	0-0	11	Kelly 55	2,332
44	18	EL	A	Northampton Town	L 0-2	0-0	12		(3,832)
45	25	EL	A	Fulham	L 1-2	1-0	12	Hathaway 10	(4,941)
46	A 1	EL	H	Hereford United	L 0-1	0-1	12		2,410
47	8	EL	H	Bury	D 2-2	1-1	13	Curran 44, Moore 90	1,969
48	15	EL	A	Hartlepool United	D 1-1	0-0	14	Hancox 90	(1,770)
49	18	EL	H	Exeter City	D 0-0	0-0			4,155
50	22	EL	A	Preston North End	W 1-0	0-0	13	Hancox 60	(9,173)
51	29	EL	A	Mansfield Town	D 2-2	1-1	13	Darby 18, Barrow 77	(3,216)
52	M 6	EL	H	Gillingham	W 3-1	1-0	13	Hancox 13, Kelly 50, Buckle 60	2,638
53									
54									
55									
56									
57									
58									
59									
60									

Best Home League Attendance: 4,739 v Fulham   **Smallest:** 1,492 v Scarborough   **Av Home Att:** 2,973

Goal Scorers: Compared with 1993-94: -464

League (54): Hancox 9, Hathaway 5, Okorie 5, Sturridge 5, Darby 4, Trollope 4, Barrow 3, Buckle 3, Goodridge 3, Kelly 3, Curran 2, Moore 2, Opponents 2, Byng, Hodges, O'Riordan, Stamps

C/Cola Cup (4): Hancox 3, Goodridge
FA Cup (3): Hancox, Hathaway, Okorie
AW Trophy (3): Darby, Laight, Moore

Bayes	Hodges	Stamps	O'Riordan	Barrow	Curran	Trollope	Buckle	Hancox	Okorie	Goodridge	Hathaway	Darby	Moore	Kelly	Burton	Byng	Laight	Brass	Sturridge	Povey	Colcombe	Hawthorne	Referee	
1	2	3	4*	5	6	7	8	9•	10	11	S1	S2											G. Barber	1
1	2	3		5	6	7	8	9	10	11	4												R. Harris	2
1	2	3	4*	5	6	7	8	9	10	11	S1												C. Wilkes	3
1	2	3		5	6	7	8	9	10	11	4												P. Vanes	4
1		3	4	5	6	7	8	9	10*	11		S1	2										P. Rejer	5
1	2	3		5	6	7	8*	9	10	11	4•	S2		S1									M. Brandwood	6
1		3	4•	5	6†	7	8	9*	10	11	S2	S1	2										S. Dunn	7
1	S1	3		2	6	7	8		10	11	9*	5		4									P. Richards	8
1•		3		2	6†	7	8	9*	10	11	S2		5		S*								A. Flood	9
	2	3*		6		7	8	9	10•	11	4	S2	5		S1								J. Holbrook	10
				2	6	7	8	9	10	11			5	3	4								P. Foakes	11
	S2			2	6	7	8*	9	10	11		S*	5	3	4•								G. Singh	12
	2*			6		7	8•	9	4	11	S*	10	5	3			S2						J. Lloyd	13
1				2*		7	S1	8		10	11		5	3	6	9•	S2						N. Barry	14
1					6	7	8	9	10	11	4		5	3	2								M. Bodenham	15
1	S1				6	7	8	9	10	11•	4		5	3	2*								G. Pooley	16
1					6	7		9	10	11*	S1	8	5	3	4			2					G. Singh	17
1					6	7		9	10	S1	11	8•	5	3*	4		S2	2					S. Dunn	18
1	8	3		6		7*		S1		11	10		5	4		9		2					M. Pierce	19
1	8	3		6		7		S1		11*	10		5	4		9		2					K. Breen	20
1	S2	3	S1	6		7		9•	8	11*	10		5	4				2					P. Rejer	21
1	S1	3•	4	6	2	7		9	8*	S2	10		5	11				2					D. Gallagher	22
1	9		4	6		7	8		11		10		5	3				2					J. Rushton	23
1	9*		4	6	2	7	8	S1	11		10		5	3				2					M. Bodenham	24
1	9•		4*	6		7	8	11	S2		10		5	3				2					P. Vanes	25
1			4	6		7	8	S1	9	11	10		5	3*				2					M. Reed	26
1	S1		4	6		7	8	11	9*		10		5	3			S2	2					S. Mathieson	27
1†	4*			6		7	8	S1	S2	11•	10	9	5	3•				2					M. Reed	28
1	S1		4	6	2			7	8	11	10*			5	3				9				J. Holbrrok	29
1	S1		4	6	2			7	8*	11	10			5	3				9				S. Dunn	30
	S1		4	6	2*			7	8	11	10			5	3				9				C. Wilkes	31
			4	6	2			7	8	11	10			5	3				9				J. Brandwood	32
1	S1		4	6	2			7	8	11*	10			5	3				9				R. Furnandiz	33
1	S1		4	6	2			7	8	11	10			5	3				9	5*			K. Cooper	34
1	S1	5		6	2		S2	7		11	10•	8*		3					9	S2	4		U. Rennie	35
1	5*			6	2*		4	7		11	10•	8				S1			9	S2	3		R. Harris	36
1	7		4	6			8	S1	11		10		5	3					9		2		M. Riley	37
1	S2	7	4	6			5	9*	8	11•	10	S1		3					9		2		T. Heilbron	38
1	7		4	6				11	S1	8*	10	9		3					9		2		J. Rushton	39
1	7		4	6				11	S1	8*	10	9		3	5†		S*				2*		G. Barber	40
1	7*		4	6			8		11	10	9	5		3		11	S2			7*	2		P. Vanes	41
1	S2	7	4	6			8	S1		10	9	5•		3				11		7	2		K. Leach	42
1	S1	7	4	6	5		8	S2		10	9	3				11•				7*	2		K. Lynch	43
1		2	4	6*	5		8			10	S2	7•		3		11						S1	A. Butler	44
1	7*		4	6	4		8		11	10	S1	5	6				S2						J. Holbrook	45
1	7*	2•		6	4			11		10		5		3		9				S1			C. Wilkes	46
1	7	3		6	4		8	11		10		5				9					2		K. Breen	47
1	7	2		6	4		8	5		11*	10	S1		3		9							S. Dunn	48
1		2		6	4		8	7		11	10	9		5	3		S2			S1			A. Flood	49
1	11*	2		6	4		8	7		10•	9	5		3			S2			S1			E. Lomas	50
1	S1	2		6	4		8	7		10	9	5		3						11*			J. Brandwood	51
																								52
37	15	23	23	40	27	18	30	29	26	27	33	13	30	32	7	6	4	7	10	5	10	1	League Appearances	
13	2	1					2	7	1		3	5	11		1	1	6		3		1		League Sub Appearances	
3	2			3	4	4	4	4	4	4	3		2	2	2								C/Cola Cup Appearances	
4	2+1	1		3	4	2	4	3	1+3	3+1	2+1	4	1	4	4			2					FA Cup Appearances	
1	1			5	1	2	1	2	2	1+1	1+1	2	2	2	1		0+2			2			AW Trophy Appearances	

† = Sent Off

Also Played: Thornley SGK((9)), Nicholson 4S2(9), Davis 1(10,11,12,13), Winstone 4(14),S2(16), Morah 9(45),9•(46), Tucker SGK(28), Pettinger 1(31,32,33)

Players on Loan: Davis (Luton Town), Brass (Burnley), Sturridge (Derby County), Pettinger (Leeds United), Morah (Cambridge United)

TORQUAY UNITED

RECORDS AND STATISTICS

CLUB RECORDS

RECORD LEAGUE VICTORY
9-0 v Swindon Town, Div 3S, 8.3.1952
Record Cup Victory and Most Goals Scored in a Cup Tie: 7-1 v
Northampton Town(h), FA Cup 1st Round, 14.11.1959 (all goals
scored by Torquay-born players:Graham Bond (3), Ernie Pym (3),
and Tommy Northcott)
6-0 v Canterbury City, FA Cup Round 1, 1964-65

RECORD LEAGUE DEFEAT
2-10 v Fulham, Div 3S, 7.9.1931   2-10 v Luton Town, Div3S,
2.9.1933   1-9 v Millwall, Div 3S, 29.8.1927
Record Cup Defeat: 0-7 v Southend United, Leyland Daf Sth Q-
Final, 26.02.1991

MOST LEAGUE POINTS
(3pts a win) 77, Div 4, 1987-88
(2pts a win) 60, Div 4,1959-60

MOST LEAGUE GOALS
89, Div 3(S), 1956-57

RECORD TRANSFER FEE RECEIVED
£185,000 from Manchester United for Lee Sharpe, June 1988

RECORD TRANSFER FEE PAID
£60,000 to Dundee for Wes Saunders, July 1990

BEST PERFORMANCES
League: 2nd Div 3S 1956-57
FA Cup: 4th Round 1948-49,1954-55, 1970-71, 1982-83, 1989-90
League Cup: Never past 3rd Round

HONOURS
Sherpa Van Trophy Finalists 1989

LEAGUE CAREER
Elected to Div 3S 1927   Original Members of Division 4 1958
Promoted to Div 3 1960   Relegated to Div 4 1962
Promoted to Div 3 1966   Relegated to Div 4 1972
Promoted to Div 3 1991   Relegated to Div 4/3 1992

INDIVIDUAL CLUB RECORDS

MOST APPEARANCES FOR CLUB
Dennis Lewis (1947-59): League 443 + FA Cup 30 Total473

MOST CAPPED PLAYER
Gregory Goodridge, Barbados International

RECORD GOALSCORER IN A MATCH
Robin Stubbs 5 v Newport County, 8-3, Div 4,19.10.1963

RECORD LEAGUE GOALSCORER IN A SEASON
Sammy Collins, 40, Div 3S, 1955-56   In All Competitions: Sammy
Collins 42 (League 40 + FA Cup 2)

RECORD LEAGUE GOALSCORER IN A CAREER
Sammy Collins 204, 1948-58   In All Competitions: 219 (League
204 + FA Cup 15)

OLDEST PLAYER IN A LEAGUE MATCH
David Webb, 38 years 8 months v Crewe Alexandra, Div 4,
5.1.1985
YOUNGEST PLAYER IN A LEAGUE MATCH
David Byng, 16 years 36 days v Walsall, Div3, 14.8.1993

PREVIOUS MANAGERS

(Since 1946): John Butler   John McNeil   Bob John   Alex Massie
Eric Webber   Frank O'Farrell   Allan Brown   Jack Edwards
Malcolm Musgrove   Frank O'Farrell   Mike Green   Frank O'Farrell
Bruce Rioch   David Webb   John Sims   Stuart Morgan   Cyril
Knowles   David Smith   John Impey   Ivan Golac   Paul Compton

ADDITIONAL INFORMATION
Previous League: Southern League
Previous Name: Torquay Town (1910), Amalgamated with
Babbacombe in 1920

Club Colours: Yellow with navy blue & white hoops & white trim,
navy shorts with white trim, yellow socks with navy blue top
Change Colours: Blue & white stripes, white shorts
Reserves League: Avon Insurance Football Combination Div.2

LONGEST LEAGUE RUNS

of undefeated matches:	15 (1960, 1990)	of league matches w/out a win:	17 (1938)
of undefeated home matches:	31 (1956-57)	of undefeated away matches:	7 (1976, 1990)
without home win:	11 (1961)	without an away win:	28 (1991-1992)
of league wins:	6 (1953, 1990)	of home wins:	13 (1966-67)
of league defeats:	8 (1948, 1971)	of away wins:	5 (1959)

THE MANAGER

DON O'RIORDAN . . . . appointed May 1993.

PREVIOUS CLUBS
As Manager. . . . . None.
As Asst.Man/Coach . . . . None.
As a player . . . . Derby County, Doncaster (Loan), P.N.E., Tulsa (USA), Carlisle Utd, Middlesbrough, Grimsby,
. . . . Notts County, Mansfield (Loan), Torquay.

HONOURS
As a Manager . . . . None.
As a Player . . . . 1 cap for Eire U21s.

TORQUAY UNITED

PLAYERS NAME Honours	Ht	Wt	Birthdate	Birthplace Transfers	Contract Date	Clubs	APPEARANCES League	L/Cup	FA Cup	Other	GOALS Lge	L/C	FAC	Oth
G O A L K E E P E R S														
Ashley Bayes	6.1	12.9	19.04.72	Lincoln	05.07.90	Brentford (T)	4	5	2	1				
E: Y.1.				Free	13.08.93	Torquay United	69	3	6	4				
D E F E N D E R S														
Lee Barrow	5.11	12.5	01.05.73	Belper	09.07.91	Notts County (T)								
				Free	03.08.92	Scarborough	11	2		1				
				Free	18.02.93	Torquay United	74+1	5	6	3	5			
Christopher Curran	5.11	11.9	17.09.71	Birmingham	13.07.90	Torquay United	127+6	12	5	8	3			
Tom Kelly	5.10	11.10	28.03.64	Bellshill		Queen of the South								
				Free	14.08.85	Hartlepool United	14+1	2		1				
				Free	16.07.86	Torquay United	116+4	7+1	7+1	16				
				Free	01.07.89	York City	35	4	1	3	2			1
				£15,000	22.03.90	Exeter City	76+12	5	5	6	9	1		
				Free	14.01.93	Torquay United	83+3	2	6	5	8			
M I D F I E L D														
Paul Buckle	5.8	10.8	16.12.70	Hatfield	01.07.89	Brentford (T)	42+15	5+1	3+1	6+5	1			
Div.3'92.				Loan		Wycombe Wanderers			1					
				Free	03.02.94	Torquay United	46+2	4	3	3	5			
Richard Hancox	5.10	13.0	04.10.68	Wolverhampton		Stourport Swifts								
				Free	18.03.93	Torquay United	35+11	4	1+3	2	9	3	1	
Donald O'Riordan	5.11	12.0	14.05.57	Dublin	01.05.75	Derby County (A)	2+4	0+1		1				
Ei: u21.1.				Loan	21.01.78	Doncaster Rovers	2							
				£30,000		Tulsa Roughnecks								
				£30,000	13.10.78	Preston North End	153+5	10	8	8		1		
				£30,000	08.08.83	Carlisle United	84	4	4	18				
				£55,000	08.08.85	Middlesbrough	41	2	1	2	2		1	1
				Free	22.08.86	Grimsby Town	86	6	6	3	14			
				£16,000	13.07.88	Notts County	102+7	5+1	6	16+2	5	1	2	1
				Loan	28.09.89	Mansfield Town	6							
				Free	12.02.93	Torquay United	70+1	2	5	3	3			
F O R W A R D S														
Ian Hatherway	5.8	10.6	22.08.68	Wordsley		Bedworth								
				£8,000	08.02.89	Mansfield Town	21+23	1+1	1	3+1	2			1
					22.03.91	Rotherham United	5+8			0+1	1			
				Free	30.07.93	Torquay United	71+8	5	6	3+3	12		1	
Mark Hall	5.7	11.7	13.01.73	Islington		Tottenham H. (T)								
				Free	20.08.91	Southend United	4+8							
				Loan	13.09.93	Barnet	3	1		1				
				Free	08.95	Torquay United								
Ellis Laight	5.10	11.0	30.06.76	Birmingham		Torquay United (T)	4+7			0+2				1
Scott Stamps	5.11	11.0	20.03.75	Birmingham	06.07.93	Torquay United (T)	30+3	2	1	1	1			

PLAINMOOR GROUND
Torquay, Devon TQ1 3PG
Tel: 01803 328 666

Capacity 6,490
Covered Standing 4,131
Seating 2,359

First game ....(As Torquay Town) v St Austell, 2-0, 03.09.1910.
First floodlit game ....v Birmingham City (F) 2-3, 22.11.1954.

ATTENDANCES
Highest..21,908 v Huddersfield, FAC 4th Rnd, 29.1.1955.
Lowest...601 v Swansea, AMC, 2.12.1986.
....967 v Chester, Division 4, 2.5.1984.

OTHER GROUNDS..None.

MATCHDAY TICKET PRICES

Seats & Terraces
Category 'A' games £8
Juv/OAP £5

Category 'B' games £6
Juv/OAP £3

Category 'C' games £4
Juv/OAP £1

Ticket Office Telephone no. 01803 328 666

CLUBCALL
0891 66 45 65

Calls cost 39p per minute cheap rate and 49p per
minute at all other times.
Call costings correct at time of going to press.

HOW TO GET TO THE GROUND

From the North
Use A38 then A380 to Kingskerswell. In 1 mile at roundabout take
1st exit. In 1 mile turn left (A3022) sign posted Babbacombe. In 0.8
miles turn left then right into Westhill Road and Warbro Road for
Torquay United FC.

From the West
Use A380 into Torquay town centre then follow signs to Teignmouth
(A379) into Lymington Road, then turn right into Upton Hill, keep for-
ward into Bronshill Road. Take 2nd turning on left into Derwent Road
and at end turn right then turn right again into Marnham Road for
Torquay United FC.

Car Parking
Street parking. Coaches park at Lymington Road Coach Station.

Nearest Railway Station
Torquay (01752 221 300)

MATCHDAY PROGRAMME

Programme Editor . . . . David Turner.

Number of pages . . . . 32.

Price . . . . £1.20.

Subscriptions . . . . Home only £29, Away only £29, Home & away £47.

Local Newspapers . . . . Herald Express, Western Morning News.

Local Radio Stations . . . . BBC Radio Devon, Geminin Radio.

WIGAN ATHLETIC
(The Latics)
ENDSLEIGH LEAGUE DIVISION 3
SPONSORED BY: JJB SPORTS

Back Row (L-R): Ian Benjamin, John Butler, Neil Ogden, Chris Lightfoot, Simon Farnworth, David Felgate, Martin Haley, David Miller, Mark Leonard, John Robertson. **Middle Row:** Joe Hinnigan (Coach), Paul Tait, Roberto Martinez, Ian Kilford, Tony Kelly, Paul West, John Doolan, Andy Lyons, Michael Millett, David Crompton (Yth Dev. Officer), Alex Cribley (Coach/Physio). **Front Row:** Tony Black, Jesus Seba, Neill Rimmer, Graham Barrow (Manager), Andy Farrell, Isidro Diaz, Matthew Carragher.

Photo: Derek Davies.

In view of the club's struggle during the previous four seasons, this campaign was a vast improvement both in terms of results and the ambition for the future, as the team finished a creditable fourteenth in the league after one stage being five points adrift at the foot of the table.

The turning point in the club's fortune arrived in September, when former player Graham Barrow returned to Springfield Park as manage after an absence of eight years in place of the sacked Kenny Swain. A member of the successful Freight Rover Trophy side of ten years ago, Barrow had guided Chester City to promotion the previous season before his controversial departure.

At this stage the Latics had lost their opening five league, and with money tight, the new manager turned to tried and trusted players recruiting seasoned campaigners Mark Leonard, Joe Jakub, Andy Farrell, Ian Benjamin and David Miller to preserve their Football League status. In November, the Latics embarked on a league run of only two defeats in eighteen matches, resulting in boss Graham Barrow deservedly winning the Manager of the Month for February.

The only setbacks during this period were in the two cup competitions. Non-League Altrincham provided one of the shocks of the second round of the FA Cup with a 1-0 victory, courtesy of a goal by ex-latic's winger Chris Sharett. In the Auto Windscreen Trophy, after progressing through to the 3rd Round, Crewe Alexandra gained revenge for their first round Coca-Cola defeat with a 3-1 victory.

Late February saw local millionaire businessman Dave Whelan take control of the club. A former professional footballer with Blackburn Rovers his career ended following a broken leg sustained in the 1960 FA Cup final. His company JJB Sports, the club's main sponsors were floated on the Stock Exchange this year netting the new Chairman £50 million pounds.

After the impressive run of results to the end of March, which had seen a climb to the highest position in several years, defeats against clubs in the top eight positions ended any dreams of a play-off place.

Andy Lyons was again the leading goalscorer with fifteen League goals, while team captain Neill rimmer won both Supporters Association Player of the Year awards. The continuing effective work by Youth Development officer Dave Crompton were reflected by former trainees John Robertson being named 'Players Player of the Year' and Matty Carragher winning the young player of the year for the second consecutive season.

With the future of the club now in safe hands, aspirations have been raised not only by a financial saviour, but by a manager in whom the supporters have total trust. Money is now available to spend in the transfer market and a new stadium at Robin Park is planned for the start of the 1997-98 season

GEOFFREY LEA.

WIGAN ATHLETIC

Division Three: 14th **FA Cup:** 2nd Round **Coca-Cola Cup:** 2nd Round **Auto Windscreen Trophy:** 3rd Round

M	DATE	COMP.	VEN	OPPONENTS	RESULT	H/T	LP	GOAL SCORERS/GOAL TIMES	ATT.
1	A 13	EL	A	Carlisle United	L 1-2	0-1		Walling 72 (og)	(6,231)
2	16	CC 1/1	A	Crewe Alexandra	L 1-2	0-1		Gavin 50	(3,054)
3	20	EL	H	Gillingham	L 0-3	0-1	22		1,514
4	23	CC 1/2	H	Crewe Alexandra	W 3-0	0-0		Gavin 71, Rennie 79, Carragher 85	1,421
5	27	EL	A	Fulham	L 0-2	0-1	22		(4,241)
6	31	EL	H	Chesterfield	L 2-3	1-2		Morton 23, Gavin 79	1,231
7	S 3	EL	H	Barnet	L 1-2	1-1	22	Gavin 24	1,438
8	10	EL	A	Hereford United	W 2-1	0-1	21	Rennie 55 (pen), Rimmer 89	(2,771)
9	13	EL	A	Lincoln City	L 0-1	0-0	22		(2,030)
10	17	EL	H	Carlisle United	L 0-2	0-0	22		3,003
11	21	CC 2/1	A	Aston Villa	L 0-5	0-2			(12,433)
12	24	EL	A	Scunthorpe United	L 1-3	0-1	22	McKearney 46	(2,602)
13	O 1	EL	H	Scarborough	D 1-1	1-1	22	Kilford 20	1,403
14	5	CC 2/2	H	Aston Villa	L 0-3	0-1			2,633
15	8	EL	A	Doncaster Rovers	L 3-5	1-3	22	Leonard 42, 50, Benjamin 90	(2,060)
16	15	EL	H	Rochdale	W 4-0	4-0	22	Kilford 6, 32, Srong 20, Benjamin 37	2,118
17	18	AWT 1	A	Rochdale	L 0-1	0-0			(1,004)
18	22	EL	A	Northampton	L 0-1	0-0	22		(6,379)
19	29	EL	H	Colchester United	L 1-2	0-2	22	Robertson 77	1,621
20	N 5	EL	A	Hartlepool United	W 1-0	1-0	22	McKearney 19	(1,683)
21	8	AWT 1	H	Blackpool	W 1-0	1-0		Leonard 3	(1,161)
22	12	FAC 1	H	Spennymoor United	W 4-0	3-0		Leonard 17, Carragher 37, 45, Kilford 87	2,183
23	19	EL	H	Darlington	W 4-1	2-1	20	Strong 21, Lyons 34, 77,85	1,785
24	26	EL	A	Torquay United	D 0-0	0-0	19		2,509
25	29	AWT 2	A	Rotherham United	W 3-1	2-0		Rimmer 17, Leonard 39, Kilford 90	(1,587)
26	D 3	FAC 2	A	Altrincham	L 0-1	0-1			(3,020)
27	10	EL	A	Gillingham	W 1-0	0-0	18	Leonard 61	(2,257)
28	17	EL	H	Fulham	W 1-1	1-0	18	Leonard 5	1,791
29	26	EL	A	Bury	D 3-3	2-2	19	Lyons 40, 45, Leonard 56	(3,616)
30	J 7	EL	H	Northampton Town	W 2-1	1-1	17	Rimmer 42, Kilford 62	1,911
31	14	EL	A	Mansfield Town	L 3-4	0-1	18	Kilford 48, Rimmer 62, Lyons 85	(2,618)
32	24	EL	H	Preston North End	D 1-1	1-0	16	Lyons 43	3,618
33	28	EL	A	Colchester United	W 1-0	0-0	16	Doolan 71	(3,067)
34	F 4	EL	H	Torquay United	D 1-1	0-1	16	Miller 85	1,609
35	7	AWT 3	H	Crewe Alexandra	L 1-2	0-2		Farrell 65	2,063
36	11	EL	A	Darlington	W 3-1	1-0	16	Rodwell 12, Benjamin 57, Lyons 82	(1,780)
37	18	EL	H	Mansfield Town	L 0-2	0-4	16		1,884
38	21	EL	A	Exeter City	W 4-2	2-1	16	Lyons 9, McKearney 11 (pen), Benjamin 48, 63	(2,370)
39	25	EL	A	Scarborough	W 1-0	1-0	15	Lyons 38	(1,416)
40	28	EL	H	Hartlepool United	W 2-0	1-0	13	McKearney 42, Lyons 56	1,452
41	M 18	EL	A	Chesterfield	D 0-0	0-0	16		(3,808)
42	25	EL	A	Barnet	D 1-1	1-1	15	McKearney 39	(2,362)
43	29	EL	H	Hereford United	D 1-1	0-0	15	Benjamin 75	1,492
44	A 1	EL	H	Lincoln City	L 0-1	0-1	15		(1,696)
45	4	EL	H	Scunthorpe United	D 0-0	0-0	14		1,307
46	8	EL	H	Exeter City	W 3-1	2-0	12	Miller 40, Lyons 42, Rimmer 72	1,417
47	11	EL	H	Walsall	W 1-0	1-0	12	Lyons 28	2,176
48	15	EL	A	Preston North End	L 0-1	0-1	12		(10,238)
49	18	EL	H	Bury	L 0-3	0-1	13		2,531
50	22	EL	A	Walsall	L 0-2	0-0	13		(3,508)
51	29	EL	A	Rochdale	L 0-1	0-1	15		(1,949)
52	M 2	EL	H	Doncaster	W 3-2	0-0	14	Lyons 50, 77 (pen), Miller 72	1,576
53									
54									
55									
56									
57									
58									
59									
60									

Best Home League Attendance: 3,618 V Preston **Smallest:** 1,231 v Chesterfield **Av Home Att:** 1,837

Goal Scorers: **Compared with 1993-94:** -60

League (53): Lyons 15, Benjamin 6, Kilford 5, Leonard 5, McKearney 5, Rimmer 4, Miller 3, Gavin 2, Strong 2, Doolan, Morton, Rennie, Robertson, Rodwell, Opponent
C/Cola Cup (4): Gavin 2, Carragher, Rennie
FA Cup (4): Carragher 2, Kilford, Leonard
AW Trophy (4): Leonard 2, Farrell, Kilford, Rimmer

Farnworth	Rennie	Wright	West	Robertson	Kilford	Campbell	Morton	Gauin	Rimmer	Lyons	Strong	Duffy	Statham	Patterson	Carragher	Doolan	Adekola	Whitney	Tait	Mckearney	Jakub	Leonard	Farrell	Benjamin	Miller	Referee	
1	2	3•	4*	5	6	7	8	9		10	11	12	14	S												S. Mathieson	1
1	2	3		5	6	7	8	9*		10	11	4	12	S	S											U. Rennie	2
1	4	3*		5	6	7	8	9		10	11	12		S		2	S									J. Winter	3
1	2	3		5	6	7	8	9			11	4		S		10	S									J. Kirkby	4
1	2	3*		5	6	7	8	9			11	4	12	S		10										G. Barber	5
1	2	3•		5	6	7	8	9			11*	14	12	S		10										T. Heilborn	6
1	2	S		5	6		8	9			3	12	S		10			7	11*							N. Barry	7
1	2	3		5	6		8*	9	10		4		S		11			7	12	S						P. Rejer	8
1	2	3		5	6		8*	9	10		4		S		11			7		12						M. Riley	9
1	2			5	6		8*	9	10		4		S		11					12	3	7				R. Furnandiz	10
1	2			5	6	7	8	9	10		4		S		11					12	3*					G. Ashby	11
1	2			5	6	7	8	9	10		4*		S		11			14		12*		3				E. Poulain	12
1	S			5	6	8			12	10	4		S		2					8	3	9*	7	11		D. Allison	13
1	12			5	6	7	14	9	10	11•	4		S		2*					3	8					P. Jones	14
1	12					8	7*		14		11	4•		S		2				3	9	6	10	5		A. Flood	15
1	S					7				10	11	4		S		2			12	3	9	6	8*	5		P. Wright	16
1	5					7		8*		10	11	4		S		2		12		3	9	6				W. Burns	17
1						12	7			10	11	4				2*		14		3•	9	6	8	5		J. Rushton	18
1	14					5	7				11	4		S		2•		12		3*	9	6	8	10		K. Lynch	19
1	2					5	7				11		S		S	8		S		10	3	9	6		4	A. Butler	20
1*	2					5	7				11	14		12		8		S		10	3	9	6		4•	E. Wolstenholme	21
1	2					5	7				11		S		S	8		12		10	3	9*	6		4†	U. Rennie	22
1	2*					5	7				11	12		S		8		S		10	3	9	6		4	N. Barry	23
1						5	7			10	11	4		S		2		S		8	3	9	6	S		P. Vanes	24
1						5	7			10	11	2		S		8		S		3	9	6		4	T. Heilborn	25
1						5	7			10	11	2*		S		8		S		3	9	6	12	4		A. Dawson	26
1						5	7			10	11	S		S		2		S		8†	3	9	6		4	R. Harris	27
1						5	7			10	11	12		S		2		14		8•	3•	9	6		4	K. Lupton	28
1	14					5				10	11			S		2	8•	7		12	3	9	6		4	P. Harrison	29
1	S					5	7			10	11			S		8	2	S		3	9	6		4	I. Cruikshanks	30
1	12	3				5	7			10†	11			S		8*	2•			9		6	14	4		P. Rejer	31
1	3					5				10	11*			S		2	S		8		9	6	12	4		E. Lomas	32
1	3					5	7				11	S		S		2	10		8		9	6	S	4		P. D'Urso	33
1	3					5				10	11			S		2		8	S	9	6*	12	4			M. Riley	34
1	3•					5				10	11			S		2*	7		8	12	9		6	14	4	J. Brandwood	35
1	S					5				10	11			S		2	S	8	3		6	9	4			J. Watson	36
1						5				10	11			S		2•	14	8	3		6	9	4			J. Winter	37
1	12					5	8*			10	11			S		2	7	S	6	3		9	4			K. Cooper	38
1	S	3				5	7			10	11			S		2	S	8		6	9	4				T. Heilborn	39
1	3					5	7			10	11			S		2		8	14	12	9•	4				J. Lloyd	40
1	11					5				10						2	7	3	S	8	9	6		4		E. Wolstenholme	41
1	11*					5	7			10				S		2	12	3		8	9	6	13	4		J. Holbrook	42
1						5	8			10				S		2	S	3	11*	9	6	12	4			K. Lupton	43
1						5	8			10				S		2	12	3	S	9	6*	11	4			T. West	44
1						5	8			10	11*			S		2	S	3		9	6	S	4			S. Mathieson	45
1						5	8			10	11			S		2	S	3	12	9	6		4			A. Flood	46
1						5	8			10	11			S		2	S	3	S	9	6		4			D. Allison	47
1						5	8			10	11			S		2	12	3	S	9	6*	11	4			J. Watson	48
1						5	8			10	11			S		2	12	3	S	9	6		4			K. Breen	49
1*						5	8			10	11			12		2	15	3		7•	9	6•		4		A. Dawson	50
S						5	8•			10	11			1		2	14	3			9		12	4		P. Richards	51
1						5	8				11			S		2		3				6	10	4		I. Cruikshanks	52
41	11	14	1	39	35	7	9	9		33	32	12		1	41	6	1+3	12	1	17	16	28	30	12	31	League Appearances	
3	1							3				5	4	1			7		4	4		1	1	5		League Sub Appearances	
4	3+1	2		4	4	4	3+1	4		3	3	4	0+1		3			0+1	2		1					C/Cola Cup Appearances	
2	1			2	2			1		2	1				2			1	2	2	2	0+1	2			FA Cup Appearances	
4	2	1		3	3	1		3	4	2+1		0+1		4	1	0+1		2	3+1	4	4	0+1	3			AW Trophy Appearances	

Also Played: Rodwell 7(32,33,34,36,37), Furlong 12(37), Black 7(43,44,45,46*,47,48,49*,51,52*), Millett 14(50),6*(51),12(52), Ogden S (41), 12 (45), Ormsby S (4,5,9,10,11) 4(6,7), Harford 7(7,8,9)
Players on Loan: Harford (Blackburn Rovers), Rodwell (Scarborough), Whitney (Huddersfield)

WIGAN ATHLETIC   RECORDS AND STATISTICS

CLUB RECORDS

RECORD LEAGUE VICTORY
7-2 v Scunthorpe Utd, (a), Div 4, 12.3.1982 5-0 v Peterborough Utd, (h), Div 4, 19.1.1982 5-0 v Swansea City, (h), Div 3, 18.1.1986 6-1 v Swansea City (a),Div 3,6.4.1991
Most Goals Scored in a Cup Tie: 6-0 v Carlisle United, FA Cup Rnd 1, 24.11.1934 6-0 v Rochdale, Freight Rover Trophy (Northern Section), 28.1.1986

RECORD LEAGUE DEFEAT
0-5 v Bristol Rovers, Div 3, 26.2.1983 1-6 v Bristol Rovers, Div 3, 3.3.1990
Record Cup Defeat: 0-5 v Chelsea (h), FA Cup Round 3 replay, 26.1.1985

MOST LEAGUE POINTS
(3pts a win) 91, Div 4, 1981-82
(2pts a win) 55, Div 4,1978-79, 1979-80

MOST LEAGUE GOALS
83, Div 3, 1985-86

RECORD TRANSFER FEE RECEIVED
£350,000 from Coventry City for Peter Atherton, August 1991

RECORD TRANSFER FEE PAID
£87,500 to Chester City for Chris Lightfoot, July 1994.

BEST PERFORMANCES
League: 4th Div 3 1985-86 & 1986-87
FA Cup: 6th Round1986-87
League Cup: 4th Round 1981-82

HONOURS
Freight Rover Trophy 1985

LEAGUE CAREER
Elected to Div 4 1978   Promoted to Div 3 (now Div 2) 1982
Relegated to Div 3 1992-93

INDIVIDUAL CLUB RECORDS

MOST APPEARANCES FOR CLUB
Kevin Langley (1982-86 & 1990-1994): League 307+10 +FA Cup 27+1 + League Cup 21 + Other Competitions 27 Total 382+11 sub
MOST CAPPED PLAYER
None
RECORD GOALSCORER IN A MATCH
Paul Jewell 4 v Aldershot, Div 3, 1.3.1988
RECORD LEAGUE GOALSCORER IN A SEASON
Warren Aspinal 21, Div 3, 1985-86 In All Competitions: Warren Aspinal 27 (League 21 + Cup Competitions 6)
RECORD LEAGUE GOALSCORER IN A CAREER
Peter Houghton 62, 1978-83 In All Competitions: Peter Houghton 68 (League 62 + FA Cup 3 + League Cup 3)

OLDEST PLAYER IN A LEAGUE MATCH
Roy Tunks, 36 years 276 days v Blackpool, Div3, 24.10.1987
YOUNGEST PLAYER IN A LEAGUE MATCH
Steve Nugent, 16 years 132 days v Leyton Orient, Division 3, 16.9.1989

PREVIOUS MANAGERS

Charlie Spencer 1932-37 Jimmy Milne 1946-47 Bob Pryde 1949-52 Ted Goodier 1952-54 Walter Crook 1954-55 Ron Suart 1955-56 Billy Cooke 1956 Sam Barkas 1957 Trevor Hitchen 1957-58 Malcom Barrass 1958-59 Jimmy Shirley 1959 Pat Murphy 1959-60 Allenby Chilton 1960 Johnny Ball 1961-63 Allan Brown 1963-66 Alf Craig 1966-67 Harry Leyland 1967-68 Alan Saunders 1968 Ian McNeill 1968-70 Gordon Milne 1970-72 Les Rigby 1972-74 Brian Tiler 1974-76 Ian McNeill 1976-81 Larry Lloyd 1981-83 Harry McNally 1983-85 Bryan Hamilton 1985-86 Ray Mathias 1986-89 Bryan Hamilton 1989-91 Dave Philpotts 1991-93, Kenny Swain 1993-94.

ADDITIONAL INFORMATION
Previous Name: None.
Previous League: Northern Premier.

Club Colours: White shirts with broad blue & narrow green striped sleeves, blue shorts with white & green trim, blue & white socks.
Change Colours: Yellow shirts with blue pin stripes, yellow shorts, yellow socks.
Reserves League: Pontins League Division Three.

LONGEST LEAGUE RUNS

of undefeated matches:	21 (1981-82)	of league matches w/out a win:	14 (1989)
of undefeated home matches:	25 (1985-86)	of undefeated away matches:	11 (1986)
without home win:	6 (1988, 1989)	without an away win:	15 (1988)
of league wins:	6 (1986, 1993)	of home wins:	8 (1978-79)
of league defeats:	7 (1993)	of away wins:	4 (1987, 1988)

THE MANAGER

Graham Barrow . . . . appointed September 1994.

PREVIOUS CLUBS
As Manager. . . . . Chester City.
As Asst.Man/Coach . . . . Chester City (Player).
As a player. . . . . Altrincham, Wigan Athletic,Chester City.

HONOURS
As a Manager . . . . None.
As a Player . . . . Freight Rover Trophy, 1982.

WIGAN ATHLETIC

PLAYERS NAME / Honours	Ht	Wt	Birthdate	Birthplace / Transfers	Contract Date	Clubs	APPEARANCES League	L/Cup	FA Cup	Other	GOALS Lge	L/C	FAC	Oth
G O A L K E E P E R S														
Simon Farnworth	5,11	11,0	28,10,63	Chorley	05.09.81	Bolton Wands (A)	113	11	6	8				
E: S.				Loan	11.09.86	Stockport County	10	2						
Loan Tranmere R., 9.1.87, & Lge App.				Free	12.03.87	Bury	105	11	3	5				
				Free	01.07.90	Preston North End	81	6	3	7				
				Free	27.07.93	Wigan Athletic	124	10	6	10				
David Felgate	6.1	13.3	04.03.60	B. Festinig	01.08.78	Bolton W. (J)								
W: 1, S. SVT'89.				Loan	07.10.78	Rochdale	35							
				Loan	27.09.79	Crewe Alexandra	14							
Loan 09.03.80 Rochdale 12 Lge App.				£25,000	05.09.80	Lincoln City	198	16	10	2				
Loan 01.12.84 Cardiff City 4 Lge App.				£27,000	23.02.85	Grimsby Town	36	2	1					
Loan 14.02.86 Bolton W. 15 Lge App., & 4 Oth App.				£15,000	17.02.87	Bolton Wanderers	223	14	17	27				
				Free	27.07.93	Bury								
Free 12.08.93 Bolton, Free 12.08.93 Wolves				Free	01.10.93	Chester City	71+1	2	6	5				
				Free	08.95	Wigan Athletic								
Mark Statham	6.2	12.2	11.11.75	Barnsley	22.03.93	Nottingham Forest								
				Free	13.07.94	Wigan Athletic	1+1			0+1				
D E F E N D E R S														
John Butler	5.11	11.7	07.02.62	Liverpool		Prescot Cables								
AGT'92. Div.2'93.				£100	15.01.82	Wigan Athletic	238+7	17+1	20+1	18	15		2	
				£100,000	23.12.88	Stoke City	258+4	19	11	26+1	7			2
				Free	08.95	Wigan Athletic								
Matthew Carragher	5.9	10.7	14.01.76	Liverpool	25.11.93	Wigan Athletic (T)	68+5	3	6	5+1	1	2		
John Doolan	5.9	10.12	10.11.68	South Liverpool		Knowsley United								
				Free	18.03.92	Wigan Athletic	27+11	4		2				
Chris Lightfoot	6.1	12.0	01.04.70	Warrington	11.07.88	Chester City (T)	263+14	15+2	16+2	14+2	31	1	1	5
				£87,500	08.95	Wigan Athletic								
Michael Millett			22.09.77	Wigan	28.09.94	Wigan Athletic (T)	1+2							
John Robertson	6.2	12.8	08.01.74	Liverpool	06.07.92	Wigan Athletic (T)	94+4	10	6+1	8+1	3			
M I D F I E L D														
Andy Farrell	5.11	11.0	07.10.65	Colchester	21.09.83	Colchester Utd (A)	98+7	9	8	6	5			
Div.4'92.				£13,000	07.08.87	Burnley	237+20	17+4	19+2	27+3	19	1		3
				£20,000	22.09.94	Wigan Athletic	30+1	1	2	4				1
Tony G Kelly	5.10	13.2	01.10.64	Prescott	30.09.82	Liverpool (A)								
FRT'85.				Free		Prescot Cables								
				Free	04.01.84	Wigan Athletic	98+3	4	10	12	15	2	1	4
				£80,000	26.04.86	Stoke City	33+3	2	5	1	4			
				£60,000	13.07.87	West Bromwich A.	26	2	1	1	1			
Loan 22.09.88 Chester C. 5 Lge, 2 LC App.				Loan	24.10.88	Colchester United	13		4	3	2			
				£30,000	28.01.89	Shrewsbury Town	100+1	8	7	4	15	1	1	
				£100,000	15.08.91	Bolton Wanderers	103+3	9	15+3	9	5	2		1
				Free	23.09.94	Port Vale	3+1	1			1			
Free 31.10.94 Millwall 1+1 Lge App.				Free	25.11.94	Wigan Athletic								
				Free	09.12.94	Peterborough Utd	12+1			1				
				Free	08.95	Wigan Athletic								
Ian Kilford	5.10	10.5	06.10.73	Bristol	03.04.91	Nottingham Forest	0+1							
				Loan	23.12.93	Wigan Athletic	42+1	4	2+1	3	8		1	1
Neill Rimmer	5.6	10.3	13.11.67	Liverpool	14.04.84	Everton (A)	0+1							
E: Y1, S.				Free	13.08.85	Ipswich Town	19+3	3		1+1	3			
				Free	04.07.88	Wigan Athletic	157+3	14	9	14	10	1	2	2
F O R W A R D S														
Ian Benjamin	5.11	13.1	11.12.61	Nottingham	26.05.79	Sheffield Utd (A)	4+1	1+1			3			
E: Y.3. Div.4'87.				£100,000	31.08.79	West Bromwich A.	1+1							
Free 05.02.82 Notts County				Free	12.08.82	Peterborough Utd	77+3	7+1	5		14	1		
				Free	20.08.84	Northampton Town	147+3	12	9	9	58	2	3	5
				Free	29.10.87	Cambridge United	20+5		2		2		1	
				Free	28.07.88	Chester City	18+4	2	2	2	3		1	1
				Free	02.02.89	Exeter City	30+2	2	4+1	4	4	1		1
				Free	02.03.90	Southend United	122	8	2	7	33	1		4
				£50,000	20.11.92	Luton Town	7+6	2	2		2			
					24.09.93	Brentford	13+2	0+1	1	2	2			
				Free	30.09.94	Wigan Athletic	12+5		0+1	0+1	6			
Tony Black	5.8	11.0	15.07.69	Barrow		Bamber Bridge								
					22.03.95	Wigan Athletic	9							
Mark Leonard	5.11	11.10	27.09.62	St Helens		Witton Albion								
via Everton 24.02.82				Loan	24.03.83	Tranmere Rovers	6+1							
				Free	01.06.83	Crewe Alexandra	51+3	4	2	3+1	15	2		
				Free	13.02.85	Stockport County	73	5	1	2	23	2		3
				£40,000	27.09.86	Bradford City	120+37	13+5	6+3	6+5	29	6	1	3
27.03.92 Rochdale 9 Lge App. 1 gl.				£50,000	13.08.92	Preston North End	19+3	2			1			
				Free	13.08.93	Chester City	28+4	2	3	3	9		1	
					14.10.94	Wigan Athletic	28+1		2	4	5		1	2
Andrew Lyons	5.10	11.0	19.10.66	Blackpool		Fleetwood Town								
				£15,000	26.10.92	Crewe Alexandra	7+4	1		1+1	2	1		
					01.10.93	Wigan Athletic	65	3	4	4	26			
Neil Ogden	5.10	10.4	29.11.75	Billinge	18.03.94	Wigan Athletic	1+4		0+1					
David Miller	5.11	11.2	08.01.64	Burnley	11.01.82	Burnley (A)	27+5	2	1	2+1	3			
Loan 18.03.83 Crewe 3 Lfe App.				Free	16.07.85	Tranmere Rovers	25+4	1	4	2	1		1	
via Colne Dynamoes (Free)				Free	18.12.86	Preston North End	50+8	6	0+1	7+2	2			
Loan 16.02.89 Burnley 4 Lge App.				£30,000	14.09.89	Carlisle United	108+1	6	4	7	7			
				£25,000	31.03.92	Stockport County	72+6	5	5+2	12+2	1			
Loan 06.10.94 Wigan Athletic					05.11.94	Wigan Athletic	31		2	3	3			

ADDITIONAL CONTRACT PLAYERS: Diaz Isidro - Balaguer -Free 08.95. Roberto Marinez - Balaguer - Free 08.95. Jesus Seba - Real Zaragoza- Free 08.95.

SPRINGFIELD PARK
Wigan, Lancashire WN6 7BA
Tel: 01942 244 433

Capacity 8,666
Covered Standing 3,000
Seating 1,257

First game ....Not known.
First floodlit game ....Not known.

ATTENDANCES
Highest ....27,500 v Hereford Utd, 2.12.1953.
Lowest ....983 v Bury, AMC, 19.10.1993.

OTHER GROUND ....None.

MATCHDAY TICKET PRICES

Phoenix Stand £8
Juv/OAP £6

Heinz Family Enclosure £8
Schoolchild (accompanied) £3

Family Ticket
1+1 . . . . £10
1+2 . . . . £15
2+1 . . . . £19
2+2 . . . . £22

Ground £6.50
Children/OAP £4
Primary schoolchild/juv Latics £1.50

Ticket Office Telephone no. 01942 44433

CLUBCALL 0891 12 16 55

Calls cost 39p per minute cheap rate and 49p per
minute at all other times.
Call costings correct at time of going to press.

HOW TO GET TO THE GROUND

From the North
Use motorway M6 until junction 27. Leave motorway and follow signs Wigan
(A5029). In 0.3 miles turn right (B5206). In 1.1 miles turn left into Springfield
Road for Wigan Athletic FC.

From the East
Use A557, sign posted Wigan, into town centre then turn left into Market Street
and at end turn left into Parsons Walk (B5375). In 0.7 miles turn right into
Springfield Road for Wigan Athletic FC.

From the South
Use motorway M6 until junction 25. Leave motorway and follow signs into Wigan
(A49). Turn left into Market Street and at end turn left into Parsons Walk
(B5375). In 0.7 miles turn right in Springfield Road for Wigan Athletic FC.

Car Parking
Parking in nearby side streets.

Nearest Railway Station
Wigan Wallgate or Wigan Northwestern (01942 242 231)

MATCHDAY PROGRAMME

Programme Editor . . . . D Davies.

Number of pages . . . . 32.

Price . . . . £1.40.

Subscriptions . . . . £39 inc. P&P.

Local Newspapers . . . . Wigan Observer, Wigan Evening Post,
. . . . Wigan Reporter.

Local Radio Stations . . . . Radio Piccadilly, Radio Manchester,
. . . . Red Rose Radio, Fortune Radio.

ENGLAND'S INTERNATIONAL MATCHES AND TEAMS
1946-1995

1946-47

1. Northern Ireland   A   W   7-2   **Goalscorers: Carter, Finney, Langton, Lawton, Mannion (3).**

Swift	Scott	Hardwick	W Wright	Franklin	Cockburn	Finney	Carter	Lawton	Mannion	Langton

2. Republic of Ireland   A   W   1-0   **Goalscorers: Finney.**

Swift	Scott	Hardwick	W Wright	Franklin	Cockburn	Finney	Carter	Lawton	Mannion	Langton

3. Wales   H   W   3-0   **Goalscorers: Lawton, Mannion (2).**

Swift	Scott	Hardwick	W Wright	Franklin	Cockburn	Finney	Carter	Lawton	Mannion	Langton

4. Holland   H   W   8-2   **Goalscorers: Carter (2), Finney, Lawton (4), Mannion.**

Swift	Scott	Hardwick	W Wright	Franklin	Johnston	Finney	Carter	Lawton	Mannion	Langton

5. Scotland   H   D   1-1   **Goalscorers: Carter.**

Swift	Scott	Hardwick	W Wright	Franklin	Johnston	S Matthews	Carter	Lawton	Mannion	Mullen

6. France   H   W   3-0   **Goalscorers: Carter, Finney, Mannion.**

Swift	Scott	Hardwick	W Wright	Franklin	Lowe	Finney	Carter	Lawton	Mannion	Langton

7. Switzerland   A   L   0-1

Swift	Scott	Hardwick	W Wright	Franklin	Lowe	S Matthews	Carter	Lawton	Mannion	Langton

8. Portugal   A   W   10-0   **Goalscorers: Finney, Lawton (4), S Matthews, Mortensen (4).**

Swift	Scott	Hardwick	W Wright	Franklin	Lowe	S Matthews	Mortensen	Lawton	Mannion	Finney

1947-48

9. Belgium   A   W   5-2   **Goalscorers: Mortensen, Lawton (2).**

Swift	Scott	Hardwick	Ward	Franklin	W Wright	S Matthews	Mortensen	Lawton	Mannion	Finney

10. Wales   A   W   3-0   **Goalscorers: Finney (2), Lawton, Mortensen.**

Swift	Scott	Hardwick	P Taylor	Franklin	W Wright	S Matthews	Mortensen	Lawton	Mannion	Finney

11. Switzerland   H   W   6-0   **Goalscorers: Haines (2), Hancocks (2), Milburn, J Rowley**

Ditchburn	Ramsey	Aston	W Wright	Franklin	Cockburn	S Matthews	J Rowley	Milburn	Haines	Hancocks

12. Scotland   H   L   1-3   **Goalscorer: Milburn**

Swift	Aston	J Howe	W Wright	Franklin	Cockburn	S Matthews	Mortensen	Milburn	Pearson	Finney

13. Sweden   A   L   1-3   **Goalscorer: Finney**

Ditchburn	Shimwell	Aston	W Wright	Franklin	Cockburn	Finney	Mortensen	Bentley	J Rowley	Langton

14. Norway   A   W   4-1   **Goalscorers: Finney, Morris, Mullen, Opponents**

Swift	Ellerington	Aston	W Wright	Franklin	Dickinson	Finney	MOrris	Mortensen	Mannion	Mullen

15. France   A   W   3-1   **Goalscorers: Morris (2)**

Williams	Ellerington	Aston	W Wright	Franklin	Dickinson	Finney	Morris	J Rowley	Mannion	Mullen

1949-50

16. Eire   H   L   0-2

Williams	Mozley	Aston	W Wright	Franklin	Dickinson	P Harris	Morris	Pye	Mannion	Finney

17. Wales   A   W   4-1   **Goalscorers: Milburn (3), Mortenson**

Williams	Mozley	Aston	W Wright	Franklin	Dickinson	Finney	Mortenson	Milburn	Shackleton	Hancocks

18. Northern Ireland   A   W   9-2   **Goalscorers: J Froggatt, Mortensen, Pearson (2), J Rowley (4)**

Streten	Mozley	Aston	Watson	Franklin	W Wright	Finney	J Rowley	Pearson	J Froggatt

19. Italy   H   W   2-0   **Goalscorers: J Rowley, W Wright**

Williams	Ramsey	Aston	Watson	Franklin	W Wright	Finney	Mortensen	J Rowley	Pearson	J Froggatt

20. Scotland   A   W   1-0   **Goalscorers: Bentley**

Williams	Ramsey	Aston	W Wright	Franklin	Dickinson	Finney	Mannion	Mortenson	Bentley	Langton

21. Portugal   A   W   5-3   **Goalscorers: Finney (4), Mortensen**

Williams	Ramsey	Aston	W Wright	W H Jones	Dickinson	Milburn	Mortensen	Bentley	Mannion	Finney

22. Belgium   A   W   4-1   **Goalscorers: Bentley, Mannion, Mortensen, Mullen**

Williams	Ramsey	Aston	W Wright	W H Jones	Dickinson	Milburn*	Mortensen	Bentley	Mannion	Finney	Mullen*

23. Chile   N   W   2-0   **Goalscorers: Mannion, Mortensen**

Williams	Ramsey	Aston	W Wright	L Hughes	Dickinson	Finney	Mannion	Bentley	Mortenson	Mullen

24. USA N L 0-1

Williams	Ramsey	Aston	W Wright	L Hughes	Dickinson	Finney	Mannion	Bentley	Mortensen	Mullen

25. Spain N L 0-1

Williams	Ramsey	Eckersley	W Wright	L Hughes	Dickinson	S Matthews	Mortensen	Milburn	E Baily	Finney

1950-51

26. Northern Ireland A W 4-1 — Goalscorers: E Baily (2), J Lee, W Wright

Williams	Ramsey	Aston	W Wright	Chilton	Dickinson	S Matthews	Mannion	J Lee	E Baily	Langton

27. Wales H W 4-2 — Goalscorers: E Baily (2), Mannion, Milburn

Williams	Ramsey	L Smith	Watson	L Compton	Dickinson	Finney	Mannion	Milburn	E Baily	Medley

28. Yugoslavia H D 2-2 — Goalscorers: Lofthouse (2)

Williams	Ramsey	Eckersley	Watson	L Compton	Dickinson	Hancocks	Mannion	Lofthouse	E Baily	Medley

29. Scotland H L 2-3 — Goalscorers: Finney, Hassall

Williams	Ramsey	Eckersley	Johnston	J Froggatt	W Wright	S Matthews	Mannion	Mortensen	Hassall	Finney

30. Argentina H W 2-1 — Goalscorers: Milburn, Mortensen

Williams	Ramsey	Eckersley	W Wright	J Taylor	Cockburn	Finney	Mortensen	Milburn	Hassall	Metcalfe

31. Portugal H W 5-2 — Goalscorers: Finney, Hassall, Milburn (2), Nicholson

Williams	Ramsey	Eckersley	Nicholson	J Taylor	Cockburn	Finney	Pearson	Milburn	Hassall	Metcalfe

1951-52

32. France H D 2-2 — Goalscorers: Medley, Opponents

Williams	Ramsey	Willis	W Wright	Chilton	Cockburn	Finney	Mannion	Milburn	Hassall	Medley

33. Wales A D 1-1 — Goalscorers: E Baily

Williams	Ramsey	L Smith	W Wright	Barrass	Dickinson	Finney	T Thompson	Lofthouse	E Baily	Medley

34. Northern Ireland H W 2-0 — Goalscorers: Lofthouse (2)

Merrick	Ramsey	L Smith	W Wright	Barrass	Dickinson	Finney	Sewell	Lofthouse	Phillips	Medley

35. Austria H D 2-2 — Goalscorers: Lofthouse, Ramsey

Merrick	Ramsey	Eckersley	W Wright	J Froggatt	Dickinson	Milton	Broadis	Lofthouse	E Baily	Medley

36. Scotland A W 2-1 — Goalscorers: Pearson (2)

Merrick	Ramsey	Garrett	W Wright	J Froggatt	Dickinson	Finney	Broadis	Lofthouse	Pearson	J Rowley

37. Italy A D 1-1 — Goalscorers: Broadis

Merrick	Ramsey	Garrett	W Wright	J Froggatt	Dickinson	Finney	Broadis	Lofthouse	Pearson	Elliott

38. Austria A W 3-2 — Goalscorers: Lofthouse (2), Sewell

Merrick	Ramsey	Eckersley	W Wright	J Froggatt	Dickinson	Finney	Sewell	Lofthouse	E Baily	Elliott

39. Switzerland A W 3-0 — Goalscorers: Lofthouse (2), Sewell

Merrick	Ramsey	Eckersley	W Wright	J Froggatt	Dickinson	R Allen	Sewell	Lofthouse	E Baily	Finney

1952-53

40. Northern Ireland A D 2-2 — Goalscorers: Elliott, Lofthouse

Merrick	Ramsey	Eckersley	W Wright	J Froggatt	Dickinson	Finney	Sewell	Lofthouse	E Baily	Elliott

41. Wales H W 5-2 — Goalscorers: Bentley, J Finney, Froggatt, Lofthouse (2)

Merrick	Ramsey	L Smith	W Wright	J Froggatt	Dickinson	Finney	R Froggatt	Lofthouse	Bentley	Elliott

42. Belgium H W 5-0 — Goalscorers: Elliott (2), Lofthouse (2), R Froggatt

Merrick	Ramsey	L Smith	W Wright	J Froggatt	Dickinson	Finney	Bentley	Lofthouse	R Froggatt	Elliott

43. Scotland H D 2-2 — Goalscorers: Broadis (2)

Merrick	Ramsey	L Smith	W Wright	Barrass	Dickinson	Finney	Broadis	Lofthouse	R Froggatt	J Froggatt

44. Argentina A D 0-0

Merrick	Ramsey	Eckersley	W Wright	Johnston	Dickinson	Finney	Broadis	Lofthouse	T Taylor	Berry

45. Chile A W 2-1 — Goalscorers: Lofthouse, T Taylor

Merrick	Ramsey	Eckersley	W Wright	Johnston	Dickinson	Finney	Broadis	Lofthouse	T Taylor	Berry

46. Uruguay A L 1-2 — Goalscorer: T Taylor

Merrick	Ramsey	Eckersley	W Wright	Johnston	Dickinson	Finney	Broadis	Lofthouse	T Taylor	Berry

47. USA A W 6-3 — Goalscorers: Broadis, Finney (2), R Froggatt, Lofthouse (2)

Ditchburn	Ramsey	Eckersley	W Wright	Johnston	Dickinson	Finney	Broadis	Lofthouse	R Froggatt	J Froggatt

1953-54

48. Wales A W 4-1 — Goalscorers: Lofthouse (2), Wilshaw (2)

Merrick	Garrett	Eckersley	W Wright	Johnston	Dickinson	Finney	Quixall	Lofthouse	Wilshaw	Mullen

49. FIFA — H — D — 4-4 — Goalscorers: Mortensen, Mullen (2), Ramsey
Merrick — Ramsey — Eckersley — W Wright — Ufton — Dickinson — S Matthews — Mortensen — Lofthouse — Quixall — Mullen

50. Ireland — H — W` — 3-1 — Goalscorers: Hassall (2), Lofthouse
Merrick — Rickaby — Eckersley — W Wright — Johnston — Dickinson — S Matthews — Quixall — Lofthouse — Hassall — Mullen

51. Hungary — H — L — 3-6 — Goalscorers: Mortensen, Ramsey, Sewell
Merrick — Ramsey — Eckersley — W Wright — Johnston — Dickinson — S Matthews — E Taylor — Mortensen — Sewell — Robb

52. Scotland — A — W — 4-2 — Goalscorers: R Allen, Broadis, Mullen, Nicholls
Merrick — Staniforth — R Byrne — W Wright — H Clarke — Dickinson — Finney — Broadis — R Allen — Nicholls — Mullen

53. Yugoslavia — A — L — 0-1
Merrick — Staniforth — R Byrne — W Wright — Owen — Dickinson — Finney — Broadis — R Allen — Nicholls — Mullen

54. Hungary — A — L — 1-7 — Goalscorer: Broadis
Merrick — Staniforth — R Byrne — W Wright — Owen — Dickinson — P Harris — Sewell — Jezzard — Broadis — Finney

55. Belgium — N — D — 4-4 — Goalscorers: Broadis (2), Lofthouse (2)
Merrick — Staniforth — R Byrne — W Wright — Owen — Dickinson — S Matthews — Broadis — Lofthouse — T Taylor — Finney

56. Switzerland — N — W — 2-0 — Goalscorers: Mullen, Wilshaw
Merrick — Staniforth — R Byrne — McGarry — W Wright — Dickinson — Finney — Broadis — T Taylor — Wilshaw — Mullen

57. Uruguay — N — L — 2-4 — Goalscorers: Finney, Lofthouse
Merrick — Staniforth — R Byrne — McGarry — W Wright — Dickinson — S Matthews — Broadis — Lofthouse — Wilshaw — Finney

1954-55

58. Northern Ireland — A — W — 2-0 — Goalscorers: Haynes, Revie
Wood — Foulkes — R Byrne — Wheeler — W Wright — Barlow — S Matthews — Revie — Lofthouse — Haynes — Pilkington

59. Wales — H — W — 3-2 — Goalscorers: Bentley (3)
Wood — Staniforth — R Byrne — Phillips — W Wright — Slater — S Matthews — Bentley — R Allen — Shackleton — Blunstone

60. West Germany — H — W — 3-1 — Goalscorers: R Allen, Bentley, Shackleton
Williams — Staniforth — R Byrne — Phillips — W Wright — Slater — S Matthews — Bentley — R Allen — Shackleton — Finney

61. Scotland — H — W — 7-2 — Goalscorers: Lofthouse (2), Revie, Wilshaw (4)
Williams — Meadows — R Byrne — Armstrong — W Wright — Edwards — S Matthews — Revie — Lofthouse — Wilshaw — Blunstone

62. France — A — L — 0-1
Williams — P Sillett — R Byrne — Flowers — W Wright — Edwards — S Matthews — Revie — Lofthouse — Wilshaw — Blunstone

63. Spain — A — D — 1-1 — Goalscorer: Bentley
Williams — P Sillett — R Byrne — Dickinson — W Wright — Edwards — S Matthews — Bentley — Lofthouse — Quixall — Wilshaw

64. Portugal — A — L — 1-3 — Goalscorer: Bentley
Williams — P Sillett — R Byrne — Dickinson — W Wright — Edwards — S Matthews — Bentley — Lofthouse* — Wilshaw — Blunstone — Quixall*

1955-56

65. Denmark — A — W — 5-1 — Goalscorers: Bradford, Lofthouse (2), Revie (2)
Baynham — Hall — R Byrne — McGarry — W Wright — Dickinson — Milburn — Revie — Lofthouse — Bradford — Finney

66. Wales — A — L — 1-2 — Goalscorer: Opponents
Williams — Hall — R Byrne — McGarry — W Wright — Dickinson — S Matthews — Revie — Lofthouse — Wilshaw — Finney

67. Northern Ireland — H — W — 3-0 — Goalscorers: Finney, Wilshaw (2)
Baynham — Hall — R Byrne — Clayton — W Wright — Dickinson — Finney — Haynes — Jezzard — Wilshaw — Perry

68. Spain — H — W — 4-1 — Goalscorers: Atyeo, Finney, Perry (2)
Baynham — Hall — R Byrne — Clayton — W Wright — Dickinson — Finney — Atyeo — Lofthouse — Haynes — Perry

69. Scotland — A — D — 1-1 — Goalscorer: Haynes
R Matthews — Hall — R Byrne — Dickinson — W Wright — Edwards — Finney — T Taylor — Lofthouse — Haynes — Perry

70. H — Brazil — W — 4-2 — Goalscorers: Grainger (2), T Taylor (2)
R Matthews — Hall — R Byrne — Clayton — W Wright — Edwards — S Matthews — Atyeo — T Taylor — Haynes — Grainger

71. Sweden — A — D — 0-0
R Matthews — Hall — R Byrne — Clayton — W Wright — Edwards — Berry — Atyeo — T Taylor — Haynes — Grainger

72. Finland — A — W — 5-1 — Goalscorers: Astall, Haynes, Lofthouse (2), Wilshaw
Wood — Hall — R Byrne — Clayton — W Wright — Edwards — Astall — Haynes — T Taylor* — Wilsahw — Grainger — Lofthouse*

73. West Germany — A — W — 3-1 — Goalscorers: Edwards, Grainger, Haynes
R Matthews — Hall — R Byrne — Clayton — W Wright — Edwards — Astall — Haynes — T Taylor — Wilshaw — Grainger

1956-57

74. Northern Ireland — A — D — 1-1 — Goalscorer: S Matthews
R Matthews — Hall — R Byrne — Clayton — W Wright — Edwards — S Matthews — Revie — T Taylor — Wilshaw — Grainger

75.	Wales	H	W	3-1	Goalscorers: Brooks, Finney, Haynes

Ditchburn · Hall · R Byrne · Clayton · W Wright · Dickinson · S Matthews · Brooks · Finney · Haynes · Grainger

76.	Yugoslavia	H	W	3-0	Goalscorers: Brooks, T Taylor (2)

Ditchburn · Hall · R Byrne · Clayton · W Wright · Dickinson · S Matthews · Brooks · Finney · Haynes* · Blunstone · T Taylor*

77.	Denmark	H	W	5-2	Goalscorers: Edwards (2), T Taylor (3)

Ditchburn · Hall · R Byrne · Clayton · W Wright · Dickinson · S Matthews · Brooks · T Taylor · Edwards · Finney

78.	Scotland	H	W	2-1	Goalscorers: Edwards, Kevan

Hodgkinson · Hall · R Byrne · Clayton · W Wright · Edwards · S Matthews · T Thompson · Finney · Kevan · Grainger

79.	Eire	H	W	5-1	Goalscorers: Atyeo (2), T Taylor (3)

Hodgkinson · Hall · R Byrne · Clayton · W Wright · Edwards · S Matthews · Atyeo · T Taylor · Haynes · Finney

80.	Denmark	A	W	4-1	Goalscorers: Atyeo, Haynes, T Taylor (2)

Hodgkinson · Hall · R Byrne · Clayton · W Wright · Edwards · S Matthews · Atyeo · T Taylor · Haynes · Finney

81.	Eire	A	D	1-1	Goalscorer: Atyeo

Hodgkinson · Hall · R Byrne · Clayton · W Wright · Edwards · Finney · Atyeo · T Taylor · Haynes · Pegg

1957-58

82.	Wales	A	W	4-0	Goalscorers: Finney, Haynes (2), Opponents

Hopkinson · D Howe · R Byrne · Clayton · W Wright · Edwards · Douglas · Kevan · T Taylor · Haynes · Finney

83.	Northern Ireland	H	L	2-3	Goalscorers: A'Court, Edwards

Hopkinson · D Howe · R Byrne · Clayton · W Wright · Edwards · Douglas · Kevan · T Taylor · Haynes · A Court

84.	France	H	W	4-0	Goalscorers: R Robinson (@), T Taylor (2)

Hopkinson · D Howe · R Byrne · Clayton · W Wright · Edwards · Douglas · R Robson · T Taylor · Haynes · Finney

85.	Scotland	A	W	4-0	Goalscorers: R Charlton, Douglas, Kevan (2)

Hopkinson · D Howe · Langley · Clayton · W Wright · Slater · Douglas · R Charlton · Kevan · Haynes · Finney

86.	Portugal	H	W	2-1	Goalscorers: R Charlton (2)

Hopkinson · D Howe · Langley · Clayton · W Wright · Slater · Douglas · R Charlton · Kevan · Haynes · Finney

87.	Yugoslavia	A	L	0-5	

Hopkinson · D Howe · Langley · Clayton · W Wright · Slater · Douglas · R Charlton · Kevan · Haynes · Finney

88.	USSR	A	D	1-1	Goalscorer: Kevan

McDonald · D Howe · T Banks · Clamp · W Wright · Slater · Douglas · R Robson · Kevan · Haynes · Finney

89.	USSR	N	D	2-2	Goalscorers: Finney, Kevan

McDonald · D Howe · T Banks · Clamp · W Wright · Slater · Douglas · R Robson · Kevan · Haynes · Finney

90.	Brazil	N	D	0-0	

McDonald · D Howe · T Banks · Clamp · W Wright · Slater · Douglas · R Robson · Kevan · Haynes · A'Court

92.	Austria	N	D	2-2	Goalscorers: Haynes, Kevan

McDonald · D Howe · T Banks · Clamp · W Wright · Slater · Douglas · R Robson · Kevan · Haynes · A'Court

92.	USSR	N	L	0-1	

McDonald · D Howe · T Banks · Clayton · W Wright · Slater · Brabrook · Broadbent · Kevan · Haynes · A'Court

1958-59

93.	Northern Ireland	A	D	3-3	Goalscorers: R Charlton (2), Finney

McDonald · D Howe · T Banks · Clayton · W Wright · McGuinness · Brabrook · Broadbent · R Charlton · Haynes · Finney

94.	USSR	H	W	5-0	Goalscorers: R Charlton, Haynes (3), Lofthouse

McDonald · D Howe · G Shaw · Clayton · W Wright · Slater · Douglas · R Charlton · Lofthouse · Haynes · Finney

95.	Wales	H	D	2-2	Goalscorers: Broadbent (2)

McDonald · D Howe · G Shaw · Clayton · W Wright · Flowers · Clapton · Broadbent · Lofthouse · Haynes · A'Court

96.	Scotland	H	W	1-0	Goalscorer: R Charlton

Hopkinson · D Howe · G Shaw · Clayton · W Wright · Flowers · Douglas · Broadbent · R Charlton · Haynes · Holden

97.	Italy	H	D	2-2	Goalscorers: Bradley, R Charlton

Hopkinson · D Howe · G Shaw · Clayton · W Wright · Flowers · Bradley · Broadbent · R Charlton · Haynes · Holden

98.	Brazil	A	L	0-2	

Hopkinson · D Howe · Armfield · Clayton · W Wright · Flowers · Deeley · Broadbent · R Charlton · Haynes · Holden

99.	Peru	A	L	1-4	Goalscorer: Greaves

Hopkinson · D Howe · Armfield · Clayton · W Wright · Flowers · Deeley · Greaves · R Charlton · Haynes · Holden

100.	Mexico	A	L	1-2	Goalscorer: Kevan

Hopkinson · D Howe · Armfield · Clayton · W Wright · McGuinness*Holden' · Greaves · Kevan · Haynes · R Charlton · Flowers*, Bradley'

102.	USA	A	W	8-1	Goalscorers: Bradley, R Charlton (3), Flowers (2), Haynes, Kavan

Hopkinson · D Howe · Armfield · Clayton · W Wright · Flowers · Bradley · Greaves · Kevan · Haynes · R Charlton

1959-60

103. Wales   A   D   1-1   Goalscorer: Greaves

Hopkinson	D Howe	A Allen	Clayton	T Smith	Flowers	Connelly	Greaves	Clough	R Charlton	Holliday

104. Sweden   H   L   2-3   Goalscorers: R Charlton, Connelly

Hopkinson	D Howe	A Allen	Clayton	T Smith	Flowers	Connelly	Greaves	Clough	R Charlton	Holliday

105. Northern Ireland   H   W   2-1   Goalscorers: Baker , Parry

R Springett	D Howe	A Allen	Clayton	Brown	Flowers	Connelly	Haynes	Baker	Parry	Holliday

106. Scotland   A   D   1-1   Goalscorer: R Charlton

R Springett	Armfield	Wilson	Clayton	Slater	Flowers	Connelly	Broadbent	Baker	Parry	R Charlton

107. Yugoslavia   H   D   3-3   Goalscorers: Douglas, Greaves (2), Haynes

R Springett	Armfield	Wilson	Clayton	Swan	Flowers	Douglas	Haynes	Baker	Greaves	R Charlton

108. Spain   A   L   0-3

R Springett	Armfield	Wilson	R Robson	Swan	Flowers	Brabrook	Haynes	Baker	Greaves	R Charlton

109. Hungary   A   L   0-2

R Springett	Armfield	Wilson	R Robson	Swan	Flowers	Douglas	Haynes	Baker	Viollet	R Charlton

1960-61

110. Northern Ireland   A   W   5-2   Goalscorers: R Charlton, Douglas, Greaves (2), R Smith

R Springett	Armfield	McNeil	R Robson	Swan	Flowers	Douglas	Greaves	R Smith	Haynes	R Charlton

111. Luxembourg   A   W   9-0   Goalscorers: R Charlton (3), Greaves (3), Haynes, R Smith

R Springett	Armfield	McNeil	R Robson	Swan	Flowers	Douglas	Greaves	R Smith	Haynes	R Charlton

112. Spain   H   W   4-2   Goalscorers: Douglas, Greaves, R Smith (2)

R Springett	Armfield	McNeil	R Robson	Swan	Flowers	Douglas	Greaves	R Smith	Haynes	R Charlton

113. Wales   H   W   5-1   Goalscorers: R Charlton, Greaves (2), Haynes, R Smith

Hodgkinson	Armfield	McNeil	R Robson	Swan	Flowers	Douglas	Greaves	R Smith	Haynes	R Charlton

114. Scotland   H   W   9-3   Goalscorers: Douglas, Greaves (3), Haynes (2), R Robson, R Smith (2)

R Springett	Armfield	McNeil	R Robson	Swan	Flowers	Douglas	Greaves	R Smith	Haynes	R Charlton

115. Mexico   H   W   8-0   Goalscorers: R Charlton (3), Douglas (2), Flowers, Hitchens, R Robson

R Springett	Armfield	McNeil	R Robson	Swan	Flowers	Douglas	Kevan	Hitchens	Haynes	R Charlton

116. Portugal   A   D   1-1   Goalscorer: Flowers

R Springett	Armfield	McNeil	R Robson	Swan	Flowers	Douglas	Greaves	R Smith	Haynes	R Charlton

117. Italy   A   W   3-2   Goalscorers: Greaves, Hitchens(2)

R Springett	Armfield	McNeil	R Robson	Swan	Flowers	Douglas	Greaves	Hitchens	Haynes	R Charlton

118. Austria   A   L   1-3   Goalscorer: Greaves

R Springett	Armfield	Angus	Miller	Swan	Flowers	Douglas	Greaves	Hitchens	Haynes	R Charlton

1961-62

119. Luxembourg   H   W   4-1   Goalscorers: R Charlton (2), Pointer, Viollet

R Springett	Armfield	McNeil	R Robson	Swan	Flowers	Douglas	Fantham	Pointer	Viollet	R Charlton

120. Wales   A   D   1-1   Goalscorer: Douglas

R Springett	Armfield	Wilson	R Robson	Swan	Flowers	Connelly	Douglas	Pointer	Haynes	R Charlton

121. Portugal   H   W   2-0   Goalscorers: Connelly, Pointer

R Springett	Armfield	Wilson	R Robson	Swan	Flowers	Connelly	Douglas	Pointer	Haynes	R Charlton

122. Northern Ireland   H   D   1-1   Goalscorer: R Charlton

R Springett	Armfield	Wilson	R Robson	Swan	Flowers	Douglas	J Byrne	Crawford	Haynes	R Charlton

123. Austria   H   W   3-1   Goalscorers: Crawford, Flowers, Hunt

R Springett	Armfield	Wilson	Anderson	Swan	Flowers	Connelly	Hunt	Crawford	Haynes	R Charlton

124. Scotland   A   L   0-2

R Springett	Armfield	Wilson	Anderson	Swan	Flowers	Douglas	Greaves	R Smith	Haynes	R Charlton

125. Switzerland   H   W   3-1   Connelly, Flowers, Hitchens

R Springett	Armfield	Wilson	R Robson	Swan	Flowers	Connelly	Greaves	Hitchens	Haynes	R Charlton

126. Peru   A   W   4-0   Goalscorers: Greaves (3), Flowers

R Springett	Armfield	Wilson	Moore	Norman	Flowers	Douglas	Greaves	Hitchens	Haynes	R Charlton

127. Hungary   N   L   1-2   Goalscorer: Flowers

R Springett	Armfield	Wilson	Moore	Norman	Flowers	Douglas	Greaves	Hitchens	Haynes	R Charlton

128. Argentina   N   W   3-1   Goalscorers: R Charlton, Flowers, Greaves

R Springett	Armfield	Wilson	Moore	Norman	Flowers	Douglas	Greaves	Peacock	Haynes	R Charlton

129. Bulgaria   N   D   0-0

R Springett	Armfield	Wilson	Moore	Norman	Flowers	Douglas	Greaves	Peacock	Haynes	R Charlton

130. Brazil   N   L   1-3   Goalscorer: Hitchens

R Springett | Armfield | Wilson | Moore | Norman | Flowers | Douglas | Greaves | Hitchens | Haynes | R Charlton

---

1962-63

131. France   H   D   1-1   Goalscorer: Flowers

R Springett | Armfield | Wilson | Moore | Norman | Flowers | Hellawell | Crowe | Charnley | Greaves | A Hinton

132. Northern Ireland   A   W   3-1   Goalscorers: Greaves, O'Grady (2)

R Springett | Armfield | Wilson | Moore | Labone | Flowers | Hellawell | F Hill | Peacock | Greaves | O'Grady

133. Wales   H   W   4-0   Goalscorers: Connelly, Greaves, Peacock (2)

R Springett | Armfield | G Shaw | Moore | Labone | Flowers | Connelly | F Hill | Peacock | Greaves | Tambling

134. France   A   L   2-5   Goalscorers: R Smith, Tambling

R Springett | Armfield | Henry | Moore | Labone | Flowers | Connelly | Tambling | R Smith | Greaves | R Charlton

135. Scotland   H   L   1-2   Goalscorer: Douglas

G Banks | Armfield | G Byrne | Moore | Flowers | Douglas | Greaves | R Smith | Melia | R Charlton

136. Brazil   H   D   1-1   Goalscorer: Douglas

G Banks | Armfield | Wilson | Milne | Norman | Moore | Douglas | Greaves | R Smith | Eastham | R Charlton

137. Czechoslovakia   A   W   4-2   Goalscorers: R Charlton, Greaves (2), R Smith

G Banks | Shellito | Wilson | Milne | Norman | Moore | Paine | Greaves | R Smith | Eastham | R Charlton

138. East Germany   A   W   2-1   Goalscorers: R Charlton, Hunt

G Banks | Armfield | Wilson | Milne | Norman | Moore | Paine | Hunt | R Smith | Eastham | R Charlton

139. Switzerland   A   W   8-1   Goalscorers: J Byrne (2), R Charlton (3), Douglas, Kay, Melia

R Springett | Armfield | Wilson | Kay | Moore | Flowers | Douglas | Greaves | J Byrne | Melia | R Charlton

---

1963-64

140. Wales   A   W   4-0   Goalscorers: R Charlton, Greaves, R Smith (2)

G Banks | Armfield | Wilson | Milne | Norman | Moore | Paine | Greaves | R Smith | Eastham | R Charlton

141. Rest of World   H   W   2-1   Goalscorers: Greaves, Paine

G Banks | Armfield | Wilson | Milne | Norman | Moore | Paine | Greaves | R Smith | Eastham | R Charlton

142. Northern Ireland   H   W   8-3   Goalscorers: Greaves (4), Paine (3), R Smith

G Banks | Armfield | R Thomson | Milne | Norman | Moore | Paine | Greaves | R Smith | Eastham | R Charlton

143. Scotland   A   L   0-1

G Banks | Armfield | Wilson | Milne | Norman | Moore | Paine | Hunt | J Byrne | Eastham | R Charlton

144. Uruguay   H   W   2-1   Goalscorers: J Byrne (2)

G Banks | Cohen | Wilson | Milne | Norman | Moore | Paine | Greaves | J Byrne (2) | Eastham | R Charlton

145. Portugal   A   W   4-3   Goalscorers: J Byrne (3), R Charlton

G Banks | Cohen | Wilson | Milne | Norman | Moore | P Thompson | Greaves | J Byrne | Eastham | R Charlton

146. Eire   A   W   3-1   Goalscorers: J Byrne, Eastham, Greaves

Waiters | Cohen | Wilson | Milne | Norman | Moore | P Thompson | Greaves | J Byrne | Eastham | R Charlton

147. USA   A   W   10-0   Goalscorers: R Charlton, Hunt (4), Paine (2), Pickering (3)

G Banks | Cohen | R Thomson | M Bailey | Norman | Flowers | Paine | Hunt | Pickering | Eastham* | P Thompson | R Charlton *

148. Brazil   A   L   1-5   Goalscorer: Greaves

Waiters | Cohen | Wilson | Milne | Norman | Moore | P Thompson | Greaves | J Byrne | Eastham | R Charlton

149. Portugal   N   D   1-1   Goalscorer: Hunt

G Banks | R Thomson | Wilson | Flowers | Norman | Moore | Paine | Greaves | J Byrne | Hunt | P Thompson

150. Argentina   N   L   0-1

G Banks | R Thomson | Wilson | Milne | Norman | Moore | P Thompson | Greaves | J Byrne | Eastham | R Charlton

---

1964-65

152. Northern Ireland   A   W   4-3   Goalscorers: Greaves (3), Pickering

G Banks | Cohen | R Thomson | Milne | Norman | Moore | Paine | Greaves | Pickering | R Charlton | P Thompson

153. Belgium   H   D   2-2   Goalscorers: Pickering, Opponents

Waiters | Cohen | R Thomson | Milne | Norman | Moore | P Thompson | Greaves | Pickering | Venables | A Hinton

154. Wales   H   W   2-1   Goalscorers: Wignall (2)

Waiters | Cohen | R Thomson | M Bailey | Flowers | Young | P Thompson | Hunt | Wignall | J Byrne | A Hinton

155. Holland   A   D   1-1   Goalscorer: Greaves

Waiters | Cohen | R Thomson | Mullery | Norman | Flowers | P Thompson | Greaves | Wignall | Venables | R Charlton

156. Scotland   H   D   2-2   Goalscorers: R Charlton, Greaves

G Banks | Cohen | Wilson | Stiles | J Charlton | Moore | P Thompson | Greaves | Bridges | J Byrne | R Charlton

157. Hungary — H — W 1-0 — Goalscorer: Greaves
G Banks, Cohen, Wilson, Stiles, J Charlton, Moore, Paine, Greaves, Bridges, Eastham, Connelly

158. Yugoslavia — A — D 1-1 — Goalscorer: Bridges
G Banks, Cohen, Wilson, Stiles, J Charlton, Moore, Paine, Greaves, Bridges, Ball, Connelly

159. West Germany — A — W 1-0 — Goalscorer: Paine
G Banks, Cohen, Wilson, Flowers, J Charlton, Moore, Paine, Ball, M Jones, Eastham, Temple

160. Sweden — A — W 2-1 — Goalscorers: Ball, Connelly
G Banks, Cohen, Wilson, Stiles, J Charlton, Moore, Paine, Ball, M Jones, Eastham, Connelly

1965-66

161. Wales — A — D 0-0
R Springett, Cohen, Wilson, Stiles, J Charlton, Moore, Paine, Greaves, Peacock, R Charlton, Connelly

162. Austria — H — L 2-3 — Goalscorers: R Charlton, Connelly
R Springett, Cohen, Wilson, Stiles, J Charlton, Moore, Paine, Greaves, Bridges, R Charlton, Connelly

163. Northern Ireland — H — W 2-1 — Goalscorers: Baker, Peacock
G Banks, Cohen, Wilson, Stiles, J Charlton, Moore, P Thompson, Baker, Peacock, R Charlton, Connelly

164. Spain — A — W 2-0 — Goalscorers: Baker, Hunt
G Banks, Cohen, Wilson, Stiles, J Charlton, Moore, Ball, Hunt, Baker*, Eastham, R Charlton, Hunter*

165. Poland — H — D 1-1 — Goalscorer: Moore
G Banks, Cohen, Wilson, Stiles, J Charlton, Moore, Ball, Hunt, Baker, Eastham, G Harris

166. West Germany — H — W 1-0 — Goalscorer: Stiles
G Banks, Cohen, K Newton*, Moore, J Charlton, Hunter, Ball, Hunt, Stiles, G Hurst, R Charlton, Wilson*

167. Scotland — A — W 4-3 — Goalscorers: R Charlton, Hunt (2), G Hurst
G Banks, Cohen, K Newton, Stiles, J Charlton, Moore, Ball, Hunt, R Charlton, G Hurst, Connelly

168. Yugoslavia — H — W 2-0 — Goalscorers: R Charlton, Greaves
G Banks, Armfield, Wilson, Peters, J Charlton, Hunter, Paine, Greaves, R Charlton, G Hurst, Tambling

169. Finland — A — W 3-0 — Goalscorers: J Charlton, Hunt, Peters
G Banks, Armfield, Wilson, Peters, J Charlton, Hunter, Callaghan, Hunt, R Charlton, G Hurst, Ball

170. Norway — A — W 6-1 — Goalscorers: Connelly, Greaves (4), Moore
R Springett, Cohen, G Byrne, Stiles, Flowers, Moore, Paine, Greaves, R Charlton, Hunt, Connelly

171. Denmark — A — W 2-0 — Goalscorers: J Charlton, Eastham
Bonetti, Cohen, Wilson, Stiles, J Charlton, Moore, Ball, Greaves, G Hurst, Eastham, Connelly

172. Poland — A — W 1-0 — Goalscorer: Hunt
G Banks, Cohen, Wilson, Stiles, J Charlton, Moore, Ball, Greaves, R Charlton, Hunt, Peters

173. Uruguay — H — D 0-0
G Banks, Cohen, Wilson, Stiles, J Charlton, Moore, Ball, Greaves, R Charlton, Hunt, Connelly

174. Mexico — H — W 2-0 — Goalscorers: R Charlton, Hunt
G Banks, Cohen, Wilson, Stiles, J Charlton, Moore, Paine, Greaves, R Charlton, Hunt, Peters

175. France — H — W 2-0 — Goalscorers: Hunt (2)
G Banks, Cohen, Wilson, Stiles, J Charlton, Moore, Callaghan, Greaves, R Charlton, Hunt, Peters

176. Argentina — H — 1-0 Goalscorer: G Hurst
G Banks, Cohen, Wilson, Stiles, J Charlton, Moore, Ball, G Hurst, R Charlton, Hunt, Peters

177. Portugal — H — 2-1 Goalscorers: R Charlton (2)
G Banks, Cohen, Wilson, Stiles, J Charlton, Moore, Ball, G Hurst, R Charlton, Hunt, Peters

178. West Germany — H — 4-2 Goalscorers: G Hurst (3), Peters
G Banks, Cohen, Wilson, Stiles, J Charlton, Moore, Ball, G Hurst, R Charlton, Hunt, Peters

1966-67

179. Northern Ireland — A — W 2-0 — Goalscorers: Hunt, Peters
G Banks, Cohen, Wilson, Stiles, J Charlton, Moore, Ball, G Hurst, R Charlton, Hunt, Peters

180. Czechoslovakia — H — D 0-0
G Banks, Cohen, Wilson, Stiles, J Charlton, Moore, Ball, G Hurst, R Charlton, Hunt, Peters

181. Wales — H — W 5-1 — Goalscorers: J Charlton, R Charlton, G Hurst (2), Opponents
G Banks, Cohen, Wilson, Stiles, J Charlton, Moore, Ball, G Hurst, R Charlton, Hunt, Peters

182. Scotland — H — L 2-3 — Goalscorers: J Charlton, G Hurst
G Banks, Cohen, Wilson, Stiles, J Charlton, Moore, Ball, Greaves, R Charlton, G Hurst, Peters

183. Spain — H — W 2-0 — Goalscorers: Greaves, Hunt
Bonetti, Cohen, K Newton, Stiles, Labone, Moore, Ball, Greaves, G Hurst, Hunt, Hollins

184.	Austria	A	W 1-0	Goalscorer: Ball							
Bonetti	K Newton	Wilson	Mullery	Labone	Moore	Ball	Greaves	G Hurst	Hunt	Hunter	

1967-68

185.	Wales	A	W 3-0	Goalscorers: Ball, R Charlton, Peters						
G Banks	Cohen	K Newton	Mullery	J Charlton	Moore	Ball	Hunt	R Charlton	G Hurst	Peters

186.	Northern Ireland	H	W 2-0	Goalscorers: R Charlton, G Hurst						
G Banks	Cohen	Wilson	Mullery	Sadler	Moore	P Thompson	Hunt	R Charlton	G Hurst	Peters

187.	USSR	H	D 2-2	Goalscorers: Ball, Hunt						
G Banks	C Knowles	Wilson	Mullery	Sadler	Moore	Ball	Hunt	R Charlton	G Hurst	Peters

188.	Scotland	A	D 1-1	Goalscorer: Peters						
G Banks	K Newton	Wilson	Mullery	Labone	Moore	Ball	G Hurst	Summerbee	R Charlton	Peters

189.	Spain	H	W 1-0	Goalscorer: R Charlton						
G Banks	C Knowles	Wilson	Mullery	J Charlton	Moore	Ball	Hunt	Summerbee	R Charlton	Peters

190.	Spain	A	W 2-1	Goalscorers: Hunter, Peters						
Bonetti	K Newton	Wilson	Mullery	Labone	Moore	Ball	Peters	R Charlton	Hunt	Hunter

191.	Sweden	H	W 3-1	Goalscorers: R Charlton, Hunt, Peters						
Stepney	K Newton	C Knowles	Mullery	Labone	Moore	Bell	Peters	R Charlton*	Hunt	Hunter	G Hurst*

192.	West Germany	A	L 0-1							
G Banks	K Newton	C Knowles	Hunter	Labone	Moore	Ball	Bell	Summerbee	G Hurst	P Thompson

193.	Yugoslavia	N	L 0-1							
G Banks	K Newton	Wilson	Mullery	Labone	Moore	Ball	Peters	R Charlton	Hunt	Hunter

194.	USSR	N	W 2-0	Goalscorers: R Charlton, G Hurst						
G Banks	T wright	Wilson	Stiles	Labone	Moore	Hunter	Hunt	R Charlton	G Hurst	Peters

1968-69

195.	Romania	A	D 0-0							
G Banks	T Wright*	K Newton	Mullery	Labone	Moore	Ball	Hunt	R Charlton	G Hurst	Peters	McNab*

196.	Bulgaria	H	D 1-1	Goalscorer: G Hurst						
West	K Newton*	McNab	Mullery	Labone	Moore	F Lee	Bell	R Charlton	G Hurst	Peters	Reaney

197.	Romania	H	D 1-1	Goalscorer: J Charlton						
G Banks	T Wright	McNab	Sties	J Charlton	Hunter	Radford	Hunt	R Charlton	G Hurst	Ball

198.	France	H	W 5-0	Goalscorers: O'Grady, G Hurst (3), F Lee						
G Banks	K Newton	Cooper	Mullery	J Charlton	Moore	F Lee	Bell	G Hurst	Peters	O'Grady

199.	Northern Ireland	A	W 3-1	Goalscorers: G Hurst, F Lee, Peters						
G Banks	K Newton	McNab	Mullery	Labone	Moore	Ball	F Lee	R Charlton	G Hurst	Peters

200.	Wales	H	W 2-1	Goalscorers: R Charlton, F Lee						
West	K Newton	Cooper	Moore	J Charlton	Hunter	F Lee	Bell	Astle	R Charlton	Ball

201.	Scotland	H	W 4-1	Goalscorers: G Hurst (2), Peters (2)						
G Banks	K Newton	Cooper	Mullery	Labone	Moore	F Lee	Ball	R Charlton	G Hurst	Peters

202.	Mexico	A	D 0-0							
West	K Newton*	Cooper	Mullery	Labone	Moore	Ball	Ball	R Charlton	G Hurst	Peters	T Wright*

203.	Uruguay	A	W 2-1	Goalscorers: G Hurst, F Lee						
G Banks	T Wright	K Newton	Mullery	Labone	Moore	F Lee	Bell	G Hurst	Ball	Peters

204.	Brazil	A	L 1-2	Goalscorer: Bell						
G Banks	T Wright	K Newton	Mullery	Labone	Moore	Ball	Bell	R Charlton	G Hurst	Peters

1969-70

205.	Holland	A	W 1-0	Goalscorer: Bell						
Bonetti	T Wright	E Hughes	Mullery	J Charlton	Moore	F Lee*	Bell	R Charlton	G Hurst	Peters	P Thompson*

206.	Portugal	H	W 1-0	Goalscorer: J Charlton						
Bonetti	Reaney	E Hughes	Mullery	J Charlton	Moore	F Lee	Bell*	Astle	R Charlton	Ball	Peters*

207.	Holland	H	D 0-0							
G Banks	K Newton	Cooper	Peters	J Charlton	Hunter	F Lee*	Bell	M Jones'	R Charlton	Storey-Moore	Mullery*,G Hurst'

208.	Belgium	A	W 3-1	Goalscorers: Ball (2), G Hurst						
G Banks	T Wright	Cooper	Moore	Labone	E Hughes	F Lee	Ball	Osgood	G Hurst	Peters

209.	Wales	A	D 1-1	Goalscorer: F Lee						
G Banks	T Wright	E Hughes	Mullery	Labone	Moore	F Lee	Ball	R Charlton	G Hurst	Peters

210. Northern Ireland   H   W   3-1   Goalscorers: R Charlton, G Hurst, Peters

G Banks | K Newton* | E Hughes | Mullery | Moore | Stiles | Coates | Kidd | R Charlton | G Hurst | Peters | Bell*

211. Scotland   A   D   0-0

G Banks | K Newton | E Hughes | Stiles | Labone | Moore | P Thompson* | Ball | Astle | G Hurst | Peters | Mullery*

212. Colombia   A   W   4-0   Goalscorers: Ball, R Charlton, Peters (2)

G Banks | K Newton | Cooper | Mullery | Labone | Moore | F Lee | Ball | R Charlton | G Hurst | Peters

213. Ecuador   A   W   2-0   Goalscorers: Kidd, F Lee

G Banks | K Newton | Cooper | Mullery | Labone | Moore | F Lee* | Ball | R Charlton' | G Hurst | Peters | Kidd*, Sadler'

214. Romania   N   W   1-0   Goalscorer: G Hurst

G Banks | K Newton* | Cooper | Mullery | Labone | Moore | F Lee* | Ball | R Charlton | G Hurst | Peters | T Wright*, Osgood'

215. Brazil   N   L   0-1

G Banks | T Wright | Cooper | Mullery | Labone | Moore | F Lee* | Ball | R Charlton' | G Hurst | Peters | Astle*, Bell'

216. Czechoslovakia   N   W   1-0   Goalscorer: A Clarke

G Banks | K Newton | Cooper | Mullery | J Charlton | Moore | Bell | R Charlton* | Astle | A Clarke' | Peters | Ball*, Osgood'

217. West Germany   N   L   2-3   Goalscorers: Mullery, Peters

Bonetti | K Newton | Cooper | Mullery | Labone | Moore | F Lee | Ball | R Charlton' | G Hurst | Peters' | Bell*, Hunter'

1970-71

218. East Germany   H   W   3-1   Goalscorers: A Clarke, F Lee, Peters

Shilton | E Hughes | Cooper | Mullery | Sadler | Moore | F Lee | Ball | G Hurst | A Clarke | Peters

219. Malta   A   W   1-0   Goalscorer: Peters

G Banks | Reaney | E Hughes | Mullery | McFarland | Hunter | Ball | Chivers | Royle | Harvey | Peters

220. Greece   H   W   3-0   Goalscorers: Chivers, G Hurst, F Lee

G Banks | Storey | E Hughes | Mullery | McFarland | Moore | F Lee | Ball* | Chivers | G Hurst | Peters | Coates*

221. Malta   H   W   5-0   Goalscorers: Chivers (2), A Clarke, F Lee, Lawler

G Banks | Lawler | Cooper | Moore | McFarland | E Hughes | F Lee | Coates | Chivers | A Clarke | Peters* | Ball*

222. Northern Ireland   A   W   1-0   Goalscorer: A Clarke

G Banks | Madeley | Cooper | Storey | McFarland | Moore | F Lee | Ball | Chivers | A Clarke | Peters

223. Wales   H   D   0-0

Shilton | Lawler | Cooper | T Smith | Lloyd | E Hughes | F Lee | Coates* | G Hurst | Coaters | Peters | A Clarke*

224. Scotland   H   W   3-1   Goalscorers: Chivers (2), Peters

G Banks | Lawler | Cooper | Storey | McFarland | Moore | F Lee* | Ball | Chivers | G Hurst | Peters | A Clarke*

1971-72

225. Switzerland   A   W   3-2   Goalscorers: Chivers, G Hurst, Opponents

G Banks | Lawler | Cooper | Mullery | McFarland | Moore | F Lee | Madeley | Chivers | G Hurst* | Peters | Radford*

226. Switzerland   H   D   1-1   Goalscorer: Summerbee

Shilton | Madeley | Cooper | Storey | Lloyd | Moore | Summerbee* | Ball | G Hurst | F Lee' | E Hughes | Chivers*, Marsh'

227. Greece   A   W   2-0   Goalscorers: Chivers, G Hurst

G Banks | Madeley | E Hughes | Bell | McFarland | Moore | F Lee | Ball | Chivers | G Hurst | Peters

228. West Germany   H   L   1-3   Goalscorer: F Lee

G Banks | Madeley | E Hughes | Bell | Moore | Hunter | F Lee | Ball | Chivers | G Hurst* | Peters | Marsh*

229. West Germany   A   D   0-0

G Banks | Madeley | E Hughes | Storey | McFarland | Moore | Ball | Bell | Chivers | Marsh* | Hunter' | Summerbee*, Peters'

230. Wales   A   W   3-0   Goalscorers: Bell, E Hughes, Marsh

G Banks | Madeley | E Hughes | Storey | McFarland | Moore | Summerbee | Bell | MacDonald | Marsh | Hunter

231. Northern Ireland   H   L   0-1

Shilton | Todd | E Hughes | Storey | Lloyd | Hunter | Summerbee | Bell | MacDonald* | Marsh | Currie' | Chivers*, Peters'

232. Scotland   A   W   1-0   Goalscorer: Ball

G Banks | Madeley | E Hughes | Storey | McFarland | Moore | Ball | Bell | Chivers | Marsh* | Hunter | MacDonald*

1972-73

233. Yugoslavia   H   D   1-1   Goalscorer: Royle

Shilton | M Mills | Lampard | Storey | Blockley | Moore | Ball | Channon | Royle | Bell | Marsh

234. Wales   A   W   1-0   Goalscorer: Bell

Clemence | Storey | E Hughes | Hunter | McFarland | Moore | Keegan | Chivers | Marsh | Bell | Ball

235. Wales   H   D   1-1   Goalscorer: Hunter

Clemence | Storey | E Hughes | Hunter | McFarland | Moore | Keegan | Bell | Chivers | Marsh | Ball

236. Scotland   A   W   5-0   Goalscorers: Chivers1, A Clarke (2), Shannon, Opponents
Shilton   Storey   E Hughes   Bell   Madeley   Moore   Ball   Channon   Chivers   A Clarke   Peters

237. Northern Ireland   A   W   2-1   Goalscorers: Chivers(2)
Shilton   Storey   Nish   Bell   McFarland   Moore   Ball   Channon   Chivers   Richards   Peters

238. Wales   H   W   3-0   Goalscorers: Channon, Chivers, Peters
Shilton   Storey   E Hughes   Bell   McFarland   Moore   Ball   Channon   Chivers   A Clarke   Peters

239. Scotland   H   W   1-0   Goalscorer: Peters
Shilton   Storey   E Hughes   Bell   McFarland   Moore   Ball   Channon   Chivers   A Clarke   Peters

240. Czechoslovakia   A   D   1-1   Goalscorer: A Clarke
Shilton   Madeley   Storey   Bell   McFarland   Moore   Ball   Channon   Chivers   A Clarke   Peters

241. Poland   A   L   0-2
Shilton   Madeley   E Hughes   Storey   McFarland   Moore   Ball   Bell   Chivers   A Clarke   Peters

242. USSR   A   W   2-1   Goalscorers: Chivers, Opponents
Shilton   Madeley   E Hughes   Storey   McFarland   Moore   Currie   Channon^   Chivers   A Clarke*   Peters'   M'cDonald*,Hunter', Sumerbe^

243. Italy   A   L   0-2
Shilton   Madeley   E Hughes   Storey   McFarland   Moore   Currie   Channon   Chivers   A Clarke   Peters

---

1973-74

243. Austria   H   W   7-0   Goalscorers: Bell, Channon (2), Chivers, A Clarke (2), Currie
Shilton   Madeley   E Hughes   Bell   McFarland   Hunter   Currie   Channon   Chivers   A Clarke   Peters

244. Poland   H   D   1-1   Goalscorer: A Clarke
Shilton   Madeley   E Hughes   Bell   McFarland   Hunter   Currie   Channon   Chivers*   A Clarke   Peters   Hector*

245. Italy   H   L   0-1
Shilton   Madeley   E Hughes   Bell   McFarland   Moore   Currie   Channon   Osgood   A Clarke*   Peters   Hector*

246. Portugal   A   D   0-0
Parkes   Nish   Pejic   Dobson   Watson   Todd   Bowles   Channon   MacDonald*   Brooking   Peters   Ball*

247. Wales   A   W   2-0   Goalscorers: Bowles, Keegan
Shilton   Nish   Pejic   E Hughes   McFarland   Todd   Keegan   Bell   Channon   Weller   Bowles

248. Northern Ireland   H   W   1-0   Goalscorer: Weller
Shilton   Nish   Pejic   E Hughes   McFarland*   Todd   Keegan   Weller   Channon   Bell   Bowles'   Hunter*, Worthington'

249. Scotland   A   0-2
Shilton   Nish   Pejic   E Hughes   Hunter*   Todd   Channon   Bell   Worthington'   Weller   Peters   Watson*, MacDonald'

250. Argentina   H   D   2-2   Goalscorers: Channon, Worthington
Shilton   E Hughes   Lindsay   Todd   Watson   Bell   Keegan   Channon   Worthington   Weller   Brooking

251. East Germany   A   D   1-1   Goalscorer: Channon
Clemence   E Hughes   Lindsay   Todd   Watson   Dobson   Keegan   Channon   Worthington   Bell   Brooking

252. Bulgaria   A   W   1-0   Goalscorer: Worthington
Clemence   E Hughes   Todd   Watson   Lindsay   Dobson   Brooking   Bell   Keegan   Channon   Worthington

253. Yugoslavia   A   D   2-2   Goalscorers: Channon, Keegan
Clemence   E Hughes   Lindsay   Todd   Watson   Dobson   Keegan   Channon   Worthington*   Bell   Brooking   MacDonald*

1974-75

254. Czechoslovakia   H   W   3-0   Goalscorers: Bell (2), Channon
Clemence   Madeley   E Hughes   Dobson*   Watson   Hunter   Bell   G Francis   Worthington'   Channon   Keegan   Brooking*, Thomas'

255. Portugal   H   D   0-0
Clemence   Madeley   Watson   E Hughes   Cooper*   Brooking   G Francis   Bell   Thomas   Channon   A Clarke'   Todd*, Worthington'

256. West Germany   H   W   2-0   Goalscorers: Bell, MacDonald
Clemence   Whitworth   Gillard   Bell   Watson   Todd   Ball   MacDonald   Channon   Hudson   Keegan

257. Cyprus   H   W   5-0   Goalscorers: MacDonald (5)
Shilton   Madeley   Watson   Todd   Beattie   Bell   Ball   Hudson   Channon*   MacDonald   Keegan   Thomas*

258. Cyprus   A   W   1-0   Goalscorer: Keegan
Clemence   Whitworth   Beattie*   Watson   Todd   Bell   Thomas   Ball   Channon   MacDonald   Keegan'   E Hughes*, Tueart'

259. Northern Ireland   A   D   0-0
Clemence   Whitworth   E Hughes   Bell   Watson   Todd   Ball   Viljoen   MacDonald*   Keegan   Tueart   Channon*

260. Wales   H   D   2-2   Goalscorers: Johnson (2)
Clemence   Whitworth   Gillard   G Francis   Watson   Todd   Ball   Channon*   Johnson   Viljoen   Thomas   Little*

261. Scotland   H   W   5-1   Goalscorers: Beattie, Bell, G Francis (2), Johnson
Clemence   Whitworth   Beattie   Bell   Watson   Todd   Ball   Channon   Johnson   G Francis   Keegan*   Thomas*

262. Switzerland A W 2-1 Goalscorers: Channon, Keegan
Clemence Whitworth Todd Watson Beattie Bell Currie G francis Channon Johnson* Keegan MacDonald*

263. Czechoslovakia A L 1-2 Goalscorer: Channon
Clemence Madeley Gillard G Francis McFarland* Todd Keegan Channon' MacDonald A Clarke Bell Watson*, Thomas'

264. Portugal A D 1-1 Goalscorer: Channon
Clemence Whitworth Beattie G Francis Watson Todd Keegan Channon MacDonald' Brooking Madeley* A Clarke*, Thomas'

265. Wales A W 2-1 Goalscorers: Kennedy, P Taylor
Clemence Cherry* M Mills Neal P Thompson Doyle Keegan Channon' Boyer Brooking Kennedy Clement*, P Taylor'

266. Wales A W 1-0 Goalscorers: P Taylor
Clemence Clement M Mills Towers B Greenoff P Thompson, Keegan G francis Pearson Kennedy P Taylor

267. Northern Ireland H W 4-0 Goalscorers: Channon (2), G Francis, Pearson
Clemence Todd M Mills P Thompson B Greenoff R Kennedy Keegan' G Francis Pearson Channon P Taylor* Towers*, Royle'

268. Scotland A L 1-2 Goalscorer: Channon
Clemence Todd M Mills P Thompson McFarland' R Kennedy Keegan G Francis Pearson* Channon P Taylor Cherry*, Doylet'

269. Brazil N L 0-1
Clemence Todd Doyle P Thompson Doyle G Francis Cherry Brooking Keegan Pearson Channon

270. Italy N W 3-2 Goalscorers: Channon (2), P Thompson
Rimmer* Clement Neal' P Thompson Doyle Towers Wilkins Brooking Royle Channon Hill Corrigant*, M Mills'

271. Finland A W 4-1 Goalscorers: Channon, Keegan (2), S Pearson
Clemence Todd M Mills P Thompson Madeley Cherry Keegan Channon S Pearson Brooking G Francis

1976-77

272. Eire H D 1-1 Goalscorer: Pearson
Clemence Todd Madeley Cherry McFarland Greenhoff Keegan Wilkins Pearson Brooking George* Hill*

272. Finland H W 2-1 Goalscorers: Royle, Tueart
Clemence Todd Beattie P Thompson Greenoff Wilkins Keegan Channon Royle Brooking* Tueart' M Mills*, Hill'

273. Italy A L 0-2
Clemence Clement* M Mills B Greenoff McFarland E hughes Keegan Channon Bowles Cherry Brooking Beattie*

274. Holland H L 0-2
Clemence Clement Beattie Doyle Watson Madeley' Keegan Greenoff* T francis Bowles Brooking Todd*, S Pearson'

275. Luxembourg H W 5-0 Goalscorers: Channon (2), T Francis, Keegan, Kennedy
Clemence Gidman Cherry Kennedy Watson E Hughes Keegan Channon Royle* T francis Hill Mariner*

276. Northern Ireland A W 2-1 Goalscorer: Channon
Shilton Cherry M Mills Greenhoff Watson Todd Wilkins* Channon Mariner Brooking Tueart Talbot*

277. Wales H L 0-1
Shilton Neal M Mills Greenhoff Watson E Hughes Keegan Channon Pearson Brooking* R Kennedy Tueart*

278. Scotland H L 1-2 Goalscorer: Channon
Clemence Neal M Mills Greenhoff* Watson E Hughes T Francis Channon Pearson Talbot R Kennedy' Cherry*, Tueart'

279. Brazil A D 0-0
Clemence Neal Cherry B Greenhoff Watson E Hughes Keegan T Francis Pearson* Wilkins' Talbot Channon*, R Kennedy'

280. Argentina A D 1-1 Goalscorer: Pearson
Clemence Neal Cherry B Greenhoff* Watson E Hughes Keegan Channon Pearson Wilkins Talbot R Kennedy*

281. Uruguay A D 0-0
Clemence Neal Cherry B Greenhoff Watson E Hughes Keegan Channon Pearson Wilkins Talbot

1977-78

282. Switzerland H D 0-0
Clemence Neal Cherry McDermott Watson E Hughes Keegan Channon* T Francis R Kennedy Callaghan' Hill*, Wilkins'

283. Luxembourg A W 2-0 Goalscorers: R Kennedy, Mariner
Clemence Cherry Watson' E Hughes R Kennedy Callaghan McDermott* Wilkins T Francis Mariner G Hill Whymark*, Beattie'

284. Italy H W 2-0 Goalscorers: Brooking, Keegan
Clemence Neal Cherry Wilkins Watson E Hughes Keegan' Coppell R Latchford* Brooking P Barnes Pearson*, T Francis'

285. West Germany A L 1-2 Goalscorer: S Pearson
Clemence Neal M Mills Wilkins Watson E Hughes Keegan* Coppell S Pearson Brooking P Barnes T Francis*

286. Brazil H D 1-1 Goalscorer: Keegan
Corrigan M Mills Cherry B Greenhoff Watson Currie Keegan Coppell R Latchford T Francis P Barnes

287. Wales A W 3-1 Goalscorers: P Barnes, Currie, R Latchford
Shilton M Mills Cherry* B Greenhoff Watson Wilkins Coppell T Francis R Latchford' Brooking P Barnes Currie*, Mariner'

288. Northern Ireland	H	W 1-0	Goalscorer: Neal

Clemence Neal M Mills Wilkins Watson E Hughes Currie Coppell Pearson Woodcock B Greenhoff

289. Scotland	A	W 1-0	Goalscorer: Coppell

Clemence Neal M Mills Currie Watson E Hughes* Wilkins Coppell Mariner' T Francis P Barnes B Greenhoff*, Brooking

290. Hungary	H	W 4-1	Goalscorers: P Barnes, Currie, T Francis, Neal

Shilton Neal M Mills Wilkins Watson* E Hughes Keegan Coppell T Francis Brooking P Barnes B Greenhoff*, Currie'

1978-79

291. Denmark	A	W 4-3	Goalscorers: Keegan (2), Latchford, Neal

Clemence Neal M Mills Wilkins Watson E Hughes Keegan Coppell Latchford Brooking P Barnes

292. Eire	A	D 1-1	Goalscorer: Latchford

Clemence Neal M Mills Wilkins Watson* E Hughes Keegan Coppell Latchford Brooking P Barnes' P Thompson*, Woodcock

293. Czechoslovakia	H	W 1-0	Goalscorer: Coppell

Shilton Anderson Cherry P Thompson Watson Wilkins Keegan Coppell Woodcock* Currie P Barnes Latchford*

294. Northern Ireland	H	W 4-0	Goalscorers: Keegan, Latchford (2), Watson

Clemence Neal M Mills Currie Watson E Hughes Keegan Coppell Latchford Brooking P Barnes

295. Northern Ireland	A	W 2-0	Goalscorers: Coppell, Watson

Clemence Neal M Mills P Thompson Watson Wilkins Coppell Wilkins Latchford Currie P Barnes

296. Wales	H	D 0-0	

Corrigan Cherry Sansom ' Watson E Hughes Keegan* Wilkins Latchford McDermott Cunningham Coppell*, Brooking'

297. Scotland	H	W 3-1	Goalscorers: P Barnes, Coppell, Keegan

Clemence Neal M Mills P Thompson Watson Wilkins Keegan Coppell Latchford Brooking P Barnes

298. Bulgaria	A	W 3-0	Goalscorers: P Barnes, Keegan, Watson

Clemence Neal M Mills P Thompson Watson Wilkins Keegan Coppell Latchford* Brooking P Barnes' T Francis*, Woodcock'

299. Sweden	A	D 0-0	

Shilton Anderson Cherry McDermott* Watson E Hughes Keegan T Francis' Latchford Woodcock Cunningham Wilkins*, Brooking'

300. Austria	A	L 3-4	Goalscorers: Coppell, Keegan, Wilkins

Shilton' Neal M Mills P Thompson Watson Wilkins Keegan Coppell Latchford' Brooking P Barnes Clemence*, T Francis', Cunningham^

1979-80

301. Denmark	H	W 1-0	Goalscorer: Keegan

Clemence Neal M Mills P Thompson Watson Wilkins Coppell McDermott Keegan Brooking P Barnes

302. Northern Ireland	A	W 5-1	Goalscorers: T Francis (2), Woodcock (2), Opponents

Shilton Neal M Mills P Thompson Watson Wilkins Keegan Coppell T Francis Brooking* Woodcock McDermott*

303. Bulgaria	H	W 2-0	Goalscorers: Hoddle Watson

Clemence Anderson Sansom P Thompson Watson Wilkins Reeves Hoddle T Francis Kennedy Woodcock

304. Eire	H	W 2-0	Goalscorer: Keegan (2)

Clemence Cherry Sansom P Thompson Watson Robson Keegan McDermott Johnson Woodcock* Cunningham Coppell*

305. Spain	A	W 2-0	Goalscorers: T Francis, Woodcock

Shilton Neal* M Mills P Thompson Watson Wilkins Keegan Coppell T Francis' R Kennedy Woodcock E Hughes*, Cunningham'

306. Argentina	H	W 3-1	Goalscorers: Johnson (2), Keegan

Clemence Neal* Sansom P Thompson Watson Wilkins Keegan Coppell Johnson' Woodcock R Kennedy^ Cherry*, Birtles', Brooking^

307. Wales	A	L 1-4	Goalscorer: Mariner

Clemence Neal* Cherry P Thompson Lloyd' R Kennedy Coppell Hoddle Mariner Brooking Barnes Sansom*, Wilkins'

308. Northern Ireland	H	D 1-1	Goalscorer: Johnson

Corrigan Cherry Sansom E Hughes Watson Wilkins Reeves* Wilkins Johnson Brooking Devonshire Mariner*

309. Scotland	A	W 2-0	Goalscorers: Brooking, Coppell

Clemence Cherry Sansom P Thompson Watson Coppell McDermott Johnson Mariner* Brooking E Hughes*

310. Australia	A	W 2-1	Goalscorers: Hoddle, Mariner

Corrigan Cherry Lampard Talbot Osman Butcher Robson* Hoddle Mariner Armstrong^ B Greenhoff*, Ward' Devonshire^

311. Belgium	N	D 1-1	Goalscorers: Wilkins

Clemence Neal Sansom P Thompson Watson Wilkins Keegan Coppell* Johnson' Woodcock Brooking McDermott*, R Kennedy'

312. Italy	A	L 0-1	

Shilton Neal Sansom P Thompson Watson Wilkins Keegan Coppell Birtles* R Kennedy Woodcock Mariner*

313. Spain	N	W 2-1	Goalscorers: Brooking, Woodcock

Clemence Anderson M Mills* P Thompson Watson Wilkins McDermott Hoddle' Keegan Woodcock Brooking Cherry*, Mariners'

1980-81

314. Norway H W 4-0 **Goalscorers: Mariner, McDermott (2), Woodcock**
Shilton Anderson Sansom P Thompson Watson Robson Gates McDermott Mariner Woodcock Rix

315. Romania A L 1-2 **Goalscorer: Woodcock**
Clemence Neal Sansom P Thompson Watson Robson Rix McDermott Birtles' Woodcock Gates* Cunningham*, Coppell'

316. Switzerland H W 2-1 **Goalscorers: Mariner, Opponents**
Shilton Neal Sansom Robson Watson M Mills Coppell McDermott Mariner Brooking* Woodcock Rix*

317. Spain H L 1-2 **Goalscorer: Hoddle**
Clemence Neal Sansom Robson Butcher Osman Keegan T Francis* Mariner Brooking' Hoddle P Barnes*, Wilkins'

318. Romania H D 0-0
Shilton Anderson Sansom Robson Watson Osman Wilkins Brooking Coppell T Francis Woodcock* McDermott*

319. Brazil H L 0-1
Clemence Neal Sansom Robson Martin Wilkins Coppell McDermott Withe Rix P Barnes

320. Wales H D 0-0
Corrigan Anderson Sansom Robson Watson Wilkins Coppell Hoddle Withe* Rix P Barnes Woodcock*

321. Scotland H L 0-1
Corrigan Anderson Sansom Wilkins Watson* Robson Coppell Hoddle Withe Rix Woodcock* Martin*, T Francis'

322. Switzerland A L 1-2 **Goalscorer: McDermott**
Clemence M Mills Sansom Wilkins Watson' Osman Robson Keegan Mariner T Francis* McDermott*, P Barnes'

323. Hungary A W 3-1 **Goalscorers: Brooking (2), Keegan**
Clemence Neal M Mills P Thompson Watson Robson Keegan McDermott Mariner Brooking* T Francis Wilkins*

1981-82

324. Norway A L 1-2 **Goalscorer: Robson**
Clemence Neal M Mills P Thompson Osman Robson Keegan T Francis Mariner* Hoddle' McDermott Withe*, P Barnet'

325. Hungary H W 1-0 **Goalscorer: Mariner**
Shilton Neal M Mills P Thompson Martin Robson Keegan Coppell* Mariner Brooking McDermott Morley*

326. Northern Ireland H W 4-0 **Goalscorers: Hoddle, Keegan, Robson, Wilkins**
Clemence Anderson Sansom Wilkins Watson Foster Keegan Robson T Francis* Hoddle Morley' Regis*, Woodcock'

327. Wales A W 1-0 **Goalscorer: T Francis**
Corrigan Neal Sansom P Thompson Butcher Robson Wilkins T Francis* Withe Hoddle' Morley McDermott*, Regis'

328. Holland H W 2-0 **Goalscorers: Mariner, Woodcock**
Shilton Neal Sansom P Thompson Foster Robson Wilkins Devonshire* Mariner' McDermott Woodcock Rix*, Barnes'

329. Scotland A W 1-0 **Goalscorer: Mariner**
Shilton M Mills Sansom P Thompson Butcher Robson Keegan* Coppell Mariner' Brooking Wilkins McDermott*, T Francis'

340. Iceland A D 1-1 **Goalscorer: Goddard**
Corrigan Anderson Neal Watson Osman McDermott Hoddle Devonshire* Withe Regis' Morley Perryman*, Goddard'

341. Finland A W 4-1 **Goalscorers: Mariner (2), Robson (2)**
Clemence M Mills Sansom P Thompson Martin Robson* Keegan Coppell' Mariner Brooking^ Wilkins Rix*, T Francis', Woodcock^

342. France N W 3-1 **Goalscorers: Mariner, Robson (2)**
Shilton M Mills Sansom* P Thompson Butcher Robson Coppell T Francis Mariner Rix Wilkins Neal*

343. Czechoslovakia N W 2-0 **Goalscorer: T Francis, Opponents**
Shilton M Mills Sansom P Thompson Butcher Robson* Coppell T Francis Mariner Rix Wilkins Hoddle*

344. Kuwait N W 1-0 **Goalscorer: T Francis**
Shilton Neal M Mills P Thompson Foster Hoddle Coppell T Francis Mariner Rix Wilkins

345. West Germany N D 0-0
Shilton M Mills Sansom P Thompson Butcher Robson Coppell T Francis* Mariner Rix Wilkins Woodcock*

346. Spain A D 0-0
Shilton M Mills Sansom P Thompson Butcher Robson Rix* T Francis Mariner Woodcock' Wilkins Brooking*, Keegan'

1982-83

347. Denmark A D 2-2 **Goalscorers: T Francis (2)**
Shilton Neal Sansom Wilkins Osman Butcher Morley* Robson Mariner T Francis Rix Hill*

348. West Germany H L 1-2 **Goalscorer: Woodcock**
Shilton Mabbutt Sansom P Thompson Butcher Wilkins R Hill Regis Mariner* Armstrong' Devonshire^ Woodcock*, Blissett', Rix^

349. Greece A W 3-0 **Goalscorers: S Lee, Woodcock (2)**
Shilton Neal Sansom P Thompson Martin Robson S Lee Mabbutt Mariner Woodcock Morley

350. Luxembourg	H	W 9-0	**Goalscorers: Blissett (3), Chamberlain, Coppell, Hoddle, Neal, Woodcock, Opponents**

| Clemence | Neal | Sansom | Robson | Martin | Butcher | Coppell* | S Lee | Woodcock | Blissett | Mabbutt' | Chamberlain*, Hoddle' |

351. Wales — H — W 2-1 — **Goalscorers: Butcher, Neal**

Shilton | Neal | Statham | S Lee | Martin | Butcher | Mabbutt | Blissett | Mariner | Cowans | Devonshire

352. Greece — H — D 0-0

Shilton | Neal | Sansom | S Lee | Martin | Butcher | Coppell | Mabbutt | T Francis | Woodcock* | Devonshire' | Blissett*, Rix'

353. Hungary — H — W 2-0 — **Goalscorers: T Francis, Withe**

Shilton | Neal | Sansom | S Lee | Martin | Butcher | Mabbutt | T Francis | Withe | Blissett | Cowans

354. Northern Ireland — A — D 0-0

Shilton | Neal | Sansom | Hoddle | Roberts | Butcher | Mabbutt | T Francis | Withe | Blissett* | Cowans | J Barnes*

355. Scotland — H — W 2-0 — **Goalscorers: Cowans, Robson**

Shilton | Neal | Sansom | S Lee | Roberts | Butcher | Robson* | T Francis | Withe' | Hoddle | Cowans | Mabbutt*, Blissett'

356. Australia — A — D 0-0

Shilton | Thomas | Statham* | Williams | OSman | Butcher | Barham | Gregory | Blissett' | T Francis | Cowans | J Barnes*, Walsh'

357. Australia — A — W 1-0 — **Goalscorer: Walsh**

Shilton | Neal | Statham* | Barham | Osman | Butcher | Gregory | T Francis | Walsh | Cowans | J Barnes | Williams*

358. Australia — A — D 1-1 — **Goalscorer: T Francis**

Shilton* | Neal' | Pickering | S Lee | Osman | Butcher | Gregory | T Francis | Walsh^ | Cowans | J Barnes | Spink*, Thomas', Blissett^

1983-84

359. Denmark — H — L 0-1

Shilton | Neal | Sansom | S Lee* | Osman | BUtcher | Wilkins | Gregory | Mariner | T Francis | J Barnes' | Blissett*, Chamberlain'

360. Hungary — A — W 3-0 — **Goalscorers: Hoddle, S Lee, Mariner**

Shilton | Gregory | Sansom | S Lee | Martin | Butcher | Robson | Hoddle | Mariner | Blissett* | Mabbutt | Withe*

361. Luxembourg — A — W 4-0 — **Goalscorers: Butcher, Mariner, Robson (2)**

Clemence | Duxbury | Sansom | S Lee | Martin | Butcher | Robson | Hoddle | Mariner | Woodcock* | Williams | J Barnes*

362. France — A — L 0-2

Shilton | Duxbury | Sansom | S Lee* | Roberts | Butcher | Robson | Stein' | Walsh | Hoddle | Williams | J Barnes*, Woodcock'

363. Northern Ireland — H — W 1-0 — **Goalscorer: Woodcock**

Shilton | Anderson | A Kennedy | S Lee | Roberts | Butcher | Robson | Wilkins | Woodcock | T Francis | Rix

364. Wales — A — L 0-1

Shilton | Duxbury | A Kennedy | S Lee | Martin* | Wright | Wilkins | Gregory | Walsh | Woodcock | Armstrong' | Fenwick*, Blissett'

365. Scotland — A — D 1-1 — **Goalscorer: Woodcock**

Shilton | Duxbury | Sansom | Wilkins | Roberts | Fenwick | Chamberlain* | Robson | Woodcock' | Blissett | J Barnes | Hunt*, Lineker'

366. USSR — H — L 0-2

Shilton | Duxbury | Sansom | Wilkins | Roberts | Fenwick | Chamberlain | Robson | T Francis* | Blissett | J Barnes' | Hateley*, Hunt'

367. Brazil — A — W 2-0 — **Goalscorers: J Barnes, Hateley**

Shilton | Duxbury | Sansom | Wilkins | Watson | Fenwick | Robson | Chamberlain | Hateley | Woodcock* | J Barnes | Allen*

368. Uruguay — A — L 0-2

Shilton | Duxbury | Sansom | Wilkins | Watson | Fenwick | Robson | Chamberlain | Hateley | Allen* | J Barnes | Woodcock*

369. Chile — A — D 0-0

Shilton | Duxbury | Sansom | Wilkins | Watson | Fenwick | Robson | Chamberlain* | Hateley | Allen | J Barnes | S Lee*

1984-85

370. East Germany — H — W 1-0 — **Goalscorer: Robson**

Shilton | Duxbury | Sansom | Williams | Wright | Butcher | Robson | Wilkins | Mariner* | Woodcock | J Barnes | Hateley*, T Francis'

371. Finland — H — W 5-0 — **Goalscorers: Hateley (2), Robson, Sansom, Woodcock**

Shilton | Duxbury* | Sansom | Williams | Wright | Butcher | Robson' | Wilkins | Hateley | Woodcock | J Barnes | G Stevens*, Chamberlain'

372. Turkey — A — W 8-0 — **Goalscorers: Anderson, J Barnes (2), Robson (3), Woodcock (2)**

Shilton | Anderson | Sansom | Williams* | Wright | Butcher | Robson | Wilkins | Withe | Woodcock* | J Barnes | G Stevens*, Francis'

373. Northern Ireland — A — W 1-0 — **Goalscorer: Hateley**

Shilton | Anderson | Sansom | Steven | Martin | Butcher | Robson | Wilkins | Hateley | Woodcock* | J Barnes | T Francis*

374. Eire — H — W 2-1 — **Goalscorers: Lineker, Steven**

Bailey | Anderson | Sansom | Steven | Wright | Butcher | Robson | Wilkins | Hateley* | Lineker | Waddle | Hoddle*, Davenport'

375. Romania — A — D 0-0

Shilton | Anderson | Sansom | Steven | Wright | Butcher | Robson | Wilkins | Mariner* | T Francis | J Barnes' | Lineker*, Waddle'

376. Finland — A — D 1-1 — **Goalscorer: Hateley**

Shilton | Anderson | Sansom | Steven* | Fenwick | Butcher | Robson | Wilkins | Hateley | T Francis | J Barnes | Waddle*

377. Scotland A L 0-1

Shilton | Anderson | Sansom | Hoddle* | Fenwick | Butcher | Robson | Wilkins | Hateley | T Francis | J Barnes' | Lineker*, Waddle'

378. Italy N L 1-2 Goalscorer: Hateley

Shilton | Stevens | Sansom | Steven* | Wright | Butcher | Robson | Wilkins | Hateley | T Francis' | Waddle^ | Hoddle*, Lineker', J Barnes^

379. Mexico A L 0-1

Bailey | Anderson | Sansom | Hoddle* | Fenwick | Watson | Robson | Wilkins' | Hateley | T francis | J Barnes' | K Dixon*, Reid' Waddle^

380. West Germany N W 3-0 Goalscorers: K Dixon (2), Robson

Shilton | Stevens | Sansom | Hoddle | Wright | Butcher | Reid | Robson* | K Dixon | Lineker' | Waddle | Bracewell*, J Barnes'

381. USA A W 5-0 Goalscorers: K Dixon (2), Lineker (2), Steven

Woods | Anderson | Sansom* | Hoddle' | Fenwick | Butcher | Robson^ | Bracewell | K Dixon | Lineker | Waddle" | Watson*, Steven', Reid^

J Barnes"

1985-86

382. Romania H D 1-1 Goalscorer: Hoddle

Shilton | Stevens | Sansom | Reid | Wright | Fenwick | Robson | Hoddle | Hateley | Lineker* | Waddle' | Woodcock*, J Barnes'

383. Turkey H W 5-0 Goalscorers: Lineker (3), Robson, Waddle

Shilton | Stevens | Sansom | Hoddle | Wright | Fenwick | Robson* | Wilkins | Hateley' | Lineker | Waddle | Steven*, Woodcock'

384. Northern Ireland H D 0-0

Shilton | GStevens | Sansom | Hoddle | Wright | Fenwick | Bracewell | Wilkins | K Dixon | Lineker | Waddle

385. Egypt A W 4-0 Goalscorers: Cowans, Steven, Wallace, Opponents

Shilton | Stevens | Sansom | Cowans | Wright | Fenwick | Steven | Wilkins | Hateley | Lineker | Wallace

386. Israel A W 2-1 Goalscorer: Robson (2)

Shilton* | Stevens | Sansom | Hoddle | Martin | Butcher | Robson | Wilkins | Dixon' | Beardsley^ | Waddle | Woods*, Woodcock', J Barnes^

387. USSR A W 1-0 Goalscorer: Waddle

Shilton | Anderson | Sansom | Hoddle | Wright | Butcher | Cowans* | Wilkins | Beardsley | Lineker | Waddle' | Hodge*, Steven'

388. Scotland H W 2-1 Goalscorers: Butcher, Hoddle

Shilton | Stevens | Sansom | Hoddle | Watson | Butcher | Wilkins* | T Francis | Hateley | Hodge' | Waddle | Reid*, G Stevens'

389. Mexico N W 3-0 Goalscorers: Beardsley, Hateley (2)

Shilton | Anderson | Sansom | Hoddle | Fenwick | Butcher | Robson* | Wilkins' | Hateley^ | Beardsley | Waddle" | G Stevens*, Steven'

K Dixon^, J Barnes"

390. Canada A W 1-0 Goalscorer: Hateley

Shilton* | Stevens | Sansom | Hoddle | Martin | Butcher | Hodge | Wilkins' | Hateley | Lineker^ | Waddle" | Woods*, Reid', Beardsley^

J Barnes"

391. Portugal N L 0-1

Shilton | Stevens | Sansom | Hoddle | Fenwick | Butcher | Robson* | Wilkins | Hateley | Lineker | Waddle' | Hodge*, Beardsley'

392. Morocco N D 0-0

Shilton | Stevens | Sansom | Hoddle | Fenwick | Butcher | Robson* | Wilkins | Hateley' | Lineker | Waddle | Hodge*, G Stevens'

393. Poland N W 3-0 Goalscorer: Lineker (3)

Shilton | Stevens | Sansom | Hoddle | Fenwick | Butcher | Hodge | Reid | Beardsley* | Lineker' | Steven | Waddle*, K Dixon'

394. Paraguay N W 3-0 Goalscorers: Beardsley, Lineker (2)

Shilton | Stevens | Sansom | Hoddle | Martin | Butcher | Hodge | Reid* | Beardsley' | Lineker | Steven | G Stevens*, Hateley'

395. Argentina N L 1-2 Goalscorer: Lineker

Shilton | Stevens | Sansom | Hoddle | Fenwick | Butcher | Hodge | Reid* | Beardsley | Lineker | Steven' | Waddle*, J Barnes'

1986-87

396. Sweden A L 0-1

Shilton | Anderson | Sansom | Hoddle | Martin | Butcher | Steven* | Wilkins | K Dixon | Hodge | J Barnes' | Cottee*, Waddle'

397. Northern Ireland H W 3-0 Goalscorers: Lineker (2), Waddle

Shilton | Anderson | Sansom | Hoddle | Watson | Butcher | Robson | Hodge | Beardsley* | Lineker | Waddle | Cottee*

398. Yugoslavia H W 2-0 Goalscorers: Anderson, Mabbutt

Woods | Anderson | Sansom | Hoddle | Wright | Butcher | Mabbutt | Hodge* | Beardsley | Lineker | Waddle' | Wilkins*, Steven'

399. Spain A W 4-2 Goalscorer: Lineker (4)

Shilton* | Anderson | Sansom | Hoddle | Adams | Butcher | Robson | Hodge | Beardsley | Lineker | Waddle | Woods*, Steven'

400. Northern Ireland A W 2-0 Goalscorers: Robson, Waddle

Shilton* | Anderson | Sansom | Mabbutt | Wright | Butcher | Robson | Hodge | Beardsley | Lineker | Waddle | Woods*

401. Turkey A D 0-0

Woods | Anderson | Sansom | Hoddle | Adams | Mabbutt | Robson | Hodge* | Allen' | Lineker | Waddle | J Barnes*, Hateley'

402. Brazil H D 1-1 Goalscorer: Lineker

Shilton | Stevens | Pearce | Reid | Adams | Butcher | Robson | J Barnes | Beardsley | Lineker* | Waddle | Hateley*

403. Scotland — A — D — 0-0

Woods	Stevens	Pearce	Hoddle	Wright	Butcher	Robson	Hodge	Beardsley	Hateley	Waddle

1987-88

404. West Germany — A — L — 1-3 — Goalscorer: Lineker

Shilton	Anderson	Sansom*	Hoddle'	Adams	Mabbutt	Reid	J Barnes	Beardsley	Lineker	Waddle^	Pearce*, Webb', Hateley^

405. Turkey — H — W — 8-0 — Goalscorers: J Barnes (2), Beardsley, Lineker (3), Robson, Webb

Shilton	Stevens	Sansom	Stevens*	Adams	Butcher	Robson	Webb	Beardsley'	Lineker	J Barnes	Hoddle*, Regis'

406. Yugoslavia — A — W — 4-1 — Goalscorers: Adams, J Barnes, Beardsley, Robson

Shilton	Stevens	Sansom	Steven	Adams	Butcher	Robson*	Webb'	Beardsley	Lineker	J Barnes	Reid*, Hoddle'

407. Israel — A — D — 0-0

Woods	Stevens	Pearce	Webb	Watson	Wright*	Allen'	McMahon	Beardsley	J Barnes	Waddle	Fenwick*, Harford'

408. Holland — H — D — 2-2 — Goalscorers: Adams, Lineker

Shilton	Stevens	Sansom	Steven	Adams	Watson*	Robson	Webb'	Beardsley^	Lineker	J Barnes	Wright*, Hoddle' Hateley^

409. Hungary — A — D — 0-0

Woods	Anderson	Pearce*	Steven	Adams	Pallister	Robson	McMahon	Beardsley	Lineker^	Waddle	Stevens', Hateley', Cottee^
											Hoddle"

410. Scotland — H — W — 1-0 — Goalscorer: Beardsley

Shilton	Stevens	Sansom	Webb	Watson	Adams	Robson	Steven*	Beardsley	Lineker	J Barnes	Waddle*

411. Colombia — H — D — 1-1 — Goalscorer: Lineker

Shilton	Anderson	Sansom	McMahon	Wright	Adams	Robson	Waddle*	Beardsley'	Lineker	J Barnes	Hoddle*, Hateley'

412. Switzerland — A — W — 1-0 — Goalscorer: Lineker

Shilton*	Stevens	Sansom	Webb	Wright	Adams'	Robson^	Steven"	Beardsley	Lineker	J Barnes	Woods*, Watson', Reid^,
											Waddle"

413. Eire — N — L — 0-1

Shilton	Stevens	Sansom	Webb*	Wright	Adams	Robson	Waddle	Beardsley'	Lineker	J Barnes	Hoddle*, Hateley'

414. Holland — N — L — 1-3 — Goalscorer: Robson

Shilton	Stevens	Sansom	Hoddle	Wright	Adams	Robson	Steven*	Beardsley'	Lineker	J Barnes	Waddle*, Hateley'

415. USSR — N — L — 1-3 — Goalscorer: Adams

Woods	Stevens	Sansom	Hoddle	Watson	Adams	Robson	Steven	McMahon*	Lineker'	J Barnes	Webb*, Hateley'

1988-89

416. Denmark — H — W — 1-0 — Goalscorer: Webb

Shilton*	Stevens	Pearce	Rocastle	Adams'	Butcher	Robson	Webb	Harford^	Beardsley"	Hodge	Woods*, Walker', Cottee^
											Gascoigne"

417. Sweden — H — D — 0-0

Shilton	Stevens	Pearce	Webb	Adams*	Butcher	Robson	Beardsley	Waddle	Lineker	J Barnes'	Walker*, Cottee'

418. Saudi Arabia — A — D — 1-1 — Goalscorer: Adams

Seaman	Sterland	Pearce	M.Thomas*	Adams	Pallister	Robson	Rocastle	Beardsley'	Lineker	Waddle^	Gascoigne*, A Smith'
											Marwood^

419. Greece — A — W — 2-1 — Goalscorers: J Barnes, Robson

Shilton	Stevens	Pearce	Webb	Walker	Butcher	Robson	Rocastle	A Smith*	Lineker	J Barnes	Beardsley*

420. Albania — A — W — 2-0 — Goalscorers: J Barnes, Robson

Shilton	Stevens	Pearce	Webb	Walker	Butcher	Robson	Rocastle	Waddle*	Lineker	J Barnes	Beardsley*, A Smith'

421. Albania — H — W — 5-0 — Goalscorers: Beardsley (2), Gascoigne, Lineker, Waddle

Shilton	Stevens*	Pearce	Webb	Walker	Butcher	Robson	Rocastle'	Beardsley	Lineker^	Waddle	Parker*, Gascoigne'

422. Chile — H — D — 0-0

Shilton	Parker	Pearce	Webb	Walker	Butcher	Robson	Gascoigne	Clough	Fashanu*	Waddle	Cottee*

423. Scotland — A — W — 2-0 — Goalscorers: Bull, Waddle

Shilton	Stevens	Pearce	Webb	Walker	Butcher	Robson	Steven	Fashanu*	Cottee'	Waddle	Bull*, Gascoigne'

424. Poland — H — W — 3-0 — Goalscorers: J Barnes, Lineker, Webb

Shilton	Stevens	Pearce	Webb	Walker	Butcher	Robson	Waddle*	Beardsley'	Lineker	J Barnes	Rocastle*, A Smith'

425. Denmark — A — D — 1-1 — Goalscorer: Lineker

Shilton*	Parker	Pearce	Webb'	Walker	Butcher	Robson	Rocastle	Beardsley^	Lineker	J Barnes"	Seaman*, McMahon'
											Bull^, Waddle"

1989-90

426. Sweden — A — D — 0-0

Shilton	Stevens	Pearce	Webb*	Walker	Butcher	Beardsley	McMahon	Waddle	Lineker	J Barnes'	Gascoigne*, Rocastle'

427. Poland A — D 0-0
Shilton, Stevens, Pearce, McMahon, Walker, Butcher, Robson, Rocastle, Beardsley, Lineker, Waddle

428. Italy H — D 0-0
Shilton*, Stevens, Pearce', McMahon^, Walker, Butcher, Robson", Waddle, Beardsley", Lineker, J Barnes — Beasant*, Winterburn', Hodge^, Phelan", Platt"

429. Yugoslavia H — W 2-1 — Goalscorer: Robson (2)
Shilton*, Parker, Pearce, Thomas, Walker, Butcher, Robson, Rocastle, Bull, Lineker, Waddle — Beasant*, Dorigo', Platt^, McMahon", Hodge"

430. Brazil H — 1-0 — Goalscorer: Lineker
Shilton*, Stevens, Pearce, McMahon, Walker, Butcher, Platt, Waddle, Beardsley', Lineker, J Barnes — Woods*, Gascoigne'

431. Czechoslovakia H — W 4-2 — Goalscorers: Bull (2), Gascoigne, Pearce
Shilton*, Dixon, Pearce', Steven, Walker^, Butcher, Robson", Gascoigne, Bull, Lineker, Hodge — Seaman*, Dorigo', Wright^, McMahon^

432. Denmark H — W 1-0 — Goalscorer: Lineker
Shilton*, Stevens, Pearce', McMahon^, Walker, Butcher, Hodge, Gascoigne, Waddle", Lineker", J Barnes — Woods*, Dorigo', Platt^, Rocastle", Bull"

433. Uruguay H — L 1-2 — Goalscorer: Lineker
Shilton, Parker, Pearce, Hodge*, Walker, Butcher, Robson, Gascoigne, Waddle, Lineker', J Barnes — Beardsley*, Bull'

434. Tunisia A — D 1-1 — Goalscorer: Bull
Shilton, Stevens, Pearce, Hodge*, Walker, Butcher', Robson, Waddle^, Gascoigne, Lineker", J Barnes — Beardsley*, Wright', Platt^, Bull"

435. Eire N — D 1-1 — Goalscorer: Lineker
Shilton, Stevens, Pearce, Gascoigne, Walker, Butcher, Waddle, Robson, Beardsley, Lineker*, J Barnes' — McMahon*, Bull'

436. Holland N — D 0-0
Shilton, Parker, Pearce, Wright, Walker, Butcher, Robson*, Waddle', Gascoigne, Lineker, J Barnes — Platt*, Bull'

437. Egypt N — W 1-0 — Goalscorer: Wright
Shilton, Parker, Pearce, Gascoigne, Walker, Wright, McMahon, Waddle*, Bull', Lineker, J Barnes — Platt*, Beardsley'

438. Belgium N — W 1-0 — Goalscorer: Platt
Shilton, Parker, Pearce, Wright, Walker, Butcher, McMahon*, Waddle, Gascoigne, Lineker, J Barnes — Platt*, Bull'

439. Cameroon N — W 3-2 — Goalscorers: Lineker (2), Platt
Shilton, Parker, Pearce, Wright, Walker, Butcher*, Platt, Waddle, Gascoigne, Lineker, J Barnes — Steven*, Beardsley'

440. West Germany N — D 1-1 — Goalscorer: Lineker — West Germany won 4-3 on penalties.
Shilton, Parker, Pearce, Wright, Walker, Butcher*, Platt, Waddle, Gascoigne, Lineker, Beardsley — Steven*

441. Italy A — L 1-2 — Goalscorer: Platt
Shilton, Stevens, Dorigo, Parker, Walker, Wright*, Platt, Steven, McMahon', Lineker, Beardsley — Waddle*, Webb'

1990-91

442. Hungary H — W 1-0 — Goalscorer: Lineker
Woods, Dixon, Pearce*, Parker, Walker, Wright, Platt, Gascoigne, Bull', Lineker, J Barnes — Dorigo*, Waddle'

443. Poland H — W 2-0 — Goalscorers: Beardsley, Lineker
Woods, Dixon, Pearce, Parker, Walker, Wright, Platt, Gascoigne, Bull*, Lineker', J Barnes — Beardsley*, Waddle'

444. Eire A — D 1-1 — Goalscorer: Platt
Woods, Dixon, Pearce, Adams, Walker, Wright, Platt, Cowans, Beardsley, Lineker, McMahon

445. Cameroon H — W 2-0 — Goalscorer: Lineker (2)
Seaman, Dixon, Pearce, Steven, Walker, Wright, Robson*, Gascoigne', I Wright, Lineker, J Barnes — Pallister*, Hodge'

446. Eire H — D 1-1 — Goalscorer: Dixon
Seaman, Dixon, Pearce, Adams*, Walker, Wright, Robson, Platt, Beardsley, Lineker', J Barnes — Sharpe*, I Wright'

447. Turkey A — W 1-0 — Goalscorer: Wise
Seaman, Dixon, Pearce, Wise, Walker, Pallister, Platt, G Thomas*, A Smith, Lineker, J Barnes — Hodge*

448. USSR H — W 3-1 — Goalscorers: Platt, A Smith
Woods, Stevens, Dorigo, Wise*, Parker, Wright, Platt, G Thomas, A Smith, I Wright, J Barnes — Batty*, Beardsley'

449. Argentina H — D 2-2 — Goalscorers: Lineker, Platt
Seaman, Dixon, Pearce, Batty, Walker, Wright, Platt, G Thomas, A Smith, Lineker, J Barnes* — Clough*

450. Australia A — W 1-0 — Goalscorer: Opponents
Woods, Parker, Pearce, Batty, Walker, Wright, Platt, G Thomas, Clough, Lineker*, Hirst' — Wise*, Salako'

451. New Zealand A — W 1-0 — Goalscorer: Lineker
Woods, Parker, Pearce, Batty*, Walker, Barrett, Platt, G Thomas, Wise, Lineker, Walters' — Deane*, Salako'

452. New Zealand A — W 2-0 — Goalscorers: Hirst, Pearce
Woods, Charles, Pearce, Wise, Walker, Wright, Platt, G Thomas, Deane*, I Wright, Salako, Hirst

453.	Malaysia	A	W	4-2	Goalscorers: Lineker (4)						
Woods	Charles	Pearce	Batty	Walker	Wright	Platt	GThomas	Clough	Lineker	Salako	

1991-92

454.	Germany	H	L	0-1							
Woods	Dixon	Dorigo	Batty	Pallister	Parker	Platt	Steven*	A Smith	Lineker	Salako'	Stewart*, Merson'
455.	Turkey	H	W	1-0	Goalscorer: A Smith						
Woods	Dixon	Pearce	Batty*	Walker	Mabbutt	Robson	Platt	A Smith	Lineker	Waddle	
456.	Poland	A	D	1-1	Goalscorer: Lineker						
Woods	Dixon	Pearce	Gray*	Walker	Mabbutt	PLatt	G Thomas	Rocastle	Lineker	Sinton'	A Smith*, Daley'
457.	France	H	W	2-0	Goalscorers: Lineker, Shearer						
Woods	R Jones	Pearce	Keown	Walker	Wright	Webb	G Thomas	Clough	Shearer	Hirst*	Lineker*
458.	Czechoslovakia	A	D	2-2	Goalscorers: Keown, Merson						
Seaman	Keown	Pearce	Rocastle*	Walker	Mabbutt'	Platt	Merson	Clough^	Hateley	J Barnes"	Dixon*, Lineker', Stewart^ Dorigo"
459.	CIS	A	D	2-2	Goalscorers: Lineker, Steven						
Woods*	Stevens	Sinton'	Palmer	Walker	Keown	Platt	Steven^	Shearer"	Lineker	Daley	Martyn*, Curle', Stewart^ Clough"
460.	Hungary	A	W	1-0	Goalscorer: Webb						
Martyn*	Stevens	Dorigo	Curle'	Walker	Keown	Webb^	Palmer	Merson"	Lineker"	Daley	Seaman*, Sinton', Batty' A Smith", I Wright"
461.	Brazil	H	D	1-1	Goalscorer: Platt						
Woods	Stevens	Dorigo*	Palmer	Walker	Keown	Daley'	Steven^	Platt	Lineker	Sinton"	Pearce*, Merson', Webb^ Rocastle"
462.	Finland	A	W	2-1	Goalscorer: Platt (2)						
Woods	Stevens*	Pearce	Keown	Walker	Wright	Platt	Steven'	Webb	Lineker	J Barnes^	Palmer*, Daley', Merson^
463.	Denmark	N	D	0-0							
Woods	Curle*	Pearce	Palmer	Walker	Keown	Platt	Steven	A Smith	Lineker	Merson'	Daley*, Webb'
464.	France	N	D	0-0							
Woods	Batty	Pearce	Palmer	Walker	Keown	Platt	Steven	Shearer	Lineker		
465.	Sweden	N	L	1-2	Goalscorer: Platt						
Woods	Batty	Pearce	Keown	Walker	Palmer	Platt	Webb	Sinton*	Lineker	Daley	Merson*, A Smith'

1992-93

466.	Spain	A	L	0-1							
Woods	Dixon	Pearce	Ince	Walker	Wright	White^	Platt	Clough	Shearer	Sinton"	Bardsley*, Palmer', Merson^, Dean"
467.	Norway	H	D	1-1	Goalscorer: Platt						
Woods	Dixon*	Pearce	Batty	Walker	Adams	Platt	Gascoigne	Shearer	I Wright'	Ince	Palmer*, Merson'
468.	Turkey	H	W	4-0	Goalscorers: Gascoigne (2), Pearce, Shearer						
Woods	Dixon	Pearce	Palmer	Walker	Adams	Platt	Gascoigne	Shearer	I Wright	Ince	
469.	San Marino	H	W	6-0	Goalscorers: Ferdinand, Palmer, Platt (4)						
Woods	Dixon	Dorigo	Palmer	Walker	Adams	Platt	Gascoigne	Ferdinand	J Barnes	Batty	
470.	Turkey	A	W	2-0	Goalscorers: Gascoigne, Platt						
Woods	Dixon*	Sinton	Palmer	Walker	Adams	Platt	Gascoigne	J Barnes	I Wright'	Ince	Clough*, Sharpe'
471.	Holland	H	D	2-2	Goalscorers: J Barnes, Platt						
Woods	Dixon	Keown	Palmer	Walker	Adams	Platt	Gascoigne*	Ferdinand	J Barnes	Ince	Merson*
472.	Poland	A	D	1-1	Goalscorer: I Wright						
Woods	Bardsley	Dorigo	Palmer*	Walker	Adams	Platt	Gascoigne'	Sheringham	J Barnes	Ince	I Wright*, Clough'
473.	Norway	A	L	0-2							
Woods	Dixon	Pallister	Palmer	Walker*	Adams	Platt	Gascoigne	Ferdinand	Sheringham'	Sharpe	Clough*, I Wright'
474.	United States	A	L	0-2							
Woods	Dixon	Dorigo	Palmer*	Pallister	Ince	Clough	Sharpe	Ferdinand'	J Barnes	Walker*, I Wright'	
475.	Brazil	D	1-1	Goalscorer: Platt							
Flowers	Barrett	Dorigo	Walker	Pallister	Batty*	Ince'	Clough^	I Wright	Sinton	Sharpe	Platt*, Palmer', Merson^
476.	Germany	N	L	1-2	Goalscorer: Platt						
Martyn	Barrett	Sinton	Walker	Pallister*	Ince	Platt	Clough'	Sharpe^	J Barnes	Merson	Keown*, I Wright', Winterburn^

1993-94

477.	Poland	H	W	3-0	Goalscorers: Ferdinand, Gascoigne, Pearce					
Seaman	Jones	Pearce	Ince	Pallister	Adams	Platt	Gascoigne	Ferdinand	Wright	Sharpe

478.	Holland	A	L	0-2						
Seaman	Parker	Dorigo	INce	Pallister	Adams	Platt	Palmer*	Shearer	Merson'	Sharpe	Sinton*, I Wright'

479.	San Marino A	W	7-1	Goalscorers: Ferdinand, Ince (2), I Wright (4)						
Seaman	Dixon	Pearce	INce	Pallister	Walker	Platt	Ripley	Ferdinand	I Wright	Sinton

480.	Denmark	H	W	1-0	Goalscorer: Platt					
Seaman	Parker	Le Saux	Ince*	Adams	Pallister	Platt	Gascoigne'	Shearer	Beardsley	Anderton	Batty*, Le Tissier'

481.	Greece	H	5-0	W	Goalscorers: Anderton, Beardsley, Platt (2), Shearer					
Flowers	Jones*	Le Saux	Richardson	Bould	Adams	Platt	Merson	Shearer	Beardsley'	Anderton^	Pearce*, I Wright', Le Tissier^

482.	Norway	H	D	0-0						
Seaman	Jones	Le Saux	Ince*	Bould	Adams	Platt	Wise	Shearer	Beardsley	Anderton'	Le Tissier*, I Wright'

1994-95

483.	United States	H	W	2-0	Goalscorer: Shearer (2)					
Seaman	Jones	Le Saux	Venison	Adams	Pallister	Platt	J Barnes	Shearer*	Sheringham'	Anderton	Ferdinand*, I Wright'

484.	Romania	H	D	1-1	Goalscorer: Lee					
Seaman	Jones*	Le Saux	Ince	Adams	Pallister	Lee'	I Wright^	Shearer	J Barnes	Le Tissier	Pearce*, Wise', Sheringham^,

485.	Nigeria	H	W	1-0	Goalscorer: Platt					
Flowers	Jones	Le Saux	Lee*	Howey	Ruddock	PLatt	Beardsley'	Shearer^	J Barnes	Wise	McManaman*, Le Tissier' Sheringham^

486.	Eire	A		0-1	Game abandoned after 27 minutes.					
Seaman	Barton	Le Saux	Ince	Adams	Pallister	Platt	Beardsley	Shearer	Le Tissier	Anderton

487.	Uruguay	H	D	0-0						
Flowers	Jones	Le Saux*	Venison	Adams	Pallister	Platt	Beardsley'	Sheringham^	J Barnes	Anderton	McManaman*, Barmby' Cole^

488.	Japan	H	W	2-1	Goalscorers: Anderton, Platt					
Flowers	Neville	Pearce	Batty*	Scales	Unsworth	Platt	Beardsley	Shearer	Collymore^	Anderton	McManaman*, Gascoigne' Sheringham^

489.	Sweden	H	D	3-3	Goalscorers: Anderton, Platt, Sheringham					
Flowers	Barton	Le Saux	J Barnes*	Cooper	Pallister'	Platt	Beardsley'	Shearer	Sheringham	Anderton	Gascoigne*, Scales', Barmby^

490.	Brazil	H	L	1-3	Goalscorer: Le Saux					
Flowers	Neville	Pearce	Batty*	Cooper	Scales'	Platt	Le Saux	Shearer	Sheringham^	Anderton	Gascoigne*, Barton', Collymore^

EURO - '96 - DATES & VENUES

FIRST ROUND

Saturday	June	8th	Wembley Stadium	3.00
Sunday	June	9th	Leeds United FC	2.30
		9th	Manchester United FC	5.00
		9th	Sheffield Wednesday FC	7.30
Monday	June	10th	Aston Villa FC	4.30
		10th	Newcastle United FC	7.30
Tuesday	June	11th	Liverpool FC	4.30
		11th	Nottingham Forest FC	7.30
Thursday	June	13th	Aston Villa FC	7.30
		13th	Newcastle United FC	4.30
Friday	June	14th	Liverpool FC	7.30
		14th	Nottingham Forest FC	4.30
Saturday	June	15th	Wembley Stadium	3.00
		15th	Leeds United FC	6.00
Sunday	June	16th	Manchester United FC	3.00
		16th	Sheffield Wednesday FC	6.00
Tuesday	June	18th	Aston Villa FC	7.30
		18th	Newcastle United FC	4.30
		18th	Wembley Stadium	7.30
		18th	Leeds United FC	4.30
Wednesday	June	19th	Liverpool FC	7.30
		19th	Nottingham Forest FC	4.30
		19th	Manchester United FC	7.30
		19th	Sheffield Wednesday	4.30

QUARTER-FINALS

Saturday	June	22nd	Liverpool FC	6.30
		22nd	Wembley Stadium	3.00
Sunday	June	23rd	Manchester United FC	3.00
		23rd	Aston Villa FC	7.30

SEMI-FINALS

Wednesday	June	26th	Manchester United FC	4.00
		26th	Wembley Stadium	7.30

FINAL

Sunday	June	30th	Wembley Stadium	7.00

CLUB INDEX

Printed and bound by Unwin Brothers Ltd.,
The Gresham Press, Old Woking, Surrey GU22 9LH
A Member of the Martins Printing Group